A
CHECKLIST OF
AMERICAN IMPRINTS
for
1840

Items 40-1—40-7198

compiled by

CAROL RINDERKNECHT
and
SCOTT BRUNTJEN

The Scarecrow Press, Inc.
Metuchen, N.J., & London
1990

*R
015.73
Sh 7
1840

Library of Congress Catalog No. 64-11784

ISBN 0-8108-2376-4

65.00

These volumes have been improved by incorporating the ideas presented by reviewers of earlier editions of *The Checklist*.

The type size has been increased by twenty percent. The page headings include most if not all of the entire main entry of the first complete item on the page. These two changes should improve the readability and ease of use of this and future volumes.

The entry numbers have taken a new form. Prior to the beginning of the 1840's, each entry was numbered sequentially. The numbers had no meaning. One review of the indexes for the 1830's noted that it would be helpful to know which volume to examine after finding the entry in the index. Beginning with the volume for 1840, the entry number has as a prefix two digits representing the year. Thus 40-1 is the first item for the 1840 volume and 41-2 is the second item in the 1841 *Checklist*. When the indexes are compiled for the decade of the 1840's, the user will not have to examine the entry numbers on the spines of the individual *Checklists* to find the correct volume.

One reviewer questioned how the location symbols were constructed and where one could find a table listing the library represented by the symbol. The *Checklist* uses the National Union Catalog (NUC) symbol for the library. This system was developed by Frank Petersen in the 1920's. Petersen's system was expanded by Douglas C. Mc-Murtrie, the primary leader of the American Imprints Inventory; the governmental agency which listed most of the raw material that the compilers use in identifying the items for each volume of the *Checklist*. A further discussion of McMurtrie, The American Imprints Inventory, and the NUC symbols can be found in *Douglas C. Mc-Murtrie, Bibliographer and Historian of Printing* by Scott Bruntjen and Melissa L. Young published by Scarecrow Press in 1979. A fairly complete list of NUC symbols is appended to volume 200 of *The National Union Catalog, pre-1956 Imprints* published by Mansell in 1972.

Previous editions of the *Checklist* used "dash-on entries" for representing the same author in the second and subsequent items in the same volume. This technique is well documented for use in bibliographies but the compilers found it confusing when one author, such as the City of New York, might have fifty entries in a volume. The reader was forced to look back to the first entry to determine the author of the item. Beginning with 1840, the author is provided in full for each entry. As this is a reference work to be used one item at a time, this change should make it easier for the reader.

Carol R. Rinderknecht and Scott Bruntjen

Eldora, Colorado

October, 1990

A

A'Beckett, Gilbert Abbott, 1811-1856. The Siamese twins. A farce in one act. By Gilbert Abbott a Beckett. New York: Samuel French & co. [1840] 17 p. OCl. 40-1

Abbot, Joseph Hale, 1802-1873. An attempt to determine by experimental research the true theory of the pneumatic paradox. An article from the American Journal of Science and Arts. By Joseph Hale Abbot. Boston, MA: C. C. Little & J. Brown, 1840. 25 p. CtHT; IaDaP; MeB; MH; PU. 40-2

Abbot, Joseph Hale, 1802-1873. ... A description of several new electromagnetic & magnetic electric instruments & experiments... [Boston, MA: s. l., 1840] 8 p. MH; MH-BA. 40-3

Abbott, Alvin. A blow at the serpent's head. Original poems against the vices of the tongue with others on intemperance, revenge, etc... New Haven, CT: s. l., 1840. 24 p. CtY. 40-4

Abbott, Jacob, 1803-1879. Jonas a judge; or, law among the boys. By the author of the Rollo Books, Jonas's stories, &c., &c. Boston, MA: William D. Ticknor, 1840. 179 p. DLC; GDecCT; InU; MHi; NbCrD. 40-5

Abbott, Jacob, 1803-1879. Jonas a judge; or, law among the boys. By the author of the Rollo Books, Jonas's stories, &c., &c. New York: Clark &

Maynard, Publishers [1840] 179 p. CtY; DLC; MB; MH; PP. 40-6

Abbott, Jacob, 1803-1879. The Mount Vernon reader. A course of reading lesson... designed for middle classes. By the Messrs. Abbott. New York: Published by Collins, Keese & Co., 1840. 252 p. CSmH; DLC; MB; MH; PLFM. 40-7

Abbott, Jacob, 1803-1879. The Mount Vernon reader; A course of reading lessons designed for senior classes, by the Messrs. Abbott. Boston, MA: W. Crosby & Co., 1840. 162 p. INormN; MH; NNC. 40-8

Abbott, Jacob, 1803-1879. Rollo's correspondence. By the author of Rollo Learning To Talk, To Read, At Work, At Play, At School, At Vacation &c. Boston, MA: William Crosby and Co., 1840. 189 p. DLC; MeB; MH; NNU; PPULC. 40-9

Abbott, Jacob, 1803-1879. Rollo's philosophy. Water... By Jacob Abbott. [Rollo series] Boston, MA: Phillips [184-?] 192 p. OOxM. 40-10

Abbott, Jacob, 1803-1879. Rollo's travels. By the author of Rollo learning to talk, to read, at work, at play, at school, at vacation &c. Boston, MA: W. Crosby and Company, 1840. 189 p. DLC; MH; MHi; MiD; NhLac. 40-11

Abell, T. P. Universalist belief. A dis-

course preached in the Universalist
Church, Castine, Me., on the afternoon
of March 8, 1840. By Rev. T. P. Abell.
Boston, MA: A. Tompkins, 1840. 16 p.
MeHi; MMeT-Hi; MWA; RPB. 40-12

Abercrombie, John, 1780-1844. In-
quiries concerning the intellectual
powers and the investigation of truth.
From the 2nd Edinburgh ed. New York:
Harper & brothers, 1840. 376 p. DLC;
KyU; PPULC; PU. 40-13

Abercrombie, John, 1780-1844. The
philosophy of the moral feelings. By John
Abercrombie... From the 2d Edinburgh
ed. New York: Harper & brothers, 1840.
236 p. CtY; IaCrC; MWelC; ScAb; ViR.
40-14

Abolition!! Infatuation of Federal Whig
Leaders of the South. The South
Betrayed! Read the following clear exposition of the dangers to which your
property and your lives are exposed by
the ambition or treachery of political
leaders, etc. [S. l.: s. l., 1840] 7 p. PPL;
PPULC; Vi; ViU. 40-15

About plants. With many engravings.
Worcester: J. Gout, jr. [184-?] 24 p. DLC.
40-16

Abstract from the statement of the condition of the several Banks in Conn., on
the last Saturday of March, 1840. [New
Haven, CT: s. l., 1840] PHi. 40-17

Abt, Franz, 1819-1885. ... In the eye
there lies the heart... New York;
Philadelphia, PA: Dubois & Warriner;
A. Fiot [184-?] 3 p. ViU. 40-18

Academy of natural Sciences of
Philadelphia. Act of incorporation and
by-laws of the Academy of Natural Scien-
ces of Philadelphia. Philadelphia, PA: T.
K. and P. G. Collins, printers, 1840. 12 p.
PHi; PPULC; PU. 40-19

Ackley, Alvan. Hell, a place of future
punishment. Being the substance of
three sermons delivered to the Baptist
congregation, Greenport, Long Island,
Dec. 29, 1839, by Alvan Ackley. New
London: Ebenezer Williams, printer,
1840. 22 p. CtY; MMeT-Hi; NBLiHi;
NCH-S. 40-20

Act suspending the operation of the
sundry acts of this commonwealth
prohibiting the incorporated banking institutions from issuing bills less than five
dollars. [S. l.: s. l., 1840] 4 p. PHi. 40-21

Acton, Henry. Three lectures on the
supposed apostolical succession and
authority of a Christian priesthood;
delivered in George's Chapel, Exeter...
[S. l.: s. l., 1840] 96 p. ICMe; NNUT. 40-
22

Adair, Robert. Memoir of Rev. James
Patterson... by Robert Adair... With an
introduction and chapter on field preach-
ing, by Rev. D. L. Carroll. Philadelphia,
PA: H. Perkins, 1840. 324 p. IEG; KyDC;
MiU; NbOM; ViU. 40-23

Adam, Adolphe Charles, 1803-1856.
Beneath cool shades reposing. [Assis au
pied d'un hetre pastoral] in the admired
opera "Le Postillion de Lonjumeau.
Composed by A. Adam. Philadelphia,
PA; New Orleans; Charleston, SC: A.
Fiot; B. Casey; Geo. Oates [184-?] 3 p.
ViU. 40-24

Adam, Alexander, 1741-1804. Adam's
Latin grammar, with some improve-

ments, and the following additions: Rules for the right pronunciation of the Latin language; a metrical key to the Odes of Horace; a list of Latin authors, arranged according to the different ages of Roman literature; tables showing the value of the various coins, weights and measures used among the Romans, by Benjamin A. Gould. Boston, MA: Hilliard, Gray & Co., 1840. 299 p. MH; NNC; OOxM; PPAN; WaPS. 40-25

Adam, William. The law and custom of slavery in British India, in a series of letters to Thomas Fowell Buxton, esq. Boston, MA: Weeks, Jordan and co., 1840. 279 p. InU; MeB; MH; MWiW; NbCrD. 40-26

Adams, Abigail [Smith] 1744-1818. Letters of Mrs. Adams, the wife of John Adams. With an introductory memoir by her grandson, Charles Francis Adams. Boston, MA: C. C. Little and J. Brown, Pub., 1840. 447 p. CSmH; IaGG; OrU; RBr; WaPS. 40-27

Adams, Abigail [Smith] 1744-1818. Letters of Mrs. Adams, the wife of John Adams. With an introductory memoir by her grandson, Charles Francis Adams. Second edition. Boston, MA: C. C. Little and J. Brown, Pub., 1840. 2 v. AU; GU; IaB; LNT; MiU. 40-28

Adams, Charles, pub. The log cabin and hard cider melodies; a collection of popular and patriotic songs, respectively dedicated to the friend of Harrison and Tyler. Boston: Charles Adams, 1840. 72 p. InHi; MB; MH; MHi. 40-29

Adams, Daniel, 1773-1864. ... Arithmetic, in which principles of operating with numbers are analytically explained,

and synthetically applied, thus combining the advantages to be derived both from the inductive and synthetic mode of instructing... Designed for the use of schools and academies in the United States. By Daniel Adams. Keene, NH: J. & W. Prentiss, 1840. 262 p. C-S; DAU; KyU; NjR; OBerB; OClWHi. 40-30

Adams, Daniel, 1775-1864. The monitorial reader. Designed for the use of academies and schools and as a monitor to youth, holding up to their view models whereby to form their own characters. Keene, NH: J. J. W. Prentiss, 1840. MB; NN; TxDam. 40-31

Adams, John, 1786-1856. A treatise on the principles and practice of the action of ejectment, and the resulting action for mesne profits... From the 3rd London ed... New York: Published by Gould, Banks & co. [etc.] 1840. 544 p. GU-L; NbCrD; OClW; RPL; WMMU. 40-32

Adams, John Greenleaf, 1810-1887. The Christian's triumph; including happy death scenes, illustrative of the power of the Gospel. Drawn from facts. By John G. Adams. Boston, MA: A. Tompkins, 1840. 216 p. DLC; IaMP; ICMe; PU; RPB. 40-33

Adams, John Greenleaf, 1810-1887. Practical hints to believers in the Gospel of universal grace and salvation. By John G. Adams. Boston, MA: Published by Thomas Whittemore, 1840. 271 p. DLC; IaMp; MH; MMeT-Hi; NCas. 40-34

Adams, John Quincy, pres. U. S., 1767-1848. Discourse on education, delivered at Braintree, Oct. 24, 1839. By John Quincy Adams. Boston, MA: Perkins &

4 Adams, John Quincy

Marvin, 1840. 36 p. CtY; ICU; MeB; MWA; NjP. 40-35

Adams, John Quincy, pres. U. S., 1767-1848. Speech of the Hon. John Quincy Adams, in relation to the navy pension fund. Delivered in the House of Representatives, on the 28th of December, 1840. [Washington, DC: s. l., 1840] 8 p. CU; DLC; MH; MWA; WHi. 40-36

Adams, John Quincy, pres. U. S., 1767-1848. Substance of the speech of John Quincy Adams, together with a part of the debate in the House of Representatives of the United States, upon the bill to ensure the more faithful execution of the laws relating to the collection of duties on imports. Boston, MA: printed by Perkins & Marvin, 1840. 30 p. InHi; MWA; OCLaw; PHi; WHi. 40-37

Adams, Nehemiah, 1806-1878. My baptism. From "The Baptized Child," by Nehemiah Adams. Revised by the Committee of Publication. Second edition. Boston, MA: Sabbath School Society Depository, 1840. 32 p. MBC; MPeHi. 40-38

Addison, James, 1672-1719. Selections from the Spectator: embracing the most interesting papers, by Addison, Steele, and others. New York: Harper, 1840. 2 v. LNH; NCas; OClW; RPE; WHi. 40-39

Addison County, Vt. Courts. Rules of Addison County court. Adopted Dec. term, 1840. Middlebury, VT: Office of the People's Press, printed by Eph. Maxham [1840] 8 p. VtMidSM. 40-40

An address of the democratic members of the legislature to the democratic party

in the state of Maine. [Augusta, ME.] : s. l. [1840?] 8 p. MH; NNC. 40-41

Address of the Hickory Club to the people of Louisiana, New Orleans, March 25, 1840. [S. l.: s. l. 1840?] 1 p. MdHi. 40-42

Address of the Roman Catholics to their fellow citizens of the city and state of New York. New York: H. Cassidy, printer, 1840. 14 p. NNC. 40-43

An address, showing, by well authenticated documents, the wasteful and extravagant manner in which the President and his subordinate offices have been squandering the money of the people. Columbus, OH: Jonathan Phillips, 1840. 16 p. OClWHi. 40-44

Address to the Democracy of the state of New York [unanimously adopted at a meeting of the Democratic members of the legislature, May 4, 1840] Albany, NY : s. l., 1840. 96 p. NN. 40-45

Address to the Democratic Republican electors of the state of New York. Washington, DC:printed at the Globe office, 1840. 22 p. A-Ar; MBC; MdHi; MH; TxDaM; TxU. 40-46

An address to the Mechanics and Laboring Classes. By a Mechanic. New York: s. l., 1840. 48 p. NHi. 40-47

Address to the people of the slave holding states, by the Democratic Republican members of Congress from those states. [Washington, DC: s. l., 1840] 16 p. DLC; GU; MB; NcU; PPL; TxU; V. 40-48

Address to the workingmen of the United States. [Washington, DC: s. l.,

1840] 16 p. DLC; MBC; MdHi; OClWHi. 40-49

Address to working men, on the low prices of wages, by a mechanic. New York: s. l., 1840. 4 p. InHi; NHi; NNC; PPL. 40-50

Adhemar, Ab. Comte d'. Vole, vole, ma gondole... Philadelphia, PA: s. l. [184-?] 5 p. MB. 40-51

Adirondack Iron and Steel Co., New York Papers... relative to... McIntyre Essex Co. New York: s. l., 1840. p. NjP; SG. 40-52

Advance guard of democracy. v. 1, no. 1-24; Apr. 23-Oct. 16, 1840. [Nashville, TN: J. H. Harris, 1840] 368 p. DLC. 40-53

... Adventures of Goody Twoshoes. Albany, NY: Published by Gray, Sprague & co. [1840?] 15 p. No Loc. 40-54

Advice to Sabbath School children. Andover, MA: s. l. [184-?] 16 p. MH. 40-55

Advice to Sabbath School children. Northampton: J. Metcalf, 1840. 23 p. MH. 40-56

Adyelott, Benjamin Parham, 1795-1880. The duties of American citizens. An address by Rev. B. P. Aydelott, D. D., President of Woodward College. Cincinnati, OH: Pugh, 1840. ICU; KyLo; MBAt; OClWHi; PU. 40-57

Affecting and thrilling anecdotes respecting the hardships and sufferings of our brave and venerable forefathers. Numerous woodcuts. Boston, MA: s. l. [1840-45] p. No Loc. 40-58

Affections Gift: for the instruction and amusement of the young. With engravings. By a lady. Hartford, CT: Brown and Parsons, 1840. 82 p. No Loc. 40-59

African Methodist Episcopal Church. The doctrines and discipline of the African Methodist Church. 5th ed. Brooklyn, NY: George Hogarth, 1840. 223 p. DLC; MH; NB. 40-60

African Methodist Episcopal Church. Minutes. Philadelphia, PA: s. l., 1840-52. p. DLC. 40-61

African Methodist Episcopal Church. Minutes of conferences, 1839-40. Brooklyn, NY: s. l., 1840. p. DLC. 40-62

Agawam quick step. Composed and arranged for the piano forte, by D. A. A. Boston, MA: H. Prentiss [184-?] 2 p. DLC; ICN; MB. 40-63

Agawam quick step. Composed and arranged for the piano forte, by D. A. A. New York: Wm. Hall & son [184-?] 2 p. MB; ViU. 40-64

Agnew, Emily C. Geraldine: a tale of conscience. By E. C. A. Philadelphia, PA: published by Eugene Cummiskey, 1840. p. NGH. 40-65

Aguilar, Grace. The women of Israel. By Grace Aguilar, author of "Woman's friendship"... New York; Philadelphia, PA: D. Appleton & Co.; Geo. S. Appleton, 1840. 270 p. NcWsS. 40-66

Aikin, John, 1747-1822. The juvenile budget opened; being selections from the writings of Doctor John Aikin, by Mrs. Sarah J. Hale. School Library

Juvenile series. Boston, MA: Marsh, Capen, Lyon, Webb, 1840. 288 p. InCW; MB; MBol; MFalm; PU. 40-67

Aikin, John, 1747-1822. The juvenile budget reopened; being further selections from the writings of Doctor John Aikin. With copious notes... Boston, MA: Marsh, Capen, Lyon, Webb, 1840. 250 p. InCW; MB; TxGeoS. 40-68

Aikin, John, 1747-1822. Select works of the British poets, in a chronological series from Ben Jonson to Beattie. With biographical and critical notices. 10th edition. Philadelphia: T. Wardle, 1840. 807 p. CSt; MiU; NcD; OClW; PLF. 40-69

Aikin, William E. A., 1807-1888. An introductory lecture. Delivered before the medical class of the University of Maryland, September, 1840. By William E. A. Aikin, M. D., Professor of Chemistry and Pharmacy. Baltimore, MD: Printed by John Murphy [1840] 32 p. DLC; DNLM; MB; MdBLC; MdBM; MdBP; MdHi; MdW; MH-M; PPL. 40-70

Aikin, William E. A., 1807-1888. Notice of the Daguerreotype. By William E. A. Aikin, M. D., Professor Chemistry and Pharmacy, University of Maryland. Baltimore, MD: Printed by John Murphy, 1840. 16 p. Md; MdBP; MdHi; MH; NjR. 40-71

Aikin, William E. A., 1807-1888. Theory of daguerreotype process. [Baltimore, MD: s. l., 1840?] 4 p. DLC; MB. 40-72

Aimard, Gustave. The border rifles. A tale of the Texan war. Philadelphia, PA:

T. B. Peterson & Bros. [1840?] 172 p. ICN; NN. 40-73

Aimard, Gustave. The freebooters, a story of the Texan war. Complete and unabridged ed. Philadelphia, PA: T. B. Peterson & Brotherss [1840?] 162 p. NN. 40-74

Aimard, Gustave. The gold-finders, a romance of California. New York: E. D. Long & Co. [1840] 130 p. NN. 40-75

Aimard, Gustave. The prairie-flower. Philadelphia, PA: s. l. [1840?] 165 p. NN. 40-76

Ainsworth, Robert, 1660-1743. New abridgment of dictionary, English and Latin... For the use of grammar schools... With corrections & improvements by Charles Anthon. New American ed. Philadelphia, PA: Cowperthwait, 1840. 406 p. PU. 40-77

Ainsworth, William Harrison, 1805-1882. The tower of London. New York: George Routledge & Sons, 1840. p. InAndC. 40-78

Ainsworth, William Harrison, 1805-1882. The tower of London. Philadelphia, PA: Geo. Barrie & Sons, 1840. 317 p. KyCov. 40-79

Ainsworth, William Harrison, 1805-1882. The works of W. H. Ainsworth. With illustrations by George Cruishank. New York: Nottingham Society, 1841. 8 v. NcD; PU. 40-80

Alabama. Report of the Select Committee to whom was referred the communication of the Secretary of State, together with the accompanying documents, relative to the proposed amendments to the constitution, providing for biennial sessions of the Legislature and for other purposes. [Tuscaloosa, AL: s. l., 184-?] No Loc. 40-81

Alabama. General Assembly. Joint Examining Committee on the Condition of the State Bank and Branches. Report of the Joint Examining Committee on the Condition of the State Bank and Branches. With an exhibit of the debt incurred by the state for the banking capital and a statement of condition of the debts due the state bank and branches. Tuscaloosa, AL: Hale & Phelan, 1840. 15 p. GEU. 40-82

Alabama. Governor, 1837-1841 [A. P. Bagby] Message of His Excellency, Gov. Bagby, to the Legislature of Alabama, at the commencement of the annual session, November 2, 1840. Tuscaloosa, AL: printed by Hale & Phelan, 1840. 15 p. TxU. 40-83

Alabama. Laws, statutes, etc. Acts passed at the annual session of the General Assembly of the State of Alabama... on the first Monday in December, 1839. Tuscaloosa, AL: Hale and Phelan, Printers, 1840. 192 p. DLC; In-SC; MH-L; NNB; RPL. 40-84

Alabama. Legislature. Commission Appointed to Examine the Condition of the Branch Bank of the State of Alabama at Huntsville. Reort of the commissioners appointed by the governor to examine the condition of the branch of the Bank of the State of Alabama at Huntsville... Tuscaloosa, AL: Hale & Phelan, 1840. 8 p. GEU. 40-85

Alabama. Legislature. Committee Ex-amining the Condition of the State Bank and Branches. Report of the Joint Examining Committee on the condition of the state bank and branches. With an exhibit of the debt incurred by the State for banking capital; and a statement of the condition of the debts due the State Bank and branches. Tuscaloosa, AL: s. l., 1840. 15 p. A-Ar; NN. 40-86

Alabama. Legislature. House of Representatives. Committee on Ways and Means. Report of the Committee of Ways & Means. [Montgomery, AL: s. l., 1840] 4 p. MH. 40-87

Alabama. Legislature. House of Representatives. Journal of the House of Representatives, at the Annual Session of the General Assembly of the State of Alabama. Begun and held in the City of Tuscaloosa, on the first Monday in December, 1840. [Tuscaloosa, AL: Hale & Eaton, printers, 1840] 376 p. A-SC. 40-88

Alabama. Legislature. House of Representatives. Rules of the House of Representatives. [Tuscaloosa, AL: s. l., 1840] No Loc. 40-89

Alabama. Legislature. Joint Examining Committee on the Condition of the State Bank and Branches. Report of the Joint Examining Committee on the condition of the state bank and branches. With an exhibit of the debt incurred by the state for banking capital; and a statement of the condition of the debts due the state bank and branches. Tuscaloosa, AL: Hale & Phelan, 1840. 15 p. GEU; MB; NN. 40-90

Alabama. Legislature. Judiciary Committee. Report of the Judiciary Committee in relation to the eligibility of certain officers to seats in the House of Representatives. Tuscaloosa, AL: Hale & Eaton, state printers, 1840. 7 p. TxU. 40-91

Alabama. Legislature. Senate. Journal of the Senate at a session of the General Assembly of the State of Alabama. Begun and held in the City of Tuscaloosa, on the first Monday in December, 1839. Tuscaloosa, AL: Hall and Eaton, State Printers, 1840. 336 p. A-SC; ICU. 40-92

Albany. Chamberlain's Office. The Chamberlain's report to the Common Council, of the receipts and expenditures from May 1st, 1839 to May 1st, 1840. Albany, NY: Hoffman, White & Visscher, printers, 1840. 14 p. NN; NNS. 40-93

Albany. Chamberlain's Office. Report of the Chamberlain of the City of Albany, made pursuant to a resolution of the Common Council, passed July 6, 1840, requiring him to report the location & value of all the real estate owned by said city. Albany, NY: Printed by Hoffman, White & Visscher, 1840. 15 p. NNC; WHi. 40-94

Albany. New York Young Men's Association for Mutual Improvement in the City of Schenectady, N. Y. Annual report of the president of the Young Men's Association for Mutual Improvement in the City of Albany... February 3, 1840... Albany, NY: Printed by J. Munsell, 1840. 13 p. CSmH; MHi; MWA; NjR; NN. 40-95

Albany. Phrenological Society. Constitution. Albany, NY: s. l., 1840. 8 p. CtY. 40-96

Albany County, N. Y. Court of Com-

mon Pleas. Rules... Adopted June term, 1840. Albany, NY: Printed by Hoffman, White & Visscher, 1840. 18 p. NN. 40-97

Albany and West Stockbridge Railroad Company. Act of incorporation of the Albany and West Stockbridge rail-road company, and additional acts; together with the proceedings of the Common Council of Albany. Albany, NY: Printed by C. Van Benthuysen, 1840. 23 p. CSmH; DBRE; ICU; MH-BA; NjP. 40-98

Albany and West Stockbridge Railroad Company. By-laws adopted July 29, 1840. Albany, NY: s. l., 1840. 4 p. CtY; DBRE; MH-BA; MWA; NN. 40-99

Albany City Temperance Society. Mr. Delavan's correspondence... Albany, NY: s. l., 1840. No Loc. 40-100

Albany Medical College, Albany, N. Y. Catalogues and circulars.... Albany, NY: printed by Joell Munsell, 1840. MB; NN; OO; PHi; PPL-R. 40-101

Albert, Charles Louis Napoleon d', 1809-1886. The coquette polka. Boston, MA: Ditson [184-?] 5 p. MB. 40-102

Albert, Charles Louis Napoleon d', 1809-1886. The serenading of good luck polka. [For piano forte] Boston, MA: Reed and Co. [184-?] 2 p. MB. 40-103

Alcott, William Andrus, 1798-1859. Abuses of the eye. Boston, MA: s. l., 1840. MB; MBM; MH-M. 40-104

Alcott, William Andrus, 1798-1859. The first foreign mission... Boston, MA: s. l. [1840?] DLC. 40-105

Alcott, William Andrus, 1798-1859. Health in common schools. By Dr. Wm. A. Alcott. Boston, MA: George W. Light, 1840. 31 p. MHi; MWA; WHi. 40-106

Alcott, William Andrus, 1798-1859. The house I live in... Boston, MA: George W. Light, 1840. 264 p. MFiHi. 40-107

Alcott, William Andrus, 1798-1859. The library of health, and teacher on the human constitution. Wm. A. Elcott, ed. Boston, MA: published by George W. Light, 1840. 384 p. MNBedf; NRivHi; OMC. 40-108

Alcott, William Andrus, 1798-1859. Travels of our Saviour, with some of the leading incidents of his life. Written for the Massachusetts Sabbath School Society & revised by the Committee on Publication. Boston, MA: Massachusetts Sabbath School Society, 1840. 311 p. DLC; InCW; MoSpD; OO. 40-109

Alcott, William Andrus, 1798-1859. The young house-keeper; or, Thoughts on food and cooking. 5th stereotype edition. Boston, MA: George W. Light, 1840. p. MNF. 40-110

Alcott, William Andrus, 1798-1859. The young husband, or duties of the man in the marriage relation. 5th ed. Boston, MA: s. l., 1840. 388 p. DLC; DSG; DNLM. 40-111

Alcott, William Andrus, 1798-1859. The young wife; or, duties of woman in marriage relations. By Wm. A. Alcott. Stereotype ed. Boston, MA: G. W. Light, 1840. 376 p. P; PPFr. 40-112

Alcott, William Andrus, 1798-1859. The young woman's guide to excellence. 3d ed. Boston, MA: s. l., 1840. MB; NjMD. 40-113

Alcott, William Andrus, 1798-1859. Young woman's guide to excellence. 4th ed. Boston, MA: s. l., 1840. 356 p. MAnA; MBC; OO; TxDaM. 40-114

Aldrich, Elisha F. The propulsion of vessels of war, and those for ocean, lake & canal navigation, by steam, or any other appropriate moving power. New York: G. Mitchell, printer [184-?] 14 p. DLC; MdBP. 40-115

Alexander, Archibald, 1772-1851. Christ's gracious invitation to the laboring and heavy laden. By A. Alexander. Philadelphia, PA: Presbyterian Board of Publication, 1840. 12 p. CtHC; MB; MsSC. 40-116

Alexander, Archibald, 1772-1851. The duty of catechetical instruction. By the Rev. Archibald Alexander, D. D., professor of didactic and polemic theology in the Theological Seminary at Princeton, New Jersey. Philadelphia, PA: Presbyterian Board of Publication, James Russell, publishing agent, 1840. 12 p. CtHC; MB; NjPT; OMtV; PPM. 40-117

Alexander, Archibald, 1772-1851. Evidences of the authenticity, inspiration and canonical authority of the Holy Scriptures. By Archibald Alexander. New edition. Philadelphia, PA: Joseph Whitham, 1840. 382 p. ArBaA; ODaB; PPWe; TNP; WM. 40-118

Alexander, Archibald, 1772-1851. Future punishment. Princeton, NJ: Nassau Hall Tract Society [184-?] 36 p. NN. 40-119

Alexander, Archibald, 1772-1851. A treatise on justification by faith. By Archibald Alexander, D. D., professor of didactic and polemic theology in the Theological Seminary at Princeton, New Jersey. Philadelphia, PA: Presbyterian Board of Publication, James Russell, pubishing agent, 1840. 50 p. CtHC; MB. 40-120

Alexander, Henry. An exposition of book-keeping, by single or double entry... Baltimore, MD: Printed by R. Neilson, 1840. 24 p. DLC; MdHi. 40-121

Alexander, John Henry, 1812-1867. Contributions to the history of the manufacture of iron. [Part first: Report on the manufacture of iron; addressed to the Governor of Maryland. Part second: An elementary treatise on iron-making, by S. Rogers. Now... first pubished, with notes, and an appendix, by John H. Alexander] Baltimore, MD: s. l., 1840-44. p. ICJ. 40-122

Alexander, John Henry, 1812-1867. Report on the manufacture of iron; addressed to the Governor of Maryland; by J. H. Alexander, topographical engineer of the state. Printed by order of the Senate. Annapolis, MD: W. McNeir, printer to the Senate, 1840. 269 p. CtY; DLC; MBAt; NNE; PPAmP. 40-123

Alexander, John Henry, 1812-1867. Report on the manufacture of iron; addressed to the Governor of Maryland; by J. H. Alexander, topographical engineer of the state. Printed by order of the Senate. Baltimore, MD: T. Lucas, jr., 1840. 269 p. ICJ; Md; MdBP; MH-BA; LNHT. 40-124

Alexandria, N. J. Presbyterian Church.

Application to be received... under the Third Presbytery of Philadelphia. Philadelphia, PA: s. l., 1840. p. PPPrHi. 40-125

Alexandria, Va. Protestant Episcopal Theological Seminary in Virginia. Catalogue of the officers, students, and alumni of the Theological Seminary of the Protestant Episcopal Church in the Diocese of Virginia, session of 1839-1840, with the course of studies, etc. Washington, DC: s. l., 1840. 14 p. NNG. 40-126

Alford, Julius C., 1799-1863. Address of J. C. Alford, William C. Dawson, Richard W. Habersham, Thos. Butler King, E. A. Nesbit, and Lott Warren, representatives from the State of Georgia, in the 26th Congress of the United States to their constituents, May 27, 1840. [Washington, DC: s. l., 1840] 31 p. DLC; GU; NcU; PPL; ViU. 40-127

Alford, Julius C., 1799-1863. Letter from a portion of the Representatives of the State of Georgia, in the 26th Congress of the United States, to the Governor of Georgia, on the controversy between Georgia & Maine. Washington, DC: Gales & Seaton, 1840. 8 p. GSDe; MdBP; PPL. 40-128

Alford, Julius C., 1799-1863. Speech of Mr. J. C. Alford, of Georgia, on Abolition Petitions. Delivered in the House of Representatives, January 22, 1840. Washington, DC: printed by Gales and Seaton, 1840. 14 p. DLC; MdHi; MWA. 40-129

Alford, Julius C., 1799-1863. Synopsis of the speech against the sub-treasury bill. Delivered in the House of

Representatives, June, 1840. Rockville, MD: s. l., 1840? DLC; NNC. 40-130

Allen, John William, 1802-1887. Remarks of Mr. John W. Allen, of Ohio, on the Sub-treasury bill, in Committee of the Whole, Mr. Banks, of Virginia, in the Chair. Delivered in the House of Representatives, June 24, 1840. Washington, DC: Madisonian Office, 1840. 16 p. CtY; NNC; OClWHi; PKsL; PPULC. 40-131

Allen, Joseph, 1790-1873. Questions on select portions of the four Evangelists. Part second... By Joseph Allen. Boston, MA: Benjamin H. Greene, 1840. 118 p. MH; MoSpD. 40-132

Allen, William, 1803-1879. Speech... on the report of the select committee in re on [?] to the assumption of the debts of the states by the federal government. Senate... Feb. 11, 1840. Washington, DC: s. l., 1840. 14 p. MiD-B; NN; ViU. 8 40-133

Allen, William Henry, 1808-1882. A baccalaureate address, delivered before the senior class, Dickinson college, Carlisle, Pennsylvania, July 8th, 1840. By William H. Allen... Philadelphia, PA: T. K. & P. G. Collins, printers, 1840. 21 p. IEG; MBC; MH; NcU; PU. 40-134

Allingham, Jack Till, fl. 1799-1810. The weathercock. A farce in two acts. New York: s. l. [1840] 28 p. IU; MH; NIC. 40-135

Almanac for the year of Our Lord 1840. Being bissextile or leap year. Arranged after the system of the German Calendar, containing: the rising, setting, and eclipses of the sun and moon; the phases, signs, and southings of the moon; the aspects of the planets; with the rising, setting, and southing of the most conspicuous planets and fixed stars; the time of high water at Philadelphia; the equation of time; and other miscellanies, etc., etc. Carefully calculated for the meridian of Philadelphia. By John Ward, of New Jersey. Notes to the reader... S. l.: s. l. [1840] 34 p. NCH. 40-136

Almanack for 1841. Anson Allen. Hartford, CT: Henry Benton [1840] MWA. 40-137

Alpha Delta Phi. Catalogue of the society, 1840. New Haven, CT: Hamlen, 1840. 15 p. Mi; MokU. 40-138

Alston, Philip William Whitmel, 1813-1847. An address delivered at the laying of the corner-stone of Immanuel church, La Grange. By the Rev. Philip W. Alston... Published by request of the rector and vestry of Immanuel church. Memphis, TN: Enquirer Office, 1840. 9 p. CSmH; NNG; T. 40-139

American almanac. Boston, MA: Folsom, Wells, & Thurston, printer; David H. Williams, publisher, 1840. 334 p. IaHA. 40-140

The American almanac 1840... Cambridge, MA: Folsom, Wells, & Thurston, 1840. 334 p. RP. 40-141

The American almanac for the year 1841. Boston, MA: Pub. by David Williams [1840] 312 p. MWHi. 40-142

American and Foreign Anti-Slavery Society. The annual report... New York: American and Foreign Anti-Slavery

Society, 1840-56? v. C; DLC; MiU; OClWHi; PHi; TxU. 40-143

American Anti-slavery Society. Address to the friends of constitutional liberty on the violation of the right of petition. New York: Amer. Anti-Slavery Soc., 1840. 12 p. CtMW; ICN; MH; MH-AH; PU. 40-144

The American anti-slavery almanac for 1840. Boston, MA; New York: published by Am. Anti-Slavery Soc. and J. A. Collins [1840] 48 p. ArU; CtHWatk; MH; MWA; NUtHi; RNHi. 40-145

American Art Union, N. Y. Catalogue of the sixth exhibition... 1840. New York: s. l., 1840. 12 p. MBAt; NIC. 40-146

American Art Union, N. Y. Transactions of the Apollo Association for the promotion of the fine arts in the United States for the year 1840. New York: H. Ludwig, 1840. 28 p. MBAt; MdBP; MdHi. 40-147

American Baptist Almanac. Almanac and Baptist register for... 1841... Philadelphia, PA: Pub. by the American Baptist Publication and S. School Society... Pr. by King & Baird [1840] 36 p. GDecCT; MeHi; MHi; PPM; ViRU. 40-148

American Board of Commissioners for Foreign Missions. Maps of missions of the American board of commissioners for foreign missions. Boston, MA: s. l. [1840] 15 p. DLC; OrU; WHi-Mss. 40-149

American Board of Commissioners for Foreign Missions. On receiving donations from holders of slaves. Boston, MA:

Printed by Perkins and Marvin [1840?] 20 p. CtY; KHi; MiD-B; MWA; TxU. 40-150

American Board of Commissioners for Foreign Missions. Progress & state of the mission of the Sandwich Islands. [Boston, MA: s. l., 1840?] 24 p. ICN; MB; NN. The American book of beauty. Hartford, CT: s. l. [184-?] p. MB. 40-151

The American boundary question... By an American citizen. New Haven, CT: Printed for the author by W. Storer, jun., 1840. 36 p. CtY; DLC; MiD-B. 40-152

American comic almanack. Boston, MA: S. N. Dickinson, 1842. MWA. 40-153

The American Farmer's Almanac for the year 1840. Boston, MA: Published and sold by Allen & Company, 1840. 36 p. MeBaHi; RnHi. 40-154

The American farmer's companion; or, Cabinet of agricultural knowledge:containing a variety of useful information on husbandry, breeding, the dairy, orcharding, gardening, and all the economy of a farm. V. 1, no. 1-7, Jan. -July, 1840. Philadelphia, PA: s. l., 1840. 212 p. DLC. 40-155

American Institute of the City of New York. Library. Report of the committee appointed May 7, 1840, to investigate all charges of improper conduct against all officers & members of the Institute & report thereon. [New York: s. l., 1841] 27 p. NIC. 40-156

The American Joe Miller. Philadelphia, PA: Carey & Hart, 1840. 219 p. DLC; LNH; MWA; NcD; NN. 40-157

American Life Insurance and Trust Company, Baltimore. Report of the committee of trustees of the American Life Insurance and Trust Company, appointed for the purpose of examining the books, vouchers and documents in the office, and of ascertaining the state of its affairs, on the 30th June 1840. New York: Carvill & Co., 1840. 14 p. MdHi. 40-158

American medical almanac. By J. V. C. Smith. Boston, MA: Marsh, Caper, Lyon & Webb, 1840. ICU; MB; MWA. 40-159

American medical almanac for 1841. Comp. by J. U. C. Smith. Boston, MA: Otis, Broadus & Co. [1840] MWA. 40-160

The American medical almanac for 1841. Designed for the daily use of practising physicians, surgeons, students and apothecaries; being also a pocket memorandum and account book and general medical directory of the United States and the British provinces. Continued annually. Boston, MA: Otis, 1840-41. 2 v. MH-M. 40-161

American miniature almanacs. Allen's edition. Boston, MA: Allen & Co., 1840. MWA. 40-162

The American naval and patriotic songster. In honour of Hull, Jones, Decatur, Perry, &c. &c. &c. &c... By a gentleman from New York. New York: N. C. Nafis, 1840. 108 p. DLC; ICN; InU; NBuG. 40-163

American naval battles; being a complete history of the battles fought by the navy of the United States, from its establishment in 1794 to the present time...

Boston, MA: Gaylord, 1840. 278 p. CSmH; IHi; MiD; MWA; OUrC. 40-164

The American orator's own book:a manual of extemporaneous eloquence including a course of discipline and also practical exercises. Philadelphia, PA: Kay & Troutman, 1840. 279 p. MH; NcW; PAtM. 40-165

American oratory; or, selections from the speeches of eminent Americans. Compiled by a member of the Philadelphia Bar. Philadelphia, PA: Edward C. Biddle, 1840. 531 p. AB; MoKR; NRU; OClW; PU. 40-166

American Philosophical Society, Philadelphia. Bulletins. Philadelphia, PA: The Society, 1840-. v. PPL; PPULC. 40-167

American Philosophical Society, Philadelphia. Proceedings of the American Philosophical Society, held at Philadelphia, for promoting useful knowledge. Philadelphia, PA: The Society, 1840-. 9 v. CtMW; ICU; KU; NjP; OClW. 40-168

The American repertory of arts, sciences, and manufactures. Ed. by James J. Mapes... V. 1-4, Feb., 1840-Jan., 1842. New York; Boston, MA: W. A. Cox; Weeks, Jordan & Co. [etc., etc.] 1840-42. 4 v. CtY; IaAS; MH; OClWHi; PPAmP. 40-169

American Seamen's Friend Society, Boston. Circular, May 29, 1840. S. l.: s. l., 1840? 2 p. MHi. 40-170

American Silk Society. Journal of the American Silk Society and rural economist. By Gideon B. Smith, editor.

Baltimore, MD: Published by the Society; printed by John D. Toy, 1840. 2, 358 p. FOA; ICMcHi. 40-171

American Statistical Association. Constitution and by-laws of the American Statistical Associaton, with a list of officers, fellows and members, and an address. Boston, MA: printed by Perkins & Marvin, 1840. 24 p. MBC; MHi; MWA; Nh; PHi. 40-172

American Sunday School Union. Bread from God. Philadelphia: American Sunday School Union [1840?] 11 l. RPB. 40-173

American Sunday School Union. Introduction to Bible chronology, written for the American Sunday School Union and revised by the committee on publication. Philadelphia, PA: American Sunday School Union [1840] 144 p. CtHC; MA; NN; PReaAT; ScCliTO. 40-174

American Sunday School Union. Reports and mischief they do. Philadelphia [184-?] 23 p. N. 40-175

American Sunday School Union. Scenes of childhood. For children four or five years old. Philadelphia [184-?] 16 p. MB; ViU. 40-176

American Sunday School Union. Scripture prints; or, The child's sabbath, pleasantly and profitably employed. Prepared for the American Sunday School Union and revised by the committee of publication. Philadelphia [184-?] 20 l. RPB. 40-177

American Sunday School Union. Second reading book. Prepared for the American Sunday School Union and revised by the committee of publication. Philadelphia [184-?] 24 p. RPB. 40-178

American Sunday School Union. The Sunday school teacher. Philadelphia, 1840. 61 p. DLC; MH. 40-179

American Temperance Union. Report of the executive committee of the American Temperance Union, 1840... New York: Printed by S. W. Benedict, 1840. 84 p. MNBedf; MoKu; PLT. 40-180

American Tract Society. Easy lessons for the little ones at home. [New York: Published by the American Tract Society [184-?] 96 p. WHi. 40-181

American Tract Society. The enormity of the slave-trade and the duty of seeking the moral and spiritual elevation of the colored race. Speeches of Wilberforce, and other documents and records... New York: s. l. [184-?] p. CtY. 40-182

American Tract Society. Happy voices. New hymns and tunes. With many popular and sterling old ones. For the Home Circle and Sabbath Schools. New York: Published by the American Tract Society [184-?] 176 p. WHi. 40-183

American Tract Society. Liederbuch fur die Jugend. Youth's songs. Anhange von Melodieen. New York: Herausgegeben von der Amerikanischen Tractat Gesellschaft [184-?] 240 p. WHi. 40-184

American Tract Society. The lost mechanical mystery. [New York: Amer. Tract Soc., 184-?] 4 p. NN. 40-185

American Tract Society. The temperance volume, embracing the temperance tracts of the American Tract Society. New York: American Tract Society [1840?] v. CtY. 40-186

American Tract Society. Usefulness of tracts. [New York: s. l., 184-?] p. CtHT. 40-187

Americanischer Stadt und Land Calendar auf das 1841ste Jahr Christi... Philadelphia, PA: Gedruckt und zu haben bey Conrad Zentler [1840] 28 p. PReaHi. 40-188

Americanischer Stadt und Land Calendar for 1841. Philadelphia, PA: Conrad Zentler [1840] p. MWA. 40-189

Americanischer Unabhangig keits Kalender... 1840. Philadelphia, PA: C. F. Stollmeyer [1840] p. MWA. 40-190

The American's guide: comprising the Declaration of Independence; the Articles of Confederation; the Constitution of the United States, and the Constitutions of several states compromising the Union. Philadelphia, PA: Hogan & Thompson, 1840. 419 p. AB; NUt; PU-Penn; RAp. 40-191

Der Amerikanisch Deutsche Hausfreund und Baltimore Calendar for 1841. Baltimore, MD: Johann T. Hanzsche [1840] p. MWA. 40-192

Ames, John F. The Mnemosynum. Intended to aid not only students and professional men, but every other class of citizen in keeping a list of incidents, facts, and in such a manner that they may be recalled at pleasure... Utica, NY: Orren Hutchinson, 1840. 150 p. NN; NNC; RPB. 40-193

Amherst College. Catalogue of the officers and students of Amherst College, for the academical year, 1840-41. Amherst, MA: J. S. & C. Adams, 1840. 24 p. CoU; MdBJ; MeB; NN; TNP. 40-194

Amherst College. Commencement. Order of exercises... Amherst, MA: s. l., 1840. p. MBC; MH. 40-195

The amiable Louisa. New York: The American Tract Society [184-?] 17 p. OO. 40-196

The Amorous Intrigues and Adventures of Aaron Burr. New York: published for the Proprietors [184-?] 100 p. CSmH. 40-197

Amory, John H. Alnomuc: or, the golden rule, a tale of the sea. Boston, MA: James B. Dow, 1840. p. CtY; MdBP; PU; RPB; ViU. 40-198

Amory, John H. Old Ironside. The story of Shipwreck. Boston, MA: s. l., 1840. MB; MH. 40-199

The Amulet. A Christmas and New Year's or holiday present. With nine beautiful steel engravings. Boston, MA: Otis, Broaders and company [184-?] 3 p. ViU. 40-200

Amussat, Zulema, 1796-1856. Lectures on retention of urine, caused by strictures of the urethra, and on the diseases of the prostate. Edited by A. Petit. Translated from the French by James P. Jervey. Philadelphia, PA: Haswell, Barrington & Haswell, 1840. 103 p. CtY; ICJ; MdBJ; MoSW-M; NBMS; NhD. 40-201

Ancient Briton's Benefit Society. By-laws of the American Briton's Benefit Society of the city of Utica. Utica, NY: printed by R. W. Roberts, 1840. 13 p. NUt. 40-202

Andersen, Hans Christian. The sandhills of Jutland. Boston, MA: Ticknor and Fields, 1840. 267 p. NN. 40-203

Anderson, Alexander, 1794-1869. Speech of Mr. Anderson, of Tennessee, on the several motions to print the report of the militia committee of the Senate; and, also, the letter of details of the Secretary of War. Senate of the United States, June 10th and 16th, 1840. [Washington, DC: s. l., 1840] 16 p. CtY; MdHi; NNC. 40-204

Anderson, Charles, 1814-1895. An address. Delivered before the Society of Alumni of Miami University, at their anniversary, August 13th, 1840. Oxford, OH: Printed by John B. Peat, 1840. 37 p. CSmH; DU; MHi; OUr; PPPrHi. 40-205

Anderson, Christopher, 1782-1852. The family book. The genius and design of the domestic constitution, with its untransferable obligations and peculiar advantages. By Christopher Anderson. From the Edinburgh ed. New York: Robert Carter, 1840. 422 p. GDecCT. 40-206

Anderson, Rufus, 1796-1880. The Christian missionary desiring to be with Christ. A sermon preached at Westborough, Me., June 30, 1840, at the funeral of Rev. Ephrain Spaulding, a missionary of the American Board of Coms. for Foreign Missions. By Rufus Anderson, D. D. Boston, MA: Printed by Crocker & Brewster, 1840. 22 p. CtSoP; ICP; MH-AH; MWA; OO; RPB. 40-207

Anderson, Rufus, 1796-1880. The work of missions to be progressive; a sermon on the present crisis in the missionary operations of the American Board of Commissioners for Foreign Missions. Boston, MA: Crocker & Brewster, 1840. 22 p. IaDuU; MeHi; MH; OO; WHi. 40-208

Anderson, Rufus, 1796-1880. The work of missions to be progressive; a sermon. By Rufus Anderson... 2d ed. Boston, MA: Crocker & Brewster, 1840. 22 p. MWA; NjR; PHi. 40-209

Anderson, William, 1799-1873. An apology for millennial doctrine, in the form in which it was entertained by the primitive church... By William Anderson. Philadelphia, PA: Orrin Rogers, E. G. Dorsey, printer, 1840. 52 p. CBPSR; DLC; ICP; MWA; PPM. 40-210

Andover, Mass. First Universalist Church. The confession of faith and form of church government of the First Universalist Church in Andover. [Andover, MA?: J. N. Bang, printer, 1840] 8 p. MAnHi. 40-211

Andover Theological Seminary. Catalogue of the officers and students of the Theological Seminary, Andover, Mass., Jan., 1840. Andover, MA: Printed by Gould, Newman and Saxton, 1840. 11 p. MiD-B. 40-212

Andover Theological Seminary. Outline of the course of study pursued by the students of the Theological Seminary, Andover, in the Department of Christian Theology. With references to the principal books in the library pertaining to that department. For the use of the students. [Andover, MA: s. l., 1840] 48 p. IEG; MB; MH; NNUT. 40-213

Andrews, Ethan Allen, 1787-1858. First lessons in Latin; or, an introduction to Andrews and Stoddard's Latin grammar. Boston, MA: Crocker and Brewster, 1840. 216 p. InU; MH; MiU. 40-214

Andrews, Ethan Allen, 1787-1858. The first part of Jacobs and Doring's Latin reader: adapted to Andrews and Stoddard's Latin grammar. By Prof. E. A. Andrews. Fifth edition. Boston, MA: Crocker and Brewster, 1840. 266 p. MH; MiD; NN; NT; OMC. 40-215

Andrews, Ethan Allen, 1787-1858. A grammar of the Latin language. For the use of schools & colleges. 7th edition. Boston, MA: Crocker and Brewster, 1840. 323 p. MH; PPL; ScCliTO; ViU; WU. 40-216

Andrews, John C. Empire state quadrille, in which are introduced The Cracovienne, Rory O'Moore, O Jenny is my own love, Lady Frances & Jim a long Josey... [For the piano forte] New York: Hewett & Jacques [184-?] 6 p. MB. 40-217

Andrews, John C. Somebody's coming, but I'll not tell who. Sung with great applause by Miss Jane A. Andrews. Written, composed & dedicated to Miss Eveline Hayner, by John C. Andrews. [For piano & guitar] New York: Firth Pond & Co. [184-?] 5 p. ViU. 40-218

Andrews, John C. The Trojan grand march & quick step. Composed by John C. Andrews. Baltimore, MD: F. D. Benteen [184-?] 2 p. ViU. 40-219

Andrews, Landaf F. W. The salvation of the world; or, Christianity and Universalism identified in a discourse. By L. F. W. Andrews. Philadelphia, PA: Printed by John H. Gihon and Co., 1840. 16 p. PPM. 40-220

Andrews, Landaf F. W. Speech on the sub-treasury bill. In the House of Representatives [of the United States] June 25, 1840. Washington, DC: printed by Hales & Seaton, 1840. 13 p. M. 40-221

Andrews, Silas Milton. The Sabbath at home. By the Rev. Silas M. Andrews. Philadelphia, PA: Presbyterian Board of Publication, 1840. 18 p. CtHC; MeBat; NjP. 40-222

Andrews, William. Introduction and variations to the air "The Swiss Boy." Philadelphia, PA: G. Willig, 184-? 25 p. NN. 40-223

Andry, Felix, b. 1808. Manual of diagnosis of diseases of the heart. Translated by Samuel Kneeland. Boston, MA: s. l., 1840. PPHa; PPULC. 40-224

Anecdotes and characteristics of Napoleon Bonaparte. Tr. and comp. from writings of Napoleon himself, and from the memoirs and military works of Bourrienne, Las Cases... &c. By an American. Philadelphia, PA; New York: C. F. Stollmeyer, 1840. 102 p. CtY; MBBC; OCl; PLFM; PU. 40-225

Anecdotes for the family and the social circle. Selected for the American Tract Society. New York: The Society [184-?]

406 p. CU; DLC; MH; TxDaM; ViU. 40-226

Anecdotes of the emperor Napoleon and his times. From the most approved French authorities. Edited by an American. Buffalo, NY: A. W. Wilgus, 1840. 252 p. MNan; NNUT; NStC; PLF. 40-227

Angell, Joseph Kinnicut, 1794-1857. Law of watercourses. 4th ed. Boston, MA: s. l., 1840. p. PU-L. 40-228

Angell, Joseph Kinnicut, 1794-1857. A treatise on the law of private corporations aggregate. 2nd ed., rev., corrected & enl. Boston, MA: s. l., 1840. PPB; PPULC. 40-229

Angell, Joseph Kinnicut, 1794-1857. Treatise on the law of watercourses. With an appendix, containing forms of declaration. Rev. ed. Boston, MA: C. C. Little & J. Brown, 1840. 224, 31 p. DLC; PPULC; PU-L. 40-230

Angell, Joseph Kinnicut, 1794-1857. A treatise on the law of watercourses; with an appendix, containing forms of declaration, etc. By Joseph K. Angell. Third edition. Revised and containing references to many new adjudged cases. Boston, MA: Charles C. Little and James Brown, 1840. 224, 31 p. GAWW; MH-L; NIC-L; RHi; TU. 40-231

Angell, Oliver, 1787-1858. Angell's union, no. 3; or, child's third book. Being the third of a series of spelling & reading books in 6 numbers. 11th ed. Philadelphia, PA: Marshall, Williams & Butler, 1840. 206 p. MH; TxU-T; ViU. 40-232

Angell, Oliver, 1787-1858. Angell's union series. The union, number two; or,

child's second book. Being the second of a series of spelling and reading books, in six numbers. By Oliver Angell, A. M. Eleventh edition. Philadelphia, PA: Marshall, Williams & Butler, 1840. 136 p. NNC; PReaHi. 40-233

Angell, Oliver, 1787-1858. The select reader, or union, no. 6. Designed for the higher classes in academies and schools. Being the sixth of a series of common school classes. Philadelphia, PA: Marshall, Williams & Butler, 1840. 504 p. DLC; PV; ViU. 40-234

Angell, Oliver, 1787-1858. The select reader, or union no. 6... sixth of a series of common school classics. By Oliver Angell, A. M. Revised stereotype edition. Philadelphia, PA: Marshall, Williams & Butler, 1840. 504 p. ICBB; ICU; MH; PSC-Hi. 40-235

Angell, Oliver, 1787-1858. The union no. i-vi... By Oliver Angell. Revised stereotype edition. Philadelphia, PA: Marshall, Williams & Butler, 1840. v. ICU. 40-236

Angell, Oliver, 1787-1858. The union, no. 4; containing lessons for reading and spelling... Revised stereotype ed. Philadelphia, PA: Marshall, Williams & Butler, 1840. 252 p. MH; MHolliHi; PPe-Schw. 40-237

Anguera, J. de. Slighted love, A song [S. or T.] ... With an accompaniment for the piano forte or guitar... Boston, MA: Bradlee [1841] 3 p. MB. 40-238

The Annualette, a Christmas and New Year's gift for children. Boston, MA: Samuel G. Simpkins, 1840. 137 p. ICN; ICU; MH; MWA; RPB. 40-239

Answer of the Whig members of the legislature of Massachusetts, constituting a majority of both branches, to the address of His Excellency Marcus Morton. Delivered in the convention of the two houses, January 22, 1840. Boston, MA: Printed by Perkins & Marvin, 1840. 36 p. CtY; ICMe; MBC; OClWHi; WHi. 40-240

Anthon, Charles, 1797-1867. First Latin lessons, containing the most important parts of the grammar of the Latin language, together with appropriate exercises in the translating and writing of Latin, for the use of beginners. By Charles Anthon. New York: Harper and Brothers [1840] 367 p. IBloW; NjPT; OO; ScCMu; TxU-T. 40-241

Anthon, Charles, 1797-1867. A grammar of the Greek language. For the use of schools and colleges. New York: Harper & Brothers, 1840. 284 p. MH; NNC; ODaV; TBriK. 40-242

Anthony, Darius. The substance of a sermon, delivered in the Methodist Episcopal church, in Fayetteville, Onondaga Co., N. Y., on Sabbath evening, March 16th, 1840; also on another occasion. By Rev. Darius Anthony. Cazenovia, NY: gPr. at the Union Herald office, 1840. 16 p. NNUT. 40-243

Anti-slavery hymns. New York: Anti-slavery office, 1840? 18 p. IU; NBuG. 40-244

Apostolic Fathers. English. Doane. The rector's Christmas offering to the parishioners of St. Mary's church, 1840; Poly-carp, Ignatius, Clement; apostolical fathers. Burlington, NJ: J. L. Powell, 1840. 2 v. in 1. NNG. 40-245

An appeal to the American people: being an account of the persecutions of the Church of Latter Day Saints; and the Barbarities Inflicted on them by the Inhabitants of the state of Missouri. By Authority of said church. Second edition, revised. Cincinnati, OH: Printed by Shepard & Stearns, 1840. 60 p. CtY; PCC; PPULC. 40-246

Appeal to the citizens of Philadelphia against the city councils. Philadelphia, PA: s. l., 1840? 11 p. NN. 40-247

Appeal to the democratic electors of the county of Lewis, who, with the undersigned, supported the election of Gen. Jackson & Martin Van Buren. [Lewis Co., NY: n. p., 1840] 16 p. ViU. 40-248

Appleton's dictionary of machines, mechanic's engine-work, and engineering. Illustrated with four thousand engravings on wood. In two volumes. New York: D. Appleton and company, 1840. 2 v. MdBLC. 40-249

Apuntamientos para la introduccion a las ciencias morales y politicas. Por un joven Americano. New York: Imprenta de Don Juan de la Granja, 1840. 151 p. MdBS-P. 40-250

The Arabian Nights Entertainment. Consisting of One Thousand and One Stories. Told by the Sultaness of the Indies, to divert the Sultan from the execution of a bloody vow he had made to marry a lady every day and have her put to death the next morning, to avenge himself for the disloyalty of his first Sultaness. Boston, MA: Printed and published by Charles Gaylord, 1840. 2 v. ICBB. 40-251

The Arabian Nights Entertainment. Consisting of One Thousand and One Stories. Told by the Sultaness of the Indies, to divert the Sultan... Translated from the Arabian MSS. In two volumes. Ninth American from the 18th English edition. Exeter, NH: published by J. and B. Williams, 1840. 2 v. NNS. 40-252

The Arabian Nights Entertainment. Embellished with nearly one hundred engravings. Complete in one volume. New edition. Philadelphia, PA: s. l., 1840. 518 p. MHi. 40-253

Archbold, John Frederick, 1785-1870. Archbold's summary of the law relative to pleading & evidence in criminal cases; with the statutes, precedents of indictments, &c. & the evidence necessary to support them. By John Jervis. 4th American from the 7th London ed., enl. with the decisions to the present time. New York: Gould, Banks, & Co. [etc., etc.] 1840. 701 p. Ct; CU-Law; IaU-L; N-L; WaU. 40-254

Archbold, John Frederick, 1785-1870. Pleading and evidence in criminal cases. With precedents of indictments, &c. and the evidence necessary to support them. By John Jervis. 4th American from the 7th London ed. New York: s. l., 1840. 701 p. MH-L. 40-255

Archer, Thomas. Asmodeus, or the little devil's share. A drama in two acts. New York: S. French [184-?] 32 p. MH; OU. 40-256

The Argus, Albany. Argus extra, January, 1840. Governor Seward's message, its misrepresentations and perversions exposed. Albany, NY: The Argus, 1840. 20 p. NN. 40-257

Arkansas. General Assembly. Journals of the 3d session of the General Assembly of the State of Arkansas... Little Rock, AR: s. l., 1840. 542, 52 p. ArL. 40-258

Arkansas. General Assembly. Report on the Judiciary. Report of the committee on the Judiciary in relation to the title of the State of Arkansas to the lots on which the publish buildings are situate; and also the memorial of Wm. Russell, of St. Louis County, Mo.; to the General Assembly of the State of Arkansas. [Little Rock, AR: s. l., 1840] 30 p. MoSHi; PPL. 40-259

Arkansas. Laws, statutes, etc. Acts passed at the third session of the General Assembly of the State of Arkansas, which was begun and held at the capitol, in the City of Little Rock, on Monday, the second day of November, one thousand eight hundred and forty; and ended on Monday, the twenty-eighth day of December, one thousand eight hundred and forty. Published by authority. Little Rock, AR: George H. Burnett, 1840. 176 p. A-SC; DLC; MiU-L; Or-SC; RPL. 40-260

Arkansas. Real Estate Bank. Revised rules and regulations, adopted by the Central Board of the Real Estate Bank of Arkansas, at their meeting in May, 1840. In force from May 15, 1840; together with the charter, and other laws relating to the bank, a list of stockholder, &c., &c., &c. Printed in pursuance of the orders of the said board, for the use of the stockholders, officers, &c. Little Rock, AR: Printed by Stone & McCurdy, 1840. 72 p. LNSCR. 40-261

Arkansas. Supreme Court. Reports of the cases argued and determined in the

Supreme Court of the State of Arkansas... V. 1-183; 1837-1831. Little Rock, AR: s. l., 1840-1925. 183 v. CSfBar; MnU; NIC-L. 40-262

Armistead, Jesse S. The work of the Holy Spirit on the hearts of men. By the Rev. Jesse S. Armistead. Philadelphia, PA: Presbyterian Board of Publication [184-?] 16 p. GDecCT. 40-263

Armstrong, John, 1758-1843. Notices of the war of 1812. By John Armstrong... New York: Wiley & Putnam, 1840. 2 v. CSmH; NjN; OHi; PPi; Vi. 40-264

Armstrong, John, 1758-1843. A treatise on agriculture, comprising a concise history of its origin and progress; the present condition of the art abroad and at home; and the theory and practice of husbandry. To which is added, a dissertation on the kitchen and fruit garden. By John Armstrong. With notes by J. Buel. New York: Harper and brothers, 1840. 282 p. CU; NbOM; NGlc; OClW; P. 40-265

Armstrong, William. The aristocracy of New York: who they are and what they were; being a social and business history of the city for many years. By an Old Resident. New York: s. l., 184-? 32 p. MHi. 40-266

Arnell, James Morrison, 1808-1850. Sensibility not piety; a sermon delivered at the funeral of Mrs. Mary Ann Looney, wife of Col. David Looney, of Columbus, Tenn., July 18, 1840. Columbus, TN: s. l., 1840. 16 p. MWiW; T. 40-267

Arnold, Dr. The way-worn traveller. An admired duett. Sung by Mrs. Burke & Mr. Jefferson with abounded applause in the Moutaineers. Composed by Dr. Arnold. Philadelphia, PA: G. Willig [184-?] 2 p. ViU. 40-268

Arnold, Samuel George, 1806-1891. The life of George Washington, first President of the United States... Revised by the editors. New York: Published by T. Mason and G. Lane, 1840. 228 p. MB; MoS; NjMD; OClWHi; PHi. 40-269

Arnold, Samuel George, 1806-1891. Memoir of Hannah More. With brief notices of her work, contemporaries, etc. By S. G. Arnold. New York: Carlton & Porter, 1840. 184 p. CoU; DLC. 40-270

Arnold, Thomas, 1795-1842. The history of Rome. By Thomas Arnold, D. D., Late Regius Professor of Modern History in the University of Oxford, Head Master of Rugby School, and Member of the Archeological Society of Rome. Three volumes in one. Reprinted entire from the last London edition. New York: D. Appleton & Co., 1840. 670 p. IP; ViNew. 40-271

Arnoult, E. For sale: New Metz, Dr. E. Arnoult's late residence and farm on the banks of the Ohio River... 16 miles to Louisville. New York: Printed by Lesueur & Co., 1840. 14 p. CSmH; MB; MHi; NN. 40-272

Around the world; a narrative of a voyage in the East India squadron, under Commodore George C. Read. By an officer of the U. S. Navy... New York; Boston, MA: C. S. Francis; J. H. Francis, 1840. 2 v. KWiU; MBAt; MPiB; Nh-Hi; RPAt. 40-273

Arthur, John M. Address delivered to the Union literary society of Miami University at its fifteenth anniversary,

August 12, 1840. By Rev. J. M. Arthur, A. M. Oxford, OH: Printed by John B. Peat, 1840. 25 p. OUr. 40-274

Articles of Agreement for the publication of "Barnaby Rudge" between Charles Dickens and Richard Burtby. [S. l.: s. l., 1840] MH. 40-275

Artists' & Amateurs' Association for the Encouragement of the Arts of Design, Philadelphia. Catalogue of exhibition. Philadelphia, PA: s. l., 1840. PHi; PPAmP; PPULC. 40-276

Artists' Fund Society of Philadelphia. Fifth exhibition catalog. Philadelphia, PA: s. l., 1840. p. OCHP. 40-277

Aschenback, L. Ashland duetts. A collection of six waltzes and two gallopades. Respectfully dedicated to the ladies of the United States. Arranged for two performers on the piano forte by L. Aschenback. Baltimore, MD: George Willig, Junr. [184-?] 11 p. ViU. 40-278

Asher & Adams new topographical atlas and gazetteer of New York. Comprising a topographical view of the several counties of the state. Together with a railroad map, geological and metosological maps, and alphabetical gazeteer, giving a concise description and location of Cities, villages, post offices, railroad stations, landings, &c., including a Fine Copper Plate Railroad Map of the United States and territories, Drawn on the Polyconic Projection, expressly for this work. Compiled from the latest Astronomical Observations, Official Surveys and Records of the United States and territories, as well as from counties, towns, and personal observations. Engraved on copper plate and lithographed from original drawings. New York; Indianapolis, IN: Asher & Adams; Asher, Adams and Higgins [1840] 79 p. No Loc. 40-279

Aspin, Jehoshaphat. Picture of the world; or, a description of the manners, customs, and costumes of all nations. New and enlarged edition. Hartford, CT: P. Canfield, 1840. 256 p. DSI; MWA; NcD; OCl; WHi. 40-280

Associate Presbyterian Church of North America. The book of disciples of the Associate Pres. Ch. of N. A. Philadelphia, PA: Young, 1840. 90 p. PPPrHi; PPULC. 40-281

Associate Reformed Synod of New York. History, catalogue and arrangements of the Theological Seminary of the Associate Ref. synod of N. Y., at Newburgh... address of the Rev. J. McCarrell, D. D. Newburgh, NY: Spalding, 1840. p. PPPrHi. 40-282

Association of American Geologists and Naturalists. Abstract of the proceedings. V. 1-6, 1840-1845. Boston, MA: s. l., 1840-45. 6 v. PPAN; PU; PPWa. 40-283

Association of American Geologists and Naturalists. Reports of the... meetings, embracing its proceedings and transactions. V. 1-3, 1840-1842. Boston, MA: s. l., 1840-42. 3 v. MCM. 40-284

Association of Friends for Promoting the Abolition of Slavery. Report on the conditionof the people of British India. S. l.: s. l., 1840. 1 p. PHi; PPULC. 40-285

Association of the Defenders of Baltimore in 1814. Constitution and report. S. l.: s. l., 1841? 12 p. MdHi. 40-286

An astronomical diary... farmer's almanac for the year 1841... By Thomas Spofford. Boston, MA: n. pr., n. pub. [1840] 36 p. MWA; NjR. 40-287

An astronomical diary... the farmers' almanac for the year 1841. Calculated for New York... By Thomas Spofford. New York: David Felt & Co., n. pr. [1840] 36 p. NjR. 40-288

Atherley, Edmond Gibson. A practical treatise of the law of marriage and other family settlements. By Edmond Gibson Atherley, Esq., Philadelphia, PA; New York: John S. Littell; Halsted and Voorhies, 1840. 315, 226 p. Ct; IaU-L; LNL-L; MoU; NbCrD; PP. 40-289

Atherton, Charles Gordon, 1804-1853. Speech in the House of Representatives, May 27th, 1840, in Committee of the Whole on the state of the Union, on the bill to provide for the collection, safekeeping, transfer, and disbursement of the public revenue. Washington, DC: s. l., 1840. 16 p. DLC; IU; MdHi; MWA; ViU. 40-290

Atherton, Charles Gordon, 1804-1853. Speech of Mr. Atherton, of New Hampshire, on the general appropriation bill. Delivered in Committee of the Whole on the state of the Union, in the House of Representatives, Monday, April 23 and 24, 1840. Washington, DC: printed at the Globe Office, 1840. 15 p. CtY; IU; MH; Nh; MiU-C. 40-291

Atlantic and St. Lawrence Rail Road. Specification of the manner of grading or forming the road-bed of the Atlantic & St. Lawrence R. R. [Portland, ME: s. l., 184-?] MB. 40-292

Atlantic Dock Company, Brooklyn. Prospectus of the Atlantic Dock Company, New York, August 1st, 1840. New York: s. l., 1840. 16 p. NBLiHi; MHi. 40-293

Attention! The people!! A. Lincoln, esq'r., of Sangamon County, one of the electoral candidated, will address the people this evening!! at early candlelighting, at the old court room. [Riley's building] ... Thursday, April 9th, 1840. [Alton, IL: s. l., 1840] p. CSmH. 40-294

Attention!!! Pioneer Fire Company! You are hereby notified to attend the regular monthly meeting of said company at the Engine House, This Day at 4 o'clock P. M. J. H. Alexander, Sec'y., Monday, May 11, 1840. S. l.: s. l., 1840. p. ICHi. 40-295

Atwater, Caleb. The military fame of Gen. Wm. Henry Harrison acquired in the battles of Tippecanoe, Fort Meigs and the Thames. Cincinnati, OH: s. l., 1840. 16 p. MB. 40-296

Atwood, Anthony, 1801-1888. A manual of Christian baptism; or, the nature, subjects, and mode of this divine ordinance pointed out and defended. Philadelphia, PA: s. l., 1840. 226 p. MoFuWc; PCC; PPM; WaPS; WHi. 40-297

Auber, Daniel Francois Espirit, 1782-1871. [L'ambassadrice] Sultan Misapouf. "C'est en vain. "From the opera L'ambassdrice. Music by D. F. Auber. [Avec accompagnement de piano. Paroles de Scribe et Vernoy de Saint George] Boston, MA: Reed [184-?] 10 p. MB. 40-298

Auber, Daniel Francois Espirit, 1782-

1871. L'Aragonaise valse. Chantee par Mme. Damoureau & Melle. Calve dans l'opera Le domino noir. Musique de D. F. E. Auber. Philadelphia, PA; New York: A. Fiot; W. Dubois [184-?] 2 p. ViU. 40-299

Auber, Daniel Francois Espirit, 1782-1871. La Bayadere Waltz; or, The White sulphur Spring Waltz. For the piano forte. Music by Auber. Baltimore, MD: F. D. Benteen [184-?] 2 p. ViU. 40-300

Auber, Daniel Francois Espirit, 1782-1871. Cavatina brillante le Sultan Misapouf de l'opera L' Ambassadrice Chantee par Mademoiselle Calve et Madame Cinti Damorean. Musique d'-Auber... Philadelphia, PA: George Willig [184-?] 9 p. DLC; PPCI; PPULC; ViU. 40-301

Auber, Daniel Francois Espirit, 1782-1871. Come o'er the moonlit sea. Duett [A. A.] The accompaniment arranged for the Spanish guitar by Francis Weiland. Philadelphia, PA: Willig [184-?] 4 p. MB. 40-302

Auber, Daniel Francois Espirit, 1871. Dark eye'd one. Sung by Mr. Horn. Written by J. R. Planche. Music by Auber. Baltimore, MD: F. D. Benteen [184-?] 2 p. ViU. 40-303

Auber, Daniel Francois Espirit, 1782-1871. Fra-Diavolo, or, The inn of Terracina. A comic opera in three acts. Composed by Auber. Written and the music adapted by Rophino Lacy... Philadelphia, PA; New York: Turner & Fisher [1840?] 64 p. CtY; NN. 40-304

Auber, Daniel Francois Espirit, 1782-1871. [Fra Diavolo] 'Tis tomorrow, or

Oui, c'est demain. The favorite song... in the opera of Fra Diavolo. By Auber. [The words by Scribe. With accompaniment for piano forte] Philadelphia, PA: George Willia [184-?] 6 p. MB. 40-305

Auber, Daniel Francois Espirit, 1782-1871. Galop favori. Sur des motifs de l'-Opera D'Auber Les diamans de la Couronne par F. Burgmuller. Philadelphia, PA; New York: A. Fiot; W. Dubois [184-?] 3 p. ViU. 40-306

Auber, Daniel Francois Espirit, 1782-1871. Garde a vous. The admired song from the opera of La Fiancee. The poetry by I. R. Planche, Esq'r. The music by Auber. Adapted to the English state by T. Cooke, director of music at the Theatre Royal Drury Lane. New York: Firth & Hall [184-?] 3 p. ViU. 40-307

Auber, Daniel Francois Espirit, 1782-1871. Gustave ou le bal masque. Air favori de l'opera d'Auber, Gustave. Arrange pour le piano par Duvernoy. Boston, MA: Reed [184-?] 2 p. MB. 40-308

Auber, Daniel Francois Espirit, 1782-1871. ... Hence discontent waltz... Philadelphia, PA: A. Fiot [184-?] 5 p. ViU. 40-309

Auber, Daniel Francois Espirit, 1782-1871. Mansaniello. Auber's celebrated overture to Masaniello... Arranged for the piano forte, with an accompaniment for the flute [ad lib] by J. F. Burrowes. New York: Mesier [184-?] 10, 3 p. MB. 40-310

Auber, Daniel Francois Espirit, 1782-1871. Mansaniello. Behold! how brightly breaks the morning... the celebrated barcarolle. The music by D. F. E. Auber. Words by Scribe and Dalavigne. [With accompaniment for the piano forte] 4th ed. New York: Hewitt [184-?] 6 p. MB. 40-311

Auber, Daniel Francois Espirit, 1782-1871. March from Masaniello. Arranged by Chaulieu. New York: Dubois & S. [184-?] 2 p. MB. 40-312

Auber, Daniel Francois Espirit, 1782-1871. Melange sur des motifs de Fra Diavolo de D. F. E. Auber. Pour le piano forte par Adolphe Adam. Philadelphia, PA: Kretschmar & Nunns [184-?] 14 p. ViU. 40-313

Auber, Daniel Francois Espirit, 1782-1871. My sister dear. Sung by Mr. Sinclair in the opera of Masaniello. Composed by Auber. New York; Philadelphia, PA: s. l. [184-?] 2 p. ViU. 40-314

Auber, Daniel Francois Espirit, 1782-1871. Overture, of the celebrated opera, Fra Diavolo. Composed by D. F. E. Auber. Arranged for the piano forte by Ch. Rummel. Philadelphia, PA: Geo. Willig [184-?] 11 p. ViU. 40-315

Auber, Daniel Francois Espirit, 1782-1871. Overture to the favorite opera of Masaniello. For the piano forte. Composed by Al. F. E. Auber. New York: published by Hewitt & Jaques [184-?] 10 p. WHi. 40-316

Auber, Daniel Francois Espirit, 1782-1871. La Parisienne. Auber's Heroic air... La Parisienne... Arranged for one or two performers on the piano forte by Chas. Arnold. New York: Mesier [184-?] 3 p. MB. 40-317

Auber, Daniel Francois Espirit, 1782-1871. La Parisienne, marche nationale.

Paroles de Casimir Delavigne. [With piano forte accomp.] New York: Bourne [184-?] 3 p. MB. 40-318

Auber, Daniel Francois Espirit, 1782-1871. La Parisienne, marche nationale. Variation characteristiques pour le piano forte. Philadelphia, PA: Krestschmar & Nunns [184-?] 15, 2 p. MB. 40-319

Auber, Daniel Francois Espirit, 1782-1871. Quadrilles & waltz from the opera of L'ambassadrice. Arranged for the piano forte by Adelaide De V. New York: Hewitt & Jaques [184-?] 7 p. MB. 40-320

Auber, Daniel Francois Espirit, 1782-1871. Valse de mignonette. Sur un motif d' Auber. Composee & dediee a Madlle. Mary Moore par Henry Knecht. Baltimore, MD: F. D. Benteen [184-?] 2 p. ViU. 40-321

Auber, Daniel Francois Espirit, 1782-1871. When morning's light is gently breaking. Barcarole [T.] in Masaniello. Boston, MA: Ashton [184-?] 4 p. MB. 40-322

Auber, Daniel Francois Espirit, 1782-1871. Young Agnes beauteous flower. Serenade. In Auber's celebrated opera of Fra Diavolo. Sung by Mr. Wilson. Arranged by R. Lacy. Philadelphia, PA: Geo. Willig [184-?] 3 p. ViU. 40-323

Auber, Daniel Francois Espirit, 1782-1871. Zanette; a grand overture performed with repturous applause at Niblo's garden. Composed and arranged for the piano forte. New York: published by Firth & Hall [184-?] 11 p. MB; WHi. 40-324

Auber and Weiland, F. The set of fashionable quadrilles, from Auber's celebrated opera of Gustavus the third, or the masked ball, as danced at Biblos and Charrauds assemblies. Arranged for the piano forte. New York: published by Hewitt and Jaques, 1840. p. MBNEC. 40-325

Auburn Academy. Annual catalogue of the Trustees, Instructors & Students of the Auburn Academy, for th year ending February 17th, 1840. Auburn, NY: Printed by Allen and Lounsbury, 1840. 12 p. N. 40-326

Auburn Theological Seminary. Catalogue of the officers and students in the Theological Seminary, at Auburn [N. Y.] 1839-40. Auburn, NY: Printed by Miller and Stow, 1840. 8 p. MBC; N; NAuT. 40-327

Audubon, John James, 1785-1851. The birds of America, from drawings made in the United States and their territories... New York; Philadelphia, PA: J. J. Audubon; J. B. Chevalier, 1840-44. 7 v. CSmH; MnU; PPAmP; WaS; WHi. 40-328

Augusta, Me. South Congregational Church. Report of a committee to the Congregational Church in the South Parish, Augusta, Me., Feb., 1840. Augusta, ME: Severance & Dorr, printers, 1840. 14 p. CSmH; MH. 40-329

Augusta Gallopade. [For the piano forte] [Boston, MA: Prentiss, 184-?] 1 p. MB. 40-330

Auld Robin Gray, with recitative & vocal embellishments, as sung with the greatest applause by Mrs. French. New

York: published by W. Dubois [184-?] 4 p. WHi. 40-331

Austin, John Mather, 1805-1880. Review of Miller's destruction of the world. Boston, MA: s. l., 1840. p. PPL; PPULC. 40-332

Austin, John Mather, 1805-1880. A voice to youth, addressed to young men and young ladies. By Rev. J. M. Austin. 4th ed. Utica, NY: Grosh and Hutchinson, 1840. 424 p. DLC. 40-333

Austin, Stephen Fuller, 1793-1836. General Austin's map of Texas with part of the adjoining states. Compiled by Stephen F. Austin. Philadelphia, PA: H. H. Tanner, 1840. p. TxU. 40-334

Austin Lyceum, Austin, Tx. Constitution abd by-laws of the Austin Lyceum, instituted February 12, 1840. Austin, TX: Printed at the Gazette office, 1840. 22 p. TxU. 40-335

Ein Auszug bes Pilgers Reise... New Berlin, PA: C. Hammer, 1840. 93 p. PReaAT. 40-336

Authentic view of the Bar Room in the Log Cabin, Broadway, New York, headquarters of the 14th Ward Tippecanoe Club. S. l.: s. l. [1840] p. MHi. 40-337

Auxiliary Bible Society in Worcester County. Report of the Auxiliary Bible Society, in Worcester County. With an account of the annual meeting, held in Worcester, Nov. 4, 1840. Worcester: Lewis Metcalf, printer, 1840. 16 p. MWA. 40-338

Awful calamities; or, The shipwrecks of December, 1839, being a full account of the dreadful hurricanes of Dec. 15, 21 and 27 on the coast of Massachusetts... and also the dreadful disaster at Gloucester. Boston, MA: Press of Howe, 1840. 24 p. IaDaP; LNH; MBC; MWA; NNA. 40-339

Awful calamities; or, The shipwrecks of December, 1839... on the coast of Massachusetts; in which were lost more than 90 vessels, and nearly 200 dismasted, driven ashore or otherwide damaged, and more than 150 lives destroyed... 2nd ed. Boston, MA: Press of J. Howe, 1840. 24 p. MH; MiD-B. 40-340

Awful calamities; or, The shipwrecks of December, 1839, being a full account of the dreadful hurricanes of Dec. 15, 21 & 27 on the coast of Massachusetts... 3d ed. Boston, MA: Press of J. Howe, 1840. 24 p. MMal; MNF; MWA; N; NjP. 40-341

Awful calamities; or, The shipwrecks of December, 1839, being a full account of the dreadful hurricanes of Dec. 15, 21 & 27 on the coast of Massachusetts... 4th ed. Boston, MA: Press of J. Howe, 1840. 24 p. Ct; MSo; NN; RWe. 40-342

Awful calamities; or, The shipwrecks of December, 1839, being a full account of the dreadful hurricanes of Dec. 15, 21 & 27, on the coast of Massachusetts... comprising also a particular relation of the shipwreck of the following vessels: Barque Lloyd, brigs Pocahontas, Rideout and J. Palmer, and sons. Deposite, Catharine Nichols and Miller. And also the dreadful disasters at Gloucester. 5th

ed. Boston, MA: Press of J. Howe, 1840. 24 p. DLC; M; NNUT. 40-343

Awful calamities; or, The shipwrecks of December, 1839, being a full account of the dreadful hurricanes of Dec. 15, 21 & 27, on the coast of Massachusetts... and also the dreadful disasters at Gloucester. 6th ed. Boston, MA: Press of J. Howe, 1840. 24 p. MWo; MWA. 40-344

Awful calamities; or, The shipwrecks of December, 1839... on the coast of Massachusetts... 7th ed. Boston, MA: J. Howe, 1840. 24 p. PHi; WHi. 40-345

Awful carflagration of the strains beat Lexington in L. I. Sound, Jan. 13, 1840, about 140 persons lost their lives... Boston, MA: Moore, 1840. p. MB. 40-346

Aykroyd, J. The American and New Orleans favorite waltzes. For the piano forte. Philadelphia, PA: Blake [184-?] 2 p. MB. 40-347

Aylesworth, Sylvester, 1789-1857. A register of the Aylesworth family, beginning with Arthur... through the male line... to the seventh generation, by Sylvester Aylesworth, of the fifth generation... Utica, NY: Bennett, Backus & Hawley, 1840. 12 p. DLC; MBNEH. 40-348

Ayling, Thomas. The Victoria quadrilles. For the piano forte. New York: The Author [184-?] 7 p. MB. 40-349

B

Bacon, Henry. The Christian comforter; a gift for the afflicted & bereaved, by Henry Bacon. Boston, MA: Able Tompkins, 1840. 216 p. MBUGG; MHoly; MMeT-Hi; MsOK; OTU. 40-350

Bacon, Leonard, 1802-1881. An appeal to the Congregational ministers of Connecticut against a division. With an appendix, containing short notes on Mr. Calhoun's letters. By Leonard Bacon... New Haven, CT: B. L. Hamlen, 1840. 144 p. CSmH; IaDuU; MH-AH; PHi; RPB. 40-351

Bacon, Leonard, 1802-1881. The goodly heritage of Connecticut. A discourse in the First Church in New Haven, on Thanksgiving Day, Nov. 19, 1840. By Leonard Bacon... New Haven, CT: printed by B. L. Hamlen, 1840. 24 p. Ct; MAnP; MWA; NjR; PPPrHi. 40-352

Bacon, Leonard, 1802-1881. Seven letters to the Rev. George A. Calhoun, concerning the Pastoral union of Connecticut & its charges against the ministers & churches. New Haven, CT: Hamlen, 1840. 131 p. CSmH; IaDuU; MWA; OClW; PPPrHi. 40-353

Bacon, Leonard, 1802-1881. Views and reviews, no. 1-11, January & May, 1840... New Haven, CT: Durrie, 1840. 2 v. CtHT; MB; MH-AH; MWA. 40-354

Bacon, William Thompson. Poems, by William Thompson Bacon. 3d ed. Boston, MA: Weeks, Jordon & Co., 1840. 214 p. CtY; MH; MPiB; Nh. 40-355

Badger, George Edmund, 1795-1866. Speech delivered at the great Whig meeting in the county of Granville, on Tuesday, the third day of March, 1840. Raleigh, NC: Register, 1840. 24 p. DLC; NcU; PHi; Vi. 40-356

Bagioli, Antonio. Il lablro sincero Arietta. [Con accompanimento di piano.] New York: Bagiolo [184-?] 5 p. MB. 40-357

Bailey, Ebenezer. First lessons in algebra... easy introduction to that science... for academies and common schools. By Ebenezer Bailey. Boston, MA: Jenks & Palmer, 1840. 252 p. MeHi; MH; MiU; OMC; NPV. 40-358

Bailey, J. T. An historical sketch of the city of Brooklyn, and the surrounding neighborhood, including the village of Williamsburgh, and the towns of Bushwick, Flatbush, Flatlands, New Utrecht and Gravesend... account of the battle of Long Island. Brooklyn, NY: Pub. by the author, 1840. 72 p. CSmH; ICU; MiU-C; NjR; PPM. 40-359

Baines, Peter Augustine, Bp. The substance of a discourse, delivered at Bradford, England, by the Rt. Rev. Dr. Baines, Bishop of Siga. Baltimore, MD: published by the Catholic Tract Society,

1840. 24 p. DLC; MdBLC; MdBS; Md-CatS; MdW; MWo; NNF. 40-360

Baines, Rev. Faith of the Catholic Church unchanged and unchangeable, shown from the very form of her institution. Extract of a letter of the Rt. Rev. Dr. Baines. Baltimore, MD: Published by the Catholic Tract Society, Nurphy, printer, 1840. 24 p. Md-B; MdBLC; NNG. 40-361

Baker, Conrad. An address, delivered before the members of the Phrenakosmian Society of Pennsylvania College, at the celebration of their ninth anniversary, Feb. 21, 1840. Gettysburg, PA: printed by H. C. Neinstedt, 1840. 21 p. DLC; InU; MiD-L; NCH; OSW; PPL. 40-362

Baker, I. State House Boston. New York: s. l. [184-?] p. MB. 40-363

Balch, William S. A manual for Sunday schools, to which is added a collection of hymns. By Wm. S. Balch. 2nd edition. Boston, MA: A. Tompkins, 1840. 144 p. ICMe; In; MdBS; MMeT-Hi. 40-364

Balestier, Joseph Neree. Annals of Chicago; a lecture delivered before the Chicago Lyceum, Jan. 21, 1840. [With notes] Chicago, IL: Edward H. Rudd, 1840. 24 p. ICHi; MB; MBAt; MH; NN. 40-365

Balfe, Michael William. The music of the Bohemian Girl, consisting of six songs and three pieces. New York; Philadelphia, PA: s. l. [184-?] 15 p. MH. 40-366

Balfe, Michael William. Then you'll remember me. A ballad in the opera of

The Bohemian girl. Composed by M. W. Balfe. Philadelphia, PA; New York: A. Fiot; W. Dubois [184-?] 4 p. ViU. 40-367

Balfe, Michael William. Then you'll remember me. From the opera of The Bohemian girl. Composed by M. W. Balfe. Louisville, KY; Cincinnati, OH; Baltimore, MD: D. P. Faulds & Co.; Peters, Field & Co.; W. C. Peters & Co. [184-?] 2 p. ViU. 40-368

Ballantine, Elisha, 1809-1886. Address delivered in the chapel of the Ohio University, on Christmas day, 1839... Professor of the Greek language and literature, and teacher of Hebrew, French, and German. Athens, OH: printed by A. Van Vorhes, 1840. 16 p. NjPT; OHi; OWervO. 40-369

Ballantine, Elisha, 1809-1886. Literary character of the Bible; an address delivered before the literary societies of Marietta college... at the annual commencement, Aug. 29th, 1840. Marietta, OH: printer Isaac Maxon, 1840. 19 p. CSmH; ICP; OClWHi; OMC; PPPrHi. 40-370

Ballard, Joseph. A sermon... in Lowell, on the Sabbath following the funeral of Alvah Mansur, Esq., who died... Nov. 1, 1840... Lowell, MA: Leonard Huntress, printer, 1840. 12 p. MH; MiD-B; MW. 40-371

Ballou, Hosea, 1771-1852. A review of some of Professor Stuart's arguments in defence of Endless Misery, published in the American Biblical Repository, July, 1840. By Hosea Ballou, pastor of the second Universalist Society in Boston. Boston, MA: A. Tomkins... [J. N. Bang, pr.] 1840. 72 p. IGK; MB; MBUPH; MMeT-Hi; NCas. 40-372

Ballou, Hosea, 1771-1852. A series of lecture sermons, delivered at the Second Universalist meeting in Boston. By Hosea Ballou... Revised by the author. Third edition... Utica, NY: Orren Hutchinson, 1840. 375 p. IaMp; MH; MMeT-Hi; OHi; PPM. 40-373

Baltimore. The Church of the Lord Jesus Christ. The Church of the Lord Jesus Christ worshipping in North Street, Baltimore, to all the brethren to whom this communication may come. Baltimore, MD: Printed by Samuel Sands, 1840. 23 p. MdHi. 40-374

Baltimore. First Presbyterian Church. Historical discourse... First Presbyterian Congregation. Boston, MA: s. l., 1840. PPL. 40-375

Baltimore. Harrison Association of Baltimore. Constitution and by-laws of the Harrison Associatin of Baltimore. Instituted April, 1840. Baltimore, MD: Printed by Jos. Robinson, 1840. 14 p. MdHi. 40-376

Baltimore Directory for 1840-1; containing in addition to a register of all the householders, a variety of business cards; a list of streets, lanes, wharves, alleys &c. &c. and [or without an engraved plan of the city.] Baltimore, MD: Baltimore Directory Office, 1840? 374 p. MdBLC; MdBB. 40-377

Baltimore [Ecclesiastical province] Council(1837) Pastoral letter of the most reverend the Archbishop of Baltimore, and the right reverend, The Bishops of the Roman Catholic Church, in the United States of America; asembled in provincial council in the City of Baltimore, in the month of May, 1840, to the clergy and laity of their charge. Baltimore, MD: Fielding Lucas, Jr., 1840. 27 p. DLC; MdBLC; MdHi; PPL. 40-378

Baltimore Mercantile Library Association. The first annual report of the board of directors of the Mercantile Library Association, November, 1840. Baltimore, MD: Printed by John Murphy, 1840. 13 p. MB; MdHi; ScHi. 40-379

Bancroft, George, 1800-1891. Address at Hartford, before the delegates to the Democratic convention of the Young Men of Connecticut, on the evening of February 18, 1840, by George Bancroft. Puboished in conformity to a vote of the Convention. [Hartford, CT: s. l., 1840] 16 p. CtSoP; MiD-B; MWA; PHi; WHi. 40-380

Bangor, Me. Theological Seminary. Catalogue of the Theological Seminary, Bangor, Maine, 1839-40. Bangor, ME: S. S. Smith, printer, 1840. 12 p. MeB. 40-381

Bangs, Nathan, 1778-1862. Centenary sermon, New York, October 25, 1839, on the one hundredth year of Methodism. New York: Harper & Brothers, 1840. 26 p. PHi; RPB. 40-382

Bangs, Nathan, 1778-1862. An original Church of Christ; or, a scriptural vindication of the orders and powers of the ministry of the Methodist Episcopal Church, by Nathan Bangs, D. D. Second edition, revised. New York: published by T. Mason and G. Lane, 1840. 388 p. ArCH; CoDI; GEU-T; OBerB; WaTC. 40-383

Bank of Louisville, Louisville, Ky. Correspondence between the President and Directors of Mother Bank of the Bank of Kentucky and the Branch at Maysville, touching the removal of $100, 000 of the Capital of the Branch at the City of Maysville. [Frankfort, KY: s. l., 1840] 49 p. WHi. 40-384

Bank of Maine. List of stockholders in the banks of Maine... Augusta, ME: Wm. R. Smith & Co., printers to the State, 1840. 102 p. MeHi; MeLewB; MeU. 40-385

Bank of the State of Alabama. Reports of the commissioners and of the president and cashier of the bank of the state of Alabama, together with the various documents referred to in said report. Tuscaloosa: Hale & Phelan, 1840. 23 p. GEU. 40-386

Bank of the State of Alabama, Mobile. Liabilities of the president and directors and members of the General Assembly to the bank of the State of Alabama, November 9th, 1840. Also, a statement of the amount paid to valueless sixteenth sessions. Tuscaloosa, AL: Hale & Phelan, 1840. 7 p. GEU. 40-387

Bank of the State of Alabama, Mobile. Report of the president of the branch of the Bank of the State of Alabama. Together with the accompanying documents referred to in said report. Tuscaloosa, AL: Hale & Phelan, 1840. 18 p. GEU. 40-388

Bank of the United States. General statement of the Bank of the United States, its agencies, &c. Read in the House of Representatives, Feb. 18, 1840.

Harrisburg, PA: Holbrook, Henlock & Bratton, printers, 1840. 1 p. P. 40-389

Bank of Virginia. By-laws of the Bank of Virginia. To which are appended the act establishing general regulations for the incorporation of banks and subsequent acts respecting the banks of this Commonwealth. Richmond, VA: Printed by Shepherd and Colin, 1840. 71 p. Vi. 40-390

Banks, John, 1793-1864. Address delivered before the Franklin and Washington literary societies of Lafayette college, by Hon. John Banks. Easton, PA: Printed by Hetrich & Maxwell, 1840. 24 p. DLC; MnSM; NjPT; PHi; PU. 40-391

Baptist almanac for 1841. Philadelphia, PA: American Baptist Publication and S. School Society [1840] p. MWA. 40-392

Baptists. Alabama. Choctaw Association. Minutes of the second anniversary meeting of the Choctaw Baptist Association, held with the Gainsville Church, September 18, 19, and 21, 1840. Livingston, Ala., Printed at the office of the "Voice of Sumpter. "1840. 11 p. MoSM. 40-393

Baptists. Alabama. Mulberry Association. Minutes of the thirteenth annual session of the Mulberry Baptist Association, begun and held with the Chesnut Creek Church, Autauga County, Alabama, September 26-29, 1840. Wetumpka: Printed at the Argus Office, 1840. 8 p. NHC-S. 40-394

Baptists. Connecticut. Ashford Association. Minutes of the sixteenth anniversary of the Ashford Baptist

Association, held with the Baptist Church in Mansfield, Conn., May 27 and 28, 184?. Hartford: Walter S. Williams, printer, 1840. 15 p. NCH-S; PCA. 40-395

Baptists. Connecticut. Hartford Association. Minutes of the fifty-first anniversary of the Hartford Baptist Association, held with the Second Baptist Church. Hartford: Burr & Williams, printer, 1840. 11 p. Ct; NHC-S. 40-396

Baptists. Connecticut. New London Association. Minutes of the New London Baptist Association, held with the Baptist church in New London, Ct. September 30 and October 1, 1840. New London: Printed by Ebenezer Williams, 1840. 16 p. NHC-S; PCA. 40-397

Baptists. Connecticut. State Convention. Seventeenth annual meeting of the Connecticut Baptist Convention, held at Essex, June, 1840. Hartford: Burr & Williams, printer, 1840. 42 p. CtHWatk; PCA. 40-398

Baptists. Connecticut. Stonington Union Association. Minutes of the twenty-third anniversary of the Stonington Union Association, held at Preston, June 17 and 18, 1840. New London: Printed by Ebenezer Williams, [1840?] 11 p. CBB; NHC-S; PCA; RWe. 40-399

Baptists. Georgia. Convention. Minutes of the nineteenth anniversary of the Georgia Baptist convention, held at Penfield, Greene County, Georgia, on May 1, 2 and 4, 1840. Washington, Ga.: Printed by M. J. Kappel, 1840. 23 p. ICU; NcD; PCA. 40-400

Baptists. Georgia. Ebenezer Association. Minutes of the Primitive Ebenezer

Association, held with the Mount Olive Church in Wilkinson County, Georgia, commencing September 26, 1840. Milledgeville: Park and Rogers, printers, 1840. 8 p. PCA. 40-401

Baptists. Georgia. Edisto Association. Minutes of the Edisto Baptist Association, at its sixth anniversary. Augusta: Brown and M'Cafferty, 1840. 15 p. DLC. 40-402

Baptists. Georgia. Ellijay Association. Minutes. [S. l.: s. l., 1840-] v. PCA. 40-403

Baptists. Georgia. Georgia Association. Minutes of the Georgia Baptist Association, held at Bethesda, Greene County, Georgia, on October 16, 17 and 19, 1840. Washington, Ga.: Printed at the Christian Index office 1840. 14 p. NHC-S. 40-404

Baptists. Georgia. Ocmulgee Association. Minutes of the Ocmulgee Baptist Association, convened with the Hebron Church, Jasper County, Georgia, from September 12-15, 1840. [Milledgeville: Grantland? 1840] 8 p. PCA. 40-405

Baptists. Georgia. Upatoie Association. Minutes of the Upatoie Association, held with the Mount Paron Church, Muscogee County, Ga., September 12, 13 and 14, 1840. Columbus, Ga., 1840. 4 p. PCA. 40-406

Baptists. Illinois. Blue River Association. Minutes of the eighth annual meeting of the Blue River Association of United Baptists, held at the Perry Church, Pike County, Illinois, August 21 and days following, 1840. Winchester, Ill: S. A. Adams, printer, 1841 8 p. ISB; NHC-S. 40-407

Baptists. Illinois. Colored Association. Minutes [2] ... Alton Church, Madison County. August 21-24 [1840] Alton: Parks Job Office, 184?. 8 p. ISB. 40-408

Baptists. Illinois. Edwardsville Association. Minutes of the twelfth annual meeting of the Edwardsville Baptist Association, held with the Baptist Church, Hillsborough, Montgomery County, Illinois, May 21, 22 and 23, 1841. Louisville: Printed by J. Eliot & Co. 184?. 8 p. MHi; NHC-S; PCA. 40-409

Baptists. Illinois. Illinois Convention. Minutes of the fifth annual meeting of the Illinois Baptist Convention, held at Bloomington... October 10-14, 1839; with the report of the executive committe. Belleville, Ill.: Printed at the Mercury Office, 1840. 30 p. IaIS; ICU; NHC-S; PCA; PPEB. 40-410

Baptists. Illinois. North District Association. Minutes of the twelfth annual meeting of the North Distrcit Baptist Association Frends to Humanity, held with the White Hall Church, Greene County, Illinois, September 11, and days following. Alton: Printed at Parks' Job Office, 1840. 7 p. IaIS; NHC-S; NRCR-S. 40-411

Baptists. Illinois. Rock River Association. Minutes of the anniversary. Rockford, 1840-1888. 48 v. in 3 v. IRo; PCA. 40-412

Baptists. Illinois. Second Colored Association. Minutes of the Second Colored Baptist Association, and friends of Harmony, Held with Alton Church, Madison County, Ill., August 21, 22, 23, 24, 1840. Alton: Printed at Parks' Job Office, 1840. 8 p. IRo; PCA. 40-413

Baptists. Illinois. South District Association. Minutes... September 18, 1840. Belleville: Advocate Office, 1840. Baptists. Illinois. Illinois River Association. Fifth annual session of the Illinois River Baptist Association, held in the Baptist meeting house, in Lowell, LaSalle County, September 18, 19 and 20, 1840. Ottawa: Weaver & Hise, printers, 1840. 16 p. NHC-S. 40-414

Baptists. Indiana. Curry's Prairie Association. Minutes of the seventh annual meeting at First Priarie Creek Church, Middletown, Vigo County, Ia., September 11, 12, and 13, 1841. Mount Carmel, Ill.: W. D. Latshaw, printer, 1840. 4 p. NHC-S. 40-415

Baptists. Indiana. General Association. Proceedings of the eighth anniversary of the General Association of Baptists in Indiana. Held at the Baptist meeting House in Greencastle, October 1, 2 and 3, 1840. Franklin, Ind.: Printed by J. R. Kerr, 1840. 20 p. ICU; In; OClWHi; PCA. 40-416

Baptists. Iowa. Des Moines River Association. Minutes of the convention, met to form the Des Moines River Association of Regular Baptists, held with the Little Cedar Church, in Van Buren County, I. T. June 6, 7 and 8, 1840. Burlington: Printed by James G. Edwards, 1840. 8 p. IAIB. 40-417

Baptists. Kentucky. General Association. Minutes of the... of the Kentucky Foreign Bible Society, and of the Roberts Fund and China Mission Society. Louisville, 1840. 60 p. CSmH; MHi. 40-418

Baptists. Kentucky. Long Run Association of Baptists. Minutes of the Thirty-seventh annual meeting of the Long Run Association of Baptists, Brashear, Creek, Ky., September, 1840. Louisville, Ky., 1840. 8 p. MHi. 40-419

Baptists. Maine. Barnstable Association. Minutes of the Barnstable Baptist Association, held with the church in Brewster, August 12 & 13, 1840. Yarmouth: Printed by W. S. Fisher & Company, 1840. 15 p. PCA. 40-420

Baptists. Maine. Bowdoinham Association. Minutes of the fifty-fourth anniversary of the Bowdoinham Association, holden at Litchfield, September 22, 23 and 24, 1840. Hallowell: Glazier, Masters and Smith, 1840. 10 p. PCA. 40-421

Baptists. Maine. Cumberland Association. Minutes of the twenty-ninth anniversary of the Cumberland Baptist Association, held in... Freeport, Me. 1840. Portland: Charles Day and Company, Printers, 1840. 13 p. MeB; MeHi; PCA. 40-422

Baptists. Maine. Penobscot Association. Minutes of the Penobscot Baaptist Association, held in the Baptist meeting house, Charlseston, September 15, 16 and 17, 1840. Hallowell: Glazier, Masters and Smith, 1841. 8 p. MeBa; PCA. 40-423

Baptists. Maryland. Baltimore Association. Minutes of the Baltimore Association... Held by appointment at the Baptist meeting house of the Second Baptist Church, Baltimore, Md., May 15, 16 and 17, 1840. Washington: P. Force, printer, 1840. 13 p. MdHi. 40-424

Baptists. Maryland. Maryland Baptists Union Association. Minutes of the fifth meeting of the Maryland Baptist Union Association. Held in the Baptist Meeting House, Pikesville, Md., October 22d and 23d, 1840. Baltimore, MD: Richard J. Matchett, printer, 1840. 16 p. PCA; ViRu. 40-425

Baptists. Massachusetts. Baptist Conventtion. Thirty-eighth report of the Massachusetts Baptist convention, presented by the board of directors at Boston, May 23, 1840. Boston: William D. Ticknor, 1840. 26 p. MBevHi. 40-426

Baptists. Massachusetts. Berkshire County Association. Minutes of the thirtenth anniversary of the Berkshire Baptist Associaton, held in the Baptist Church, Lanesborough, October 14 and 15, 1840. Pittsfield: Printed by Phineas Allen and son, 1840. 8 p. MPiB; PCA. 40-427

Baptists. Massachusetts. Boston Association. The twenty-ninth anniversary of the Boston Baptist Association, held in the meeting house of the Baptist church in Watertown, September 16 & 17, 1840. Boston: Press of Putnam & Hewes, 1840. 22 p. LNB; MiD-B; PCA. 40-428

Baptists. Massachusetts. Franklin County Association. Minutes of the Franklin County Baptist Association, held at the Baptist meeting house in Deerfield, Mass., September 9 and 10, 1840. Greenfield: Phelps & Ingersoll, 1840. 8 p. PCA. 40-429

Baptists. Massachusetts. Salem Association. Minutes of the thirteenth anniversary of the Salem Baptist

Associaton, held in the Worthen Street Baptist Meeting House, in Lowell, September 23 & 24, 1840. Lowell: Leonard Huntress, printer, 1840. 24 p. TxFwSB. 40-430

Baptists. Massachusetts. Taunton Association. The fifth session of the Taunton Baptist Associaton, held in the meeting house of the First Baptist Church in Swansea, August 26 and 27, 1840. Providence: H. H. Brown, Printer, 1840. 24 p. MoSM. 40-431

Baptists. Massachusetts. Worcester Association. Minutes of the Sabbath schoool teachers convention held at Grafton, Mass., October 13, 1840. Worcester, printed by Spooner and Howland, 1840. 12 p. MiD-B. 40-432

Baptists. Massachusetts. Worcester Association. Minutes of the Worcester Baptist Association, held with the Baptist church in Westborough, August 20 & 21, 1840. Worcester: Printed by Spooner & Howland, 1840. 24 p. MiD-B; MNtcA; PCA. 40-433

Baptists. Mississippi. Mississippi Association. Minutes of the thirty-third anniversary of the Mississippi Baptist Association, held with the Ebenezar Church, Amite County, Mississippi, October 3, 4, and 5th, 1840. Liberty, Ms: Printed by Tothill and Eisely, 1840. 15 p. MoLiWJ. 40-434

Baptists. Mississippi. Mississippi Association. Proceedings of the fourth annual meeting of the convention of the Baptist denomination of the state of Mississippi, held in Wahalak, Kemper County, Mississippi, May 1840. New Orleans:

Printed at the Bulletin office, 1840. 28 p. MoSM; NRAB. 40-435

Baptists. Mississippi. Pearl River Association. Minutes of the twenty-first annual meeting of the Pearl River Baptist Association; convened at Hebron, Lawrence County, Mississippi on September 12, 13 and 14. 1840. NHC-S. 40-436

Baptists. Mississippi. Pearl River Association. Minutes of the twenty-first annual meeting of the Pearl River Baptist Association, convened at Hebron, Lawrence County, Mississippi, on September 12, 13, and 14, 1841. Monticello: M. H. Smith, Printer, 1840. 13 p. NHC-S. 40-437

Baptists. Mississippi. State Convention. Proceedings of the fourth annual meeting of the convention of the Baptist demonination of the state of Mississippi, held in Wahalak, Kemper County, Mississippi, May 1840. New Orleans: Printed at the Bulletin Office, 1840. 28 p. LNB; NHC_S; NRAB. 40-438

Baptists. Mississippi. Union Baptist Association. Minutes of the Union Baptist Association, held at County Line Church, Copiah County, Mississippi, October 10, 11, and 12, 1840. Raymond: King & North, printers, 1840. 14 p. MoSM. 40-439

Baptists. Missouri. Blue River Association. Minutes of the Blue River Association of United Baptists held at the high point meeting house, Johnson County, Missouri on the third Saturday in September, 1840 and two succeeding days. Independence: Printed at the Chronicle office, 1840. 3 p. MoLiWJ. 40-440

Baptists. New York. Buffalo Association. Minutes of the twenty-fifth anniversary of the Buffalo [formerly Holland Purchase] Baptist Association, held with the Springville Church, in Springville on September 9 and 10, 1840. Lodi: Printed by Edwin Hough, 1840. 16 p. NHC-S; PCA. 40-441

Baptists. New York. Education Society. Twenty-third annual meeting of the Baptist Education Society of the state of New York; held at Hamilton, August 18, 1840. Utica: Bennett, Backus & Hawley, 1840. 24 p. DLC; MWA; NRCR. 40-442

Baptists. New York. Fairfield County Association. Minutes of the third session of the Fairfield County Baptist Association, held with the Second Baptist church in Danbury, Conn. October 14 and 15, 1840. New York: Robert Sears, printer, 1840. 16 p. NHC-S. 40-443

Baptists. New York. Mohawk Baptist Association. Minutes. [S. l.: s. l., 1840-] v. PCA. 40-444

Baptists. New York. Monroe Association. Minutes of the thirteenth anniversary of the Monroe Baptist Association, held in the Chapel of the Baptist church in Wheatland, September 30 and October 1, 1840. Rochester: Printed by Shepard & Strong, 1840. 16 p. NRC-R. 40-445

Baptists. North Carolina. Three Forks Baptist Association. Minutes. [S. l.: s. l., 1840-] v. PCA. 40-446

Baptists. Ohio. Cleveland or Rocky River Association. Minutes of the ninth anniversary of the Rocky River Baptist Association, convened at Richfield,

Summit County, Ohio, June 17, 18, 1840. Cleveland: F. B. Peniman, printer, 1840. 16 p. CSmH; OClWHi. 40-447

Baptists. Ohio. Columbus Association. Minutes of the twenty-second anniversary... held with the McKean Church, in Licking County, O., on September 9 and 10, 1840. [Colophon]: Printed at the Olentangy gazette office, [1840] 15 p. CSmH; KyLoS; PCA. 40-448

Baptists. Ohio. Geouga Association. Minutes of the sixth anniversary of the Geouga Baptist Association, convened at the Baptist meeting house of Mentor and Willoughby Plains, Lake County, Ohio, on June 10 and 11, 1840. Chardon, Ohio: Printed by Joseph W. White, 1840. 8 p. OClWHi; PCA. 40-449

Baptists. Ohio. Huron Association. Minutes of the nineteenth anniversary of the Huron Baptist Association, held with the church in Norwalk, Huron County, Ohio, July 1 & 2, 1840. Norwalk, Ohio: S. & C. A. Preston, Printers, 1840. 14 p. OClWHi. 40-450

Baptists. Ohio. Lorain Association. Minutes of the second anniversary of the Lorain Baptist Association, held with the Church in Avon, June 24 & 25, 1840. Elyrn, Ohio: Charles Chaney, Printer, 1840. 12 p. OClWHi. 40-451

Baptists. Ohio. Mad River Association. Minutes of the twenty-eighth anniversary of the Mad River Baptist Association, held with the Myrletree Church, September 18, 19, & 20, 1840. Springfield: Gallagher and Halsey, 1840. 12 p. CSmH; NN; PCA. 40-452

Baptists. Ohio. Maumee River Association. Minutes of the sixth anniversary of the Sandusky River Baptist Association, held with the Second Church in Reed, Seneca County, Ohio, September 16 & 17, 1840. Tiffin, Ohio: H. Cronise and Company, printers, 1840. 7 p. OClWHi. 40-453

Baptists. Ohio. Miami Association. Minutes of the Miami Association of Regular Baptists, held with the Baptist Church at Middletown, September 9, 10, 1840. Lebanon: Printed at the office of the Western Star, 1840. 8 p. OClWHi; PCA. 40-454

Baptists. Ohio. Portage Association. Minutes of the Portage Baptist Association, held with the church in Bedford, September 30 & October 1, 1840. Ravenna, Ohio, 1840. 11 p. OClWHi. 40-455

Baptists. Ohio. Salem Association. Minutes of the Salem Baptist Association, held at Graham's station, September 26, 27, and 28, 1840. Gallipolis: Printed by William Nash, 1840. 4 p. OClWHi. 40-456

Baptists. Ohio. Scioto Assocaition. Minutes of the Scioto Baptist Association, held with the Walnut Creek Church, Baltimore, September 26 and 28, 1840. Lancaster: Printed by C. H. Brough, 1840. 8 p. OClWHi; PCA. 40-457

Baptists. Ohio. Trumbull Association. Minutes of the first anniversary of the Trumbull Baptist Association, held at the Baptist meeting house in Hubbard, October 16 & 17, 1840. Warren, Ohio: Printed at the Job office by J. Palm, 1840. 8 p. OCLWHi. 40-458

Baptists. Ohio. Wooster Association.

Minutes of the first anniversary of the Wooster Regular Baptist Association, held in the meeting house of the Baptist Church, Massillon, O. September 23 & 24, 1840. Wooster: Printed by Milller and Carpenter, 1840. 15 p. CSmH; MoSM; OClWHi. 40-459

Baptists. Ohio. Wooster Association. Minutes of the 1st-8th anniversary of the Wooster Baptist Association. Wooster: Printed by Milller and Carpenter, 1840-1847. 2 v. CSmH. 40-460

Baptists. Ohio. Zoar Regular Association. Minutes of the fourteenth anniversary of the Zoar Regular Baptist Association, holden with the Harmony Church, Monroe County, Ohio. September 4, 5, 6, and 7, 1840. St. Clairsville, Ohio: Printed by Heaton and Gressinger, 1840. 15 p. MoSM. 40-461

Baptists. Pennsylvania. Monongahela Association. Minutes of the eigth anniversary of the Monongahela Baptist Association, held with the Forks Cheat Church, Monongahela County, Va., September 13, 14, 15, 1840. Mount Pleasant, Pa.: S. Siegfried, printer, 1840. 12 p. PCA. 40-462

Baptists. Pennsylvania. Philadelphia Association. Minutes of the one hundred thirty-third anniversary of the Philadelphia Baptist Association, held by appointment in the meeting house of the Spruce Street Church, Philadelphia, October 6, 7, 8, 1840. Philadelphia: King and Baird, printer, 1840. 32 p. PCA. 40-463

Baptists. Rhode Island. Warren Association. Minutes of the Warren Baptist Association, held with the Pine Street Baptist Church in Providence, on

Sepember 9 and 10, 1840. Providence: H.
H. Brown, printer, 1840. 16 p. DLC;
NRAB; RHi; RWe. 40-464

Baptists. Tennessee. Nolachucky Association. Proceedings of the thirteenth
anniversary of the Nolachucky Association, convened at Buffalo Creek meeting
house, Grainger County, Tenn., on September, 1840. [Knoxville, Tn: Jas. C.
Moses and Company, printers, 1840. 4 p.
NHC-S. 40-465

Baptists. Tennessee. State Convention.
Proceedings of the Baptist State Conven-
tion, held with the Baptist Church in
Nashville, October 9-13, 1840. Colum-
bia, Tn: A. Fuller, printer, 1840. 48 p.
MoSM; NHC-S. 40-466

Baptists. Texas. Union Association.
Minutes of the first session of the Union
Baptist Association, begun and held in
the town of Travis, in Western Texas, October 8, 1840. Houston: Telegraph Press,
1840. 16 p. TxFwSB. 40-467

Baptists. Vermont. Addison County Association. Minutes of the seventh anniversary of the Addison County Baptist
Association, held at Whiting, September
23 & 24, 1840. Brandon, Vermont:
Telegraph Print., 1840. 7 p. PCA. 40-468

Baptists. Vermont. Vermont Association. The fifty-fifth anniversary of the
Vermont Baptist Association, held in the
Baptist meeting house in Hubbardton,
October 7 and 8, 1840. Brandon, Vermont: Telegraph Print. 1840. 8 p. PCA.
40-469

Baptists. Virginia. Albemerle Association. Minutes of the Albemarle Baptist
Association; held at Mount Moriah, M.

H. Amherst County, Va., on August 15,
16, 17, 1840. Richmond: Printed by William Sands, 1840. 8 p. ViRU. 40-470

Baptists. Virginia. Columbia Association. Minutes of the twenty-first annual
meeting of the Columbia Baptist Association; held by appointment. Zoar
meeting house, Fauquier County, Virginia. August 20, 21, and 22, 1840.
Fredericksburg: Printed at the Herald
office, 1840. [2] -3-16 p. ViRU. 40-471

Baptists. Virginia. Dan River Association. Minutes of the second session of the
Dan River Baptist Association; held with
the Clover Church on August 29, 30, and
31, 1840. Richmond: Printed by William
Sands, 1840. 16 p. NcU; ViRU. 40-472

Baptists. Virginia. General Association.
Proceedings of the seventeenth annual
meeting of the General Association of
Virginia held at the First Baptist Church,
Richmomd, Va., June 5-8, 1840. [n. p.,
1840] 28 p. ViRU. 40-473

Baptists. Virginia. Grand Lodge.
Proceedings of a grand annual communication of the Grand Lodge of Virginia, begun and held in the Mason's hall,
in the city of Richmond, December 14,
1840. Richmond: Printed by John Warrock, 1840. 31 p. NNFM; OCM. 40-474

Baptists. Virginia. Salem Union Baptist
Association. Minutes of the Salem Uion
Baptist Association, held by appoint-
ment with Front Royal Church, Warren
County, Virginia. Richmond: Printed by
William Sands at the Religious Herald,
1840. 24 p. ViRu. 40-475

Baptists. Virginia. Shiloh Baptist Association. Annual minutes of the Shiloh

Baptist Association, held with the church at Mount Lebanon, Rappahannock County, Va., on September, 1840. Richmond: Printed by William Sands at the Herald Office, 1840. 24 p. ViRu. 40-476

Baptists. Virginia. Virginia Portsmouth Association. Minutes of the fiftieth session of the Virginia Portsmouth Baptist Association, held at High Hills Meeting House, Sussex County, May 20, 21, and 22, 1840. Portsmouth: Printed at the office of the Old Dominion, 1840. 16 p. ICU; PCA; ViRU. 40-477

Baptists. Wisconsin Territory, Central Association. Minutes of the second anniversary of the Central Baptist Association of Wisconsin, held at Southport, September 30, and October 1, 1840. Southport: C. Latham Sholes, Printer, 1840. 8 p. NcU; ViRU. 40-478

Barber, John Warner, 1798-1885. Historical collections; being a general collection of interesting facts, traditions, relating to the history and antiquities of every town in Massachusetts, with geographical descriptions, by John Warner Barber. Worcester, MA: Dorr, Howland & Co., 1840. 624 p. CSmH; MBev; MnDu; NNUT; TxH. 40-479

Barber, John Warner, 1798-1885. A history of the Amistad Captives: being a circumstantial account of the capture of the Spanish Schooner Amistad, by the Africans on board; their voyage, and capture near Long Island, New York; with biographical sketches of each of the surviving Africans. Also an account of the trials had on their case, before the District and Circuit Courts of the United States, for the District of Columbia. Compiled from authentic sources, by

John W. Barber, Mem. of the Connecticut Hist. Soc. New Haven, CT: Published by E. L. & J. W. Barber, Hitchcock & Stafford, printers, 1840. 32 p. DLC; MnHi; MWA; OClWHi; PHC. 40-480

Barcarolle waltz. Baltimore, MD: F. D. Benteen [184-?] 1 p. ViU. 40-481

Barker, Benjamin. Mornilva; or, the outlaw of the forest, a romance of "Lake" Wenham. Boston, MA: United States Publishing Co., 184-? 58 p. IaU. 40-482

Barnard, Charlotte. Maggie's welcome. [Song. Accomp. for piano forte] By Claribel [pseud, of C. Barnard] Boston, MA: Ditson & Co. [184-?] 5 p. MB. 40-483

Barnard, Daniel Dewey, 1797-1861. Speech of Mr. Barnard, of New York, against abandoning or suspending the prosecutions of works of internal improvements. Delivered in the House of Representatitves, February 14, 1840. Washington, DC: Gales & Seaton, 1840. 16 p. M; MB; MBAt; OClWHi. 40-484

Barnard, Daniel Dewey, 1797-1861. Speech of Mr. Barnard, of New York, on the sub-treasury bill. Delivered in the House of Representatives, being in committee of the whole on the State of the Union, June 12, 1840. Washington, DC: printed by Gales and Seaton, 1840. 22 p. M; MB; MWA. 40-485

Barnard, Daniel Dewey, 1797-1861. Speech of Mr. Barnard, of New York, on the treasury note bill. Delivered in the House of Representatives, being in committee of the whole, March 25, 1840. Washington, DC: printed by Gales and

Seaton, 1840. 16 p. DLC; IU; MB; MWA; RPB. 40-486

Barnard Memorial, Boston. Proceedings. Boston, MA: s. l., 1840-79. v. DLC; MH. 40-487

Barnes, Albert, 1798-1870. An oration on the progress and tendency of science. Delivered before the Connecticut Alpha Phi, Beta, Kappa, at New Haven, August 18, 1840. By Albert Barnes. Philadelphia, PA: Printed by I. Ashmead, 1840. 40 p. CtY; MHi; MWA; NNC; PHi. 40-488

Barnes, Albert, 1798-1870. A pastor's appeal to the youngster, the benefits of having been born in a Christian land & or being early educated to God. Philadelphia, PA: Perkins, 1840. 58 p. PPPrHi. 40-489

Barnes, Albert, 1798-1870. The progress and tendencies of science; an address delivered before the Diagnothian and Goethean Societies of Marshall College, at Mercersburg, Pa., September 29, 1840. By Albert Barnes. Philadelphia, PA: Printed by L. Ashmead, 1840. 40 p. CSmH; MH; NjR; OClWHi; PHi. 40-490

Barnett, John. Moonlight, music, love and flowers. A duet. Written by Harry Stae Van Dyk. Composed by John Barnett. Boston, MA: Parker & Ditson [184-?] 5 p. ViU. 40-491

Barns, William. A sermon on the greatness and government of God. By Rev. William Barns. Harrisburg, PA: printed by Barrett & Parke, 1840. 40 p. MMeT-Hi; NNUT; PHi; PPL-R. 40-492

Barringer, Daniel Moreau, 1807-1873. An address, delivered before the alumni and graduating class of the University of N. C., Wednesday, June 3, 1840. By Daniel M. Barringer, esq. Raleigh, NC: Printed at the office of the Raleigh Star, 1840. 26 p. DE; MoS; NN; NcD; NcWfC; WHi. 40-493

Barrow, John, 1764-1848. Description of Pitcairn's Island and its inhabitants, with an authentic account of the Mutiny of the ship, Bounty, and of the subsequent fortunes of the mutineers. New York: Harper & Brothers, 1840. 303 p. CtY; InRch; OAU; PPM; WM. 40-494

Barrow, John, 1764-1848. A memoir of the life of Peter the Great. New York: Harper & Brothers, 1840. 320 p. InRch; LNH; MeLewB; NjR; P. 40-495

Barry, A. C. A sermon, at the opening of the new Universalist church, in Homer, N. Y. By A. C. Barry. New York: Universalist Union Press, 1840. 16 p. MMeT-Hi. 40-496

Barthelemy, Peter. Rev. Anthony Verren, pastor of the French Episcopal Church of the Saint Espirit, at New York, judged by his works. New York: s. l., 1840. CSfCW; DLC; MBAt; MdBD; OC. 40-497

Bartlett and Welford, New York. Catalogue of a select collection of rare and curious old books, comprising a great variety of desirable and important works both English and foreign, suited for public or private libraries, including some modern editions and American works relating to the history and antiquities of this country. New York: printed by Robert Craighead, 1840. 58 p. InGrD; MHi; PPAmP; RPJCB. 40-498

Barton, Cyrus. ... Defence of Cyrus Barton, against the attacks of Hon. Isaac Hill upon the establishment of the New Hampshire Patriot and state gazette. [Concord, NH: s. l., 1840?] 16 p. CSmH; MB; MiD-B; MWA. 40-499

Bates, Elisha, 1780-1861. Doctrine of Friends: or, principles of religion held by the Society of Friends. 4th ed. Providence, RI: s. l., 1840. 320 p. DLC; ICU; MWA. 40-500

Bates, Stephen. Party and its experiments, a poem, delivered before the Harrison Democrats of East Boston, on Tuesday, Sept. 8, 1840, by Stephen Bates. Boston, MA: Weeks, Jordan & Company, 1840. 24 p. CtHT; DLC; MB; MWA; RPB. 40-501

Battle, William Horn. An address delivered before the Philomathesian and Euzelian Societies of Wake Forest College, June 18, 1840. By Wm. Horn Battle. Raleigh, NC: Printed at the office of the Raleigh Register, 1840. 16 p. NcD; NcWfC. 40-502

Battleborough waltz, and quickstep. Arranged for the piano forte. Baltimore, MD: F. D. Benteen [184-?] 2 p. ViU. 40-503

The batture [sic] question examined, by a member of the Louisiana bar. New Orleans, LA: F. Cook and A. Levy, 1840. 52 p. LNHT; OrSC; TxU. 40-504

Bauge, Francois George. A Progressive course of fencing... Baltimore, MD: W. Wooddy, 1840. 8 p. DLC. 40-505

Baugs & Co., New York. Catalogue...

valuable books... New York: Osborn, 1840. 16 p. PPAmP. 40-506

Baxter, George Addison, 1771-1841. Parity: the scriptural order of the Christian ministry. A sermon... By Rev. G. A. Baxter... Lynchburg: printed by Fletcher & Toler, 1840. 23 p. CSmH; NcMHi; NjR; PPPrHi. 40-507

Baxter, Richard, 1615-1691. Call to the unconverted. By Richard Baxter. New York: American Tract Society; D. Fanshaw, printer [1840] 144 p. NjP. 40-508

Baxter, Richard, 1615-1691. A call to the unconverted. New York: American Tract Society [1840?] 159 p. DLC. 40-509

Baxter, Richard, 1615-1691. A call to the unconverted, to which are added several valuable essays. By Richard Baxter. New York: Carter, 1840. 220 p. DLC; In. 40-510

Baxter, Richard, 1615-1691. Life and death of the Rev. Joseph Alleine... Written by the Rev. Richard Baxter, his widow, Mrs. Theodosia Alleine, and other persons. To which are added his Christian letters... with a recommendatory preface by Alexander Duff... From the last Edinburgh ed. New York: Robert Carter; [Sam'l. Adams, printer] 1840. 276 p. GDecCT; InCW; NjR; PPL-R; ScCoT. 40-511

Baxter, Richard, 1615-1691. The Saints' Everlasting rest. Abridged by Benjamin Fawcett. New York: American Tract Society [184-?] 540 p. CBPSR. 40-512

Baxter, Richard, 1615-1691. The Saints' Everlasting rest, by the Rev. Richard

Baxter. Abridged by Benjamin Fawcett, A. M. New York: published by the American Tract Society; Fanshaw, printer [184-?] 271 p. CSt; MH. 40-513

Baxter, Richard, 1615-1691. The Saints' Everlasting rest. By the Rev. Richard Baxter. Abridged by Benjamin Fawcett, A. M. New York: American Tract Society [184-?] 445 p. CtMW; DLC; FU; MiD-B; ViU. 40-514

Baxter, Richard, 1615-1691. The Saints' Everlasting rest: or, a treatise of the blessed state of the saints, etc., extracted from the works of Mr. Richard Baxter, by John Wesley, M. A. New York: pub. by T. Mason and G. Lane; J. Collord, printer, 1840. 333 p. MsJMC; ScOrC. 40-515

Baxter, Richard, 1615-1691. Tragywyddol orphwysfa y saint; neu draethawd ar wynfydedig gyflwr y saint yn y mwynhad o Dduw yn y nefoedd. New York: Gymdeithas draethodol Americanaidd [184-?] 431 p. CBPSR. 40-516

Bay State Democrat, July 1 - Dec. 31, 1840, 1842-44. Boston, MA: s. l., 1840-44. v. MBAt. 40-517

Bayard, James. A brief exposition of the Constitution of the United States. With an appendix containing the Declaration of Independence, and the Articles of Confederation, and a copious index. By James Bayard. 2d ed. Philadelphia, PA: Hogan & Thompson, 1840. 178 p. AU; CSmH; ICU; MeB; PPWa. 40-518

Bayard, James Asheton, 1799-1880. Addresses to the people of Delaware relative to General Harrison's opinion on abolition. Georgetown, DE: s. l., 1840. PPULC. 40-519

Bayard, Jean Francois ALfred, 1796-1853. The youthful queen; [or, Christine of Sweden. A comedy in two acts.] New York: French [184-?] 36 p. MB. 40-520

Bayard, Samuel, 1767-1840. Letters on the Sacrament, Lord's Supper. By Samuel Bayard, Esq., a ruling Elder in the Presbyterian church at Princeton, N. J. To which is added an appendix. Second edition, revised and improved. Philadelphia, PA: William L. Martien, 1840. 219 p. NcCJ; NN; OWoC; PPPrHi; ScCMu. 40-521

Bayard, Samuel John, d. 1879. A short history of the life and services of Gen. William Henry Harrison. Seneca Falls, NY: Fuller & Bloomer, printer, 1840] 20 p. DLC; MNH. 40-522

Bayle-Mouillard, Elizabeth Felicie (Conard), Mme., 1796-1865. The gentleman and lady's book of politeness and propriety of deportment, dedicated to the youth of both sexes. By Mme. Celnart. Translated from the sixth Paris edition, enlarged and improved. Fifth American edition. Philadelpia, PA: published by Griff & Elliot, 1840. 214 p. DLC; KPea. 40-523

Bayley, William. Balmy sweetness... Boston, MA: s. l. [184-?] 3 p. MB. 40-524

Bayley, William. The fable of the bees... New York: G. Vale, 1840. 8 p. NN. 40-525

Bayly, Thomas Haynes, 1797-1839. The Barrack Room. A Musical Burletta in

Two Acts. New York: s. l. [184-?] 32 p. MH. 40-526

Bayly, Thomas Haynes, 1797-1839. Comfortable service. An entirely original farce in one act. Philadelphia, PA: s. l. [184-?] 32 p. MB. 40-527

Bayly, Thomas Haynes, 1797-1839. Fly away, pretty moth. A ballad. New York: s. l. [184-?] 3 p. MB. 40-528

Bayly, Thomas Haynes, 1797-1839. Long, long ago. A ballad. Composed by Thos. H. Bayly, Esqr. New York: Firth & Hall [184-?] 2 p. ViU. 40-529

Bayly, Thomas Haynes, 1797-1839. Long, long ago. A ballad. Composed by Thos. H. Bayly, Esqr. Philadelphia, PA: Ld. Meignen & Co. [184-?] 2 p. MB; ViU. 40-530

Bayly, Thomas Haynes, 1797-1839. No! ne'er can thy home be mine. Duett. Written and adapted to a Canzonetta Fiorentina by T. H. Bayly, Esq.... Baltimore, MD: Frederick D. Benteen [184-?] 5 p. ViU. 40-531

Bayly, Thomas Haynes, 1797-1839. No! ne'er can thy home be mine. Duett. Written and adapted to a Canzonetta Fiorentina by T. H. Bayly, Esq.... Philadelphia, PA; Boston, MA; New York: J. E. Gould, successors to A. Fiot; Oliver Ditson and C. C. Clapp & Co.; Berry & Gordon [184-?] 5 p. ViU. 40-532

Bayly, Thomas Haynes, 1797-1839. No! ne'er can thy home be mine. Duett. Written and adapted to a Canzonetta Fiorentina by T. H. Bayly. Philadelphia, PA; New Orleans, LA: Lee & Walker; W. T. Mayo [184-?] 5 p. ViU. 40-533

Bayly, Thomas Haynes, 1797-1839. Oh, no I never shall forget. Song. New York: Atwill [184-?] 2 p. MB. 40-534

Bayly, Thomas Haynes, 1797-1839. Perfection, or the Cork Leg; a farce in one act. Oh, no I never shall forget. Song. New ed., revised and improved. New York: Atwill [184-?] 2 p. MH. 40-535

Bayly, Thomas Haynes, 1797-1839. ... Perfection; or, The maid of muster. A farce in one act. By Thoams Haynes Bayly. With the stage business, cast of characters, costumes, relative positions, etc. New York: S. French, [etc., etc., 184-?] 35 p. CSt; MH. 40-536

Bayly, Thomas Haynes, 1797-1839. The Swiss cottage, or, Why don't she marry? A musical burletta in two acts. New York; Philadelphia, PA: Turner and Fisher [184-?] 22 p. MH; NN. 40-537

Bayly, Thomas Haynes, 1797-1839. Tom Noddy's secret... Baltimore, MD: J. Robinson [Co.] 1840? 27 p. DLC; MH; RPB. 40-538

Bayly, Thomas Haynes, 1797-1839. Tom Noddy's secret. Philadelphia, PA: . l. [184-?] MB. 40-539

Bayly, Thomas Haynes, 1797-1839. Tom Noddy's secret; a farce in one act... New York: Samuel French [1840] 22 p. OCl. 40-540

Bear, James. The Christian minister's affectionate advice to a married couple... including a letter from the Rev. Henry Venn... New York: Amer. Tract Society [184-?] 96 p. NN. 40-541

Bear, John W., b. 1800. Speech of John

W. Baer, the Buckeye blacksmith, delivered at Easton, Monday, August 3, 1840. Easton, PA: Printed by A. H. Senseman, 1840. 8 p. CSmH; DLC; IaHi; PPL. 40-542

Beaumont, Francis, 1584-1616. ... The bridal. A tragedy in five acts. Adapted for representation [with three original scenes, written by James Sheridan Knowles, esq.] from the Maid's tragedy of Beaumont and Fletcher... New York: S. French & son, [etc., etc., 184-?] 67 p. CSt. 40-543

Beaumont, Francis, 1584-1616. The works of Beaumont and Fletcher. With an introduction by George Darley... New ed. New York; London: G. Routledge and sons [1840] v. MdBG. 40-544

Beaver Meadow Railroad and Coal Company. The act incorporating the Beaver Meadow Railroad and Coal Company, and the supplements thereto. February 20, 1833. Phildelphia, PA: C. A. Elliott, Pr., 1840. 24 p. PHi; PPM. 40-545

Bedford, G. S. A general introductory lecture to a course of lectures on popular anatomy and physiology, delivered... Nov. 25, by Dr. G. S. Bedford... [S. l.: J. Winchester, printer, 1840] 24 p. NNNAM. 40-546

Beebe, Roswell. Memorial of Roswell Beebe addressed to the General Assembly of the State of Arkansas. With an appendix. Little Rock, AR: Printed by G. H. Burnett, 1840. 336 p. Ar-Hi. 40-547

Beecher, Henry Ward, 1813-1887. An address delivered before the Platonean society of the Indiana Asbury University, September 15, 1840. By Henry Ward Beecher... Indianapolis, IN: printd by William Stacy, 1840. 28 p. InGDU; MWA; NNG. 40-548

Beene, Jesse. Letter of Jesse Beene, of Dallas, in defence of his course in the Democratic Convention, held in Tuscaloosa in December, 1839, and against the charges brought against him by the Whig meeting in Cahawba, on the 16th March, 1840. Cahawba: Printed by Stuart & Richardson, 1840. 16 p. OClWHi. 40-549

Beene, Jesse. Letters of Jesse Beene, in answer to invitations to become a candidate for governor. Cahawba: Printed by Richardson & Hardy, 1840. 8 p. A-Ar; TxU. 40-550

Beethoven, Ludwig, 1770-1827. Azalia, or Almack's waltz. Composed for the piano forte. Boston, MA: Ditson [184-?] 2 p. MB. 40-551

Beethoven, Ludwig, 1770-1827. Beethoven's dream; Grand Waltz. Composed for the piano forte. Baltimore, MD: F. D. Benteen [184-?] 2 p. ViU. 40-552

Beethoven, Ludwig, 1770-1827. Beethoven's last waltz; or, the celebrated Clara waltz. Baltimore, MD: F. D. Benteen [184-?] 2 p. MB; ViU. 40-553

Beethoven, Ludwig, 1770-1827. Beethoven's waltz. No. 3. New York: Atwill [184-?] 1 p. ViU. 40-554

Beethoven, Ludwig, 1770-1827. The bird let loose. The celebrated trio, as sung at the oratorios; the words by Thos. Moore, esq.; music by Beethoven. New

York: Firth & Hall [184-?] 3 p. ViU. 40-555

Beethoven, Ludwig, 1770-1827. The celebrated last, or Clara waltz. Arranged for the piano forte. Philadelphia, PA: Lee and Walker [184-?] 2 p. ViU. 40-556

Beethoven, Ludwig, 1770-1827. Grand waltz. Composed for the piano forte. New York: Torp [184-?] 2 p. MB. 40-557

Beethoven, Ludwig, 1770-1827. Rosalie. Cantata. Sung by Mr. Horn at the musical fund concert. Adapted by him to the celebrated Adelaida of Beethoven. New York: Dubois & Stodart [184-?] 8 p. ViU. 40-558

Beethoven, Ludwig, 1770-1827. Sonatas. Piano forte. Sonalten fur das Pianoforte. Sonatine. No. 30. Metronomised and fingered by Ch. Czerny. Boston, MA: Russell & Co. [184-?] 5 p. MB. 40-559

Beethoven, Ludwig, 1770-1827. ... Sonate pathetique. von L. Van Beethoven, Op. 13. New York?: s. l. [184-?] 18 p. CSmH. 40-560

Beethoven, Ludwig, 1770-1827. Songs: Music, love & wine. [Solo and chorus.] [Philadelphia, PA?: s. l. [184-?] 2 p. MB. 40-561

Beethoven, Ludwig, 1770-1827. Souvenir d'affection. Waltz. [For piano forte.] Boston, MA: Reed [184-?] 2 p. MB. 40-562

Beethoven, Ludwig, 1770-1827. Spirit waltz. Boston, MA: Oliver Diston [184-?] 1 p. MB; ViU. 40-563

Beethoven, Ludwig, 1770-1827. The spirit waltz. [For the piano forte.] Boston, MA: Reed [184-?] 1 p. MB. 40-564

Beginning to do good; the mehshowayoree society, written for the New England Sabbath School Union, and revised by the committee of publication. Boston, MA: New England S. S. Union, 1840. 72 p. No Loc. 40-565

Begone dull care. A celebrated trio [A cappella.] Boston, MA: Bradlee [184-?] 2 p. MB. 40-566

Beith, Alexander, 1799-1891. Sorrowing, yet rejoicing. New York: s. l., 1840. MB. 40-567

Beldeny, G. H. Letters to the people of the United States. Published semimonthly. In six series. From the 15th August to 1st November, 1840. By Concivis. New York: s. l., 1840. CtY; ICN; MBAt; MiD-B. 40-568

Beleke, Caspar J. A grammar of the German language, systematically arranged on a new plan, brief, comprehensive and practical. By Caspar J., Beleke. Philadelphia, PA: Geo. Mentz & Son, Publisher, 1840. 228 p. DLC; MiU; NjP; PPA; ViU. 40-569

Belknap, Jeremy, 1744-1798. American biography, by Jeremy Belknap, with addition and notes by F. M. Hubbard. In three volumes. New York: Harper & Brothers, 1840. 3 v. MiEM; N; Nh; OCl. 40-570

Bell, Charles, 1774-1842. The hand, its mechanism and vital endowments as ... design. New York: Harper, 1840. 213 p. DSG; ICJ; MH; MiD; NCH. 40-571

Bell, Charles, 1774-1842. ... Institutes of surgery: arranged in the order of the lectures delivered in the University of Edinburgh. By Sir C. Bell... Philadelphia, PA: A. Waldie, 1840. 446 p. ArU-M; CSt; MeB; PPA; TxU. 40-572

Bell, Fanny. Long, long ago! Arranged with variations for the piano forte by Fanny Bell. Boston, MA: Oliver Ditson [184-?] 5 p. ViU. 40-573

Bell, Henry Glassford, 1803-1874. Life of Mary Queen of Scots. By Henry Glassford Bell, esq. New York: Published by Harper & Brothers, 1840. 276 p. GEU; InRch; OAU; ScCoB; WU. 40-574

Bell, John, 1797-1869. Mr. Bell's suppressed report in relation to difficulties between the Eastern and Western Cherokee. Washington, DC: Gales & Seaton [1840] 23 p. DLC; NN; OkHi. 40-575

Bell, John, 1797-1869. Speech of Mr. Bell, of Tennessee, on the bill to secure the freedom of elections. Delivered in the House of Representatives April, 1840. Washington, DC: Gales & Seaton [1840] 39 p. CtY; MB; MHi; NjR; OCHP; Tx. 40-576

Bell, John, 1797-1869. Speech on the Cumberland Road, in the House of Representatives [of the U. S.] Feb. 17, March 2, 1840. Washington, DC: pr. by Gales & Seaton [1840] 24 p. M; OClWHi; T. 40-577

Bell, John, 1797-1869. Speech... on the Sub-Treasury bill. Delivered in the House of Representatives... 1840. Washington, DC: Gales & Seaton [1840]

43 p. A-Ar; Ct; MB; OClWHi; OkHi. 40-578

Bell, Luther Vose, 1806-1862. Design for the "Butler Hospital for the Insane." [Providence, RI: s. l., 184-?] 22 p. DLC; MB; PPULC. 40-579

Bell, Luther Vose, 1806-1862. An hour's conference with fathers and sons in relation to a common and fatal indulgence of youth. Boston, MA: Whipple & Damrelle, 1840. 88 p. MB; MH-M. 40-580

Bell, Robert, 1800-1867. ... Tempter. A comedy in five acts. By Robert Bell. With the stage business, cast of characters, relative positions, etc. New York: S. French, 184-? 78 p. CSt. 40-581

Bellak, James. Linda polka. Composed for the piano forte and dedicated to Miss Caroline Elfelt, by James Bellak. Philadelphia, PA; New Orleans, LA: Lee & Walker; W. T. Mayo [184-?] 2 p. ViU. 40-582

Belle of Baltimore, containing a collection of the most popular nigger melodies. New York; Boston, MA: T. W. Strong [184-?] 190 p. No Loc. 40-583

Bellini, Vincenzo, 1801-1835. Angels of peace and gladness. Written by J. L. Himens, esq. Composed by Bellini. Boston, MA: Oliver Ditson [184-?] 5 p. ViU. 40-584

Bellini, Vincenzo, 1801-1835. "As I view these scenes so charming," [English & Italian words.] In the celebrated opera La Sonnambula, by Bellini. Baltimore, MD: Geo. Willig, Junr. [184-?] 8 p. ViU. 40-585

Bellini, Vincenzo, 1801-1835. ...
Beatrice di tenda. Composees pour le
piano par Henri Herz. Op. 124...
Philadelphia, PA; New York: A. Fiot; W.
Dubois [184-?] 11 p. MB; ViU. 40-586

Bellini, Vincenzo, 1801-1835. [Beatrice
di tenda.] Romanza Beatrice di Tenda.
[Ah! non pensar che piano.] Music di
Bellini. [Parole di F. Romani. Con ac-
compagnamento di piano forte.] New
York: Baglioli [184-?] 3 p. MB. 40-587

Bellini, Vincenzo, 1801-1835. Cantina...
from the opera Il perata de Bellini...
Philadelphia, PA: Kutseleman & Nems
[184-?] 9 p. MB. 40-588

Bellini, Vincenzo, 1801-1835. Casta
diva. Gentle goddess [Ah! bella a me
ritorna. Songs. Songs. S. Accomp. for
piano forte. From the opera of Norma.]
Boston, MA: Ditson [184-?] 11 p. MB.
40-589

Bellini, Vincenzo, 1801-1835. Come
brave with me the sea love. [Suoni la
tromba intrepido] From the opera Il
puritani. Composed by Bellini. Baltimore, MD: Geo. Willig, jr. [184-?] 5 p.
ViU. 40-590

Bellini, Vincenzo, 1801-1835. Deh!
conte, conte li prendi. Duetto [S. and A.]
in the celebrated opera "La Norma."
[Pianoforte accomp.] Philadelphia, PA:
Fiot, Meignen & Co. [184-?] 15 p. MB.
40-591

Bellini, Vincenzo, 1801-1835. False one
I love thee still. Ah! Perche non posse or-
diarte. Sung by Mr. Wood, in the
celebrated opera La Sonnambula. Composed by V. Bellini. Baltimore, MD: F.
D. Benteen [184-?] 3 p. ViU. 40-592

Bellini, Vincenzo, 1801-1835. [Giuliet-
ta e Romeo.] Romanza. Oh quante volte,
oh quante. Musica del celebre maestro
Bellini. [Con accompagnamento di
piano...] New York: s. l. [184-?] 9 p. MB.
40-593

Bellini, Vincenzo, 1801-1835. Hear me,
Norma. The celebrated duett, from the
opera, La Norma, by Bellini. Baltimore,
MD: F. D. Benteen [184-?] 7 p. ViU. 40-
594

Bellini, Vincenzo, 1801-1835. [I
puritani] Qui la voce. It was here in accents sweetest, from the opera, I
Puritani. [Music by Bellini. Words by
Pepoli, with accompaniment by piano
forte.] Boston, MA: Ditson & Co. [184-
?] 9 p. MB. 40-595

Bellini, Vincenzo, 1801-1835. La sonnambula. An opera in three acts.
Philadelphia, PA: Turner & Fisher [184-
?] 38 p. ICU; MB. 40-596

Bellini, Vincenzo, 1801-1835. La Sonnambula... Philadelphia, PA: Fiot, Meignen & Co. [184-?] 4 p. MB. 40-597

Bellini, Vincenzo, 1801-1835. Les
plaisers du salon. A set of quadrilles from
[the] opera of La Straniera. Arranged for
the piano forte by Charles Czerny. New
York: Hewlitt and Jaques [184-?] 6 p.
MB. 40-598

Bellini, Vincenzo, 1801-1835. Pot Pour-
ri. From the opera La Sonnambula, by
Bellini. Arranged for the piano by Carl
Czerny. Boston, MA: H. Wade [184-?] 7
p. ViU. 40-599

Bellini, Vincenzo, 1801-1835. Son ver-
gin vezzosa in vesta di spasa. Arrag'd. for

the bridal "Polacca" in the opera of I Puritani. [S. or T. Accomp. for piano forte.] Boston, MA: Ditson [184-?] 9 p. MB. 40-600

Bellman, Henry. Orphean waltz. [For the pianforte.] Baltimore, MD: Willig [184-?] 2 p. MB. 40-601

Beman, Nathan Sidney Smith, 1785-1871. The gospel adapted to the wants of the world. A sermon, preached in Providence, R. I., Sept. 9, 1840, by Nathan S. S. Beman, D. D. Boston, MA: Printed by Crocker and Brewster, 1840. 31 p. CtY; ICU; MeBat; MWA; PPPrHi. 40-602

Beman, Nathan Sidney Smith, 1785-1871. The gospel adapted to the wants of the world. A sermon. Providence, Sept., 9, 1840. New York: s. ol., 1840. 15 p. MH-AH. 40-603

Benedict, Julius. By the sad sea waves. Ballad. Sung by Jenny Lind; composed by J. Benedict. Louisville, KY; Cincinnati, OH; New Orleans, LA: David P. Faulds; W. C. Peters & sons; W. T. Mayo [184-?] 2 p. ViU. 40-604

Benedict, Julius. By the sad sea waves. [Song, A. or Bar. Accomp. for piano forte.] Boston, MA: Reed & Co. [184-?] 4 p. MB. 40-605

Benevolent Fraternity of Churches, Boston, Mass. The quarterly report of the executive committee, and the semi-annual reports of the ministers at large... Oct. 4, 1840. Boston, MA: s. l., 1840. 1 v. IaHi; MHi; MWA; OClWHi. 40-606

Benham's New Haven city directory.

New Haven, CT: s. l., 1840-. v. 1-. CU; MH; NBuG; NN; OClWHi. 40-607

Benjamin, Asher, 1773-1845. The architect; or, Practical house carpenter... By Asher Benjamin... Boston, MA: B. B. Munsey & Co., 1840. 119 p. RP. 40-608

Benjamin, Asher, 1773-1845. Practice of architecture. Containing the five orders of architecture and an additional column and entablature, with all their elements and details explained and illustrated, for the use of carpenters and practical men. With sixty plates. By Asher Benjamin, architect... Fourth edition. Boston, MA: published by Perkins and Marvin, 1840. 96 p. CtB; DLC; MA. 40-609

Benjamin, Judah Philip, 1811-1884. Digest of the reported decision of the Superior court of the late territory of Orleans, and of the Supreme court of the state of Louisiana. Originally compiled by J. P. Benjamin and T. Slidell... and now revised and enlarged by Thomas Slidell. New Orleans, LA: E. Johns & co., 1840. 758 p. CtY; DLC; LNHT; NcD; PPB. 40-610

Bennett, S. A few remarks by way of reply to an anonymous scribbler, calling himself a philanthropist, disabusing the Church of Jesus Christ of Latter Day Saints of the slanders and falsehoods which he has attempted to fasten upon it. By S. Bennett. Philadelphia, PA: Brown, Bicking & Guilbert, printers, 1840. 16 p. CU; DLC; MH. 40-611

Bennett, William Sterndale. To Chloe in sickness. [Song. Accomp. for piano forte.] Boston, MA P:Diston [184-?] 5 p. MB. 40-612

Benquo, pseud. A hist[ory] at banking...
Richmond, VA: Printed by P. D. Bernard, 1841 CSmH; CtY; NHi. 40-613

Benson, Joseph, 1749-1821. The life of the Rev. John W. de la Flechere, compiled from the narratives of Rev. Mr. Wesley; the biographical notes of Rev. Mr. Gilpin; from his own letters, and other authentic documents, many of which were never before published. New York: T. Mason and G. Lane, 1840. 356 p. CtY; NN; NNG; OCY; TBrik. 40-614

Bent, Nathaniel T. The past: a fragment. Written for The Ladies' Fair, at Mechanics Hall, February, 1840. By Nathaniel T. Bent. New Bedford, MA: printed by Benjamin Lindsey, 1840. 10 p. MNBedf. 40-615

Bentham, Jeremy, 1748-1832. Theory of legislation, by Jeremy Bentham. Translated from the French of Etienne Dumont, by R. Hildreth. Boston, MA: Weeks, Jordan & Co., 1840. 2 v. CSf; InNd; MB; MeAu; NjP. 40-616

Bentley, Rensselaer. English spelling book, containing the rudiments of the English language. By Rensselaer Bentley. Poughkeepsie, NY: William Wilson, 1840. 156 p. NP; NPV. 40-617

Bentley, Rensselaer. The pictorial spelling book, containing an improved method of teaching the alphabet, and likewise spelling and pronunciation, by the use of pictures: interspersed with a variety of useful and interesting reading lessons, illustrated with numerous engravings... New York: s. l., 1840. CtY. 40-618

Benton, Thomas Hart, 1782-1858. Mr.

Benton's speech. Federal falsehood exposed. [Auburn, NY: s. l., 1840?] 8 p. NN. 40-619

Benton, Thomas Hart, 1782-1858. Remarks of Mr. Benton, of Missouri, on the annual expenditures of the government. In Senate, Thursday, May 7, 1840. [S. l.: s. l., 1840] 8 p. MiD-B; MiU-C; ViU. 40-620

Benton, Thomas Hart, 1782-1858. Remarks of Mr. Benton, of Missouri, on the annual expenditures of the government. [Washington, DC: s. l., 1840] 7 p. MdHi; MiU-C; MoHi; OO. 40-621

Benton, Thomas Hart, 1782-1858. Speech of Mr. Benton, of Missouri, on his motion to strike out from the 19th and 20th sections of the independent subtreasury bill, the causes which permitted the reception and disbursement of bills, notes, or paper issued under the authority of the United States and in support of the bill. Senate, U. S., January 16, 1840. Washington, DC: Globe office, 1840. 16 p. InHi; MdHi; NjN; NSmb; OClWHi. 40-622

Benton, Thomas Hart, 1782-1858. Speech of Mr. Benton, of Missouri, on Mr. Benton's resolutions against the constitutionality and expediency of assuming or providing for the payment of the state debts, or diverting the land revenue to that object. Delivered in the United States Senate, January 6, 1840. Washington, DC: s. l., 1840. 16 p. CtY; GEU; MeB; MdBJ. 40-623

Benton, Thomas Hart, 1782-1858. Speech of Mr. Benton, of Missouri, on the bill for the armed occupation of Florida; and in reply to Messrs. Crittenden, Preston, and Strange. Senate, U. S., Jan. 12, 1840. Washington, DC: printed at the Globe office, 1840. 15 p. MeB; MoHi. 40-624

Benton, Thomas Hart, 1782-1858. Speech of Mr. Benton, of Missouri, on the repeal of the Salt Tax. Delivered in the Senate... April 22, 1840. Washington, DC: printed at the Globe office, 1840. 23 p. DLC; MdHi; MH; NN. 40-625

Benton, Thomas Hart, 1782-1858. Speech on public lands. Washington, DC: s. l., 1840. MBAt. 40-626

Benton, Thomas Hart, 1782-1858. Speeches on independent treasury bill. Washington, DC: printed at the Globe Office, 1840. 16 p. NjN. 40-627

Bentzel-Sternan, Christian Ernst, Graf von, 1767-1849. Geist aus den Werken, von Ch. E. Graf v. Bentzel-Sternan und Dr. Friedrich Ehrenberg... New York; Hildburghausen: Druck und Verlag des Bibliographischen Instituts [184-?] 173 p. CtY. 40-628

Berg, Joseph Frederick, 1812-1871. The ancient land marks, being the substance of a discourse preached Sept. 29, 1839... on the centenary anniversary of the organization of the German Reformed Church on Race Street, Phila. Phialdelphia, PA: printed at the Office of the Christian Observer, 1840. 162 p. IEG; MoWgT; NjPT; PLT; PPPrHi. 40-629

Berg, Joseph Frederick, 1812-1871. Lectures on Romanism. By Joseph F. Berg. With an introduction by W. C. Brownlee, D. D. Phialdelphia, PA: D. Weidner; D. Ashmead, printer, 1840. 300 p. CtY; NjP; OCoC; PLT; RPB. 40-630

Bernard, David. Zion's harp. A collection of hymns and spiritual songs, designed for social, conference, and prayer meetings, and seasons of revival. By David Bernard, Pastor of the Baptist Church in Norristown, Pa. [Quotation.] Philadelphia, PA: David Clark, 1840. 429 p. PCA. 40-631

Bernard, William Boyle, 1807-1875. His last legs. A farce in two acts. New York: W. Taylor & Co. [184-?] p. MH; PPL; PPULC; PU. 40-632

Bernard, William Boyle, 1807-1875. The Irish attorney; or, Galway practice in 1770. New York: S. French [184-?] 38 p. MH; MnU; NN. 40-633

Bernard, William Boyle, 1807-1875. The nervous man and the man of nerve. A farce in two acts. By William Boyle Bernard. With the stage business, cast of characters, costumes, relative positions, &c. New York: S. French & Son [184-?] 45 p. CSt. 40-634

Bernard, William Boyle, 1807-1875. ... The passing cloud. A romantic drama in two acts. By Boyle Bernard. With stage business, cast of characters, costumes, relative positions, etc. New York: S. French & son [etc., etc., 184-?] 59 p. CSt. 40-635

Berquin, Arnaud, 1747 or 9-1791. The Child's Friend: being selections from the various works of Arnaud Berquin. Adapted to the use of American readers, with a sketch of his life and writings. Boston, MA: Marsh, Capen, Lyon, and Webb, 1840. 252 p. DLC; MFalm; MLow; MTop. 40-636

Berquin, Arnaud, 1747 or 9-1791. Louisa's tenderness to the little birds, in winter... Portland, ME: Bailey & Noyes [ca. 1840?] 16 p. CtY. 40-637

Berrian, Hobart. A brief Sketch of the Origin and Rise of the Workingmen's Party in the City of New York. Washington, DC: s. l. [1840] 16 p. MH. 40-638

Bertini, Henri Jerome, 1798-1876. A Progressive and complete method for the piano-forte... Boston, MA: Published by Oliver-Ditson... Charles C. Clapp and Co. [184-] 191 p. CSmH. 40-639

Bethel and Sabbath Convention, Cincinnati. Proceedings of the Bethel and Sabbath Convention: held at Cincinnati, November 19, 1840. With reasons for the establishment of lines of Sabbath-keeping and temperance boats on the canals and rivers of the West. By the Standing Committee. Cincinnati, OH: Printed at the Cincinnati Observer Office, 1840. 15 p. MBC; NNUT; PPPrHi. 40-640

Bethune, George Washington, 1805-1862. An Address before the Philomathean Society of the University of Pennsylvania, Nov. 30th, 1940. Philadelphia, PA: Printed for the Philomathean Society, 1840. 38 p. DCL; NN; PHC; PHi; PPL. 40-641

Bethune, George Washington, 1805-1862. The British Female Poets: with biographical and critical notices. New York: Hurst & Co., 1840. 490 p. OCh. 40-642

Bethune, George Washington, 1805-1862. The child Samuel. A discourse delivered at the opening of the Chapel of the New York Orphan Asylum, at Bloomingdale, by George W. Bethune... New York: printed for the Orphan Asylum Society, 1840. 20 p. NjR; NNG; NNS; PPPrHi. 40-643

Bethune, George Washington, 1805-1862. The prospects of art in the United States. An address before the Artists' Fund Society of Philadelphia, at the opening of their exhibition, May, 1840. By George W. Bethune... Philadelphia, PA: John C. Clark, printer, 1840. 45 p. CSmH; MBAt; MWA; PPM; RPB. 40-644

Bethune, George Washington, 1805-1862. The prospects of art in the United States. An address before the Artists' Fund Society of Philadelphia, at the opening of their exhibition, May, 1840. Philadelphia, PA: Printed for the Artists' Fund Society, 1840. 45 p. CSmH; DLC; MBAL; NBuG; OO. 40-645

Beverly, Mass. Town of Beverly, expenses from March, 1839 to March, 1840. Salem, MA: Salem Register Press, 1840. 8 p. MBev. 40-646

Beyer, Ferdinand, 1803-1863. Fantaisies variations & rondeaux pour le piano forte sur des motifs favoris de l' Opera La Sonnambula de Bellini. Composees par Ferd. Beyer. Op. 53. Boston, MA: Geo. P. Reed [184-?] 15 p. ViU. 40-647

Beyer, Ferdinand, 1803-1863. Hail Columbia. Rondino. [For piano forte] Philadelphia, PA: Tiot. [184-?] 5 p. MB. 40-648

Beyer, Ferdinand, 1803-1863. Le premier debut. 24 instructive recreations for the piano consisting of rondos and variations. [No. 1-5.] Boston, MA: Detson [184-?] 11 p. MB. 40-649

Beyer, Ferdinand, 1803-1863. Les progre's des jeunes eleves. Ferd. Beyer. Pour le piano La Norma. Air tyrolien I Puritani....Op. 88. Boston, MA: G. P. Reed [184-?] 7 p. MB; ViU. 40-650

Beyer, Ferdinand, 1803-1863. ... Rondeau Tyrolien, pour le piano fortepar F. Beyer. Philadelphia, PA; New York: A. Fiot; W. Dubois [184-?] 3 p. ViU. 40-651

Beyer, Fred. Star Spangled Banner... Philadelphia, PA; New York: A. Fiot; W. Dubois [184-?] 5 p. ViU. 40-652

Bible. An alphabet of lessons for children. New York: American Tract Society, [184-?] 15 p. IaU; NN. 40-653

Bible. Die Bibel, oder, Die ganze Heilige Schrift des Alten und Neuen Testaments nach der Dutchen Vebersetzung D. Martin Luther's. Handausgabe mit Nonpareil-Schrift. Mit dem Bildnisse unsers Herrn und Heilandes Jesu Christe. Hildburghausen Amsterdam; Philadelphia, PA: Druck und Verlag vom Bibliographischen Institut, 1840. 540, 159 p. KNB. 40-654

Bible. Die Bibel, oder, Die ganze Heilige Schrift des Alten und Neuen Testaments nach Dr. Martin Luther's uebersetzung... Zwolfte auflage. Philadelphia, PA: Mentz, 1840. 972, 320 p. IEG; P. 40-655

Bible. The Bible; or, the New Testament of the Lord and Saviour Jesus Christ. Translated by Dr. Martin.

Philadelphia, PA: George B. Mentz and Son, 1840. 2 v. in 1. OkWo. 40-656

Bible. The book of Joshua... Translated from the original Hebrew into English. New York: pub. by W. M. Nash & W. S. Gould, 1840. 267 p. CtMW; MWA; PPA; PPins; TxD-W; WNaE. 40-657

Bible. The book of Psalms. Translated into English verse. By George Burgess. New York: F. J. Huntington and Co., 1840. 276 p. Ct; ICU; MdBD; PPPrHi; WNaE. 40-658

Bible. The book of Psalms. Translated into English verse. Hartford, CT: L. Skinner, printer, 1840. 276 p. RP. 40-659

Bible. The book of Psalms, translated out of the original Hebrew. Philadelphia: Presbyterian Board of Publication, [184-?] 320 p. NN. 40-660

Bible. The books of the Old and New Testament canonical and inspired. With remarks on the Apocrypha. By Robert Haldane. With an appendix. First American edition. Boston, MA: American Doctrinal Tract Society, 1840. 191 p. MWA; NNUT; PPWe; RPB; WHi. 40-661

Bible. Comprehensive commentary on the Holy Bible. consisting the text according to the authorized version. With marginal references, Matthew Henry's commentary condensed, but containing the most useful thoughts. The practical observations of Rev. Thomas Scott, D. D... Notes selected from Scott, Doddridge, Gill... Edited by Rev. William Jenks, D. D... Engravings on wood and steel... Acts-Revelation. Brattleboro, VT: Published by the Brattleboro

Typographical Company, 1840. 774 p. IaDuU; MBC; PReaAT. 40-662

Bible. The devotional family Bible. With practical and experimental reflections on each verse of the Old and New Testaments and rich marginal references. By the Rev. Alexander Fletcher... New York: G. Virtue [184-?] 2 v. ViU. 40-663

Bible. The English version of Bagster's Polyglot Bible, containing the Old and New Testaments with a copious and original selection of references to parallel and illustrative passages. Boston: H. L. Hastings, [184-?] 603, 190, 66 p. CLU. 40-664

Bible. English version of the Polyglott Bible, containing the Old and New Testaments. Concord, NH: s. l., 1840. 190 p. MBC; MH; Nh-Hi. 40-665

Bible. The English version of the Polyglott Bible, containing the Old and New Testaments. With marginal readings... a critical introduction... by Rev. Joseph A. Warne... Brattleboro, VT: Brattleboro Typographic Company, 1840. 3, 82, 68, 7, 705, 1, 216, 2, 63, 2, 84 p. No Loc. 40-666

Bible. The English version of the Polyglott Bible, containing the Old and New Testaments... Stereotyped by Henry Wallis and L. Roby. Concord, NH: published by Roby, Kimball and Merrill, [1840] 2 v. MH-AH; MSpe; OrU. 40-667

Bible. The English version of the Polyglott Bible, the Old and New Testaments, Apocrypha and Brown's Concordance. Boston, MA: Gaylord, 1840. IaFairP. 40-668

Bible. English version of the Polyglott Bible. With marginal readings. Together with a copious selection of references to parallel and illustrative passages. Exhibited in a manner hitherto unattempted. Springfield, MA: G. & C. Merriam, 1840. 856, 259 p. CtHWatk; NHem; MWHi; NNUT; OC. 40-669

Bible. Epistles of John. Translated into the Cherokee language. Tsani tsuwowelanelvhi tsunandodi. Park Hill: s. l., 1840. 20 p. DLC. 40-670

Bible. The Epistles of John in the Ojibwa language. Boston, MA: printed for the American Board of Commissioners for Foreign Missions by Crocker & Brewster, 1840. 30 p. MBGCT; MH-AH; NN; PPAmP. 40-671

Bible. An exposition of the gospels of St. Matthew and St. Mark, and some other detached parts of the Holy Scripture. By the Rev. Richard Watson. New York: T. Mason and G. Lane, 1840. 538 p. ABBS; GAGTh; OBerB; PReaAT; TJaL. 40-672

Bible. An exposition of the Old and New Testaments... Philadelphia, PA: E. Barrington & G. D. Haswell [184-?] p. NN. 40-673

Bible. A harmony of the four evangelists in the words of the authorized version, according to Creswell's "Harmonia Evangelica."In parallel columns, having marginal references and occasional notes. With an accompanying chart of Our Lord's life and ministry. Compiled by Robert Minpress. New York: Dodd [184-?] 180 p. CBPac. 40-674

Bible. Holy Bible; containing the Old

and New Testaments. Concord, NH: s. l., 1840. 259 p. Nh-Hi. 40-675

Bible. The Holy Bible; containing the Old and New Testaments. The text carefully printed from the most correct copies of the present authorized translation, including the marginal readings and parallel texts. With a commentary and critical notes. Designed as a help to a better understanding of the sacred writings. By Adam Clarke, LL. D., F. S. A. & c. A new edition, with the author's final corrections... New York: T. Mason & G. Lane, 1840. 6 v. ArEs; CtY-D; KWS; MdBG. 40-676

Bible. The Holy Bible; containing the Old and New Testaments. Together with the Apocrypha. Translated out of the original tongues and the former translations diligently compared and revised. Philadelphia, PA: Kimber and Sharpless [184-?] 570, 770 p. DLC; N; NN; OClW; TxU. 40-677

Bible. The Holy Bible; containing the Old and New Testaments. Together with the Apocrypha. Translated out of the original tongues and the former translations diligently compared and revised. With Canne's marginal notes and references. To which are added an index; an alphabetical table of all the names in the Old and New Testaments, with their significations; tables of scripture weights, measures, and coins, etc. Concord, NH: Published by Roby, Kimball, and Merrill, 1840. 767 p. NRMA. 40-678

Bible. The Holy Bible; containing the Old and New Testaments. Together with the Apocrypha. Translated out of the original tongues, and with the former translations diligently compared and revised. With Canne's marginal notes and references. To which are added an index; an alphabetical table of all the names... with their significations; tables of scripture weights... &c. Cooperstown, NY: published by H. & E. Phenney, 1840. 576, 4, 99, 2, 768, 35 p. DLC; MAshlHi; N; NLitf; NN. 40-679

Bible. The Holy Bible; containing the Old and New Testaments. Together with the Apocrypha. Translated out of the original tongues, and with the former translations diligently compared and revised. With Canne's marginal notes and references. To which are added an index. Concord, NH: Published by Roby, Kimball and Merrill, 1840. 576, 96, 768 p. MMhHi. 40-680

Bible. Holy Bible; containing the Old and New Testaments. Together with the Apocrypha... with Canne's marginal notes and refrences. To which are added an index... Concord, NH: Roby, Kimball and Merrill, 1840. 768 p. CSmH; MHa; Nh-Hi; NRMA; TxH. 40-681

Bible. The Holy Bible; containing the Old and New Testaments, translated from the original tongues, and with the former translation dilligently compared and revised. New York: Cornish Lamport & Company, [184-?] 829 p. ViU. 40-682

Bible. The Holy Bible; containing the Old and New Testaments. Translated out of the original tongues and the former translations diligently compared and revised. New York: Published by the American Bible Society, D. Fanshaw, printers, 1840. 852 p. MFai; NNUT; PAtM; WEau. 40-683

Bible. The Holy Bible; containing the Old and New Testaments. Translated out of the original tongues and the former translations diligently compared and revised. New York: Stereotyped by Smith and Valentine for the American Bible Society, D. Fanshaw, printers, 1840. 979 p. MAnHi. 40-684

Bible. The Holy Bible; containing the Old and New Testaments. Translated out of the original tongues and the former translations diligently compared and revised. 49th edition. New York: Published by the American Bible Society, D. Fanshaw, printers, 1840. 832, 254 p. NN. 40-685

Bible. The Holy Bible; containing the Old and New Testaments. Translated out of the original tongues and with the former translations diligently compared and revised. New York: American Bible Society, D. Fanshaw, printers, 1840. 669 p. DLC; IClay; NbCrD; TxAbC. 40-686

Bible. Holy Bible; containing the Old and New Testaments. Translated out of the original tongues and with the former translations diligently compared and revised. New York: printed by D. Fanshaw for the American Bible Society, 1840. 251 p. OMC. 40-687

Bible. The Holy Bible... New York: Pub. by the American Bible Society, printed by D. Fanshaw, 1840. 824, 251 p. MWinchrHi. 40-688

Bible. The Holy Bible. Translated from the Latin Vulgate diligently compared with the Hebrew, Greek and other editions in divers language. The Old Testament first published by the English College at Douay, A. D. 1609; and the New Testament first published by the English College at Rheims, A. D. 1582. New York: John Doyle, 1840. 968 p. GAU. 40-689

Bible. The Holy Bible. Translated from the Latin vulgate. O. T. first published by English College at Doway, A. D. 1609. N. T. at English College at Rhemes, 1502. 1st stereotype from the 5th Dublin edition. Philadelphia, PA: Pub. by Eugene Cummiskey, 1840. 691, 191 p. CSmH; NN; NNAB; PU; WaTC. 40-690

Bible. The Holy Bible. Translated from the Latin vulgate. O. T. first published by English College at Doway, A. D. 1609. N. T. at English College at Rheimes, A. D. 1582. With annotations, references, and an historical index, etc. New York: s. l., 1840. MBAt. 40-691

Bible. The Holy Bible... With Canne's marginal notes and references. To which are added an index; an alphabetical table of all the names in the Old and New Testaments... tables of weights... etc. Stereotyped edition. Philadelphia, PA: I. M. Moses, 1840. 768 p. PP. 40-692

Bible. Improved metr. tr. of Psalms of David. Philadelphia, PA: s. l., 1840. MB. 40-693

Bible. He keine diatheke. Novum Testamentum Graecum. Ad exemplar Roberti Stephani Aucuratissime editum... Philadelphia, PA: Ed. Barrington and George D. Haswell [184-?] 369 p. WHi. 40-694

Bible. Lessons for schools taken from the Holy Scriptures. Philadelphia, PA: American Sunday School Union, 1840? 300 p. NN. 40-695

Bible. The ministry of Jesus Christ: compiled and arranged from the four gospels, for familes and Sunday schools. Boston: Weeks, Jordan & Co., 1840. 13-204 p. MB; MWA. 40-696

Bible. Das Neue Testament unsurus Herrn und Heilandes Jesu Christi. 4th edition. New York: Stereotypiet von H. M. Rees for die Amerikanische Bibel-Gesellschaft, 1840. 472 p. CtHT; NNAB. 40-697

Bible. Das Neue Testament unsurus Herrn und Heilandes Jesu Christi. Nach Uebersetzung Dr. Martin Luther. Philadelphia, PA: Geo. W. Mentz, 1840. 504 p. DLC; MiU. 40-698

Bible. Das Neue Testament unsurus Herrn und Heilandes Jesu Christi. Nach Uebersetzung Dr. Martin Luther. Mit erklarungen und Nutzanwendungen. Fur unstudirte. Herausgfegeben von Daniel Dobler... Lebanon, PA: Gedruckt von Samuel Miller, 1840. 428 p. MH; PReaAT; ScCoT; WHi. 40-699

Bible. A new hieroglyphic Bible with 400 cuts. New York: Blakeman & Mason, [184-?] 106 p. ICU. 40-700

Bible. The New Testament. New York: For the American and Foreign Bible Society, 1840. 423 p. NHC-S. 40-701

Bible. The New Testament. Stereotype edition. New York; Pittsburgh, PA: Luke Loomis [1840?] 226 p. NNC; NNC-Atf. 40-702

Bible. The New Testament. Arranged in historical and chronological order. Revised, divided into paragraphs, punctuated... by Rev. T. W. Coit. Boston, MA: s. l., 1840. MdBP. 40-703

Bible. The New Testament. Arranged in historical and chronological order. With copious notes on the principal subjects in theology... By the Rev. George Townsend... The whole revised... by the Rev. T. W. Coit... Boston, MA: Published by Perkins and Marvin, 1840. 455, 472 p. GDecCT; KyLoS; OrPD; PCC. 40-704

Bible. The New Testament illustrated. Hartford: S. Andrus and Son, [184-?] 344 p. NN. 40-705

Bible. New Testament of Our Lord and Saviour Jesus Christ. Ed. 16. New York: s. l., 1840. 403 p. IU. 40-706

Bible. New Testament of Our Lord and Saviour Jesus Christ. Philadelphia, PA: Bible Asso. of Friends, 1840. 386 p. No Loc. 40-707

Bible. The New Testament of Our Lord and Saviour Jesus Christ. By Adam Clarke, LL. D. A new edition with the author's final corrections. New York: published by T. Mason and G. Lane, 1840. 920 p. KWi; NcWilA. 40-708

Bible. The New Testament of Our Lord and Savior Jesus Christ. Translated from the Latin Volgate diligently compared with the original Greek, and first published by the English College at Rhemes, A. D. 1582. With annotations, references, and a historical and chronological index. Newly revised and corrected accoring to the Clementin edition of the Scriptures. Approved by Dr. Conwell, Bishop of Philadelphia. From the fifth Dublin edition. Philadelphia,

PA: Published by Eugene Commiskey, 1840. 191 p. NRSB. 40-709

Bible. The New Testament of Our Lord and Savior Jesus Christ. Translated from the Latin vulgate... with annotations, references and an historical and chronological index... Philadelphia, PA: E. Cummiskey, 1840. 429 p. IaDuC; ICU; NBuCC; TNL; TxSaUr. 40-710

Bible. New Testament of Our Lord and Saviour Jesus Christ. Translated out of the original Greek. Concord, NH: John F. Brown, 1840. 383 p. MiU; Nh-Hi. 40-711

Bible. The New Testament of Our Lord and Saviour Jesus Christ. Translated out of the original Greek, and with the former translations diligently compared and revised. New York: Stereotyped by Smith & Valentine for the American Bible Society, printed by D. Fanshaw, 1840. 342 p. No Loc. 40-712

Bible. The New Testament of Our Lord and Saviour Jesus Christ. Translated out of the original Greek, and with the former translations diligently compared and revised. New York: Stereotyped by Smith & Valentine for the American Bible Society, printed by D. Fanshaw, 1840. 429 p. MTemnHi. 40-713

Bible. The New Testament of Our Lord and Saviour Jesus Christ. Translated out of the original Greek, and with the former translations diligently compared and revised. New York: D. Fanshaw, 1840. 340 p. IaMp. 40-714

Bible. The New Testament of Our Lord and Saviour Jesus Christ. Translated out of the original Greek, with former trans-lations diligently compared and revised. New York: American Bible Society, 1840. 344 p. CBPac; GEU-T. 40-715

Bible. The New Testament of Our Lord and Saviour Jesus Christ. Translated out of the original Greek, with the former translations diligently compared and revised. Cooperstown, NY: H. E. Phinney, 1840. 576, 99, 579, 768 p. MAshlHi. 40-716

Bible. The New Testament of Our Lord and Saviour Jesus Christ. Translated out of the original Greek, with the former translations diligently compared and revised. Stereotyped edition. Concord, NH: Roby, Kimball and Merrill, 1840. 263 p. MSpe. 40-717

Bible. The New Testament of our Lord and Saviour Jesus Christ translated from the original Greek. New Haven: S. Babcock, [184-?] 288 p. NN. 40-718

Bible. The New Testament of our Lord and Saviour Jesus Christ translated out of the Latin Vulgate... and first published by the English college of Rhemes, anno 1582. Utica: Printed for T. Davis, 1840. 14-344 p. DGU; NN. 40-719

Bible. The New Testament of our Lord and Saviour Jesus Christ translated out of the original Greek and with the former translations dilgently compared and revised. Utica: Printed for T. Davis, 1840. 14-344 p. OC. 40-720

Bible. The New Testament of our Lord and Saviour Jesus Christ translated out of the original Greek. Newburyport: J. G. Tiltson, 1840. 450 p. MB; NN. 40-721

Bible. The New Testament of our Lord

and Saviour Jesus Christ translated out of the original Greek. Philadelphia: Stereotyped for the Bible Society of Philadelphia, 1840. 352 p. NNAB. 40-722

Bible. The New Testament of our Lord and Saviour Jesus Christ translated out of the original Greek. Philadelphia: W. S. Young, 1840. 159 p. NN. 40-723

Bible. The New Testament of our Lord and Saviour Jesus Christ with the references and marginal readings of the polyglott Bible. New York: C. Wells, 1840. 742 p. MB; NN. 40-724

Bible. Notes, critical and practical on the book of Genesis... by George Bush. 5th ed. Andover, MA: Gould & Newman, 1840. 2 v. IU; MMeT; OCl; TJaL; VtU; WaPS. 40-725

Bible. Notes, critical and practical on the book of Genesis... Designed as a general help to Biblical reading and instruction. 4th ed. Andover, MA: Gould, Newman & Saxton, 1840. 2 v. MNtCA; MTop. 40-726

Bible. Notes, critical and practical on the book of Jesus. Designed as a general help to Biblical reading and instruction y George Bush. 2d edition. Boston, MA: H. A. Young & Co. [184-?] 221 p. OU. 40-727

Bible. Notes, critical, explanatory, and practical on the book of the prophet Isaiah. With a new translation. By Albert Barnes... Boston, MA: Crocker & Brewster, 1840. 3 v. CU; KyDC; NNUT; OClW; PU; ScDuE. 40-728

Bible. Notes, critical, illustrative, and

practical on the Bible. By George Bush. New York; Chicago, IL: Ivison, Phinney & Co.; S. C. Griggs & Co., 1840-69. 20 v. ODW. 40-729

Bible. Notes, explanatory & practical, on the Gospels. Designed for Sunday School teachers and Bible classes. By Albert Barnes. With an index, a chronological table, tables of weights, etc. 25th ed., rev. New York: Harper & brothers, 1840. 2 v. ICMBI; KEmC; MBelc; NBuG; NSchHi. 40-730

Bible. Notes, explanatory & practical, on the second Epistle to the Corinthians and the Epistle to the Galations. By Albert Barnes. New York: Homer Franklin, 1840. 398 p. CoU; LNB; MiU; NbOM; WHi. 40-731

Bible. Notes, illustrative and explanatory, on the Holy Gospels, arranged according to Townsend's chronological New Testament, by Joseph Longking. New York: Carlton & Porter, [1840-1842] Bible. Notes, illustrative and explanatory, on the Holy Gospels, arranged according to Townsend's chronological New Testament, by Joseph Longking. New York: G. Lane & P. P. Sandford, 1840-1844. 4 v. DLC; ViU. 40-732

Bible. Notes... on Romans... New York: s. l., 1840. PPT-L. 40-733

Bible. Novum Testamentum ad exemplar millianum, cum emendationibus et lectionibus griesbachii, praecipuis vocibus ellipticis, thematibus omnium vocum difficiliorum, atque locis scripture parallelis. Studio et Labore Gulielmi Greenfield Hauc editionem primam Americanam Josephus P. Engles, A. M. Philadelphia, PA: Sumptibus Henrici

Perkins, 1840. 281 p. MiEalC; NbCrD; NNMHi. 40-734

Bible. Osagiitiuin au Jesus, gibinibotauat iniu mejiizhinebizinijin. In the Ojibwa language. Boston, MA: printed for the American Board of Commissioners for Foreign Missions by Crocker & Brewster, 1840. MBAt. 40-735

Bible. The Polyglott Bible... Springfield, MA: G. & C. Merriam, 1840. 856, 259 p. NN. 40-736

Bible. Polyglott family testament... With the marginal readings, etc. [Polyglott School Testament] Keene, NH: H. J. & J. W. Presntiss, 184?. 422 p. NN. 40-737

Bible. Promises of scripture. Baltimore: J. N. Lewis, 1840. 250 p. MiU. 40-738

Bible. Psalms of David, carefully imitated in the language of the New Testament, and applied to the Christian state and worship in the United States, being an improvement on the old version of the Psalms of David. New York: C. Wells, 1840. 573 p. CSansS. 40-739

Bible. The Psalms of David, imitated in the language of the New Testament, and applied to the Christian state and worship. By Isaac Watts, D. D... Cooperstown, NY: Published by H. and E. Phinney, 1840. 282 p. Nh; NPV. 40-740

Bible. Psalms, in metre... Selected from the Psalms of David. New York: New York Bible and Common Prayer Book Society, 1840. 51, 48 p. DLC; KMK; MMeT; NNG. 40-741

Bible. Psalms, in metre... Selected from the Psalms of David. Suited to the feasts and fasts of the church and other occasions of public worship.. Philadelphia, PA: s. l., 1840. 43 p. MH. 40-742

Bible. Psalms, in metre... Selected from the Psalms of David. Suited to the feasts and fasts of the Church and other occasions of public worship. Philadelphia, PA: Herman Hooker, 1840. 105 p. InRchE; LNH; MiU-C; MH; PPF. 40-743

Bible. Psalms, in metre... Selected from the Psalms of David. With hymns... Philadelphia, PA: H. F. Anners, 1840. 55 p. NNG. 40-744

Bible. Psalms, in metre. Suited to the feasts and fasts of the church, and other occasions of public worship... Philadelphia, PA: Hooker, 1840. 43 p. MB; NjP. 40-745

Bible. Psalms, in metre... with hymns... Philadelphia, PA: Anners, 1840. 2 pt in 1. NjP. 40-746

Bible. Psalms. Translated into English verse by George Burgess. New York: F. J. Huntington and Co., 1840. NjMD. 40-747

Bible. Der Psalter des Konigs und Propheten David, verdeutscht von Dr. Martin Luther. Mit kurzen Summarien oder Inhalt jedes Psalmen... Philadelpyia, PA: Mentz, 1840. 251 p. P. 40-748

Bible. A Sagiitiuin au Jesus, gibinibotauat iniu mejiizhiuebizinijin. In the Ojibwa language. Boston, MA: ABCFM, 1840. 21 p. MH-And. 40-749

Bible. Scripture portions for the afflicted, especially the sick. With reflections from various authors. Philadelphia, PA: Presbyterian Board of Publication, William S. Martien, publishing agent, 1840. [5]-209 p. GDecCT; NNUT; NWM; ScCliP. 40-750

Bible. Specimens of an improved metrical translation of the Psalms of David. Intended for the use of the Presbyterian Church in Australia and New Zealand. With preliminary dissertation and notes, critical and explanatory. By John Dunmore Lang. Philadelphia, PA: Printed by Adam Waldie, 1840. 231 p. GDecCT; NNUT, PPL; ViRut. 40-751

Bible. Thoughts of peace for the Christian sufferer. A selection of short passages from scripture and sacred poetry. From the 4th London edition. Philadelphia: H. Hooker, 1841? 238 p. RPB; ViU. 40-752

Bible stories and pictures, from the Old and New Testaments. New Haven, CT: Published by S. Babcock [1840?] 16 p. MiU. 40-753

Bickersteth, Edward, 1786-1850. The time to favour Zion; or, an appeal to the Gentile churches in behalf of the Jews. By the Rev. E. Bickersteth... Philadelphia, PA: Orrin Rogers, 1840. 47 p. CBPSR; MBC; MWA; OO; PHi. 40-754

Bicknell, Robert T. Bicknell's counterfeit detector and bank note list. Philadelphia, PA: Miller, 1840. 48 p. MnH; OO. 40-755

Biddle, Richard, 1796-1847. Remarks of Mr. Biddle, of Pennsylvania, upon the resolution relative to the Cumberland Road, made in the House of Representatives, February 8, 1840. [S. l.: s. l., 1840?] 6 p. DLC. 40-756

Biddle, Richard, 1796-1847. Remarks of Mr. Biddle, on abolition petitions, delivered in the House of Representatives, Jan. 16, 1840. Washington, DC: Gales and Seaton, 1840. 8 p. DLC. 40-757

Biddleford, Me. First Congregational Church. Confession and covenant of the First church in Biddleford. Portland, ME: s. l. [1840?] 6 p. CSmH. 40-758

Biegler, Augustus. Anatomy and physiology of the brain and nervous system, an essay read to the Albany Phrenological Society, April 3, 1840. By Aug. P. Biegler, M. D. Albany, NY: Printed by C. Van Benthuysen, 1840. 22 p. DLC; MB; MWA; NjR; NNNAM. 40-759

Bigelow, Andrew, 1795-1877. A pastor's retrospect: two discourses on the completion of seven years' ministry in Taunton. [S. l.: s. l.] 1840. 32 p. MBC; MH; MHI; NN; RPB. 40-760

Bigelow, Jacob, 1787-1879. A collection of plants of Boston and its vicinity... by Jacob Bieglow, M. D. 3d ed., enl. and containing a glossary of botanical terms. Boston, MA: C. C. Little and J. Brown, 1840. 468 p. KBB; MiToC; MNBedf; MSaP; MSo. 40-761

Bigelow, Jacob, 1787-1879. Florula bostoniensis. A collectinof plants of Boston and its vicinity... by Jacob Bieglow... 3d ed., enl. and containing a glossary of botanical terms. Boston, MA: C. C. Little and J. Brown, 1840. 468 p. DLC; MH-AH; MiU; MWA; RPB; WV. 40-762

Bigelow, Jacob, 1787-1879. The useful arts considered in connexion with the applications of science. New York: Harper, 1840. 2 vols. in 1. MCM; MtH. 40-763

Bigelow, Jacob, 1787-1879. The Useful Arts; considered in connexion with the Applications of Science: with numerous engravings. Boston, MA: Marsh, Capen, Lyon and Webb, 1840. 2 v. CU; InCW; MeBa; MH; WaPS. 40-764

Bigelow, John P. Abstract exhibiting the condition of the banks in Mass., on the first Saturday of Oct., 1840. Prepared from official returns, by John P. Bigelow. Boston, MA: DUtton and Whenworth, state ptrs., 1840. 51 p. MiD-B. 40-765

Bijou minstrel: containing all the choice, fashionable and popular songs, as sung at the concerts, in private circles, etc., many of which have never before been offered to the public in book form. Philadelphia, PA; New York: Turner & Fisher, 1840. 338 p. TxU. 40-766

Billard, Charles Michael, 1800-1832. A treatise on the diseases of infants... by C. M. Billard. Second American, translated from the third French edition. New York: T. & H. G. Langley, 1840. 611 p. Ia; LNOP; MnU; PPCP; WMAM. 40-767

Billings, C. H. New custom house, Boston: view and plans. Boston, MA: s. l., 1840. MB. 40-768

Binney, Amos, 1802-1878. Missionary hymns; a choice selection to aid the general cause of missions. Boston, MA: published by D. S. King, 1840. 80 p. DLC; MBNMHi. 40-769

Binney, Amos, 1802-1878. The theological compend... by Amos Binney... New York: T. Mason & G. Lane, 1840. 128 p. DLC; NNMHi; TxD-T. 40-770

Binney, Amos, 1802-1878. The theological compend containing a system of divinity, or, a brief view of the evidences, doctrines, morals, and institutions of Christianity... by Amos Binney. Cincinnati, OH: Hitchcock & Walden, 1840. 128 p. InHu; KSalW; NcGI; OSW. 40-771

Binney, Amos, 1802-1878. A theological compend containing a system of divinity, or, a brief view of the evidences, doctrines, morals, and institutions of Christianity. Designed for the benefit of families, Bible classes, and Sunday schools. By Rev. Amos Binney, of the New England conference. New York: Carlton and Porter, 1840. 128 p. CtY-D; MBNMHi; MiU; NcGI; TChU. 40-772

Binney, Horace. 1780-1878. Letter to the Public Ledger. Philadelphia, PA: s. l., 1840. PPL; PPULC. 40-773

Binney, Horace, 1780-1875. Remarks upon Mr. Binney's letter, of January 3, 1840, to the presidents of the councils of the city of Philadelphia. By the writer of the letter. Philadelphia, PA: C. Sherman & co., printers, 1840. 31 p. DLC; IU; MH; MWA; PPL. 40-774

Binns, John, 1772-1860. Binn's Justice: digest of the laws and judicial decisions of Pennsylvania by J. Binns. Philadelphia, PA; Pittsburgh, PA: James Kay, Jun. & Bro.; C. H. Kay & Co., 1840. 556 p. CoU; DLC; PPB; PU; WaU-L. 40-775

Binns, John, 1772-1860. ... Digest of the laws and judicial decisions of Pennsylvania, touching the authority and duties of justices of the peace... 1st ed. Philadelphia, PA; Pittsburgh, PA: J. Kay, junr., and bro.; C. H. Kay & Co., 1840. 556 p. CU-Law; MH-L; OCoSc; PPB; PPi. 40-776

Biographical sketches of eccentric characters. Cooperstown, NY: H. & E. Phinney [1840?] 443 p. CtY; IU; MH; NBuG; PPULC. 40-777

Biography of the Savior and His Apostles, with a portrait of each. New York: Taylor & Dodd, 1840. 108 p. DLC; ICRL; IU; OO; WHi. 40-778

Biot, Jean Baptiste, 1774-1862. An elementary treatise on analytical geometry. Tr. from the French by J. B. Biot, for the use of the cadets of the Virginia Military Institute, at Lexington, Va.; and adapted to the present state of mathematical instruction in the colleges of the United States by Francis H. Smith. New York: Wiley, 1840. 212 p. InCW; NCH; OMC; TNP; WBeloC. 40-779

Birch, Samuel. The adopted child. A musical drama in two acts. Boston, MA: W. V. Spencer [184-?] 24 p. MH. 40-780

Bird stories and dog stories. Cincinnati, OH: William T. Truman [184-?] 16 p. NN. 40-781

Bird waltz. Baltimore, MD: S. Carusi [184-?] 2 p. ViU. 40-782

Birgham, Amariah, 1798-1849. An enquiry concerning the diseases and functions of the brain, spinal cord and nerves.

New York: s. l., 1840. 327 p. DLC; ICJ; MnU; OClWHi; PPCP. 40-783

Bishop, Henry Rowley, 1786-1855. Be mine dear maid, as sung by Mr. C. E. Horn. Composed & arranged for the piano forte by H. R. Bishop. Baltimore, MD: Geo. Willig Junr. [184-?] 3 p. ViU. 40-784

Bishop, Henry Rowley, 1786-1855. Bid me discourse. [Song, words from Shakespeare's Venus and Adonis composed by Henry R. Bishop. With accomp. for piano forte. In the Key of G.] Philadelphia, PA: Klemm [184-?] p. MB. 40-785

Bishop, Henry Rowley, 1786-1855. ....The bloom is on the Rye. As sung by Mr. Edward Sheppard. The poetry by Fitzball. Composed by Henry R. Bishop. New York: Firth & Hall [184-?] 4 p. ViU. 40-786

Bishop, Henry Rowley, 1786-1855. Cortez, or, the conquest of Mexico. O, there's a mountain palm! [Song with accompaniment for piano forte.] Sung in the historical drama of Cortez... Composed by Henry R. Bishop. [The words by J. R. Planche.] Boston, MA: Hewitt [184-?] 3 p. MB. 40-787

Bishop, Henry Rowley, 1786-1855. [Evenings in Greece] To Greece we give our shining blades. Trio. [S. T. B.] From Moore's Evenings in Greece. Composed by Henry R. Bishop. [With accomp. for piano forte.] Philadelphia, PA: Blake [184-?] 3 p. MB. 40-788

Bishop, Henry Rowley. 1786-1855. Feast of roses. [Song. A.] Arranged for the Spanish guitar by A. Schmitz.

Philadelphia, PA: Willig [184-?] 2 p. MB. 40-789

Bishop, Henry Rowley. 1786-1855. Feast of roses. Words by Thomas Moore, Esq.; arranged for the piano forte. New York: William Hall & son [184-?] 2 p. ViU. 40-790

Bishop, Henry Rowley, 1786-1855. Hark! hark! each Sparton hound. Boston, MA: s. l. [184-?] p. MB. 40-791

Bishop, Henry Rowley, 1786-1855. Home sweet home, arrang'd with variations for the piano forte by Valentine. Boston, MA: Geo. P. Reed [184-?] 4 p. ViU. 40-792

Bishop, Henry Rowley, 1786-1855. Home, sweet home! Written by J. Howard Payne, Esqr. Arranged by Henry R. Bishop. Baltimore, MD: F. D. Benteen [184-?] 3 p. ViU. 40-793

Bishop, Henry Rowley, 1786-1855. If I speak to three in friendship's name. [Song] written by T. Moore, Esq. Arranged for the piano forte by H. R. Bishop. Boston, MA: Bradlee [184-?] 2 p. MB. 40-794

Bishop, Henry Rowley, 1786-1855. In tears the heart oppress'd.... Boston, MA: s. l. [184-?] p. MB. 40-795

Bishop, Henry Rowley, 1786-1855. Isabel. Spanish serenade [Bar.] Philadelphia, PA: Willig [184-?] 2 p. MB. 40-796

Bishop, Henry Rowley, 1786-1855. "Je ne scais Quoi! "Sung by Mr. Braham, in the comic opera called Englishman in India, at the Theatre Royal Drury Lane. Composed by Henry R. Bishop.

Philadelphia, PA: John G. Klemm [184-?] 2 p. ViU. 40-797

Bishop, Henry Rowley, 1786-1855. A kiss! there's nobody nigh. Duetto, sung by Miss E. Jefferson and Mr. Hutchins, in the operatic comedy of The Rencontre, at the Philadelphia theatre. Composed by Henry R. Bishop; the poetry by J. R. Planche, Esqr.; arranged by H. Willis. Philadelphia, PA: Geo. Willig [184-?] 4 p. ViU. 40-798

Bishop, Henry Rowley, 1786-1855. The leaf and the fountain. Boston, MA: Ditson [184-?] 5 p. MB; WyU. 40-799

Bishop, Henry Rowley, 1786-1855. Lo! hear the gentle lark. [Song. S. accomp. for piano forte] New York: Firth & Hall [184-?] 7 p. MB. 40-800

Bishop, Henry Rowley. 1786-1855. A mistletoe bough. A ballad. [Accomp for piano forte] Boston, MA: Ditson [184-?] p. MB. 40-801

Bishop, Henry Rowley, 1786-1855. Row gently here: a Venetian air. Written by T. Moore. Arranged by Henry R. Bishop [Song with accomp. for piano forte] New York: Riley [184-?] 2 p. MB. 40-802

Bishop, Henry Rowley, 1786-1855. The sashing white sergeant. [Song. S. or T. Accomp. for piano forte.] New York: Dubois and Stodart [184-?] 3 p. MB. 40-803

Bishop, Henry Rowley, 1786-1855. Should he upbraid. [Song with an accompaniment for the piano forte] Boston, MA: Bradlee [184-?] 5 p. MB. 40-804

Bishop, Henry Rowley, 1786-1855.

Sleep gentle lady. [Serenade. S. A. B.]
New York: Hewitt [184-?] 5 p. MB. 40-
805

Bishop, Henry Rowley, 1786-1855.
Teach O! teach me to forget. Written by
T. H. Bayly, esq.; the music arranged by
Henry R. Bishop. Louisville, KY: Perters
& Webb [184-?] 2 p. ViU. 40-806

Bishop, Henry Rowley, 1786-1855.
Teach, oh teach me to forget. A favorite
ballad. Poetry by Thos. Haynes Bayly;
music by Henry R. Bishop. Boston, MA:
Oliver Ditson & Co. [184-?] 2 p. ViU. 40-
807

Bishop, Henry Rowley, 1786-1855.
Teach, oh teach me to forget. A favorite
ballad. Poetry by Thos. Haynes Bayly;
music by Henry R. Bishop. New York:
Atwill [184-?] 2 p. ViU. 40-808

Bishop, Henry Rowley, 1786-1855. Tell
me where content to find. Duetto. Sung
by Mrs. Sequin & Mr. Manvers, at the
theatres & public concerts, the poetry by
M. Virtue, esq.; the music composed by
Henry R. Bishop, Mus. Bac. Oxon. New
York: Hewitt & Jaques [184-?] 7 p. ViU.
40-809

Bishop, Henry Rowley, 1786-1855.
They have given thee to another. A bal-
lad (A.)arranged for the Spanish guitar
by George H. Derword. New York:
Firth, Hall and Pond [184-?] 2 p. MB;
ViU. 40-810

Bishop, Henry Rowley, 1786-1855.
Thou! oh! thou hast lov'd me dearest.
Sung by Mr. Sinclair, In the Opera of The
Tyrolese peasant. Composed & arranged
by Henry R. Bishop. Philadelphia, PA:
Geo. Willig [184-?] 2 p. ViU. 40-811

Bishop, Henry Rowley, 1786-1855.
Though from our cheerful homes... Boston, MA: s. l. [184-?] 3 p. MB. 40-812

Bishop, Henry Rowley, 1786-1855. To
Greece we give our shining blades. From
Moore's evenings in Greece. Composed
by Henry R. Bishop. Philadelphia, PA: A.
Foit [184-?] 3 p. ViU. 40-813

Bishop, Henry Rowley, 1786-1855. Yes!
'tis the Indian drum! The celebrated
round, composed and arranged for three
voices by Henry R. Bishop. Boston, MA:
C. Bradlee [184-?] 5 p. ViU. 40-814

Bishop, Henry Rowley, 1786-1855. The
young muleteers of Grenada. A glee for
three voices by Thomas Moore. [Ar-
ranged by Henry R. Bishop. With accompaniment for the piano forte] New York:
Bancroft [184-?] 8 p. MB. 40-815

Bishop, Robert Hamilton. An address
delivered to the graduates of Miami
University, August 13th, 1840... Oxford,
OH: John B. Peat, 1840. 17 p. MiD-B;
NjPT; NN; OClWHi; OUr; PPPrHi. 40-
816

Bissell, Thomas. Le Deum. [For 4
voices, with organ.] Boston, MA: Ditson
& co. [184-?] 9 p. MB. 40-817

Black, Edward Junius. Edward J. Black,
to his constituents, and particularly to the
State Rights party of Georgia.
[Washington, DC: Printed by Blair &
Rives, 1840?] 16 p. GSDe; GU;
OClWHi. 40-818

Black, Edward Junius. Speech of Edward J. Black, of Georgia, on the independent treasury bill. Delivered in the
House of Representatives on the 15th

and 16th of June, 1840. [Washington, DC: Printed by Blair & Rives, 1840] 30 p. GSDe; MdHi. 40-819

Black River Literary and Religious Institute. Catalogue and circular... year ending Feb. 8, 1840. Watertown, NY: Printed by Knowlton & RIce, 1840. 16p. NN. 40-820

Blackaller, Henry. A liturgy; or, manual of Sunday School devotion and instruction. Adapted to the capacities of children. Boston, MA: J. B. DOw, 1840. 174 p. ICBB; MBD; MCET; Nh; PPL. 40-821

Blackford, Martha. The Scottish Orphans. A moral tale founded on a historical fact and calculated to improve the minds of young people. To which is added Arthur Monteith, being a continuation of the "Scottish Orphans." By Mrs. Blackford, author of the "Eskdale Herd boy" and other popular works for youth. Philadelphia, PA: Published by John B. Perry, 1840. 216 p. Md; PU. 40-822

Blackstone, William, 1723-1780. Commentaries on the laws of England. In four books. With an analysis of the work. By Sir. William Blackstone... With a life of the author, and notes, by Christian, Chitty, Lee, Hovenden, and Ryland; and also references to American cases by a member of the New York bar. From the 18th London ed. New York: W. E. Dean [etc] 1840. 2 v. IaMpI; LNB; OClW; PU-L; ViU. 40-823

Blackwood, Mrs. Price. "By gone hours, "written by the Hon. Mrs. Norton; music by Mrs. Price Blackwood. Baltimore,

MD: F. D. Benteen [184-?] 2 p. ViU. 40-824

Blackwood, Mrs. Price. 'Tis sad to think upon the joyous days of old. By gone hours. Words by the Hon. Mrs. Norton. Music by Mrs. Blackwood. Philadelphia, PA: George Willig [184-?] 2 p. ViU. 40-825

Blagden, George Washington, 1802-1884. An address delivered before the associated choirs of the Evangelical Churches, Boston, in the Bowdoin Street Church, October 24, 1840. By George W. Blagden, Pastor of the Old South Church. Boston, MA: Perkins and Marvin, 1840. 22 p. ICMe; MeHi; MiD-B; MWA; RPB. 40-826

Blair, Hugh, 1718-1800. An abridgment of lectures on rhetoric. New edition. New York: W. E. Dean, 1840. 90 p. No Loc. 40-827

Blair, Hugh, 1718-1800. Dr. Blair's lectures on Rhetoric. Abridged. With questions. New York: W. E. Dean, 1840. 268 p. KyU; MH; N; PPL. 40-828

Blair, Robert, 1699-1746. The grave. A poem. New York: s. l., 184-? 5 p. MB. 40-829

Blake, James, 1688-1753. ... Annals of the town of Dorchester... 1750. Boston, MA: D. Clapp, 1840. 95 p. OClWHi. 40-830

Blake, John Lauris, 1788-1857. A general biographical dictionary... By Rev. J. L. Blake. 3d ed. Philadelphia, PA; New York: J. Kay Jun. and brother; A. V. Blake, 1840. 1096 p. FSa; IaCrM; MoS; OCl; PCC. 40-831

Blake, John Lauris, 1788-1857. A general biographical dictionary, comprising a summary account of the most distinguished persons of all ages, nations, and professions... 4th ed. Philadelphia, PA: pub. by James Kay, Jun. and bro. [etc.] 1840. 1096 p. MiD-B; MWA; NbCrD; NNG; ScCoT. 40-832

Blake, John Lauris, 1788-1867. Conversations on the evidences of Christianity: in which the leading arguments of the best authors are arranged, developed, and connected with each other. New York: Gould, Newman, Saxton, 1840. 274 p. MBC; Nh-Hi. 40-833

Blake, John Lauris, 1788-1867. The historical reader, designed for the use of schools and families. On a new plan. "History serves to amuse the imagination; to interest the passions; to improve the understanding; and to strengthen the sentiments of virtue and piety." Stereotyped By T. H. Carter & Co. Boston. Concord, NH: Published by John F. Brown, 1840. 372 p. ICBB. 40-834

Blake, John Lauris, 1788-1867. The young orator; and New York class book, especially designed to prevent dullness and monotony in the reading and declamation of schools, by the Rev. J. L. Blake, D. D. Ninth edition. New York: Published by Robinson, Pratt, & Co., and by A. V. Blake, 1840. 252 p. MH; NAlf. 40-835

Blake, John Lauris, 1788-1867. The young orator; and New York class book, especially designed to prevent dullness and monotony in the reading and declamation of schools, by the Rev. J. L. Blake, D. D. Tenth edition. New York: Published by Robinson, Pratt, 1840. 288 p. MH; MLy. 40-836

Blanchor, F. Fanny Grey. Popular ballad. Arranged for the Spanish guitar, by F. Blanchor. Philadelphia, PA: George Willig [184-?] 2 p. ViU. 40-837

Bland, Theodorick, 1742-1790. The Bland papers: being a selection from the manuscripts of Colonel Theodorick Bland, Jr. To which are prefixed an introduction, and a memoir of Colonel Bland... Ed. by Charles Campbell... Petersburg, VA: Printed by E. & J. C. Ruffin, 1840-43. 2 v. in 1. ICU; MWA; RJa; ScC; ViW; WHi. 40-838

Blantchor, F. La receation du jeune quitariste. A collection of admired cotillions partly composed and arranged for the Spanish guitar, and respectfully dedicated to his pupils, by Fr. Blantchor. Philadelphia, PA: George Willig [184-?] 3 p. ViU. 40-839

Blessington, Marguerite Power Farmer Gardiner, 1789-1849. The belle of a season... illus. from drawings by A. E. Chalon... under the superintendence of Mr. Charles Heath. London; New York: Longman, Orme, Brown, Green and Longmans; Appleton and Co., 1840. 93 p. CtY. 40-840

Blewitt, Jonathan. The age of Indian rubber. [Song. With accompaniment for the piano forte. Words written by J. E. Carpenter. Music composed by J. Blewitt] [Boston, MA: s. l., 1841?] 4 p. MB. 40-841

Blewitt, Jonathan. The merry little fat man. Boston, MA: Ditson [184-?] 5 p. MB. 40-842

Blewitt, Jonathan. "Wery pekorliar, "or, the lisping lover. Comic song [T.] Arranged for the piano forte. [Boston, MA: s. l., 184-?] 3 p. CtY; MB. 40-843

Bliss, Albert A. Speech of Albert A. Bliss, of Lorain, on the resolution instructing our senators, and requesting our representatives to vote for the independent treasury bill. Delivered in the House of Representatives of Ohio, January 24, 1840. Elyria, OH: Printed at the Atlas office, 1840. 26 p. OClWHi. 40-844

Bliss, Leonard, 1811-1842. ... Practical grammar of the English language; introductory lessons. 2d ed. Louisville, KY: Morton, 1840. 72 p. MH. 40-845

Bliss, Leonard, Jr. An address on the uses of history, delivered before the Philomathean Society of the Washington County Seminary, at Salem, Ia., March 26th, 1840... Louisville, IA: Prentice and Weissinger, 1840. 19 p. MH; NN. 40-846

Bliss Lansingburgh almanac. Troy, NY: Luther Bliss [1840] MWA. 40-847

Bliss Lansingburgh almanac for 1841. Luther Bliss. Lansingburgh, NY: Luther Bluss [1840] MWA. 40-848

Blockcey, John. Hark 'tis the Moorish evening drum, notturno for 1 or 2 voices [A. A. Accomp. for piano forte] Boston, MA: Reed [1840?] 5 p. MB. 40-849

Blockcey, John. Hearts and homes. [Song, the accomp.] arranged for the guitar by N. P. B. Curtiss. Boston, MA: Wade [1840?] 2 p. MB. 40-850

Blockcey, John. List! to the convent bells. Notturno, for one or two voices. Composed by John Blockley. Baltimore, MD: Saml. Carusi [1840?] 3 p. ViU. 40-851

Blockcey, John. "Love not. "Ballad. The poetry by The Hon. Mrs. Norton; the music composed by J. Blockley; arranged with an accompt. for the Spanish guitar, by C. M. Sola. New York: Hewitt & Jacques [184-?] 2 p. ViU. 40-852

Blockcey, John. Love not, Written by Mrs. Norton, composed for the piano forte by Blockley. Boston, MA: Bradlee [184-?] 2 p. MB. 40-853

Blockcey, John. Love not, written by Mrs. Norton; composed for the piano forte by Blockley. New York: Firth Pond & Co. [184-?] 2 p. ViU. 40-854

Blockcey, John. Love not, Written by Mrs. Norton. Composed for the piano forte by Blockley. Philadelphia, PA: Geo. Willig [184-?] 2 p. MB; ViU. 40-855

Blockley, John. The moon is beaming o'er the lake. Notturno for two voices. Composed by John Blockley... New York: W. Dubois [184-?] 7 p. ViU. 40-856

Blockley, John. My childhood's home. A ballad. [With accompaniment for piano forte] Poetry by the Honble. Mrs. Norton. Music by John Blockley... New York: Firth & Hall [184-?] 5 p. MB. 40-857

Blockcey, John. "Yesterday. "A ballad. The poetry written by Miss M. A. Browne. The music composed by John

Blockley. Philadelphia, PA: George Willig [184-?] 5 p. ViU. 40-858

Blois, John T. Gazetteer of the State of Michigan. In three parts, containing a general view of the state, a description of the face of the country... Reprint edition. Detroit, MI; New York: Sidney L. Rood & Co.; Robinson Pratt & Co., 1840. 418 p. ICU. 40-859

Bluff, Harry. Our navy. Extracts from the Lucky bag, on the reorganization of the navy. Washington, DC: Printed at the Madisonian Office, 1840. 16 p. DLC. 40-860

Blundell, James, 1790-1877. ... Observations on some of the more important diseases of woman. By James Blundell... ed. by T. Castle. Philadelphia, PA: A. Waldie, 1840. 215 p. CSt-L; GU0M; MB; NBuU-M; ViU. 40-861

Blunt, E. G. W. Chart of the South Atlantic ocean... New York: s. l., 1840. RPB. 40-862

Blunt, Henry, 1794-1843. Lectures upon the history of Our Lord and Saviour Jesus Christ. By the Rev. Henry Blunt, A. M. Second American edition. Philadelphia, PA: Herman Hooker, 1840. 447 p. IEG; InID; MBC; NCH; RNR. 40-863

Blunt, Henry, 1794-1843. Sermons preached in Trinity Church, Upper Chelsea. By the Rev. Henry Blunt, A. M. First American from the fourth London edition. Philadelphia, PA: Herman Hooker, 1840. 287 p. CSansS; IES; MdBE; PPA; WNaE. 40-864

Blunt, Walter, 1802-1868. Dissenters baptisms and church burials. Strictures

upon the decision of the late Sir John Nicholl... Exeter, PA: s. l., 1840. 227 p. CtY; PPM. 40-865

Board of Aldermen, March 30, 1840. Supplemental report of the late Water Commissioners, laid on the table and ordered to be printed for the use of the members. Thomas Bolton, Clerk. Utica, NY?: s. l., 1840. NUtHi. 40-866

Boardman, Andrew. An essay on the means of improving medical education and elevating medical character, by Andrew Boardman, M. D. Philadelphia, PA: Printed by Haswell, Barrington and Haswell, 1840. 23 p. MB; MBAt; MMeT-Hi; NBuU-M; NNNAM. 40-867

Bochsa, Robert Nicholas Charles, 1789-1856. Bochsa's Celebrated march describing the advance & retreat of a military band. For the piano forte. Arranged by S. T. Rosenberg. New York: Dubois & Bacon [184-?] 5 p. MB. 40-868

Bochsa, Robert Nicholas Charles, 1789-1856. The Cracovienne, arranged as a quick step. [Anon. For the piano forte.] Boston, MA: Reed [184-?] 2 p. MB. 40-869

Bochsa, Robert Nicholas Charles, 1789-1856. The Cracovienne. [For the piano forte.] Danced by Madlle. Fanny Elssler... Composed by N. C. Bocsha [sic.] New York: Firth & Hall [184-?] 6 p. MB. 40-870

Bochsa, Robert Nicholas Charles, 1789-1856. A new and improved method of instruction for the harp, in which the principles of fingering and the various means of attaining a finished excution on that instrument are clearly explained and illustrated by numerous examples and exercises. Boston, MA: Ditson [184-?] 68 p. MB. 40-871

Bochsa, Robert Nicholas Charles, 1789-1856. One little word before we part. Ballad. Composed by N. C. Bochsa. Baltimore, MD: Geo. Willig, Jr. [184-?] 2 p. ViU. 40-872

Bogatzky, (Karl) Heinrich von, 1690-1774. Golden treasury. New York: R. Carter [184-?] 384 p. MH; PPULC; PU; ViU. 40-873

Bogue, David, 1750-1825. Essay on the divine authority of the New Testament. By David Bogue. Rev. ed. New York: American Tract Society [184-?] 252 p. CBPSR; CSansS; CU; MH. 40-874

Bohlman-Saurzeau, Henri. La Chasse infernale quadrille fantastique. Compose pour le piano forte par Henri Bohlman-Sauzeau. Philadelphia, PA; New York: A. Fiot; W. Dubois [184-?] 6 p. ViU. 40-875

Bohlman-Saurzeau, Henri. Diabolique quick step, composed by Henry Bohlman. Boston, MA: O. Ditson [184-?] 2 p. ViU. 40-876

Bohuszewicz, E. B. Boston waltzes and cotillion. [For the piano forte.] Boston, MA: Parker & Ditson [184-?] 2 p. MB. 40-877

Boieldieu, Francois Adrien. [La Dame Blanche] The evening parting hymn. [Song] Poetry by Dr. T. Gray. Music from "The White Lady" by Boieldieu. Arranged... by Geo. Kingsley. [With accompaniment for the piano forte] Boston, MA: Bradlee [184-?] 3 p. MB. 40-878

Boieldieu, Francois Adrien. The much admired overture to the opera "La Dame Blanche. "For the piano forte. Composed by A. Boieldieu. Baltimore, MD: Geo. Willig, Jr. [184-?] 10 p. ViU. 40-879

Bolmar, Antoine. A book of the French verbs, wherein the model verbs and several of the most difficult are conjugated. Philadelphia, PA: Lea and Blanchard, 1840. 173 p. NN. 40-880

Bolmar, Antoine. A collection of colloquial phrases, on every topic to maintain conversation... By A. Bolmar. A new edition, revised and corrected. Philadelphia, PA: Lea & Blanchard, 1840. 208 p. DLC; MH; MWA; OO; PPW; ViU. 40-881

Bonaparte's march crossing the Rhine, composed and arranged for the piano forte. Boston, MA: Ditson [184-?] 1 p. MB. 40-882

Bond, Thomas Emerson, 1782-1856. Address delivered before the Delta Phi and Athenaean literary societies of Newark college... Baltimore, MD: Woods & Crane, printers, 1840. 24 p. CSmH; DLC; NjPT; OClWHi; PPPrHi. 40-883

Bond, William Key, d. 1864. Speech of Mr. Bond, of Ohio, on the treasury note bill. Delivered in the House of Representatives, March 18, 1840. [Washington, DC: s. l., 1840] 31 p. DLC; IU; MB; OClWHi; PPL. 40-884

Bond, William Key, d. 1864. To the clergy and laity of P. E. Ch. in Ohio. [S. l.: s. l., 1840?] p. CtHT. 40-885

Bonnell, George William. Topographical description of Texas. To which is added an account of the Indian tribes. Austin, TX: Wing & Brown, 1840. 150 p. CSmH; ICN; MHi; TxGR; WHi. 40-886

Bonny lassie songster. New York: J. Slater, 184-? 32 p. DLC. 40-887

Bonnycastle, John, 1750?-1821. An introduction to mensuration and practical geometry. Philadelphia, PA: Kimber & Sharples, 1840. 288 p. ICU; NPStA. 40-888

The book of accidents; or, Warnings to the heedless. New Haven, CT: Published by S. Babcock, 1840. 8 p. CtY; MiU; PPULC. 40-889

Book of Bible stories. A present for a good scholar. New Haven, CT: S. Babcock, 1840? p. MH. 40-890

Book of Mormon. The book of Mormon. Translated by Joseph Smith, jr. Third edition... Nauvoo, IL; Printed by Robinson and Smith, 1840. 571 p. ICP; KyBvU; MWA; NCH; PHi. 40-891

The book of remarkable characters and events. Hartford, CT: s. l. [184-?] p. MB. 40-892

The book of shipwrecks, and narratives of maritime discoveries and the most popular voyages, from the time of Columbus to the present day. Embelloished with engravings. Boston, MA: Charles Gaylord, 1840. 492 p. MH; NcWsS. 40-893

The book of the seasons, a gift for the young. Autumn. Boston, MA: William Crosby and Company, 1840. 70 p. MBSPN; MH; PPL; PPULC. 40-894

Book of trees. New York: M. Day & Co.; Baker, Crane & Co. [184-?] 32 p. CtY. 40-895

Booth, Abraham, 1734-1806. The reign of grace, from its rise to its consummation. With a memoir of his life and writings. Philadelphia, PA: American Baptist Publication Society [184-?] p. ICNBT; KKcB; MH; MiU; PPULC. 40-896

Booth, Junius Brutus, 1796-1852. Ugalina. A tragedy in three acts. New York: S. French [1840?] 27 p. CtY; LNH; MH; OCl; RPB. 40-897

Booth, Junius Brutus, 1796-1852. Ugalina. A tragedy in three acts. Philadelphia, PA: Turner & Fisher [1840?] p. MiU; NN; NNC; PPULC. 40-898

Boothbay, Maine. Congregational Church. The articles of faith, covenant and ecclesiastical rules and principles, adopted by the Congregational church in Boothbay, Maine. Bath: E. Clarke, printer, 1840. 27 p. M; MBC; MHi. 40-899

Borguno, Agustin. Believe me if all those endearing young charms. Irish melodies. Boston, MA: Oliver Diston [184-?] 2 p. ViU. 40-900

Bosche, Eduard Theodor. Allgemeine beschreibung der erde und ihrer bewohner; nebst einer kurzen darstellung der himmelskorper. Mit vielen abbildungen und einer illuminirten weltkarte. Bearb... von Eduard Theodor Bosche... Philadelphia, PA: Leineweber und Rex, 1840. 793 p. DLC; MoS; PHi; PPM; WStfSF. 40-901

Bosovitz, Frederick. Souvenir de Vienne. Galop de concert [pour piano] Op. 26. New York: Harris [184-?] 9 p. MB. 40-902

Boston, Thomas, 1677-1732. Human nature in its fourfold state... By Thomas Boston. Third Phila. edition. Philadelphia, PA: Towar and J. & D. M. Hogan, 1840. 400 p. PReaAt. 40-903

Boston. Boy's Monitorial School. A report upon the boy's monitorial school with a catalogue of the pupils. George Fowle, principal. Boston, January, 1840. Boston, MA: Clapp and Son's Press [1840] 14 p. MnU. 40-904

Boston. Common Council. Rules and orders of the Common Council of the City of Boston, 1840. Boston, MA: John H. Eastburn, City Printer, 1840. 86 p. MiD-B. 40-905

Boston. First Free Congregational Church. Brief history of the first free Congregational church, with the articles of faith... and a list of its members. Boston, MA: Dow and Jackson, printers, 1840. 48 p. ICN; M. 40-906

Boston. Foreign Library. Catalogue of the Foreign Library. Boston, MA: printed by S. N. Dickinson, 1840. 12 p. MB. 40-907

Boston. Hollis Street Church. Correspondence between a committee and the Pastor of Hollis Street Society, upon the subject of a Second Ecclesiastical Council, from Oct. 26 to Nov. 12, 1840. Boston, MA: s. l., 1840. 23 p. No Loc. 40-908

Boston. Hollis Street Church. Cor-

respondence between a committee and the pastor of Hollis Street Society, upon the subject of a second ecclesiastical council, from Oct. 26, to Nov. 12, 1840. Boston, MA: S. N. Dickinson, 1840. 23 p. CBPac; ICMc; MB; NNP; OCHP. 40-909

Boston. Hollis Street Church. Proceedings in the controversy between a part of the proprietors and the pastor of Hollis street church, Boston, 1838 and 1839. Boston, MA: Dickinson [1840?] 60 p. CBPac; MB; MH; MH-AH; TNF. 40-910

Boston. Hollis Street Church. Reply of the friends of Rev. John Pierpont, to a proposal for dissolving the pastoral connection between him and the Society in Hollis Street. Boston, MA: s. l., 1840. 8 p. CBPac; MH; MiD-B; MWiW; NNP. 40-911

Boston. Hollis Street Church. Special meeting of the proprietors of Hollis street meeting house, March 9th, 1840. [Boston, MA: W. W. Clapp & Son, 1840] 15 p. CtHT; DLC; MHi; MiD-B; NNP. 40-912

Boston. Mayor (Jonathan Chapman) Address of the Mayor to the City Council of Boston, January 6, 1840. [Boston, MA: s. l., 1840] 18 p. MHi. 40-913

Boston. Ordinances. An act for supplying the city of Boston with pure water. [Boston, MA: s. l., 1840] 12 p. MHi. 40-914

Boston. Public Schools. Order of exercises. Voluntary declaration at the English High School, July 22, 1840. [Bos-

ton, MA: S. N. Dickinson, Printer, 1840]
MBB. 40-915

Boston. School Committee. Report of
the school committee on the expeniency
of introducing musical instruction into
the public schools. Boston, MA:
Academy of Music, 1840. 16 p. MB; MHi.
40-916

Boston. School for Young Ladies. Mrs.
H. J. Finn, Mrs. Hopkins, and daughter,
propose opening a school for young
ladies on Monday, the 14th of September, [1840] [S. l.: s. l., 1840] 1 p. MHi. 40-
917

Boston. Suffolk Street Chapel. Order of
services at the dedication, Wed., Feb. 5,
1840. [Boston, MA: s. l., 1840] p. MBAt;
MHi. 40-918

Boston. Suffolk St. Chapel. Services at
the dedication of the chapel. Boston,
MA: s. l., 1840 MBAt. 40-919

Boston. Warren Street Church. Liturgy
for the use of the church at the Warren
Street Chapel in Boston. Boston, MA: s.
l., 1840. 509 p. CBPac; ICMe; MBC;
MWHi. 40-920

Boston Academy of Music. Anniversary
Concert, May 27, 1840. [Boston, MA: s.
l., 1840] 4 p. MHi. 40-921

Boston Academy of Music. The Boston
academy's collection of church music,
consisting of the most popular Psalm and
hymn tunes, anthems, sentences, chants,
etc. old and new... Published under the
direction of the Boston academy of
music. 8th ed. Boston, MA: Published by
J. H. Wilkins and R. B. Carter, 1840. 357

p. MAnHi; MH; MnM; NIC; PPPrHi;
RPB. 40-922

Boston Academy of Music. Concert by
the juvenile choir... at the Odeon... May
16, 1840. [Boston, MA: s. l., 1840] 12 p.
MHi. 40-923

Boston almanac and business directory.
Boston, MA: DIckinson, 1840. CtMW;
MS. 40-924

Boston almanac and business directory.
Boston, MA: Sampson, Murdock & Co.,
1840-. v. CtMW. 40-925

The Boston almanac, for the year 1840.
Boston, MA: S. N. Dickinson; Published
by Thomas Groom; Printed at the Office
of the Rotary Card Press [Dickinson's]
1840. 132 p. MWo. 40-926

The Boston almanac, for the year 1841.
Boston, MA: Published by Dickinson's,
1840. 120 p. MBevHi; MWeyHi. 40-927

The Boston almanac, for the year 1841.
By S. N. Dickinson. Boston, MA:
Published by Thomas Groom. Printed at
the office of the Rotary Card Press, 1840.
120 p. IaHi; MHa; MoSpD; MMal;
MWA. 40-928

Boston and Portland Railroad Corporation. Report of a committee appointed to
investigate the doings of... (n.) [Boston,
MA: s. l., 1840] 56 p. MH-BA. 40-929

Boston and Portland Railroad Corporation. Report of a committee of stockholders of the Boston and Portland
rail-road, with a brief description of the
road, and a statement of its costs, income
and future prospects. Anvoer, MA:

Gould, Newman and Saxton, 1840. 7 p. MB; MBAt; MH-BA; MLaw. 40-930

Boston and Worcester Railroad Corporation. Report of a committee of directors of the Boston and Worcester rail-road corporation. On the proposition of the directors of the Western rail-road, to reduce the rates of fare and freight on the two railroads. With the correspondence on that subject... Boston, MA: Printed by S. N. Dickinson, 1840. 32 p. CtY; ICU; MBAt; MiD-B; PU. 40-931

Boston Athenaeum. Catalogue of books added to the Boston Athenaeum, since the publication of the catalogue in January, 1827. Boston, MA: Eastburn's Press, 1840. 178 p. MH; MnHi; MWA; NCH. 40-932

Boston Athenaeum. Catalogue of the fourteenth exhibition of paintings in the Athenaeum Gallery. Boston, MA: Eastburn's Press, 1840. 12 p. MNF. 40-933

The Boston collection of instrumental music: containing marches, quicksteps, waltzes... arranged for brass, wooden & stringed instruments. Boston, MA: Diton [184-?] 184 p. MB; RPB. 40-934

Boston comic almanac. Boston, MA: J. Fisher, 1840. MWA. 40-935

Boston directory; containing names of inhabitants, occupants, places of business and homes and city register. Boston, MA: Charles Stimpson, Jr., 1840. 451 p. IaHA; PPL; WHi. 40-936

Boston Marine Society. Constitution and laws of the Boston Marine Society, instituted in the year 1742; incorporated

in the year 1754... Boston, MA: Marden & Co. printers, 1840. 53 p. MMhHi. 40-937

Boston Society of the New Jerusalem. Documents of the Boston society of the New Jerusalem comprising a brief sketch of its history, its origination for 1840 and a list of its members. Boston, MA: Printed for the Society, 1840. 12 p. OUrC. 40-938

Bosworth, N. Treatise on the rifle, musket, pistol & fowling piece: embracing projectiles & sharp-shooting also the manufacture of guns, & the preparation of the materials suited to their construction... New York: Redfield, 1840. 113 p. PPFrankI. 40-939

Botta, Carlo Giuseppi Guglielmo, 1766-1837. History of the war of independence of the United States of America. By Charles Botta....Translated from the Italian, by George Alexander Otis, esq. 8th ed., rev. and cor. New Haven, CT: T. Brainard, 1840. 2 v. ArBaA; LNH; MBC; NjMD; TxWB. 40-940

Botta, Carlo Giuseppi Guglielmo, 1766-1837. History of the war of independence of the United States of America. Translated from the Italian, by George Alexander Otis, Esq. 9th ed., rev. and cor. New Haven, CT: T. Brainard, 1840. 2 v. LNL. 40-941

Botts, John Minor, 1802-1869. Speech of Mr. Botts, of Virginia, on the New Jersey contested election. Delivered in the House of Representatives, January 9, 1840. Washington, DC: Printed by Gales and Seaton, 1840? 16 p. CSmH; Ct;

CtHT-W; CtY; KSalW; M; MBevHi; NjR; OClWHi; Vi; WHi. 40-942

Boucicault, Dion, 1822?-1890. ... Old heads and young hearts. A comedy in five acts. By Dion Boucicault. With the stage business, cast of characters, costumes, relative positions, etc. New York: S. French [184-?] 73 p. CSt; DLC; MH; NN. 40-943

Bouhours, Dominique, 1628-1702. Life of St. Ignatius, founder of the Society of Jesus; to which is afixed a sketch of the Institute of the Jesuits. From the French. By a Catholic clergyman. Philadelphia, PA: E. CUmmiskey, 1840. 419 p. ArLSJ; MiDU; MoSU; OCX; ScU. 40-944

Bounding billows. A favorite song. Arranged for the piano forte. New York: Jas. L. Hewitt & Co. [184-?] 1 p. ViU. 40-945

The bouquet. Or spirit of English poetry. Third edition. Philadelphia, PA: Thomas T. Ash and Company [184-?] p. CSmH. 40-946

Bourdon, Louis Pierre Marie, 1779-1854. Elements of algebra. Tr. from the French of M. Bourdon... Adapted to the course of mathematical instruction in the United States, by Charles Davies... Rev. ed. Philadelphia, PA: A. S. Barnes & Co., 1840. 358 p. CtHT; MiEalC; NjP; OOxM; PPL; TxShA. 40-947

Bowditch, Henry Ingersoll, 1808-1892. Remarks, relative to Dr. Paines commentaries upon the writings of M. Louis. Boston, MA: Clapp, 1840. 32 p. MB; MBAt; MBM; PU. 40-948

Bowditch, Nathaniel Ingersoll, 1805-

1861. Memoir of Nathaniel Bowditch. By his son. Originally prefixed to the 4th volume of the Mecanique Celeste. 2d edition. Boston, MA: Charles L. Little and James Brown, pub., 1840. 172 p. GU; MB-FA; MBev; NNUT; WHi. 40-949

Bowdoin College. Catalogue of the officers and students of Bowdoin College and the Medical School of Maine. Brunswick, NJ: s. l., 1840. MBAG; Me; MeHi. 40-950

Bowdoin College. Catalogus senatus academici... Collegio Bowdoineusi... Brunswick, NJ: E. Typis Josephi Griffin, 1840. 46 p. CtY; DLC; ICJ; MeHi; PPULC. 40-951

Bowen, Abel, 1790-1850. The naval monument containing official and other accounts of all the battles fought between the navies of the United States and Great Britain during the late war. Boston, MA: published by George Clark, 1840. 326 p. CSmH; LU; MdBJ; MDeeP; MMal; OHi. 40-952

Bowen, Benjamin B., compiler. Daisies and dew-drops. A memorial to the blind. Boston, MA: John H. Eastburn, printer, 1840. 64 p. MMhHi. 40-953

Bowen, Benjamin B., compiler. Daisies and dew-drops, a memorial of the blind. Compiled by B. B. Bowen, late a pupil of the Institution for the Blind at Boston, Mass. Lowell, MA: A. Watson, Printer, 1840. 64 p. ICBB; MWA; MWatP. 40-954

Bowen, Benjamin B., compiler. Daisies and dew-drops. Memorial to the blind. New York: D. Murphy, 1840. 60 p. MBNMHi. 40-955

Bowie, Thomas F. Remarks of... at the Convention of tobacco planters of the United States. Upper Marlboro: Wilson, 1840. 12 p. P. 40-956

Boyce, J. A sermon preached... on the fourteenth of October, 1839... Columbia, SC: Printed at the Southern Chronicle Office, 1840. 12 p. CSmH. 40-957

Boyer, Abel, 1667-1729. Boyer's French dictionary, comprising all the additions and improvements of the latest Paris and London editions... Boston, MA: Hilliard, Gray and Co., 1840. 780 p. CBPSR; CoPu; GAuY; MH; WAsN. 40-958

Boyle, Isaac. An historical memoir of the Boston Episcopal Charitable Society. By Isaac Boyle... Boston, MA: [I. R. Butts] 1840. 31 p. LNH; MB; MWA; WHi. 40-959

Boyle, Isaac. Historical view of the Council of Nice. Bound up with Ecclesiastical History of Eusebius Pamphilua. Philadelphia, PA: s. l., 1840. 59 p. NjNbS; OClW; ODW. 40-960

The boys' and girls' own primer, or, First step to learning. Baltimore, MD: Wm. Raine [1840?] p. MH. 40-961

The boys' own primer. With engravings. By a friend to youth. Cincinnati, OH: Truman and Smith [184-?] 16 p. MiU. 40-962

The Boy's Talisman; A Christmas and New Year's Gift. Boston, MA: Benjamin H. Greene, 1840. 133 p. MHi; RPB; TxU. 40-963

Brace, Jacob, jr. A key to Brace's principles of English grammar, containing the corrected exercises, and a full account of the method of teaching the grammar. Arranged on the plan of Lennie's key. By Joab Brace, Jr. Philadelphia, PA; Boston, MA: Henry Perkins; Ives and Dennet, 1840. 108 p. CtHWatk; KyU; MB; MH; MiU. 40-964

Brace, Jacob, Jr. The principles of English grammar. With copious exercises in parsing and syntax. Arranged on the basis of Lennie's grammar, by Joab Brace, Jr. Philadelphia, PA; Boston, MA: H. Perkins; Ives and Dennet, 1840. 144 p. CtHWatk; CtY; DLC. 40-965

Brackenridge, Henry Marie, 1786-1871. History of the late war between the United States and Great Britain. Philadelphia, PA: J. Kay, Jun. and brother, [184-?] 298 p. MLy. 40-966

Bradbury, Thomas. The mystery of Godliness, wherein the Deity of Christ is improved. By the Rev. Thomas Bradbury. Philadelphia, PA: Presbyterian Board of Publication, 1840. 2 v. GDecCT; MBC; NcU; PPM; ViRut. 40-967

Bradbury Academy, Bradford, Mass. Catalogue of the officers and members of Bradford Academy, Bradford, Massachusetts, for the year ending November 20, 1840. Haverhill, MA: from the Essex Banner Press, 1840. 12 p. MB; MHa. 40-968

Bradford, Alden, 1765-1843. History of the federal government for fifty years, from March, 1789, to March, 1839. By Alden Bradford... Boston, MA: S. G. Simpkins, 1840. 180 p. Ct; InND; LNH; MPiB; O; PPAmP. 40-969

Bradford, James. Address delivered at Rowley, Massachusetts, September 5th, 1839, at the celebration of the second centennial anniversary of the settlement of the town, embracing its ecclesiastical history from the beginning... Boston, MA: Ferdinand Andrews, 1840. 54 p. MSaE; MWA; O; PPPrHi; RPB; WHi. 40-970

Braham, John. When they bosom heaves the sigh. A duett (S. and T.)... in the... opera of Narensky. [Accomp. for piano.] Philadelphia, PA: Nunns [184-?] 6 p. MB. 40-971

Brainard, Dyar Throop, 1790-1863. The annual address to the candidates for degrees and licenses, in the Medical institution of Yale College, January 21, 1840. New Haven, CT: s. l., 1840. 16 p. MB; NBMs; OClM; PPAmP. 40-972

Brainerd, David, 1718-1747. The life of Rev. David Brainerd, chiefly extracted from his diary. By President Edwards. Somewhat abridged... New York: Published by the American tract society [184-?] 360 p. CSmH; IAIS; GDecCT. 40-973

Brainerd, Thomas. Influence of theatres; a lecture on the nature and tendency of the stage, delivered in the Third Presbyterian church of Philadelphia, Sept. 6th, 1840. Philadelphia, PA: s. l., 1840. 16 p. ICU; MB; MWA; PPPrHi. 40-974

Braithwaite's retrospect of practical medicine and surgery. Vols. 1-80. American edition. New York: s. l., 1840-79. 80 v. GDecCT; GU; MBP; OClM; Tx-DaBm; WaPS. 40-975

Braman, Milton Palmer, 1799-. Obstacles to the success of the gospel. A sermon preached at the dedication of the new meeting house, erected by the first religious society in North Danvers... 1839... Salem: Ives & Jewett, 1840. 50 p. CSmH; MiD-B; MWA; OClWHi; RPB. 40-976

Branagan, Thomas, b. 1774. The guardian genius of the Federal Union; or, Patriotic admonitions on the signs of the times, in relation to the evil spirit of party, arising from the root of all evils, human slavery. By Thomas Branagan. Being a part of the Beauties of Philanthropy, by a philanthropist. 2nd. ed. New York: Published for the author, 1840. 186 p. ArU; NcD; WHi. 40-977

Brandling, Mary. I pray for thee; or, The farewell. A duett as sung by Mr. & Mrs. Wood. Written & composed by Miss Mary Brandling, and dedicated to her sister. Philadelphia, PA: Geo. W. Hewitt & Co. [184-?] 7 p. ViU. 40-978

Brandreth, Benjamin, 1807-1880. Purgatin: or, The Brandrethian Method of treating diseases and curing them with one and the same universal medicine, the efficacy of which has been fully tested, beyond the power of malice or misrepresentation to dispute, with an attempt to explain the cause and origin of all diseases. By Benjamin Brandreth, M. D. New York: Published by the author, 1840. 39 p. MWA. 40-979

Brantly, W. T. The covenant of circumcision, no just plea for infant baptism. By W. T. Brantly. Philadelphia, PA: s. l., 1840. 16 p. NjPT; PCA. 40-980

Bready, J. Hall. The annual address

delivered before the Union philosophical and Belles Letters societies of Dickinson College, Carlisle, Pa., July 8, 1840. By J. Hall Bready. Philadelphia, PA: J. Crissy, printer, 1840. 35 p. MH; MnHi; NCH; NjR; OOxM; PPL; TxU. 40-981

Breck, Joseph. West Point: or, A tale of treason, an historical drama in three acts. Dramatized from Ingraham's Romance of American history. Baltimore: Bull & Tuttle, 1840. 21 p. MdHi; NIC; RPB. 40-982

Breck, Joseph, 1794-1873. Catalogue of vegetable, herb, tree, flower and grass seeds... By Joseph Breck & Co. Eighth edition. Boston, MA: New England Farmer Office, 1840. 84 p. MB; MHi; MiD-B. 40-983

Breckinridge, Robert Jefferson, 1800-1871. A full report of the trial of the Rev. Robert J. Breckinridge, on an indictment for a libel on James L. Macquire, overseer of the Alms house of Baltimore city and county. Published under the superintendence of a member of the Baltimore bar, Baltimore City Court, February term, 1840. Baltimore, MD: J. Reilly, 1840. 36 p. MdBE; MdHi; MH-L; Mi-L. 40-984

Breckinridge, Robert Jefferson, 1800-1871. Second defense Louisville, 1841. Baltimore, MD: s. l., 1840. 687 p. No Loc. 40-985

Breckinridge, Robert Jefferson, 1800-1871. Speech... delivered in the courthouse at lexington, Ky., on the 12th day of October, 1840, in reply to "The speech of Robert Wickliffe." Lexington, KY: N. L. & J. W. Finnell, ptrs., 1840. 32 p.

CSmH; ICMe; KyU; MdBP; MWA; OClWHi. 40-986

Breckinridge, Robert Jefferson, 1800-1871. The state of Maryland vs. Robert J. Breckinridge; Indictment for libel. Baltimore, MD: s. l., 1840? p. ViU. 40-987

Breese, Sidney. Speech of Sidney Breese, of Clinton County, in defence of the measures of the national administration; in favor of an independent treasury; and against a national bank. Delivered before the people of Montgomery, by request of a Committee of Democratic citizens of that county, on the eleventh of April, eight hundred and forty. Published by the Committee. Vandalia: John McDonald, printer, 1840. 43 p. MWA. 40-988

Bremer, Fredrika, 1801-1865. Brothers and sisters; a tale of domestic life. Translated from the original unpublished manuscript by Mary Howitt. New York: Harper & Bros. [184-?] p. MH. 40-989

Brentwood, N. H. Congregational Church. Articles of faith and form of covenant, adopted by the Congrgational Church in Brentwood, N. H., May 2, 1839. Exeter, NH: s. l., 1840. 12 p. NBLIHI. 40-990

Brewster, David, 1781-1868. ... Letters on natural magic addresses... New York: Harper & Brothers, 1840. 314 p. P; ViR. 40-991

Brewster, David, 1781-1868. The life of Sir Isaac Newton, by Sir David Brewster, LL. D. and F. R. S. New York: pub. by Harper bros., 1840. 322 p. CU; ICMe; MLow; NNNG; PWaybu. 40-992

Bricher, T. Come to the forest. Duet [S. A. Accomp. for the piano forte.] Boston, MA: Reed & Co. [184-?] 5 p. MB. 40-993

Bricher, T. Come to the forest. Duet [S. A. Arranged for the guitar by N. P. B. Curtiss.] Philadelphia, PA: s. l. [184-?] 5 p. MB. 40-994

Bricher, T. Hall's quick step... dedicated to Orderly, John Hall. Boston, MA: s. l. [1840] 2 p. KU; MHi. 40-995

Bridgeman, Thomas, d. 1850. Extracts from the eighth edition of Bridgeman's Young gardener's assistant relative to an alleged discovery on "terraculture," as described in Senate document, no. 23, of the third session of the 25th Congress... New York: D. Mitchell, printer, 1840. 12 p. DLC; MB. 40-996

Bridgeman, Thomas, d. 1850. The florist's guide. New York: Bridgeman, 1840. 179 p. IaFair. 40-997

Bridgeman, Thomas, d. 1850. The florist's guide; containing practical directions for the cultivation of annual, biennial, and perennial flowering plants... 3d ed., enl. and improved, by T. Bridgeman. New York; Boston, MA: for sale by T. Bridgeman; J. Beck and Co. [etc., etc.] 1840. 180 p. Ct; IU; MWA; PLFM; RPAt; TxU. 40-998

Bridgeman. Thomas, d. 1850. The Florists' guide, containing practical directions for cultivation of annual, biennial, and perennial flowering plants, of different classes, herbaceous and shrubby, bulbous, fibrour, and tuberous-rooted; including the double dahlia; with a monthly calendar, containing instructions for the management of greenhouse plants throughout the year. By T. Bridgeman, gardener, seedsman, and florist. Third ed., enlarged and improved. New York: s. l., 1840. 172 p. CoCsLTG; NIC-Ar. 40-999

Bridgeman, Thomas, d. 1850. Kitchen gardener's instructor, containing a catalogue of garden & herb seeds with practical directions under each head, for the cultivation of culinary vegetables and herbs. New York: Bridgeman, 1840. 144 p. NN; NNNAm; PPULC; PU-V; ViU. 40-1000

Bridgeman, Thomas, b. 1850. The young gardener's assistant; containing a catalogue of garden and flower seeds, with practical directions under each head, for the cultivation of culinary vegetables and flowers... 8th ed. New York: s. l., 1840. 408 p. CtY; MNH; NcD; OMC; RPAt. 40-1001

Bridgewater, Mass. State Normal School. Catalogues, 1840. [Bridgewater, MA: s. l., 1840] p. MBC. 40-1002

A bridal gift. By the editor of "A parting gift to a christian friend. "... from the fourth London edition. Hartford, CT: Brown and Parsons, 1840. 204 p. MB; MHa. 40-1003

A brief biographical sketch of I. A. Van Amburgh and an illustrated and descriptive history of the animals contained in the mammoth menagerie. New York: S. Booth [184-?] 79 p. MH. 40-1004

A brief enquiry into the true basis of the credit system; and into the true basis of bank credit, as part thereof. Petersburg, VA: Edmund and Julian C. Ruffin, 1840. 24 p. CSmH; DLC; Vi. 40-1005

A brief examination of the expediency of repealing the naturalization. Originally published in the Native American newspaper, New Orleans. New Orleans, LA: s. l., 1840. 19 p. MBAt; MdBP; MnHi. 40-1006

A brief sketch of the life and services of Gen. William Henry Harrison, by a young gentleman of this city. Buffalo, NY: Published by N. R. Stimson; Printed by A. Dinsmore, 1840. 35 p. NBu; Vi. 40-1007

A brief statement of the Unitarian belief. Hallowell, ME: Glazier, Masters & Smith, 1840. 4 p. MeHi. 40-1008

A brief statement of the Unitarian belief. Portland, ME: Sanborn & Foster, printers, 1840. 4 p. CBPac; ICMe; MBAU; OO. 40-1009

Brigham, Amariah, 1798-1849. An inquiry concerning the diseases and functions of the brain, the spinal cord, and the nerves. By A. Brigham, M. D. New York: G. Adlard, 1840. 327 p. CSt-L; IaDuU; NCH; OClM; TxU. 40-1010

Bright, William. Bright's single stem, dwarf and renewal system of grape culture, adapted to the vinyard, the grapery, and the fruiting of vines in pots, on trellises, abrors, etc... New York: Saxton, Parker, 1840. 123 p. PBa. 40-1011

Bright, William. Bright's single stem, dwarf and renewal system of grape culture, adapted to the vinyard, the grapery, and the fruiting of vines in pots, on trellises, abrors, etc... Philadelphia, PA: Author, 1840. 123 p. PBa. 40-1012

Brighton, Mass. School Committee.

[1st] -25th report, 1839/40-62/63. Waltham, MA; Cambridge, MA: s. l., 1840-63. v. M; MBC; MH; 40-1013

Bring flowers, the poetry, by Mrs. Hemans. Baltimore, MD: Geo. Willig Jr. [184-?] 2 p. ViU. 40-1014

Brisbane, Albert, 1809-1890. Social destiny of man, or, Association & reorganization of industry. Philadelphia, PA: C. F. Slollmeyer, 1840. 480 p. CoU; DLC; IaU; MB; OOxM; PPA. 40-1015

Brisbane, William Henry, 1803-1878. ... Address delivered at the anti-slavery convention, assembled in Hamilton, Ohio, July 3d, 1840, to which is added the constitution of the Butler county Anti-slavery society. [Cincinnati, OH: s. l., 1840] 8 p. OCHP; WHi. 40-1016

Brisbane, William Henry, 1803-1878. A letter from William Henry Brisbane to the Baptist denomination in South Carolina. Cincinnati, OH: Samuel A. Alley, printer, 1840. 8 p. CtY; InU; NjPT; OCHP; RPB. 40-1017

Brisbane, William Henry, 1803-1878. Speech of the Rev. W. H. Brisbane... delivered before the Female anti-slavery society of Cincinnati, Feb. 12, 1840. Hartford, CT: Samuel A. Alley, 1840. 16 p. CtMW; IU; MB; OClWHi. 40-1018

Brisbane, William Henry, 1803-1878. Speech of the Rev. Wm. H. Brisbane, lately a slaveholder in South Carolina; containing an account of the change of his views on the subject of slavery. Delivered before the Ladies' anti-slavery society of Cincinnati, Feb. 12, 1840. Hartford, CT: S. S. Cowles, 1840. 12 p. CtSoP; ICN; MdBJ; OO; PHC. 40-1019

Bristol, Rhode Island. Petition of Mark Anthony D'Wolf and others to the Hon. court of probate of the town of Bristol, Rhode Island. Bristol?1840? 34 p. RPB. 40-1020

Bristol Academy, Taunton, Mass. Laws... Taunton, MA: I. Amsbury, Jr., 1840. 21 p. NN. 40-1021

British Guiana. Imigration Society Inducements to emigrate to British Guiana. Boston, MA: s. l., 1840. CCHP. 40-1022

Britten, Emma [Hardings] Modern American spiritualism: a twenty year record of the communion between earth and the world of spirits. By Emma Hardings. New York: The Author, 1840. 565 p. MdBP. 40-1023

Broad, John Samuel. The minister's parting resolution & advice. A sermon. Preached in the Church of All Saints, Northampton... S. l.: s. l., 1840. 34 p. CtY. 40-1024

Broaddus, Andrew, 1770-1848. "Holding forth the word of Life. "A sermon, delivered before the Virginia Baptist Education Society, Richmond, June 6th, 1840. By A. Broaddus. Richmond, VA: Printed at the Office of the Religious Herald, 1840. 12 p. NcD; Vi; ViRU. 40-1025

Broaddus, Andrew, 1770-1848. The Virginia selection of psalms, hymns, and spiritual songs... Richmond, VA: Smith & Palmer, 1840. 730 p. DLC; TxU. 40-1026

Broaddus, William F. Substance of an Address on Temperance; delivered by William F. Broaddus, at the Session of the Shiloh Association, and furnished by request of that body, for publication in the minutes. Richmond, VA: Printed by William Sands at the Herald Office, 1840. 8 p. MWA; ViRU. 40-1027

Brocklesby, John, 1811-1889. Elements of meteorology. New York: Woodford Co., 1840. 240 p. WBeloC. 40-1028

Brockway, John Hall, 1801-1870. Speech on the sub-treasury bill. In the House of Representatives [of the U. S.] June 2, 1840. Washington, DC: pr. by Gales & Seaton, 1840. 18 p. CtSoP; CtY; CU; M; MBevHi; MWA. 40-1029

Brooke, Henry J. Annals of the Revolution; or, A history of the Doans. Philadelphia, PA; New York: J. B. Perry; Nafis & Cornish, 184?. 84 p. OCLWHi; PBL; PHi; PPULC. 40-1030

Brooke, John T. The doctrine of a special providence; briefly tested by scripture and reason. A discourse, by Rev. John T. Brooke, rector of Christ Church, Cincinnati. Cincinnati, OH: A. Pugh, 1840. 15 p. CSmH; ICU; MdBD; NjR; ViRU. 40-1031

Brooke, Samuel. Slavery opposed to Christianity. Cincinnati, OH: s. l., 1840. MBAt. 40-1032

Brookes, Richard, fl. 1750. New universal gazetteer, containing a description of the principal nations, empires, kingdoms, states... of the known world... the whole remodelled and the historical and statistical department brought down to the present period, by John Marshall. Philadelphia, PA: Marshall, 1840. 816 p. CtHT; MB; MiD; OCo. 40-1033

Brookline. Report of the School Committee of the Town of Brookline, March 2, 1840. Boston, MA: s. l., 1840. 15 p. MH. 40-1034

Brooklyn. First Presbyterian Church. Manual, 1840 and '82. Brooklyn, NY: s. l., 1840-42. 2 v. CtY; NBLiHi. 40-1035

Brooklyn. First Presbyterian Church. Manual for the communicants of the First Presbyterian Church, Brooklyn. Compiled and published by order of session... [New York: s. l., 1840] 25 p. CtY. 40-1036

Brooklyn. First Presbyterian Church. A narrative of the difficulties in the First Presbyterian Church, of Brooklyn, N. Y., in the years 1838, 1839 & 1840. [Brooklyn, NY: s. l., 1840] 38 p. MHi; NB; NjPT; NN; NSmb. 40-1037

Brooklyn. Ordinances, etc. Acts relating to The City of Brooklyn, and the ordinances thereof: together with an appendix, containing the old charters, statistical information, & c. &c. Brooklyn, NY: A. Spooner & Son, Printers, 1840. 283 p. CSmH; MH-L' NB; NN; NSmB. 40-1038

Brooklyn City Library. Act of Incorporation, By-laws and catalogue of the Brooklyn City Library... Brooklyn, NY: s. l., 1840. 80 p. MH; WHi. 40-1039

Brooklyn Daily News and Long Island Times. March 2, 1840-Dec. 27, 1843. Brooklyn, NY: s. l., 1840-43. 6 v. NBLiHi. 40-1040

Brooklyn directory and yearly advertiser, for 1840-1....Compiled by T. & J. W. Leslie, and W. F. Chichester. Brooklyn, NY: Stationers' Hall Works, 184-. 310 p. NNA. 40-1041

Brooklyn Tippecanoe Glee Club. Brooklyn Tippecanoe Song Book. Being a Selection of the Most Approved Songs, from the Various Collections recently published and Popular Songs, not included in other editions. Compiled by the Brooklyn Tippecanoe Glee Club. Second Edition. Brooklyn, NY: A. Spooner & Son, 1840. No Loc. 40-1042

Brooks, Joshua William, 1790-1882. Essay on the advent and Kingdom of Christ, and the events connected therwith. By Rev. J. W. Brooks. Philadelphia, PA: Orrin Rogers, 1840-41. 115 p. CoDI; GDecCt; MiU; MWA; OO. 40-1043

Brooks, Nathan Covington, 1809-. The literary amaranth; or, Prose and poetry... By N. C. Brooks. Philadelphia, PA: Kay, 1840. 264 p. CtY; MWA; NjP; PPL-R; WU. 40-1044

Brooks, Nathan Covington, 1809-1898. The utility of classical studies: an address. By N. C. Brooks, A. M. The uncertainty of literary fame: a poem, by C. W. Thomson. Pronounced before the Philomanthaen society of Penn. College... Pub. by the society. Baltimore, MD: printed by John Murphy, 1840. 47 p. MdBP; MH; OSW; PPL; ScCoT; TxU. 40-1045

Brough, William, 1826-1870. The Corsair. New York: s. l. [184-?] p. MB. 40-1046

Brougham and Vaux, Henry Peter Brougham, 1778-1868. Discourses on the objects and uses of science and literature with preliminary observations, by A. Potter, D. D. New York: Harper & Bro., 1840. 332 p. CtB; ICartC; NGlc; OrP; PPGP. 40-1047

Brougham and Vaux, Henry Peter Brougham, 1778-1868. Historical sketches of statesmen who flourished in the time of George III, to which is added Remarks on Party and an appendix by Henry lord Brougham, F. R. S. In two volumes. Vol. I. A New edition First Series. Philadelphia, PA: Lea and Blanchard, 1840. 2 v. NcD; OU; PHC; PU; ViU. 40-1048

Brougham and Vaux, Henry Peter Brougham, 1778-1868. Historical sketches of statesmen who flourished in the time of George III. By Henry lord Brougham. Philadelphia, PA: Lea and Blanchard, 1840-44. 3 v. CtHT; CtY; PHatU; PPULC. 40-1049

Brougham and Vanx, Henry Peter Brougham, 1778-1868. Letters and speeches on various subjects, by Henry, Lord Brougham... Philadelphia, PA: Carey & Hart, 1840. 2 v. AU; CtY; ICU; KyLxT; PPA. 40-1050

Broughton, Rhoda. Nancy: a novel. New York: s. l., 1840. MH. 40-1051

Brown, Aaron Vail, 1795-1859. Speech... on the bill introduced by Mr. Bell, to secure the freedom of elections, and to provide for the faithful administration of the executive patronage, House of Representatives, May 19, 20, 1840. Washington, DC: Printed by Blair and Rives, 1840. 21 p. IU; MdHi; WHi. 40-1052

Brown, Addison. What shall we do? Sermon, Brattleboro, Vt., March, 1840.

Brattleboro, VT: s. l., 1840. ICN; MBAt; Vt. 40-1053

Brown, Albert Gallatin. Speech of Mr. Brown, of Mississippi, on the general appropriation bill. Delivered in committee of the whole, in the House of Representatives, April 17, 1840. Washington, DC: Globe Office, 1840. 14 p. IaHi; MsJs; NcU; OCHP; TxU. 40-1054

Brown, Alexander Enos, d. 1865. Address delievered before the members of the Franklin Literary Society of Lafayette College, on the evening of the 20th of December 1839, at the dedication of their hall. Easton, PA: J. P. Hetrich, 1840. 8 p. PHi; PLT. 40-1055

Brown, Bedford. Speech on the motion to print the report of the Secretary of the Treasury on the expenditures of the government. Delivered in the Senate of the United States, May 7, 1840. Washington, DC: Blair & Rives, 1840. NcU. 40-1056

Brown, Benjamin N. Defence of infant baptism. A discourse, in defence of infant baptism: delivered in the William Street Church, Baltimore, January 26, 1840. By Rev. Benjamin N. Brown, Pastor of William Street Station. Published by request. Baltimore, MD: Isaac P. Cook; R. J. Matchett, printer, 1840. 16 p. MdHi. 40-1057

Brown, Erastus. The trial of Cain, the first murderer, by rule of court; in which a Predestinarian, a Universalist and an Arminian [sic] argue as attorneys. By Erastus Brown. Poetry. Boston, MA: s. l., 1840. 36 p. NjPT; PU. 40-1058

Brown, Erastus. The trial of Cain, the

irst murderer, by rule of court; in which a predestinarian, a Universalist and an Arminian argue as attorneys at the bar; he two former as prisoner's counsel, the atter as attorney-general. In poetry... Lowell, MA: Printed for the purchaser, 1840. 32 p. CtY; NjPT; PU; RPB. 40-1059

Brown, Francis H. The Cracovienne valtz. Arranged for the piano forte. New York: Hewlitt & Jacques, 1840. 2 p. CtY; MB. 40-1060

Brown, Francis H. The fountain waltz. Composed & respectfully dedicated to nifs Mary Cunningham by Francis H. Brown. Boston, MA: Oliver Diston [184-3 p. ViU. 40-1061

Brown, Francis H. Evening song to the irgin at sea. A duett. The words by Mrs. Hemans; the music by her sister. Louisville, KY: David P. Faulds [184-?] 3 p. ViU. 40-1062

Brown, Francis H. Round Hill Quick Step. Respectfully dedicated to the adies of Northampton by the officers of he New England Guards. Music composed by Francis H. Brown. Boston, MA: Geo. P. Reed, 1840. MB; MNF; MNS. 0-1063

Brown, Gould, 1791-1857. The institute of English grammar, methodically arranged; with examples for parsing, quesins for examination, false syntax for correction, exercises for writing, observations for the advanced student, & a key o the oral exercises; to which are added appendixes. New York: S. S. & W. Wood, 184-? 311 p. CtY; DLC; OClWiti; PU; Pu-Penn. 40-1064

Brown, Isaac. A sermon delivered before the First Universalist Society... By Isaac Brown. Boston, MA: J. N. Bang, 1840. 16 p. MMeT; MMeT-Hi. 40-1065

Brown, James. American slavery, in its moral and political aspects, comprehensively examined; to which is subjoined on epitome of ecclesiastical history, shewing the mutilated state of modern christianity, by James Brown. Oswego, NY: Printed by G. Henry, 1840. 102 p. IaU; NjR; OO; RP; ViU. 40-1066

Brown, James. Grammarian. An exegesis of English syntax. Designed to enable teachers, pupils, and others to comprehend fully, the present popular system of English grammar, as presented by Murray. Philadelphia, PA; Pittsburgh, PA: J. Key; C. H. Kay & Co., 1840. DLC; MiU; PPULC; PU. 40-1067

Brown, James. Writer on education. American slavery, in its moral and political aspects, comprehensively examined; to which is subjoined an epitome of ecclesiastical history, by James Brown... Oswego, NY: Printed by G. Henry, 1840. 102 p. OClWHi. 40-1068

Brown, James. Writer on education. On the means and manifestations of a genuine revival of religion, an address delivered... Edinburgh, Scotland, on November 19, 1839.. Second edition. Oxford, OH: J. M. Christy, 1840. 25 p. OClWHi. 40-1069

Brown, John, 1722-1787. Brown's Concordance of the Old and New Testaments. New York: Hurst and Co., pub., 1840. 220 p. NcGA. 40-1070

Brown, John Newton, 1803-1868.

Emily, and other poems. By J. Newton Brown... Concord, NH: I. S. Boyd, 1840. 276 p. CSmH; NhD; OO; PHi; TxU. 40-1071

Brown, Matilda A. True friendship. [Song, with accompaniment for piano forte.] Boston, MA: Ditson [184-?] 2 p. MB. 40-1072

Brown, Milton, 1804-1883. Speech of Mr. Milton Brown, of Tennessee, on the bill introduced by Mr. Bell, to secure the freedom of elections, and to provide for the faithful administration of the executive patronage. House of Representatives, May 19, 20, 1840. Washington, DC: Printed by Blair and Rives, 1840. 21 p. MdHi; TxU. 40-1073

Brown, Solyman, 1790-1876. Dentologia: a poem on the diseases of the teeth and their proper remedies. With notes, practical, historical, illustrative, and explanatory, by Eleazar Parmly. New York: [American Journal of Dental Science] 1840. 104 p. CU; IU; NBMS; NBuG; NNN; PPCP; TNN. 40-1074

Brown, Solyman. 1790-1876. Llewellen's dog. A ballad. By Solyman Brown, M. D. From the "Young Ladies' Journal of Literature and Science" for December, 1840. Edited by Mrs. Almira Spencer King. New York: s. l., 1840. 12 p. MWA; RPB. 40-1075

Brown, Thomas. Lectures on the philosophy of the human mind. By Thomas Brown, M. D. Two volume edition. Boston, MA: Glazier Masters and Smith, Hallowell, 1840. 538 p. GMM; KyLxT; OCl; ScCoB; Tu-M. 40-1076

Brown, William H., 1796-1867. Early history of the state of Illinois; A lecture delivered before the Chicago Lyceum on the 8th day of December, 1840. Chicago, IL: Halcomb and W. printers, Saloon Building, 1840. 16 p. ICHi; MBC. 40-1077

Brown University, Providence, R. I. Catalogue of the officers and students of Brown University, for the academical year, 1840-41. Providence, RI: Knowles and Vose, 1840. 22 p. DLC; Nh; NRAB. 40-1078

Browne, Arthur, 1756?-1805. A compendious view of the civil law and of the law of admiralty... By Arthur Browne... First American from the second London edition, with great additions. New York: Halsted and Voorhies, 1840. 2 v. KyLxT; NcD; PP; ViU; WaU. 40-1079

Browne, Augusta. The American bouquet. Consisting of the national airs Star spangled banner, Hail Columbia, & Yankee Doodle with variations... [For the piano forte.] Philadelphia, PA: Osborn's Music Saloon [184-?] 4 p. MB. 40-1080

Browne, Augusta. The messenger bird. Duett [S. A. Accomp. for piano forte] Philadelphia, PA: Fiot [184-?] 4 p. MB. 40-1081

Browne, Augusta. The seaman's night song. [With accompaniment for piano forte.] Boston, MA: Bradlee & Co. [184-?] 5 p. MB. 40-1082

Browne, Augusta. Variations on a favorite air from the opera of La Zangara... composed for the piano forte or harp..... by Mis Augusta Browne.

Philadelphia, PA: Published by G. E. Blake [184-?] 5 p. WHi. 40-1083

Brownell, Thomas Church, 1779-1865. Religion of the heart and life, comp. from the works of the best writers on experimental and practical piety. With an introductory chapter prefixed to each volume. Hartford, CT: Huntington, 1840. 5 v. Ct; GAGTh; MCET; NNG; OC; PWbO. 40-1084

Browning, Elizabeth Barrett, 1806-1861. Poems, by Elizabeth Barrett Browning from the last London edition, corrected by the author. New York: C. S. Francis and Co., 1840. 2 v. WMSMA. 40-1085

Brown's almanack for 1841. Boston, MA: Amos Head [1840] MWA. 40-1086

Brown's improved almanack, pocket memorandum, and account book for... 1840... Published annually. No. III. Concord, NH: Published by John F. Brown, 1840. 71 p. MWA; NhHi. 40-1087

Brownson, Augusta. The pilgrim fathers. Words by Mrs. Hemans; music by Miss Brown, sister of Mrs. Hemans. Baltimore, MD: F. D. Benteen [184-?] 5 p. ViU. 40-1088

Brownson, Orestes Augustus, 1803-1876. Brownson's defence. Defence of the article on the laboring classes. From the Boston quarterly review. By O. A. Brownson. Boston, MA: Benjamin H. Greene, 1840. 94 p. ICU; MBAt; MH-L; MWA; PU. 40-1089

Brownson, Orestes Augustus, 1803-1876. Charles Elwood; or, the infidel converted. By O. A. Brownson. Boston,

MA: C. C. Little and J. Brown, 1840. 262 p. CtY; ICU; MB; MiGr; MWA; NNUT. 40-1090

Brownson, Orestes Augustus, 1803-1876. The laboring classes. An article from the Boston Quarterly Review. Boston, MA: B. H. Greene, 1840. 24 p. CtY; IaU; MWA; MiD-B; NjPT. 40-1091

Brownson, Orestes Augustus, 1803-1876. The laboring classes, an article from the Boston quarterly review. 2d edition. Boston, MA: B. H. Greene, 1840. 24 p. MdBJ; MH; OFH. 40-1092

Brownson, Orestes Augustus, 1803-1876. The laboring classes, an article from the Boston quarterly review. By O. A. Brownson. Third edition. Boston, MA: Benjamin H. Greene, 1840. 24 p. MBC; MH; MH-AH; MWA; VtU. 40-1093

Brownson, Orestes Augustus, 1803-1876. The laboring classes, an article from the Boston quarterly review. Ed. 4. Boston, MA: B. H. Greene, 1840. 24 p. MH; MH-BA; MWA; PU. 40-1094

Brownson, Orestes Augustus, 1803-1876. An oration before the democracy of Worcester and vacinity, delivered at Worchester, Mass., July 4, 1840. Boston, MA; Worcester, MA: E. Littlefield; M. D. Phillips, 1840. 38 p. CtY; DLC; ICN; MWA; RPB. 40-1095

Brownson, Orestes Augustus, 1803-1876. The Rich Against the Poor. The Labouring Classes. New York: Applegate, 1840. 23 p. CtY; MBNMHi; NN; PPULC. 40-1096

Bruce, James C. An address delivered

before the society of alumni of the University of Virginia, by James C. Bruce. Richmond, VA: Printed by P. D. Bernard, 1840. 28 p. Vi; ViU. 40-1097

Brunson, Alfred, 1795-1882. The sweet singer of Israel; a collection of hymns & spiritual songs, usually sung at camp, prayer & social meetings, & in revivals of religion; selected & compiled, at the request of the publishers, by Alfred Brunson & Charles Pitman. New ed. Pittsburgh, PA: C. H. Kay & Co., 1840. 320 p. AmSSchU; IEG; MdBD; NNUT; RPB. 40-1098

Brunswick and Florida Railroad Co. Circular, Brunswick and Florida railroad company. Instalment... [Issued by board of directors] Brunswick, Ga., March 16th, 1840. Brunswick, GA: . l., 1840. 2 p. MHi. 40-1099

Brunswick waltz. [For the piano forte.] Boston, MA: Bradlee [184-?] 1 p. MB. 40-1100

Bryan, James. An introductory lecture. To a course on the principles and practice of surgery. Delivered in the Vermont adacemy of medicine, March 12th, 1840, by James Bryan... Rutland, VT: H. T. White & co., printers, 1840. 12 p. DLC; DSG; MWA; NNNAM. 40-1101

Bryant, Edwin. What I saw in Calif. New York: s. l., 1840. NB. 40-1102

Bryant, William Cullen, 1794-1878. Poems, by William Cullen Bryant. 6th ed. New York: Harper & brothers, 1840. 276 p. DLC; MBAt; MnU; OO; TxH. 40-1103

Bryant, William Cullen, 1794-1878.

Selections from the American poets. By William Cullen Bryant. New York: Harper & brothers, 1840. 316 p. CtMW; DLC; MWA; NNebg; TxU. 40-1104

Bryon, George Gordon Noel Byron, 1788-1824. ... Sardanapolus, king of Assyria. A tragedy in five acts. By Lord Byron. Adapted for representation by Charles Kean. New York: S. French [etc., etc., 184-?] 62 p. CSt; DLC; MB. 40-1105

Bryon, George Gordon Noel Byron, 1788-1824. ... Werner. A tragedy in five acts. By Lord Byron. With the stage business, cast of characters, costumes relative positions, etc. New York: S. French & son, [etc., etc., 184-?] 75 p. CSt. 40-1106

Bryon, George Gordon Noel Byron, 1788-1824. The works of Lord Byron, including the suppressed poems. Also a sketch of his life. By J. W. Lake. Philadelphia, PA: Griff and Elliot, 1840. 764 p. CtY. 40-1107

Bryon, George Gordon Noel Byron, 1788-1824. Works in verse and prose, including his letters, journals, etc., with a sketch of his life. New York: A. V. Blake, 1840. MH; NjR; PPL; PPULC. 40-1108

Buchanan, James, 1791-1868. Mr. Buchanan's answer to the misrepresentations of Mr. Davis's speech; vindicating himself and the Democratic party from the unfounded aspersion of designing to destroy the banks and reduce the wages of labor and the value of property. [Delivered in the Senate, Friday, March 6, 1840] Worcester, MA: Bartlett & co., printers [1840] 12 p. DLC; MB; MBAt; MH-BA. 40-1109

Buchanan, James, 1791-1868. Opening

speech of the Hon. James Buchanan, of Pennsylvania, in the case of McLeod; and also his reply to Messrs. Rives, Choate, Huntington & Preston. Washington, DC: s. l., 1840. 16 p. CSmH; MBAt; MdHi; NjR; TxU. 40-1110

Buchanan, James, 1791-1868. Remarks of Mr. Buchanan of Pennsylvania, in defence of the administration of Mr. Van Buren against the charge of extravagance in expending the Public money. Delivered in the Senate of the U. S. Friday, January 22, 1841. Washington, DC: Printed at the Globe office, 1840. 14 p. TxU. 40-1111

Buchanan, James, 1791-1868. Remarks of Mr. Buchanan of Pennsylvania, in reply to Mr. Davis, of Massachusetts, against the Independent treasury bill. Senate U. S. March 3, 1840. Washington, DC: Printed at the Globe office, 1840. 8 p. CtY; MdBJ; MiUC; PPL; TxU. 40-1112

Buchanan, James, 1791-1868. Speech of Mr. Buchanan, of Pennsylvania, in defence of the administration of Mr. Van Buren against the charge of extravagance in expending the public money. Delivered in the Senate of the United States, Friday, February 22, 1841. Washington, DC: Globe Office, 1840. 14 p. CSmH; P; TxU; WaPS. 40-1113

Buchanan, James, 1791-1868. Speech of Mr. Buchanan, of Pennsylvania. In Senate... January 22, 1840. -On the independent treasury bill, in reply to Mr. Clay, of Kentucky. [Washington, DC: Blair and Rives, 1840] 16 p. MBAt; OClWHi; PHi; Tx; ViU. 40-1114

Buchanan, James, 1791-1868. Speech of

the Hon. James Buchanan, of Pennsylvania, in the United States Senate, on the independent treasury bill. Taunton, MA: Published by the Democratic Association, Edmund Anthony, printer, 1840. 24 p. CSmH. 40-1115

The Buckeye song. A favorite patriotic ballad, as sung at the Tippicanoe Associations, with great applause. Partly written and arranged for the Piano forte by a member of the Fifth Ward Club. New York: Thomas Birch, 1840. 3 p. ViU. 40-1116

Buckingham, James Silk, 1786-1855. Mr. Buckingham's defence reply to the letters of Palestinensis in the New York Overver. [New York: s. l., 1840] 36 p. OC. 40-1117

Buckingham, James Silk, 1786-1855. Public address, delivered by Mr. Buckingham, in defence of his lectures on Palestine, against the criticisms of the Reverend Eli Smith, published anonymously in the New York Observer, in 1839. Delivered... Jan., 1840. New York: s. l. [1840] 36 p. CtHT; MH; PHi; PPPrHi; WHi. 40-1118

Buckminster, William. Practical farmer; or, Spirit of the Boston cultivator; containing a collection of valuable essays on practical agriculture, etc. By William Buckmister. Boston, MA: David H. Williams, 1840. 300 p. GHi; MWA; NIC; NRom; WaPS. 40-1119

Buckstone, John Baldwin, 1802-1879. The dead shot; a farce in one act. New York: S. French & Son [184-?] 27 p. MH. 40-1120

Buckstone, John Baldwin, 1802-1879.

The Irish lion; a farce in one act. New York: W. Taylor & Co. [184-?] 26 p. MH. 40-1121

Buckstone, John Baldwin, 1802-1879. The Irish lion; a farce in one act. Philadelphia, PA; New York: Turner & Fisher [184-?] 50 p. MiU; IU. 40-1122

Buckstone, John Baldwin, 1802-1879. A kiss in the dark; a farce in one act. New York: Dramatic Pub. Co. [1840?] NBUG. 40-1123

Buckstone, John Baldwin, 1802-1879. A kiss in the dark; a farce in one act. New York: S. French & Son [184-?] 20 p. MH; MWA; NN; PPULC. 40-1124

Buckstone, John Baldwin, 1802-1879. A kiss in the dark; a farce in one act. New York: W. Taylor & Co. [184-?] 20 p. MH. 40-1125

Buckstone, John Baldwin, 1802-1879. ... Leap year; or, The ladies' privilege. A comedy in three acts. By J. Baldwin Buckstone. With the stage business, cast of directors, costumes, relative positions, etc. New York: T. H. French & Son [184-?] 74 p. CSt; IaU; MB; NN; PPULC. 40-1126

Buckstone, John Baldwin, 1802-1879. Luke the labourer; A dramatic drama in two acts. New York: W. Taylor & Co. [184-?] MH. 40-1127

Buckstone, John Baldwin, 1802-1879. Mischief-making. An interlude in one act. New York: S. French & Son [184-?] 20 p. MH. 40-1128

Buckstone, John Baldwin, 1802-1879. Rural felicity; A comedy in two acts. With original cast... as marked by J. B. Wright... New York: French [184-?] 86 p. MB. 40-1129

Buckstone, John Baldwin, 1802-1879. The scholar. A comedy in two acts. With description of costume, cast... New York: French [184-?] p. MB. 40-1130

Buckstone, John Baldwin, 1802-1879. The snapping turtles, or matrimonial masquerading; A dialogue in one act. New York: R. M. De Witt [184-?] 18 p. MH. 40-1131

Buckstone, John Baldwin, 1802-1879. Weak points; A comedy in two acts. New York: Happy Hours Company [184-?] 40 p. MH. 40-1132

Buel, Jesse, 1778-1839. The Farmer's Companion; or, Essays on the principles and practices of American husbandry. With the address, prepared to be delivered before the Agricultural and Horticultural Societies of New Haven County, Connecticut, and an appendix containing tables and other matter useful to the farmer. By the late Hon. Jesse Buel... Boston, MA: Marsh, Capen, Lyon, and Webb, 1840. 336 p. CoCsC; InCW; MB; MeU; NIC. 40-1133

Buel, Jesse, 1778-1839. The Farmer's Companion; or, Essays on the principles and practices of American husbandry. With the address, prepared to be delivered before the Agricultural and Horticultural Societies of New Haven County, Connecticut, and an appendix containing tables and other matter useful to the farmer. By the late Hon. Jesse Buel... 2d. ed. Boston, MA: Marsh, 1840. 303 p. DLC; MBHo; NcD; NIC-A; PPFrankI. 40-1134

Buel, Jesse, 1778-1839. The farmer's instructor; consisting of essays, practical directions, and hints for the management of the farm and the garden. New York: Harper & brothers, 1840. 2 v. DNAL; MWA; NbOM; NjN; OClW. 40-1135

Buffalo city directory; containing a list of the names, residence and occupation of the heads of families, householders, & c., on the first of May, 1840. Faxon & Graves, publishers. Horatio N. Walker, compiler. Buffalo, NY: Faxon & Graves, printers, 1840. 178 p. MH; NBuG. 40-1136

Buffon, George Louis Leclerc, 1707-1788. Buffon's natural history of man, the globe, and of quadrupeds. With additions from Cavier, Lacepede, and other eminent naturalists... Abridged ed. Cooperstown, NY: H. & E. Phinney, 1840. 2 v. LNT; NLock. 40-1137

Bufford, John H. [View of Boston from Chelsea] Boston, MA: Prentiss, 1840. MB. 40-1138

Bugard, Bertrand Francis. French practical translator; or, Easy method of learning to translate French into English. 4th ed. Boston, MA: Munroe & Francis, 1840. 278 p. ICartC; KEmC; MH; NNC. 40-1139

Buist, Robert, 1805-1880. The American flower garden directory; containing practical directions for the culture of plants in the flower garden, hot-house, green-house, rooms, or parlour windows, for every month in the year. With a description of the plants most desirable in each, the nature of the soil, and situation best adapted to their growth, the proper season for transplant-ing, &c. Instructions for erecting a hot-house, green-house, and laying out a flower garden. Also, table of soils most congenial to the plants contained in the work. The whole adapted to either large or small gardens, with instructions for preparing the soil, propagating, planting, pruning, training, and fruiting the grape vine. With descriptions of the best sorts for cultivating in the open air. By Robert Buist. New ed., with numerous additions. Philadelphia, PA: Carey and Hart, 184?. 379 p. DLC; MSaP; MWA; OO; RPB. 40-1140

Bulfinch, Charles, 1763-1849. Memorial of Charles Bulfinch, et. al., praying that their title to certain lands in the territory of Oregon may be confirmed. January 13, 1840. [Washington, DC: Blair & Rives, 1840?] 14 p. CU-B; ICN; MBAt; WaSp. 40-1141

Bullard, Mrs. E. Child's book on natural history... Maulmainm: s. l., 1840. MH. 40-1142

Bullions, Peter, 1791-1864. The principles of Greek grammar. New York: Pratt, Woodford, 184-? 308 p. ICU. 40-1143

Bunker Hill declaration. Sept. 10, 1840. [Boston, MA: s. l., 1840] 12 p. DLC; MB; MH; WHi. 40-1144

Bunn, Alfred, 1796?-1860. The stage, both before and behind the curtain. From "Obsevations taken on the spot." By Alfred Bunn... Philadelphia, PA: Lea & Blanchard, 1840. 2 v. in 1. CSmH; MWA; NjP; OU; PPA. 40-1145

Bunyan, John, 1628-1688. Eins Christens reize naar de eeuwigheid voorstellende onder verscheidene zinnebeelden den ganschen staat van eene boetvaardige en godzoekende ziele, uit het Engelsch vertaald. New York [American Tract Society, 1840?] 254 p. MiGr. 40-1146

Bunyan, John, 1628-1688. Le pelerinage du chretien a la eite celeste... New York: Am. Tract, 184-? p. MBAt; MH-L. 40-1147

Bunyan, John, 1628-1688. Le pelerinage du chretien a la cite celeste, decrit sous la similitude d'un songe. [Pt. I] New York: La Societe Americaine des Traites [1840?] 235 p. CtY; IaPeC; ICU; ViU. 40-1148

Bunyan, John, 1628-1688. Pilgrim's progress delivered under the similitude of a dream. New York: American Tract Society [184-?] 603 p. IU; MH. 40-1149

Bunyan, John, 1628-1688. Pilgrim's progress. With notes by T. Scott. Hartford, CT: Andrus & Judd [184-?] 368 p. MB. 40-1150

Bunyan, John, 1628-1688. Pilgrim's progress. With notes by T. Scott. Middletown, CT: Hunt & Noyes, 1840. 384 p. CtY. 40-1151

Bunyan, John, 1628-1688. Pilgrim's Progress... Boston, MA: Am. Tract, 184-? 384 p. DLC; MB. 40-1152

Bunyan, John, 1628-1688. Pilgrim's progress... New York: Am. Tract, 1840? 232 p. NN. 40-1153

Bunyan, John, 1628-1688. Pilgrim's progress... New York: Am. Tract, 1840? 376 p. MB; WHi. 40-1154

Bunyan, John, 1628-1688. Pilgrim's progress... New York: Am. Tract, 1840? 651 p. MB. 40-1155

Bunyan, John, 1628-1688. The Pilgrim's progress from this world to that which is to come, delivered under the similitude of a dream. New York: Published by American Tract Society, D. Fanshaw printer, 184-? 603 p. DLC; MB; WHi 40-1156

Buona notte, a favorite Italian song, arranged for the piano forte. Philadelphia PA: Geo. Willig [184-?] 2 p. ViU. 40-1157

Burder, George, 1752-1832. Twelve sermons to the aged, by Rev. George Burder... New York: American Tract Society [1840] 144 p. No Loc. 40-1158

Burder, George, 1752-1832. Village sermons; or, fifty-two plain & short discourses on the principal doctrines of the Gospel. New York: American Tract Society [184-?] 571 p. NN; ViU. 40-1159

Burder, George, 1752-1832. Village sermons; or, one hundred and one plain and short discourses on the principal doctrines of the Gospel. Intended for the use of families, Sunday schools, or companies assembled for religious instruction in country villages. By George Burder....To which is added to each sermon a short prayer.... Philadelphia, PA Grigg and Elliott, 1840. 476 p. IaDL; IU NOssMF. 40-1160

Burder, Samuel. Oriental customs, or An illustration of the sacred scriptures by an explanatory application of the customs and manners of the eastern nations and especially the Jews, therein alluded to, together with observations on many difficult and obscure texts, collected from the most celebrated travellers, and the most eminent critics. Philadelphia, PA: W. W. Woodward, 1840. MH. 40-1161

Burditt, Benjamin A. Andrews' Quick Step. [For the piano forte.] Boston, MA: Reed, 1840. 2 p. MB. 40-1162

Burford, Robert, 1791-1861. Description of a view of Rome, ancient and modern, with the surrounding country. Taken from the tower of the Capitol... Painted by Robert Burford, from drawings taken by himself in 1837. New York: Printed by W. Osborn, 1840. 16 p. DLC; MWA; OCIWHi; NRom; PPM. 40-1163

Burford, Robert, 1791-1861. Description of a view of the Bay of Islands, New Zealand, and the surrounding country, now exhibiting at the Panorama, Broadway... New York. Painted by Robert Burford, from drawings taken by Augustus Earle, esq. New York: Printed by W. Osborn, 1840. 12 p. CtY; DLC; NN; OCIWHi; PHi. 40-1164

Burford, Robert, 1791-1861. Description of a view of the great temple of Karnak, and the surrounding city of Thebes, now exhibiting at the Panorama... painted by Robert Burford, from drawings taken in 1834, by F. Catherwood. Philadelphia, PA: Merrihew and Thompson, printers, 1840. 16 p. DLC; MBAt; PHi; RPB. 40-1165

Burgess, Ebenezer, 1790-1870. Our fathers honorable and useful to their posterity. Boston, MA: s. l., 1840. MB; RPB. 40-1166

Burgess, Geroge, 1809-1866. A sermon preached in Christ Church, Hartford, on the Second Sunday after Epiphany, 1840, being the Sunday after the loss, by fire, of the Steamboat Lexington, on Lond Island Sound. Hartford, CT: L. Skinner, 1840. 15 p. Ct; CtSoP; MWA; RHi. 40-1167

Burgmueller, Friedrich, 1806-1874. Bolero. Sur un motif favori de l'Opera Le Domino Noir. Compose pour le piano. Et dedie a son ami Ernest Dejazet par Fred. Burgmuller. Philadelphia, PA: A. Fiot [184-?] 10 p. ViU. 40-1168

Burgmueller, Friedrich, 1806-1874. La Corbeille de Roses. Basket of roses. 4 morceaux... pour piano. Par Frederic Burgmuller. No. 1. Boston, MA: Reed [184-?] p. MB. 40-1169

Burgmueller, Friedrich, 1806-1874. ... Cracovienne. Burgmuller... Baltimore, MD: Geo. Willig, Junr. [184-?] 5 p. ViU. 40-1170

Burgmueller, Friedrich, 1806-1874. Fantaisie brillante. Pour le piano. Sur Erani. Il Proscritto par Fre'd. Burgmiller. Op. 92. Philadelphia, PA: George Willig [184-?] 11 p. ViU. 40-1171

Burgmueller, Friedrich, 1806-1874. Old Dan Tucker. A celebrated banjo song. Arranged for the piano-forte. The Ball-Room March. By Burgmuller. [S. l.: s. l., 184-?] p. ViU. 40-1172

Burgmueller, Friedrich, 1806-1874. Rondino sur la polka favorite, pour le piano. Compose par F. Burgmeller. Op. 89. Baltimore, MD: G. Willig, Jr. 184-?] 6 p. ViU. 40-1173

Burgmueller, Friedrich, 1806-1874. Souvenir de Schoenbrunne. Grande walze brillante pour le piano. [Brunswick, NJ: s. l., 184-?] 11 p. MB. 40-1174

Burke, Edmund, 1809-1882. Speech of Mr. Burke, of New Hampshire, in the independent treasury bill. Delivered in the Committee of the Whole in the House of Representatives, June 13, 1840. [Washington, DC: s. l., 1840] 16 p. CtY; MdHi; NjR; TxU. 40-1175

Burlington silk record. Burlington, NJ: n. pub., n. pr., 1840-. v. 1-. MH-BA; NjP. 40-1176

Burnam, Curtis Field. Valedictory oration before the senior class in Yale College. New Haven, CT: s. l., 1840. 18 p. ICN; MB; MBC. 40-1177

Burnap, George Washington, 1802-1859. Lectures to young men on the cultivation of the mind, the formation of character, and the conduct of life. Delivered in Masonic Hall, Baltimore. By George W. Burnap... Baltimore, MD: J. Murphy, 1840. 144 p. DLC; MdHi; OSW; PU; RPAt. 40-1178

Burne, John. A treatise on the causes and consequences of habitual constipation. Philadelphia, PA: Haswell, 1840. 257 p. CtMW; MdBM; PPA. 40-1179

Burne, John. A treatise on the causes and consequences of habitual constipation, Philadelphia, PA: Haswell, Barrington, and Haswell, 1840. 164 p. LNOP; NBMS; NhD; RNR; WMAM. 40-1180

Burne, John. A treatise on the causes

and consequences of habitual constipation. Philadelphia, PA: Haswell, Barrington, and Haswell, 1840. 164, 192 p. ICJ; Nh. 40-1181

Burne, John. A treatise on the causes and consequences of habitual constipation. Philadelphia, PA; New Orleans, LA: Haswell, Barrington, and Haswell; John J. Haswell and co., 1840. 164 p. CSt-L; MeB; NcD; OC; P. 40-1182

Burnet, David Gouverneur, 1789-1870. Message of the President on the subject of our Mexican relations... Dec. 16, 1840. [Austin, TX: s. l., 1840] 4 p. Tx; TxU. 40-1183

Burnet, Jacob, 1770-1853. Notices of the public services of General William Henry Harrison. [Cincinnati, OH?: s. l., 1840?] 7 p. DLC. 40-1184

Burnet, Jacob, 1770-1853. Speech of Judge Burnet, of Ohio, in the Whig National Convention, giving a brief history of the life of Gen. Wm. H. Harrison... Erie, PA: Sterrett & Shaner, 1840. 12 p. PMA. 40-1185

Burnett, William. The gospel ministry, a sermon, preached at the installation of the Rev. Alexander Wilson as pastor of the Associate Reformed congregation, of Cadiz, O., January 24, 1840. By William Burnett, president of Franklin college. Pittsburgh, PA: Published by the congregation, 1840. 21 p. CSmH; PPULC. 40-1186

Burney, Sarah Harriet. Renunciation:a romance of private life. By Miss Burney [sic] In two volumes. Philadelphia, PA: Lea & Blanchard, 1840. 2 v. MBAt; MPeal; OC; PFal; RPB. 40-1187

Burnham, Georgiana N. O worship not the beautiful. Words by Lucy Linwood. Music by Georgiana N. Burnham. [Song with accompaniment for the piano forte.] Boston, MA: Diton [184-?] 2 p. MB. 40-1188

Burns, Robert, 1759-1796. Highland Mary. A Scotch ballad, by Robert Burns... New York: E.] Boston, MA: Diton [184-?] 2 p. MB. 40-1189

Burns, Robert, 1759-1796. Highland Mary. A Scotch ballad, by Robert Burns... New York: Engraved & printed by E. Riley [184-?] 2 p. ViU. 40-1190

Burns, Robert, 1759-1796. The poetical works of Robert Burns. With a sketch of his life, by James Curie [!] M. D. With many additional poems and songs and an enlarged and corrected glossary... New York: E. Kearny [184-?] 2 v. in 1. DLC; IU. 40-1191

Burr, Charles Chauncey, 1817-1883. Discourse on revivals in the Universalist Church, Portland, Apr. 5. Portland, ME: s. l., 1840. MBAt. 40-1192

Burr, David H., 1803-1875. The American Atlas. Exhibiting the Post Offices, Post Roads, Rail Roads, Canals, and the Physical and Political Divisions of the United States of America... [S. l.: n. p., 184-?] 13 Roads, Rail Roads, Canals, and the Physical and Political Divisions of the United States of America... [S. l.: n. p., 184-?] 13 p. MBAt; ViU. 40-1193

Burr, David H., 1803-1875. Atlas of the state of New York... Ithaca, NY: s. l., 1840. unp. CtSoP. 40-1194

Burr, Samuel Jones. The life and times of William Henry Harrison, by S. J. Burr... New York; Philadelphia, PA: L. W. Random; R. W. Pomeroy, 1840. 304 p. ICHi; NCH; NjMD; OFH; WHi. 40-1195

Burr, Samuel Jones. Life and times of William Henry Harrison. Edition 3. New York: Ransom, 1840. 300 p. DeWi; IaGG; IaU; InLPU; NT. 40-1196

Burr, Samuel Jones. The life and times of William Henry Harrison, by S. J. Burr... 8th ed. New York; Philadelphia, PA: L. W. Ransom; R. W. Pmeroy, 1840. 300 p. Ia; MWA; NcU; OO; ViL. 40-1197

Burrell, George Pratt. A letter to the Hon. Henry Clay, of Kentucky, containing a brief reply to some statements of Joseph John Gurney, in relation to Jamaica. By George Pratt Burrell... New York: Narine & Co's Print., 1840. 23 p. DLC; NcD; NN; RP. 40-1198

Burrill, Alexander Mansfield, 1807-1869. The practice of the Supremem Court of the state of New York in personal actions, with an appendix of practical forms. New York: s. l., 1840. 2 v. MH-L; NNIA; PPB; PPULC. 40-1199

Burrill, ALexander Mansfield, 1807-1869. A treatise on the practice of the Supreme court of the state of New York in personal actions; with an appendix of practical forms. By Alexander M. Burrill... New York: Halsted and Voorhies, 1840. 2 v. DLC; MH-L; NjR; NN; WHi. 40-1200

Burritt, Elijah Hinsdale, 1794-1838. The geography of the heavens and class book of astronomy, accompanied by a celestial atlas. With and introduction by Thomas Dick. 5th ed. New York: F. J. Huntington and Co., 1840. MBAt; MH; PPULC. 40-1201

Burroughs, Stephen, 1765-1840. Memoirs of the notorious Stephen Burroughs; containing many incidents in the life of this wonderful man, never before published. Stereotype ed., newly cor. and rev. Boston, MA: C. Gayl, 1840. 2 v. in 1. IU; LNH; MBBC; MWA; PHi. 40-1202

Burrowes, John Freckleton, 1787-1862. The Cinderella waltz... Philadelphia, PA: Edgar [184-?] 7 p. MB. 40-1203

Burton, I. W. Speech of the Honorable I. W. Burton, on the "bill providing for sectioning and selling the lands formerly owned and occupied by the Cherokees." Houston, TX: printed at the Telegraph Office, 1840. 16 p. TxWFM. 40-1204

Bush, George. Notes critical and practical on the book of Genesis. 5th ed. New York: s. l., 1840. 2 v. VtU. 40-1205

Bush, James Miles, 1808-1875. An introductory lecture to the dissecting class of Transylvania University, Lexington, Nov. 9th, 1840. By James M. Bush, M. D. Lexington, KY: N. L. & J. W. Finnell, printers, 1840. 12 p. DNLM; DSG; KyU. 40-1206

Bushnell, George W. An address, delivered before the Youths' Lyceum, at their first semi-annual exhibition. By Master Geo. W. Buchnell. [Published by request] Utica, NY: C. C. P. Grosh, printer, 1840. 12 p. NUt. 40-1207

Bustis, George. The argument of Mr.

Eustis, one of the counsel for the defendants, in the Batture case. New Orleans, LA: William M'Kean, 1840. 24 p. LNH. 40-1208

Butler, Andrew Pickens. Remarks on the resolution of Mr. Waddy Thompson, jr., to amend the rules relative to the reception & disposal of Abolition Petitions, House of Rep., Jan. 21, 1840. Washington, DC: s. l., 1840. 7 p. MdHi; PU. 40-1209

Butler, Benjamin Franklin, 1795-1858. ... Jeffersonian Democracy, definied and vindicated. By Benjamin F. Butler in opposition to its definition by Daniel Webster... [New York] no printer [1840] 8 p. IaU; MBC; MiD-B; NHi. 40-1210

Butler, Benjamin Franklin, 1795-1858. Legal opinion of the honorable Benj. F. Butler... on the rights and privileges of the N. Y. & Harlem R. R. Co... New York: Printer by C. C. & E. Childs, jr., 1840. 10 p. NN. 40-1211

Butler, Clement Moore, 1810-1890. "The grass withereth, the flower fadeth. "A sermon preached in Zion Church, Palmyra, on the second Sunday after Christmas, January 5, 1840. By Rev. C. M. Butler... Palmyra, NY: H. Spencer, printer, 1840. 15 p. CSmH; MdBD; NCanHi; NGH. 40-1212

Butler, Henry. Scholar's companion; containing exercises in the orthography, derivation & classification of English words. 7th ed. Philadelphia, PA: H. Perkins, 1840. 274 p. MH; PHi. 40-1213

Butler, John J. An eulogy upon the character of George Swan. Delivered before the Miami Chapter of the Alpha

Delta Phi... March, 1840. Oxford, OH: Published by order of the society, 1840. 15 p. CBPSR; MBAt; NCH; OClWHi; OHi. 40-1214

Butler, John J. Thoughts on the Benevolent Enterprises... By John J. Butler... Dover: Published by the Trustees of the Freewill Baptist Connection, 1840. 175 p. MeLewB; NHC-S. 40-1215

Butler, Joseph, bp. of Durham, 1692-1752. The analogy of religion, natural and revealed, to the constitution and course of nature. By Joseph Butler, LL. D. With an introductory essay, by Albert Barnes. New stereotype edition. New York: Homer Franklin, 1840. 348 p. ICartC; LNB; OkU; PPEB; WHi. 40-1216

Butler, Samuel, bp. of Lichfield and Coventry, 1774-1839. Geographia classics; pr the application of ancient geography to the classics, by Samuel Butler. With questions on the maps by John Frost. 4th American from the last London ed. Philadelphia, PA: Lea & Blanchard, 1840. 262 p. GMM; InU; MdBD; ScNC; ViU. 40-1217

Butler, William Orlando, 1791-1880. Speech of W. O. Butler, of Kentucky, in Committee of the Whole, in reply to Mr. Biddle and Mr. Hunt, upon the appropriation for surpressing hostilities in Florida. Delivered in the House of Representatives, June 11, 1840. Washington, DC: Printed by Blair and Rives, 1840. 30 p. CSmH; FSaW; ICN; MdHi; OClWHi. 40-1218

Buttner, Johann Gottfried. Kurz geschichte der reformation, von Dr. Johann

Gottfried Buttner. Pittsburg: Bei Victor Scriba, 1840. 132 p. MoWgT; P. 40-1219

Buxton, Thomas Fowler, 1786-1845. The African slave trade. By Thomas Fowell Buxton, Esq..... New York: Reprinted from the London edition. Published by the American Anti-Slavery Society, 1840. 2 v. CSto; KHi; MeHi; NNUT; RP. 40-1220

Buxton, Thomas Fowler, 1786-1845. The African slave trade. Part II. The remedy... By Thomas Fowell Buxton, Esq..... New York: Reprinted from the London edition [John Murray] Published by the S. W. Benedict, 1840. 259 p. CSfCW; GEU; ICU; NeD; OClWHi. 40-1221

Byberry Library Company, Philadelphia. Constitution of Byberry Library Company. Catalogues. Philadelphia, PA: Richard, 1840. PSC-Hi; PPULC. 40-1222

Byfield, Shadrach, b. 1789. A narrative of a light company soldier's service in the 41st Regiment of Foot during the late AC. 40-1223

Byfield, Shadrach, b. 1789. A narrative of a light company soldier's service in the 41st Regiment of Foot during the late American War. Together with some adventures amongst the Indian tribes from 1812 to 1814. Bradford: J. Bubb, 1840. 87 p. An-Ct; CSmH; NN; PHi. 40-1224

Bynum, Jesse Atherton, 1797-1868. Speech of Mr. Bynum, of North Carolina, on the resolution of Mr. Thompson, of South Carolina, on the subject of abolition. In the House of Representatives, January 25, 1840. Washington, DC:

Globe Office, 1840. 32 p. KHi; MB; NcU; OCHP; TxU. 40-1225

Byron, George Gordon Noel Byron, 178?-1824. The works of Lord Byron, in verse and prose. Including his letters, journals, etc. With a sketch of his life. New York: A. V. Blake, 1840. 627 p. CtHT; MdBJ; PPL; OWor; RNPL. 40-1226

C

C. Little & Brown & Company. A catalogue of law books published and for sale by C. C. Little and J. Brown. Boston, MA: s. l., 1840. MB. 40-1227

Cachucha. Arranged for the guitar by A. Schmitz. Philadelphia, PA: Fiot [184-?] 2 p. MB. 40-1228

The cachucha; or, Come, o come! castanets are gaily sounding. Sung by Madame Vestris; arranged by S. Nelson. Philadelphia, PA: Burns & co. [184-?] 7 p. ViU. 40-1229

[La Cachucha.] The original castanet Spanish dance, La cachucla as danced by Fanny Elssler. [For piano forte.] Boston, MA: Prentiss, 1840. 5 p. MB; ViU. 40-1230

Caesar, C. Julius. Caesar. Transl. by William Duncan. New York: Harper, 1840. 2 v. ICU; InLW; OCX; PU. 40-1231

Cahoane, Sarah S. Visit to Grand-papa; or, a Week at Newport. New York: Taylor and Dodd, 1840. 213 p. DLC; MBC; MWA; OCHP; RHi. 40-1232

Caldwell, Charles, 1772-1853. Thoughts on the character and standing of the mechanical profession: a discourse, ... January 14, 1840. Louisville, KY: Prentice and Weissinger, 1840. 34 p. DSG; InU; MoHi. 40-1233

Calhoun, George Albion, 1788-1867. Letters to the Rev. Leonard Bacon, in reply to his attack on the pastoral union and theological institute of Connecticut. By Rev. George A. Calhoun. Hartford, CT: E. Geer, 1840. 84 p. CU; IaU; MAnP; MWA; TxHuT. 40-1234

Calhoun, John Caldwell, 1782-1850. Life and character of John C. Calhoun. With illustrations containig notices of his father, uncles, and their brave conduct in Amer. Revolution. New York: s. l., 1840. 24 p. PHi. 40-1235

Calhoun, John Caldwell, 1782-1850. Speech of Mr. Calhoun of S. C. on seizure of Negroes... Mar. 13, 1840. [Washington, DC: s. l., 1840] 8 p. CtY; DLC; MuI-C; NcD; ViU. 40-1236

Calhoun, John Caldwell, 1782-1850. Speech of Mr. Calhoun, of South Carolina, on the report of Mr. Grundy, of Tennessee, in relation to the assumption of the debts of the states by the federal government. Senate, U. S. February 5, 1840. Washington, DC: Printed at the Globe Office, 1840. 14 p. CU; ICU; MBAt; MiD-B; NcU. 40-1237

Calhoun, John Caldwell, 1782-1850. Speech of Mr. Calhoun, of South Carolina, the following resolutions were taken up for consideration: Resolved, that a ship... on the high seas, in time of peace, engaged in a lawful voyage, is according to the laws of nations, under the exclusive jurisdiction of the State to which her flag belongs; as much as if constituting a part of her own domain... In Senate, March 13, 1840. [Washington, DC: s. l., pr, 1840] 8 p. CtY; DLC; MdHi; MH. 40-1238

Calhoun, John Caldwell, 1782-1850. Speech relative to ships or vessels on the high seas in time of peace. Senate, March, 1840. [Washington, DC: s. l., pr, 1840] 8 p. WHi. 40-1239

Calhoun, John Caldwell, 1782-1850. Speech... on the bankrupt bill. Senate, June 2, 1840. [Washington, DC: s. l., pr, 1840] 8 p. ICP; MH; MiD-B; P; WHi. 40-1240

Calvert, George Henry, 1803-1889. Cabiro: a poem. By George H. Calvert, author of "Counth Julian, a tragedy" and translator of Schiller's "Don Carlos." Cants I and II. Baltimore, MD: N. Hickman, 1840. 36 p. CSmH; MB; MdHi; MH. 40-1241

Calvert, George Henry, 1803-1889. Count Julian; a tragedy, by George H. Calvert... Baltimore, MD: N. Hickman, 1840. 69 p. CSmH; DLC; MH; NBuG; RHi. 40-1242

Calvert, George Henry, 1803-1889. Miscellany of verse and prose, by George H. Calvert... Baltimore, MD: N. Hickman, 1840. 47 p. CSmH; MdBP; MH; NN. 40-1243

Calvin, Jean, 1509-1564. Calvin on secret providence, by Jean Calvin, tr. by James Lillie. New York: R. Carter & Bros., 1840. 118 p. ICP; DLC; NjNbS; OO; WaU. 40-1244

Cambell, David. Illustrations of prophecy; particularly the evening and morning visions of Daniel, and the ... visions of John, by David Cambell. Boston, MA: pub. by the author, 1840. 414 p. MBC; MeB; MWA; NNUT; OClW. 40-1245

Cambridge, Mass. Cambridgeport Parish Sunday School. Annual meeting... Christmas Eve., 1840. Order of Exercises. Boston, MA: Broadside, 1840. MHi. 40-1246

Cambridge, Mass. Second Baptist Church. The declaration of faith and covenant of the Second Baptist Church, Cambridge, 1840. Boston, MA: Press of Jonathan Howe, 1840. 24 p. MH; MHi. 40-1247

The campaigns of Napoleon Bonaparte, embracing the events of his unexampled military career, from the siege of Toulon to the battle of Waterloo....compiled from distinguished authors by an American.... Boston, MA: Printed and published by Charles Gaylord, 1840. 422 p. DLC; MdBLC; MNe; NcAS; NHem. 40-1248

Campbell, Alexander, 1788-1866. Address delivered before the Charlottesville lyceum... Charlottesville, VA: R. C. Novel, 1840. 30 p. NcD; PP; TxU; ViU. 40-1249

Campbell, Alexander, 1788-1866. Christian system, in reference to the union of Christians, and a restoration of primitive Christianity, as plead in the current reformation. By A. Campbell. 3d ed. Bethany, VA: Prined by A. Campbell; published by Forrester & Campbell, Pittsburgh, 1840. 354 p. CtHT; ICP; OClWHi; PCA; PPPrHi. 40-1250

Campbell, Alexander, 1788-1866. Discussion of the doctrines of endless misery and universal salvation in an epistolary correspondence between Alexander Campbell... and Dolphus Skinner. Utica, NY: C. C. P. Grosh, 1840. 436 p. IaDmD; LNB; NcD; NNUT; PPPrHi; WU. 40-1251

Campbell, David. Appendix, consisting of maps and diagrams showing the local and chronological outlines of the evening and morning visions of Daniel, etc. Boston, MA: Published by the author, 1840. 25 p. MH. 40-1252

Campbell, George Washington, 1768-1848. Republicanism, a sermon, delivered at the dedication of the Congregational meeting-house in Newbury, Vermont, Nov. 13, 1840. Haverhill: John R. Reding, 1840. 18 p. MiD-B; MBAt; MWA; NCH; Nh; RPB. 40-1253

Campbell, John, 1766-1840. Voyages to and from the Cape of Good Hope; with an account of the journey into the interior of South Africa. By the Rev. John Campbell. Intended for the young. 1st American ed. Philadelphia, PA: Presbyterian board of publication, 1840. 271 p. CU; MWiW; NNMr; OSW; ViRut. 40-1254

Campbell, Thomas, 1777-1844. A poem delivered before the Mechanics apprentices library association, at their 20th anniversary, Feb. 22, 1840. By Thomas Campbell, a member of the association. [Boston, MA: s. l., 1840? 4 p. CSmH; MHi. 40-1255

Campbell, William Bowen. Speech... on the sub-treasury bill... House... June 27, 1840. Washington, DC: s. l., 1840. 24 p. MiD-B. 40-1256

The Campbell's are coming; or, Hob Nob. Baltimore, MD: G. Willig [184-?] 1 p. ViU. 40-1257

Campbells are coming, The cheat & Come haste to the wedding. Baltimore, MD: F. D. Benteen [184-?] 1 p. ViU. 40-1258

Canandaigua Academy. Catalogue of the trustees, teachers and students, of Canandaigua Academy, Canandaigua: for the year ending April 8, 1840... Canandaigua, NY: Printed by Geo. L. Whitney, 1840. 8 p. NCanHi. 40-1259

Canfield, Thomas. The useful christian. Philadelphia, PA: American Sunday School Union, 1840. 227 p. ODaB. 40-1260

Cantier, Felix. Farewell my Fatherland. Baltimore, MD; New Orleans, LA: F. D. Benteen; Wm. F. Mayo [184-?] 5 p. ViU. 40-1261

Cantier, Felix. Jenny Lind's song, Farewell my fatherland [Lebe wohl mein Vaterland. With accompaniment for the piano forte.] Boston, MA: Ditson [184-?] 5 p. MB. 40-1262

Caperton, Hugh, 1821- Address delivered before the Philademic Society of Georgetown College... on the 4th July, 1840, by Hugh Caperton... To which are prefixed the remarks of John H. O'Neill... Washingtonk, DC: Gales and Seaton, 1840. 16 p. MWH; PPL; PPULC; ViU. 40-1263

Cardon, Louis, 1747-1805. Ah vous dirai je mamman. French air, with variations for the harp or piano, by Cardon Fils. Baltimore, MD: F. D. Benteen [184-?] 5 p. ViU. 40-1264

Carey, Henry Charles, 1793-1879. Answers to the questions: What constitutes currency? What are the causes of unsteadiness of the currency? and Waht is the remedy?By H. C. Carey... Philadelphia, PA: Lea & Blanchard, 1840. 81 p. CU; InU; MB; MWA; NjP; PPAmP. 40-1265

Carey, Henry Charles, 1793-1879. Causes which Retard Increase in The Numbers of Mankind. Philadelphia, PA: Carey, Lea & Blanchard, 1840. 91 p. InGrD. 40-1266

Carey, Mathew, 1760-1829. A View of the Ruinous Consequences of a Dependence on FOreign Markets for the Sale of ... Flour, Cotton, and Tobasso. Read before ... the Board of Manufacturers of the Pennsylvania Society for... Promotion of American Manufacturers. Philadelphia, PA: s. l., 1840. 42 p. MHi. 40-1267

Carleton, William, 1794-1869. O'Sullivan's love... a legend of Edenmore. Philadelphia, PA: s. l., 184-? 103 p. NN. 40-1268

Carlyle, Thomas, 1795-1881. Chartism. By Thomas Carlyle. "It never smokes but there is fire." Old proverb. Boston, MA: Charles C. Little and James Brown, 1840. 113 p. CtHT; LNH; MDeeP; NjP; PU. 40-1269

Carlyle, Thomas, 1795-1881. Heroes and hero worship. By Thomas Carlyle.

Chicago, IL: Donohue Henneberry & Co., 1840. 345 p. No Loc. 40-1270

Carlyle, Thomas, 1795-1881. Heroes and hero worship. By Thomas Carlyle. New York: Home Book Co., 1840. 347 p. FTa; OkCla. 40-1271

Carlyle, Thomas, 1795-1881. Heroes & Hero-Worship. By Thomas Carlyle. New York: Hurst & Co. Pub. [1840] 192 p. OkAlv; UOM. 40-1272

Carlyle, Thomas, 1795-1881. Heroes, Hero Worship and the Heroic in History. By Thomas Carlyle. New York: A. L. Burt Company, 1840. 302 p. MiJa; NBuSM; NGlc; NIC-LA; TxSa-C. 40-1273

Carlyle, Thomas, 1795-1881. Heroes, Hero Worship and The Heroic History. By Thomas Carlyle. New York: The F. M. Lutpon Publishing Company, 1840. 184 p. No Loc. 40-1274

Carlyle, Thomas, 1795-1881. Heroes, Hero-worship and the Heroic in History. By Thomas Carlyle. New York: Frederick A. Stokes & Brothers, 1840. 286 p. WvWelT. 40-1275

Carlyle, Thomas, 1795-1881. Heroes, Hero-Worship and the Heroic in History. By Thomas Carlyle. New York: Thomas Y. Crowell & Co., 1840. 241 p. IndS; KyLoYMH. 40-1276

Carlyle, Thomas, 1795-1881. Heroes, hero-worship and the heroic in history. By Thomas Carlyle. New York: William L. Allison [1840] 184 p. LStBA; MoS; WvWelt. 40-1277

Carlyle, Thomas, 1795-1881. On

heroes, hero-worship, and the heroic in history. Boston, MA: Estes & Lauriat, Printer John Wilson & Son, 1840. 461 p. No Loc. 40-1278

Carlyle, Thomas, 1795-1881. On heroes, hero-worship, and the heroic in history. New York: Cromwell & Co., 1840. 344 p. C-S; IaHmton; LAlS. 40-1279

Carlyle, Thomas, 1795-1881. On heroes, hero-worship, and the heroic in history. New York: Frederic A. Stokes Company, 1840. 286 p. GCed; MDr. 40-1280

Carlyle, Thomas, 1795-1881. On heroes, hero-worship, and the heroic in history. New York: Lovell Bros. & Co., 1840. 235 p. PPE; PPPL; PPT; PPTU; PPUL. 40-1281

Carlyle, Thomas, 1795-1881. On heroes, hero-worship, and the heroic in history. New York: The Mershon Co., 1840. 345 p. PWaybuGHi. 40-1282

Carlyle, Thomas, 1795-1881. Past and Present. New York: Lovell Bros. & Co., 1840? p. IaHmton. 40-1283

Carlyle, Thomas, 1795-1881. Sartor resartus; the life and opinions of Herr Teufelsdrockh. In three books. 3d American, from the 2d London ed., rev. and cor. by the author. Boston, MA; Philadelphia, PA: J. Munroe and Company; J. Kay, jun. & brother, 1840. 305 p. AU; MeB; MH; NjP; ViU. 40-1284

Carolina and Georgia Almanac 1841. By Robert Grier.... Augusta, GA: Thomas Richard [1840] p. CtY; MWA; ViU. 40-1285

Carolina planter... V. 1, Jan. 15, 1840-Jan. 13, 1841. Columbia, SC: A. S. Johnston, 1840-41. 416 p. DLC. 40-1286

Carpenter, James. Speech of Mr. James S. Carpenter, on the resolutions of Mr. Fisher, of Hardin. House of Representatives, Ohio, Feb. 24, 1840. [Medina: s. l., 1840] 16 p. OClWHi. 40-1287

Carulli, Gustavo, 1800-1877. Young love. Italian air. Arr. for piano forte by J. Chadwick. New York: s. l., 1840. CtY. 40-1288

Caruthers, William Alexander, 1800-1846. The Drunkard; from the cradle to the grave. A lecture delivered before the Savannah Temperance Society, at the First Presbyterian Church, Jan. 15, and repeated Feb. 26. By William A. Caruthers, M. D. Printed under the direction of the Board of Managers of the S. T. Society. Savannah: W. T. Williams, 1840. 27 p. NCD; NN. 40-1289

Carver, Robert. Christian Hope. A sermon preached in Berlin, August 13, 1839, at the funeral of Mrs. Ann W. Park.... Portland: Ptd. at the Argus office, 1840. 20 p. ICU; MiD-B; MW; RPB. 40-1290

Carvosso, William. The great efficacy of simple faith in the atonement of Christ, exemplified in a memoir of Mr. William Carvosso, sixty years a class-leader in the Wesleyan Methodist connection; written by himself and ed. by his son. Louisville, KY: Pub. by John Early for the Methodist Episcopal church, south [184-?] GEU. 40-1291

Carvosso, William. The great efficacy of simple faith in the atonement of Christ, exemplified in a memoir of Mr. William

Carvosso, sixty years a class-leader in the Wesleyan Methodist connection; written by himself and ed. by his son. New York: T. Mason and G. Lane, 1840. 348 p. MH; NNUT; OO. 40-1292

Cary, H. C. Duration of the presidential term. Philadelphia, PA: s. l., 1840. MB. 40-1293

Case, Josiah L. Biographical sketch of Rev. Josiah L. Case, late pastor of the Congregational Church and Society, Kingston, N. H. Boston, MA: s. l., 1840. 12 p. MBC; MWA; NBLIHI. 40-1294

Cass, Lewis, 1782-1866. France, its king, court, and government. By an American. New York; London: Wiley & Putnam, 1840. 191 p. ICN; LNH; MiGr; Nh-Hi; PPi. 40-1295

Casserly, Patrick S. To the Editor of the North American Review. New York Editors and New England Critics. [In a Review of Casserly's Edition of Jacobs' Greek Reader.] [New York: s. l., 184-?] 16 p. MH. 40-1296

Catalogue of a rich collection of rare & valuable London books, comprising works on theology, curious editions of classics, ... to be sold at auction, by Royal Gurley, at the New York Long Room, 169 Broadway, on Saturday evening, February 8th, at half past 6 o'clock. New York: Printed by Charles Vinten, 1840. 8 p. CtMW. 40-1297

Catalogue of Goods to be sold at Auction... Portland: Arthur Shirley, printer, 1840. 6 p. MeHi; My. 40-1298

Catechetical assistant, for the use of parents & Sabbath-school teachers...

Philadelphia, PA: Pres. bd. of pub., 1840. NT; PPPrHi. 40-1299

Cathcart, Robert, of Pennsylvania. A pastoral letter of the church under the case of Harrisburg Presbytery. Philadelphia, PA: Printed by I. Ashmead & Co., 1840. 14 p. P; PHi; PPPrHi. 40-1300

Cathcart, Robert, of Pennsylvania. A pastoral letter of the church under the case of Harrisburg Presbytery. Philadelphia, PA: Printed at the office of the Christian Observer, 1840. 12 p. CBPSR; PHi; PPPrHi. 40-1301

Cathcart, Robert, of Pennsylvania. A pastoral letter of the church under the case of Harrisburg Presbytery. 2nd ed. Philadelphia, PA: Printed at the office of the Christian Observer, 1840. 12 p. OClWHi; PHi; PPPrHi. 40-1302

Catholic claims. Review of the proceedings of the Catholics, on their application for a division of the school fund. By a citizen. New York: s. l., 1840. PPPrHi. 40-1303

Catholic Tract Society of Baltimore. Catholic tracts. Baltimore, MD: Catholic Tract Society, 1840-42. p. PLatS; PPL-R. 40-1304

Catholic Tract Society of Baltimore. The Inspiration and the canon of scripture. Baltimore, MD: Published monthly by the Catholic Tract Society, 1840. 24 p. DLC; MdBLC; MdCatS. 40-1305

Catholic Tract Society of Baltimore. On the original texts and translations of the Bible. Baltimore, MD: published monthly by the Catholic Tract Society, 1840. 24

p. DLC; DCU-H; MdBLC; MdCatS. 40-1306

Cattanio, P. A. Der geographisches Bildersaal. Philadelphia, PA: Gorton, 1840. MSaP; NjP; PPG. 40-1307

Cattanio, P. A. Der geographisches Bildersaal, oder, All-gemeiner ueberblick des markuerdigsten allerlaender. Philadelphia, PA: Fagan, 1840. PPG; PPULC. 40-1308

Caulkins, Francis Manwaring, 1795-1869. The children of the Bible: as examples, and as warnings. New York: American Tract Society. D. Fanshaw, printer [184-?] 46 p. CSmH; NN; PPeSchw; WHi. 40-1309

Caulkins, Francis Manwaring, 1795-1869. The child's hymn book. Selected by F. M. Caulkins for the American Tract Society. New York: American Tract Society [184-?] 208 p. MB. 40-1310

Caulkins, Frances Manwaring, 1795-1869. Eve and her daughters of Holy Writ; or, Women of the Bible. New York: Published by the American Tract Society [184-?] 144 p. WHi. 40-1311

Causten, James H. Letter on Bolk's veto of the French Spoliation bill. Washington: s. l., 1840. PPL; PPULC. 40-1312

Cayuga County Medical Society. Medical fee-bill, as revised and reported by the committee, and adopted by the Cayuga county medical society, at its annual meeting, in Auburn, June 4, 1840, to regulate the charges of physicians and surgeons in the county of Cayuga. Auburn, NY: Oliphant & Skinner, book

and fancy job printers, 1840. 10 p. IENM; NCH. 40-1313

Cecil, Catharine. Memoirs of Mrs. Hawkes, late of Islington; including remarks in conversation and extracts from sermons and letters of the late Rev. Richard Cecil. By Catharine Cecil. Third American edition, with additions. Philadelphia, PA: Washington J. Simon, 1840. 484 p. CtY; DLC; MWA; PPA; ViU. 40-1314

Cecil, Richard, 1748-1810. A friendly visit to the house of mourning. By Rev. Richard Cecil. Philadelphia, PA: Presby. bd. of pub., 1840. 96 p. CSamS; NjPT. 40-1315

The Cedar Hill Repository. Edited by the principal of the Young Ladies' Lyceum Inst., Cedar Hill, No. 1. Philadelphia, PA: s. l., 1840. 46 p. PHi. 40-1316

The celebrated one finger'd sliding waltz. Baltimore, MD: F. D. Benteen [184-?] 2 p. ViU. 40-1317

The celebrated Saratoga polka, as taught by Korponay. New York: Firth & Hall [184-?] 2 p. ViU. 40-1318

Cellerier, J. E. The authenticity of the New Testament. Translated from the French of J. E. Cellerier, Jr... With notes and references by a Sunday School teacher. 2nd ed. Boston, MA: Weeks, Jordan and Co., 1840. 254 p. GMar; IaDL; MBC; MMeT. 40-1319

Central Railroad and Banking Co. of Georgia. Semi-annual report of the engineer of the Central rail-road and banking company of Georgia, to the president, directors and stockholders.

Savannah, GA: s. l., 1840. 8 p. WHi. 40-1320

Cervantes Saavedra, Miguel de, 1547-1616. The life and exploits of the ingenious gentleman Don Quixote de la Mancha. Translated by Charles Jarvis. To which is prefixed a life of the author. [Philadelphia, PA: J. Crissy, 1840] 4 v. CtHT-W; MH; TNP. 40-1321

Cervantes Saavedra, Miguel de, 1547-1616. The life and exploits of the ingenious gentleman Don Quixote de la Mancha. Translated from the original Spanish of Miguel de Cervantes Saavedra, by Charles Jarvis, esq. In four volumes. Exeter: J. & B. Williams, 1840-41. 4 v. DLC; KyBgW; MH; TJaU. 40-1322

Chabert, J. X. Medical notice, by J. X. Chabert, M. D., known as the Fire King. New York: s. l. [184-?] 45 p. NNNAM. 40-1323

Chadbourne, Thomas, 1791-1864. A brief account of the application and uses of the instruments called abdominal supporters. Concord, NH: Panoply office print, 1840. 8 p. MiDW-M. 40-1324

Challoner, Bishop, V. A. L. Memoirs of missionary priests and other catholics of both sexes that have suffered death in England on religious accounts from the year 1577 to 1684. Philadelphia, PA: Published by Michael Kelly, 1840. 2 v. ArLSJ; IaDmDC; GDecCT; MB; WMMU. 40-1325

Challoner, Richard, 1691-1781. An abstract of the history of the Old and New Testaments... Revised by the Very Rev. John Power, V. G... 3ed American ed.

New York: McSweeny, 1840. 232 p. MdBS. 40-1326

Chalmers, Thomas, 1780-1847. Discourses on the Application of Christianity to the Commercial and Ordinary Affairs of Life. New York: s. l., 1840. 377 p. OO. 40-1327

Chalmers, Thomas, 1780-1847. On the Miraculous and Internal Evidences of the Christian Revelation, and an authority of its records. New York: Rob't Carter, cl., 1840. 2 v. OO. 40-1328

Chalmers, Thomas, 1780-1847. Sketches of Moral and Mental philosophy; their connection with each other; and their bearings on doctrinal and practical christianity... New York: Robert Carter, 1840. 420 p. CtY; GEU; IaDuU; MWelC. 40-1329

Chalmers, Thomas, 1780-1847. The works of Thomas Chalmers.... New York: Robert Carter, 1840. 7 v. MiU; NjMD; RPaw; ViU; WBelC. 40-1330

Chalmers, Thomas, 1780-1847. The works of Thomas Chalmers, D. D., L. L. D. Third uniform edition. New York: Robert Carter, 1840. 404 p. CtHT; IaDuU; MH; ViU. 40-1331

Chalmers, Thomas, 1780-1847. The works of Thomas Chalmers.... Third Uniform edition. New York: Robert Carter, 1840. 7 v. CBPSR; MWelC. 40-1332

Chalmers, Thomas, 1780-1847. [His] Works. Complete in one volume. Philadelphia, PA: s. l. [184-?] CtY; MH. 40-1333

Chamberlain, N. B. A catalogue of philosophical and astronomical instruments, manufactured and sold by N. B. Chamberlain, No. 2 & 9 School Street, Boston. Boston, MA: Isaac R. Butts, printer, 1840. 72 p. IaPeC; KyLxT; MHi. 40-1334

Chambers, Juliet Bell. The spell is broken. Ballad. Written & composed by Juliet Bell Chambers. Baltimore, MD: F. D. Benteen [184-?] 2 p. ViU. 40-1335

Chambers, Robert, 1802-1871. Vestiges of the natural history of creation. With a sequel. New York: Harper [184-?] 303 p. CBPSR; MB. 40-1336

Chamier, Frederick, 1796-1870. The Spitfire. By Captain Chamier... Philadelphia, PA: Carey and Hart, 1840. 2 v. in 1. DLC; MoU; NHem; RPB; WGr. 40-1337

Champneys, Benjamin. Address delivered at the common school celebration, May 1, 1840. Lancaster, PA: Forney, 1840. 26 p. NjR; P; PHDHi; PLFM. 40-1338

Channing, William Ellery, 1780-1842. Christian views of human suffering. 1st series, No. 152. By William E. Channing, D. D. Boston, MA: James Munroe & Co., printer, 1840. 30 p. CBPac; ICMe; MeB; MWA; RPB. 40-1339

Channing, William Ellery, 1780-1842. A discourse occasioned by the death of the Rev. Dr. Follen. By William E. Channing. Boston, MA: J. Munroe and company, 1840. 29 p. CtY; ICN; MWA; MiD-B; PPAmP. 40-1340

Channing, William Ellery, 1780-1842.

A discourse occasioned by the death of the Rev. Dr. Follen. 2nd ed. Boston, MA: J. Munroe & Co., 1840. 29 p. CtSoP; MH-AH; MWo; NcD; PHi; PPM. 40-1341

Channing, William Ellery, 1780-1842. Emancipation. By William E. Channing. Boston, MA: E. P. Peabody, 1840. 111 p. CSmH; LNH; MB; MBBC; MWA; NjP; NNUT; PHC; RPB; TxU. 40-1342

Channing, William Ellery, 1780-1842. Lectures on the elevation of the labouring portion of the community. By William E. Channing. Boston, MA: W. D. Ticknor, 1840. 80 p. ICU; LNH; MdBJ; MWA; PPAmP. 40-1343

Channing, William Ellery, 1780-1842. Letter of the Rev. William E. Channing to the Standing Committee of the proprietors of the Meeting-house in Federal Street, in the town of Boston, read at the annual meeting, May 6, 1840... Boston, MA: J. Dowe, 1840. 80 p. MB; MBAt; MH; MWA; RNR. 40-1344

Channing, William Ellery, 1780-1842. The power of Unitarian Christianity to produce an enlightened and fervent piety. Boston, MA: s. l., 1840. 43 p. CBPac; MDeeP; MeBat; MHi; MMet-Hi. 40-1345

Channing, William Ellery, 1780-1842. The works of William E. Channing, D. D. Boston, MA: James Munroe and Company, 1840. 7 v. PPA; PPULC. 40-1346

Chants of the Episcopal Church, original and selected, harmonized for four voices, provided with an organ or piano forte accompaniment, by W. H. W. Darley... and J. C. B. Standbridge.

Philadelphia, PA: Lee & Walker [1840]
46 p. NNU-W. 40-1347

Chapin, Alonzo Bowen, 1808-1858. On
the study of the Celtic languages. From
the New York Review for April, 1840, by
A. B. Chapin, M. A., Mem. Conn. Acad.
Arts and sciences... New York: published
by Alexander V. Blake, 1840. 32 p. MH;
MWA; PPAmP; RP; TxH. 40-1348

Chapin, Edwin Hubbell, 1814-1880. An
address on true greatness, published as
delivered before the Madison debating
society [at the request of the society] by
E. H. Chapin. Richmond, VA: Printed by
P. D. Bernard, 1840. 23 p. CSmH;
NcWfC. 40-1349

Chapin, Edwin Hubbell, 1814-1880. A
discourse on the burning of the steamboat Lexington, preached in the first Independent Christian church, March 8th
and 15th. Richmond, VA: Printed by
James C. Walker, 1840. 11 p. ViU. 40-
1350

Chapin, Edwin Hubbell, 1814-1880.
Duties of young men, exhibited in six lec-
tures... By E. H. Chapin. Boston, MA:
Abel Tompkins and B. B. Muzzey, 1840.
212 p. IEG; MB; MMeT-Hi; NhPet;
ScCliTO. 40-1351

Chapin, Edwin Hubbell, 1814-1880. An
oration, delivered fourth of July, 1840, at
the invitation of the Richmond Light
Dragoons, the Washington Grenadiers
and the Scarlet Guard... Richmond, VA:
Printed by Peter D. Bernard, 1840. 8 v.
CSmH; MiU; PPL; PPULC; ViU. 40-
1352

Chapin, Edwin Hubbell, 1814-1880.
Responsibilities of a republication

government. A discourse, preached fast
day, April 8th. [S. l.] A. Tompkins, pub.,
184-? p. CSmH; ICU; MB; NN. 40-1353

Chapin, Edwin Hubbell, 1814-1880.
Tracts for an honest inquirer. No. 1.
Universaliam: what it is not and what it
is. A sermon by Rev. E. H. Chapin, D. D.
Boston, MA: Published and for sale by
James M. Lisher [184-?] 16 p. CBPSR.
40-1354

Chapin, Edwin Hubbell, 1814-1880.
Universalism: what it is not, and what it
is. A discourse preached in the Indepen-
dent Christian Church, Richmond, Va...
Utica, NY: O. Hutchinson, C. C. P.
Grosh, printer, 1840. 23 p. CSmH;
NNUT; NUt. 40-1355

Chapin, Horace Billings, 1792-1840.
Love of the gift, not love to the giver. A
thanksgiving sermon, delivered Dec. 28,
1839, at Lewiston Falls, by Rev. Horace
B. Chapin, pastor of the Congregational
church. Published by request. Portland,
ME: Arthur Shirley, printer, 1840. 27 p.
CSmH; MeHi; MH-AH; MWA; RPB.
40-1356

Chapin, John R. Description of Dr.
Chapin's instrument for the treatment of
prolapsus uteri, by external support. New
York: s. l., 1840. 6 p. DLC; DNLM;
MBM; MH-M; NNNAM. 40-1357

Chapin, William, 1802-1888. A complete reference gazeteer of the United
States of North America; containing a
general view of the United States, and of
each state and territory, and a notice of
the various canals, railroads, and internal
improvements... together with all the
Post Offices in the United States... the
whole forming a complete manual of

reference on the geography and statistics of the United States. New York: Phelps and Ensign, 1840. 347 p. CoU; In; KyHi; MWA; NNF; TxU. 40-1358

Chaplin, Connecticut. Church of Christ. A brief historical sketch of the Church of Christ in Chaplin, Connecticut. Hartford, CT: s. l., 1840. 56 p. CtY; MiD-B; MWA; NBLIHI. 40-1359

Chapman, John Gadsby, 1808-1884. The picture of the baptism of Pocahontas:Painted by order of Congress, ... by J. G. C. [Historical sketch and extracts from contemporary writers, relating to the subject of the picture.] Washington: P. FOrce, 1840. 22 p. CSfCW; DLC; KHi; MB; PHi. 40-1360

Chapman, Maria Weston, 1806-1885. Pinda: a true tale... New York: American anti-slavery society, 1840. 23 p. MH; OO. 40-1361

Chapman, Maria Weston, 1806-1885. Right and Wrong in Massachusettts. Boston, MA: Henry L. Devereaux, printer, 1840. CSmH; MB; NcD; PPL; PPULC. 40-1362

Chaptal de Chauteloup, Jean Antoine Claude, 1756-1832. Chymistry applied to agriculture. By M. le comte Chaptal... with a preliminary chapter on the organization, structure, etc., of plants; by Sir Humphrey Davy. And an essay on the use of lime as a manure, by M. Puvis; with introductory observations to the same, by James Renwick... tr. and ed. by Rev. William P. Page. New York: Harper & brothers, 1840. 359 p. CSt; GWay; MB; MiU; NcU; PU. 40-1363

Charleston, S. C. Apprentices Library Society. Catalogue of the books belonging to the Apprentices' Library society of Charleston, S. C. Charleston, SC: printed by B. B. Hussey, 1840. 336 p. DLC; ScC; ScCC. 40-1364

Charleston, S. C. Citizens. Proceedings of a public meeting... On the 28th August, 1840; in relation to the persecution of the Jews in the East, also the proceedings of a meeting of the Israelites of Charleston, convened at the hall of the Hebrew orphan society, on the following evening, in reference to the same subject. Charleston, SC: Hayden & Burke, printers, 1840. 32 p. ScU. 40-1365

Charleston, S. C. Ordinances, etc. Ordinances of the city of Charleston, from the 24th May, 1837, to the 18th March, 1840. Together with such of the acts and parts of acts of the legislature of South Carolina, as relate to Charleston, from December, 1837, to December, 1839, inclusive. Published by a resolution of Council. Charleston, SC: Printed by B. R. Getsinger, 1840. 255 p. DLC; NN; WHi. 40-1366

Charleston Library Society, Charleston, S. C. Rules and by-laws of the Charleston Library Society. Charleston, SC: B. B. Hussey prtr., 1840. 15 p. GU; ScC; ScCC. 40-1367

Charlestown, Mass. Emmon's Charlestown Directory... [Charlesstown, MA: s. l., 1840. 107 p. MBNEH; MHi. 40-1368

Charlestown, Mass. Order ot Exercises for the Dedication of the New Brick School House [Charlestown, Mass.] , on Tuesday, April 21, 1840. [Charlston, MA: n. p., 1840?] p. MHi. 40-1369

Charlestown, Mass. School Committee. Annual report of the school committee of Charlestown... 1840, 1846, 1848. [Charlston, MA: s. l., 1840-48. 3 v. CSmH; MB. 40-1370

Charlestown, Mass. Workingmen. Third grand rally of the workingmen of Charlestown, Mass, held October 23, 1840. [Charlestown, MA: s. l., 1840] 18 p. DLC; MH; Mh-BA; MiD-B. 40-1371

The charming woman. A popular ballad arranged for the Spanish guitar, and respectfully dedicated to John P. Collord, by L. T. B., Esq. New York: Firth, Pond & Co. [184-?] 2 p. ViU. 40-1372

Charnock, Stephen, 1628-1680. Discourses upon the existence and attributes of God, by Stephen Charnock, B. D. First American edition. Philadelphia, PA: Presbyterian Board of Publication, 1840. 2v. IaGG; KyLoP; LNB; MWA; PPWe. 40-1373

Charnock, Stephen, 1628-1680. The doctrine of regeneration. Selected from the writings of the Rev. Stephen Charnock... Philadelphia, PA: Presbyterian Board of Publication, 1840. 323 p. AFIT; KyLoP; MWA; NjPT; ODaB; PPM. 40-1374

Chase, Enoch. Tables of advance on British sterling; by which British sterling is reduced to dollars and cents, with advance thereon from five to one hundred per cent. By Enoch Chase. Boston, MA: Josiah Loring, 1840. 84 p. LNL; LNH; MH. 40-1375

Chautauqua County Common School Institute. First annual report of the Chautauqua county common school institute, held at a meeting of the society in Fredonia, January 1, 1840. By B. J. Seward, chairman of the executive committee. Buffalo, NY: printed at Steele's press, 1840. 24 p. NBu. 40-1376

Chavliev, Charles. The yellow hair'd laddie, Scotch air. With an introduction & variations for the piano forte. New York: Hewitt [184-?] 6 p. MB. 40-1377

Chazotte, Peter S. Historical sketches of the revolution and the foreign and civil wars in the Island of St. Domingo. With a narrative of the entire massacre of the White Population... by Peter S. Chazotte, esq., an eyewitness. New York: Wm. Applegate, 1840. 71 p. PPM. 40-1378

The Cheat Come Haste to the Wedding the Waterman. [Pianoforte music.] Boston, MA: Ditson [184-?] 1 p. MB. 40-1379

Cheever, George Barrell, 1807-1890. American common-place book of poetry. Boston, MA: s. l., 184-? p. MB. 40-1380

Cheever, George Barrell, 1807-1890. The American common-place book of prose, a collection of eloquent and interesting extracts from the writings of American authors. By G. B. Cheever. Cooperstown, NY: E. Phinney, 1840. 468 p. MtBiP; MtBilP; PU. 40-1381

Cherokee almanac. Park Hill: s. l., 1840-60. 5 v. MBAt. 40-1382

Cherokee almanac for 1840. Park Hill, OK: s. l., 1840. PPAmP. 40-1383

Cherokee Nation. The constitution and laws of the Cherokee nation: passed at

Tah-le-quah, Cherokee nation, 1839. Washington: printed by Gales and Seaton, 1840. 36 p. ICN; MHi; MnU; PPM; Tx. 40-1384

Cherokee Nation. Memorial of the delegates and representatives of the Cherokee Nation, West; referred Apr. 1, 1840. [Washington, DC: s. l., 1840. MBAt. 40-1385

Cherokee Nation. Memorial of the delegation, [Feb. 28, 1840, Washington] [Washington, DC: s. l., 1840. MBAt. 40-1386

Cherokee primer. Park Hill: Mission press. J. Canday, printer, 1840. 24 p. DLC; MB; NcWsM. 40-1387

Cherry, Andrew, 1762-1812. ... The soldier's daughter, a comedy, in five acts. With the stage business, cast of characters, costumes, relative positions, etc. By A. Cherry. New York: S. French [etc., etc., 184-?] 73 p. CSt; MB. 40-1388

Cherry, John William, 1824-1889. Shells of ocean. A song. Written by J. W. Lake. [Accomp. for piano] Philadelphia, PA: Lee & Walker [184-?] 6 p. MB. 40-1389

Cherry Valley, New York. The Centennial celebration at Cherry Valley, Otsego co., N. Y., July 4th, 1840. The address of William W. Campbell, esq. and Gov. W. H. Seward, with letters, toasts, &c. &c. New York: Taylor & Clement, 1840. 59 p. CSmH; ICN; MBAt; MH; PHi. 40-1390

Chesapeake and Delaware canal. Tolls to be paid and regulations to be observed by vessels navigating the Chesapeake and Delaware canal. Philadelphia, PA: William Stavely and co., 1840. NjR. 40-1391

Chesapeake and Ohio Canal Company. By the House of Delegates, Feb. 14, 1840. Communication from Francis Thomas, president of the Chesapeake and Ohio canal company, to the governor of Maryland. [S. l.: s. l., 1840?] 76 p. MdHi; WHi. 40-1392

Chesapeake and Ohio Canal Company. [Document V.] By the House of Delegates, Feb. 14, 1840. Communication from Francis Thomas, President of the Chesapeake and Ohio Canal company, to the governor of Maryland. [Annapolis, MD: s. l., 1840] 76 p. WHi. 40-1393

Chesapeake and Ohio Canal Company. Letter from Francis Thomas, president of the Chesapeake and Ohio canal company, to William A. Spencer, chairman of the Committee of Ways and Means. By the House of delegates, Feb. 19, 1840. [Annapolis, MD: s. l., 1840?] 6 p. WHi. 40-1394

Chesapeake and Ohio Canal Company. Proceedings... of the Chesapeake and Ohio canal company, in relation to the present condition of the work on the line of the canal... Washington, DC: Printed by Gales and Seaton, 1840. 27 p. DLC; MdHi; NNE; OClWHi; ViU. 40-1395

Chesapeake and Ohio Canal Company. Report from the committee on internal improvements transmitting a communication from Francis Thomas as president of the C. & O. C. Co. to the governor of Maryland. Annapolis, MD:

G. & W. Johnston, 1840. 76 p. DLC. 40-1396

Chesapeake and Ohio Canal Company. Report of the general committee of the stockholders of the Chesapeake and Ohio canal company, presented on the 21st of July, 1840. Washington, DC: Printed by Gales and Seaton, 1840. 20 p. MdHi. 40-1397

Chester, Albert Tracy, 1812-1892. A serman delivered at the funeral of Hon. Anson Brown who died at Ballston Spa, June 14, 1840. Saratoga Springs, NY: G. M. Davison, 1840. 20 p. CSmH; MH-AH; N; PPPrHi; PPULC. 40-1398

Chicken Little. Remarkable story of Chicken Little. Roxbury: s. l., 1840. MB. 40-1399

Child, David Lee, 1794-1874. The culture of the beet, and manufacture of beet sugar. By David Lee Child. Boston, MA; Northampton: Weeks, Jordan & Co.; J. H. Butler, 1840. 156 p. IU; MiGr; MWA; NNS; OClW; PU. 40-1400

Child, Lydia Maria Francis, 1802-1880. The history of the condition of women in various ages and nations. By Mrs. D. L. Child... Third edition. Boston, MA: Otis, Broaders & Co., 1840. 298 p. MoSW; MSbo; MWelC; NUt. 40-1401

Child, Lydia Maria Francis, 1802-1880. The little girl's own book... New York: S. Colman, 1840. 288 p. MnU; RPB. 40-1402

Childs, George. Elementary drawing-book; a series of easy progressive lessons for young beginners. New and improved ed. Philadelphia, PA: J. T. Bowen [1840?] 2 p. MH. 40-1403

Childs, Isaac, fl. 1757. The vision of Isaac Child. With explanatory notes from another hand. To which is prefixed a biographical sketch of his life. Philadelphia, PA: John Simmons, 1840. 26 p. In-RchE; MH; PHi; PSC-Hi. 40-1404

The Child's book of natural history. Boston, MA: Henshaw [184-?] 64 p. MB. 40-1405

The child's cabinet of beasts and birds. Northampton: John Metcalf, 1840. 22 p. CtY; MH. 40-1406

Child's first lessons, or, Infant primer. New Haven, CT: S. Babcock [184-?] ICU; MH; NN. 40-1407

The childs first primer, or, A. B. C. Book. New York: H. & S. Raynor [184-?] p. DLC; ICU; MH. 40-1408

The Child's Own Book. Boston, MA: s. l., 1840. 620 p. PHi. 40-1409

The Child's own Sunday book; or Sabbath-day lessons for little children. New Haven, CT: S. Babcock [184-?] p. CtY; MH; NNC. 40-1410

The child's pictorial music book. Hartford, CT: E. B. & E. C. Kellogg, 1840. 24 p. CTHWatk; NRU. 40-1411

Child's prayer and hymn book for the use of Catholic Sunday schools throughout the United States. 10th ed. rev. & enl. Baltimore, MD: J. Murphy [184-?] 221 p. RPB. 40-1412

Chillicothe Female Seminary.

Catalogue of the officers and members of the Chillicothe Female Seminary, Ohio, for three terms, from September, 1839 to May, 1840. Chillicothe, OH: Prnted by Wm. C. Jones, 1840. 12 p. OClWHi. 40-1413

Chillingworth, William, 1602-1644. The works of W. Chillingworth, containing his book entitled "The religion of Protestants, a safe way to salvation," together with his sermons, letters, discourses, controversies. 1st American from the 12th English ed. Philadelphia, PA: Published by Herman Hooker for Robert Davis, 1840. 764 p. CBPac; GEU-T; OrPD; PPP; ScSp. 40-1414

Chinn, Thomas W. Letter to Thomas W. Chinn to Hon. Thomas Gibbs Morgan, president of the Whig convention of the second congressional district in the state of Louisiana, convened at the town of Baton Rouge, on the 20th of January 1840. Wasington, DC: Printed by J. Gideon, Jr [1840] 14 p. LNH; LNHT; LU; MHi. 40-1415

Chittenden, Thomas C. Speech on the sub-treasury bill. In the House of Representatives of the United States, June 27, 1840. Washington, DC: s. l. [1840] 16 p. FedResBk; M. 40-1416

Chitty, Joseph, 1776-1841. A treatise on pleading with a collection of precendents, and an appendix of forms adapted to the recent pleading and other rules and with practical notes... By Joseph Chitty, Esq., ...with notes and additions, by John A. Dunlap, Esq., and additional notes and references to later decisions by E. D. Ingraham, Esq. Springfield, MA: G. and C. Merriam, 1840. 3 v. Ia. 40-1417

Chitty, Joseph, 1776-1841. A treatise on the parties to actions, and on pleading, with second and third volumes containing precedents of pleadings... By Joseph and Thomas Chitty... Springfield, MA; New York: G. and C. Miriam; Collins and Harmay, 1840. 3 v. CSdCL; LU; MdBP; NcEcEN; OTU. 40-1418

Choctaw Nation. Chahta yakni nan vlhpisa nishkoboka, micha anumpa vlhpisa aiena, Jonathan Cogswell vt. chahta anumpa atoshdi tok. Park Hill: Cherokee Nation, John Candy, printer, 1840. 39 p. MH-L. 40-1419

Choctaw Nation. Constitutin and laws of the Choctaw nation. Park Hill: Cherokee Nation, 1840. DLC; MBAt; MH. 40-1420

The Christian almanac for New England for the year of Our Lord 1840. Boston, MA: Published for the American Tract Society and for Gould, Kendall & Lincoln, 1840. 49 p. RNHi. 40-1421

Christian Baptism and Church Communion. A Conversation between two Laymen, on the Subjects and Mode of Christian Baptism and Church Communion, forming a complete Manual. Cleveland, OH: s. l., 1840. 137 p. RHi. 40-1422

Christian biography. No. 1. The life of the Rev. John Newton... written by himself....No. 2. The life of Archbishop Leighton....No. 3. The life of the Rev. C. F. Swartz, missionary... in India. Also: Sermons to the aged. New York: American Tract Society [1840] 236 p. DLC; NcCJ; PWmpDS. 40-1423

The Christian keepsake and missionary

annual. Edited by the Rev. John A. Clark. Philadelphia, PA: William Marshall and co. [1840] p. DLC; KyBC; MWA; RWe; ViU. 40-1424

The Christian library. [New York: s. l., 1840?-185-?] v. DLC; MH; ViW. 40-1425

The Christian parlor book: devoted to literature, morals, and religion. New York: Geo. Pratt, 184-? v. TxU. 40-1426

Christian register and almanac for 1841. Exeter, NH: A. R. Brown [1840] p. MWA; NhHi. 40-1427

The christian's guide to heaven: or, a manual of spiritual exercises for catholics. New York: John Kenedy, 1840. 255 p. MdBD. 40-1428

A Christmas of New Year's present. Hartford, CT: Silas Andrus [184-?] 248 p. NNC. 40-1429

Chronicle of events, discoveries and improvements for the popular diffusion of useful knowledge with an authentic record of facts, illustrated with maps and drawings. Boston, MA: s. l., 1840-42. 3 v. MnHi. 40-1430

Church, Benjamin, 1639-1718. The History of Phillip's war, commonly called the great Indian war, of 1675 and 1676. Also of the French and Indian wars at the Eastward, in 1689, 1690, 1692, 1696, and 1704. 2d ed., with plates. Exeter, NH: J. & B. Williams, 1840. 360 p. CSmH; IU; NN; OkU; PU. 40-1431

Church, Benjamin, 1734-1776. Correspondence and orders relating to the trial and imprisonment of Dr. Benjamin

Church on the charge of treasonable correspondence with the British, 1775-1776. Washington, DC: s. l. 1840-46. 15 p. DLC. 40-1432

The Church Almanac for 1841. New York: Protestant Episcopal Tract Society [1840] 36 p. MBC; NBuDD; OrPD. 40-1433

The church almanac for the year of Our Lord 1841... New York: published by the Protestant Episcopal Tract Society [1840?] 36 p. IEG; MWA; NjR; NNA; WHi. 40-1434

The church the nursing mother of her people. [New York: Published by the Protestant Episcopal Tract Society, 1840] 8 p. DLC; IEG; InID; NN; WHi. 40-1435

Churchill, Fleetwood, 1808-1878. Observations on the diseases incident to pregnancy and childbirth. Philadelphia, PA: Adam Waldie, 1840. 88 p. ArU-M; MdBJ; Nh; PPCP; WMAM. 40-1436

Cicero, Marcus Tullius. C. Cornelii Taciti Germania, Agricola, et De oratoribus dialogus. Accedunt notae Anglicae, cura C. K. Dillaway. Ex editione Oberliniana. Boston, MA: Perkins, 1840. 177 p. KAStB; MBBC; NCanHi; NNC; PU. 40-1437

Cicero, Marcus Tullius. The orations, translated by Duncan, the offices by Cockman, and the Cato and Laelius by Melmoth. New York: Harper & Brothers, 1840. 3 v. ICP; OCX; ScC; WStfSF. 40-1438

Cicero, Marcus Tullius. Select orations of Cicero with English notes critical and explanatory, and historical, geographical, and legal indexes. A new edition, with improvements. New York: Harper & Brothers, 1840. 518 p. GMM; KyLoS; TChU; ViRU; WAsN. 40-1439

Cicero, Marcus Tullius. Works. New York: Harper & Bros., 1840. InLW. 40-1440

Cincinnati. Address and the proceedings of the Festival, held in the City of Cincinnati, January 29th, 1840, in commemoration of the Revolutionary Services of that wonderful advocate of civil liberty, Thomas Paine. Cincinnati, OH: s. l., 1840. NHi. 40-1441

Cincinnati. Chamber of Commerce. Constitution and By-Laws of the... instituted October 1839. Cincinnati, OH: s. l., 1840. 16 p. OCHP. 40-1442

Cincinnati. Ninth Street Baptist Church. Act of incorporation, deed of trust and by-laws. Cincinnati, OH: s. l., 1840. 12 p. NHC-S. 40-1443

Cincinnati. Third Presbyterian Church Sabbath School. The Juvenile Temperance Society of the Third Presbyterian Church Sabbath School, Cincinnati. Formed July 15, 1838. [Constitution as amended July, 1839, and Annual Report of the Society, May 15, 1840.] [Cincinnati, OH?: s. l., 1840?] p. ICU. 40-1444

Cincinnati. University. Medical College of Ohio. Doc. No. 40. Annual Report of the Trustees of the Medical college of Ohio. Presented by Mr. Faran. In Senate, December 30, 1839. [Columbus, OH: s. l., 1840.] 14 p. WHi. 40-1445

Cincinnati. Woodward high school & college. Annual Circular and Catalogue of the Woodward College and of the High School. Cincinnati, OH: s. l., 1840. 8 p. OCHP. 40-1446

Cincinnati and White-water canal company. Report of the president to the stockholders in the Cincinnati and White-water canal company. January 8th, 1840. Cincinnati, OH: Gazette printers, 1840. 20 p. MiU; OClWHi. 40-1447

Cincinnati Daily Gazette. Carrier's address, Cincinnati. Address of the Carriers of the Cincinnati Daily Gazette to their patrons, Jan. 1, 1840. Cincinnati, OH: s. l., 1840. 8 p. OCHP. 40-1448

Cincinnati Directory. The Cincinnati, Covington, Newport and Fulton Directory, for 1840:comprising the names of householders, heads of families, and those engaged in business, together with the state or country of their birth, &c. rule, by David Henry Shaffer. Cincinnati, OH: Printed by J. S. & R. P. Donogh [1840?] 520 p. OClWHi; ViU. 40-1449

Circular on contemplated Whig frauds. Philadelphia, PA: s. l., 1840. PPL. 40-1450

Circular to the Whig electors. Philadelphia, PA: s. l., 1840. PPL. 40-1451

A Citizen of Saratoga Springs, etc. Saratoga, NY: s. l., 1840. MB. 40-1452

The Citizen soldier, a military paper, devoted to the interests of the militia. Major J. Swett, jr., editor. v. 1; July 22, 1840-July 30, 1841. Windsor, VT: Swett and Jackman, 1840-41. 412 p. Ct; CtY; MdBLC; MbHi; NWM. 40-1453

Citizen's and farmers almanac. By C. F. Engelmann. Baltimore, MD: J. T. Hanzeche, 1840. MWA. 40-1454

Citizen's and farmer's almanac for 1841. Original calculations by Charles F. Engelmann. Baltimore, MD: John T. Hanzsche [1840] p. MWA. 40-1455

City Point School and classical Mercantile & Literary Inst., S. Boston. Scrapbook. [Boston, MA: Prospectuses, 184-?] p. MB. 40-1456

The civil service of William Henry Harrison, with extracts from his addresses, speeches, and letters, and a sketch of his life. [Philadelphia, PA: C. Sherman & co., 1840?] 48 p. DLC; RPB. 40-1457

Claggett, Rufus. American expositor, or intellectual definer. Designed for the use of schools. Boston, MA: Gould, Kendall & Lincoln, 1840. MH. 40-1458

Claims of the gospel ministry to an adequate support. Philadelphia, PA: Presbyterian board of publication; William S. Martien, publishing agent, 1840. 16 p. CtHC; McSC. 40-1459

The claims of the Holy Week: a plain address to Churchmen. New York: Printed by A. Hanford, 1840. 12 p. NSmb. 40-1460

Clapisson, Louis, 1755-1820. The conscripts return. Ouvrez! ouvrez! Paroles de A. Richomme. Musique de Lo. Clappison. The English translation by Mrs. Mary E. Hewitt. New York: James L.

Hewitt & co., Firth & Hall [184-?] 6 p. NN; ViU. 40-1461

Clapp, Eliza Thayer. Words in a Sunday school. [S. l.: n. p., 184-?] p. MH. 40-1462

Clara: a story for children. Written by the Lady of the New Church [pseud.] Boston, MA: s. l., 1840. MBAt. 40-1463

Clare De Kitchen. Philadelphia, PA: Geo. Willig [184-?] 1 p. ViU. 40-1464

Clark, Abraham. The friends and acquaintances of Mr. Abraham Clark, are respecfully invited to attend the Funeral of his sister Harriet Clark, from his residence, above the steam saw-mill, Tomorrow Evening at 3 o'clock. Religious exercises by the Rev. Mr. Henderson may be expected, Saturday, Oct. 17, 1840. [Clarksville, AR: s. l., 1840] p. No Loc. 40-1465

Clark, Alva. A new system of astronomy, in questions and answers. For the use of schools and academies. By Alva Clark, A. B. Seventh edition. New York: R. Lockwood; S. W. Benedict, printer, 1840. 72 p. MPiB; NcWsHi; NcWsS. 40-1466

Clark, Daniel Kinnear, d. 1896. Railway Machinery: a treatise on the Mechanical Engineering of Railways....By Daniel Kinnear Clark. New York: C. E. Blackie and Son, 1840. 230 p. MoU. 40-1467

Clark, John Alonzo, 1801-1843. Glimpses of the old world; or, Excursions on the continent and in the island of Great Britain. By John Alonzo Clark... Philadelphia, PA: Marshall, 1840. 2 v. CtMW; KWiU; MiU; NjP; PU. 40-1468

Clark, John Alonzo, 1801-1843. A walk about Zion; By Rev. John A. Clark, D. D. revised and enlarges....Fourth edition. Philadelphia, PA: Marshall, Williams & Butler, 1840. 244 p. KSalW; NCH; OWor. 40-1469

Clark, John Chamberlain. Letter of the Hon. John C. Clark, of New York, to his constituents, on the necessity of efficient political action and organization. Washington, DC: s. l., 1840. 7 p. CtHWatk; CtY; MiU-L; MWA. 40-1470

Clark, Noah B. Second annual catalogue of Noah B. Clark's seminary for the year ending April 10th, 1840. Hartford, CT: Case, 1840. CtHT-W. 40-1471

Clark, Willis Gaylord, 1810-1841. An address on the characters of Lafayette and Washington. Pronounced before the Washington society of Lafayette College, Easton, Pa., on July 4, 1840. By Willis Gaylord Clark. Philadelphia, PA: J. Crissy, printer, 1840. 24 p. CtY; DLC; MB; MiGr; PLERC-Hi. 40-1472

Clarke, Adam, 1760?-1832. Account of the religious & literary life of Adam Clarke... written by one who was intimately acquainted with him from his boyhood to the sixtieth year of his age. Ed. by the Rev. J. B. B. Clarke. New York: Mason, 1840. 223 p. CtMW; DLC; CBB; NjPT; TxU. 40-1473

Clarke, Adam, 1760?-1832. Christian theology, by Adam Clarke, LL. D., F. A. S. Selected from his published and unpublished writings and systematically arranged. With a life of the author, by Samuel Dunn. New York: Mason &

Lane, 1840. 438 p. IaMp; NcD; NNMHi; PCC; TJoT. 40-1474

Clarke, Francis Gedney, 1792-1843. A synthetic and inductive system of bookkeeping by double entry, designed particularly for schools and academies... by F. G. Clarke... Portland; Boston, MA: Published by S. H. Colesworthy; B. B. Mussey, 1840. 82 p. DLC; MH. 40-1475

Clarke, James Freeman, 1810-1888. Letter to the Unitarian Society in Louisville. By Rev. J. F. Clarke. Louisville, KY: Morton & Griswold, printers, 1840. 15 p. ICU; MH; MWA. 40-1476

Clarke, Martha J. The child's first catechism... Providence, RI: s. l., 1840. 18 p. RPB. 40-1477

Clarke, Mary. A Concise History of the Life amours of Thos. S. Hamblin, late manager of the Bowery Theatre... Philadelphia, PA: s. l. [184-?] p. MB. 40-1478

Clarke, Samuel, 1684-1850. Collection of the sweet assuring promises of Scripture, or the believer's inheritance. Baltimore, MD: Lewis, 1840. 250 p. MiU; NN; OO. 40-1479

Clarke, Samuel, 1791-1859. A tribute to the memory of Mrs. Susannah Adams, widow of the late Hon. Benj. Adams, of Uxbridge, who died Oct. 13, 1840, aged 73; and of Miss Sarah W. Capron, only daughter of the late Charles S. Capron, of Uxbridge, who died Oct. 12, 1840, aged 17. Boston, MA: printed by James Munroe and company, 1840. 18 p. MB; MWA; NjR; NNC; RHi. 40-1480

Clarkson, Thomas, 1760-1846. An essay

on the doctrines and practices of the early Christians, as they relate to war... Boston, MA: s. l. [184-?] p. MBAt. 40-1481

Clay, Cassius Marcellus, 1810-1903. A Review of the Late Canvass, and R. Wickliffe's Speech on the Negro Law. Sept. 25. Lexington: s. l., 1840. 18 p. CtY; KyU; MH; NIC; PPPrHi. 40-1482

Clay, Clement Comer, 1789-1866. Remarks of Mr. Clay, of Alabama, Senate, Thursday, April 16, 1840, [on] the "bill supplementary to the act, entitled "an act to grant pre-emption rights to settlers on the public lands, approved June 22d, 1838, having been taken up for cinsideration, and the amendments, reported by the committee on the public lands, having been adopted by the Senate..." [Washington, DC: s. l., 1840] 8 p. CtY; MdHi; TxU. 40-1483

Clay, Clement Comer, 1789-1866. Speech of Mr. Clay, of Alabama, Mr. Poinsett's report. In Senate, Saturday, June 13, 1840, on the motion of Mr. Roane to print 20, 000 copies of the report to the committee on the militia. [Washington, DC: s. l., 1840] 16 p. CtY; MdHi; TxU. 40-1484

Clay, Clement Comer, 1789-1866. Speech of Mr. Clay, of Alabama, on the bill for the armed occupation of Florida. Senate, U. S., January 14, 1840. [Washington, DC: printed at the Globe office, 1840] 7 p. MdHi; TxU. 40-1485

Clay, Clement Comer, 1789-1866. Speech... on the permanent prospective pre-emption bill... In Senate... January 15, 1840. [Washington, DC: s. l., 1840] 15 p. MHi. 40-1486

Clay, Henry, 1777-1852. The Life and Speeches, delivered mainly in the Senate and House of the United States, between 1810 and 1842 Inclusive, including his Valedictory in the Senate and last Lexington Speech. With explanatory Notes. New York: s. l., 184- 2 v. MBr; MH. 40-1487

Clay, Henry, 1777-1852. Speech of H. Clay, of Kentucky, on the bill commonly called the Sub-treasury bill; describing its true character; proving its pernicious tendency upon the interests of the country; and establishing that it lays the foundations of a government bank... Delivered in the Senate of the United States, the 20th January, 1840. [Washington, DC: s. l., 1840] 16 p. CtSoP; CtY; DLC; MWA; OClWHi. 40-1488

Clay, Henry, 1777-1852. Speech of the Hon. Henry Clay, on the bill Sub-treasury bill. Delivered in the Senate of the United States, January 20, 1840. Boston, MA: published by George Oscar Bartlett, 1840. 23 p. CSmH; MBAt; MdBJ; MWA; MWey. 40-1489

Claybaugh, Joseph, 1803-1855. Address at the Theological Sem'y. Oxford, OH: s. l., 1840. IaU; PPL-R; PPPrHi. 40-1490

Clemenceau de Saint-Jullien, Alfred de, 1821? La sicilienne. Nouvelle danse de salon. Composee par Markowski; musique [pour le piano forte] d'Alfred de St. Julien. Philadelphia, PA: Lee & Walker [184-?] 5 p. MB. 40-1491

Cleveland, Edwards. The glory of a house of worship. A sermon preached at the dedication of the Congregational meeting-house, in Stoneham, Thursday, Oct. 22, 1840... Stoneham: Willey, 1840.

20 p. CSmH; ICN; MBC; Mh-AH; MiD-B. 40-1492

Cleveland, Henry Russell, 1808-1843. An address delivered before the Harvard Musical Association, at the annual meeting on commencement day, Aug. 26, 1840. Boston, MA: published by request, 1840. 14 p. CtY; MB; MH. 40-1493

Cleveland, Henry Russell, 1808-1843. A letter to the Hon. Daniel Webster, on the causes of the destruction of the steamer Lexington, as discovered in the testimony before the Coroner's Jury in New York. By A Traveller. Boston, MA: Charles C. Little and James Brown, 1840. 46 p. DLC; MB; MMal; MWA; NIC; RPE. 40-1494

Cleveland, Richard Jeffry, 1773-1860. In the forecastle; or, Twenty-five years a sailor. New York: Hurst & Co., 1840? 407 p. IaCll; ICN; NjR; NN. 40-1495

Cleveland, First Wesleyan Methodist Church. Constitution, articles, and covenant of the Wesleyan Methodist Church, Cleveland. Cleveland, OH: Francis B. Penniman, 1840. 18 p. OClWHi. 40-1496

Clifford, Nathan. Speech of Mr. Clifford, of Maine, on the Resolution of Mr. Campbell, of South Carolina, concerning the New Jersey disputed election. Delivered in the House of Representatives, January 10 and 11, 1839. Washington, DC: Printed at the Globe Office, 1840. 16 p. IU; MBAt; MdHi. 40-1497

Clifton, William. Auld Lang Syne. A favorite Scotch ballad. Arranged as a song and trio by William Clifton. Boston, MA: Published by Oliver Ditson, 1840. 4 p. KU. 40-1498

Clifton, William. The carrier dove. A favorite song or duet... Arranged as a duet [S. A.] with symphonies and accompaniments for the piano forte. Boston, MA: Ditson [184-?] 3 p. MB. 40-1499

Clifton, William. The pilot on the deep. Ballad. New York: Birch [184-?] 2 p. MB. 40-1500

Clifton, William. The rose will cease to blow. Written by Robert Guylott, Esqr., and sung with great applause by Mr. Salmon. Arranged for the piano forte by William Clifton. Boston, MA: Oliver Ditson [184-?] 4 p. ViU. 40-1501

Clifton's instructions for the piano forte. Containing the rudiments of music, scales, exercises & rules for fingering, to which is added a number of the late popular airs, arranged as lessons. Baltimore, MD: F. D. Benteen [184-?] 19 p. ViU. 40-1502

Clinch, Joseph Hart, d. 1884. The captivity in Babylon, and other poems. By the Rev. Joseph H. Clinch, A. M. Boston, MA: James Burns, 1840. 115 p. CtHT; ICU; MBAt; RPB; TxU. 40-1503

A Cloud of witnesses for the royal Prerogatives of Jesus Christ; or, The last speeches and testimonies of those who suffered for the truth in Scotland in the years 1681 to 1688... New York: Publication society of the First Reformed Presbyterian church, Piercy & Reed press, 1840. 396 p. CSanS; IaHoL; PWW; TxBrdD. 40-1504

Clowes, John. Geist des gebetes des

Herrn und der zehn Gebote... nebst an-
leitung "Was uns noth thut" und einen an-
hang von lehrsatzen aus der neuen
kirche. Harrisburg, PA: Gedruckt bey
Joseph Ehrinfried, 1840. 71 p. PBa; PHi;
PLT; PLERC-Hi; PPG. 40-1505

Coates, Reynell, 1802-1886. Physiology
for schools. By Reynell Coates...
Philadelphia, PA: Marshall, Williams,
and Butler, 1840. 333 p. CtY; DLC; Ia-
FayU; MH; NN. 40-1506

Coates, Reynell, 1802-1886. Syllabus of
a course of popular lectures on physiology, with an outline of the principles
which govern the gradual development
of the faculties of jmind and body. By
Reynell Coates... Philadelphia, PA: C.
Sherman & co., printers, 1840. 23 p. CtY;
IaHi; MBC; MWA; PHi. 40-1507

Cobb, Lyman, 1800-1864. Cobb's spelling book, being a just standard for
pronouncing the English language...
Designed to teach the orthography and
ortheopy [sic] of J. Walker. By Lyman
Cobb... Rev. ed. Newark, NJ: B. Olds,
1840. 168 p. NjR. 40-1508

Cobb, Lyman, 1800-1864. Cobb's spell-
ing book, being a just standard for
pronouncing the English language...
Designed to teach the orthography and
ortheopy [sic] of J. Walker. By Lyman
Cobb... Rev. ed. Ithaca, NY: Mack,
Andrus and Woodruff, 1840. MH; TxU-
T. 40-1509

Cobb, Lyman, 1800-1864. Cobb's spelling book, being a just standard for
pronouncing the English language...
Designed to teach the orthography and
ortheopy [sic] of J. Walker. By Lyman
Cobb... Rev. ed. St. Clairsville, OH:

Heaton & Gressinger, 1840. 168 p. OCo.
40-1510

Cobbett, William, 1763-1835. Advise to
young men, and [incidentally] to young
women, in the middle and higher ranks
of life, in a series of letters, to a youth, a
bachelor, a lover, a husband, a citizen or
a subject. Huntsville, IA: T. Adamson,
1840. 323 p. InHi; InU; IU. 40-1511

Coburn, J. Milton. A discourse on the
suffering and death of Saints... at the en-
tombing of Mrs. Susan Hobbs, March 29,
1840. By J. Milton Coburn... Dover, NH:
Printed by George Wadleigh, 1840. 14 p.
Nh-Hi; PCA; RPB. 40-1512

Cocke, Stephen F. A funeral sermon, on
the death of Col. William Anderson, late
of Botetourt county, Va., preached in the
Presbyterian church at Fincastle, Sept.
15th, 1849, by Rev. Stephen F. Cocke.
Richmond, VA: Bernard R. Wren, 1840.
16 p. CSmH; Vi; ViRut; ViRVal. 40-
1513

Coe, Benjamin Hutchins, 1799-1883.
Easy lessons in landscape drawing, with
sketches of animals & rustic figures &
directions for using the lead pencil.
Designed for schools. Hartford, CT:
Robins & Folger, 1840. 4 p. DLC. 40-
1514

Coe, David Denton, 1814-1895. Statistics of the class of 1837, Yale. [New
Haven, CT: s. l.] 1840. PPAmP; PPULC.
40-1515

Coe, Joseph. The true American; containing the inaugural addresses together
with the first annual addresses and messages of all the Presidents of the United
States from 1789 to 1839; the declaration

of Independence and Constitution of the United States, etc., by Joseph Coe. Concord, NH: I. S. Boyd, 1840-41. 2 v. CSmH; InU; MPiB; NhD; TNF. 40-1516

Cogswell, William, 1787-1850. Theological class book, containing system of divinity in form of question and answer. Accompanied with scripture proofs, designed for the benefit of theological classes and the higher classes in Sabbath schools. Boston, MA: Crocker & Brewster, 1840. CtHWatk; MB; MH. 40-1517

Coit, John Calkins, 1799-1863. Substance of an address on the Semicentenary celebration Dec. 1839, before the Presbyterian church in Cheraw. [With appendix.] Columbia, SC: s. l., 1840. 72 p. CSmH; MBAt; NjPT; PPPrHi; RPB. 40-1518

Coke, Thomas, 1747-1814. .... A sermon preacher at Baltimore, Maryland, before the General Conference of the Methodist Episcopal church, Dec. 27, 1784, at the ordination of the Rev. Francis Asbury, to the office of a superintendent... New York: T. Mason & G. Lane, 1840. 15 p. CtMW; MH; MiD-B; MWA; RPB. 40-1519

Coke, Thomas, 1747-1814. Substance of a sermon, at Baltimore, Maryland, before the General Conference of the Methodist episcopal church, Dec. 27, 1784, at the ordination of Francis Asbury; [with charge.] New York: Harper & Brothers, 1840. 41 p. RPB. 40-1520

Colas, Maria de. Chant du Berger, for the piano. Baltimore: George Willig, [184-?] 5 p. ViU. 40-1521

Colburn, Warren, 1793-1833. Arithmetic upon the inductive method of instruction. Being a sequel to intellectual arithmetic. By Warren Colburn, A. M. Boston, MA: published by Hilliard, Gray & co., 1840. 245 p. InCW; MB; MH; MNS. 40-1522

Colburn, Warren, 1793-1833. Intellectual arithmetic. Boston, MA: s. l., 1840. MB. 40-1523

Colburn, Warren, 1793-1833. Intellectual arithmetic, upon the inductive method of instruction. Portland: s. l., 1840. MBC. 40-1524

Colburn, Warren, 1793-1833. An introduction to Algebra on the inductive method of instruction. Boston, MA: Hilliard, Gray & Co., 1840. MH. 40-1525

Colburn, Warren, 1793-1833. Key Containing answers to the examples in the sequel to intellectual arithmetic. Boston, MA: Hilliard, Gray & Co., 1840. 70 p. MB; MH. 40-1526

Colby Junior College, New London, N. H. Catalogue of the officers and students of New London Academy, Chester County, Pa., 1839-40. Baltimore, MD: Printed by John Murphy, 1840? 15 p. MBC; MdBLC. 40-1527

Cole, Benjamin H. Easy lessons in landscape drawing... Hartford, CT: s. l., 1840. DLC. 40-1528

Cole, George F. O'er the far blue mountain. [Song, A., the accomp.] arranged for the guitar by H. N. Gilles. Baltimore, MD: Willig [184-?] 2 p. MB. 40-1529

Cole, Thomas, 1801-1848. Cole's pictures of the voyage of life, now exhibiting at the new building at Leonard St. & Broadway, New York. New York: Osborn, 1840. 2 L. NN. 40-1530

Coleridge, Samuel Taylor, 1772-1834. Aids to reflection. By Samuel Taylor Coleridge. With a preliminary essay, By James Marsh, D. D. From the fourth London edition....Edited by Henry Nelson Coleridge, M. A. Boston, MA: Crocker & Brewster, 1840. 357 p. MeB; MnSM. 40-1531

Coledirge, Samuel Taylor, 1772-1834. Aids to reflection, by Samuel Taylor Coleridge. With a preliminary essay, by James Marsh, D. D. Edited by Henry Belson Coleridge, esq., M. A. From the fourth London edition, New York: Newman & Saxton, 1840. 357 p. FDeS; IaGG; MeB; NcSaIL; ScSp. 40-1532

Coleridge, Samuel Taylor, 1772-1834. The works of Samuel Taylor Coleridge, prose and verse... Philadelphia, PA: T. Cowperthwait & co., 1840. 546 p. CtHT; ILM; MiOC; PHi; WaU. 40-1533

Coles, George, 1792-1858. History and character of Methodism; a centenary sermon preached in the Duane-Street Church, New York, Oct. 25, 1839. New York: s. l., 1840. 40 p. IEG; PHi; PPULC; ODW. 40-1534

Coles, George, 1792-1858. Lectures on the book of proverbs. New York: s. l., 1840. 1 v. DLC. 40-1535

Coles, George, 1792-1858. The Sunday school orator. By George Coles. New York: s. l., 1840. IEG. 40-1536

Colesworth, Daniel Clement, 1810-

1893. A touch of the times. Portland: s. l., 1840. DLC; NNHisT; RPB. 40-1537

Colgate University. Hamilton, N. Y. Catalogue of the corporation, officers, and students of Hamilton College. Clinton, 1840-41. [Utica, NY: Press of Bennett, Backus & Hawley, 1840] 20 p. NCH. 40-1538

Colgate University, Hamilton, N. Y. Laws of Hamilton Literary and Theological Institution. [Hamilton, NY?] s. l., 1840. MH. 40-1539

Colgate University. Hamilton, N. Y. Laws of Hamilton Literary and Theological Institution. [Utica, NY: Press of Bennett, Backus & Howley, 1840] 12 p. MB; NNUT; NRC-R. 40-1540

Collectanea Sacra Latina: an introduction to the use of sacred Latin in schools. New York: Printed by William Osborn, 1840. 54 p. CtHT; MB; NNC; NSmb; ViAl. 40-1541

A collection of patriotic Harrison & Tippicanoe songs... Philadelphia, PA: s. l., 1840. PPL-R. 40-1542

Collection of piano music. Philadelphia, PA: A. Fiot [184-?] p. NCD. 40-1543

A collection of political speeches made in the United States Congress and elsewhere, bound together with the above title. Washington, DC: Printed at the Globe office, 1840. v. NcU. 40-1544

College of Physicians of Philadelphia. Charter, ordinances, and by-laws of the College of Physicians of Philadelphia Philadelphia, PA: C. Sherman & co.

printers, 1840. 23 p. DLC; DSG; OCGHM. 40-1545

Collins, John A. To the Abolitionists of Mass. Boston, MA: Dow & Jackson [184-?] 3 p. MB. 40-1546

Collin's Irish Longester. New York; Philadelphia, PA: Turner [184-?] 32 p. DLC. 40-1547

Collot, Alexander G., b. 1796. Progressive French dialogues & phrases:consisting of a systematic collection of conversation on familiar subjects, also of select idioms & proverbs. Arranged in progressive order of difficulty, & calculated to facilitate the study of the French language... Philadelphia, PA: James Kay, Jr. & brothers, 1840. 226 p. DLC; ICP; MH; OFH; WaU. 40-1548

Colman, George, 1732-1794. ... The clandestine marriage. A comedy in five acts. By George Colman, the elder. With the stage business, cast of characters, costumes, relative positions &c. New York: S. French [etc., etc., 184-?] 82 p. CSt; NIC. 40-1549

Colman, George, 1762-1836. ... The heir at law. A comedy in five acts. By George Colman, the younger. New York: S. French [etc., etc., 184-?] 71 p. CSt. 40-1550

Colman, George, 1762-1836. The iron chest. A play in three acts. By George Colman, the younger. With the stage business, cast of characters, costumes, relative positions, &c. New York: S. French [184-?] 68 p. CSt; MH. 40-1551

Colman, George, 1762-1836. The mountaineers. A play in three acts. With the stage business, cast of characters, costumes, relative publications, etc. New York: S. French and Sons, [184-?] [5] -57 p. CSt; MH. 40-1552

Colman, George, 1762-1836. ... The poor gentleman. A comedy in five acts. By George Colman, the younger. With the stage business, cast of characters, costumes, relative positions, &c. As performed at the Park theatre. New York: S. French [etc., etc., 184-?] 72 p. CSt. 40-1553

Colman, George, 1762-1836. The review. Philadelphia, PA: s. l. [184-?] p. MB. 40-1554

Colman, Henry, 1785-1849. Agricultural addresses delivered at New Haven, Norwich, and Hartford, Connecticut, at the country cattle shows in the year 1840. Boston, MA: Dutton and Wentworth, 1840. 72 p. DLC; MBH; MHi; PPL; PPULC. 40-1555

Colquitt, Walter Terry, 1799-1885. Circular. To the people of Georgia, and especially to the State Rights Party. Milledgeville, GA: [n. p., 1840?] 16 p. DLC; GU; NcD; TxU ViU 40-1556

Colquitt, Walter Terry, 1799-1885. Remarks of Hon. W. T. Colquitt, of Georgia, against reception of abolition petitions, in H. Rep., Jan. 17, 1840. [S. l.: s. l., 1840] 16 p. PHi. 40-1557

Colquitt, Walter Terry, 1799-1885. Reply to the editors of the Georgia Journal [of Millegeville] and the Chronicle and Sentinel [of Augusta] [S. l.: s. l., 1840] 16 p. GU-De. 40-1558

Colquitt, Walter Terry. 1799-1885.

Speech of Mr. Colquitt, of Georgia, against the reception of abolition petitions. Washington, DC: printed by Blair and Rives, 1840. 7 p. CtHWatk; GU; MdHi. 40-1559

Colquitt, Walter Terry. 1799-1885. Speech of Mr. Colquitt, of Georgia, in committee of the whole, on the independent treasury bill. Delivered in the House of Representatives, June 20, 1840. Washington, DC: printed by Blair and Rives, 1840. 32 p. GU; MdHi; TxU. 40-1560

Colton, Calvin, 1789-1857. American Jacobism. Being a sequel to the "Crisis of the country. "By Junius [pseud.] ... [New York: s. l., 1840] 8 p. DLC; MBAt; MH; MiD-B; RP. 40-1561

Colton, Calvin, 1789-1857. Colonization and abolition contrasted. Philadelphia, PA: H. Hooker [184-?] 16 p. CSmH. 40-1562

Colton, Calvin, 1789-1857. The crisis of the country. By Junius [pseud.] [Entered according to Act of Congress, by T. K. and P. G. Collins, in the Clerk's Office of the Court of the Eastern District of Pennsylvania.] New York; Boston, MA: s. l., 1840? 16 p. Ct; MBAt; OO. 40-1563

Colton, Calvin, 1789-1857. The crisis of the country. By Junius [pseud.] New York: E. Benson [1840?] 16 p. CSmH; DLC; NIC; NN; OO. 40-1564

Colton, Calvin, 1789-1857. The crisis of the country. By Junius [pseud.] Philadelphia, PA: T. K. and P. G. Collins, 1840? 16 p. DLC; MiU-C; Nh; OClWHi; PMA; RP. 40-1565

Colton, Calvin, 1789-1857. The crisis of the country. By Junius [pseud.] 2d ed. [Philadelphia, PA: T. K. and P. G. Collins, 1840?] 16 p. CtHT; DLC; MiD-B; NIC. 40-1566

Colton, Calvin, 1789-1857. The Junius papers.] [New York: E. Benson, 1840?] 4 nos. in 1 v. ICU. 40-1567

Colton, Calvin, 1789-1857. Our presidential term. New York: E. Benson [1840] 12 p. MH; MH-BA; MiD-B; NcU; NN. 40-1568

Colton, Calvin, 1789-1857. Reply to Webster. A Letter to Daniel Webster, of Massachusetts, a member of the Senate of the United States, in reply to his legal opinion to Baring, Brothers & co. upon the illegality and unconstitutionality of state bonds and loans of state credit. New York: s. l., 1840. 79 p. Ct; InHi; MH; MiGr; PU. 40-1569

Colton, Calvin, 1789-1857. The right of petition. New York: s. l., 1840. CtY; MBAt; MdBP; MH; OClWHi. 40-1570

Colton, Calvin, 1789-1857. Sequel to The crisis of the country. By Junius [pseud.] [New York: R. Bogert, 1840] 8 p. CtY; MBAt; MH; MiD-B; PPL. 40-1571

Colton, Charles Caleb, 1780?-1832. Lacon; or, Many things in few words. Addressed to those who think. By the Rev. C. C. Colton, A. M. With an index. Revised edition. New York: E. Kearny [184-?] 504 p. DLC. 40-1572

Colton, George Hooker, 1818-1847. Hymn [sung at Presentation Day Exercises, 1840] [New Haven, CT?: s. l., 1840] 1 p. CtY. 40-1573

Colton, Joseph Hutchins, 1800-1893. The western tourist and emigrant's guide, with a gazetteer of the states of Ohio, Michigan, Indiana, Illinois, and Missouri, and the territories of Wisconsin, and Iowa; describing all the principal stage routes, canals, railroads, and the distances between towns. New York: J. H. Colton, 1840. 180 p. ICHi; MiD-B; MoS; VtBrt. 40-1574

Columbia, Conn. Congregational Church. Catalogue of the officers & members of the Congregational church, Columbia, Conn., together with a confession of faith, adopted by said church, June 7th, 1840. Hartford, CT: Elihu Geer, 1840. 8 p. Ct. 40-1575

Columbia Hose Company. Constitution and by-laws. Philadelphia, PA: s. l., 1840. 22 p. PHi. 40-1576

Columbia University. Statutes of Columbia college, revised and passed by the board of trustees, May, 1836... An historical sketch of the college. New York: Printed for Columbia college, by R. Craighead, 1840. 39 p. CBPSR; NNNAM; PPPrHi. 40-1577

Columbian Almanac. Philadelphia, PA: Jos. McDowell, 1840. MWA. 40-1578

The Columbian riddler, or, entertaining puzzle book. Newark, NJ: printed and published by Benjamin Olds, 1840. 22 p. NjR. 40-1579

Columbus, Mississippi. Baptist Church. Manual of the Baptist Church in Columbus, Mississippi. New Orleans: Printed by S. M. Stewart, 1840. 7 p. NRAB. 40-1580

Columbus, O. Second Presbyterian Church. Constitution of the Second Presbyterian church of Columbus, Ohio:together with a summary of the confession of faith. [Columbus, OH: C. Scott, printer, 1840] 12 p. OClWHi; OMC. 40-1581

Combe, Andrew, 1797-1847. The physiology of digestion considered with relation to the principles of dietics. By Andrew Combe... From the 3rd Edinburgh rev. and enl. ed. with illustrations. New York: Harper & brothers [184-?] 287 p. CSt-L; MB; NRU-M; OHi; ScAb. 40-1582

Combe, Andrew, 1797-1847. The principles of physiology applied to the preservation of health, and to the improvement of physical and mental education. By Andrew Combe. From the 7th Edinburgh ed. New York: Harper & Brothers, 1840. 396 p. CtY; MH; OClM; PPM; ScC. 40-1583

Combe, Andrew, 1797-1847. The principles of physiology applied to the preservation of health, and to the improvement of physical and mental education. By Andrew Combe. From the 7th Edinburgh ed. New York: Harper & Brothers, 1840. 291 p. CoFcS; IaMp. 40-1584

Combe, Andrew, 1797-1847. Treatise on the physiological and moral management of infancy. By Andrew Combe, M. D....With notes and a supplementary chapter by John Bell, M. D..... Philadelphia, PA: Carey & Hart, 1840. 307. IEN-

M; MoSU-M; OCo; PPiU-D; RPM. 40-1585

Combe, Andrew, 1797-1847. Treatise on the physiological and moral management of infancy. By Andrew Combe, M. D....With notes and a supplementary chapter by John Bell, M. D..... 2d. ed. Philadelphia, PA: Carey & Hart, 1840. 307 p. Ia; MHi; MWA; NBMS; PU. 40-1586

Combe, George, 1788-1858. An address delivered at the anniversary celebration of the birth of Spurzheim, and the organization of the Boston Phrenological Society, Dec. 31, 1839. Boston, MA: Marsh, Capen, Lyon and Webb, 1840. 28 p. ICBB; MH; MiD-B; NN; Vi. 40-1587

Combe, George, 1788-1858. Constitution of man considered in relation to external objects. With additional chapter on the harmony between phrenology and revelation, by Joseph A. Warne. 10th Am. from the latest Eng. ed., cor. & enl. Boston, MA: Wm. D. Ticknor, 1840. CtY; MB; MdBM; MiU; MNF; VtBrt. 40-1588

Combe, George, 1788-1858. Lectures on moral philosophy; delivered before the Philosophical Association at Edinburgh in the winter session of 1835-1836, by George Combs. Boston, MA: Marsh, Capen, Lyon and Webb, 1840. 138 p. CtY; FDU; MeB; MWA; RNR. 40-1589

Combe, George, 1788-1858. Lectures on Phrenology. 3d ed., with corrections & additions. New York: Fowler & Wells [1840] 391 p. CtY-M. 40-1590

Combe, George, 1788-1858. Moral philosophy; or, the duties of man con-sidered... Boston, MA: Marsh, Capen, Lyon and Webb, 1840. ICMe; MBAt. 40-1591

Come haste to the wedding. Baltimore, MD: S. Carusi [184-?] 1 p. ViU. 40-1592

Come sing me that sweet air again. [Song, S., with guitar accompaniment.] Philadelphia, PA: Lee & Walker [184-?] 5 p. MB. 40-1593

Come to the Sunset Tree, or Tyrolese evening hymn. Philadelphia, PA: Willig, 1840. 2 p. MB. 40-1594

Come with thy lute to the fountain. Duett for soprano & contralto. Adopted to a favorite German air with a piano forte. Philadelphia, PA: A. Fiot, 1840. NN; ViU. 40-1595

Comer, Thomas. The Ariel waltz. Composed for the piano forte. Boston, MA: Reed [184-?] 2 p. MB. 40-1596

Comer, Thomas. Boston musical institute's collection of church music; comprising a great variety of psalm & hymn tunes, anthems, chants, sentences & other set pieces, original & selected from the most eminent composers. Boston, MA: Otis, Broaders & co., 1840. 352 p. MB; NNUT; PPrHi. 40-1597

Comer, Thomas. The Boston musical institute's collection of church music....By T. Comer... Second edition. Boston, MA: Otis, Broaders & Co., 1840. 352 p. MeHi. 40-1598

Comly, John, 1773-1850. ....Comly's reader and book fo knowledge: with exercises of spelling and defining....By John

Comley. Philadelphia, PA: Thomas L. Bonsal, 1840. 212 p. PLFM. 40-1599

Comly, John, 1773-1850. Comly's spelling book, revised and improved. Philadelphia, PA: W. Marshall and Co., 1840. MH. 40-1600

Commerce dictionary. Philadelphia, PA: s. l., 1840. 2 v. MWA. 40-1601

Commercial & political crises of 1840. By a Jeffersonian. New York: s. l., 1840. MH-BA; NN; PPL; PPULC. 40-1602

Common almanac for 1840... Watertown, NY: Rice, 1840. 82 p. NNHist. 40-1603

The Commonwealth of Pennsylvania, ex relatione Paul Daniel Gonzalve Grand d'Hauteville. Report of the d'-Hauteville case: The Commonwealth of Pennsylvania, at the suggestion of Paul Daniel Gonsalve Grand d'Hauteville, versus David Sears, Miriam C. Sears, and Ellen Sears Grand d'Hauteville. Habeas corpus for the custody of an infant child. Philadelphia, PA: Printed by W. S. Martien, 1840. 295 p. Ct; DLC; MH; PHi; WaU. 40-1604

Comstock, John Lee, 1789-1858. The flora belle, or, Gems from nature. With twenty-five illustrations, colored. By J. L. Comstock, A. M. New York: T. L. Magagnos [184-?] 384 p. DLC; OU; RPB. 40-1605

Comstock, John Lee, 1789-1858. A system of natural pyhilosophy, in which the principles of mechanics, hydrostatics, hydraulics, pneumatics, acoustics optics, astronomy, electricity, etc., are fully explained... etc... by J. L. Comstock.

Stereotyped from the 53d ed. New York: Robinson, Pratt & Co., 1840. 340 p. MdBS; MH; MoS; NIC; TNJU. 40-1606

Comstock, Joseph. The Tongue of Time and Star of the States: A system of human nature, with the phenomena of the heavens and earth... Hartford, CT: s. l., 1840. 487 p. CtHT; MB; MHi; REd; RPB. 40-1607

Comstock, William, 1804-1882. The life of Samuel Comstock, the terrible whaleman. Containing an account of the meeting and massacre of the officers of the ship Globe, of Nantucket... By his brother, William Comstock. Boston, MA: James Fisher, 1840. 115 p. DLC; M; MB; Nh-Hi. 40-1608

Concone, Guiseppe, 1810-1861. Fifty lessons in singing, for the middle register of the voice. Boston, MA: Ditson [1840] MB-FA. 40-1609

Concord. Hillsborough Bridge Congregatonal Church. Articles of faith and form of covenant, adopted by Hillsborough Bridge Congrgational Church. Concord: Printed at the Christian Panoply Office, 1840. 11 p. MBC. 40-1610

Concord, N. H. First Congregational Church. Manual for the use of the members... Congregational Church in Concord. [S. l.: n. p., 184-?] 20 p. CtY; CtY-D. 40-1611

Cone, Spencer Wallace, 1819-1888. The proude ladye, and other poems... New York: Wiley & Putnam [etc.] 1840. 144 p. CSmH; MB; NjP; PPL; RPB. 40-1612

Confessions, trials, and biographical sketches of the most cold blooded murderers, who have been executed in this country from its first settlement down to the present time... Containing also accounts of various other daring outrages... Boston, MA: George N. Thompson, 1840. 408 p. CSmH; DLC. 40-1613

Congdon, Charles Taber, 1821-1891. Flowers plucked by a traveller on the journey of life. By Charles T. Congdon... Boston, MA: Published by George W. Light, 1840. 72 p. CSmH; ICU; MBL; RPB; TxU. 40-1614

Congregational Board of Publication. Doctrinal tracts. A collection of tracts issued by the American Doctrinal Tract Society. Boston, MA: Published by the American Doctrinal Tract Society, 184-? Nos. 1-45. WHi. 40-1615

Congregational churches in Maine. Slavery vs. the Bible. A correspondence between the general Conference of Maine and the Presbytery of Tombechbee, Mississippi. Worchester: Spencer and Howland, 1840. 158 p. NN; OClWHi. 40-1616

Congregational churches in Maine. York county conference. Constitution and by-laws, of the York county conference of churches, as revised and presented to the conference, at its semi-annual meeting at Acton, Oct. 1, 1839. Portland, ME: Alfred Merrill, printer, 1840. 8 p. CSmH. 40-1617

Congregational Churches in Ohio. Congregational Church. Articles of faith & covenant, Adopted Jan. 1, 1840. Marietta, OH: Tyler, 1840. OCHP; OClWHi. 40-1618

Congregational Churches in Ohio. Western Reserve-General Association of Congregationalists. Confession of faith & constitution. Lorain, OH: Ravinna Cabinet & Visitor Pr.; Congl. Assoc. Records, 1840. 7 p. MBC; OO; PPPrHi. 40-1619

Congregetional churches in Vermont. General convention. Extracts from the minutes of the General convention... at their session at Burlington, Sept., 1840. Windsor: Ptd. at the Chronicle Press, 1840. 16 p. MiD-B. 40-1620

Congregational churches in Wisconsin. General convention. Jubilee memorial of the Convention, with sketches historical and biographical, 1840-1890. [Madison, WI: s. l., 1840-90] v. CtY. 40-1621

Congregational Churches of Connecticut. Minutes of the General Association of Connecticut, at their Meeting in New Haven, June, 1840; with an Appendix, ontaining the Report on the State of Religion &c. Hartford, CT: E. Gleason, printer, 1840. 44 p. NcMHi. 40-1622

Congregational Churches of Massachusetts. Minutes at their meeting in Ipswich, June, 1840. With the narrative of the state of religion, and the Pastoral letter. Boston, MA: pr. by Crocker & Brewster, 1840. 51 p. IEG; VtMidSM. 40-1623

Congregational Churches of New York. Minutes of the General Association of New York, Hamilton, Aug. 27, 1840 Hamilton, NY: s. l., 1840. 26 p. MHi. 40 1624

Congregational Union of Scotland. Ad

dress of the Congregational Union in Scotland to their fellow Christians in the United States on the subject of American slavery. New York: American & Foreign Anti-Slavery Society, 1840. 12 p. ICU; MH; NIC; NN; TxU. 40-1625

Connecticut. General Assembly. Committee on the state prison. Report... to the Legislature of Connecticut, May session, 1840... Hartford, CT: Babcock & Wildman, Printers, 1840. 5 p. CtY. 40-1626

Connecticut. General Assembly. Joint standing committee on banks. General assembly, May session, 1840. The joint standing committee on banks... report... Hartford, CT: s. l., 1840. 4 p. CtY. 40-1627

Connecticut. House of Representatives. Journal of the house of representatives of the state of Connecticut, May session, 1840. Published by order of a resolution of the house of representatives. Hartford, CT: Printed by Case, Tiffany & Co., 1840. 126 p. Mi. 40-1628

Connecticut. Laws, statutes, etc. Public Acts of the State of Connecticut, passed May session, 1840. Published agreeably to a resolve of the General Asssembly, under the superintendence of the Secretary of State. Hartford, CT: Printed by Case, Tiffany & Co., 1840. 48 p. Ky; MdBB; Nv; T; Wa-L. 40-1629

Connecticut. Laws, statutes, etc. Resolves and private acts, of the State of Connecticut, passed May session, 1840. Published agreeably to a resolve of the General Asssembly, and prepared under the superintendence of the Secretary of

State. State of Connecticut, SS: Office of the secretary of state, June, 1840. Hartford, CT: Printed by Case, Tiffany & Co., 1840. 96 p. ArSC; IaU-L; MdBB; NNL; Wa-L. 40-1630

Connecticut. Laws, statutes, etc. The statute laws of the state of Connecticut, relative to the city of Hartford & by-laws of said city, passed since March 1st, 1834... Hartford, CT: J. B. Eldredge, 1840. 30 p. Ct. 40-1631

Connecticut. Senate. Journal of the Senate of the State of Connecticut, May session, 1840. Published in conformity to a resolution of the state. Hartford, CT: printed by Case, Tiffany & Co., 1840. 94 p. CtSoP; DLC; IU; Mi. 40-1632

Connecticut. State Prison. Report of the directors, warden, &c., of the COnnecticut State Prison, to the Legislature of the State, at its May session, 1840. Printed by order of the Assembly. New Haven, CT: Babcock & Wildman, printers, 1840. 36 p. Ct; NBu. 40-1633

The conspiracy of the office holders unmasked. Boston, MA: s. l., 1840. MB. 40-1634

The Contrast; or Sketches from Real Life, showing the true source of Happiness. New York: Printed and published by J. F. Trow, 1840. 72 p. NN; NPla. 40-1635

The Contrast; or Sketches from Real Life, showing the true source of Happiness. New York: W. W. Dodd, 1840. 72 p. ICN. 40-1636

Controversy between the author of "Baptizo defined" and the Rev. Mr.

Kelly... Albany, NY: Pr. for the author, 1840. MB; MBC; NjPT; NN. 40-1637

Controversy between the Rev. R. J. Breckinridge, D. D., and Dr. S. Annan. Baltimore, MD: Publication Rooms, 1840. 45 p. KyU; MdHi; PPL; PPPrHi. 40-1638

Conversations about the Babe of Bethlehem. Written for the Massachusetts Sabbath School Society, and revised by the committee of publication. Boston, MA: Massachusetts Sabbath School Society, 1840. 72 p. DLC. 40-1639

Conversations on the South Sea missions Island of Rarotonga. By the author of Conversations on the life of Carey.... New York: T. Mason & G. Lane for the Sunday School Mission of the United Episcopal Church, 1840. 3 v. in 1. INS. 40-1640

Converse, John Kendrick, 1801-1880. The history of slavery, and means of elevating the African race. A discourse, delivered before the Vermont colonization society, at Montpelier, Oct. 15, 1840. By J. K. Converse, pastor of the First Congregational Church, Burlington, Vt. Burlington, VT: Chauncey Goodrich, 1840. 24 p. CtHT; MiD-B; MWA; TxU; VtU. 40-1641

Conversion of the Earl of Rochester. Philadelphia, PA: Presbyterian Board of Publication [184-?] 28 p. GDecCT. 40-1642

The converted child... Philadelphia, PA: American Sunday-school union [1840] 148 p. NNC. 40-1643

Conway, Mass. Congregational Church.

The confession of faith, and covenant of the Congregational Church in Conway, Mass... Northampton: s. l., 1840. 16 p. MBC; MConw; MiD-B; WHi. 40-1644

Cook, Charles. The trial, life, and confession of Charles Cook, who was indicted, tried, and convicted of the murder of Mrs. Catherine Merry, on the 22d day of September last, sentenced to be executed at Schenectady on the 18th December, 1840. Schenectady, NY: E. M. Packard, 1840. N-L; NSchHi. 40-1645

Cook, Eliza. ... Washington, Star of the West. Philadelphia, PA: A. W. Auner, song publisher [184-?] CSmH. 40-1646

Cook, Eliza. Washington, Star of the West. As sung by Mr. Quayle. Philadelphia, PA: O. Delestatius... Grattan & bro., Job printers [184-?] CSmH. 40-1647

Cook, Russell S., 1811-1864. Rept. of a western tour. [New York: s. l., 184-?] 16 p. DLC; MB; NN. 40-1648

Cook, T. D. A discourse on the burning of the Steamboat Lexington, on Long-Island Sound, January 13, 1840. By Rev. T. D. Cook, pastor of the First Universalist Society of Utica, N. T. Utica, NY: O. Hutchinson, 1840. 23 p. NSmb; NUt. 40-1649

Cooke, Eleutheros. An address, in commemoration of the brillant and glorious defence of Fort Meigs... in 1813: embracing a sketch of the civil and military services of General William Henry Harrison. Delivered on the site of the fort, at the request of the Ohio Central Commmittee, June 11th, 1840

[Published by the Committee of arrangements of the Fort Meigs Celebration.] Perrysburg: H. T. Smith, 1840. 21 p. NN. 40-1650

Cooke, R. Farewell to the Nymph of my heart. Sung by Mr. Ed. Sheppard. Composed by R. Cooke. New York: Firth & Hall [184-?] 3 p. ViU. 40-1651

Cooke, T. Come soldier come, the much admired duett in the opera of the National Guard. Composed by Auber, adapted to the English stage by T. Cooke. New York: E. Riley [184-?] 8 p. MNF. 40-1652

Cooke, Thomas Simpson, 1782-1848. Love's ritornella. [Song, the accomp.] arranged for the guitar by S. Meignen. Philadelphia, PA: Fiot [184-?] 2 p. MB. 40-1653

Cooke, Thomas Simpson, 1782-1848. The wolf is out. [Song. B. Pianoforte accomp.] New York: Atwill [184-?] 7 p. MB. 40-1654

Cookman, George G., 1800-1841. Speeches delivered on various occasions, by George G. Cookman, of the Baltimore Annual Conference, and Chaplain to the Senate of the United States. New York: George Lane, 1840. 139 p. CtMW; DLC; MdBP; NjMD; ODaB. 40-1655

Coolidge and Haskell. Catalogue of furniture... to be sold, Apr. 22, 1840. Boston, MA: Eastburn, 1840. 8 p. MB. 40-1656

Cooper, J. W. The experiences botanist or Indian physician; being a new system of practice, founded on botany... by J. W. Cooper... Lancaster, PA: Printed for the author and publisher, John Bear, printer, 1840. 303 p. OCLoyd; PLFM; PPL; St-TeachC; WU-M. 40-1657

Cooper, James. Speech of Mr. Cooper, of Pennsylvania, on the Sub-Treasury Bill. Delivered in the House of Representatives, June 22, 1840. Washington, DC: printed by Gales and Seaton, 1840. 23 p. M; MWA; PHi. 40-1658

Cooper, James Fenimore, 1789-1851. The Bravo; a tale. New ed. Philadelphia, PA: Lea & Blanchard, 1840. 2 v. CtY. 40-1659

Cooper, James Fenimore, 1789-1851. History of the navy of the United States of America. By J. Fenimore Cooper. 2d edition. Philadelphia, PA: Lea & Blanchard, 1840. 2 v. GHi; MSaP; PP; TU; WaS. 40-1660

Cooper, James Fenimore, 1789-1851. Mercedes of Castile; or, the voyage to Cathay. By the author of "The bravo," "The headsman." Philadelphia, PA: Lea & Blanchard, 1840. 2 v. CSmH; MH-AH; MWA; OHi; RPAt. 40-1661

Cooper, James Fenimore, 1789-1851. Notions of the Americans picked up by a travelling bachelor. Philadelphia, PA: Lea & Blanchard, 1840. 2 v. CtHWatk; IaU; ICU; IEN; NDg; OMC. 40-1662

Cooper, James Fenimore, 1789-1851. The pathfinder. By James Fenimore Cooper. New York: A. L. Burt company, publishers, 1840. 430 p. IaCrest; NcLoC. 40-1663

Cooper, James Fenimore, 1789-1851. The pathfinder. By James Fenimore

Cooper. Philadelphia, PA: Lea and Blanchard, 1840. 2 v. CU; DLC; InU; PPGi; ViU. 40-1664

Cooper, James Fenimore, 1789-1851. The pathfinder; or, the inland sea. By the author of "The Pioneers," "Last of the Mohicans," "Prairie," etc. First edition. Philadelphia, PA: Lea & Blanchard, 1840. 2 v. DLC; LNH; MWA; NN; PU. 40-1665

Cooper, James Fenimore, 1789-1851. The pioneers, or the sources of the Susquehanna; a descriptive tale. By the author of "The Spy." Philadelphia, PA: Lea and Blanchard, 1840. 2 v. CtY; NHerCHi. 40-1666

Cooper, James Fenimore, 1789-1851. The Redskin, or, Indian & Injin. New York: G. P. Putnam's Sons, 1840. 506 p. WvWeo. 40-1667

Cooper, James Fenimore, 1789-1851. The Spy: A Tale of the Neutral Ground... [anon.] Philadelphia, PA: Lea & Blanchard, 1840. 2 v. CtY. 40-1668

Cooper, James Fenimore, 1789-1851. Travelling bachelor, or notions of the Americans. New York: Stringer & Townsend [1840?] 2 v. in 1. MB; NN. 40-1669

Cooper, Mark Anthony. Speech of Mr. Cooper, of Georgia, on the resolution of Mr. W. Thompson, of South Carolina, on the reception of abolition petitions. Delivered in the House of Representatives, January 16, 1840. Washington, DC: Printed at the Globe Office, 1840. 8 p. GU; MBC; MiD-B; MiU-L; PPL. 40-1670

Cooper, Mark Anthony. Speech... In the House... June, 1840... on the bill to establish an independent treasury. [Washington, DC: s. l., 1840] 16 p. MBAt. 40-1671

Cooper, Samuel A. The Light guard's quick step. [For piano forte.] Hartford, CT: Goodwin, 1840. 2 p. KU; MB. 40-1672

Cooper, Thomas, 1759-1839. The fabrication of the Pentateuch proved, by the anchoronisms, contained by those books. By Thomas Cooper, LL. D. Second edition. Granville, NJ: George H. Evans, 1840. 16 p. IU; LNH; NcAS; PPL. 40-1673

Coote, Clement T., d. 1849. An address on the life and character of Abraham Howard Quincy, delivered at the request of the grand lodge of the District of Columbia, in the foundry meeting house at Washington city, on the fifteenth of November, 1840. [Washington, DC: P. Force, printer, 1840] 41 p. DLC; MdHi; MH. 40-1674

Corbould, Edward Henry, 1815-1905. Gems of beauty displayed ina series of twelve highly finished engravings of various subjects. From designs by Edward Corbould... with fanciful illustrations, in verse, by the Countess of Blessington... New York: Appleton and co., 1840. 11 p. CFrt; MeB; MWA; PU; ViU. 40-1675

The Corenanlet. Vol. 1. [Pt. of Vol. 2 & 3] Philadelphia, PA: s. l., 1840. v. MB. 40-1676

The Corinthian waltz. Baltimore, MD: Geo. Willig [184-?] 1 p. ViU. 40-1677

The cork leg. Comic song. [Bar. accomp. for piano forte.] New York: Bancroft [184-?] 3 p. MB. 40-1678

Cormenin, Louis Marie de Lahaye, Viscount de, 1788-1868. Complete history of the Popes of Rome fr. St. Peter... to Pius IX, including the history of Saints, Martyes, Fathers of the Church, religious orders, Cardinals, Inquisitions, Schisms and the Great Reformers. Philadelphia, PA: s. l. [1840] 432 p. PPP. 40-1679

Cornell, Robert C. Reply to the Trustees of the Public School Society to the address of the Roman Catholics. New York: Day Co., 1840. 7 p. CtHT-W. 40-1680

Cornish, Samuel F., d. 1859? The colonization scheme considered in its rejection by the colored people, in its unfitness for christianizing the aborigines of Africa and for putting a stop to the African slave trade. Newark, NJ: s. l., 1840. 27 p. ICU; MH-AH; MW; MWA; OCHP; PPiW. 40-1681

Correspondence between the Presbyterians and Congregationalists of Lebanon [N. Y.] Pittsfield: s. l., 1840. 8 p. MBC. 40-1682

A correspondence on the subject of the excommunication of Mr. Levi Hermance, formerly a members of the Baptist Church, at Auburn, in consequence of a letter addressed to... James Johnston, pastor of said church. Auburn, NY: printed by Oliphant & Skinner, 1840. 12 p. DLC; ICU; NNUT. 40-1683

Corri, Haydn, of Dublin, 1785-1860. Wha'll be King but Charlie. The woods by Sir Walter Scott. Symphonies and accompaniments by P. K. Moran. New York: Riley [184-?] 3 p. MB. 40-1684

Cortes, Hernando, 1485-1547. The Despatches of Hernando Cortes to Charles V. Now first translated into English. New York: s. l., 1840. 431 p. PHi. 40-1685

Corwin, Thomas, 1794-1865. Speech of Mr. Corwin, of Ohio, in reply to General Crary's attack on General Harrison. Delivered in the House of Representatives, February 15, 1840. Washington, DC: Printed by Gales & Seaton, 1840. 16 p. CtY; IaHi; MWA; Nh-Hi; OO. 40-1686

The Cottages of the Alps, or, life and manners in Switzerland, by the author of "Peasant life in Germany." New York: Charles Scribner, 1840. 422 p. MLow. 40-1687

Cotten, Edward R. Life of the Hon. Nathaniel Macon, of North Carolina, in which there is displayed striking instances of virtue, enterprise, courage, generosity, and patriotism. His public life... by Edward R. Cotten... Baltimore, MD: printed by Lucas & Deaver, 1840. 272 p. CU; ICN; MB; NcD; Vi. 40-1688

Cottin, Marie Risteau, called Sophie, 1770-1807. Elizabeth; or, The exiles of Siberia, a tale. From the French of Madame Cottin. Boston, MA: C. Gaylord, 1840. MH. 40-1689

Coues, Samuel Elliott. Remarks on the Bunker-hill monument, addressed to the ladies engaged in getting up the fair for its completion. By Elliott [pseud.] ... Portsmouth, NH: Printed by C. W.

Brewster, 1840. 12 p. CSmH; ICU; MB; MH; Nh-Hi. 40-1690

Count Roderic's Castle; or, Gothic Times. Philadelphia, PA: s. l., 1840. 137 p. PHi. 40-1691

Cour Supreme. Municipalite Numero Deux, EDe la cite de la Nouvelle-Orleans. De manderesse vs. La Compagnie de la Presse a Cotton D'Orleans, Defenderesse. Replique. [S. l.: s. l., 1840] 240 p. LNHT; NN. 40-1692

A course of lectures on the Jews. By ministers of the established church in Glasgow. Philadelphia, PA: Presbyterian Board of Publication. WIlliam S. Martin, Printer, 1840. 499 p. CSansS; GDecCT; KyLoP; ODaB; PAnL. 40-1693

Covel, James, Jr. A concise dictionary of the Holy Bible. By Rev. Jornes Covel, Jr.... New York: Published by T. Mason and G. Lane, for the Sunday School Union of the Methodist Episcopal Church....J. Collord, printer, 1840. 536 p. NbCrD. 40-1694

Covert, Bernard. Court and Dodge's Collection of songs, duetts, glees, choruses, &c., as sang by them and J. B. Gough, at their temperence concerts throughout the union. Boston, MA: Ditson [184-?] 46 p. MB. 40-1695

Covert, Bernard. A new medley. A song arranged from popular airs. By B. Covert. [With accompaniment for the piano forte.] Boston, MA: Ditson [184-?] 7 p. MB. 40-1696

Cowles, Henry, 1803-1881. Holiness of Christians in the present life... Professorin Oberlin Theological Seminary.

Oberlin, OH: [J. Steele] 1840. 124 p. CBPSR; MH; OCl; OO; OSW. 40-1697

Cowper, William, 1731-1800. The poems of William Cowper on the Innter Temple. Complete in one volume. New York: Pubished by C. Wells; Piercy & Read, printers, 1840. 491 p. MBBC; NbHC; ScSp. 40-1698

Cowper, William, 1731-1800. The poetical works of William Cowper, with a biographical notice by the Rev. H. F. Cary... New York: Leavitt & Allen [1840?] 2 v. in 1. CLU; NN; OCl; ScC; Vt-Wood. 40-1699

Cox, Gersham F. Remains of Melville B. Cox, late missionary to Liberia: with a memoir. By the Rev. Gersham F. Cox... New York: T. Mason and G. Lane, 1840. 250 p. FNp; KyBgW; NcD; PPM; TxDaM. 40-1700

Cox, John. A millenarian's answer of the hope that is in him; or, A brief statement and defence of the doctrine of Christ's pre-millenial advent and personal reign on earth... Philadelphia, PA: Orrin Rogers, 1840. 48 p. CBPSR; ICU; MMeT-Hi; MWA; NbOP; NjPT. 40-1701

Cox, Samuel Hanson, 1793-1881. A squint at a "Co-Presbyter," in the New York Evangelist of November 10th, 1838, and a glance at the minutes of the High School Synod, which was organized in Newburgh, October 17, 1838... By Trio. N. V. D. et S. S. S. New York: Goshen, 1840. 16 p. CtY; MBC; NjR; PPL; PPPrHi. 40-1702

Coxe, Arthur Cleveland, 1818-1896. Athanasion, an ode pronounced before the associate alumni of Washington College in Christ Church, Hartford, on the day before commencement, 1840. Hartford, CT: published by the Association, 1840. 32 p. CtY; INC; NNC; RPB; ViU. 40-1703

Coxe, Arthur Cleveland, 1818-1896. Christian ballads... New York: Wiley and Putnam, 1840. 138 p. CtY; In; MWA; PPPrHi; TxU. 40-1704

Coxe, Margaret. Life of John Wycliffe, D. D. Columbus, OH: D. D. Gambier; printed by Thomas R. Raymond; pubished by Isaac N. Whiting, 1840. 272 p. IEG; MAm; OEaC; PPM; RPB. 40-1705

Coxe, Margaret. The young lady's companion: in a series of letters, by Margaret Coxe... 2d ed. Columbus, OH: Isaac N. Whiting, 1840. 348 p. GHi; MeBat; OC; PP. 40-1706

Coxe, Richard Smith, 1792-1865. Letter to James Buchanan, Nov. 18, 1840. by R. S. Coxe, et. al. Washington, DC: s. l., 1840. 2 p. PHi. 40-1707

Coyne, Joseph Stirling, 1803-1868. Box and Cox married and settled; an original farce in one act. New York: W. Taylor & Co., etc., etc. [184-?] 20 p. MH. 40-1708

Coyne, Joseph Stirling, 1803-1868. Wanted - 1000 spirited young milliners for the gold diggings; a farce in one act. New York: Roorbache [184-?] p. MB. 40-1709

Crabb, George Whitfield. Speech of George W. Crabb... against the subtreasury bill. Delivered in the House of Representatives, June 27, 1840.

Washington, DC: Printed by Gales and Seaton, 1840. 31 p. DLC; GEU; M. 40-1710

The Cracovian maid, a Polish melody. [Song, the accomp.] arranged for the guitar by Adolph Schmitz. Philadelphia, PA: Fiot [184-?] p. MB. 40-1711

The Cracovienne dance. Composed and arranged for the piano forte. Boston, MA: Ditson [184-?] p. MB. 40-1712

Craik, George Lillie, 1798-1866. The Pursuit of knowledge under difficulties. Illustrated by anecdotes. Revised edition. Boston, MA: Published by Marsh, Capen, Lyon and Webb, c1840. 2 v. FNp; InCW; Me; MeU; OHi; ScAb. 40-1713

Craik, George Lillie, 1798-1866. Pursuit of knowledge under difficulties, its pleasures and rewards. New York: Harper, 1840. 2 v. CtMW; KyDC; MHi; NBuG; OO. 40-1714

Cramer, H. Serenade from Don Juan. Divertissement by H. Cramer. Baltimore, MD: Geo. Willig, Junr. [184-?] 2 p. ViU. 40-1715

Cramer, Johann Baptist. Cramer's Turkish march. [For the piano forte.] Boston, MA: Bradlee [184-?] 2 p. MB. 40-1716

Cramp, John Mockett, 1796-1881. The Reformation in Europe. By the author of "The Council of Trent." With a chronology of the Reformation. New York: The American Tract Society [184-?] 432 p. DLC; NcD. 40-1717

Cranch, Christopher Pearse, 1813-1892. A poem, delivered in the First Congregational church in the town of Quincy, May 25, 1840, the two hundredth anniversary of the incorporation of the town. By Christopher Pearse Cranch. Pub. by request. Boston, MA: J. Munroe and company, 1840. 26 p. CtY; ICMe; MMal; MWA; Nh-Hi; OO; TxU. 40-1718

Craven, John Thomas. Oh! I should like to marry. Comic song. Boston, MA: Ditson [184-?] 2 p. MB. 40-1719

Creagh, William. Scripture cathecism, being a compend of sacred history, in the form of questions and answers. by William H. Creagh. New York: F. Mason & G. Lane, 1840. 136 p. DLC. 40-1720

Creagh, William. Scripture cathecism, being a compend of sacred history, in the form of questions and answers. by William H. Creagh. New York: Nelson and Phillips, 1840. NjMD. 40-1721

Creigh, Thomas. A sermon:"The present distress"....delivered April 5, 1840, by Thomas Creigh. Chambersburg, PA: n. pub., Pritts and Catlin, printers, 1840. 16 p. NjPT; PPL; PPPrHi. 40-1722

Crescenti, G. Art of singing... Philadelphia, PA: s. l. [184-?] p. MB. 40-1723

Crichton, Andrew, 1790-1855. The history of Arabia, ancient and modern. By Andrew Crichton. In two volumes. New York: Published by Harper & Brothers, 1840. 2 v. MH; NAlf; NcHil; TxU; ViR. 40-1724

The crisis met. A reply to Junius. [New York: s. l., 1840] 16 p. CtY; MH; MiD-B; NcD; OClWHi; PPL. 40-1725

The crisis, or A few thoughts on the subject of slavery. [New York: H. Parks, printer, 184-?] 10 p. MH; NN. 40-1726

Crockett, David, 1786-1836. Life of Martin Van Buren. New York: s. l., 184-? 209 p. MWA. 40-1727

Crockett, John Wesley. Speech of Mr. Crockett, of Tennessee, on the subtreasury bill. Delivered in the House of Representatives, in committee of the whole, June 16, 1840. Baltimore, MD: Duff Green [1840] 21 p. MBAt; OClWHi; T; TxU. 40-1728

Crockett almanac for 1841. Boston, MA: J. Fisher [1840] p. MWA. 40-1729

Crockett almanac for 1841. Nashville, TN: Ben Harding [1840] p. MsJS; MWA; PHi. 40-1730

Crockett's Harrison almanac, 1841. New York: Elton [1840] 24 p. CSmH; InLPU; MWA. 40-1731

Croly, George, 1780-1860. ... Life and times of His Majesty George the Fourth. With anecdotes of distinguished persons of the last 50 years. By the Rev. George Croly. New and improved edition. New York: Harper & Brothers, 1840. 414 p. CtY; InRch; MH; ScDuE; TJaU. 40-1732

Croly, George, 1780-1860. Salathiel; [the wandering Jew] A story of the past, the present and the future. By George Croly. Philadelphia, PA: Peterson, 1840. 232 p. NjP. 40-1733

Cromwell, Oliver, 1599-1658. Cromwell's letters and speeches, by Oliver Cromwell. Ed. by Thomas Carlyle. New York: Colyer, 1840. 2 v. in 1. PPA. 40-1734

Cromwell, Oliver, 1599-1658. Cromwell's letters and speeches, by Oliver Cromwell. Ed. by Thomas Carlyle. New York: Wiley & Putnam, 1840. 2 v. in 1. MBBCHJ. 40-1735

Cromwell, Oliver, 1599-1658. Oliver Cromwell's letters and speeches with elucidations, by Thos. Carlyle. New York: Colyer, 1840. PPA. 40-1736

Crookshank, N. Observations on the milk sickness, sick stomach, or gastroenteritis. By Dr. N. Crookshank... Cincinnati, OH: Looker & Graham, printers, 1840. 12 p. IEN-M; NNNAM; OC. 40-1737

Crosby, Daniel, 1799-1843. The death scene of the aged saint. A sermon preached December 8, 1839, in the Winthrop Church, Charlestown on the occasion of the death of Deacon Amos Tufts. Boston, MA: Marden & Co., printers, 1840. 16 p. MHi. 40-1738

Crosby, Daniel. 1799-1843. Sermon preached December 8, 1839, in the Winthrop Church, Charlestown, on the occasion of the death of Deacon Amos Tufts. Boston, MA: s. l., 1840. 16 p. MBC; Nh-Hi. 40-1739

Crosby, L. V. H. The dying child. Music composed... by L. V. H. Crosby. Words by Theodore A. Gould. Boston, MA: Reed & Co. [184-?] 5 p. MB. 40-1740

Crosby, L. V. H. The wild old woods. Quartette as sung by the Harmoneons. The music composed & most respectfully dedicated to F. S. Allen, Esq.,

Springfield, Ms., By L. V. H. Crosby. Boston, MA: Oliver Ditson [184-?] 3 p. ViU. 40-1741

Cross, Joseph Warren. The ascension; a sermon, by Rev. Joseph Cross, pastor of the Methodist Episcopal Church in Cazenovia, N. Y. Cazenovia, NY: Printed at the "Union Herald Office, 1840. 22 p. KyLx; MBC; MoS; NjR; ViRut. 40-1742

Cross, Joseph Warren. [Dedication] Sermon, Stow, July 8, 1840. Lancaster: s. l., 1840. 24 p. RPB. 40-1743

Cross, Joseph Warren. Salvation by grace alone. Sermon at the dedication of a house of worship of Jehovah, Father, Son, and Holy Ghost, in Stow, July 8, 1840. Lancaster: Marsh, Capen, Lyon, and Webb, 1840. 24 p. MBAt; MBC; MBNMHi; MWA; NN. 40-1744

Croswell, Harry, 1778-1858. Rudiments of the Church. In Three parts. By the Rev. Harry Croswell, D. D., Rector of the Parish of Trinity Church, New Haven, Conn. New Haven, CT: S. Babcock, 1840. 176 p. CtY; InID; NNUT. 40-1745

Crouch, Frederick William Nicholls, 1808-1896. Atherlie. Ballad. Sung by Madame Caridori Allen; the music composed by F. W. N. Crouch. New York: Hewitt & Jacques [184-?] 3 p. ViU. 40-1746

Crouch, Frederick William Nicholls, 1808-1896. The union of Kathleen Mavourneen & Dermot, Asthore. Written by Mrs. Crawford; music by F. N. Crouch. Boston, MA: Oliver Ditson [184-?] 4 p. ViU. 40-1747

Crow, Chapman, crow! or, Van Buren's last song. A new comic Whig song & chorus. Arranged for the piano forte. New York: Atwill, 1840. 31 p. MB. 40-1748

Crowe, Eyre Evans. The history of France. By Eyre Evans Crowe. New York: published by Harper & Bros., 1840. 3 v. InRchE; MB; MDeeP; Nh-Hi; ViRU. 40-1749

The Cruiser, or 'tis thirty years ago. Boston, MA: s. l. [184-?] 40 p. MB. 40-1750

Cubi y Soler, Mariano, 1801-1875. A new Spanish grammar, adapted to every class of learners. Ed. 6, with corrections and improvements. Baltimore, MD: Lucas [1840] 294 p. CU; NCH; NjP; PPAmP; RPB. 40-1751

Cubi y Soler, Mariano, 1801-1875. A new Spanish grammar, adapted to every class of learners. By Mariano Cubi I. Solder.... 7th edition. Baltimore, MD: Fielding Lucas, Jr., 1840. 294 p. MH; NIC; PWmpDS; ViU. 40-1752

Cubi y Soler, Mariano, 1801-1875. Phrenology. A lecture delivered before the Woodville lyceum association... Boston, MA: Marsh, Capen, Lyon, and Webb, 1840. 24 p. CtY; LU; MBAt; MdHi; WHi. 40-1753

Cubi y Soler, Mariano, 1801-1875. The Spanish translator; or, A practical system for becoming acquainted with the Spanish written language, through the medium of the English. By Mariano Cubi Soler... Third edition.... Baltimore, MD: Fielding Lucas, Jr., 184?. 279 p. DLC; MAnP; MB; MoSU; TxSaO. 40-1754

Cubi y Soler, Mariano, 1801-1875. Traductor ingles; o, sistema practico i teorico para aprender a traducir la lengua inglesa par medio de la espanola... Cambridge, MA: Impr. de Folsom, Wells, i Thurston [1840] 304 p. DLC; MH; NIC; PPAmP; RPAt. 40-1755

The cultivator's almanac and cabinet of agricultural knowledge for the year 1840. Boston, MA: Pub. by H. B. Williams, 1840. 124 p. MBAt; MiU-C; MHi; NjR; WHi. 40-1756

Cultivator's almanac and cabinet of agricultural knowledge for 1841. Boston, MA: Pub. by H. B. Williams, 1840. MWA. 40-1757

Culverwell, Robert James, 1802-1852. Physiology of the passions... of the human reproductive powers... New York: Christie's [184-?] 38 p. NN; PPL. 40-1758

Culverwell, Robert James, 1802-1852. Physiology of the passions; the study of health. A new & original medico-physiological work, on the physiology of the passions; illustrative of the rise, progress, attainment, & decline of the human reproductive powers... From the thirty-second London edition. Boston, MA: Saxton, Peirce & co., 184-? p. PU. 40-1759

Cumberland almanac, for the year of our Lord 1841; being the first after bis-sextile or leap year, and 65th and 66th of American Independence. Containing the motions of the sun and moon--the true phases and aspects of the planets--the rising and setting of the sun--the rising and setting of the moon--solar and lunar eclipses, etc. Calculated for the horizon of Nashville, Tenn., latitude 36o9'43" N. --longitude 86o47'15" from London. And with slight variation, will answer for Kentucky, Mississippi and Alabama. By William L. Willeford, A. M. Nashville, TN: Printed and published by S. Nye & Co. [1840] 36 p. T. 40-1760

Cumberland Co., N. J. Cedarville Baptist Church. The articles of faith and covenant, of the Cedarville Baptist Church, Cumberland County, New Jersey. Philadelphia, PA: Published by David Clark, 1840. 12 p. PCA. 40-1761

Cumberland Presbyterian Church. The confession of faith of the Cumberland Presbyterian Church in the Untied States of America. Revised and adopted by the General Assembly at Princeton, Ky., May, 1829. [Nashville, TN?] : Published by Cumberland Presbyterian Board of Publication, 1840? 286 p. ArBaA; CSaT; IaManc. 40-1762

Cumings, Samuel. The western pilot, containing charts of the Ohio River and of the Mississippi from the mouth of the Missouri to the Gulf of Mexico. Cincinnati, OH: G. Conclin, 1840. DLC; FMU; IU; NN; OCl. 40-1763

Cummings, Jacob Abbot, 1773-1820. First lessons in geography and astronomy... New Haven, CT: s. l., 1840. 82 p. CtY. 40-1764

Cummings, Jacob Abbot. 1773-1820. The pronouncing spelling book, adapted to Walker's critical pronouncing dictionary... Revised and improved from the fourth edition. Concord, NH: s. l., 1840. MBevHi; OCLWHi; RPB. 40-1765

Cunningham, Allan, 1784-1842. The lives of the most eminent British painters and sculptors. By Allan Cunningham. In three vols. New York: Pub. by Harper and brothers, 1840-44. 5 v. Ia; IU; OO; NN; TxH. 40-1766

Cunningham, John William. Velvet cushion... a tale. New York: s. l., 1840. NN-As. 40-1767

Cuninghame, William. d. 1849. The political destiny of the earth, as revealed in the Bible. By William Cuninghame, Esquire, of Lainshaw in the county of Ayr. Philadelphia, PA: Orrin Rogers; G. Dorsey, printer, 1840. 48 p. ICU; MBC; MiU; MWA; NbOP; OO. 40-1768

Cuninghame, William, d. 1849. The political destiny of the earth, as revealed in the Bible, and The Pre-Millennial Advent of Messiah demonstrated from the Scriptures... From the 3d Lond. ed. Philadelphia, PA: O. Rogers, 1840. 48, 44 p. CtY; DLC; ICU; MiU; NjPT. 40-1769

Cuninghame, William, d. 1849. Pre-Millennial advent of Messiah demonstrated from the Scriptures... ed. 8. Philadelphia, PA: Rogers, 1840. 44 p. CtY; ICU; NjPT; OO. 40-1770

Curd, William P. Pedigrees and likenesses of Berkshire & Irish grazien hogs. Lexington, KY: Finnell & Lambert, 1840. 28 p. DLC. 40-1771

Curtis, George William, 1824-1892. Nile notes, by George William Curtis. New York: Harper & Brothers, 1840. 307 p. IaPeC. 40-1772

Curtis, Newton Mallory. Bryan Blonday; or, The blue ranger of the Mohawk...

New York: Dick, 1840. 105 p. NjP. 40-1773

Curtiss, N. P. B. O no we never mention her. Arranged as a waltz by N. P. B. Curtiss. Boston, MA: Oliver Ditson [184-?] 2 p. ViU. 40-1774

Curtiss, N. P. B. The seraphine waltz. Composed and respectfully dedicated to Dr. C. S. Cartee of Charlestown, by N. P. B. Curtiss. Boston, MA: Henry Prentiss [184-?] 2 p. ViU. 40-1775

Cushing, Caleb, 1800-1879. Brief sketch of the life and public services, civil and military, of William Henry Harrison, of Ohio... Augusta: Printed by Severance and Dorr, 1840. 32 p. MeHi; NN. 40-1776

Cushing, Caleb, 1800-1879. The Harrison Medal. Letters of Mr. Cushing, of Massachusetts, concerning the Resolution for presenting a Medal and the Thanks of Congress to General William Henry Harrison... Washington, DC: s. l., 1840. 8 p. MBAt; MH. 40-1777

Cushing, Caleb, 1800-1879. Outlines of the life and public services, civil and military, of William Henry Harrison of Ohio. Boston, MA: Eastburn's press, 1840. 24 p. CaBViP; DLC; InU; MWA; PHi. 40-1778

Cushing, Caleb, 1800-1879. Outlines of the life and public services, civil and military, of William Henry Harrison of Ohio. Boston, MA: Weeks, Jordan & Company, 1840. 71 p. CtY; DLC; MWA; OClWHi; OO; ViU. 40-1779

Cushing, Caleb, 1800-1879. Outlines of the life and public services, civil and

military, of William Henry Harrison. Boston, MA: William D. Ticknor, 1840. 36 p. MnU. 40-1780

Cushing, Caleb, 1800-1879. Outlines of the life and public services, civil and military, of William Henry Harrison of Ohio. Newark, NJ: printed at the Daily and sentinel office, 1840. 32 p. DLC; MMaL; MWA; NN. 40-1781

Cushing, Caleb, 1800-1879. Outlines of the life and public services, civil and military, of William Henry Harrison of Ohio. Washington, DC: T. Allen, 1840. 21 p. DLC; MHi; MWA; OU; TxU. 40-1782

Cushing, Caleb, 1800-1779. Sketch and public services of Wm. H. Harrison of Ohio. Augusta, ME: Severance & Dorr, 1840. 32 p. NN. 40-1783

Cushing, Caleb, 1800-1879. Speech of Mr. Cushing, of Massachusetts, on the sub-treasury bill. Delivered in the House of Representatives, May 20 and 21, 1840. Washington, DC: s. l., 1840. 23 p. DLC; MH; MHi; MWA; OClWHi. 40-1784

Cushing, Eliza Lanesford [Foster] Esther, a sacred drama; with Judith, a poem. By Mrs. E. L. Cushing. Boston, MA: J. Dowe, 1840. 118 p. CtY; ICU; MH; PU; RPB. 40-1785

Cutter, George Washington, 1801-1863. Elskwatawa; or, The moving fires, and other poems. Indianapolis, IN: Stacy & Williams, 1840. 113 p. In. 40-1786

Czerny, Carl, 1791-1857. The admired Swiss air "The Swiss drover boy, "with easy and brilliant variations! Composed for the piano forte. Boston, MA: Ditson [184-?] 6 p. MB; NcD. 40-1787

Czerny, Carl. ... Alexis waltz. Baltimore, MD: F. D. Benteen [184-?] 5 p. ViU. 40-1788

Czerny, Carl. ... Duke of Reichstadt's waltz... Baltimore, MD: Frederick D. Benteen [184-?] 5 p. ViU. 40-1789

Czerny, Carl. ... Exercise dans les tons les moins usites... Baltimore, MD: Frederick D. Benteen [184-?] 7 p. ViU. 40-1790

Czerny, Carl. Fantasie on two popular airs "On yonder rock" & "Tis Tomorrow" from Auber's celebrated of Foa Diavolo. [For the piano forte.] New York: Dubius & Bacon [184-?] 9 p. MB. 40-1791

Czerne, Carl. Ireland. 3 popular Irish airs. Arranged as rondos for the piano forte by C. Czerny. No. 2. Philadelphia, PA: Fiot [184-?] 5 p. MB. 40-1792

Czerny, Carl. Odblee concerto, an air by Mozart, arranged as a rondo for the piano forte by Czerny. Boston, MA: Reed [184-?] 4 p. MB. 40-1793

Czerny, Carl. Rondeau sur un tema de l'opera La sonnambula de Bellini, arrange pour le piano forte par Charles Czerny. New York: Dubois & Bacon [184-?] 8 p. MB. 40-1794

Czerny, Carl. Vienna march, arranged as a duett... by J. T. Gordon. [For piano forte.] Boston, MA: Ditson [184-?] 2 p. MB. 40-1795

Czerny, Carl. A Viennoise waltz. For the piano forte. Philadelphia, PA: Fiot [184-?] 2 p. MB. 40-1796

Czerny, Charles. 24 studies for the left hand. Composed for the piano forte, Ch. Czerny. No. 1. Op. 718. Boston, MA: Geo. P. Reed [184-?] 8 p. ViU. 40-1797

Czerny, Charles. ... 101 preparatory lessons of moderate difficulty expressly composed to facilitate the instruction of youth on the piano forte, by Charles Czerny. To which are added 20 five fingered exercises and six new studies for the left hand alone. Boston, MA: Oliver Ditson [184-?] 17 p. ViU. 40-1798

Czerny, Charles. ... Bohemian melody... Baltimore, MD: F. D. Benteen [184-?] 4p. ViU. 40-1799

Czerny, Charles. ... Bohemian melody... Baltimore, MD: F. D. Benteen [184-?] 5 p. ViU. 40-1800

Czerny, Charles. Czerny's indispensable exercises. The pianist's daily & indispendable exercises, or, collection of the most useful scales & passages in all the major & minor keys, by Charles Czerny. Baltimore, MD; New Orleans, LA: F. D. Benteen; W. T. May [184-?] 13 p. ViU. 40-1801

Czerny, Charles. Etudes de la velocite. Pour le piano forte en Trente Exercises. Pour developper la souplesse de la dexterite des doigts, et parvenir a executer les passages les plus rapides. par Charles Czerny. No. 1... Philadelphia, PA: A. Fiot [184-?] 17 p. ViU. 40-1802

Czerny, Charles. Fautasie on two popular airs "On Yonder rock" & "Tis tomorrow," from Auber's celebrated opera

of Fra. Diavolo. Composed by Charles
Czerny. Philadelphia, PA: George Willig
[184-?] 9 p. ViU. 40-1803

Czerny, Charles. The Linden waltz. Ar-
rnaged for the piano forte, by Charles
Czerny. Baltimore, MD: G. Willig Jr.
[184-?] 2 p. ViU. 40-1804

Czerny, Charles. ... Octaves et austres
intervalles eloignes... Baltimore, MD:
Frederick D. Benteen [184-?] 5 p. ViU.
40-1805

Czerny, Charles. ... Pour acquerir de la
facilite dans le feu... Baltimore, MD:
Frederick D. Benteen [184-?] 7 p. ViU.
40-1806

Czerny, Charles. ... Swiss air... Baltimore, MD: F. D. Benteen [184-?] 5 p.
ViU. 40-1807

Czerny, Charles. Tyriolian air. With

brilliant & easy variations for the piano
forte by Charles Czerny. Philadelphia,
PA: Geo. W. Hewitt & Co. [184-?] 5 p.
ViU. 40-1808

Czerny, Charles. Variations elegantes,
pour servie d' etude composees pour le
pianopar Ch. Czerny. Op. 706... No. 11.
Pour acquerir de la seuplesse dans
l'executien des passages rapides... Baltimore, MD: G. Willig Jr. [184-?] 7 p.
ViU. 40-1809

Czerny, Charles. Waltzes di Bravura.
Compose pour le piano forte, par C.
Czerny. Set. No. 1. Philadelphia, PA:
George Willig [184-?] 5 p. ViU. 40-1810

Czerny, Charles. Was it not at one. A
popular song as sung by the Rainer Family. Varied by C. Czerny. Baltimore, MD:
G. Willig [184-?] 5 p. ViU. 40-1811

D

D'Albert, Charles. The bridal or Wedding polka. Composed for the piano forte by Charles D'Albert. Baltimore, MD; New Orleans, LA: F. D. Benteen; W. T. Mayo [184-?] 5 p. ViU. 40-1812

D'Oyley, Charles W. An examination of the argument of David Hume, Esq., on miracles. Being the substance of a lecture delivered at Maysville and other parts of Kentucky, by Charles W. D'Oyley, of South Carolina. Maysville, KY: Printed by Stanton and Crookshanks, 1840. 14 p. KyLx. 40-1813

Daily foor for Christians. Being a promise, and another Scriptural portion, for every day in the year: together with a verse of a hymn. [Stereotyped by F. Lucas, Jr.] Baltimore, MD: Tract Depository [184-?] 192 p. MB; MdHi. 40-1814

Dalrymple, J. S. The Naiad queen; or, The revolt of the Naiads. A grand romantic operatic spectacle in three acts. New York; London: Samuel French [1840?] 27 p. C; OCl. 40-1815

Dalzel, Andrew, 1742-1805. ... Avalexta! Ellnvixa, nocova, or, Collectanea Graeca minora. With notes partly compiled and partly written by Andrew Dalzel... 6th American ed. New York: W. E. Dean, 1840. 299 p. CU; OrPD; OU; PEaL. 40-1816

Dalzel, Andrew, 1742-1805. ... The prose selections of Dalzel's collectanea Graeca major. For the use of schools and colleges. With English notes, prepared by C. S. Wheeler... Boston, MA; Philadelphia, PA: Hilliard, Gray, and company; Kimber and Sharpless, 1840. / 364, 160 p. CSt; MH; NjMD; TSewU; ViU. 40-1817

Dame, Charles. Mode and subjects of baptism. Two sermons, on the mode and subjects of Christian baptism, preached at Falmouth, July 5, 1840. Portland, ME: A. Shirley, 1840. 34 p. LNB; MBC; NHCS; NjPT; PPPrHi. 40-1818

Damon, David, 1787-1843. Miracles as an evidence of Christianity. An address delivered before the ministerial conference in Berry St., Boston, May 27, 1840. Boston, MA: Little and Brown, 1840. 24 p. CtY; DLC; MH; NcD; RPB. 40-1819

Damon, Norwood, b. 1816. Haying Hayed. A discourse. Delivered before the First Congregational Society in Sudbury, Mass... By Norwood Damon... Boston, MA: Charles C. Little and James Brown, 1840. 12 p. MB; MBAU; MH; MHi. 40-1820

Damon, Norwood. b. 1816. Remarks on the Importance of Obedience to Law... Delivered... December 30, 1839... Boston, MA: Charles C. Little and James Brown, 1840. 16 p. DLC; MBAt; MH. 40-1821

Damphoux, Edward. St. Joseph's manual. Baltimore, MD: s. l., 1840. 464 p. MWA. 40-1822

Dana, Edmund P. A Voice from Bunker-Hill, and the Fathers of the Revolutionary War, in favor of the Hero of North Bend. 2nd ed. Bunker Hill: s. l., 1840. 25 p. CtY; DLC; MH; MiD-B; MWA. 40-1823

Dana, Joshua Markham. Incidents in the history of Vermont... as sung before the Freemen of Chlais, Vt... S. l.: s. l., 1840. VtHi. 40-1824

Dana, Richard Henry, 1815-1882. Two Years Before the Mast. Boston, MA: Fields, Osgood and Company, 1840. 470 p. No Loc. 40-1825

Dana, Richard Henry, 1815-1882. Two Years Before the Mast. Boston, MA: Houghton Mifflin and Co., 1840. 362 p. IaAS; NJam; OkAt. 40-1826

Dana, Richard Henry, 1815-1882. Two Years Before the Mast. Illustrated. Chicago, IL: Montogmery & Co., publishers, 1840. 362 p. CoMv. 40-1827

Dana, Richard Henry, 1815-1882. Two years before the mast. [Harvard Classics, V. 23] New York: Collier, 1840. 424 p. ScGrvGWC. 40-1828

Dana, Richard Henry, 1815-1882. Two Years Before the Mast. New York; Boston, MA: H. M. Caldwell Company, 1840. 362 p. IaAS; KyLoSX. 40-1829

Dana, Richard Henry, 1815-1882. Two years before the mast. New York: International Book Co., 1840. 362 p. IaSlB. 40-1830

Dana, Richard Henry, 1815-1882. Two years before the mast. New York; New Orleans, LA: J. J. Little and Co.; Unversity Publishing Co., 1840. 180 p. NcLoC. 40-1831

Dana, Richard Henry, 1815-1882. Two years before the mast. A personal narrative of life at sea. Boston, MA: The Book-lovers Library, 1840. IaMarion. 40-1832

Dana, Richard Henry, 1815-1882. Two Years Before the Mast. A Personal Narrative of life at Sea. New York: A. L. Burt, 1840. 363 p. GAuY; IaBed; MB; OJa; RWoH. 40-1833

Dana, Richard Henry, 1815-1882. Two years before the mast. A personal narrative of life at sea. New York: American Publishers Co. [1840] 362 p. LNB. 40-1834

Dana, Richard Henry, 1815-1882. Two years before the mast. A personal narrative of life at sea, New York: F. M. Lupton publishing company, 1840. 372 p. GCed; InPla; MAr; MiCass; RReaAt. 40-1835

Dana, Richard Henry, 1815-1882. Two years before the mast. A personal narrative of life at sea. New York; Boston, MA: Hurst and Company, 1840. KyOwSF. 40-1836

Dana, Richard Henry, 1815-1882. Two years before the mast. A personal narrative of life at sea. New York: Harper & brothers, 1840. 483 p. CU; InHi; MH-AH; NBuCC; RPB. 40-1837

Dana, Richard Henry, 1815-1882. Two years before the mast. A personal narrative of life at sea. New York: Lovell

Coryell & co., 1840. 362 p. CHay; CoMo; GNe; MBele. 40-1838

Dana, Richard Henry, 1815-1882. Two Years Before the Mast. A Personal Narrative of life at Sea. New York: New York Book Co., 1840. 180 p. NcSo. 40-1839

Dana, Richard Henry, 1815-1882. Two years before the mast. A personal narrative, by R. H. Dana. Philadelphia, PA: Henry Altemus Co., 1840. 430 p. MiDo. 40-1840

Dana, William Coombs. An address delivered on the Fifty-first anniversary of the Orphan House, in Charleston, S. C., October 16, 1840, by Rev. W. C. Dana. Charleston, SC: printed by B. B. Hussey, 1840. 20 p. MeBaT; NcU; NIC; PPL. 40-1841

Dance, Charles, 1794?-1863. Naval engagements. A comedy in two acts. New York: M. Douglas [184-?] 48 p. MH. 40-1842

Dance, Charles, 1794?-1863. Naval engagements. A comedy in two acts. New York: S. French and Son [184-?] 48 p. MH. 40-1843

Dance, Charles, 1794?-1863. Naval engagements. A comedy in two acts. New York: W. Taylor & Co. [184-?] 48 p. MH. 40-1844

Dance, Charles, 1794?-1863. Who speaks first? A farce, in one act. New York: S. French and Son [184-?] 28 p. MH. 40-1845

The danger of riches. Written for the Am. S. S. U. and revised by the Committee of Publication. Philadelphia, PA:

Am. Sunday School Union [1840] p. DLC. 40-1846

Darley, William Henry Westray, 1801-1872. Chants of the Episcopal Church, original and selected, harmonized for four voices... By W. H. W. Darley & J. C. B. Standbridge. Philadelphia, PA: Williams, 1840. 46 p. PPCI; PPL; PHi; RPB. 40-1847

Darnes, William P. A full and accurate report of trial, by William P. Darnes, or an indictment found by the Grand Jury of the County of St. Louis, at the September term, 1840... on a charge of manslaughter for the death of Andrew J. Davis. Saint Louis: s. l., 1840. 248 p. DLC; MH; NcD; PP; PPL. 40-1848

The Dartmouth. Conducted by students of Dartmouth College. Hanover: Chronicle Press, F. A. Allen, printer, 1840-44. v. 1-5; Nov., 1839-July, 1844. DLC; Nh; Nh-Do; NjP; PU. 40-1849

Dartmouth college. A catalogue of the officers and students of Dartmouth College, September, 1840. Concord, NH: Printed by Asa McFarland, opposite the state house, 1840. 25 p. KHi; MHaHi; Nh. 40-1850

Dartmouth college. Catalogue of the officers and members of the Society of United Fraternity... Dartmouth College, 1840. Concord, NH: Printed by Asa Mc-Farland, for the Society, 1840. 56 p. MeLewB; NBLiHi; Nh. 40-1851

Dartmouth college. Catalogue senatus academici collegii Darmuthensis, in republica Neo-Hantonieusi, eorumque omnium qui in eodem munera et officia gesserunt, aut alicujus gradus laurea exornati fuerunt. Boston, MA: Typis Perkins et Marvin, 1840. 74 p. Ct; MNS. 40-1852

Dartmouth College. United Fraternity. Catalogue of the officers and members of the Society of United Fraternity... Dartmouth College... Concord, NH: n pub., printed by Asa McFarland, 1840. 56 p. NjR. 40-1853

Daughters of the American Revolution, Ohio. Early marriage bonds of Ohio, copied by the Daughters of the American revolution, compiled under the direction of of Mrs. Rufus W. Russell, Mrs. Peter J. Blosser and Mrs. Ase Clay Messenger. Ottawa County, 1840-1880. [S. l.: s. l., 1840-80] 144 p. O. 40-1854

The daughter's own book; or, practical hints from a father to his daughter. Sixth ed. Philadelphia, PA: Griff & Elliot, 1840. 240 p. NPalk; VtMidSM. 40-1855

Davezac, Augustus. Marius [from the Democratic Review] New York: s. l., 1840. PPL. 40-1856

David, Felicieu Cesar, 1810-1876. Bird of Spring (Les hirondelles) [Song with accomp. for piano forte] The English version by Thos. Gliphant, Esq. New York: Firth, Hall and Pond [184-?] 4 p. MB. 40-1857

David, J. C. David's Chemical-astro-geographical system of botany. [New York: s. l., 184-?] p. NN. 40-1858

Davidson, Robert, 1808-1876. An excursion to the Mammoth Cave and the barrens of Kentucky. With some notices of the early settlement of the state. By the Rev. R. Davidson. Philadelphia, PA:

Thomas Cowperthwait and co., 1840. 148 p. ICU; KyU; MWA; OFH; TxDaM. 40-1859

Davidson, Robert, 1808-1876. An excursion to the Mammoth Cave and the barrens of Kentucky. With some notices of the early settlement of the state. Lexington, KY: A. T. Skillman & son, 1840. 148 p. ICP; MB; MiD-B; NjPT; WHi. 40-1860

Davidson, Robert. A reply to the mate manifesto. By R. Davidson. Lexington, KY?: s. l. [1840] 24 p. PPL-R. 40-1861

Davies, Charles, 1798-1876. Arithmetic, designed for academies and schools... Philadelphia, PA: A. S. Barnes and Co. [1840] 340 p. CtHWatk; CtY; MH; OCo. 40-1862

Davies, Charles, 1798-1876. Elements of Algebra. Translated from the French of M. Boardon. Revised and adapted to the course of mathematical introduction in the U. S. Rev. ed. Philadelphia, PA: A. S. Barnes & Co., 1840. 358 p. MiEM; MH; NjP; PPL; ViU. 40-1863

Davies, Charles, 1798-1876. Elements of analytical geometry: embracing the equations of the point, the straight line, the conic sections, and surfaces of the first and second order. Rev. ed. New York: A. S. Barnes & Co., 1840. 352 p. NjP. 40-1864

Davies, Charles, 1798-1876. Elements of analytical geometry; embracing the equations of the point, the straight line, the conic sections and surfaces of the first and second order, by Charles Davies... 2e ed., rev. and cor. Philadelphia, PA: A. S

Barnes and Co. [1840] 352 p. CtHT; CtY; MdBS; OClW; TxHR; ViU. 40-1865

Davies, Charles, 1798-1876. Elements of descriptive geometry, with their application to spherical trigonometry, spherical projections, and warped surfaces. 2nd ed. Philadelphia, PA: A. S. Barnes & Co., 1840. 174 p. MdBP; MH; MWM. 40-1866

Davies, Charles, 1798-1876. Elements of surveying, with a description of the instruments and the necessary tables, including a table of natural sines. 4th ed. Philadelphia, PA: Published by A. S. Barnes & Co., 1840. 334 p. MBBCHS; MH; RPB. 40-1867

Davies, Charles, 1798-1876. Elements of the differential and integral calculus, by Charles Davies... 2d ed., revised and corrected. Philadelphia, PA: A. S. Barnes and Co., 1840. 283 p. LNH; MdBJ; MnHi; NjR; OOxM. 40-1868

Davies, Charles, 1798-1876. First lessons in algebra, embracing the elements of science. By Charles Davies. Hartford, CT; New York; Philadelphia, PA; Boston, MA; Baltimore, MD: A. S. Barnes and Co.; Wiley & Putnam; Collins, Keese and Co.; Thomas Cowperthwait and Co.; Perkins and Marvin; Cushing and Sons, 1840. 252 p. CoU; DLC; MDeeP; OMC; TNP. 40-1869

Davies, Charles, 1798-1876. First lessons in arithmetic. Designed for beginners, by Charles Davies. Hartford, CT: A. S. Barnes and Co., 1840. 132 p. CtHWatk; CtY; DLC; MH; NBuT. 40-1870

Davies, Charles, 1798-1876. First lessons in geometry, by Charles Davies.

Hartford, CT; New York; Philadelphia, PA; Boston, MA; Baltimore, MD; Louisville, KY: A. S. Barnes and Co.; Robinson, Pratt and Co.; COllins, Keese and Co.; Thomas Cowperthwait and Co.; Perkins and Marvin; Cushing and Bro.; Morton and Griswold, 1840. 252 p. CtHWatk; InJ; NjMD; OHi; ScCliTO. 40-1871

Davies, Charles, 1798-1876. First lessons on Algebra, embracing the elements of the science. Hartford, CT: Barnes, 1840. 252 p. DLC; MWHi; OO. 40-1872

Davies, Charles, 1798-1876. First lessons on Algebra, embracing the elements of the science. Philadelphia, PA: A. S. Barnes Co., 1840. 252 p. DLC. 40-1873

Davies, Charles, 1798-1876. First lessons on geometry, with practical applications in mensuration & artificers work & mechanics. Hartford, CT: Barnes, 1840. 252 p. PU. 40-1874

Davies, Charles, 1798-1876. Key to Davies' Mental and Practical Arithmetic. For the use of teachers only. Hartford, CT: published by Alfred S. Barnes & Co., 1840. 278 p. CTHWatk; RKi. 40-1875

Davies, Charles, 1798-1876. Mental & Practical Arithmetic. Designed for the use of academies & schools. Hartford, CT: Barnes, 1840. 334 p. CTHWatk; CtMW; MNBedf. 40-1876

Davies, Charles, 1798-1876. A treatise on shades and shadows, and linear perspective. 2d ed. Philadelphia, PA: A. S. Barnes and co., 1840. 159 p. MBU-A; MtU; OClJC; TxU; WM. 40-1877

Davis, Ashabel, b. 1791. Antiquities of

America, the first inhabitants of Central America, and the discovery of New England by the Northmen, five hundred years before Columbus. Lectures delivered in New York, Washington, Boston, and other cities. The first has been given eighteen times in the most dintinguished institutions of New York and Brooklyn, the first year. By A. Davis. Boston, MA: s. l., 1840. 21 p. No Loc. 40-1878

Davis, Ashabel, b. 1791. Antiquities of America, the first inhabitants of Central America, and the discovery of New England by the Northmen, five hundred years before Columbus. Lectures delivered in New York, Washington, Boston, and other cities. The first has been given eighteen times in the most dintinguished institutions of New York and Brooklyn, the first year. By A. Davis. 21st edition, with important additions. Buffalo, NY: Jewett, Thomas & Co., 1840. 32 p. MdHi. 40-1879

Davis, Ashabel, b. 1791. Lecture on the antiquities of central America and on the discovery of New England by the Northmen, delivered in [several] cities. 6th edition, with aditions. New York; Boston, MA: Bartlett and company; Dutton & Wentworth, 1840. 23 p. FSa; MnHi; MWA; NN; PHi. 40-1880

Davis, Ashabel, b. 1791. A lecture on the discovery of America by the Northmen, five hundred years before Columbus, delivered in New York, New Haven, Philadelphia, Baltimore, Washington, and other cities. Also some of the first literary institutions of the Union. By A. Davis. Fifth edition, with improvements. New York; Boston, MA:

Bartlett and company, 1840. 23 p. IC; MH; MWA; NN; OO; PHi. 40-1881

Davis, David Daniel, 1777-1841. ... Acute hydrocephalus, or water in the head, as inflammatory disease, and curable equally by the same means with other diseases of inflammation. By David D. Davis... Philadelphia, PA: Printed by Adam Waldie, 1840. 126 p. CtY; ICU; PPA; NcD; RPM; ScU. 40-1882

Davis, Emerson, 1798-1866. The mind and its developments; a lecture delivered before the American Institute of Instruction, at its annual session, held in Springfield, Aug., 1839. Boston, MA:Marsh, Capen, Lyon and Webb, 1840. MBAt; MH; MWiU. 40-1883

Davis, Emerson, 1798-1866. The teacher taught; or, The principles and modes of teaching... Boston, MA: March, Capen, Lyon and Webb, 1840. 79 p. DLC; MB; PU; RPB. 40-1884

Davis, George Thomas, 1810-1871. Reply of Mr. Davis, of Massachusetts, to the charge of misrepresenting Mr. Buchanan's argument in favor of the hard money system, and the consequent reduction of wages. Delivered in the Senate of the United States, March 6, 1840. Washington, DC: Government Printing Office, 1840. 8 p. CtY; DLC; IU; MWA; RPB. 40-1885

Davis, Gustavus Fellows. A familiar dialogue between Peter and Benjamin on the subject of close communion. Philadelphia, PA: Lippincott Press, 1840. 12 p. MNtCA; RPB. 40-1886

Davis, J. Memoir of the Rev. Christmas Evans, a minister of the Gospel, in the principality of Wales. By J. Davis. Mount Pleasant, PA: J. Davis and Siegfried, 1840. 719 p. CBB; KyLoS; NNUT; ODaB; PCA. 40-1887

Davis, James, commissioner. Report of Doctor James Davis, Commissioner to ascertain the Southern Boundary of the Territory of Iowa. Made to Governor Lucas, January 15, 1839. Burlington, IA: Printed by J. H. M; Kenny, 1840. 27 p. IaCrM; NN. 40-1888

Davis, James M. An address, delivered in the Fifth Presbyterian Church... city of Pittsburgh. By Rev. James M. Davis. Pittsburgh, PA: printed by Alexander Jaynes, 1840. 17 p. MeBaT; NjR. 40-1889

Davis, John, 1787-1854. Reply of John Davis, of Massachusetts, to Mr. Buchanan, of Pennsylvania, on the reduction of wages and of the value of property. Delivered in the Senate of the United States, January 23, 1840. Rochester, NY: Shepard & Strong, 1840. 15 p. DLC; NRU. 40-1890

Davis, John, 1787-1854. Reply ... to Mr. Buchanan, of Pennsylvania, on the Reduction of Wages. Delivered in the Senate of the United States, January 23, 1840. Washington, DC: s. l., 1840. 12 p. ?Hi. 40-1891

Davis, John, 1797-1854. Reply to Buchanan on the reduction of wages and f the value of property, in the Senate of he U. S., Jan. 23, 1840. Washington, DC: rinted at the Madisonians office, 1840. 0 p. DLC; ICU; MHi; PPL; WHi. 40-892

Davis, John, 1787-1854. Reply of John

Davis, of Massachusetts, to Mr. Buchanan, of Pennsylvania, on the reduction of wages. Delivered in the Senate of the United States, January 23, 1840. Together with extracts from the speeches of Messrs. Buchanan, Walker, Benton, and Calhoun. Washington, DC: Madisonian Office, 1840. 24 p. IaHi. 40-1893

Davis, John, 1787-1854. Reply of Mr. Davis, of Massachusetts, to the charge of misrepresenting Mr. Buchanan's argument in favor of the hard-money system, and the consequent reduction of wages. Delivered in the Senate of the United States, March 6, 1840. Washington, DC: Printed by Gales and Seaton, 1840. 8 p. CtY; IU; MHi; MWA; RPB. 40-1894

Davis, John, 1787-1854. Reply... to Mr. Buchanan, of Pennsylvania, on the reduction of wages and of the value of property. Delivered in the Senate of the United States, January 23, 1840... Washington, DC: Printed at the Madisonian office, 1840. 30 p. DLC; PPL; TxU; WHi. 40-1895

Davis, John, 1787-1854. Speech of Mr. Davis on the independent treasury bill. In the House of Representatives, June 27, 1840. Washington, DC: GPO, 1840. 8 p. MdHi; MiD-B; MiU-C; TxU. 40-1896

Davis, John, 1787-1854. Speech of Mr. Davis of Massachusetts, on the sub-treasury bill. Delivered in the Senate of the United States, January 23, 1840. Washington, DC: Gales and Seaton, 1840. 16 p. CtY; IU; MdHi; MH; OClWHi. 40-1897

Davis, John, 1787-1854. Speech of Mr. Davis of Massachusetts on the Sub-treasury bill, in the Senate of the United States, January 23, 1840. Published by the Whiz Republican Association of Boston. Second ed. of 10, 000 copies [Imp.] Boston, MA: J. H. Eastburn, printer, 1840. 16 p. CSfCW; CSt; KHi. 40-1898

Davis, John, 1787-1854. Speech of Mr. Davis of Massachusetts on the Sub-treasury bill, in the Senate of the United States, January 23, 1840. 3d ed. Boston, MA: Published by the Whig Republication Association of Boston, 1840. 16 p. CtY. 40-1899

Davis, John, 1787-1854. Speech of Mr. Davis on the sub-treasury bill, in the Senate of the United States, January 23, 1840. 7th ed. Boston, MA: published by the Whig Republication Association of Boston [1840?] 16 p. MHi; WHi. 40-1900

Davis, John, 1787-1854. Sub-treasury bill. Reply of Mr. Davis, of Massachusetts, to Mr. Buchanan, of Pennsylvania, on the reduction of wages and of the value of property... Washington, DC: Printed by Gales and Seaton, 1840. 16 p. IaHi; MHi; MiD-B; NcD; WHi. 40-1901

Davis, John Francis, 1795-1890. The Chinese: a general description of the Empire of China and its inhabitants. By John Francis Davis, esq. New York: Harper & brothers, 1840. 2 v. C-S; InRch; MeB; NjN; ViR. 40-1902

Davis, John Wesley. Speech of Mr. Davis, of Indiana, on an appropriation for the Cumberland Road. In the House of Representatives, April 30, 1840. Washington, DC: s. l., 1840. 7 p. ICHi; MdHi; MH; MiU-C; MoSHi. 40-1903

Davis, Nathan Smith, 1817-1904. Prize dissertation on diseases of the spinal solumn... by Nathan S. Davis, M. D.... Albany, NY: Printed by J. Munsell, 1840. 64 p. MB; NNNAM. 40-1904

Davison, Gideon Miner, 1791?-1869. The traveller's guide through the middle and northern states and the provinces of Canada. By G. M. Davison. 8th ed. Saratoga Springs, NY; New York: G. M. Davison; S. S. & W. Woods, 1840. 395 p. CtY; MnHi; MWA; OCl; RBr. 40-1905

Davy, Isaac, 1782-1835. ... Rob Roy Macgregor; or, "Auld lang syne. "An opertic play in three acts. By I. Pocock. New York: S. French [etc., etc., 184-?] 60 p. CSt. 40-1906

Davy, John, 1763-1824. "Poor Tom Bowling." [Song. T.]" Boston, MA: Ditson [184-?] 5 p. MB. 40-1907

Davy, John, 1763-1824. "Poor Tom Bowling. "Written by Dibdin; arranged by John Davy. Boston, MA: Parker & Ditson [184-?] 2 p. ViU. 40-1908

Davy, John, 1790-1868. ... Researches, physiological and anatomical. By John Davy. Philadelphia, PA: A. Waldie, 1840. 436 p. ArU-M; CSt-L; ICU-R; PPA; ViRA. 40-1909

Davy, John, 1790-1868. Researches, physiological and anatomical. By John Davy. Philadelphia, PA: W. Waldie, publisher, 1840. 162 p. DLC; MBAt; MnU; PP; WU-M. 40-1910

Dawson, Moses. Sketches of the life of Martin Van Buren, President of the United States, by Moses Dawson... Cincinnati, OH: Published by J. W. Ely,

1840. 216 p. DLC; InHi; KyHi; MH; OClWHi. 40-1911

Dawson, Reuben. Address to the people of Kentucky, on the subject of emancipation. [Signed by Reuben Dawson, and four others.] [S. l.: n. p. 184-?] 12 p. MH. 40-1912

Day, George Edward, 1815-1905. A geneological register of the descendants in the male line of Robert Day, of Hartford, Conn... New Haven, CT: Printed by W. Storer, jun., 1840. 44 p. CtSoP; DLC; MBNEH; MH; MWA. 40-1913

Day, Jeremiah, 1773-1867. An introduction to algebra; being the first part of a course of mathematics. Adapted to the method of instruction in the American colleges. By Jeremiah Day, D. D., LL. D., president of Yale College. Thirty-eighth edition. New Haven, CT; New York: Durie and Peck; Keese & Co., 1840. 332 p. NbPorT; NIC; NjNbR. 40-1914

Day, Thomas, 1777-1855. A digest of the reported cases decided by the Supreme Court of Errors of the State of Connecticut from 1786 to 1838, inclusive, . With tables of the names of the cases and of the titles. Hartford, CT: Day, 1840. 507 p. CtY; DLC; NcD; PPB; PUL. 40-1915

Day's New York pocket almanac for 1841. New York: M. Day [1840] p. MWA. 40-1916

De Charms, Richard, 1796-1864. Reasons & principles for a Middle convention of the New Jerusalem in the United States. Philadelphia, PA: Brown,

Bickering & Guilbert, 1840. 72 p. MCNC; PBa. 40-1917

De Charms, Richard, 1796-1864. Sermons illustrating the doctrine of the Lord, and other fundamental doctrines of the New Jerusalem Church. By Richard De Charms... Philadelphia, PA: Brown, Bicking & Guilbert, 1840. 376 p. CtSoP; ICBB; NNUT; OkU; PBa. 40-1918

De Pauw University, Greencastle, Ind. Address delivered by Governor Wallace and President Simpson, at the Indiana Asbury University, September 16, 1840. Indianapolis, IN: Printed by W. Stacy, 1840. CSmH; DLC. 40-1919

De Pauw University, Greencastle, Ind. Second annual catalogue of the officers and students... Indianapolis, IN: s. l., 1840. 16 p. In; InGDU. 40-1920

De Tocqueville, Alexis. Report made to the Chamber of Deputies, on the abolition of slavery... Cambridge, MA: Cambridge Press, Metcalf, Torry and Ballou, 1840. 54 p. RP. 40-1921

De Veaux, Samuel, 1789-1852. Legend of the whirlpool. Buffalo, NY: press of Thomas & co., 1840. 24 p. CSmH; MH; NBuG; NN; PPL. 40-1922

Dean, Amos, 1803-1868. Eulogy on the life and character of the late Judge Jesse Buel... before the New York agricultural society... by Amos Dean, Esq... Albany, NY: Printed by Charles Van Benthuysen, 1840. 29 p. ICN; MBAt; NCH; NjR; PHi. 40-1923

Dean, Amos, 1803-1868. Manual of medical jurisprudence. By Amos Dean,

Esq... Albany, NY: Printed by J. Munsell, 1840. 58 p. Ct; CtY; DSG; NBMS; NNN. 40-1924

Dean, Paul. The instability of ministerial life. A discourse, delivered at Bulfinch Street, on taking leave of the Society, May 24, 1840. By Paul Dean. To which is appended Mr. Dean's letter and proceedings of the Society. Boston, MA: Samuel G. Simpkins, 1840. 23 p. DLC; ICMe; MiD-B; MMeT-Hi; MWA. 40-1925

Deapier, A. E. Report of the Debate on Baptism which was held at Bellville, Hendricks County, Ind., from 4th to 7th Sept., 1839, between John O. Kane of Crawfordsville, Ia., and W. Mangues, Editor of the Regular Baptist, taken down and engrossed by A. E. Drapier. Indianapolis, IN: s. l., 1840. 144 p. IN; NjR; WHi. 40-1926

Dearborn, Henry Alexander Scammell, 1783-1851. An address delivered before the Berkshire Agricultural Society at Pittsfield [Mass.] , October 8, 1840. [Pittsfield, MA] : Printed by P. Allen and son, 1840. 24 p. DLC; MB; MHi; NN. 40-1927

Dearborn, Henry Alexander Scammell, 1783-1851. Digest of the militia laws of the United States and Massachusetts, May, 1840. Boston, MA: Dutton and Westworth, State printers, 1840. 48 p. MBVAFCC. 40-1928

Dearborn, Henry Alexander Scammell, 1783-1851. Militia laws of the United States and of the commonwealth. Boston, MA: s. l., 1840. 119 p. No Loc. 40-1929

Dearborn, Nathaniel, 1786-1852. The chess player. Illustrated with engravings and diagrams. Containing Franklin's essay on the morals of chess; Introduction to the rudiments of chess, by George Walker, teacher. To which are added the three games played at one and the same time by Philidor, sixty openings, mates and situations, by W. S. Kenney, teacher. With remarks, anecdotes, etc., etc., and an explanation of the round chess board. Boston, MA; New York: N. Dearborn; W. A. Colman [etc., etc.] 1840. 155 p. CtY. 40-1930

Dearborn, Nathaniel, 1786-1852. New map of Massachusettts. Compiled from the latest and best authorities and corrected by permission from the survey ordered in 1830. Carefully revised and additions made in 1839. 3d edition. Boston, MA: s. l., 1840. MB. 40-1931

Dearborn, Nathaniel. New map of the vicinity of Boston, with the dates of settlement, population in 1840 and distance from the capital. From the latest and most approved authorities, [by] Nathaniel Dearborn... [Boston, MA: s. l., 1840] p. NNUT. 40-1932

Dearborn, William L. A report of the survey of a rail road route from Portland to Lake Champlain, which is included within the State of Maine. By William L. Dearborn, Civil Engineer. Augusta, ME: Wm. R. Smith & Co., printers to the State, 1840. 42 p. ICJ; ICN; MeHi; MeU; MH. 40-1933

Dearle, Edward. O ask me not to sing tonight. [Song. With accomp. for piano forte] Boston, MA: Bradlee [184-?] 2 p. MB. 40-1934

The Death of Christ; a Tract for Good Friday, Protestant Episcopal Church Tracts. New York: s. l., 1840. EG. 40-1935

Deavernog, Jean Baptiste. Fifteen studies for the piano. Boston, MA: Ditson [184-?] p. No Loc. 40-1936

Debate on the claim of the Catholics to a portion of the common school fund... 2d ed. New York: pub. by the proprietor of the N. Y. Freeman's Journal, 1840. MiDU. 40-1937

Dedham, Massachusetts. First Church. ... Sermons by the pastors of the first church in Dedham, in XVIIth and XVIIIth centuries; with a centennial discourse by the present pastor... Ebenezer Burgess. Boston, MA: Published by Perkins & Marvin, 1840. 517 p. ICN; MH-AH; MWA; Nh-Hi; WHi. 40-1938

The dedication of the abolitionists refuted in a letter from J. W. Tyson the Harrison candidate. Philadelphia, PA: s. l., 1840. PPL. 40-1939

Deems, Charles Force, 1820-1893. The triumph of peace, and other poems... New York: published by D. Fanshaw, 1840. 96 p. GEU; MH; NcD; NNC; PHi. 40-1940

Deer Island and the city institutions [by . H. W.] from the Daily evening traveler. Boston, MA: s. l., 184-?] 8 p. MH. 40-1941

A defence of some important doctrines the gospel. In twenty-six sermons; eached at the Lime-street lecture. By veral eminent ministers. Philadelphia, A: Presbyterian board of publication,

William S. Martien, publishing agent, 1840. 476 p. CtY-D; GDecCT; IU; ScCOT; ViRUt. 40-1942

Defence of the N. J. dissent; being a brief answer to a pamphlet recently published by the family of the late Noah Webster. [S. l.: n. p., 184-?] p. DLC; MB; MH. 40-1943

Defoe, Daniel, 1661-1731. The life and adventures of Robinson Crusoe... Philadelphia, PA: W. A. Leary & Co. [1840?] 2 v. in 1. CtY. 40-1944

Degrand, Peter Paul Francis, d. 1855. An address on the advantages of low fares & low rates of freight... by a meeting of gentlemen friendly to internal improvements held in Boston, Dec. 3, 1840. Boston, MA: Dutton & Wentworth, printers, 1840. 39 p. CSmH; ICJ; MH-BA; NN; PPL. 40-1945

Degrand, Peter Paul Francis, d. 1855. Extracts on low fares on railroads. [Boston, MA: s. l., 1840] p. MBAt. 40-1946

Degrand, Peter Paul Francis, d. 1855. To the people of Massachusetts and to the friends of railroads throughout the union, extracts on low fares on railroads. Boston, MA: s. l., 1840. 39 p. MB; NNC. 40-1947

Delaware Academy, Delhi, N. Y. Catalogue, 1840. Delhi, NY: Anth. M. Paine, printer, 1840. v. CSmH. 40-1948

Delaware and Raritan canal company. Report of the Joint board of directors to the stockholders of the Delaware and Raritan canal, and Camden and Amboy rail road and transportation companies, on the completion of their works; with the proceedings of the stockholders at their meeting on the 29th of January, 1840. Princeton, NJ: Robert E. Horner, printer, 1840. 35, 12 p. CSmH; DLC; ICU; MH-BH; Nj; NN; PPL; WU. 40-1949

Delaware Vigilant Society. Constitution of the Delaware Vigilant society. New York: printed by William Worts, 1840. 11 p. NjR. 40-1950

Dell, William. The doctrine of Baptisms, reduced, from its ancient and modern corruptions; and restored to its primitive soundness and integrity... First pr. 1652. Philadelphia, PA: Richards, 1840. PPPrHi; PSC-Hi. 40-1951

Dellet, James. Remarks of Mr. Dellet, of Alabama, on the civil and diplomatic appropriation bill. Delivered in the committee of the whole, in the House of Representatives, April 25 and 27, 1840. Washington, DC: Gales & Seaton, 1840. 31 p. A-Ar; CtY; GEU; NjR; ViU. 40-1952

Democratic Association, Washington, D. C. Address of the Democratic Association of the District of Columbia to the people of the United States. [Washington, DC: s. l., 1840] 16 p. DLC. 40-1953

Democratic Association, Washington, D. C. Circular, Washington, Sept. 23, 1840. [Washington, DC: s. l., 1840] p. ViU. 40-1954

Democratic medley. Election returns in Phila., and a list of the officers of the general government, with their salaries. Philadelphia, PA: s. l., 1840. PPL. 40-1955

Democratic Party. Arkansas. Pulaski Co. Address of the Democratic citizens of the county of Pulaski, to the people of Arkansas. Adopted May 5, 1840. Little Rock, AR: Printed by E. Cole, 1840. 16 p. TxU. 40-1956

Democratic Party. Illinois. Address of the democratic republican citizens of the State of Illinois, assembled at Springfield, June 4, 1840, to the people of Illinois. [Springfield, IL: Walters & Weber, 1840] 8 p. MH. 40-1957

Democratic Party. Masschusetts. Proceedings of the democratic legislative concerns, held in Boston, March, 1840. [Boston, MA: Beales & Greene, 1840] 16 p. CtY; MBevHi; MH; NIC. 40-1958

Democratic Party. Masschusetts. 4th Congressional District, 1840. A circular to each democratic voter in the town. District No. 4. [S. l.: n. p., 1840] 15 p. MiU-C. 40-1959

Democratic Party. National Party. Baltimore, 1840. Proceeding of the National Democratic convention, held in the city of Baltimore, on the 5th of May, 1840. Embracing resolutions, expressive of the sentiments of the Democratic party of the union; and an address, in support of the principles and measures of the present national administration. Baltimore, MD: Printed at the office of the Republican, 1840. 24 p. DLC; MdHi; PU; TMeC; TxDaM. 40-1960

Democratic Party. New York. Lewis County. To the democratic electors of the county of Lewis, who, with the undersigned supported the election of Gen Jackson and Martin Van Buren. [Lowville, NY: s. l., 1840] 14 p. NNC. 40-196?

Democratic Party. New York. New York (City). General Committee of Young Men. Address of the Democratic Republican young men's committee of the city of New York to the Republican young men of the state. [New York: printed by J. W. Bell, 1840] 8 p. DLC; N. 40-1962

Democratic Party. Ohio. Convention, 1840. Proceedings of the Democratic state convention, held in Columbus on the eighth of January, 1840; with an address to the people of Ohio. Columbus, OH: S. & M. H. Medary, 1840. 16 p. CtY; MiD-B; OCHP; OClWHi. 40-1963

Democratic Party. Tennessee. Central Corresponding Committee. Address to the republican people of Tennessee, by the Central corresponding committee of the state. [No. 1] Nashville, TN: Printed for the Committee, 1840. 24 p. DLC; T; WHi. 40-1964

Democratic Party. Tennessee. Central Corresponding Committee. Address to the republican people of Tennessee, by the Central corresponding committee of the state. [No. 2] Nashville, TN: Printed for the Committee, 1840. 40 p. DLC; TxU; WHi. 40-1965

Democratic Party. Tennessee. State Convention. Voice of the Southwest. Proceedings of the Democratic State Convention of Tennessee at Nashville, February 11, 1840. Nashville, TN: Union Press, 1840. 12 p. MoSM; NN; T. 40-1966

Democratic Party. Virginia. Convention. Proceedings of the Democratic state convention held at Charlottesville, Va., Sept. 9-10, 1840. [Charlottesville,

VA?: s. l., 1840?] 29 p. CSmH; DLC; ICU; PPL; Vl. 40-1967

Democratic Party. Virginia. Convention, Richmond, 1840. Proceedings of the Democratic Republican convention held at Richmond, Feb. 20, 1840. [Portsmouth, VA: Old Dominion office, 1840] 16 p. NcD; Vi; ViU. 40-1968

Democratic Party. Virginia. Electoral ticket. For president, Martin Van Buren. 23 District. [Richmond, VA: s. l., 1840?] p. ViU. 40-1969

The Democrat's Almanac and People's Register for 1840... New York: pub. at the office of the Evening Post, 1840. 72 p. CoCsC; MBaHi; Tx; WHi. 40-1970

The Democrat's Almanac and People's Register for 1841. Boston, MA: s. l. [1840] p. MAtt; MB; MH; MnHi; MWA. 40-1971

The Democrat's Almanac and People's Register for 1841. 2d ed. Boston, MA: E. Littlefield, n. pr. [1840] 36 p. CoCsC; InH; NjR; WHi. 40-1972

Demosthenes. The orations of Demosthenes. Translated by Thomas Leland, D. D. In two volumes. New York: Published by Harper & Brothers, 1840. 282 p. GAuY; KMK; MH; NNebg; OrU; OZaN. 40-1973

Dempster, William Richardson, 1809-1871. I cosma lo'l lives less! Ballad. Written by Catherine H. Watermass. The music composed by Wm. R. Dempster. Philadelphia, PA: s. l., 184?. 7 p. NN. 40-1974

Dempster, William Richardson, 1809-

1871. I have left my native mountains. Ballad. Composed & arranged for the piano forte by Wm. R. Dempster. New York: James L. Hewitt & Co. [184-?] 3 p. ViU. 40-1975

Dempster, William Richardson, 1809-1871. The May queen. Cantata in three parts. [Solo voice. With piano accompaniment] Poetry by Alfred Tennyson. Music composed... by William Dempster. Boston, MA: Ditson [184-?] 3 pts. in 1 v. NRU-Mus. 40-1976

Denison, Charles Wheeler, 1809-1881. Christ of no reputation. A sermon, preached at the public recognition of the West Baptist church, Providence, R.I., in the meeting-house of the Roger Williams church, on Thursday, October 1, 1840, by Charles W. Denison... Providence, RI: Knowles & Vose, printers, 1840. 24 p. CSmH; DLC; RPB. 40-1977

Denkwurdige Ereignisse im Leben des Andreas Bernardus Smolnikar. B. III. New York: s. l., 1840. 856 p. NjPT. 40-1978

Dennery, Adolphe Philippe, 1811-1899. ... Ernestine. A drama in two acts. From the French of MM. Dennery and Clement. Tr. and adapted by William Robertson... New York: S. French [184-?] 27 p. CSt; DLC; ICU. 40-1979

Dennis, Rodney Gove. Christ seen by every eye, and a paster's farewell address to his people. Two sermons, preached to the Congregational church and society, in Somers, June 30, 1839. By Rodney Gove Dennis. Hartford, CT: Printed by Elihu Geer, 1840. 23 p. Ct; CtSoP; MBC; ViU. 40-1980

DePinna, Jochua. What fairy like music. A gondola duett. [S. and T. Accompaniment] arranged for the guitar by Adolph Schmitz. Philadelphia, PA: Fiot [184-?] 2 p. MB; ViU. 40-1981

DePinna, Jochua. What fairy like music. A gondola, song or duet. The poetry by Mrs. B. Wilson. Composed and arranged by J. De Pinna. Boston, MA: Oliver Diston [184-?] 3 p. ViU. 40-1982

DePinna, Jochua. What fairy like music. A gondola, song or duet. Words by Mrs. C. B. Wilson. Music by J. De Pinna. New York: Firth & Hall [184-?] 3 p. MB; ViU. 40-1983

Derby, John Barton, 1793?-1867. The sea. By J. B. Derby. Boston, MA: n. pub.; printed for the author by Kidder & Wright, 1840. 16 p. CtY; NjR; RPB. 40-1984

Detmold, William, 1808-1894. An essay on club foot and some analogous diseases, by W. Detmold, M. D. From the New York journal of medicine and surgery... New York: George Adlard, 1840. 64 p. LNT-M; MdBM; NjD; NjP; OClW; RPM. 40-1985

Devanant, William, Sir, 1606-1668. My lodging is on the cold ground. The celebrated song in the "Rivals. "Composed by Sir William Davenant. Boston, MA: Oliver Ditson [184-?] 2 p. ViU. 40-1986

Development of Protestantism. Cincinnati, OH: s. l. [184-?] 70 p. MB. 40-198?

Devereaux, Leonardo. The Maltese boatman's song. For one, two, or three voices. [With accompaniment for the piano forte] New York: Dubois & Stodart [184-?] 4 p. MB. 40-1988

Devereaux, Leonardo. The Maltese boatman's song. [Song and chorus] Philadelphia, PA: Willig [184-?] 4 p. MB. 40-1989

Devereaux, Leonardo. The Swiss herdsman. Sung by Madame Vestris. Composed and arranged by L. Devereaux. [Words by Charles Jeffreys. With accompaniment for the piano forte] New York: Mesier [184-?] 4 p. MB. 40-1990

Devereaux, Leonardo. The wings of a dove. As sung with great applause by Mrs. Wood. Written by Charles Jeffreys. Arranged by L. Devereaux. New York: Firth & Hall [184-?] 2 p. ViU. 40-1991

Dew, Thomas Roderick, 1802-1846. The great question of the day. Letter from President Thomas R. Dew of William and Mary College, Virginia, to a representative in Congress from that State on the subject of the financial policy of the administration and the laws of credit and trade. Originally published in the Madisonian. Washington, DC: T. Allen, 1840. 16 p. MWA; NcD; PPAmP; TxU; WHi. 40-1992

Dewees, William Potts, 1768-1841. A treatise on the diseases of females. By William P. Dewees... 7th ed., rev. and corr. Philadelphia, PA: Lea & Blanchard, 1840. 591 p. CtY; MdUM; NbU-M; TNV; ViU. 40-1993

Dewey, Orville, 1794-1882. Discourses and discussions in explanation and defense on unitarianism. By Orville Dewey, pastor of the Church of the Mes-

siah, in New Yrok. Boston, MA: published by Joseph Dowe, 1840. 307 p. CBPac; ICMe; MeB; MPiB; OO. 40-1994

Dewey, William. Plot of the city of Richmond, Wayne County, Indiana. Drawn from the original surveys. Cincinnati, OH: Klauprech & Menzel, 1840. In. 40-1995

DeWitt, William Radcliffe, 1792-1867. Profanity and intemperance, prevailing evils. Harrisburg, PA: s. l., 1840. 14 p. CtY; MBC; Mh-AH; PPPrHi. 40-1996

Dexter, Henry Stanley. Communication of the Canal Commissioners transmitting a communication of H. S. Dexter. Albany, NY: s. l., 1840. 24 p. NN. 40-1997

Dexter, Henry Stanley. Observations on calcareous mortars and cements, by H. S. Dexter, civil engineer. Albany, NY: Printed by Thurlow Weed, printer to the state, 1840. 24 p. CSmH; DLC; NNE. 40-1998

The Dial, a magazine for literature, philosophy, and religion. July, 1840-April, 1844. Boston, MA; London: Weeks, Jordan and Company; Wiley and Putnam, 1840-44. 4 v. Ct; IaSc; LNH; MB; NjR. 40-1999

The Diamond. no. 1-12, May, 1840-March, 1841; 2d ser., no. 1-12, April, 1841-April, 1842. New York: G. Vale, 1840-42. 2 v. CtHWatk; DLC; ICN; LNH. 40-2000

Dick, Thomas, 1774-1857. The Christian philosopher; or, the connectin of science and philosophy with religion.

Philadelphia, PA: Biddle, 1840. 350 p. OO. 40-2001

Dick, Thomas, 1774-1857. Dick's Works. Philadelphia, PA: Biddle, 1840. 7 v. KyU; NWM; OCX. 40-2002

Dick, Thomas, 1774-1857. An essay on the sin and the evils of covetousness; and the happy effects which would flow from a spirit of christian beneficence. Illustrated by a variety of facts, selected from sacred & civil history & other documents. Philadelphia, PA: Edward C. Biddle, 1840. 304 p. NcD. 40-2003

Dick, Thomas, 1774-1857. On the improvement of society by the diffusion of knowledge; or, An illustration of the advantages which would result from a more general dissemination of rational and scientific information among all ranks. By Thomas Dick... [Harper's stereotype ed.] New York: Harper & Brothers, 1840. 442 p. DLC; ICMe; MeB; MiD. 40-2004

Dick, Thomas, 1774-1857. On the mental illumination and moral improvement of mankind; or, An inquiry into the means by which a general diffusion of knowledge and moral principal may be promoted. Illustrated with engravings. By Thomas Dick, LL. D. Philadelphia, PA: Edward C. Biddle, 1840. 422 p. KyU. 40-2005

Dick, Thomas, 1774-1857. The practical astronomer. By Thomas Dick. New York: Harper & Bros., 1840. 437 p. NGH. 40-2006

Dick, Thomas, 1774-1857. The sidereal heavens and other subjects connnected with astronomy, as illustrative of the character of the Deity and of an infinity of words... By Thomas Dick... New York: Harper & Brothers, 1840. 432 p. CtY; MB; MeAu; NbOM; RJa. 40-2007

Dick, Thomas, 1774-1857. The works of Thomas Dick, LL. D. Four volumes in one. Viz: An essay on the improvement of society. The philosophy of a future state. The philosophy of religion. The christian philosopher, or, the connection of science and philosophy with religion. Hartford, CT: Sumner and Goodman, 1840. 668 p. NcRP. 40-2008

Dickens, Charles, 1812-1870. The chimes; a goblin story of some bells that rang an old year out and a new year in. By Charles Dickens, esq. S. l.: n. pub., 1840? 32 p. DLC. 40-2009

Dickens, Charles, 1812-1870. Dickens works: Old curiosity chop; Sketches by Boz; Hard times; A message from the sea; Master Murphy's clock; Miscellaneous. New York: Collier, 1840. NcDurC; NdDiT. 40-2010

Dickens, Charles, 1812-1870. The life and adventures of Martin Chuzzlewit. By Charles Dickens. New York: J. Winchester [184-?] 150 p. DLC; ViLC. 40-2011

Dickens, Charles, 1812-1870. The old curiosity shop, by Charles Dickens. New York: Published by F. M. Lupton Publishing Co., 1840. 399 p. KAn; NcSo; WMau. 40-2012

Dickens, Charles, 1812-1870. The old curiosity shop, by Charles Dickens. Philadelphia, PA: T. B. Peterson & Bros., 1840. 630 p. NCenv; NTSJ; TxEagpM. 40-2013

Dickens, Charles, 1812-1870. The old curiosity shop, hard times, and the holly tree inn. By Charles Dickens. New York: Aldine book publishing co. [1840?] 832 p. LShD. 40-2014

Dickens, Charles, 1812-1870. The old curiosity shop. Hard times, and the holly tree in. By Charles Dickens. Illustrated by S. Green. New York: Frank F. Lowell and company, 1840. 832 p. LAlS; ViHop. 40-2015

Dickens, Charles, 1812-1870. The old curiosity shop. Hard times and the Holly Tree Inn. By Charles Dickens. New York: International Book Company, 1840. 832 p. No Loc. 40-2016

Dickens, Charles, 1812-1870. The old curiosity shop. By Charles Dickens, with illustrations. Boston, MA: DeWolfe, Fiske & Co., Publishers, 1840. 435 p. KyLoBTr. 40-2017

Dickens, Charles, 1812-1870. The old curiosity shop. By Charles Dickens. New York: A. L. Burt co., 1840. 295 p. No Loc. 40-2018

Dickens, Charles, 1812-1870. The old curiosity shop. Master Humphrey's Clock and Miscellanies. By Charles Dickens. New York: G. W. Carleton & Co., 1840. No Loc. 40-2019

Dickens, Charles, 1812-1870. The old curiosity shop. With illustrations. By Charles Dickens. New York: George Rutledge & sons, 1840. 435 p. OCStR. 40-2020

Dickens, Charles, 1812-1870. The old curiosity shop. By Charles Dickens. New York: Thomas Y. Crowell & Co., 1840. 463 p. NdDiT; WyU. 40-2021

Dickens, Charles, 1812-1870. The old curiosity shop. By Charles Dickens. Philadelphia, PA: Macrae, Smith Company, 1840. 618 p. WyU. 40-2022

Dickens, Charles, 1812-1870. Oliver Twist. By Charles Dickens. [Boz] ... Philadelphia, PA: Lea & Blanchard, 1840. 212 p. CtY; MH. 40-2023

Dickens, Charles, 1812-1870. The posthumous papers of the Pickwick club. By Charles Dickens. With illustriont by Crowquill [pseud.] 4th ed. New York: J. Van Amringe [etc.] 1840. 609 p. DLC; MB. 40-2024

Dickens, Charles, 1812-1870. Sketches, by Boz, illustrative of every-day life and every-day people. By the author of "The Pickwick papers," "Oliver Twist," and "Nicholas Nickleby." With twenty illustrations by George Cruikshank. New edition, complete. Philadelphia, PA: Lea & Blanchard, 184?. 268 p. CtY; DLC; GA; MBAt; MLei. 40-2025

Dickerson, A. C. A sermon on regeneration effected by the Spirit of God. Preached in the Presbyterian Church, Bowling Green, Ky., 8th March, 1840. By A. C. Dickerson. Bowling Green, KY: Macey, 1840. 15 p. NjPT; PPPrHi; TxU. 40-2026

Dickinson, Daniel Stevens. Remarks in the [New York] Senate, Jan. 11, 1840, upon resolutions to refer the governor's message. [Albany, NY: s. l., 1840] 8 p. MH. 40-2027

Dickinson College, Carlisle, Pa.

Catalogue of the officers and students of Dickinson College, Carlisle, Pa., 1840-41. Carlisle, PA: Collens, 1840. 24 p. MB; MdHi; MHi; NcD. 40-2028

Dickinson College, Carlisle, Pa. Catalogus Senatus Academici, et eorum, qui Munera et Officia Academica gesserunt quique alicujus gradus laurea donati sunt, in Collegio Dickinsoniensi... Carlisle, PA: s. l. [1840] 31 p. MH. 40-2029

Dickson, David, 1583-1663. The sum of saving knowledge: or a brief sum of Christian doctrine, contained in the holy scriptures, and held forth in the confessions of faith and catechisms of the Presbyterian Church. Philadelphia, [184-?] 36 p. GDecCT. 40-2030

Dickson, Samuel Henry, 1798-1872. Address read to the Temperance Society of Ashville, Buncombe County, North Carolina, July, 1839. By Professor Samuel Dickson. Greenville, TN: Published by the Society; printed at the office of the Greenville Mountaineer, 1840. 16 p. NN. 40-2031

A dictionary of select and popular quotations, which are in daily use; taken from the Latin, French, Greek, Spanish, and Italian languages; together with copious collection of law-maxims and law-terms. Translated into English with illustrations, historical and idiomatic. 6th American ed., cor., with additions. Philadelphia, PA: Grigg & Elliott, 1840. 312 p. MdBE; RPA. 40-2032

Diefenbach, Daniel. Der seig Jesu in einer erklarung uber das gottliche geheimniss der erlosung... New Berlin, PA: Gedruckt in der Evangelischen

Gemeinschaft, 1840. 360 p. P; PLERC-Hi; PLT; PPG. 40-2033

Dielman, Henry. The wrecker's daughter. A quick step. Arranged for the piano forte by H. Dielman. Baltimore, MD: Geo. Willig, Junr. [184-?] 2 p. ViU. 40-2034

Digges, Daniel C. Address delivered before the Philodemic Society of Georgetown College... at the annual commencement, held July 28th, 1840. By Daniel C. Digges. Georgetown: Charles C. Fulton, 1840. 12 p. MWH. 40-2035

Dillard, Ryland T. Funeral oration on the death of President Giddings; delivered by the Rev. Ryland T. Dillard, at the request of the treusteed of Georgetown College, in Georgetown, on the fifth day of January, 1840. Louisville, KY: printed at the office of the Baptist Banner, 1840. 16 p. KyLoS; MB; MH; RPB; ViRU. 40-2036

Dillaway, Charles Knapp, d. 1889. Roman antiquities and ancient mythology... By Charles K. Dillaway. 4th edition. Boston, MA: Gould, Kendall and Lincoln, 1840. 144 p. ICPNA; MB; NcGu. 40-2037

Dillingham, William S. United States' historical and statistical index... from the administration of Washington... to... 1840. New York: s. l., 1840. CtY; Mit-BA NjR. 40-2038

Dimond, William, fl. 1800-1830. The broken sword. New York: s. l. [1840] p. MB. 40-2039

Discipulus. Serious thoughts on the two tables of the law. By Discipulus. Boston

MA: s. l., 1840. 40 p. MBAt; MBC; MNtCA. 40-2040

A discourse at the opening of the chapel of the N. Y. orphan asylum, Bloomingdale, Nov. 19, 1839. New York: s. l., 1840. 20 p. MH-And. 40-2041

Discourse on the death of Rev. Thomas Jones. S. l.: s. l., 184-? 8 p. MW. 40-2042

Disneg, David Tierman. Argument in the matter of application by Randolph Coyle and John Delafield to enter as public land fractional section number 11. [S. l.: Donaldson & Armstrong, 184-?] p. MH; OClWHi. 40-2043

Disraeli, Isaac, 1766-1848. Clamities and quarrels of authors with some inquirires respecting their moral and literary characters... New York: Armstrong, 1840. 2 v. in 1. CU; IaFairP; MFmT; WA. 40-2044

Disraeli, Isaac, 1766-1848. The literary character; or, The history of men of genius drawn from their own feelings and confessions... Edited by Disraeli, son of the Right Hon. B. Disraeli. New York: A. C. Armstrong and son, 1840. 592 p. FU; IQ; PPD; PWbg; WA. 40-2045

District of Columbia. ... Memorial of the corporation of the City of Washington on the subject of the Smithsonian bequest, February 5, 1840... [Washington, DC: Blair and Rives, printers, 1840?] p. p. CU-B; IaU-L; MiD-B; TxU. 40-2046

District of Columbia. Citizens. The remonstrance of the citizens of the District of Columbia by their delegates in convention, to the people of the United States, and to the legislatures of the several states, against oppressions, manifold and grevious, suffered from the misrule of the now ruling majority in Congress. August, 1840. Washington, DC: National intelligencer office, 1840. 15 p. DLC; GEU; MdHi; OClWHi; WHi. 40-2047

Disturnell, John, 1801-1877. Europe with part of Asia and Africa. New York: s. l., 1840. MH. 40-2048

Disturnell, John, 1801-1877. Guide to the city of New York: containing an alphabetical list of streets, etc., accompanied by a new & correct map. New York: Tanner & Disturnell, 1840. 15 p. N; NN. 40-2049

Dix, Dorothea Lynde, 1802-1887. Conversations on common things. 8th ed. Boston, MA: s. l., 1840. CtHWatk; MB. 40-2050

Dix, John Adams, 1798-1879. Address before the democracy of Herkimer County, on the 4th July, 1840. [S. l.: n. p., 1840] 11 p. MH; NN; PPL. 40-2051

Doane, George Washington, 1799-1859. An appeal to parents for female education on Christian principles; with a prospectus of St. Mary's hall, Green Bank, Burlington, New Jersey. That our daughters may be as the polished corners of the temple. Fourth edition. Burlington: J. L. Powell, Missionary Press, 1840. 15 p. AU; DE; Md. 40-2052

Doane, George Washington, 1799-1859. Bishop Doane's farewell correspondence with the diocese of Maryland. Baltimore, MD: s. l., 1840. 8 p. DLC; NNG; OClWHi. 40-2053

Doane, George Washington, 1799-1859. A brief narrative. [Burlington, NJ] : s. l., 1840. 14 p. DLC; MH; NN. 40-2054

Doane, George Washington, 1799-1859. Episcopal address to the annual convention of the diocese of New Jersey, May 27, 1840. By the Rt. Rev. George Washington Doane, D. D., Bishop of the Diocese. Burlington, NJ: At the Missionary Press, 1840. 43 p. MdBD; MWA; NBuDD; NGH; PPL. 40-2055

Doane, George Washington, 1799-1859. The faith once delivered to the Saints. The sermon before the Northern Convocation of the Clergy of the Diocese of New Jersey... New Brunswick... Oct. 28, 1840. By the Rt. Rev. George W. Doane... Burlington, NJ: J. L. Powell, printer [1840] 28 p. CtHT; MWA; NjR; PHi; RPB. 40-2056

Doane, George Washington, 1799-1859. Isiah's prospect of the church; the sermon at the consecration of Rev. E. Gadsden, bishop of South Carolina, in Trinity Church, Boston, on the first Sunday of the Trinity. Burlington, NJ: J. L. Powell, 1840. 28 p. MH; NN; RPB. 40-2057

Doane, George Washington, 1799-1859. Pastoral letter, to the clergy and laity of the diocese of New Jersey, on the rights and duties of church wardens and vestrymen. [S. l.: s. l., 1840?] 8 p. DLC; NNG. 40-2058

Doddridge, Philip, 1702-1751. The rise and progress of religion in the soul illustrated in a course of serious and practical addresses suited to persons of every character and circumstance: with a devout medication, or prayer, subjoined to each chapter. By Philip Doddridge, D. D. New York: American tract society [184-?] 452 p. CSansS; IaU; MiD-B; TxD-T; ViU. 40-2059

Dods, John Bovee. Thirty short sermons on various important subjects both doctrinal and practical, by John Bovee Dods. Boston, MA: Thomas Whittemore, 1840. 348 p. MH; MMeT-Hi. 40-2060

Doehler, Theodore. Fantaisie brillante. Pour le piano, sur des motifs de l'opera "L'elisire d'amore" de Donizetti. Boston, MA: Ditson [184-?] 11 p. MB. 40-2061

Doehler, Theodore. Grand caprice. [Pour piano] Op. 37. [Boston, MA: s. l., 184-?] 27 p. MB. 40-2062

Doehler, Theodore. Valse brillante, pour le piano forte. Composee et dediee a Madame Cinti Damorean, par Th. Dohler. New York; Philadelphia, PA: W. Dubois; A. Fiot [184-?] 5 p. MB; ViU. 40-2063

Doggett, John, Jr. Doggett's New York business directory, for 1840/41-1846/47. [1st] -4th publications. New York: J. Doggett, jr. [1840-46] 4 v. CSmH. 40-2064

Dole, Benjamin. An address to the people of Massachusetts, on the subject of the license law of 1838, and its repeal. By Benjamin Dole. Second edition, enlarged. Boston, MA: Printed by Kidder & Wright, 1840. 72 p. CBPSR; MBAt; MBC; MWA; NN. 40-2065

Done, Joshua, d. 1848. "There's no smile like thine," a ballad, composed by

Joshua Done. Philadelphia, PA: A. Fiot [184-?] 5 p. ViU. 40-2066

Donizetti, Gaetano, 1797-1848. Anna Bolena... [Libretto, Ital. By F. Romani & Eng.] New York: s. l., 1840. 75 p. CtY. 40-2067

Donizetti, Gaetano, 1797-1848. Beauties from Donizetti's opera of Lucrezia Borgia. Arranged for the piano forte, by C. Czerny... New York: Firth & Hall184-?] 7 p. ViU. 40-2068

Donizetti, Gaetano, 1797-1848. Belisario... Baltimore, MD; New Orleans, LA: F. D. Benteen; W. T. Mayo [184-?] 9 p. ViU. 40-2069

Donizetti, Gaetano, 1797-1848. Bouquet de melodies. Ges from Donizetti's opera, Linda di chamounix. For the piano by Ferd. Beyer. Baltimore, MD; New Orleans, LA: F. D. Benteen; W. T. Mayo [184-?] 11 p. ViU. 40-2070

Donizetti, Gaetano, 1797-1848. ... The celebrated duett in the opera of Linda, as played by the Steyermarkische musical company. Composed and arranged for the piano forte by Donizetti. Boston, MA: G. P. Reed [184-?] 5 p. ViU. 40-2071

Donizetti, Gaetano, 1797-1848. ... Child of the Regiment. Boston, MA; New York; Montreal; Philadelphia, PA; Cincinnati, OH: Oliver Ditson & Co.; C. C. Clapp & Co.; S. T. Gordon; H. Prince; Beck & Lawton; Traux & Badlwin [184-?] 5 p. ViU. 40-2072

Donizetti, Gaetano, 1797-1848. [Coll. of songs and duets from some of the Donzetti operas.] Boston, MA; Paris: s. l., 184-?-185-?] 34 in 1. MB. 40-2073

Donizetti, Gaetano, 1797-1848. [Com' e bello, quale incanto.] Boston, MA: s. l. [184-?] p. MB. 40-2074

Donizetti, Gaetano, 1797-1848. Fatal Goffredo. Recitvo. E. Jo L'udia Ne suoi bei Carmi. Aria. In the opera of Tasso, as sung with unbounded applause by Madame Caradore Allan. Composed by Signor Donizetti. New York: James L. Hewitt & Co. [184-?] 11 p. ViU. 40-2075

Donizetti, Gaetano, 1797-1848. La favorita. The favorite. A lyrical drama in four acts. The music by Donizetti. New York: French [184-?] 52 p. MB. 40-2076

Donizetti, Gaetano, 1797-1848. La figlia del reggimento. [Conrien partir] Romanza per voce di sopriano. [Con accompagnamento di piano] de G. Donizetti. [Parole di Baynard e St. Georges] [Boston, MA: s. l., 184-?] 11 p. MB. 40-2077

Donizetti, Gaetano, 1797-1848. ... La fille du Regiment. Italian gems from Donizetti's oepras. Arranged for the piano forte by A. Le Carpentier. Philadelphia, PA: Klemm & Brother [184-?] 1, 5 p. ViU. 40-2078

Donizetti, Gaetano, 1797-1848. Il guiramento. The vow. Nocturne for two voices. [S. T. Accomp. for piano forte] From the Nuits d'ete a Pausilippe. Boston, MA: Reed & Co. [184-?] 5 p. MB. 40-2079

Donizetti, Gaetano, 1797-1848. I'll pray for three. "Spargi d' Amaro." The popular song in Lucia de Lammermoor. Composed by Donizetti. Boston, MA: Oliver Ditson [184-?] 9 p. ViU. 40-2080

Donizetti, Gaetano, 1797-1848. In questo simplice. Cavatina tivolese [S. or T. Accomp. for piano forte] del operetta giocosa Betly. Boston, MA: Ditson & Co. [184-?] 11 p. MB. 40-2081

Donizetti, Gaetano, 1797-1848. It is better to laugh than be sighing. Il Segretto, air from Donizetti's popular opera, Lucretia Borgia. Written and adapted by G. Linley. Baltimore, MD: F. D. Benteen [184-?] 5 p. ViU. 40-2082

Donizetti, Gaetano, 1797-1848. It is better to laugh than to be sighing. Music by G. Donizetti. Words by George Linley... New York: Chas. Mangus [1840?] p. NBuG. 40-2083

Donizetti, Gaetano, 1797-1848. Life has no power. New York: William A. Pond & Co. [184-?] 7 p. ViU. 40-2084

Donizetti, Gaetano, 1797-1848. ... List what I say. Baltimore, MD: Miller & Beacham, successors to F. D. Benteen [184-?] 7 p. ViU. 40-2085

Donizetti, Gaetano, 1797-1848. [Lucia di Lammermoor.] Oh for an eagle's pinions. [Perche non ho del vento. Cavatina for soprano in the opera Lucia de Lammermoor. [Music] by G. Donizetti. [Words by S. Cammarano. With accompaniment for piano forte.] Philadelphia, PA: Fiot [184-?] 9 p. MB. 40-2086

Donizetti, Gaetano, 1797-1848. Lucretia Borgia. Make me no fancy chaplet... Boston, MA: Reed [184-?] p. MB. 40-2087

Donizetti, Gaetano, 1797-1848. Make me no gaudy chaplet. The favorite Canzonetta in the opera Lucrezia Borgia. Composed by Donizetti. Arranged by W. H. Callcott. Baltimore, MD: George Willig, Jr. [184-?] 5 p. ViU. 40-2088

Donizetti, Gaetano, 1797-1848. Make me no gaudy chaplet. [Song from the opera Lucrezia Borgia. With accomp.] arranged for the guitar by John E. Gould. Boston, MA: Reed [184-?] 3 p. MB. 40-2089

Donizetti, Gaetano, 1797-1848. [Mariano Faliero] Thro' all the heaven. [On che in cielo] Barcarolle in the opera Mariano Faliero. [With accompaniment for piano forte] Composed by Donizetti. [The words by G. E. Bidera] Philadelphia, PA: Fiot [184-?] 2 p. MB. 40-2090

Donizetti, Gaetano, 1797-1848. Oh summer night. Com e Gentil. Serenade, in the Opera Don Pasquale. By Donizetti. Philadelphia, PA: A. Fiot [184-?] 5 p. ViU. 40-2091

Donizetti, Gaetano, 1797-1848. Polonaise favorite "O Luce di quest' anima. "Chantee par Mme. Persiani dans l'opera Linda di Chamounix de Donizetti. Arrangee pour le piano par Henri Herz. Baltimore, MD; New Orleans, LA: F. D. Benteen; W. T. Mayo [184-?] 9 p. ViU. 40-2092

Donizetti, Gaetano, 1797-1848. Rataplan. [Adapted by Charles W. Clover. Song. Accomp. for piano forte.] Boston, MA: s. l. [184-?] 5 p. MB. 40-2093

Donizetti, Gaetano, 1797-1848. ... Rataplan, rataplan. Op. 117... Boston,

MA: Miller & Beacham, wsuccessors to F. D. Benteen [184-?] 7 p. MB; ViU. 40-2094

Donizetti, Gaetano, 1797-1848. [Roberto Deveux. Cavatina nell opera Robert d'Evreux, del M. Donizetti. [A te diro. Con accompagnamento di piano. Parole di S. Cammarano.] New York: Bagioli [184-?] 2 p. MB. 40-2095

Donizetti, Gaetano, 1797-1848. ... Song of the drum... Boston, MA: Oliver Ditson [184-?] 5 p. ViU. 40-2096

Donizetti, Gaetano, 1797-1848. ... "Tho to other lands I wander." Aria... Composed by Signor Donizetti... New York: Firth & Hall; Firth, Hall & Pond [184-?] 7 p. ViU. 40-2097

Donnegan, James, fl. 1841. A new Greek and English lexicon; principally on the plan of the Greek and German lexicon of Schneider. The words alphabetically arranged... By James Donnegan, M. D. First American, from the second London edition... Boston, MA; New York: Published by Hilliard, Gray & co.; G. & C. Carvill & co., 1840. 1413 p. ArSeH; NN; ODaB; OrUM; ViU. 40-2098

Dorcas Benevolent Society of West Baltimore Station. Constitution and by-laws of the Dorcas benevolent society of W. Baltimore station, M. E. church. Baltimore, MD: Printed by Richard J. Matchett, 1840. 3 p. MdHi. 40-2099

Dorchester, Mass. The Auditor's second Printed Report of the Receipts and Expenditures of the Town of Dorchester... from March 21, 1839 to March 21, 1840... Boston, MA: Albert Morgan, printer, 1840. 23 p. MH. 40-2100

Dorchester, Mass. Annual report of the finances of the town. Boston, MA: s. l., 1840- p. PPAmP. 40-2101

Dorchester, Mass. Regulations of the school committee. Boston, MA: s. l., 1840-58. p. MB; PPAmP. 40-2102

Dorchester, Mass. Third Church. Order of exercises at the dedication of the church erected by the Third Religious Society in Dorcester, October 28th, 1840. Boston, MA: S. N. Dickinson, printer, 1840. MHi. 40-2103

Dorigo, Felice. A chi d'amor sospira. Canzonetta. The poetry by A. G. Music composed & arranged for the piano or harp... by Felice Dorigo. Phildelphia, PA: Fiot, Meignen & Co. [184-?] 3 p. MB. 40-2104

Dorr, Benjamin, 1796-1869. The recognition of friends in another world. By the Rev. Benjamin Dorr, D. D., Rector of Church. Third edition. Philadelphia, PA: R. S. H. George, 1840. 96 p. MB; NN; ScCoT. 40-2105

Doty, James D. vs. Stevens T. Mason and others, in relation to the title to the Town of Madison. In Chancery. Bill and answer. Madison: s. l., 1840. 16 p. MBAt; WHi. 40-2106

Doty, James Duane, 1799-1865. To the people of Wiskinsin. [Washington, DC: n. pr., 1840] 14 p. MiU-C. 40-2107

Douglass, L. F. Map exhibiting the relative situation of Jersey City Harsimus,

Pavonia and Hoboken. Jersey City: s. l., 1840. 1 p. PHi. 40-2108

Dove, John, fl. 1830. A biographical history of the Wesley family, more particularly its earlier branches. Hamilton, OH: Adams, 1840. 299 p. MdBP; NNG; PPL; TxHuT. 40-2109

Dowling, John, 1807-1878. An expositon of the prophecies supposed by William Miller to predict the second coming of Christ in 1843. With a supplementary chapter upon the true Scriptural doctrine of a millennium prior to the judgment. Providence, RI: G. P. Daniels, 1840. 232 p. CtHT-W; CtY; MB; MBBCHS; MH; MH-AH; MHi; MnU; MnSS; MWA; NRAB; NsSalL; PCC; RLa; RP. 40-2110

Downing, Charles, fl. 1839. Address of Charles Downing, of Florida, to his constituents. Washington, DC: Printed at the Madisonian office, 1840. CSmH. 40-2111

Drake, Benjamin, 1794-1841. The life & adventures of Black Hawk, with sketches of Keokuk, the Sac & Fox Indians & the late Black Hawk War. 6th edition, improved. Cincinnati, OH: G. Conclin, 1840. 288 p. MeB; NjP. 40-2112

Drake, Daniel. An introductory discourse to a course of lectures on clinical medicine and pathological anatomy; delivered at the opening of the new Clinical Ampithestre of the Louisville Marine Hospital, November 5th, 1840. Louisville, KY: Printed by Prentice and Weissinger, 1840. 16 p. IEN-M; MBAt; OCGHM; TxU. 40-2113

Drake, J. G. Pensez a moi. A favorite song, composed & arranged for the piano forte. By Mr. Drake. Boston, MA: C. Bradlee [184-?] 2 p. ViU. 40-2114

Drake, James G. Away! away we bound o'er the deep. Song. The words and air by Mr. Drake. The symphonies & accompaniments by T. V. Wiesenthal. Baltimore, MD: George Willig, Jr. [184-?] 2 p. ViU. 40-2115

The dream. [Song] Adapted to the Swedish melody by Karl Muller. Boston, MA: Reed [184-?] p. MB. 40-2116

Dressler, Raphael. 12 recreations; or, Popular airs for piano and flute... Boston, MA: O. Ditson [184-?] p. NN. 40-2117

Dreyschoek, Alexander, 1818-1869. La campanella, impromptu pour la piano forte... Boston, MA: E. H. Wade [184-?-1850?] p. NN. 40-2118

Drinkard, William M. Oratin on the life & character of Patrick Henry, before the Patrick Henry Society of William & Mary College, by Wm. M. Drinkard of Petersburg, on May 29, 1840. Richmond, VA: printed by P. D. Barnard, 1840. 16 p. DLC; PPL; ViU. 40-2119

Dromgoole, George C. Speech of Mr. [George] Dromgoole, of Virginia, on the New Jersey disputed election in reply to Mr. Sergeant, of Pennsylvania. Delivered in the House of Representatives December 14, 1839. Washington, DC: Printed at the Globe Office, 1840. 13 p. MdHi; NcU; PU; Vi. 40-2120

A drop of hard cider on the Tippecanoe roarer. New York: s. l. [184-?] p. MWA. 40-2121

The drunkard's funeral sermon; the substance of an address before an annual union temperance meeting. By a clergyman of Massachusetts. Woburn: s. l., 1840. 47 p. M; MH; NcD; Nh. 40-2122

Ducanga, Victor Henri Joseph Brahain, 1783-1833. ... Therese, the orphan of Geneva. A drama, in three acts. Tr. from the French, altered and adapted to the English state, by John Howard Payne... As performed at the New York theatres. New York: S. French & son [etc., etc.], 184-? 33 p. CSt. 40-2123

Dumanoir, Philippe Francois Pine, 1806-1865. Don Caesar de Bazan; a drama in three acts. New York: W. Taylor & co. [184-?] 47 p. CSt; MH. 40-2124

Dun, Finlay. I have come from a happy land. Arranged as a duet by Finlay Dun. Boston, MA: published by Oliver Ditson, 1840. 4 p. KU. 40-2125

Dunbar, George T. Rapport of Mr. Geo. T. Dunbar, ingenious de L' etat de la Louisiane, adresse a Mr. Felix Garola, president de la Compagnie de dessechement de la Nouvelle - Orleans sur le dessechement des Terres Bosses au dela de la Rue Claiborne, et un Memoire sur le meme siyet, adresse au Conseil de la Municipalile No. Un. par Charles Lesseps... New Orleans, LA: Brusle & Lesseps, Mars., 1840. 20 p. AU; LU. 40-2126

Dunbar, John Richard Woodcock, 1805-1871. Circulars. Private medical Institute of Baltimore. Baltimore, MD: s. l., 1840. 10 p. PPCP. 40-2127

Duncan, Alexander, 1788-1852. Remarks of Mr. Duncan, of Ohio, on the

bill to continue in force the bank charters in the District of Columbia. Delivered in the House of Representatives, July 3, 1840. Washington, DC: Blair & Rives, 1840. 15 p. CSmH; CtY; NNC; VtBrt. 40-2128

Duncan, Alexander, 1788-1852. Speech of Mr. Duncan, of Ohio, on the bill to authorize the issue treasury notes. Delivered in the Committee of the Whole, House of Representatives, March 26, 1840. Washington, DC: Globe Office, 1840. 16 p. OClWHi; PHi. 40-2129

Duncan, Alexander, 1788-1852. Speech of Mr. Duncan, of Ohio, on the general appropriation bill for 1840. Delivered in the House of Representatives, April 10, 1840. New York: Printed at the Evening Post Office [1840] 24 p. DLC; IaHi; MoSHi. 40-2130

Duncan, Alexander, 1788-1852. Speech of Mr. Duncan, of Ohio, on the general appropriation bill for 1840. Delivered in the House of Representatives, April 10, 1840. New York: Printed at the New Era Office by Jared W. Bell [1840] 23 p. CoFcS; DLC; OClWHi; WHi. 40-2131

Duncan, Alexander, 1788-1852. Speech of Mr. Duncan, of Ohio, on the general appropriation bill for 1840. Delivered in the House of Representatives, April 10, 1840. Washington, DC: Printed at the Globe Office, 1840. 22 p. DLC; InHi; MeB; MWA; WHi. 40-2132

Duncan, Alexander, 1788-1852. Speech of Mr. Duncan, of Ohio, on the subject of the New Jersey election for members of the twenty-sixth Congress. Delivered in the House of Representatives, January 9,

1840. Washington, DC: s. l., 1840. 24 p. CtY; MdHi; MH; OCHP; PHi. 40-2133

Duncan, Alexander, 1788-1852. Speech... on the bill to authorize the issue of treasury notes. Delivered in the Committee of the Whole... House... March 26, 1840. Washington, DC: s. l., 1840. 22 p. MBAt; MdHi; MH; MiD-B. 40-2134

Duncan, James. A treatise on slavery, in which is shown forth the evil of slaveholding both from the light of nature and divine revelation. Vevay, Indiana Register Office. [2d ed.] New York: reprinted and publihsed by the American Anti-Slavery Society, 1840. 136 p. MH; OO. 40-2135

Dunham, Samuel Astley. History of Spain and Portugal. By Samuel Astley Dunyham. New York: Published by Harper & Bros., 1840. 5 v. CLSU; Me; MWH; NcU; NRU. 40-2136

Dunlap, William. A history of New York. For schools. By William Dunlap. New York: Harper & Brothers, 1840. 2 v. GAuY; NMam; P; RWoH. 40-2137

Dunlap, William. History of the New Netherlands, Province of New York, and State of New York, to the adoption of the Federal Constitution. New York: Carter & Thorp, 1840. 2 v. Ia; NGH; NjR; NNS; NSmB. 40-2138

Dunn, L. A. The scholar's guide. To a practical knowledge of sacred geography, upon the classification system, by L. A. Dunn & A. Webster. Sanbornton, NH: Printed by J. C. Wilson, 1840. 36 p. CSmH. 40-2139

Durell, Edward. Scenic beauties of the

island of Jersey, by Philip John Ouless, to which are added descriptive, topographical & historical explanations by Edward Durell. [S. l.: s. l., 1840] 56 p. MH. 40-2140

Durfee, Job, 1790-1847. "What cheer;" or, Roger Williams in banishment. A poem... With a recommendatory preface, by the Rev. John Eustace Giles, Leeds. Providence, RI: Leeds, 1840. 196 p. CtSoP; GHi; InCW; MH; TNP. 40-2141

Dusenberg, William C. St. Matthew's Hall for the education of young gentlemen... Belvidere: Printed by W. B. Brittain, 1840. MdBD; MH; NN. 40-2142

Duval, P. S. Map of the Railroad Routes to Phila. Philadelphia, PA: s. l., 184-? 1 p. PHi. 40-2143

Duvernoy, Jean Baptiste, 1802-1880. Duvernoy's exercises. Ecole du Mecanisme, 15 etudes pour le piano. Composees exprefsement pour preceder celles de la velocite De Czerny, par J. B. Duvernoy... [no. 1...] Baltimore, MD: F. D. Benteen [184-?] 11 p. ViU. 40-2144

Duvert, Felix Augustus, 1795-1876. Used up. New York: s. l. [184-?] 38 p. MB. 40-2145

Duveyrier, Anne Honore Joseph, Baron, 1797-1865. Secret Service. A Drama in Two Acts. From the French of Messrs. Melesville and Duveyrer, by J. R. New York: s. l. [184-?] 46 p. MH. 40-2146

Dwight, Elizabeth B. James and his mother; or, conversations on Constantinope. Boston, MA: s. l., 1840. 57 p. DLC; Nh-Hi. 40-2147

Dwight, Harrison Gary Otis. Memoir of Mrs. Elizabeth B. Dwight, including an account of the plague of 1837. By Rev. H. G. O. Dwight, missionary to Constantinople. With a sketch of the life of Mrs. Judith S. Grant, missionary to Persia. New York: M. W. Dodd, 1840. 323 p. CSmH; MBC; MiD; MWA; NbCrD. 40-2148

Dwight, Nathaniel, 1770-1831. The lives of the signers of the Declaration of Independence. By N. Dwight, esq. A new ed. New York: Harper & Brothers, 1840.

373 p. CoD; MDeeP; MWA; NBuG; PU. 40-2149

Dwight, Theodore, 1796-1866. The history of Connecticut, from the first settlement to the present time. By Theodore Dwight, jr. New York: Harper & brothers [1840] 450 p. CtB; IaU; MnU; NcU; PAnL. 40-2150

Dymond, Jonathan, 1796-1828. Oaths; their moral character, and effects, extracted from "Essay on the Principles of Morality," &c., by Jonathan Dymond. Philadelphia, PA: published by the Tract Association of Friends [184-?] 12 p. WHi. 40-2151

E

East, John. My Savior; or, devotional meditations, in prose and verse, on the names and titles of the Lord Jesus Christ. 3d ed. Boston, MA: Daw, 1840. In. 40-2152

The East Boston directory, containing the names, occupations, places of business & residences of the inhabitants, by George Adams. Boston, MA: Boston Directory Office, 184-? v. MH. 40-2153

East Tennesse University, Knoxville, Tenn. Catalog of the officers and students of East Tennessee University: 1840. Knoxville, TN: Jas. C. Moses & Co., 1840. 18 p. MBC; MdBD; T; TKL-Mc; TU. 40-2154

East Tennesse University, Knoxville, Tenn. A System of Punctuation. Prepared for the Students of East Tennessee University, April, 1840. [Knoxville, TN] : Jas. C. Moses & Co., 1840. 8 p. TU. 40-2155

Eastern Railroad Company. Report of the committee appointed at a meeting of the stockholders of the Eastern Railroad Co. to examine into the past doings and present condition of said company and to report at an adjourned meeting, to be held at Boston, May 21, 1839. Boston, MA: Dutton & Wentworth, 1840. 20 p. CSt; DLC; MBAt; MiU; PPi. 40-2156

Easton, Mass. Congregational Church of Christ. The confession of faith and covenant. Boston, MA: s. l., 1840. 8 p. MBC. 40-2157

Easy lessons for infant classes in Sunday Schools. Ed. 4, rev. & enl. Worcester: s. l., 1840. CtHT-W. 40-2158

Eaton, Amos, 1776-1842. North American botany; comprising the native and common cultivated plants, north of Mexico; genera arranged according to the articifial and natural methods. 8th ed., with the additions and the properties of plants, from Lindley's New medical flora. Troy, NY: Elias Gates, 1840. 625 p. CtY; NcD; PPAmP; RPB; WyU. 40-2159

Eaton, Amos, 1776-1842. North American botany, comprising the native & common cultivated plants North of Mexico: genera arranged according to the artificial & natural methods... by Amons Eaton & John Wright. Ed. 2, enl. Troy: Gates, 1840. 625 p. PU. 40-2160

Eaton, John Henry, 1790-1856. Memoirs of Andrew Jackson... Compiled by a citizen of Massachusetts. Philadelphia, PA: T. K. and P. G. Collins, printers, 1840. 334 p. KyOw; MoFayC. 40-2161

Eberle, John, 1787-1838. Notes of lectures on the theory and practice of medicine, delivered in the Jefferson medical college, at Philadelphia. 3d ed., cor. Philadelphia, PA: Grigg & Elliott,

1840. 248 p. CSt-L; ICU; KyLxT; NBMS; NjP. 40-2162

Economical cookery; designed to assist the housekeeper in retrenching her expenses, by the exclusion of spiritous liquors from the cookery. Newark, NJ: printed & published by Benjamin Olds, 1840. 144 p. NjP; NjR. 40-2163

Eddowes, John, bookseller. Catal. of old books on sale. Shrewsbury: s. l., 1840. 388 p. MB. 40-2164

Edgeworth, Maria, 1767-1849. The parent's assistant; or, stories for children... complete in one volume. A new edition. New York: Harper & Brothers, 1840. 455 p. NGlc. 40-2165

Edgeworth Ladies' Seminary. Catalogue of the officers and members of the Edgeworth Ladies' Seminary, for the year ending September, 1840. Also several particular to said Seminary. Pittsburgh, PA: Johnston & Stockton, 1840. 24 p. OClWHi; PPM. 40-2166

Edwards, Bela Bates, 1802-1852. Memoir of Rev. Elias Cornelius. 2nd ed. Boston, MA: Harper and bros., 1840. NjMD. 40-2167

Edwards, Bela Bates, 1802-1852. Fessenden & Co.'s encyclopedia, religious knowledge, or dictionary, the Bible. By Rev. B. B. Edwards. Brattleboro, VT: Published by the Brattleboro Typographic Company, 1840. 1280 p. KyPr; MeLew; ScCoB; TJaU. 40-2168

Edwards, George Cunningham, 1787-1837. A treatise on the powes and duties of justices of the peace and town officers, in the state of New York, under the revised statutes, with practical forms. By George C. Edwards. 4th ed., rev. and improved, by D. McMaster. Ithaca, NY: Mack, 1840. CtY; DLC; MH-L; OMC; WHi. 40-2169

Edwards, Jonathan, 1703-1758. Careful and strict inquiry into the modern prevailing notions of that freedom of the will, which is supposed to be essential to moral agency. Andover, MA: Gould, 1840. 2 v. MBGT. 40-2170

Edwards, Jonathan, 1703-1758. An inquiry into the modern prevailing nations respecting that freedom of will, which is supposed to be essential to moral agency, virtue and vice, rewards and punishment, praise and blame, by Jonathan Edwards, A. M. With an index. Andover, MA: Gould, Newman and Saxton, 1840. 432 p. CtMW; GAU; KWiU; LNB; MAnP; ViU. 40-2171

Edwards, Justin, 1787-1853. Permanent Sabbath documents. By the Rev. Justin Edwards, D. D. Philadelphia, PA: s. l. [184-?] 54 p. GDecCT. 40-2172

Edwards, Justin, 1787-1853. The family and the Sabbath, being Sabbath manual. New York: American Tract Society [184-?] 48 p. MH. 40-2173

Edwards, Justin, 1787-1853. The proper mode of keeping the Sabbath; being the fourth number of the Sabbath Manual. New York: American Tract Society [184-?] p. MH. 40-2174

Edwards, Justin, 1787-1853. The Sabbath manual. New York: American Tract Society [184-?] 131 p. CBPac. 40-2175

Ehrlich, S. The Francis waltz. For the

piano forte. Philadelphia, PA: Fiot, Mugnian & Co. [184-?] 1 p. MB. 40-2176

Eight reasons why ministers should promote Sabbath schools, by a clergyman. Philadelphia, PA: American Sunday School Union [184-?] 12 p. WHi. 40-2177

Eights, J. Outlines of the geol. structure of Lake Superior mineral region. Albany, NY: s. l., 1840. MB. 40-2178

Eland, Samuel R. Worcester Guards quick step. As performed by the Boston Brigade Band, Sept. 19th, 1840. Composed and respectfully dedicated to the Officers and Members of the Worcester Guards, by Samuel R. Leland. Boston, MA: Henry Prentiss, 1840. 3 p. ViU. 40-2179

The elements of socialism. Compiled by the author of "An essay Towards A Science of Consciousness." Birmingham: Published by Watts, Snowhill, 1840. 28 p. ICMe; ICU; NPV. 40-2180

The elephant as he exists in a wild state, and as he has been made subservient in peace and in war to the purposes of man. New York: Harper & Brothers, 1840. 300 p. NGlc. 40-2181

Eliot, George. The Mill of the Floss. By George Eliot. Chicago, IL: Donohoe, Henneberry & Co., 1840. 2 v. CoOrd. 40-2182

Ellet, Charles, 1810-1862. Report and plan for a wire suspension bridge, proposed to be constructed across the Mississippi river at Saint Louis. By Charles Ellet, jr... Philadelphia, PA: W. Stave-

ly & co., printers, 1840. 58 p. CtY; ILM; MdBP; NNC; PPWa. 40-2183

Ellet, Charles, 1810-1862. The laws of trade applied to the dtermination of the most advantageous fare for passengers on rail roads. Philadelphia, PA: s. l., 1840. 16 p. CtY; ICU; MH-BA; NNE; ViU. 40-2184

Ellet, Elizabeth Fries (Lummis) 1818-1877. The pioneer women of the West. Philadelphia, PA: s. l., 184-? 434 p. MW. 40-2185

Ellet, Elizabeth Fries (Lummis) 1818-1877. Rambles about the country. By Mrs. E. F. Ellet. Boston, MA: Marsh, Capen, Lyon, and Webb, 1840. 257 p. Ia; MLow; MWA; NcD; OMC. 40-2186

Ellet, Elizabeth Fries (Lummis) 1818-1877. Scenes in the life of Joanna of Sicily. By 'Mrs. E. F. Ellet. Boston, MA: Marsh, Capen, Lyon and Webb, 1840. 256 p. CtY; ICU; MiD; MWA; RPAt. 40-2187

Elliott, David, 1787-1874. Life of the Rev. Elisha Macurdy... Alleghany: s. l., 1840. N. 40-2188

Elliott, Jesse Duncan, 1782-1845. Defence of Commodore Jesse Duncan Elliott, of the United States Navy, read by the Hon. Geo. Mifflin Dallas, before the naval court martial at Philadelphia, June 20, 1840. With letters and documents explanatory of portions of the defence. Philadelphia, PA: Mifflin & Parry, 1840. 28 p. CSmH; DLC; MBAt; MH; PPB. 40-2189

Ellis, Brabazon. Dr. Hook's test of controversy, examined... A sermon... With an appendix, containing a correspondence between the author and Dr. Hook. Manchester: s. l., 1840. 24 p. CtY. 40-2190

Ellis, George Edward, 1814-1894. A collection of Psalms and hymns for the sanctuary. Compiled for the Harvard Church, Charlestown. Boston, MA: s. l. 184-? 90 p. MHi. 40-2191

Ellis, George Edward, 1814-1894. Collected writings. Boston, MA: s. l., 1840-92. 4 v. MB. 40-2192

Ellis, George Edward, 1814-1894. An individual faith. By Rev. Geo. E. Ellis. Boston, MA: James Munroe & Co.; I. R. Butts, printer, 1840. 28 p. ICMe; MB; MeB; MH-AH; MMeT-Hi. 40-2193

Ellis, George Edward, 1814-1894. Two discourses, delivered in Harvard Church, Charlestown, Sunday, March 15, 1840, on the commencement of his ministry. By George E. Ellis. Printed by request for the use of the society. Boston, MA: William Crosby & Co., 1840. 47 p. CBPac; ICN; MBB; MnHi; PPAmP. 40-2194

Ellis, William. Polynesian researches during a residence of nearly eight years in the Society & Sandwich Islands, by William Ellis. New York: Harper & Brothers, 1840. 4 v. MLanc; NNebg. 40-2195

Ellsworth, Henry William, 1814-1864. The American swine breeder. A practical treatise on the selection, rearing, and fattening of swine. Boston, MA: Weeks, Jordan & Co., 1840. 304 p. DNAL; ICJ; MdBP; MWA; NGH. 40-2196

Ellsworth, Henry William. 1814-1864. American swine breeder, a practical treatise on the selection, rearing, and fattening of swine. Philadelphia, PA: s. l., 1840. In; M. 40-2197

Ellsworth, William Wolcott, 1791-1868. Speech from His Excellency, Wm. W. Ellsworth, Governor of Connecticut (1838-41) to the Legislature of the State, May, 1840. New Haven CT: Babcock and Wildman, printers, 1840. 16 p. CSmH; CtSoP; MH; PHi; PPL. 40-2198

Elton's comic all-my-nack, 184?. New York: Published by the Booksellers generally in the U. S. [1840] p. MWA; WHi. 40-2199

Elwyn, John Langdon. Some account of John Langdon. Portsmouth: s. l., 1840. 34 p. MiD-B; Nh-Hi; NhM. 40-2200

Ely, Thomas. Sermon on mode of baptism, May, 1840, before the church and congrgation to which the author ministers. New Bedford, MA: s. l., 1840. 26 p. MB; NHCS; NjPT. 40-2201

Emerson, Benjamin Dudley. The first class reader; a selection for exercises in reading, from standard British and American authors. In prose and verse... by B. D. Emerson. Claremont, NH: Claremont Manufacturing Company, 1840. 276 p. ICMcHi; MH; Nh-Hi; OClWHi; VtMidbC. 40-2202

Emerson, Frederick, 1788-1857. North American arithmetic, part first for the young learners. Claremont, NH: Claremont Manufacturing Company, 1840. MB; NN. 40-2203

Emerson, Frederick, 1788-1857. The North American arithmetic, part II, uniting oral and written exercises in corresponding chapters. By Frederick Emerson, late principal in the department of arithmetic, Boylston School, Boston. Windsor: Nathan C. Goddard, 1840. 190 p. DLC. 40-2204

Emerson, Frederick, 1788-1857. The North American arithmetic, part third, for advanced scholars. By Frederick Emerson. Boston, MA: Jenks and Palmer, 1840. 288 p. KEmT; MeB; MH; PMA; RPB. 40-2205

Emerson, Gouveneur. Lecture on the advantages derived from cultivating the arts and sciences. By G. Emerson, M. D., December 8, 1939. Philadelphia, PA: Printed by A. Waldie, 1840. 22 p. DeWi; MBC; PPAmP; PPM; TxDaM. 40-2206

Emerson, Joseph, 1777-1833. Questions adapted to Whelpley's compend of history. By Joseph Emerson. Tenth edition. New York: Collins, Keese & Co., W. E. Dean, printer, 1840. 69 p. ArPb; OBerB. 40-2207

Emerson, Joseph, 1777-1833. Questions and supplement to Goodrich's history of the U. S. By Joseph Emerson, principal of Female Seminary in Wethersfield, Ct. New edition, revised and adapted to the enlarged edition of the history. Claremont, NH: Claremont Manufacturing Co., 1840. 188 p. MWhitv; NN. 40-2208

Emmons, Samuel Bulfinch. The book of promises; or, The universalist's daily pocket companion. Being a collection of scripture promises arranged under their proper heads. Boston, MA: James M. Usher [1840] 128 p. MH-AH; MHi; NCaS. 40-2209

Emmons, Samuel Bulfinch. The book of promises; or, the universalist's daily pocket companion; being a collection of scripture promises arranged under their proper heads. Boston, MA: T. Whittemore, 1840. MH; MHi; MMeT-Hi; MPiB; NCaS; TxGR. 40-2210

Emory, John, 1789-1835. A defense of Our Fathers and of the Original Organization of the Methodist Espicopal Church against the Rev. Alexander M'Caine and others. With historical and critical notices of early American Methodism. Fifth edition. New York: T. Mason and G. Lane, 1840. 154 p. ICU; MBC; NjMD; OBerB; TJoT; WHi. 40-2211

Encyclopedia Americana. A popular dictionary... including a copious collection of original articles in American biography; on the basis of the seventh edition of the German conversation lexicon. Edited by Francis Lieber, assisted by E. Wigglesworth and T. G. Bradford. New edition. Philadelphia, PA: Thomas Cowperthwait & Co., 1840. 13 v. IU; ODaUB; MsJMC. 40-2212

Engelbrecht, J. C. "Good-bye," or Farewell, farewell is a lonely sound. Ballad. Composed & arranged for the piano forte by J. C. Engelbrecht. Baltimore, MD: F. D. Benteen [184-?] 5 p. ViU. 40-2213

England, John. Reply to an invitation to a Democratic dinner. Charleston: s. l., 1840. PPL. 40-2214

Engles, Joseph Patterson, 1795-1864. Catechism for young children, being an introduction to the shorter catechism... Written for the Presbyterian Board of

Publication. Philadelphia, PA: Presbyterian Board of Publication, 1840. 32 p. IaDaP; MH-AH; NcD; ViRU; WHi. 40-2215

Engles, William Morrison, 1797-1867. A caution against prevailing errors: being a conversation between a Presbyterian pastor and his parishioner. By Wm. M. Engles. Philadelphia, PA: Presbyterian board of publication, 1840. 36 p. CtHC. 40-2216

Engles, William Morrison, 1797-1867. Qualifications and duties of ruling elders in the Presbyterian Church. By the Rev. Wm. M. Engles. Philadelphia, PA: Presbyterian board of publication, 1840. 24 p. CtHC; MsJMC; OMtv; PPM. 40-2217

Entz, John F. Exchange and cotton trade between England and the U. S.; containing performa accounts on cotton purchased in the principal markets of the Union and shipped to Liverpool... New York: Clayton, 1840. 62 p. GU; ICU; MNH; MH; ScC. 40-2218

Episcopacy weighed in balances of the Holy Scriptures, and found wanting. A tract on church government. In three parts. By the author of The seven last plagues... Erie, PA: Printed by Hiram A Beebe, 1840. 29 p. NbOP. 40-2219

Equitable Safety Marine & Fire Insurance Co. Act of incorporation & by laws. Boston, MA: s. l., 1840. OCHP. 40-2220

Equitable Safety Marine & Fire Insurance Co. The constitution of the ... incorporated by the Legislature of Massachusetts, April 6, 1839. Boston,

MA: s. l., 1840. 30 p. MB; MHi; NNIns. 40-2221

Ercilla y Zuniga, Alonso de, 1533-1594. La Araucana, poema de Don Alonso de Ercilla y Zuniga. En un tomo. New York; Paris: Roe Lockwood & son; Baudry, Libreria Europea, 1840. 216 p. CtY. 40-2222

Eine Erzaeblung von dem Seligen Tode der Caroline Hanna Smith. New Berlin, PA: C. Hammer, 1840. 32 p. PReaAt. 40-2223

Esling, Catherine Harbeson [Waterman] b. 1812. The religious offering. Edited by Miss Catherine H. Waterman. Philadelphia, PA: William Marshall and Co., 1840. 288 p. InU; KU; MoU; NjR; PU. 40-2224

Esquiroe, Jean Etienne Dominique, 1772-1840. On mental diseases. [From the Edinburgh Medical and Surgial Journal.] [Philadelphia, PA: Haswell, Barrington, and Haswell, 1840] 30 p. CSt-L; CtY; KU-M; MBM; PPL. 40-2225

... An essay on the formation, government, and manner of conducting Sabbath schools. Written for the New York City Sunday School Society of the Methodist Episcopal church. New York: Published for the Tract society of the Methodist Episcopal church [184-?] 16 p. MnU. 40-2226

Estate of John Nicholson and Peter Baynton. Philadelphia, PA: s. l., 1840-42. p. PHi. 40-2227

Etiquette for gentlemen; or, Short rules and reflextions for conduct in society. By a gentleman. [2d ed.] Philadelphia, PA:

Lindsay and Blakiston [184-?] 224 p. Ct; MH. 40-2228

Ettling, Emile. Mazuska des concerts Vivienne. [Pour piano] Philadelphia, PA: Fiot [184-?] 7 p. MB. 40-2229

Etzler, John Adolphus. Description of the Naval Automation invented by J. A. Etzler. Philadelphia, PA: s. l., 184-? 16 p. NN; PHi; PPF. 40-2230

Euler, Leonhard, 1707-1783. Letters of Euler on different subjects in natural philosophy. Addressed to a German princess. With notes, and a life of Euler, by David Brewster... Containing a glossary of scientific term [s] with additional notes, by John Griscom... New York: Harper & brothers, 1840. 2 v. CtY; ICMe; InRch; PPFrankl. 40-2231

Eurn, William. A short expose on quackery, or, Introductin of his own to physicians and country merchants. Philadelphia, PA: s. l., 1840. 18 p. DLC; PPL. 40-2232

Eusebius Pamphilus. The ecclesiastical history of Eusebius Pamphilus... Translated from the original, by Rev. C. F. Cruse, A. M....And an historical view of the council of Nice. With a translation of documents by the Rev. Isaac Boyle, D. D. Philadelphia, PA: R. Davis and brothers, 1840. CMenSP; CoDI; MBC; MMeT; NMidt; PNt. 40-2233

Evangelical Lutheran Joint Synod of Ohio and adjacent states. Eastern District. Minutes of the 5th. convention... Canton, OH: Saxton, 1840. v. ICN. 40-2234

Evangelical Lutheran Ministerium of

Pa. and Adjacent States. Minutes of the German Evangelical Lutheran Synod of Pennsylvania. Baltimore, MD: Publication Rooms, 1840. 30 p. No Loc. 40-2235

Evangelical Lutheran Ministerium of the State of New York. Minutes of the forty-fifth synod of the Evangelical Lutheran Ministerium of the state of New York, and adjacent states and counties... Baltimore, MD: Publication rooms, n. pr., 1840. 19 p. NjR. 40-2236

Evangelical Lutheran Synod. 15th sess. Proceedings of the fifteenth session of the Evangelical Lutheran Synod of West Pennsylvania. Convened at York, York County, from the 3d to the 9th October, 1839. Gettysburg, PA: Printed by H. C. Neinstedt, 1840. 48 p. ScCoT. 40-2237

Evangelical Lutheran Synod and Ministerium of the S. S. 17th Meeting. Minutes... convened at St. Paul's Church, Newberry, S. C., on Saturday, the 14th of November, 1840, and continued its session, on the 10th, 17th and 18th instant. Baltimore, MD: Publication rooms, n. pr., 1840. 35 p. ScCoT. 40-2238

Evangelisches Liederbuchlein fur Sonntagsifchulen. New Berlin, PA: C. Hammer, 1840. 48 p. PReaAT. 40-2239

Evans, Oliver, 1755-1819. Young millwright & miller's guide. 10th ed. with additions & corrections by F. P. Jones. Philadelphia, PA: Lea, 1840. 392 p. MH-BA; OUxM; PU; ViU. 40-2240

Evengelical Lutheran Synod of West Pennsylvania. Verhandlungen der Sechzehnten Sitzung der Evangelisch-Lutherischen Synode von West pennsylvanien. Gehalten zu Pittsburgh,

Oct. 1-5, 1840. Gettysburg, PA: s. l., 1840. 38 p. PHi. 40-2241

Evengelical Tract Society. Tracts on holiness, no. 1-2, 5-6, 8. [Boston, MA: Evangelical Tract Society, 184-?] p. OO. 40-2242

The evening museum; a collection of deeply interesting tales and legends, together with several affecting narratives and surprising adventures. By Gaylord. Boston, MA: C. Gaylord, 1840. FJ; InU; MB; NN; RPB. 40-2243

Everest, Charles William, 1814-1877. The moss-rose, a parting token. Ed. by C. W. Everest. Hartford, CT: G. Robins, Jr., 1840. 184 p. CtHWatk; MH; RPB; WKenHi. 40-2244

Everett, Edward, 1794-1865. Importance of practical education and useful knowledge; being a selection from his orations and other discourses, by Edward Everett. Boston, MA: Marsh, Capen, Lyon and Webb, 1840. 419 p. CSt; MdBG; Me; MPiB; NIC. 40-2245

Everett, Edward, 1794-1865. Lives of John Stark, Charles Brockden Brown, Richard Montgomery, and Ethan Allen. New York: Harper and Brothers, 1840. 356 p. NAlbi; NBuCC; NLock. 40-2246

Everett, Edward, 1794-1865. A memoir of Mr. John Lowell, Jr., delivered as the introduction to the lectures on his foundation, in the odeon, 31st December, 1839; repeated in the Marlborough chapel, 2nd January, 1840... Boston, MA: Charles C. Little and James Brown, 1840. 74 p. CBPac; MH; NjR; PPL; RPB. 40-2247

The Evergreen: a monthly magazine of new and popular tales and poetry... v. 1-2: Jan. 1840-June 1841. New York: J. Winchester, 1840-41. 2 v. CtY; LNH; MiU; PP; ViU. 40-2248

The evidence of the Divinity of the Saviour, Part 1. New York: [published by the Protestant Episcopal Tract Society, 1840] 8 p. IEG; InID; NjR; WHi. 40-2249

An examination of the independent treasury bill. Washington, DC: s. l., 1840. PPL. 40-2250

The excellence and dignity of Religion. Baltimore, MD: Published by the Catholic Tract Society, Murphy, printer, 1840. 12 p. DLC; ICRL; MdBLC; Md-CatS; PLatS. 40-2251

Excursions in Egypt and Syria, by the crew of the United States ship Delaware in 1834. Hartford, CT: s. l., 1840. 36 p. Ct; CtHWatk. 40-2252

Exercises on the shorter catechism; in which the answers are minutely dissected, &, by a paraphrase & explanatory notes, may be explained & re-constructed by the learner; to which are added select proofs & the whole rev., by the Committee on Publication. 1st American, from the 6th Edinburgh ed. Boston, MA: Sabbath school society, 1840. 90 p. Ct; MBC; MMeT; MWA; OMC. 40-2253

Exeter Female Academy, Exeter, N. H. Catalogue, 1840/41-41/42. [S. l.: s. l., 1840?] p. MH. 40-2254

The expediencey of a uniform bankrupt

law. New York: n. pub., n. pr., 1840. 25 p.
NjR. 40-2255

Explanation of the church catechism or
a summary of Christian doctrine and
practice. From a tract by a Presbyter of
the United Diocese of Dunkeld and
Dunblane... [New York: pub. by the
Protestant Episcopal Tract Society,
1840] 16 p. DLC; IEG; InID; VtMidSM.

40-2256

Ezell, Robert A. Speech, delivered
before the Democratic association of
Warren, N. C., by Robert A. Ezell.
Printed by order of the Association.
Richmond, VA: Printed by Shepherd
and Colin, 1840. 29 p. NcWfC; NcU;
TxU. 40-2257

F

F., W. H. Affection waltz. Composed & arranged for the piano forte by W. H. F. Baltimore, MD: F. D. Benteen [184-?] 2 p. ViU. 40-2258

Faber, Frederick William, 1814-1863. The ancient things of the Catholic Church, altered from a tract by the Rev. Frederic W. Faber... New York: Published by the Protestant Episcopal Tract Society, 1840. 12 p. DLC; IEG; InID; PPL; WHi. 40-2259

Faber, Frederick William, 1814-1863. The Reformation, and the duty of keeping to its principles. Adapted from a tract by the Rev. Frederick W. Faber. New York: Published by the Protestant Episcopal Tract Society, 184?. 8 p. IEG; InID. 40-2260

Faber, George Stanley, 1773-1854. The difficulties of Romanism. By George Stanley Faber... with an introductory essay by the Rev. John Coleman... Philadelphia, PA: R. S. H. George, 1840. 342 p. CtHT; InID; GDecCT; NGH; OrPD; RPAt. 40-2261

Faber, George Stanley, 1773-1854. The doctrine of election. New York: Charles Henry, 1840. 376 p. OrPD. 40-2262

Faber, George Stanley, 1773-1854. Practical treatise on the ordinary operations of the holy spirit. Philadelphia, PA: Brown, 1840. 220 p. IBLoW; PP. 40-2263

Faber, George Stanley, 1773-1854. The primitive doctrine of election; or, An historical inquiry into the ideality and causation of scriptural election as received and maintainted in the primitive Church of Christ. By George Stanley Faber. st American ed. New York: C. Henry, 1840. 376 p. C-S; MH-AH; NjPT; OrPD; PPP; WNaE. 40-2264

The factory boy; or, the child of providence. By a lady. Written for the New England S. S. union, and revised by the committee of publication. Third edition. Boston, MA: New England Sabbath school union, 1840. 141 p. WHi. 40-2265

Fair, John. The Elegchios, or a Refutation of Walter Balfour's Inquiry into the Scriptural Import of the Words Sheol, Hades, Tartarus, and Gehenna, all translated "Hell" in our common English version. In four chapters. By John Fair. Albany, NY: s. l., 1840. 77 p. MWA; NjR. 40-2266

A familiar conversation upon an old subject between U and I. By a citizen of Mass. Second edition. Brookfield, MA; Boston, MA: E. and L. Merriam, printers; Crocker and Brewster, 1840. 94 p. LNB; MBC; MWHi; NCH-S. 40-2267

A familiar conversation upon an old subject, between U and I. By a citizen of Mass. 2nd ed. Brookfield, MA: E. & L.

Merriam, printers, 1840. 94 p. CSmH;
NRAB; RPB. 40-2268

Family book of rare and valuable
recipes, to which is added, the complete
family doctor. Compiled by an eminent
physician. New York: Turner and Fisher
[184-?] 22 p. WHi. 40-2269

The family christian almanac for the
United States. Calculated for the horizon
and meridian of Boston, New York, Baltimore & Charleston. Adapted to four
parallele of latitude and for use in every
part of the country. For the year of Our
Lord and Savious Jesus Christ 1841. Boston, MA: Published by Gould, Kendall &
Lincoln; D. Fanshaw, printer, 1840. 36 p.
MNBedf. 40-2270

The family christian almanac for the
United States... for the year of Our Lord
and Savious Jesus Christ 1841... New
York: Published by the American Tract
Society, D. Fanshaw, printer [1841] 35 p.
MPeHi; MWA; MWHi; NjR; WHi. 40-
2271

Family instructor; or, a manual of the
duties of domestic life. New York: Harper, 1840. 300 p. NICIA; P; PJA. 40-2272

The family physician and farmer's com-
panion. [Syracuse, NY] : Printed for M.
Baldwin, the blind man [184-?] 24 p. CtY;
MBCo; MH; NN; MiU-C. 40-2273

Family receipts; being a compilatin
from several publications... Sold at L. H.
Redfield's bookstore. Syracuse, NY: T.
A. Smith & co., printers [1840?] 59 p. NN.
40-2274

Fanning, Edmund. ... Memorial of Edmund Fanning, respectfully soliciting a
loan from Congress to the support and
advancement of commerce, the fisheries,
etc., by exporatin in the SOuth seas.
February 5, 1840... [Washington, DC: s.
l., 1840?] 11 p. CU-B. 40-2275

Farmer, George O. The Norfolk guards
quick step. As performed by the Boston
Brigade Band. Composed and respectfully dedicated to the officers and members of the Norfolk Guards, by Geo. O.
Farmer. [Boston, MA: Oakes and Swan,
1840] 3 p. MB; MHi; MNe. 40-2276

Farmer, George O. Song of the fisher's
wife. [With accompaniment for the piano
forte.] [Boston, MA: Oakes and Swan,
1840] 3 p. CtY; MB. 40-2277

Farmer, John, 1798-1859. Map of the
surveyed part of Michigan. Engraved by
S. Stiles & Co. New York: Pub. by J. H.
Colton, 1840. IGK; Mi. 40-2278

Farmer's almanac. By David Young.
New York: Collins, Keese & Co., [1840]
No Loc. 40-2279

The farmer's almanac... 1841... By
Thomas Spofford. New York: David Felt
and Company, [1840] [36] p. WHi. 40-
2280

The farmer's almanack, calculated on a
new and improved plan, for the year
1841. By Robert B. Thomas. Boston:
Jenks and Palmer, [1840] (46) p. CoU;
MWA; NjR; PHi; RNHi. 40-2281

Farmer's almanac for 1841. By David
Young. Newark, N. J.: Benjamin Olds,
[1840] 40-2282

Farmer's almanac for 1841. By David

Young. New York: H. & S. Raynor, [1840] 40-2283

Farmer's almanac for 1841. By David Young. New York: Poinier & Snell, [1840] 40-2284

Farmer's almanac for 1841. Calculations by John Ward. Philadelphia, Pa.: M'Carty and Davis, [1840] 40-2285

Farmer's almanac for the year 1840. New York: David Felt and Company, 1840. 35 p. NHuntHi. 40-2286

The farmer's almanack... for the year of our Lord, 1840... No. 48. Boston: Carter, Hendee and Co., [1840] 40-2287

The farmer's almanack... for the year of our Lord, 1841. Calculated for the state of Maineby Robert B. Thomas. Portland, Me.: H. J. Little, [1840] (48) p. MMhHi. 40-2288

Farmer's almanack. By Dudley Leavitt. Concord: Marsh, Capen and Lyon, 1840. Farmer's almanac for... 1841. By Thomas Spofford. Boston, [1840] 36 p. MBilHi; MHi. 40-2289

Farmer's and mechanics almanack for the year of our Lord 1841. By Charles Frederick Egelmann. Philadelphia: George W. Mentz & son, [1840] 34 p. MWA; WHi. 40-2290

Farmer's and planter's almanac for 1841. Salem, N. C.: Blum & son, [1840] No Loc. 40-2291

The farmer's cabinet; devoted to agriculture, horticulture, and rural economy. Philadelphia: Kimber & Sharpless, 1840. 384 p. MdBD. 40-2292

The farmer's calendar, for the year 1841. By Charles F. Egelmann. Baltimore: Cushing and Brother, [1840] (32) p. MWA; NjR. 40-2293

Farrar, Eliza Ware (Rotch)1791-1870. The youth's letter-writer; or, The epistolary art made plain and easy to beginners, through the example of Henry Moreton. By Mrs. John Farrar... 4th stereotype ed. Boston, MA: Broaders & co. [etc., etc.] 1840. 170 p. CtY; MiD; NbU. 40-2294

Farrar, John, 1779-1853. Elementary treatise on the application of trigonometry to orthographic & stereographic projection, dialing... with logarithmic & other tables... For the use of students of the University at Cambridge, New England. 4th edition. Boston, MA: Hilliard, 1840. 155 p. MeB; MH; OCY; OO; PU. 40-2295

Farrell, John, d. 1848. The dumb girl of Genoa; or, The bandit merchant, a melodrama in 3 acts... New York: S. French [1840] 21 p. C. 40-2296

Facts for the people; or, Every one's book. No. 10. [S. l.: s. l., 184-?] p. MBAt; ViU. 40-2297

Fauquier County, Va. Second address of the Central Committee of Fauquier to the people of that County on the Army Bill. Washington, DC: printed at the Madisonian Office, 1840. 34, 11, 8 p. DLC; MdBP; MoS; NBuG; NcD. 40-2298

Favorite Swiss waltz. For the harp or piano forte. New York: Firth & Hall [184-?] 1 p. ViU. 40-2299

Fay, Theodore Sedgwick, 1807-1898. The countess Ida. A tale of Berlin. By the author of Norman Leslie. In two volumes. New York: Harper & brothers, 1840. 2 v. FOA; IU; LNH; MeB; NIC. 40-2300

The fear of God and human respect. Translated from the French. Baltimore, MD: Catholic Tract Society, 1840. 12 p. MdBLC; PLatS. 40-2301

Felch, Walton. A phrenological chart, and table of combinations. By W. Felch, Lecturer on the Science of Phrenology. Second edition. Brookfield, MA: E. and L. Merriam, printers, 1840. 47 p. ICN; MB; MWA. 40-2302

Felton, Cornelius Conway, 1807-1862. Greek reader for the use of schools; containing selections in prose & poetry, with English notes & a lexicon. Adapted particularly to the Greek grammar of E. A. Sophocles. Hartford, CT: Huntington, 1840. 442 p. CSt; IEG; MH; NNC; PU. 40-2303

Female Charitable Society of Amoskeag. Constitution. Manchester: s. l., 1840. 8 p. Nh-Hi. 40-2304

Female Education and Missionary Association. Reports of the Female Education and Missionary Association, and the Executive Committee of the Young Men's Missionary Society, of St. Luke's Church. Read at the Annual Celebration of the Societies, held in that Church on Sunday evening, February 2, 1840. New York: Printed by William Osborn, 1840. 26 p. MdBD. 40-2305

Fendall, P. R. Speech at meeting Feb.,

1840. [Washington, DC: s. l., 1840] p. MB. 40-2306

Fenelon, Francois de Salignae de La Mothe, 1651-1715. Les avdenturesde Telemaque, fils d'Ulysse. Par Fenelon. Par A. Bolmar. Nouvr. ed. soigneusement rev. et cor. sur l'edition de Didot, A. Paris. Philadelphia, PA: Lea & Blanchard, 1840. 2 v. DLC; MH; NjMD; PPL; ViL. 40-2307

Fenelon, Francois de Salignac de la Mothe, 1651-1715. Key to the first eight books of the adventures of Flemachus, the son of Ulysses, with the help of which any person can learn how to translate French and English. By A. Bolmar.... Philadelphia, PA: Lea and Blanchard, 1840. 222 p. IaSIB; NN. 40-2308

Fenning, Daniel. The improved edition of Fenning's Universal spelling book; or, A new and easy guide to the English language. Stereotype ed. New York: McFeeter and brother [1840?] 144 p. MH. 40-2309

Fernald, Woodbury M. Universalism against Partialism: in a series of lectures delivered in Newburyport, Mass. By Woodbury M. Fernald. Boston, MA: B. B. Mussey, 1840. 270 p. CU; MBUPH; MNe; Nh; OHi. 40-2310

Ferrari, Giacomo Gotfredo, 1759-1842. Instruction book for the voice. With accomp. for the piano. Boston, MA: Ditson [184-?] 51 p. MB. 40-2311

Fessenden, Thomas Green, 1771-1837. ... The complete farmer & rural economist; containing a compendiu: epitome of the most important branche of agricultural and rural economy. B

Thomas G. Fessenden. 5th ed., rev., improved and enlarged. Boston, MA: Otis, 1840. 345 p. MdW; NcRA; NN; PU; RPAt. 40-2312

Fessenden, Thomas Green, 1771-1837. ... The new American gardener, containing practical directions on the culture of fruits and vegetables, including landscape and ornamental gardening, grapevines, silk, strawberries, &c., &c. 14th ed. Boston, MA; Philadelphia, PA: s. l., 1840. 306 p. CtY; KyBC; MB-FA; NLew; ViRU. 40-2313

Feuchtwanger, Lewis. The mad dog; or, Hydrophobia, with all its various symptoms, causes, and remedies, minutely described. By Dr. Lewis Feutchtwanger. New York: Wm. Applegate, 1840. 16 p. MB; MWA; NjR; PPL. 40-2314

A few flowers worthy of general culture. An effort to win for hardy plants a recognition of their great wealth of beauty. Pittsburgh, PA: B. A. Elliott co., 1840. 112 p. LNH. 40-2315

Fez, Conrad. Wreckers daughter, a quick step... [For piano forte.] 3d ed. Boston, MA: Prentiss, 1840. 3 p. MB. 40-2316

Fez, Conrad. Wreckers daughter. 5th ed. Boston, MA: Prentiss, 1840. 3 p. MAm. 40-2317

Fez, Conrad. Wreckers daughter. 6th ed. Boston, MA: Prentiss, 1840. MB. 40-2318

Field, Barnum. The American school geography, with an atlas. 11th ed. Boston,

MA: Gould, Kendall & Lincoln, etc., etc., 1840. MH. 40-2319

Fillmore, Millard, pres. U. S., 1800-1874. Letter of Mr. Fillmore & Speeches in Congress of Mr. Rives, Dromgoole, Fisher, Brown & Duncan on the N. J. contested election. Washington, DC: s. l., 1840. PPL. 40-2320

Fillmore, Millard, pres. U. S., 1800-1874. Letter to his constituents, and his remarks in the House of Representatives on the New Jersey contested election, Mar. 6-7, 12, 1840. [S. l.: n. p. [1840] 16 p. M; MHi; PPL. 40-2321

Fillmore, Millard, pres. U. S., 1800-1874. Letters to Mr. Cadwallader, Esq., in regard to the Van Buren administration and the hoped for election of Harrison. [Washington, DC: n. p., 1840] 3 p. IEN-M. 40-2322

Finden, William, 1787-1852. The book of the boudoir; or, The Court of Queen Victoria. A series of portraits of the British nobility, from original paintings by eminent artists, engraved under the superintendance of W. and E. Finden. Second series. London; Philadelphia, PA: Tilt and Bogue; Carey & Hart [184-?] 36 p. MWA; PP; RPB; ViU. 40-2323

Fine, John, 1784-1867. Letter to his constituents, Aug., 1840. [S. l.: s. l., 1840] p. DLC; MBAt; NcD; OClWHi; TxU. 40-2324

Finley, James Bradley, 1781-1856. History of the Wyandott mission at Upper Sandusky, Ohio, under the direction of the Methodist Episcopal Church. By Rev. James B. Finley... Cincinnati, OH: Pub. by J. F. Wright and L. Swormstedt for the Methodist Episcopal Church, 1840. 432 p. CoD; IaHA; OHi; PPiU; TxH. 40-2325

Finney, Charles Grandison, 1792-1875. Skeletons of a course of theological lectures. By Rev. C. G. Finney, Professor of didactic Palemic and pastoral theology, in the Oberlin Collegiate Institute. Oberlin, OH: James Steele, 1840. 248 p. ArCH; IaGG; KyLoP; MiOC; OWoC. 40-2326

Finney, Charles Grandison, 1792-1875. Views of sanctification. By Rev. Charles G. Finney... Oberlin, OH: James Steele, pr. and pub., 1840. 206 p. KyBC; MWiW; NbOM; PPPrHi; ScCoT. 40-2327

Fiorini, G. E. The nightingale. Arranged as a rondino, for the piano forte, by G. E. Giorini. Philadelphia, PA: John G. Klemm [184-?] 3 p. ViU. 40-2328

The Firemen's songster. Philadelphia, PA: Perry [184-?] 94 p. MB. 40-2329

First Social Reform Society, New York (City) Address to the people of Rhode Island who are denied the right of suffrage. New York: s. l., 1840. 8 p. RPB. 40-2330

Fischer's hornpipe & College hornpipe. Baltimore, MD: F. D. Benteen [184-?] 1 p. ViU. 40-2331

Fishbough, William. The Government of God, considered with reference to natural laws, and the nature of rewards and punishments explained. By Rev. William Fishbough. Taunton: I. Amsbury, Jr., printer, 1840. 16 p. MiD-B; MMeT; MMeT-Hi. 40-2332

Fisher & Brother, Philadelphia, Pa.

Great and free songster. Philadelphia, PA: s. l. [184-?] 2 p. MB. 40-2333

Fisher & Brother, Philadelphia, Pa. Nancy Till songster. Philadelphia, PA: s. l. [184-?] 2 p. MB. 40-2334

Fisher & Brother, Philadelphia, Pa. Ocean songster. Philadelphia, PA: s. l. [184-?] 2 p. MB. 40-2335

Fisher, Charles, 1789-1849. Remarks on the bill for issuing five millions of treasury notes... Washington, DC: Blair, 1840. 7 p. NcU; NNC. 40-2336

Fisher, Charles, 1789-1849. Speech on the resolution offered by Mr. Johnson, of Tennessee, instructing the committee of elections to report forthwith... Washington, DC: Globe, 1840. 8 p. MB; MdHi; NcU. 40-2337

Fisher, George, 1795-1873. Memorials of George Fisher, late secretary to the expeditionof Gen. Jose Antonio Mexia, against Tampico, in November 1835. Presented to the 4th & 5th Congresses of the Republic of Texas, praying for relief in favor of members of the said exposition. Houston, TX: printed at the Telegraph office, 1840. 27 p. CU; DLC; RPB; TxH; TxWB. 40-2338

Fisk, Benjamin Franklin, d. 1832. A Grammar of the Greek language. Stereotype edition. Boston, MA: Hilliard, Gray & Co., 1840. 263 p. MoKR; NCas; PHi. 40-2339

Fitch, Charles, 1804-1843. Letter to the Newark presbytery... by Charles Fitch. Newark, NJ: Aaron Guest, 1840. 20 p. MBNMHi; NGH; NjPT; OClWHi. 40-2340

Fitch, Charles, 1804-1842. Reasons for withdrawing from the Newark Presbytery. Newark, NJ: Aaron Guest, 1840. 14 p. NCH; NjPT; OClWHi. 40-2341

Fitch, Eleazar Thompson, 1791-1871. Account of the meeting of the members of the class which graduated at Yale college in 1810, held at New Haven, August 18, 1840. New Haven, CT: s. l., 1840. 14 p. Ct; CtY; MBC; MH. 40-2342

Fitch, J. P. Watertown directory for 1840, arranged in three parts. 1. A short account of the settlement of Watertown. 2. A list of the officers of the town... 3. List of the names of citizens of Watertown and the villages of Pamelia and Juheville... Watertown, NY: Printed by Knowlton & Rice, 1840. 55 p. CSmH; MWA; NN; WHi. 40-2343

Fitchburg, Mass. Christ Church. Articles of faith, form of covenant, principles of discipline, and rules of practice. Adopted by the Christ Church in Fitchburg, Mass., 1824. Fitchburg, MA: J. Garfield, printer, 1840. 12 p. MBC; MWA. 40-2344

Fithian's silk grower's almanac. Philadelphia, PA: M. Fithian, 1840. 31 p. DLC; MWA; PHi. 40-2345

Fitz, Asa, b. 1810. The multiplication table, set to music, in a variety of pleasing tunes. Boston, MA: D. S. King, 1840. 16 p. MH; RPB. 40-2346

Fitz, Asa, b. 1810. My little singing book; designed for the use of Sabbath and juvenile singing schools. Boston, MA: D. S. King, 1840. 67 p. CtMW; MH. 40-2347

Fitzgerald, Mrs. Edward. I remember how my childhood fleeted by. A ballad. Words by W. M. Praed, Esqr.; the music Composed by Mrs. E. Fitzgerald. Boston, MA: Geo. P. Reed [184-?] 3 p. ViU. 40-2348

Fitzgerald, Mrs. Edward. I remember how my childhood fleeted by. A ballad. Words by Winthrop M. Praed, Esqr.; the music Composed by Mrs. Edwd. [sic] Fitzgerald. New York: Atwill, publisher [184-?] 3 p. WHi. 40-2349

Fitzgerald, Mrs. Edward. I remember how my childhood fleeted by. Sung by Mr. Horn. Compoesd by Mrs. E. Fitzgerald. Baltimore, MD: F. D. Benteen [184-?] 3 p. ViU. 40-2350

Flavel, John. 1630?-1691. A blow at the root of antinomianism. By the Rev. John Flavel. Philadelphia, PA: William S. Martien, 1840. 124 p. CSansS; GDecCT; OWoC; PPL; TxAuPT; ViRut. 40-2351

Flavel, John, 1630?-1691. Christ knowking [sic] at the door of sinners' hearts; or, A solemn entreaty to receive the Saviour and his gospel in this day of mercy. Rev. ed. New York: [American Tract Society, 1840?] 400 p. MiGr. 40-2352

Flavel, John, 1630?-1691. Divine conduct; or, the mystery of providence wherein the being and efficacy of providence are assorted and vindicated, the method of Providence, as it passes through the several stges of our lives opened. Philadelphia, PA: Presbyterian Board of Publication [1840] 252 p. ICU; MiU; MBuG; PPL; ViU. 40-2353

Flavel, John, 1630?-1691. The fountain

of life; or, A display of Christ in his essential and meditorial glory. Rev. and somewhat abridged [ed.] New York: [American Tract Society, 1840?] 559 p. IU; KyU; MiGr. 40-2354

Flavel, John, 1630?-1691. The method of grace in the Holy Spirit's applying to the souls of men the eternal redemption contrived by the Father and accomplished by the Son. 1st American ed., and somewhat abridged. New York: [American Tract Society, 1840?] 560 p. MiGr; WHi. 40-2355

Flavel, John, 1630?-1691. A treatise on keeping the heart; or, The Saint indeed. By Rev. John Flavel. Written A. D. 1667. Boston, MA: Published by the American Tract Society, 1840. 192 p. No Loc. 40-2356

Fleetwood, John. The life of our Lord and Saviour Jesus Christ... by the Rev. John Fleetwood... To which is added, Evidences of Christianity by P. Doddridge; The Golden grove... by Jeremy Taylor; Meditations upon the Lord's prayer, by Sir Matthew Hale; Sermons... by the Rev. Hugh Blair... New York: R. Martin [1840?] 785 p. NNG. 40-2357

Fletcher, Alexander, 1787-1860. Excellence of the Bible, illustated, etc., Moorfields, Christmas, 1840; annual sermon to S. S. children. [S. l.: s. l., 184-?] p. MBAt. 40-2358

Fletcher, Alexander, 1787-1860. Guide to family devotion... With an appendix of prayers and hymns... New York: Virtue, 1840. 761 p. CtHWatk; PP. 40-2359

Fletcher, James, 1811-1832. The history of Poland from the earliest period to the present time. With a narrative of the recent events. New York: Harper & Brothers, 1840. 339 p. InRch; MH; MMe; NUtHi; ScDuE; ViR. 40-2360

Fletcher, John, 1579-1625. ... The clear brother. A play in five acts. Altered from Beaumont and Fletcher. Also the stage business, casts of characters, costumes, relative positions, etc. New York: S. French [184-?] 72 p. CSt. 40-2361

Fletcher, John, d. 1848. An address to such as inquire. What must we do to be saved? New York: B. Waugh and T. Mason; J. Collaid, printer, [1840] 74 p. NjR. 40-2362

Fletcher, John, d. 1848. A comparative view of the grounds of the Catholic and Protestant Churches. By the Rev. John Fletcher, D. D.... Baltimore, MD: Fielding Lucas, Jr. [1840] 366 p. MWH. 40-2363

Fletcher, John, Phrenologist. The Mirror of Nature, part 1, presenting a brief sketch of the science of Phrenology. Baltimore, MD: s. l., 1840. MH. 40-2364

Fletcher, John William, 1729-1785. An appeal to matter of fact and common sense; or, A rational demonstration of man's corrupt and lost state. New York: Published by T. Mason and G. Lane, for the Methodist Episcopal church, at the Conference office; J. Collord, printer, 1840. 214, 74 p. CtY-D; IEG; RPB. 40-2365

Flint, Timothy, 1780-1840. Biographical memoir of Daniel Boone, the first settler of Kentucky: interspersed with incidents in the early annals of the country. By Timothy Flint. Cincinnati

OH: O. G. Conclin, 1840. 252 p. DLC; MoU; OFH. 40-2366

Flohr, G. D. Sermons and essays in two parts. The first part containing popular and evangelistic sermons. By the late Rev. G. D. Flohr. The second containing sermons and essays for the most part by living ministers. Baltimore, MD: J. T. Tabler, 1840. 408 p. KKcBT; NcElon; OSW; ScCoT; TxAuPT. 40-2367

Flood, Edwin. There is a dream of bye-gone days. Written by S. Farquharson, Esq. Music by Edwin Flood. Baltimore, MD; New Orleans, LA: F. D. Benteen; W. T. Mayo [184-?] 2 p. ViU. 40-2368

Florian, Jean Pierre Claris de, 1775-1794. History of the Moors of Spain. Translated from the French original. To which is added a brief notice of Islamism. New York: pub. by Harper & Brothers, 1840. 296 p. ArLC; IaDmU; Me; NCaS; ViU. 40-2369

Florian, Jean Pierre Claris de, 1755-1794. William Tell; or, Switzerland delivered. By the Chevalier de Florian, member of the royal academies of Paris, Madrid, &c., &c. A Posthumus Work. To which is prefixed, The life of the author, by Jauffret. Translated from the French, by William B. Heweston. Author of "The blind boy," "The fallen minister" & c. Concord, NH: Published by Luther Roby, 184?. 143 p. MiD-B. 40-2370

Florian, Jean Pierre Claris de, 1755-1794. William Tell; or, Switzerland delivered. By the Chevalier de Florian, member of the royal academies of Paris, Madrid, Florence, &c., &c. To which is prefixed, The life of the author, by Jauffret. Translated from the French, by W.

B. Heweston. Author of "The blind boy," "The fallen minister" & c. Ithaca, NY: Mack, Andrus & Woodruff, 1840. 108 p. MeB. 40-2371

Florida (territory). Laws, statutes, etc. Acts and resolutions of the legislative council of the territory of Florida, passed at its eighteenth session... 1840... Tallahassee:B. F. Whitner, jr., printer, Star office, 1840. 76, 10 p. FU; InSC; Mi-L; Nj; RPL. 40-2372

Florida (territory). Laws, statutes, etc. A journal of the proceedings of the Legislative Council of the territory of Florida, at the eighteenth [-twentieth] session. Begun and held at the city of Tallahassee, on Monday the sixth day of Jan. 1840 [-the 3d day of Jan. 1842] Tallahassee: s. l., 1840-42. 3 v. C; FJ. 40-2373

Florida (territory). Laws, statutes, etc. A journal of the proceedings of the Senate of the territory of Florida, at its First Session... Tallahassee, FL: S. S. Sibley, Printer, 1840. 529 p. No Loc. 40-2374

Florida (territory). Laws, statutes, etc. A journal of the proceedings of the Senate of the territory of Florida, at its Second Session. Begun and held at the city of Tallahassee, on Monday the sixth day of Jan. eighteen hundred and forty. Tallahassee, FL: J. B. Webb, Printer, Star Office, 1840. FJ. 40-2375

Florida (territory). Laws, statutes, etc. Resolutions of the legislative council of the territory of Florida. Tallahassee:B. F. Whitner, jr., printer, Star office, 1840. 56 p. Nv. 40-2376

Florida (territory). Laws, statutes, etc.

Rules of the Supreme Court for the Southern Judicial District in Florida. In admiralty. [The law of salvage; being a judgment in the case of the ship Montgomery, by W. Marvin. Reprinted from Hunt's Merchant's Magazine.] New York: s. l., 1840. NHi. 40-2377

Flotow, Friederich von, 1812-1883. The last rose of summer, with easy variations, by A. Mine. Boston, MA: Geo. P. Reed [184-?] 2 p. ViU. 40-2378

Flow on gentle streamlet. [Song with accompaniment for guitar.] Philadelphia, PA: Lee & Walker [184-?] 1 p. MB. 40-2379

Flower, Eliza, 1803-1846. Wert thou like me. Aunt Lyle's song from musical. Illustrations of the Waverly novels. Composed by Miss Eliza Flower. [With accompaniment for the piano forte.] Philadelphia, PA: Fiot, Merguen & Co. [184-?] 2 p. MB. 40-2380

Flowers for a juvenile garland. New Haven, CT: Published by S. Babcock, 1840. 8 p. CtY; DLC; N; RPB; WHi. 40-2381

Folsom, Nathaniel. A dissertation on the second coming and kingdom of our Blessed Lord and Savior, Jesus Christ, upon the earth, by Nathaniel Folsom and John Truair. Cazenovia, NY: printed at the Union Herald Office, 1840. 92 p. MNtCA; WHi. 40-2382

Folsom, Nathaniel Smith, 1806-1890. The scriptural doctrine of Our Lord Jesus Christ and the Holy Spirit, in their relation to God the Father... Boston, MA: James Munroe and company, 1840.

84 p. CBPac; ICMe; MH-AH; MWA; WHi. 40-2383

Fontaine, A. de, b. 1798. Book of prudential revelation; or, the golden bible of nature and reason with the confidential doctor at home. Boston, MA: s. l., 1840. 507, 53 p. OO. 40-2384

Foot, Joseph Ives, 1796-1840. An address. Prepared by Rev. Joseph I. Foot, D. D., for his inauguration as President of Washington College, East Tennessee. Knoxville, TN: J. C. Moses and Company, 1840. 12 p. MB; NjR; NN; Thi; TxU. 40-2385

Forbes, Darius. Duties of Universalists. An occasional sermon, delivered before the Maine convention of Universalists, at its session in Albion, June 24, 1840. By Rev. Darius Forbes... Pub. by request of convention. [Albion, ME: s. l., 1840] 17 p. MiD-B; MMeT. 40-2386

Forde, William, 1796-1850. L' anima dell'opera. A collection of cavatinas & favorite pieces by the most celebrated composers. Arranged for the piano & flute. Boston, MA: s. l. [184-?-5-?] 20 pts. in 1 v. NN. 40-2387

The Forecastle Songster. New York: R. Marsh [184-?] 226 p. NRES. 40-2388

Foreign Evangelical Society. Annual reports: 1st-10th. Merged with Am. Prot. Society & Christian Alliance to form American & Foreign Christian Union. New York: s. l. [1840-49] v. 1-10. CtY; ICP; MeBat; PPPrHi; WHi. 40-2389

Forget me not songster. Containing a choice collection of old ballad songs

Boston, MA: J. S. Locke & Co. [1840?]
256 p. IU; MiU; RPB. 40-2390

Forget me not songster. Containing a choice collection of old ballad songs. Philadelphia, PA: Turner & Fisher [184-?] 255 p. DLC; ViU. 40-2391

Forget me not songster. Containing a choice collection of old ballad songs. Philadelphia, PA: W. A. Leary, Jr. [184-?] 256 p. RPB. 40-2392

Forget me not songster. Containing a choice collection of old ballad songs, as sung by our grandmothers. Embellished with Numerous Engravings. New York: Nafis & Cornish, 1840. 256 p. DLC; MH; NcU; WaU. 40-2393

Forman, John. Sermons, preached on various occasions. By the late Rev. John Forman, of the Protestant Episcopal Church of Maryland. With a short biographical sketch by his son. Baltimore, MD: D. Brunner, 1840. 192 p. IEG; Md; MdBD; ViAl. 40-2394

Forry, Samuel, 1811-1844. Statistical researches relative to the etiology of pulmonary and rheumatic diseases... extracted from the American Journal of the Medical Sciences. Philadelphia, PA: T. K. & P. G. Collins, printers, 1840. 41 p. DLC; DNLM; NBMS; PPHa; WU-M. 40-2395

Forsch, Johann August. Die gemeinde der vernunftglaubigen zu New York; ihre grundsatze und ansichten constitution, katechismus, gesangbuch. Nach einem beschlusse der gemeinde zum frucke befordert. New York: N. Y. Staatszeitung, 1840. MH. 40-2396

Forsyth, John, 1780-1841. Address to the people of Georgia. Fredericksburg, VA: s. l., 1840. 8 p. DLC; GU-De; OClWHi; PPL. 40-2397

Fort Meigs Club, Baltimore, Md. To the voters of Maryland. [Baltimore, MD: s. l., 1840] 16 p. CtY; MdHi; MH. 40-2398

Forward, Walter. Speech of Walter Forward to the Association of the Pittsburgh Board of Trade on the occasion of the fifth anniversary. Pittsburgh, PA: Printed at the Advocate Office, 1840. 16 p. ICU; MBAt; PHi; PSeW. 40-2399

Fosdick, David, 1813-1892. A grammar of the French language, with an appendix. By David Fosdick, Jr. Andover, MA: published by Gould, Newman and Saxton [etc.] 1840. 402 p. MAnP; WBeloC. 40-2400

Fosdick, David, 1813-1892. Introduction to the French language; comprising a French grammar, with an appendix of important tables and other matters; a French reader... and a vocabulary adopted to the selections. Andover, NY: Gould, Newman and Saxton [etc.] 1840. 402 p. DLC; OO. 40-2401

Foster, Benjamin Franklin. The clerk's guide or commercial instructor. By B. F. Foster. Second edition. Boston, MA: Published by Perkins & Marvin, 1840. 252 p. CtHWatk; MNBedf; MTa. 40-2402

Foster, Benjamin Franklin. Elementary copy-books... No. 2. Boston, MA: Perkins & Marvin, 1840. MH. 40-2403

Foster, Benjamin Franklin. Exercises in current-hand writings... Designed to facilitate the labour of the teacher to enable young learners to acquire an elegant rapid & mastery use of the pen. Boston, MA: Perkins & Marvin, 1840. MH; NN; NNC. 40-2404

Foster, Benjamin Franklin. A Practical Summary of the Law and Usage of Bills of Exchange and Promissory Notes... To which are added rates of commission and storage; equation of payments; and general information connected with the business of the counting-house. 2nd ed. Boston, MA: Perkins & Marvin, 1840. IC; MH. 40-2405

Foster, Benjamin Franklin. Theory & practice of book-keeping. Boston, MA: s. l., 1840. MB. 40-2406

Foster, Hannah [Webster] 1759-1840. The coquette; or, The history of Eliza Wharton. A novel founded on fact. By a lady of Massachusetts. 30th ed. Boston, MA: G. Gaylord, 1840. 246 p. CLU; DLC; MBC; MH; MWelC; NIC. 40-2407

Foster, John, 1770-1843. Essays in a series of letters. By John Foster, author of "An Essay on Popular Ignorance." New York: Robert Carter & Brothers, 1840. 352 p. NcMfC. 40-2408

Foster, John, 1770-1843. Living for immortality... being an introductory essay to Doddridge's Rise and progress of religion in the soul. By John Foster. Boston, MA: James Loring, 1840. 213 p. CtY; InCW; MWiW; PPM; RPAt. 40-2409

Foster, Stephen Collins, 1826-1864. Old Uncle Ned. An Ethiopian melody. Arranged with symphinoes & accompaniments for the piano forte by R. O.

Wilson. Baltimore, MD: Willig [184-?] 5 p. MB. 40-2410

Foster, W. C. Substance of the speech of W. C. Foster, delivered at a meeting of the democratic republicans of Monroe County, held at the court house in Bloomington, March 14, 1840. Pub. at the request of said meeting. Terre Haute, IN: G. A. Chapman, printer, 1840. 18 p. ICHi. 40-2411

Foster, William. An address to the mechanic and laboring classes, by a mechanic. New York: s. l., 1840. 8 p. MH-BA. 40-2412

Four letters respectfully dedicated to the working men of America. [Philadelphia, PA: s. l., 1840] 8 p. MH. 40-2413

Fowle, William Bentley, 1795-1865. The improved guide to English spelling; in which by the aid of a simple, yet particular, classification, the use of all figures and marks to indicate the pronunciation is rendered unnecessary, and the progress of the pupil greatly aided by association... Boston, MA: H. B. Williams, 1840. CtY; MH. 40-2414

Fowler, Andrew. An Exposition of articles of religion of the Protestant Episcopal Church in the United States of America... added some useful extracts. Charleston, SC: Pub. by Andrew Fowler, 1840. 192 p. NNUT; OC; ScC; TxU; WM. 40-2415

Fowler, Orson Squire. Fowler's practical phrenology. By O. S. Fowler, A. B. 1st ed. Philadelphia, PA; New York: O. S. Fowler; S. N. Fowler, 1840. 480 p. CtY; IaGG; MB; MCarv; MWA; Nh. 40-2416

Fox, John, 1516-1587. Algemeine Geschichte des Christlichen Marterthums. Philadelphia, PA: George W. Mentz und Sohr; T. Howe, 1840. 934 p. ICN; PLT. 40-2417

Fox, John, 1516-1587. Book of martyrs; Being a complete history of the lives and sufferings and death of Christ as martyes. By John Fox. Boston, MA: Charles Gaylord, 1840. 515 p. MB; NjMD; NjR. 40-2418

Fox, John, 1516-1587. A universal history of Christian martyrdom, from the birth of our blessed Saviour to the latest periods of persecution... now cor. throughout, with copious and important additions relative to the recent persecutions in the South of France. New ed. Philadelphia, PA: Biddle, 1840. 2 v. in 1. CtHT; MH. 40-2419

Fox, Thomas Bailey, 1808-1876. Christianity, the basis of true philanthropy. A discourse delivered at the 4th anniversary of the Warren St. Chapel, January 26, 1840. Boston, MA: printed by Tuttle, Dennett & Chisholm, 1840. 16 p. DLC; MHi. 40-2420

Fox, Thomas Bailey, 1808-1876. Christianity, the true basis of true philanthropy. A discourse. Delivered... January 26, 1840. Boston, MA: Printed by Tuttle, Dennett & Chisholm, 1840. 12 p. CtHWatk; MBAt; MBAU; MiD-B; NjPT. 40-2421

Fox, Thomas Bailey, 1808-1876. Hints to Sunday school teachers in a series of familiar lectures. By a pastor. Boston, MA: J. Munroe and Co., 1840. 100 p. MB-W; MH; MMeT; MNotn. 40-2422

Fox, Thomas Bayley, 1808-1876. The ministry of Jesus Christ. Compiled and arranged from the four Gospels, for families and Sunday schools. With notes and questions... By T. B. Fox... Second edition. Boston, MA; Portsmouth: Weeks, Jordan and company; John W. Foster, 1840. 264 p. CBPac; MB; MBAU; MMeT; MWA 40-2423

Fox, Thomas Bayley, 1808-1876. The one thing needful... By Rev. Thomas B. Fox. Tracts... American Unitarian Association... Boston, MA: James Munroe & company, 1840. 13 p. CBPac; ICMe; MCon; MeBat; MMeT-Hi; MNF. 40-2424

Fox, Thomas Bailey, 1808-1876. Questions on the "Ministry of Jesus Christ" for Sunday schools. Boston, MA: Weeks, Jordan and Company, 1840. 70 p. IEG; MB-W; PPL. 40-2425

Francis, C. P. Grand Russia march. Arranged for the piano forte. New York: Hall [184-?] 2 p. MB. 40-2426

Francis, Convers, 1795-1863. Life of John Eliot, the apostle to the Indians, by Convers Francis. New York: Harper & Brothers, 1840. 357 p. MMe; Nh-Hi; RPE; WGrNM. 40-2427

Franklin, Benjamin, 1706-1790. Life of Benjamin Franklin, containing the autobiography with notes and a continuation, by Jared Sparks. Boston, MA: Hilliard, Gray, and Company, 1840. NjNbS; NRU; PLF. 40-2428

Franklin, Benjamin, 1706-1790. Memoirs of Benjamin Franklin. Written by himself... Selected... from all his published productions, and comprising whatever is most entertaining and valuable to the general reader. New York: Harper & Brothers, 1840. 2 v. CtMW; FTa; KyDC; PAtM. 40-2429

Franklin, Benjamin, 1706-1790. Memoirs of Benjamin Franklin. Written by himself and continued by his grandson and others. Philadelphia, PA: McCarty and Davis, 1840. 2 v. CSt; ICN; MAb; MiGr; PHi. 40-2430

Franklin, Benjamin, 1706-1790. The works of Benjamin Franklin; containing several political and historical tracts not included in any former edition, and many letters, official and private, not hitherto published; with notes and a life of the author. Boston, MA: Hilliard, Gray, and Company, 1840. 10 v. CBPSR; MiD; ODaU; ScU; ViPet. 40-2431

Franklin Almanac. By Chas. F. Egelmann. Baltimore, MD: J. N. Lewis, 1840. MWA. 40-2432

Franklin Almanac. Calculated by John Armstrong. Pittsburgh, PA: Johnston & Stockton, 1840. MWA. 40-2433

The Franklin Almanac and Western New York Calendar for the year of Our Lord 1840, being the 64th and 65th Year of Amerian Independence. Calculated for the meridian of Rochester, Lat. 43o 8' 17" N., Lon. 49" 12" W. of Wash. City. Rochester, NY: Printed and published by David Hoyt, 1840. 24 p. NRHi; NRMA; NRU. 40-2434

The Franklin Almanac for the year 1840....By John Ward. Phialdelphia, PA: M'Carty & Davis, n. pr., 1840. 36 p. NjR. 40-2435

Franklin Almanac for 1841. New York: J. Pease and Son, [1840] 40-2436

Franklin Almanac for 1841. Calculations by John Ward. Philadelphia, PA: s. l. [1840] p. MWA. 40-2437

The Franklin Almanac for the year 1841... by John Foulke. Philadelphia, PA: Thomas L. Bonsal, n. pr. [1840] 35 p. NjR. 40-2438

Franklin Fire Company. Constitution and By-Laws. Philadelphia, PA: s. l., 1840. 18 p. PHi. 40-2439

Franklin Institute, Philadelphia, Penna. Constitution & by-laws of the Franklin Institute of the State of Pennsylvania for the promotion of the mechanic arts; with the act of incorporation. Philadelphia, PA: J. Crissy, printer, 1840. 24 p. CtY; PHi; PPAmP. 40-2440

The Franklin Magazine Almanac for 1841. Calculations by John Armstrong. Pittsburgh, PA: Franklin Magazine Alamanac [1840] p. MWA; PHi. 40-2441

The Franklin primer or lessons in spelling and reading. Adapted to the understandings of children. Composed and published by a committee appointed for the purpose of the School Convention of Franklin County. 26th edition. Greenfield, MA; Boston, MA: Phelps & Ingersoll; stereotyped by Lyman Thurston & Co., 1840. 54 p. MMhHi; MNS; NNC. 40-2442

Frankford, Pa. Friends' Asylum for the Insane. Rules for the management of the Asylum: 1 mo. 20, 1840. Philadelphia, PA: s. l., 1840. 12 p. PHi. 40-2443

Frederick, Md. The Evangelical Lutheran Church. The constitution of the Evangelical Lutheran church of Frederick, Md. Adopted at a meeting of the congregation on the 15th of February, 1840. Frederick, MD: Printed by Ezekiel Hughes, 1840. 16 p. MdHi; PPL. 40-2444

Freedom's gift: or, Sentiments of the free. Hartford, CT: S. S. Cowles, 1840. 108 p. CtY; DLC; ICN; MH; OClWHi. 40-2445

Freeman, George Washington, bp., 1789-1858. Appendix to the documents printed by the vestry connected with the resignation of the rector of the church. Raleigh, NC: s. l., 1840. NcU; PPL. 40-2446

Freeman, J. J. Persecution of the Christians in Madagascar. New York: Harper & Bros., pub., 1840. 298 p. IaPeC. 40-2447

Freeman, W. H. Matrimonial sweets. Comic duet. Boston, MA: Bradlee [184-?] 3 p. MB. 40-2448

Freeman, W. H. Matrimonial sweets. Comic duet. New York: Hewitt [184-?] 3 p. MB. 40-2449

The freeman's almanac for 1841... By Joseph Ray. Cincinnati, OH: G. Guilford and Ely & Strong [1840] p. MWA. 40-2450

The freeman's almanac for the year 1840... By Elisha Divelle. Cincinnati, OH: G. Guilford and Ely & Strong, 1840. 20 p. OC. 40-2451

Freemasons. Alabama. Minutes of the grand royal arch chapter of the state of Alabama; A. D. 1839-A. L. 5839-R. A. M. 2369. Tuscaloosa: Hale and Eaton, printers, 1840. 203-214 p. LNMas. 40-2452

Freemasons. Connecticut. Proceedings of the M. W. grand lodge of the state of Connecticut, at their annual communication in New Haven, May 13, 1840. New Haven: printed by William Storer, 1840. 24 p. NNFM. 40-2453

Freemasons. Georgia. Proceedings of the Right worshipful grand lodge of the state of Georgia, at an annual communication held on the 3d, 4th, 5th, 6th, and 7th, of Nov'r., A. L. 5840 1840... Milledgeville, GA: printed at the Georgia Journal office, 1840. 22 p. NNFM. 40-2454

Freemasons. Kentucky. Proceedings of grand chapter of masonic lodge, in Kentucky, meeting held in 1840. Lexington, Ky.: N. L. & J. W. Finnell, 1840. 15 p. IaCrM; NNFM. 40-2455

Freemasons. Kentucky. Proceedings of the grand lodge of Kentucky, at a grand annual communication, in the city of Louisville, commencing August 20-31, 5840. Louisville, Ky.: Penn and Eliot, printers, 1840. 72 p. IaCrM; NNFM. 40-2456

Freemasons. Maryland. Proceedings of the grand royal arch chapter of the state of Maryland, ... Baltimore; on May 20, 1840. Baltimore: Printed by Jos. Robinson, 1840. 17 p. DLC; NIC; NNFM. 40-2457

Freemasons. Massachusetts. Proceedings of the grand royal arch chapter of

Massachusetts, Boston, September, 1840. Boston: John B. Hammatt, 1840. 15 p. MWA; NNFM; OCM. 40-2458

Freemasons. Mississippi. Extracts from the proceedings of the M. W. grand lodge of the state of Mississippi, begun and held at the masonic hall in the city of Natchez, on Monday, February 3, 1840-A. L. 5840. Natchez: Daily Courier, 1840. 112 p. IaCrM; MBFM; NNFM; MsFM. 40-2459

Freemasons. New Hampshire. Journal of the proceedings of the grand royal arch chapter of New Hampshire... Concord, June, 1839, 1840. Concord: Printed by Asa M'Farland, 1840. 11 p. NNFM. 40-2460

Freemasons. New York. By-laws of Columbian Encampment, no. 1, of Knights Templars and the appendent orders, held in the city of New York. Revised November, A. D., 1840; and of the Order 722. New York: J. Van Norden and Co., pr., 1840. 11 p. IaCrM. 40-2461

Freemasons. New York. Constitution of the grand encampment of Knights Templars and the appendant orders for the state of New York. New York, 1840. 20 p. IaCrM; InHi; NNFM; PPFM; WHi. 40-2462

Freemasons. New York. Extracts from the proceedings of Grand Encampment of the State of New York, at their meetings held at the Howard House, city of New York, June 7th, 1839, May 1st, 1840, and June 5th and 6th, 1840. New York: J. Van Norden and Co., pr., 1840. 11 p. NNFM. 40-2463

Freemasons. New York. Proceedings of

Grand Commandery of Masonic Lodge in New York. Meetings held in 1839 and 1840. New York: J. Van Norden and Co., pr., 1840-45. 11 p. IaCrM. 40-2464

Freemasons. New York. Transactions of the Rt. worshipful grand lodge... of free and accepted masons of the State of New York. New York: J. M. Marsh, pr., 1840. 23 p. NNFM; OCM. 40-2465

Freemasons. North Carolina. Proceedings of the grand lodge of ancient York masons of North Carolina. A. L. 5839. Raleigh: Printed by T. Loring, 1840. 25 p. NcHiC; NNFM. 40-2466

Freemasons. Ohio. Journal of the proceedings of the Grand Council of Royal and Select Masters for the State of Ohio at the annual grand communication, held in Lancaster, Y. D., 1840. Lancaster, OH: n. pr., 1840. 16 p. LNMas. 40-2467

Freemasons. Ohio. Masonic funeral service for use of Nova Caesara Lodge, no. 2. Cincinnati, OH: Printed at the Republican Office, 1840. 12 p. MBFM. 40-2468

Freemasons. Pennsylvania. By-laws of lodge no. 43, Ancient York Masons, Lancaster, Pennsylvania. Lancaster, Pa.: Forney, printer, 1840. 9 p. IaCrM; PPFM. 40-2469

Freemasons. Tennessee. Proceedings of the grand lodge of the state of Tennessee, at the Masonic hall, in the city of Nashville, on Monday, October 5, 5840, A. D. 1840. Nashville, Tn: Printed by B. R. M'Kennie, 1840. [3] , 4-23 p. IaCrM; MBFM; NNFM. 40-2470

Freemasons. Tennessee. Proceedings of the grand royal arch chapter of the state of Tennessee, October, 1840. Nashville, Tn: Cameron & Fall, Printers, 1840. 11 p. DSG; MBFM; T. 40-2471

Freemen's ticket... For President, James G. Birney, of New York. For Vice-President, Thomas Earl, of Pennsylvania... Address, Lowville, October 5, 1840... [Lowville, NY?: s. l., 1840] p. NN. 40-2472

French, Henry. An address delivered before the students of Phillips Exeter Academy, at a regular meeting of their temperence society, May 2, 1840. By Henry French. Exeter, NH: Printed at F. Grant's office, 1840. 28 p. MB; MdBJ; MH; Nh. 40-2473

Frey, Joseph Samuel Christian Frederick, 1773-1850. Judah and Israel; or, The restoration and conversion of the Jews and the Ten Tribes. Prefixed by the author's narrative and his portrait. 3d edition, enlarged. New York: D. Fanshaw, 1840. 310 p. IU; MeBat; MiU; MWA; TWcW. 40-2474

Frey, Joseph Samuel Christian Frederick, 1773-1850. Joseph and Benjamin; a series of letters on the controversy between Jews and Christians. Comprising the most important doctrines of the Christian religion. By Joseph Samuel, F. C. Frey... Seventh edition. New York: Daniel Fanshaw, 1840. 2 v. IU; MeBat; MWA; NjR; NNUT. 40-2475

Frey, Joseph Samuel Christian Frederick, 1771-1850. Report of the late agency of the Rev. J. S. C. F. Frey, presented to the Bd. of Mgrs. of the American Society for ameliorating the condition of the Jews. New York: Fanshaw, 1840. 36 p. ICU; MH-AH; NjR; PPDrop; PPPrHi. 40-2476

Friedel, Louise Beate Augustine [Utrecht] d. 1818. Letters a Sophie, on les derniers accents de la tendresse-maternelle, par Mme. Louise Augustine Friedel. Nouvelle edition, par Louis Friedel. New Orleans, LA: Chez L'auteur, 1840. 179 p. AU; NjR; PPL. 40-2477

Friedel, Louise Beate Augustine [Utrecht] d. 1818. Petit Cuisiniere habite a L'Art d'appreter les economic ecrit sous la dictee de Mlle. Jeannette... New Orleans, LA: Chez L'auteur, 1840. 140 p. AU; NjR; PPL. 40-2478

Friedheim, John. Calathumpian quick step... Performed by the Harmony Band at Mrs. Pelby's benefit, March 2d, 1840. Boston, MA: s. l. [1840] 3 p. MHi. 40-2479

Friends' Almanac. Philadelphia, PA: s. l., 1840. PPAmP. 40-2480

Friends' Almanac for 1841. By Joseph Foulke. Philadelphia, PA: Elijah Weaver [1840] p. MWA. 40-2481

Friends of Temperance. Massachusetts. Report and Resolutions adopted at a Meeting of the Friends of Temperance, held at the Lyceum, New Bedford, May 30, 1840. New Bedford, MA: Press of Benjamin Lindsey, 1840. 12 p. MNBedf. 40-2482

Friends of Temperance. Order of exercises for the juvenile celebratin of the Seventh Simultaneous meeting of the friends of Temperance throughout the world at the Marlboro Chapel, Wendesday, February 26, 1840. Boston, MA: s. l., 1840. 2 p. MHi. 40-2483

Friends, Society of. Memorial and remonstrance of the committees appointed by the Yearly Meetings of Friends of Genesee, New York, Philadelphia and Baltimore, to the President of the United States; in relation to the Indians in the State of New York. New York: Mercein & Post's Press, 1840. 19 p. MdBP; MH; PHi; PSC-Hi; WHi. 40-2484

Friends, Society of. Memorial of the Society of Friends in Pennsylvania, New Jersey and Delaware, on the African slave-trade. Washington, DC: Blair & Rives, 1840. 3 p. NjR. 40-2485

Friends, Society of. Proceedings of the Society of Friends in the case of William Bassett. Worcester, MA: Published by Joseph S. Wall, 1840. 24 p. MB; MWHi; NjR; PSC-Hi. 40-2486

Friends, Society of. Society of Friends in the U. S., their views of the anti-slavery question, and treatment of the people of colour. Compiled from original correspondence. Darlington, SC?: Wilson, 1840. 26 p. NCH. 40-2487

Friends, Society of. Baltimore Yearly Meeting. Appendix to the "... defence of the Religious Society of Friends in the City of Baltimore... against certain charges circulated by Joseph J. Gurney. "By a member of the society. Baltimore, MD: Wm. Woody, 1840. 12 p. MBBC; MdHI; MH; PHi; PSC-Hi. 40-2488

Friends, Society of. Baltimore Yearly

Meeting. Review of a pamphlet entitled "A defence of the religious Society of Friends who constitute the Yearly Meeting of Baltimore, against certain charges circulated by Joseph J. Gurney." Baltimore, MD: J. D. Toy, 1840. 15 p. IEG; MBBC; MH; PHC; WHi. 40-2489

Friends, Society of. (Hicksite) Committees on Indians Concerns Appointed by the Four Yearly Meetings of Friends of Genesse, New York, Philadelphia, and Baltimore. Memorial and remonstrance of the committees to the President of the United States in relation to the Indians in the State of New York. New York: Mercien & Post's Press, 1840. 19 p. MH. 40-2490

Friends, Society of. (Hicksite) Joint Committee on Indian Affairs. The case of the Seneca Indians in the state of New York. Illustrated by facts. Printed... by direction of the joint committees on Indian affairs, of the four Yearly meetings of Friends of Genesee, New York, Philadelphia, and Baltimore... Philadelphia, PA: Merrihew and Thompson, printers, 1840. 256 p. CtY; ICN; MnU; PHC; WHi. 40-2491

Friends, Society of. (Hicksite) New York Yearly Meeting. Committee of Indians Affairs. The case of the Seneca Indians in the state of New York. Illustrated by facts. Printed by direction of the jt. com. on Indian Affairs, of the four yearly meetings of Friends of Genessee, N. Y., Phila., Baltimore. Baltimore, MD: Merrihew and Thompson, printers, 1840. 256 p. DLC; MnHi; NIC; OCU; PPiU; WaU. 40-2492

Friends, Society of. (Hicksite) Reports

on burials and marriages. [Philadelphia, PA?] : s. l., 1840. 8 p. PHi. 40-2493

Friends, Society of. Indiana Yearly Meeting. At Indiana Yearly Meeting, held at White Water in Wayne County, Indiana, on 1st day of the 10th month, 1840. [Richmond, IN?] : s. l., 1840? 26, 5 p. ICU; In; InRE; WHi. 40-2494

Friends, Society of. Joint Committee on Indian Affairs. Memorials and remonstrance... in relation to the Indians in the State of New York. New York: Mercein & Posts Press, 1840. 19 p. CSmH; MB; MH; N; PHC. 40-2495

Friends, Society of. New England Yearly Meeting. Friends or Quakers. Rules of discipline of the yearly meeting held on Rhode Island for New England. New Bedford, MA: s. l., 1840. 136 p. CtY; MWA; MNtCA; PSC-Hi; RPB. 40-2496

Friends, Society of. New England Yearly Meeting. Meeting of Sufferings. A declaration of the views of the Society of Friends in relation to church government... Providence, RI: Knowles and Vose, 1840. 31 p. DLC; PHC; MBC. 40-2497

Friends, Society of. New England Yearly Meeting. Report on the Memorials of the seneca Indians and others, accepted November 21, 1840, in the council of Massachusetts. Boston, MA: s. l., 1840. 28 p. DeWi; PSC-Hi. 40-2498

Friends, Society of. New England Yearly Meeting. Rules of discipline of the yearly meeting, held in Rhode Island for New England. Printed by direction of the meeting. New Bedford, MA: B. Lindsey

& Co., printers, 1840. 156 p. MSy. 40-2499

Friends, Society of. New England Yearly Meeting. Views of the Society of Friends in relation to civil government. Cincinnati, OH: A. Pugh, Printer, 1840. 12 p. CtY. 40-2500

Friends, Society of. New England Yearly Meeting. Views of the Society of Friends in relation to civil government. Providence, RI: Printed by Knowles and Vose, 1840. 15 p. DLC; MBC; MWA; NIC; PHC. 40-2501

Friends, Society of. New York Monthly Meeting. Account of the times of holding the yearly meeting of Friends, held in New York, and the meetings constituting it. New York: M. Day & Co., 1840. 27 p. InRchE; MH; PHC; PSC-Hi. 40-2502

Friends, Society of. New York Monthly Meeting. An address on the subject of theatrical amusements from the monthly meeting of Friends to its members. New York: M. Day & Co., 1840. 12 p. MH; MH-AH; PHC. 40-2503

Friends, Society of. New York Monthly Meeting. The memorial of the monthly meeting of Friends held in New York concerning our beloved friend, Sarah Waring. New York: M. Day & Co., 1840. 12 p. MH; PSC-Hi. 40-2504

Friends, Society of. Newton Preparative Meeting. Concord Quarter. Men's Minutes. Newton, MA: s. l., 1840-1909. 2 v. PSC-Hi. 40-2505

Friends, Society of. Ohio Yearly Meeting. The Minutes of Ohio yearly meeting, held at Mountpleasant... [St. Clairsville,

OH: printed by Easton & Gressinger, 1840. 24 p. MiD-B. 40-2506

Friends, Society of. Ohio Yearly Meeting of Women Friends. Minute of advice from Ohio yearly meeting of women Friends. To the quarterly and monthly meeting within its limits. [St. Clairsville, OH: printed by Easton & Gressinger, 1840. 4 p. OClWHi. 40-2507

Friends, Society of. Philadelphia Yearly Meeting. Extracts from the minutes of the Yearly Meeting of Friends, held in Philadelphia, by adjournments, from the Eleventh of the Fifth Month to the Fifteenth of the same, inclusive. Philadelphia, PA: Printed by John Richards, 1840. 24 p. No Loc. 40-2508

Friends, Society of. Philadelphia Yearly Meeting. Memorial of the Society of Friends in Pennsylvania, N. J. & Delaware on the African slave trade. Philadelphia, PA: J. and W. Kite, 1840. 7 p. DLC; ICN; MdBJ; PHC; TxU. 40-2509

Friends, Society of. Rhode Island Yearly Meeting. Rules of discipline of the Yearly meeting, held on Rhode Island for New England. Printed by direction of the meeting. New Bedford, MA: s. l., 1840. CtHWatk. 40-2510

Friendship's gift. Boston, MA: s. l. [1840] 2 v. MB. 40-2511

Friendship's offering: A Christmas, New Year and birthday present... [V. 1-15] ; 1841-55. Philadelphia, PA: Marshall, Williams, and Butler [etc., etc., 1840-55] 15 v. CtY; ICU; KU; NbU; TNP. 40-2512

Frost, J. Class book of nature; comprising lessons on the universe, the three kingdoms of nature & the form & structure of the human body... Ed. 5. Hartford, CT: s. l., 1840. 283 p. CtMW; InCW; MNan. 40-2513

Frost, John, 1800-1859. Indian wars of the United States, from the discovery to the present time. From the best authorities. By William V. Moore [pseud.] Philadelphia, PA: R. W. Pomeroy, 1840. 321 p. DLC; MWA; NjP; OClWHi; RPB. 40-2514

Frothingham, Nathaniel Langdon, 1793-1870. The memory and example of the just. A sermon. Preached on All Saints' Day to the First Church. Boston, MA: Printed by Joseph T. Buckingham, 1840. 15 p. ICMe; MBC; MWA; RPB; VtU. 40-2515

Frothingham, Nathaniel Langdon, 1793-1870. The new idolatry. A sermon, preached to the First Church, on Sunday, 22nd November, 1840. By its Minister, N. L. Frothingham. Boston, MA: Printed by J. T. Buckingham, 1840. 15 p. CtY; ICMe; MnHi; MWA; OO. 40-2516

A full account of Henry Clay's duels. Compiled from official documents. Also Polk's and Clay's opinion on the tariff, and a table showing the votes at the presidential elections of 1832, '36, and '40. [Philadelphia, PA: Office of "The Pennsylvanian, "1840?] 8 p. OO. 40-2517

A full and particular account of all the circumstances attending the loss of the steambost Lexington, in Long Island Sound, on the night of January 13, 1840, as elicited in the evidences of the witnesses examined before the Jury of Inquest. Held in New York immediately after the lamentable event. [Copyright secured accordint to law] Providence, RI: H. H. Brown and A. H. Stillwell, 1840. 32 p. DLC; MiU-C; MNe; NcD; PHi; OO. 40-2518

A full description of the daguerreotype process... New York: M. Daguerre, 1840. 16 p. NjR. 40-2519

Fuller, Daniel. A familiar expostion of the constitution of Pennslyvania. For the use of schools and of the people. By Daniel Fuller. Philadelphia, PA: Published by Iruah Hunt, 1840. 105 p. MB; P; PHi; PReaHi; PU. 40-2520

Fuller, Henry. Casper's inquiry; a dialogue, in four parts... adapted to the present crisis. By Henry Fuller. Philadelphia, PA: s. l., 1840. 36 p. DLC; PPM. 40-2521

Fuller, Richard, 1804-1876. Letters concerning the Roman chancery, by the Rev. Richard Fuller of Beauford, North Carolina, and the Right Rev. John England... Baltimore, MD; Charleston, SC: Published by Fielding Lucas, Jr.; John P. Beale, 1840. 276 p. ICU; MiD; NcAS; PV; ScU. 40-2522

Fulton, William Savin. Speech of Mr. Fulton, of Arkansas, on the report of the Select Committee on the assumption of the debts of the States by the Federal government. Senate... United States, March 3, 1840. Washington, DC: Globe office, 1840. 8 p. MdHi; NNC; PHi. 40-2523

El Fureidis. By the author of "The Lamplighter" and "Mabel Vaughan." Boston, MA: Ticknor and Fields, 1840. 379 p. MdW. 40-2524

Furness, William Henry, 1802-1896. A discourse. Delivered on the morning of the Lord's Day, January 19, 1840, in the First Congregational Unitarian Church, occasioned by the loss of the Lexington. Philadelphia, PA: C. A. Elliot, 1840. 16 p. MBAt; MH-AH; MHi; MWA; NNG; PPM. 40-2525

Furness, William Henry, 1802-1896. Domestic worship. Philadelphia, PA: James & Jay jun. & Brothers, etc., etc., 1840. 275 p. DLC; MB; MH; MWA; PPAmP. 40-2526

The future destiny of Israel. By a clergyman of the Church of England. From the second London edition. Philadelphia, PA: E. G. Dorsey, printer, 1840. 15 p. CBPSR; ICP; MMeT-Hi; MsJMC; NbOP; OO. 40-2527

Fyler, Fanny. An outline of the history of the British church from the earliest times to the period of the Reformation... shwoing by an appeal to historical facts her antiquity and independence of the Church of Rome. New York: pub. by the Prot. Episcopal Tract Society [184-?] 40 p. WHi. 40-2528

G

Gadsden, Christopher Edwards, 1785-1852. A discourse on the occasion of the death of the Right Rev. Nathaniel Bowen. Charleston, SC: A. E. Miller, 1840. 50 p. ICN; MWA; NNG; RPB; ScCC. 40-2529

Gage, Thomas, 1774-1842. The history of Rowley, anciently, including Bradford, Boxford, and Georgetown, from the year 1639 to the present time... With an address, delivered September 5, 1839, at the celebration of the second centennial anniversary of its settlement. By J. Bradford. Boston, MA: F. Andrews, 1840. 483 p. CtY; ICN; MH-AH; NhD; OCHP. 40-2530

Gaines, Edmund Pendleton, 1777-1849. Memorial of Edmund Pendleton Gaines, to the Senate and House of Representatives of the United States, in Congress assembled. Memphis, TN: Enquirer Office, 1840. 30 p. BrMus; DNA; InHi; MB; MBAt; MiD-B; NWM; PPAmP; TNP; TxU. 40-2531

Galbraith, John, 1794-1860. Speech on the independent treasury bill. In the House of Representatives, June 12, 1840. [Washington, DC: s. l., 1840] 20 p. MiU-C; WHi. 40-2532

Gale, Charles James, 1805-1876. A treatise on the law of easements. By C. C. Gale, esq., and T. D. Whatley. With American notes by E. Hammond. New York: Halsted & Voorhies, 1840. 352 p. CU; MPiB; NjP; RPL; WU-L. 40-2533

Gale, Wakefield. The soul returning unto its rest. A sermon. Preached at the re-opening of the Congregational Meeting-house in Rockport, Massachusetts, January 1, 1840. By Wakefield Gale. Printed by request. Boston, MA: printed by Perkins & Marvin, 1840. 20 p. CtY; ICN; MBC; MNe. 40-2534

Galena gazette and advertiser: extra [concerning the disputed boundary between the states of Illinois and territory of Wisconsin; proceedings of the citizens' committee, Galena, Ill., 1st February, 1840. [Galena, IL?: s. l., 1840?] p. ICHi. 40-2535

Galland, Isaac, 1790-1858. Iowa emigrant; containing a map and general description of Iowa Territory... Chillicothe, OH: s. l., 1840. 32 p. IaCrM; ICN; NN; OFH; WHi. 40-2536

Gallatin, Albert, 1761-1849. Peace with Mexico. By Albert Gallatin. New York: Bartlett & Welford [184-?] 34 p. CSfCW; TxU. 40-2537

Gallatin, Albert, 1761-1849. The right of the U. S. of Amer. to the Northeastern boundary claimed by them. Principally extracted from the statement laid before the King of the Netherlands & rev. by A. G....With an appendix & eight maps.

New York: S. Adams, pr., 1840. 179 p. CSt; ICU; MdBE; PPA; RPB. 40-2538

Gallaudet, Thomas Hopkins, 1787-1851. The child's book of the soul. Two parts in one. New York: Published by the American Tract Society [184-?] 155 p. WHi. 40-2539

Gallaudet, Thomas Hopkins, 1787-1851. The child's book of the soul. Two parts in one... 5th ed., with questions. Hartford, CT: s. l., 1840. 2 v. in 1. CtY; MBAt. 40-2540

Gallaudet, Thomas Hopkins, 1787-1851. Hoike Akua. He palala ia a hoike ana ma na mea i haraia aia no he Akua, he mana loa kona a me ka ike Kupanaha. Lahaina-luna Mea pai palapala: no ke lulanui, 1840. 178 p. CaBViPA; DLC. 40-2541

Gallaudet, Thomas Hopkins, 1787-1851. The practical spelling-book, with reading lessons. By T. H. Gallaudet and Horace Hooker. Hartford, CT: Belknap and Hamersley [1840] 166 p. InCW; MH; NNC; NRU; OO. 40-2542

Gallaudet, Thomas Hopkins, 1787-1851. Samuel, including the life of Saul, by Rev. T. H. Gallaudet. New York: published by the American Tract Society, D. Fanshaw, printer, 1840. 198 p. RNR. 40-2543

Gallaudet, Thomas Hopkins, 1787-1851. Scripture biography for the young. With critical illustations and practical emarks. Samuel. Including the life of Saul. New York: Published by the American Tract Society, D. Fanshaw, printer, 1840. 198 p. MBAt; MH; MnM; ijMD; WHi. 40-2544

Gallup, Joseph A. Observations made during a visit to the Clarendon Springs, Vt... by Joseph A. Gallup, M. D. Windsor: printed by Tracy & Severance, 1840. 14 p. MH-M; NNNAM; Vt; VtU; VtMidbC. 40-2545

Galt, John, 1779-1839. All the voyages round the world, from the first by Magellan in 1520 to that of Freycinet in 1820; now first collected by Capt. Samuel Prior [pseud.] New York: William H. Colyer, 1840. 418 p. CtHT; MWet; NBuG; NCH; NN; PU. 40-2546

Gammage, Smith P., 1810-1893. Fact not fiction; or, the remarakable history of Mrs. Louisa Liscum. With an appendix. By Rev. S. P. Gammage. New York: Wm. C. Martin, print., 1840. 72 p. DLC; NN; NSm; NSmb. 40-2547

Gannal, Jean Nicholas, 1791-1852. History of embalming, and of preparations in anatomy, pathology, and natural history, including an account of a new process for embalming. By J. N. Gannal... Tr. from the French. With notes and additions, by R. Harlan, M. D. Philadelphia, PA: J. Dobson, 1840. 264 p. CtMW; KyLo; NhD; PPi; ViU. 40-2548

Gannett, Ezra Stiles, 1801-1871. The arrival of the Britannia. A sermon delivered... by Ezra S. Gannett... Boston, MA: Joseph Dowe, 1840. 23 p. CtSoP; ICMe; MBC; MeHi; MiD-B; MWA; PCC. 40-2549

Gannett, Ezra Stiles, 1801-1871. The Spring. A sermon for children, preached in the Federal Street meeting house, April 26, 1840. Boston, MA: s. l., 1840. DLC; MB; MH; PPAmP. 40-2550

Gannett, Ezra Stiles, 1801-1871. Unitarian Christianity: What it is, and what it is not. A discourse delivered at the installation of Rev. John Parkman as pastor of the First Unitarian Church and Society in Dover, N. H., Apr. 22, 1840. Boston, MA: William Crosby and Co., 1840. 56 p. ICMe; MH; MiD-B; Nh; PHi. 40-2551

Gardner's Hartford city directory for 1840. With a complete list of city officers, officers of the First Department, of the several corporations in the City of Hartford, &c. &c. Published annually. No. 3, May, 1840. Hartford, CT: Printed by Case, Tiffany & Co., 1840. 65 p. Ct. 40-2552

Garidel, L. A. Large sale of real estate [situated in the second municipality] at Banks arcade, on Monday, 3rd. of August, 1840, by L. A. Garidel, Hewlett and Cenas, and Joseph A. Beard. New Orleans, LA: Greene & Fishbournes, lithographers, 1840. 3 p. LNHT. 40-2553

Garland, Hugh A. Address of the Hon. Hugh A. Garland before the Democratic mass convention held at New Brunswick, N. J., October 8th, 1840... Published by request of the committee. New Brunswick, NJ: Lewis R. Stelle, 1840. 16 p. MBC; Nj; PHi. 40-2554

Garland, Hugh A., 1805-1854. An oration pronounced in Castle Garden, July 27, 1840, by Hugh A. Garland, of Virginia, in celebration of the second declaration of independence or the passage of the independent treasury bill. New York: W. G. Boggs [1840] 31 p. MdH; NN; Vi; ViN; ViU. 40-2555

Garland, James, 1791-1885. Letter of

James Garland to his constituents. 2d edition. [Washington, DC: s. l., 1840] 30 p. CtY; NcD; OClWHi; PPL. 40-2556

Garland, James, 1791-1885. Letter to his constituents [Apr., 1840, advocating the election of W. H. Harrison to the presidency.] [Washington, DC: s. l., 1840] 31 p. M. 40-2557

Garland, James, 1791-1885. Speech of Hon. James Garland, of Virginia, on the resolution of Mr. Thompson, of South Carolina, for the rejection of abolitionist petitions. Delivered in the House of Representatives of the United States, January 21, 1840. Washington, DC: Madisonian Office, 1840. 14 p. CtY; MBC; MdHi; MiU-C; OClWHi. 40-2558

The Garland for 1840; a Christmas, New Year and birthday present. Added t. p. in colors. Boston, MA: J. A. Noble, 1840. 331 p. ICU; MWHi; NNF; WU. 40-2559

Garrard, Daniel. An address to the young men of Kentucky, comprising a bief review of the military services of General William Henry Harrison, during the late war between Great Britain and the United States. By Daniel Garrard, of Clay County, Ky. Frankfort, KY: Printed by Robinson & Adams, 1840. 29 p. ICU; MoSM; OC. 40-2560

Garrison, Edwin William, 1804-1840. Memoir of Mrs. Rebekah P. Pinkham, late consort of Rev. E. Pinkham, of Sedgwick, Me... By E. W. Garrison. Portland, ME: printed by the Zions Advocate office, 1840. 160 p. DLC; MeB; MeBa; MWA; OrU. 40-2561

Gaskell, Elizabeth Cleghorn (Stevenson)1810-1865. The life of Charlotte Bronte, by E. C. Gaskell. Two volumes, complete in one. New York: D. Appleton and Company, 1840. 2 v. NAlf. 40-2562

Gaylord, Willis, 1792-1844. American husbandry; being a series of essays on agriculture compiled principally from "The Cultivators" and "The Genesee Farmer" with additions. By Willis Gaylord and Luther Tucker. New York: Harper and Brothers, 1840. 2 v. IP; MWA; NGlc; OOxM-S; P. 40-2563

Geist des gebetes des Herrn und der zehn gebote in morgan und adondgebeten. Harrisburg, PA: s. l., 1840. 71 p. DLC; PSt. 40-2564

The gem; a Christmas & New Year's present for 1840. Philadelphia, PA: s. l. [1840] 287 p. KU; MWA; NcD. 40-2565

The gem; a Christmas & New Year's present... Philadelphia, PA: Henry F. Anners; [Adam Waldie, pr., 1840-42] 2 v. NjR. 40-2566

The gem; or, Young ladies' commonplace book. Changed title for 1840 from "The Gem, a Christmas & New Year's present" for that year. Philadelphia, PA: s. l. [1840] p. MBAt. 40-2567

Der Gemeinschaftliche Gesangbuch. 6th ed. Philadelphia, PA: George W. Mentz & Son, 1840. PPeSchw. 40-2568

Gems. From Bellini's celebrated opera, La Norma, arranged as waltzes for the piano forte, by J. D. Baldenecker, author of "Potpourris," "Norma," "Anna Balena" $c... Philadelphia, PA: George Willig [184-?] 5 p. ViU. 40-2569

Gems of American poetry, by distinguished authors. New York: A. and C. B. Edwards, 1840. 253 p. ICHi; MiD; NcAS; RPB; ViU. 40-2570

Genealogy & biography of the first settlers of Hartford. [Hartford, CT: s. l., 184-?] 48 p. MB. 40-2571

General Association of Connecticut. Minutes of the General Association of Connecticut, at their meeting in New Haven, June, 1840. With an appendix, containing the report of the state of religion, etc., etc. Hartford, CT: E. Gleason, printer, 1840. 44 p. MoWgT. 40-2572

General Association of Massachusetts. Minutes of the General Association of Massachusetts at their meeting in Ipswhich, June, 1840, with the narrative of the State of Relgiion and the pastoral letter. Boston, MA: Printed by Crocker and Brewster, 1840. 49 p. IEG. 40-2573

General Harrison in Congress. [Washington, DC: Office of the National Intelligencer, 1840] 32 p. CtY; DLC; MH; OClWHi; RPB. 40-2574

The Genesee farmer & gardener's journal: a monthly journal devoted to agriculture & horticulture, domestic and rural economy. Rochester, NY: Bateman & Crossman, 1840. ICMcHi; NN; NRU; NRHi; PU. 40-2575

The Genesee farmer:a monthly journal devoted to agriculture & horticulture, domestic and rural economy... vol. 1 - 1840. Rochester, NY: J. Harris [etc.] 1840-65. 26 v. Cu-B; IU; Mh-BA; OCl; PPHor. 40-2576

Genesee Wesleyan Seminary, Lima, N. Y. Catalogue of the Officers and Students of the Genesee Wesleyan Seminary, Lima, N. Y. For the year ending September 30, 1840. Rochester, NY: William Alling, Printer, 184?. 22 p. NLG. 40-2577

Geneva Lyceum. Catalogue of Geneva Lyceum, 1839-40. Geneva, NY: Ira Merrell, Printer, 1840. 12 p. NGH. 40-2578

Geneva Medical College. Annual circular of the Medical Institution of Geneva College. June 1840. Geneva, NY: Ira Merrell, Printer, 1840. 15 p. NGH; NNNAM; PPL. 40-2579

Geneva Medical College. Catalogue of the trustees, officers, and medical class. Session 1839-40. Geneva, NY: Ira Merrell, Printer, 1840. 12 p. NGH. 40-2580

Genius of liberty. v. 1., Dec. 19, 1840-. Lowell, IL: The Board of Managers of the La Salle County Anti-Slavery Society [1840-] v. CSt; DLC; IEN; InU; NjP. 40-2581

Gentry, Meredith Poindexter. Speech on the bill to secure the freedom of elections, and in reply to Watterson, in the House of Representatives [of the U. S.] May 19, 1840. Washington, DC: pr. by Gales & Seaton, 1840. 31 p. DLC; M; T. 40-2582

George, William. An essay on angling, by a member of the Worcester Anglers' Society. Worcester, MA: Printed at the Guardian Off., 1840. 44 p. CtY; ICN; MH; NN. 40-2583

Georgetown College, Ky. The laws of Georgetown college, Kentucky, revised 1840. Georgetown, KY: s. l., 1840. 20 p. MHi. 40-2584

Georgia. General Assembly. Acts of the General assembly of the State of Georgia, passed in Milledgeville at an annual session in November and December, 1839. Published by authority. Milledgeville, GA: Grieve & Orme, State printers, 1840. 245 p. GHi; IaU-L; MdBB; Nj; Wa-L. 40-2585

Georgia. General Assembly. House of Representatives. Journal of the House of Representatives of the State of Georgia, at an annual session of the General assembly, begun and held in Milledgeville, the seat of government, in November and December, 1839. Milledgeville, GA: Grieve & Orme, State printers, 1840. 450 p. G-Ar; GMilvC; NNFM. 40-2586

Georgia. General Assembly. Senate. Journal of the Senate of the State of Georgia, at an annual session of the General assembly, begun and held in Milledgeville, the seat of government, in November and December, 1839. Milledgeville, GA: Grieve & Orme, State printers, 1840. 384 p. G-Ar; GMilvC; NcU. 40-2587

Georgia. Governor, 1837-1839 (Gilmer) Annual message of Governor Gilmer, to both branches of the General assembly of the state of Georgia, November 5, 1839. [Milledgeville, GA: s. l., 1840?] p. GEU. 40-2588

Georgia Historical Society. Collections of the Georgia Historical Society. Vol. I . Savannah, GA: printed for the Society 1840-. v. InU; MeHi; NjR; OkHi; ScCC 40-2589

The Georgia, Carolina, and Alabama planters' and merchants; almanac for 1841... Augusta, GA: Browne & Mc-Cafferty [1840] p. GSDe. 40-2590

Geramb, Marie Joseph, 1772-1848. Pilgrimage to Jerusalem and Mt. Sinai. Philadelphia, PA: Carey & Hart, 1840. 2 v. InNd; MiD; NjMD; PPA; RPAg. 40-2591

Geramb, Marie Joseph, 1772-1848. A Pilgrimage to Palestine, Egypt and Syria. By Marie-Joseph de Geramb, monk of La Trappe. Philadelphia, PA: s. l., 1840. 2 v. PPL-R. 40-2592

Geramb, Marie Joseph, 1772-1848. Visit to Rome. By Rev. Father Baron Geramb, Abbot and procurator-general of La Trappe. Philadelphia, PA: published by Michael Kelly, 1840. 271 p. InNd; LNX; MBBC; MoSU; PPL. 40-2593

Gettysburg College. Annual announcement of lectures. Philadelphia, PA: s. l., 1840. MHi; PHi; PP; PPCP; PPL; PPL-R; PU. 40-2594

Gettysburg College. Annual catalogue of the officers and students in Pennsylvania College. S. l.: s. l., 1840. 19 p. PHi; OSW. 40-2595

Gettysburg College. Medical Department. 1st annual announcement, Medical Department of Penn. College, 1840/41. Gettysburg, PA?: s. l., 1840? p. MH. 40-2596

Gettysburg College. Theological Seminary of the United Lutheran Church in America. Catalogue. Gettysburg, PA: s. l., 1840. 12 p. MeB; PPLT; PU. 40-2597

Gettysburg College. Theological Seminary of the United Lutheran Church in America. General catalogue & constitution. Gettysburg, PA: s. l., 1840. 11, 20 p. MBC; N. 40-2598

Gibbon, Edward, 1737-1794. The history of the decline and fall of the Roman Empire... With notes by H. H. Milman. New York: Harper, 1840. 4 v. CtHC; KyHop; MdBJ; OClW; PPL; ScDuE. 40-2599

Gibbons, William. Practical logic, or, An assistant to theme writers. Designed for academies, public schools. Published by William Gibbons. Cleveland, OH: Printed by Sanford & Litt, 1840. 100 p. DLC; OClWHi. 40-2600

Gibson, George R. Address at the installation of the officers of Vincennes Lodge, No. 1, on the 24th of June, 1840. By George R. Gibson. Vincennes, IN: Printed by Elihu Stout and Son, 1840. 14 p. MBFM; NNFM. 40-2601

Gibson, Robert. The theory and practice of surveying. By Robert Gibson. Philadelphia, PA: Published by A. S. Barnes and Co., 1840. 412 p. MdW; PBL; TxD-T. 40-2602

Gibson, Robert. The theory and practice of surveying; containing all the instructions requisite for the skilled practice of this art, with a new set of accurate mathematical tables. By Robert Gibson. Illustrated by copper plates. Newly arranged, improved and enlarged with useful selections by James Ryan. Hartford, CT: A. S. Barnes and Co., 1840. 248, 73, 91 p. NcAS; PBL. 40-2603

Giddings, Joshua Reed, 1795-1864.

Speech... in answer to Mr. Duncan, on the bill providing for the civil and diplomatic expenses of government for the year 1840... House... April 11, 1840. [Washington, DC?: s. l., 1840?] 16 p. MdHi; MiD-B; OClWHi. 40-2604

Gidu. [In the Grebs language] [Fair Hope, AL: s. l., 1840] 10 p. CtY. 40-2605

Gift for the holidays. Philadelphia, PA: American Sunday School Union, 1840. DLC; MB; MH; MnU; PD. 40-2606

A gift for the young. Boston, MA: W. Crosby and Company, 1840. 66 p. MH. 40-2607

Giger, George Musgrave, 1822-1865. Note book of lectures on architecture by A. B. Dod. Baltimore, MD: s. l., 1840. 149 p. PPPrHi. 40-2608

Gilder, J. Leonard. Illustrations of divine providence: a sermon preached... on occasion of the celebration of the centenary of Wesleyan Methodism. New York: s. l., 1840. 16 p. CtMW; IEG; MBNMHi. 40-2609

Giles, Charles, 1783-1867. Convention of drunkards: a satirical essay on intemperance, to which are added, three speeches on the same subject; an oration on the anniversary of American independence; and an ode on the completion of the Erie canal... 2d ed. New York: Scofield and Voorhies, 1840. 126 p. ICN; WHi. 40-2610

Gillette, A. D. A sermon. Delivered before the Bucks County Bible Society in the Hill-Town Baptist Meeting House... By A. D. Gillette... Philadelphia, PA: King and Baird, printers, 1840. 16 p.

MNtCA; NHC-S; PCA; PCC; PHi. 40-2611

Gilman, Caroline Howard, 1794-1888. Love's progress. By the author of "The recollections of a New England housekeeper." New York: Harper & Brothers, 1840. 171 p. CSmH; MH; PPL-R; ScU; TxU. 40-2612

Gilman, Caroline Howard, 1794-1888. Oracles from the poets; a fanciful diversion for the drawing room. By Caroline Gilman... New York: Wiley and Putnam, 1840. 242 p. LNH. 40-2613

Gilman, Chandler Robbins. Introductory address to the students in medicine of the College of Physicians and Surgeons of the University of State of New York... Delivered November. 6, 1840, by Chandler R. Gilman. New York: the students, 1840. 24 p. MB; NBMS; NNC; NNN; NNNAM. 40-2614

Gilmanton Theological Seminary, N. H. Catalogue of the officers and students of the Theological Seminary, Gilmanton, N. H. Gilmanton, NH: Alfred Prescott, 1840. 12 p. CBPSR; Nh-Hi. 40-2615

Gilmanton Theological Seminary, N. H. Exercises of the Rhetorical Society, 1840-1843. Gilmanton, NH: s. l. [1840-45] v. Nh-Hi. 40-2616

Gilmer, Thomas Walker, 1802-1844. [Letter dated, Executive Department, Nov. 12th, 1840] [Richmond, VA?: n. p., 1840] p. ViU. 40-2617

Gilpin, Joshua, vicar of Wrockwardine. A monument of parential affection to a dear and only son. New York: Published by T. Mason and G. Lane, 1840. 94 p. MsAb. 40-2618

Ginal, Heinrich. Rede gehalten ber der feierlichen Eroffnung der deutschen evangelischen kirche in Philadelphia. By Heinrich GInal. Philadelphia, PA: n. pub., n. pr., 1840. 14 p. NjPT. 40-2619

Girard almanac for 1841. Philadelphia, PA: Thomas L. Bonsal [1840] p. MWA. 40-2620

Girard College, Philadelphia. Appeal against the conduct of Councils... Philadelphia, PA: s. l., 1840. PPL. 40-2621

Girard College, Philadelphia. Communication from the board of trustees to the select & common councils of Philadelphia. Presented July 16, 1841. Philadelphia, PA: Bailey, 1840?. 22 p. MBC; PPAmP; PPFrankI; PHi. 40-2622

Girard College, Philadelphia. Magnetic Observatory. Ordinary meteorological observations. Philadelphia, PA: s. l. [1840-45] 3 v. OHi. 40-2623

Girard College, Philadelphia. Report of the special committee appointed by the common council on a communication fr. the board of trustees... read... Aug. 27, 1840. Philadelphia, PA: s. l., 1840. 53 p. PPFrankI. 40-2624

Girardin, Delphine Gay, 1804-1855. The clockmaker's hat; a farce. Adapted from "Le chapeau d'un horologer" by Mme. Emile de Girardin, and translated by William Robertson. New York: S. French [184-?] 14 p. MH. 40-2625

Gleig, George Robert, 1796-1888. The

life of Oliver Cromwell, by Rev. G. R. Gleig. Sanbornton, NH: C. Lane, 1840. 161 p. CtY; MWA; Nh-Hi; NRMA; OClWHi; OO. 40-2626

Glengall, Richard Butler, 1794-1858. The Irish tutor, or New lights; a farce in one act. New York: S. French [184-?] 20 p. CSmH; MH; NIC; OU; PPL. 40-2627

Glenn, James. The real nature of the electric fluid... and also, a cause assigned for the polarity of the magnet... Morrisville, NY: printed by J. & E. Norton, 1840. 16 p. CtY; MBM; NjR. 40-2628

Glentworth, James B. A statement of the frauds on the elective franchise in the City of New York... in 1838 and 1839... New York: s. l., 1840. MB; MBAt; NHi. 40-2629

Gloucester County, N. J. Citizens. Appeal to the people of the County of Gloucester to their fellow citizens of N. J. on the subject of public horse racing. Camden, NJ: P. G. Gray, 1840. 28 p. NjR; PHC. 40-2630

Glover, Charles William, 1806-1863. Cheer up my own Jeannette. Composed by Charles W. Glover. Boston, MA: Oliver Ditson [184-?] 3 p. ViU. 40-2631

Glover, Charles William, 1806-1863. ... Conscripts departure... Boston, MA: Oliver Ditson [184-?] 5 p. IaU; ViU. 40-2632

Glover, Charles William, 1806-1863. I'm a merry laughing girl. Composed for the piano forte by C. W. Glover. Baltimore, MD: Miller & Beacham, successors to F. D. Benteen [184-?] 5 p. ViU. 40-2633

Glover, Charles William, 1806-1863. Jeannette & Jeannot. [The conscript's departure] Written by Charles Jeffreys; composed by Chas. W. Glover. Baltimore, MD: F. D. Benteen [184-?] 11 p. NcD. 40-2634

Glover, Charles William, 1806-1863. Jeannette & Jeannot. [The conscript's departure] Written by Charles Jeffreys; composed by Chas. W. Glover. Baltimore, MD; Cincinnati, OH: G. Willig Jr.; Mason, Colburn & Co. [184-?] 2 p. ViU. 40-2635

Glover, Charles William, 1806-1863. Little gipsy Jane. [Song. Accomp. for piano forte] New York: Berry & Gordon [184-?] 5 p. MB. 40-2636

Glover, Charles William, 1806-1863. The royal gems: a set of waltzes, arranged by C. W. Glover. Boston, MA: Published by Oliver Ditson [184-?] 6 p. WHi. 40-2637

Glover, Charles William, 1806-1863. The soldier's return. [Song with accompaniment for piano forte] Words by Charles Jeffereys [sic] Music by Charles W. Glover. Boston, MA: Ditson [184-?] 9 p. MB. 40-2638

Glover, Charles William, 1806-1863. The melodies of many lands. Written by Charles Jefferies; composed by Charles W. GLover. New York; Boston, MA; Cincinnati, OH: Wm. Hall & son; G. P. Reed; L. Lemaire [184-?] 2 p. MB; ViU. 40-2639

Glover, Stephen, 1812-1870. Annie o' the banks o' the Dee, song of the day dreamer, written by Mrs. Crawford.

Music by Stephen Glover. Boston, MA: Oliver Ditson [184-?] 5 p. WHi. 40-2640

Glover, Stephen, 1812-1870. Ask me no more to sing that song of gladness. [Song. Accomp. for piano forte] Boston, MA: Oliver Ditson [184-?] 4 p. MB. 40-2641

Glover, Stephen, 1812-1870. Charity: "Meek and lowly. "Sacred song. Written by Charles Jeffreys; composed by Stephen Glover. Baltimore, MD; New Orleans, LA: F. D. Benteen [184-?] 3 p. ViU. 40-2642

Glover, Stephen, 1812-1870. ... Charity... Written by Charles Jeffreys; composed by Stephen Glover. Boston, MA: Oliver Ditson [184-?] 5 p. ViU. 40-2643

Glover, Stephen, 1812-1870. The dream is past. Song written by E. Fitz Aubin, Esqr. Composed by S.] Glover. Philadelphia, PA: A. Fiot [184-?] 2 p. ViU. 40-2644

Glover, Stephen, 1812-1870. Dreams of childhood. Poetry by W. Jones, esq. Music by S. Glover. Boston, MA: Oliver Ditson [184-?] 2 p. ViU. 40-2645

Glover, Stephen, 1812-1870. Give me a cot in the valley I love. Ballad. Written by Charles Jeffreys; music by S. Glover. Boston, MA: Oliver Ditson [184-?] 4 p. ViU. 40-2646

Glover, Stephen, 1812-1870. A home that I love. A popular ballad. Poetry by Charles Jeffreys; music by Stephen Glover; arranged for the guitar by Saml. Carusi. Louisville: Peters, Webb & Co. [184-?] 3 p. ViU. 40-2647

Glover, Stephen, 1812-1870. A home that I love. A popular ballad. Poetry by Charles Jeffreys; music composed & arranged for the piano forte by Stephen Glover. Baltimore MD: Saml. Carusi [184-?] 5 p. ViU. 40-2648

Glover, Stephen, 1812-1870. A home that I love. [Song. Accomp for piano forte] 4th edition. New York: Firth & Hall [184-?] 7 p. MB; WHi. 40-2649

Glover, Stephen, 1812-1870. Listen! 'tis the woodbird's song. Vocal duett. [S. A. Acomp for piano forte] New York: Firth & Hall [184-?] 9 p. MB. 40-2650

Glover, Stephen, 1812-1870. Music and her sister song. Song. Words by Richard Ryqn, Esq. Music by Stephen Glover... Baltimore, MD; New Orleans LA: F. D. Benteen; W. T. Mayo [184-?] 7 p. ViU. 40-2651

Glover, Stephen, 1812-1870. My heart of sad to day. Words by Charles Jeffreys; music by Stephen Glover. Boston, MA: Oliver Ditson [184-?] 4 p. ViU. 40-2652

Glover, Stephen, 1812-1870. Sister since I met thee last. Song. Written by Mrs. Hemans. Composed by Stephen Glover. New York: Firth, Hall & Pond and Firth & Hall [184-?] 7 p. ViU; WHi. 40-2653

Glover, Stephen, 1812-1870. The song of Blanche Alpen. The words written by Charles Jeffreys. The music composed by Stephen Glover. Baltimore, MD; New Orleans, LA: F. D. Benteen; W. T. Mayo [184-?] 5 p. ViU. 40-2654

Glover, Stephen, 1812-1870. The song of Blanche Alpen. The words written by

Charles Jeffreys. The music composed by Stephen Glover. Philadelphia, PA: George Willig [184-?] 5 p. ViU. 40-2655

Glover, Stephen, 1812-1870. The song of charity. Boston, MA: s. l. [184-?] p. MB. 40-2656

Glover, Stephen, 1812-1870. ... The valley of Chamouni: ballad. Words by E. Enoch; music by Stephen Glover. New York: Pub. by Firth Pond & Co. [184-?] 5 p. WHi. 40-2657

Glover, Stephen, 1812-1870. Walter and Florence. The subject from Mr. Charles Dickens, tale, "Dombry and Son." The music by Stephen Glover. Boston, MA: Published by Oliver Ditson [184-?] 5 p. WHi. 40-2658

Glover, Stephen, 1812-1870. What are the wild waves saying? Duett between Paul and Florence in "Dombry and Son. "The music by Stephen Glover. Philadelphia, PA; New York: J. E. Gould; T. S. Berry [184-?] 5 p. ViU. 40-2659

Gluck, Christoph Willibald Ritter von. Che faro senza Euridice. I have lost my Euridice. Cavatina [S. or T. Accomp. for piano forte] Boston, MA: Ditson [184-?] 7 p. MB. 40-2660

Glynn, James. Chart of the Entrance of Cape Fear River, with continuation. Washington, DC: s. l., 1840. 9 p. PHi. 40-2661

Glynn, James. Continuation of the survey of Cape Fear river... Washington, DC: s. l., 1840. RPAt. 40-2662

Go-ahead. The Crockett almanac for

1841. Boston, MA: published by J. Fisher [1840] 36 p. MHi. 40-2663

Go ahead! The Crocket Almanac, 1841, containing adventures, exploits, sprees & Scarapes in the west, & life and manners in the backwoods. Nashville, TN: Published by Ben Harding [1840] 36 p. MHi; MWA; MsJS; T. 40-2664

Go thou and dream! Arranged for the piano by C. Meineke. Baltimore, MD: G. Willig, Jr. [1840] 2 p. ViU. 40-2665

Godman, John, 1782-1847. A sermon delivered before His Excellency Edward Everett, Governor, the Honorable Council, and the Legislature of Massachusetts at the annual election, January 1, 1840. By John Godman, D. D., pastor of the Second Church in Dorchester. Boston, MA: Dutton and Wentworth, 1840. 32 p. CtY; ICMe; MeHi; MWA; NjR. 40-2666

Goethe, Johann Wolfgang von, 1749-1832. Faust: a dramatic poem, by Goethe. Translated into English prose, with notes, etc., by A. Hayward, Esq. First American from the third London edition. Loweell, MA: Daniel Bixby, 1840. 317 p. LNH; MNBedf; MWA; NcU; WHal. 40-2667

Goggin, William Lefwich, 1807-1870. Speech of Mr. Goggin, of Virginia, on The Treasury Note Bill. Delivered in the House of Representatives of the United States in Committee of the Whole on the State of the Union, March 25, 1840. Washington, DC: Printed by Gales and Seaton, 1840. 23 p. M; MWA. 40-2668

Goin, Thomas, 1803-1847. Remarks on the home squadron and naval school. By a gentleman of New York, formerly connected with the city press [Thomas Goin] New York: Printed by J. P. Wright, 1840. 40 p. CU; DLC; MH; NjR; NN. 40-2669

Goldsbury, John, 1795-1890. American common-school reader and speaker; being a selection of pieces in prose and verse, with rules for reading and speaking. Boston, MA: C. Tappan [184-?] 428 p. DLC; MB. 40-2670

Goldsmith, Oliver, 1728-1774. Goldsmith's Roman history. Abridged by himself, for the use of schools. Stereotyped by B. & J. Collins, New York. First edition, divided into sections, for a class-book. Hartford, CT: Andrus and Judd [184-?] 316 p. RPB. 40-2671

Goldsmith, Oliver, 1728-1774. Goldsmith's Roman history. Abridged by himself, for the use of schools. Stereotyped by B. & J. Collins, New York. First edition, divided into sections, for a class-book. Ithaca, NY: Mack, Andrus & Woodruff, 1840. 316 p. DLC; NIC; NWM. 40-2672

Goldsmith, Oliver, 1728-1774. Goldsmith's Roman history. Abridged by himself, for the use of schools. Revised and corrected... By William Grimshaw. Improved ed. Philadelphia, PA: Grigg & Elliott, 1840. 316 p. MH. 40-2673

Goldsmith, Oliver, 1728-1774. The Grecican history, from the earliest state to the death of Alexander the Great. By Dr. Goldsmith. Ithaca, NY: Mack, Andrus & Woodruff, 1840. 316 p. IEG; ViU. 40-2674

Goldsmith, Oliver, 1728-1774. The history of Greece, from the earliest state to the death of Alexander the Great. To which is added a summary account of the affairs of Greece, from the period to the sacking of Constantinople by the Ottomans. New York: Harper & Brothers, 1840. 2 v. InU; LN; NjR; RJa; ScGrw. 40-2675

Goldsmith, Olivier, 1728-1774. The history of Rome, by Dr. Goldsmith. Edited for the school district library by H. W. Herbert, author of "The brothers," "Cromwell," etc. New York: Harper & Brothers, 1840. 340 p. MLow; NNebg; NNG; P; RKi. 40-2676

Goldsmith, Oliver, 1728-1774. The miscellaneous works of Oliver Goldsmith. With an account of his life and writings. Edited by Washington Irving. Complete in one volume. Philadelphia, PA: J. Crissy, 1840. 527 p. CtY; IaDuC; LStBA; MBC; NP. 40-2677

Goldsmith, Oliver, 1728-1774. Pinnock's Improved Edition of Dr. Goldsmith's abridgement of the history of Rome. To which is prefixed an introduction to the study of Roman history and a great variety of valuable information added throughout the work on the manners, institutions, and antiquities of the Romans. With numerous biographical and historical notes. First American, corrected and revised from the twelfth English edition. Philadelphia, PA: F. W. Greenough, 1840. 395, 36 p. COCA; MnWh; OHi. 40-2678

Goldsmith, Oliver, 1728-1774. ... She stoopes to conquer. A comedy in five acts. By Dr. Goldsmith. With the stage business, cast of characters, costumes, relative positions, etc. New York: S.

French [etc., etc., 184-?] 66 p. CSt; ViU. 40-2679

Goldsmith, Oliver, 1728-1774. The Vicar of Wakefield, a tale. To which is annexed the deserted village. Exeter: J. & B. Williams, 1840. 288 p. MWA. 40-2680

Gooch, Richard Barnes, 1820-1849. The anniversary address of the Jefferson society, of the University of Virginia, delivered on the 13th April 1840, by Richard Barnes Gooch, of Richmond. Published by order of the Jefferson society. Charlottesville, VA: James Alexander, printer, 1840. 15 p. DLC; TxU; ViU. 40-2681

Gooch, Robert, 1784-1830. A practical compendium of midwifery; being the course of lectures on midwifery and on the diseases of women and infants. Delivered at St. Bartholomew's Hospital... Prepared for publication by George Skinner. 3rd American ed. Philadelphia, PA: s. l., 1840. 339 p. CSt-L; GEU-M; ICU-R; MdBJ; PPCP. 40-2682

Good, John Mason, 1764-1827. Book of nature; to which is prefixed a sketch of the author's life. Hartford, CT: Belknap & Hamersley, 1840. 467 p. MH; ScC. 40-2683

Good advice for boys & girls. Worcester: s. l. [184-?] p. MB. 40-2684

Good Intent Hose Company, Philadelphia. Constitution and by-laws. Philadelphia, PA: s. l., 1840. 22 p. PHi. 40-2685

Goodale, Montgomery S. Christian satisfied. Sermon, funeral of Mr. Joseph

Clezbe. Amsterdam, NY: s. l. [1840] 12 p. RPB. 40-2686

Goode, Patrick Gaines, 1798-1862. Speech of the Hon. Patrick G. Goode, of Ohio, in reply to Mr. Cary's attack upon General Harrison, delivered in the House of Representatives in the United States, February, 1840... [Washington, DC: Smith, 1840] 16 p. MiGr; MoS; OClWHi. 40-2687

Goode, Patrick Gaines, 1798-1862. Speech on the continuation of the Cumberland Road, in the House of Representatives [of the U. S.] Feb. 15, 1840... Washington, DC: pr. by Gales & Seaton, 1840. 16 p. M. 40-2688

Goode, Patrick Gaines, 1798-1862. A statement of the expenditures of government, exhibiting the prodigality & extravagance of the present administration taken from the speech of Mr. Goode of Ohio. Delivered in the House of Representatives, April 27, 1840. [Washington, DC: s. l., 1840?] 4, 2 p. DLC; Nh. 40-2689

Goodell, William, 1792-1878. One more appeal to professors of religion, ministers and churches who are not enlisted in the struggle against slavery. By William Goodell, abolitionist. Boston, MA: s. l., 184-? 8 p. MH; OO. 40-2690

Goodheart, Mrs. The progressive primer. Copy Right. Concord: J. F. Brown [1840?] p. MH. 40-2691

Goodman, John R. ... Penna. biography; or, Memoirs of eminent Pennsylvania. With occasional extracts, in prose and verse, from their writings... to which is prefixed as required introduction the life of Wm. Penn... Philadelphia, PA: J. Crissy, 1840. 276 p. DLC; ICP; MdBE; PLFM; PPWa. 40-2692

Goodrich, Charles Augustus 1790-1862. History of the United States of America on a plan... Rev. and enl. from the 65th edition. Boston, MA: Jenks & Palmer [184-?] p. MH; OO. 40-2693

Goodrich, Charles Augustus, 1790-1862. Lives of the signers of the Declaration of Independence. By Rev. Charles A. Goodrich. 8th edition. New York: Thomas Mather, 1840. 460 p. CtHT; IaDa; MDux; MWHi; NFai. 40-2694

Goodrich, Charles Augustus, 1790-1862. Questions on enlarged and improved edition of Goodrich's school history. Boston, MA: Jenks & Palmer [1840?] p. MH. 40-2695

Goodrich, Charles Augustus, 1790-1862. Religious ceremonies and customs, or the forms of worship... on the basis of the celebrated and splendid works of Bernard Picart... by Charles A. Goodrich. Louisville, KY: R. H. Brockway, 1840. 576 p. CTHWatk; MnSM; OClWHi; VtMidbC. 40-2696

Goodrich, Charles Augustus, 1790-1862. The universal traveller: designed to introduce readers at home to an acquaintance with the arts, customs, and manners of the principal modern nations of the globe... By Charles A. Goodrich. New York: James, 1840. 504 p. CLCo; NCH; NHem; RBr; ScCliTO. 40-2697

Goodrich, Chauncey Allen, 1790-1860. Lessons in Latin parsing... 3d ed. New Haven, CT: Durrie & Peck, 1840. MH. 40-2698

Goodrich, Samuel Griswold, 1793-1860. Abinoji aki tibajimouin. In the Ojibwa language. Boston, MA: printed for the American Board of Commisioners for Foreign Missions by Crocker & Brewster, 1840. 139 p. MB; MBGCT; MH; MnHi; PPAmP. 40-2699

Goodrich, Samuel Griswold, 1793-1860. Biography of eminent men, statesmen, heroes, authors, artists, and men of science, of Europe and America, Part II. New York: published by Cornish Lamport & Co., 1840. 286 p. MPiB. 40-2700

Goodrich, Samuel Griswold, 1793-1860. The child's botany. Boston, MA: Jenks and Palmer, 1840. ICU; MH. 40-2701

Goodrich, Samuel Griswold, 1793-1860. The first book of history, for chldren and youth, by the author of Peter Parley's tales... Revised edition. Boston, MA: Charles J. Hendee and Jenks and Palmer, 1840. 183 p. LU; MAnHi; MBU-E. 40-2702

Goodrich, Samuel Griswold, 1793-1860. The Fourth reader, for the use of schools. By S. G. Goodrich. Louisville, KY: Morton and Griswood [1840?] 324 p. KyHi. 40-2703

Goodrich, Samuel Griswold, 1793-1860. Moral tales: a selection of interesting stories. New York: Natfis & Cornish 1840] p. CSmH; DLC; KEmT; MB; MBAt. 40-2704

Goodrich, Samuel Griswold, 1793-1860. Peter Parley's arithmetic. [Vignette] With engravings. Boston, MA: Jenks & Palmer [1840] 144 p. DAU; hMHI. 40-2705

Goodrich, Samuel Griswold, 1793-1860. Peter Parley's Bible dictionary, containing illustrations of arts, manners, customs, birds, beasts, fishes, reptiles, insects and other things mentioned in the Bible. By Samuel Griswold Goodrich. Boston, MA: B. B. Mussey [1840] 208 p. MH-AH; NP. 40-2706

Goodrich, Samuel Griswold, 1793-1860. Peter Parley's Bible gazetteer, containing illustrations of Bible geography. Boston, MA: Mussey [1840] 192 p. KyPr; MH; MH-And; NN. 40-2707

Goodrich, Samuel Griswold, 1793-1860. Peter Parley's book of anecdotes. Illustrated by engravings. Philadelphia, PA: Thomas, Cowperthwait & Co. [1840] 144 p. CtY; ICU; NGos. 40-2708

Goodrich, Samuel Griswold, 1793-1860. Peter Parley's common school history. Illustrated by engravings. 7th ed. Philadelphia, PA: Marshall, Williams & Butler, 1840. MH. 40-2709

Goodrich, Samuel Griswold, 1793-1860. Peter Parley's common school history. Illustrated by engravings. 8th ed. Philadelphia, PA: Marshall, Williams & Butler, 1840. MH. 40-2710

Goodrich, Samuel Griswold, 1793-1860. Peter Parley's farewell. By S. G. Goodrich. New York: S. Colman, 1840. 324 p. DLC; MH; MLow; NPlaK; OSW. 40-2711

Goodrich, Samuel Griswold, 1793-1860. Peter Parley's illustration of astronomy. By Samuel Griswold Goodrich. Boston, MA: B. B. Mussey, 1840. 160 p. MH; NN; NP. Goodrich, Samuel Griswold, 1793-1860. Peter

Parley's illustrations of the Animal Kingdom; beasts, birds, fishes, reptiles and insects. Boston, MA: B. B. Mussey, 1840. 160 p. InU; KyPr; MH; NN. 40-2712

Goodrich, Samuel Griswold, 1793-1860. Peter Parley's illustration of commerce. By Samuel Griswold Goodrich. Boston, MA: B. B. Mussey, 1840. 152 p. NP. 40-2713

Goodrich, Samuel Griswold, 1793-1860. Peter Parley's illustration of the vegetable kingdom, trees, plants, and shrubs. By Samuel Griswold Goodrich. Boston, MA: B. B. Mussey, 1840. 330 p. CtHWatk; InU; NjPat. 40-2714

Goodrich, Samuel Griswold, 1793-1860. Peter Parley's illustrations of history. Boston, MA: B. B. Mussey, 1840. 152 p. InU; KyPr; NhM; NjN. 40-2715

Goodrich, Samuel Griswold, 1793-1860. Peter Parley's method of telling about geography to children. With nine maps and 75 engravings. New York: F. J. Huntington & Co., 1840. 120 p. IaBo; NN. 40-2716

Goodrich, Samuel Griswold, 1793-1860. Peter Parley's wonders of the earth, sea and sky. New York: S. Colman, 1840. CSmH; DLC; ICU; NBuG. 40-2717

Goodrich, Samuel Griswold, 1793-1860. A pictorial geography of the world, comprising a system of universal geography, popular and scientific... and illustrated by more that one thousand engravings... With a copious index, answering the purpose of a gazetteer. By S. G. Goodrich. 2d ed. Boston, MA: Otis, Broaders and Company, 1840. 2 v. [1008 p.] KU; MnHi; OCl; PPAmP; ViU. 40-2718

Goodrich, Samuel Griswold, 1793-1860. A pictorial geography of the world, comprising a system of universal geography, popular and scientific... With a copious index, answering the purpose of a gazetteer, by S. G. Goodrich. Third ed. Boston, MA: Otis, Broaders and Company, 1840. 2 v. MH; OCHP; PHi; PPWa; TxHR. 40-2719

Goodrich, Samuel Griswold, 1793-1860. The second book of history, including the modern history of Europe, Africa, and Asia. 35th edition. Boston, MA: C. J. Hendee, etc., 1840. MH. 40-2720

Goodrich, Samuel Griswold, 1793-1860. Short stories; or, A Selection of Interesting Tales... [anon.] New York: Nafis & Cornish [1840] 191 p. InU; MBAt; MH; PU; WU. 40-2721

Goodrich, Samuel Griswold, 1793-1860. Third reader for the use of schools. [Comprehensive readers.] Louisville, KY: Morton, 1840. PU. 40-2722

Goodrich, Samuel Griswold, 1793-1860. Third reader. 5th ed. Boston, MA: s. l., 1840. CTHWatk. 40-2723

Goodrich, Samuel Griswold, 1793-1860. The token and atlantic souvenir; a Christmas and New Year's present. Edited by S. G. Goodrich. Boston, MA: Otis, Brooders & Co., 1840. 304 p. ICN; KU; MWHi; NPV; TxDaM. 40-2724

Goodwin, Thomas. The return of prayers, by Thomas Goodwin... Philadelphia, PA: Presbyterian board of publication, William S. Martien, publishing agent, 1840. 229 p. CtHC; NjPT; TWcW; ViRut. 40-2725

Goody Two Shoes. The history of Goody Two Shoes; or, Life of Margery Meanwell. New York: Elton [184-?] 24 p. ICU. 40-2726

Gordon, Stanhope. Dear Normandie. [Song. Accomp for piano forte.] Boston, MA: Ditson [184-?] 5 p. MB. 40-2727

Gore, Catherine Grace Francis Moody, 1799-1861. The abbey, and other tales. Philadelphia, PA: s. l., 1840. 2 v. DLC; MB; MdBP. 40-2728

Gore, Catherine Grace Francis Moody, 1799-1861. The maid of Croissey; or [sic] Theresa's Vow. A Drama in Two Acts. New York: Samuel French [184-?] p. No Loc. 40-2729

Gore, Catherine Grace Francis Moody, 1799-1861. The maid of Croissey; or [sic] Theresa's Vow. A Drama in Two Acts. New York: Wm. Taylor & Company [184-?] 34 p. MH. 40-2730

Gore, Catherine Grace Francis Moody, 1799-1861. Preferment; or, My Uncle the Earl. By Mrs. Charles Gore... In two volumes... New York: Harper & Brothers, 1840. 2 v. GU; LU; MB; NNC; PU; RPE. 40-2731

Goria, Alexandre Edouard, 1823-1860. Nadiejda. Esperance, mazurka. Originale. Pour le piano par A. Goria. Op. 18... Baltimore, MD; New Orleans, LA: D. Benteen & co.; W. T. Mayo [184-] 5 p. ViU. 40-2732

Goria, Alexandre Edouard, 1823-1860. Olga Mazurka. Pour piano par A. Goria.

Philadelphia, PA; New York: A. Fiot; W. Dubois [184-?] 5 p. ViU. 40-2733

The gospel harmony, chronologically arranged in separate lessons, for Sunday schools and Bible classes. By a layman. Utica, NY: B. S. Merrill, publisher, 1840. 222 p. IaDuU; NUt; NUtHi; NN; OO. 40-2734

Gottschalk, Louis Moreau, 1829-1869. Bamboula; fantaisie pour piano. Op. 2. Boston, MA: O. Ditson [184-?] 17 p. WHi. 40-2735

Gouge, William M., 1796-1863. A short history of paper-money and banking in the United States, including an account of provincial and continental paper-money. To which is prefixed an inquiry into the principles of the system... William M. Gouge. 3rd edition. New York: The Evening Post, 1840. 64 p. CtY; NjP. 40-2736

Gouge, William M., 1796-1863. A short history of paper-money and banking in the United States, including an account of provincial and continental paper-money... By William M. Gouge. Fourth edition. New York: Office of the Evening Post, n. pr., 1840. 49 p. InHi; MH-BA; MiGr; NjR; WHi. 40-2737

Gould, Hannah Flagg, 1789-1865. The rising monument. [Poem.] Newburyport: s. l., 1840. MB. 40-2738

Gould, Nathaniel Duren. The sacred minstrels; a collection of psalm tunes, chants, anthems, sentences, and selected pieces. Boston, MA: s. l., 1840. 352 p. CtHWatk; MB; MHi. 40-2739

Gould, W. C. An appeal, with a brief account of the sentiments of five members of the Pres. Church, Newark, termed modern Perfectionists. By W. C. Gould and G. C. Stewart. Newark: s. l., 1840. MBAt. 40-2740

Gould's stenographic reporter; published monthly in the city of Washington, and devoted to the recording of important trials... also miscellaneous speeches of American statesmen... v. 1-v. 3, no. 1, 1840-1842? Washington: M. T. C. Gould, 1840-42? 3 v. DLC; NBu; NN; NTSC; Vi. 40-2741

Gouraud, Francois. Description of the Daguereotype process; or, A summary of M. Gouraud's public lectures, according to the principles of M. Daguerre; with a description of a provisory method for taking human portraits. Boston, MA: Dutton and Wentworth's print., 1840. 16 p. MBAt; MdAN; MU. 40-2742

Graeff, Johann Georg. The fairy's song. [S.] Philadelphia, PA: Klemm [184-?] 3 p. MB. 40-2743

Graff, Frederick, 1774-1847. Plans, sections & elevations of Fairmount water works. Philadelphia, PA: s. l., 1840. PPF; PPFrankI. 40-2744

Grafton, Mass. Normal School. Catalogue of the Grafton Normal School, Grafton, Mass., November, 1840. Worcester, MA: s. l., 1840. 6 p. MWA. 40-2745

Graham, James, 1793-1851. Speech of Mr. James Graham, of North Carolina, on the Sub-treasury bill, delivered in the House of Representatives, June 30th, 1840. Washington, DC: Printed by J.

Gideon, jr., 1840. 20 p. DLC; IU; MdBJ; NcU; PHi. 40-2746

Graham, James, 1793-1851. To the freemen of the Twelfth Congressional district of N. C. [Washington, DC: s. l., 1840] 8 p. NcU. 40-2747

Graille, J. J. The Prince Augustus of Portugal's favorite waltz, composed for the piano forte... New York: Published by J. L. Hewitt & Co. [184-?] 3 p. WHi. 40-2748

Grambs, Frederick C. Saratoga Lake waltz. Arranged for the piano and most respectfully dedicated to Miss Caroline Content by F. C. Grambs. Philadelphia, PA; New York: A. Fiot; W. Dubois [184-?] 2 p. MB; ViU. 40-2749

Grand Gulf Railroad & Banking Company. Charter of the Grand Gulf Railroad & Banking Co. granted by act of the Legislature of Mississippi. Philadelphia, PA: Ptd. by J. C. Clark, 1840. 21 p. CtY; MiD-B; NN; PHi; ViU. 40-2750

Grant, Dunca. The duty of children to love and sek Christ. By the Rev. Duncan Grant, A. M., Minister of Forres... First American from the sixth Edinburgh edition. Philadelphia, PA: Presbyterian Board of Publication, James Russell, publishing agent, 1840. 192 p. NjPT; ViRut. 40-2751

Grant, James, 1802-1879. Walks and wanderings in the world of literature. Philadelphia, PA: Carey & Hart, 1840. 2 v. MB; MPeaI; PP; PRea; ScC. 40-2752

Grant, Robert. A new theory for an independent treasury, for the people; or an explanation of the causes of the lat fluctuations in our currency, with a proposition for an efficient remedy. By Robert Grant. Bangor, ME: S. S. Smith, printer, 1840. 36 p. IU; MH-BA; MdBJ; P; PU. 40-2753

Grattan, Thomas Colley. High-ways and by-ways; or, Tales of the roadside, picked up in the French provinces by a walking gentleman. New ed., rev. Boston, MA: George Roberts, 1840. 3 v. CtY; LNH; MB; NN; PP. 40-2754

Gratton, Thomas Colley, 1792-1864. History of the Netherlands. By T. Colley Grattan. Philadelphia, PA: Harper & Brothers, 1840. 300 p. InRchE; LN; MB; MHoly; NP. 40-2755

Graves, William Jordan. Speech of Mr. Graves, of Kentucky, on the treasury note bill. Delivered in the House of Representatives, March 26, 1840. [Washington, DC?: s. l., 1840?] 40 p. ICU; MoS; NNC; TxU. 40-2756

Gray, Alonzo, 1808-1860. Elements of chemistry; containing the principles of the science, both experimental and theoretical... By Alonzo Gray... Andover, NY: Gould, Newman & Saxon, 1840. 359 p. IP; MnU; MPiB; PU; VtU. 40-2757

Gray, Asa, 1810-1888. Notices of European Herbaria, particularly most interesting to the North American botanist. [S. l.: s. l., 1840] 18 p. CSt; DLC; Mh-A; PPAN. 40-2758

Gray, Francis Calley, 1790-1856. Poem spoken at Cambridge before the Phi Beta Kappa Society of Harvard Univesity, Aug. 27, 1840. Boston, MA: C. C. Little and J. Brown, 1840. 36 p. ICMe; MH; CHP; RPB; TxU. 40-2759

Gray, Thomas, 1716-1771. Elegy written in a country churchyard. New York: Cassettl, Petter, Galpin and Co. [1840] 26 p. AzU. 40-2760

Grayson, F. W. S. "There are times in life's dull dream." [Song.] Arranged for the guitar by Ld. Meignen. Philadelphia, PA: Meignen & Co., 1840. 2 p. MB; ViU. 40-2761

Great Britain. Courts. Reports of cases argued and determined in the several courts of law & equity in England, during 1839. Jurist ed. New York: Halsted & Voorhies, 1840. 2 v. C; DLC-P4; FTU; MiDU-L; NNLI. 40-2762

The great contest. What the two political parties are struggling for. S. l.: n. pr. [1840] 3 p. MH. 40-2763

Great meeting of Democratic Merchants, at the Merchants' Exchange, New York. New York: s. l., 1840. 44 p. MBC. 40-2764

Great western almanac for 1841. Calculations by C. F. Engelmann. Philadelphia, PA: Jos. McDowell [1840] p. MWA; NjR. 40-2765

Green, Beriah, 1794-1874. A right minded minority. A valedictory address to the senior class of the Oneida Institute, delivered Sept. 9, 1840. Whitesboro: Oneida Institute, 1840. 16 p. MiD-B; NCH; OClWHi. 40-2766

Green, Charles C. The Nubian slave, by Charles C. Green. [Boston, MA: Lane & Scott's lith., 184-?] 7 p. DLC; MWA; NNC; OClWHi. 40-2767

Green, Horace, 1802-1866. An introductory address before the students and trustees of the Vermont academy of medicine. Delivered at the opening of that institution, Casstleton, March 11, 1840. By Horace Green, M. D. Rutland, VT: H. T. White and co., printers, 1840. 17 p. DLC; MWA; NBMS; NN; NNNAM. 40-2768

Green, J. ... The little fish. Music by J. Green. Boston, MA: Oliver Ditson [184-?] 2 p. ViU. 40-2769

Green, Richard W. An arithmetical guide; in which the principles of numbers are inductively explained... 4th ed. enl. Philadelphia, PA: H. Perkins, 1840. 288 p. DAU; DLC; MiU; PPM. 40-2770

Green, Richard W. An inductive algebra, in which the most useful elements of the science are theoretically investigated and practically applied... Philadelphia, PA; New York: H. Perkins; R. Lockwood [etc., etc.] 1840. 303 p. CTHWatk; DLC; NNC; OClWHi. 40-2771

Greene, Charles Gordon, 1804-1866. The identity of the old Hartford convention Federalists with the modern Whig, Harrison party. Carefully illustrated by living specimens, and dedicated to the young men of the Union. Boston, MA: s. l., 1840. 18 p. DLC; MeB; MH; MiD-B; NIC. 40-2772

Greene, Charles Gordon, 1804-1866. Whigery is Federaliam. From the Boston morning post, extra. The identity of the old Hartford convention Federalists with the modern Whig, Harrison party. Carefully illustrated by living specimens, and dedicated to the young men of the Union.

Boston, MA: s. l., 1840. 23 p. DLC; MH; MiU-C; NcD; PU. 40-2773

Greene, Roscoe Goddard. A practical grammar of the English language. 10th ed. Portland, ME: W. Hyde, 1840. 139 p. DLC. 40-2774

Greenleaf, Abner. Remarks prepared for a meeting of the Democratic Republicans of Portsmouth, in Jefferson Hall, October 31, 1840, by Abner Greenleaf. But omitted at the suggestion of the author, to give place to an Address from Abel Cushing, Esq., of Massachusetts. Published at the request of the meeting. Portsmouth, NH: Abner Greenleaf, Jr... printer, 1840. 64 p. MWA. 40-2775

Greenleaf, Jeremiah, 1791-1864. A new universal atlas; comprising separate maps of all the principal empires, kingdom and states throughout the world: and forming a distinct atlas of the United States... A new ed. rev. and cor. to the present time. Brattleboro, VT: Printed by G. R. French, 1840. 64 p. CtHC; CTHWatk; MB; MnHi; ScU. 40-2776

Greenleaf, Simon, 1783-1853. A collection of cases overruled, denied, doubted, or limited in their application... 3d ed. New York: Halsted and Voorhies, 1840. 467 p. MnU; NcD; PU-L; TxWB-L; Vt. 40-2777

Green's Connecticut Annual Register and United States Calendar, for 1840. To which is prefixed An Almanac... Sold by all booksellers in the state. East Windsor CT: Published by Samuel Green, 1840 176 p. Ct. 40-2778

Greenwood, Francis William Pitt

1797-1843. A Collection of Psalms and Hymns for Christian worship. Twenty-ninth edition. Boston, MA: s. l., 1840. MBilHi. 40-2779

Greenwood, Francis William Pitt, 1797-1843. A Sermon on the death of John Lowell, LL. D. Delivered in King's Chapel, Boston, March 22, 1840. By F. W. P. Greenwood, D. D. Boston, MA: C. C. Little and J. Brown, 1840. 36 p. CtSoP; MeHi; MWA; PHi; WHi. 40-2780

Gregg, Josiah, 1806-1850? Commerce of the Prairies. New York: Langley, 1840. 2 v. OMC. 40-2781

Gregory, George, 1754-1808. Concise history of the Christian church from its first establishment to the present time... comp. fr. the works of Dr. G. Gregory by Martin Ruter. New York: Mason, 1840. 446 p. ArSsJ; KBB; PPM; PU; TNT. 40-2782

Gregory, Henry. Sermon preached at the opening of the third annual convention of the diocese of western New York. Utica, NY: Hobart Press, 1840. 22 p. CSmH; IEG; MWA; NBuDD; NUt. 40-2783

Gregory, John. A Commemorative Address to the Young Men of Quincy, Pronounced May 25, 1840, on the Second Centennial Anniversary of The Original incorporation of the town. By John Gregory. Quncy, MA: Published by John A. Green, 1840. 28 p. ICMe; MQ. 40-2784

Gregory, John, 1724-1773. A Father's egacy to his daughters. By Dr. Gregory. Lowell, MA: A. Watson, 1840. 67 p. MLexHi; MWA. 40-2785

Gregory, Olinthus Gilbert, 1774-1841. Letters to a friend... by Olinthus Gregory, D. D. From the fourth London ed., rev. and slightly abridged. New York: American Tract Society [184-?] 480 p. CBCDS; CBPSR; WHi. 40-2786

Grenhow, Robert, 1800-1854. Memoir, historical and political, on the Northwest coast of North America, and the adjacent territories... By Robert Greenhow... New York; London: Wiley and Putnam, 1840. 228 p. CtY; ICN; MiD; NIC; WaSp. 40-2787

Grenhow, Robert, 1800-1854. Memoir, historical and political, on the Northwest coast of North America, and the adjacent territories... By Robert Greenhow... Washington, DC: Blair and Rives, printers, 1840. 228 p. CoD; ICN; MdBP; OrHi; WaS. 40-2788

Grey, Elizabeth Caroline. The duke. A novel. By Mrs. Grey. Philadelphia, PA: Lea & Blanchard, 1840. 2 v. LNH; MB; MBL; MB-FA; WU. 40-2789

Grey, Elizabeth Caroline. The young Prima Donna: a Romance of the Opera. By Mrs. Grey. Philadelphia, PA: Lea & Blanchard, printers, Griggs & Co., 1840. 2 v. MH; MPiB; MsNF; NjP; PU. 40-2790

Griffin, Gerald, 1803-1840. Gisippus; or, The forgotten friend. A play in five acts. By Gerald Griffin, esq. With the stage business, cast of cahracters, costumes, relative positions, etc. New York: S. French & Son [etc., etc., 184-?] 71 p. CSt; CtY; NN; OCl. 40-2791

Griffin, John, 1769-1834. Memoir of Capt. James Wilson, containing an account of his residence in India, his conversion to Christianity, his missionary voyage to the South Seas & his peaceful death. Philadelphia, PA: Presbyterian Board of Publication, 1840. 138 p. MBC; NjP; NjPT. 40-2792

Griffin, Sarah Lawrence, Mrs. The Southern second class book: designed for the middle class in the schools. Macon, GA: Benjamin F. Griffin, 1840. GA. 40-2793

Griffith, John. Life of Capt. James Wilson. Containing an account of his residence in India; his conversion to Christianity; his missionary voyage to the South Seas; and his peaceful death. Abriadged from the memoir by Rev. John Griffith. Philadelphia, PA: Presbyerian Board of Publication; William S. Martien, publishig agent, 1840. 138 p. ICP; MsJMC; NcMHi; NjPT. 40-2794

Grigg, John, 1792-1864. Grigg's Southern and Western Songster... Philadelphia, PA: Grigg and Elliot, 1840. 324 p. NPlaK; ScMar. 40-2795

Grillet, F. J. Map of the railroad routes to Philadelphia. Philadelphia, PA: s. l., 184-? 1 p. PHi. 40-2796

Grimaldi, Joseph, 1779-1837. Life of Joseph Grimaldi; the noted English clown. Written out from Grimaldi's own manuscript and notes... By Charles Dickens... Philadelphia, PA: T. B. Peterson [184-?] 192 p. ICU; NN. 40-2797

Grimes, James Stanely, 1807-1903. Outlines of Grime's new system of phrenology. Albany, NY: J. Munsell, printer, 1840. 12, 44 p. CtY; LNH; MBAt; NjR; WHi. 40-2798

Grimm, Jacob Ludwig Karl, 1785-1863. Grammer Grethel; or, German fairy tales and popular stories from the collection of M. M. Grimm and other sources. By Jacob Ludwig Karl Grimm and Karl Wilhelm Grimm. [Translated by E. Taylor] Edited by Mr. [E. L. C.] Follen. Boston, MA: s. l., 1840. 2 v. MBAt; RPB. 40-2799

Grimshaw, William, 1782-1852. History of England, from the first invasion by Julius Caesar to the accession of William the Fourth in 1830. Philadelphia, PA: Published by Grigg & Elliott, 1840. 318 p. ScCC. 40-2800

Grimshaw, William, 1782-1852. History of France, from the foundation of the monarchy to the death of Louis XVI. Philadelphia, PA: Published by Grigg & Elliott, 1840. 302 p. IU; NcD; ODW. 40-2801

Grimshaw, William, 1782-1852. History of the United States, from their first settlement as colonies to the period of the fifth census in 1830... By William Grimshaw. Philadelphia, PA: Grigg & Elliott, 1840. 326 p. MH; MStoc. 40-2802

Grimshaw, William, 1782-1852. Questions adapted to Grinshaw's history of the United States. Revised & improved Philadelphia, PA: Grigg & Elliott, 1840 88 p. PHi. 40-2803

Grindrod, Ralph Barnes, 1811-1883 Bacchus; an essay on the nature, causes effects and cure, of intemperence, b Ralph Barnes Grinrod. Edited by Char les A. Lee, A. M., M. D. First America from the third English edition. Ne York: J. & H. G. Langley, 1840. 512 CtY; InCW; MH; PPM; RNR. 40-280

Griscom, John Hopkins, 1809-1874. Animal mechanism and physiology; being a plain and familiar exposition of the structure and functions of the human system. By John H. Griscom. Illustrated with numerous woodcuts by Butler. New York: Harper & brothers, 1840. 357 p. CtY; IU; NhD; NUtHi. 40-2805

Griscom, John Hopkins, 1809-1874. Spinal irritation, its history, diagnosis, pathology, and treatment. Illustated by cases. An essay read before the New York Medical and Surgical Society, Nov. 3, 1849, by John H. Griscom, M. D....From the N. Y. Journal of Medicine and Surgery. New York: Printed by Hopkins & Jennings, 1840. 52 p. NBMS; NNNAM. 40-2806

Griswold, Alexander Viets. The order and duty of bishops; a sermon preached in St. Paul's church, Baltimore, Sept. 17, 1840... by the Rt. Rev. Alexander V. Griswold... Baltimore, MD: Printed by Joseph Robinson, 1840. 19 p. MBD; MdHi; NGH; PHi. 40-2807

Griswold, Rufus Wilmot, 1815-1857. The poetry of the affections. New York: s. l. [184-?] p. MB; NBuG. 40-2808

Groke, I. A. Bunker Hill march. [For piano forte.] Respectfully dedicated to the Battle Monument Association. Philadelphia, PA: Blake, 1840. MB. 40-2809

Groom, Mrs. Over the sea. Song. [Pianoforte accomp.] Boston, MA: Ditson & Co. [184-?] 5 p. MB. 40-2810

Grosh, Aaron Burt, 1803-1884. Inquiry nto the teachings of the Holy Scriptures. n two lectures. I. Partialism not taught in the Bible. II. Scripture proofs of Universaliam. Utica, NY: Hutchinson, 1840. 48 p. NUt. 40-2811

Grosh, Aaron Burt, 1803-1884. The ministry. The station, duties and teachings of the minister required at the present age. Delivered at the ordination of Rev. J. T. Goodrich in Oxford, N. Y., September 1, 1840, by Rev. A. B. Grosh. To which are added the charge and address to the society of Revs. O. Whiston and A. C. Barry. Utica, NY: O. Hutchinson, 1840. 26 p. No Loc. 40-2812

Grosh, Aaron Burt, 1803-1884. A sermon. Delivered at the dedication of the Universalist Meeting House in Litchfield, Herkimer County, N. Y., on January 22, 1840. By A. B. Grosh. Utica, NY: O. Hutchinson, 1840. 17 p. NUt. 40-2813

Grosse, William. O'er the waters by Moonlight. Written by Charles Jeffreys. Composed by Wm. Grosse. New York: Firth & Hall [184-?] 5 p. ViU. 40-2814

Grosvenor, Godfrey J. Geneva, March 5, 1840. Dear Sir: Mr. Coffin, who had most of the Legal Agencies at this place, died yesterday. It will probably be necessary for you, and other Attornies in your vicinity, to have another Agent here. I shall be happy to serve you in that capacity. My terms will be the same as Mr. Coffin's. Respectfully yours, G. J. Grosvenor, Esquire, Attorney and Counsellor, etc. Geneva, NY: s. l., 1840. NHi. 40-2815

Grover, John C. New tea, coffee, and grocery store, 398 Washington St., Boston. John C. Grover respectfully informs the inhabitants of Boston... S. l.: s. l., 184-? p. MHi. 40-2816

Groves, John. A Greek and English Dictionary... by the Rev. John Groves, with corrections and additional matter by the American editor. Boston, MA: Hilliard, Gray and Company, 1840. 102 p. ArCH; ICN; MH; NjNbS. 40-2817

Grund, Francis Joseph, 1805-1863. Aufruf an die deutschen wahler. General Harrison's leben und wirken. Von Franz J. Grund. Philadelphia, PA: Gedruckt bei C. F. Stollmeyer, 1840. 30 p. InU; MiD-B; MWA; OClWHi; PPG. 40-2818

Grundy, Felix, 1777-1840. Speech of Mr. Grundy. Delivered in the Senate of the United States on the 4th and 5th of March, 1840, in favor of the report of the Select Committee against the assumption by the general government, of the states' debts contracted for local internal improvements and other state purposes. [Washington, DC?: s. l., 1840?] 16 p. CtY; MH; MiU-C; P; ViU. 40-2819

Guernsey, Wellington. I'll hang my harp on a willow tree. [Song.] Arr. for the piano forte. Boston, MA: Ditson [184-?] 2 p. MB. 40-2820

Guglielmi, Pietro Alessandro, 1728-1804. Gratias agimus tibi. Anthem, S. or T., with piano forte accomp. Arranged also with English words... Boston, MA: Ditson [184-?] 9 p. MB. 40-2821

A guide to devotion for the use of the blind. Boston, MA: By the Pres. Bd. of Pub., 1840. PPL-R. 40-2822

Guide to the city of New York and guide between N. Y. & Wash. With new and correct maps. New York: s. l., 1840. PPL. 40-2823

Guizot, Francois Pierre Guillaume, 1787-1874. Essay on the character and influence of Washington in the revolution of the United States of America... Boston, MA: J. Munros & Co., 1840. 188 p. CtY; MLy; OClWHi; PPA; ScU. 40-2824

Guizot, Francois Pierre Guillaume, 1787-1874. General history of civilization in Europe, from the Fall of the Roman Empire to the French Revolution. Tr. from the French. Ed. by Francois Pierre Guillaume Guizot. 2d Amer. from the 2d. English ed. New York: Appleton, 1840. 346 p. GU; IaGG; MeB; NNC; WMMD. 40-2825

Gully, James Manby, 1808-1883. The water cure in chronic diseases; an exposition of the causes, progress, and termination of various chrinoc diseases of the digestive organs, lungs, nerves, limbs, and skin; and of their treatment by water, and other hygienic means. By James Manby Gully... New York: Fowler and Wells [184-?] 405 p. CU; IU-M; NN. 40-2826

Gung'l, Josef, 1810-1889. Fest march; or, La Victorie. Triumphal march as played by the Steyermarkische band. Composed by J. Gung'l. Baltimore, MD; New Orleans, LA: F. D. Benteen; W. T. Mayo [184-?] 2 p. MB; ViU. 40-2827

Gung'l, Josef, 1810-1889. Fest march; or, La Victorie. Triumphal march as played by the Steyermarkische band. Composed by J. Gung'l. Boston, MA: Ditson [184-?] 2 p. MB. 40-2828

Gung'l, Josef, 1810-1889. Rail road galop. Composed and arranged for the piano forte. Boston, MA: Reed [184-?] 3 p. MB. 40-2829

Gung'l, Josef, 1810-1889. Sounds from home, a set of admired waltzes. As performed by the Steyermarkische musical company. Composed by J. Gung'l. Baltimore, MD; New Orleans, LA: F. D. Benteen; W. T. Mayo [184-?] 5 p. ViU. 40-2830

Gung'l, Josef, 1810-1889. Sounds from home. A set of waltzes, played by Steyermarkische company... by Gung'l. Boston, MA: Oliver Ditson [184-?] 4 p. MB; ViU. 40-2831

Gung'l, Josef, 1810-1889. ... Warrior's joy. [Fest march. Gung'l.] Baltimore, MD: George Willig [184-?] 3 p. ViU. 40-2832

Gunn, John C. Gunn's Domestic guide, or Poor man's friend, describing in plain language the diseases of men, women and children... Louisville, KY: Pool and Wilson, 1840. 786 p. NNF. 40-2833

Gunn, John C. Gunn's Domestic medicine, or Poor man's friend. The last revised addition. Louisville, KY: Allston Mygatt, 1840. 893 p. DNLM; DSG; GMilvC; LNT-M. 40-2834

Gunn, John C. Gunn's Domestic medicine, or Poor man's friend... diseases of men, women, and children... and their cure... also contains medicinal roots and herbs of the United States... First rev. ed., enl. Philadelphia, PA: published by G. V. Raymond, 1840. 893 p. LStB; MBM; MBevHi; MoU; WU-M. 40-2835

Gurney, Joseph John, 1788-1847. Brief remakrs on impartiality in the interpretation of scripture, by J. J. Gurney [Jos. John] Norwich, NY; New York: Printed for Isaac T. Hopper, 1840. 16 p. MH; PHi; PSC-Hi. 40-2836

Gurney, Joseph John, 1788-1847. Essay on the habitual exercise of love to God. By Joseph John Gurney. From the fifth English edition. Philadelphia, PA; Boston, MA: Henry Perkins and Marvin, 1840. 242 p. CtHC; InCW; MB; NjR; PSC-Hi. 40-2837

Gurney, Joseph John, 1788-1847. Familiar lectures to Henry Clay, of Kentucky, describing a winter in the West Indies. By Joseph John Gurney. New York: Press of M. Day & Co., 1840. 203 p. DeWi; ICU; MWA; PPA; TxU. 40-2838

Gurney, Joseph John, 1788-1847. Four lectures on the evidences of Christianity, delivered in Southwark, 1834... 1st American ed. Philadelphia, PA: J. Dobson; E. G. Dorsey, pr., 1840. 194, 2 p. MB; MNS; PPFr; PSC-Hi; ScCoT. 40-2839

Gurney, Joseph John, 1788-1847. Impartiality in the Interpretation of Scripture. New York: s. l., 1840. PSC-Hi. 40-2840

Gurney, Joseph John, 1788-1847. A Letter to the followers of Elias Hicks... By Joseph John Gurney. Baltimore, MD: Woods & Crane, printers, 1840. 18 p. MH; MMeT-Hi; NcGu; PHC; PSC-Hi. 40-2841

Gurney, Joseph John, 1788-1847. Letters describing a winter in the West Indies, by Joseph John Gurney. New York:

Mahlon Day, 1840. MBBCHS; NjR. 40-2842

Gurney, Joseph John, 1788-1847. Observations on the distinguishing views and practices of the Society of Friends. By Joseph John Gurney. 1st American from the 7th London edition. New York: Mahlon Day & Co., 1840. 338 p. InRch-E; MWA; OClWHi; PHC; PRB. 40-2843

Gurney, Joseph John, 1788-1847. Remarks on impartiality in interpretate of scripture. New York: s. l., 1840. PSC-Hi. 40-2844

Gurney, Joseph John, 1788-1847. Sermon and prayer... delivered in Burlington, New Jersey, at the Friends meeting, on the afternoon of Fourth-day, the 22nd of 7th mo., 1840. [Burlington, NJ?: s. l., n. p., 184-?] 12 p. DLC; OCHP; PHC; PPFr; PPL; WHi. 40-2845

Gurney, Priscilla, 1785-1821. Hymns selected from various authors. 3d Amer. from 9th London ed. Philadelphia, PA: Henry Longstreth [184-?] 276 p. MNan; PPL. 40-2846

Guthrie, William. The Christian's great interest; or, the trail of a saving interest in Christ and the way to attain it, by William Guthrie. With an introductory essay by Thomas Chalmers. Philadelphia, PA: Presbyterian Board of Publication, 1840. 322 p. GAIN; ICP; TWoW; ViRut; TxAuPT; WM. 40-2847

Gutierrez de Estrada, Jose Maria, 1800-1867. Carta dirigida al Escmo. Senor Presidente de la Republica sobre la necesidad de buscar en una convencion el posible remedio de los malos que acerca del mismo asunto, por J. M. Gutierrez Estrada... New Orleans, LA: Imprenta Francesa, 1840. 72 p. CtY; NN. 40-2848

Gutzlaff, Charles. Two letters on the Chinese system of writing, by C. Gutzlaff & P. S. Du Ponceau. Philadelphia, PA: Young, 1840. 29 p. MH-AH; PPAmP. 40-2849

Guyonneau de Pambour, Francois Marie, comte, b. 1795. A new theory of the steam engine and the mode of calculation by means of it, of the effective power &c. of every kind of steam engine, stationary or locomotive. Philadelphia, PA: Carey & Hart, 1840. 48 p. PPL; RNR; WU-E. 40-2850

Guyonneau de Pambour, Francois Marie, comte, b. 1795. A practical treatise on locomotive engines upon railways... founded on a great many new experiments... with many different engines... To which is added, an appendix, showing the expense of conveying goods, by locomotive engines, on railroads. And "A new theory of the steam engine." By the Chev. F. M. G. de Pambour... 2d American ed. Philadelphia, PA: Carey & Hart, 1840. 304, 48 p. DLC; IU; MB; NjP; RNR. 40-2851

Gwynne, Walter. Report on the completion of the Wilmington & Raleigh railroad... Fayetteville, AR: Edward J Hale, printer, 1840. 16 p. NcU; NjR. 40-2852

H

Habermann, Johann, 1516-1590. Doct. Johann Habermann's Christliches Gebet-Buchlein, enthaltend Morgen- und Abendsegen auf alle Tage in der Woche. Nebst andern schonen Geben- ten. Wie auch Doctor Neuman's Kern aller Gebete, und schonen Morgen- abend-und andern Liedern, nebst ange- hangtem Geistlichen Stundenwecker. Harrisburg, PA: Gedruckt und zu haben bey G. S. Peters, 1840. 144 p. DeU; KHesC; PSt. 40-2853

Habersham, Richard Wylly, 1786-1842. Speech on the Treasury note bill. Delivered in the House on March 24, 1840. Washington, DC: Gales and Seaton, 1840. 8 p. DLC. 40-2854

Hadaway, T. H. Hadaway's select songster; being a collection of the most approved new and fashionable sentimen- tal and comic songs... Philadelphia, PA: J. H. Gihon & co., 1840. 263 p. MH; MnHi; NBuG. 40-2855

Hadley, William Hobart. The American citizen's manual of reference; being a comprehensive historical, statis- tical, topographical & political view of the United States of N. American & of the several states & territories. New York: Applegate's Double Monarch Cylinder Press, 1840. 102 p. CtY; NBu. 40-2856

Hadley, William Hobart. The American citizen's manual of reference;

being a comprehensive historical, statis- tical, topographical, and political view of the United States of North America, and of several states and territories. Carefully comp. from the latest authorities and pub. by W. Hobart Hadley. New York: Printed by S. W. Benedict, 1840. 102 p. CtY; IaDm; MWA; NjP; PPL; RPB. 40- 2857

Hadyn, Joseph, 1732-1809. The crea- tion, with verdure clad. [Aria S.] from Creation. [Accomp. for piano forte] Bos- ton, MA: Ditson [184-?] 7 p. MB; NN. 40-2858

Hagarty, Joseph P. I think of thee. Bal- lad. Poetry by Capt. Cholmely E. Dering. Music by J. P. Hagarty. [With accompani- ment for the piano forte.] Boston, MA: Ditson [184-?] 5 p. MB. 40-2859

Hagerstown town and country al- manack for 1841. By John F. Egelmann. Hagerstown, MD: J. Gruber [1840] p. MWA. 40-2860

Hague, Thomas. The meteorological al- manac and spring quarter horoscope; containing extensive weather predic- tions, with a farmers; and ship masters' guide, and a table of days to be chosen for any new undertaking or enterprise during the months of April, May and June, 1840. By Thomas Hague. Philadel- phia, PA: Prined by J. H. Gihon & Co. [1840] 24 p. DLC; PHi. 40-2861

Hague, William, 1808-1887. A guide to conversation on the New Testament... Gospel of John... Boston, MA: GOuld, Kendall and Lincoln, 1840. 142 p. ViRU. 40-2862

Hague, William. 1808-1887. Public worship. A discourse delivered at the dedication of the Baptist Church in Bowdoin Square, Boston, November 5, 1840. By William Hague, pastor of the Church in Federal Street, Boston. Published by request. Boston, MA: Gould Kendall & Lincoln, 1840. 38 p. CtY; ICN; MHi; NHC-S; PCA. 40-2863

Hahnemann, Samuel, 1705-1843. Organon of homoepathic medicine... Ed. 3. New York: s. l., 1840. 230 p. OCHP. 40-2864

Haight, Benjamin Isaacs, 1809-1879. An address delivered before the Philolexian society, of Columbia College, May 17th, 1840, being the anniversary of the society, by Benjamin Haight. New York: W. C. Martin, print, 1840. 31 p. CtHT; DLC; MWA; NjPT; PHi. 40-2865

Haight, Benjamin Isaacs. 1809-1879. The two aspects of death: a sermon, preached in All Saints' church, New York, on the second Sunday after Trinity, MDCCCXL. By Benjamin I. Haight... New York: J. Van Norden & co., 1840. 14 p. MdBD; NNG; NNS; OrPD; RNR. 40-2866

Haight, Sarah Rogers, Letters from the Old world. By a lady of New York. New York: Harper & brothers, 1840. 2 v. ArBaA; DLC; ICU; PPA; TxGR. 40-2867

Haight, Sarah Rogers. Letters from the Old world. By a lady of New York. Second edition. New York: Harper, 1840. 2 v. LNH; MoK; NIC; NNC; OO. 40-2868

Hail Columbia, Happy Land. A national song. Written to the Presidents march, by F. Hopkinson, Esqr. Louisville, KY: W. C. Peters [184-?] 2 p. ViU. 40-2869

Haines, John Thomas, 1799-1843. The Wizard of the Wave; or The Ship of the Avenger. A Grand Nautical Drama, in Three Acts. New York: S. French [184-?] 48 p. CtY; MH. 40-2870

Haining, Samuel. Mormonism weighed in the balances of the sanctuary, and found wanting:the substance of four lectures. Douglas: printed for the author, 1840. 66 p. CtY; CU-B; MH; NN. 40-2871

Haldane, Robert, 1764-1842. The books of the Old and New Testaments, canonical and inspired with remarks on the apocrypha. 1st edition with an appendix. Boston, MA: Am. doctrinal tract soc., 1840. 191 p. CtHC; MWA; RPB; Wa. 40-2872

Haldeman, Samuel Stehman, 1812-1880. ... A monagraph of freshwater univalve mollusca of the United States, including notices of species in other parts of North America. By S. Stehman Haldeman... Philadelphia, PA: s. l., 1840-44. 7 parts. CtY; ICU; MH; OCU. 40-2873

Haldeman, Samuel Stehman, 1812-1880. Monograph of the limniades, or freshwater univalve shells of North America. Philadelphia, PA: J. Dobson

1840-44. 8 parts. CtY; ICU; MSaP; OClW; PPWa. 40-2874

Haldeman, Samuel Stehman, 1812-1880. Supplement to number one of "A monograph of the Limniades, or freshwater univalve shells of North America," containing descriptions of apparently new animals in different classes, and the names and characters of the subgenera in Paludina and Anculosa. By S. S. Haldeman. [Philadelphia, PA: s. l., 1840] 3 p. DLC; PPWi. 40-2875

Hale, Mary Whitwell, 1810-1862. Poems. by Mary W. Hale. Boston, MA: W. D. Ticknor, 1840. 216 p. DLC; InU; MoSM; NNC; RPB. 40-2876

Hale, Salma, 1787-1866. History of the United States, from their first settlement as colonies to the close of the administration of Mr. Madison in 1817. By Salma Hale... New York: Harper & brothers, 1840. 2 v. CtHC; CtY; MnU; OClWHi; PSC; RPAt. 40-2877

Hale, Salma, 1787-1866. ... History of the United States, from their first settlement as colonies, to the close of the war with Great Britain in 1815. To which are added questions, adapted to the use of schools... Cooperstown, NY: H. & E. Phinney, 1840. 298, 26 p. ICHi; MeB; MiU-C; NGH; RPB; WHi. 40-2878

Hale, Sarah Josepha Buell, 1788-1879. Flora's interpreter: or, the American book of flowers and sentiments... 9th ed. improved. Boston, MA: Marsh, Capen, Lyon and Webb, 1840. 262 p. ICU; MH; NjP; OClSoM; RPB. 40-2879

Haliburton, Thomas Chandler, 1796-1865. The clockmaker; or, The sayings

and doings of Samuel Slick, of Slickville. 1st and 2d ser. New York: W. H. Colyer, 1840. 240 p. DLC; GEU; MH; OMC; PHi. 40-2880

Haliburton, Thomas Chandler, 1796-1865. The clockmaker; or, The sayings and doings of Samuel Slick, of Slickville... 3d ser. Philadelphia, PA: Lea and Blanchard, 1840. 215 p. DLC; LNH; MdBE; OHi; PHi. 40-2881

Haliburton, Thomas Chandler, 1796-1865. Judge Halliburton's Yankee stories. With illustrations. Philadelphia, PA: Lindsey and Blakiston [184-?] 192 p. NcU. 40-2882

Haliburton, Thomas Chandler, 1796-1865. The letter bag of the Great Western; or, Life in a steamer... by the author of "The sayings and doings of Samuel Slick." New York: W. H. Colyer, 1840. 112 p. CtHT; NNC; OC; PAtM; TxH. 40-2883

Haliburton, Thomas Chandler, 1796-1865. The letter bag of the Great Western; or, Life in a steamer... by the author of "The sayings and doings of Samuel Slick," &c., &c. Philadelphia, PA: Lea & Blanchard, 1840. 189 p. MB; IaDu; GHi; MdBG; MWA; TxU. 40-2884

Haliburton, Thomas Chandler, 1796-1865. Sam Slick Comic all-my-nack. New York: s. l., 1840. MH; MWA. 40-2885

Hall, A. G. A funeral sermon, occasioned by the death of Geo. B. Benjamin and J. Eaton, members of Fire Company No. 1... Rochester, NY: Printed by Welles and Hayes, 1840. 20 p. NN; NRHi; ViU. 40-2886

Hall, Addison. A sermon, delivered at the Seventeenth Annual Meeting of the General Association of Virginia, June 6th, 1840. By Addison Hall. Richmond, VA: Printed at the office of the Religious Herald, 1840. 14 p. NcWfC; ViRU; ViU. 40-2887

Hall, Anna Maria [Fielding] 1800-1881. Marian; or, A young maid's fortunes... New York: Harper & Brothers, 1840. 2 v. CtHT; MBL; MLow; PPL-R; TJo. 40-2888

Hall, B. F. A discourse on spiritual influence. Louisville, KY: Penn, 1840. PPPrHi; PPPD. 40-2889

Hall, Edward Brooks, 1800-1866. Hymns for social worship... New York: s. l. [1840] p. MBC. 40-2890

Hall, Edward Brooks, 1800-1866. The Temperance reform: being a review of Rosonna, or scenes in Boston, [by Mrs. Hannah F. Lee.] From the Christian Examiner for March, 1840. Boston, MA: J. Munroe and Co., 1840. 14 p. MB; MMeT; NjP. 40-2891

Hall, Edward Brooks, 1800-1866. Temperance reform: a review of Rosonna, or scenes in Boston. 3d ed. Boston, MA: s. l., 1840. MBAt. 40-2892

Hall, Edwin, 1802-1877. An exposition of the law of baptism, as it regards the mode and the subjects. By Edwin Hall. New York: Gould, Newman and Saxton, 1840. 216 p. CtHC; DLC; GDecCT; NbCrD; WBeloC. 40-2893

Hall, Edwin, 1802-1877. An exposition of the law of baptism, as it regards the mode and the subjects. By Edwin Hall.

First edition. Norwalk, CT: John A. Weed, 1840. 216 p. CtSoP; DLC; NNUT; OMC. 40-2894

Hall, Edwin, 1802-1877. An exposition of the law of baptism, as it regards the mode and the subjects. By Edwin Hall, A. M., pastor of the First Congregational Church, Norwalk, Conn. Second edition with an appendix. Norwalk, CT; New York: Published by John A. Weed; Gould, Newman and Saxton, 1840. 220 p. Ct; MBC; NHCS; OO; PCA. 40-2895

Hall, Foley. Ever of thee. Ballad. By Foley Hall. Baltimore, MD: George Willig [184-?] 5 p. ViU. 40-2896

Hall, Frederick, 1780-1843. Letters from the east and from the west. By Frederick Hall... Washington City; Baltimore, MD: F. Taylor and W. M. Morrison; F. Lucas, jr., 1840. 168 p. KyLo; MdBP; NNUT; OCo; TxD-T. 40-2897

Hall, John. New & concise method of handrailing, upon correct principles, simplified to the capacity of every practical carpenter... Baltimore, MD: Murphy, 1840. 23 p. CtY; LN; MdBP; MoSU; NNC; P. 40-2898

Hall, John, architect. A series of select and original modern designs for dwelling houses, for the use of carpenters and builders; adapted to the style of building in the United States. With twenty-four plates. By John Hall... Baltimore, MD: John Murphy, 1840. 31 p. MdBP; NUt; ViU. 40-2899

Hall, John, architect. Series of select & original modern designs for dwelling houses, for the use of carpenters and builders; adapted to the style of building in the U. S. Ed. 2. Baltimore, MD: Murphy, 1840. 31 p. MdBP; P; ViRVal. 40-2900

Hall, John, 1783-1847. The reader's guide containing a notice of the elementary sounds of the English language, instructions for readings... and lessons for practice. 6 ed. Hartford, CT: Robins & Falger, 1840. 333 p. CtY; MH; RPB. 40-2901

Hall, John, 1783-1847. Reader's manual... Hartford, CT: s. l., 1840. CtHWatk; MH. 40-2902

Hall, John, 1806-1894. The cabinet maker's assistant, embracing the most modern style of cabinet furniture... Baltimore, MD: printed by J. Murphy, 1840. 40 p. In; MiD; MiD-T; NN. 40-2903

Hall, John H. The word baptizo defined and the mode of baptism proved from the Scriptures. In three parts. Albany, NY: Weare C. Little, 1840. 124 p. LNH; MCET; MPiB; NN; OCHP; WHi. 40-2904

Hall, Louisa Jane Park, 1802-1892. Alfred. By the author of "Trials of a school girl." Boston, MA: James Munroe & Co., 1840. 4, 16, 8 p. MB; MVh. 40-2905

Hall, Rufus, 1744-1818. A journal of the life, religious exercises, and travels in the work of the ministry of Rufus Hall, late of Northampton, Montgomery county, in the state of New York. Byberry; Philadelphia, PA: Published by John and Isaac Cowly; J. Richards, printer, 1840. 176 p. NBF; NBLiHi; PSC-Hi; WHi. 40-2906

Hall, Samuel Read, 1795-1877. The

child's book of geography... 6th ed. New York: Published by Robinson Pratt & co., 1840. 112 p. MHa; NPV. 40-2907

Hall, Willard, 1780-1875. Lecture on the Banking System, delivered before the Franklin Lyceum, Wilmington, De., By Hon. Willard Hall. Wilmington, DE: Printed by Porter & Naff, 1840. 36 p. MdBJ; PPPrHi; PU. 40-2908

Hall, William M. The apiarian; or, A practical treatise on the management of bees; with the best method of preventing the depredations of the bee moth, by William M. Hall. New Haven, CT: Hitchcock & Stafford, printers, 1840. 48 p. CtHWatk; MB; MBH; MWA; TxU; WU. 40-2909

Hallam, Henry, 1777-1859. View of the state of Europe during the middle ages. By Henry Hallam... From the 7th ed. Paris, etc... New York: Harper & Brothers, 1840. 2 v. MH; NOg; OPosm. 40-2910

Hallatt, George. Infidel Socialism calmly considered; and proved to be... absurd. Norwich: s. l., 1840. 67 p. CtY. 40-2911

Halleck, Fitz-Greene, 1790-1867. Selections from the British poets. In two volumes. New York: Harper & brothers, 1840. 2 v. DLC; ICU; FTa; NhPet; OCY. 40-2912

Hallock, B. B. Letters to Rev. E. F. Hatfield in review of two lectures against Universalism, delivered by him in the Seventh Presbyterian church, Broome street, on Sunday evenings, January 5th and 12th... New York: Universalist

Union Press, 1840. 94 p. MMeT-Hi; NCas; NNUT; WHi. 40-2913

Halvorson, H. The enamored musician; a Scandinavian serenade... arranged for the piano forte. Boston, MA: Ditson [184-?] 3 p. MB. 40-2914

Hamilton, Frank Hastings, 1813-1886. Introductory lecture before the surgical class of Geneva Medical College, December 1, 1840. By Frank H. Hamilton. Geneva, NY: Printed by I. Merrell, 1840. 20 p. DLC; MHi; NCH; NNC; NNNAM. 40-2915

Hamilton, John Church, 1792-1882. Life of Alexander Hamilton. By his son, John C. Hamilton. New York: D. Appleton & Co., 1840. 2 v. MbBJ; MWA; NNS; OWoC; PPi. 40-2916

Hamilton Literary & Theological Institution. Laws of Hamilton Literary and Theological Institution. Utica, NY: Bennett, Backus & Hawley, 1840. 12 p. NNUT; NRCR. 40-2917

The Hamlet. A poem for the ladies' fair, Port Henry, N. Y. Middlebury, VT: pr. by Eph. Maxham, 1840. 24 p. VtMidSM. 40-2918

Hammond, Elisha, 1780-1851. Treatise on the law of contracts for the payment of specific articles and of the law of tender generally. With an appendix of forms by a counsellor at law. [Boston, MA] : Merriam, printer, 1840. 84 p. KuBC; MH; NB. 40-2919

Hammond, Elisha, 1780-1851. A treatise on the law of fire insurance, and insurance on inland waters. In two parts. With an appendix of forms. By Elisha Hammond. New York: Halsted & Voorhies, 1840. 182 p. CU; DLC; LNH; MdBB; PP. 40-2920

Hammond, Jabez Delano, 1778-1855. The history of political parties in the state of New York; from the ratification of the federal constitution to December, 1840. Albany, NY: Van Benthaugen [1840-42] 3 v. CSt; NAl; PPA; WM. 40-2921

Hammond, Jabez Delano, 1778-1855. The history of political parties in the state of New York; from the ratification of the federal constitution to December, 1840. 4th ed. Cooperstown, NY: Phinney, 1840-48. 3 v. I; Wl. 40-2922

Hamner, James G. Discourse delivered in the Fifth Presbyterian Church of Baltimore on Sabbath morning, June 28th, 1840. Baltimore, MD: Woods and Crane, printers, 1840. 16 p. CtHC; MdBE; MdHi; NIC; PPL. 40-2923

Hance, J. F. Haste idle time. Polacca [S.] Baltimore, MD: Willig [184-?] 4 p. MB. 40-2924

Hance, J. F. The much admired Amaranth waltz. Arranged for the piano forte by J. F. Hance. Philadelphia, PA: George Willig [184-?] 2 p. ViU. 40-2925

Hance, J. F. The opera waltz. [The motives from Il Barbrere] Arranged for the piano forte by J. F. Hance. New York: Dubois & Stodart [184-?] 3 p. ViU. 40-2926

Hancock, N. H. First Church. Articles of faith and covenant, adopted by the First Church in Hancock, N. H. Amherst, MA: R. & R. D. Boylston, 1840. 1 p. MBC. 40-2927

The Hand-Book of carving with hints on the etiquette of the dinner table. Boston, MA: s. l., 1840. 32 p. MH. 40-2928

Handel, Georg Friedrich, 1685-1759. ... Angels ever bright and fair, from Theodora. Composed by Handel. Boston, MA: Parker & Ditson [184-?] 4 p. ViU. 40-2929

Handel, Georg Friedrich, 1685-1759. Holy, Holy, Lord God Almighty. [Anthem, solo. Accomp. for piano forte] Boston, MA: Parker & Ditson [184-?] 4 p. MB. 40-2930

Handel, Georg Friedrich, 1685-1759. Oh! had I Jubal's lyre. Boston, MA: Parker & Ditson [184-?] 5 p. MB. 40-2931

Handel and Haydn Society, Boston. The Creation... Feb. 2d, 1840... [Boston, MA: s. l., 1840] 4 p. MHi. 40-2932

Handel and Haydn Society, Boston. Massachusetts collections of psalmody by the Boston Handel and Haydn Society. Consisting of... psalm and hymn tunes, anthems, sentences, chants... Boston, MA: Wilkins, 1840. 319 p. ICN; MBAt; MBevHi; MHi; MS. 40-2933

Hanover College, Hanover, Ind. A catalogue of the Officers and Students of Hanover College. Madison: s. l., 1840. 14 p. In; InHC; InU; MHi. 40-2934

Hansman, C. F. Daylight love if pass'd away. [Song. A., the accomp. arranged for the Spanish guitar...] Philadelphia, PA: s. l. [184-?] 3 p. MB. 40-2935

The Happy Family. A Reading Book for Youth. Translated from the French. Philadelphia, PA: Eugene Cummiskey, 1840. 108 p. MdW; OCX. 40-2936

Haraden, David T. Massachusetts Quick Step. Composed by D. T. Haraden. Boston, MA: Henry Prentiss, 1840. 3 p. MB; MBNEC. 40-2937

Hard cider; a poem descriptive of the Nashville Convention. Louisville, KY: s. l., 1840. 56 p. MB; MH. 40-2938

Hard cider and log cabin almanac for 1841. New York: Turner & Fisher [1840] p. DLC; InHi; InLPU; MWA. 40-2939

Harding, Jesper. General William Henry Harrison... Philadelphia, PA: s. l., 1840. 15 p. CtY. 40-2940

Hare, George Emlen. Christ to return: A practical exposition of the prophecy recorded in the 24th and 25th chapters of the Gospel according to St. Matthew... by G. Emlen Hare... Philadelphia, PA: H. Hooker, 1840. 132 p. GDecCT; NCH; OrPD; PHi. 40-2941

Hare, Robert, 1781-1858. A brief exposition of the science of mechanical electricity, or electricity proper; subsuduary to the course of chemical instruction in the University of Pennsylvania... by Robert Hare. Philadelphia, PA: J. G. Auner, 1840. 144 p. CtHT; DSG; MB; NBuU-M; PU; TNP. 40-2942

Hare, Robert, 1781-1858. Communication faite a la Societe philosophi que americanine dans une de ses seances de 1839 au sujet des trombes et relativement a une memoire de Mr. Peltier sur la cause de ces meteores... accompagnee de la traduction d'un memoire sur les causes trombles publie par la meme auteur... Philadelphia, PA: s. l., 1840. 12 p. CtY; DLC; PPAmP. 40-2943

Hare, Robert, 1781-1858. A compendium of the course of chemical instruction in the Medical department of the University of Pennsylvania. By Robert Hare... In two parts. 4th ed., with amendments and additions. Philadelphia, PA: J. G. Auner, 1840-43. 2 v. in 1. CtMW; MdUM; MH; NN; PU. 40-2944

Hare, Robert, 1781-1858. Course of medical instruction. Philadelphia, PA: Printed by John C. Clark, 1840. 598 p. PPiAM. 40-2945

Hare, Robert, 1781-1858. Notices of Tornadoes. [New Haven, CT: s. l., 1840] p. NN. 40-2946

Hare, Robert, 1781-1858. Objections to the nomenclature of the celebrated Berzelius, with suggestions respecting a substitute, in a letter to Professor Silliman. First published in 1834 and republished in Silliman's journal for 1835, vol. XXVII. By Robert Hare... Also a letter from the dinstinguished Swedish chemist abovementioned, in reply; with a concluding examination of the suggestions in that letter, by the author of the Obejctions. Republished from the Journal of pharmacy for April, 1837. Philadelphia, PA: Printed by J. C. Clark, 1840. 23 p. CtY; DSG; MB; NBuU-M; NNC; PU. 40-2947

Hare, Robert, 1781-1858. On the origin and progress of galvanism or voltaic electricity. Philadelphia, PA: s. l., 1840. 80 p. CtY; PCC. 40-2948

Hare, Robert, 1781-1858. A verbal communication, respecting source experiments made by him to ascertain the comparative heating or cooling influence of changes of destiny resulting from changes in pressure in dry air & air replete from aquerous vapor. Philadelphia, PA: s. l., 1840. 6 p. DNLM; DSG; NN. 40-2949

Harkness, James. God dwelling with men on the earth. A sermon [on I Kings vii. 27] preached... on the opening of the Reformed Protestant Dutch Church, Franklin Street, which was burnt Sept. 22, 1840. New York: Carter, 1840. MH-AH; PPPrHi. 40-2950

Harmer, O. Congregational Church. The articles of faith and covenant of the Congregational Church in Harmar, O. Adopted at the organization of the church, January 1, 1840... Marietta, OH: G. W. Tyler & Co., printers, 1840. 20 p. OCHP; OClWHi. 40-2951

The Harmonist: being a collection of tunes from the most approved authors. Adapted to every variety of metre in the Methodist hymn-book. And, for particular occasions, a selection of anthems, pieces and sentences. New ed. - rev. and greatly enl. New York: G. Lane & P. P. Sanford, 1840. 383 p. KMK; NcU; NN; OCl; TxU. 40-2952

Harmony Grove Cemetary. Order of exercises at the consecration of Harmony Grove Cemetary... June 13, 1840. Salem: Salem Observer Press [1840] p. MPeHi. 40-2953

Harney, John H. ... An algebra upon the inductive method of instruction... 3d ed. Louisville: Morton & Griswold [1840] 288 p. ICartC; MH; OSW. 40-2954

Harney, John H. ... An algebra upon the inductive method of instruction. By John H. Harney. 4th ed. Louisville, KY: Morton & Griswold [1840] 288 p. NjR; NNC. 40-2955

Harney, John H. An algebra upon the inductive method of instruction. By John H. Harney. 6th ed. Louisville, KY: Morton and Griswold [1840] 288 p. KSalW; KyLxT; OO. 40-2956

Harney, John H. An algebra upon the inductive method of instruction. By John H. Harney. 8th ed. Louisville, KY: Morton & Griswold [1840] 288 p. CtY; Im-PerM; OClWHi. 40-2957

Harney, John H. Algebra upon the inductive method of instruction. 10th ed. Louisville, KY: Morton & Griswold [1840] p. In; PPM; TxD-T. 40-2958

Harris, John, 1802-1856. The Witnessing Church. A sermon. By Rev. John Harris... New York: Published by T. Mason and G. Lane for the Methodist Epsicopal Church at the Conference Office, J. Collord, printer, 1840. 86 p. ViU. 40-2959

Harris, Nicholas. A complete system of practical bookkeeping, exemplified in six sets of books: journalized daily, weekly, & monthly; by single & double entry. Applicable to all kinds of business, both individual & partnership concerns. Accompanied with the various forms of bills, mercantile letters, etc. in daily use in the counting room... 2d ed. Hartford, CT; New York; Philadelphia, PA: Brown & Parsons [etc.] 1840. 230 p. Ct; MB; NNC; PU. 40-2960

Harris, Nicholas. Tables of interest and discount, and business man's assistant... Hartford, CT: Spalding & Storrs, 1840. DLC; MH. 40-2961

Harris, William Cornwallis, 1807-1848. Adventures in Africa during a tour of two years through that country. From the 10th London ed., revised & corr. Philadelphia, PA: T. B. Peterson [184-?] 392 p. CtY; DLC; IEN; NcD; PHC. 40-2962

Harrisburg, Portsmouth, Mount Joy and Lancaster Railroad Co. Annual report of Messrs. A. J. Pleasonton, John Moss, Richard Ronaldson and John Sharp, Jr., directors... of the Harrisburg, Portsmouth, Mountjoy and Lancaster railroad company... Philadelphia, PA: T. K. & P. G. Collins, printers, 1840. 36 p. DBRE; DLC; PPG; PPL. 40-2963

Harrisburg, Portsmouth, Mount Joy and Lancaster Railroad Co. A letter from A. J. Pleasonton, president of the... company to the Hon. James Nill... exhibiting the affairs & condition of the said company... Philadelphia, PA: Collins, 1840. 17 p. CtY; DLC; MH-BA; PPAmP. 40-2964

Harrison, Hannah. Some of the mysterious and wonderful dealings of God, with Mrs. Nancy Woodney... Wooster, OH: Printed by D. N. Sprague, 1840. 26 p. OO. 40-2965

Harrison, Robert, 1796-1858. The Dublin dissector, or manual of anatomy; comprising a description of the bones, muscles, vessels, nerves, and viscera; also the relative anatomy of the different regions of the human body, together with the elements of pathology. By Robert Harrison. With additions by Robert

Watts, jr. 1st American, from the fifth enl. Dublin ed. New York; Philadelphia, PA: J. & H. G. Langley; Haswell, Barrington and Haswell, 1840. 541 p. DLC; ICJ; MBM; MsH; PPCB. 40-2966

Harrison, Robert, 1796-1858. Manual of anatomy. Also the relative anatomy of the different regions of the human body, together with the elements of pathology, by Robert Harrison, A. M. M. D. T. C. D. New York: J. & H. G. Langley, 1840. 541 p. MB; MLow. 40-2967

Harrison, William Henry, 1773-1841. A discourse on the aborigines of the Valley of the Ohio... Boston, MA: Ticknor, 1840. 47 p. ICHi; Nh; NjR; PHi; WHi. 40-2968

Harrison, William Henry, 1773-1841. Gen. Harrison's speech at Fort Meigs. [Orange, NJ: s. l., 1840] 8 p. MHi; OClWHi; PHi; RPB. 40-2969

Harrison, William Henry, 1773-1841. Gen. Harrison's speech at the Dayton convention, September 10, 1840. [Boston, MA: Gould, Kendell & Lincoln, 1840] 8 p. GEU; MH; OClWHi; RPB. 40-2970

Harrison, William Henry, 1773-1841. General Harrison's speech at Columbus, Ohio. Delivered June 5, 1840. [Tuscaloos, AL?: Monitor Office, 1840?] 8 p. GEU. 40-2971

Harrison, William Henry, 1773-1841. General William H. Harrison, candidate of the people for President of the United States. Lowell, MA: pub. by William Wyman; Pub. by A. B. F. Hildreth, office of the Literary Souvenir, 1840. 16 p. MWo; OClWHi; PHi. 40-2972

Harrison, William Henry, 1773-1841. Harrison and reform. Montpelier, VT: s. l., 1840. 2 p. VtU. 40-2973

Harrison, William Henry, 1773-1841. Life with a history of the wars with the British and Indian. Philadelphia, PA: W. Marshall & Co., 1840. 218 p. MiPh. 40-2974

Harrison, William Henry, 1773-1841. To the farmers and working men! Democracy of the country! [Campaign document] S. l.: n. p., 1840. 15 p. WHi. 40-2975

The Harrison almanac, 1841. New York: published by J. P. Giffing; stereotyped by R. C. Valentine, 1840. 36 p. CSf; IHi; MWA; PPM; WaS; WHi. 40-2976

The Harrison and log cabin song book. Columbus: I. N. Whiting, 1840. 105 p. InHi; MB; MiD; OMC; RPB. 40-2977

Harrison and Reform Citizens of East Boston, one & all, who are tired of hard times... You are requested to assemble at the ward room June 4th. Boston, MA: Easburn Press, 1840. 14 p. InU. 40-2978

Harrison Calendar auf das Jahr 1841. Philadelphia, PA: Georg. W. Mentz und Sohn [1840] p. DLC; MWA; PPG; PPeSchw. 40-2979

Harrison Club, Boston. The constitution and by-laws... with a list of its members... Boston, MA: n. pub., 1840. 8 p. MB; MH; MnHi; MWA; OCHP. 40-2980

Harrison Club, Boston. Harrison melodies. Original and selected. Pub.

under the directon of the Boston Harrison Club. Boston, MA: Weeks, Jordan & Company, 1840. 72 p. DLC; NN; OClWHi; OO; ViU. 40-2981

Harrison Club, Boston. New York fraud; the conspiracy of the office holders unmasked. New York: N. Y. Committee of the Boston Harrison Club [1840?] 24 p. M; MH; MiD-B; OClWHi. 40-2982

Harrison Democrat. Roxbury, MA: s. l., 1840-. v. MMedHi; NN. 40-2983

Harrison Glee Club. A new collection of songs, glees and catches. Arranged and sung by the Harrison Glee Club. Buffalo, NY: Published by the club; Press of Thomas & Co., 1840. 36 p. NBuHi; OClWHi. 40-2984

The Harrison medal minstrel. Comprising a collection of the most popular and patriotic songs, illustrative of the enthusiastic feelings of a grateful but power-ridden people towards the gallant defenders of their country... Philadelphia, PA: Grigg & Elliott; M'Carty & Davis [etc.] 1840. 192 p. Ct; InHi; NjR; PPL-R; RPB. 40-2985

The Harrison, Tippecanoe, and Patriotic Songster. Dayton, OH: Sold by T. barrett, J. Wilson, printer, 1840. 64 p. No Loc. 40-2986

Harrison's Tippecanoe songster. New York: [pub. by] Turner and Fisher [1840] 63 p. RPB. 40-2987

Harrodeu, David T. Massachusetts quick step. [For the piano forte] Boston, MA: Prentiss, 1840. MB. 40-2988

Harsley, William. Retire, my love. [Glee, A. T. T. B.] Boston, MA: s. l., 184-?] 4 p. MB. 40-2989

Hart, Luther, 1783-1834. Plain reasons for relying on Presbyterian ordination, in a letter to a friend. By Luther Hart. First published as a tract by a Doctrinal Tract Society, in the year 1818. Hartford, CT: Elihu Geer, print., 1840. 50 p. Ct; MBC; MeHi; MH-AH; PPPrHi. 40-2990

Hartford. Center Church. Historical celebrations, Tuesday, April 21, 1840. Order of exercises... Hartford, CT? n. p. [1840] 4 p. CtHC. 40-2991

Hartford. Public High School. Catalogue of the trustees, instructors and pupils of the Hartford Grammar school, for the year ending August 6th, 1840. Hartford, CT: Printed by Elihu Geer, 1840. 12 p. CTHWatk. 40-2992

Hartford. Public High School. Daily and weekly report... Hartford, CT: Printed by Elihu Geer, 1840. 8 p. Ct; CTHWatk. 40-2993

Hartford Female Seminary, Hartford, Conn. Regulations of the Hartford female seminary... [Hartford, CT: s. l., 1840] 14 p. Ct. 40-2994

Hartford Theological Seminary, Hartford, Conn. General catalogue of the theological institute of Connecticut at East Windsor... 1840. Hartford, CT: Elihu Geer, 1840. 12 p. NNUT. 40-2995

Harvard University. Arrangement of lectures & Recitations for the second term of 1839-40. Cambridge, MA: Printed by Folsom, Wells, and Thurston, 1840. 13 p. DHEW; MBC; MHi. 40-2996

Harvard University. Arrangement of lectures and recitations in Harvard University for the first term of the academic year, 1840-41. Cambridge, MA: s. l., 1840. KHi. 40-2997

Harvard University. A catalogue of the officers and students of Harvard University, for the academical year 1840-41. Cambridge, MA: Folsom, Wells, and Thurston, printers to the University, 1840. 39 p. KHi; MNoanHi; MS. 40-2998

Harvard University. Harvard Musical Association. By-laws. [Boston, MA] : s. l., 1840. 8 p. MHi. 40-2999

Harvard University. Law School. [Circular to all who have at any time been connected with the school...] [Cambridge, MA: s. l., 1840] 1 p. MH-L. 40-3000

Hascall, J. Summary view of all the Protestant missions in the world, by J. Hascall and D. Wise. Boston, MA: S. N. Dickinson, 1840. 23 p. MBNMHi; NjR. 40-3001

Hastings, John. d. 1854. Speech of Mr. John Hastings, of Ohio, in Committee of the Whole, on the independent treasury bill. Delivered in the House of Representatives, Thursday, June 25, 1840. Washington, DC: Printed by Blair and Rives, 1840. 24 p. InHi; MdHi; MiU-C; TxU; WHi. 40-3002

Hastings, Thomas, 1784-1872. The Christian psalmist or Watts' Psalms and hymns, with copious selections from other sources. The whole carefully revised and arranged, with directions for musical expression. New York: D. Fan-

shaw, printer and publisher, 1840. 634 p. CtY; NBLIHI; VtMidSM. 40-3003

Hastings, Thomas, 1784-1872. The Manhattan collection of psalms and hymn tunes and anthems. Compiled & composed under the special patronage of the New York Academy of Sacred Music, and adapted to the use of classes, choirs & congregations. New York: D. Fanshaw, 1840. 352 p. ICN; KMK; NNUT; MiU. 40-3004

Hastings, Thomas, 1784-1872. The sacred lyre. A collection of psalm and hymn tunes, anthems, and set pieces. Compiled and composed under the patronage of the New York Academy of Sacred Music. By Thomas Hastings. New York: Daniel Fanshaw, 1840. 352 p. CtMW; MHi; NjR; NNeb; OO. 40-3005

Hatfield, Edwin Francis, 1807-1883. Freedom's lyre; or Psalms, hymns, and sacred songs for the slave and his friends. Comp. by Edwin F. Hatfield. New York: S. W. Benedict, 1840. 265 p. DLC; MWA; NBuG; OO; RPB. 40-3006

Hatfield, Edwin Francis, 1807-1883. Freedom's lyre; or Psalms, hymns, and sacred songs for the slave and his friends. Comp. by Edwin F. Hatfield. 2d ed. New York: S. W. Benedict, 1840. 265 p. CtY; OClWHi, TxU. 40-3007

Hatton, John Liptrot, 1801?-1886. Come live with me and be my love. [Song, with piano forte accompaniment.] Music by J. L. Hatton. Words by C. Marlower. Boston, MA: Russell & Fuller [184-?] 7 p. MB. 40-3008

Hatton, John Liptrot, 1801?-1886. Sweet love, good night to thee. [Song, S.

or T. Accomp. for piano.] Boston, MA: Ditson & Co. [184-?] 5 p. BPL; MB. 40-3009

Hawes, Joel, 1789-1867. Reason's for not embracing the doctrine of universal salvation, in a series of letters to a friend. New York: American Tract Society [184-?] 133 p. MiUL; NcD. 40-3010

Hawes, Joel, 1789-1867. Sermon, occasioned by the death of Mrs. Delia Williams. Delivered 28th of June, 1840. Hartford, CT: s. l., 1840. 23 p. CtY-D; CtHC; MB; MH-AH; RPB. 40-3011

Hawes, Josiah J., 1808?-1901, photographer. [Portrait of Wendell Phillips.] Daguerreotype. [Boston, MA: s. l., 184-?] p. BPL. 40-3012

Hawes, Maria Billington, 1816-1886. I'll speak of thee, I'll love thee too. Ballad. Sung by Mrs. Seguin; words by Maurice M. C. Dowling; music by Maria B. Hawes... New York: Atwill [184-?] 4 p. ViU. 40-3013

Hawes, Maria Billington, 1816-1886. Thou art lovlier. Song. The poetry by Richard Howitt; the music by Maria B. Hawes. Philadelphia, PA; New York: A. Fiot; W. Dubois [184-?] 3 p. ViU. 40-3014

Hawes, Richard, 1797-1877. Speech of Mr. Richard Hawes, of Kentucky, on the Sub-Treasury Bill. Delivered... June 30, 1840. Washington, DC: Printed by Gales & Seaton, 1840. 30 p. IC; ICJ; NN; NNC. 40-3015

Hawks, Francis Lister, 1798-1866. Adventures of Daniel Boon, by the author of "Uncle Phillips conversations." New York: Appleton, 1840. VtNofN. 40-3016

Hawks, Francis Lister, 1798-1866. The early history of the Middle states... By Lambert Lilly, schoolmaster [pseud.] Boston, MA: W. D. Ticknor, 1840. 167 p. MiD-B; NbU; ViW. 40-3017

Hawks, Francis Lister, 1798-1866. Evidences of Christianity; or, Uncle Philip's conversations about the truth of the Christian religion. New York: Harper & brothers, 1840. MBAt; MiD. 40-3018

Hawks, Francis Lister, 1798-1866. The history of New England. Illustrated by tales, sketches, and anecdotes... by Lambert Lilly, schoolmaster [pseud.] Boston, MA: W. D. Ticknor, 1840. 184 p. ICN; NcAs. 40-3019

Hawks, Francis Lister, 1798-1866. History of the United States. Uncle Philip's conversations with the children of Massachusetts. New York: Harper & brothers, 1840. 2 v. DLC; NGlc; NNia; P; RKi. 40-3020

Hawks, Francis Lister, 1798-1866. The history of the Western states, illustrated by tales, sketches and anecdotes... By Lambert Lilly, schoolmaster [pseud.] Boston, MA: W. D. Ticknor, 1840. 167 p. IEN-M; LU; MiU-C; ViW. 40-3021

Hawks, Francis Lister, 1798-1866. The lost Greenland; or, Uncle Philip's conversations with the children about the lost colonies of Greenland. New York: Harper, 1840. 180 p. DLC; NGlc; NICLA; NR; RWoH. 40-3022

Hawks, Francis Lister, 1798-1866. The

monuments of Egypt; or, Egypt, a witness for the Bible. New York: George Putnam, 1840. GMM; PPAN. 40-3023

Hawley, Jesse. An essay on the enlargement of the Erie Canal... By Jesse Hawley. Lockport, NY: Printed at the Courier office, 1840. 16 p. DLC; MiD-B; NBu; NNE; PPL. 40-3024

Hawthorne, Nathaniel, 1804-1864. The marble faun: or, the romance of Monte Beni... Boston, MA: Ticknor, 1840. 2 v. MdBLC. 40-3025

Hayden, William. The national Whig song. Adapted to a popular air. By William Hayden. Boston, MA: Parker & Ditson, 1840. 3 p. InThT; MB; MNF. 40-3026

Haydn, Joseph, 1732-1809. Piercing eyes... [Cauzonet, T...] Boston, MA: Parker & Ditson [184-?] 3 p. MB. 40-3027

Haynes, Lemuel, 1753-1833. Universal Salvation, a very ancient doctrine; a sermon, delivered at Rutland West Parish, Vt., in the yeqr 1805. 13th ed. Newburyport: Re-published by request, 1840. 5 p. NN. 40-3028

Haynes, Thomas Wilson. Baptist cyclopedia. Charleston: s. l., 1840. v. NN. 40-3029

Hays, Isaac, 1796-1879. Outlines of human physiology; designed for the use of the higher classes in common schools. 3d ed. Boston, MA: Marsh, Capen, Lyon & Webb, 1840. 378 p. RPB. 40-3030

Hayward, John, 1781-1862. The family visitor. Boston, MA: Weeks, Jordan and co., 1840. 224 p. MPlyA; RP; RPB; WRichM. 40-3031

Hayward, John, 1781-1862. The family visitor. 2d edition. Boston, MA: Otis, Broaders and Company, 1840. 224 p. Ct; Nh. 40-3032

Hayward, John, 1781-1862. The family visitor. By John Hayward, author of the New England Gazetteer, etc., etc. Third edition. Boston, MA; New York; Philadelphia, PA; Baltimore, MD: Otis, Broaders and Company; Tanner and Disturnell; William Marshall and Company; Cushing and Brothers, 1840. 224 p. CtY; Ia; IEG. 40-3033

Hayward, W. Catalogue of W. Hayward's collection of paintings by the ancient and modern masters; now exhibiting at Corinthian Gallery. Boston, MA: Eastburn's Press, 1840. 13 p. IaDaP; MB; MBAt. 40-3034

Haywood, John. The duty and authority of justices of the peace in the State of Tennessee. Compiled by John Haywood, Esq., attorney at law. Copyright secured according to law. Nashville, TN: Printed and sold by Thomas G. Bradford, 1840. 379 p. TKL-Mc. 40-3035

Hazard, Thomas Robinson, 1797-1886. Facts for the laboring man:by a laboring man... [no. 1-12] Newport, RI: J. Atkinson, printer, 1840. 102 p. IaU; MiD-B; NcU; RNH; WHi. 40-3036

Hazard's United States commercial and statistical register, containing documents, facts, and other useful information, illustrative of the history and resources of the American union, and of each state... Philadelphia, PA: Printed by

Wm. F. Geddes, 1840-42. 6 v. DLC; MB; MWA; NcD; PPL; WaU-L. 40-3037

Hazeltine, Miron James, 1824-1907? Beadle's dime chess instructor... by Miron J. Hazeltine... New York: Beadle and Co. [1840] 80 p. CtY. 40-3038

Hazen, Edward. The speller and definer; or, class book, No. 2. Designed to answer the purpose of a spelling book, and to supersede the necessity of the use of a dictionary as a class rook. By E. Hazen. Stereotyped by J. Fagan, Philadelphia. New York: Baker, Crane & Co; Mahlon Day & Co. [184-?] 214 p. ViU. 40-3039

Hazen, Edward. The Symbolical Spelling Book. In Two Parts. Part the First. Containing 288 Engravings. By E. Hazen, author of "The Speller and Definer" and "The Panorama of Professions and Trades." Within an oval circle of leaves. Baltimore, MD: Published by Joseph N. Lewis, 1840. 140 p. ICBB. 40-3040

Hazen, James A., 1813-1862. Sermon preached at the funeral of Mrs. Delia M. Spelman, So. Wilbraham, Mass., Apr. 28, 1840. Springfield, MA: S. Bowles, 1840. CtHC; RPB. 40-3041

Hazlitt, William, 1778-1830. Eloquence of the British Senate. A selection of speeches of parliamentary speakers from the beginning of the reign of Charles I to the present time. Brooklyn, NY: T. Kerr, 1840. 2 v. MH. 40-3042

Hazlitt, William, 1778-1830. Lectures on the dramatic literature of the age of Elizabeth. By William Hazlitt. Ed. by his son. 3d ed. Philadelphia, PA: Lippincott,

1840. 333 p. CtY; DLC; MdBP; MnS; OOxM. 40-3043

Hazzard favorite waltz. Arranged for the piano forte by J. G. Osbourn. Philadelphia, PA: Geo. Willig [1840-?] 1 p. ViU. 40-3044

Head, Francis Bond, Sir, 1793-1875. Life and adventures of Bruce, the African traveller. By Sir Francis Bond Head. New York: Harper & brothers, 1840. 382 p. CtB; MWA; NBuCC; PPGi; WaU. 40-3045

The Heart, that loves fondest of any. A favorite song, composed & arranged with an accompaniment for the piano forte. Philadelphia, PA: Willig [184-?] 2 p. MB. 40-3046

Heath, Charles. The heroines of Shakespeare; comprising the principal female characters in the plays of the great poet. Engraved under the direction of Mr. Charles Heath from drawings by eminent artists. New York: John Wiley, 1840. NRHi. 40-3047

Hebrew Sunday School of Phildelphia. Second Annual examination of the Sunday School for Religious Instruction of Israelites in Phila. held at the Synagogue Mikveh Israel on Sunday the 29th of March, 1840, 24th. of Veadar, 5600. Together with a prayer by Isaac Leeser... and an address by Moses M. Nathan. Philadelphia, PA: s. l., 1840. 28 p. PPDrop. 40-3048

Hedge, Frederic Henry, 1805-1890. Practical goodness, and true religion. By Rev. F. H. Hedge. Printed for the American Unitarian Association. Bos-

ton, MA: James Munroe and Co., 1840.
16 p. DLC; MCon; PHi. 40-3049

Hedge, Frederic Henry, 1805-1890.
Practical goodness, the true religion. A
sermon preached at Union Street
Church, March 1, 1840... Bangor, ME:
Printed by Samuel S. Smith, 1840. 15 p.
ICMe; MBAU; MDeeP; MeHi; MeBat.
40-3050

Hedge, Levi. Elements of logick...
Stereotyped edition. Boston, MA: Hil-
liard, Gray & Company, 1840. 178 p.
MNan; NjP; NBu; TNP; WNaE. 40-3051

Heerbrugger, Emil. L'union. Two
waltzes & a rondo. Composed for the
guitar. Philadelphia, PA: Fiot [184-?] 3 p.
MB. 40-3052

Heerbrugger, Emil. Swiss air, with
variations for the guitar. Composed and
dedicated to Thos. L. Budd, Esqr., of
Nashville, by his friend Emil Heerbrugger. Philadelphia, PA: Fiot, Meignen &
co. [184-?] 2 p. ViU. 40-3053

Heerbrugger, Emil. Three favorite
waltzes. Arranged for the guitar.
Philadelphia, PA: Willig [184-?] 2 p. MB.
40-3054

Heidelberg Catechism. Catechismus
oder kurzer unterricht Christlicher
lehre... sammt Haul-Tafel... Philadelphia, PA: Heransgegeben von G. B.
Mentz and Sohn, 1840. 128 p. PLT; PPe-
Schw. 40-3055

Heidelberg Catechism. The Heidelberg
catechism or method of instruction in the
Christian religion. Comp. by A. Snyder.
New York: s. l., 1840. VtU. 40-3056

Heidelberg Catechism. The Heidelberg
cat., together with the Constitution &
Discipline of the German Ref. Ch. in the
U. S. of Am. Revd. & cor. approved by
the synod of said ch. 3d. ed. Chambersburg, PA: s. l., 1840. 94 p. DLC;
NcMHi. 40-3057

Heinen, Henry. Gesundheits-
Schaltzkammer oderkurze und richtige
Anwissung zur erhaltung du Gesheit und
Abwendung mancher Krankheiten so
wie auch gute und silornen Gesundheit...
2 aufl. Philadelphia, PA: Lippincott,
1840. 118 p. DNLM; PPC; PPCP. 40-
3058

Heinrich, Anton Philipp, 1781-1861.
An elegiac impromptu fantasia for the
piano forte. A tribute to the memory of
Daniel Schlesinger. New York: The
Author, 1840. 5 p. MB. 40-3059

Heinrich, Anton Philipp, 1781-1861.
The Elssler dances for the piano forte.
New York: The Author, 1840. 3, 7, 3 p.
MB. 40-3060

Heinrich, Anton Philipp, 1781-1861.
The nymph of the Danuba. A grand
serenade [for the piano forte.] New
York: The Author, 1840. 5 p. MB. 40-
3061

Hemans, Felicia Dorothea [Browne]
1793-1835. Hymns for childhood on the
works of nature and other subjects for the
use of children, by Mrs. Felicia Hemans.
Philadelphia, PA: Henry F. Anners,
1840. 64 p. DLC; IEG; LNH; MBev;
TxD-T. 40-3062

Hemans, Felicia Dorothea [Browne]
1793-1835. The works of Mrs. Hemans,
with a memoir by her sister, and an essay

onher genius, by Mrs. Sigourney... Philadelphia, PA: Lea & Blanchard, 1840. 7 v. CtY; MBAt; RPAt; ViL; WvF. 40-3063

Hemmenway, J. Miss Billing's waltz, for the piano forte. Philadelphia, PA: Bacon & co. [184-?] 3 p. MB. 40-3064

Hempel, Carl Julius. Christenthum and Civilisation. New York: A. G. Neumann, 1840. 39 p. NN; PPG. 40-3065

Hempstead. Samuel H. Speech of Samuel H. Hempstead, esq., on the impolicy and unconstitutionality of creating a National bank, and the expediency and necessity of establishing the Independent treasury system. Delivered in the Council hall, in Little Rock, before a Democratic meeting of the county of Pulaski, March 23, 1840. Little Rock, AR: Printed by Edward Cole, printer to the state, 1840. 16 p. ArU; MH-BA; TxU. 40-3066

Henderson, John, 1795-1857. Letter to the legislature of the state of Mississippi, Dec. 28, 1840, in reply to resolutions passed by the Mississippi legislature censuring him for his opposition to the Independent treasury bill, and requesting his resignation from the U. S. Senate. [Washington, DC: s. l., 1840] 16 p. MB; MHi; MiU-C; WHi. 40-3067

Henderson, Thomas, 1789-1854. Hints on the medical examination of recruits for the army; and on the discharge of soldiers from the service on surgeon's certificate. Adapted to the service of the United States. Philadelphia, PA; New Orleans, LA: Haswell, Barrington, and Haswell; John J. Haswell & co., 1840. 44, 192, 99, 58, 117, 113 p. ArU-M; KyLxT; MB; PPAmP; WHi. 40-3068

Hengstenberg, Ernest Wilhelm, 1802-1869. Commentary on Ecclesistes, with other treatises... tr. from the German by D. W. Simon. Philadelphia, PA: Smith, 1840. 488 p. NCH; ViRU. 40-3069

Henry, Caleb Sprague, 1804-1884. The position and duties of the educated men of the country. A discourse pronounced before the Euglossian and Alpha Beta Delta Societies of Geneva College, Aug. 5, 1840. New York: Robert Craighead, pr., 1840. 46 p. CtY; MBC; MeB; NjR; PPM. 40-3070

Henry, Matthew, 1662-1714. The communicant's companion; or, instructions for the right receiving of the Lord's Supper. By the Rev. Matthew Henry, author of the "Commentary," etc. Carefully edited and abridged by Howard Malcom. Philadelphia, PA: Herman Hooker, 1840. 244 p. ICBB; KyHe; NN; PCA; PPRETS. 40-3071

Henry, Matthew, 1662-1714. The life of the Rev. Philip Henry, by his son, the Rev. Matthew Henry. Abridged for the Board. Philadelphia, PA: Presbyterian Board of Publication, 1840. 258 p. CtHC; KyLoP; NbOP; NNUT; ViRut. 40-3072

Henry, Robert. The cultivation of the fine arts... An address... Columbia, SC: s. l., 1840. 15 p. A-Ar; DLC. 40-3073

Henry, Thomas Carlton, 1790-1827. Letters to an anxious inquirer, designed to relieve the difficulties of a friend under serious impressions, by T. Carlton Henry, D. D. With a biographical sketch of the author. 3d ed. Philadelphia, PA:

Presbyterian board of publication, William S. Martien, 1840. 308 p. CSansS; DLC; GEU-T; NjPT; ViRut. 40-3074

Henry, Thomas Carlton, 1790-1827. Letters to an anxious inquirer, designed to relieve the difficulties of a friend under serious impressions, by T. Carlton Henry, D. D. With a biographical sketch of the author. 4th ed. Philadelphia, PA: Presbyterian board of publication [1840] 309 p. MH; NcD; TWcW; WvU. 40-3075

Henshaw, John Prentiss Kewley, 1792-1852. Theology for the people: in a series of discourses on the catechism of the P. E. church. Baltimore, MD: Daniel Brunner [Printed by Joseph Robinson] 1840. 575 p. ICU; NNUT; MdHi; OrPD; PPM. 40-3076

Henz, Henri. Grand fantasie from favorite motifs of Lucia di Mamermoor... New York: Firth & Hall [184-?] 19 p. MB. 40-3077

Hermann, J. Wex. St. Clair waltz. Composed for the guitar. Baltimore, MD: Benteen [184-?] 1 p. MB. 40-3078

"Hero of Tippecanoe; "or, the story of the life of William Henry Harrison. Related by Captain Miller to his boys. New York: s. l. [1840] 121 p. MdBE; MFiHi; MiD-B; MWA; OMC. 40-3079

Herodotus. Herodoti Orientalia Antiquoiora; comprising mainly such portions of Herodotus as give a connected history of the east to the fall of Bablyon and the death of Cyrus the Great. By Herman M. Johnson, D. D... A new revised edition. New York: D. Appleton & Co., 1840. 185 p. KyLoSH. 40-3080

Herodotus. Herodotus. Translated from the Greek, with notes and life of the author by the Rev. William Beloe. Philadelphia, PA: Thomas Wardle, 1840. 489 p. GAuY; GDecCT; IEG; LNT; MB. 40-3081

Heroes of the revolution. With fine portraits. Worcester, MA: Published by J. Grout, jr. [1840?] 24 p. NN. 40-3082

Herring, James, 1794-1867. The national portrait gallery of distinguished Americans. Conducted by James B. Longacre... and James Herring... Under the superintendence of the American Academt of Fine Arts. Philadelphia, PA: James B. Longacre, 1840. 4 v. NcAS. 40-3083

Herring, James, 1794-1867. Oration on the origin, design and duties of Freemasonry. Pronounced at the Second Street Presbyterian Church in the city of Troy on June 24, 1840... Troy, NY: Published by Apollo Lodge, 1840. 22 p. IaCrM; MBAt; MH; NNFM. 40-3084

Herschel, John Frederick William, 1792-1871. A preliminary discourse on the study of natural philosophy. New ed. New York: Harper & brothers, 1840. 279 p. MB; MWiW; PHC; PU; ViU. 40-3085

Herschel, John Frederick William, 1792-1871. A preliminary discourse on the study of natural philosophy. By John Frederick William Hershel... A new edition. Philadelphia, PA: Lea & Blanchard, 1840. 279 p. CtHT; DLC; MBBC; ViU. 40-3086

Herschel, John Frederick William, 1792-1871. A treatise on astronomy. A

new ed. Philadelphia, PA: s. l., 184-? p.
NNUT. 40-3087

Herz, Henri, 1803-1888. Cavatina du
Pirate de Bellini. Tu vedrai la sventurata,
variee. Pour le piano. Op. 68. Baltimore,
MD: Cole [184-?] 11 p. MB. 40-3088

Herz, Henri, 1803-1888. Les elegances.
A favorite set of quadrilles. To which is
added a grand waltz. For the piano forte.
Baltimore, MD: Cole [184-?] 21 p. MB.
40-3089

Herz, Henri, 1803-1888. Empress
Henrietta's waltz. Composed for the
piano forte by H. Herz. New York: Firth,
Hall & Pond [184-?] 2 p. ViU. 40-3090

Herz, Henri, 1803-1888. Empress.
Henrietta's waltz. [For piano forte] Boston, MA: Ditson [184-?] 2 p. MB. 40-
3091

Herz, Henri, 1803-1888. First set of
quadrilles. Baltimore, MD: s. l. [184-?] p.
MB. 40-3092

Herz, Henri, 1803-1888. Gen.
Harrison's quickstep. Subject from Herz.
Arr. for the piano forte by Cle. Zeuner.
Boston, MA: Parker & Ditson, 1840. 2 p.
MB. 40-3093

Herz, Henri, 1803-1888. Herz's exercises and scales for the piano forte. Written expressly to form the hand of the
pupil and to acquire an easy method, A
perfect execution, by Henry Herz. Baltimore, MD; New Orleans, LA: F. D.
Benteen; W. T. Mayo [184-?] 15 p. ViU.
40-3094

Herz, Henri, 1803-1888. Inspruck
Waltz. Arranged for the piano forte by H.

Herz. Philadelphia, PA: A. Fiot [184-?] 1
p. ViU. 40-3095

Herz, Henri, 1803-1888. Lutine. Valse
brillante. Pour le piano. Composee par
Henri Herz. Op. 145... Philadelphia, PA:
George Willig [184-?] 7 p. ViU. 40-3096

Herz, Henri, 1803-1888. ... La
Parisienne. Marche nationale. Varia-
tions caracteristiques pour le piano forte
par Henry Herz. Opus. 53... Baltimore,
MD: Frederick D. Benteen [184-?] 15 p.
ViU. 40-3097

Herz, Henri, 1803-1888. La Parisienne,
marche. Philadelphia, PA: s. l. [184-?] p.
MB. 40-3098

Herz, Henri, 1803-1888. La Polka.
Nouvelle danse nationale, Allemande.
Arrangee pour le piano avec introduc-
tion et Finale, par Henri Herz... Op. 135.
Philadelphia, PA; New York: A. Fiot; W.
Dubois [184-?] 9 p. ViU. 40-3099

Herz, Henri, 1803-1888. Rondo Turc.
Composee pour le piano forte, par Henri
Herz... New York: Dubois & Bacon [184-
?] 7 p. ViU. 40-3100

Herz, Henri, 1803-1888. The second set
of quadrilles; Les elegances. A favorite
set of quadrilles. Added a grand waltz for
the piano forte. Baltimore, MD: Cole
[184-?] 21 p. MB. 40-3101

Herz, Henri, 1803-1888. Souvenir de
Paris, fantaisie sur un theme favori de
l'opera Gustave III. Musiqie de Auber.
Compose par Henri Herz. [Pour le piano
forte.] Philadelphia, PA: Nunns. [184-?]
13 p. MB. 40-3102

Herz, Henri, 1803-1888. 'Tis the last

rose of summer. Irish air, with variations. For the piano forte, by Henry Herz. Baltimore, MD: F. D. Benteen [184-?] 5 p. ViU. 40-3103

Herz, Henri, 1803-1888. 'Tis the last rose of summer, the celebrated Irish air. With an introduction and variations for the piano forte. Boston, MA: Bradlee [184-?] 4 p. MB. 40-3104

Herz, Henri, 1803-1888. Tis the last rose of summer. With an introduction and variations by Henri Herz. Louisville, KY; Cincinnati, OH: W. C. Peters & co.; Peters & Field [184-?] 4 p. ViU. 40-3105

Herz, Henri, 1803-1888. Valse favorite de la Reine d' Angleterre. Composee pour le piano forte par Henri Herz. Philadelphia, PA: G. Willig [184-?] 4 p. ViU. 40-3106

Herz, Henri, 1803-1888. Variations brillantes, Avec introduction & finale alla militare. Pour le piano forte. Fur la cavatine favorite de La violette de carafa. Composies par Henri Herz. Op. 48. Philadelphia, PA: Kretschmar & Nunns. [184-?] 17 p. ViU. 40-3107

Herz, Henri, 1803-1888. Variations brillantes, Avec introduction and [sic] finale alla militare. Pour le piano forte. Fur la cavatine favorite de La violette de carafa. [Op. 48] Philadelphia, PA: Lee and Walker [184-?] 17 p. MB. 40-3108

Herz, Henri, 1803-1888. Variations for the piano forte. By Henri Herz. Boston, MA: Published by Geo. P. Reed [1840] 13 p. KU. 40-3109

Herz, Henri, 1803-1888. A waltz rondo

for the piano forte. New York: Hewitt [184-?] 5 p. MB. 40-3110

Herz, Henri, 1803-1888. We have lived and loved together. Composed y Henri Herz. New York: Published by F. Riley & Co., 1840. 4 p. KU; MB; ViU. 40-3111

Herz, Henri, 1803-1888. Why are you weeping? Ballad. [Accomp. for piano] Boston, MA: Parker & Ditson [184-?] 4 p. MB. 40-3112

Herz, Jacques Simon, 1794-1880. Valse brillante sur un motif de l'Opera Dom Sebastian de Donizetti. Pour le piano par Jacques Herz... New York; Philadelphia, PA: Wm. Dubois; A. Fiot [184-?] 11 p. ViU. 40-3113

Hesser, Jupiter Zeus. Congress grand march by J. Z. Hesser. Brooklyn, NY: P. K. Weizel [184-?] 2 p. ViU. 40-3114

Hesser, Jupiter Zeus. Congress grand march. Composed & arranged for the piano forte by J. Z. Hesser. Louisville: G. W. Brainard & Co. [184-?] 2 p. ViU. 40-3115

Hesser, Jupiter Zeus. Congress grand march. Composed & arranged for the piano forte by J. Z. Hesser. New York: E. Riley & Co. [184-?] 2 p. ViU. 40-3116

Hewett, George. Private record of the life of the Right Honorable General Sir George Hewett, bt., G. C. B. Newport: Printed by W. W. Yelf, 1840. 115 p. DLC. 40-3117

Hewitt, John Hill, 1801-1890. Hewitt's Quick Step... Arranged for the piano forte by T. Rebhun. New York: [Hewitt & Co., 184-?] 3 p. MB. 40-3118

Hewitt, John Hill, 1801-1890. Hewitt's quick step... 10th ed. New York: s. l. [184-?] p. MB. 40-3119

Hewitt, John Hill, 1801-1890. [Military] Hewitt's Quick Step, as performed by the Jefferson Guards Band. Arranged for the piano forte and dedicated to Lieut. James L. Hewitt, and the officers and members of the New York Light Guard by T. Rebhun. [2nd ed.] New York: Hewitt & Jacques, 1840. 3 p. MB. 40-3120

Hewitt, Nathaniel, 1788-1867. A discourse delivered before the general association of Connecticut at its annual meeting, New Haven, June, 1840. By Nathaniel Hewitt... Hartford, CT: n. pub., Elihu Geer, printer, 1840. 26 p. CtY; DLC; IaU; MWA; NjPT. 40-3121

Hewlett, Joseph L. In the court for the trial of impeachments and the correction of errors, Horatio G. Onderdonk, administrator, and Sarah D. Schenck, administratrix... of Abraham H. Schenck, deceased... ads. H... case on the part of the respondents. Manhasset, NY: s. l., 1840. 66 p. NBLIHI. 40-3122

Hews, George. Freeman's quick step... performed... 10th September... dedicated to the Bunker Hill Whig Convention of 1840... With lithograph. Boston, MA: s. l. [1840] 3 p. MHi. 40-3123

Hews, George. Webster's quick step. Composed & arranged for the piano forte by George Hews. New York: Firth & Hall [184-?] 2 p. ViU. 40-3124

Hews, George. Webster's quick step. Composed & arranged [for] piano forte by George Hews. Washington, DC: C. Carusi [184-?] 2 p. ViU. 40-3125

Hews, George. The Whig waltz. Composed for the piano forte. Boston, MA: Parker & Ditson [1840] 2 p. MB. 40-3126

Heyworth, J. Animadversions on Captain Marryart's diary in America, in letters to a friend, 1840. [Zanesville, OH: s. l., 1840?] 24 p. OHi. 40-3127

Hickok, John Hoyt, 1792-1841. Evangelical musick; or, The sacred minstrel and sacred harp united... By J. H. Hickok and C. Fleming... 13th ed. Philadelphia, PA: Whetham, 1840. 312 p. NjP; PHi; PPPrHi. 40-3128

Hickok, John Hoyt, 1792-1841. The social lyrist: a collection of sentimental, patriotis, and pious songs, set to music, arranged for one, two, and three voices. By J. H. Hickok. Harrisburg, PA: W. O. Hickok, 1840. 144 p. DLC; IaHA; MdBG; P; PAtM; RPB. 40-3129

Higbee, Elias. "Latter-day Saints," alias Mormons. The position of the Latter-day Saints, commonly known as Mormons, stating that they have purchased lands of the general government, from which they have been driven... and have suffered other wrongs, for which they pray Congress to provide a remedy... for Memorialists, Elias Higbee and Robert B. Thompson... [Washington, DC: s. l., 1840] 13 p. NNUT; ViU. 40-3130

Higgins, William Mullinger. The earth, its physical condition and most remarkable phenomenon. New York: Harper & Bros., 1840. 408 p. IEG; MLow; NjR; OCY; ScDuE. 40-3131

Hildebertus. The hymn of Hildebert and the Ode of Xavier with English versions. Auburn, NY: H. Ivison, jr., 1840. 35 p. NCH; OHi; PPPrHi; WBeloC. 40-3132

Hildreth, Richard, 1807-1865. Banks, banking, and paper currencies. In three parts. I. History of banking and paper money. --II. Argument for open competition in banking. --III. Apology for one-dollar notes. By R. Hildreth... Boston, MA: Whipple & Damrell, 1840. 209 p. DLC; ICU; MdBJ; PU; TxU. 40-3133

Hildreth, Richard, 1807-1865. The contrast: or, William Henry Harrison versus Martin Van Buren... Boston, MA: Weeks, Jordan & company, 1840. 72 p. DLC; InHi; MB; OClWHi; PHi. 40-3134

Hildreth, Richard, 1807-1865. Despotism in America; or, An inquiry into the nature and results of the slave-holding system in the U. S., by the author of "Archy Moore." Boston, MA: Whipple & Damrell, 1840. 186 p. CSf; KyLo; MBC; NcU; RPB; TxU. 40-3135

Hildreth, Richard, 1807-1865. Despotism in America; or, An inquiry into the nature and results of the slave-holding system in the United States. 2d ed. Boston, MA: Anti-Slavery Society, 1840. 186 p. IGK; MB; MiD-B; MWA; OO; PHi. 40-3136

Hildreth, Richard, 1807-1865. A letter to Andrew Norton on miracles as the foundation of religious faith. Boston, MA: Weeks, Jordan & co., 1840. 52 p. CBPac; DLC; MH; MWA; NjPT. 40-3137

Hildreth, Richard, 1807-1865. A letter to Emory Washburn, Wm. M. Rogers, & 78 other dissentients from the resolution touching political action, adopted at the State Temperance Convention. Boston, MA: The Office of the Boston Spy, 1840. 16 p. CtY; MB; MHi; OCHP; PPL. 40-3138

Hildreth, Richard, 1807-1865. A letter to his excellency Marcus Morton, on banking and currency. By R. Hildreth... Boston, MA: Printed by Kidder & Wright, 1840. 16 p. CtY; DLC; MH; NNC; PPL. 40-3139

Hildreth, Richard, 1807-1865. A letter to Mr. Wm. M. Rogers touching political action. Boston, MA: Kidder & Wright, 1840. 16 p. MMeT. 40-3140

Hildreth, Richard, 1807-1865. The people's presidential candidate; or, the life of William Henry Harrison, of Ohio... Boston, MA: Weeks, Jordan & co., 1840. 126 p. DLC; ICN; IU; OHi. 40-3141

Hildreth, Richard, 1807-1865. The people's presidential candidate; or, the life of William Henry Harrison, of Ohio. By Richard Hildreth. [2d ed.] Boston, MA: Weeks, Jordan & co., 1840. 126 p. InU; MnM; OClWHi. 40-3142

Hildreth, Richard, 1807-1865. The people's presidential candidate; or, the life of William Henry Harrison, of Ohio. By Richard Hildreth. [3d ed.] Boston, MA: Weeks, Jordan & co., 1840. 126 p. OClWHi; TxU. 40-3143

Hildreth, Richard, 1807-1865. The people's presidential candidate; or, the life of William Henry Harrison, of Ohio. By Richard Hildreth. [4th ed.] Boston,

MA: Weeks, Jordan & co., 1840. 126 p.
Ia; IC; MiD-B; MWA; OO. 40-3144

Hildreth, Richard, 1807-1865. The
people's presidential candidate; or, the
life of William Henry Harrison, of Ohio.
By Richard Hildreth. [6th ed.] Boston,
MA: Weeks, Jordan & co., 1840. 126 p.
KHi; MBNEH; MWA; WHi. 40-3145

Hildreth, Richard, 1807-1865. The
people's presidential candidate; or, the
life of William Henry Harrison, of Ohio.
By Richard Hildreth. [7th ed.] Boston,
MA: Weeks, Jordan & co., 1840. 126 p.
MnHi; P. 40-3146

Hildreth, Richard, 1807-1865. The
slave; or, Memoirs of Archy Moore
[pseud.] By Richard Hildreth. 2d ed. Boston, MA; New York: Massachusetts
Anti-slavery Society; American Anti-
slavery Society, 1840. 2 v. in 1. CtY; ICU;
MBC; OClWHi. 40-3147

Hildreth, Richard, 1807-1865. The
slave; or, Memoirs of Archy Moore
[pseud.] 3d ed. Boston, MA: Anti-slavery
Society, 1840. CtY; GAU; MWA; Nh-
Hi; TNF. 40-3148

Hildreth, Richard, 1807-1865. Strictures on Governor Morton's Message....
Second Edition. Boston, MA: Printed by
Cassady & March, 1840. 16 p. MH; NNC.
40-3149

Hildreth, Samuel Prescott, 1783-1863.
Genealogical and bographical sketches
of the Hildreth family, from the year 1652
down to the year 1840... Marietta, OH: s.
l., 1840. 334 p. NBLiHi; OClWHi; OMC;
WHi. 40-3150

Hill, Alonzo, 1800-1871. A discourse on

the life and character of the Rev.
Nathaniel Thayer, D. D., pastor of the
First Congregational church and society
in Lancaster. Delivered at his interment,
June 29, 1840. By Alonzo Hill... Wor-
cester: Printed by Spponer & Howland,
1840. 40 p. CtSoP; MBC; MWA; OCHP;
PPAmP. 40-3151

Hill, Frederic Stanhope, 1805-1850.
The Shoemaker of Toulouse. New York:
s. l. [184-?] p. MB; NCU. 40-3152

Hill, Stephen Prescott, 1806-1884.
Theatrical amusements. A premium
tract. [Philadelphia, PA: Baptist General
Tract Society, 184-?] 28 p. MH. 40-3153

Hill's New Hampshire patriot, August
12, 1840, Jan. 13, 1841, Mar. 10, June 16,
July 7, July 20-Aug. 3, Aug. 17, 24, Sept.
7, 14, Oct. 26-May 12, 1842, June 16-July
14, Aug. 11, 1842. Concord, NH: s. l.,
1840-42. v. CtY; MBAt. 40-3154

Hill's Tennessee, Alabama, Mississippi,
and Arkansas Almanack for 1841. By J.
B. Hill. Fayetteville, TN: E. Hill [1840]
74 p. MWA. T. 40-3155

Hillsborough Bridge, N. H. Congregational Church. Articles of faith and form
of covenant. Concord, NH: s. l., 1840. 11
p. MBC. 40-3156

Hillyard, Clark. Practical farming and
grazing; with observations on the breeding & feeding of sheep & cattle. 3rd edition. Northampton: T. E. Dicey, 1840.
168 p. DLC; MH-BA; NIC. 40-3157

Hilmara, F. ... Kralowe Hradecks.
Polka, by Hilmara. Newport, polka, arranged by Thorbecke. Philadelphia, PA;

New York: A. Fiot; W. Dubois [184-?] 3
p. ViU. 40-3158

Hime, B. Wilt thou meet me there love.
[Song, S. or T.] Arranged for the Spanish
guitar, by A. Schmitz. Philadelphia, PA:
Fiot [184-?] 2 p. MB. 40-3159

Himes, Joshua Vaughan, 1805-1895. A
pictorial chart of Daniel's visions. Boston, MA: s. l., 184?. p. MBAt. 40-3160

Hines, David Theodore. The life, adventures and opinions of David Theo.
Hines, of South Carolina, master of arts,
and sometimes, doctor of medicine... in a
series of letters to his friends. Written by
himself... New York: Bradley & Clark,
1840. 195 p. CtMW; GEU; MiD-B; TxU;
WHi. 40-3161

Hinkle & Drury. Colored drawings of
the locomotive engine, Charlestown.
[Boston, MA: s. l., 184-?] p. MB. 40-3162

Hinton, Isaac Taylor, 1799-1847. A history of baptism, both from the inspired
and uninspired writings, by Isaac Taylor
Hinton... Philadelphia, PA: American
Baptist Publications and S. S. Society,
1840. 372 p. GMM; MH-AH; PHi; TJaU;
WHi. 40-3163

Hints to the honest tax payers of the City
of Boston. Signed Temperance. [Boston,
MA: s. l., 184-?] p. MH. 40-3164

A historical account of the circum-
navigation of the globe... and of the
progress of discovery in the Pacific
Ocean, from the voyage to Magellan to
the death of Cook. New York: Harper &
Brothers, 1840. 366 p. CtY; InRch; KyLx;
NjR; OClWHi. 40-3165

Historical Epitome of the State of
Louisiana, with an Historical notice of
New-Orleans, views and descriptions of
public buildings. New Orleans, LA: s. l.,
1840. MH; OMC. 40-3166

Historical notices of Hartford.
[Hartford, CT: s. l., 184-?] 24 p. MB. 40-
3167

History and anecdotes of the elephant.
New Haven, CT: Printed and published
by S. Babcock, 1840. 16 p. CtY; ICU;
MH; NN; RPB. 40-3168

History and horros of the Helderberg
war, one of the most ferocious atrocious
and tremendiocious conflicts ever known
in any Kingdom or principality of the
world. By a continentaler. Albany, NY: s.
l., 1840. 28 p. MB; MBAt. 40-3169

The History and refutation of the
charge of "Bargain intrigue and corrup-
tion," against Mr. Clay, in his vote for
John Quincy Adams. [S. l.: n. p., 1840?]
16 p. MiD-B. 40-3170

History of American missions to the
heathen from their commencement to
the present time. Worcester, MA:
Spooner & Howland, 1840. paging not
continuous. FSa; IaG; MBC; MWA; PU.
40-3171

History of Honest Roger. New York:
American Tract Society [184-?] 48 p. NN;
ViU. 40-3172

History of Jack the Giant Killer.
Philadelphia, PA: Turner & Fisher, 1840.
OMC. 40-3173

The history of Switzerland from B. C.
110 to A. D. 1830. New edition. New

York: Harper & Brothers, 1840. 288 p. ICBB; MB; NcDaD; NGlc; ScDuE. 40-3174

History of the Delaware and Iroquois Indians, formerly inhabiting the middle states... Written for the American Sunday School Union. Philadelphia, PA: American Sunday School Union, 184-? p. NN. 40-3175

History of the Puritans in England... New York: s. l., 1840. 508 p. NN. 40-3176

Hitchcock, David K. Preservation of the teeth; a family guide, being familiar observations on their structurel and diseases. With practical illustrations and engravings, embracing the modern improvements in dentistry. Boston, MA: Ives, 1840. 92 p. IEN-D; MB; MdUM; NNN; PPiU-D. 40-3177

Hitchcock, E. Key of Hitchcock's new method of teaching book-keeping. Philadelphia, PA: published by the author [ca. 1840?] 56 p. MiU. 40-3178

Hitchcock, Edward, 1793-1864. Elementary Geology. By Edward Hitchcockl, Professor of Chemistry and Natural History in Amherst College and Geologist to the State of Mass. Amherst, MA; Boston, MA; New York; Philadelphia, PA: Published by J. S. & C. Adams; Crocker and Brewster; F. J. Huntington and Co., Gould, Newman and Saxton; Thomas Cowperthwait and Co., Marhall and Co., 1840. 329 p. CtSoP; ICU; MiU; OO; RPAt. 40-3179

Hitchcock, R. An oration, delivered before the students of Wesleyan academy, on the Fourth of July, 1840...

Springfield: Printed by Merriam, Wood and Co., 1840. 14 p. CtY; Nh-Hi. 40-3180

Hoare, Clement, 1789-1849. A practical treatise on the cultivation of the grape vines on open walls. Boston, MA: W. D. Ticknor, 1840. ICJ; MB; NIC; OO; PPL. 40-3181

Hoare, Clement, 1789-1849. A practical treatise on the cultivation of the grape vine on open walls. Second American ed. Boston, MA: s. l., 1840. 144 p. ICJ; MNan; NCH; OO; RPAt. 40-3182

Hob, nob; or, The Campbells are comin' and The morning star. New York: Firth & Hall [184-?] 1 p. ViU. 40-3183

Hobart, John Henry, 1775-1830. A companion for the altar; or, Week's preparation for the Holy Communion: consisting of a short explanation of the Lord's Supper and medications and prayers proper to be used before and during the receiving of the Holy Communion; according to the form prescribed by the Protestant Episcopal Church in the United States of America. Thirteenth edition. New York: Published by the Swords, Stanford and Co., 1840. 244 p. CtHT; MoS; VtMidSM. 40-3184

Hobart, John Henry, 1775-1830. A companion for the festivals and fasts of the Protestant Episcopal Church in the United States of America, principally selected and altered from Nelson's companion for the festivals and casts of the Church of England with forms of devotion. 8th ed. New York: Swords, Stanford and Co., 1840. 331 p. MH; NNC. 40-3185

Hobart College, Geneva, N. Y.

Catalogue of the Officers and Students of Geneva College for the Academical Year 1839-40. Geneva, NY: Printed by Stow and Frazee, 1840. 34 p. CtY; MBC; MiU; N; NGH. 40-3186

Hobbs, John William, 1799-1877. Song of the captive Greek girl. As sung by Mrs. Franklin. Poetry by Miss Pardoe. Music by J. W. Hobbs. Boston, MA: Oliver Ditson [184-?] 5 p. ViU. 40-3187

Hoch-Deutsche German taun Calender. Philadelphia, PA: Wm. W. Walker, by Carl F. Engelmann, 1840. MWA. 40-3188

Hodge, Charles, 1797-1878. A commentary on the Epistle to the Romans, by Charles Hodge... abridged by the author, for the use of Sunday-schools and Bible-classes. 3d ed. Philadelphia, PA; Boston, MA: H. Perkins; Ines & Dennet, 1840. 352 p. NWatt; OkEnS; PWaybu. 40-3189

Hodge, Charles, 1797-1878. The constitutional history of the Presbyterian church in the United States of America. By Charles Hodge... Part II... Philadelphia, PA: William S. Martien, 1840. 516 p. MnSM. 40-3190

Hodge, Hugh Lenox, 1796-1873. Introductory Lecture to the Course on Obstetrics and Diseases of Women and Childre. Delivered in the University of Pennsylvania, Nov. 2, 1840. Philadelphia, PA: L. R. Bailey, 1840. 16 p. DNLM; DSG; PHi; PU. 40-3191

Hodge, Paul Rapseys. The steam engine, its origin and gradual improvement, from the time of hero to the present day... By P. R. Hodge... New York: D. Appleton & Co. [H. Ludwig, printer] 1840. 254 p. DLC; IU; MiD; NjR; PU. 40-3192

Hodge, Paul Rapseys. The steam engine, its origin and gradual improvement, from the time of hero to the manufactures, locomotion and navigation. By P. R. Hodge... New York: D. Appleton & Co., 1840-41. 254 p. MiDT; NBu; NNCoCi; OC. 40-3193

Hodgson, Francis, 1805-1877. An examination of the system of new divinity; or, new school theology. By Rev. Francis Hodgson... [Quotation] New York: published by George Lane, for the Methodist Episcopal Church, 1840. 416 p. DLC; IEG; LNB; MsJMC; NcMHi. 40-3194

Hodson, George Alexander, d. 1863. Child of the West. Highland ballad. Words by F. W. N. Bayley. Music by G. A. Hodson. Baltimore, MD: Published by F. D. Benteen [184-?] 3 p. ViU. 40-3195

Hodson, George Alexander, d. 1863. The lake of Como. [Morning] To Como's lake. Arranged for the piano forte, by G. A. Hodson. Baltimore, MD: Geo. Willig, Jr. [184-?] 3 p. ViU. 40-3196

Hodson, George Alexander, d. 1863. ... My home, my happy home. A ballad. Composed expressly for Mademoiselle Jenny Lind. Philadelphia, PA: E. Ferrett & Co. [184-?] 3 p. NN; ViU. 40-3197

Hodson, George Alexander, d. 1863. ... My home, my happy home. Philadelphia, PA; New York: A. Fiot; W. Dubois [184-?] 5 p. ViU. 40-3198

Hodson, George Alexander, d. 1863

My mountain home. Ballad. As sung with great applause by Mrs. Wood. Composed by G. A. Hodson. Baltimore, MD: Geo. Willig, Junr. [184-?] 2 p. ViU. 40-3199

Hodson, George Alexander, d. 1863. My mountain home. Ballad. Sung with enthusiastic applause by Miss Coveney; the poetry by I. Donoghue, esq. Composed by G. A. Hodson. New York: Dubois & Stodart [184-?] 3 p. ViU. 40-3200

Hodson, George Alexander, d. 1863. "My pretty gazelle. "Composed by G. A. Hodson. Boston, MA: Geo. Willig, Junr. [184-?] 3 p. MiU-C; NN; ViU. 40-3201

Hodson, George Alexander, d. 1863. Oh! give me back my Arab steed. Ballad. Sung by Madame Feron. Composed by G. A. Hodson. New York: Dubois & Stodart [184-?] 3 p. ViU. 40-3202

Hodson, George Alexander, d. 1863. Wi' my love I'll march away. Sung with unbounded applause by Miss Clasa Fisher; composed by G. A. Hodson. Philadelphia, PA: John G. Klemm [184-?] 3 p. ViU. 40-3203

Hoffman, Charles Fenno, 1806-1884. Greyslaer: A romance of the Mohawk. By the author of "A Winter in the West." New York: Harper & Brothers, 1840. 2 v. CtSoP; IEN; MWA; NjP; PU. 40-3204

Hoffman, Ernest Teodor Amadeus. Signor Formica. Novelle, von E. T. A. Hoffmann. New York: Verlag der Buchhandlung von W. Radde, 1840. 92 p. CtMW; InGrD; MoS; OU; TNJU. 40-3205

Hoffman, Ogden. Speech on the motion

to report a bill appropriating $150, 000 to each of the states of Ohio, Indian, and Illinois for the continuation of the Cumberland Road. In the House of Representatives [of the United States] Feb. 12, 1840. Washington, DC: Printed by Gales & Seaton, 1840. 15 p. CtY; DLC; MH; MWA; PHi. 40-3206

Hoffmann, Ernest Theodor Amadeus, 1776-1822. Die Rauber: Abenteuer zweier Freunde auf einem Schloss in Bohmen, von E. T. A. Hoffmann. New York: W. Radde, 1840. 48 p. CtMW; InGrD; OU; TNJU. 40-3207

Hoffman's Albany Directory and City Register for the year 1840/41. Compiled and published by L. G. Hoffman... Albany, NY: printed by L. G. Hoffman, 1840. v. MBNEH. 40-3208

Hofland, Barbara Wreaks Hoole, 1770-1844. Farewell tales. Boston, MA: J. H. Francis, etc., etc. [184-?] MH. 40-3209

Hofland, Barbara Wreaks Hoole, 1770-1844. Farewell tales. Boston, MA: Roberts Bros. [184-?] 216 p. MB; MiD-W. 40-3210

Hofland, Barbara Wreaks Hoole, 1770-1844. Farewell tales. Founded on facts. By Mrs. Hofland, author of.... New Edition. New York: W. E. Dean [1840?] 3 p. ViU. 40-3211

Hofland, Barbara Wreaks Hoole, 1770-1844. The helpless orphans & other stories. Boston, MA: Shepard, Clark & Brown [1840] 176 p. ICU. 40-3212

Hoge, James. A reply to the letter of A. Leonard to the Presbytery of Columbus. [S. l.: s. l., 1840] p. PPPrHi. 40-3213

Hohnstock, Adele. The celebrated concert polka. Performed with great applause by Miss Adele Hohnstock. Baltimore, MD; New Orleans, LA: F. D. Benteen; W. T. Mayo [184-?] 5 p. ViU. 40-3214

Holbrook, Josiah, 1788-1854. Easy lessons in geometry. Intended for infant and primary schools, but useful in academies, lyceums and families. 11th ed. Boston, MA: Jenks & Palmer, 1840. CTHWatk; DLC; MB. 40-3215

Holcombe, Hosea. A history of the rise and progress of the Baptists in Alabama. With a miniature history of the denomination. Philadelphia, PA: King and Baird, 1840. 375 p. GU; KyLoS; MH-AH; MoSHi; PHi; ViRU. 40-3216

Holden, Charles. Influence and duties of mechanics; an address... [Portland: s. l., 1840] 18 p. DLC. 40-3217

Holdrich, Joseph. Poor Robert... New York: G. Mason & G. Lane, 1840. 31 p. DLC. 40-3218

Holford, George Peter, 1768-1839. The destruction of Jerusalem, an irresistable proof of the divine origin of Christianity. Philadelphia, PA: William S. Martien, 1840. 106 p. GDecCT; NjPT. 40-3219

Holiday present; being a variety of stories for children. Newark, NJ: s. l., 1840. NJl; NjP. 40-3220

Hollick, Frederick, b. 1818. The matrons manual of midwifery & the diseases of women during pregnancy & in child birth... 4th ed. New York: T. W. Strong [etc., etc., 1840] 458 p. IEN-M; IU. 40-3221

Hollister, Gideon Hiram, 1817-1881. A poem, by Gideon Hiram Hollister. And the valedictory oration by Curtis Field Burnam, pronounced before the senior class in Yale College, July 1, 1840. Published by request of the class. New Haven, CT: Hitchcock & Stafford, printers, 1840. 36 p. CSmH; MBC; PHi; RPB; TxU. 40-3222

Holliston Academy, Holliston, Mass. Catalogue of the officers and students. Dedham, MA: Printed by H. Mann, book & job printer, 1840. 12 p. MHolliHi. 40-3223

Holmes, John, 1773-1843. The statesman; or, Principles of legislation and law. By John Holmes... Augusta, ME: Severance & Dorr, printers, 1840. 510 p. DLC; MB; MeU; MWA; RPB. 40-3224

Holmes, Oliver Wendell, 1809-1894. The autocrat of the breakfast table... Boston, MA: James Munroe & Co., 1840. 359 p. RPB. 40-3225

Holst, Matthias von. The first cottage rondo. [For piano forte.] Boston, MA: Ditson [184-?] 4 p. MB. 40-3226

Holthaus, Peter Diedrich. Wanderings of a Journey man Tailor Through Europe and the East... By P. D. Holthaus New York: J. Winchester, 184-? 97 p. OC. 40-3227

Holyday present, being a variety of stories for children... Newark, NJ: Benjamin Olds, 1840. 127 p. NjN. 40-3228

Home, John, 1722-1808. ... Douglas. A tragedy in five acts. By Rev. Dr. Home New York: S. French [184-?] 55 p. CSt; MB. 40-3229

Home; its joys and its sorrows. A domestic tale. By Uncle Author... New York: Taylor and Dodd, 1840. 96 p. LNH; NcWsS. 40-3230

The home of the lost child. A tale of the asylum of the Good Shepard, Hammersmith... Baltimore, MD: Fielding Lucas, Jr. [184-?] 232 p. MBEmm. 40-3231

Homeopathic Examiner. The Homeopathic examiner... Vol. 1-3, new series, vol. 1-2; 1840-1843, Aug. 1845-July 1847. New York; London: s. l., 1840-47. v. CoCsC; ICJ; MdBM; OU; PPHa. 40-3232

Homerus. Homer. Translated by Alexander Pope, Esq. In three volumes. New York: Harper and brothers, 1840. 3 v. CtY; MeB; NUt; OCX; PP. 40-3233

Homo, Benjamin. A letter concerning Thomas Wilson Dorr, addressed to the Hon. T. Anthropos of Providence, R. I.... Providence, RI: s. l., 1840. 15 p. RHi. 40-3234

Honestas, pseud. A defence of the Lehigh coal and navigation company, from assaults made upon its interests by X. Philadelphia, PA: J. Harding, printer, 1840. 66 p. CtY; DBRE; MH-BA; OClWHi. 40-3235

Hood, George, 1807-1882. Can all learn to sing? by George Hood. [Boston, MA: Boston Academy of Music, 1840] p. MB; MHi. 40-3236

Hood, Thomas, 1799-1845. Up the Rhine... With Comic illustrations. 2nd ed. Philadelphia, PA: Porter and Coates [1840] 339 p. KyBgW; MB; PPi; TxU; WaS. 40-3237

Hood, Thomas, 1799-1845. Whims and Waifs. New York: s. l., 1840. OClStM. 40-3238

Hook, James, 1746-1827. Within a mile of Edinburg town. Scotch ballad. Sung [by] Madame Sontag, newly arranged for the piano forte. Baltimore, MD: Miller & Becham, successors to F. D. Benteen [184-?] 3 p. ViU. 40-3239

Hooker, Edward William, 1794-1875. Love to the doctrines of the Bible, an essential element of Christian character. Philadelphia, PA: Presb. board, 1840. 18 p. CtHC; OMtv; PPM; WHi. 40-3240

Hooker, Edward William, 1794-1875. Memoir of Mrs. Sarah Lanman Smith. Boston, MA: Published by Perkins & Marvin, 1840. 396 p. InCW; MH; NRU; TxHuT; WBeloC. 40-3241

Hooker, Edward William, 1794-1875. Memoir of Mrs. Sarah Lanman Smith, late of the mission in Syria, under the direction of the American Board of Commissioners for Foreign Missions. 2d ed. Boston, MA: Perkins and Marvin, etc., etc., 1840. 396 p. CtHC; MBL; PPiW; TxHuT; WHi. 40-3242

Hooker, Edward William, 1794-1875. Memoir of Mrs. Sarah L. Huntington Smith, late of the American mission in Syria. Third edition. New York: Perkins & Marvin, 1840. 396 p. MeAu; MHi. 40-3243

Hooker, Herman. The family book of devotion; containing daily morning and evening prayers for four weeks...

Philadelphia, PA: Published by Edward C. Biddle; printed by T. K. & P. G. Collins, 1840. 207 p. MB; MBC; PPM. 40-3244

Hooper, Edward James, b. 1803. The practical farmer, gardiner, and housewife; or, Dictionary of agriculture, horticulture, and domestic economy... Also with remarks on the cultivation of some select flowers and ornamental shrubs. By James Hooper. Cincinnati, OH: G. Conclin, 1840. 544 p. CSt; OClWHi; RPAt. 40-3245

Hooper, John. The present crisis; or, a correspondence between the Signs of the Times in which we live, and the Prophetic Declarations of Holy Scripture. By Rev. John Hooper, of Westbury, Eng... Boston, MA: Published by Dow & Jackson, 1840. 16 p. ICU; MWA. 40-3246

Hooper, Lucy, 1816-1841. Scenes from real life. An American tale. New York: J. P. Griffing, 1840. 83 p. CU; DLC; N. 40-3247

Hoosac Tunnel... Boston, MA: s. l., 184-? 8 p. MB. 40-3248

Hooton, Charles, 1813?-1847. Colin Clink. Containing the Contentions, Dissentions, Loves, Hatreds, Jealousies, Hypocrisies, and Vicisstudes, incident to his Chequered life. Philadelphia, PA: s. l., 1840-41. 2 v. CtY; MH; MHa; NIC; PHi. 40-3249

Hooton, James. Boston Light Infantry's grand march. [For the piano forte.] Boston, MA: Reed [184-?] 2 p. MB. 40-3250

Hooton, James. Castle march. [For the

piano forte.] Boston, MA: Bradlee [184-?] 1 p. MB. 40-3251

Hooton, James. Ladies cavalcade... quick step... Boston, MA: Wm. H. Oakes, 1840. 3 p. NN. 40-3252

Hooton, James. The popular melody of Old Rosin the beau. Arranged as an easy lesson by James Hooton. Boston, MA: Oliver Ditson [184-?] 2 p. ViU. 40-3253

Hooton, James. Variations for the piano forte on a favorite dance, The soldiers joy. Composed & dedicated to Miss Martha Strang, of St. Andrews, N. B., by James Hooton. Boston, MA: C. Bradlee [184-?] 7 p. MB; ViU. 40-3254

Hooton, James. Variations for the piano forte on a favorite dance, The soldier's joy. Composed & dedicated to Miss Martha Strang, of St. Andrews, N. B., by James Hooton. Boston, MA: Oliver Ditson [184-?] 6 p. ViU. 40-3255

Hopkins, Erastus. Family, a religious institution; or, Heaven its model. Troy, NY: Elias Gates, 1840. 204 p. DLC; MBC; MWA; NbCrD; NT; OO. 40-3256

Hopkins, George Washington, 1804-1861. Letter of George W. Hopkins, of Russell, to Col. James H. Piper, of Wythe, Va. [Dated March 16, 1840] Washington, DC: s. l., 1840. 32 p. DLC; MBAt; MBC; NcD; OClWHi. 40-3257

Hopkins, George Washington, 1804-1861. Letter of George W. Hopkins, of Russell, to Col. James H. Piper, of Wythe. Washington, DC: s. l., 1840. 47 p. DLC; MoSM; NCH; NcU; TxU. 40-3258

Hopkins, George Washington, 1804-

1861. Speech of Mr. Hopkins, of Virginia, on the general appropriation bill. Delivered in Committee of the Whole, in the House of Representatives, April 22, 1840. Washington, DC: printed at the Globe Office, 1840. 15 p. DLC; IU; MiGr. 40-3259

Hopkins, Mark, 1802-1887. An address, delivered in South Hadley, Mass., July 30, 1840, at the Third Anniversary of the Mt. Holyoke Female Seminary. Northampton, MA: Printed by John Metcalf, 1840. 23 p. CtHC; MB; NCH; OCl; PPPr-Hi. 40-3260

Hopper, Isaac Tatem, 1771-1852. Expositon of the proceedings of John P. Darg, Henry W. Merritt, and others, in relation to the robbery of Darg, the elopement of his alleged slave, and the trial of Barney Corse, who was unjustly charged as an accessary. New York: I. T. Hopper, 1840. 39 p. CtY; DLC; NIC-L; OClWHi; PHi. 40-3261

Horatius Flaccus, Quintus. Horace. Translated by Philip Francis, D. D. With an appendix, containing translations of various odes, etc... New York: Harper and brothers, 1840. 2 v. IEG; MoSpEA; PMy; PV. 40-3262

Horatius Flaccus, Quintus. The works of Horace. With English notes, critical and explanatory, by Charles Anthon, LL. D. A new edition, with corrections and improvements. New York: Harper and brothers, 1840. 681 p. CtY; GDecCT; Ky-CovV; ScC; ViU. 40-3263

Horn, Charles Edward, 1786-1849. Child of earth with the golden hair. Titania's love, from Song of the fairies.

Composed by C. E. Horn. Boston, MA: C. Bradlee [184-?] 5 p. ViU. 40-3264

Horn, Charles Edward, 1786-1849. The deep, deep sea. Cavatina. Composed for the piano forte by C. E. Horn. Boston, MA: C. Bradlee [184-?] 5 p. MB; ViU. 40-3265

Horn, Charles Edward, 1786-1849. [The devil's bridge.] 'Tis but fancy's sketch, the celebrated picture song... in the devil's bridge. [The music by C. E. Horn and J. Braham. The words by S. J. ARnold. With accompaniment for piano forte.] Boston, MA: Bradlee [184-?] 2 p. MB. 40-3266

Horn, Charles Edward, 1786-1849. Follow a shadow. Round for 3 voices. Boston, MA: s. l. [184-?] 3 p. MB. 40-3267

Horn, Charles Edward, 1786-1849. I know a bank whereon the wild thyme blows. A popular duet. Baltimore, MD: Willig [184-?] 7 p. MB. 40-3268

Horn, Charles Edward, 1786-1849. I know a bank whereon the wild thyme blows. Boston, MA: s. l. [184-?] p. MB. 40-3269

Horne, Thomas Hartwell, 1780-1862. A compendious introduction to the study of the Bible; being an analysis of: An introduction to the critical study and knowledge of the Holy Scriptures." In four separate volumes by the same author. By Thomas Hartwell Horne. New York: Mason and Lane, 1840. 391 p. GDecCT; IaPeC; KSalW; OCl; PPLT. 40-3270

Horne, Thomas Hartwell, 1780-1862. An introduction to the critical study and knowledge of the Holy Scriptures. New edition from the eighth London ed. Philadelphia, PA: Joseph Whetham, 1840. 2 v. IEG; MB; MH. 40-3271

Horner, William Edmonds, 1793-1853. Home book of health & medicine, a popular treatise on the means of avoiding & curing diseases & of preserving the health & vigour of the body... By a physician of Philadelphia. Philadelphia, PA: Biddle, 184?. 456 p. UofPEngTS. 40-3272

Horner, William Edmonds, 1793-1853. A treatise on special and general anatomy. By William E. Horner... 5th ed., rev. and improved. Philadelphia, PA: Lea & Blanchard, 1840. 2 v. CU; LNT-M; NcU; PPCP; ViNoM. 40-3273

Horsford, Eben Norton, 1818-1893. Report on the phrenological classification of J. Stanley Grimes. By E. N. Horsford... Albany, NY: n. pub., Printed by J. Munsell, 1840. 28 p. CtY; DLC; NjR; WHi. 40-3274

Horton, George Moses, 1798-1880. Two poems. Chapel Hill, NC: s. l., 1840. NcU. 40-3275

Horton, Jotham. A tribute to James Stetson Wilson: Containing an account of his life, Christian experience, happy death, miscellaneous writings and selections from H. K. White... Lowell, MA; Boston, MA: E. A. Rice Company; D. S. King, 1840. 144 p. DLC; MWA. 40-3276

Hosmer, George Washington, 1804-1881. An address, delivered before the Erie County Common School Education Society at Buffalo, N. Y., Feb. 3, 1840. By George W. Hosmer. Buffalo, NY:

Printed at Steele's Press, 1840. 23 p. ICMe; NBu; NNUT. 40-3277

Household remedies for various diseases; sun and moon phases, calendar for year, etc., etc. Compiled by Geo. R. Perkins. Watertown, NY: Printed by Knowlton & Rice, 1840-47. 2 v. WGrNM. 40-3278

The Housekeeper's almanac; or, The young wife's oracle, for 1840. New York: Elton, 1840. MB; MWA; NBuG; NIC. 40-3279

Houston, Russell. An address, delivered before the Philo-rhetorican & Neatrophian societies at Jackson college, on the eleventh of March, 1840. By Russell Houston, esq... [Published by request of the societies] Columbia, TN: Printed on the Observer Press, 1840. 21 p. T; TKL-Mc. 40-3280

How shall lawyers be paid? Or some remarks from two acts recently passed on the subject of the costs of legal proceedings, in a letter to John Anthon, Esq... New York: Alexander S. Gould, 1840. 31 p. MH; NN; PPL. 40-3281

Howard, Edward, d. 1841. Jack ashore. By the author Ratlin [!] the reefer, etc... Philadelphia, PA: Carey and Hart, 1840. 2 v. CtY; DLC; MnU; PU; RPB. 40-3282

Howard, Franklin Bryant. Account of [the death] of Franklin Bryant Howard, a scholar of Grace Church Sunday School, Boston [who died, 24th February, 1840] [Boston, MA: s. l., 1840?] 8 p. MB; MBAt; MWA; WaS. 40-3283

Howard, H. R. The life and adventures of John A. Murrall, the great western and pirate. With twenty-one spirited illustrative engravings. Philadelphia, PA: T. B. Peterson and Brother [184-?] 126 p. NcU. 40-3284

Howard, Nathaniel. Vocabulary, English and Greek... By Nathaniel Howard. Philadelphia, PA: s. l., 1840. 167 p. NjP. 40-3285

Howard, Tilghman Ashurst, 1797-1844. Outline of the remarks of Mr. Howard, of Indiana, in the House of Representatives, Feb. 12, 1840, on the proposition to instruct the com. of Ways and Means... [S. l.: n. p., 1840] 8 p. IU; MdHi; MiD-B; MiU-C; OClWHi. 40-3286

Howe, Eber D., d. 1798. History of Mormonism or a faithful account of that singular impostition and delusion. With sketches of the characters of its propagators. Painesville: Author, 1840. 290 p. ICHi; MWA; NbHi; OClWHi; OHi. 40-3287

Howe, Elias, 1820-1892. The fairy bell waltz. Arranged for the Spanish guitar by Thomas Crouch. New York: Firth, Pond & Co. [184-?] 2 p. MB. 40-3288

Howe, Elias, 1820-1892. Howe's 100 Scotch songs. Words and music. Boston, MA: Howe [184-?] p. MB. 40-3289

Howe, Henry, 1816-1893. Memoirs of the most eminent American mechanics; also, lives of distinguished European mechanics; together with a collection of anecdotes, description &c., relating to the mechanic arts. Illustrated by fifty engravings. By Henry Howe. New York: Harper & brothers, 1840. 482 p. CtB; KTW; MdBE; MiGr; PHi; WU-EM. 40-3290

Howe, John Moffat, 1806-1885. To Consumptives. Information respecting the practice of F. H. Ramadge, M. D. Also an account of several cases in relation to this practice, to which it has been beneficial in this country, with other corrabative testimony. New York: pub. by author, 1840. 48 p. DLC; DNLM; MBNMHi; NcD. 40-3291

Howe, Luke. The Use and Application of an Improved Apparatus for particular Fractures and Dislocations of the Extremities. Illustrated by Cuts and Cases, with Remarks. By Luke Howe, M. D. Republished from the Boston Medical and Surgical Journal. Boston, MA: D. Clapp, Jr., 1840. 16 p. DNLM; DSG. 40-3292

Howe, William. An address, delivered at the Berry Street Church before the [Boston] Society for the Prevention of Pauperism, March 1, 1840. Boston, MA: s. l., 1840. 21 p. DLC; IU; MBAt; MHi; MiU. 40-3293

Howitt, Mary Botham, 1799-1888. Hope on! Hope ever! or, The boyhood of Felix Law. By Mary Howitt... Boston, MA: James Munroe and Company, 1840. 225 p. MBilHi; MH; MNan; MWA; RJa. 40-3294

Howitt, Mary Botham, 1799-1888. Love and money, an everyday tale. New York: J. Winchester [1840?] 52 p. MdBP; MH. 40-3295

Howitt, Mary Botham, 1799-1888. My juvenile days, and other tales. By Mary Howitt. New York; Philadelphia, PA: D. Appleton & Co.; George S. Appleton, 1840. ScCliTO. 40-3296

Howitt, Mary Botham, 1799-1888. Strive and thrive: a tale. Boston, MA: James Munroe & Co., 1840. CtY; MH; RPAt. 40-3297

Howitt, William, 1792-1879. The boy's country book of amusements, pleasures, and pursuites... Edited by William Howitt. From the London edition. New York: published by Samuel Colman, 1840. 356 p. CU; DLC; MWA; NNS; PU. 40-3298

Howland, S. A. Steamboat disasters and railroad accidents in the United States. To which are appended accounts of recent shipwrecks, fires at sea, etc. By S. A. Howland. Worcester, MA: Dorr, Howland & Co., 1840. 408 p. AB; ICJ; MWA; NjR; OClWHi. 40-3299

Howland, S. A. Steamboat disasters and railroad accidents in the United States. To which is appended accounts of recent shipwrecks, first at sea, thrilling incidents, &c. By S. A. Howland. Second edition. Worcester, MA: Published by Dorr, Howland & Co., 1840. 398 p. AB; CSf; MBAt; MWH; WU. 40-3300

Hoxse, John. The Yankee tar. An authentic narrative of the voyages and hardships of John Hoxse, and the cruises of the U. S. Frigate Constellation... written by himself... Northampton: printed by John Metcalf, for the author, 1840. 200 p. DLC; MBAt; MDeeP; NjR; NNA. 40-3301

Hubbard, David, 1806-1874. Letter of Hon. David Hubbard to the voters of the second Congressgional district of the state of Alabama. Washington, DC: printed at the Globe office, 1840. 7 p. DLC; MiU-C; ViU. 40-3302

Hubbard, David, 1806-1874. Speech of Hon. David Hubbard, to the voters of the Second Congressional district of the State of Alabama. Washington City, March, 1840. Washington, DC: Printed at the Globe Office, 1840. 7 p. MdHi; MiU-C; NjR; NNC; TxU. 40-3303

Hubbard, David, 1806-1874. Speech of the Hon. David Hubbard, of Alabama, on the independent treasury bill. Delivered in the House of Representatives, June 27, 1840. Washington, DC: P. Force, 1840. 15 p. DLC; MdHi; TxU. 40-3304

Hubbard, Henry, 1784-1857. Speech of Mr. Hubbard, of New Hampshire, on Mr. Grundy's report in relation to the assumption of the debts of the states by the federal government. Delivered in Senate, Tuesday, February 18, 1840. [Washington, DC: s. l., 1840] 16 p. CtY; DLC; MiGr; TxU. 40-3305

Hubbard, Henry, 1784-1857. Speech of Mr. Hubbard, of New Hampshire, on the bill to authorize the issue of treasury notes. Delivered in Senate, U. S., Marcm [sic] 30, 1840. [Washington, DC: printed at the Globe Office, 1840] 13 p. MdHi; NNC; TxU. 40-3306

Hubbard, Henry, 1784-1857. Speech on the bankrupt bill. In the Senate of the United States, May 25, 1840. Washington, DC: printed at the Globe Office, 1840. 15 p. IU; MdHi; MH-BA; NjR; OClWHi. 40-3307

Hubner. Biblische Historien aus dem alten und neuen Testamente... Philadelphia, PA: Herausgegeben von George W. Mentz und Sohn, 1840. 484 p. PPeSchw; RPeaHi. 40-3308

Hudson, Charles, 1795-1881. Questions on select portions of Scripture, designed for the higher classes in Sabbath schools. By Charles Hudson. Boston, MA: B. B. Mussey and Abel Tompkins, 1840. 178 p. MH; MMeT-Hi. 40-3309

Hudson Academy, Hudson, Ohio. Catalogue... year ending March, 1839-40. Cayahoga Falls, OH: Printed by S. F. Wetmore, 1840. 11 p. NN. 40-3310

Hudter, Louisa H. The Swiss girl, as sung with rapturous applause by M'lle Lovarney. Composed by G. Linley. Boston: Oliver Ditson, [184-?] 5 p. ViU. 40-3311

Hughes, John, 1797-1864. Debate before the Common Council on the Catholic petition respecting common school fund & the public school system of education in the City of New York. 2nd ed. New York: Freeman's Journal, 1840. MdW. 40-3312

Hughes, John, 1797-1864. Kirwan unmasked. A review of Kirwan, in six letters, addressed to the Rev. Nicholas Murray, D. D., of Elizabethtown, N. J. By the Right Rev. John Hughes, D. D., Bishop of New York. New York: Edward Dunigan & Brother, n. d. 72, 36 p. MH; MiDSH; MiU. 40-3313

Hughes, Mary Robson. Pleasing & instructive stories for young children. Philadelphia, PA: T. T. Ash [184-?] 105 p. NN. 40-3314

Hughes, Thomas, 1822-1896. School days at Rugby. Boston, MA: s. l., 1840. MSbri. 40-3315

Hughes, William. The messenger bird...

New York: Dubois & Stodard, 184-? 6 p. MB. 40-3316

Hull, Laurens, 1779-1865. Annual address, delivered before Medical Society of the State of New York, Fe., 1840. Albany, NY: s. l., 1840. 15 p. CtY; MHi; MWA. 40-3317

Hullah, John Pyke, 1812-1884. Come with thy lute to the fountain. Duett for soprano & contralto. Adapted to a favorite German air, with a piano forte accompaniment by J. P. Hullah... New York; Philadelphia, PA: Wm. Dubois; A. Fiot [1840] 8 p. NN; ViU. 40-3318

Humboldt, Alexander Freiherr von, 1769-1859. Travels and researches of Alexander von Humboldt; being a condensed narrative of his journeys in the equinoctical regions of America and in Osiatic Russia... il. map. New York: Harper [1840?] 367 p. MB. 40-3319

Humbugs of speculation. A satirical poem, embracing several historical sketches of speculative operations, national and individual during the last four years. By a citizen of Saratoga Springs... Saratoga Springs, NY: s. l., 1840. 12 p. IU; MBC; MH; NN; TxU. 40-3320

Hume, David, 1711-1776. The history of England, from the invasion of Julius Caesar, to the revolution in 1688. By David Hume, esq. With notes and references exhibiting the most important differences between this author and Dr. Lingard. Philadelphia, PA: M'Carty and Davis, 1840. 2 v. CU; IU; FStP; KyHi; WHi. 40-3321

Hume, James Nelson. The downfall of alcohol, being two addresses on temperance, delivered at sundry places, by the Rev. Jas. Nelson Hume. Boston, MA: Printed by D. H. Ela, 1840. 24, 24 p. IEG; MWA. 40-3322

Hume, James Nelson. Temperance vs. Intemperance:An address, or Concise Treatise on the Nature & Effects of Alcohol. Delivered in... Montpelier, Vt... Feb. 25th, 1840. by the Rev. James Nelson Hume... Boston, MA: Printed by D. H. Ela, 1840. 24 p. MBNMHi; MWA. 40-3323

Humor; tales of Boston. Vol. I. Boston, MA: s. l. [1840] 192 p. MWA. 40-3324

Humorist tales; a selection of interesting stories. Boston, MA: Shepard, Clark & Brown [184-?] 192 p. ICU; NN; PSt. 40-3325

Humphrey, Heman, 1779-1861. Domestic education. By H. Humphrey, D. D. Amherst, MA: J. S. and C. Adams, 1840. 239 p. IaMp; MH-AH; NhPet; PU; RPB. 40-3326

Hunt, Benjamin Faneuil, 1792-1857. Speech of Col. Benj. Faneuil Hunt, of Charleston, South Carolina, delivered at the request of the Democratic Republicatin General Committee, at the Mass Meeting of the Mechanics and Working Men of New York, in reply to the doctrines of Daniel Webster, on the Currency and a National Bank. Reported and published by James Rees, at the Office of the New Era. New York: J. Rees [1840] 8 p. MWA; MWo; NN. 40-3327

Hunt, Hiram Paine, 1796-1865. Speech of Hon. Hiram P. Hunt, of New York, on the subject of the reception of abolition petitions and papers. Delivered in the House of Representatives of the United States, January 23, 1840. Washington, DC: Printed at the Madisonian office, 1840. 15 p. MdHi; RP. 40-3328

Hunt, Hiram Paine, 1796-1865. Speech of Mr. Hunt, of New York, in the House of Representatives, on the expenses of the Florida war, July 11, 1840. Troy, NY: Printed by James M. Stevenson, 1840. 22 p. N. 40-3329

Hunt, Hirem Paine, 1796-1865. Speech of Mr. Hunt, of New York, on the Sub-Treasury Bill, Delivered in ... June 3, 1840. Washington, DC: Printed by Gales & Seaton, 1840. 15 p. DLC; OCl; OClWHi. 40-3330

Hunt, Randell, d. 1892. Argument Randell Hunt, esq., in the Batture case. New Orleans, LA: William M'Kean, 1840. 175 p. LNHT; LU. 40-3331

Hunt, Thomas Poage, 1794-1876. The cold water army... Boston, MA: Whipple & Damrell, 1840. 36 p. MH; MnU; NN; PU. 40-3332

Hunten, Franz, 1793-1878. ... Air Suisse Varie... Philadelphia, PA: A. Fiot [184-?] 5 p. MB; ViU. 40-3333

Hunten, Franz, 1793-1878. Air tyroliene barie. [Pour le piano] New York: Dubois & Stodart [184-?] 11 p. MB. 40-3334

Hunten, Franz, 1793-1878. Les Bords du Rhin. Grande Valse brillante, pour piano, par, Francois Hunten. Op. 120. Solo... Philadelphia, PA; New Orleans, LA: A. Fiot; W. T Mayo [184-?] 9 p. MB; ViU. 40-3335

Hunten, Franz, 1793-1878. The bride. New York: Riley & Co. [184-?] 7 p. MB. 40-3336

Hunten, Franz, 1793-1878. ... La Cachucha. A national Spanish dance. Arranged for the piano forte by F. Hunten. Baltimore, MD: G. Willig [1840?] 5 p. ViU. 40-3337

Hunten, Franz, 1793-1878. Callopade quadrille. Arranged for the piano forte. Boston, MA: Ditson [184-?] 2 p. MB. 40-3338

Hunten, Franz, 1793-1878. ... Danse espagnole... Composed and arranged by Francoise Hunten. New York: Firth, Hall & Pond & Firth & Hall [184-?] 6 p. ViU. 40-3339

Hunten, Franz, 1793-1878. Le diademe. Variations brillantes sur en theme de Donezetto. Philadelphia, PA: Fiot [184-?] p. MB. 40-3340

Hunten, Franz, 1793-1878. The emerald grande valse brillante. Composed & arranged for the piano forte by F. Hunten. Baltimore, MD: Frederick D. Benteen [184-?] 7 p. ViU. 40-3341

Hunten, Franz, 1793-1878. The emerald grande valse brillante, as performed by Dodworth's corner band. Composed by Francois Hunten. Op. 128. New York: Firth, Hall & Pond [1840?] 6 p. ViU. 40-3342

Hunten, Franz, 1793-1878. F. Huenten's celebrated instructions. New York: Hewitt & Co. [184-?] p. MB. 40-3343

Hunten, Franz, 1793-1868. Favorite march from Rossini's opera "William Tell. "With brillant variations for two performers on the piano forte. Composed by F. Hunten. Op. 40. Baltimore, MD: G. Willig, Jr. [184-?] 19 p. ViU. 40-3344

Hunten, Franz, 1793-1878. Gallopade quadrille. Composed for the piano forte, by F. Hunten. Baltimore, MD; New Orleans, LA: F. D. Benteen; W. T. Mayo [1840?] 2 p. ViU. 40-3345

Hunten, Franz, 1793-1878. Joys that we've tasted. With variations. For pf. Baltimore, MD: s. l. [184-?] p. CtY. 40-3346

Hunten, Franz, 1793-1878. Melodie de Mercante. With variations for the piano forte, by Francois Hunten. Boston, MA: Oliver Ditson [184-?] 5 p. ViU. 40-3347

Hunten, Franz, 1793-1878. A new and improved edition of Hunten's Celebrated instructions for the piano forte, in which is introduced a series of popular airs. Philadelphia, PA: A. Fiot [1840?] 67 p. MH. 40-3348

Hunten, Franz, 1793-1878. La Norma de Bellini. [Variations pour le piano] Baltimore, MD: Cole [184-?] 7 p. MB. 40-3349

Hunten, Franz, 1793-1878. Palagne. [For piano forte] Philadelphia, PA: Fiot, Meignam & Co. [184-?] 5 p. MB. 40-3350

Hunten, Franz, 1793-1878. The Pearl waltz. Composed by F. Hunten. Baltimore, MD: F. D. Benteen [184-?] 2 p. ViU. 40-3351

Hunten, Franz, 1793-1878. Les perles...

New York: Hewitt & Co. [184-?] p. MB. 40-3352

Hunten, Franz. 1793-1878. La rose. By F. Hunten. Boston, MA: Published by Geo. P. Reed, 1840. 14 p. KU. 40-3353

Hunten, Franz, 1793-1878. Les topazes. [No. 1.] Grande valse brillante, composee pour piano forte par Francoise Hunten. Op. 129. New York: Firth, Hall & Pond & Firth & Hall [184-?] 7 p. ViU. 40-3354

Hunten, Franz, 1793-1878. ... 'Twere vain to tell thee. A Swiss air with variations. Composed for the piano forte, by Francois Hunten. Baltimore, MD: Geo. Willig, Junr. [184-?] 5 p. ViU. 40-3355

Hunten, Franz, 1793-1878. Variations on the favorite air, See oh! Norma... Philadelphia, PA: Fiot [184-?] 9 p. MB. 40-3356

Hunten, Franz, 1793-1878. Vive la danse: galoppe et marche. [for pf.] Boston, MA: s. l., 1840. CtY. 40-3357

Hunter, J. A home that I iove. Arranged as a waltz for the piano forte by J. Hunter. Baltimore, MD: F. D. Benteen [184-?] 2 p. ViU. 40-3358

Hunter, J. B. To the voters of Fairfax. [By J. B. Hunter] [Fairfax County, VA: s. l., 1840] p. NbHi. 40-3359

Hunter, John, 1728-1793. Observations on certain parts of the animal economy... by John Hunter. With notes by Richard Owen. Philadelphia, PA: Haswell, Barrington and Haswell, 1840. 480 p. ArU-M; KyU; LNOP; MeB; MoSW-M. 40-3360

Hunter, John, 1728-1793. A treatise on the blood, inflammation, and gunshot wounds, by John Hunter, F. R. S. With notes by James F. Palmer... Philadelphia, PA; New Orleans, LA: Haswell, Barrington and Haswell; John J. Haswell & Co., 1840. 611 p. CSt; KyLxT; MH-M; NBMS; PPA. 40-3361

Hunter, Robert Mercer Taliaferro, 1809-1887. Letter of... to his constituents. Washington, DC: s. l., 1840. 8 p. DLC; NcD. 40-3362

Huntting, James Murdock. A sermon; containing a general history of the parish of Westfield, N. J., preached Jan. 1, 1839, in the Presbyterian Church of that place. By James M. Huntting... Elizabethtown, NJ: H. H. Hassey, pr., 1840. 31 p. MWA; Nj; NNUT; OClWHi; PPPrHi. 40-3363

Hurlbut, E. P. Civil office and political ethics. With an appendix, containing familiar law relating to husband and wife, parent and child, guardian and ward, wills, executors, and administrators. By E. P. Hurlbut. New York: Taylor & Clement, 1840. 208 p. MDeeP; MLow; NcD; NNLI. 40-3364

Huston, Robert M. Introductory lecture to the course of obstetrics and diseases of women and children... by R. M. Huston, M. D. Philadelphia, PA: Printed by Wm. F. Geddes, 1840. 22 p. DLC; DSG; MHi; PHi; PP. 40-3365

Hutchins' Improved almanac. By David Young. New York: Poinier & Snell, 1840. MWA. 40-3366

Hutchins' Improved almanac for the year 1841. By David Young. Elizabethtown, NJ: Henry Kiggins, n. pr. [1840] 34 p. MWA; NjR. 40-3367

Hutchins' Improved almanac for the year 1841. By David Young. Somerville, NJ: S. L. B. Baldwin, n. pr. [1840] 35 p. NjR. 40-3368

Hutchins' Improved almanac for the year 1841... Calculated for the horizon and meridian of New Jersey... By David Young. New Brunswick, NJ: J. Terhune, n. pr. [1840] 35 p. MWA; NjR. 40-3369

Hutchins' Improved for 1841. By David Young. New York: Charles Small [1840] 34 p. MWA. 40-3370

Hutchins' Improved for 1841. By David Young. New York: H. & S. Raynor [1840] 34 p. MWA; NjMo; NjR. 40-3371

Hutchins' Improved for 1841. Rahway,

NJ: John Pearson [1840] p. MWA. 40-3372

Hutchinson, Graham. Objections to Mr. Espy's theory of rain, hail, etc. Philadelphia, PA: s. l. [184-?] p. NN. 40-3373

Hymers, John. A treatise on the theory of algebraical equations. 2d ed. Cambridge, MA: Parker, 1840. 216 p. IRA; MsU; OO; PU. 40-3374

Hymns for little children. Northampton: Metcalf, 1840. 24 p. MB. 40-3375

Hymns, collects, anthems, and selections to be sung in churches and Sunday Schools. [Compiled by E. W., Jr.] Boston, MA: s. l., 1840. MoS. 40-3376

I

I'm a pilgrim. Adapted to Buona Notte, an Italian song, arranged for the piano forte. Baltimore, MD; New Orleans, LA: F. D. Benteen; Wm. T. Mayo [184-?] 2 p. ViU. 40-3377

Ide, Jacob, 1785-1880. A sermon prached at the ordination of Rev. Samuel Hunt... in Natick... Boston, MA: Ptd. by John S. March, 1840. 28 p. MBC; MiD-B. 40-3378

Ide, Jacob, 1785-1880. The virtuous woman commended; a sermon... occasioned by the death of Mrs. Hannah Miller, wife of Nathaniel Miller. by Jacob Ide. Providence, RI: n. pub., n. pr., 1840. 29 p. DLC; MBC; MH-AH; PHi; RPB. 40-3379

Ide, Jacob, 1785-1880. A sermon prached at the ordination of Rev. Daniel J. Poor, to the pastoral care... in Foxborough, March 11, 1840... By Jacob Ide, D. D., pastor... Medway. Boston, MA: Ptd. by John S. March, 1840. 21 p. MiD-B; MWA; OClWHi; PPM; RPB. 40-3380

If I speak to thee in friendship's name. Written by T. Moore, esqr. Arranged for the piano forte by H. R. Bishop. New York: Wm. Hall & son [184-?] 2 p. ViU. 40-3381

Illinois. General Assembly. House. Journal of the House of the twelfth General assembly... convened by proclamation of the Governor, being their first session, begun and held in the city of Springfield, Nov. 23, 1840. Springfield: Wm. Walters, public printer, 1840. 570 p. IHi; ILM; NN. 40-3382

Illinois. General Assembly. Senate. Journal of the Senate of the twelfth General assembly... convened by proclamation of the Governor, being their first session, begun and held in the city of Springfield, Nov. 23, 1840. Springfield: Wm. Walters, public printer, 1840. 455 p. DLC; ILM; IU; MiU; WHi. 40-3383

Illinois. State house commissioners. ... Communication from A. G. Henry and William Herndon, state house commissioners... Springfield, IL: Wm. Walters, public printer, 1840. 4 p. Nb. 40-3384

Illinois. State house commissioners. ... Communication from Archibald Job, one of the state house commissioners. Springfield, IL: Wm. Walters, public printer, 1840. 3 p. No Loc. 40-3385

Illinois and Michigan Canal. Chief engineer of. Report estimating the damages to the canal which would arise from a suspension of the work. Made by the chief enegineer of the Illinois and Michigan canal, in reply to a resolution of the House. Springfield, IL: Wm. Walters, public printer, 1840. 9 p. Nb; Nj; WHi. 40-3386

Illinois College, Jacksonville, Ill. Catalogue of the officers and students... 1839-40. Jacksonville, IL: Goudy's Job Office, 1840. 16 p. IHi; IJC. 40-3387

The illustrated book of songs for children. The illustrations [from designs by Birket Foster] New York: Gregory [184-?] 64 p. MB. 40-3388

Imitatio Christi. An extract of the Christian's pattern; or, A treatise on the Imitation of Christ. Written in Latin by Thomas a Kempis. By John Wesley... Baltimore, MD: J. N. Lewis, 1840. 208 p. IEG; MdHi; MdW; MiEalC. 40-3389

Importance of a Register Law to the purity of the Election Franchise. By a Citizen of Kentucky. Louisville, KY: s. l., 1840. 16 p. MHi. 40-3390

In days of old. A favorite patriotic ballad, as sung at the Tippecanoe associations, with great applause, partly written and arranged for the piano forte by a member of the Fifth Ward Club. [S. l.: s. l., 1840?] 3 p. ViU. 40-3391

In the court for the trial of impeachments and correction of errors, Ezra White vs. the people of the State of New York. Case on the part of the plaintiff in error. D. Graham, Jr., for the plaintiff in error. J. R. Whiting for defendants in error. New York: Printed by Bryand & Boggs, 1840. 128 p. InHi. 40-3392

Index to the Subjects Contained in the Old and New Testaments... New York: s. l., 184-? 14 p. NN. 40-3393

Indian Anecdotes and Barbarites, being Description of Their Customs and Deeds of Cruelty, with an Account of the Cap-tivity, Sufferings and Heroic Conduct of Many who have fallen into their Hands, or who have defended Themselves from Savage Vengeance. All Illustrating the General Traits of Indian Character... [Numerous woodcuts] Palmer, MA: Printed for M. Baldwin, the Blind Man [184-?] 29 p. CtY; NN. 40-3394

The Indian chief's march. Genl. Gate's march. Baltimore, MD: Geo. Willig Jr. [184-?] 1 p. ViU. 40-3395

Indiana. General Assembly. House. Committee the State Bank. Report of Mr. Fisher, from the Committee... February 4, 1840. [Indianapolis, IN: s. l., 1840] 85 p. NNC. 40-3396

Indiana. General Assembly. House. Journal of the House of Representatives at the Twenty-fifth Session of the General assembly of the State of Indiana, commenced at Indianapolis, on Monday, The Seventh Day of December, 1840. [Indianapolis, IN: Osborn & Chamberlain, Printers to the State, 1840] 915 p. InLB; LU; WHi. 40-3397

Indiana. General Assembly. Senate. Documents of the Senate of Indiana, twenty-fourth session. Indianapolis, IN: Douglas and Noel, state printers, 1840. 298 p. InFtw; InSbNHi; MnHi. 40-3398

Indiana. General Assembly. Senate. Journal of the Senate of the state of Indiana, during the twenty-fifth session of the General Assembly. Indianapolis, IN: Douglas and Noel, state printers, 1840. 715 p. In-SC; LU. 40-3399

Indiana. Governor. [David Wallace] Governor's message, delivered to the General Assembly of the State of Indiana, December 8, 1840. Indianapolis, IN: Osborn & Chamberlain, 1840. In; WHi. 40-3400

Indiana. Governor. [Samuel Bigger] Communication from the Governor, enclosing resolutions of the State of Indiana, in relation to the North-eastern boundary. Indianapolis, IN: s. l., 1840. 5 p. MiD-B. 40-3401

Indiana. Governor. [Samuel Bigger] Inaugural address [of Gov. Samuel Bigger] delivered to the General Assembly of the State of Indiana, Dec. 9, 1840. Indianapolis, IN: s. l., 184?. 14 p. WHi. 40-3402

Indiana. Laws, statutes, etc. General laws of the state of Indiana, passed at the twenty-fifth session of the General Assembly. Begun December, 1840. Indianapolis, IN: Douglas & Noel, state printers, 1840. 245 p. A-SC; Ar-Hi; Ar-SC; Az; DLC; IaHi; IaU-L; In-SC; L; MCWL; Mi-L; Mo; MoHi; Ms; NNLI; Nb; Nc-S; Nv; OCLaw; R; RPL; Sc; T. 40-3403

Indiana. Laws, statutes, etc. Laws of a local nature passed and published at the twenty-fourth session of the General Assembly of the state of Indiana. Held at Indianapolis, on the first Monday in December, one thousand eight hundred and thirty-nine. By authority. Indianapolis, IN: Douglass and Noel, state printers, 1840. 267 p. IaHi; In-SC; Mi-L; Nj; Wa-L. 40-3404

Indiana. Selecting Commissioners. Report of the Selecting Commissioners to the governor [relating to the lands the state is entitled to on the Wabash and Erie Canal east of the Tippecanoe River,

Aug. 12, 1840] Indianapolis, IN: s. l., 1840. 14 p. WHi. 40-3405

Indiana. University. Address by a Committee of the Trustees [of Indiana University] to the People of Indiana. Indianapolis, IN: s. l., 1840. 15 p. ICU; DLC; In; InU; MHi; NjP; NNC; PU; RPB. 40-3406

Indiana. University. Annual circular. Bloomington, IN: s. l., 1840-1932. v. MB. 40-3407

Indiana. University. Catalogue... Bloomington, IN: Drefrees, 1840. 14 p. InU; MB. 40-3408

Indiana. University. [Diploma for B. A. degree and certificate of the Athenian society presented to J. R. Cravens, 1840] Bloomington, IN: n. pub., 1840. InU. 40-3409

Inducements to the colored people of the U. S. to emigrate to British Guiana, comp. fr. statements & documents furnished by Mr. Edw. Carbery, agent of the "Immigration society of British Guiana," and a proprietor in that colony. By a friend to the colored people. Boston, MA: Printed for distribution, Kidder and Wright, 1840. 24 p. IaHi; MWA; OClWHi; PPL; WHi. 40-3410

The infant school primer. Compiled by the published for small children and approved by Samuel W. Seton. New York: G. F. Cooledge [184-?] p. MH; PSC-Hi. 40-3411

The influence of the slave power. [Signed A teller of the truth] [Boston, MA: s. l., 184-?] 4 p. MH. 40-3412

Information for the Legislature and people of the State of Pennsylvania, and professional men throughout the U. S., in relation to various systems of superstitions, frauds & particularly those inflicted upon the credulous by pretended doctors in medicine. Philadelphia, PA: s. l. [184-?] 32 p. DNL-M; NN. 40-3413

Inglis, Henry David, 1795-1835. The miser, or The confessions of an avaricious man. Boston, MA: J. N. Bradley & Co. [1840?] 24 p. MH. 40-3414

Inglis, Henry David, 1795-1835. Rambles in the footsteps of Don Quixote... Philadelphia, PA: Lea & Blanchard, 1840. 180 p. MnM; MWA; PP; RBr; TSewU. 40-3415

Inglis, Paul. A letter to mechanics and working men on the wages of labor. By Paul Inglis, carpenter. New York: s. l., 1840. 16 p. DLC; ICU; MiU-C; NjR; NN. 40-3416

Ingraham, Joseph Holt. 1809-1850. Arnold; or, the British spy. A tale of treason and treachery. New York: s. l., 184-? 38 p. IU. 40-3417

Ingraham, Joseph Holt, 1809-1850. The dancing feather; or, the amateur freebooters: a romance of New York. New York: Burgess & Garrett [184-?] 92 p. CtY. 40-3418

Ingraham, Joseph Holt, 1809-1850. Lafitte... New York: s. l. [1840] p. DLC. 40-3419

Ingraham, Joseph Holt, 1809-1850. Paul Perril, the merchant's son; or, the adventures of a New England boy launched upon life. Boston, MA: s. l. [184-?] p. CtHWatk. 40-3420

Ingraham, Joseph Holt, 1809-1850. The silver bottle; or, the adventures of "Little Marlboro" in search of his father. Boston, MA: s. l. [184-?] 2 v. in 1. RPB. 40-3421

Inquiry into the alleged tendency of the separation of convicts, one from the other, to reduce disease and derangement, by a citizen of Pennsylvania. Philadelphia, PA: J. Biddle, 1840. 160 p. LNT. 40-3422

The Insinuator... [Schenectady, NY: Union College, 1840] 21 p. NN. 40-3423

The Iris, or literary messenger... Vol. 1, November, 1840-October, 1841... New York: The Proprietors, 1840-. v. CtY; DLC; MH; NjR; PPPrHi. 40-3424

Insurance & Trust Company of Illinois. Charter of the Insurance & Trust Company of Illinois, incorporated A. D. 1839. Kaskaskia, IL: Printed at the Republican Office, 1840. 7, 4 p. IHi. 40-3425

Investigator and expositor. v. 1-. Troy, OH: s. l., 1840-. v. OClWHi. 40-3426

Iowa [Territory] Governor, 1838-1841 [Robert Lucas] Governor's message, delivered at the 4th session of the Iowa Legislature. Burlington, IA: s. l., 1840. 7 p. IaCrM. 40-3427

Iowa [Territory] Laws, statutes, etc. Acts and joint resolutions passed at the regular session of the... [several sessions of the territorial Legislature- 47th; 1840/1937] General Assembly of the State of Iowa... Des Moines, IA:

Published by the State of Iowa, 1840-1937. 42 v. Ok. 40-3428

Iowa [Territory] Laws, statutes, etc. Laws of the territory of Iowa, enacted at the session of the legislature which commenced on the first Monday of November, A. D. 1839. Published by authority. Burlington, IA: John H. M'Kenny, 1840. 227 p. Az; IaU-L; MWCL; Wa-L. 40-3429

Iowa [Territory] Laws, statutes, etc. Laws of the territory of Iowa. Passed at the extra asession of the Legislative Assembly. Begun and held in the city of Burlington on the first Mondayin July, in the year of our Lord one thousand eight hundred and forty. Published by authority. Burlington, IA: John H. M'Kenny, 1840. 80 p. IaU-L; MWCL; Nb; RPL; Wa-L. 40-3430

Iowa [Territory] Legislative Assembly. Council. Council File... No. [1] Mr. Parker. A Bill to repeal the acts herein mentioned. [Acts in regard to the acts of the Territories of Michigan and Wisconsin in force in the Territory of Iowa. Also the statutes of England] [S. l.: n. p., 1840] p. IaHA. 40-3431

Iowa [Territory] Legislative Assembly. Council. Council File... No. 1 [3] Mr. Hempstead. A bill to provide for the expression of opinion of the people of the Territory of Iowa as to taking preparatory steps for their admission into the Union. [S. l.: n. p., 1840] p. IaHA. 40-3432

Iowa [Territory] Legislative Assembly. Council. Council File... No. 1 [4] Mr. Hempstead. A bill to amend an act entitled "An act for the appointment and

duties of Sheriff." [S. l.: n. p., 1840] p. IaHA. 40-3433

Iowa [Territory] Legislative Assembly. Council. Council File... No. 1 [5] Mr. Parker. A bill to establish the Seat of Justice in Scott County. [S. l.: n. p., 1840] 2 p. IaHA. 40-3434

Iowa [Territory] Legislative Assembly. Council. Council File... No. [2] Mr. Parker. A Act to define the Jurisdiction of the several Counties in this Territory that front upon the Mississippi River. [S. l.: n. p., 1840] p. IaHA. 40-3435

Iowa [Territory] Legislative Assembly. Council. Council File... No. [3] Joint Resolution to provide for the publishing the Reports of the Supreme Court and for other purposes. [S. l.: n. p., 1840] p. IaHA. 40-3436

Iowa [Territory] Legislative Assembly. Council. Council File... No. [4] Mr. Hastings, Nov. 9, 1840. A bill to amend "An Act subjecting real and personal estate to executions." [S. l.: n. p., 1840] p. IaHA. 40-3437

Iowa [Territory] Legislative Assembly. Council. Council File... No. [5] Mr. Hempstead. Joint Resolution to provide for the Auditing of certain accounts. [S. l.: n. p., 1840] p. IaHA. 40-3438

Iowa [Territory] Legislative Assembly. Council. Council File... No. [5] Mr. Springer, Nov. 9, 1840. A Bill providing for the service of writs by copy in certain cases. [S. l.: n. p., 1840] p. IaHA. 40-3439

Iowa [Territory] Legislative Assembly. Council. Council File... No. [6] Mr. Springer, Nov. 9, 1840. A Bill additiona to "An Act regulating practices in the District Courts of the Territory of Iowa." [S. l.: n. p., 1840] p. IaHA. 40-3440

Iowa [Territory] Legislative Assembly. Council. Council File... No. [7] Mr. Kirkpatrick, Nov. 11, 1840. A Bill to amend an act providing for and regulating General Elections in this Territory. [S. l.: n. p., 1840] p. IaHA. 40-3441

Iowa [Territory] Legislative Assembly. Council. Council File... No. [9] Mr. Hastings, Nov. 12, 1840. A Bill to amend an act regulating conveyances. [S. l.: n. p., 1840] p. IaHA. 40-3442

Iowa [Territory] Legislative Assembly. Council. Council File... No. [10] Mr. Payne. A Bill to authorize Peter Brewer, his heirs or assigns, to erect a dam across Skunk River. [S. l.: n. p., 1840] p. IaHA. 40-3443

Iowa [Territory] Legislative Assembly. Council. Council File... No. [11] Mr. Payne. A Bill to authorize James Wilson, his heirs or assigns, to build a dam across Skunk River in Jefferson County. [S. l.: n. p., 1840] p. IaHA. 40-3444

Iowa [Territory] Legislative Assembly. Council. Council File... No. [12] Mr. Greene, Nov. 18, 1840. A Bill establishing and regulating Medical Societies. [S. l.: n. p., 1840] 2 p. IaHA. 40-3445

Iowa [Territory] Legislative Assembly. Council. Council File... No. [13] Mr. Bainbridge, Nov. 18, 1840. A Bill to incorporate the Iowa Mining and Smelting Company. [S. l.: n. p., 1840] p. IaHA. 40-3446

Iowa [Territory] Legislative Assembly.

Council. Council File... No. [17] Mr. Hempstead. A Bill to grant upon certain conditions lots of land in Iowa City for church purposes. [S. l.: n. p., 1840] p. IaHA. 40-3447

Iowa [Territory] Legislative Assembly. Council. Council File... No. [22] Mr. Coop, Dec. 2, 1840. A Bill supplementary to an act concerning Water Crafts found adrift Lost Goods and Stray Animals, approved January 22, 1839. [S. l.: n. p., 1840] p. IaHA. 40-3448

Iowa [Territory] Legislative Assembly. Council. Council File... No. [25] Mr. Parker, Dec. 8, 1840. A Bill relative to Incorporated Religious Societies. [S. l.: n. p., 1840] p. IaHA. 40-3449

Iowa [Territory] Legislative Assembly. Council. Council File... No. [27] Mr. Parker, Dec. 9, 1840. A Bill to re-locate the seat of Justice in Clinton County. [S. l.: n. p., 1840] p. IaHA. 40-3450

Iowa [Territory] Legislative Assembly. Council. Council File... No. [29] Mr. Parker, Dec. 14, 1840. A Bill to amend "An Act concerning Grand and Petit Jurors." [S. l.: n. p., 1840] p. IaHA. 40-3451

Iowa [Territory] Legislative Assembly. Council. Council File... No. [32] Mr. Greene, Dec. 14, 1840. A Bill to amend "An Act to regulate ferries, approved December 20th, A. D. 1838." [S. l.: n. p., 1840] p. IaHA. 40-3452

Iowa [Territory] Legislative Assembly. Council. Council File... No. [42] Mr. Greene, Dec. 23, 1840. A Bill relative to Improvements on Unsurveyed Lands. [S. l.: n. p., 1840] p. IaHA. 40-3453

Iowa [Territory] Legislative Assembly. House. H. R. File... No. 1. Mr. Miller, Nov. 5, 1840. A memorial to Congress relative to the completion of the penitentiary. [S. l.: n. p., 1840] p. IaHA. 40-3454

Iowa [Territory] Legislative Assembly. House. H. R. File... No. 3. Mr. Browning, Nov. 10, 1840. A bill to amend an Act concerning Grand and Petit Jurors, approved January 4th, 1839. [S. l.: n. p., 1840] p. IaHA. 40-3455

Iowa [Territory] Legislative Assembly. House. H. R. File... No. 5. Mr. Walworth, Nov. 11, 1840. Memorial to Congress for an appropriation to improve and continue the Military road from Dubuque to the Missouri Line. [S. l.: n. p., 1840] p. IaHA. 40-3456

Iowa [Territory] Legislative Assembly. House. H. R. File... No. 6. Mr. Felkner, Nov. 11, 1840. A Bill to amend an act directing the valuation and sale of Lots in Iowa City and to provide for executing deeds to the same. [S. l.: n. p., 1840] p. IaHA. 40-3457

Iowa [Territory] Legislative Assembly. House. H. R. File... No. 14. Mr. Langworthy, Nov. 16, 1840. Memorial for an appropriation to improve the Rapids of the Mississippi River. [S. l.: n. p., 1840] 2 p. IaHA. 40-3458

Iowa [Territory] Legislative Assembly. House. H. R. File... No. 18- [5] Extra Session. Mr. Coop, July 17, 1840. A bill amendatory of "An Act subjecting real and personal estate to execution, approved January twenty-five, eighteen hundred and thirty-nine." [S. l.: n. p., 1840] p. IaHA. 40-3459

Iowa [Territory] Legislative Assembly. House. H. R. File... No. 18- [6] Extra Session. Mr. Churchmen, July 17, 1840. A bill relative to writs of scire facias upon judgements in the District Court. [S. l.: n. p., 1840] p. IaHA. 40-3460

Iowa [Territory] Legislative Assembly. House. H. R. File... No. 18- [7] Extra Session. Mr. Hastings, July 17, 1840. A bill to district Musquetine county for the election of County Commissioners. [S. l.: n. p., 1840] p. IaHA. 40-3461

Iowa [Territory] Legislative Assembly. House. H. R. File... No. 20. Mr. Wilson of J., Nov. 17, 1840. A bill prohibiting Vice and Immorality. [S. l.: n. p., 1840] p. IaHA. 40-3462

Iowa [Territory] Legislative Assembly. House. H. R. File... No. 24. Mr. Isett, Dec. 1, 1840. A bill supplementary to an act defining the duties of County Surveyor's, approved December 25, 1838. [S. l.: n. p., 1840] p. IaHA. 40-3463

Iowa [Territory] Legislative Assembly. House. H. R. File... No. 32. Mr. Toole, Nov. 20, 1840. [A memorial to Congress for appropriations to improve certain Territorial Roads] [S. l.: n. p., 1840] p. IaHA. 40-3464

Iowa [Territory] Legislative Assembly. House. H. R. File... No. 33. Mr. Teeple, Nov. 20, 1840. A bill to amend the act organizing a Board of County Commissioners in each county in the Territory. [S. l.: n. p., 1840] p. IaHA. 40-3465

Iowa [Territory] Legislative Assembly. House. H. R. File... No. 36. Mr. Porter, Nov. 26, 1840. A memorial to Congress for an appropriation to improve the Territorial Road from the City of Burlington to the town of Fairfield in the county of Jefferson. [S. l.: n. p., 1840] p. IaHA. 40-3466

Iowa [Territory] Legislative Assembly. House. H. R. File... No. 38. Mr. Mason, Nov. 27, 1840. A bill relative to Mechanic's Liens, and for other purposes. [S. l.: n. p., 1840] p. IaHA. 40-3467

Iowa [Territory] Legislative Assembly. House. H. R. File... No. 43. Mr. Browning, Dec. 3, 1840. An act to amend an act concerning Executions, approved January 25, 1839. [S. l.: n. p., 1840] p. IaHA. 40-3468

Iowa [Territory] Legislative Assembly. House. H. R. File... No. 62. Mr. Toole, Dec. 14, 1840. A bill to provide for Assessing and Collecting County Revenue. [S. l.: n. p., 1840] p. IaHA. 40-3469

Iowa [Territory] Legislative Assembly. House. H. R. File... No. 65. Mr. Miller, Dec. 11, 1840. [December15, laid on table until first Monday of January next, and ordered to be printed] A bill to establish a Territorial road from Burlington to the mouth of the Des Moines River. [S. l.: n. p., 1840] p. IaHA. 40-3470

Iowa [Territory] Legislative Assembly. House. H. R. File... No. 81. Mr. Walworth, Dec. 15, 1840. Memorial to Congress, on the subject of Post Roads in the Territory of Iowa. [S. l.: n. p., 1840] p. IaHA. 40-3471

Iowa [Territory] Legislative Assembly. House. H. R. File... No. 90. Mr. Isett, Dec. 18, 1840. A bill to confer on certain Associations of the citizens of this Territory, the powers and immunities of cor-porations or bodies politic in law. [S. l.: n. p., 1840] p. IaHA. 40-3472

Iowa [Territory] Legislative Assembly. House. H. R. File... No. 175. Extra Session. Mr. Summers, July 16, 1840. A bill to change the time of holding the district Courts in the Third Judicial District. [S. l.: n. p., 1840] p. IaHA. 40-3473

Iowa [Territory] Legislative Assembly. House. H. R. File... No. 177. Extra Session. Mr. Hall, July 16, 1840. A bill in relation to that portion of country which is attached to the several organized counties in this Territory for Judicial Purposes. [S. l.: n. p., 1840] p. IaHA. 40-3474

Iowa [Territory] Legislative Assembly. House. H. R. File... No. 178. Extra Session. Mr. Hall, July 16, 1840. A bill to district Van Buren county for the election of County Commissioners. [S. l.: n. p., 1840] p. IaHA. 40-3475

Iowa [Territory] Legislative Assembly. House. H. R. File... No. 179. Extra Session. Mr. Langworthy, July 16, 1840. A bill to amend "An Act for opening and regulating roads and highways, approved January 17, 1840." [S. l.: n. p., 1840] p. IaHA. 40-3476

Iowa [Territory] Legislative Assembly. House. H. R. File... No. 181. Extra Session. Mr. Leffler, July 17, 1840. A bill to provide for the survey of a Territorial Road. [S. l.: n. p., 1840] p. IaHA. 40-3477

Iowa [Territory] Legislative Assembly. House. H. R. File... No. 183. Extra Session. Mr. Brewer, July 17, 1840. A bill to legalize the establishment of a Territorial Road from the ferry landing opposite Oquawka in Illinois to Napoleon in Johnson County. [S. l.: n. p., 1840] p. IaHA. 40-3478

City in Johnson County. [S. l.: n. p., 1840] p. IaHA. 40-3484

Iowa [Territory] Legislative Assembly. House. H. R. File... No. 188. Extra Session. Mr. Rich, July 20, 1840. A bill to attach that part of the Half Breed tract lying in Van Buren county to the County of Lee for Judicial purposes. [S. l.: n. p., 1840] p. IaHA. 40-3479

Iowa [Territory] Legislative Assembly. House. H. R. File... No. 195. Extra Session. Mr. Bailey, July 20, 1840. A bill to authorize the Boards therein named to take charge of the School Lands in this Territory. [S. l.: n. p., 1840] p. IaHA. 40-3485

Iowa [Territory] Legislative Assembly. House. H. R. File... No. 190. Extra Session. Mr. Biggs, July 20, 1840. A bill directing the valuation and sale of Lots in Iowa City and to provide for executing deeds for the same. [S. l.: n. p., 1840] p. IaHA. 40-3480

Iowa [Territory] Legislative Assembly. House. H. R. File... No. 196. Extra Session. Mr. Rich, July 20, 1840. A bill to authorize Joseph Wasson to erect a dam across English river in Washington County. [S. l.: n. p., 1840] p. IaHA. 40-3486

Iowa [Territory] Legislative Assembly. House. H. R. File... No. 191. Extra Session. Mr. Mintun, July 20, 1840. A bill to amend an act relative to Wills and Testaments, executors, administrators and the settlement of estates. [S. l.: n. p., 1840] p. IaHA. 40-3481

Iowa [Territory] Legislative Assembly. House. H. R. File... No. 197. Extra Session. Mr. Mintun, July 20, 1840. A bill to alter and repeal a part of the ninth section of an act entitle"An act to provide for the appointment of Justices of the Peace to prescribe their powers and duties and to regulate their proceedings." [S. l.: n. p., 1840] p. IaHA. 40-3487

Iowa [Territory] Legislative Assembly. House. H. R. File... No. 192. Extra Session. Mr. Hall, July 20, 1840. A bill to amend an act entitled "An act relating to the office of Recorded of Deeds &..." [S. l.: n. p., 1840] p. IaHA. 40-3482

Iowa [Territory] Legislative Assembly. House. H. R. File... No. 198. Extra Session. Mr. Rich, July 21, 1840. A bill to divorce Harriett Knapp. [S. l.: n. p., 1840] p. IaHA. 40-3488

Iowa [Territory] Legislative Assembly. House. H. R. File... No. 193. Extra Session. Mr. Owens, July 20, 1840. A bill to enforce the observance of the Sabbath. [S. l.: n. p., 1840] p. IaHA. 40-3483

Iowa [Territory] Legislative Assembly. House. H. R. File... No. 199. Extra Session. Mr. Leffler, July 21, 1840. A bill to provide for the payment of contingent expenses of the offices of Auditor and Treasurer. [S. l.: n. p., 1840] p. IaHA. 40-3489

Iowa [Territory] Legislative Assembly. House. H. R. File... No. 194. Extra Session. Mr. Summers, July 20, 1840. A bill to establish a Territorial Road from the town of Lyons in Clinton county to Iowa

Iowa [Territory] Legislative Assembly. House. H. R. File... No. 204. Extra Session. Mr. Hawkins, July 22, 1840. A bill to amend an act entitled "An act to provide for the erection of a Penitentiary and establishing and regulating prison discipline for the same." [S. l.: n. p., 1840] p. IaHA. 40-3490

Iowa [Territory] Legislative Assembly. House. H. R. File... No. 205. Extra Session. Mr. Leffler, July 22, 1840. A bill to provide for the sale of Town lots in Fairfield, the County seat of Jefferson County. [S. l.: n. p., 1840] p. IaHA. 40-3491

Iowa [Territory] Legislative Assembly. House. H. R. File... No. 207. Extra Session. Mr. Churchman, July 23, 1840. A bill relative to taxation. [S. l.: n. p., 1840] p. IaHA. 40-3492

Iowa [Territory] Legislative Assembly. House. H. R. File... No. 209. Extra Session. Mr. Hastings, July 27, 1840. A memorial to the President of the United States relative to the payment of the annuities of the Sac and Fox Indians. [S. l.: n. p., 1840] p. IaHA. 40-3493

Iowa [Territory] Legislative Assembly. House. H. R. File... No. 210. Extra Session. Mr. Mintun, July 23, 1840. A bill to repeal an act to regulate the mode of petitioning the Legislature in certain cases. [S. l.: n. p., 1840] p. IaHA. 40-3494

Iowa [Territory] Legislative Assembly. House. Journal of the House of Representatives of the Second Legislative Assembly of the Territory of Iowa. Begun and held at the City of Burlington, inthe County of Des Moines, on the fourth day of November, one thousand eight hundred and thirty-nine. [Burlington, IA: Printed by J. Gardiner Ed-

wards, 1840] 284 p. Ia; IaDa; IaHA. 40-3495

Iowa [Territory] Legislative Assembly. Journal of the Council. [S. l.: n. p., 1840] 5 v. IaAS. 40-3496

Iowa [Territory] Legislative Assembly. Journals of the Council, 1840-43. [S. l.: n. p., 1840-43] 5 v. IaB. 40-3497

Iowa [Territory] Secretary. Communication from the Secretary of the Territory, made in compliance with a resolution of the House of Representatives on the subject of liabilities of the Territory. Burlington, IA: J. H. M'Kenny, Jr., 1840. 6 p. ICN. 40-3498

Iowa [Territory] Supreme Court. Reports of the decisions of the Supreme Court of Iowa from the organization of the territory in July, 1838, to December, 1839, inclusive. Published by order of the Legislature. By William J. A. Bradford. Rules of pratice in... Galena: Printed by William C. Taylor, 1840. 62 p. IaCrM; MokB. 40-3499

Irish eloquence, the speeches of the celebrated Irish orators Philips, Curran, and Gratton, to which is added the pwoerful appeal of Robert Emmet, at the close of his trial for high treason. Selected by a member of the bar. Philadelphia, PA: s. l., 1840. 370 p. MBS; MdBE; MW; NP; RPA. 40-3500

Irraragorra, Guillermo. Gov. Tacon's march. Boston, MA: Ashton [184-?] 3 p. MB. 40-3501

Irving, Josiah. The history of Howard University. By Josiah Irving. Cambridge, MA: J. Owen, 1840. 2 v. NcD. 40-3502

Irving, Washington, 1783-1859. The Alhambra: a series of tales and sketches of the Moors and Spaniards. By the author of "The sketch book." In two volumes. A new ed. Philadelphia, PA: Lea & Blanchard, 1840. 2 v. CtY; MB; Nox; ViU. 40-3503

Irving, Washington, 1783-1859. A chronicle of the Conquest of Granada. By Fray Antonio Agapida [pseud.] A new edition. Philadelphia, PA: Lea & Blanchard, 1840. 2 v. InStmaS; NNS; NOx; OMC; PWe. 40-3504

Irving, Washington, 1783-1859. A history of New York from the beginning of the world to the end of the Dutch dynasty. Philadelphia, PA: Lea & Blanchard, 1840. 2 v. DLC; MB; NIC. 40-3505

Irving, Washington, 1783-1859. A history of New York, from the beginning of the world to the end of the Dutch Dynasty... By Diedrich Knickerbocker [pseud.] A new edition. Philadelphia, PA: Lea and Blanchard, 1840. 2 v. GEU; InFtw; LNL; MB; NNS; PReaA. 40-3506

Irving, Washington, 1783-1859. Life and Voyages of Christopher Columbus. By Washington Irving. Philadelphia, PA: Lea & Blanchard, 1840. 2 v. GNe; IHi; OClW; PPFr. 40-3507

Irving, Washington, 1783-1859. The life of Oliver Goldsmith. With selections from his writings... New York: Harper, 1840-41. 2 v. PMA. 40-3508

Irving, Washington, 1783-1859. The sketch book of Geoffrey Crayon, gent... In two volumes. A new ed. Philadelphia,

PA: Lea & Blanchard, 1840. 2 v. in 1. MH; MSbri; NbHi; NNS; NOx. 40-3509

Irving, Washington, 1783-1859. Tales of a traveller. By Geoffrey Crayon, gent. [pseud.] New ed. Philadelphia, PA: Lea & Blanchard, 1840. 2 v. NcW; NNS; ViU. 40-3510

Irving, Washington, 1783-1859. Works. New York: s. l., 1840. 2 v. MSbri. 40-3511

Irving, Washington, 1783-1859. The works of Washington Irving. Containing the Sketch Book, Tales of A Traveller, Knickerbocker's History, A Chronicle of New York, The Conquest of Granada, Bracebridge Hall, The Alhambra. Philadelphia, PA: Lea and Blanchard, 1840. 2 v. GMWa; MeBa; OEaC; PU; ScDuE. 40-3512

Is slavery sanctioned by the Bible? Boston, MA: American Tract Society [184-?] 24 p. WHi. 40-3513

Iucho, Wilhelm. Come where the violets blow, a duett for two voices [S. and T. With piano forte accompy.] New York: Firth & Hall, 1840. 7 p. MB; ViU. 40-3514

Ives, Levi Silliman, 1797-1867. Humility, a ministerial qualification. An address to the students of the general theological seminary of the Protestant Episcopal Church in the United States. Delivered... New York, June 28, 1840. New York: Swords, Stanford & Co., 1840. 22 p. InID; MWA; OrU; RPB; TxDaM. 40-3515

J

J. A. Q. Proudly will I meet thee. Ballad. Arranged for the piano, by J. A. Q. Baltimore, MD: F. D. BEnteen & Co. [184-?] 2 p. ViU. 40-3516

J. E. D. All hands ahoy! A song written and composed on board the U. S. Frigate Constitution at Sea. Words by J. E. D. The Music by F. I. L. New York: James L. Hewitt & Co. [184-?] 2 p. ViU. 40-3517

Jack Tar's songster. Philadelphia, PA: s. l. [184-?] 2 p. MB. 40-3518

Jackson, Charles Thomas, 1805-1880. Report on the geological and agricultural msurvey of the State of Rhode Island, 1839. Providence, RI: R. Cranston & Co., 1840. 312 p. DLC; GAU; MWA; PPF; RLa. 40-3519

Jackson, Daniel, b. 1790. Alonzo and Milissa, or the Unfeeling Father. A tale founded on fact. [Illus. a wreath of roses, an arrow, a heart, a bugle, and a plume] Boston, MA: Published by Charles Gaylord, 1840. 187 p. ICBB; MeU. 40-3520

Jackson, Isaac Rand, d. 1843. General William Henry Harrison, candidate of the people for President of the United States. Baltimore, MD: Printed by Samuel Sands, 1840. 16 p. DLC; KyHi; MdHi; MH; WHi. 40-3521

Jackson, Isaac Rand, d. 1843. General William Henry Harrison, candidate of the people for president of the United States. Philadelphia, PA: Jester Harding; stereotyped by L. Johnson, 1840. 15 p. DLC; NjR; NN; PPSchw. 40-3522

Jackson, Isaac Rand, d. 1843. Lebensgeschichte des Generals Harrison... Aus dem Englischen des I. R. Jackson. Philadelphia, PA: Marschall, Williams, und Butler, 1840. 32 p. CtY; KyDC; MiD-B; RP; WHi. 40-3523

Jackson, Isaac Rand, d. 1843. The life and public services of William H. Harrison... Philadelphia, PA: published by Croome, Meignelle, 1840. In. 40-3524

Jackson, Isaac Rand, d. 1843. The life of William Henry Harrison [of Ohio] ... Fourth edition. Philadelphia, PA: Marshall, Williams, und Butler, 1840. 222 p. CtSoP; DLC; IU; MBAt; MiD-B. 40-3525

Jackson, Isaac Rand, d. 1843. The life of William Henry Harrison [of Ohio] the people's candidate for the Presidency. With a history of the wars with the British and the Indians on our northwestern frontier. 2nd edition. Philadelphia, PA: W. Marshall and Company, 1840. 218 p. DeWi; ICU; KHi; MnHi; NUt; PPAmP. 40-3526

Jackson, Isaac Rand, d. 1843. The life of William Henry Harrison, of Ohio, the people's candidate for the presidency, with a history of the wars with the British and Indians of our northwestern frontier. Philadelphia, PA: W. Marshall and company, 1840. 212 p. KyBgW; MnHi; NjP; ODaB; PU. 40-3527

Jackson, Isaac Rand, d. 1843. The life of William Henry Harrison [of Ohio] the people's candidate for the Presidency. With a history of the wars with the British and the Indians on our nortyh-west frontier. 3rd edition. Philadelphia, PA: Marshall, Williams, und Butler, 1840. 218 p. CSt; InU; MB; NcW; OClWHi. 40-3528

Jackson, Isaac Rand, d. 1843. The life of William Henry Harrison [of Ohio] the people's candidate for the Presidency. With a history of the wars with the British and Indians on our Northwestern Frontier. By Isaac R. Jackson. Fifth edition. Philadelphia, PA: Marshall, Williams, und Butler, 1840. 222 p. InHi; NNC; OCHP; PPL-R; RPB. 40-3529

Jackson, Isaac Rand, d. 1843. Sketch of the life and public services of General William Henry Harrison, candidate of the people for president of the United States... To which is annexed an appendix. Philadelphia, PA: C. Sherman & Co., 1840. 60 p. AU; CoU; DLC; MWA; NcU. 40-3530

Jackson, Isaac Rand; d. 1843. Sketch of the life and public services of General William Henry Harrison, candidate of the people for president of the United States... published by the Young Men's Tippecanoe Association of New Orleans. New Orleans, LA: The Picayune, 1840. 16 p. DLC; LNH; LU. 40-3531

Jackson, Isaac Rand, d. 1843. Sketch of the life and public services of General

William Henry Harrison, candidate of the people for president of the United States... To which is annexed an appendix. To which is added Gen. Harrison's letter to Harmar Denny. Steubenville, OH: J. & R. C. Wilson [1840?] 32 p. NN. 40-3532

Jackson, Isaac Rand, d. 1843. Sketch of the life and public services of General William Henry Harrison, candidate of the people for president of the United States... To which is annexed an appendix. Washington City: Jacob Gideon, Jr., 1840. 15 p. DLC; IaHi; MH; PU; WHi. 40-3533

Jackson, Isaac Rand, d. 1843. A sketch of the life and public services of William Henry Harrison, with an appendix... Columbus, OH: I. N. Whiting, 1840. 49 p. DLC; MH; MnHi; OCHP; PPPrHi. 40-3534

Jackson, Isaac Rand, d. 1843. A sketch of the life and public services of William Henry Harrison, commander in chief of the north western army during the war of 1812. Hartford, CT: J. H. Eldredge, 1840. 32 p. CtB; DLC; InHi; Mi. 40-3535

Jackson, John, 1809-1855. Considerations on the impropriety of Friends participating in the administration of political governments. Philadelphia, PA: J. Richard, 1840. 12 p. MdToH; OClWHi; PHi; PSC-Hi. 40-3536

Jackson, John B. The Knoxville harmony of music made easy, which is an intersting selection of hymns and psalms... Composed by John B. Jackson... 2d ed. Pumpkintown, TN: Printed by Johnson & Edwards, 1840. 260 p. TKL; TKL-MC. 40-3537

Jackson, Samuel. Address to the medical graduates of the University of Pennsylvania. Delivered April 3, 1840, by Samuel Jackson, M. D., Professor of the Institutes of Medicine in the University. Published by the graduates. Philadelphia, PA: T. K. & P. G. Collins, printers, 1840. 21 p. DLC; MB; NNNAM; PPM; TxU. 40-3538

Jackson, Samuel C. The license law vindicated. A discourse, delivered at the annual Thanksgiving, November 28, 1839, by Rev. Samuel C. Jackson. Andover, MA: William Peirce, 1840. 32 p. MAnP; MB; MeB; NN; RPB. 40-3539

Jackson, Thomas, 1783-1873. The centenary of Wesleyan Methodism; a brief sketch of the rise, progress, and present state of the Wesleyan Methodist socities throughout the world. By Thomas Jackson, president of the [British] conference. New York: T. Mason & G. Lane, publisher, 1840. 279 p. CBPSR; CtY; IEG; KMK; PPiW; TMeG. 40-3540

Jackson, Thomas, 1783-1873. A memorial of the Wesleyan Centenary; extracted from "The Centenary of Wesleyan Methodism, "by Thomas Jackson. Revised by the editors. New York: Published by T. Mason and G. Lane, for the Sunday School Union of the Methodist Episcopal Church, at the Conference Office, 1840. 128 p. IEG; MsJS; NcD. 40-3541

Jacksonville Mechanics Union. The Constitution and by-laws of the Jacksonville [Ill.] Mechanics Union. Jacksonville, IL: Printed by Goudy's Job Office, 1840. 24 p. IHi. 40-3542

Jacobs, Friedrich, 1764-1847. The Greek reader, by Frederic Jacobs. With English notes, critical and explanatory, a metrical index to Homer and Anacreon, and a copious lexicon, by Charles Anthon... A new ed. New York: Harper & Brothers, 1840. 614 p. CtHC; MB; NNC; OO; RNR. 40-3543

Jacobs, Friedrich, 1764-1847. The Greek reader. By Frederic Jacobs. Tenth, from the ninth German edition, corrected and improved. New York: W. E. Dean, printer and publisher, 1840. 311 p. CtB; KyBC; OO. 40-3544

Jacobs, Friedrich, 1764-1847. Latin reader, the first part of, by Prof. E. A. Andrews. Boston, MA: Corcker & Brewster, 1840. 266 p. OCX. 40-3545

Jacocks, John H., 1778-1848. Toleration. No. 2. New Haven, CT: s. l., 1840. 12 p. CtY; MB. 40-3546

Jamaica. Remarks on emigration to Jamaica. Addressed to the coloured class of the United States. New York: James Van Norden & Co., printers, 1840. 16 p. InHi. 40-3547

Jamaica, L. I. First Presbyterian Church. Manual. Jamaica, NY: s. l., 1840. 32 p. NBLIHI. 40-3548

James, Augustus. In Chancery. Before the Chancellor. Augustua James & Elizabeth, his wife, vs. William James and other. In partition. Further supplemental bill. Pruyn & Martin, Solicitors. Albany, NY: Alfred Southwick, printer, 1840. 31 p. NjR. 40-3549

James, George Payne Rainsford, 1801?-1860. Arrah Neil; or, Times of old.

A romance. New York: J. Winchester [184-?] 160 p. OrU. 40-3550

James, George Payne Rainsford, 1801?-1860. Forest days; A romance of old times. New York: Harper and brothers [184-?] p. MH. 40-3551

James, George Payne Rainsford, 1801?-1860. The forgery; A tale. New York: Harper and brothers [184-?] p. CtY; MH. 40-3552

James, George Payne Rainsford, 1801?-1860. The gentleman of the old school. [New York: s. l., 1840?] p. NN. 40-3553

James, George Payne Rainsford, 1801?-1860. Henry of Guise; or, The States of Blois, by G. P. R. James, esq. In two volumes. New York: Harper and Brothers, 1840. 2 v. CtMW; MBoy; MH; OMC; TJoV. 40-3554

James, George Payne Rainsford, 1801?-1860. Henry of Guise; or, The states of Blois. by G. P. R. James, Esq., author of "The Gentleman of the Old School," "The Huguenot," "The Gipsy," "The Robber," "Richelieu," &c. New York: Harper & Bros., 1840. 2 v. CtY; MH; NcD. 40-3555

James, George Payne Rainsford, 1801?-1860. History of Chivalry. New York: s. l., 1840. 342 p. PU. 40-3556

James, George Payne Rainsford, 1801?-1860. The history of chivalry. By G. P. R. James, esq., author of "Del'-Orme," "Darnley," "Richelieu"... Harper's stereotype edition. New York: Harper and Brothers, 1840. 342 p. ICMe; InRch; NNefi; PU; ScDuE. 40-3557

James, George Payne Rainsford, 1801?-1860. The king's highway. A novel. By G. P. R. James... New York: Harper & brothers, 1840. 2 v. CtHT; CtY; DLC; NUt; OSW; PNt. 40-3558

James, George Payne Rainsford, 1801?-1860. The man at arms; or, Henry de Cerons. A romance. New York: Harper & brothers, 1840. 2 v. DLC; MH; NN; OCl; PNt. 40-3559

James, George Payne Rainsford, 1801?-1860. ... Richelieu. A tale of France... Sandbornton, NH: C. Lane, 1840-41. 2 v. in 1. MiU; NBuG. 40-3560

James, John Angell, 1785-1859. The anxious enquirer after salvation, directed and encouraged. New York: D. Appleton & Co., 1840. 176 p. MH; MWA; PPPrHi. 40-3561

James, John Angell, 1785-1859. An earnest minstry the want of the times. With an introduction by Rev. J. B. Condit, D. D. 2d. ed. New York: Dodd, 1840. 288 p. PPPrHI. 40-3562

James, John Angell, 1785-1859. Happiness, its nature and sources described and mistakes concerning it corrected. Philadelphia, PA: Amer. Sunday school union [184-?] 95 p. PU. 40-3563

James, John Angell, 1785-1859. The young man from home. New York: American Tract Society [184-?] 187 p. WHi. 40-3564

James, John Angell, 1785-1859. The young man from home, by John Angell James... [quotation] New York: D. Appleton & Co., 1840. 187 p. CtY; DLC; IaMp; LU; ODaB. 40-3565

James River and Kanawha Company, Richmond. Regulations for the James River and Kanawha canal, and laws for its protection, together with tables of tolls, weights and distances. Richmond: Printed by Shepherd and Colin, 1840. 23 p. MH; Vi. 40-3566

Jameson, Anna Brownell [Murphy] 1794-1860. Characteristics of women, moral, poetical and historical. By Mrs. Anna Brownell [Murphy] Jameson. Boston, MA: William D. Ticknor & co., 1840. 348 p. NjMD. 40-3567

Jameson, Anna Brownell [Murphy] 1794-1860. The heroines of Shakespeares: their moral, poetical and historical characteristics. Philadelphia, PA: J. E. Potter & co. [184-?] 384 p. NN. 40-3568

Jameson, Anna Brownell [Murphy] 1794-1860. Memoirs of celebrated female sovereigns. By Mrs. Jameson... New York: Harper & brothers, 1840. 2 v. CtY; InRch; NNC; OAU; OC. 40-3569

Jameson, Anna Brownell [Murphy] 1794-1860. Winter studies and summer rambles in Canada. New York: Wiley & Putnam [184-?] 2 v. in 1. MB; NN. 40-3570

Jameson, John. Speech of Mrs. Jameson, of Missouri, on the general appropriation bill. Delivered in Committee of the Whole, in the House of Representatives, April 21, 1840. Washington, DC: Printed at the Globe Office, 1840. 15 p. IU; KHi; MiU-C; OClWHi; WHi. 40-3571

Jameson, Robert, 1774-1854. Narrative of discovery and adventure in Africa, from the earliest ages to the present time... New York: Printed by J. & J. Harper, 1840. 359 p. ICJ; InRch; NCas; ViR. 40-3572

Jamieson, Alexander. A grammar of rhetoric and polite literature; comprehending the principles of language and style... with rules for the study of composition and eloquence. Illustrated with appropriate examples, selected chiefly from the British classics... By Alexander Jamieson, LL. D. 20th ed., stereotyped. New Haven, CT: A. H. Maltby, 1840. 306 p. InThR; MBAt; NN; OCl; OO. 40-3573

Jane and Eliza. Newark, NJ: Ptd. for the publisher, 1840. 12 p. MiD-B; NjN; NPV. 40-3574

Janes, Edmund Storer, 1807-1876. The agency of the spirit in the promotion of Christianity; a sermon, delivered in... New York, Oct. 25, 1839... New York: Published by T. Mason and G. Lane... at the Conference office, 1840. 40 p. CtMW; IEG; N; NNC. 40-3575

Janeway, Jacob Jones, 1774-1858. Exposition of a portion of the Epistle to the Romans, in the form of questions and answers... By J. J. Janeway. Philadelphia, PA: s. l., 1840. 137 p. NjP. 40-3576

Janeway, Jacob Jones, 1774-1858. Historical discourseprepared from the semi-centenary Sabbath and del'd. on that day at the request of Session of the Pres. Ch. in New Brunswick... New Brunswick, NJ: Terhune, 1840. 28 p. MBC; MH-AH; Nj; PPPrHi; RPB. 40-3577

Janeway, Jacob Jones, 1774-1858. The scriptural doctinre of the Atonement, illustrated and defended... Philadelphia, PA: Presbyterian Board of Publication, William S. Martien, publishing agent, 1840. 24 p. CtHC; NjPT; OMtv; PPM; WHi. 40-3578

Janeway, James, 1636?-1674. Life of the Rev. John Janeway. Abridged for the board. Philadelphia, PA: Pres. Bd. Pub., 1840. 32 p. MA; PPPrHi. 40-3579

Janeway, James, 1636?-1674. The Saint's encouragement to dilligence in Christ's service. Philadelphia, PA: Presbyterian Board of Publication, 1840. 155 p. CLamB; NNUT; NWM; OClW; ViLxM. 40-3580

Janius. Letters of Junius. Two volumes in one. New edition. Boston, MA: Sanborn, Saxon & co., 1840. 214 p. PPM. 40-3581

Janius. The letters of Junius. New York: Campe and Co. [184-?] 317 p. CtY. 40-3582

Janney, Samuel Macpherson, 1801-1880. A Teacher's Gift, consisting of Original essays in prose and verse, and Translations from the French. By S. M. Janney. Philadelphia, PA: T. Ellwood Chapman, 1840. 170 p. DLC; PHC; PSC-Hi; ViW. 40-3583

Janurin, Mary W. The best story; or, an hour with the children. Boston, MA: Published by the American Tract Society [184-?] 16 p. WHi. 40-3584

Jarratt, Devereux, 1733-1801. ... Life of the Rev. Devereux Jarratt. Abridged from an account of himself in a series of letters to the Rev. John Coleman. By the Rt. Rev. Wm. Meade... Richmond, VA: Printed at the Office of the Southern Churchman [1840?] 56 p. DLC; NcU; NjR; NNG; TxDaM. 40-3585

Jarvis, William, 1770-1859. Speech of Hon. Wm. Jarvis, at the Whig convention at Windsor, July 4, 1840. Windsor, VT: The "Times" press, 1840. 24 p. DLC; MeHi. 40-3586

Java march. [For piano forte] New York: Hall [184-?] 1 p. MB. 40-3587

Jay, William, 1769-1853. Exercises for the closet. For every day in the year. New York: R. Lockwood, 1840. 2 v. in 1. NN. 40-3588

Jay, William, 1769-1853. Morning exercises for the closet. For every day in the year. By William Jay. [5 lines of quote] Baltimore, MD: Published by Plaskitt & Cugle, 1840. 421 p. Nh; OSW. 40-3589

Jay, William, 1769-1853. Prayers for the use of families... New York: Lerritt & Allen [184-?] 249 p. DLC. 40-3590

Jay, William, 1769-1853. Standard works... Comprising all of his works known in this country; and also, several which have not, heretofore, been presented to the American public. From a copy furnished by the author to the publisher... Baltimore, MD: Plaskitt & Cugle, 1840. 3 v. CBPSR; IaVin; MokWS; NCH; OWoC. 40-3591

Jay, William, 1789-1858. An inquiry into the Character and Tendency of the American Colonization and American Anti-Slavery Societies... Third edition. New York: s. l., 1840. MB. 40-3592

Jay, William, 1789-1858. An inquiry

into the character and tendency of the American colonization... 10th ed. New York: Amer. Anti-slavery Soc., 1840. 206 p. CtHC; MPeHi; MWA; NNUT; WHi. 40-3593

Jay, William, 1789-1858. Inquiry into the Character and Tendency of the American Colonization and American Anti-Slavery Societies... 16th ed. New York: Harper, 1840. 266 p. IaFair. 40-3594

Jefferson & Lake Pontchartrain Railway Company. Act of incorporation... and report of the committee of the commissioners, presented Aug. 8, 1840. New Orleans, LA: F. Cook & A. Levy, 1840. 16 p. AU; NN; PPAmP. 40-3595

Jefferson College, Cannonsburg, Pa. Catalogue of... Jefferson College, Cannonsburgh, Pa., July, 1840. Pittsburgh, PA: Printed by William Allinder, 1840. 15 p. MdHi; NjP; PPPrHi; PWW. 40-3596

Jefferson College, Cannonsburg, Pa. Philo Literary Society. Catalogue of the members and library of the Philo Literary Society of Jefferson College, Cannonsburgh, Pa., from its formation, August 23, 1797, to July 4, 1840. Pittsburgh, PA: A. Jaynes, 1840. 32 p. DLC; MnSM; OCHP; PPL; PWW. 40-3597

Jefferson College, Washington, Miss. The charter and statutes of Jefferson college, Washington, Mississippi, as revised and amended: together with a historical sketch of the institution from its establishment to the present time; to which is prefixed a list of the trustees, officers and faculty, the acts of Congress and of the Legislature relating to the institution,

and a cattalogue of its library, apparatus, &c... Natchez, MS: Printed at the book and job office, 1840. 90 p. DLC; MH; KyLoF; LU; MBC; MsJS; MsJPED; MsWJ; N; PHi; RPB; TxU. 40-3598

Jefferson, Thomas, Pres. U. S., 1743-1826. A manual of parliamentary practice. Composed originally for the use of the Senate of U. S. New York: Clark & Maynard, 1840. 196 p. AzU; InBra; NjP; PP; ViU. 40-3599

Jefferson, Thomas, Pres. U. S., 1743-1826. A manual of parliamentary practice. Composed originally for the use of the Senate of the United States, by Thomas Jefferson. With references to the practice and rules of the House of Representatives... And accompanied with copious indices. Philadelphia, PA: Hogan and Thompson, 1840. 204 p. A-Ar; CoD; MWA; NjP; ViU. 40-3600

Jeffreys, Charles, 1807-1865. Come o'er the moonlit sea. Duett [S. A.] Written by Charles Jeffreys. Adapted to a celebrated air by Auber, and arranged by L. Devereux. [With accompaniment for piano forte] New York: Hewitt & Co. [184-?] 9 p. MB. 40-3601

Jeffreys, Charles, 1807-1865. I welcome thee with gladness. [A bello a me ritorno] From the opera La Norma. Written by C. Jeffreys; arranged by S. Nelson. Boston, MA: Oliver Ditson [184-?] 4 p. ICN; ViU. 40-3602

Jeffreys, Henry. The Religious objections to tetotalism. By Archdeadon Jeffreys. New York; London: Office of the American Temperance Union; John Snow, Pasternoster-Row, 1840. 32 p. MdBD; MWA; NjPT; NN; PPL. 40-3603

Jenifer, Daniel. 1791-1855. Remarks of the Hon. Daniel Jenifer at the opening of the Convention of Tobacco Planters of the United States, held at Washington City, Dec. 15, 1840. Washington, DC: National Intelligencer Office, 1840. 16 p. CU; MB; MWA; OClWHi; PPi. 40-3604

Jenifer, Daniel, 1791-1855. Speech of Mr. Jenifer, of Maryland, on the proposition to print the testimony in relation to the New Jersey contested election. Delivered... March 11, 12, 13, 14 and 17, 1840. Washington, DC: s. l., 1840. 32 p. CtY; DLC; MBAt; MdHi; NjR. 40-3605

Jenkins, E. Chartism unmasked. By the Rev. E. Jenkins... 19th ed. Merthyn Tydvil: Printed and published by J. E. Dibb, 1840. 35 p. MdBJ. 40-3606

Jeremy, George. Equity jurisprudence of the high court of chancery. New York: Halsted & Voorhies, 1840. 568 p. C; MWCL; PU-L. 40-3607

Jeremy, George. A treatise on the equity jurisprudence of the high court of chancery. By George Jeremy... 2d American, from the last London ed. New York: Halsted & Voorhies, 1840. 568 p. CU; Nj; OCLaw; PP; WaU. 40-3608

Jerrold, Douglas William, 1803-1857. Black-eyed Susan; or, "all in the downs." A nautical & domestic melo-drama in 3 acts. New York: Clayton [184-?] 43 p. MB; MH; NcD; PU. 40-3609

Jerrold, Douglas William, 1803-1857. Mrs. Caudle's curtain lectures. By "Punch" [pseud.] Cincinnati, OH: U. P. James [184-?] 144 p. FMU; OC; ViU. 40-3610

Jerrold, Douglas William, 1803-1857. ... The rent day; a domestic drama. In three acts. By Douglas Jerrold. With stage business, cast of characters, costumes, relative position, &c., as originally performed by Mr. Janes Wallack at Drury Lane. New York: T. H. French [etc., etc., 184-?] 48 p. CSt; MH; NN; OU; PSt. 40-3611

Jervey, James P. Strictures of the urethra. Philadelphia, PA: s. l., 1840. PPGenH; PhGenlHos. 40-3612

Jervis, John Bloomfield, 1795-1885. J-S's dream. [New York: s. l., 1840] p. MB; NBuG; RPB; ViU. 40-3613

Jesse, John Heneage, 1815-1874. Memoirs of the court of England during the reign of the Stuarts, including the protectorate. By John Heneage Jesse. Philadelphia, PA: Lea and Blanchard, 1840. 4 v. in 2. FTU; MeBa; MWA; OCY; PPA. 40-3614

Jewel or token of friendship. 3d edition. New York: s. l., 1840. v. WHi. 40-3615

Jewett, Charles, 1807-1879. The license system illustrated... Boston, MA: Whipple & Damrell, 1840? p. MB. 40-3616

Jewett, Charles, 1807-1879. Temperance poem. Delivered before the Massachusetts Temperance Convention at the Marlboro Chapel, Feb. 12, 1840. By Charles Jewett, M. D. 4th ed. Boston, MA; Providence, RI; : Published by Cassady & March, Temperance Press; R. J. Johnson & Smith, 1840. 15 p. MH; MH-AH; MoKU; NNC; RPB; WHi. 40-3617

Jewett, Charles, 1807-1879. ... Temperance toy... by Charles Jewett...

Boston, MA: Whipple & Damrell, 1840. 15 p. DLC. 40-3618

Jewett, Charles, 1807-1879. The vision. A poem. [Boston, MA: s. l., 1840?] p. MB. 40-3619

Jewett, Charles, 1807-1879. The youth's temperance lecturer. By Dr. Charles Jewett. Boston, MA: Whipple & Damrell, 1840. 32 p. DLC; NN. 40-3620

Jewett, John P. The business man's aid; or, Tables of interest, together with many other useful tables, convenient for reference. Salem: published by John P. Jewett, 1840. 24 p. MWA. 40-3621

Jewett, M. Augustus. Oration delivered before the citizens of Vigo County, Indiana, in the court-house in Terre Haute, July 4, 1840. Terre Haute, IN: s. l., 1840. 12 p. In; InFtwL; InFWL. 40-3622

Jewett, Milo P. The mode and subjects of baptism... 3rd ed., revised. Boston, MA: Gould, Kendall & Lincoln, 1840. 129 p. A-Ar; NCH; OClWHi; PPPrHi; TBrik. 40-3623

Jewett, Paul. The New England farrier, or, Farmers' receipt book; a selection of valuable receipts for the cure of diseases in horse, cattle, sheep and swine with directions to farmers for choosing good stock. 22 edition. Boston: Charles Gaylord, 1840. 9-214 p. OMC. 40-3624

Jewitt, John Rodgers, 1788-1821. Narrative of the adventures and sufferings of John R. Jewitt, only survivor of the crew of the ship Boston, during a captivity of nearly three years among the savages of Nootka sound... [Edited by Richard

Alsop] New York: Printed for the publisher [1840?] 166 p. NN. 40-3625

Jim along Josey. [Voice & pf.] New York: s. l., 1840. CtY. 40-3626

John Anderson my Jo. A beautiful Scotch air & ballad. Arranged for the piano forte [by John Watson] Boston, MA: Ditson [184-?] 5 p. MB. 40-3627

John Anderson my Jo. A Scotch air. Sung by Mr. Sinclair. Arranged by Kozeluch. New York: Firth & Hall [184-?] 2 p. ViU. 40-3628

John Anderson my jo. A Scotch air. Sung by Sinclair; arranged by Kozeluch. Baltimore, MD: Geo. Wilig, Jr. [184-?] 3 p. ViU. 40-3629

Johns, John, Bp., 1796-1876. An address, delivered before the American Whig and Cliosophic societies of the College of New Jersey, September 29, 1840. By the Rev. John Johns... Princeton, NJ: Printed by J. Bogart, 1840. 26 p. CtHC; IEG; MH; MnHi; NcD; NcMHi; NjP; NjR; NN; NNC; OC; OCHP; PHi; PPL; PPPrHi; TNJ; TxU. 40-3630

Johnson's Pocket Almanac. Philadelphia, PA: Willard Johnson, 1840. MWA. 40-3631

Johnson, Alexander Bryan, 1786-1867. Religion in its relation to the present life. In a series of lectures. Delivered before the Young Men's Associatin of Utica, by A. B. Johnson, and pub. at their request. New York: Harper [1840] 180 p. CBPac; DLC; LU; MH-AH; PPA. 40-3632

Johnson, Edwin Ferry. Table of quantities, for tracing railroad curves. With illustrations. By Edwin F. Johnson... New York: The Railroad Journal Office, 1840. 21, 11 p. DLC; MB; NNE. 40-3633

Johnson, Evan Malbone, 1791-1865. Missionary failtures, the reason for renovated exertions. A sermon... on occasion of a collection for the benefit of St. Mary's church, Wallabout. By Evan M. Johnson. [Brooklyn, s. l., 1840?] 16 p. MH; MHi; NNG. 40-3634

Johnson, Francis, musician. Deux quadrilles de contre danses pour le piano forte. Composes & arranges sur des motifs de l'opera de Bellini, La somnambula, part Francis Johnson. Philadelphia, PA: Fiot, Meignen & Co. [184-?] 7 p. MB. 40-3635

Johnson, James, 1777-1845. The economy of health; or, The stream of human life, from the cradle to the grave. With reflections, moral, physical, and philosophical, on the septennial phases of human existence. By James Johnson, M. D., physician extraordinary to the king. Third edition. New York: Harper & brothers, 1840. 282 p. TChU; TSewU. 40-3636

Johnson, Laura. Botanical teacher for North America; in which are described the indigenous and common exotic plants, growing north of the Gulf of Mexico, by Laura Johnson... Second edition... Troy, NY: Published by Elias Gates, N. Tuttle, printer, 1840. 268 p. CoFcS; CtY; MH; NCH; NNNBG. 40-3637

Johnson, Reverdy, 1796-1876. The memorial of Reverdy Johnson, of the city of Baltimore, to the legislature of Maryland. With an appendix. Baltimore,

MD: Printed by J. Murphy, 1840. 20, 46 p. DLC; MBAt; MdHi; MH-L; PHi. 40-3638

Johnson, Samuel, 1709-1784. The history of Rasselas, prince of Abyssinia, a tale... By Samuel Johnson... New York: D. Appleton & co. [184-?] 12, 172 p. NjP; NN; ViU. 40-3639

Johnson, Samuel, 1709-1784. The life and writings of Samuel Johnson. New York: Harper & brothers, 1840. 2 v. CtMW; MH; NbOM; OFH. 40-3640

Johnson, Samuel, 1709-1784. The works of Samuel Johnson, LL. D. With an essay of his life & genius by Arthur Murphy, esq. In two volumes. First complete American edition. New York; Boston, MA; Philadelphia, PA: Alexander V. Blake, publisher; sold by Collins, Keese & Co.; Otis, Broaders & co.; Thomas, Cowperthwait & co., 1840. 2 v. KyU; Nh-Hi; OC; OO; TJaU. 40-3641

Johnson, Walter Rogers, 1794-1852. Description of a specimen of engraving, by the original inhabitants of North America. With a notice of some incidents in the history of the early settlers on the west branch of the Susquehanna River. By Walter R. Johnson, A. M., member of the Historical Society of Pennsylvania... Read at a meeting of the society, May 1st, 1837. Philadelphia, PA: s. l., 1840. 11 p. DLC; IU; MdBJ; MH; MWA; NCH; RPB. 40-3642

Johnson, Walter Rogers, 1794-1852. A lecture, introductory to a course on chemistry and natural philosophy, in the Medical Department of Pennsylvania College. Delivered November 3, 1840. By Walter R. Johnson... Published by request of the class. Philadelphia, PA: L. R. Bailey, printer, 1840. 24 p. DLC; MH; PPAN; PHi; PPL. 40-3643

Johnson, Walter Rogers, 1794-1852. Notice of a report of a geological, mineralogical, and topological examination of the coal fields... [New Haven, CT: etc., 1840] 149 p. MH; MH-Z. 40-3644

Johnson, Walter Rogers, 1794-1852. Report of a geological, mineralogical, and topological examination of the coal fields of Carbon Creek, the property of the Towanda rail road and coal company, Bradford County, Pa. Philadelphia, PA: J. C. Clark, 1840. 47 p. DLC; ICT; P; PHi; PPAmP. 40-3645

Johnson, William Cost, 1806-1860. Remarks in reply to certain charges against Ge. Harrison, in the House of Representatives [of the United States] March 1840. By William C. Johnson. Washington, DC: printed by Gales & Seaton, 1840. 8 p. M. 40-3646

Johnson, William Cost, 1806-1860. Speech of William Cost Johnson, of Maryland, on the subject of the rejection of petitions for the abolition of slavery... Delivered in the House of Representatives, Jan. 25, 27, 28, 1840. Washington, DC: Printed by Gales and Seaton, 1840. 63 p. DLC; MBC; MdBJ; MWA; OClWHi. 40-3647

Johnson, William Cost, 1806-1860. Speech of William Cost Johnson, of Maryland, on the subtreasury bill. Delivered in the House of Representatives, June 25, 1840. Washington, DC: Printed by Gales and Seaton, 1840. 48 p. CtY; KSalW; MBAt. 40-3648

Johnson, William Lupton, 1802-1873. Awakening out of sleep; the rector's offering for 1840, being a pastoral address to the parishoners of Grace church, Jamaica, Long Island. New York: Percy & Reed, printers, 1840. 20 p. MdBD; NBLIHI; NNQ; NSmb. 40-3649

Johnson, William Lupton, 1802-1873. The Incarnate God; the rector's Christimas offering for 1841, being a second pastoral address to the parishoners of Grace church, Jamaica, Long Island. Flushing, NY: Printed at St. Thomas' Hall Press, by Charles R. Lincoln, 1840. 32 p. MWA; NBLiHi; NIC; NSmb. 40-3650

Johnson and Waaners' Almanac for the year 1841. Being the first after Bissextile, or Leap Year. Seal Justice and Liberty carefully circulated for the Latitude and Meridian of Philadelphia. Philadelphia, PA: Sold by W. A. Leary, 1840? 27 p. IaDaP. 40-3651

Johnston, James Finley Weir, 1796-1855. Chemistry of common life... by James F. Johnston... New York: D. Appleton & co., 1840. 2 v. NWM. 40-3652

Johnston, John, 1806-1879. A manual of chemistry, on the basis of Dr. Turner's elements of chemistry, containing in a condensed form all of the most important facts & principles of the science... Middletown, CT: Barnes & Saxe, 1840. 453 p. CtY; DLC; MB. 40-3653

Johnston, William, of Chester Co., Pa. The good samaritan; or, sick man's friend... containing the botanical medical practice. Philadelphia, PA: W. A. Leary, 1840. 287 p. MdW; PLFM; PPCP. 40-3654

Johnstone, Christian Isobel, 1781-1857. Lives and voyages of Drake, Cavendish, and Dampier; including an introductory view of the earlier discoveries in the South Sea and the history of the bucaniers. With portraits on steel. New York: Harper & Brothers, 1840. 332 p. CtY; IaFair; InRch; KSalW; MMN. 40-3655

Johnstone, John Beer, 1803-1891. The sailor of France; or, The republicans of Brest. An original drama in two acts. New York: French [184-?] 22 p. IaU; MB; MH; NN. 40-3656

Jones, Benjamin S. Abolitionrieties; or, remarks on some of the members of the Pennsylvania State Anti-Slavery Society for the Eastern District, and the American Anti-Slavery Society, most of whom were present at the annual meetings, held in Philadelphia and New York in May, 1840. S. l.: s. l., 1840. DHU; DLC; ICN; MB. 40-3657

Jones, Elijah. A sermon, delivered in Hallowell, June 24, 1840, before the Maine Missionary Society... By Elijah Jones. Portland, ME: Alfred Merrill, printer, 1840. 46 p. CBPSR; IaGG; MBC; MeLewB; MH-AH. 40-3658

Jones, George [alias Count Joannes] 1810-1879. Oration on the national independence, Richmond, Va., July 4, 1840, before the Franklin Society, at the City-Hall. Written and pronounced by George Jones, tragedian... Richmond, VA: Published at the request of the Franklin Society, by Smith & Palmer, 1840. 43 p. DLC; MH; Vi. 40-3659

Jones, John Winston, 1791-1848. Speech of Mr. Jones, of Virginia, on the bill making appropriations for the civil and diplomatic expenses of the government for the year 1840. Delivered in the House of Representatives of the United States, April 11, 1840. Washington, DC: Blair and Rives, 1840. 23 p. CoFcS; MdHi; NcU; OClWHi; ViU. 40-3660

Jones, Thomas P., 1774-1848. Conversations on natural philosophy, in which the elements of that science are familiarly explained, and adapted to the comprehension of young pupils. Illustrated with plates. By the author of "Conversations on Chemistry" and "Conversations on Political Economy." Improved by appropriate questions. For the examination of Scholars; Also by illustrative notes, and a Dictionary of Philosophical Terms. By Rev. J. L. Blake, D. D., Rector of St. Matthew's Church, and Principal of a Literary Seminary, Boston, Mass. Boston stereotype edition. Boston, MA: Gould, Kendall & Lincoln, 1840. 276 p. KyU. 40-3661

Jones, Thomas P., 1774-1848. Conversations on natural philosophy, in which the elements of that science are familiarly explained. Illustrated with plates. By the author of "Conversations on Chemistry," &c. With corrections, improvements, and considerable additions in the body of the work, by Dr. Thomas P. Jones, professor of Mechanics, in the Franklin Institute, of the State of Pennsylvania. Philadelphia, PA: Grigg and Elliot, 1840. 215 p. MdBS-P. 40-3662

Jones, William Alfred, 1817-1900. The Analyst; a collection of miscellaneous papers. New York: Wiley & Putnam, 1840. 174 p. DLC; FU; MB; PPL; WaU. 40-3663

Jonny Boker, or De Broken Yoke in de coaling ground. The original banjo song as sung with great applause at the Tremont Theatre, by J. W. Sweeny. Boston, MA: Henry Prentiss, 1840. 3 p. MB. 40-3664

Josephus, Flavius. The works of Flavius Josephus, the learned and authentic Jewish historian, and celebrated Warrior, ... Translated from the original Greek, according to Havercamp's accurate edition. Together with explanatory notes and observations. With engravings, by the late William Whiston, A. M. From the last London edition of 1827. Philadelphia, PA: Grigg & Elliot, 1840. 2 v. CtHC; ICU; NjPT; OrAlc. 40-3665

Josselyn, Lewis. An appeal to the people. Proof of an alliance between American Whigs and British Tories to put down Martin Van Buren and put up William Henry Harrison. Boston, MA: Bay State Democratic Office, 1840. 14 p. CtY; M; MBAt; TxU. 40-3666

The Journal of Lewis and Clarke to the mouth of the Columbia River beyond the Rocky Mountains, in the years 1804-5 &6. Giving a faithful description of the River Missouri and its source; of the various tribes of Indians through which they passed; manners and customs; soil; climate; commerce; gold and silver mines; animal and vegetable productions; &c. Revised, corr., and illustrated with numerous wood cuts. To which is added a complete dictionary of the Indian tongue. New ed., with notes. Dayton, OH: B. F. Ells, 1840. 240 p. ICU; MWA; OrHi; PHi; WHi. 40-3667

Julio, Joseph. Palermo march. For the

piano forte. Philadelphia, PA: Fiot, 1840. 2 p. MB. 40-3668

Jullien, Louis Antoine, 1812-1860. The celebrated polkas, as danced... in London, Paris, Vienna, etc. 2d. ed. Boston, MA: Oakes [184-?] 6 p. MB. 40-3669

Jullien, Louis Antoine, 1812-1860. Deux polkas. Pour le piano. By Jullien. New York: Millet's music saloon [184-?] 4 p. ViU. 40-3670

Jullien, Louis Antoine, 1812-1860. The fourth polka. Composed for the piano forte on National, Bohemian & Hungarian melodies, by Jullien. New York: Firth & Hall [184-?] 2 p. ViU. 40-3671

Jullien, Louis Antoine, 1812-1860. Isabella polka. For the piano forte by Jullien. Baltimore, MD; New Orleans, LA: F. D. Benteen; W. T. Mayo [184-?] 2 p. ViU. 40-3672

Jullien, Louis Antoine, 1812-1860. Julien's celebrated polka. Composed on National Polish, Bohemian melodies, by Julien. Philadelphia, PA: George Willig [184-?] 2 p. ViU. 40-3673

Jullien, Louis Antoine, 1812-1860. Jullien's Chimes. Quadrilles. By Jullien. Philadelphia, PA: E. Ferrell & Co., 1840. 7 p. KU. 40-3674

Jullien, Louis Antoine, 1812-1860. L'echo du Mout Blanc polka. Boston, MA: Reed & Co., 184-? 7 p. MB. 40-3675

Juvenile forget-me-not. New York: Leavitt & Allen [184-?] p. MB. 40-3676

The Juvenile forget-me-not; a

Christmas and New Year's present. Boston, MA: S. Colman [184-?] 192 p. WU. 40-3677

The juvenile forget-me-not; a Christmas, New Year's and birth day present for 1841... Philadelphia, PA: H. F. Anners [1840] 180 p. DLC; NjR; OCh. 40-3678

Juvenile hymns. A present for a good girl. Buckville, NY: B. Maynard [1840?] 18 p. N. 40-3679

Juvenile Minstrel. Boston, MA: s. l., 1840. MB; NN. 40-3680

K

Kalkbrenner, Friedrich Wilhelm Michael, 1785-1849. Rondo sur un motif de L'Orgie. Musique de Carafa, pour le piano part F. Kalkbrenner. Philadelphia, PA: Klemn & brother [184-?] 9 p. ViU. 40-3681

Kalliwoda, Johann Wenzel, 1801-1866. Pestal [sic] or, the prison song, Yes the die is cast. Arranged for the piano forte by John R. Ling. Boston, MA: Reed & Co. [184-?] 5 p. MB. 40-3682

Kames, Henry Home, 1696-1732. Elements of criticism... with analyses, and translations of ancient and foreign... Edited by Abraham Mills. New ed. New York: F. J. Huntington and Co., 1840. 504 p. MeBat; NGH; NN; NNiaU; WaPS. 40-3683

Kathleen O Moore. A much admired song as sung by Miss Louisa Gillingham. Composed and arranged for the piano forte. Baltimore, MD: George Willig, Jr. [184-?] 2 p. ViU. 40-3684

Katy Darling. Sung by Master Adams of Kundel's nightingale troupe. Favorite song. Composed for the piano forte. Baltimore, MD; New Orleans, LA: F. D. Benteen; W. T. Mayo [184-?] 5 p. ViU. 40-3685

Kay, James. Kay's infant and primary school reader and speller. No. I. Philadelphia: J. Kay, jun. and Brother, etc, 1840. 94 p. MH. 40-3686

Keene, N. H. First Congregational Church. Confession of faith and catalogue of officers and members. Keene, NH: s. l., 1840. 25 p. CtY; NBLi-Hi; Nh-Hi. 40-3687

Keese, John, 1805-1856. The poets of America. Illustrated by one of her painters... Ed by John Keese. New York: S. Colman, 1840-42. 2 v. CSr; InU; MiDU; TxU; ViU. 40-3688

Keese, John, 1805-1856. The poets of America. 4th ed. New York: Samuel Colman, 1840-42. 2 v. Ia; MnHi; NBLIHI. 40-3689

Keightley, Thomas, 1789-1872. The history of England. By Thomas Keightley. Rev. and ed. with notes and additions, by Joshua Toulmin Smith... Boston, MA: Hilliard, Gray, and company, 1840. 2 v. CtMW; GAuY; InCW; MoK; Nh-Hi; ViU. 40-3690

Keightley, Thomas, 1789-1872. The history of England, from the earliest period to 1839. by Thomas Keightley... From the second London edition... New York: Harper & Brothers, 1840. 5 v. IEN; LNL; Me; NbOM; RPaw. 40-3691

Keightley, Thomas, 1789-1872. History of the Roman empire, from the accession of Augustus to the end of the empire of the West; being a continuation of the history of Rome. New York: Leavitt &

Allen, 1840. 438 p. CSfU; MiK; ScDuE. 40-3692

Kelley, John Clawson, b. 1793. Dr. Kelley's new system of medicine treatment of disease upon plain and rational principles; new theory based upon obvious and known existence of unequivocal facts; the vital organs... and how they may be restored to a healthy state. New York, 1840. 24 p. DLC; DNLM; DSG; RNHi; RNHS. 40-3693

Kellogg & Co.'s Alabama Almanac for the year 1840; being bissextile or leap year, and until July 4th, the sixty-fourth of American independence. Adapted to the latitude and meridian of Mobile. North latitude 30o 43', longitude 88o 21' west from Greenwich. By David Young, Philom. Mobile, AL: Published by J. S. Kellogg & co., 1840. 47 p. No Loc. 40-3694

Kelly, Michael, 1764?-1826. Here's a health to thee Tom Moore; my boat is on the shore. A ballad. Sung by Mr. Keene; the words by Lord Byron; composed by Michael Kelly. New York: Firth & Hall [184-?] 3 p. ViU. 40-3695

Kelly, Michael, 1764?-1826. The lady and the devil; a musical drama in two acts. Boston, MA: W. V. Spencer [184-?] 22 p. MH. 40-3696

Kendall, Amos, 1789-1869. Mr. Kendall's address to the people of the United States. [Washington, DC: s. l., 1840] 7 p. DLC; NNC; OClWHi; PPL; WHi. 40-3697

Kennaday, John, 1800-1863. Sermon before the Sunday School Teacher's Union of the M. E. Church of Phila.,

1839. Philadelphia, PA: Thomas V. Baker, pr., 1840. 15 p. ICT; NjPT; PHi. 40-3698

Kennedy, Grace, 1782-1825. The Abbey of Innismoyle:a story of another century. Philadelphia, PA: G. B. Peterson & Bros. [184-?] 173 p. NN. 40-3699

Kennedy, Grace, 1782-1825. Anna Rose, a story for chldren. Philadelphia, PA: s. l. [184-?] 160 p. CTHWatk. 40-3700

Kennedy, John Pendleton, 1795-1870. Quodlibet: containing some annals thereof... edited by Solomon Second throughts [pseud.] From original mss. indited by him, and now made public at the request and under the patronage of the great New light democratic central committee of Quodlibet. Philadelphia, PA: Lea & Balnchard, 1840. 350 p. GU; MWA; NNC; OO; PU. 40-3701

Kenney, James, 1780-1849. Raising the wind; a farce in two acts. New York: Longworth, 1840. 47 p. DeWi. 40-3702

Kenney, James, 1780-1849. Raising the wind; a farce in two acts. New York: W. Taylor and Co. [184-?] 32 p. MH; NIC. 40-3703

Kenney, James, 1780-1849. Sweet hearts and wives; a comedy in three acts. By James Kenney. With the stage business, cast of characters, costumes, relative positions, etc. New York: S. French [184-?] 61 p. CSt. 40-3704

Kenney, James, 1780-1849. Sweet hearts and wives; a comedy in three acts New York: W. Taylor & Co. [184-?] 61 p MB; MH. 40-3705

Kenney, Lucy. A history of the present Cabinet. Benton in ambush for the next presidency. Kendal coming in third best. Gather all your strength and oused [!] the Cossacks, draw their teeth in time, unless they should devour you. An expositon of Martin Van Buren's reign. Washington, DC: s. l., 1840. 8 p. DLC; MoSHi; PHi. 40-3706

Kenney, Lucy. The strongest of all government is that which is most free... An address to the people of the United States, by Lucy Kenney. [Washington, DC?: s. l., 1840?] 12 p. DLC. 40-3707

Kenrick, Peter Richard. The month of May; or, Reflections for each day of the month on the different titles applied to Holy Mother of God, in litany of Loretto. Principally designed for the month of May... Philadelphia, PA: Eugene Cummiskey, 1840. 247 p. CSfU; MdBS; MH; NTCH; WNaE. 40-3708

Kent, James, 1763-1847. Commentaries on American law. 4th ed. New York: the author, 1840. 4 v. DLC; KyU; OU; PU-L; WaU-L. 40-3709

Kent, James, 1763-1847. A course of reading, drawn up by the Hon. James Kent... for the use of the members of the Mercantile Library Association... New York: Wiley and Putnam, 1840. 69 p. CU; DLC; MWA; RKi; WHi. 40-3710

Kent Academy. Catalogue... 1839-40. Providence, RI: Printed by Knowles and Vose, 1840. 8 p. MH. 40-3711

Kentucky. Auditor's Office. Circular of the second auditor, to the clerk of the State of Kentucky. Frankfort, KY: A. G. Hodges, 1840. 14 p. KyU. 40-3712

Kentucky. Board of Internal Improvement. Report of the Board of Internal Improvement made in compliance with a resolution of the House of Representatives of the State of Kentucky, of December 9, 1839. [Frankfort, KY: s. l., 1840] 277 p. KyU-L; MB. 40-3713

Kentucky. Board of Internal Improvement. Report of the Joint Committee appointed to settle with Green and Barren River Commissioners. [Frankfort, KY: s. l., 1840] 9 p. KyLo. 40-3714

Kentucky. General Assembly. Reports Communicated to both branches of the Legislature of Kentucky, at the December Session, 1840. Frankfort, KY: A. G. Hodges, State Printer, 1840. 558 p. InU; Ky. 40-3715

Kentucky. General Assembly. Reports of the Treasurer of the State, Made in compliance with a resolution of the House of Representatives of December 16, 1839... State of Kentucky, Treasurer's Office, January 6th, 1840. Frankfort, KY: s. l., 1840. 14 p. KyU-L. 40-3716

Kentucky. General Assembly. House. Committee on the Expenditures of the Board of Internal Improvement. Report of the Committee on the Expenditures of the Board of Internal Improvement. Frankfort, KY: s. l. [1840] 51 p. KyU; MHi; NIC. 40-3717

Kentucky. General Assembly. House. Committee on the Sinking Fund. Report of the Committee on the Sinking Fund, February 12, 1840. Frankfort, KY: s. l., 1840. 36 p. InU; IU; MHi. 40-3718

Kentucky. General Assembly. House. Journal of the House of Representatives of the Commonwealth of Kentucky. Begun and held in the town of Frankfort, August 19, 1840. Frankfort, KY: A. G. Hodges, state printer, 1840. 596 p. InU; KY; KyBrCL; KyHi; KyU-L. 40-3719

Kentucky. General Assembly. Joint Committee on Banks. Report of the Joint Committee on Banks Communicated to the Legislature, Jan. 28, 1840. Frankfort, KY: A. G. Hodges, State Printer [1840?] p. InU. 40-3720

Kentucky. General Assembly. Senate. Journal of the Senate of the Commonwealth of Kentucky. Begun and held in the town of Frankfort, on Wednesday, the 19th day of August, 1840, called session. Frankfort, KY: A. G. Hodges, state printer, 1840. 494 p. KyHi; KyLo; KyRMCL; KyU-L. 40-3721

Kentucky. Governor [R. P. Letcher] Message of Governor Letcher to the Legislature of Kentucky, December session, 1840. Frankfort, KY: Hodges, 1840. 14 p. MH; TxU. 40-3722

Kentucky. Laws, statutes, etc. Acts of the general assembly of the Commonwealth of Kentucky. December session, 1839. C. A. Wickliffe, lieutenant and acting governor. Published by authority. Frankfort, KY: A. G. Hodges, 1840. 319 p. A-SC; IaU-L; KyHi; MdBB; Wa-L. 40-3723

Kentucky almanac, for the year of Our Lord, 1840... By Dam'l D. M'Cullough, A. M. Lexington, KY: Noble & Dunlop, Printers, 1840. 32 p. OC. 40-3724

Kenyon College, Gambier, O. Catalogue of the library and names of members of the Philomathesian society

of Kenyon college, from its formation in 1827 to 1840. Gambier, OH: printed by Thomas R. Raymond, 1840. 44 p. DLC; MB; OHi. 40-3725

Ker, John Bellenden. Essay on the archaeology of our popular phrases, terms, and nursery rhymes. Andover, MA: King, 1840. 2 v. CtSoP; MnHi; NB; NjMD; P. 40-3726

Ker, Leander. Slavery consistent with Christianity. By the Rev. Leander Kerr [!] Baltimore, MD: Printed by Sherwood & Co., 1840. 31 p. DLC; NcU; PHi; PPL. 40-3727

Kerr, Lewis. An expositon of the criminal laws of the state of Louisiana; or, Kerr's expositon of the criminal laws of the "territory of Orleans."Revised with additions and additional forms for the use of magistrates... Plaquemine, LA: printed by J. H. Peoples, 1840. 85 p. DLC; LNHT; MH-L; OCLaw. 40-3728

Keystone Agricultural Almanac, for 1840... Philadelphia, PA: William W. Walker [1840] 34 p. MH. 40-3729

Keystone Agricultural Almanac, for 1841. Philadelphia, PA: William W. Walker [1840] p. MWA; NjR. 40-3730

Kiallmark, George, 1781-1835. Araby's daughter. Ballad, from Moore's "... Lalla Rookh... "The melody by [?] with symphonies & accompaniments [for the piano forte] by G. Kiallmark. [Boston, MA] : Hewitt & Co. [184-?] 3 p. MB. 40-3731

Kiallmark, George, 1781-1835. Fleuve du Tage. Arranged with variations for the piano forte by G. Kiallmark. Boston,

MA: G. P. Reed [184-?] 6 p. ViU. 40-3732

Kiallmark, George, 1781-1835. Hinda's appeal to her lover. Written by T. Moore. Composed by G. Kiallmark. New York: Published by Dubois & Stodart [184-?] 3 p. ViU. 40-3733

Kimball Union Academy, Plainsfield, N. H. Catalogue of the trustees, instructors and students... Newport, NH: s. l., 1840. 23 p. MeHi; MiD-B. 40-3734

Kimball, Heber Chase, 1801-1868. Journal of Heber C. Kimball, an elder of the Church of Jesus Christ of Latter Day Saints. Giving an account of his mission to Great Britain, and the commencement of the work of the Lord in that land. Also the success which has attended the labors of the elders to the present time. By R. B. Thompson... Nauvoo, IL: Printed by Robinson and Smith, 1840. 60 p. CSmH; DLC; MH. 40-3735

Kinderhook Academy, Kinderhook, N. Y. Catalogue... year ending March 1, 1840. Kinderhook, NY: Published by P. Van Schaack, 1840. 16 p. CSmH; NN. 40-3736

King, David. Erysipelas, its causes and treatment. By David King, M. D... Boston, MA: D. Clapp, Jr., 1840. 20 p. DSG; MBM; NNN; NNNAM; RPA. 40-3737

King, Grace. Grace King; or, Recollections of events in the life and death of a pious youth. With extracts from her diary. Published for the benefit of youth. Revised by the editors. New York: T. Mason and G. Lane, for the Sunday School Union of the Methodist Epis-

copal Church, 1840. 228 p. DLC; MWA; NNMHi; ODW; Or. 40-3738

King, H. Directions for making collections in natural history. Prepared for the National Institution for the Promotion of Science, by H. King, M. D. Washington, DC: Printed by Gales and Seaton, 1840. 24 p. IEN-M; MdHi; MiGr; MWA; PPM. 40-3739

King, John W. Federalism; or, The question of exclusive power, the true issue in the present monetary and political discussions in the United States... Cincinnati, OH: Shepart & Stearns, 1840. 68 p. InHi; MB; MH; PU; TxU. 40-3740

King, Matthew Peter, 1773-1823. The minute gun at sea. Boston, MA: s. l. [184-?] p. MB. 40-3741

King, Matthew Peter, 1773-1823. The minute gun at sea. Duett [S. T. Pianoforte accomp.] New York: Hewitt & Co. [184-?] 4 p. MB. 40-3742

King, Thomas Butler. Speech on the bill additional to the act on the subject of treasury notes. Delivered in the House of Representatives, March 18, 1840. 16 p. IU; KSalW; MBAt; MiD-B. 40-3743

King's Rochester City Directory and Register, 1841; containing the names, occupation, and place of residence of all heads of families, firms, and those doing business in the city, in correct alphabetical arrangement; also much other useful and interesting matter. Rochester, NY: Printed by Welles and Hayes, 1840. 168 p. NRHi; NRU. 40-3744

Kingsbury, Harmon, d. 1868. The Sabbath; a brief history of laws, petitions, remonstrances, and reports, with facts and arguments, relating to the Christian Sabbath... New York: Robert Carter, 1840. 391 p. CtMW; GDecCT; MH-AH; PPiW; VtU; WHi. 40-3745

Kingsbury, Oliver Richmond, 1809-1889. Hymns for social worship. Selected from Watts, Doddridge, Newton, Cowper, Steele, and others... New York: American Tract Society [1840] 468 p. DLC; IaDuU; MShM; PPPrHi; VtMidSM. 40-3746

Kingsley, George, 1811-1884. The social choir... Vol. I. 9th ed. Boston, MA: s. l., 1840. CtHWatk. 40-3747

Kinne, Asa. Questions and answers on law, alphabetically arranged, with references to the most approved authorities, by Asa Kinne. New York: Collins, Keese & Co., 1840. 2 v. NcD; RPL. 40-3748

Kinne, Asa. Questions and answers on law, alphabetically arranged, with references to the most approved authorities, by Asa Kinne. Second edition. New York: Published by Collins, Keese & Co., 1840. 616 p. In-SC; MdBS; MiDU-L; Ms; MWiW. 40-3749

Kinne, Asa. The most important parts of Kent's commentaries, reduced to questions and answers. 2nd ed. New York: W. E. Dean, 1840. 249 p. Ia; MdBS; MiD; PPM; WaU. 40-3750

Kinney, Hannah [Hanson] Trial of Mrs. Hannah Kinney for alleged Murder of her husband, George T. Kinney, by poison. Before the Supreme Court of Massachusetts, Dec. 21st to Dec. 26th...

for the Prisoner; By a member of the Bar. Boston, MA: s. l., 1840. 62 p. CtHC; MBBC; MHi; PP; Vi; WaU. 40-3751

Kinnicutt, Thomas, 1800-1858. An oration, delivered before the Society of United Brothers, of Brown University, September 1, 1840. By Thomas Kinnicutt, of Worcester, Massachusetts. Published by request of the Society. Providence, RI: Knowles and Vose, printers, 1840. 32 p. CtY; MBAt; MBAU; MBC; MHi; MiD-B; MWHi; NCH; NN; NNC; RNHi; RPaw; WHi. 40-3752

Kip, William Ingraham, 1811-1893. Our national sins; a sermon... twentieth Sunday after Trinity MDCCCXL. By Wm. Ingraham Kip, M. A.... Albany, NY: Printed by J. Munsell, 1840. 21 p. CU-B; MiD; NNG; OClWHi; PHi. 40-3753

Kip, William Ingraham, 1811-1893. Sermon on sexagesima Sunday, 1840. Albany, NY: s. l., 1840. 24 p. RPB. 40-3754

Kip, William Ingraham, 1811-1893. The Manifestation of the truth; a sermon, preached in St. Paul's Church in the City of Albany... after the consecration of the edifice... Albany, NY: Printed by J. Munsell, 1840. 24 p. DLC; MBC; MiD; NNG; OClWHi. 40-3755

Kirk, Edward Norris, 1802-1874. Sermons on different subjects. Delivered in England and America... with an introducton by Samuel Hanson Cox... New York: Printed by J. F. Trow, 1840. 316 p. CtY-D; MoSpD; NbOP; TChU; ViRut. 40-3756

Kirk, Edward Norris, 1802-1874. Sermons on different subjects. Delivered in England and America, by Rev. Edward

Norris Kirk, A. M., late pastor of the Fourth Presbyterian Church, Albany, N. Y. Second edition revised. New York; Philadelphia, PA; Boston, MA: Gould, Newman & Saxton; Henry Perkins; Ives & Dennett, 1840. 367 p. CtY; MBevHi; NbCrD; NUtHi; OO. 40-3757

Kirk, Edward Norris, 1802-1874. Sermons on different subjects delivered in England and America....With an introduction by Samuel Hanson Cox. Ed. 3., revised. New York: Gould, Newman & Saxton, 1840. 367 p. MWA; NhD; OMC. 40-3758

Kirk, Wheateley. There is an isle, a bonny isle. Ballad. Written by Robert Baker, Esqr. Composed by Wheateley Kirk. Philadelphia, PA: George Willig [184-?] 2 p. ViU. 40-3759

Kirkham, H. B. Traveller's guide of the Hudson River. Published by H. B. Kirkham, for the proprietor, and for sale on all the steamboats and at all the principal hotels in the United States. [New York: s. l., 184-?] p. NN. 40-3760

Kirkham, Samuel. English grammar in familiar lectures: Accompanied by a compendium... an appendix, and a key to the exercises... By Samuel Kirkham. 105th ed. Baltimore, MD: Plaskitt & Cugle, 1840. 228 p. ICN; MdHI; MiU; TU; ViU. 40-3761

Kirkham, Samuel. English grammar in familiar lectures: embracing a new systematic order of parsing, a new system of punctuation, exercise in false syntax, and a system of philosophical grammar. To which are added a compendium, an appendix, and a key to the exercises designed for the use of schools and

private learners. By Samuel Kirkham. 50th ed., enl. and improved. Rochester, NY: Published by William Alling, 1840. 228 p. DLC; NRU; OCl; OFH. 40-3762

Kirkham, Samuel. English grammar in familiar lectures... To which are added a compendium, an appendix, and a key to the exercises designed for the use of schools and private learners. By Samuel Kirkham. Stereotyped by Wm. Hagar & Co., New York. Forty-ninth edition, enlarged and improved. Rochester, NY: Published by William Alling, 1840. 228 p. NNC; OClWHi; OO; PLFM. 40-3763

Kirkham, Samuel. An essay on elocution, designed for the use of school and private learners... 3rd edition, enl. and improved. Baltimore, MD: J. W. Woods, printer, 1840. 357 p. TNP. 40-3764

Kirkham, Samuel. An essay on elocution, designed for the use of school and private learners. By Samuel Kirkham... 3d edition, enlarged and improved. New York: Robinson, Pratt & Co., 1840. 357 p. CStcr. 40-3765

Kirkland, Caroline Matilda [Stansbury] 1801-1864. A new home -- who'll follow?or, Glimpses of western life. By Mrs. Mary Clavers [pseud.] 2d ed. New York; Boston, MA: C. S. Francis; J. H. Francis, 1840. 337 p. DLC; MWA; PPi; ScC. 40-3766

Kirkpatrick, John L. Oration, delivered before the Philistorian Society of Georgetown College, D. C., on the Feb. 22, 1840, to which are prefixed the remarks of W. L. Warren, previous to his reading the Farewell Address at Washington. Washington, DC: Jacob Gideon, Jr.,

1840. 16 p. MdHi; MWH; OCX; PPM. 40-3767

Kitchel, Harvey Denison, 1812-1895. An appeal for discussion and action on the slavery question. By H. D. Kitchel... Hartford, CT: Printed by L. Skinner, 1840. 28 p. CtY; DLC; MWA; NN; OClWHi. 40-3768

Kleine biblische historien aus dem alten und neuen Testament. Mit vielen bunten Bilderngeziert. Harrisburg, PA: Peter, 1840. 18 p. PU; ViHarEM. 40-3769

Knaebel, S. Sigourney's quick step. Dedicated to Captain H. H. Sigourney, the officers & members of the New England Guards... Composed & arranged... for the brass band. Boston, MA: Prentiss [184-?] 3 p. MB. 40-3770

Knaebel, S. Twelfth waltz, as played by the brass band. Composed by S. Knaebel. Baltimore, MD: F. D. Benteen [184-?] 2 p. ViU. 40-3771

Knaebel, S. Twelfth waltz. For the piano forte. Boston, MA: Ashton & Co. [184-?] 2 p. MB. 40-3772

Knapp, F. H. A few brief remarks concerning the proper management of the teeth. Baltimore, MD: J. Murphy, 1840. 12 p. DLC. 40-3773

Knapp, Jacob, 1799-1874. Restricted and mixed communion. New York: s. l., 1840. 12 p. NHCS. 40-3774

Knauff, George P. Mount Elba waltz. Composed & dedicated to Miss Virginia A. B. Shields, by Geo. P. Knauff. Bal-

timore, MD: F. D. Bentee & co. [184-?] 1 p. ViU. 40-3775

Knauff, George P. Virginia cotillions. Composed for the piano forte, and dedicated to the ladies of Virginia, by Geo. P. Knauff. No. 1... Baltimore, MD; New Orleans, LA: F. D. Benteen & co.; W. T. Mayo [184-?] 5 p. ViU. 40-3776

Kneass, Nelson. Old Aunty Brown. [Song. Altered from a melody by Nelson Kneass] Arranged by Wm. Cumming. Guitar accomp. Cincinnati, OH: Peters & Field [184-?] 5 p. MB. 40-3777

Knecht, Henry. Fairy waltz. Composed & respectfully dedicated to Miss Mary Morton Clark [of Petersburg, Va.] by Henry Knecht. Baltimore, MD: F. D. Benteen [184-?] 3 p. ViU. 40-3778

Knecht, Henry. Fairy waltz. Composed and respectfully dedicated to Miss Mary Morton Clark [of Petersburg, Va.] by Henry Knecht. New York: Firth, Pond & co. [184-?] 3 p. ViU. 40-3779

Knecht, Henry. Mobile grand march. [For the piano forte] New York: Hewitt & Jaques [184-?] 2 p. MB. 40-3780

Knight, Abel F. Boston independent company of cadets' grand march. [For the piano forte.] [Boston, MA: Prentiss, 184-?] 2 p. MB. 40-3781

Knight, Abel F. Camp-Sargent quick step, performed at the encampment of the Boston Light Infantry, Springfield, Mass., July, 1840. [For the piano forte] Boston, MA: Reed, 1840. 3 p. MB. 40-3782

Knight, Abel F. The Maryland cadet's

quick step. [For the piano forte] Boston, MA: Prentiss [184-?] 3 p. MB. 40-3783

Knight, Charles, 1791-1873. Natural history:the elephant as he exists in a wild state, & as he has been made subservient in peace & in war to the purpose of man. New York: Harper, 1840. 300 p. MWA; NGlo; P. 40-3784

Knight, I. P. Rock in the cradle of the deep. The words by Mrs. Williard of Troy. The music by I. P. Knight. New York: C. E. Horn, 1840. 7 p. No Loc. 40-3785

Knight, Joseph Philip, 1812-1887. Beautiful Venice! An admired ballad. [Accomp. for piano forte] Philadelphia, PA: Fiot [184-?] 3 p. MB. 40-3786

Knight, Joseph Philip, 1812-1887. Beautiful Venice! Ballad... [the accomp. arranged for the guitar by R. Culver] Philadelphia, PA: Lee & Walker [184-?] 3 p. MB. 40-3787

Knight, Joseph Philip, 1812-1887. The gipsy's [sic] invitation. A cavativa. The poetry by J. B. Phillips. Boston, MA: Parker & Ditson, 1840. 5 p. MB; MNF. 40-3788

Knight, Joseph Philip, 1812-1887. Go, forget me. Poetry by Rev. Charles Wolfe. [New York: James L. Hewitt & co., 184-?] 6 p. ViU. 40-3789

Knight, Joseph Philip, 1812-1887. The Grecian daughter. Ballad. Sung by Miss Sherreff. Written by Haynes Bayle. Music composed by J. P. Knight. [New York: Atwill?184-?] p. ViU. 40-3790

Knight, Joseph Philip, 1812-1887. I wish

I were a child again. Ballad. By Jos. P. Knight. Philadelphia, PA: A. Fiot & Co., 1840. 5 p. KU. 40-3791

Knight, Joseph Philip, 1812-1887. I'm queen of a fairy band. Cavatina. [S. Accomp. for piano forte] Boston, MA: Ditson184-?] 5 p. MB. 40-3792

Knight, Joseph Philip, 1812-1887. O swift we go! sleighing song... by J. T. Fields. [Voice & pf.] Boston, MA: s. l., 1840. CtY. 40-3793

Knight, Joseph Philip, 1812-1887. The prairie lea. A song. Poetry by Dr. J. K. Mitchell; the music composed & dedicated, Dr. C. H. Stedman. Boston, MA: Oakes & Swan, 1840. 7 p. MiU-C. 40-3794

Knight, Joseph Philip, 1812-1887. Rocked in the cradle of the deep. Words by Mrs. Williard of Troy. The music by J. P. Knight. [New York: C. E. Horn, 1840] 33-36 p. NcD. 40-3795

Knight, Joseph Philip, 1812-1887. Shall I sing you a song of the past?Ballad [S. or T. Accomp. for piano forte] Boston, MA: Oakes [184-?] 5 p. MB; NcD. 40-3796

Knight, Joseph Philip, 1812-1887. ... She wore a wreath of roses. A ballad. Sung by Mrs. Wood. The music composed by Joseph Philip Knight. New York: Firth & Hall [184-?] 7 p. ViU. 40-3797

Knight, Joseph Philip, 1812-1887. ... She wore a wreath of roses. A ballad, sung by Mrs. Wood; the poetry by Thomas Haynes Bayly, Esqr.; the music composed and dedicated to Miss Norcott, by John Philip Knight. Second edition. New

York: Atwills music saloon [184-?] 6 p. ViU. 40-3798

Knight, Joseph Philip, 1812-1887. Sleeping for sorrow; a sacred song. The poetry by Dr. J. K. Mitchell; the music by Joseph Philip Knight. Boston, MA: Wm. H. Oakes, 1840. 6 p. WHi. 40-3799

Knight, Nehemiah Rice. Speech on the resolution to restore the duty on umbrellas and parasols. In the Senate of the United States, Mar. 11, 1840. By Nehemiah R. Knight. [Washington, DC: s. l., 1840] 9 p. M; RPB. 40-3800

Knill, Richard, 1787-1857. The missionary's wife; or, A brief account of Mrs. Loveless, of Madras, the first American missionary to foreign lands. By Richard Knill. Philadelphia, PA: Presbyterian Board of Publciation, James Russell, publishing agent, 1840. 24 p. CtHC; MsSC. 40-3801

Knodle, E. A classifying word-book, in some parts of which, words are classed according to meaning... Compiled by E. Knodle. Baltimore, MD: Printed by John Murphy, 1840. 273 p. MdBP; MdHi; PLPM. 40-3802

Knowles, James David, 1798-1838. Memoir of Mrs. Ann H. Judson, late missionary of Burma; including a history of the American Baptist mission in the Burman Empire. Twenty-fourth thousand, with a continuation of the history of the mission. Boston, MA: Gould, Kendell & Lincoln, 1840. 395 p. GMM; MBNEH; MCon. 40-3803

Knowles, James Sheridan, 1784-1862. ... John of Procida; or, The bridals of Messina. A tragedy in five acts... Philadel-

phia, PA; New York: Turner & Fisher [1840?] 68 p. CtY; MH. 40-3804

Knowles, James Sheridan, 1784-1862. ... Love. A play in five acts. By James Sheridan Knowles. With the stage business, cast of characters, costumes, relative positions, etc. 1st American ed. Baltimore, MD; New York: H. A. Turner; Turner & Fisher [184-?] 78 p. DLC; OCU; OU; PU-F. 40-3805

Knowles, James Sheridan, 1784-1862. ... Love. A play in five acts. By James Sheridan Knowles. With the stage business, cast of characters, costumes, relative positions, etc. 1st American ed. New York: S. French [etc., etc., 184-?] 60 p. CSt. 40-3806

Knowles, James Sheridan, 1784-1862. ... Love. A play in five acts. By James Sheridan Knowles. With the stage business, cast of characters, costumes, relative positions, etc. 1st American ed. Philadelphia, PA; New York: Turner & Fisher [184-?] 78 p. ViU. 40-3807

Knowles, James Sheridan, 1784-1862. The Love-chase. A comedy in 5 acts. New York: Taylor & Co. [184-?] 67 p. MB; MWA; PPL. 40-3808

Knowles, James Sheridan, 1784-1862. The maid of Mariendorpt. A play in five acts. Boston, MA: J. Fisher, etc. [1840?] 72 p. MH. 40-3809

Knowles, James Sheridan, 1784-1862. ... Old maids. A play in five acts, by James Sheridan Knowles... Correctly printed from the most approved acting copy. Philadelphia, PA; Boston, MA: Turner & Fisher; J. Fisher, etc. [184-?] 84 p. ICU; MB; MH; NN; ViU. 40-3810

Knowles, James Sheridan, 1784-1862. ...
Virginius. A tragedy in five acts, by James
Sheridan Knowles. With the stage busi-
ness, cast of characters, costumes, rela-
tive positions, etc., as performed by Mr.
Forrest, Mr. Macready, and other
eminent tragedians. New York: S.
French [etc., etc., 184-?] 72 p. CtY; MB;
NIC; PU. 40-3811

Knowles, James Sheridan, 1784-1862.
The wife, a tale of Mantua. A play in five
acts. By James Sheridan Knowles. With
the stage directions and corrections as
played at the Park Theatre. J. B. Addis,
prompter. New York: S. French [184-?]
68 p. CSmH; CSt; MH. 40-3812

Knowles, James Sheridan, 1784-1862.
The wife, a tale of Mantua. A play in five
acts. New York: W. Taylor & Co. [184-?]
12 p. CSt; MH; NIC; PSt; RPB. 40-3813

Knowles, James Sheridan, 1784-1862. ...
William Tell. A play in three acts. By
James Sheridan Knowles. As acted by
Mr. Forrest. With the stage business, cast
of characters, costumes, relative positions, etc. New York: S. French [184-?]
50 p. CSt; MB; MWA; NN; OCl. 40-3814

Koch, Albrecht Karl. A short description of fossil remains, found in the state
of Missouri by the author. Written &
published by Albert Koch, proprietor of
the St. Louis Museum. Saint Louis, MO:
Churchill & Stewart, printers, 1840. 8 p.
MHi; NL. 40-3815

Koczwara, Franz, d. 1791. The battle of
Prague. A favorite sonata for the piano
forte. Composed by F. Kotzwara. Boston,
MA: C. Bradlee [184-?] 10 p. ViU. 40-
3816

Koczwara, Franz, d. 1791. The battle of
Prague. A favorite sonata for the piano
forte. Composed by Kotzwara. New
York: Firth & Hall [184-?] 11 p. ViU. 40-
3817

Koenig. Eclipse polka. [For piano forte]
New York: Firth, Pond & Co. [184-?] 7
p. MB. 40-3818

Kollock, Shepard K. The doctrine of the
perseverance of the Saints. Illustated,
proved and applied, by Rev. Shepard K.
Kollock. Philadelphia, PA: Presbyterian
Board of Publication, James Russell,
publishing agent, 1840. 20 p. CtHC;
MsJMC; OMtv; PPM; WHi. 40-3819

Kotzebue, Augustus Friedrich Ferdinand von, 1761-1819. ... The stranger.
A play in five acts. By Augustus Frederic
Ferdinand von Koezebue. With state
directions, and costumes, marked and
corrected by J. B. Addis, prompter. New
York: S. French [184-?] 59 p. CSt. 40-
3820

Kotzeluch, Leopold Antonin Tomas,
1752-1818. Bonnie Doon, a favorite
song, written by R. Burns. Arranged for
the piano forte by Kotzeluch. Baltimore,
MD: Geo. Willig [184-?] 2 p. ViU. 40-
3821

Krebs, Karl August, 1804-1880.
Dearest, I think of thee. Ballad, from the
gems of German songs. Music by C.
Krebs. Baltimore, MD: F. D. Benteen
[184-?] 3 p. ViU. 40-3822

Kriss Kringle's Christmas tree. A
holiday present for boys and girls. New
York; Philadelphia, PA: E. Ferrett & co.,
1840. 160 p. LNH. 40-3823

Krummacher, Friedrich Wilhelm, 1796-1868. Dew of Israel & the lily of God; or, a glimpse of the kingdom of grace. Fr. the 2d London ed. New York: Carter, 1840. 262 p. InCW; NTEW; OClW; PPLT; TKC. 40-3824

Krummacher, Friedrich Wilhelm, 1796-1868. Elias der Thisbiter, nach seinem aussern und inneruleben... New York: Amerikanische traktat-geselschaft [184-?] 707 p. ICU. 40-3825

Krummacher, Friedrich Wilhelm, 1796-1868. Elisha. By F. W. Krummacher... Translated from the German, without alteration or omission. Philadelphia, PA: Joseph Whetham, 1840. 408 p. MDeeP; OClW; PP; WHi. 40-3826

Kuffner, Joseph, 1776-1856. Ragozi's waltz. For the piano forte. Composed by Joseph Kuffner. Philadelphia, PA; Klemm & brother [184-?] 2 p. ViU. 40-3827

Kuhe, Wilhelm, 1823-1912. Le Feu Follet. Scherzo capricciose. [For piano forte] Philadelphia, PA: Gould [184-?] 7 p. MB. 40-3828

Kunst, P. J. An American Dictionary of the English and German Languages, containing all the words in general use; designating the various parts of speech in both languages with the orthography, accentuation, division and plan for pronunciation according to Webster, and with the genders and plurals of the German nouns, the division of words into syllables, the separation of compound nouns by double-hyphens according to theoir foundation, by P. J. Kunst. Part 1. English and German. [Part 2. German and English] Harrisburg, HA: printed and published by G. S. Peters; Stereotyped at the "Harrisburg Stereotype Foundry, "1840. 416, 397 p. ArL; CoHi; NbOC. 40-3829

Kurtz, Benjamin. Arguments derived from sacred scripture and sound reason, exhibiting the necessity and advantages of infant baptism... by Benjamin Kurtz, D. D. Baltimore, MD: Printed at the publication rooms, 1840. 370 p. GDecCT; MBC; NbOP; ODaB; PAtM; TxDaM. 40-3830

L

L'Homond, Charles Franquois, 1727-1794. Elements of French grammar... Translated [by H. W. Longfellow] 5th edition. Boston, MA: J. Munroe & Co., 1840. DLC; MBC; MH; PU; WaU. 40-3831

La Blanche, Luigi, 1794-1858. Complete method of singing... with examples. From the French. Boston, MA: Ditson [184-?] 102 p. ICN; MB. 40-3832

Labaree, Benjamin, 1801-1883. Lecture. Education demanded by the peculiar character of our civil institutions. [S. l.: s. l., 184-?] 32 p. MH. 40-3833

Labarraque, Antoine Germain, 1777-1850. Instructions and observations concerning the use of the chlorides... Ed. 3. New Haven, CT: William Storer, 1840. 30 p. CtY; DLC; MH-AH; MWA; NNNAM. 40-3834

Labitzky, Joseph, 1802-1881. The Aurora waltzes. Composed & arranged for the piano forte by Labitzky. Baltimore, MD; New Orleans, LA: F. D. Benteen; W. T. Mayo [184-?] 4 p. ViU. 40-3835

Labitzky, Joseph, 1802-1881. Les Clochettes:Polka, pour le piano, par Labitzky. Philadelphia, PA; New York: A. Fiot; W. Dubois [184-?] 2 p. MH; ViU. 40-3836

Labitzky, Joseph, 1802-1881. The elfen waltz. Composed and dedicated to the Emperor & Empress of Russia, by J. Labitzky. Baltimore, MD: G. Willig, Jr. [184-?] 2 p. ViU. 40-3837

Labitzky, Joseph, 1802-1881. The elfin waltz. For the piano forte. Composed & dedicated to the Emperor & Empress of Russia, by J. Labitzky. Baltimore, MD; New Orlenas, LA: F. D. Benteen; W. T. Mayo [184-?] 2 p. ViU. 40-3838

Labitzky, Joseph, 1802-1881. ... The evergreen gallop... New York; Philadelphia, PA: Wm. Duboi; A. Fiot [184-?] 7 p. ViU. 40-3839

Labitzky, Joseph, 1802-1881. Jessamine waltzes. From Labitsky's celebrated waltzes and gallopades as performed at Nibles and at the assemblies & private parties. New York; Philadelphia, PA: Wm. Dubois; A. Fiot [184-?] 9 p. ViU. 40-3840

Labitzky, Joseph, 1802-1881. Tremolo waltzes. Boston, MA: Marsh [184-?] 9 p. MB. 40-3841

Laborre, T. She is thine. An admired ballad. Sung by Mrs. Wood. Composed by T. Laborre. Arranged for the guitar by L. Meignen. Philadelphia, PA: Burns & co. [184-?] 1 p. ViU. 40-3842

Labourers in the east; or, memoirs of eminent men who were devoted to the service of Christ in India. Containing abridged biographies of the Rev. Dr. Buchanan, Rev. Henry Martyn, and Rev. David Brown. Philadelphia, PA: Presbyterian Board of Publication, James Russell, Publishing Agent, William S. Martieu, Printer, 1840. 304 p. CSt; GDecCT; ICP; NjPT; ViRut. 40-3843

Lacey, Michael Rophino, 1795-1867. ... The two friends. A domestic drama, in two acts. By Rophino Lacey. New York: S. French [184-?] 39 p. CSt; MB; MH. 40-3844

Lacordaire, Jean Baptiste Henri, 1802-1861. Apology for the Order of St. Dominic. By the Abbe H. Lacordaire... Philadelphia, PA: Eugene Cummiskey, 1840. 143 p. CMenSP; LU; MdW; MoSU; PV; TNV. 40-3845

Ladd, William, 1778-1841. An essay on a congress of nations, for the adjustment of international disputes, and for the promotion of peace without resort to arms. Boston, MA: American Peace Society, 1840. 190 p. MH. 40-3846

Ladd, William, 1778-1841. An essay on a congress of nations, for the adjustment of international disputes, without resort to arms. Containing the substance of the rejected essay on that subject. With original thoughts and a copious appendix. By William Ladd. Boston, MA: Whipple and Damrell, 1840. 192 p. DLC; IaGG; MiD; Nh-Hi; WHi. 40-3847

The Lady's album, a gift for all seasons... New York: Nafis & Cornish [184-?] 348 p. C-S; DLC; ICU; MiL; NcU. 40-3848

The lady's and gentleman's athenaeum. New York: s. l., 184-? 32 p. NN. 40-3849

The lady's annual; a Christmas and New year's gift. New York: s. l. [184-?] p. MBAt. 40-3850

The Lady's Annual Register and Housewife's Memorandum-book for 1840. By Caroline Gilman... Boston, MA; New York; Philadelphia, PA: Otis, Broaders and Co.; Collins, Keese and Co.; Thomas, Cowperthwait & Co., 1840. 108 p. No Loc. 40-3851

Lady's Annual Register and Housewife's Memorandum-book for 1841. By Caroline Gilman. Boston, MA: William Crosby and Company [1840] p. MWA. 40-3852

Laila; a juvenile opera. Taunton: Republican Job Printing Rooms, [184-?] Broadside. NN. 40-3853

Lamartine, Alphonse de, 1790-1869. Additional memoirs of my youth. By A. De Lamartine... New York: Harper Brothers, 1840. 49 p. NRviHi. 40-3854

Lame John; or, The charitable poor man. Written for the American S. S. Union and revised by the Com. of Pub. Philadelphia, PA: American S. S. Union 1840. 137 p. AmSSchU; NjP; PAnL; ScCliTO. 40-3855

LaMennais, Hagues Felicite Robert de. People's own book. Tr. fr. the French by Nathaniel Greene. Boston, MA: Littlefield, 1840. 175 p. PU. 40-3856

Lammson, James H. The progress of the North West... S. l.: s. l., 1840? 40 p. WePS. 40-3857

Lamoille County, Vt. Justice Court. A record of the Justice Court of Lamoille

County, state of Vermont, in the year 1840, which were trials on notes of default, Defaults of Account trials and confessions. Morrisville, VT: s. l., 1840. VtMorr. 40-3858

Lancaster, John. The life of Lady Darcy Maxwell, of Pollock, late of Edinburgh. Compiled from her voluminous diary and correspondence... by the Rev. John Lancaster... New York: T. Mason and G. Lane, 1840. 407 p. CtY-D; ICN; LNH; PReaAT. 40-3859

Lancaster, Pa. Common Schools. Rules and regulations of the common schools of Lancaster. Lancaster, PA: s. l., 1840-45. 10 p. PHi. 40-3860

Lancaster, Pa. Theological Seminary. Address delivered at the inauguration of Rev. J. W. Nevin as professor of theology in the Theological Seminary of the German Reformed Church, Mercersburg, Pa., May 20, 1840. Chambersburg, PA: Printed at the office of publication of the German Reformed Church, 1840. 28 p. DLC; NN; PSt; MoKU. 40-3861

Lancaster, Pa. Theological Seminary. Andreden gehalten bei der Einsetzung des Ehrw. J. W. Nevin als Professor der Theologie in dem Theologischen seminar der Deutsch-Reformirten Kirche, Mercersburg, Penn., May 20, 1840. Chambersburg, PA: Gedrukt in der Druckerei der Deutsch-Reformiten Kirsche, 1840. 32 p. DLC. 40-3862

Lancaster City Temperance Society, Lancaster, Pa. Minutes. Lancaster, PA: s. l. 1840. NN. 40-3863

Land wirths und Seidenbauers Calen-dar, 1840. Lancaster, PA: Johann Bar [1840?] p. MWA. 40-3864

Land Without a Sabbath; A history of France when the fearful experiment was made in 1793, of abolishing the Sabbath... New York: Prepared for the American Sabbath Enterprise [184-?] p. CSmH. 40-3865

Landon, Letitia Elizabeth, 1802-1838. The works of L. E. Landon. Philadelphia, PA: Published by E. L. Carey and A. Hart, 1840. 579 p. CSmH; IaK; MWA; NAvon; NRU. 40-3866

Lane, A. Address to the Whigs of Lancaster... Lancaster, PA: s. l., 1840. unp. MLanc. 40-3867

Lane Theological Seminary, Cincinnati, O. Catalogue of the officers and students of Lane Theological Seminary, Cincinnati, Ohio, 1839-40. Cincinnati, OH: Hefley, Hubbell & Co., 1840. 16 p. MBC; MHi. 40-3868

Lang, John Dunmore, 1799-1878. The moral and religious aspect of the future American of the Southern hemisphere; or, A letter to the members of the Pres. Churches... in U. S. A. New York: Van Norden, 1840. 27 p. ICU; MHi; NCH; PPPrHi; ScC. 40-3869

Lang, John Dunmore, 1799-1878. Specimens of an improved metrical translation of the Psalms of David, intended for the use of the Presbyterian Church in Australia and New Zealand. With a preliminary dissertation and notes, critical and explanatory. By John Dunmore Lang. Philadelphia, PA: Printed by Adam Waldie, 1840. 230 p. KyLoP; MWA; PPPrHi. 40-3870

Langley, J. Catalogue of works on medicine and anatomy and the collateral sciences. By Langley. New York: J. & H. G. Langley, publishers, William Osborn, printer, 1840. 23 p. MsH. 40-3871

Lankester, Edwin, 1814-1874. Vegetable substances used for the food of man... New York: Harper & brothers, 1840. 271 p. C; KyLx; MB; MWiW; NGlc. 40-3872

Lanner, Joseph Franz Carl, 1801-1843. Morning star waltz. Arranged for the piano by F. Beyer. Boston, MA: Wade [184-?] 7 p. MB. 40-3873

Lape, Thomas. An extract of a sermon. Delivered in the Evangelical Lutheran Zions Church, Athens, N. Y.... Baltimore, MD: publication rooms, n. pr., 1840. 12 p. NjR. 40-3874

Lapham, Increase Allen, 1811-1875. A catalogue of plants found in the vicinity of Milwaukee, Wisconsin Territory. Milwaukee, WI: Printed by the Advertiser Office, 1840. 23 p. MBHo; NN. 40-3875

Lapham, Increase Allen, 1811-1875. A Documentary History of the Milwaukee and Rock River Canal. Milwaukee, WI: Printed at the Office of the Advertiser, 1840. 151 p. DNA; OCHP; W; WHi; WM. 40-3876

Lapham, Increase Allen, 1811-1875. Paper on the number, locality, and times of removal of the Indians in Wisconsin. Milwaukee, WI: s. l., 1840. 27 p. MWA. 40-3877

Lapham, Increase Allen, 1811-1875. Supplement to Catalogue of plants...

[Milwaukee, WI: s. l., 1840] 23 p. NN; WHi; WM. 40-3878

Lardner, William. The watcher. Arranged for one or two voices. Composed & respectfully dedicated to Mrs. Sarah J. Hale by Dr. William Lardner. Boston, MA: Oliver Ditson [184-?] 3 p. ViU. 40-3879

Lardner, William. The watcher. Arranged for one or two voices. Written by Mrs. Sarah J. Hale; composed by Dr. Wm. Lardner. Baltimore, MD; New Orleans, LA: F. D Benteen; Wm. T. Mayo [184-?] 2 p. ViU. 40-3880

Lardner, William. The watcher. Words by Mrs. S. J. Hale; music by Dr. Lardner. Philadelphia, PA: E. Ferrett & co. [184-?] 2 p. ViU. 40-3881

The Lass O'Gowrie. Sung by Mr. Wilson. [Philadelphia, PA: E. Ferrett & co., 184-?] 1 p. ViU. 40-3882

A late visit to some of the principal hospitals, prisons, &c. in France, Scotland and England. Philadelphia, PA: s. l., 1840. PPL; PPL-R. 40-3883

Latrobe, Benjamin Henry. Description of a new form of edge rail to be called the Z rail... By Benj. H. Latrobe. Baltimore, MD: n. p., 1840. 27 p. CSmH; LNMus; NN; WU-En. 40-3884

Latrobe, John Hazlehurst Boneval, 1803-1891. The justices' practice under the laws of Maryland, including the duties of a constable. With an appendix, containing a collection of forms used in conveyancing. A synopsis of the law of evidence-of-promisory notes- of the statutes of limitations, with an explana-

tion of law terms... 3d ed., rev., enl. &
imp. Baltimore, MD: Pub. by Fielding
Lucas, Jr., John Murphy, pr., 1840. 502 p.
IaDmD-L; MdHi; MH-L; OCLaw;
TMeC. 40-3885

Latrobe, John Hazlehurst Boneval,
1803-1891. Manual labour school. Address on the subject of a manual labour
school. By John H. B. Latrobe, esq., and
an address to the citizens of Baltimore.
Baltimore, MD: Printed by J. D. Toy,
1840. 20 p. DLC; MdHi; MWA; PHi;
PPM. 40-3886

Latta, Samuel Arminius, 1804-1852.
The ladies guide to health; or Woman's
private counsellor, and... nurse's manual.
Cincinnati, OH: E. Morgan & Co., 1840.
286 p. No Loc. 40-3887

Laurel Hill Cemetery, Philadelphia, Pa.
Regulations of the Laurel Hill cemetery,
on the river Schuylkill, near Philadelphia; the acts of incorporation by the
legislature of Pennsylvania in 1837; and
a catalogue of the proprietors of lots.
Philadelphia, PA: s. l., 1840. CtY; MB;
MBAt; MHi; PPAmP. 40-3888

The laurel wreath. A Christmas and
New Year's gift. New York: Leavitt and
Allen, 1840. 264 p. Ia-L-B. 40-3889

The lavender girl. Boston, MA: Ditson
[184-?] 1 p. MB. 40-3890

Law, William, of Georgia. A discourse
delivered before the Georgia Historical
Society, Savannah, on Wednesday,
February 12, 1840. By William Law.
Savannah, GA: Published by a resolution
of the Society, 1840. 43 p. DLC; GU-De;
MWA; NcD; PPAmP. 40-3891

Lawrence, Edward Alexander, 1808-
1883. The mission of the church, or Systematic Beneficence. New York: s. l.
[184-?] p. MH. 40-3892

Lawrence, Margaret Oliver Woods,
1813-1901. Blossoms of chldhood. New
York: Gen. Prot. Epis. S. S. U., 1840. 155
p. DLC; NN; NNC. 40-3893

Lawrence Gallopadee. Arranged for
the guitar by F. Weiland. Philadelphia,
PA: Lee and Walker [184-?] 1 p. MB. 40-
3894

Laycock, Thomas, 1812-1876. An essay
on hysteria; being an analysis of its ir-
regular and aggravated forms; including
hysterical hemorrhage and hysterical is-
churia... By Thomas Laycock... Philadelphia, PA; New Orleans, LA: Haswell,
Barrington, and Haswell; J. J. Haswell &
Co., 1840. 192 p. CSt; ICJ; KyLxT; MH-
M; OC. 40-3895

Leach, John, 1724-1799. A journal kept
by John Leach, during his confinement
by the British, in Boston gaol [sic] in
1775... [Boston, MA: s. l., 184-?] 140 p.
WHi. 40-3896

Leake and Watts Children's Home,
Younkers, N. Y. Last will and testament
of John G. Leake; act of incorporation of
the Leake and Watts orphan house... as-
signment to release by and by-laws of the
trustees. New York: s. l., 1840. 20 p.
MWCL; NNC; PHi. 40-3897

Lear, Tobias, 1762-1816. Last words of
Gen. Washington. [Philadelphia, PA: s.
l., 1840] 7 p. MBAt; NBuG. 40-3898

Leavitt, Joshua, 1794-1873. American
lessons in reading and speaking. An-

dover, MA: Gould, Newman & Saxton, etc., etc., 1840. CtHWatk; MH; PPL. 40-3899

Leavitt, Joshua, 1794-1873. The Christian lyre; a collection of hymns and tunes, adapted for social worship, prayer meetings and revivals of religion. By Joshua Leavitt. Twenty-fifth edition, revised. Andover, MA: Published by Gould, Newman & Saxton, etc., etc., 1840. var. pag. MdBD; MWA; NjPT; NBLIHI; RPB. 40-3900

Leavitt, Joshua, 1794-1873. The financial power of slavery. The substance of an address delivered in Ohio, in September, 1840. [S. l.: s. l., 1840] 4 p. NIC. 40-3901

Lectures on the Points in Controversy between Romanists and Protestants. By the Hon. and Rev. B. W. Noel... Philadelphia, PA: Presbyterian Board of Publication, James Russell, Publishing Agent, 1840. 336 p. IaHoL; KyLoP; MWiW; PPPrHi; ViRut. 40-3902

Lee, Charles Alfred, 1801-1872. An account of a filaria in a horse's eye. With remarks... [New Haven, CT: s. l., 1840] p. DSG; NN. 40-3903

Lee, Charles Alfred, 1801-1872. The elements of geology, for popular use; containing a description of the geological formations and mineral resources of the United States. By Charles A. Lee... New York: Harper & Brothers, 1840. 375 p. CSt; GU; InCW; MH; NCH. 40-3904

Lee, Charles Alfred, 1801-1872. Human physiology for the use of elementary schools. 3d ed. New York: American Common School depository, 1840. 336 p.

AU; MH; NcD-MC; PPCP; ViU. 40-3905

Lee, David, d. 1849. Now to the lists, of the field of the cloth and gold. Song. New York: Bourne [184-?] 5 p. MB. 40-3906

Lee, Eliza [Buckminister] Delusion; or, The witch of New England... [anon.] Boston, MA: Hilliard, Gray and Company, 1840. 160 p. CtY; DLC; MB; MH; MnU; NcD; OMC; RPB. 40-3907

Lee, George Alexander, 1802-1851. Away, away to the mountain's brow. A cavatina, as sung with unbounded applause by Miss Hughes. Composed by Alexander Lee. New York: Hewitt [184-?] 4 p. ViU. 40-3908

Lee, George Alexander, 1802-1851. Away, away to the mountain's brow. Cavatina. Sung with unbounded applause by Miss Hughes. Composed by Alexr. Lee. Baltimore, MD: Geo. Willig, Jr. [184-?] 4 p. ViU. 40-3909

Lee, George Alexander, 1802-1851. Away, away to the mountain's brow. A celebrated cavatina, as sung by Miss Hughes at the Park Theatre, the music composed by Alexander Lee. Boston, MA: Oliver Ditson [184-?] 4 p. ViU. 40-3910

Lee, George Alexander, 1802-1851. Come o'er the heather, as sung with unbounded applause by Mr. Pearman. The words and arrangement by Alexr. Lee. Baltimore, MD: Geo. Willig, Junr. [184-?] 2 p. ViU. 40-3911

Lee, George Alexander, 1802-1851. I'll be no submissive wife. Ballad. Composed by Alexander Lee. Baltimore, MD: F. D. Benteen [184-?] 3 p. ViU. 40-3912

Lee, George Alexander, 1802-1851. In my own sweet native vale. Ballad from the operetta, The Fairy of the Lakes. Composed & arranged for the piano forte by Alexander Lee. New York: E. Riley & co. [184-?] 5 p. ViU. 40-3913

Lee, George Alexander, 1802-1851. Napolitaine, I am dreaming of thee. [Song. Accompaniment for piano forte] Boston, MA: Ditson [184-?] 5 p. MB. 40-3914

Lee, George Alexander, 1802-1851. Oh, 'twas sweet to hear her singing. Song. Boston, MA: Reed [184-?] 5 p. MB. 40-3915

Lee, George Alexander, 1802-1851. Pretty maidens, come wonder with me. Ballad. Boston, MA: Reed [184-?] 3 p. MB. 40-3916

Lee, George Alexander, 1802-1851. Soldier's tear. As sung by Miss Watson, at Niblo's concerts. Words by Thoms. H. Bayley. Music by Alexander Lee. New York: Firth & Hall [184-?] 3 p. MB; ViU. 40-3917

Lee, George Alexander, 1802-1851. The soldier's tear. Composed by A. Lee. Philadelphia, PA: Fiot, Meignen & co. [184-?] 2 p. ViU. 40-3918

Lee, George Alexander, 1802-1851. The soldier's tear. Song. Baltimore, MD: Willig, Jr. [184-?] 2 p. MB. 40-3919

Lee, George Alexander, 1802-1851. What's the steer, Kimmer? [Voice & pf.] Boston, MA: Prentiss [184-?] 5 p. CtY; MB. 40-3920

Lee, George Alexander, 1802-1851. When the dew is on the grass. [Song. With accompaniment for piano forte] Boston, MA: Reed [184-?] 3 p. MB. 40-3921

Lee, Hannah Farnham Sawyer. Stories for the people. Boston, MA: Whipple & Damrell, 1840. MB-FA. 40-3922

Lee, John. Letter to the Hon. Judge Story, LL. D., discovering and correcting the errors of Blackstone and his editor on the theory of human genealogy and kindred. Cambridge, MA: Metcalf, Torry & Ballou, 1840. 32 p. CtY; DLC; MBC; MH-L; MWA. 40-3923

Lee, Leroy Madison. Advice for a young convert; in a series of letters on practical Christianity, by Rev. Leroy M. Lee. New York: published by T. Mason & G. Lane, for the Methodist Episcopal Church, at the Conference Office, J. Collord, printer, 1840. 399 p. LU; MnSH; OBerB; TxHuT. 40-3924

Lee, Mary Elizabeth, 1813-1849. Social evenings; or, Historical tales for youth. By Mary E. Lee. Boston, MA: Marsh, Capen, Lyon, and Webb, 1840. 260 p. DLC; InCW; MB; PU; ScU. 40-3925

Lee, N. K. M. Cook's own book and house-keepers register... Boston, MA: Munroe & Francis, 1840. 300 p. KMK; MWA; NN; RPB. 40-3926

Lee, William, 1778-1863. The excellent properties of Brandy & Salt as an efficient medicine in several dangerous diseases incident to mankind. Philadelphia,

PA: C. A. Elliott, 1840. DLC; DNLM; DSG; IEN-M; OCHP. 40-3927

Lee, William States. A sermon, preached before the Charleston Union Presbytery, at the opening of their session in Charleston, November 17th, 1840. By the Rev. William States Lee... Charleston, SC: Printed by B. B. Hussey, 1840. 16 p. GDecCT; MBC; PPPrHi; RPB; ScU. 40-3928

Leet, Isaac, 1802-1844. Speech of Mr. Leet, of Pennsylvania, on the Independent treasury bill. Delivered in Committee on the Whole, in the House of Representatives, June 2, 1840. Washington, DC: Printed at the Globe Office, 1840. 13 p. IaHi; MiU-C; TxU; WHi. 40-3929

Lefebure-Wely, Louis James Alfred. Les cloches du monastere. Nocturne pour piano. Boston, MA: Ditson [184-?] 7 p. MB. 40-3930

LeFevre, Clement Fall, 1797-1882. The Lexington calamity. A sermon delivered in the Bleeker-St. [Universalist] Church on Feb. 9th, and repeated Feb. 16, 1840. 2nd ed. New York: s. l., 1840. 23 p. MH; MHi; MMeT-Hi. 40-3931

LeFevre, Clement Fall, 1797-1882. Sunday school hymn book designed for Universalist Sunday schools throughout the United States. New York: s. l., 1840. 64 p. PHi. 40-3932

Legare, John B. Valedictory oration of the Clariosophic society, delivered in the chapel of the South Carolina college by John B. Legare, Jr., December 1, 1840. Columbia, SC: I. C. Morgan, 1840. 15 p. TxU. 40-3933

Leggett, William, 1801-1839. A collection of the political writings of William Leggett, by Theodore Sedgwick, Jr. Selected and arranged with a preface. New York: s. l., 1840. 409 p. DLC; ICRL; MdBP; MH-L; PU. 40-3934

Leggett, William, 1801-1839. A collection of the political writings of William Leggett. Selected and arranged with a preface by Theodore Sedgwick, Jr... New York: Taylor & Dodd, 1840. 2 v. CS; CtY; IaDmD; LNT; MWA; PWW. 40-3935

Lehigh Coal and Navigation Company. Defence of the Lehigh Coal & Navigation Company, from the Assaults made upon its Interests by X. Philadelphia, PA: Jesper Harding, printer, 1840. 66 p. ICJ; MB; MH. 40-3936

Lehigh Coal and Navigation Company. Exposure of... Philadelphia, PA: s. l., 1840. 32 p. PHi. 40-3937

Lehigh Coal and Navigation Company. A history of the Lehigh Coal and Navigation Company. Pub. by order of the Board of Managers. Philadelphia, PA: Printed by W. S. Young, 1840. 68 p. DLC; ICU; MnU; PPAmP; RPB. 40-3938

Lehmann, C. The geranium waltz. Composed & respectfully dedicated to Miss Elizabeth Hodges by C. Lehmann. Baltimore, MD: F. D. Benteen [184-?] 2 p. ViU. 40-3939

Lehmanowski, Louis Ferdinand. The fall of Warsaw... Annapolis, MD: printed by G. s. M; Kiernan, 1840. 59 p. DLC; MH; MnU; NBuG; PPL. 40-3940

Leicester Academy, Massachusetts Catalogue of the trustees, instructors and students of Leicester Academy, Massachusetts, for the year ending August 12, 1840. Worcester, MA: Printed at the Spy Office, 1840. 12 p. MWHi. 40-3941

Leigh, Percival, 1813-1889. The comic English grammar, a new and facetious introduction to the English tongue. Illustrations by J. Leech. New York: Dick & Fitzgerald [184-?] p. MH. 40-3942

Leighton, Robert. Life of archbishop Lieghton, with brief extracts from his writings. New York: American Tract Society, 1840. 60 p. CtHT; DeWi; IEG; MFiHi; MH; NRSB. 40-3943

Leiris, Mathilde. Geographie par demandes et par responses, a l'usage des colleges et ecoles de la Louisiane. Nouvelle ed., rev. et. augm. par Mme. Leiris. New Orleans, LA: s. l., 1840. 120 p. LNT; LU. 40-3944

Leiser, Isaac. Prayer at 2d Annual Examination of the Sunday School for Israelites in Philadelphia, March 29, 1840. Philadelphia, PA: s. l., 1840. OCHP. 40-3945

Lemoine, Henri, 1786-1854. The Lawrence waltz. Composed for the piano forte. Boston, MA: Prentiss [184-?] MB. 40-3946

Lemoine, Henri, 1786-1854. The Lawrence waltz. Composed for the piano forte. Philadelphia, PA: Fiot [184-?] 2 p. MB. 40-3947

Lemon, Mark, 1809-1870. Grandfather Whitehead. An original drama in two acts. New York: M. Douglas [184-?] 38 p. CSt; MH; NIC. 40-3948

Lemon, Mark, 1809-1870. ... Mind your own business. A drama in three acts. By Mark Lemon. New York: S. French & son [etc., etc., 184-?] 72 p. CSt; MB. 40-3949

Lempriere, John, 1765-1824. Bibliotheca classica; or, Dictionary of all the principal names & terms relating to the geography, topography, history, literature, mythology of antiquity and of the ancients with a chronological table... Rev. by Lorenzo L. Da Ponte and John D. Ogilby. 10th ed. New York: Dean, 1840. 803 p. DLC; GAAD; MB; MH; PPiW; TxU. 40-3950

Leonard, Levi Washburn, 1790?-1864. North American spelling book. 16th revised edition. Keene, NH: G. Tilden, etc., etc., 1840. MH. 40-3951

Leonard, Levi Washburn, 1790?-1864. North American spelling book. 17th revised edition. Keene, NH: G. Tilden, etc., etc., 1840. MH. 40-3952

Lerow, George L. The politician's manual, containing the Declaration of... Independence, the Constitution of the United States and of New York... together with... tables, political and statistical... Second edition. Poughkeepsie, NY: William Wilson, 1840. 175 p. MB; MiD-B; MiGr; NOg. 40-3953

Leslie, Eliza, 1787-1858. Birth day stories, by Miss Eliza Leslie. Philadelphia, PA: Henry F. Anners, printed by King and Baird [1840] 179 p. DLC; MBev; MH; RPB. 40-3954

Leslie, Eliza, 1787-1858. Companion to Miss Leslie's cookery, the housebook; or, a manual of domestic economy, by Miss

Leslie... containing directions for laundry work, removing stains, waiting on company, caring... Philadelphia, PA: s. l. [1840] 436 p. No Loc. 40-3955

Leslie, Eliza, 1787-1858. Directions for cookery, in its various branches. By Miss Leslie. 10th ed... Philadelphia, PA: E. L. Carey & A. Hart, 1840. 468 p. DLC; MdBP; NIC; PP. 40-3956

Leslie, Eliza, 1787-1858. The house book; or, a manual of domestic economy, by Miss Leslie... Philadelphia, PA: Carey and Hart [1840] 428 p. PMA. 40-3957

Leslie, Eliza, 1787-1858. ... The house book; or, A manual of domestic economy. 3d ed. Philadelphia, PA: Carey & Hart, 1840. 436 p. MH; MsNF; MWA; OClW; ViU. 40-3958

Leslie, Eliza, 1787-1858. The house book; or, a manual of domestic economy. 5th ed. Philadelphia, PA: Carey and Hart [1840] 436 p. MH; NcGU; NIC; PP; ViU. 40-3959

Leslie, John, 1766-1832. ... Narrative of discovery and adventure in the polar seas and regions... by Professor Leslie, Professor Jameson and Hugh Murray... New York: Harper & Brothers, 1840. 373 p. CU; LRuL; MMe; PPM; ViR. 40-3960

Lesser, Isaac, 1806-1868. The claims of the Jews to an equality of rights. Illustrated in a series of letters to the editor of the Philadelphia Gazette. Philadelphia, PA: s. l. [1840] 99 p. CtY; DLC. 40-3961

Lesser, Isaac, 1806-1868. Second annual examination of Sunday School of

Mikvih Israel, March 29, 1840, with prayer by I. Lesser, and an address by Moses N. Nathan. Philadelphia, PA: s. l. [1840] 28 p. PHi; PPDrop. 40-3962

Lessons of profit and stories of truth. By the author of "A Teacher's Gift." Boston, MA: New England Sabbath School Union, 1840. 142 p. No Loc. 40-3963

Lester, Charles Edwards, 1815-1890. The Ivory Crucifix, or Statue of Christ, carved... by a monk... on exhibition at the Lafarge Buildings. New York: s. l. [184-?] 12 p. CtY. 40-3964

Let me live remove'd from noise. Airmark my Alford. Baltimore, MD: John Cole [184-?] 1 p. ViU. 40-3965

A letter addressed to the Chairman of the Committee of the Legislature on the license law, by Homo [pseud.] Boston, MA: printed for the author [1840] 8 p. DLC. 40-3966

The letter of General Harrison to the Secretary of War, giving an official account of the affair at Tippecanoe, in 1811, with the remarks of Humphrey Marshall, Esq., on that letter and the transactions it relates to as published in his "History f Kentucky." Cincinnati, OH: printed by Dawson and Fisher, 1840. 16 p. OHiHL; PHi; PPL. 40-3967

Letter on the controversy between Georgia and Maine respecting fugitive slaves. Washington, DC: s. l., 1840. PPL. 40-3968

Letter to a New Hampshire land owner, upon the constitutionality of granting the power of taking private property to railroad corporations. Portsmouth, NH: s. l.

1840. 8 p. DBRE; MH; MH-BA; Nh-Hi; NN. 40-3969

Letter to a Romanist, on the scriptures. As the sole rule of our faith and practice; in answer to Tract No. 6, issued by the Romish church. Published by request. Baltimore, MD: Printed by Sherwood & co., 1840. 12 p. MdBD; Md-Hi. 40-3970

A Letter to everybody. [Boston, MA: s. l., 184-?] 18 p. MH. 40-3971

A Letter to Guilian C. Verplanck, on the reform of the judicial system of this state. By a member of the New York Bar, December, 1839. New York: University Press, John F. Trow, printer, cc1840. 43 p. CtY; IaU-L; MPiB; NbHi; NN. 40-3972

The Letter Writer; containing a great variety of letters on the following subjects: relationship, business, love, courtship, and marriage, friendship, and miscellaneous letters, law forms, etc. Boston, MA: pub. by Charles Gaylord, 1840. 144 p. InGrD; FStPHi; MA; WRichM. 40-3973

Letters to a disbeliever in revivals. Northampton: s. l., 1840. PPL-R. 40-3974

Leutner. The gipsy polka, as performed by the Steyermark Company. [Baltimore, MD; New Orleans, LA: F. D. Benteen; W. T. Mayo, 184-?] 2 p. ViU. 40-3975

Leutner. The gipsy polka. As performed by the Steyermark Company. Composed by Leutner. New York: Gould & Berry [184-?] 2 p. ViU. 40-3976

Levenu, Louis Henry, 1818-1859. On the banks of Guadalquiven. Ballad. Song in the opera of Loretta. [Accomp. for piano forte] Boston, MA: Ditson [184-?] 5 p. DLC; MB. 40-3977

Lever, Charles James, 1806-1872. Arthur O'Leary, his wanderings and ponderings, by his friend Henry Lorrequer [pseud.] Philadelphia, PA: Peterson [184-?] 221 p. KyHop; NNC. 40-3978

Lever, Charles James, 1806-1872. Charles O'Malley. The Irish Dragoon. By Charles Lever. [pseud.] With illustrations by Phiz. Philadelphia, PA: Carey and Hart, 1840-41. 392 p. DeGE; MdBP; NRU. 40-3979

Lever, Charles James, 1806-1872. The confessions of Harry Lorrequer. With numerous illustrations by Phiz [pseud.] Philadelphia, PA: Carey and Hart, 1840. 402 p. DLC. 40-3980

Lever, Charles James, 1806-1872. The confessions of Harry Lorrequer. With numerous illustrations by Phiz [pseud.] Second American ed. Philadelphia, PA: Carey and Hart, 1840. 402 p. CoU; DeGE; NN. 40-3981

Leverett, Frederick Percival, 1803-1836. A new and copious lexicon of the Latin language; compiled chiefly from the magnum totius latinitatis lexicon of Facciolate and Forcellini, and the German works of Scheller and Luenemann. Ed. by F. P. Leverett. Boston, MA: J. H. Wilkins and R. B. Carter [etc.] 1840. 2 v. in 1. ABBS; FOA; MiDU; MnU; TxAuPT. 40-3982

Leverett, Frederick Percival, 1803-1876. The new Latin tutor; or, Exercises in etymology, syntax and prodosy. Compiled chiefly from the best English works.

Philadelphia, PA: U. Hunt [184?] 350 p. ViU. 40-3983

Levings, Noah, 1796-1849. Anti-universaliam; being the substance of a sermon, preached in the North Second-St. Methodist Episcopal Church, on the evening of March 8, 1840, against modern universalism. By Rev. N. Levings. Troy, NY: N. Tuttle, printer, 1840. 40 p. IEG; MWA; NjR; NN; NT. 40-3984

Lewes, George Henry, 1817-1878. The physiology of common life. By George Henry Lewes... In two volumes. New York: D. Appleton & co., 1840. 2 v. NjR. 40-3985

Lewes, George Henry, 1817-1878. Three sisters and her three fortresses. New York: Harper & Bros., 184-? 163 p. DLC. 40-3986

Lewis, Alonzo, 1794-1861. The practical analyst; or, A treatise on Algebra, containing the most useful parts of that science, illustrated by a copious collection of examples. Designed for the use of schools. By Enoch Lewis. 3d ed. Philadelphia, PA: Kimber and Sharpless, 1840. DLC; InLPU; PPL; PSC-Hi; TxU-T. 40-3987

Lewis, Jason. Universalist belief: a friendly epistle to the clergymen of the various Christian sects who hold the doctrine of endless punishment. By Ev. Jason Lewis. Utica, NY: O. Hutchinson, 1840. 24 p. NUt. 40-3988

Lewis, William H. Address, delivered before the Philodemic Society of Georgetown College, D. C., Feb. 22, 1840, to which are prefixed the remarks of William S. Walker, of Mississippi, previous

to his reading the Farewell Address of Washington. Washington, DC: Gales & Seaton, 1840. 21 p. MsWJ; MWH; NN; OCX; PPL; TxDaM. 40-3989

Lewiston Falls, Me. Congregational Church. Articles of faith and covenant... Congregational Church at Lewiston Falls, January 3d and February 21st, 1840... Lewiston Falls, ME?: s. l., 1840. 10 p. MeHi. 40-3990

Lexington, Mass. Order of exercises at the dedication of the Church, lately erected at Lexington [East Village] January 15, 1840... Boston, MA: Office of the Rotary Press [S. N. Dickinson] 1840? p. MH. 40-3991

Liberty or slavery? [Cincinnati, OH: s. l., 184-?] MB. 40-3992

Liddell, Henry George, 1811-1898. A Greek-English lexicon... By Henry George Liddell, M. A. New York: Harper Brothers Publishers, 1840. 1705 p. McSC. 40-3993

Liebe, Edward Ludwig, 1819-1900. Gertrude's dream waltz. Thranen waltzer. Composed for the piano forte by Beethoven. Philadelphia, PA; New York: A. Fiot; W. Dubois [184-?] 2 p. ViU. 40-3994

Lieber, Francis, 1800-1872. Great events described by distinguished historians, chroniclers, and other writers. Translated by Francis Lieber. Boston, MA: Marsh, Capen, Lyon & Webb, 1840. 415 p. CtY; MB; MTop; RPA; ScU. 40-3995

Lieber, Francis, 1800-1872. On international copyright, in a letter to the Hon.

W. C. Preston... by Francis Lieber. New York: Wiley & Putnam, 1840. 67 p. DLC; MHi; NNC; OWoC. 40-3996

Liebig, Justus Freiherr von, 1803-1873. Professor Liebig's complete works on chemistry. Philadelphia, PA: Peterson, 1840. MBU-M; OCGHM; OM; PPCP. 40-3997

Life and Adventure of the Renowned Tom Thumb. New York: Turner & Fisher, 1840. OMC. 40-3998

The life and sketches of curious and odd characters. Boston, MA: Gaylord, 1840. 192 p. MB; MdBLC; MH; MWA. 40-3999

Life in a log cabin with hard cider. [A political pamphlet...] Philadelphia, PA: M. B. Robertson, 1840. 8 p. NN. 40-4000

Life let us cherish. Lord Wellington... New York: Firth & Hall [184-?] 1 p. NN; ViU. 40-4001

... The life of Christopher Columbus, the discoverer of America. Boston, MA: B. H. Green, 1840. 223 p. WHi. 40-4002

Life of General Scott. New York: C. A. Alvord, printer, 184-?] 32 p. CU; CU-B. 40-4003

The life of George Washington. Illus. by tales, sketches and anecdotes adapted to the use of schools with engravings. Philadelphia, PA: Thomas, Cowperthwait & Co., 1840. 174 p. MB; MiU-C; OMC; PHi; ScCh; TNP. 40-4004

Life of Lieut. Col. Blockader, born 1664, died 1729. [Philadelphia, PA] : Presbyterian Board of publication, 1840.

118 p. GDecCT; ICP; NjPT; NNUT; NWM. 40-4005

The life of Major General Andrew Burn of the Royal Marines. 1st edition. Philadelphia, PA: Published by Presbyterian Board of Publication, 1840. 242 p. GDecCT; ICBB; NcDaD; NjPT; PPPrHi; ViRut. 40-4006

The life of Major-general William Henry Harrison: comprising a brief account of his important civil and military services and an accurate description of the council at Vincennes with Tecumseh, as well as the victorires of Tippecanoe, Fort Meigs, and the Thomas. Philadelphia, PA: Grigg and Elliot [etc., etc.] 1840. 96 p. IaU; MiD; MnHi; OSW; RPB. 40-4007

The life of Our Savior. New Haven, CT: Published by S. Babcock, 1840. 8 p. CtY; MHi; MiD. 40-4008

The life of the beautiful and accomplished danseuse, Mademoiselle Fanny Elssler. New York: s. l., 1840. DLC. 40-4009

The life of the Rev. C. F. Swartz, missionary of Trichinopoly and Tanjore in India. New York: Published by the American Tract Society, 1840. 60 p. CtHT; IEG; MNt; MoIn; NbOM. 40-4010

Life of the Rev. George Trosse, of Exeter, England. Philadelphia, PA: Presbyterian board of publication, 1840. 124 p. CSmH; MWA; NNUT; OClW. 40-4011

The life of Washington. Batavia, NY:

W. A. Seaver, 1840. 1 p. CSmH; DLC. 40-4012

The light and truth of slavery. Aaron's history. [Worcester, MA: s. l., 184-?] 48 p. DHU; DLC; MH; MiD-B. 40-4013

Lighton, William Beebey, b. 1805. Narrative of the life and sufferings of Rev. William B. Lighton... Written by himself... Emebllished with engravings. Rev. ed. Boston, MA: Published by the author, printed by S. N. Dickinson, 1840. 228 p. CtMW; DLC; MH; PPL-R; TJoT. 40-4014

Lighton, William Beebey, b. 1805. Narrative of the life and sufferings of Rev. William B. Lighton... 2d ed. Boston, MA: Printed by S. N. Dickinson, 1840. 258 p. MdHi. 40-4015

Lincoln, Abraham, 1809-1865. Speech of Mr. Lincoln at a political discussion, in the hall of the House of Representatives, December, 1839... [Springfield, IL: s. l., 1840] 10 p. CSmH. 40-4016

Lincoln, Almira Hart Lincoln, 1793-1884. Lectures on Botany, practical, elementary and physiological. With an appendix. 10th edition. New York: Published by F. J. Huntington & Co., 1840. 246, 186 p. MBHo; MBP; MSaP; ScC. 40-4017

Lincoln, Levi. 1782-1868. Remarks of Mr. Lincoln, of Massachusetts, in the U. S. House of Representatives, April 6, 1840, in reply to Mr. Ogle, upon... the general appropriation bill... Boston, MA: published at No. 1 Devonshire Street, 1840. 8 p. CSmH; IaHi; MHi; MiD-B; TxU. 40-4018

Lincoln, Levi, 1782-1868. Speech in reply to Mr. Ogle on the general appropriation bill. Delivered in Committee of the Whole... in the House of Representatives, April 16, 1840. Washington, DC: s. l., 1840. 8 p. IU; NcD; NjR; NN; ViU. 40-4019

Lincoln, Luther Barker, 1802-1855. The means of cultivating a classic taste in our common schools; a lecture delivered before the American Institute of Instruction, at its annual session, held in Springfield, August, 1839. Boston, MA: Marsh, Capon, Lyon and Webb, 1840. MDeeP; MH; MWA. 40-4020

Lindsly, Harvey. Medical science and the medical profession in Europe and the United States. An introductory lecture, by Harvey Lindsly... November, 1840. Washington, DC: Peter Force, 1840. 35 p. DLC; IEN-M; MHi; NNNAM; PPL; TNL. 40-4021

Lineback, Charles F. An oration delivered in St. John's day, June 24, 1840, before a large assembly of members of the Ancient and Honourable Fraternity of Free and Accepted Mason and citizens of the city of New York in the church corner of Broome and Norfolk streets [at the request of Munn Lodge no. 5] New York; C. C. and E. Child, printers, 1840. 12 p. IaCrM; NNFM. 40-4022

Lingard, John, 1771-1851. Catechistical instructions on the doctrines and worship of the Catholic Church... by John Lingard, D. D. New York: Patrick S. Casserly & Sons [1841] 139 p. DLC; MdBS; MH-AH; MoSU. 40-4023

Linley, George, 1798-1865. Come to the dance. A favorite song. Written, composed and arranged for the piano forte by George Linley... Philadelphia, PA: A. Fiot [184-?] 5 p. ViU. 40-4024

Linley, George, 1798-1865. The corsair's farewell. Song. [Bar. Accomp. for piano forte.] New York: Riley [184-?] 3 p. MB. 40-4025

Linley, George, 1798-1865. The dining gentleman. Written and composed by George Linley, Esqr. Most respectfully dedicated to all lovers of good company. New York: Firth & Hall [184-?] 5 p. ViU. 40-4026

Linley, George, 1798-1865. The heart of they Norah is breaking for thee. An Irish ballad. Sung by Mr. John Templeton. Written and composed by George Linly [!] Esq. New York: Atwill [184-?] 5 p. ViU. 40-4027

Linley, George, 1798-1865. I do not ask to offer. A song. Boston, MA: Ditson & Co. [184-?] 5 p. MB. 40-4028

Linley, George, 1798-1865. I mourn thee in silence. [Song. With accompaniment for piano forte] Boston, MA: Ditson [184-?] 5 p. MB. 40-4029

Linley, George, 1798-1865. I've left the snow-clad hills. [Song. By G. Linley. With accopaniment for piano forte] New York: Holt [184-?] 6 p. MB. 40-4030

Linley, George, 1798-1865. Kate O'Shane. Composed by George Linley. Philadelphia, PA: Osbourns music saloon [184-?] 5 p. ViU. 40-4031

Linley, George, 1798-1865. The night before the bridal. [Song. Accomp. for piano forte] Boston, MA: Ditson [184-?] 4 p. MB. 40-4032

Linley, George, 1798-1865. Passing away. Song. Boston, MA: Ditson [184-?] 2 p. MB. 40-4033

Linley, George, 1798-1865. Thou art gone from my gaze; or, The Spirit of love keeps a watch over me. Ballad. Words & music by G. Linley... Philadelphia, PA; New York: A. Fiot; W. Dubois [184-?] 5 p. ViU. 40-4034

Linley, George, 1798-1865. To meet again with thee. A favorite ballad... arranged for piano forte. Philadelphia, PA: Meignen & Co. [184-?] 5 p. MB. 40-4035

Linley, George, 1798-1865. Years have roll'd since we did part; or, To meet again with thee. A favorite ballad. Written, composed and arranged for the piano by George Linley. Philadelphia, PA: Lee & Walker [184-?] 3 p. ViU. 40-4036

Linter, Ricardo. Jenny's Lind's English polka. [For piano forte] Boston, MA: Ditson [184-?] 5 p. MB. 40-4037

Litchfield, Edwin Clark. Motives to effort in America. Address before the Young Men's Association for mutual improvement in West Troy. Troy, NY: s. l., 1840. 31 p. MBC; NCH; NIC. 40-4038

The Literalist. A collection of essays on the second coming of Christ and related subjects. Philadelphia, PA: Orrin Rogers, 1840-42. 5 v. CtHC; DLC; ICU; NjPT; PWW. 40-4039

The Literary casket. A gift for all sessions. New York: Moore & Atkins [1840?] 206 p. MB. 40-4040

Literary Institute and Gymnasium, Pembroke, N. H. Catalogue of the officers, instructors and students of the peoples Literary Institute and Gymnasium, at Pembroke, N. H... Concord, NH: printed by Asa McFarland, 1840. 22 p. MHaHi. 40-4041

Literary pearl and weekly village messenger. Vol. I, no. 1-13 [Nove. 18, 1840-Feb. 13, 1841] Charlton, NY: s. l., 1840-41. v. MH. 40-4042

The Literary repository. Devoted to polite literature; such as moral and sentimental tales, original communications, biography, traveling sketches, amusing miscellany, humorous and historical anecdotes, poetry, &c... v. 1, Jan. 1, 1840-Dec. 12, 1840. Lowell, MA: YHoldrett, 1840. v. ICN. 40-4043

Literary Souvenir; a Christmas and New Year's present for MDCCCXL. Philadelphia, PA: E. L. Carey and A. Hart, 1840. 226 p. CtMW; KKcBT; PPL; ScC; ViRU. 40-4044

Littell's select reviews of foreign literature. Philadelphia, PA: E. Littell & Co., 1840. 440 p. KyLoN; PHi; PP. 40-4045

Little Bally of the Sabbath School... New York: Amer. Tract Soc. [184-?] 16 p. MB. 40-4046

Little Bally of the Sabbath School... Portland, ME: Bailey & Noyes [ca. 1840?] 16 p. CtY. 40-4047

The little book of trades, describing some plain things. New Haven, CT: Published by S. Babcock, 1840. 8 p. CtY. 40-4048

Little Helen; or, A day in the life of a naughty girl. New Haven, CT: S. Babcock, 1840. 16 p. CtY. 40-4049

The little keepsake; or, Easy lessons in words of one syllable. New Haven, CT: Published by S. Babcock [184-?] 16 p. CtY. 40-4050

Little Lucy; or, The plesant day; an example for little girls. New Haven, CT: Printed and published by S. Babcock, 1840. 16 p. CtY; MH; NN; NUt. 40-4051

Little present. Northampton: J. Metcalf, 1840. 8 p. ICU; MiHi. 40-4052

The Little Sisters; or, Emma and Caroline. New Haven, CT: Published by S. Babcock [1840?] 16 p. CtY. 40-4053

Little Sophie. The Bethrothed. A Christmas story. By Sophia Little. Pawtucket: Printed by R. W. Potter, 1840. 48 p. RHi; RPaw. 40-4054

A little story for a little boy. Northampton: J. Metcalf, 1840. 8 p. WHi. 40-4055

Little Susan and her lamb. Boston, MA: s. l. [184-?] p. MB. 40-4056

A little toy for girl or boy. New York: Printed and sold by Mahlon Day [184-?] 8 p. NN. 40-4057

Lives and exploits of the most distinguished voyagers, adventurers, and discoverers in Europe, Asia, Africa, American, the South Seas, and Polar Regions... Illustrated by nuemerous engavings... by J. A. St. John, Sir Hugh Murray, and others. Hartford, CT:

Huntington, 1840. 660 p. CtMW; MLow; NbU; NNA. 40-4058

Lives of Alexander Wilson and Captain John Smith. New York: Published by Harper and Brothers, 1840. 403 p. NAlbi. 40-4059

The Lives of Christopher Columbus, the doscovered of America, and Americus Vespucuis, the Florentine. With engravings. Boston, MA: Marsh, Capen, Lyon & Webb, 1840. 278 p. DLC; ICN; MH; MTew; PLFM. 40-4060

Lives of Robert Fulton, Joseph Warren, Henry Hudson, and Father Marquette. New York: Harper & Brothers, 1840. 386 p. MSbo; NAlbi; NGlc; NLock. 40-4061

Lives of Sir William Phils, Israel Putnam, Lucretia Maria Davidson, and David Rittenhouse. New York: Harper & Brothers, 1840. 398 p. NAlbi; NLock; RPE. 40-4062

The Lives of Vasso Nuniz... and Francisco Pizarro... Boston, MA: Marsh, Capen, Lyon and Webb, 1840. 276 p. DLC; ICN; MH; MWA. 40-4063

Livius, Titus. The history of Rome. By Titus Livius. Translated from the original, with notes and illsutations, by George Bake, A. M... A new edition, carefully corrected and revised. Philadelphia, PA: Thomas Wardle, 1840. 2 v. DLC; GAuY; MdBD; NNF. 40-4064

Locke, John, 1632-1704. Locke's Essays on Human Understanding, by John Locke. [S. l.: Published by James Kay, Junr. and Brothers, 1840] 523 p. ArGe. 40-4065

Lockhart, John Gibson. History of Napoleon Buonaparte, by J. G. Lockhart. New York: Harper and brothers, 1840. 2 v. DLC; GMM; IEG; InRch; KyU. 40-4066

Loco-Focoism; as displayed in the Boston Magazine against Schools and Ministers... [Albany, NY: s. l., 1840] 32 p. MB; NjR. 40-4067

Loder, Edward James, 1813-1865. Ah, no! you'll not forget me! From the grand opera of Giselle; or, The night dancers. Composed by Edward I. Loder. New York: Atwil [184-?] 4 p. ViU. 40-4068

Loder, Edward James, 1813-1865. I'll be gay, while I may. Cavatina. Composed by Edward J. Loder. Boston, MA: Oliver Ditson [184-?] 6 p. MB; ViU. 40-4069

Loder, Edward James, 1813-1865. Oh little daisy growing wild. Ballad in the old English style. Sung by Mrs. Loder. Composed by E. J. Loder. New York: Hewitt & Jaques [184-?] 6 p. ViU. 40-4070

Loder, Edward James, 1813-1865. The old house at home. A ballad. From the opera of Francis the First... [the accomp.] arranged for the guitar by Henry Chadwick. Boston, MA: Ditson [184-?] 2 p. MB. 40-4071

Loder, Edward James, 1813-1865. Philip, the Falconer. Song. Written by W. H. Bellamy, Esqre.; composed by Edward J. Loder. Philadelphia, PA; New York; Cincinnati, OH; Boston, MA: E. Ferrett & co. [184-?] 6 p. ViU. 40-4072

Loder, Edward James, 1813-1865. A song of the Oak. The poetry by H. T. Chorley, esq.; music by Edward J. Loder.

3d edition. New York: Atwill [184-?] 5 p. ViU. 40-4073

Loder, George, 1816-1868. Camp Glee. Composed and dedicated to the New York City Guards Glee Club, and performed by the Class of the New York Vocal Institute in presence of the Mayor and corporation, by George Loder. New York: J. L. Hewitt [184-?] 5 p. ViU. 40-4074

Lodi-Manufacturing Company, Lodi, N. Y. An Act to incorporate the Lodi Manufacturing Company... passed 6th February, 1840... New York: Printed by H. Cassidy, 1840. 35 p. MB; MH-BA; NN. 40-4075

Loeke, Richard Adams, 1800-1871. Magnetism and astronomy. A lecture. [New York, 184-?] 8 p. NN. 40-4076

The Log cabin. v. 1 [no. 10-14, 17-27] July 4-Aug. 1, 22-Oct. 31, 1840. New York: s. l., 1840-41. 2 v. in 1. CtMW; DLC; ICU; PHi; VtBrt. 40-4077

The Log cabin advocate. From the commencement, Vol. 1, no. 1, Baltimore, March 21st to Dec. 15th, 1840. The issue of Dec. 15th, 1840, contains the electoral vote on the election of President Wm. Henry Harrison, and with portraits. Baltimore, MD: s. l., 1840. v. DLC; GEU. 40-4078

Log cabin anecdotes. Illustrated incidents in the life of Gen. William Henry Harrison. New York: s. l., 1840. v. MBAt; RPB. 40-4079

The Log cabin minstrel; or, Tippecanoe songster, containing a selection of songs, original and selected... Compiled, published and arranged by a member of the Roxbury Democratic Whig association. Roxbury: Pub. at the Patriot and Democrat office, 1840. 60 p. MB; MH; OClWHi. 40-4080

The Log cabin patriot. V. 1 [no. 1-12] Aug. 7-Nov. 17, 1840. East Bridgewater, MA: s. l., 1840. 48 p. DLC. 40-4081

The Log cabin song book. A collection of popular and patriotic songs... dedicated to the friends of Harrison and Tyler... New York: Log Cabin Office, 1840. 72 p. DLC; In; MiD-B; PU; RPB; WHi. 40-4082

The Log cabin song book. A compendium selection of the most popular Tippecanoe melodies. Springfield, OH: J. R. Crain, 1840. 96 p. RPB. 40-4083

The Log cabin songster; being a collection of the most popular Tippecanoe song. Respectfully dedicated to the friends of Harrison & democracy. Steubenville, OH: Printed by J. & R. C. Wilson, 1840. 64 p. RPB. 40-4084

Lohman, Anna Trow, 1812-1878. Trial of Madame Restell. [New York, 184-?] 48 p. ViU. 40-4085

Long Island Railroad Company. Act to incorporate the Long Island Railroad Company. Passed Apr. 24, 1834. [Albany, NY: s. l., 1840] 16 p. CSmH; MB; Mh-BA; NBHi; NN. 40-4086

Longfellow, Henry Wadsworth, 1807-1882. Manual de proverbes dramatiques. 3d ed. Boston, MA: Munroe et compagnie, 1840. 333 p. MB; MSa; NN; NRU; PPL; ViU. 40-4087

Longfellow, Henry Wadsworth, 1807-1882. The song of Hiawatha, by Henry Wadsworth Longfellow. Boston, MA: Ticknor & Fields, 1840. 316 p. NBebg. 40-4088

Longfellow, Henry Wadsworth, 1807-1882. Voices of the Night. 2d ed. Cambridge, MA: J. Owen, 1840. 144 p. MB; NjP; OClW; PLFM; RPB. 40-4089

Longfellow, Henry Wadsworth, 1807-1882. Voices of the Night. 3d ed. Cambridge, MA: John Owen, 1840. 144 p. MB; MBAt; PPL-R. 40-4090

Longfellow, Henry Wadsworth, 1807-1882. Voices of the Night. 4th ed. Cambridge, MA: published by John Owen, 1840. 144 p. MHW; NRU; NRU-W. 40-4091

Longstreet, Augustus Baldwin, 1790-1870. Address delivered before the faculty and students of Emory College, Oxford, Ga., by A. B. Longstreet. Augusta, GA: W. T. Thompson, printer, 1840. 22 p. CtY. 40-4092

Longstreet, Augustus Baldwin, 1790-1870. Georgia scenes, characters, incidents, etc., in the first half century of the republic. By a creative Georgian. With the original illustrations. New edition from new plates. New York: Harper & brothers, publishers [1840] GFtv; InU; OkEnP; TxLocC; ViRJ. 40-4093

Longstreet, Augustus Baldwin, 1790-1870. Georgia scenes, characters, incidents, etc., in the first half century of the republic. By a creative Georgian. With original illustrations. 2nd ed. New York: Harper & brothers, 1840. AB; GEU; KyU; MWA; RPA. 40-4094

Longworth's American almanac, New York Register, and city directory, for the sixty-fifth year of American independence... New York: published by Thomas Longworth, 1840. 732, 36 p. MBNE; NjR; NNMuCN; NNS; RNHi. 40-4095

Loomis, Aretas, 1790-1857. A sermon on the mode of Christian baptism; delivered at Bennington East Village, Vt. December 29, 1839. Troy: printed at the Budget office, 1840. 15 p. NBuG. 40-4096

Loomis, D. W., Mrs. A memoir of Harriet Eliza Snow... Boston, MA: Mass. S. S. Society, 1840. 288 p. InCW; DLC; MBC; MH; MWA. 40-4097

Loomis' Magazine Almanac for 1841. Calculations for Sanford C. Hill. Pittsburgh, PA: Luke Loomis [1840] p. MnHi; MWA; PSeW; WHi. 40-4098

Lord, John. A sermon on the duty of public worship; preached at New Marlborough, Mass., February 23, 1840. By Rev. John Lord, A. M. Published by request. Lenox, MA: Charles Montague, printer, 1840. 24 p. MBC; MH-AH; MPiB. 40-4099

Lord McDonald's Reed. Baltimore, MD: Willig's music store [184-?] 1 p. ViU. 40-4100

Lossing, Benson John, 1813-1891. History of the fine arts. By Benson J. Lossing. New York: Harper and bros., 1840. 330 p. MCli; NcWsS; NN; UU; VtWinds. 40-4101

Lossing, Benson John, 1813-1891. Outline history of the fine arts. Embracing a view of the rise, progress, and influence of the arts among different nations, ancient and modern, with notices of the character and works of many celebrated artists... By Benson J. Lossing. New York: Harper and brothers, 1840. 330 p. GMM; IaDaA; KyHi; NhD; RPA. 40-4102

Lothrop, Samuel Kirkland, 1804-1886. A sermon preached at the church in Brattle Square, on Sunday morning, January 19, 1840, on the destruction of the Lexington, by fire, January 13th. By S. K. Lothrop, pastor of the church. Published by request. Third edition. Boston, MA: John H. Eastburn, printer, 1840. 24 p. CBPac; CtSoP; ICMe; MeB; MWA; Nh. 40-4103

Louel, H. The dawn waltz. Composed for the piano forte. Boston, MA: Ditson [184-?] 3 p. MB. 40-4104

Louisiana. Laws, statutes, etc. Acts passed at the second session of the fourteenth Legislature of the State of Louisiana, began and held in the City of New Orleans, on the 6th day of January, 1841. Published by authority. New Orleans, LA: Bullitt, Mange & co., State Printer, 1840?. 142 p. IaU-L; MdBB; Nv; T; Wa-L. 40-4105

Louisiana. Legislature. Joint Committee on Banks & Banking. Documents relative to the investigation of Banks, by the Joint Committee of the House of the Louisiana Legislature, 1840. [New Orleans, LA: s. l., 1840] 191 p. LNHT; LU. 40-4106

Louisiana Merchant's & Planter's Almanac, for the year of our Lord and Savior 1841. By Thomas Spofford. New York: Published by David Felt & Co., 1840. 30 p. NcU. 40-4107

Louisville, Ky. Catholic Benevolent Society. The Constitution of the Catholic Benevolent Society, of Louisville, Kentucky, 1840. Louisville, KY: s. l., 1840. 12 p. MHi. 40-4108

Louisville, Ky. Church of Christ. Constitution of the Church of Christ, in the Unitarian Society, adapted June 14, 1840. Boston, MA: H. L. Devereux, 1840. 11 p. MBC; MH. 40-4109

Louisville, Ky. Medical Institute. Catalogue of the officers and students of The Medical Institute of the City of Louisville, Jan., 1840. Louisville, KY: Prentice & Weissinger, 1840. 16 p KyU; MBAt; MHi. 40-4110

Louisville Church of Christ in a constitution adopted January 4, 1840. Boston, MA: s. l., 1840. 24 p OCHP. 40-4111

Louisville march and quick step. Composed for & dedicated to Mrs. A. Bowen, by W. C. P. New York: FIrth & Hall [184-?] 2 p. NcD; ViU. 40-4112

Love-spell waltz. Arranged for the guitar. By B. G. Ginoud. New York: Christmore [184-?] 1 p. MB. 40-4113

Lovell, George William, 1804-1878. ... Look before you leap; or, Wooing and weddings. A comedy in five acts. By George W. Lovell... With the stage business, cast of characters, costumes, relative positions, etc. New York: S. French & son [etc., etc., 184-?] 79 p. CSt; MH 40-4114

Lover, Samuel, 1797-1868. The angel

wing. [Song. With accompaniment for piano forte] Boston, MA: Ditson [184-?] 5 p. MB. 40-4115

Lover, Samuel. 1797-1868. Atwill's collection of Lover's songs. Written and composed by Samuel Lover. New York: Atwill's Music Salon, [184-?] 12 v. in 1. NN. 40-4116

Lover, Samuel. 1797-1868. Dear love and native land, farewell; song. Written and adapted to an admired Irish air. by Samuel Lover. Philadelphia: A. Fiot, [184-?] 2 l. DLC; MH. 40-4117

Lover, Samuel, 1797-1868. The fairy boy. From the Songs of the superstitions of Ireland. Written & composed by S. Lover, Esqr. Philadelphia, PA: A. Fiot [184-?] 5 p. ViU. 40-4118

Lover, Samuel, 1797-1868. The fairy boy. From the Songs of the superstitions of Ireland. Written & composed by S. Lover. [With accompaniment for the piano forte] Philadelphia, PA: Willig [184-?] 5 p. MB; MH. 40-4119

Lover, Samuel, 1797-1868. The fountain and the flower; ballad. Written and composed by Samuel Lover. New York: Firth and Hall [184-?] 7 p. DLC; ViU. 40-4120

Lover, Samuel, 1797-1868. The four-leaved shamrock. Song. With accompaniment for te piano forte] New York: Firth & Hall [184-?] 7 p. MB. 40-4121

Lover, Samuel, 1797-1868. Gondolier, row! Barcarole, in the musical drama of the Greek boy, Written and composed by Samuel Lover. New York: Hewitt and James [184-?] 5 p. NcD. 40-4122

Lover, Samuel, 1797-1868. Hark to my lute. Serenade. Written & composed by Samuel Lover, Esq. New York: Firth & Hall [184-?] 5 p. ViU. 40-4123

Lover, Samuel, 1797-1868. The land of the west. From the Songs of Rory O'More. Song. Written, composed and arranged for the piano forte by Saml. Lover, Esq. Baltimore, MD: Geo. Willig, Junr. [184-?] 5 p. ViU. 40-4124

Lover, Samuel, 1797-1868. The land of the west. From the Songs of Rory O'More. Song. The accomp. for the guitar by L. Meignen] Philadelphia, PA: Fiot [184-?] 3 p. MB. 40-4125

Lover, Samuel, 1797-1868. The Maydew. A popular ballad from the songs of the superstitions of Ireland. As sung by Mrs. Wood. Composed by S. Lover. Philadelphia, PA: Lee & Walker [184-?] 5 p. ViU. 40-4126

Lover, Samuel, 1797-1868. The Maydew. Sung by Mrs. Wood. Taken from the songs of the superstitions of Ireland. Written & composed by Samuel Lover, Esq. Boston, MA: C. Bradlee [184-?] 5 p. ViU. 40-4127

Lover, Samuel, 1797-1868. Molly Bawn. Irish ballad. Sung by M. Balfe in the comic operetta of Il Paddy Whack in Italia. Written & composed by Samuel Lover, Esq. Boston, MA: Oliver Ditson [184-?] 5 p. MB; ViU. 40-4128

Lover, Samuel, 1797-1868. My dark hair'd girl. Ballad. With symphonies & accompaniments by Charles E. Horn. Words and melody by Samuel Lover, Esqr. Baltimore, MD: F. D. Benteen [184-?] 3 p. ViU. 40-4129

Lover, Samuel, 1797-1868. My dark hair'd girl. Ballad... The symphonies & accompaniments by Charles E. Horn. [With accompaniment for the piano forte] Philadelphia, PA: Blake [184-?] 2 p. MB. 40-4130

Lover, Samuel, 1797-1868. My mother dear. A favorite ballad. Written & composed for the piano forte. Boston, MA: Ditson [184-?] 2 p. MB. 40-4131

Lover, Samuel, 1797-1868. Oh! don't you remember? Sung with great applause by Mr. Walton & Miss de Bar in the White Horse of the Peppers. Also by Messrs. Howard & Dempster at their concerts. Written & adapted by Samuel Lover, Esqr. Philadelphia, PA: John F. Nunns [184-?] 7 p. ViU. 40-4132

Lover, Samuel, 1797-1868. Rory O'Moore. A favorite ballad. As sung by Tyrone Power, Esqr. Partly composed and arranged by Samuel Lover. Boston, MA: Oliver Ditson [184-?] 3 p. ViU. 40-4133

Lover, Samuel, 1797-1868. Rory O'Moore. An Irish melody. [Song. With accompaniment for piano forte] Boston, MA: Prentiss [184-?] p. MB. 40-4134

Lover, Samuel, 1797-1868. Under the rose... [Song. With accompaniment for piano forte] Arranged by Chas. E. Horn. Boston, MA: Bradlee [184-?] 2 p. MB. 40-4135

Lover, Samuel, 1797-1868. What will you do, love? [Song. With accompaniment for piano forte] Philadelphia, PA: Lee & Walker [184-?] 7 p. MB. 40-4136

Lover, Samuel, 1797-1868. Widow Machree. From the songs of Handy Andy. Sung by Henry Phillips. Written & composed by Samuel Lover, Esqr. Baltimore, MD: F. D. Benteen [184-?] 3 p. ViU. 40-4137

Lover, Samuel, 1797-1868. The Widow Machree. Written & composed by Samuel Lover. Boston, MA: Oliver Ditson [184-?] 4 p. ViU. 40-4138

Lover, Samuel, 1797-1868. Widow Machree. Sung with enthusiastic applause by Mr. Collins. Also by the author in his Irish Evenings. Written & composed by Samuel Lover. Philadelphia, PA; New York: A. Fiot; W. Dubois [184-?] 5 p. ViU. 40-4139

Lowell, Joshua Adams, 1801-1874. Speech of Lowell, of Maine, on the independent treasury bill... In the House of Representatives, May 27th and 28th, 1840. [S. l., n. p., 1840] 15 p. MdHi; MiU-C; ViU. 40-4140

Lowell, Mass. Charter. The charter and the revised ordinances of the City of Lowell; together with sundry laws of the Commonwealth. Published under the authority of the City Council. Lowell MA: Leonard Huntress, Printer, 1840 133 p. MLow. 40-4141

Lowell, Mass. John Street Church. By laws and act of incorporation of the proprietors of the John St. Church Lowell, Mass. Lowell, MA: s. l., 1840. 1' p. MBC. 40-4142

Lowell, Mass. Missionary Society. Firs Annual Report of the Treasurer an Secretary. Lowell, MA: s. l., 1840. 23 MHi. 40-4143

Lowell, Mass. Municipal register, 1840-69. Lowell, MA: s. l., 1840-69. 4 v. MB. 40-4144

Lowell, Mass. Rules and Orders of the City Council and list of Officers of the City of Lowell. Lowell, MA: L. Huntress, 1840. 16 p. MLow. 40-4145

Lowell, Mass. Worthen St. Baptist Church. Persons belonging to the church, Sept. 1, 1840. Lowell, MA: A. B. F. Hildreth, 1840. 16 p. MH. 40-4146

Lowell Dispensary. Act of Incorporation, Constitution and By-Laws of the Lowell Dispensary... Lowell, MA: Leonard Huntress, Printer, 1840. 9 p. MH. 40-4147

Lowrie, J. C. Two years in upper India. New York: Carter, 1840. 40-4148

Lube, Denis George. An analysis of the principles of equity pleading, containing a compendium of the pratice of the High court of Chancery, and the foundatoin of its rules. By D. G. Lube... With notes and references to American cases. By J. D. Wheeler... 1st American from the last London ed. New York; Albany, NY: Banks, Gould & Co., 1840. Ct; MAnP; NcU; PU-L; WaU-L. 40-4149

Lucas, F., Jr., firm, Bookseller. Lucas illustrations. [Baltimore, 184-?] 48 l. MdBP; NIC. 40-4150

Lucas, Frederick, 1812-1855. Reasons for becoming a Roman Catholic; addressed to the Society of Friends. Cincinnati, OH: Catholic Society for the Diffusion of Religious Knowledge, 1840. 80 p. DGU; MdBS; MoSU; OCX; PPL. 40-4151

Luckey, Samuel, 1791-1869. The Wesleyan Methodists, a Christian church. A sermon, preached in... New York, Oct. 25, 1839... By S. Luckey, D. D. New York: Published by T. Mason and G. Lane... at the Conference office, J. Collord, printer, 1840. 40 p. NNMHi. 40-4152

Lucy Long and Mary Blans. Baltimore, MD; New Orleans, LA: F. D. Benteen; W. T. Mayo [184-?] 1 p. ViU. 40-4153

Lucy Long's nigga humming bird. New York and Philadelphia: Turner and Fisher [1840?] 40 p. NBu. 40-4154

Ludlow, Henry Gilbert. Our happy form of government. A thanksgiving sermon, preached in the Church Street Church, New Haven, Nov. 19, 1840. New Haven, CT: Printed by B. L. Hamlen, 1840. 23 p. CtY; MB; MHi; OCl; PPPr-Hi. 40-4155

Ludwick Institute, Philadelphia. The constitution of the Philadelphia Society for the Establishment and Support of Charity Schools. Incorporated the eighth day of September, 1801. Philadelphia, PA: Printed by Order of the Society, 1840. 18 p. MnHi; PHi; PPM; PU; WHi. 40-4156

Lunn, Joseph, 1784-1863. ... Fish out of water; a farce in two acts. By Joseph Lunn... correctly printed from the most approved acting copy... New York; Philadelphia, PA: Turner & Fisher [184-?] 38 p. CtY; MB; PU; RPB; ViU. 40-4157

Lunt, William Parson, 1805-1857. Two discourses, delivered September 29, 1839, on occasion of the two hundredth anniversary of the gathering of the First

Congregational Church, Quincy. By William P. Lunt. Boston, MA: James Munroe and Company, 1840. 147 p. CBPac; ICU; MNBedf; MNtcA; PHi; WHi. 40-4158

Luther, Martin, 1483-1546. A commentary on Saint Paul's epistle to the Galatians. Philadelphia, PA: S. S. Miles, 1840. n. p. ICP; MnSM; NcWsS; NjNbS; PLT. 40-4159

Luther, Martin, 1483-1546. Small catechism. Tr. from the original pub. by the General Synod of the Lutheran Church. 3d ed. Baltimore, MD: Pub. Rooms, 1840. 72 p. PPLT. 40-4160

Lyell, Charles, 1797-1875. Principles of Geology; or, The modern changes of the earth and its inhabitants... Boston, MA: Hilliard, Gray & Co., 1840. 3 v. ICU. 40-4161

Lynch, Eugene H. Address delivered before the Philomathean society of Mount Saint Mary's college, by Eugene H. Lynch, esq. Baltimore, MD: Printed by John Murphy, 1840. 27 p. GAM-R; MdHi; MH; OCX; PPL; RPB. 40-4162

Lynch, William Francis, 1801-1865. Narrative of the United States' expedition to the River Jordon and the dead sea. Philadelphia, PA: Lea & Blanchard, 1840. MB-FA. 40-4163

Lyon, James A. The reiterated charges made by Rev. J. W. Cunningham, answered and refuted by Rev. James A. Lyon, pastor of the Presbyterian Church at Rogersville, E. Ten. Jonesboro, TN: printed at the Sentinel office, 1840. 30 p. KyLoS; PPPrHi; T. 40-4164

Lyon, James A. To the public! Richmond, Nov. 1, 1840. Handbill, with letter from W. H. Harrison, denying his authorship of a letter written to Arthur Tappan and others, in which he is made to avow himself an Abolitionist. [Richmond, VA: s. l., 1840] p. ViU. 40-4165

Lytton, Edward George Earle Lytton Bulwer-Lytton, 1803-1873. Ernest Maltravers. Alice; or, the mysteries. By Edgar Bulwer Lytton. Boston, MA: Aldine Book Publishing Co. 1840. 2 v. IRivfT; MLud. 40-4166

Lytton, Edward George Earle Lytton Bulwer-Lytton, 1803-1873. Ernest Maltravers. By E. G. Lytton, E. Lytton, & B. Lytton, 1st baron. Boston, MA: Printed by Dana Estes & Co., 1840. 407 p. UOW; WaU. 40-4167

Lytton, Edward George Earle Lytton Bulwer-Lytton, 1803-1873. Ernest Maltravers. Chicago, IL: Rand McNally & Co., 1840. 455 p. KyCov. 40-4168

Lytton, Edward George Earle Lytton Bulwer-Lytton, 1803-1873. Ernest Maltravers. New York: E. P. Dutton & Co., publishers, 1840. 440 p. NSy. 40-4169

Lytton, Edward George Earle Lytton Bulwer-Lytton, 1803-1873. Ernest Maltravers, and Alice, or, the mysteries. By Edward Bulwer Lytton. New York: Lovell, Coryell & Company, 1840. 853 p. PL; WyU. 40-4170

Lytton, Edward George Earle Lytton Bulwer-Lytton, 1803-1873. Ernest Maltravers. New York: G. Routledge, 1840. 406 p. IaWav; MMel; TxHuT. 40-4171

Lytton, Edward George Earle Lytton Bulwer-Lytton, 1803-1873. Eugene Aram. A serious drama in 3 acts. Boston, MA: Estes, 1840. 106 p. MB. 40-4172

Lytton, Edward George Earle Lytton Bulwer-Lytton, 1803-1873. Eugene Aram. A tale, by Edward Bulwer Lytton [Lord Lytton] New York: Hurst & company, publishers [1840] 392 p. IU; LU; MH; MsAb; TNY. 40-4173

Lytton, Edward George Earle Lytton Bulwer-Lytton, 1803-1873. Eugene Aram. A tale, by the Right Hon. Lord Lytton. With a frontispiece by Hablot [!] K. Browne. New York: Published by George Routledge and Sons, 1840. 296 p. MoCg. 40-4174

Lytton, Edward George Earle Lytton Bulwer-Lytton, 1803-1873. Godolphin. New York: Harper, 1840. 2 v. CtY; IaU; MH; NcD; PU. 40-4175

Lytton, Edward George Earle Lytton Bulwer-Lytton, 1803-1873. Harold. The last days of the saxon kings. By Edward Bulwer Lytton. New York: A. L. Burt Company, publishers, 1840. 427 p. PPPCity 40-4176

Lytton, Edward George Earle Lytton Bulwer-Lytton, 1803-1873. Harold. The last days of the saxon kings. By the Hon. Lord Lytton. New York: Published by George Routledge and Sons, 1840. 338 p. MoCg. 40-4177

Lytton, Edward George Earle Lytton Bulwer-Lytton, 1803-1873. The lady of Lyons; or, Love and pride. A play in five acts. By Lord Lytton... New York: S. French [184-?] 59 p. CSt; NN. 40-4178

Lytton, Edward George Earle Lytton Bulwer-Lytton, 1803-1873. ... The lady of Lyons; or, Love and pride. A play in five acts. By Lord Lytton... Philadelphia: PA: s. l. [184-?] 63 p. PBm. 40-4179

Lytton, Edward George Earle Lytton Bulwer-Lytton, 1803-1873. [The last days of Pompeii] Buy me flowers. Sung by the blind girl. New York: Hewitt & Co. [184-?] 3 p. MB; MBAt. 40-4180

Lytton, Edward George Earle Lytton Bulwer-Lytton, 1803-1873. Money; a comedy in five acts. By Sir Edward Bulwer Lytton. New York: T. H. French, etc., etc. [1840] 72 p. MH; NIC; NNC; OCl. 40-4181

Lytton, Edward George Earle Lytton Bulwer-Lytton, 1803-1873. My novel; or, Varieties in English life. By Edward Bulwer Lytton. New York: George Routledge and Sons, 1840. 460 p. LAlS; NcEcCN. 40-4182

Lytton, Edward George Earle Lytton Bulwer-Lytton, 1803-1873. Novels. New York: George Routledge & Sons, 1840-72. 25 v. NTaM. 40-4183

Lytton, Edward George Earle Lytton Bulwer-Lytton, 1803-1873. Paul Clifford. By Sir Edward Bulwer Lytton. New York: George Routledge & Sons, 1840. 460 p. LAlS; MQ; MoCg. 40-4184

Lytton, Edward George Earle Lytton Bulwer-Lytton, 1803-1873. Richelieu; or, The conspiracy, a play in five acts. By Lord Lytton. New York: S. French [184-?] 69 p. CSt. 40-4185

Lytton, Edward George Earle Lytton Bulwer-Lytton, 1803-1873. Richelieu;

or, The conspiracy! A play in five acts. By
E. Lytton Bulwer. 1st American from the
5th London ed. New York: Turner &
Fisher, etc., etc. [184-?] 96 p. MH. 40-
4186

Lytton, Edward George Earle Lytton
Bulwer-Lytton, 1803-1873. Rienzi, the
last of the Roman tribunes. New York:
George Routledge & Sons, 1840. 509 p.
REd. 40-4187

Lytton, Edward George Earle Lytton
Bulwer-Lytton, 1803-1873. Rienzi, the
pilgrims of the Rhine... Boston, MA: Aldine bk. pub. co. [1840] 2 v. in 1. GAGT.
40-4188

Lytton, Edward George Earle Lytton
Bulwer-Lytton, 1803-1873. Rienzi. The
Pilgrims of the Rhine, and the coming
race. New York: University Press, 1840.
2 v. in 1. PLeb. 40-4189

Lytton, Edward George Earle Lytton
Bulwer-Lytton, 1803-1873. ... The sea-
captain, or, the birthright! A drama in
five acts. By Sir E. Lytton Bulwer... 1st
American ed. Philadelphia, PA; New
York: Turner & Fisher [ca. 1840] 68 p.
CSt; DLC; IU; PBL; PU-F. 40-4190

Lytton, Edward George Earle Lytton
Bulwer-Lytton, 1803-1873. What will he
do with it? By Edward Bulwer-Lytton
[Pisistratus Caxton, pseud.] New York:
George Routledge and sons, 1840. 2 v.
LAlS. 40-4191

Lytton, Rosina Doyle [Wheeler] Bulwer-Lytton, baroness, 1802-1882. The
budget of the Bubble family. By Lady
Bulwer. New York: Harper & brothers,
1840. 2 v. LNH; MH; TxU; ViAl. 40-
4192

M

McAllister, Matthew Hall, 1800-1865. Addres to the Democratic republican convention of Georgia. Delivered... at Milledgeville, on 4th July, 1840. [Milledgevill, GA: Standard of union print., 1840] 12 p. GHi; NN; PPL. 40-4193

M'Allum, Daniel, 1794-1827. Remains of the late Rev. Daniel M'Alum, M. D., with a memoir. Rev. and slightly abridged by the editors. New York: T. Mason & G. Lane, for the Methodist Episcopal church, 1840. 307 p. DLC; ICP; NjMD; OPDaB; TxDaM. 40-4194

M'Arthur, John. Address delivered to the Union literary society of Miami university, at its fifteenth anniversary, August 12, 1840... Oxford, OH: Printed by John B. Peat, 1840. 25 p. CSmH; ICU; MiGr; OClWHi; RPB. 40-4195

Macartney, James, 1770-1843. A treatise of inflammation. By James Macartney, M. D. Philadelphia, PA: Haswell, Barrington, and Haswell, 1840. 117, 36 p. CSt-L; GEU-M; ICJ; MdBM; PPCP. 40-4196

McBlair, Charles Henry. Proceedings of the Naval general court martial in the case of Lieutenant C. H. McBlair, convened at the Navy Yard, Philadelphia, May 4th, 1840. Baltimore, MD: Printed by James Lucas & E. K. Deaver, 1840. 44 p. DLC; MdAN; MdHi; PPL; Vi. 40-4197

McCabe, James Dabney, 1808-1875. An address, delivered in Edenton on the 24th June, 1839, A. L. 5839, at the request of the officers and members of Uninity lodge, no. 54, Edenton... [Edenton, NC: s. l., 1840] p. ICN. 40-4198

McCahon, Alexander. Strictures and remarks upon some parts of a book published by Rev. J. P. Miller, Argyle, N. Y., entitled "Biographical sketches, &c.," being the substance of an address delivered to the Associate Reformed Congregation of Spier's Spring... Pittsburgh, PA: Alex. Jaynes, 1840. 42 p. InU; NcMHi; OClWHi; PPPrHi. 40-4199

McCarter's Carolina and Georgia almanac. S. l.: J. J. McCarter & Co., 1840. MWA. 40-4200

McCartney, Washington, 1812-1856. Discourse before the students of Lafayette College on the study of mathematics. Easton, PA: Printed by Hetrich & Maxwell, 1840. 20 p. CSmH; DLC; NN; PHi; PPPrHi. 40-4201

MacCaulay, Thomas Babington Macaulay, 1800-1859. Critical and miscellaneous essays, by T. Babington Macaulay. Boston, MA: Weeks, Jordan and Company, 1840-44. 5 v. CtHT; LNB; MH; OrPD; PU. 40-4202

McCheyne, Robert Murray, 1813-1843.

A castaway. By the Rev. Robert Murray McCheyne. Philadelphia, PA: Presbyterian board of publication [184-?] 8 p. GDecCT. 40-4203

McClintock, James, b. 1809. Annual lecture. Introductory lecture to the winter course of anatomy, in the Philadelphia School of anatomy... by James M'Clintock, M. D....published by the class. Philadelphia, PA: Charles A. Elliott, printer, 1840. 16 p. DLC; MHi; NNNAM; PLT. 40-4204

McClintock, Thomas. Letter from Thomas McClintock to the Association of Friends for Promoting the Abolition of Slavery, etc. Philadelphia: Printed by Merrihew and Thompson, 1840. 8 p. DLC; PPFr; PSC-Hi. 40-4205

McClintock, William L. A narrative of the discovery of the fate of Sir John Franklin and his companions, by Capt. M'Clintock, R. N., LL. D. Boston, MA: Ticknor & Fields, 1840. 374 p. NNebg. 40-4206

McClintock, William L. The voyage of the Fox in Arctic seas. Boston, MA: Ticknor & Fields, 1840. 374 p. MLanc. 40-4207

McClusky, John. Address delivered to the Literary Soc. of Franklin College... 1840. St. Clairsville, OH: Heaton, 184?. 22 p. DLC; PPPrHi. 40-4208

McCoy, Isaac, 1784-1846. History of the Baptist Indian Missions; embracing remarks on the former and present condition of the aboriginal tribes; their settlement within the Indian territory and their future prospects. Washington: W. M. Morrison, New York: H. and S.

Raynor, 1840. 369 p. DLC; IaU; GU; MWA; PPAmP. 40-4209

McCrie, Thomas, 1772-1835. The life of Andrew Melville, the Scottish reformer. Abridged for the Board, from McCrie's "Life of Melville." Philadelphia, PA: Presbyterian Board of Publication [1840] 117 p. ICP; MiU; NNUT; PPPrHi. 40-4210

McCrie, Thomas, 1772-1835. The life of Andrew Melville, the Scottish reformer. Abridged for the Board, from McCrie's "Life of Melville." Philadelphia, PA: William S. Martien [1840] 104 p. GDecCT; KyLoS; NcD; RNR; ViRut. 40-4211

McCrie, Thomas, 1772-1835. Life of John Knox. First American edition. Philadelphia, PA: Presbyterian Board of Publication [1840] p. RNR. 40-4212

McCulloch, John Ramsay, 1789-1864. A dictionary, practical, theoretical, and historical of commerce and commercial navigation. By J. R. M'Culloch... Ed. by Henry Vethake... Philadelphia, PA: T. Wardle, 1840-41. 2 v. CtMW; MB; MoS. 40-4213

M'Cullough, Samuel D. Picture of the heavens, for the use of schools and private families; being a full and distinct explanation of the different celestial phenomena, divested of methematical formulae. With tables for determining the moon's age, calculating the eclipses... Lexington, KY; Cincinnati, OH: J. B. & R. P. Donogh, 1840. 143 p. CL; KyLx; KyRE; MB; OMC; TNP. 40-4214

McDougall, Frances Harriet Whipple Greene, 1805-1878. The envoy. From free hearts to the free. Pawtucket, R. I.:

Juvenile Society, 1840. [7] -112 p. DLC; ICN; MeB; MWA; PHi. 40-4215

McDougall, Frances Harriet Whipple Greene, 1805-1878. Memoirs of Elleanor Eldridge. Providence: Printed by B. T. Albro, 1840. 9-128 p. CtY; DLC; NNC; RPB; TxU. 40-4216

M'Dougall, William R. An address, on the subject of education, delivered December 11th, by William R. M'Dougall, A. B., before the trustees of the Liberty Institution, at Lebanon, Wilson County, Tenn. [Lenanon, TN: Printed by W. P. M'Clain, Chronicle Office, 1840] 12 p. CSmH; NNUT. 40-4217

McDuffie, George, 1790-1851. Anniversary oration of the State Agricultural Society of South Carolina... on the 26th November, 1840... Columbia, SC: A. S. Johnston, 1840. 31 p. DNLM; ScC. 40-4218

McDuffie, George, 1790-1851. A eulogy upon the life and character of the late Hon. Robert Y. Hayne; delivered on the 13th February 1840, at the Circulare Church, by appointment of the citizens of Charleston. By George M'Diffie... Charleston, SC: Printed by W. Riley, 1840. 63 p. CU; ICN; NcAS; OFH; ScCC. 40-4219

M'Elhiney, Thomas. Rules and principles, with useful information to serve as a guide throughout the world. By Thomas M'Elhiney, Esq., Attorney and Counsellor at law, author of the 4th July oration, &c. Kittanning, PA: n. pr., 1840. 24 p. LNHT; PHi; PWW. 40-4220

M'Elroy's Philadelphia directory for 1840: Containing names of inhabitants, their occupations, places of business and dwelling-houses; also a list of the streets, lanes, alleys, etc... Third edition. Philadelphia, PA: Published by A. M'Elroy; Printed by Isaac Ashmead & Co., 1840. 52 p. KHi. 40-4221

McEwen, James Frisbie. New Year's sermon. A sermon, preached at Topsfield, January 7, 1840. Salem: Printed at the Gazette Office, 1840. 22 p. CtSoP; MBC; MH-AH; RPB. 40-4222

McGuffey, William Holmes, 1800-1873. ... The electic fourth reader, containing elegant extracts in prose and poetry... 14th ed., enl., imp., & ster. Cincinnati, OH: Truman and Smith, 1840. 324 p. OClWHi. 40-4223

McGuffey, William Holmes, 1800-1873. ... The electic fourth reader, containing elegant extracts in prose and poetry... 17th ed., enl., imp., & ster. Cincinnati, OH: Truman and Smith, 1840. 324 p. OClWHi. 40-4224

McGuffey, WIlliam Holmes, 1800-1873. Electic reader for review, adapting it to the use of schools. Prepared for the electic series. Cincinnati, OH: Published by Truman & Smith, 1840. 336 p. DLC; ICN; KyCov; MiU; WaPS. 40-4225

McGuffey, William Holmes, 1800-1873. ... The fourth electic reader, containing elegant extracts in prose and poetry, from the best American and English writers. With copious rules for reading, and directions for avoiding common errors. 13th ed., enlarged, improved, and stereotyped. Cincinnati, OH: Truman and Smith, 1840. 324 p. OCl. 40-4226

McGuffey, William Holmes, 1800-1873. McGuffey's newly revised first reader... Enl. & greatly imp. Cincinnati, OH: Winthrop B. Smith, 1840? 104 p. OClWHi. 40-4227

McGuffey, William Holmes, 1800-1873. Revised and improved electic third reader, containing selections in prose and poetry from the best American and English writers... 26th ed. Cincinnati, OH: Truman and Smith, 1840. 165 p. DLC; In; OClWHi. 40-4228

Machias, Me. First Congregational Church. Confession of faith and covenant... Boston, MA: s. l., 1840. 21 p. MBC. 40-4229

Machold, G. The Indian girl. Ballad. The words by Lois B. Adams. The music by G. Machold. New York: James L. Hewitt & Co. [184-?] 3 p. MB; ViU. 40-4230

M'Jilton, John Nelson, 1805-1875. The path of life. An address, delivered before the Washington and Franklin Literary Societies of Lafayette College... at the annual commencement, Sept. 22, 1841... Baltimore, MD: Printed by John Murphy, 184?. 35 p. MdBD; MH; NjPT; PEaL; PHi. 40-4231

M'Jilton, 1805-1875. Poems... Boston, MA; New York; Baltimore, MD: Otis, Broaders & Co.; Wiley and Putnam; Cushing & Bro., 1840. 360 p. MB; MdBJ; NBuG; PPM; TxU. 40-4232

M'Kendree College. Fourth annual catalogue of the officers and students. August 20, 1840. Lebanon, IL: Printed at the "Great Western" Office, 1840. 16 p. MH; NN. 40-4233

Mackenzie, Alexander Slidell, 1803-1848. The life of Commodore Oliver Hazard Perry. New York: Harper and brothers, 1840. 2 v. DLC; MB; MeB; MWA; PPA. 40-4234

Mackintosh, James, Sir, 1765-1832. The history of England. New York: Harper & bros., 1840. GEU; MB; NcU; NjNbS; ODW. 40-4235

McIlvaine, Charles Pettit, 1799-1873. Justification by faith; a charge delivered before the clergy of the Protestant Episcopal Church in the dioceses of Ohio... Sept. 13, 1839, with an appendix. By Rt. Rev. Charles P. McIlvaine, D. D.... Columbus, OH: Isaac N. Whiting, 1840. 156 p. DLC; MBD; MiU; NjP; NNUT; OClWHi. 40-4236

McIntyre, N. Y. Papers and documents relative to the iron ore veins, water power and wood land, &c., &c., in and around the village of McIntyre, in the Town of Newcomb, Essex County... New York.... New York: P. Miller, printer, 1840. 54 p. WHi. 40-4237

McKay, James Iver, 1793-1853. Speech of Mr. McKay, of North Carolina, on the General Appropriateion bill. Delivered in Committee of the Whole, in the House of Representatives, April 22, 1840. Washington, DC: Printed at the Globe Office, 1840. 24 p. IU; MeB; NcU; NNC; OClWHi; ViU. 40-4238

McKeen, Silas. Slavery in the Bible; a correspondence between the general conference of Maine, and the presbytery of Tombecbee, Miss... Worcester, MA: Spooner & Howland, 1840. 158 p. MBC. 40-4239

McKinstry, William C. The Colorado navigator, containing afull description of the beds and banks of the Colorado river, from the City of Austin to its mouth... Matagorda, TX: Printed at the Office of the Colorado Gazatte, 1840. 22 p. DLC; Tx: TxU. 40-4240

McLaren, Donald Campbell, 1794-1882. The psalms of holy scripture, the only songs of Zion. An appeal to the churches in behalf of the ordinance of God. By Donald C. McLaren... Geneva, NY: Merrell, 1840. 60 p. CSmH; ICU; NN; PPPrHi. 40-4241

Maclay, Archibald, 1778-1860. An address delivered before the Saratoga Baptist Association, at Middletown, Saratoga County, N. Y., June 28, 1838. By Archibald Maclay, A. M. New York: printed by John Gray, 1840. 16 p. MB; NCH. 40-4242

Maclay, William Brown. Address, delivered at the Democratic Republic celebration of the sixty-fourth anniversary of the independence of the United States, July 4, 1840. Poughkeepsie, NY: s. l., 1840. 24 p. ICU; NN; NNC. 40-4243

Maclure, William, 1763-1840. Catalogue of mineralogical and geological specimens at New Harmony, Indiana. Collected in various parts of Europe and America, by William Maclure... Arranged for distribution at the request of Miss Maclure and Alexander Maclure, his executors. By David Dale Owen, M. D. New Harmony, IN: s. l., 1840. 15 p. DLC; MH-Z; NN; OClWHi; PHi. 40-4244

McMahon, J. H. Address, delivered in commemoration of the anniversary of Saint John the Baptist, on Wednesday, 24th June, A. L. 5840, before the companions and brethren of Washington Chapter No. 13, and Memphis Lodge No. 91, by J. H. McMahon, Grand Scribe of State of Tennessee. Memphis, TN: Printed at the Enquirer Office, 1840. 16 p. MBFM. 40-4245

M'Naughton, James. Case of sudden death from rupture of the spermatic vein... Albany, NY: n. pub., printed by J. Munsell, 1840. 8 p. NjR. 40-4246

McNeile, Hugh, 1795-1879. Prospects of the Jews; or, a series of popular lectures on the Prophecies relative to the Jewish nationa, by the Rev. Hugh M'Neile, A. M., minister of St. Jude's Church, Liverpool. [Quotation] With a preface and notes not in former edition. From the second London edition. Philadelphia, PA: Orrin Rogers, E. G. Dorsey, printer, 1840. 135 p. CtHC; ICP; KyLoP; ViAl; WHi. 40-4247

McNeile, Hugh, 1795-1879. Sermons on the second advent of the Lord Jesus Chrust. By the Rev. Hugh M'Neile, A. M., minister of St. Jude's Church, Liverpool. Philadelphia, PA: Orrin Rogers, E. G. Dorsey, printer, 1840. 122 p. CtHC; MMeT-Hi; MWA; OO; WHi. 40-4248

Macomb, ALexander, 1782-1841. The practice of courts martial. New York: S. Colman, 1840. 154 p. CU; DLC; NjP; MWCL; ViU-L; WaWW. 40-4249

McRoberts, Samuel, 1799-1834. To the members of the General Assembly of Illinois. [n. p.] 1840. 7 p. DLC. 40-4250

Madden, Richard Robert, 1798-1886. A letter to Wm. E. Channing, D. D. In reply to one addressed to him by R. R. Madden, on the abuse of the flag of the United States in the Island of Cuba, for promoting the slave trade. By a calm observer. Boston, MA: I. R. Butts, printer; William D. Ticknor, publisher, 1840. 36 p. CtY; MH; MnU; MWA; PPAmP. 40-4251

Madison, James, 1751-1836. The papers of James Madison, purchased by order of Congress; being his correspondence and reports of debates during the Congress of the Confederation and his reports of debates in the federal convention, now published from the original manuscripts... under the superintendence of Henry D. Gilpin. Washington, DC: Langtree & O'Sullivan, 1840. 3 v. PPA; RNR; TxGR; ViPet; Wa. 40-4252

Magie, David, 1795-1865. Heaven's chief attraction; a sermon at the funeral Rev. Abraham Brown. Elizabethtown, NY: Edward Sanderson, 1840. 22 p. CtY; RPB. 40-4253

Maginnis, John Sharp, 1805-1852. An inaugural address, delivered in the chapel of the Hamilton Literary and Theological Institution, August 21, 1839. Utica, NY: Bennett, Backus & Hawley, 1840. 26 p. MH-AH; MNtcA; OO; PCC; TxU. 40-4254

The Magnet. Devoted to arts, science, and mechanism. v. 1, no. 1 [July 4, 1840] New York: s. l., 1840. NN. 40-4255

The Magnolia; or, Southern Apalachian. A literary magazine and monthly review. Charleston, S. C.: P. C. Pendleton, 1840. 6 v. DLC; GEU; NcU; NjP; ViU. 40-4256

Maguire, Thomas. The authentic report

of the discussion, which took place at the lecture room of the Dublin institution between the Rev. Thomas Maguire and Rev. Richard T. P. Pope... New York: Pub. by John Doyle, 1840. 309 p. ICLay; MdCatS; OCIJC; OSW. 40-4257

Mahan, Asa. 1800-1889. Abstract of a course of lectures on mental and moral philosophy... Oberlin, OH: Printed by James Steele, 1840. 305 p. MiD; NbCrD; NN; OO. 40-4258

Mahan, Asa, 1800-1889. Scripture doctrine of Christian perfection; with other kindred subjects. By Rev. Asa Mahan. Third ed. Boston, MA: D. S. King, 1840. 193 p. MeBat; PLT. 40-4259

Mahan, Asa, 1800-1889. Scripture doctrine of Christian perfection; with other kindred subjects. Illus. and confirmed in a series of discourses designed to throw light on the way of holiness. Ed. 4. Boston, MA: King, 1840. 193 p. IEG; MBAt; MWA; PCC; VtMidSM. 40-4260

Mahan, Dennis Hart. Composition of Armies. West Point, NY: s. l., 184-? 32 p. NWM. 40-4261

Mahan, Dennis Hart. Notes on architecture. By D. H. Mahan. West Point, NY: s. l., 184-? 16 p. NWM. 40-4262

Mahan, Dennis Hart. Notes on attack and defence of permanent words. By D. H. Mahan. West Point, NY: s. l., 184-? 36 p. NWM. 40-4263

Mahan, Dennis Hart. Notes on mines. By D. H. Mahan. West Point, NY: s. l., 184-? 40 p. NWM. 40-4264

The maid of Florence; or, A woman's

vengeance! A pseudo-historical tragedy in five acts. With entrances and exits and a description of the costume. Embellished with a fine wood engraving. Philadelphia, PA; New York: Turner & Fiher [!] 1840. 76 p. DLC; RPB. 40-4265

Maine. Commissioners to Revise the Public Laws. Report of the Commissioners appointed to revise the public laws of the State of Maine. Augusta, ME: Printers to the state, 1840. v. p. M. 40-4266

Maine. Communication from the Governor, enclosing resolutions to the State of Maine, relating to the Northeastern Boundary. [S. l.: s. l., 1840] 5 p. MiD-B. 40-4267

Maine. Governor, 1839-41. Message of Governor Fairfield, to both branches of the legislature of the state of Maine, January, 1840. Augusta, ME: Smith & Robinson, printers, 1840. 24 p. MBAt; MeB; MeHi; MeLR; MiU-C. 40-4268

Maine. Laws, statutes, etc. An act relating to County Officers. Augusta, ME: Wm. R. Smith & Co., printers to the State, 1840. 5 p. MeB. 40-4269

Maine. Laws, statutes, etc. An act to incorporate the Farmers' Bank. Augusta, ME: Wm. R. Smith & Co., printers to the State, 1840. 10 p. MeB. 40-4270

Maine. Laws, statutes, etc. Acts and Resolves, passed by the Twentieth Legislature of the State of Maine, January session, 1840. Published by the Secretary of State, agreeable to resolve of June 28, 1820, and February 26, 1840. Augusta, ME: Wm. R. Smith & Co., printers to the State, 1840. 254 p. A-SC; MeLR; MeU; OrSC; Wa-L. 40-4271

Maine. Laws, statutes, etc. The powers and duties of the town officer, as contained in the statutes of the State of Maine... also the powers and duties of plantation & parish officers... 4th ed., improved. Hallowell, ME: Glazier Masters & Smith, 1840. 321 p. NN. 40-4272

Maine. Laws, statutes, etc. Report of commissioners, appointed to revise the public laws. Augusta, ME: s. l., 1840. 91 p. OCLaw. 40-4273

Maine. Legislature. A report of the Survey of a Railroad Route from Portland to Lake Champlain, which is included within the State of Maine. By William L. Dearborn, Engineer. Augusta, ME: Wm. R. Smith & Co., printers to the State, 1840. 37 p. MeB. 40-4274

Maine. Legislature. Documents printed by order of the Legislature of the State of Maine... 1840. Augusta, ME: Wm. R. Smith & Co., printers, 1840. 84 p. MeHi; MeLewB; MeU. 40-4275

Maine. Legislature. Private or special laws of the State of Maine, from 1836 to 1839, inclusive. Vol. III. Published agreeably to a resolve of March 16, 1840. Augusta, ME: Wm. R. Smith & Co., printers, 1840. 685 p. Me-LR. 40-4276

Maine. Legislature. Commissioners Appointed to Revise the Public Laws. Report of the Commissioners appointed to revise the public laws of the State of Maine. Augusta, ME: Wm. R. Smith & Co., printers to the State, 1840. 198 p. MeU. 40-4277

Maine. Legislature. House. An act relating to the Booms on the Aroostook, St. John and Fish Rivers. Twentieth Legislature. No. 34. Augusta, ME: Severence & Dorr, printers to the State, 1840. 5 p. MeB. 40-4278

Maine. Legislature. House. An act relating to a State Valuation. Twentieth Legislature. No. 32. Augusta, ME: Severence & Dorr, printers to the State, 1840. 21 p. MeB. 40-4279

Maine. Legislature. House. An act relating to the Wild Lands in Maine. Twentieth Legislature. No. 20. Augusta, ME: Severence & Dorr, printers to the State, 1840. 5 p. MeB. 40-4280

Maine. Legislature. House. An act to assessing a tax on this State. Twentieth Legislature. No. 22. Augusta, ME: Severence & Dorr, printers to the State, 1840. 39 p. MeB. 40-4281

Maine. Legislature. House. An act to incorporate the Allagash Company. Twentieth Legislature. No. 12. Augusta, ME: Severence & Dorr, printers to the State, 1840. 7 p. MeB. 40-4282

Maine. Legislature. House. An act to incorporate the Ebeme Company. Twentieth Legislature. No. 16. Augusta, ME: Severence & Dorr, printers to the State, 1840. 7 p. MeB. 40-4283

Maine. Legislature. House. An act to regulate Attachment on Mesne Process. Twentieth Legislature. No. 26. Augusta, ME: Severence & Dorr, printers to the State, 1840. 5 p. MeB. 40-4284

Maine. Legislature. House. Documents accompanying the Governor's Message.

Twentieth Legislature. No. 1. Augusta, ME: Severence & Dorr, printers to the State, 1840. 6 p. MeB. 40-4285

Maine. Legislature. House. Donations granted to Literary Institutions and Primary Schools. Twentieth Legislature. No. 6. Augusta, ME: Severence & Dorr, printers to the State, 1840. 5 p. MeB. 40-4286

Maine. Legislature. House. List of notes due to the State of Maine for lands. [S. l.: n. pr. [1840] p. MBAt. 40-4287

Maine. Legislature. House. Report and resolve relating to Bounty to Fishing Vessels. Twentieth Legislature. No. 33. Augusta, ME: Severence & Dorr, printers to the State, 1840. 12 p. MeB. 40-4288

Maine. Legislature. House. Report of a Minority of the Committee on Elections. Twentieth Legislature. No. 9. Augusta, ME: Severence & Dorr, printers to the State, 1840. 5 p. MeB. 40-4289

Maine. Legislature. House. Report of the Committee on Elections. Twentieth Legislature. No. 8. Augusta, ME: Severence & Dorr, printers to the State, 1840. 14 p. MeB. 40-4290

Maine. Legislature. House. Report of the Committee on Finance. Twentieth Legislature. No. 10. Augusta, ME: Severence & Dorr, printers to the State, 1840. 7 p. MeB. 40-4291

Maine. Legislature. House. Report of the Committee on Public Buildings, relating to the Insane Hospital. Twentieth Legislature. No. 14. Augusta, ME:

Severence & Dorr, printers to the State, 1840. 12 p. MeB. 40-4292

Maine. Legislature. House. Report of the Committee on State Lands. Twentieth Legislature. No. 29. Augusta, ME: Severence & Dorr, printers to the State, 1840. 14 p. MeB. 40-4293

Maine. Legislature. House. Report of William P. Parrott, on the Construction of the Aroostook Boom. Twentieth Legislature. Augusta, ME: Severence & Dorr, printers to the State, 1840. 12 p. MeB. 40-4294

Maine. Legislature. House. Resolve providing for the choice of electors. Twentieth Legislature. No. 24. Augusta, ME: Severence & Dorr, printers to the State, 1840. 8 p. MeB. 40-4295

Maine. Legislature. House. Resolves relating to the Public Domain. Twentieth Legislature. No. 21. Augusta, ME: Severence & Dorr, printers to the State, 1840. 6 p. MeB. 40-4296

Maine. Legislature. House. Rules and orders of the House of Representatives of the State of Maine... 1840. Augusta, ME: Smith & Robinson, printers to the State, 1840. 84 p. MeHi; MeLR; MeU. 40-4297

Maine. Legislature. Senate. An Act for the Preservation of Fish. Twentieth Legislature. No. 11. Augusta, ME: Smith & Robinson, Printers to the State, 1840. 7 p. MeB. 40-4298

Maine. Legislature. Senate. An act for the relief of Insolvent Debtors. Twentieth Legislature. No. 2. Augusta, ME:

Smith & Robinson, Printers to the State, 1840. 43 p. MeB. 40-4299

Maine. Legislature. Senate. An act further Regulating Divorces. Twentieth Legislature. No. 13. Augusta, ME: Smith & Robinson, Printers to the State, 1840. 5 p. MeB. 40-4300

Maine. Legislature. Senate. An act regulating to Banks and Banking. Twentieth Legislature. No. 23. Augusta, ME: Smith & Robinson, Printers to the State, 1840. 17 p. MeB. 40-4301

Maine. Legislature. Senate. An Act relating to Sheriffs' bonds. Twentieth Legislature. No. 31. Augusta, ME: Smith & Robinson, Printers to the State, 1840. 5 p. MeB. 40-4302

Maine. Legislature. Senate. An act to incorporate The Moosehead and Wilson Stream Canal and Sluiceway Company. Twentieth Legislature. No. 18. Augusta, ME: Smith & Robinson, Printers to the State, 1840. 5 p. MeB. 40-4303

Maine. Legislature. Senate. Annual Report of the Inspectors of the State Prison. Twentieth Legislature. No. 5. Augusta, ME: Smith & Robinson, Printers to the State, 1840. 17 p. MeB. 40-4304

Maine. Legislature. Senate. Report and bill of the Committee on Finance. Twentieth Legislature. No. 35. Augusta, ME: Smith & Robinson, Printers to the State, 1840. 12 p. MeB. 40-4305

Maine. Legislature. Senate. Report and bill of the Committee on the Militia of the State of Maine. Twentieth Legislature. No. 35. Augusta, ME: Smith &

Robinson, Printers to the State, 1840. 106 p. MeB. 40-4306

Maine. Legislature. Senate. Report and Bill relating to the Seboomook Sluiceway. Twentieth Legislature. No. 15. Augusta, ME: Smith & Robinson, Printers to the State, 1840. 15 p. MeB. 40-4307

Maine. Legislature. Senate. Report of the Warden of the State Prison. Twentieth Legislature. No. 4. Augusta, ME: Smith & Robinson, Printers to the State, 1840. 10 p. MeB. 40-4308

Maine. Legislature. Senate. Reports on the Petition of William Emerson. Twentieth Legislature. No. 25. Augusta, ME: Smith & Robinson, Printers to the State, 1840. 14 p. MeB. 40-4309

Maine. Legislature. Senate. Rules and orders to be observed in the Senate of the State of Maine... 1840. Augusta, ME: Smith & Robinson, printers to the state, 1840. 36 p. MeLewB. 40-4310

Maine. Legislature. Senate. Rules and orders to be observed in the Senate of the State of Maine... 1840. Augusta, ME: Smith & Robinson, printers to the state, 1840. 83 p. MeB. 40-4311

Maine. Schools. Abstract from the returns of Common Schools... in Maine for the year 1839. By Phillip C. Johnson. Augusta, ME: Wm. R. Smith & Co., printers, 1840. 28 p. MeHi. 40-4312

Maine. Secretary of State. Abstract from the returns of Common Schools, made by the several cities, towns, and plantations in Maine, for the year 1839... Augusta, ME: Wm. R. Smith & Co.,

printers to the state, 1840. 28 p. MeH; MeLR; MeU; MH; Nh. 40-4313

Maine. State Hospital. Augusta. System of Regulations for Maine Insane Hospital. Augusta, ME: W. R. Smith & co., printers, 1840. 12 p. DLC; MnU. 40-4314

Maine. State Prison Inspectors. Annual report. Augusta, ME: s. l., 1840. PHi. 40-4315

Maine Anti-Slavery Society. The annual report of the executive committee of the Maine anti-slavery society, 1840. Brunswick, ME: Press of Joseph Griffin, 1840. 48 p. MA. 40-4316

The Maine Farmer's Almanac... 1841. By Daniel Robinson. Belfast, ME: H. G. O. Washburn & co. [1840] 46 p. WHi. 40-4317

The Maine Farmer's Almanac for the year of Our Lord 1841. By Daniel Robinson. Gardener, ME: William Palmer [etc., 1840] p. CSmH. 40-4318

The Maine Farmer's Almanac for the year of our Lord 1841. By Daniel Robinson. Waterville, ME: Printed by Merrill & Crowell, 1840. 48 p. MMeT. 40-4319

Maine Farmer's Almanack. By Daniel Robinson. Augusta, ME: R. D. Price, 1840. MWA. 40-4320

Maine Farmer's Almanack. By Daniel Robinson. Bangor, ME: Smith & Fenno, 1840. MWA. 40-4321

Maine Farmer's Almanack for 1841. By Daniel Robinson. Hallowell, ME: C. Spaulding [1840] p. MWA. 40-4322

Maine Farmer's Almanack for 1841. By Daniel Robinson. Portland, ME: William Hyde [1840] p. MeHi; MWA. 40-4323

Malcolm, Howard, 1799-1879. A dictionary of the most important names, objects and terms found in the Holy Scriptures. Intended principally for sunday school teachers and Bible classes. Boston: Gould, Kendall and Lincoln, 1840. 309 p. MH; NcD. 40-4324

Malcolm, Howard, 1799-1879. The extent and efficacy of the atonement. By Howard Malcom, president of Georgetown College, Kentucky. Second edition. New York: Robert Carter, 1840. 136 p. ICP; KyLo; MiU; PPiW; TxAbH. 40-4325

Malcolm, Howard, 1799-1879. Travel in south-eastern Asia, embracing Hindustan, Malaga, Siam, and China, with notices of numerous missionary stations, and a full account of the Burman empire. With dissertations, tables, etc., by Howard Malcolm. Fifth ed. Boston, MA: Gould, Kendall and Lincoln, 1840. 2 v. CSmH; KyHi; MH; PWWJS; TNP. 40-4326

Malcolm, Howard, 1799-1879. Travel in south-eastern Asia, embracing Hindustan, Malaga, Siam, and China, with notices of numerous missionary stations, and a full account of the Burman empire. With dissertations, tables, etc., by Howard Malcolm. 6th ed. Boston, MA: Gould, Kendall and Lincoln, 1840. 2 v. SfA; MNe; NGlc; OAU; ScCoB. 40-4327

Malder, James Gaspard. The silent rewell. A ballad. [Accompaniment for piano forte] Boston: Parker and Ditson, [184-?] 3 p. MB. 40-4328

Malibran, Maria Felicita Garcia, 1808-1836. There is no home like my own. [Song. A. Accomp. arranged for the guitar by L. Meignen] Boston, MA: Reed [184-?] 2 p. MB. 40-4329

Malibran, Maria Felicita Garcia, 1808-1836. There is no home like my own. Tyrollien. Words from The Bijou. Music by Madame Milibran. New York: Firth & Hall [184-?] 3 p. ViU. 40-4330

Malibran, Maria Felicita Garcia, 1808-1836. There is no home like my own. Tyrollien. Words from The Bijou. Music composed by Madame Milibran. Philadelphia, PA: George Willig [184-?] 3 p. MB; ViU. 40-4331

Mallard, John B. A short account of the Congregational church, at Midway, Georgia... Savannah, GA: Purse, 1840. 28 p. DLC; GDC; GHi; GU; GU-De; MH; NcD. 40-4332

Mallory, Richard P. A panoramic view from Bunker Hill monument. Engraved by James Smillie, from a drawing by R. P. Mallory. Boston, MA: L. Stevens [184-?] 16 p. MH. 40-4333

Malon, Cesar, 1787-1864. The watchmaker and his family. New York: s. l., 1840. 31 p. CtY; NN. 40-4334

Man, George Flagg, 1807-1885. The geranium leaf: an original tale. Boston, MA: Marsh, Capen, Lyon & Webb, 1840. 69 p. CU; MB; MH; RPB. 40-4335

The man is not bought! He is still in the slave pen in the court house. [Circular regarding a fugitive slave] [Boston, MA: s. l., 184-?] p. MHi. 40-4336

Manchester Medical Society. Constitution, by-laws, code of medical ethics, and fee-table. Manchester, NH: s. l., 1840. 18 p. No Loc. 40-4337

Mandeville, Henry, 1804-1858. An address on perseverance, as a means of success in life; its limits, the habits of thought, feeling, and action adverse to its practice; and its effects. Delivered before the literary societies of Hamilton College at the commencement, July 29, 1840, by H. Mandeville... Utica, NY: Bennett, Backus & Hawley, 1840. 32 p. ICP; MBC; MWA; NjR; OO. 40-4338

Manhattan Company, New York. Report of the commissioners appointed to investigate the condition of the Manhattan company:together with the minutes of their proceedings, and various statements relative thereto, March 14, 1840. New York: Printed by J. P. Wright, 1840. 24, 50 p. DLC; MB; NN; NNC; WHi. 40-4339

The Maniac beauty. [Boston, MA: s. l., 184-?] 66 p. DLC; MB. 40-4340

A manifesto, containing a plain statement of facts relative to the acts of the general assembly, together with the sentiments of the undersigned members of the Synod of Kentucky. [Lexington, Ky., 1840. Fleming, Robert. The fulfilling of the scripture, for confirming believers and convincing unbelievers. Philadelphia: Presbyterian Board of Publication, 1840. [13] -376 p. CSt; MB; NNUT; OO; ViRut. 40-4341

Mann, Horace, 1796-1859. Lecture of education. By Horace Mann... Boston, MA: Marsh, Capen, Lyon and Webb, 1840. 62 p. ICU; MBC; MWA; NCH; RPB. 40-4342

Mann, Jonathan B. An appeal to the administration. [Boston, MA: s. l., 1840] 8 p. DLC. 40-4343

A map of the canals & railroads of Pa., N. J., & adjoining states, showing county, towns, villages, mills, iron works, forts & post offices. Also battle grounds, places of worship, public houses, roads, ferries & water falls, including canals completed or in progress, contemplated canals, railroads & proposed railroads, Scale of Amer. miles 50 to a degree. Philadelphia, PA: s. l., 1840. AmSwdHMus. 40-4344

Map of the Half Breed Sac & Fox Reservation. New York; E. Jones [1840?] p. No Loc. 40-4345

Map of the railroads of Mass. running west from Boston. Boston, MA: s. l., 184-? p. MB. 40-4346

Map of the Troy and Greenfield Railroad and its connections. Boston [184-?] Map of the Troy and Greenfield Railroad and its connections. Boston [184-?] Marryat, Frederick, 1792-1848. Complete works of Captain F. Marryat Philadelphia: J. Harding, 1840. 2 v. MH 40-4347

[Map showing] the end of Boston wharf from which restrictions are to be taken off. [Boston, MA] : C. Cook [184-?] p MB. 40-4348

Map showing the proposed railroad from Boston to Burlington... from Hale map of New England. Map of the rai road from Boston to Slanstead. Boston, MA: s. l. [184-?] p. MB. 40-4349

Marcailhou, Gatien, d. 1856. La belle Agnes. Valse pour le piano, par G. Marcailhou... New York: Firth, Pond & Co. [184-?] 7 p. ViU. 40-4350

Marcailhou, Gatien, d. 1856. Bouton de rose [Rose bud] ... and Grand waltz. By G. Marcailhou. Philadelphia, PA; New York: A. Fiot; W. Dubois [184-?] 7 p. ViU. 40-4351

Marcailhou, Gatien, d. 1856. ... Les Bruyeres... Op. 111... Philadelphia, PA; New York: A. Fiot; W. Dubois [184-?] 7 p. ViU. 40-4352

Marcailhou, Gatien, d. 1856. Fenella. A brillant waltz. By G. Marcailhou. Philadelphia, PA; New York: A. Fiot; W. Dubois [184-?] 9 p. ViU. 40-4353

Marcailhou, Gatien, d. 1856. ... Indiana. Pour le piano... Op. 111. Philadelphia, PA; New York: A. Fiot; W. Dubois [184-?] 5 p. NN; ViU. 40-4354

Marcailhou, Gatien, d. 1856. ... Le torrent... Op. 111. Philadelphia, PA; New York: A. Fiot; W. Dubois [184-?] 7 p. ViU. 40-4355

Marcet, Jane Haldimand, 1769-1858. Conversations on natural philosophy, in whch the elements of that science are familiarly explained... with corrections, improvements, and considerable additions in the body of the work; appropriate questions, and a glossary, by Dr. Thomas P. Jones. Philadelphia, PA: Grigg and Elliot, 1840. 220 p. MH; ViU. 40-4356

Marcet, Jane Haldemand, 1769-1858.

Scenes in nature; or, Conversations for children on land and water. By Mrs. T. H. Marcet. Boston, MA: Marsh, Capen, Lyon and Webb, 1840. 324 p. DLC; InCW; MnS; MTop; PU. 40-4357

March, Daniel, 1816-1902. Yankee land and the Yankee... Hartford, CT: Printed by Case, Tiffany and Burnham, 1840. 33 p. CtMW; IC; MiD; MnHi; OC; TxU. 40-4358

March in the lady of the lake & Indian march in Columbus. Baltimore, MD: F. D. Benteen [184-?] 1 p. ViU. 40-4359

Maretzek, Max, 1821-1897. The flower dance of the Viennoise children. New York: Atwill [184-?] 7 p. ViU. 40-4360

Maretzek, Max, 1821-1897. ... Harvest fete, as performed at the principal theatres; music by Maretzek. No. 2. Baltimore, MD; New Orleans, LA: Frederick D. Benteen; Wm. T. Mayo [184-?] 7 p. ViU. 40-4361

Marietta College, Marietta, O. Library. Catalogue of the Officers and Students in Marietta College, 1840-41. [S. l.: s. l., 184-?] 23 p. ICHi; MBC; MH; OMC. 40-4362

Marietta College, Marietta, O. Library. Laws of Marietta college... Marietta, OH: G. W. Tyler & Co., 1840. 56 p. DLC; MB; MWA. 40-4363

The Mariner's Chronicle of shipwrecks, fires, famines, and other disasters at sea... together with an account of the whale fishery, sketches of nautical life, steam boat disasters... Boston, MA: printed and published by Charles Gaylord, 1840. 2 v. MBGCT; MeBa; MHBA. 40-4364

The Mariner's library, or voyager's companion. Containing narratives of the most popular voyages, from the time of Columbus to the present day... Boston, MA: C. Gaylord, 1840. 492 p. DLC; MBAt; MH; MNBedf. 40-4365

Mark, W. Whisperings of Fancy. Boston, MA: J. Philipson, pub., 1840. 208 p. IaPeC. 40-4366

Mark, W. The whisperings of Fancy. New York: Harper & Bros., Pub., 1840. 192 p. IaPeC. 40-4367

Marryat, Frederick, 1792-1848. The complete works of Captain Marryat. Sandbornton N. H.: C. Lane, 1840. 2 v. in one. CtY. 40-4368

Marryat, Frederick, 1792-1848. Jacob Faithful; or, The adventures of a waterman. New York: Nafis and Cornish, [184-?] 2 v. in one. CtY. 40-4369

Marryat, Frederick, 1792-1848. Jacob faithful; or, The adventures of a waterman. Sandbornton, NH: s. l., 1840. 2 v. Nh-Hi. 40-4370

Marryat, Frederick, 1792-1848. Japhet in search of a father, by the author of "Peter Simple." Cincinnati, OH: James, 1840. 2 v. in 1. OC. 40-4371

Marryat, Frederick, 1792-1848. ... The king's own... Sandborton, NH: Charles Lane, 1840. 2 v. PLFM; TNP. 40-4372

Marryat, Frederick, 1792-1848. The mission; or, Scenes in Africa. Written for young people. By Captain Marryat... With illustrations by Sir John Gilbert. New edition. New York: G. Routledge & sons [184-?] 446 p. CSf; DLC; TxSaO. 40-4373

Marryat, Frederick, 1792-1848. Novels and tales. Philadelphia, PA: Smith & Co. [184-?] p. MB; MsU. 40-4374

Marryat, Frederick, 1792-1848. Pacha of many tales. Sandbornton, NH: C. Lane, 1840. 2 v. in 1. CtY; DLC; MH. 40-4375

Marryat, Frederick, 1792-1848. Poor Jack. By Capt. Marryat, C. B. author of "Peter Simple," "Jacob Faithful," &c., &c., &c... Philadelphia, PA: Carey & Hart, 1840. 2 v. LNB; MAnP. 40-4376

Marryat, Frederick, 1792-1848. Second series of A diary in America, with remarks on its institutions. By Capt. Marryat, author of Peter Simple. Philadelphia, PA: T. K. & P. G. Collins, 1840. 300 p. ICU; KyHi; MH; NjR; PFal; ScP. 40-4377

Marryat, Frederick, 1792-1848. Snarleyyow; or, The dog fiend. New York: Nafis and Cornish, [184-?] 2 v. ViU. 40-4378

Marryat, Frederick, 1792-1848. The works of Captain Marryat. Complete in two volumes; containing Peter Simple, Jacob Faithful, The naval officer, Japhet in search of his father, The king's own, Newton Foster, The Pacha of many tales, Pirate, and three others, Mr. Midshipman Easy, Snarleyyow, The phantom ship... Philadelphia, PA: s. l., 1840. 2 v. CSf; ICHi; ICU; MeBa; TCH. 40-4379

Marry-it, Captain, pseud. Lie-ary on America! with yarns on its Institutions. By Captain Marri-it, C. S. [A parody of

Capt. Marry at's "A Diary in America."] Boston, MA: pub. for the author, 1840. 36 p. DLC. 40-4380

Marsh, F. Star polka. Composed for the piano and respectfully dedicated to Miss Mary Rice, by F. Marsh. Philadelphia, PA; New Orleans, LA: Lee & Walker, successors to George Willig; W. T. Mayo [184-?] 2 p. ViU. 40-4381

Marsh, John, 1788-1868. The bow of primose. An address, delivered before the new York Marine Temperance Society, at the erection of a new flag, on the anniversary of American Independence, July 4th, 1840. by John Marsh. New York: Published by request of the Society, 1840. 20 p. CSPSR; CtHC; MB; MdBD; NjR; OMC. 40-4382

Marsh, John, 1788-1868. An epitome of general ecclesiastical history from the earliest period to the present time. With a history of the Jews from the destruction of Jerusalem to the present day. 5th edition. New York: J. Tilden and Co., 1840. 26-462 p. NN; OO. 40-4383

Marshall, Henry, 1775-1851. On the enisting, discharging and pensioning of soliers, with the official documents of hese branches of military duty. With the egulations for the recruiting service in he Army and Navy of the United States nd a preface by W. S. W. Ruschenerger. From the 2nd London ed. hiladelphia, PA: Waldie, 1840. 209 p. St-L; MdBJ; NcD; PPM; ViU. 40-4384

Marshall, John, 1755-1835. The life of eorge Washington, Commander in ief of the American forces, during the ar which established the independence his country, and first President of the

United States. Comp. under the inspection of the Honourable Bushcod Washington, from original papers. 2d ed., rev. and cor. by the author. Philadelphia, PA: J. Crissy and Thomas Cowperthwait and Co., 1840. 2 v. DLC; IaW; MB; MdBS; TJoT. 40-4385

Marshall, John, 1755-1835. Opinions of the late Chief Justice of the United States concerning freemasonry. Boston, MA: [n. pub., n. pr.] 1840. 4 p. DLC; MH; NjP; PHi; WHi. 40-4386

Marshall, Thomas Francis, 1801-1864. Letters to the Editors of the Commonwealth containing the argument in favor of the constitutionality of the law of 1833, "Prohibiting the importation of slaves into this commonwealth," and also defending the propriety and policy of that law in reply to a pamphlet by Robert Wickliffe, son, and to the views taken by other enemies of the law. [Frankfort, KY: A. G. Hodges, 1840] p. NN; PSt; TxFTC. 40-4387

Marshall, Thomas Francis, 1801-1864. Letters to the Editors of the Commonwealth containing the argument in favor of the constitutionality of the law of 1833, "Prohibiting the importation of slaves into this commonwealth," and also defending the propriety and policy of that law in reply to a pamphlet by Robert Wickliffe, son, and to the views taken by other enemies of the law. [Louisville, KY: s. l., 1840] 37 p. MH-And. 40-4388

Marshall College, Mercersburg, Pa. Catalogue and addresses before societies, etc. Chambersburg, PA: s. l., 1840-48. p. ICJ. 40-4389

Martin, William. Oh! dear what can the

matter be, with variations for the piano forte, by Wm. Martin. Baltimore, MD; New Orleans, LA: F. D. Benteen; W. T. Mayo [184-?] 6 p. ViU. 40-4390

Martin, William. The Young mother's delight in the guidance of her chil'd intellect. Also, the duties of mothers, by E. N. Kirk. Boston, MA: s. l., 1840. 216 p. CtY; KyBC; MeBat; MH; MWA. 40-4391

Martinet, Antoine, 1802-1871. Religion in society, placed within the reach of every mind; or, The solution of great problems. New York: D. & J. Sadlier & Co., 1840. 2 v. OClStM; OCX. 40-4392

Martomeai, Jarroet, 1802-1876. Devotional exercises: consisting of reflections and prayers, for the use of young persons. To which is added a guide to the study of the Scriptures. From the 3d Lond. ed. Boston, MA: Otis, Broaders, 1840. 132 p. CBPSR; MeBAt; MWA. 40-4393

Marvin, Richard P. Speech of Mr. Marvin, of New York, on the sub-treasury bill. Delivered in the House of Representatives, June 9, 1840. Washington, DC: Printed by Gales and Seaton, 1840. 37 p. MiD-B; MWA; NNC; PPL; TxU. 40-4394

Maryland. General Assembly. House. Journal of proceedings of the House of Delegates to the State of Maryland, December, 1839. By authority. [Annapolis, MD: Geo. & Wm. Johnson, printers, 1840] 851 p. MdBB; MdHi; MdLR. 40-4395

Maryland. General Assembly. House. Journal of proceedings of the House of Delegates of the State of Maryland,

December session, 1840. S. l.: s. l., 1840. 597 p. MdBB. 40-4396

Maryland. General Assembly. House. Report from the Select Committee to whom was referred a bill entitled, "An Act to provide for the election of the levy court of Caroline and Frederick counties. "By the House of Delegates, Feb. 29, 1840. [Annapolis, MD: s. l., 1840] 3 p. WHi. 40-4397

Maryland. General Assembly. House. Committee on Banking Institutions. Report from the Committee to whom was referred a bill entitled, "An Act for the better regulatin of the banking institutions of the state, with proposed amendments from the Senate. [Annapolis, MD: s. l., 1840] 8 p. WHi. 40-4398

Maryland. General Assembly. House. Committee on Colored Population. Report of the Committee on colored population. By the House of delegates, Feb. 26, 1840. [Annapolis, MD: s. l., 1840] 26 p. MdHi; WHi. 40-4399

Maryland. General Assembly. House. Committee on Currency. Report of the Committee on the currency, together with the answers of the banks to the interrogatories of said committee. [Annapolis, MD: s. l., 1840] 134 p. MdHi; WHi. 40-4400

Maryland. General Assembly. House Committee on Eastern Shore R. R. Co Mr. Owen's report of evidence taken before the select committee on the E. S Railroad, in reference to M. Duval' claim against said company. By th House of delegates, March 16, 1840. [Ar napolis, MD: s. l., 1840] 23 p. WHi. 40-4401

Maryland. General Assembly. House. Committee on Eastern Shore R. R. Co. Report of the minority of the Committee on the Eastern Shore rail road company. [Annapolis, MD: s. l., 1840] 8 p. WHi. 40-4402

Maryland. General Assembly. House. Committee on Education. Report of the committee on education. By the House of delegates, March 13, 1840. [Annapolis, MD: s. l., 1840] 6 p. WHi. 40-4403

Maryland. General Assembly. House. Committee on Grievances & Courts of Justice. Report of the committee of grievances and courts of justice, relative to the attendance of judges of the court of appeals and county courts. [for 1839] [Annapolis, MD: s. l., 1840] 11 p. WHi. 40-4404

Maryland. General Assembly. House. Committee on Internal Improvement. A report from the committee on Internal improvement, transmitting a communication from the Chesapeake & Ohio Canal company, relative to the salaries, extra allowance, etc. of the officers of said company... Mar. 20, 1840. [Annapolis, MD: s. l., 1840] 24 p. ViU; WHi. 40-4405

Maryland. General Assembly. House. Committee on Internal Improvement. A report in part from the committee on Internal improvement, in relation to the Chesapeake & Ohio Canal. By the House of delegates, Mar. 4, 1840. [Annapolis, MD: s. l., 1840] 18 p. DLC; ViU; WHi. 40-4406

Maryland. General Assembly. House. Committee on Judicial Proceedings. Report of the Majority on the committee on Judicial proceeedings, to which was referred a bill to provide for the election of County Clerks and Registers of Wills, by the people. [Annapolis, MD: William M'Neir, printer, 1840] 7 p. MdLR. 40-4407

Maryland. General Assembly. House. Committee on Library. Report from the committee on the Library on the manuscript in the library relating to the early history of the State. [Annapolis, MD: s. l., 1840] p. WHi. 40-4408

Maryland. General Assembly. House. Committee on Lotteries. Communication from J. S. Williams, late lottery commissioner... [and report of the majority of the standing committee on lotteries, etc.] By the House of delegates, March 17, 1840. [Annapolis, MD: s. l., 1840] 24 p. WHi. 40-4409

Maryland. General Assembly. House. Committee on Lotteries. Report from the committee on lotteries. By the House of delegates, Feb. 28, 1840. [Annapolis, MD: s. l., 1840] 7 p. WHi. 40-4410

Maryland. General Assembly. House. Committee on Ways and Means. Report of the committee on Ways and Means, on the finances of the State. By the House of delegates, Mar. 3, 1840. [Annapolis, MD: s. l., 1840] 16 p. WHi. 40-4411

Maryland. General Assembly. Senate. Journal of proceedings of the Senate of Maryland, at December session, eighteen hundred and thirty-nine. By authority. Annapolis, MD: William

M'Neir, printer, 1840. 356 p. MdBB; MdHi; MdLR. 40-4412

Maryland. General Assembly. Senate. Proceedings of the Senate of Maryland, in executive session, 1839. Annapolis, MD: William M'Neir, printer, 1840. 82 p. MdLR. 40-4413

Maryland. General Assembly. Senate. Report of the Majority of the Committee on Internal Improvement. Annapolis, MD: William M'Neir, printer, 1840. 21 p. MdLR. 40-4414

Maryland. General Assembly. Senate. Committee on Colored Population. Report of the Committee on Colored Population submitting answers from the Board of Managers for removing free people of color in obedience to an order of the Senate. Annapolis, MD: William M'Neir, printer, 1840. 27 p. MdLR; WHi. 40-4415

Maryland. General Assembly. Senate. Committee on Internal Improvement. Report of the Majority [and] minority of the Committee on on Internal Improvement. [Annapolis, MD: s. l., 1840] 21, 4 p. WHi. 40-4416

Maryland. General Assembly. Senate. Committee on Judicial Proceedings. Report of the Committee on Judicial proceedings to which was referred so much of the Governor's message as relates to a Convention [to revise the constitution] [Annapolis, MD: s. l., 1840] 13 p. WHi. 40-4417

Maryland. Governor. Annual message from the Governor, to the Legislature of Maryland, December session, 1839. [An-napolis, MD: Wm. Johnston, printer, 1840] 14 p. MBAt; MdLR. 40-4418

Maryland. Governor. Communication from the Governor of Maryland, made to the President of the United States, in pursuance of an Act of Assembly 1838, in relation to the Chesapeake & Ohio Canal. [Annapolis, MD: Wm. Johnston, printer, 1840] 6 p. ViW; WHi. 40-4419

Maryland. Governor. Executive communication to the House of Delegates, relative to the contract between the Baltimore & Ohio R. R. Co. and the Barings, Bros. Co., for the sale of the State's bonds. [Annapolis, MD: s. l., 1840] 43 p. PHi; WHi. 40-4420

Maryland. High court of chancery. Reports of cases decided in the High court of chancery of Maryland. By Theodorick Bland. Baltimore, MD: s. l., 1840-57. 3 v. Ar-SC; CSfU; MdBE; NbU-L; ODaL. 40-4421

Maryland. Laws, statutes, etc. The general public statutory laws & public local law of Maryland, from 1692 to 1839, inclusive, with annotations thereto and a copious index, by Clement Dorsey... Baltimore, MD: John D. Toy, 1840. 3 v. CSt; DeWi; Ia; MdBJ; NcD. 40-4422

Maryland. Laws, statutes, etc. Laws... made and passed at a session of Assembly... begun Monday, December 30th, 1839, and ended the 21st of March, 1840. Annapolis, MD: Printed by William M'Neir, 1840. 475 p. IaU-L; MdBB; NNLI; R. 40-4423

Maryland medical and surgical journal and official organ of the medical department of the army and navy of the United

States. v. 1-3, 1839-1843. Published under the auspices of the medical and surgical faculty of Maryland. Baltimore, MD: s. l., 1840-43. 3 v. DLC; ICJ; MdBJ; MoSMed; PU. 40-4424

The Maryland pocket annual for the year of Our Lord 1841. Annapolis, MD: Printed by J. Hughes, 1840. v. MdBE; MdHi; MdW. 40-4425

Mary's home. [anon.] [Boston, MA: Sabbath school co., 1840] 36 p. DLC. 40-4426

"Mary's tears," from Moore's sacred melodies. The music by O. Shaw. Baltimore, MD: F. D. Benteen [184-?] 2 p. ViU. 40-4427

Maryland. Electors of U. S. Pres. & Vice Pres. Proceedings of the electors of President and Vice-President of the United States of America, in and for the State of Maryland, December, 1840. Annapolis, MD: William M'Neir, printer, 1840. 8 p. MdHi. 40-4428

Masini, Francesco, 1804-1863. I moti d'amore. Arietta. [An accomp. agnamento di piano] Philadelphia, PA: Fiot [184-?] 2 p. MB. 40-4429

Mason, Cyrus. The oration on the thirteenth anniversary of the American Institute. Delivered by Cyrus Mason, at the Broadway Tabernacle, October 15th, 1840. Second edition. New York: D. Appleton & Co., 1840. 38 p. GDecCT; MH; MWA; NjR; NNC. 40-4430

Mason, Henry M. An address delivered May 21, 1840 in Easton, Md... Easton, MD?: E. G. Dorsey, printer, 1840. 16 p.

CtHC; CtHT; MdBD; MdHi; NGH. 40-4431

Mason, John, 1646?-1694. Select remains of the Rev. John Mason, M. A., rector of Water Stratford, Buckinghamshore, who died A. D. 1694. Recommended by Dr. Watts. Abridged. New York: The American Tract Society [184-?] 189 p. WHi. 40-4432

Mason, Lowell, 1792-1872. Asaph; or, The choir book. By Lowell Mason. New York: Mason Bros. [etc., etc., 184-?] 384 p. ICU. 40-4433

Mason, Lowell, 1792-1872. The Boston Glee book, consisting of an extensive collection of glees, madrigals, and rounds. Selected from the works of the most admired composers. Together with many new pieces from the German, arranged expressly for this work. By Lowell Mason and George J. Webb. Boston, MA: J. H. Wilkins & R. B. Carer, and G. W. Palmer & Co., 1840. 264 p. CtHC; NUtHi. 40-4434

Mason, Lowell, 1792-1872. Church Psalmody: a collection of Psalms and Hymns, adapted to public worship. Selected from Dr. Watts and other authors. Boston, MA; Philadelphia, PA: published by Perkins & Marvin; Henry Perkins, 1840. 576 p. DLC; NIC. 40-4435

Mason, Lowell, 1792-1872. The juvenile singing school. By Lowell Mason & G. J. Webb, Professors in the Boston Academy of Music. Boston, MA: J. H. Wilkins & R. B. Carter [1840] 128 p. IEG; MDevC; MHi; MPeHi. 40-4436

Mason, Lowell, 1792-1872. Little songs for little singers. Published under the

sanction of the Boston Academy of
Music. Boston, MA: Perkins & Marvin
[1840] 96 p. IaHi; MH; MH-AH. 40-
4437

Mason, Lowell, 1792-1872. Manual of
Christian psalmody; a collection of
psalms and hymns for public worship.
Boston, MA: Perkins and Marvin, 1840.
DLC; PPL-R. 40-4438

Mason, Lowell, 1792-1872. The modern
psalmist:a collection of church music,
comprising the most popular psalm and
hymn tunes and occasional pieces in
general use... By distinguished
European authors, including, also, com-
positions by the editor never before
published ... Boston, MA: J. H. Wilkins
and R. B. Carter, 1840. 352 p. CtY; ICN;
MWA; NNUT; OrP. 40-4439

Mason, Lowell, 1792-1872. The musical
library, a collection of vocal and instrumental music, original and selected,
consisting of songs, duets, glees, marches, waltzes, variations, etc., Beethoven,
von Weber, Mozart, Rossini Rinck...
Edited by Lowell Mason and George J.
Webb. Boston, MA: Ditson [184-?] 196
p. NRU-Mus. 40-4440

Mason, Lowell, 1792-1872. The sacred
harp or electic harmony; a collection of
church music... By Lowell Mason and
Timothy B. Mason. New ed., rev. and cor.
Boston, MA: s. l., 1840. 232 p. CtY. 40-
4441

Mason, Lowell, 1792-1872. The sacred
harp or electic harmony; a collection of
church music... By Lowell Mason and
Timothy B. Mason. New ed., rev. and cor.
Cincinnati, OH: Published by Truman

and Smith, 1840. 232 p. CtY; DLC; ICN;
TKL-Mc. 40-4442

Mason, M. M. The Southern first class
book; or, Exercises in reading and
declamation. Selected principally from
American authors, and designed for the
use of schools and academies in the
Southern and Western states. By M. M.
Mason, A. B., principal of the Vineville
Academy. Macon, GA: B. F. Griffin and
John M. Cooper, 1840. 336 p. CTHWatk;
PU-Penn. 40-4443

Mason, Samson, 1793-1869. Charge
against Gen. Harrison for voting to sell
white men for debt. Speech on the
general appropriation bill, in the House
of Representatives [of the U. S.] Apr. 24,
1840. [Washington, DC: s. l., 1840] 8 p.
DLC; M; OC; OClWHi. 40-4444

Mason, Samson, 1793-1869. Speech on
the obligation of the U. S., founded on
compacts with Ohio, Indiana, Illinois,
and Missouri, to construct the Cumberland Road, in the House of Representatives, Feb. 11, 1840. Washington, DC: pr.
by Gales & Seaton, 1840. 16 p. DLC; IU;
M; MiU; OClWHi. 40-4445

Mason, Stevens Thomson, 1811-1843.
In chancery. James D. Doty vs. Stevens T.
Mason and others [Kintzing Pritchette
and Moses M. Strong] in relation to the
Title to the Town of Madison. Bill and
Answer. Madison: Josiah A. Noonan,
printer, 1840. 16 p. MBAt; WHi. 40-4446

Mason, Timothy Battelle, 1801-1861.
The sacred harp; or Beauties of church
music. Vol. II: a new collection of psalm
and hymn tunes... collected and arranged
by T. B. Mason. Boston, MA: Robinson,

1840. 279 p. CtMW; MBC; MoS; OC. 40-4447

Mason, Timothy Battelle, 1801-1861. The sacred harp; or Beauties of church music. Vol. II: a new collection of psalm and hymn tunes, anthems, ... sentences and chants, derived from the highest sources of the musical talent of Europe and America... Cincinnati, OH: Truman, 1840. 279 p. CtY; ICN. 40-4448

Massachusetts. Annual reports of the railroad corporations in Mass., 1839-1869. Boston, MA: n. pub., n. pr., 1840-70. 31 v. MBAt; NjR; NNL. 40-4449

Massachusetts. In the House, March 6, 1840. The joint special committee, to whom were referred the petition of Spencer Vining and 272 others of Abington... and many other petitions... relating to slavery. [Boston, 1840] 7 p. MB; Nh. 40-4450

Massachusetts. Map of the railroads of Mass. Boston, MA: s. l. [184-?] p. MB. 40-4451

Massachusetts. Minority report of the Committee on Education [regarding the abolition of the Board of Education and the normal schools] Boston, [1840] 22 p. MiU-C; Nh; NIC. 40-4452

Massachusetts. New map of Mass., corrected from the survey... Boston, MA: N. Dearborn, 1840. MB. 40-4453

Massachusetts. Ordered that the committee on education consider the expediency of abolishing the Board of Education, and the Norman Schools, and report by bill or otherwise. Boston, MA: n. pub., n. pr., 1840. 23 p. NjR. 40-4454

Massachusetts. Reduction of salaries... Boston, MA: s. l., 1840. PPL. 40-4455

Massachusetts. Report [and resolves relating to slavery and the slave trade, and the admission of new states into the Union. Boston, 1840] 7 p. NIC. 40-4456

Massachusetts. Report of the commissioners for fixing the line of private property in Boston harbor. Boston, MA: s. l., 1840. 28 p. DLC; ICN; MBC; MCM; Nh. 40-4457

Massachusetts. Report of the Committee on the subject of a new canal, to the Proprietors of the Locks and Canals on Merrinac River. Boston, MA: E. N. Moore, printer, 1840. 20 p. MWo. 40-4458

Massachusetts. Report of the Joint Special Committee on laws relating to Intermarriage on intermarriages between white persons and negroes, &c. Boston, MA: s. l., 1840. 9 p. MBC; NIC. 40-4459

Massachusetts. Report on the affairs of the Western rail-road corporation, Mar. 17, 1840. Boston, MA: s. l., 1840. 36 p. DLC; M. 40-4460

Massachusetts. Report on the memorials of the Seneca Indians and others, accepted November 21, 1840, in the Council of Massachusetts. Boston, MA: n. pub., n. pr., 1840. 28 p. CoFcS; DLC; MBAt; NjR; OClWHi. 40-4461

Massachusetts. Report [regarding the abolition of the Board of Education and the normal school. Boston, [1840] 14 p. NIC. 40-4462

Massachusetts. Reports in the Legislature on the Reduction of Salaries and the Abolishing of Commissions. Boston, MA: s. l., 1840. No Loc. 40-4463

Massachusetts. Resolves relating to the exclusion of the New Jersey Representatives. Boston, MA: s. l., 1840. 27 p. MBC. 40-4464

Massachusetts. Agricultural Survey. Memorial of the commissioner for the agricultural survey of Mass., on a board of industry and statistical returns of the products of industry. Boston, MA: s. l., 1840. 16 p. MBC; Nh; NN. 40-4465

Massachusetts. Agricultural Survey. Report of the Agricultural Meeting, held in Boston, January 13, 1840, containing the Remarks... of the Hon. Daniel Webster... and of Professor Silliman, M. D. With notes by Henry Colman, Commissioner for the Agricultural Survey of the State. Salem, MA: Printed at the Gazette Office, 1840. 36, 7 p. ICJ; MH; MiD-B; NjR; PPAmP. 40-4466

Massachusetts. Bank Commissioners. Report respecting the rates of exchange. Boston, MA: n. pub. [1840] p. Nh. 40-4467

Massachusetts. Board of Inspectors, State Prison. Annual report together with the annual reports of the officers... Boston, MA: n. pub., 1840-54. v. Nh. 40-4468

Massachusetts. Bridge Commission. Report of the Agent and Committee on Charles River and Warren Bridges. Boston, MA: n. pub., 1840-43. 13, 7 p. MBC. 40-4469

Massachusetts. Commonwealth of

Mass. abstract of the returns of insurance companies, incorporated with specific capital... prepared by the Secretary of the Commonwealth. Boston, MA: Dutton and Wentworth, state pr., 1840. 12 p. NjR. 40-4470

Massachusetts. General Court. Aggregate of the returns of the several towns in each county of the commonwealth for the year 1840. [Boston, MA: State printers, 1840] 76 p. ICJ; M. 40-4471

Massachusetts. General Court. The consitution of the Equitable Safety Marine and Fire Insurance Company, incorporated by the Legislature of Massachusetts, April 6, 1839. Boston, MA: John H. Eastburn, printer, 1840. 30 p. MH-BA. 40-4472

Massachusetts. General Court. Report and bill for the establishment of a controller's office. Boston, MA: s. l., 1840. Nh. 40-4473

Massachusetts. General Court. Report and bill to abolish imprisonment for debt. Boston, MA: s. l., 1840. Nh. 40-4474

Massachusetts. General Court. Report and resolution respecting bankruptcy. [Boston, MA: s. l., 1840.] p. Nh. 40-4475

Massachusetts. General Court. Report and resolution urging the necessity of providing effective measures... [Boston, MA: s. l., 1840.] p. Nh. 40-4476

Massachusetts. General Court. Report and resolves relating to slavery and the slave trade and the admission of new states into the Union. Boston, MA: n. pub., 1840. MH. 40-4477

Massachusetts. General Court. Report of the Joint Special Committee to whom were referred petitions praying that so much of the revised statutes as relates to intermarrige between white persons and Negroes, etc. be erased. [Boston, MA: s. l., 1840.] p. MH. 40-4478

Massachusetts. General Court. Committee on Currency. Report on so much of the Governor's address as relates to the currency. [Boston, MA: s. l., 1840] 20 p. MH-BA. 40-4479

Massachusetts. General Court. Committee on Railways and Canals. Report of the Committee... [Boston, MA: s. l., 1840] 13 p. DLC. 40-4480

Massachusetts. General Court. Committee on Railways and Canals. Reports of the Boston and Lowell... [Boston, MA: s. l., 1840] 7 p. IU. 40-4481

Massachusetts. General Court. House of Representatives. House... No. 62... Order that so much of the Governor's address... Boston, MA: s. l., 1840. DLC. 40-4482

Massachusetts. General Court. House of Representatives. Minority report of the Comm. of education... Boston, MA: s. l., 1840. Nh. 40-4483

Massachusetts. General Court. House of Representatives. Minority report on the expediency of making members... Boston, MA: s. l., 1840. Nh. 40-4484

Massachusetts. General Court. House of Representatives. Report on the amendments of the Constitution. Boston, MA: s. l., 1840. Nh. 40-4485

Massachusetts. General Court. House of Representatives. Report of the Comm. on education. Boston, MA: s. l., 1840. Nh. 40-4486

Massachusetts. General Court. House of Representatives. Report on the competency of jurors and witnesses. Boston, MA: s. l., 1840. Nh. 40-4487

Massachusetts. General Court. House of Representatives. Report on the currency. Boston, MA: s. l., 1840. Nh. 40-4488

Massachusetts. General Court. House of Representatives. Report on the expediency of regulating the rate of interest. Boston, MA: s. l., 1840. Nh. 40-4489

Massachusetts. General Court. House of Representatives. Report relating to manufactures. Boston, MA: s. l., 1840. Nh. 40-4490

Massachusetts. General Court. House of Representatives. Rules and orders to be observed in the House of Representatives of the commonwealth of Massachusetts... Boston, MA: Dutton and Wentworth, state printers, 1840. 104 p. MiD-B. 40-4491

Massachusetts. General Court. House of Representatives. Special Comm. on repealing laws of interest. Boston, MA: s. l., 1840? 25 p. MH-BA. 40-4492

Massachusetts. General Court. Joint Special Committee on Petition of Jas. P. Boyce. In the House of Rep., March 6,

1840... [Boston, MA: s. l., 1840] 9 p. MB. 40-4493

Massachusetts. General Court. Joint Special Committee on Western Railroad Corporation. [Report on Railroad Corporations] [Boston, MA: s. l., 1840?] 36 p. WU. 40-4494

Massachusetts. General Court. Senate. The committee on education, to whom was recommitted their report on the petition of Benjamin Greenleaf and others. [Boston, MA: s. l., 1840. 11 p. NjR. 40-4495

Massachusetts. General Court. Valuation Committee. Valuation Commission report on manufactures. [Boston, MA: s. l., 1840] p. MB. 40-4496

Massachusetts. Governor. Report on so much of the Governor's address as relates to manufactures. [Boston, MA: n. pr., 1840] 7 p. MBC. 40-4497

Massachusetts. Governor. Special message to the Senate and House of Rep. [Boston, MA: n. pr., 1840-42] p. Nh. 40-4498

Massachusetts. Governor [Marcus Morton] Address of his Excellency Marcus Morton to the two branches of the legislature, on the organization of the government for the political year commencing January 1, 1840. [S. l.: n. pr., 1840] 16 p. CSmH; ICU; RPB. 40-4499

Massachusetts. Governor [Marcus Morton] ... A proclamation for a day of public humiliation, fasting and prayer... Thursday, the second day of April next... Given... this third day of March... one thousand eight hundred and forty... [Bos-

ton, MA: n. pr., 1840] p. M; MBC; MHi; MiU-C. 40-4500

Massachusetts. Laws, statutes, etc. Act concerning the militia. [Boston, MA: n. pr., 1840] 68 p. MBC. 40-4501

Massachusetts. Laws, statutes, etc. Act to unite the West Stockbridge Railroad Corporation and the Hudson and Berkshire Rail-road Company. Boston, MA: s. l., 1840. 4 p. MBC. 40-4502

Massachusetts. Laws, statutes, etc. A compendium and digest of the laws of Massachusetts... Boston, MA: Printed by Thomas B. Waite & Co., 1840. 750 p. Nv. 40-4503

Massachusetts. Laws, statutes, etc. Laws and Resolves passed by the Legislature of Massachusetts, in the year 1841. Published by the Secretary of the Commonwealth. Boston, MA: Dutton & Wentworth, printers to the State, 1840. 335 p. F-SC; IaU-L; MBC; NNLI; TxU-L. 40-4504

Massachusetts. Laws, statutes, etc. Militia laws of the U. S. Boston, MA: s. l., 1840. 119 p. MB. 40-4505

Massachusetts. Laws, statutes, etc. Report on the expediency of modifying or repealing all laws regulating the rate of interest. Boston, MA: s. l., 1840? 26 p. MH-L; MH-BA. 40-4506

Massachusetts. Legislature. ... Resolutions of the Legislature of Massachusetts, on the subject of the public lands, January 13, 1840. [Washington, DC: Blair & Rives, printers, 1840?] p. CU-B. 40-4507

Massachusetts. Legislature. House of Representatives. An account of the State of the Treasury of the Commonwealth of Massachusetts House, January 1, 1840. House. No. 5. Boston, MA: Dutton and Wentworth, printers to the State, 1840. 36 p. MiD-B. 40-4508

Massachusetts. Legislature. House of Representatives. Question of order, interested members, Massachusetts House of Representatives, Feb. 19, 1840. [Boston, MA: s. l., 1840] 4 p. MB; MHi. 40-4509

Massachusetts. Legislature. House of Representatives. Report of the Committee on elections in the Mass. H. of R. in the case of Daniel Bassett. [S. l.: s. l., 1840] 2 p. MBC. 40-4510

Massachusetts. Legislature. Senate. Report and resolutions as to granting aid to the School Teachers' Association... Boston, MA: s. l., 1840. Nh. 40-4511

Massachusetts. Legislature. Senate. Report and resolutions concerning the Charles river... Boston, MA: s. l., 1840. Nh. 40-4512

Massachusetts. Legislature. Senate. Report of the Joint Special Comm. concerning the small pox... [Boston, MA: s. l., 1840] 28 p. CtY-M; DLC; MBM; Nh; NN. 40-4513

Massachusetts. Legislature. Senate. Report on the expediency of a general law enabling persons to erect houses... Boston, MA: s. l., 1840. Nh. 40-4514

Massachusetts. Legislature. Senate. Reports relating to the returns of votes... Boston, MA: s. l., 1840. Nh. 40-4515

Massachusetts. Legislature. Senate. A table giving name of each city and town, with its population, by the census of 1840. Senate. No. 18. Commonwealth of Massachusetts. In Senate, January 14, 1852... Boston, MA: s. l., 1840. 28 p. MeHi. 40-4516

Massachusetts. Legislature. Senate. Committee on Public Charitable Institutions. Report respecting the New England Asylum for the Blind. [Boston, MA: s. l., 1840] 12 p. MBC; MH-M; Nh; WHi. 40-4517

Massachusetts. Militia. Divison orders; orders; and regimental orders. Braintree, Aug. 29; Boston, Sept. 4 & 18, 1840. Boston, MA: s. l., 1840. MHi. 40-4518

Massachusetts. Militia. Report of the committee on the militia, Council Chamber, April 17, 1840. Boston, MA: s. l., 1840. 12 p. MHi. 40-4519

Massachusetts. Secretary of Commonwealth. Abstract of the returns of the several registers of deeds in Mass., 1839. Boston, MA: s. l., 1840. Nh. 40-4520

Massachusetts. State Teachers' College, Bridgewater, Mass. Catalogue. [S. l.: s. l., 1840-55. v. MH. 40-4521

Massachusetts. Treasury Department. Estimate of the probable income and... [S. l.: s. l., 1840. Nh. 40-4522

Massachusetts. Zoological and Botanical Survey. Reports on the herbaceous plants and on the quadrupeds of Massachusetts. Pub. agreeably to an order of the Legislature, by the Commissioners on the Zoological and Botanical Survey of the State. Cambridge, MA: Folsom, Wells, and Thurston, printers, 1840. 80 p. MH-A; MiU; NN; ODW; PPAN. 40-4523

Massachusetts Anti-slavery Society. Anti-slavery fair... proposed by the women of the Massachusetts Anti-slavery Society. [Boston, 184-?] Broadside. NIC. 40-4524

Massachusetts Anti-Slavery Society. Catalogue of publications for sale at the depository of the Massachusetts Anti-Slavery Society... Boston, MA: Henry L. Devereux, printer, 1840. 4 p. CSmH; MeHi; MPeaHi. 40-4525

Massachusetts Anti-slavery Society. Order of services in commemeration of the life and character of Charles Follen, held in Marlboro Chapel, April 17, 1840. [Boston, 1840] Broadside. NIC. 40-4526

Massachusetts Charitable Eye & Ear Infirmary, Boston. Acts & resolves, with the by-laws of the corporation. Boston, MA: s. l., 1840. 2 v. in 1. MB. 40-4527

Massachusetts defrauded in relation to the public lands. [Boston, MA: Weeks, Jordan & Co., 1840?] 11 p. MH. 40-4528

Massachusetts Female Emancipation Society. Address... to the women of Massachusetts. [Boston, 1840] Maury, Abraham Poindexter, 1801-1848. Address on the life and character of Hugh Lawson White, delivered at Franklin, May 9, 1840. Franklin, [Tenn.] Printed at the Review Office, 1840. 15 p. DLC; MB; OFH; THi; TU. 40-4529

Massachusetts Health Insurance Com-

pany, Boston. [Prospectuc] Boston, MA: s. l., 184-? 16 p. MB. 40-4530

Massachusetts Homeopathic Medical Society. Proceedings... Vol. 1-, 1840-. Boston, MA: The Society, 1840-. v. MBU-M; MH-M; PPCP; PPHa. 40-4531

Massachusetts Medical Society. Acts of incorporation, and acts regulating the practice of physick and surgery, with the by-laws and orders. Boston, MA: Putnam & Hewes, 1840. 96 p. DLC; MB; MHi; MiDW-M. 40-4532

Massachusetts Register & Business Directory. The Massachusetts Register, and United States Calendar for 1841, and other valuable information. Boston, MA: James Loring, publisher, 1840. 250 p. MeHi; MHa; MoSpD; MTop. 40-4533

Massachusetts Sabbath School Society. A Biblical catechism No. 2. Stereotype edition. Boston, MA: Massachusetts Sabbath School Society, 1840. MH. 40-4534

Massachusetts Temperance Convention. Proceedings of the Mass. State Temperance convention, Feb. 12, 1840. Boston, MA: Printed by Whipple & Damrell, 1840. 31 p. MB; MBC; MMeT; NjR; NN. 40-4535

Massillon Rolling Mill Company, Ohio. Abstract of the reports and documents relating to the property and present condition of the Massillon Rolling Mill Co. Boston, MA: printed by Perkins & Marvin, 1840. 27 p. MH-BA. 40-4536

Massinger, Philip, 1583-1640. A new way to pay old debts. A comedy in five acts. New York: S. French [184-?] 75 p. MH; NN. 40-4537

Mather, Cotton, 1663-1728. Essays to do good addressed to all Christians, whether in public of private capacities. New York: American Tract Society [184-?] p. CSmH; DLC; FMU; MB; MH. 40-4538

Mathews, Charles [James] Used up; a petit comedy, in two acts. Translated from the French of "L'homme blase," [by F. A. Duvert and Augustin Theodore, chevalier de Lauzanne de Vaux Roussel] New York: W. Taylor & Co [184-?] 38 p. MH; NIC. 40-4539

Mathews, Cornelius, 1817-1889. The Motley book. A series of tales and sketches. By the Late Ben. Smith [pseud.] 3d ed. New York: Banj. G. Trevett, 1840. 190 p. CtY; DLC; ICU; MB; MnU; NIC; OMC. 40-4540

Mathews, Cornelius, 1817-1889. The politicians. A comedy in five acts. New York: B. G. Trevett, 1840. 118 p. DLC; MB; MH; RPB. 40-4541

Mathews, James McFarlane. What is your life? A sermon preached on the loss of the Lexington. New York: G. F. Hopkins, 1840. 20 p. MBAt; MH; MH-AH; NjR; RPB. 40-4542

Matlock, Lucius C. The history of American slavery and methodism, from 1780-1849, and history of the Wesleyan methodist connection in America. In two parts. By Lucius C. Matlock. [New York?: s. l., 1840] 368 p. ArLP. 40-4543

Matthews, John. Divine purpose displayed in the works of providence and

grace, in a series of letters to an inquiry [sic] friend. Philadelphia, PA: Presbyterian Board of Publication, 1840. 276 p. CtB; IaK; KyLo; NCH; ViRut. 40-4544

Mattison, Hiram. A discourse, in defence of the first day of the work as the Christian Sabbath. Delivered in the Seventh-Day Baptist Church, at Adams Center, N. Y., June 28, 1840. Watertown, NY: Knowlton & Rice, 1840. 36 p. MH; N; TxDaM. 40-4545

Maury, Abram Poindexter. Address of the Honorable Abram P. Maury, on the life and character of Hugh Lawson White. Delivered at Franklin, May 9, 1840. Published by request. Franklin: Printed at the Review Office, 1840. 15 p. DLC; MBAt; OFH; T; THi; TKL-Mc; TU. 40-4546

Maury, F. Treatise on Dental Art. Founded on Actual experience [vignette] by F. Maury, Dentist of the Royal Polytechnic School. Translated from the French with notes and additions by J. B. Savier, Doctor of Dental Survery. Philadelphia, PA: Lea & Blanchard, 1840. 285 p. KyLoU-D. 40-4547

Maury, Matthew Fontaine, 1806-1873. Our Navy; extracts from the Lucky Bag on the reorganization of the navy. Washington, DC: Madisonian office [1840] p. DeGE; DLC; MBAt; MH. 40-4548

May, Caroline. American female poets. Philadelphia, PA: Lindsay and Blakiston, 1840. MtStJosC. 40-4549

May, Hiram. The harp: being a collection of hymns and spiritual songs, adapted for all purposes of social and religious worship. By Rev. Hiram May... Perry, NY: American Citizen Office, 1840. 360 p. NNUT; NRU-Mus. 40-4550

May, J. G. The Lord's Prayer. Composed by J. G. May; the words by the Rev. C. E. Copyright secured according to law. Philadelphia, PA: G. Willig [184-?] 2 p. ViU. 40-4551

May, Samuel Joseph, 1797-1871. A discourse on the life and character of the Rev. Charles Follen, who perished, Jan. 13, 1840, in the conflagration of the Lexington. Delivered before the Massachusetts Anti-slavery Society, in the Marlborough Chapel, Boston, April 17, 1840. Boston, MA: Devereux, 1840. 30 p. ICMe; NcD; OClWHi; PHi; RPB. 40-4552

Mayo, Robert, 1784-1864. The affidavit of Andrew Jackson, taken by the defendants in the suit of Robert Mayo vs. Blair & Rives for a libel, analysed and refuted, by Robert Mayo... Washington, DC: Printed for the plaintiff, 1840. 23 p. ICU; MNBedf; Nh; PPB; RPB; TxU. 40-4553

Mayo, Robert, 1784-1864. The affidavit of Andrew Jackson, taken by the defendants in the suit of Robert Mayo vs. Blair & Rives for a libel, analysed and refuted, by Robert Mayo... [3d ed., with supplementary notes] Washington, DC: Printed for the plaintiff, 1840. 80 p. MdHi; Mi; RPB; TxU; Vi. 40-4554

Mayo, Robert, 1784-1864. A word in season; or, review of the political life and opinions of Martin Van Buren... 2d ed. Washington, DC: Wm. M. Morrison, 1840. 46 p. InHi; MdBJ; MdHi; MiD-B. 40-4555

Mayo, Robert, 1784-1864. Addressed to the entire Democracy of the American people... Dedicated to the Tippecanoe clubs of the Union, by a Harrison Democrat... 3d ed. Washington, DC: Wm. M. Morrison, 1840. 46 p. LNH; MH; OClWHi; PPL; WHi. 40-4556

Mazas, F. Three brilliant duetts for two violins. For the practice of the 3rd and 4th and 5th positions. Composed and carefully fingered by F. Mazas. No. 1... Philadelphia, PA: Meignen & Co [184-?] 11 p. ViU. 40-4557

Mazureau, Etienne, 1777-1849. Replique de Mr. Etienne Mazureau, avocat general, aux avocats de l'accuse dous l'offaire de l'etat de la Louisiane, contre Hyppolite Trouette, accuse d'avoir tue Paulin Prue enduel. New Orleans, LA: Stenographie par T. W. Collins, avocat.; Gaux et cie, 1840. 116 p. LNHT; L-M. 40-4558

Mazzinghi, Joseph, 1765-1844. Ye Shepherd's tell me. A celebrated glee for three voices. Composed by J. Mazzinghi. New York: F. RIley [184-?] 8 p. ViU. 40-4559

Meade, William, 1789-1862. Sermon preached on Sunday, February 16, 1840, in the chapel of the Theological Seminary of Virginia, to the students of the high school and the Fairfax Institute. Washington: Printed by J. Gideon, jr., 1840. 15 p. TxU; Vi; ViU. 40-4560

Meade, William, 1789-1862. The wisdom, moderation and charity of the English reformers, and of the fathers of the Protestant Episcopal Church in the United States. A sermon preached before Theological Seminary of Virginia

February 15, 1840. Washington: Printed by J. Gideon, jr., 1840. 28 p. Vi; ViU. 40-4561

Meadows, F. C. A new French and English pronouncing dictionary on the basis of Nugents. With many new words in general use. In two parts. I. French and English. II. English and French... by F. C. Meadows, M. A. With a selection of idiomatic phrases by George Falsom, M. A. Fourth American edition, corrected and improved. New York: Alexander V. Blake, 1840. 376 p. DLC; IU; MoMal; MsMer; NBuT. 40-4562

Mebane, A. W. Address to the people of Northampton. [S. l.: Hertford and Bertie, 1840] 15 p. NcU. 40-4563

Medical Society of the State of New York. Report of a committee of the Medical Society of the State of New York, on the subject of medical education. Albany, NY: Printed by J. Munsell, 1840. 22 p. MB; MHi; NjR; NNN. 40-4564

Meek, Alexander Beaufort, 1814-1865. The South West; Its history, character, and prospects. A discourse for the eighth anniversary of the Erosophic Society of the University of Alabama. Tuscaloosa: C. B. Baldwin, pr., 1840. 40 p. Au; DLC; NN; TNj. 40-4565

Meignen, Leopold. Au clair de la lune... Philadelphia, PA: Fiot [184-?] 4 p. MB. 40-4566

Meignen, Leopold. Beats there a heart on earth sincere. Air from the Opera, The maid of Cashmere. Arranged for the guitar by L. Meignen. Philadelphia, PA: A. Fiot [184-?] 2 p. ViU. 40-4567

Meignen, Leopold. The haunted spring, from the songs of the legends & traditions of Ireland. Arranged for the guitar by L. Meignen. Philadelphia, PA: Fiot, Meignen & co. [184-?] 2 p. ViU. 40-4568

Meignen, Leopold. Liberty for me. Liberte cherie, the admired Swiss air. Sung by Mrs. Keefen in Adam's opera, The Swiss cottage; or, Le chalet... Philadelphia, PA: Fiot, Meignen & co. [184-?] 4 p. ViU. 40-4569

Meignen, Leopold. 2d divertissment for the guitar. Philadelphia, PA: Fiot, Meignen & co. [184-?] 2 p. MB. 40-4570

Meikle, James, 1730-1799. Solitude sweetened; or, Miscellaneous meditations on various religious subjects, by James Meikle. Hartford, CT: William Andrus, 1840. 286 p. CSmH; MWA; NICLA; OU. 40-4571

Meineke, Christopher, 1782-1850. The basket Catillion; or, The Castilian Maid. Arranged as a rondo for the piano forte by C. Meineke. Baltimore, MD: G. Willig [184-?] 3 p. ViU. 40-4572

Meineke, Christopher, 1782-1850. Bird at sea. Written by Mrs. Hemans. Composed for & dedicated to Mrs. Payne by C. Meineke. Baltimore, MD: F. D. Benteen [184-?] 5 p. ViU. 40-4573

Mellen, Greenville, 1799-1841. A book of the United States, exhibiting its geography division, constitution, and government... and presenting a view of the republic generally, and of the individual states... Hartford, CT: Published by H. F. Sumner and Companye, 1840. 824 p. OClWHi. 40-4574

Memes, John S. Memoirs of the Empress Josephine. By John S. Memes, LL. D. Harper's stereotyped edition. New York: Harper & brothers, 1840. 396 p. InRch; MLow; NGlo; PScrHi. 40-4575

Memoir of Anson B. Daniels. Written for the American Sunday-School Union, and revised by the Committee of publication. Philadelphia, PA: American Sunday School Union [1840] 68 p. CtY-M; DLC; MChes; PPAmS. 40-4576

Memoir of Fanny Elssler; with anecdotes of her public and private life! Boston, MA: Fisher, 1840. 24 p. MB; NN. 40-4577

Memoir of Mary Anne Hooker... for the American Sunday School Union, and revised by the committee of publication. Philadelphia, PA: American Sunday School Union, 1840. 177 p. GMM; ICBB; MB; NcWsS; NNUT. 40-4578

Memoir of Mr. and Mrs. Wood, containing an authentic account of the principal events in the lives of these celebrated vocalists; including the marriage of Miss Paton to Lord William Lennox and the causes which led to their divorce, her subsequent marriage to Joseph Wood, and a full statement of the popular disturbance at the Park theatre, New York. Boston, MA: J. Fisher [1840] 36 p. ICU; MdHi; MH; NIC; PU. 40-4579

The Memoir of Mr. and Mrs. Wood, containing an authentic account of the principal events in the lives of these celebrated vocalists, etc. Philadelphia, PA: Turner & Fisher [1840] 36 p. CtY; ICN; MB; MBAt; MH; PU. 40-4580

Memoir of the public and private life of Fanny Elssler. New York: s. l., 1840. 24 p. MB; MWA. 40-4581

Memorial of sundry proprietors and managers of American steam vessels, on the impolicy and injustice of certain enactments contained in the law relating to steamboats... New York: s. l., 1840. 23 p. DLC; MH-BA; NN; NNC. 40-4582

Mendelssohn-Bartholdy, Felix, 1809-1847. Elijah, an oratorio. The words selected from the Old Testament, the English version by W. Bartholomew, esq. The music composed by Felix Mendelssohn Bartholdy, Op. 70. Pianoforte arrangement by the author. Boston, MA; New York: G. P. Reed & co.; Billings, Taylor & Aiken [184-?] 296 p. ViU. 40-4583

Mendelssohn-Bartholdy, Felix, 1809-1847. The moon. Der Mond. [Song with accompaniment for piano forte] Boston, MA: Richardson [184-?] 2 p. MB. 40-4584

Mendelssohn-Bartholdy, Felix, 1809-1847. The wedding march, from Shakespeare's Midsummer nights' dream. [For piano forte] 4 hands. Boston, MA: Reed & co. [184-?] 7 p. MB. 40-4585

Menzel, Wolfgang, 1798-1873. German literature. Tr. from the German of Wolfgang Menzel by C. C. Felton... Boston, MA: Hilliard, Gray and Co., 1840. 3 v. KyDC; LNP; OHi; PWW; Wa. 40-4586

Mercein, Imogen. Conversations on the geography, topography, and natural history of Palestine, by Imogen Mercein...

New York: Published by T. Mason and G. Lane, 1840. 304 p. CtMW; MH; OO. 40-4587

Mercersburg, Pa. Reformed Theological Reformed Seminary. Anreden, gehalten b ei der Einsetzung des Ehrw. J. W. Nevin, D. D., als professor der Theologie in dem Theologischen Seminar der Deutsch Reformirten Kirche, Mercersburg, Penn., May 20, 1840. Heransgegeben auf beordnung der Board der Besucher. Chambersburg, PA: Gedruckt in der Druckerei der Deutsch-Reformirten Kirche, 1840. 32 p. PJi; PLERCHi. 40-4588

Merchants' and Farmers' Mutual Fire Insurance Company of Worcester, Mass. An explanation of the plan upon which it is established. Worcester, MA: J. GCrout, jr., printer, 1840. 23 p. NNInS. 40-4589

Merchants magazine and commercial review. Vol. 1-63, July, 1839 - Dec., 1870. New York: F. Hunt [etc., etc.] 1840-70. 63 v. CoU; IU; MiD; PWW; TxU. 40-4590

Meriwether, James A., 1806-1852. Reply to Nathan Bass. Milledgeville, Ga.: Printed at the Georgia Journal Office, 1840. 44 p. GU. 40-4591

Merlin, Maria de las Mercedes [Jaruco] Contessa de. Memoirs and letters of Madame Malibran. By the Countess of Merlin. With notices of the musical drama in England. Philadelphia, PA: Carey and Hart, 1840. 2 v. CtMW; LNH; MH; MiU; PPL-R; RPA. 40-4592

Merriam, George, 1803-1880. The child's guide: comprising familiar les-

sons, designed to aid in correct reading, spelling, defining, thinking, and acting. Stereotype edition. Springfield, MA: G. & C. Merriam, 1840. 180 p. NBatHL. 40-4593

Merriam, George, 1803-1880. The village reader: designed for the use of schools. By the compilers of the Easy primer... Springfield, MA: Published by G. & C. Merriam, 1840. 300 p. CoGrS; DLC; MH; MiD-B; WHi. 40-4594

Merrick, William Duhurst, 1793-1857. Speech of Mr. Merrick, of Maryland, on the subtreasury bill. Delivered in the Senate of the United States January 23, 1840. Washington, DC: Gales and Seaton, 1840. 16 p. IaHi; MdHi; MWA; PHi; TxDaM. 40-4595

Merrill, Thomas, 1814-1849. The catastrophe; or, A tale of a New Englander: A poem. 2d ed. Newburyport, ME: printed by J. Gilman, 1840. 12 p. DLC; WHi. 40-4596

Merritt, Henry W. Trial of Henry W. Merritt, a special justice for preserving the peace in the City of New York. New York; Albany, NY: Published by Gould, Banks & Co.; Wm. & A. Gould & Co., 1840. 203 p. DLC; In-SC; Nh; O; PP. 40-4597

Merritt, Timothy, 1775-1845. The Christian's manual; a treatise on Christian perfection, with directions for obtaining that state. New York: Mason & Lane, 1840. 152 p. MB. 40-4598

Merry, Robert. Robert Marry's annual for all seasons. New York: Colman, 1840. MA; MB; MWA. 40-4599

Messia, Alonzo, 1665-1732. The devotion to the Three Hours of Agony of Jesus Christ, Our Redeemer... Originally composed at Lima in Peru in the Spanish language, by the R. F. Alphonsa Messia, S. J. Baltimore, MD: Fielding Lucas, Jr., 1840. 69 p. MdB. 40-4600

Metcalf, Theron, 1784-1875. Digest of the decisions of the courts of common law and admiralty in the United States. By Theron Metcalf and Jonathan C. Perkins. Boston, MA: Hilliard, Gray, and company, 1840. 3 v. MBU-L; MdBB; NbCrD; PP; ViU-L. 40-4601

Metcalfe, William. Bible testimony on abstinence for the flesh of animals as food; being an address delivered in the Bible Christian Church... Philadelphia, PA: J. Metcalfe & Co., Printers, 1840. 35 p. OC; PHi; PPM. 40-4602

Methodist almanac for 1841 By David Young. New York: T. Mason and G. Lane [1840] p. MWA; NjR. 40-4603

Methodist Episcopal Church. Address of the Bishops to the General Conference. 1840. Baltimore, 1840-. v. MB; Nh; WHi. 40-4604

Methodist Episcopal Church. A collection of hymns, for the use of the Methodist Episcopal church, principally from the collection of the Rev. John Wesley... Rev. and cor., with a supplement... Cincinnati, OH: Wright & Swormstedt, for the Methodist Episcopal Church, 1840. 623 p. CBPac. 40-4605

Methodist Episcopal Church. A collection of hymns, for the use of the Methodist Episcopal church, principally

from the collection of the Rev. John Wesley, A. M., revised and corrected, with a supplement. New York: T. Mason and G. Lane, publishers, J. Collard, printer, 1840. 624 p. MBNMHi; NNMHi; ViU. 40-4606

Methodist Episcopal Church. A collection of hymns. 4th ed. Fayetteville, NY: Haight Printer, 1840. 504 p. NbLW. 40-4607

Methodist Episcopal Church. The doctrines and Discipline of the Methodist Episcopal Church. Cincinnati, OH: Pub. by J. F. Wright and L. Swormstedt, for the Methodist episcopal church, 1840. CoDI. 40-4608

Methodist Episcopal Church. The doctrine and Discipline of the Methodist Episcopal Church. New York: T. Mason and G. Lane, 1840. 206 p. CBPSR; LNB; MoHi; OBerB; PMA. 40-4609

Methodist Episcopal Church. Hymn book of the Methodist Protestant Church. Compiled by Authority of the General Conference. Third edition. Baltimore, MD: Published by the Book Committee of the Meth. Prot. Church, 1840. 641 p. GEU. 40-4610

Methodist Episcopal Church. Hymns, addresses, Bible lessons, infant class exercises &c., for the annual celebration of the Sunday school of the Forsyth street M. E. church, December 25, 1840. New York: J. W. Harrison, printer, 1840. 39 p. NNMHi. 40-4611

Methodist Episcopal Church. Hymns for the use of the Methodist Episcopal Church principally from the collection of Rev. John Wesley, A. M., late Fellow of

Lincoln College, Oxford, with the tune in the harmonist affixed to each hymn. New York: J. Collord, 1840. 660 p. MBNMHi; MNt. 40-4612

Methodist Episcopal Church. Minutes of the annual conferences of the Methodist Episcopal church, for the year 1773-1828. Volume I. New York: Published by T. Mason and G. Lane, for the Methodist Episcopal church, J. Collord, printer, 1840. 574 p. GEU-T; IC; NcU; OHi; PPPrHi; TxHuT. 40-4613

Methodist Episcopal Church. Conferences. Mississippi. Minutes of the Mississippi annual conference, held in Natchez, December, 1839. Natchez, MS: s. l., 1840. 28 p. MHi. 40-4614

Methodist Episcopal Church. Conferences. New England Southern. Address of the convention of friends of sunday schools, held in Providence, R. I. May 13, 14, 1840. to the members and friends of the Methodist Episcopal Church in Rhode Island and the adjacent towns on the Providence district, with the minutes of the convention. Providence, [R. I.] : B. Cranston and Co., 1840. 19 p. CSmH. 40-4615

Methodist Episcopal Church. Conferences. New Jersey. Minutes of the New Hampshire annual conference of the Methodist Episcopal church held at Burlington, April 15, 1840. Burlington, NJ: Published by J. L. Powell [1840] 12 p. MBC; NNMHi. 40-4616

Methodist Episcopal Church. Conferences. North Ohio. Official minutes of the... annual session of the North Ohio conference... Cleveland, OH: s. l., 1840-

1911. 72 v. CSmH; DLC; IaMpI; ICU; OClWHi. 40-4617

Methodist Episcopal Church. South. Conferences. Texas. Journal. [Texas?] , 1840-1939. 100 v. IEG; NcD. 40-4618

The metropolitan Catholic almanac and Laity's directory for the year of Our Lord 1841. Baltimore, MD: Fielding Lucas, Jr., 1840. 222 p. MB; MoKCC; PHi; PPL-R; WStfSF. 40-4619

Meurer, Moritz, 1806-1877. The life of Martin Luther. Related from original authorities. With 16 engravings. By Moritz Meurer. New York: Printed and Published by H. Ludwig & Co., 1840. 694 p. PATM. 40-4620

Meyer, Heinrich, 1812-1863. 1840... Philadelphia, PA; Braunschweig: J. G. Wesselhoft; J. H. Meyer [etc., etc.] 1840. 348 p. DLC; ICJ; NhD. 40-4621

Meyer, Leopold von, 1816-1883. ... Le Carnaval de venise. Varie pour piano forte par L. De Meyer. Philadelphia, PA; New York: A. Fiot; W. Dubois [184-?] 11 p. ViU. 40-4622

Meyer, Leopold von, 1816-1883. Machmudier, ou, Marche Marocaine. Pour le piano par Leopold De Meyer, membre honoraire de la societe Philarmonique de St. Petersbourg. Oeuvre 22. New York: Chez Scharfenberg & Luis [184-?] 11 p. ViU. 40-4623

Meyer, Leopold von, 1816-1883. ... Marche triomphale d'Isly. Composee pour piano par L. De Meyer. Op. 30... Baltimore, MD: George Willig, Junr. [184-?] 11 p. ViU. 40-4624

Meyerbeer, Giacomo, 1791-1864. Ah! my child [Ah mon fils. Song, mezzo-soprano. Accomp for piano] Boston, MA: Ditson [184-?] 5 p. MB. 40-4625

Meyerbeer, Giacomo, 1791-1864. My heart with fear and trembling. [La crainte m'agite] The celebrated duet, in the opera Marguerite d' Anjou. Translated by B. S. Barclay. Composed by G. Meyerbeer... Philadelphia, PA; New York: A. Fiot; W. Dubois [184-?] 13 p. ViU. 40-4626

Miami University, Oxford, O. Triennial catalogue of the officers and graduates of Miami University, Oxford, Third March, 1840. Oxford, OH: Bishop, 1840. 42 p. NN; OClWHi; PPPXT; PWW. 40-4627

Michigan. Laws, statutes, etc. Acts of the legislature of the state of Michigan, passed at the annual session of 1840. With an appendix, containing an account of receipts and expenditures of the public moneys, from January 1 to November 30, 1840. Detroit, MI: George Dawson, state printer, 1840. 274 p. Wa-L. 40-4628

Michigan. Legislature. Documents accompanying the journal of the state of Michigan, at the annual session of 1840... [Lansing?] : George Dawson, state printer, 1840. 2 v. C. 40-4629

Middlebrook's almanac for 1841. By Elijah Middlebrook. Bridgeport, CT: John B. Sanford [1840] p. MWA. 40-4630

Middlebrook's almanac for 1841. By Elijah Middlebrook. New Haven, CT: Durrie & Peck [1840] p. MWA; NCH. 40-4631

Middlebrook's almanac for 1841. By Elijah Middlebrook. Norwalk, CT: E. and W. E. Bissell [1840] p. MWA. 40-4632

Middlesex Mechanics Association, Lowell, Mass. Catalogue of the Middlesex Mechanic Association, at Lowell, Mass., with the Act of Incorporation... Lowell, MA: Leonard Huntress, printer, 1840. 168 p. MB; MH; NN; PPL. 40-4633

Miles, Henry Adolphus, 1809-1895. Geneology of the Miles family. [Lowell, Mass.: Norton, printer, 1840] 12 p. DLC; MWA. 40-4634

Miles, Henry Adolphus, 1809-1895. On natural theology as a study in schools. A lecture delivered before the American Institute of Instruction, August, 1839. Boston, MA: s. l., 1840. MBAt; MB; MH; NcD. 40-4635

Milk for babes; or, A Catechism in verse. Northampton, MA: Metcalf, 1840. 22 p. MHolliHi; MNF. 40-4636

Mill Pond Wharf Corporation, Boston, Mass. Catalogue of 278 lots of land, belonging to the Corporation, the right of choice among which will be sold at auction, May 28, 1840. Boston, MA: printed by Crocker and Brewster, 1840. 20 p. DLC; MB; MHi; MWA; NjR. 40-4637

Miller, Alex H. Address delivered before the Wirt Institute, on the sixth of January, 1840, the second anniversary, by Alex H. Miller. Pittsburgh, PA: Jaynes [Franklin Head] 1840. 32 p. NjR; OClWHi. 40-4638

Miller, J. R. The history of Great

Britain. By J. R. Miller. Philadelphia, PA: M'Carty and Davis, 1840. 724 p. DAU; OClW. 40-4639

Miller, Jacob Welsh, 1800-1862. Speech of Mr. Miller, of Morris, on the joint resolutions, relative to the exclusion of the representatives of New Jersey from Congress. Delivered in Council, January 23, 1840. Trenton, NJ: Sherman & Harron, 1840. 12 p. NjR; OClWHi. 40-4640

Miller, John G. The great convention. Desription of the convention of the people of Ohio held at Columbus on the 21st and 22d February, 1840. By John G. Miller... Embracing the speeches of the Hon. J. C. Wright, Charles Anthony, esq., and others. Columbus, OH: Wright [1840] 40 p. MH; MiD-B; OC; OClWHi; OFH. 40-4641

Miller, Samuel, 1769-1850. The Christian education of the children and youth in the Presbyterian church. By the Rev. Samuel Miller... Philadelphia, PA: Presbyterian Board of Publication, 1840. 66 p. MWiW; NNUT; OSW; PU; TNP; ViRut. 40-4642

Miller, Samuel, 1769-1850. An essay on the nature, warrant and duties of the office of the ruling Elder, in the Presbyterian Church. By Samuel Miller, D. D. Third ed. Philadelphia, PA: Presbyterian Board of Publication, James Russell, publishing agent, 1840. 324 p. LNB; NjP; OO; PPPrHi; WHi. 40-4643

Miller, Samuel, 1769-1850. History of the early use of prelacy. By the Rev. Samuel Miller, D. D. Philadelphia, PA: Presbyterian Board of Publication

[1840?] 46 p. CU; IaDuU; MH; NcD; NjP. 40-4644

Miller, Samuel, 1769-1850. Infant baptism scriptural and reasonable, and Baptism by sprinkling or, affusion, the most suitable and edifying mode. By Samuel Miller, D. D. Philadelphia, PA: Presbyterian Board of Publication, James Russell, publishing agent, 1840. 122 p. MsSC; OO; PPM; RPB; WHi. 40-4645

Miller, Samuel, 1769-1850. Lives of Jonathan Edwards and David Brainerd. By Samuel Miller and William B. P. Peabody. Conducted by Jared Sparks. New York: Harper & Bros. [1840?] 373 p. MiU-C; MSbo; NGlc; RPE. 40-4646

Miller, Samuel, 1769-1850. Memoir of Charles Nisbet, D. D. By Samuel Miller, D. D. New York: Robert Carter [1840?] 358 p. CtHC; DLC; KyLxCB; NGH; PPAmP. 40-4647

Miller, Samuel, 1769-1850. Memoir of the Rev. John Rodgers, late pastor of the Wall Street and Brick Churches, in the city of New York. Philadelphia: Presbtyerian Board of Publication, 1840. 240 p. DLC; NcD; NjP; OClW; OOxM. 40-4648

Miller, Samuel, 1769-1850. Presbyterianism: the truly primitive and apostolical constitution of the church of Christ. By Samuel Miller. Philadelphia, PA: Presbyterian Board of Publication, 1840. 98 p. CtHC; KyLoS; MBC; NjR; PPM. 40-4649

Miller, Samuel, 1769-1850. Presbyterianism: the truly primitive and apostolical constitution of the church of Christ. By Samuel Miller, D. D. Philadelphia, PA: William S. Martien, 1840. 122 p. GDecCT; ICU; LNB; NcG; ViRut. 40-4650

Miller, Samuel, 1769-1850. Primitive and apostolical order of the church of Christ vindicated. By Samuel Miller... Philadelphia, PA: Presbyterian Bd. of Pub., 1840. 384 p. GDecCT; ICU; MH; NjP; ScDuE. 40-4651

Miller, Thomas, 1806-1873. Introductory lecture on anatomy. By Thomas Miller, M. D., professor of anatomy and physiology, Columbia College, D. C. Delivered on Thursday, the 5th of November, 1840. Washington, DC: Printed by J. Giden, Jr., 1840. 20 p. DLC; DNLM; MdUM; OC. 40-4652

Miller, Thomas, 1807-1874. Lady Jane Grey: an historical romance. Philadelphia, PA: Lea & Blanchard; Griggs & Co., 1840. 2 v. IaFair; MBL; MFai; TNP; WU. 40-4653

Miller, William, 1782-1849. Evidence from Scripture and History of the Second Coming of Christ about the year 1843; exhibited in a course of lectures. By William Miller. Boston, MA: Published by B. B. Mussey, 1840. 300 p. CtHC; IaGG; MBC; RWe; TxU. 40-4654

... Miller's Planters' & Mechanics' Almanac... 1841... calculated by David Young... 2d ed. Charleston, SC: printed, published and sold by A. E. Miller [1840] 48 p. MWA; WHi. 40-4655

Miller's Public Circulating Library. Catalogue of books belonging to Miller's Public Circulating Library, No. 38 State Street Schenectady. Schenectady, NY: Riggs & Norris, printers, 1840. 44 p. NSchHi; NSchU. 40-4656

Millville, Mass. Congregational Church. Doctrinal articles of faith-covenant... Providence, RI: s. l., 1840. 28 p. MBC. 40-4657

Milman, Henry Hart, 1791-1868. ... Fazio; or, The Italian wife. A tragedy in five acts. By the Rev. H. H. Milman. With state directions, and costumes, marked and corrected by J. B. Addis, prompter. New York: S. French, 184-? 60 p. CSt; MH. 40-4658

Milman, Henry Hart, 1791-1868. History of Latin Christianity, including that of the Popes to the Pontificate of Nicholas V. New York: Sheldon & Co., 1840. 3 v. NPee. 40-4659

Milman, Henry Hart, 1791-1868. ... The History of the Jews, from the earliest period to the present time. By Rev. H. H. Milman... New York: Harper & brothers, 1840-41. 3 v. InRch; MdAN; MdBJ. 40-4660

Milner, John, 1752-1826. A brief summary of the history and doctrine of the Holy Scriptures. By the Right Rev. Dr. Milner, V. A. F. S. A. In two parts. Philadelphia, PA: published by Eugene Cummiskey, 1840. 278 p. ICBB; InStma-S; MdW; NcBe; OClStM. 40-4661

Milner, John, 1752-1826. The end of religious controversy in a friendly correspondence, between a religious society of Protestants and a Catholic Divine. By John Milner, Bp: of Castabala. New York: Edward Dunigan and Brother [184-?] 318 p. MH. 40-4662

Milton, John, 1608-1674. Paradise lost. A poem. In twelve books. New York: C. Wells, 1840. 40-4663

Milton, John, 1608-1674. Paradise lost. A poem. In twelve books. A new edition. Boston: Stimpson and Company, [184-?] 294 p. WaPs. 40-4664

Milton, John, 1608-1674. Paradise lost. A poem. In twelve books. A new edition. Boston: Weeks, Jordan & Co., 1840. 294 p. CtY. 40-4665

Milton, John, 1608-1674. The poetical works of John Milton. With a memoir and critical remarks on his genius and writings, by James Montgomery... New York: Leavitt, 1840. 2 v. in 1. NNC; OCl. 40-4666

Milton, Mass. School reports, 1841-80. Boston, MA: s. l., 1841-1901. 4 v. MB. 40-4667

Milwaukee and Rock River Canal. A documentary history of the Milwaukee and Rock River canal. Compiled and published by order of the Board of Directors of the Milwaukee and Rock River Canal Company. Edited by I. A. Lapham. Milwaukee, WI: Printed at the office of the Advertiser, 1840. 151 p. MB; WHi. 40-4668

Minasi, Carlo. Columbine waltzes. [For pianoforte] Boston, MA: Oakes [184-?] 7 p. MB. 40-4669

Mine, Jacques Claude Adolphe, 1786-1854. ... Faucheux... New York: A. A. Van-Gelder [184-?] 7 p. ViU. 40-4670

Mine, Jacques Claude Adolphe, 1786-

1854. ... Le Fouyou... New York: A. A. Van-Gelder [184-?] 7 p. ViU. 40-4671

Miners' Free Press, Mineral Point, Wisc. Address of the Carrier to the Patrons of the Miners' Free Press, January 1, 1841. [Mineral Point, WI: s. l., 1840] p. WHi. 40-4672

Mines, Flavel S. Call to consideration in the day of adversity, by Flavel S. Mines... New York: Printed by H. Ludwig, 1840. 16 p. MB; NjR; PPPrHi. 40-4673

Miniature Almanack and Pocket Memoranda for 1841... Exeter, NH: Published by E. Fellows, 1840. MWA. 40-4674

A mirror for pretended democracy. With a report on executive patronage... May 4, 1826. [Washington, DC: s. l., 1840] 16 p. DLC; MHi; MiD-B; PPL. 40-4675

Miss Draper's Seminary. Catalogue of the members of Miss Draper's Seminary in the City of Hartford... Sept., 1839... Oct., 1840. Hartford, CT: Burr, 1840. 12 p. CtHWatk. 40-4676

Miss Lucy Long. A very popular melody. Arranged for the piano forte. Boston, MA: Ditson [184-?] 2 p. MB. 40-4677

Mississippi. Auditor's Office. Auditor's Office, Jackson, Mi., 1840. Sir: You will herein find a form for your Assessment return, which you will please to make in alphabetical order. I also send you a reference, by which you can readily make out the amount due by each persons assessed... Very respectfully &c., A. B. Saunders, Auditor. Jackson, MS: s. l., 1840. MsJS. 40-4678

Mississippi. Bank Commissioners. Report of the bank commissioners to the legislature of the State of Mississippi, delivered Jan. 4, 1840. Jackson, MS: s. l., 1840. 40 p. WHi. 40-4679

Mississippi. Governor. Message of the Governor to the legislature of the State of Mississippi. Delivered January 7, 1840. Printed by order of the House of Representatives. Jackson, MS: Printed by C. M. Price, 1840. 51 p. MB; NcD; NN; PPL; TxU. 40-4680

Mississippi. Laws, statutes, etc. Laws of the State of Mississippi, passed at a a regular session of the Legislature, held in the city of Jackson, in the months of January and February A. D. 1840. Printed by authority. Jackson, MS: C. M. Price, state printer, 1840. 301 p. Ar-SC; InSC; MdBB; MsU; NNLI. 40-4681

Mississippi. Laws, statutes, etc. The statutes of the State of Mississippi of a public and general nature... Comp. by V. E. Howard & A. Hutchinson. By authority. New Orleans, LA: E. Johns & Co., 1840. 885 p. KyU-L; Nj; OClW; RPL; WaU. 40-4682

Mississippi. Legislature. House of Representatives. Journal of the House of representatives of the State of Mississippi, at a regular session thereof held in the city of Jackson. Jackson, MS: C. M. Price, state printer, 1840. 967 p. MB; Mi; Ms; NcU; Nj; T; WHi. 40-4683

Mississippi. Legislature. Resolutions of the legislature of Mississippi, in favor of the passage of the independent treasury bill and of the bill to graduate the price of public lands to actual settlers, and approving the policy and measures of the late and present administration, March 5, 1840. Printed by order of the Senate of the United States. Washington, DC: Blair & Rives, printers, 1840. 1 p. MsJs. 40-4684

Mississippi. Legislature. Select Committee. Report of the joint select committee of the Legislature, appointed to examine the Mississippi Union Bank. Delivered February 15, 1840. Jackson, MS: C. M. Price, state printer, 1840. 258 p. MH-BA; Ms-Ar; MsWJ; PHi. 40-4685

Mississippi. Legislature. Senate. Journal of the Senate. [1840-41, 50] called sess., [1858] ; [1870] ; 1872-73; called sess., 1873; 1874; called sess., 1874; 1875-78. Jackson, MS: s. l., 1840-78. 15 v. M; Mi; MsWJ; Nj; WHi. 40-4686

Mississippi Union Bank. Charter of the Mississippi Union Bank and the Act Supplementary. Jackson, MS: Printed by A. B. Beckwith, 1840. 22 p. TxU. 40-4687

Missouri. General Assembly. Preamble and resolution respecting slavery. [Albany, 1840] 4 p. NIC. 40-4688

The Missouri delegation to their constituents. S. l.: s. l., 184-? 14 p. MdHi; TxU. 40-4689

Mitchell, D. The log cabin songster, and straight-out Harrison melodies. Columbus, OH: Printed at the Straight-out Harrison and Tyler office [1840] 105 p. MiU-C; OClWHi. 40-4690

Mitchell, Nahum, 1769-1853. History of the early settlement of Bridgewater, in Plymouth County, Massachusetts, including an extensive family register. By Nahum Mitchell. Boston, MA: Printed for the author by Kidder & Wright, 1840. 400 p. IHi; MeB; Nh-Hi; OCHP; WaSp. 40-4691

Mitchell, R. E. Farewell ode, sung at the close of the exhibition in Pembroke Academy, Nov. 4, 1840. Concord, NH: s. l., 1840. 1 p. Nh-Hi. 40-4692

Mitchell, Samuel Augustus, 1792-1868. An accompaniment to Mitchell's map of the world; on Mercator's projection: containing an index to the various countries, cities, towns, islands, etc. represented on the map. 1st edition. Philadelphia: R. L. Barnes, 1840. viii, [10] -572 p. DLC; IU; NcDaD; OClWHi; ViU. 40-4693

Mitchell, Samuel Augustus, 1792-1868. An accompaniment to Mitchell's reference and distance map of the United States; containing an index of all the counties, districts, townships, towns, in the Union. 1st edition. Philadelphia: R. L. Barnes, 1840. 344 p. DLC; NcD. 40-4694

Mitchell, Samuel Augustus, 1792-1868. Easy introduction to... geography. Philadelphia, PA: Thomas, Cowperthwait & Co., 1840. MH. 40-4695

Mitchell, Samuel Augustus, 1792-1868. Map of the State of Missouri and Arkansas and the Indian territory. Philadelphia, PA: Samuel Augustus Miller, 1840. 1 p. PHi. 40-4696

Mitchell, Samuel Augustus, 1792-1868. Mitchell's geographical reader: a system of modern geography, comprising a description of the world. Philadelphia: Thomas Cowperthwait and Co., 1840. viii, [9] - 600 p. DLC; MB; OCU; PU; ViW. 40-4697

Mitchell, Samuel Augustus, 1792-1868. Mitchell's primary geography. An easy introduction to the study of geography. Designed for the instruction for children in schools & families. By S. Augustus Mitchell. Philadelphia, PA: Thomas Cowperthwait & Co., 1840. 176 p. CtHWatk; KyBC; MH; NN; PP. 40-4698

Mitchell, Samuel Augustus, 1792-1868. Mitchell's school atlas. Revised ed. Philadelphia, PA: Pub. by Thomas Cowperthwait & Co. [1840] 6 p. MH; MNF; PPeSchw; WHi-Miss. 40-4699

Mitchell, T. R. Adieu, Adieu, my ain sweet land. The words and air by T. R. Mitchell. The symphony accompaniment by J. Watson. [S. l.: s. l., 184-?] 3 p. ViU. 40-4700

Mittermaier, Carol Joseph Anton, 1787-1867. Effet of drunkenness upon criminal responsibility and the application of punishment. By Dr. C. J. A. Mittermaier... Translated from the German by L. S. Cushing... Boston, MA: Charles C. Little and James Brown, 1840. 47 p. Nh; RPB. 40-4701

Modern standard drama. A collection of the most popular acting plays, etc... Edited by Epes Sargent. New York: Berford & Co., 1840-48. p. MMilt. 40-4702

Mogridge, George, 1787-1854. History of Thomas Broan. Revised by the committee of publication. Philadelphia, PA: American Sunday School Union [184-?] p. ViU. 40-4703

Mohawk and Hudson Railroad Company. Report on the Affairs of the Mohawk and Hudson Railroad Company... January, 1840. Schenectady, NY:

Riggs & Morris, printers, 1840. 24 p. CSmH; DLC; MiU; NN. 40-4704

Monongahela Navigation Company, Pittsburgh, Pa. Annual reports. Pittsburgh, PA: Printed by Johnston & Stockton, 1840-73. 32 v. DLC; MH; PPM; ViU; WU. 40-4705

Monongalia County Bible Society. Minutes of the meeting of the Monongalia County Bible Society Auxiliary to the American Bible Society, held in Morgantown, on the 11th day of July, 1840... Address by Rev. M. McElroy, sec'y. to contributions, G. R. C. Allen, E. G. Hudnell, Ag. to B. S. B. Va. [S. l.: s. l., 1840?] 24 p. WvU. 40-4706

Monsigny, Pierre Alexandre. Overture to the Deserter. Arranged for the piano forte. New York: Riley [184-?] 3 p. MB. 40-4707

Monson Academy, Monson, Mass. Catalogue of the trustees, instructors and students of Monson academy, for the year ending August 11, 1840. Springfield, MA: Merriam, Wood and company, printers, 1840. 16 p. MMonsA. 40-4708

Monteith, Alexander H. French without a master. A course of lessons in the French language, on the Robertsonian method. Intended for the use of all persons studying the French language without a teacher. Philaldelphia, PA: T. B. Peterson & bro. [184-?] 90 p. DLC; LNP; NN; PPins. 40-4709

Montgomery, James, 1771-1854. ... Lectures on general literature, poetry & c., delivered at the Royal Institution in 1830 and 1831... New York: Harper & brothers, 1840. 324 p. GMM; InRch; MBC; NGH; P. 40-4710

Montgomery, James, 1771-1854. The poetical works of James Montgomery. With a memoir. Boston, MA: Cambridge, MA: Houghton, Mifflin & Co.; The Riverside Press, 1840-58. 5 v. in 2. NjR; WaT. 40-4711

Montgomery, James, 1771-1854. A practical detail of the cotton manufacture of the United States of America... New York: D. Appleton & Co. [etc., etc.] 1840. 219 p. ICJ; MiU; MoS; NcD; NIC-A. 40-4712

Montgomery, William, 1789-1844. Speech of Mr. Montgomery, of North Carolina, on the bill to authorize the issue of treasury notes. Delivered in committee of the whole in the House of Representatives, April 25, 1840. Washington, DC: Printed at the Globe Office, 1840. 16 p. IaHi; MBAt; NcU; OCHP; TxU. 40-4713

Montgomery's tippecanoe almanac for the year 1841. 4th edition. Philadelphia, [1840] 79 p. OCHP. 40-4714

The Monthly chronicle of events, discoveries, improvements and opinions. Intended for the popular diffusion of useful knowledge and an authentic record of facts for future reference... V. 1-3, Apr., 1840-Dec., 1842. Boston, MA: S. N. Dickinson [etc.] 1840-42. 3 v. ICJ; MHi; MiD-B; MnHi; OCl; TJoT. 40-4715

Monticello College, Godfrey, Ill. First and second catalogues of the teachers and members... for the year ending 1839-40. Alton, IL: Parks' Book and Job Office, 1840. 21 p. IHi; MH. 40-4716

The Monument. Edited by Mrs. S. J. Hale. Boston, MA: printed by S. N. Dickinson, 1840. v. 1-. ICU; MB; MBAt; MH; NN. 40-4717

Moody, Charles Cotesworth Rinckney. War and strong drink. [Boston, MA: s. l., 184-?] p. MB. 40-4718

The moon was shining silver bright; or, Clear the track for old Kentucky. Arranged for the piano forte. Baltimore, MD: F. D. Benteen [184-?] 2 p. ViU. 40-4719

Moore, Asher, 1810-1891. The Christian's Triumph. A discourse at the funeral of Rev. Savillion W. Fuller, May 19, 1840. By Rev. Asher Moore. Philadelphia, PA: printed by J. H. Gihon &Co. [1840?] 23 p. MMeT-Hi. 40-4720

Moore, Asher, 1810-1891. A memoir of the late Rev. Savillion W. Fuller. By Rev. Asher Moore. Philadelphia, PA: Pub. & print. by J. H. Gihon & Co., 1840. 214 p. MMeT-Hi; MNF; NCaS; OClWHi; PP. 40-4721

Moore, Edward, 1712-1757. ... The gamester. A tragedy in five acts. By Edward Moore. With the stage directions, cast of characters, costumes, etc., as played at the Park theatre by Mr. and Mrs. Chas. Kean. Taken from the acting copy marked by C. Kean, esq. New York: S. French & son [etc., etc., 184-?] 56 p. CSt; MB; MH; NIC. 40-4722

Moore, Francis, Jr. Map and description of Texas, containing sketches of its history, geology, geography and statistics. With concise statements, relative to the soil, climate, productions, facilities of transportation, population of the country... Philadelphia, PA; New York: H. Tanner, Jr.; Tanner & Disturnell, 1840. 143 p. ICN; MoS; PPi; TxSa; TxSaA. 40-4723

Moore, Henry, 1751-1844. The life of Mrs. Mary Fletcher, consort and relict of the Rev. John Fletcher, vicar of Madely Salop. Comp. from her journal and other authentic documents. By Jenry Moore... New York: Mason, 1840. 398 p. CLSU; MH; NjR; OO. 40-4724

Moore, Jacob Bailey, 1797-1893. The Contract: or, Plain reasons why William Henry Harrison should be elected president of the United States, and why Martin Van Buren should not be re-elected. By an old democrat. New York: J. P. Giffing, 1840. 16 p. In; MH; MiD-B; OO; PPL. 40-4725

Moore, Jacob Bailey, 1797-1893. The laws of trade in the U. S.; being an abstract of the statutes of the several states and territories concerning debtors and creditors. By J. B. Moore. New York: H. Blake, 1840. 360 p. ICU; MB; NhD; NIC; PP. 40-4726

Moore, Martin. Memoir of Sophronia M. Laurence who died at Cohasset, Mass., November 2, 1849, aged twenty-six years. By Martin Moore, A. M., Pastor of the Secod Congregational Church in Cohasset... Boston, MA: Torrey & Blair, printers, 1840. 126 p. MBC; MHi. 40-4727

Moore, T. The dream... by T. Moore. Glee [for S. A. T. B. without acc.] New York: s. l., 1840. CtY. 40-4728

Moore, Thomas, 1779-1852. Alciphron. A poem. By Thomas Moore, Esq. 1st Am.

ed. Philadelphia, PA: Carey and Hart, 1840. 71 p. ViU. 40-4729

Moore, Thomas, 1779-1852. Come, play me that simple air again. Ballad. By Thomas Moore. New York: Firth & Hall [184-?] 5 p. ViU. 40-4730

Moore, Thomas, 1779-1852. Come, play me that simple air again. A ballad. Composed and arranged for the piano forte by Thomas Moore, Esq. Philadelphia, PA: George Willig [184-?] 5 p. ViU. 40-4731

Moore, Thomas, 1779-1852. Irish melodies, with the Original Prefactory Letter on Music; and a supplement containing a selection from his poetical works. First complete American, from the 13th London edition. New York: Linen & Fennell, 1840. InAnd; MLei; OGall; PP. 40-4732

Moore, Thomas, 1779-1852. Lalla Rookh, an oriental romance. New York: Leavitt & Allen, [184-?] xii, 13-346 p. MB. 40-4733

Moore, Thomas, 1779-1852. The life of Lord Byron and his letters and journals. By Thomas Moore, esq. Philadelphia, PA: Thomas Wardle, 1840. 609 p. IUr; KyLoU; OHi; PU; TxU. 40-4734

Moore, Thomas, 1779-1852. Love's Young dream. Written by Thomas Moore, Esq. Arranged by Sir John Stevenson. Baltimore, MD; Cincinnati, OH; Louisville, KY; Philadelphia, PA: W. C. Peters; Peter & Field; Peters Webb & Co.; E. L. Walker [184-?] 2 p. ViU. 40-4735

Moore, Thomas, 1779-1852. Oft in the stilly night. [Song. With accompaniment for piano forte. From Moore's national melodies.] Arranged by Sr. John Stevenson. Boston, MA: Reed [184-?] 3 p. MB. 40-4736

Moore, Thomas, 1779-1852. Origin of the harp. Conzonett for one or two voices. Written by Thos. Moore, Esqr. Baltimore, MD: F. D. Benteen [184-?] 4 p. ViU. 40-4737

Moore, Thomas, 1779-1852. The Poetical works of Thomas Moore, including his melodies, ballads, etc. Complete in one volume. Philadelphia, PA: J. Crissy, 1840. 431 p. NcAS; WvE. 40-4738

Moore, Thomas, 1779-1852. Poetical works of Thomas Moore, including his melodie ballads, etc. Complete in one volume. With a memoir. Philadelphia, PA: Porter & Coatts [184-?] 704 p. NN. 40-4739

Moore, Thomas, 1779-1852. To ladies' eyes. A favorite Irish melody. [Song with accompaniment for the piano forte] Boston, MA: Jackson [184-?] 2 p. MB. 40-4740

Moore, Thomas, 1779-1852. To sigh yet feel no pain. Written by Thomas Moore and adapted to a celebrated air by Haydn. [With accompaniment for the piano forte] New York: Dubois & Stodart [184-?] 2 p. MB. 40-4741

Moore, Thomas, 1779-1852. Travels of an Irish gentleman... Baltimore, MD: s. l. [184-?] p. MB. 40-4742

Moore, Thomas, 1779-1852. The young Indian maid. Written and composed by T. Moore. [Song, S. or T. Accompaniment arranged for the guitar by A. Schmitz] Philadelphia, PA: Fiot [184-?] 2 p. MB. 40-4743

The moral almanac for the year 1841... Philadelphia, PA: pub. by the Tract Assoc. of Friends [1840] 32 p. MWA; WHi. 40-4744

Moran, Peter K., d. 1831. The carrier pigeon. Written by the American bard Percival. The music compoed by P. K. Moran. Louisville, KY: W. C. Peters [184-?] 2 p. ViU. 40-4745

Moran, Peter K., d. 1831. A duett for two performers on one piano forte, in which are introduced the Tyrolese air & Copenhagen waltz. New York: Dubois & Bacon [184-?] 7 p. MB. 40-4746

Moran, Peter K., d. 1831. Kinlock of kinlock. Variations for the piano forte by P. K. Moran. Baltimore, MD: New Orleans, LA: F. D. Benteen; W. T. Mayo [184-?] 3 p. ViU. 40-4747

Moran, Peter K., d. 1831. Kinlock of kinlock. With variations for the piano forte by P. K. Moran. Baltimore, MD: Samuel Carusi [184-?] 3 p. ViU. 40-4748

Moran, Peter K., d. 1831. The Swiss waltz with variations. Boston, MA: s. l. [184-?] p. MB. 40-4749

More, Hannah, 1745-1833. The book of private devotion, a series of prayers and meditations. With an introductory essay on prayer, chiefly from [her] writings. Revised and enlarged edition. New York: Franklin, 1840. 256 p. MB; MH; MH-And. 40-4750

More, Hannah, 1745-1833. The book of

private devotion, a series of prayers and meditations. With an introductory essay on prayer, chiefly from the writings of Hannah More. Revised and enlarged from the 20th London edition. New York: J. A. Hoisington; D. Appleton [184-?] 126 p. DLC. 40-4751

More, Hannah, 1745-1833. Spirit of prayer. To which is added, Pietas quotidiana, or, Prayers and meditations, etc. New York: Swords, Stanford & co., 1840. CtHC. 40-4752

More, Hannah, 1745-1833. The works of Hannah More. First complete American edition. New York: Harper & brothers, 1840. 7 v. GMWa; KyLoS; MBrZ; ScU; TBri. 40-4753

More than one hundred reasons why William Henry Harrison should... have... support... in preference to Martin Van Buren. By a workingman. Boston, MA: printed by Tuttle, Dennett & Chisholm, 1840. 16 p. DLC; ICN; ICU; MBevHi; MBNEH. 40-4754

Morehead, James Turner, 1797-1854. An address in commemoration of the first settlement of Kentucky. Delivered at Boonesborough the 25th May, 1840, by James T. Morehead. Frankfort, KY: A. G. Hodges, state printer, 1840. 181 p. ICU; LU; OFH; TxU; WHi. 40-4755

Morgan, Sydney [Owenson] 1783-1859. Woman and her master. By Lady Sydney Morgan. Philadelphia, PA: Carey & Hart, 1840. 2 v. MH; OCY; PPA; ScSoh; WGr. 40-4756

Morison, John. Parent's friend; a manual of domestic instruction and discipline. With a prefatory address to parents in America, by Samuel Hanson Cox. New York: Gould, Newman & Saxton, 1840. 172 p. CtHC; ICBB; MB; MBC; OO. 40-4757

Morland, Alfred. I wish I'd a thousand a year! New song. [Accomp. for piano forte] Boston, MA: Reed [184-?] 5 p. MB. 40-4758

Morphy, Diego. Idiomatical dictionary, French and English, alphabetically arranged to facilitate the reading of the most popular works... By Diego Morphy... New Orleans, LA: Gaux and co., 1840. 383 p. AU; LNHT; LU. 40-4759

Morrill, Charles. New system of geography on the classification plan. Concord: s. l., 1840. 24 p. MH; Nh: Nh-Hi; WHi. 40-4760

Morris, John G. Popular exposition of the gospels, designed for the use of families, Bible classes, and Sunday schools. By John Morris and Charles A. Smith. Matthew-Mark. Baltimore, MD: Publication Rooms, 1840. 346 p. ICartC; KyLoP; OSW; PWmpDS. 40-4761

Mortimer, Favell Lee [Bevan] 1802-1878. The night of toil; or, a familiar account of the labors of the first missionaries in the South Sea Islands. By the author of the "Peep of Day..." Abridged ed. New York: American Tract Society [184-?] 236 p. MH. 40-4762

Morton, John Maddison, 1811-1891. Box and Cox, a romance of real life in one act. New York: S. French [184-?] 24 p. CtY; MH. 40-4763

Morton, John Maddison, 1811-1891. The mother and child are doing well. A farce in one act. By J. M. Morton, esq., correctly printed for the most approved acting copy, with a description of the costume and the whole of the stage business. New York; Philadelphia, PA: Turner & Fisher [184-?] 25 p. DLC; MB; NcU; RPB. 40-4764

Morton, John Maddison, 1811-1891. Slasher and crasher. A farce in one act. New York: S. French [184-?] 30 p. MH; MnS; NIC. 40-4765

Morton, John Maddison, 1811-1891. ... A thumping legacy. An original farce in one act. By John Maddison Morton... New York: S. French [184-?] 19 p. CSt; ICU; IU; MH; NN. 40-4766

Morton, Marcus, 1784-1864. Address of his excellency Marcus Morton to the two branches of the legislature on the organization of the government for the political year commencing January 1, 1840. Boston, MA: s. l., 1840. 16 p. MiD-B; PPAmP; RPB; WHi. 40-4767

Morton, Marcus, 1784-1864. Answer of the Whig members of the legislature of Massachusetts, constituting a majority of both branches to the address of his excellency, delivered in the convention of the two houses, January 22, 1840. Boston, 1840. 36 p. DLC; PPWa. 40-4768

Morton, Samuel George, 1799-1851. Catalogue of skulls of man and the inferior animals in the collection of Samuel George Morton, M. D... Philadelphia, PA: Printed by Turner & Fisher, 1840. 48 p. MdBM; MHi; Nh; PHi; PPAmP. 40-4769

Morton, Samuel George, 1799-1851. Illustrations of pulmonary consumption.

2nd edition. Philadelphia, 1840. Morehead, James Turner, 1797-1854. An address in commemoration of the first settlement of Kentucky; delivered at Boonesborough, May 25, 1840. Frankfort, Ky.: A. G. Hodges, state printer, 1840. 181 p. DLC; IGK; KyU; MdBP; TKL. 40-4770

Morton, Thomas, 1764-1838. ... A cure for the heartache. A comedy in five acts. By Thomas Morton. With the stage directions, cast of characters, costumes, etc. new York: S. French & son [etc., etc, 184-?] 66 p. CSt; MB; MH. 40-4771

Morton, Thomas, 1764-1838. ... A Roland for an Oliver. A farce in two acts. New York: S. French & son [etc., etc, 184-?] p. MB. 40-4772

Morton, Thomas, 1764-1838. ... Speed the plough. A comedy in five acts. By Thomas Morton. With the stage business, cast of characters, costumes, relative positions, etc. New York: S. French & son [etc., etc., [184-?] 67 p. CSt; NIC. 40-4773

Morton, Thomas, 1764-1838. ... Town and country. A comedy in five acts. By Thomas Morton, rsq. With the stage business, cast of characters, costumes, relative positions, etc. New York: S. French [184-?] 68 p. CSt; MH; NIC. 40-4774

Morton, Thomas, 1764-1838. ... The writing on the wall. A melodrama, in three acts. By Thomas and J. M. Morton... With the stage business, cast of characters, costumes, relative positions, etc. New York: S. French [184-?] 64 p. CSt. 40-4775

Mosby, Mary Webster [Pleasants] 1791-1844. Pocahontas. A legend. With historical and traditionary notes. By Mrs. M. M. Webster. Philadelphia, PA: H. Hooker, 1840. 220 p. DLC; MB; NcD; TxU; ViU. 40-4776

Moscheles, Ignaz, 1794-1870. Erin is my home. Ballad. As sung by Wm. R. Dempster; arranged and adapted to a Bohemian melody. By I. Moscheles. Baltimore, MD: George Willig [184-?] 2 p. ViU. 40-4777

Moscheles, Ignaz, 1794-1870. Erin is my home. Ballad. As sung by Wm. R. Dempster; arranged and adapted to a Bohemian melody. By I. Moscheles. New York: Millets music saloon [184-?] 2 p. ViU. 40-4778

Moscheles, Ignaz, 1794-1870. The Swiss boy. A ballad. With accompaniments for the piano forte. Arranged by J. Moscheles. Baltimore, MD: G. Willig, Jr. [184-?] 2 p. MB; ViU. 40-4779

Moscheles, Ignaz, 1794-1870. The switzer's song of home. Arranged for the guitar by L. Meignen. Philadelphia: Fiot, [184-?] 2 p. MB. 40-4780

Moseley, Henry. Illustrations of mechanics. By the Rev. H. Moseley, M. A., F. R. S. Revised by James Renwick, LL. D. New York: Harper & bros., 1840. 332 p. GU; MB; MLow; MnU; OMC; RKi. 40-4781

Mosheim, John Lorenz, 1694-1755. Ecclesiastical history, ancient and modern... tr. by Archibald Maaclaine, continued to the year 1826, by Charles Coote, and furnished with a dissertation on the state of the primitive church, by George Gleig.

New ed. Baltimore, MD: Plaskitt, 1840.
2 v. KKcBT; NbYC; NUt. 40-4782

Mother Goose. The only true Mother
Goose melodies. Boston, MA: s. l. [184-
?] p. MB. 40-4783

The Mother's manual containing practical hints, by a mother. Cotton Mother's
resolution of a parent... Together with introductory remarks and an appendix.
Dedicated to Christian mothers... Boston, MA: Published by Weeks, Jordan &
co., 1840. 60 p. LU; MBC; PLFM; RPB;
ViU. 40-4784

Motte, Mellish Irving. The Christian
patriot. A sermon, delivered at the South
Congregational Church, Boston, July
5th, 1840, by M. I. Motte, Philadelphia,
by request. Cambridge, MA: Folsom,
Wells & Thurston, 1840. 16 p. ICMe;
MB; MeHi; MHi; RPB. 40-4785

Motte, Mellish Irving. A sermon.
Delivered at the South Congregational
Church, June 28, 1840, by Rev. M. I.
Motte. Published by request. Boston,
MA: Printed by Tuttle, Dennett &
Chisholm, 1840. 12 p. MBAU; MHi. 40-
4786

Mount Carbon Coal Company. The
Mount Carbon coal property.
Wasington, DC: s. l., 1840. 24 p.
OClWHi; PPL-R. 40-4787

Mozart, Johann Chrysostom Wolfgang
Amadeus, 1756-1791. L'addio. The
farewell. [Song. With accompaniment
for piano forte] Boston, MA: Ditson
[184-?] 5 p. MB. 40-4788

Mozart, Johann Chrysostom Wolfgang
Amadeus, 1756-1791. Batti, batti o bel

Masetto. Aria in Il Don Giovanni. [S. Accomp. for piano forte] Boston, MA: Ditson & co. [184-?] 5 p. MB. 40-4789

Mozart, Johann Chrysostom Wolfgang
Amadeus, 1756-1791. La ci darem la
mano. Nay, bid me not resign, love. Duett
[A. B. Accomp. for piano forte] Boston,
MA: Ditson & co. [184-?] 7 p. MB. 40-
4790

Mozart, Johann Chrysostom Wolfgang
Amadeus, 1756-1791. ... Don Giovanni
de Mozart. Baltimore, MD: Geo. Willig,
Junr. [184-?] 7 p. ViU. 40-4791

Mozart, Johann Chrysostom Wolfgang
Amadeus, 1756-1791. ... Go, forget me,
who should sorrow. The music from
Mozart's celebrated opera Il Don
Giovanni. Arranged for the piano forte.
Boston, MA: Oliver Ditson [184-?] 2 p.
ViU. 40-4792

Mozart, Johann Chrysostom Wolfgang
Amadeus, 1756-1791. Life let us cherish.
Baltimore, MD: John Cole & son [184-?]
1 p. ViU. 40-4793

Mozart, Johann Chrysostom Wolfgang
Amadeus, 1756-1791. ... No. 4. A major...
Boston, MA: E. H. Wade [184-?] 13 p.
ViU. 40-4794

Mozart, Johann Chrysostom Wolfgang
Amadeus, 1756-1791. Vedrai carino.
[Song. S....for piano forte] Boston, MA:
Ditson & co. [184-?] 5 p. MB. 40-4795

Mrs. Macdonald and soldier's joy. Baltimore, MD: G. Willig Jr. [184-?] 1 p.
ViU. 40-4796

Muenscher, Joseph. The church choir;
a collection of sacred music, comprising

a great variety of psalm and hymn tunes, anthems, and chants. Arranged for the organ or piano-forte, by Joseph Muenscher. Columbus, OH: Published by Isaac N. Whiting, 1840. var. pag. MdBD. 40-4797

Muller, J. E. ... Cottage duetts, a popular collection of melodies. Arranged for two performers on the piano forte. Baltimore, MD; Cincinnati, OH: G. Willig, Junr.; W. C. Peters & sons [184-?] 3 p. ViU. 40-4798

Muller, J. E. ... Wrecher's daughter. Baltimore, MD: F. D. Benteen [184-?] 3 p. ViU. 40-4799

Muller, Johannes von, 1752-1809. The history of the world: from the earliest period to the year of Our Lord 1783, with particular reference to the affairs of Europe and her colonies. Boston, MA: Marsh, Capen, Lyon, and Webb, 1840. 4 v. IaPeC; MB; MoSpD; NhPet; TNJU. 40-4800

Murphy, Arthur, 1727-1805. ... Three weeks after marriage. A comedy in two acts. By Arthur Murphy. With the stage business, cast of characters, costume, relative positions, etc. New York: S. French & son [etc., etc., 184-?] 32 p. CSt. 40-4801

Murphy, Henry Cruse, 1810-1882. Catalogue of an American library chronologically arranged. [New York: s. l., 1840] 57 p. NNC. 40-4802

Murray, Hugh, 1779-1846. The encyclopedia of geography, comprising a complete description of the earth... by Hugh Murray. Philadelphia, PA: Lea and Blanchard, 1840. 3 v. CtMW; GEU; KHi; TxHR; WvU. 40-4803

Murray, Hugh, 1779-1846. An historical and descriptive account of British America; comprehending Canada, Upper and Lower, Nova Scotia, New Brunswick, etc., their history from the earliest settlement, their statistics, topography, commerce, fisheries, &c., &c. New York: Harper & brothers [1840] 2 v. CS; ICJ; LNH; NjR; RPA. 40-4804

Murray, John, 1741-1815. The life of Rev. John Murray, late minister of the reconciliation, and senior pastor of the Universalists, congregated in Boston; written by himself, the records contain anecdotes of the writer's infancy, and are extended to some years after the commencement of his public labors in America; to which are [sic] added a brief continuation to the closing scene. With notes and appendix by Rev. L. S. Everett. Seventh edition, stereotyped and improved. Utica, NY: Orren Hutchinson, 1840. 324 p. MB; MBC; MoS; NUt; OHi; RHi; WAsN. 40-4805

Murray, Lindley, 1745-1826. Abridgement of Murray's English grammar, with an appendix, containing exercises in orthography, in parsing, in syntax, and punctuation, designed for the younger classes of learners. Boston: R. S. Davis, 1840. 40-4806

Murray, Lindley, 1745-1826. English grammar, adapted to the different classes of learners. With an appendix, containing rules and observations for assisting the more advanced students to write with perspicuity and accuracy. New London, CT: Bolles, 1840. 232 p. MH; OC; ViAl; ViU. 40-4807

Murray, Lindley, 1745-1826. The English reader; or, Pieces in prose & verse, from the best writers; designed to assist young persons to read with propriety and effect; to improve their language and sentiments; and to inculcate some of the most important principles of piety and virtue... By Lindley Murray... Boston, MA: Published by Robert S. Davis, 1840. 264 p. KMK. 40-4808

Murray, Lindley, 1745-1826. The English reader; or, Pieces in prose & verse, from the best writers; designed to assist young persons to read with propriety and effect; improve their language and sentiments; and to inculcate the most important principles of piety and virtue. With a few preliminary observations on the principles of good reading. By Lindley Murray. Bridgeport, CT: J. E. Baldwin, 1840. 263 p. TCU. 40-4809

Murray, Lindley, 1745-1826. The English reader; or, Pieces in prose & verse, from the best writers... With a few preliminary observations on the principles of good reading. By Lindley Murray... Concord, NH: Printed & published by H. Hill & co. [184-?] 252 p. IU. 40-4810

Murray, Lindley, 1745-1826. The English reader; or, Pieces in prose & verse, from the best writers; designed to assist young persons to read with propriety and effect... With a few preliminary observations on the principles of good reading. By Lindley Murray... New London, CT; New York: W. and J. Balles; Collins, Keese & co., 1840. 252 p. IU; MWH. 40-4811

Murray, Lindley, 1745-1826. The English reader; or, Pieces in prose & verse, from the best writers; designed to assist young persons to read with propriety and effect; improve their language and sentiments; and to inculcate the most important principles of piety and virtue. With a few preliminary observations on the principles of good reading. By Lindley Murray. New York; Canandaigua, NY: C. Morse, 1840. 252 p. CSmH; MH; NRU. 40-4812

Murray, Lindley, 1745-1826. Introduction to the English reader. Appendix by I. Alger. Boston, MA: R. S. Davis, 1840. MH. 40-4813

Murray, Lindley, 1745-1826. Introduction to the English reader; or, Pieces in prose and poetry... to which are added rules, and observations for assisting children to read with propriety. By Lindley Murray. Philadelphia, PA: Published by Thomas Sutton, 1840. PScr-Hi. 40-4814

Murray, Lindley, 1745-1826. Murray's English grammar simplified; designed to facilitate the study of the English language. By A. Fisk. Hallowell, MA: Glazier, Masters & Smith, 1840. MH. 40-4815

Murrell, William Meacham. Cruise of the Frigate Columbia around the world, under the command of Commodore George C. Read... by William Meacham Murrell... Boston, MA: Benjamin B. Mussey, 1840. 230 p. AzU; MH; NhD; OCh; WHi. 40-4816

Musard, Phillippe, 1793-1859. [Baden Baden polka] The celebrated Baden Baden polka. Pas Bohemian, arranged by Musard. [For piano forte] New York:

Firth, Pond & Co. [184-?] 2 p. MB. 40-4817

Musard, Phillippe, 1793-1859. Baden Baden polka Pas Bohemian. Arranged by Musard. Baltimore, MD: F. D. Benteen [184-?] 2 p. ViU. 40-4818

Museum of foreign animals; or, history of beasts... New Haven, CT: Printed and published by S. Babcock, n. d. 16 p. CtY; DLC; MH; NN; NNC. 40-4819

Musgrave, George Washington, 1804-1882. A discourse concerning certain evils connected with the late presidential canvas. Baltimore, MD: Hanzsche, 1840. 23 p. DLC; NjP; OClWHi; PHi; TxHuT. 40-4820

Mustang waltz... [For piano forte] [New York: s. l., 184-?] p. MB. 40-4821

Mutter, Thomas Dent, 1811-1859. The salt Sulphur Springs, Monroe County, Pa... Philadelphia, PA: T. K. & P. G. Collins, printers, 1840. 32 p. ICJ; MBC; MiD-B; MnHi; PHi; WHi. 40-4822

Muzzey, Artemas Bowers, 1802-1892. The young maiden. By A. B. Muzzey... Boston, MA: William Crosy & co., 1840. 260 p. MB; MHi; NCaS; NhPet. 40-4823

My soul is one unbroken sigh; or, Thee & only three. Sung in the opera Linda di Chamounix. Baltimore, MD; New Orleans, LA: F. D. Benteen; W. T. Mayo [184-?] 2 p. ViU. 40-4824

My station & its duties, by the author of "The last day of the week." Revised by the editors. New York: Mason & Lane, 1840. 183 p. CtMW. 40-4825

Myers, Peter Hamilton, 1812-1875. Ensenore, a poem... Appeared later under the author's name. A narrative poem about the Indians of Central New York. New York: Wiley, 1840. 104 p. IaGG; ICU; NNC; PHi; TxU. 40-4826

N

Nall, Robert. The amiable young man. A discourse occasioned by the death of George Richard Wright... By Rev. Robert Nall, pastor of the Presbyterian Church at Marion, Alabama... Marion, AL: Printed at the office of the Perry Eagle, 1840. 16 p. MHi. 40-4827

Narrative of the extraordinary life of John Conrad Shafford, known by many by the name of the Dutch hermit... New York: C. L. Carpenter, publisher, 1840. 24 p. DLC; ICN; MiD-B; OClWHi; PU. 40-4828

A narrative of the horrid massacre by the Indians, of the wife and children of the Christian hermit, a resident of Missouri, with a full account of his life and sufferings, never before published. St. Lewis: L. W. Whiting and Co., 1840. 24 p. CSmH; DLC; ICN; MoSM. 40-4829

Nashville, Tenn. University. Laws of the University of Nashville, in Tennessee. New edition. Nashville, TN: Printed by B. R. M; Kennie, Whig and Steam Press, 1840. 31 p. DLC; MB; MH. 40-4830

Nathan, Moses Nathan, 1807-1883. Second annual examination of Sunday School of Mikveh Israel Synagogue, March 29, 1840. With prayer by I. Lieser and an address by M. N. Nathan. Philadelphia, PA: s. l. [1840] 28 p. OCHP; PHi. 40-4831

National almanac... By J. W. Herschell. New York: n. pub., 1840. MWA. 40-4832

National almanac & pocket calendar 1840. New York: J. W. Herschell, 184-? p. OCHP. 40-4833

National anti-slavery standard. V. 1-30, June 11, 1840-Apr. 16, 1870; new ser., v. 1, May-July, 1870; new ser., v. 1-3, July 30, 1870-Dec., 1872. New York: American anti-slavery society [etc., etc.] 1840-72. 34 v. ICU; MH; MiU; MW; PSt. 40-4834

National Convention for the Promotion of Education in the United States, Washington, D. C., 1840. Proceedings of a national convention for the promotion of educationin the United States, held at the City Hall, inthe City of Washington, May 6, 7, 8, 1840. Washington, DC: P. Force, printer, 1840. 23 p. DHELU; DLC; ICU; MnHi; RPB. 40-4835

National Institute for the Promotion of Science, Washington, D. C. Bulletin of the proceedings of the National Institution for the Promotion of Science... Washington, DC: Printed by Gales and Seaton, 1840-46. 64 p. DLC; ICJ; MdBJ; MiD; OClW. 40-4836

National Institute for the Promotion of Science, Washington, D. C. Constitution and by-laws of the National Institution for the Promotion of Science... Washington, DC: Printed by Gales and

Seaton, 1840. 14 p. MiD; MWA; OMC; PP; RPB. 40-4837

National Institute for the Promotion of Science, Washington, D. C. Pamphlets on the National Institution for the Promotion of Science... Washington, DC: s. l., 1840-45. p. Di-GS; PPAN; PU-S. 40-4838

National pictorial primer; or, The first book for children... New York: Cooledge, 184? p. PU-Penn. 40-4839

The National Primer. Philadelphia, PA; Boston, MA; Baltimore, MD: Turner & Fisher; I. Fisher; H. Turner, 1840. 23 p. MdHi; MHa; NIDHi; NjR. 40-4840

National Reform Association. Young America! Principles and objects of the Association, or Agrarian League. By a member. [New York: s. l., 184-?] 16 p. M. 40-4841

Nautical Almanac. Blunt's edition. New York: E. & G. W. Blunt, 1840. MWA. 40-4842

Navillus, pseud. Plenty of money and the United States of American independent of all foreign money markets. By Navillus. New York: S. Colman, 1840. 33 p. DLC; NN; PU. 40-4843

Nax, Joseph. Federal Hill quick march. Composed & respectfully dedicated to Miss Maria L. Whittemore of Fredericksurg, Va. by Joseph Nax. Baltimore, MD; New Orleans, LA: F. D. Benteen; W. T. Mayo [184-?] 3 p. ViU. 40-4844

Neal, John, 1793-1876. Appeal from the American press to the American people, n behalf of John Bratish Eliovich, late a

major general in the service of Her Most Catholic Majesty, the Queen of Spain... and now an American citizen. Portland, Me.: Argus Office, 1840. 48 p. CtY; MH; NN; RPB. 40-4845

Neale, William Johnson, 1812-1893. The flying Dutchman; a legend of the high seas. By the author of Cavendish, &c. Philadelphia, PA: Carey and Hart, 1840. 2 v. MH. 40-4846

Neil, William. Appendix to a document entitled "Minutes of the Reformed Dissenting Presbytery," met according to adjournment, May 18, 1840, at Cherry Fork meeting house, Adams County, O. [Wheeling?: s. l., 1840?] p. PPPrHi. 40-4847

Nelson, David, 1793-1844. The Cause and cure of infidelity: including a notice of the author's unbelief and the means of his rescue. By David Nelson, M. D. New York: American tract society [184-?] 399 p. ICRL; MH; NNUT; PPPrHi; WaS. 40-4848

Nelson, John, 1707-1774. Extract from the journal of John Nelson; being an account of God's dealing with him from his youth to the forty-second year of his age... to which is added an account of his death. New York: T. Mason and G. Lane; J. Collord, pr., 1840. 189 p. NcD; NjR; NNMHi. 40-4849

Nelson, John, 1786-1871. A Thanksgiving sermon, delivered November 28, 1839, by John Nelson, pastor of the First Congregational Society, Leicester, Mass. Published by request. Worcester, MA: Press of the Massachusetts Spy, 1840. 14 p. MB; MBAt; MBC; MWA. 40-4850

Nelson, Sidney, 1800-1862. The boy on the gate. [Song. With accompaniment for piano forte] Written by John Orton, Esq. Composed by S. Nelson. [New York: s. l., 184-?] 7 p. MB. 40-4851

Nelson, Sidney, 1800-1862. Mary of Argyle, an admired Scotch song. Composed by S. Nelson. Baltimore, MD: G. Willig, jr. [184-?] 2 p. ViU. 40-4852

Nelson, Sidney, 1800-1862. Mary of Argyle, an admired Scotch song. [Accomp. for piano forte] Boston, MA: Ditson & co. [184-?] p. MB. 40-4853

Nelson, Sidney, 1800-1862. Mary of Argyle, an admired Scotch song. Written by C. H. Jeffreys. Composed by S. Nelson. New York: C. Christmas [184-?] 2 p. DLC; MB; ViU. 40-4854

Nelson, Sidney, 1800-1862. Mary of Argyle, an admired Scotch song. Written by Ch. Jeffreys; composed by S. Nelson. Philadelphia, PA: A. Fiot [184-?] 5 p. ViU. 40-4855

Nelson, Sidney, 1800-1862. Mary of Argyle, an admired Scotch song. Written by Ch. Jeffreys; composed by S. Nelson. Philadelphia, PA: Klemm & brother [184-?] 5 p. ViU. 40-4856

Nelson, Sidney, 1800-1862. The Pilot. Ballad. [With accomp. for piano forte] Written by Thomas H. Bayly. Composed by S. Nelson. New York: Riley & Co. [184-?] 3 p. MB. 40-4857

Nelson, Sidney, 1800-1862. The rose of Allandale. Ballad. Written by Charles Jeffrey; the music by S. Nelson. Baltimore, MD: Geo. Willig, Jr. [184-?] 3 p. ViU. 40-4858

Nelson, Sidney, 1800-1862. The rose of Allandale. Ballad. Written by Charles Jeffrey; the music by S. Nelson. New York: Firth & Hall [184-?] 3 p. ViU. 40-4859

Nelson, Sidney, 1800-1862. The star spirit. Cavatina. The poetry from, A vision of fair Spirits and other poems by John Graham, Esq, Wadham College. The music composed & dedicated to Miss Alderson Douglas by S. Nelson. New York: James L. Hewitt [184-?] 5 p. ViU. 40-4860

Nelson, Sidney, 1800-1862. That friendship which fades not. [Song. Accomp. for piano forte] Philadelphia, PA: Nunns [184-?] 3 p. MB. 40-4861

Nelson, Sidney, 1800-1862. 'Tis sweet to see the blooming rose. A song. Written by C. J. Jeffreys, Esq. The music by S. Nelson. New York: James L. Hewitt [184-?] 6 p. ViU. 40-4862

Nelson, Sidney, 1800-1862. The vintager's evening hymn. For one, two, or three voices. Composed by S. Nelson. [Words by Charles Jeffreys. With accompaniment for piano forte; arranged for solo and chorus] Boston, MA: Ditson [184-?] 4 p. MB. 40-4863

Nelson, Sidney, 1800-1862. When night comes o'er the plain. Duett. Composed by S. Nelson; arranged for the guitar by F. Weiland. Philadelphia, PA; New York: A. Fiot; W. Dubois [184-?] 3 p. MB; ViU. 40-4864

Nelson, Sidney, 1800-1862. When night comes o'er the plain. Duett. Written by Charles Jeffreys. Music by S. Nelson. [With accompaniment for piano forte]

Boston, MA: Ditson [184-?] 5 p. DLC; MB. 40-4865

Nettleton, Asahel. Village hymns for social worship. Selected and original, designed as a supplement to the psalms and hymns of Dr. Watts... New York: E. Sands, 1840. 488 p. ICN; MB; MiD-B; WaPS; WBeloC. 40-4866

Neue Americanische Landwirthschafts Calender 1841. Von Carl Friedrich Egelmann. Reading, PA: Johann Ritter und Comp [1840] p. MWA. 40-4867

Neue Calender for Nord Amerika 1840. Philadelphia, PA: s. l. [1840] p. MWA; OCHP. 40-4868

Neue Calender fur die Bauern und Handwerker, 1841. Von Carl F. Engelmann. Philadelphia, PA: Georg W. Mentz [1840] p. MWA. 40-4869

Neuer Gemeinnutziger Pennsylvanischer Calender, 1841. Lancaster, PA: Johann Bar [1840] p. MWA. 40-4870

Ein Neues englisch-deutsches und deutsch-englisches Worterbuch, enthaltend alle in beiden Sprachen gebrauchliche Worter, bezeichnend die verschiedenen Redetheile in jeder Sprache, mit Angabe des Geschlechts und des Plurals der deutschen Nenworter. Bearbeitet nach den Worterbuchern von Lloyd, Nohden, Flugel und Sporschil. Philadelphia, PA: G. W. MEntz und Soh, 1840. 2 v. in 1. MH. 40-4871

Neukomm, Sigismund, Ritter von, 1778-1858. David. A sacred oratorio. By the Chevalier Sigismund Neukomm.

New York: s. l., 1840. 11 p. MBC. 40-4872

Neukomm, Sigismond, Ritter von, 1778-1858. [Das gesetz des alten bundes] Mount Sinai, or, The ten commandments, an oratorio, in two parts. The words taken from the Holy Scriptures; translated from the German. Boston: The Handel and Haydn Society, 1840. 195 p. ICN; MB; MH; NN; OCH. 40-4873

Neukomm, Sigismund, Ritter von, 1778-1858. The Lord is my Shepherd, the 23rd psalm. [Anthem, solo. Accomp. for piano forte] New York: Dubois & Stodart [184-?] 6 p. MB. 40-4874

Neukomm, Sigismund, Ritter von, 1778-1858. Mount Sinai, or The ten commandments. An oratorio in two parts. The words taken from the Holy Scriptures; translated from the German. The music composed by Sigismond Neukomm. Boston, MA: Handel and Haydn Society, 1840. MB; MH; MiK; MoS; NNG. 40-4875

Neukomm, Sigismund, Ritter von, 1778-1858. The oratorio of David... Philadelphia, PA: J. Van Court, 1840. 12 p. PPM. 40-4876

Neuman, Henry. Dictionary of the Spanish and English languages... Boston, MA: Hilliard, Gray and co., 1840. 2 v. MBGCT; NjP; WHi. 40-4877

Neuman, Henry. A pocket dictionary of the Spanish and English languages. Compiled from the last improved editions of Neuman and Baretti. In two parts: Spanish-English and English-Spanish.

Philadelphia, PA: S. Wakeling, 1840. 714 p. MdBJ; Nh; OCU; PPL; ViR. 40-4878

Nevin, John Williamson. Party spirit. An address, delivered before the Literary Societies of Washington, Pa. Chambersburg, PA: Office of Publication of the Ger. Ref. Church, 1840. 30 p. MBC; NbOP; OClWHi; PPPrHi; PWW. 40-4879

A new and complete preceptor for the flute... Compiled by the best authors. New York: Firth & Hall [1840] 40 p. No Loc. 40-4880

New Bedford, Mass. First Baptist Church. Articles of faith and covenant of the First Baptist Church, William Street, New Bedford, Mass. With a sketch of its history and a catalogue of its members. Providence, RI: H. H. Brown, printer, 1840. 60 p. RPB. 40-4881

New Bedford, Mass. North Congregational Church. Sabbath School Library. Catalogue of books belonging to the Sabbath School Library of the North Congregational Church. New Bedford, MA: printed by Benjamin Lindsey, 1840. 11 p. MNBedf. 40-4882

New Bedford & Fairbane signal book [S. l.: s. l., 1840-50] v. MH. 40-4883

The new coat; or, The first theft. Written for the Am. S. S. U., and revised by the committee of publication. Philadelphia, PA: American Sunday School Union [ca. 1840] 16 p. DLC; NN; RPB. 40-4884

The New England Almanac and farmers' friend, for the year 1841... by Nathan Daboll... New London, CT: printed and published by E. Williams [1840] 31 p. ICMcHi; NjR. 40-4885

The New England Almanac and farmers' friend, for the year 1844... By Nathan Daboll... New London, CT: published by Bolles & Williams [1840] 31 p. WHi. 40-4886

The New England Almanac and farmers' friend, for the year of Our Lord Christ, 1841... by Nathan Daboll, A. M... Norwich City, CT: published by Samuel C. Starr [1840] 31 p. MHa; RWe. 40-4887

The New England Almanac and farmers' friend, for the year of Our Lord Christ, 1841... Calculated for the meridian of New London... by Nathan Daboll, A. M... Norwich City, CT: s. l. [1840] 31 p. CtNwchA. 40-4888

The New England Almanac and farmers' friend... 1842... By Nathan Daboll, A. M... Norwich City, CT: s. l. [1840] 28 p. WHi. 40-4889

The New England Almanack, for the year of Our Lord 1840; being Bissextile or Leap year, and, until July 4th, the 64th of American Independence. By Anson Allen, Philom. Hartford, CT: Sold wholesale and retail by Henry Benton [1840] 18 p. NCH. 40-4890

The New England Almanack... Concord, NH: Published by Marsh, Capen, Lyon and Webb [1840] 46 p. MiD-B. 40-4891

The New England Almanack... for... 1841... by Dudley Leavitt... Concord, NH: Published by Marsh, Capen, Lyon and Webb [1840] 24 p. NjR; WHi. 40-4892

New England Almanack for 1841. By Nathan Daboll. New London, CT: E. Williams [1840] p. MWA. 40-4893

The New England Almanack on an improved plan, for the year 1841... by Dudley Leavitt... Concord, NH: Published by Marsh, Capen, Lyon and Webb [1840] 31, 16 p. NjR. 40-4894

New England and Long Island Almanac and Farmers' Friend for 1841. Sag Harbor, NY: O. O. Wicksham [1840] p. MWA; WHi. 40-4895

New England farmers' almanac for 1841. Truman W. Abell. Claremont, NH: Claremont Bookstore [1840] p. MWA; NhHi; WHi. 40-4896

New England farmers' almanack for 1841. By Dudley Leavitt. Exeter, NH: s. l., 1840. MH. 40-4897

The New England Primer: containing the assembly's catechism... Middlebury: Pub. by L. W. Clark [184-?] 102 p. CSmH. 40-4898

The New England primer, improved, for the more easy attaining the true reading of English. To which is added the Episcopal and the Assembly of Divines' catechisms. Embellished with cuts. New Haven, CT: S. Babcock [1840] 71 p. CtHT; MH. 40-4899

The New England primer, improved, for the more easy attaining the true reading of English. To which is added the Episcopal and the Assembly of Divines'

catechisms. New Haven: S. Babcock, [1840?] 71 p. CtY; DLC. 40-4900

The New England primer; or, An easy and pleasant guide to the art of reading. To which is added the catechism. Boston: Massachusetts Sabbath School Society, [1840?] 64 p. CtY; MH. 40-4901

The New England primer; or, An easy and pleasant guide to the art of reading. To which is added the catechism. Concord: Rufus Merrill, 1840. 64 p. MAm. 40-4902

New England Puritan. Boston, MA: s. l., 1840-49. v. 1-. CtHC; MBC. 40-4903

New England Sabbath School Union. Question book. Written for the New England Sabbath School Union and revised by the committee of publication. 7th edition. Boston, 1840. 40-4904

New England Screw Co. Charter of New England Screw Co., State of R. I. and Providence Plantations. In General Assembly, Oct. session, 1840. [Providence, RI: s. l., 1840] 8 p. RHi. 40-4905

New England Society, Augusta, Ga. Constitution and roll of members of the New England Society of Augusta, Ga., founded Feb. 14, 1826. Augusta, GA: Browne Pushny & M'Cafferty, 1840. 16 p. CSmH; CtSoP; NcD. 40-4906

New Gloucester, Me. Congregational Church of Christ. Articles of faith and covenant... Portland, ME: s. l., 1840. 16 p. MBC. 40-4907

A new guide to the public buildings... of Philadelphia... and a plan of the city and environs. Philadelphia, PA: H. Tanner, 1840. 36 p. MBevHi; PHi. 40-4908

New Hampshire. Governor. Inaugural messages. Concord, NH: State Printer, 1840-66. 2 v. M. 40-4909

New Hampshire. Laws, statutes, etc. Laws of the State of New Hampshire, passed June session, 1840. Published by authority. Concord, NH: Cyrus Barton, state printer, 1840. 462 p. IaU-L; In-SC; T; W. 40-4910

New Hampshire. Laws, statutes, etc. Laws of the State of New Hampshire, passed November session, 1840. Published by authority. Concord, NH: Cyrus Barton, 1840. 532 p. IaU-L; MiU-L; Nj; TxU-L. 40-4911

New Hampshire. Report of the Bank Commissioners in relation to the Concord Bank. Concord, NH: s. l., 1840. MH; NN. 40-4912

The New Hampshire annual Register... for the year 1840... Concord, NH: Marsh, Capen, Lyon and Webb, 1840. 144 p. MiD-B; MnHi; MWA. 40-4913

New Hampton Literary Institution, New Hampton, N. H. New Hampton Academical & Theological institution catalogue of the officers and students... year ending Nov. 1, 1840. Concord, NH: Young & Worth, 1840. CtY. 40-4914

New Haven, Conn. By-laws of the City of New Haven, May, 1840. New Haven, CT: Hitchcock & Stafford, printers, 1840. 54 p. Ct; MB; MH-L. 40-4915

New Haven, Conn. Congregational Church. Manual of the Church Street

Congregational Church of New Haven, 1840. New Haven, CT: Hitchcock and Stafford, 1840. 23 p. MiD-B. 40-4916

New Haven, Conn. First Church of Christ. Historical celebration. Tuesday, April 21, 1840. Order of exercises. [New Haven? 1840?] New Haven. New Burying Ground. Circular, to the inhabitants of New Haven. [New Haven], 1840. Broadside. CtY. 40-4917

New Haven, Conn. First Church of Christ. Report of the committee on the First ecclesiastical society of New Haven on the subject of ventilating their meeting house. New Haven, CT: B. L. Hamlen, 1840. 12 p. Ct. 40-4918

New Haven, Conn. Young Men's Institute. Statement of the origin, history, & present condition of the New Haven Young Men's Institute, & its library. Read at a public meeting in the Church St. church, Oct. 14, 1840. [New Haven, CT: s. l., 1840] 8 p. Ct; CtHC; CtY; MiD-B. 40-4919

New Haven & Northampton Co. Directors of the "New Haven and Northampton Company" to the citizens of New Haven. New Haven, CT: s. l., 1840. CtSoP. 40-4920

New Haven Directory, for the year 1840. To which are appended some Useful and Intersting Notices. Also, The Annual Advertiser. New Haven, CT: Published by James M. Patten, 1840. 136 p. Ct; CtSoP; MBNEH. 40-4921

New Jersey. Geological Survey. Description of the geology of the State of New Jersey, being a final report, by Henry D. Rogers, state geologist...

Philadelphia, PA: C. Sherman & Co., printers, 1840. 301 p. CU; Ia; MH; OCU; PPA. 40-4922

New Jersey. Governor. Message from the Governor of New Jersey with accompanying documents. By William Pennington. [Trenton, NJ: Phillips & Boswell, printers, 1840] 27 p. Nj. 40-4923

New Jersey. Governor. Special message of the Governor of New Jersey, with accompanying documents, January 14, 1840. [Trenton, NJ: Phillips, 1840] 27 p. MiU-C; NNC; RPB. 40-4924

New Jersey. Laws, statutes, etc. Acts of the sixty-fourth General Assembly of the State of New Jersey, at a session begun at Trenton on the twenty-second day of October eight hundred and thirty-nine. Being the first sitting. Trenton, NJ: n. pub.; Sherman & Hanon, pr., 1840. 164 p. In-SC; Ky; MdBB; Mi-L; Nv. 40-4925

New Jersey. Laws, statutes, etc. Acts relative to the Delaware and Raritan Canal Company, and Camden and Amboy rail road and transportation company. Passed by the legislature of the state of New Jersey. [Princeton, NJ: Printed by J. Bogart, 1840] 44 p. CSt; CSmH; DBRE; MH-BA; ICJ; MiU-T; NN; NNE; NjP; NjR; PPL. 40-4926

New Jersey. Legislative Council. Journal of the proceedings of the Legislatuve Council of the State of New Jersey, convened at Trenton... Being the first sitting of the sixty-fourth and sixty-fifth sessions. Somerville, NJ: S. L. B. Baldwin, 1840. 2 v. Nj. 40-4927

New Jersey. Legislature. Commissioners Appointed to Ascertain the Number of Lunatics and Idiots in the State. Report of the Commissioners appointed by the Governor of New Jersey, to ascertain the number of lunatics and idiots in the state... Newark, NJ: M. S. Harrison & Co., 1840. 25 p. Nj; NjR; PPL. 40-4928

New Jersey. Legislature. Commissioners On State Asylum for Lunatics. Report of the Commissioners appointed by joint resolution of March 6, 1839, to ascertain the number of lunatics in the state and to report the subject of an asylum. Newark, NJ: s. l., 1840. 46 p. PAnL. 40-4929

New Jersey. Legislature. General Assembly. Committee on Agriculture. Report of the Committee on Agriculture of the House of Assembly of the State of New Jersey, relative to an agricultural survey of the state. Trenton, NJ: Phillips & Boswell, 1840. 7 p. CSmH; NjR. 40-4930

New Jersey. Legislature. General Assembly. Committee on Elections. Address and suppressed report of the Minority of the Committee on Elections on the New Jersey Case. Presented to the House of Representatives, March 10, 1840. Together with the remarks of Mr. Fillmore. Washington, DC: Printed at the Madison Office, 1840. 16 p. InHi; MB; MH; MiD-B. 40-4931

New Jersey. Legislature. General Assembly. Committee on Elections. The New Jersey Election Case. Report of the Minority of the Committee on Elections. House of Representatives, July 16, 1840. Elizabeth Town, NJ: Printed by H. H. Hassey, 1840. 24 p. CSf; CSmH; MB; MBevHi; PPL. 40-4932

New Jersey. Legislature. General Assembly. Votes and proceedings of the sixth-fourth General Assembly of the State of New Jersey, at a session begun at Trenton... being the first sitting. Belvidere, NJ: Wilson & Brittian, 1840. 538 p. Nj. 40-4933

New Jersey. Legislature. Joint Committee of Council and General Assembly. An act to erect a part of the township of Nottingham, in the county of Mercer, into a borough to be called "the Borough of South Trenton." S. l.: n. pub., 1840. 7 p. NjT. 40-4934

New Jersey. Legislature. Select Committee on the Several Banks. Report of the select committee to whom were referred the annual statements of the several banks of the State of New Jersey... Trenton, NJ: Phillips & Boswell, printers, 1840. 21 p. Nj; NjR. 40-4935

New Jersey. State Prison, Trenton. Communication from the inspectors of the New Jersey penitentiary to the Speaker of the House of Assembly, respecting the financial concerns of the institution, February 17, 1840. Trenton, NJ: Phillips & Bowsell, 1840. 8 p. Nj. 40-4936

New Jersey. State Trustees of the School Fund. Report of the trustees of the school fund of the State of New Jersey. Trenton, NJ: n. pub., printed by Sherman & Harron, 1840-42. various paging. NjR. 40-4937

New Jerusalem Church. Book of public worship for the use of the new church signified by the New Jerusalem in the Revelation. Contains music. Prepared by order of the General Convention. Boston, MA: O. Clapp, 1840. MH; NNG. 40-4938

New Lebanon, N. Y. Presbyterian Church. Correspondence between the Presbyterians and Congregationalists of New Lebanon. Published by Sylvester P. Gilbert and Silas Churchill, jun., elders of the Presbyterian Church in New Lebanon, February, 1840. Pittsfield: printed by Phinehas Allen and son [1840] 15 p. NNUT. 40-4939

New London, Conn. First Church of Christ. A list of all those who have been members of the First Congregational Church, in New London, between the fifth day of October, 1670 & the first day of May, 1840. New London, CT: Ebenezer Williams, 1840. 64 p. Ct. 40-4940

New national primer. Entered according to the Act of Congress in the year 1840 by Turner & Fisher in the Clerk's office of the District Court of the Eastern District of Pennsylvania. New York; Philadelphia, PA: Published by Turner & Fisher, 1840. 24 p. MH. 40-4941

New Negro band songster. Philadelphia, PA: s. l. [184-?] p. MB; RPB. 40-4942

New Orleans and Nashville Railroad Company. Report by the Board of Directors of the transactions, affairs & accounts of the... company from its organization to the present time... 1840. New Orleans, LA: Gibson, 1840. 20 p. NN; PPAmP. 40-4943

New Orleans. Municipality No. 2. The municipality no. two of the City of New Orleans vs. the Orleans cotton press ompany. The argument of Isaac T. Preson, one of the counsels for the defenants. New Orleans, LA: William McKean, 1840. 118 p. L; LNH; LU; MH-.; NICL. 40-4944

New Orleans. Ordinances, etc. Digest f the ordinances and resolutions of the econd municipality of New Orleans, in orce May 1, 1840. Compiled by order of he Council. By John Calhoun... New Oreans, LA: Printed by F. Cook and A. evy, 1840. 392 p. IU; L-M; MH-L; NcD; JIC. 40-4945

New Orleans Cotton Press Co. Decisions of the Parish Court in the case f the second municipality versus the Jew Orleans cotton press company. Vith the proceedings of the council in elation to the batture question. New Oreans, LA: Printed by F. Cook & A. Levy, 840. 49 p. CtHT-W; LNH. 40-4946

New Orleans directory for 1841. Made y the United States deputy marshals, ontaining the names, professions and esidences of all the inhabitants of the ity and suburbs of New Orleans, afayette and Algiers. New Orleans, LA: Michel & Co., 1840. 366 p. AU; DLC; L; JU; PHi. 40-4947

A new picture of Philadelphia; or, The tranger's guide to the city and adjoining istricts. 4th ed. New York: s. l. [184-?] p. MH. 40-4948

The new primer. Hartford, CT: Henry 3enton [1840] 35 p. CtHWatk. 40-4949

The new settler... by an American Citizen. New Haven, CT: Printed by Wilam Storer, 1840. 11 p. CtY; IU; MB. 40-950

The New Town & Country almanac for the year of Our Lord, 1796. New York: Pub. & sold by Abraham Shoemaker; printed by Zachariah Poulson, jr., 1840. 48 p. NBuG. 40-4951

A new tract for the times, by an old fashioned churchman. New York: J. Van Norden & Co., 1840. 16 p. MB; MdBD; NNG. 40-4952

New World. A weekly family journal of popular literature, science, art and news. New York: J. Winchester, 1840-45. p. ICN; MH; NjR; PPL; WaPS. 40-4953

New York [City] Assessment of real and personal property in 1839 and 1840. New York: s. l., 1840. PPL. 40-4954

New York [City] Bedford St. Methodist Episcopal Church. Semi-Centennial services of the Bedford St. Methodist Episcopal Church, New York City... Nov. 19, 1840. New York: s. l., 1840. IEG. 40-4955

New York [City] Board of Aldermen. The important and interesting debate, on the claim of the Catholics to a portion of the common school fund; with the arguments of counsel, before the Board of aldermen of the city of New York. New York: Pub. by the proprietor of the New York freeman's journal, 1840. 57 p. DLC: NNC. 40-4956

New York [City] Board of Aldermen. ... Report of the Joint Special Committee on the communication from the mayor, relative to the New York and Albany Railroad... [New York: s. l., 1840] 156 p. CSt; NNC; NRU. 40-4957

New York [City] Board of Aldermen.

Report of the joint special committee, to whom was referred a communication from a committee of citizens of Bridgeport, relative to the Housatonic Railroad. New York: Bryant and Boggs, printers to the board, 1840. 40-4958

New York [City] Board of Aldermen. Report of the minority of the Special Committee on the subject of the ordinance creating the aqueduct department... New York: s. l., 1840. 194 p. DNLM; ICJ; Nh; NN; NNC. New York [City] Board of Aldermen. Report of the street committee, relative to the condition of the rails of the Harlaem Railroad, in the Bowery. Presented by Mr. Pollock. [New York, 1841] 1 p. DLC; MH; NN. 40-4959

New York [City] Board of Aldermen. Report of the special committee, to whom was referred the communication from the water commissioner, a report from the Croton Aquaduct commissioner and an opinion of the council in relation to the powers and duties of the water commissioners, together with accompanying documents. [New York, 1840] 40-4960

New York [City] Board of Aldermen. Report of the street committee, on the petition of the Harlaem Railroad Company, to lay their rails in Canal Street. Laid on the table and ordered to be printed for the use of the members. February 24, 1840. [New York: Bryant and Boggs, printers, 1841] 1 p. DLC; MH; NN. 40-4961

New York [City] Board of Assistant Aldermen. Communications of the comptroller, the water commissioners and the Croton aqueduct committee... on the subject of the ordinance to instruct the water commissioners. New York: s. l., 1840. 295 p. NjR; NNC. 40-4962

New York [City] Board of Assistant Aldermen. Report of the Committee on arts and sciences and schools of the Board of assistants, on the subject of appropriating a portion of the school money to religious societies, for the support of schools... New York: s. l., 1840. 391 p. Ct; DLC; MH; NjR; WHi. 40-4963

New York [City] Board of Education. ... The Bible in schools. Report to the Board of education. [New York: s. l., 1840] 12 p. DLC. 40-4964

New York [City] Commission to Investigate the Condition of the Manhattan Company. Report of the Commissioners appointed to investigate the condition of the Manhattan Company. Together with the minutes of the proceedings and various statements relative thereto, March 14, 1840. New York: Printed by J. P. Wright, 1840. 24 p. ICU. 40-4965

New York [City] Committee of Safety, 1775-1865. Proceedings of the committee, appointed by the public meeting of citizens on the subject of fires. Held at the Merchants' Exchange, Jan. 31, 1840. [New York: Coolidge & Lambert, 1840] 38 p. NN. 40-4966

New York [City] Common Council. Acts... and resolutions of the Common Council of the City of New York, in relation to the subject of the introduction of water into the City of New York. New York: P. A. Mesier, 1840. 36 p. CSmH. 40-4967

New York [City] Common Council. Address to the people of the state on the subject of municipal grievances. Adopted by the Boards of Aldermen and Assistant Aldermen and approved by the Mayor, Sept. 22, 1840. New York: Bryant and Boggs [1840] 8 p. CSmH; MH. 40-4968

New York [City] Common Council. Joint Special Committee on New York and Albany Rail Road. Report. New York: s. l. [1840] p. CSmH. 40-4969

New York [City] Common Council. Names and places of abode of the mayor and members of the Common Council and of officers holding appointments under them, 1840. New York: J. W. Bell [1840] 44 p. MH. 40-4970

New York [City] Coroner. Proceedings of the coroner, in the case of the steamer Lexington, lost by fire on the thirteenth of January, 1840. New York: s. l., 1840. 89 p. DLC; MH; NNC; RP; RPB. 40-4971

New York [City] Court of Common Pleas. ... Rules and orders of the Court of common pleas for the City and County of New York. New York: Gould, 1840. 62 p. MH-L; MiD-B; NNLI. 40-4972

New York [City] Croton Aqueduct Committee. Report of the special committee to whom was referred the communication from the Water Commissioners. A report of the Croton Aqueduct Committee... New York: Bryant and Boggs, printers [1840] 71 p. MiD-B. 40-4973

New York [City] Fifth Ward. Tippecanoe Club. Articles of association...

New York: Narine & Co., print [1840] 7 p. MiD-B. 40-4974

New York [City] Madison Street Presbyterian Church. Manual. New York: Trow, 1840-. p. PPPrHi. 40-4975

New York [City] Maternal Association. Report presented at the... annual meeting. New York: s. l., 1840-45. p. WHi. 40-4976

New York [City] Mayor. Communication... transmitting the report and resolutions of the Common Council, relative to the re-organization of the criminal courts of that city. New York: s. l., 1840. 15 p. WHi. 40-4977

New York [City] Mercantile Library Association. Constitution & by-laws and regulations. New York: J. Egbert, printer, 1840. 10 p. DLC. 40-4978

New York [City] Mercantile Library Association. A supplementary catalog of the books... New York: s. l., 1840. 386 p. NN. 40-4979

New York [City] National Academy of Design. Catalogue of the 15th annual exhibition. New York: s. l., 1840. 23 p. MBC; MdBD. 40-4980

New York [City] St. George's Church. Report of the Board of Directors of the Association of St. George's Church, New York, for the promotion of Christianity. Presented at the annual meeting of the association, Friday evening, February 7th, A. D., 1840. New York: Printed by G. F. Bunce, 1840. 11 p. NNG. 40-4981

New York [City] Second Universalist Society. The Christmas exercises of the

Sunday School attached to the Second Universalist Society in New York... New York: Union and Messenger Press, 1840. 62 p. MMeT-Hi. 40-4982

New York [City] Testimony. Relating to the great election Frauds of 1838. New York, 1840. 55 p. MBC. 40-4983

New York [City] Water Commissioners. Report of the Majority of the Special Committee on the subject of the ordinance creating the Aqueduct Department, etc. and to amend the ordinance to instruct the Water Commissioners. Document No. 31. New York: s. l., 1840. 194 p. DNLM; NNC; NRom. 40-4984

New York [City] Water Commissioners. Supplemental report of the late water commissioners, March 30, 1840. Document No. 65. New York: Bryant and Boggs, printer, 1840. 11 p. DNLM; MdHi; NN. 40-4985

New York [City] Wesleyan Methodist Episcopal Zion Church. The docrtinres and discipline of the Wesleyan Methodist Episcopal Zion Church in America, established in the City of New York, October 25th, 1820. Second edition. New York: J. M. March, printer, 1840. 159 p. MNBedf. 40-4986

New York [State] Canal Commissioners. Annual report of the commissioners of the canal fund, of the state of New York. Made February 3, 1840. Albany, NY: Thurlow Weed, printer to the state, 1840. 65 p. IaHi. 40-4987

New York [State] Canal Commissioners. Communication... comm...

Genesee Valley Canal... rept... 1840. Albany, NY: s. l., 1840. MB. 40-4988

New York [State] Canal Commissioners. ... Communication... transmitting the report of the survey in continuation of the Black River Canal... [Albany, NY: n. pub., n. pr., 1840?] 120 p. MH-BA. 40-4989

New York [State] Canal Commissioners. Report of the Canal Board respecting the canal debts and revenues and enlargement of the Erie Canal &c. In Assembly, April 11, 1840. Albany, NY: n. pub., n. pr., 1840. 51 p. MB; MHi; OCHP; NN. 40-4990

New York [State] Canal Commissioners. Report relating to survey of the several branches of the Hudson River transmitting the report and several estimates of the engineer, 1840. Albany, NY: s. l., 1840. 35 p. DLC; MB. 40-4991

New York [State] Canal Commissioners. ... Report... respecting the canal debts and revenues and enlargement of the Erie Canal &c. Albany, NY: n. pub., n. pr., 1840. MH-BA. 40-4992

New York [State] Canal Commissioners. Report... survey of a canal from the termination of the Chemung Canal to the state line. [Albany, NY: n. pub., n. pr., 1840] p. DLC; MB. 40-4993

New York [State] Canal Commissioners. Statements showing the amount of tolls collected at each office during the state canals during 1839... Albany, NY: s. l., 1840. MB. 40-4994

New York [State] Chancellor. Communication from the Chancellor, relative to the New York Life Insurance and Trust Company, transmitting report for the year ending Dec. 31, 1839. Albany, NY: s. l., 1840. 57 p. WHi. 40-4995

New York [State] Citizens. Memorial of Sundry residents of Cattaraugus County, New York, adverse to the ratification of the treaty with the New York Indians, February 10, 1840. S. l.: s. l., 1840. 2 p. NBu. 40-4996

New York [State] Citizens. Memorial of Sundry residents of the western part of New York, adverse to the ratification of the treaty with the New York Indians, February 10, 1840. [Batavia, NY: s. l., 1840?] 6 p. NBu. 40-4997

New York [State] Commissioners of the Canal Fund. Regulations respecting the issue and transfer of certificates of stock, issued by the State of New York. And also respecting the payment of interest on such certificates. Made by the Commissioners of the Canal Fund, July 27, 1840. Albany, NY: T. Weed, printer to the state, 1840. 16 p. DLC. 40-4998

New York [State] Comptroller's Office. Circular to auctioneers [including laws in relation to their duties and liabilities. Albany, 184-?] 19 p. N. 40-4999

New York [State] Comptroller's Office. Communications transmitting Sundry reports relating to the investigator of the Seaman's Fund & Retreat, Marine Hospital, etc. [Albany, NY: s. l., 1840] 94 p. MB. 40-5000

New York [State] Comptroller's Office. Report of the comptroller, in relation to the valuation of real and personal estate in the several cities and counties in the State. In Senate, January 14, 1840. Albany, NY: s. l., 1840. 38 p. WHi. 40-5001

New York [State] Court for the Trial of Impeachments and the Corrections of Errors. A report of the Opinions and Decision of the Court for the correction of errors, in the cases of Warner and Ray vs. Beers, President, etc.; and of Bolander vs. Stevens, president, etc. Given at a Special Term of the Court. Held at the Capitol in the City of Albany on the 7th day of April, 1840. New York: James Van Norden & Co., printers, 1840. 98 p. DLC; NHi; NNLI. 40-5002

New York [State] Court for the Trial of Impeachments and the Corrections of Errors. Rules and orders of the Court for the correction of errors of the State of New York, as revised & established by the court. New York: s. l., 1840. 8 p. DLC. 40-5003

New York [State] Court for the Trial of Impeachments and the Corrections of Errors. State of New York. In the Court for the trial of impeachments and the correction of errors: Carl G. Bolander, plaintiff in error vs. John A. Stevens, president of the Bank of Commerce in New York, defendant in error... Albany, NY: Hoffman, White & Visscher, 1840. 45 p. NCH; NNC-L. 40-5004

New York [State] Governor, 1838-1843. Correspondence between Governor of New York and the Executive of Virginia. [Albany, NY: s. l., 1840?] p. MH. 40-5005

New York [State] Governor. Communication from the Governor, transmitting several reports relative to the geological survey of the State. [Albany,

NY: s. l., 1840] 482 p. IaDaM; Nj; PPL; WHi. 40-5006

New York [State] Governor. Message from the Governor on the subject of the culture of silk and the manufacture of sugar from the beet root. [Albany, NY: s. l., 1840] 34 p. WHi. 40-5007

New York [State] Governor. Message from the Governor [Seward] in relation to the difficulties in the Manor of Rensselauerwyck. [Albany, NY: s. l., 1840] 39 p. NIC; WHi. 40-5008

New York [State] Governor. Message... transmitting a communication from the Governor of Virginia and proceedings of the legislature of that state in relation to certain alleged fugitives from justice. [Albany, NY: s. l., 18401] 30 p. ViU; WHi. 40-5009

New York [State] Laws, statutes, etc. An abstract of laws relating to the assessment and collection of taxes in the City of New York, June, 1840. [New York: s. l., 1840] 78 p. MH; NN; WHi. 40-5010

New York [State] Laws, statutes, etc. An act in relation to the construction of the New York and Erie Railroad. Repeals the acts of the same title, passed 18th April, 1843, wherein consistent with this act. [Albany, NY: s. l., 184-?] 1 p. CSt. 40-5011

New York [State] Laws, statutes, etc. Acts of the Legislature of the State and Resolutions of the Common Council of the City of New York in relation to the subject of the introduction of water into the City of New York. New York: P. A. Mesier, 1840. 36, 4, 2 p. NNC; NRom. 40-5012

New York [State] Laws, statutes, etc. Law of New York relating to fugitives from justice. Annapolis, MD: s. l., 1840. PPL. 40-5013

New York [State] Laws, statutes, etc. Laws of the State of New York, passed at the sixty-third session of the legislature. Begun and held in the City of Albany the 7th day of January, 1840. Albany, NY: printed by Charles Van Benthuysen, 1840. 413 p. Az; CoU; In-SC; MdBB; Wa-L. 40-5014

New York [State] Laws, statutes, etc. Report... License laws. [Albany, NY: s. l., 1840] p. MB. 40-5015

New York [State] Legislature. Assembly. Journal of the Assembly of the State of New York, at their sixty-third session. Begun and held at the capitol in the City of Albany, on the seventh day of January, 1840. Albany, NY: Printed by Thurlow Weed, printer to the state, 1840. 1622 p. NNLI. 40-5016

New York [State] Legislature. Assembly. ... Report of the select committee on so much of the Governor's message as relates to the national domain. New York: n. pub., n. pr., 1840. 20 p. NjR. 40-5017

New York [State] Legislature. Assembly. Committee on Canals and Internal Improvements. Report of the Committee on Canals and Internal Improvements, on so much of the Governor's Message as relates to internal improvements. Albany, 1840. [No. 277. In Assembly, March 28, 1840] [Albany, NY?: s. l., 1840] 28 p. WHi. 40-5018

New York [State] Legislature. Assembly. Committee on Medical Societies and

Colleges. Report of the Standing Committee on Medical Societies and Colleges, relative to the restrictions on unlicensed practitioners. [No. 346. In Assembly, May 9, 1840] [Albany, NY?: s. l., 1840] 11 p. WHi. 40-5019

New York [State] Legislature. Assembly. Committee on Railroads. Report of the Committee on Railroads, upon a resolution passed on the 6th day of March, last instituting an inquiry into the affairs of railroad companies. No. 314. In Assembly, 1840. [Albany, NY: s. l., 1840] 15 p. WHi. 40-5020

New York [State] Legislature. Assembly. Committee on Railroads. ... Report of the Majority of the Committee on Railroads, on the memorial of the president and directors of the New York and Erie Railroad Company, and several petitions of sundry citizens of the southern tier in the State. [No. 215. In Assembly] [Albany, NY?: s. l., 1840] 37 p. CSt; NN. 40-5021

New York [State] Legislature. Assembly. Committee on the System of Teaching Mechanical Trades to Prison Convicts. Report of a committee appointed by a public meeting of mechanics and others of the City of New York in relation to the system of teaching mechanical trades to state prison convicts accompanying their petition upon the same subject. No. 276. In Assembly, April 30, 1840. [Albany, NY: s. l., 1840] 15 p. MB; WHi. 40-5022

New York [State] Legislature. Assembly. Committee on Thomsonian Physicians. Report of the minority of the select committee to which was referred numerous petitions asking for a change of the law towards Thomsonian

Physicians. No. 354. In Assembly, May 12, 1840. [Albany, NY: s. l., 1840] 23 p. WHi. 40-5023

New York [State] Legislature. Senate. Documents of the Senate of the State of New York. Sixty-third session, 1840. Albany, NY: printed by Thurlow Weed, printer to the state, 1840. 4 v. NNLI. 40-5024

New York [State] Legislature. Senate. Journal of the Senate of the State of New York. At their Sixty-third session, begun and held at the capitol in the City of Albany, on the seventh day of January, 1840. Albany, NY: printed by E. Croswell, printer to the state, 1840. 642 p. NNLI. 40-5025

New York [State] Legislature. Senate. Committee on Bankrupt Law. Report of the majority of the Select Committee appointed to inquire into the correctness of the Senate Journal of Mar. 21, relative to the passage of the resolutions for a national bankrupt law. No. 127. In Senate, 1840. New York: State Printer, 1840. 34 p. WHi. 40-5026

New York [State] Legislature. Senate. Committee on Judiciary. Report of the Committee on the Judiciary on the bill declaratory of subdivision 2, of section 28, of title 10, chapter 8, of the third part of the Revised Statutes [relative to rents] No. 65. In Senate, February 4, 1840. New York: s. l., 1840. 12 p. WHi. 40-5027

New York [State] Legislature. Senate. Committee on License Laws. Report of the Select Committee on numerous petitions relative to the license laws. No. 73. In Senate, 1840. New York: State Printer, 1840. 12 p. WHi. 40-5028

New York [State] Legislature. Senate. Committee on Railroads. Report of the Committee on Railroads on the petitions for the construction of the Ogdensburgh and Champlain Railroad by the state. No. 44. In Senate, February 22, 1840. New York: s. l., 1840. 12 p. WHi. 40-5029

New York [State] Legislature. Senate. Committee on Railroads. Report of the Committee on Railroads on the petitions from the New York and Harlem, the Long Island, and the New York and Albany Railroad companies, asking aid from the state. No. 99. In Senate, March 17, 1840. New York: s. l., 1840. 16 p. WHi. 40-5030

New York [State] Secretary of State. Manual for the use of the Legislature of the State of New York... Albany, NY: s. l., 1840-19-. v. DLC; DLC; ICU; MdHi; PU. 40-5031

New York [State] State Hospital. Charter of the state hospital in the City of New York. With other documents, showing the origin and present state of the institution. New York: Printed by H. Ludwig, 1840. 24, 4 p. NNN; NNNAM. 40-5032

New York [State] Supreme Court. Reports of Cases. Albany, 1840-. v. 1-. NjP. 40-5033

New York [State] Superintendent of the Onondaga Salt Springs. Annual report of the Superintendent of the Onondaga Salt Springs. Made to the legislature... Albany, NY: . pub., Weed, Parsons & Co., printers, 1840-73. v. NjR. 40-5034

New York [State] University. Catalogue of the officers, alumni and students of the University of the City of New York, 1839-40. New York: Printed by Hopkins & Jennings, 1840. 19 p. PPM. 40-5035

New York and Albany Railroad Company. New York and Albany railroad. Sketch of the remarks made by the president of the company, at a meeting of citizens, held at the City Hall, November 10, 1840. Together with a copy of the resolutions passed at that meeting, and other information of interest on the subject of railroads generally. New York: Bryant & Boggs, printers [184?] 20 p. CSt; InHi; MH-BA; NBu; NN. 40-5036

New York and Erie Railroad Company. Facts and considerations relating to the New York and Erie Railroad. [New York: s. l., 1840] 16 p. CSt; NBu. 40-5037

New York and Erie Railroad Company. ... Petition of the New York and Erie Railroad Company. [Albany, NY?: s. l., 1840] 3 p. CSt; NN. 40-5038

New York and Erie Railroad Company. Report of Eleazar Lord, president of the New York and Erie Railroad Company, in answer to resolutions of the Assembly of 25th and 27th February and 10th March, 1840. [Albany, NY?: s. l., 1840] 31 p. CSt. 40-5039

New York and Erie Railroad Company. The specifications for the materials and construction of the Susquehannah division, New York and Erie Railroad Company; extending from Binghamton to Hornellsville... Put under contract Feb'y. 10th, 1840. To be completed July 1st, 1842. Charles B. Stuart, chief engineer. Manrow, Higinbotham & Co., contractors. Owego, NY: Printed by A.

H. Calhoun, 1840. 12 p. CSt; CtY; DBRE; MiU-T; NN. 40-5040

New York and Erie Railroad Company. To the stockholders of the New York and Erie Railroad Company. [New York: s. l., 184-?] 8 p. CSt. 40-5041

New York and Harlem Railroad Company. Petition of the New York and Harlem Railroad Company, in relation to certain rights and privileges claimed by said company, and remonstrating against granting permission to the New York and Albany Railroad Company to cross Harlem River opposite the Sixth or Seventh Avenue, etc. New York: Printed by C. C. & E. Childs, jr., 184?. 18 p. DBRE; NN; NN-P. 40-5042

New York and Harlem Railroad Company. Resolutions. [New York: s. l., 1840] 14 p. NN. 40-5043

New York annual register; containing an almanac, civil & judicial list. With political, statistical and other information respecting the State of New York and the U. S. New York: s. l., 1840. Mi; MiD; NPV; NUtHi; TxH. 40-5044

New York as it is; containing a general description of the City of New York; list of officers, public institutions, and other useful information, including the public officers & etc. of the City of Brooklyn... New York: T. R. Tanner, n. pr., 1840. 250, 2 p. NjR. 40-5045

New York Association for Improving the Condition of the Poor. A plan for the better distribution of medical attendance and medicines for the idigent sick by the Public DIspensaries in the City of New

York. New York: s. l., 1840. 12 p. MHi. 40-5046

The New York business directory, for 1840 and 1841. Wherein the names and occupations of the principal business men are alphbetically arranged and appropriately classed. To be published annually. New York: Publication Office, 1840. 214 p. MBNEH; MH; NNMuCN; WHi. 40-5047

New York Financial Gazette. Plans for a financial newspaper to be published daily. [New York: s. l., 1840] 8 p. DLC. 40-5048

New York Floating Dry Dock Co. Plan of the Floating Dry Dock and articles of association of the New York Floating Dry Dock Co., in the City of New York. New York: Alexander S. Gould, 1840. 15 p. MB. 40-5049

New York Historical Society. Library. Catalogue of books, manuscripts, maps, &c. added to the library of the New York Historical Society since Jananuary, 1839. New York: J. W. Harrison, printer, 1840. 32 p. DLC; MB; MH; NIC; WHi. 40-5050

The New York Journal of Medicine and Surgery. Vol. I-IV, July 1839-July [i. e., April] 1841. New York: C. S. Francis, 1840-41. 4 v. in 2. CtMW; ICU-R; MnU; NjR; PU. 40-5051

New York Life Insurance Company. An Act to incorporate the stockholders of the New York Insurance Company. [Passed 2d April, 1798] and the acts amending the same. New York: J. W. Oliver, printer, 1840. 36 p. NNMuCN. 40-5052

New York, Providence and Boston Railroad Company. Annual report submitted at the meeting of the stockholders of the New York, Providence and Boston Rail Road Company. Convened in the City of Providence, R. I., September 29th, 1840. By Wm. Gibbs McNeil, engineer and agent. New York: Printed by W. H. Thompson, 1840. 22 p. DBRE; IU; MdHi. 40-5053

The New York reader No. 2. Being selections in prose and poetry. For the use of schools. New York: Samuel S. & William Wood, 1840. 216 p. NWebyC. 40-5054

The New York serenading waltz. Arranged for the piano forte. Baltimore, MD: G. Willig, Jur. [184-?] 2 p. ViU. 40-5055

New York State pocket almanac for 1841:being the first after bissextile or leap year. Auburn, NY: published and sold, wholesale and retail, by Oliphant & Skinner [1840] 24 p. NN. 40-5056

The New York state tourist, descriptive of the scenery of the Mohwak & Hudson rivers... New York: A. T. Goodrich, 1840. 156 p. DLC; MB; N; NN; NRU. 40-5057

New York Visitor and Lady's Magazine. Visitors and lady's parlor magazine, The Monthly. New York: s. l., 1840-42. v. 1-3. IaLB; MH; MiD. 40-5058

Newburgh, N. Y. Citizens. Memorial statistical report and resolutions in relation to the N. Y. and Erie Railroad. Adopted... March 4, 1840. Newburgh, NY: s. l., 1840. 24 p. DBRE. 40-5059

Newcomb, Harvey, 1803-1863. The attributes of God; being a series of Sabbath evening conversations. Designed to illustrate the character of God. 2d ed. Boston, MA: Sabbath School Soc., 1840. CSto; MBC. 40-5060

Newcomb, Harvey, 1803-1863. Sabbath school teacher's aid: a collection of anecdotes for illustrating religious truth; arranged under a variety of subjects. Boston: Sabbath School Society, 1840. 333 p. DLC. 40-5061

Newcomb, Harvey, 1803-1863. Manual for maternal associations. Boston, MA: Mass. S. S. Soc., 1840. 108 p. DLC; MB; MBC. 40-5062

Newcomb, Harvey, 1803-1863. Samuel in the temple. Written for the Massachusetts Sabbath School Society, and revised by the Committee of publication. Boston: Massachusetts Sabbath School Society, 1840. 36 p. DLC; MB. 40-5063

Newcomb, Harvey, 1803-1863. The young lady's guide to the harmonious development of Christian character. 2nd edition. Boston: James B. Dow, 1840. 344 p. FMU. 40-5064

Newman, John Henry, 1801-1890. ... The church of the Fathers of St. Chrysostom Theodoret... by J. H. C. Newman. New York: Longmans, Green and Co., 1840. 487 p. FPe. 40-5065

Newman, John Henry, 1801-1890. An essay on the development of Christian doctrine. New York: s. l. [184-?] p. MH; MH-AH. 40-5066

Newport redowa, as performed at Newport & Saratoga. Arranged for the piano forte. Baltimore, MD: F. D. Benteen [184-?] 2 p. ViU. 40-5067

Newton, Robert, 1780-1854. The farewell sermon of the Rev. Robert Newton of England... Preached in the Allen Street Methodist Episcopal Church... June the 8th, 1840. To which is added the farewell address of Dr. Bangs. New York: Joseph W. Harrison, printer, 1840. 16 p. NNMHi; RPB. 40-5068

Newton, Robert, 1780-1854. Lord, I have lost the habitation of thy house & the place where thine honor dwelleth. A sermon preached... on laying the foundation stone of the Bedford St. M. E. Church, New York... New York: Piercy & Reed, 1840. 18 p. CtMW; NN. 40-5069

Nichol, John Pringle, 1804-1859. The architecture of the heavens. By J. P. Nichol. 9th ed. New York: Chapin, 1840. 158 p. CtHT. 40-5070

Nichol, John Pringle, 1804-1859. Views of the architecture of the heavens. In a series of letters to a lady. New ed., rev. and enl. New York: H. A. Chapin and company, 1840. 158 p. CtHC; MPiB; PU; TJaL; ViU. 40-5071

Nicholas, Samuel Smith, 1796-1869. Letters on the presidency, by a Kentucky Democrat. Republished from the Louisville Journal. [Louisville, KY?: s. l., 1840?] 28 p. MB; MH; NN. 40-5072

Nichols, Thomas L. Journal in jail, kept during a four months' imprisonment for libel, in the jail of Erie County. By Thomas L. Nichols. Buffalo, NY: A. Dinsmore, 1840. 248 p. CSmH; DLC; MWA; NBu; NBuG; NNC. 40-5073

Niles, William Ogden. The Tippecanoe Text-book. Compiled from Niles' Register and other authentic records, by William Ogden Niles, and respectfully dedicated to the young men of the United States. Baltimore, MD; Philadelphia, PA: Published by Duff Green and Cushing & Brother; Hogan & Thompson and T. K. & P. G. Collins, 1840. 95 p. InLPU; MiGr; MWA; NjR; PPL. 40-5074

Nisbet, Charles, 1736-1804. Extracts from lectures on the will, liberty, and necessity... to which are appended remarks and additional extracts from other writers. By M. Brown, Pres., Jefferson College. Pittsburgh, PA: William B. Stewart, 1840. 23 p. CSmH; MnSM; NNUT; PPL. 40-5075

No more shall the children of Judah sing; or, the Maid of Judah. Arranged for the piano forte. Philadelphia, PA: Osbourn's Music Saloon [184-?] 3 p. ViU. 40-5076

Noble, John S. An address delivered on the evening of June 9, 1840, before National Lodge, No. 30, I. O. of O. F., by John S. Noble. S. l.: Stationer's Hall Press, 1840. 32 p. MiD-B. 40-5077

Noel, Baptist W. 1798-1873. Essay on the union of church and state... New York: Harper & Bros., 1840. 442 p. NhD. 40-5078

Noel, Gerard Thomas. A brief inquiry into the prospects of the Church of Christ, in connexion with the 2nd advent of Our Lord Jesus Christ. Philadelphia, PA: Rogers, 1840. 125 p. CtHC; ICP; MWA; OO; WHi. 40-5079

Nord-Amerikanischer Calender fur das Jahr 1840. Philadelphia, PA: George W. Mentz und Sohn, 1840. PPG. 40-5080

Norfolk County, Mass. We have done it! Old Norfolk Redeemed! Tippecanoe Standard Extra, Dedham, Mass., Monday evening, 11 o'clock, Nov. 9, 1840. Dedham, MA: s. l., 1840. MHi. 40-5081

Norridge Female Academy, Norridgework, Me. Catalogue, July, 1840. [S. l.: s. l., 1840?] p. MH. 40-5082

North, Milo Linus. Saratoga waters; or, The invalid at Saratoga. By M. L. North. New York: M. W. Dodd, 1840. 70 p. MH; MPiB; NBuG; PPL; WHi. 40-5083

North Attleboro Baptist Church. Declaration of faith, with the church covenant together with Rules of Discipline and List of Members of the North Attleborough Baptist Church. Providence, RI: H. H. Brown, 1840. 12 p. MH. 40-5084

North Carolina. Governor. Message... in relation to the University of North Carolina. Raleigh: Thos. J. Lemay, 1840.] 8 p. MH; NN. 40-5085

North England Guards. Circular. Round-Hill Camp, July 13, 1840l. Northampton: s. l., 1840. 1 p. MHi. 40-5086

Norton, Andrews, 1786-1853. Two articles from the Princeton Review. Concerning the transcendental philosophy of the Germans and of Cousin, and its influence on opinion in this country. Cambridge, MA: J. Owen, 1840. 100 p. ICMe; LNH; MH; NjPT; PHC. 40-5087

Norton, J. T. Pensez a moi ma chere

amie! Composed and arranged for the piano forte by J. T. Norton. Cincinnati, OH: J. Church, jr. [184-?] 2 p. ViU. 40-5088

Nott, Eliphalet, 1773-1866. Counsels to young men on the formation of character and the principles which lead to success and happiness in life... By Eliphalet Nott... New York: Harper and brothers, 1840. 312 p. AFIT; MBC; NGlc; PPPrHi; TKC; WvU. 40-5089

Nottman, John, architect. Design for library Co., and athenaeum building. Plan of ground floor. Philadelphia, 1840. Nottman, John, architect. Offices. Fifth Street. Library Co. lot. Front elevation, section, and elevation, ground plan and plans of second and third floor. Philadelphia, 1840?. North Woodstock, Connecticut. First Congregational Church. Confession of faith and covenant. Woodstock, 1840. South Cove Corporation, Boston. Catalogue of 557 lots of land, and 8 wharves in the South Cove... by order of the directors of the South Cove Corporation, the right of choice... will be sold by auction, April 23, 1840. Boston: Printed by Crocker and Brewster, 1840. 26 p. DLC; MHi; NjR. 40-5090

The Novelty of popery, and the antiquity of the religion of protestants, proved by scripture and history. Philadelphia: Presbyterian Board of Publication, 1840. 204 p. CSansS; KyLoP; MBC; NNUT; ViRut. 40-5091

Noyes, William Curtis, 1805-1864. The argument of William Curtis Noyes, of the City of New York, on the question of the constitutionality of the general banking law of the state of New York, before the

Court for the correction of errors... Feb. 23 & 24, 1840. New York: Booth, 1840. 116 p. MiPh; MoS; NCH; NNC-L. 40-5092

Nuttall, Thomas, 1786-1859. A manual

of ornithology of the United States and of Canada. By Thomas Nuttall... 2d ed., with additions. Boston, MA: Hilliard, Gray and Company, 1840. 832 p. CSt; ICJ; LU; NcU; PPA. 40-5093

O

O for a thousand tongues to sing. As sung by the Indians of the Upper Canada Mission. Arranged for the piano forte. Baltimore, MD: John COle [184-?] 1 p. ViU. 40-5094

The O. K. songster [political] Philadelphia, PA: s. l., 1840. PPL. 40-5095

O'Brien's Philadelphia Wholesale Business Directory. O'Brien's commercial intelligencer... merchants' wholesale business directory. Philadelphia, PA: s. l., 1840. 111 p. PP; PPG; PPM. 40-5096

O'Connell, Daniel, 1775-1847. Letters to the Wesleyan Methodists on the occasion of their opposing the system of national education, established in England and Ireland. Harrisburg, PA: Patrick Kain, 1840. MdW. 40-5097

O'Connell, Daniel, 1775-1847. A memoir on Ireland native and Saxon... from A. D. 1172 to A. D. 1660... [New York: Greeley and McElrath, 184-?] 80 p. MnHi. 40-5098

O'Connor, Thomas, 1770-1855. Address before the Society of St. Peter, St. Peter's Church in Barclay Street in the City of New York. New York: Hugh Cassidy, 1840. DGH; NBLiHi. 40-5099

O'Connor, Thomas, 1770-1855. Speeches on the subject of the Common School Fund of the State of New York. Delivered at meetings of the Roman Catholics of the City of New York, by Thomas O'Connor, Esq. and Dr. Hugh Sweeny. New York: Hugh Cassidy, printer, 1840. 4, 36 p. IClay, NN. 40-5100

O'Halloran, Captain. Speech, delivered by Captain O'Halloran... Published by Order of the President and Members of the Committee. Saint John: Printed at the Brunswick Press by William L. Avery, 1840. 34 p. MWA. 40-5101

O'Neill, John Henry. Oration 4th July. Washington, DC: s. l., 1840. PPL. 40-5102

O'Reilly, Henry. A brief report on the rise, progress and condition of the Rochester Athenaeum-Young Men's Association... [Rochester, NY: s. l., 1840?] 20 p. DLC; MH; NR; NRHi. 40-5103

O'Sullivan, Mortimer, 1791?-1859. The Nevilles of Garretstown. A tale of 1760. New York: W. Taylor, etc., etc. [184-?] p. MH. 40-5104

Oakland College, Claiborne Co., Miss. Constitution of Oakland College... Mississippi. Natchez, MS: Office of Daily Courier, 1840. 16 p. Ms-Ar; PPPrHi. 40-5105

Oberlin College, Oberlin, O. Catalogue of the officers and students... 1840-41. Oberlin, OH: Printed by James Steele, 1840. 24 p. ICP; MHi; MiU; NN. 40-5106

Oberlin College, Oberlin, O. Laws and regulations of the Oberlin Collegiate Institute. Oberlin, OH: James Steele, 1840. 15 p. OClW; OClWHi; PPPrHi. 40-5107

Observations on the late suspensions of special payments by the Banks in Charleston. With suggestions for the Regulation of Banks. Charleston, SC: Printed by A. E. Miller, 1840. 20 p. A-Ar; DLC; ICU; NcD; ScCC. 40-5108

Obsevations on the navy pension laws of the United States... practical effect on the navy pension fund... some remarks... By an Officer of the Navy. Washington, DC: Printed at the Intelligencer Office, 1840. 15 p. DLC; MiU-C. 40-5109

Ocean songster. Philadelphia, PA: s. l., 184-? 2 p. MB. 40-5110

Odd Fellows, Independent Order of. New York. Charter, constitution, by-laws, and rules of the Niagra Lodge, No. 25, of the I. O. O. F. Adopted the 26th of December 1839. Buffalo, NY: George Zahm, Germand and English printer, 1840. 24 p. NBu; NBuHi. 40-5111

Odd Fellows, Independent Order of. New York. Constitution, by-laws, and rules of Buffalo Lodge, No. 37, of the I. O. O. F. Chartered May 6, 1840. By-laws and rules adopted 5th of June 1840. Buffalo, NY: Printed by A. Dinsmore, 1840. 32 p. WHi. 40-5112

Odd Fellows, Independent Order of. New York. Constitution of Trojan Lodge, No. 27. Troy, NY: s. l., 1840. MB. 40-5113

Odd Fellows, Independent Order of. New York. Marimers' Lodge No. 23.

Constitution and by-laws of Mariners' Lodge No. 23, of I. O. of O. F. of the state of New York. Adopted Aug. 3, 1840. Albany: Printed by J. B. Allee, 1840. 24 p. NN. 40-5114

Odd Fellows, Independent Order of. New York. Proceedings of the Grand Lodge of New York. New York: s. l., 1840. PPL. 40-5115

Ode to the memory of Commodore Perry. [With Tippecanoe, a legend of the border] S. l.: s. l., 1840. RPB. 40-5116

Oertel, John James Maxmillian. The reasons of John James Maximillian Oertel, late a Lutheran minister, for becoming a Catholic. New York: J. McLoughlin, printer, 1840. 34 p. MdBLC; MWH; PPL; RPB. 40-5117

Ogden, James De Peyster. Remarks on the currency of the United States, and present state and future prospects of the country. By Publius [psued.] New York: Wiley and Putnam, 1840. 59 p. CtHT; ICU; MdBJ; MH; PU. 40-5118

Ogle, Charles, 1798-1841. The pretended democracy of Martin Van Buren. [Boston, MA: s. l., 1840] 24 p. DLC; MBAt. 40-5119

Ogle, Charles, 1798-1841. Rede, uber die konigliche prach und die verschwendung im prasidenten-palast. Gehalten im hause den 14. April 1840. [Philadelphia, PA: s. l., 1840] 2, 27 p. MH; PPeSchw. 40-5120

Ogle, Charles, 1798-1841. Remarks of Mr. Ogle of Pennsylvania, on the civil and diplomatic appropriation bill, delivered in the House, April 14, 1840.

[Washington, 1840?] 32 p. ICN; IU; NRU; OClWHi; ViU. 40-5121

Ogle, Charles, 1798-1841. Remarks... on the civil and diplomatic Appropriation Bill, with reference to the expenditure of the President, etc. Delivered in the House of Representatives, April 14, 1840. [Washington, DC: s. l., 1840] 32 p. IU; NjR; NNUT; OClWHi; WHi. 40-5122

Ogle, Charles, 1798-1841. Speech of Mr. Ogle of Pennsylvania, on the regal splendor of the President's palace. Delivered in the House, April 14, 1840. [Boston: Weeks Jordan and Company, 1840?] 32 p. DLC; ViU. 40-5123

Ogle, Charles, 1798-1841. Speech of Mr. Ogle of Pennsylvania, on the regal splendor of the President's palace. Delivered in the House, April 14, 1840. [Washington, 1840?] 32 p. DLC; InU; NN; OCU; PHi. 40-5124

Ogle, Charles, 1798-1841. Speech of Mr. Ogle of Pennsylvania, [part II] on the pretended democracy of Martin Van Buren. Delivered in the House, April 15, 1840. [Washington?1840?] 16 p. DLC; OCU. 40-5125

Ogle, Charles, 1798-1841. Speech of Mr. Ogle of Pennsylvania, [part III] on the character and services of William Henry Harrison, delivered in the House, April 16, 1840. [Washington, 1840?] 32 p. GEU; NN; NRU; OClWHi. 40-5126

Oh the merry days when we were young. A favorite ballad... Arranged with an accompaniment for the piano forte. New York: Atwill, 1840. 5 p. DLC; MB. 40-5127

Oh! cast that shadow from thy brow. Philadelphia, PA: s. l. [184-?] p. MB. 40-5128

Ohio. General Assembly. Senate. Journal of the Senate of Ohio, at the first session of the Thirty-eighth General Assembly. Held in the City of Columbus and commencing Monday, December 2, 1839, and in the Thirty-eighth year of said state. Columbus, OH: Samuel Medary, printer to the State, 184?. 794, 89 p. O-LR. 40-5129

Ohio. General Assembly. Senate. Journal of the Senate of Ohio, at the first session of the Thirty-ninth General Assembly. Held in the City of Columbus and commencing Monday, December 7, 1840, and in the Thirty-ninth year of said state. Columbus, OH: Samuel Medary, printer to the State, 184?. 613 p. O-LR. 40-5130

Ohio. Laws, statutes, etc. An act for the protection of the canals of the State of Ohio. The regulation of the navigation thereof and for the collection of tolls. With the orders, rules, regulations and rates of tolls, as established by the Board of Public Works, March 24, 1840. Columbus, OH: S. & M. H. Medary, 1840. 45 p. OCLaw. 40-5131

Ohio. Laws, statutes, etc. Acts of a general and local nature, passed by the Thirty-eighth General Assembly of the State of Ohio. Begun and held in the City of Columbus, commencing December 2, 1839, and in the thirty-eighth year of Said State. Vol. XXXVIII. Columbus, OH: Samuel Medary, printer, 1840. 311 p. Ky; Mi-L; MWCL. 40-5132

Ohio. Laws, statutes, etc. Acts of a

general nature, passed by the Thirty-eighth General Assembly of the State of Ohio. Begun and held in the City of Columbus, commencing December 2, 1839, and in the thirty-eighth year of Said State. Vol. XXXVIII. Columbus, OH: Samuel Medary, printer to the state, 1840. 210 p. In-SC; MdBB; Nb; Nj; RPL. 40-5133

Ohio. Laws, statutes, etc. Acts of a local nature, passed by the 38th General Assembly of the State of Ohio. Begun and held in the City of Columbus, commencing Dec. 2, 1839, and in the thirty-eighth year of Said State. Vol. XXXVIII. Columbus, OH: Samuel Medary, printer to the state, 1840. 260, 50 p. IaU-L; In-SC; MdBB; Nb; NNLI; ODaL. 40-5134

Ohio. Legislature. General Assembly. Documents including messages and other communications made to the Thirty-Eighth General Assembly of the State of Ohio. Order to be printed in a separate volume, by act, passed December 16, 1836. Part 1 and 2 of Vol. for 1839-40. Columbus, OH: S. Medary, printer to the State, 1840. v. p. O. 40-5135

Ohio. Legislature. General Assembly. Executive documents... reports for 1840-1909 made to the 39th - 78th General Assembly of the State of Ohio, 1840-1910. Columbus, OH: s. l., 1840-1910. v. OAU. 40-5136

Ohio. Legislature. General Assembly. Journal of the House of Representatives of the State of Ohio. Being the First Session of the Thirty-Eighth General Assembly of. Held in the City of Columbus and commencing Monday, December 2, 1839, and in the thirty-eighth year of Said State. Columbus, OH: Samuel Medary,

printer to the state, 1840. 1046 p. O-LR. 40-5137

Ohio. Legislature. General Assembly. Journal of the House of Representatives of the State of Ohio. Being the First Session of the Thirty-Ninth General Assembly. Held in the City of Columbus and commencing Monday, December 7, 1840, and in the thirty-ninth year of Said State. Columbus, OH: Samuel Medary, printer to the state, 184?. 791, 247 p. O-LR. 40-5138

Ohio. State Hospital. Columbus. Annual report. Columbus, OH: s. l., 1840. PPAmP. 40-5139

Ohio. State Hospital. Columbus. By-laws, rules and regulations for the government of the Ohio Lunatic Asylum and the admission of patients. Also, the several acts of the General Assembly in relation to the same. Columbus, OH: s. l., 1840. 36 p. DNLM; OCHP. 40-5140

Ohio. State Library. Columbus. Catalogue of the Ohio State Library, December, 1840. Published by authority. Zechariah Mills, librarian. Columbus, OH: S. Medary, state printer, 1840. 60 p. DLC; O; OClWHi. 40-5141

Ohio. Supreme Court. Condensed reports of decisions in the Supreme Court of Ohio. Containing all the cases in the sixth and seventh volumes of Hammond's reports. With a newly arranged index. Edited by P. B. Wilcox, attorney at law. Columbus, OH: published by Isaac N. Whiting, 1840. 572 p. DLC; ICLaw; MH-L; Ms. 40-5142

Ohio Life Insurance and Trust Company. The Ohio Life Insurance and Trust

Company; make insurance on lives, grant annuities on lives and endowment for children. Capital $2,000,000, and paid in and invested in bonds and mortgages. Cincinnati, OH; New York: L'Hommedieu & Co., prs., 1840. 14 p. OCHP. 40-5143

Ohio Life Insurance and Trust Company. Tables of rates and letter of Wm. Bard to David E. Evans. Cincinnati, OH: s. l., 1840. OCHP. 40-5144

Ohio Mechanics' Institute, Cincinnati. Report of the Third Annual Fair of the Ohio Mechanics' Institute. Held during the third week in June at the Hall of the Institute in the City of Cincinnati. Cincinnati, OH: s. l., 1840. 39 p. MHi; NHi; OC; PP. 40-5145

Olcott, Thomas W. Address delivered before the Albany Phrenological Society... By Thomas W. Olcott... Published by request of the Society. Albany, NY: Printed by J. Munsell, 1840. 10 p. ICN; MHi; MWA; NjR; WHi. 40-5146

Old American comic almanac for 1840... Boston, MA: printed and published by S. N. Dickinson [1840?] p. MsJS. 40-5147

Old American comic almanac 1841. Boston, MA: printed and published by S. N. Dickinson [1840] p. MHi; MWA; WHi. 40-5148

Old plantation songster. Philadelphia, PA: s. l. [184-?] p. MB. 40-5149

Old soldiers, Jackson, Miss., Aug. 4, 1840-Oct. 13, 1840. Jackson, MS: s. l., 1840? p. MsSM. 40-5150

Oliver, Benjamin Lynde, 1788-1843. Forms of practice, or American precedents in personal and real actions, interspersed with annotations, by Benjamin L. Oliver. Second edition. Hallowell, ME: Glazier, Masters and Smith, 1840. 664 p. Ct; GU-L; MLow; PU-L; ViU; WaU. 40-5151

Oliver, George, 1782-1867. The history of initiation in twelve lectures. Comprising a detailed account of the rites and ceremonies, doctrines and discipline, of the secret and mysterious institutions of the ancient world. By the Rev. George Oliver, D. D... Uniform American edition. Philadelphia, PA: Leon Hyneman [1840] 176 p. LNMas; NR; TxWFM. 40-5152

Ollendorff, Heinrich Gottfried, 1803-1865. A key to the exercises in a new method of learning to read, write, and speak the French language. Revised edition. New York: D. Appleton & Co., 1840. 185 p. MeB. 40-5153

Olmsted, Denison, 1791-1859. An introduction to natural philosophy; designed as a text book for the use of the students of Yale College. By Denison Olmsted. 4th ed. New York: Collins, Keese and Co., 1840. 2 v. GU; MH; NcU; TNP; ViU. 40-5154

Olmsted, Denison, 1791-1859. Compendium of natural philosophy. Adapted to the use of the general reader and of schools and academies. Edition 5. New Haven, CT: s. l., 1840. IG; MWHi; OClW; OCOMI; OMC. 40-5155

Olmsted, Denison, 1791-1859. A Compendium of natural philosophy. Adapted to the use of the general reader and of schools and academies. By Denison Olmsted, A. M., Professor of Natural Philosophy and Astronomy in Yale College. Eighth edition, with numerous improvements. New Haven, CT; Boston, MA; New York; Philadelphia, PA; Charleston, SC; Mobile, AL; New Orleans, LA; Cincinnati, OH: Published by S. Babcock; F. J. Huntington and Co.; Robinson, Pratt, and Co.; Collins, Keese and Co.; Grigg and Elliott; Thomas, Cowperthwaite and Co.; S. Babcock and Co.; J. S. Kellogg and Co.; Wm. M'Kean; Truman and Smith, 1840. 360 p. IG; NStc. 40-5156

Olmsted, Denison, 1791-1859. A Compendium of astronomy. Containing the elements of the science, familiarly explained and illustrated, with the latest discoveries. Adapted to the use of schools and academies and of the general reader. By Denison Olmsted, A. M., Professor of Natural Philosophy and Astronomy in Yale College. 2d edition. New York: Collins, Keese and Co., 1840. 276 p. MB; OMC; ScCMu; VtMidbC. 40-5157

Olmsted, Denison, 1791-1859. Letters on astronomy, addressed to a lady:in which the elements of the science are familiarly explained in connection with its literary history:by Denison Olmsted... Boston, MA: Marsh, Capen, Lyon and Webb, 1840. 419 p. CU; InCw; MAbD; MHi; MnS. 40-5158

Olney, Jesse, 1798-1872. A history of the United States on a new plan. Adapted to the capacity of youth. To which is added The Declaration of Independence and the Constitution of the United States. New Haven, CT: Published by Durrie & Peck, 1840. 288 p. CSt; CtSoP; ICP; MH; MoU; RNHi. 40-5159

Olney, Jesse. 1798-1872. A practical system of modern geography; or, a view of the present state of the world... 33d edition. New York: Robinson, Pratt and Company, 1840. 288 p. MH; MnHi; NNC; OClWHi; WvU. 40-5160

Olster, Theodore. The little watchman. Der gestorte Nachtwachter. [For piano forte] [New York?: s. l., 184-?] 5 p. MB. 40-5161

On the interpretation of scripture. Baltimore, MD: Published monthly by the Catholic Tract Society, 1840. 24 p. MdBLC; MdCatS; MdHi; PPL. 40-5162

On the rule of faith. Baltimore, MD: Published monthly by the Catholic Tract Society, 1840. 12, 12 p. MdBD; MdCatS; MdW; PPL-R. 40-5163

Onderdonk, Benjamin Treadwell, 1791-1861. The change at the resurrection. A sermon preached in St. Philip's church, New York, on Tuesday, October 20, 1840, at the funeral of the Rev. Peter Williams, the rector of the church. New York: published by request of the wardens and vestrymen of St. Philip's church, 1840. 16 p. MBAt; MW; NNC; OClWHi; PPL; RP. 40-5164

Onderdonk, Benjamin Treadwell, 1791-1861. Christian unity. A sermon preached at the matriculation of students of the General Theological Seminary of the Protestant Episcopal Church on the evening of advent, November 29, 1840, in St. Peter's Church. New York, 1840. 16 p. DLC; ICRL; OClWHi; PHi; RPB. 40-5165

One hundred reasons why W. H. Harrison should & will have support of democracy for President of U. S. in preference to Mr. Van Buren... Boston, MA: s. l., 1840. 16 p. PHi. 40-5166

The only daughter; or, Down in the valley. Arranged for the piano forte. Baltimore, MD: Benteen [184-?] 2 p. ViU. 40-5167

Ontario Agricultural Society. Circular. Dated, Canandaigua, 19th June 1840. Printed letter from Oliver Phelps, corresponding secretary, in regard to forming [again] an agricultural society. [Canandaigua, NY: s. l., 1840] p. NCanHi. 40-5168

Opie, Amelia Alderson, 1769-1853. Illustrations of lying. Cooperstown, NY: s. l., 1840. 224 p. MWA. 40-5169

Opie, Amelia Alderson, 1769-1853. Tales, being illustrations of lying, in all its branches. Cooperstown, NY: H. & E. Phinney, 1840. 224 p. CtY; IaK; KU; NRCR; PHC. 40-5170

Oregon [Territory] Citizens. ... Petition of a number of citizens of the Oregon territory, praying the extention of the jurisdiction and laws of the United States over that territory... S. l.: s. l., 1840. 2 p. MdBJ. 40-5171

The Oriental annual; containing a series of tales, legends, and historical romances... 1840. London; Philadelphia, PA: C. Tilt; Carey and Hart, 1840. v. WU. 40-5172

Original Chrades. Prepared for the fair in aid of the Bunker Hill Monument, held in Boston, September, 1840. Boston, MA: Samuel N. Dickinson, 1840. 96 p. MB; MH; MLanc; MnS; RNR. 40-5173

Orme, William, 1787-1830. The life of the Rev. John Owen, D. D..Abridged from Orme's life of Owen. Philadelphia, PA: Presbyterian board of publication, 1840. 256 p. MiU; MWiW; NNUT; PPPrHi; ViRut. 40-5174

Orme, William, 1787-1830. The life of the Rev. Richard Baxter. Abridged from Orme's life of Baxter. Philadelphia, PA: Presbyterian board of publication, 1840. 216 p. DLC; GDecCT; KyLoP; TxD-T; ViRut. 40-5175

Orphean lyre. A collection of glees and catches. Arranged with piano forte accompaniment. Boston, MA: Parker, 1840. 2 v. in 1. CtHC; MFi; PU. 40-5176

Osborne, George Alexander, 1806-1893. ... La Pluie de Perles. Valse brillante. Pour piano, par Osborne... op. 61. Baltimore, MD; New Orleans, LA: F. D. Benteen; W. T. Mayo [184-?] 9 p. ViU. 40-5177

Osborne, Thomas Burr, 1798-1869. Speech of Mr. Osborne, of Connecticut, on the sub-treasury bill. Delivered in the House of Representatives of the United States in Committee of the Whole on the state of the union, June 3, 1840. Washington, DC: Printed by Gales and Seaton, 1840. 20 p. CSt; IU; MB; NNC; PHi. 40-5178

Osgood, Charles, 1808-1881. The causes, treatment and cure of fever and ague, and other diseases of bilious climates. By Charles Osgood, M. D.

Monroe, MI: Printed by E. Kendall, 1840. 14 p. MBCo; MiU. 40-5179

Osgood, Francis Sargent Locke, 1811-1850. The casket of fate. 2nd edition. Boston, 1840. 67 p. CtY; RPB. 40-5180

Osgood, Frances Sargent Locke, 1811-1850. Flower gift, a token of friendship for all seasons. With a complete floral dictionary. Chambersburg, Pa.: Shryock, Reed & Co., [1840] 276 p. ViU. 40-5181

Osgood, Samuel. The Star of Bethlehem. A discourse. Delivered in Nashua, Dec. 24, 1839. Cambridge, MA: Metcalf, Torry and Ballou, 1840. 24 p. MB; MH; MH-AH; MiD-B; Nl. 40-5182

Ostervald, Joan Frederic. Essay on the composition and delivery of a sermon. By the late J. F. Ostervald... Translated from the French and illustrated with notes by Joseph Sutcliffe... First American, from the last London edition. Baltimore, MD: Plaskitt & Cugle, 1840. 233 p. GEU-T; MBC; MdBP; NcCJ; NNUT. 40-5183

Oswald, John, 1804-1867. An etymological dictionary of the English language... By John Oswald... Philadelphia, PA: E. C. & J. Biddle, 1840. 523 p. NjP. 40-5184

Otey, James Hervey, 1800-1863. Preaching the gospel: a charge. Delivered to the clergy of the Protestant Episcopal Church in the State of Tennessee at the twelfth annual convention of the diocese, held in Lagrange, Tennessee, on Friday, May 8th, 1840... Nashville, TN: S. Nye & Co., printers, 1840. 26 . CSmH; MnHi; NGH; PPPrHi; 'SewU. 40-5185

Otway, Thomas, 1652-1685. Venice preserved. A tragedy in five acts. By Thomas Otway. With stage business, cast of characters, costumes, relative positions, &c. New York: S. French [184-?] 58 p. CSt; ICU. 40-5186

Our city clubs. By a City Poet. Philadelphia, PA: G. B. Zieber, 1840. 24 p. DLC; PPL; RPB. 40-5187

Our foreign debt, its causes and consequences. Albany, NY: s. l., 1840. PPL. 40-5188

Our globe, a universal picturesque album... [Philadelphia, PA: North American Bibliographic Institution, 184-?] 2 v. in 1. CtY; DLC; NRU; PHi; ViW. 40-5189

Out-of-door duties of Sunday School teachers. Philadelphia, PA: s. l., 1840. 58 p. MiGr. 40-5190

Outlet at Black's Eddy. Philadelphia, PA: s. l., 1840. PPL. 40-5191

Overseers of Schools of the Centre School District. Report in the Center School District and by-laws and regulations. Worcester, MA: Spooner & Howland, printers, 1840. 12 p. MBC; MH; MWHi; NN. 40-5192

Owen, pseud. Plans and motives for the extension of Sunday Schools... Philadelphia, PA: Am. Sunday School Union [184-?] 16 p. WHi. 40-5193

Owen, David Dale, 1807-1860. ... Mineral lands of the United States. Message from the President of the United States... [Washington, DC: GPO, 1840]

161 p. MH; NN; PPL; TxU; WHi. 40-5194

Owen, David Dale, 1807-1860. ... Report of a geological exploration of part of Iowa, Wisconsin, and Illinois. Made under instructions from the Secretary of the Treasury of the United States, in the autumn of the year 1839. With charts and illustrations. By David Dale Owen, principal agent to explore the mineral lands of the United States. [Washington, DC: GPO, 1840] 161 p. MH; OClW; PPi; PPins. 40-5195

Owen, Harriet Mary Brown, d. 1858. Memoir of the life and writings of Mrs. Hemans. By her sister... Philadelphia, PA: Lea and Blanchard, 1840. 317 p. CU; MH; MNe; PHi; ScSch. 40-5196

Owen, John, 1616-1683. The forgiveness of sin, illustrated in a practical exposition of Psalm 130. By John Owen, D. D., for some years Chancellor of Oxford University. New York: Published by the American Tract Society [184-?] 429 p. CBB; CSansS; IaPeC; MH; WU. 40-5197

Oxford theology. New York: Published by Alexander V. Blake, 1840. 43 p. MdBD; NNG; NRCR; PPL. 40-5198

P

P., W. C. Come to the sunset tree. Evening song of the Tyrolese peasants. The oetry by Mrs. Hemans. Composed y W. C. P. New York: Hewitt [184-?] 3 p. ViU. 0-5199

Pacini, Giovanni. Oh! fate unhappy and unset tears. Recitative and duet... in the opera of Sappho. Music by G. Pacini. Words by Salvatore Cammahano. With ccompaniment for piano forte] Boston, MA: Reed [184-?] 17 p. MB. 40-5200

Packard, Frederick Adolphus, 1794-867. Memorandum of a late visit to ome of the principal hospitals, prisons, & in France, Scotland and England. Embraced in a letter to the acting comnitee of the Philadelphia Society for aleviating the miseries of public prisons. Philadelphia: E. G. Dorsey, 1840. 33 p. CtY; DLC; NjP; PHi; PPC. 40-5201

Packard, Frederick Adolphus, 1794-867. The Sunday School teacher's dream. Written for the American Sunday School Union, and revised by the Committee of publication. Philadelphia, PA: American Sunday School Union [184-?] b. CtHC. 40-5202

Packard, Frederick Adolphus, 1794-867. The Union Bible dictionary for the use of schools, Bible classes, and families. Prepared for the American Sunday School Union, by the author of The Teacher Taught." Philadelphia, PA: American Sunday School Union [1840] 691 p. No Loc. 40-5203

Padda, John. The adieu, or we'll miss her at the morning hour. [Song. Accomp. for piano forte] New York: Hewitt & Jacques [184-?] 3 p. MB. 40-5204

Paddock, Zechariah. The continuance of brotherly love. A sermon for the times. By Rev. Z. Paddock... Utica, NY: R. Northway, printer, 1840. 23 p. CSmH; GAGTh; KSalW. 40-5205

Page, John E. Slander refuted. S. l.: s. l. [184-?] 16 p. MH. 40-5206

Paggi, GIovanni. Remembrance of Italy. Six waltzes. Composed and dedicated to the ladies of the Bunker Hill Fair. By Giovanni Paggi. Boston, MA: Henry Prentiss, 1840. 14 p. M; MB. 40-5207

Paige, Lucius Robinson, 1802-1896. Selections from eminent commentators, who have believed in punishment after death, wherein they have agreed with universalists, in their interpretation of Scriptures relating to punishment. 2d. ed. Boston, MA: Thomas Whittemore, 1840. 356 p. KyLoP; MH; MMeT-Hi; NNUT; VtFah. 40-5208

Paine, Martyn, 1794-1877. Medical and physiological commentaries. By Martyn Paine... New York: Collins, Keese & Co.

[etc., etc.] 1840-44. 3 v. GEU; KyDC; MeB; RPM; VtU. 40-5209

Paine, Martyn, 1794-1877. A reply to an attack by Henry I. Bowditch, M. D. Upon the essay on the principal writings of P. Ch. A. Louis, M. D., as contained in the medical and physiological comentaries... Boston, MA: republished from the medical and surgical journal, 1840. 56 p. KyLxT; MeBat; MPeaI; PPCP. 40-5210

Paine, Thomas, 1737-1809. The theological works of Thomas Paine... Boston, MA: printed for the advocates of common sense, 1840. 384 p. DLC; OCl; PSC-Hi; WMMU. 40-5211

Paley, William, 1743-1805. Archdeacon Paley's view of the evidences of Christianity. In three parts... with a memoir. Philadelphia, PA; Pittsburgh, PA: pub. by James Kay, Jun. and brother; C. H. Kay & Co. [184-?] 264 p. DLC; ICU; MiU; PPPrHi; WHi. 40-5212

Paley, WIlliam, 1743-1805. Paley's Natural theology, with illustrative notes & c. By Henry Lord Brougham... and Sir Charles Bell... with numerous woodcuts. To which are added, preliminary observations and notes. By A. Potter... New York: Harper and bro., 1840. 2 v. CMtV; MeB; P; PPL-R; PV; PSC. 40-5213

Paley, William, 1743-1805. A treatise on the law of principal and agent, chiefly with reference to mercantile transactions. By William Paley... Second American, from the third London edition, with considerable additions, by J. H. Lloyd... Philadelphia, PA; New York: John S. Littell; Halsted and Voorheis, 1840. 202 p. CoU; MdUL; NbCrD; OO; PP. 40-5214

Palfrey, John Gorham, 1796-1881 Academical lectures on the Jewish scrip tures and antiquities. Genesis an Prophets. Boston, MA: James Munroe & Company, 1840. 2 v. GAU; KyLoP; ME OCH; RNR. 40-5215

Palfrey, John Gorham, 1796-1881. discourse on the life and character of th Reverend John Thorton Kirkland, D. D LL. D., late president of Harvard Col lege... Cambridge, MA: John Owen, Fol som, Wells, and Thurston, printers to th university, 1840. 62 p. CU; ICN; MDeeF NCH; PHi. 40-5216

Palfrey, John Gorham, 1796-1881. discourse pronounced at Barnstable o the third of September, 1839, at th celebration of the second centennial an niversary of the settlement of Cape Coc by John Gorham Palfrey. Boston, MA Ferdinand Andrews, 1840. 43 p. MBarr 40-5217

Palfrey, John Gorham, 1796-1881. discourse pronounced at Barnstable o the third of September, 1839, at th celebration of the second centennial an niversary of the settlement of Cape Coc Boston, MA: F. Andrews, 1840. 71 p ICN; MNBedf; NNA; OC; PHi. 40-521

Palfrey, John Gorham, 1796-1881. discourse pronounced at Barnstable o the third of September, 1839, at the. second centennial anniversary of the set tlement of Cape Cod. Boston, MA: F Andrews, 1840. 50 p. CtSoP; DLC; MCB PPAmP; WHi. 40-5219

Palfrey, John Gorham, 1796-1881 Remarks concerning the late Dr. Bow ditch, by the Rev. Dr. Palfrey... Boston

MA: C. C. Little & co., 1840. 26 p. ICMe; MBBC; MH-AH; Nh; RPB. 40-5220

Palmer, Andrew. Letter to the members of the Port Lawrence Township Hickory Club of the City of Toledo... Toledo, OH: Printed by A. W. Fairbanks, 1840. 8 p. MiU-C; OClWHi. 40-5221

Palmer, E. Principles of nature... happiness & nursing. Granville, NY: s. l., 1840. MB. 40-5222

Palmer, Edward. A letter to those who think. By Edward Palmer. Worcester, MA: s. l., 1840. 18 p. ICME; MB; MWHi. 40-5223

Palmer, Thomas M., 1782-1861. The Teacher's Manual; being an exposition of an efficient and economical system of education suited to the wants of a free people. By Thomas H. Palmer, A. M.... Boston, MA: Marsh, Capen, Lyon, and Webb, 1840. 263 p. ICU; MB; NhPet; OCY; RPB. 40-5224

Paltock, Robert, 1697-1767. The life and adventures of Peter Wilkins; containing an account of his visit to the Flying Islanders... By R. S., a passenger in the Hector. Improved edition. Boston, MA: C. D. Strong, 1840. 186 p. LNH; MiU. 40-5225

Paltock, Robert, 1697-1767. The life and adventures of Peter Wilkins; containing an account of his visit to the Flying Islanders... By R. S., a passenger in the Hector. Hartford, CT: S. Andrus and Son [184-?] 186 p. MiU. 40-5226

Panarmo, Francis. The bird waltz, harp or piano forte. Composed by Francis

Panormo. Baltimore, MD: G. Willig [184-?] 3 p. MB; ViU. 40-5227

Park, Mungo, 1771-1806. The life and travels of Mungo Park: with an account of his death from the Journal of Isaac, the substance of later discoveries relative to his lamented fate, and the termination of the Niger. New York: Harper and brothers, 1840. 248 p. MoK; OClWHi; PMM; RPA; WvW. 40-5228

Park, Roswell, 1807-1869. A sketch of the history and topography of West Point and the U. S. Military Academy... Philadelphia, PA: H. Perkins, 1840. 140 p. ICN; MH; NNC; OClWHi; PU. 40-5229

Parke, Uriah. .... Key to the Farmers' A mechanics' practical arithmetic: in which the most difficult problems are solved, and notes and questions added for the illustation of the science, and pointing out its adaptation to the business purposes of life. By Uriah Parke. Zanesville, OH: Published by Arnold Lippitt; U. P. Bennett, printer, 1840. 130 p. ICartC; OClWHi; OO; TxElp. 40-5230

Parke, William Thomas. You don't exactly suit me... Ballad. [S. Accomp. for piano forte] Philadelphia, PA: Willig [184-?] p. MB. 40-5231

Parker, Langston, 1803-1871. ... The modern treatment of syphilitic deseases, both primary and secondary. Comprising an account of the new remedies; with numerous formulae for their preparation, and mode of administration... By Langston Parker... Philadelphia, PA: A. Waldie, 1840. 94 p. CSt-L; ICJ; MeB; NcD; PPA. 40-5232

Parker, Richard Green, 1798-1869. Progressive exercises in English composition. 26th stereotype edition. Boston, MA: Robt. S. Davis, 1840. 107 p. MdW; MeU. 40-5233

Parker, Richard Green, 1798-1869. Progressive exercises in English composition. 29th stereotype edition. Boston, MA: R. S. Davis, etc., etc., 184?. 107 p. InPerM; MH. 40-5234

Parker, Richard Green, 1798-1869. Progressive exercises in English composition. By R. G. Parker, A. M. Thirty-first stereotype edition. Boston, MA: Robert S. Davis, 1840. 107 p. CtY; MH; NN; OOxM; PPWi. 40-5235

Parker, Richard Green, 1798-1869. Progressive exercises in English grammar... By R. G. Parker... and Charles Fox... Boston, MA: Crocker & Brewster, 1840-47. 3 pts. in 1. ViU. 40-5236

Parker, Richard Green, 1798-1869. Progressive exercises in English grammar... By R. G. Parker... and Charles Fox... Boston, MA; New York: Crocker & Brewster; Leavitt, Lord & Co., 1840-42. 3 pt. in 1. MB. 40-5237

Parker, Richard Green, 1798-1869. Progressive exercises in English grammar... By R. G. Parker... and Charles Fox... Part I. 7th edition. Boston, MA: Crocker & Brewster, 1840. MH. 40-5238

Parker, Richard Green, 1798-1869. Progressive exercises in English grammar... Part III. With an appendix, embracing some of the elementary principles of rhetoric and logic, intimately connected with the subject of grammar. Boston, MA: Crocker & Brewster, etc., etc., 1840. 122, 2 p. CtHWatk; MH; NNC; ViU; WU. 40-5239

Parker, Samuel, 1779-1866. Journal of an exporing tour beyond the Rocky Mountains, under the direction of the American board of commissions for foreign missions, in the years 1835, '36, and '37... 2d ed. Ithaca, NY: The author, Mack, Andrus and Woodruff, printers, 1840. 400 p. MWA; NbU; OU; TxDaM; WyU. 40-5240

Parker, Samuel, 1779-1866. Journal of the exporing tour beyond the Rocky Mountains... 2nd ed. Ithaca, NY: The Author; Mack, Andrus & Woodruff, printers, 1840. 400 p. CSmH; IU; MdHi; MtU; OU. 40-5241

Parker, Samuel Parker, 1805-1880. Address delivered before the Common School Society of stockbridge, March 23, 1840. Lenox, Mass.: J. G. Stanly, 1840. 24 p. MH; NWM; RPB. 40-5242

Parker, Theodore, 1810-1860. The previous question between Mr. Andrews Morton and his alumni moved and handled in a letter to all those gentlemen... by Levi Blodgett, pseud. Boston, MA: Weeks, Gordon & Co., 1840. 24 p. CBPac; ICMe; MB; NjPT. 40-5243

Parkman, Francis, 1788-1852. A discourse delivered in the Church in Brattle Square, on Sunday, May 3, 1840, occasioned by the death of Rev. John T. Kirkland, D. D., LL. D., late President of Harvard University. By Francis Parkman, D. D., Pastor of the New North Church. Boston, MA: John H. Eastburn, printer, 1840. 30 p. ICMe; MiD-B; NjR; PPAmP. 40-5244

Parley, Peter. Fairy tales, or interesting tales. By the author of Peter Parley. New York: s. l., 1840. 192 p. CtY; MBAt; NcU; PPWi; ViU. 40-5245

Parley, Thomas. Little boy's own book. The well behaved little boy. Attentive little boy. Inattentive little boy. Covetous little boy. Dilatory little boy. Exact little boy. Quarrel little boy. Good little boy... New York: E. Dunigan [1840?] 62 p. MnU. 40-5246

Parlour magic. New York: s. l. [184-?] p. MB. 40-5247

Parmenter, William. Speech of Mr. Parmenter of Massachusetts. In the House of representatives, April 20, 1840. In committee of the whole on the state of the Union, on the civil and diplomatic appropriation bill. [S. l.: n. p., 1840] 16 p. IU; MH-BA; MiU-C; NNC; PPL. 40-5248

Parris, Virgil Delphini. Speech on the Cumberland Road, and constitutional power to make internal improvements. House of Representatives, February 11, 1840. Washington, DC: Blair and Rives, 1840. 8 p. MdHi; MH; OClWHi. 40-5249

Parrish, Isaac. An examination of the principles of the Independent treasury bill, the objections urged against it, and the antagonist or bank system of the opposition; in the speech of Isaac Parrish, of Ohio, in the House of Representatives, June 10 and 11, 1840, in committee of the whole on the state of the Union. Washington, DC: Printed at the Globe office, 1840. 24 p. DLC; NNC; OClFRB; PPL. 40-5250

Parrish, Joseph, 1779-1840. A letter from a young woman to a member of the Soc. of Hicksite Friends. With his reply. Philadelphia, PA: J. Townsend, 1840. 228 p. CtY; DLC; MH; NN; PHi. 40-5251

Parry, John, 1776-1851. I turn with delight towards thee. A ballad. Sung by Mr. Wilson. Written & composed by John Parry. New York: James L. Hewitt & Co. [184-?] 3 p. ViU. 40-5252

Parry, John, 1776-1851. A little farm well till'd. A comic glee. [For three men's voices] Arranged for the piano forte. Boston, MA: Bradlee [184-?] 3 p. MB. 40-5253

Parry, John, 1776-1851. O! merry row the bonnie bark. A ballad, founded on an Ancient Northumbrian melody. Sung by Miss Stephens. The words chiefly written and the music partly composed by John Parry. Baltimore, MD: Geo. Willig, Jr. [184-?] 3 p. ViU. 40-5254

Parry, John, 1776-1851. Villikins and his Dinah. Comic song. [With the four part chorus and accompaniment for the piano forte] Boston, MA: Ditson [184-?] 5 p. MB. 40-5255

Parry, John, 1776-1851. Wanted a governess! By John Parry, jun... Boston, MA: Oliver Ditson [184-?] 9 p. ViU. 40-5256

Parry, William Edward, Sir, 1790-1855. Three voyages for the discovery of a North-west passage from the Atlantic to the Pacific, and narrative of an attempt to reach the North Pole. By Sir W. E. Parry. New York: Harper and brothers, 1840. 2 v. ICU; KyDC; MDeeP; Nh-Hi; RPA. 40-5257

Parsons, Benjamin, 1797-1855. Anti-bacchus: an essay on the evils connected with the use of intoxicating drinks... By B. Parsons. Rev. and amended... By the Rev. John Marsh. New York: Published and sold by Scofield and Voorhies, 1840. 360 p. GDecCT; InCW; MBC; NNC; TxDaM. 40-5258

Parsons, Benjamin. 1797-1855. The Christian layman; or, The doctrine of the trinity fully considered, and adjudged according to the Bible... Mobile, AL; New York: Doubleday & Sears; C. C. Francis and Wiley & Putnam, 1840. 371 p. IEG; MH; NNC; OSW; WU. 40-5259

Parsons, Horatio Adams. 1797-1873. Steele's Niagara Guide Book; being a synopsis of Steele's book of Niagara Falls. With new and correct maps. Buffalo, NY: Published by Oliver G. Steele, 1840. 35 p. CtY; DLC; MWA; NN. 40-5260

Parsons, Horatio Adams, 1797-1873. Steele's Niagara Guide Book. Carefully revised and improved. Illustrated by maps of the falls and immediate vicinity, and of the Niagara River, from Lake Erie to Lake Ontario, and six new views. Buffalo, NY: Oliver G. Steele, 1840. 110 p. CaNSWA; DLC; Nh; NjR; PU. 40-5261

Parsons, Horatio Adams, 1797-1873. Steele's Niagara Guide Book. Carefully revised and improved. Illustrated by maps of the falls and immediate vicinity, and of the Niagara River, from Lake Erie to Lake Ontario, and six new views. Seventh edition. Buffalo, NY: Oliver G. Steele, 1840. 109 p. DLC; IU; MWA; NdFM; PPL. 40-5262

Parsons, Horatio Adams, 1797-1873.

Steele's Niagara Guide Book. Carefully revised and improved. Illustrated by maps of the falls and immediate vicinity, and of the Niagara River, from Lake Erie to Lake Ontario, and six new views. Eighth edition. Buffalo, NY: Oliver G. Steele, 1840. 110 p. DLC; MH; Nh; NjR; PU. 40-5263

Parsons, Isaac, 1790-1868. Memoir of Amelia S. Chapman. New York: American Tract Society, [1840?] 36 p. MiD; N; ViU. 40-5264

Parsons, Thomas William, 1819-1892. Prize poems. Delivered before the Bost. Lyceum, Nov. 19, 1840. [Boston, MA: s. l., 1840] p. MB; MH. 40-5265

The parting and return of three Indians, who graduated at Dartmouth College... [Boston, MA?: s. l. 1840?] 1 p. NN. 40-5266

Pas Styrien as danced by Mlle. Fanny Elssler & Mons. Sylvian. [Boston, MA: s. l. 1840] p. MH; MH-Mu. 40-5267

The passionate child. A story about little Ellen. New Haven, CT: S. Babcock, 1840. 16 p. CtY; NN; RPB. 40-5268

Paterson, Matthew Charles. An address on primary education, delivered by M. Charles Paterson, before the Columbian Peithologian society, in the chapel of Columbia college, June 3, 1840. New York: Wiley and Putnam, 1840. 42 p. IU; MH; NNC; PPL. 40-5269

Pathological Society of Philadelphia. Constitution and by-laws. Philadelphia, PA: s. l., 1840. 12 p. PHi. 40-5270

The pathway of the Saviour. Designed

for Sunday School Libraries and Bible classes, by a Friend of Children. [Four lines of verse] Boston, MA: Benjamin H. Greene, 1840. 155 p. No Loc. 40-5271

The patriarchs. Philadelphia, PA: William S. Martien, 1840. 285 p. GDecCT; MoS; MWiW; NNUT; ViRut. 40-5272

Patriotic songster. Philadelphia, PA: s. l. [184-?] p. MB. 40-5273

Patten's New Haven directory. No. 1-5. New Haven, CT: s. l., 1840-1844. 5 v. CtWat; MH. 40-5274

Paul, Jean. Schones und Gediegenes Aus Seinen Ver Schiedenen Schriften und Autsatzen... New York: Verlage Der Buchhandlung von W. Radde, 1840. 52 p. MNe; MoWgT. 40-5275

Paulding, James Kirke, 1778-1860. A life of Washington. By James K. Paulding... New York: Harper and brothers, 1840. 2 v. MiD-B; MnU; NjR; OClWHi; RPB. 40-5276

Pax, Carl Eduard, 1802-1867. Thou, thou reign'st in this bosom. Boston, MA: s. l. [184-?] p. MB. 40-5277

Paxton, James, 1786-1860. An introduction to the study of human anatomy. 3d American edition. Boston, MA: Ticknor, 1840. 2 v. IU-M; MdBM; Nh; NhD; OCir. 40-5278

Payne, John Howard, 1791-1852. ... Brutus; or, the fall of Tarquin. A tragedy in five acts. By John Howard Payne. With the stage business, cast of characters, costumes, relative positions, etc. New York: S. French [184-?] 53 p. CSt. 40-5279

Payne, John Howard, 1791-1852. ... Charles the Second; or, the merry monarch. A comedy in two acts. By John Howard Payne. With the stage business, cast of characters, costumes, relative positions, etc. The stage ed. New York: S. French [184-?] 44 p. CSt. 40-5280

Peabody, Andrew Preston, 1811-1893. Christian union; a sermon preached at the installation of Rev. Nathaniel S. Folsom, over the First Church in Haverhill, Ms., October 7, 1840. Andover: s. l., 1840. 15 p. CtSoP; ICMe; MHa; MoSpD; RPB. 40-5281

Peabody, Andrew Preston, 1811-1893. Portsmouth S. S. hymn book. Compiled for the use of the South Parish Sunday School. Portsmouth, NH: J. W. Foster, 1840. DLC; MB. 40-5282

Peabody, Andrew Preston, 1811-1893. The revival of religion. A sermon. Preached at Portsmouth, N. H., February 23, 1840. By Andrew P. Peabody, Pastor of the South Church. Published by request. Portsmouth, NH: J. W. Foster, J. F. Shores and Son, 1840. 23 p. CSmH; ICMe; MB; Nh; WHi. 40-5283

Peabody, Andrew Preston, 1811-1893. The revival of religion. A sermon preached at Portsmouth, N. H., February 23, 1840, by Andrew P. Peabody... 2d ed. Boston, MA: Weeks, Jordan & co., I. R. Butts, printer, 1840. 21 p. CBPac; MeBe-Hi; MH; NjR; PPAmP. 40-5284

Peabody, Andrew Preston, 1811-1893. The revival of religion. A sermon... Third edition. Boston, MA: Weeks, Jordan & Co.; I. R. Butts, printer, 1840. 21 p. MH-AH; MHi; NjR; RPB. 40-5285

Peabody, Andrew Preston, 1811-1893. A sermon on the end of the world... [Portsmouth, NH?: s. l., 184-?] 15 p. WHi. 40-5286

Peabody, Andrew Preston, 1811-1893. A sermon preached at the installation of Rev. Nathaniel S. Folsom, over the First Church and parish in Haverhill, Ma., Oct. 7, 1840. Andover, MA: printed by Gould, Newman and Saxon, 1840. 24 p. MHa; MHaHi; MH-AH; PPL. 40-5287

Peabody, Ephraim, 1807-1856. The moral power of Christ's character. By Rev. E. Peabody. Printed for the American Unitarian Association. Boston, MA: James Munroe & Co., 1840. 27 p. CBPac; ICMe; MDeeP; MeBat; MH. 40-5288

Peabody, Ephraim, 1807-1856. The moral power of Christ's character. By Rev. E. Peabody. Printed for the American Unitarian Association. Second edition. Boston, MA: Wm. Crosby and H. P. Nichols, 1840. 27 p. IaHi; IaPeC; MB-FA; MH-AH; PPLT. 40-5289

Peabody, Ephraim, 1807-1856. The religious culture of the young. Printed for the American Unitarian Association. Boston, MA: Wm. Crosby and H. P. Nichols [184-?] 24 p. WHi. 40-5290

Peabody, William Bourn Oliver, 1799-1847. Life of David Brainers, missionary to the Indians, by William B. O. Peabody. [New York: Harper and Brothers, 1840] 373 p. MiU-C. 40-5291

Peak, John, 1761-1842. Memoir of Mrs. Abigail Gale. Boston, MA: s. l., 1840. 65, 86 p. Nh-Hi. 40-5292

Peak, John, 1761-1842. Memoir of Mrs. Esther Peak, late consort of the writer. Boston, MA: s. l., 1840. 89, 96 p. Nh-Hi. 40-5293

Peak, John, 1761-1842. Sermon on Santification to which is added a memoir of Mrs. Gale and a memoir of Mrs. Esther Peak. 4th ed. Boston, MA: s. l., 1840. 96 p. MB; MH; NHC-S; Nh-Hi; PHi. 40-5294

Peirce, Benjamin, 1809-1880. An elementary treatise on Plane & spherical trigonometry with their applications to navigation, surveying, heights and distances, and spherical astronomy, and particularly adapted to explaining the construction of Bowditch's navigator, and the nautical almanac. By Benjamin Peirce... Boston, MA: J. Munroe and company, 1840. 428 p. ICU; MH; NjP; NNC; ViU. 40-5295

Peirce, Oliver Beale. Peirce's abridgment of grammar of English language. Boston, MA; New York; Watertown, NY: Weeks, Jordan & Co.; Robinson, Pratt and co.; Knowlton and Rice, 1840. 144 p. MNBedf; MShM. 40-5296

Peirson, Abel Lawrence, 1794-1853. On physical education; a lecture delivered before the American Institute of Instruction, August, 1839. Boston, MA: Marsh, Capen, Lyon and Webb, 1840. 26 p. IU; MBC; MH; MHi; MiD-B; OC. 40-5297

Peirson, Abel Lawrence, 1794-1853. Remarks on fractures. Read at the annual meeting of the Massachusetts medical society, May 27, 1840. By A. L. Peirson... Boston, MA: Whipple & Damrell, 1840. 367 p. CSt-L; MNT-M; MH-M; NNN; PPCP. 40-5298

Pelouze, Edward. Specimens of modern printing types cast at the letter foundry of Edward Pelouze... New York: s. l., 1840. ICN. 40-5299

Pembroke, N. H. Peoples Literary Institute and Gymnasium. Catalogue of the Officers, Instructors and Students of, for the Summer and Autumn Terms, 1840. Together with the students of Pembroke Academy for the last two terms whilst [sic] under the instruction of the Teachers of the Institute and Gymnasium. Concord, NH: Asa McFarland, 1840. 22 p. C; MH; Nh-Hi. 40-5300

Pendleton, Charles Henry. A conversation between two laymen, on the subjects & mode of Christian baptism & church communion, forming a complete manual. By Chas. H. Pendleton, member of the first Baptist Church, Cleveland. Cleveland, OH; Richmond, VA: Sanford & co.; etc., etc., 1840. 137 p. LNB; OO; PCA; RHi; RPB; RWe. 40-5301

Pengilly, Richard. The Scripture guide to Baptism; containing a faithful citation of all the passages of the New Testament which relate to this ordinance... from the 9th Lond. ed., rev. & imp. Philadelphia, PA: Amer. Bap. Pub. & S. S. Soc., 1840. 86 p. IEG; MiU; MNBedf; PPPrHi; OWervO. 40-5302

Penington, John, 1799-1867. An examination of Beauchamp Plantagenet's description of the province of New Albion... Philadelphia, PA: s. l., 1840. 33 p. MdBJ; MiU-C; PPAmP; VtU; WHi. 40-5303

Penn Mutual Life Insurance Company, Philadelphia. Specimen policies. [S. l.: s. l., 184-?] 184 p. OU. 40-5304

Pennsylvania. Auditor General. Report of the Auditor General, relative to the expenditure of public money, upon the breach on the Pennsylvania Canal, between Huntington and Hollidaysburg. Printed by order of the Senate, January 14, 1840. Harrisburg, PA: William D. Boss, printer, 1840. 137 p. P. 40-5305

Pennsylvania. Board of Canal Commissioners. Message from the Governor accompanied with the report of the Canal Comm'rs, relative to the Schuykill Inclined Plane. Harrisburg, PA: s. l., 1840. 13 p. DBRE; PHi. 40-5306

Pennsylvania. Board of Canal Commissioners. Report of the canal commissioners on the route of a railway avoiding the Schuylkill inclined plane. Harrisburg: W. D. Boas, printer, 1840. 10 p. DBRE; MiU-T; MWA; NN; PPAmP. 40-5307

Pennsylvania. Criminal Law. Summary of criminal law. By Henry Stephen, Sergeant at Law. Philadelphia, PA: John S. Little, publisher; Halsted and Voorhies, printers, 1840. 207 p. Nc-S. 40-5308

Pennsylvania. Dept. of Public Instruction. Manual for the directors and teachers of common schools in Pennsylvania. With forms of reports, plans of buildings, etc., etc. Philadelphia, PA: J. Crissy, 1840. MH; MoSU; PPL-R. 40-5309

Pennsylvania. Governor [David R. Porter] Message from the Governor, accompanied with the correspondence from the banks in the City and County of Phila., and the Harrisburg book, relating to the loan authorized by the Act of the 23rd Jan., 1840. Read in the House of

Representatives, Feb. 1, 1840. Harrisburg, PA: s. l., 1840. 13 p. PPAmP. 40-5310

Pennsylvania. Governor [David R. Porter] Message from the Governor of Pa. to both Houses of the Legislature at the commencement of the session, Jan. 1840. Harrisburg, PA: s. l., 1840. 44 p. PPAmP. 40-5311

Pennsylvania. Laws, statutes, etc. An act relating to orphan's courts and for other purposes. Approved October 13, 1840. Published by authority. Harrisburg, PA: William D. Boas, 1840. 28 p. CU-Law; P; PHi. 40-5312

Pennsylvania. Laws, statutes, etc. Compilation of the laws of Pennsylvania, relative to the internal improvements. Together with the canal and railway regulations, as established by the Board of Canal Commissioners. Harrisburg, PA: Printed by Barrett and Parke, 1840. 282 p. IaHil MH-L; PHi; PP; PU. 40-5313

Pennsylvania. Laws, statutes, etc. Law of Pa. relative to proceedings by foreign attachments. 2d ed. Philadelphia, PA: s. l., 1840. NjP. 40-5314

Pennsylvania. Laws, statutes, etc. Laws of the General Assembly of the Commonwealth of Pennsylvania, passed at the session of 1840, in the sixty-fourth year of independence, incuding ten acts and four resolutions, passed by both branches of the Legislature at the session of 1838-9. Published by authority. Harrisburg, PA: William D. Boas, 1840. 760, 28 p. Wa-L. 40-5315

Pennsylvania. Laws, statutes, etc. Rules

for regulating the practice of the Nicholson Court of Pleas for the State of Penna. Together with the act of Assembly relating to said Court. Harrisburg, PA: s. l., 1840. 24 p. PHi. 40-5316

Pennsylvania. Legislature. General Assembly. Address from a committee appointed at a meeting held in Bradford County on the subject of the North Branch Canal. Harrisburg, PA: s. l., 1840. 12 p. PHi. 40-5317

Pennsylvania. Legislature. General Assembly. Digest of the acts of Assembly relative to the first school district of the State of Pennsylvania. Harrisburg, PA: Pierson, 1840. 43 p. PU. 40-5318

Pennsylvania. Legislature. House of Representatives. Journal of the Fiftieth House of Representatives of the Commonwealth of Pennsylvania. Commenced at Harrisburg, Tuesday, the seventh day of January in the year of Our Lord, 1840, and of the Commonwealth, the sixty-fourth. Volume II. Harrisburg, PA: Holbrook, Henlock & Bratton, 1840. 523 p. Mi. 40-5319

Pennsylvania. Legislature. House of Representatives. Select Committee to Investigate. Report of the select committee appointed to investigate the management of the Columbia and Philadelphia Railroad. Mr. Mill, chairman, March 28, 1840. Harrisburg, PA: Holbrook, Henlock & Bratton, printer, 1840. 140 p. DBRE; MiU-T; NN; PHi. 40-5320

Pennsylvania. Legislature. Senate. Journal of the Senate, containing the canal commissioners report, and accompanying documents. As an appendix to

Vol. 11. Harrisburg, PA: W. D. Boas, 1840. 616 p. Mi; MiU. 40-5321

Pennsylvania. State Hospital, Harrisburg. Rules for the management of the asylum. Adopted by the Board of Managers, first mo. 20th, 1840. Philadelphia, PA: Brown, Bicking & Guilbert, printers, 1840. 12 p. TNP. 40-5322

Pennsylvania. State Temperance Convention. Address of the State Temperance Convention held at Harrisburg on the 15th, 16th and 17th of January, 1840 to the people of Pennsylvania. Harrisburg, PA: R. S. Elliott & Co., 1840. 8 p. NN; OClWHi. 40-5323

Pennsylvania. State Temperance Convention. Proceedings... held at Harrisburg, on the 15th, 16th and 17th of January, 1840. Harrisburg, PA: R. S. Elliott & Co., printers, 1840. 20 p. MB; MnHi. 40-5324

Pennsylvania. University. Catalogue of the trustees, officers & students of the University of Pennsylvania. Philadelphia, PA: s. l., 1840. 35 p. OC; Tx. 40-5325

Pennsylvania. University. Philo-mathean Society. Library. Catalogue of the books. Philadelphia, PA: s. l., 1840. 17 p. PHi; PU. 40-5326

Pennsylvania. University. School of Medicine. List of graduates for the years 1840-43, 1845-1853, 1867, 1871, 1873-76, 1888. Philadelphia, 1840-1888. Pennsylvania. Governor, 1939-1845. Message of the governor of Pennsylvania, in relation to a loan with the accompanying documents. Harrisburg: W. D. Boas, printer,

1840. 13 p. DLC; IU; NNC; PPeSchw. 40-5327

Pennsylvania Academy of the Fine Arts, Philadelphia, Pa. Exhibition catalogue... Philadelphia, PA: s. l., 1840-78. 8 v. MBMu; MH. 40-5328

The Pennsylvania and New Jersey almanac, for the year 1841... By Joseph Foulke... Philadelphia, PA: Thomas L. Bonsal, n. pr. [1840] 31 p. MWA; NjR. 40-5329

Pennsylvania Baptist Education Society. Minutes of the first anniversary... Philadelphia, PA: s. l. [1840] v. KyLoS; NRCR; PHi; PPTU; RPB. 40-5330

Pennsylvania Cavalry. First Troop. Philadelphia City Cavalry. By-laws, muster-roll & papers selected from the archives of the First Troop from Nov. 17, 1774 to Jan. 1, 1840. Philadelphia, PA: Sherman [1840] 64 p. MiD-B; NjP; PHi; PP; PU. 40-5331

Pennsylvania collection of church [music.] Containing... psalm & hymn tunes, anthems, etc... Harrisburg, PA: John Wyeth, 1840. PPPrHi. 40-5332

Pennsylvania democratic almanac. Harrisburg, PA: s. l., 1840-41. p. IaU. 40-5333

The Pennsylvania hermit; a narrative of the extraordinary life of Amos Wilson, who expired in a cave in the neighborhood of Harrisburg, Penn. Philadelphia, PA: s. l., 1840. 24 p. MHi; MiU. 40-5334

The Pennsylvania hermit; a narrative of the life of Amos Wilson. Annexed writings of Wilson while a recluse. St. John: s. l., 1840. 24 p. DLC. 40-5335

Pennsylvania Horticultural Society, Philadelphia, Pa. Catalogue of the library. Philadelphia, PA: s. l., 1840. 24 p. PPAmP; PPL; Vi. 40-5336

Pennsylvania Horticultural Society, Philadelphia, Pa. Constitution & by-laws. Philadelphia, PA: s. l., 1840. 24 p. PPAmP; PU; PPL-R; PHi; Vi. 40-5337

Pennsylvania Institution for the Deaf and Dumb, Philadelphia. The annuals reports of the board of directors... for 1839-1871. Philadelphia, PA: published by order of the contributors, E. G. Dorsey, T. K. and P. G. Collins, Crissy and Markley, E. C. Markley and Son, printer, 1840-1872. 11 pamphlets. MdBP; MnHi. 40-5338

... The People's almanac 1841. Boston, MA: printed and published by S. N. Dickinson, 1840. 36 p. MWA; WHi. 40-5339

Percival, Arthur Philip, 1799-1853. An apology for the doctrine of apostolical succession; with an appendix, on the English orders, by A. P. Perceval. New York: Protestant Episcopal tract society, 1840. 144 p. CtHC; GDecCT; MBAt; WHi; WNaE. 40-5340

Percival, Arthur Philip, 1799-1853. An essay on apostolical succession. By the Hon. Rev. A. P. Percival. Tenth edition. New York: Carlton C. Porter, 1840. 356 p. No Loc. 40-5341

Percival, James Gates, 1795-1856. New Haven Whig Song Book. Prepared for the New Haven County Mass. Convention, Thursday, Oct. 8th, 1840. New

Haven, CT: William Sotrer, 1840. 21 p. CtY; NN; RPB. 40-5342

Perkins, James Handasyd, 1810-1849. Associated action. An address. Delivered before the Oxford Chapter of the Alpha Delta Phi, August 11th, 1840. Cincinnati, OH: A. Pugh, print, 1840. 18 p. IaPeC; MH; OClWHi; OHi; OUr. 40-5343

Perkins, James Handasyd, 1810-1849. Christian civilization. An address. Delivered before the Athenian Society of the University of Ohio, at Athens, September sixteenth, 1840... Cincinnati, OH: A. Pugh, print, 1840. 26 p. MH; MiD-B; OClWHi; OWervO. 40-5344

Perkins, James Handasyd, 1810-1849. Duties of the liberal professions. An address, delivered before the Phi delta sigma society of Cincinnati college... Cincinnati, OH: Printed by Shepard & Stearns, 1840. 16 p. CSmH; IaPeC; PPPrHi. 40-5345

Perkins, Josiah. A brief account of the last moments of Rev. Aaron Leland Balch. Providence, RI: s. l., 1840. 12 p. MMet-Hi; RPB. 40-5346

Perkins, Samuel, 1767-1850. The world as it is; containing a view of the present condition of its principal nations... With numerous engravings. By Samuel Perkins. 5th ed. [New Haven, CT] : T. Belknap, 1840. 476 p. CSt; ICN; MH; MWA; PU. 40-5347

Perrin, Jean Baptiste. A selection of one hundred of Perrin's fables, accompanied with a key: containing the text, a literal and free translation... By A. Bolwar.... New edition. Philadelphia, PA: Lea &

Blanchard, 1840. 181 p. IaDuMtC; MH; MoS; NB; PPAN. 40-5348

Perry, J. The protesting Christian, standing before the judgment-seat of Christ, to answer for his protest against that parent church which Christ built upon a rock... By the Rev. J. Perry... Cincinnati, OH: Published by the Catholic Society for the Diffusion of Knowledge, 1840. 46 p. MdBS; NNF; OClWHi; OCHP. 40-5349

Pestel, P. The prison song. Boston, MA: s. l. [184-?] p. MB. 40-5350

Peters, Robert C. Practical farrier; or, farmer's guide in the management of cattle, horses, and sheep under various diseases. Chester, CT: Published by the Author, 1840. 53 p. CtHWatk; CtY. 40-5351

Peters, William Cumming, 1804-1866. The Greek March, in which is introduced an original Greek Air. Composed for & dedicated to Miss Elizabeth Lucket by W. C. Peters. New York: Hewitt & Jaques, 1840. 2 p. KU; MB; MWar; ViU; WHi. 40-5352

Peters, William Cumming, 1805-1866. Kind, kind and gentle is she. A favourite Scotch ballad. As sung with great applause by Mr. Dempster; poetry by Gabriel H. Barbour; music composed for & dedicated to Miss Mary Wood, by W. C. Peters... New York: C. T. Ceslain [184-?] 4 p. MH; ViU. 40-5353

Peters, William Cumming, 1805-1866. Lord Byron's favorite waltz. Composed by W. C. Peters. Philadelphia, PA: L. Meignen [1840] 4 p. KU. 40-5354

Peters, William Cumming, 1805-1866. The Louisville gallopade, arranged for the piano forte and dedicated to Miss Mary Mitchel by W. C. Peters. New York: Firth, Hall & Pond [184-?] 2 p. ViU. 40-5355

Peters, William Cumming, 1805-1866. O would I were a boy again. Ballad. Arranged for the guitar by W. C. Peters. Louisville, KY; Cincinnati, OH: W. C. Peters, Peters & Webster; Peters & Field [184-?] 2 p. ViU. 40-5356

Peters, William Cumming, 1805-1866. Shall we meet again, Mary. New York: s. l. [184-?] p. MB. 40-5357

Peters, William Cumming, 1805-1866. Shall we meet again, Mary. The words by F. Drake, Esqr. Arranged for the piano forte and respectfully dedicated to Miss Mary Jane Beard, by W. C. Peters. Philadelphia, PA: George Willig [184-?] 3 p. MB; ViU. 40-5358

Peterson magazine. Vol. 1-113, 1840-98. New York; Philadelphia, PA: s. l., 1840-98. 113 v. CSt; DLC; NcU; OOxM; WaSp. 40-5359

Peticolas, C. L. ... Impromtu on Jenny Lind polka, by C. L. Peticolas. Baltimore, MD; New Orleans, LA: F. D. Benteen; W. T. Mayo [184-?] 5 p. ViU. 40-5360

Petri, John F. The Cinderella waltz. Arranged in an easy manner and fingered for the piano forte by J. F. Petri. Baltimore, MD: G. Willig, Jr. [184-?] 2 p. ViU. 40-5361

Petri, John F. Introduction & variation. Avec finale sur un theme. Allemand pour le piano forte. Respectuensement didiee a Madamoiselle Flora Smith par John F. Petri. Philadelphia, PA: George Willig [184-?] 12 p. ViU. 40-5362

Pettit, Thomas McKean. Memoir of Roberts Vaux, one of the Vice-Presidents of the Historical Society of Pennsylvania. By Thomas McKean Pettit... Philadelphia, PA: s. l., 1840. 27 p. MdBJ; MiU-C; MnHi; Nh; PHi. 40-5363

Phaedrus. Phaedrus. With the appendix of Gudius. Translated by Christopher Smart, A. M... New York: Harper and brothers, 1840. 2 v. in 1. MdBP; PLFM; WStfSF. 40-5364

Phelon, B. Two lectures on the Seventh Commandment. Delivered in Bedford Street Chapel, Boston, March 15th and 22d, 1840. By Elder B. Phelon. Boston, MA: Albert Morgan, printer, 1840. 29 p. MeLewB. 40-5365

Phelps, Almira Hart Lincoln, 1793-1884. Botany for beginners; an introduction to Mrs. Lincoln's lectures on botany. For the use of common schools and the younger pupils of higher schools and academies. 6th ed. New York: F. J. Huntington & Co., 1840. 216 p. CSt; MH; MPeHi; NRHi. 40-5366

Phelps, Almira Hart Lincoln, 1793-1884. Familiar lectures on botany, explaining the structure, classification & uses of plants, practical, elementary & physiological. With an appendix containing descriptions of the plants of the United States & exotics, etc., for the use of seminaries & private students. 11th ed. New York: Huntington, 1840. 246 p. NNBG; PU-B; RNR. 40-5367

Phelps, Almira Hart Lincoln, 1793-

1884. Familiar lectures on natural philosophy. For the use of the higher schools and academies. By Mrs. Lincoln Phelps, author of "Familiar lectures on botany, chemistry, botany, and geology for beginners." 2nd edition. New York: F. J. Huntington & Co., 1840. 324 p. ArBaA; TBrik; WaPS. 40-5368

Phelps, Almira Hart Lincoln, 1793-1884. Natural philosophy for beginners. Designed for common schools and families. New York: F. J. Huntington & Co., 1840. 218 p. KyBC; NN. 40-5369

Phelps, Almira Hart Lincoln, 1793-1884. The fireside friend, or, Female student: being advice to young ladies on the important subject of education... by Mrs. Phelps... Boston, MA: Marsh, Capen, Lyon & Webb, 1840. 377 p. InCW; MdHi; NhPet; OMC; RPA. 40-5370

Phelps, Almira Hart Lincoln, 1793-1884. The fireside friend or female student; being advice to young ladies on the important subject of education. With an appendix on moral and religious education. Boston, MA: Marsh, Capen, Lyon & Webb, 1840. 377 p. DLC; ICarbT; WaWW; WHi. 40-5371

Phelps, Humphrey. Traveller's map of Michigan, Illinois, Indiana, and Ohio, by Humphrey Phelps and T. Ensign. With guide. New York: s. l., 1840. 2 p. PHi. 40-5372

Phelps and Ensign's traveller's guide through the United States; containing stage, steamboat, canal and rail-road routes, with the distances from place to place. New York: s. l., 1840. 53 p. ICHi; OO. 40-5373

Philadelphia. Citizens. Committee on an Asylum for the Insane Poor of Pennsylvania. A second appeal to the people of Pennsylvania on the subject of an asylum for the insane poor of the Commonwealth. Philadelphia, PA: Printed for the Committee, 1840. 35 p. MBAt; MH; NjPT; PPAmP; ViU. 40-5374

Philadelphia. Councils. Report of the Special Committee, appointed by the Common Council on a communication from the Board of Trustees of the Girad; Thomas S. Smith. Read in Councils, August 27, 1840. Philadelphia, PA: s. l., 1840. 53 p. DLC; P; PHi; PP; ViW. 40-5375

Philadelphia. Democratic Library & Reading Room. Constitution of the Democratic Library & Reading Room. Philadelphia, PA: s. l., 1840. PPL. 40-5376

Philadelphia. Fairmount First Presbyterian Church. Letter showing the causes of the decline and fall of the church... by a member. Philadelphia, PA: s. l., 1840. PPPrHi. 40-5377

Philadelphia. First Free Church. The confessions of faith and rules of government and discipline of the First Free Church. Philadelphia, PA: Merrihew & Tyhompson, 1840. 16 p. KyDC; MHi; NIC; PHi; PPPrHi. 40-5378

Philadelphia. House of Refuge. The design and advantages of the House of Refuge... Philadelphia, PA: s. l., 1840. 27 p. MB; MdBD; NNN; PPL-R; RPA. 40-5379

Philadelphia. List of the wealthy citizens of Phila., with their respective biographies, estimated &c. Philadelphia, PA: s. l., 1840. PPL. 40-5380

Philadelphia. Maps, views, etc. Fifth St., Phila., Plan of second & third floors of row of houses. Philadelphia, PA: s. l., 1840? p. PPL. 40-5381

Philadelphia. Medico-Churgical College. Constituton and by-laws. Philadelphia, PA: Barrington & Hasnell, 1840. DSG. 40-5382

Philadelphia. Mercantile Library Company. Catalogue of the books belonging to the Mercantile Library Company of Philadelphia. With a general index of authors and containing the constitution, rules, and regulations of the association. Accompanied by a sketch of its history. Philadelphia, PA: Printed for the Company, 1840. 182 p. MB; MdBP; MiU. 40-5383

Philadelphia. Mikveh Israel Congregation. Second annual examination of the Sunday School for religious instruction of Israelites in Phil. Held at the Synagogue Mikveh Israel, March 29, 1840... Together with a prayer by Isaac Leeser & an address by Moses N. Nathan. Philadelphia, PA: s. l., 1840. 28 p. OCH; PPAmP. 40-5384

Philadelphia. Mikveh Israel Synagogue. Persecution of the Jews in the East, proceedings of a meeting held... Aug. 27, 1840. Philadelphia, PA: Sherman, 1840. 26 p. PPAmP; PPDrop; PPL-R. 40-5385

Philadelphia. Sacular-feirer der Buchrucker-Kunst. Fest-Programm zur Vierten Sacular-feirer der Buchdrucker-Kunst. Philadelphia, PA: s. l., 1840. PPG. 40-5386

Philadelphia. St. Andrews Church. An annual statement of the parish statistics of St. Andrews Church. Prepared for the use of the congregation by Rev. J. A. Clark, rector. Philadelphia, PA: printed by William Stavely & Co., 1840. 22 p. MBD. 40-5387

Philadelphia. St. John's Church. Charter and by-laws of St. John's Church, northern liberties, Phila., 1840. Philadelphia, PA: s. l., 1840. 23 p. PHi. 40-5388

Philadelphia. St. Luke's Church. Charter & by-laws. Philadelphia, PA: King, 1840. 17 p. PU. 40-5389

Philadelphia. St. Philip's Church. Ceremony... cornerstone. Philadelphia, PA: s. l., 1840. PPL. 40-5390

Philadelphia. Select Councils. Journal of the Select Council, beginning October 11th, 1839 and ending October 8th, 1840. With an index. Philadelphia, PA: s. l., 1840. WHi. 40-5391

Philadelphia, Sixth Presbyterian Church. Catalogue of the Sabbath School Library... Philadelphia, PA: Ashmead, 1840. PPPrHi. 40-5392

Philadelphia. Water Works. Opinions of the Messrs. Meredith and Binney as to the right of the corporation of the City of Philadelphia to use the water and water power of the River Schuylkill at Fairmount Dam. Philadelphia, PA: J. Crissy, printer, 1840. 15 p. MnHi. 40-5393

Philadelphia & Erie Railroad Company. Second report of Edward Miller, engineer in chief... March 1, 1840. Philadelphia, PA: John C. Clarke, printer, 1840. 37 p. MeHi; MiD-B; MnHi; NBuG; NRoM; PPM. 40-5394

Philadelphia Artistic Fund Society. Catalog... 5th, 7th ann. exhibit, 1840. Philadelphia, PA: s. l., 1840. MB. 40-5395

Philadelphia Carpenters Company of the City & County of Philadelphia. An act to incorporate the Carpenters Company of the City and County of Philadelphia. Together with the by-laws and rules and regulations. Philadelphia, PA: Printed by John C. Clark, 1840. 24 p. MiD-B. 40-5396

Philadelphia Hose Company. Constitution, revised Dec. 18, 1839. Philadelphia, PA: s. l., 1840. 32 p. PHi. 40-5397

Philadelphia House of Refuge. The design and advantages of the House of Refuge. Philadelphia, PA: Brown, Bicking & Gilbert, 1840. 27 p. MdBD. 40-5398

Philadelphia Library Company. Design for Library Co. & Athenaeum Bldg. Plan of ground floor. John Nottman, Architect. Philadelphia, PA: s. l., 1840. PPL. 40-5399

Philadelphia Library Company. Offices, Fifth Street, Library Co. lot. Front elevation, section & elevation, ground plan & plans for second & third floors. John Nottman, Architect. Philadelphia, PA: s. l., 1840. PPL. 40-5400

Philadelphia Medical Society. Charter and by-laws. Philadelphia, PA: s. l., 1840. 23 p. PHi. 40-5401

The Philadelphia monthly album and

literary companion. Philadelphia, PA: W. P. Stagers [1840-] v. DLC; NIC. 40-5402

Philadelphia Museum Company. Charter and supplement to Charter and By-laws of the Philadelphia Museum Company. Philadelphia, PA: A. Waldie, 1840. 15 p. MH; PHi; OCHP; PPAmP. 40-5403

Philadelphia Prison Society. Philadelphia Society for alleviating the miseries of public prisons. Memorandum of a late visit to some of the pricipal hospitals, prisons &c. in France, Scotland, and England... Philadelphia, PA: E. G. Dorsey, 1840. 33 p. MdBM. 40-5404

Philadelphia Sabbath Association. Semi-centennial exercises and historical sketch... Philadelphia, PA: The Association, 1840-90. 96 p. PPPrHi. 40-5405

Philadelphia School of Anatomy. Annual announcements and catalogues for 1840-1841. Philadelphia, PA: Charles A. Elliott, 1840-. v. DLC; PPCP. 40-5406

Philadelphia Society for Promoting Agriculture. Charter and by-laws of the Philadelphia Society for Promoting Agriculture. Instituted February 14, 1809. Germantown, PA: printed by P. R. Freos & Co., 1840. 12 p. AzU; CoFcS; MdU; NjR; PPAmP; TxCsA. 40-5407

Philadelphia visitor & parlour companion of popular & miscellaneous literature, music, fashions, biography, science, the arts, etc. Philadelphia, PA: s. l. [1840-] v. PHi; PU; PP; TxU. 40-5408

Philanthropos. The duty of women to promote the cause of peace. By

Philanthropos. Boston, MA: American Peace Society, 1840. 39 p. MoSpD. 40-5409

Philip, Robert, 1791-1858. The life and opinions of the Rev. William Milne, D. D., missionary to China... By Robert Philip... New York: D. Appleton & Co., 1840. 320 p. IaDuW; MoSpD; MWiW; Nh-Hi; OMC; PCA. 40-5410

Philip, Robert, 1791-1858. The life and opinions of the Rev. William Milne, D. D., missionary to China... intended as a guide to missionary spirit. By Robert Philip... Philadelphia, PA: H. Hooker, 1840. 435 p. ICU; MiD; OO; PPiW; ViRut. 40-5411

Phillip, Lovell. Hunter's wife. Composed & arranged by Lovell Phillips. New York: Firth & Hall and J. L. Hewitt & Co. [184-?] 5 p. ViU. 40-5412

Phillips, Joseph F. Address... before the Catskill Young Men's Literary Society, by the Rev. Joseph F. Phillips... Catskill, NY: Printed at the Messenger Office, 1840. 12 p. NjR. 40-5413

Phillips, Richard, Sir, 1767-1840. An easy grammar of natural & experimental philosophy. For the use of schools. With ten engravings. By David Blair, pseud... Revised by B. Hallowell. 4th ed. Philadelphia, PA: Kimber & Sharpless, 1840. 252 p. MDux; PSC. 40-5414

Phillips, Willard. A treatise on the law of insurance. By Willard Phillips... Second edition. Boston, MA: Charles C. Little & James Brown, 1840. 2 v. C; LNT-L; MH; OCLaw; WMMU. 40-5415

Phillips, William. Campbellism exposed; or, Strictures on the peculiar tenets of Alexander Campbell, by Rev. William Phillips, to which is prefixed a memoir of the author. Cincinnati, OH: Hitchcock & Walden [n. d.] 267 p. CBPSR; IEG; MiD-B; MoKU; NNMHi. 40-5416

Phillips Academy, Andover, Mass. Catalogue of the officers and students in the English Department and teachers' seminary in Phillips Academy, Andover, Mass. Andover, MA: Printed by Gould, Newman and Saxton, 1840. OClWHi; PPL. 40-5417

Phinney's Calendar; or, Western Almanack for 1841. By George R. Perkins. Cooperstown, NY: H. & E. Phinney [1840] p. DLC; MiD-B; MWA; NN; WHi. 40-5418

Phipps, Edmund, 1808-1857. Woman's love and the world's favour; or, the Fergusons. By the Hon. Edmund Phipps... In two volumes. Philadelphia, PA: Lea & Blanchard, 1840. 2 v. CtY; NSyHi. 40-5419

Phrenological Almanac, and Physiological Guide, 1840-45. New York: s. l. [1840-44] 2 v. MB. 40-5420

Phrenological Almanac for 1841. By L. N. Fowler. New York: s. l. [1840] p. MBNEH; MWA. 40-5421

Pickard, Hannah Maynard Thompson, 1812-1844. Procrastination, or Maria Louisa Winslow. By a lady. Boston, MA: D. S. King, 1840. 115 p. CBVaU; CU; RPB. 40-5422

Pickens, A. C. Long ago! Boston, MA: s. l. [184-?] p. MB; ViU. 40-5423

Pickens, Francis Wilkinson, 1805-1869. Speech of Mr. F. W. Pickens, of South Carolina, on the two per cent fund, the Cumberland Road, and the Power of the Government to make internal improvements... [Washington, DC: Printed by Blair and Rives, 1840] 21 p. MdHi; MeB; NcD; OClWHi. 40-5424

Pickering, Ellen, d. 1843. The fright. By Ellen Pickering. In two volumes. Philadelphia, PA: Carey & Hart, 1840. 2 v. CtY; MBAt; MdW; NjR; WaPS. 40-5425

Pickering, Ellen, d. 1843. The orphan niece. A novel. [Philadelphia: T. B. Peterson, 184-?] 116 p. CtY; MdBP; NN. 40-5426

Pickering, Ellen, d. 1843. The poor cousin; A novel. [Philadelphia: T. B. Peterson, 184-?] Pickering, Ellen, d. 1843. Who shall be heir? New York: E. Ferrett & Company, 184-?] 128 p. MH; NjP. 40-5427

Pickering, Ellen, d. 1843. The quiet husband. By Miss Ellen Pickering, author of "The merchant's daughter..." In two volumes. Philadelphia, PA: E. Ferrett & Co., 1840? 112 p. NN. 40-5428

Pickering, Ellen, d. 1843. The quiet husband. By Miss Ellen Pickering. Philadelphia, PA: Carey and Hart, 1840. 2 v. DGU; DLC; MWH; OrU. 40-5429

Picket, Albert, 1771-1850. The principles of English grammar. By A. Picket and John W. Picket, A. M... Cincinnati, OH: Pub. by U. P. James, 1840. 213 p. IaHi; USlC. 40-5430

Picot, Charles, 1789-1852. First lessons in French; consisting of rules and directions for the attainment of a just pronunciation and select pieces arranged for double translation from French into English and from English into French. Philadelphia, PA: Printed by John H. Gihon & Co., 1840. 95 p. PHi; PWc. 40-5431

Pictorial A B C book. New York: J. Q. Preble [1840] p. DLC; MH. 40-5432

The picture alphabet, in prose and verse. New York: American Tract Society, [1840?] 32 p. NNC; RPB. 40-5433

The picture alphabet: or, Child's A B C. Portland [Maine] : Bailey and Noyes, [1840?] 16 p. CtY. 40-5434

Pictures of Bible history. Northampton: Metcalf, 1840. 24 p. CtY; PU-Penn. 40-5435

Pictures of the times; or, A contract between the effects of the true democratic system as displayed under Jefferson, Madison, and Jackson, and the effects of the aristocratic sub-trasury system as displayed at the present time. Philadelphia, PA: s. l., 1840. 16 p. DLC; NBLiHi; NN; NNC. 40-5436

Pierce, Franklin, President of the United States, 1804-1869. Speech... in Senate... May 1, 1840, upon claims for seven years' half pay. [By the heirs of officers engaged in the revolutionary war, etc.] [Washington, DC: s. l., 1840] 8 p. MdHi; Nh-Hi; TxU. 40-5437

Pierce, Oliver B. Pierce abridgement of the grammar of English language. Boston, MA: Weeks, Jordan & Co., 1840. 144 p. PLFM. 40-5438

Pierpont, John, 1785-1866. Airs of Palestine, and other poems... Boston, MA; London: J. Munroe and company; J. Green, 1840. 334 p. CtMW; IaGG; MeU; NRU; OC; RPA. 40-5439

Pierpont, John, 1785-1866. National humiliation: a sermon... By John Pierpont... Boston, MA: Samuel N. Dickinson, 1840. 16 p. CtHC; ICMe; MBAt; MiD-B. 40-5440

Pierpont, John, 1785-1866. National reader; a selection of exercises in reading and speaking. Designed to fill the same place in the schools of the U. S. that is held in those of Great Britain by the compilations of Murray Scott, Enfield, Mylius, Thompson, Williams. Boston, MA: David H. Williams, 1840. 276 p. MB; MH; OrU. 40-5441

Pierpont, John, 1785-1866. The National reader; a selection of exercises in reading and speaking. Designed to fill the same place in the schools of the U. S. that is held in those of Great Britain... By John Pierpont, compiler. 40th ed. New York: George P. Cooledge & Brother, 184-? 276 p. MB; MH; MiU. 40-5442

Pierpont, John, 1785-1866. The reformer and the conservative. A discourse delivered in Hollis street church, 24th Nov. 1839. Boston, MA: S. N. Dickinson, 1840. 15 p. ICMe; MBC; MH; MH-AH; MWA; NIC-L. 40-5443

Pike, John Gregory, 1784-1854. Persuives [sic] of early piety interspersed with suitable prayers. New York: pub. y

Am. Tract Society; D. Fanshaw, printer [184-?] 359 p. ViU; WHi. 40-5444

Pike, Marshall Spring. My Lucy and me. [Solo and chorus for mixed voices. With accompaniment for the piano forte] Words and melody by Marshall S. Pike and sung by the Harmonious Music composed and arranged by J. P. Ordway. Boston, MA: Ordway [184-?] 5 p. MB. 40-5445

Pike, Stephen. The teacher's assistant; or, a system of practical arithmetic... The hole designed to abridge the labour of teachers and to facilitate the instruction of youth. With corrections and additions by the author. Compiled by Stephen Pike. A new edition, revised. Philadelphia, PA: M'Carty & Davis, 1840. 198 p. NNC. 40-5446

Pilgrim, James, 1825-1879. Eveleen Wilson, the flower of Erin. An original drama in three acts. New York: French [184-?] 32 p. MB; PPL; PU. 40-5447

Pilgrim Society, Plymouth, Mass. Constitution of the Pilgrim Society as amended May, 1836. Together with a list of members. Adopted as amended. Plymouth, MA: James Thurber, printer, 1840. 8 p. MBC; MH; NBLiHi; PHi; RPB. 40-5448

Pilkington, James. The artists and mechanics repository and working man's informant; embracing chemistry, abstracts of electricity, calvanism, magnetism, mechanics, pneumatics, optics, and astronomy. Also mechanical exercises in iron, steel, lead, zinc, copper and tin soldering. Philadelphia, PA: Michael Kelley, 1840. 378, 116 p. NPtjerHi; PKsL; PU. 40-5449

Pinkney, Charles. The last serenade. [Song] Arranged for the piano forte & guitar. Baltimore, MD: Benteen [184-?] 2 p. MB. 40-5450

Pious songs. Baltimore, MD: Armstrong and Berry, 1840. 446 p. MWHi. 40-5451

The pirates' own book; or, authentic narratives of the lives, exploits, and executions of the most celebrated sea robbers... Philadelphia, PA: Thomas, Cowperthwait & Co., 1840. 432 p. NNS. 40-5452

Pitt, William, 1708-1778. Celebrated speeches of Chatham, Burke and Erskine, to which is added the argument of Mr. Mackintosh in the case of Peltier. Philadelphia, PA: Edward C. Biddle, 1840. 534 p. MWA; NICLA; OCh; TxU. 40-5453

Pixes, J. F. The Swiss boy. Steh nur auf. With variations for the voice. As sung with enthusiastic applause by Mlle. Sontag & Madame Caradori Allan. Composed for and dedicated to Mlle. Sontag by J. F. Pixis. Philadelphia, PA: A. Fiot [184-?] 10 p. ViU. 40-5454

Plan of Port Clinton. Philadelphia, PA: s. l., 1840? p. PHi. 40-5455

Planche, James Robinson, 1796-1880. ... Charles the XII. An historical drama in two acts. By J. R. Planche. With the stage business, cast of characters, costumes, relative positions, &c. New York: Samuel French [184-?] 45 p. CSt. 40-5456

Planche, James Robinson, 1796-1880. ... Faint heart never won fair lady. A comedy in one act. By J. R. Planche. With the stage business, cast of characters, costumes, relative positions, &c. New York: Samuel French [184-?] 31 p. CSt. 40-5457

Planche, James Robinson, 1796-1880. ... The follies of a night. A vaudeville comedy in two acts. By J. R. Planche. With the stage business, cast of characters, costumes, relative positions, &c. New York: Samuel French [184-?] 54 p. CSt; MH. 40-5458

Planche, James Robinson, 1796-1880. ... The invisible prince, or the island of tranquil delights. A fairy extravaganza in one act. By J. R. Planche. New York: Samuel French [184-?] 35 p. MH; NIC-L. 40-5459

Planche, James Robinson, 1796-1880. ... The loan of a lover. A vaudeville in one act. By J. R. Planche. New York: Samuel French [184-?] 29 p. MH; NN. 40-5460

Planche, James Robinson, 1796-1880. ... The pride of the market. A comic drama in three acts. By J. R. Planche. New York: W. Taylor & Co. [184-?] 47 p. MH; NIC. 40-5461

Plants and birds. Illustrated with coloured engravings. For young children. By a lady. New York: S. Colman, 1840. 112 p. DLC; MH. 40-5462

Platt, Dennis. The foundations examined; or, Plain scriptural reasons for refusing to become a Baptist... Ed. 2, rev. and enl. Skaneateles, NY: s. l., 1840. 48 p. CSansS; MBC; NAuT; NNUT. 40-5463

Playfair, John, 1748-1819. Elements of geometry; containing the first six book ofIgn 40-5464

Playfair, John, 1748-1819. Euclid... to which are added elements of plane and spherical trigonometry. By John Playfair, F. R. S., Lond. & Edin... From the last London edition, enlarged. New York: W. E. Dean, printer & publisher, 1840. 317 p. NNS; Or. 40-5465

Playfair, John, 1748-1819. Euclid... Elements of geometry; containing the first six books of Euclid... Philadelphia, PA: Marot & Walter, 1840. 320 p. OCX. 40-5466

Pleyel, Ignay, 1757-1831. ... Six favorite easy duets. Progressively arranged for two violins. Composed by Ignace Pleyel. Philadelphia, PA: G. E. Blake [184-?] 11 p. ViU. 40-5467

Plumb, David. Man. A poem. Delivered at the commencement of the Wesleyan University, August 5, 1840, by D. Plumb. Lowell, MA: L. Huntruss, printer, 1840. 16 p. NN; NNMHi; RPB. 40-5468

Plumer, William Swan, 1802-1880. Ann Eliza Williams; or, the child one hundred years old. An authentic narrative. New York: The American Tract Society [184-?] 25 p. OO. 40-5469

Plumer, William Swan, 1802-1880. The offices of Christ. Abridged from the original work of the Rev. George Stevenson, by William S. Plumer, D. D. Philadelphia, PA: William S. Martien, 1840. 150 p. GDecCT; KyLoP; MWiW; TxAuPT; ViRut. 40-5470

Plumer, William Swan, 1802-1880. Theatrical entertainments; a premium tract. Philadelphia, PA: American Baptist Publication Society [184-?] 24 p. MH. 40-5471

Plutarch. Plutarch's lives of the most select and illustrious characters of antiquity. Translated from the original Greek. With notes... by John Langhorne, D. D., and William Langhorne, A. M., and others. By William Mavor, LL. D....Complete in one volume. [2 line quote] Ithaca, NY: Mack, Andrus & Woodruff, 1840. 432 p. MdBJ; NhAndP; NIC; OWoC; ViU. 40-5472

Plutarch. Plutarch's lives. Translated from the original Greek. With notes, critical & historical, and a life of Plutarch, by John Langhorne, D. D., and William Langhorne, A. M. New York: Harper & Brothers, 1840. 4 v. ICU; MH; NBu; ScGrw. 40-5473

... Pocket almanack for the year... 1841. By Thos. Spofford. Boston, MA: Thos. Groom [1840] 48 p. MHi; PHi. 40-5474

The pocket letter writer; consisting of letters on every occurrance in life. With complimentary cards, etc. 4th ed. Providence, RI: B. Cranston & Co., 1840. 256 p. RHi; RPB; TU. 40-5475

Poe, Edgar Allan, 1809-1849. The conchologist's first book: or, A system of testaceous malacology, arranged expressly for the use of schools, in which the animals, according to Cuvier, are given with the shells... 2d ed. Philadelphia, PA: Pub. for the author, by Haswell, Barrington, and Haswell, 1840. 166 p. CtMW; CU; IaAS; MH; MNe; PU; WU. 40-5476

Poe, Edgar Allan, 1809-1849. The conchologist's first book; or, a system of testaceous malacology. Arranged expressly for the use of schools, in which animals, according to Cuvier, are given with the shells a great number of new species added, and the whole brought up, as accurately as possible, to the present condition of the science. By Edgar A. Poe. With illustrations of two hundred and fifteen shells. 3d ed. Philadelphia, PA: pub. for the Author by Haswell, Barrington and Haswell, 1840-45. 166 p. CSt. 40-5477

Poe, Edgar Allan, 1809-1849. Tales of the grotesque and arabesque, by Edgar A. Poe... Philadelphia, PA: Lea and Blanchard, 1840. 2 v. CSt; DLC; LNH; MH; OCY; RPB. 40-5478

The poet. A metrical romance of the seventeenth century. A keepsake for 1840. Philadelphia, PA: Carey and Hart, 1840. 216 p. DLC; KU; PP; RPB. 40-5479

The poetical present. With beautiful engravings. Worcester: J. Grout, Jr., 184-? 24 p. CtY; DLC; MWA; RPB. 40-5480

The poetical wreath for 1840. New York: Charles Wells, 1840. 395 p. MiU; NjR; ViU. 40-5481

Poinsett, Joel Roberts, 1779-1851. A comparison of Mr. Poinsett's plan for the re-organization of the militia with that of Gen. Harrison and both with the old law. Washington: printed at the Globe office, 1840. 15 p. MiU-C; OClWHi. 40-5482

Polack, Joel Samuel, 1807-1882. Manners and customs of the New Zealanders. With notes corroborative of their habit, usages, etc., and remarks to intending emigrants. With numerous cuts drawn on wood. New York: s. l., 1840. 2 v. RPA. 40-5483

The political mirror for 1840, showing the true cause of the present commercial distress of the nation, with the remedy. By a merchant. New York: printed for the author, 1840. 34 p. MH. 40-5484

The politician's register containing the result of the elections during 1836, 7, 8, & 40. With a list of Chief Executive Offices, names of members of Congress... Governors of the different states, time of meeting of the different legislatures, and time of holding elections... Baltimore, MD: [Pub. by James Young] 1840. 58, 1 p. DLC; MdHi; MdLR; NN; PPL. 40-5485

The Politician's register; a compilation of returns of votes cast in the several states of the Union mainly during the years 1836, 1838 & 1840 for President, members of Congress & state officers. 5th ed. New York: H. Greeley, 1840. 36 p. CtHWatk; MeHi; MH; MiD-B; MsJS; PWW. 40-5486

Politician's register. Results of elections, 1840-44. 3d ed. New York: Burgess, Stringers Co., 1840-44. p. PHi. 40-5487

Pollock, Abraham David, b. 1807. Africa and her children and her prospect; a discourse in behalf of African colonization. By A. D. Pollock... Richmond, VA: Printed by P. D. Bernard, 1840. 19 p. DLC; ViU. 40-5488

Pollock, Robert, 1798-1827. The Course of time; a poem. By Robert Pollok, A. M. With a memoir of the author...

Cincinnati, OH: James, 1840. 256 p. MiKC. 40-5489

Pollock, Robert, 1798-1827. Course of time; a poem. With a memoir of the author, by Wm. Livingstone Prall... New York: E. Kearny [184-?] 328 p. MiU; NNC. 40-5490

Pollock, Robert, 1798-1827. The course of time; a poem in ten books... With a sketch of the life of the author. New York: Piercy and Reed [1840?] 248 p. MNS. 40-5491

Pollock, Robert, 1798-1827. The course of time; a poem. With an enlarged index, a memoir of the author, an introductory notice, and an analysis prefixed to each book. Rev. ed. Boston, MA: Benjamin B. Mussey, 1840. 286 p. IU; OAU; OClW; RPB; VtWood. 40-5492

Pollock, Robert, 1798-1827. Tales of the Scottish Covenanters. New York: R. Carter, 184-? 113, 103, 115 p. OU. 40-5493

Pond, H. New at moonlight's fairy hour. [Four part song a cappella] [Boston?Ditson?184-?] 3 p. MB. 40-5494

Pons, Charles, d. 1870. Grand march. New York: Firth & Hall [184-?] 2 p. MB. 40-5495

Poole, George Ayliffe. The life and times of Saint Cyprian. Oxford, OH: Parker, 1840. 419 p. DLC; IaU; MB; NNUT; OClW. 40-5496

Poole, John, 1786?-1872. ... Married and single. A comedy in three acts. By John Poole. Also the stage business, casts of characters, costumes, relative positions, etc. New York: S. French [184-?] 48 p. CSt; MB; ViU. 40-5497

Poole, John, 1786?-1872. ... Paul Pry. A comedy in three acts. By John Poole. Also the stage business, casts of characters, costumes, relative positions, etc. New York: S. French [184-?] 69 p. CSt; CtY; MB; ViU. 40-5498

Poole, John, 1786?-1872. ... Simpson and co. A comedy in two acts. By John Poole. Also the stage business, casts of characters, costumes, relative positions, etc. New York: S. French [184-?] 39 p. CSt; DFo; IaU; NN; OCl. 40-5499

Poole, Matthew, 1624-1679. A model for the maintaining of students of choice abilities at the University. [Boston, MA: s. l., 1840?] 8 p. MHi. 40-5500

Poor Richard's Almanack, for the Northern Neck, Virginia, and for the year of Our Lord 1840; being bissextile or Leap Year, and the 64th of American Independence. By Richard Saunders, Jr. Richmond, VA: Bailie and Gallaher, printers [1840] 34 p. ViRVal. 40-5501

Poor Wills Almanac... 1841... Philadelphia, PA: Published by Joseph M'Dowell [1840] 36 p. WHi. 40-5502

Pop goes the weasel songster. Philadelphia, PA: s. l. [184-?] 221, 44 p. MB. 40-5503

Pope, Alexander, 1688-1744. The complete poetical works of Alexander Pope, Esq. With an original memoir of the author, critical and explanatory notes, and several valuable miscellaneous productions, not contained in any other edition. Edited W. C. Armstrong. New York: Published by Leavitt & Allen Brothers, 1840. 2 v. in 1. MoCg. 40-5504

Pope, Alexander, 1688-1744. Essay on man. Translated from the English by Charles Le Brun. Philadelphia, PA: s. l., 1840. 228 p. PU. 40-5505

Pope, Alexander, 1688-1744. The poetical works of Alexander Pope. To which is prefixd a life of the author. Exeter, NH: J. & B. Williams, 1840. 2 v. in 1. IU. 40-5506

Popular story of Blue-Beard; or, the effects of female curiosity. New York; Philadelphia, PA: Turner & Fisher, 1840. OMC. 40-5507

Porter, Ebenezer, 1772-1834. The Rhetorical reader, consisting of instructions for regulating the voice, with a rhetorical notation... and a course of rhetorical exercises... By Ebenezer Porter, D. D... Fifty-third ed... Andover, MA: Gould and Newman, 1840. 304 p. MAnP; MeBa; MoS; NjR; OClWHi. 40-5508

Portland, Ferdinand & Company, Cranston, R. I. ... Annual catalogue of fruit and ornamental trees... 1841-42. Providence, RI: B. Cranston & Co., 1840. 23 p. RHi; RPB. 40-5509

Portsmouth, New Hampshire. Middle Street Baptist Church of Christ. Summary declaration of the faith and practice. Boston, 1840. Portsmouth, New Hampshire. South Parish. Library. Catalogue of books belonging to the South Parish library. [Portsmouth?] C. W. Brewster, printer, 1840. 22 p. DLC. 40-5510

Portsmouth and Columbus turnpike road company. Act of incorporation of the Portsmouth and Columbus turnpike company; with the amendatory and explanatory acts, proceedings, by-laws, and general orders of the company. Chillicothe, OH: Ely., 1840. 31 p. OHi. 40-5511

Portsmouth Sacred Music Society. Act of incorporation, the constitution, and by-laws. [S. l.: n. p., 1840] 12 p. Nh-Hi. 40-5512

Potter, Alonzo, 1800-1865. Discourses on the objects and uses of science and literature, by Lord Brougham, Prof. Sedgwick, F. R. S., and the Hon. G. C. Nerplanck. With preliminary observations, etc. on reading, by A. Potter, D. D., professor of moral philosophy in Union College. New York: pubished by Harper & Brothers [1840] 332, 8 p. MB; MSbol; RKi. 40-5513

Potter, Alonzo, 1800-1865. Political economy: its objects, and principles with reference to the condition of the American people. With a summary for the use of students. By A. Potter. New York: Harper & brothers, 1840. 318 p. CU; IEG; LNB; OClW; WHi. 40-5514

Potter, Alonzo, 1800-1865. The principles of science applied to the domestic and mechanic arts and to manufacturers and agriculture. Boston, MA: Marsh, Capen, Lyon and Webb, 1840. 432 p. IaGG; LN; MB; MEab; MWHi. 40-5515

Potter, Eli. Remarks of Eli Potter, esq., at the trial of two individuals for a breach of the peace in disturbing a meeting in which a female was lecturing upon the subject of abolition... Litchfield, CT: s. l., 1840. ICN; NIC; TxU. 40-5516

Potter, Horatio, 1802-1887. The stability of the church as seen in her history and in her principles. A sermon... Albany, NY: Erastus H. Pease, 1840. 23 p. NjR. 40-5517

Poughkeepsie Engine Company. Message from the Governor [of Illinois] enclosing contract with Poughkepsie Engine Company and the protest of a draft drawn on them; enclosing the legal opinion of the Attorney General. [Springfield, IL: s. l., 1840] 6 p. WHi. 40-5518

Poulson, Charles A. American biography; scrap books consisting chiefly of newspaper cuttings. Philadelphia, PA: s. l., 1840-58. 4 v. PPL. 40-5519

Powel, J. Hare. Furniture of J. Hare Powel to be sold at his residence, Arch St. South side, West of 13th, on April 30, 1840. Philadelphia, PA: s. l., 1840. 14 p. PHi. 40-5520

Powell, Thomas. An essay on Apostolical succession, by Thomas Powell. Ninth edition. New York: Carlton & Porter [1840?] 354 p. CBCDS. 40-5521

Power, Thomas, 1786-1868. An oration delivered by request of the city authorities, before the citizens of Boston, on the sixty-fourth anniversary of American independence, July 4, 1840. By Thomas Power. Boston, MA: Eastburn, 1840. 32 p. CtSoP; MBAt; MDeeP; OO; WHi. 40-5522

Power, Tyrone, 1797-1841. How to pay the rent. A farce in one act... New York:

Samuel French [1840] 30 p. CtY; NIC; OCl. 40-5523

Power, Tyrone, 1797-1841. ... St. Patrick's eve; or, the order of the day. A drama in three acts. By Tyrone Power. With the stage business, cast of characters, relative positions, etc. New York: S. French [184-?] 50 p. ICU; MH; MiU. 40-5524

Powers, Grant, 1784-1841. Historical sketches of the discovery settlement and progress of events in the Coos Country and Vicinity... principally included between the years 1754 and 1785. Haverhill, NH: s. l. [1840] p. CU; DLC; MWA; NcD; OCl. 40-5525

The practical Christian. Published twice every calendar month. Adin Ballow, editor. Mendon, MA: s. l., 1840. v. MHaHi. 40-5526

Pratt, James. An address delivered before the Pnyxian club, at their third anniversary, Feb. 13, 1840, in Park Street Church, Portland, Me... Portland, ME: Arthur Shirley, printer, 1840. 16 p. MBC; MeHi; MnHi; RHi. 40-5527

Pratt, Parley Parker, 1807-1857. Late persecution of the church of Jesus Christ, of Latter day saints... With a sketch of their rise, progress and doctrine... New York: J. W. Harrison, printer, 1840. 215 p. CSansS; MH; MnU; OClWHi; WHi. 40-5528

Pratt, Parley Parker, 1807-1857. The millennium and other poems. To which is annexed a treatise on The regeneration and eternal duration of matter. New York: W. Molineaux, 1840. IEG; MH; MiD; MoKU; UU. 40-5529

Prayers for children and youth and for persons of all ages by omitting those parts in italics. Philadelphia, PA: s. l., 1840. 4 p. MdBD. 40-5530

Pre-emptions; federal promise contrasted with federal performance in regard to the tenants of log cabins. [Washington, DC: s. l., 1840] 3 p. MBC; NNC. 40-5531

Premord, C. The rules of a Christian life; selected from the most approved spiritual writers, in a series of letters to a lady, converted from Protestantism to the Catholic faith. By the Rev. C. Premord, A. M. First American from the second London edition. Philadelphia, PA: Eugene Cummiskey, 1840. 2 v. KyLoSL; MdW; MoSU; OCX; PV. 40-5532

Prentiss, Samuel. Speech... on the Bankrupt Bill; delivered in the Senate... June 23, 1840. Washington, DC: s. l., 1840. 20 p. M; MB. 40-5533

Presbyterian Church in the U. S. A. The constitution of the Presbyterian Church in the United States of America; containing the confession of faith, the catechisms, and the directory for the worship of God... Philadelphia, PA: Presbyterian Board of Publication, William S. Marietn, publishing agent, 1840. 536 p. GDecCT; NbOP; PPPrHi; ScDuE; ViU. 40-5534

Presbyterian Church in the U. S. A. The form of government, the discipline, and the directory for the worship. Philadelphia, PA: Pres. Bd. Pub., 1840. PPPrHi. 40-5535

Presbyterian Church in the U. S. A.

Psalms and hymns for public worship; comprising the entire selection authorized by the General Assembly of the Presbyterian Church. Philadelphia, PA: Presbyterian Board of Publication, 1840. 666 p. PPPrHi; PU; ViRut. 40-5536

Presbyterian Church in the U. S. A. Associate Reformed. Synod of the South. Minutes of the Associate Reformed Synod of the South. Held at Hopewell, Maury Co., Tenn., Oct. 12, 1840. Columbia, TN: printed on the Observer Press, 1840. 16 p. NcMHi; T. 40-5537

Presbyterian Church in the U. S. A. Board of Foreign Missions. Manual prepared for... missionaries and missionary candidates in connection with the Board of Foreign Missions. New York, 1840-. Peck, John Mason, 1789-1858. The traveller's directory for Illinois, containing sketches of the state. New York: J. H. Colton, [1840] 219 p. ICHi. 40-5538

Presbyterian Church in the U. S. A. Board of Publication. By-laws... with a list of members of the Board & of the officers & committees. Philadelphia, PA: Presbyterian Board of Publication, 1840. 8 p. PPPrHi. 40-5539

Presbyterian Church in the U. S. A. Board of Publication. Second annual report of the Presbyterian Board of Publication to the General Assembly, May, 1840. Philadelphia, PA: published for the board, 1840. 20 p. GDecCT; MnHi; OOxM; WHi. 40-5540

Presbyterian Church in the U. S. A. Board of Publication. The sin and danger of neglecting the Saviour. Philadelphia,

PA: Presbyterian Board of Publication [184-?] 16 p. GDecCT. 40-5541

Presbyterian Church in the U. S. A. General Assembly. Minutes of the General Assembly of the Presbyterian Church in the United States of America. With an appendix. Philadelphia, PA: Published by the stated Clerk of the Assembly; printed by William S. Martien, 1840. 173 p. TMeSC; TU; WHi. 40-5542

Presbyterian Church in the U. S. A. New York Synod. Minutes of the Particular Synod of New York, May, 1840. New York: Mercein & Port Press, 1840. 34 p. NcMHi. 40-5543

Presbyterian Church in the U. S. A. [Old School] Board of Publication. A series of tracts on the doctrines, order, and polity of the Presbyterian Church in the United States of America; embracing several on practical subjects. By Wm. M. Engles, Archibald Alexander, D. D., Rev. William Symington, A. Alexander, Rev. S. G. Winchester, and Richard Knill. Philadelphia, PA: Presbyterian Board of Publication, 1840. 325 p. CSansS; GDecCT; MH; ScC; ViRut. 40-5544

Presbyterian Church in the U. S. A. Presbyteries. Grand River, O. The confession of faith and covenant of the Presbytery of Grand River. Adopted February 5, 1840. Painesville, OH: P. Winchester, printer, 1840. 8 p. OClWHi. 40-5545

Presbyterian Church in the U. S. A. Presbytery of Baltimore. Correspondence between Presbytery of Baltimore and Rev. J. G. Hamner... Baltimore, MD: Publication Rooms, 1840. 30 p. MdBJ; MdHi; NjR; PPPrHi; ViU. 40-5546

Presbyterian Church in the U. S. A. Presbytery of Ohio. A pastoral letter, addressed by the Presbytery of Ohio, to the churches under its case, on the subject of ministers' salaries. Pittsburgh, PA: printed by William B. Stewart, 1840. 16 p. MnSM; NbOP; OOxM; PPL. 40-5547

Presbyterian Church in the U. S. A. Synod. Cincinnati. Extracts from the minutes of the Synod of Cincinnati at its late meeting in Dayton, Ohio, 1840, by S. Steel, stated clerk, and J. Burtt, on committee to prepare and print the minutes of the Synod. Cincinnati, OH: s. l., 1840. 8 p. ICP; ICU; R. 40-5548

Presbyterian Church in the U. S. A. Synod. Illinois. Minutes of the Commission of the Synod of Illinois. With an appendix. Published by order of the commission. Springfield, IL: S. Francois & Co., printers, 1840. 15 p. DLC. 40-5549

Presbyterian Church in the U. S. A. Synod. Mississippi. Address of the Synod of Mississippi to the churches under their care on the subject of the ministerial support and fashionable amusements. Natchez, MS: Daily Courier, 1840. PPPr-Hi. 40-5550

Presbyterian Church in the U. S. A. Synod. New York and New Jersey. A report on systematic benevolence. Adopted October, 1840. New York: William Osborn, 1840. 24 p. MBC. 40-5551

Presbyterian Church in the U. S. A. Synod. South Carolina and Georgia. Minutes of the Synod of South Carolina and Georgia at their sessions in Charleston, S. C., November, 1841?. With an ap-

pendix. Charleston, SC: Observer Office Press, 184?. 24 p. ScCliJ. 40-5552

Prescott, William Hickling, 1796-1859. History of the reign of Ferdinand and Isabella, the Catholic. By William H. Prescott. New York: Hooper, Clarke [184-?] 3 v. ICU. 40-5553

Prescott, William Hickling, 1796-1859. History of the reign of Ferdinand and Isabella, the Catholic. By William H. Prescott. 7th ed. Boston, MA: Charles C. Little and James Brown [1840] 3 v. LNB; MH; MPiB. 40-5554

Presidential and statistical chart. New York: Wm. Van Norden [184-?] p. RPB. 40-5555

Pressly, John T. An address to the students of the theological seminary of the first Associate Reformed synod of the West, at the opening of the session, Nov. 30, 1840... Pittsburgh: Printed by A. Jaynes, 1840. 24 p. MnHi; NcMHi; OClWHi; PPi; PPPrHi. 40-5556

Preyer, Gottfried. Peace, Thou art of heavenly birth. Song. Composed by G. Preyer; arranged for the guitar by Ld. Meignen. Philadelphia, PA: A. Fiot [184-?] 2 p. ViU. 40-5557

Priest, Josiah, 1788-1851. A true story of the extraordinary feats, adventures and sufferings of Matthew Calkins, Chenango Co., N. Y., in the war of the revolution-never before published. Also the deeply interesting story of the captivity of General Patchin, of Schoharie Co., N. Y., when a lad: by Brant and his Indians. In the same war: written from the lips of the respective heroes abovenamed. The spirit of evil and the spirit of good: a Saginaw tale; from Schoolcraft's researches. And the story of Conrad Mayer, the hunter... By Priest. Lansinburgh, NY: Printed by W. B. Harkness, 1840. 38 p. DLC; ICN; NN; WHi. 40-5558

Prime, Benjamin Young, 1684-1846. Muscipula sive Cambromyomachia: the Mouse-trap; or, The battle of the Welsh and the Mice. In Latin and English, with other poems. By an American. New York: N. W. Dodd, 1840. 96 p. MWA; NBuDD; NjR; PHi; TxU. 40-5559

Princeton Theological Seminary. Catalogue of the officers and students of the theological seminary, at Princeton, New Jersey, 1840-1841. Princeton, NJ: printed by Robert E. Hornor, 1840. 12 p. GDC; GDecCT; MB; MBC; NbOP; Nh; NjP. 40-5560

Princeton University. American Whig Society. Catalogue of the American Whig Society, instituted in the College of New Jersey, 1769. Princeton, NJ: printed by Robert E. Hornor, 1840. 36 p. CSmH; ICN; MB; PU; WM. 40-5561

Princeton University. Cliosophic Society. Catalogue of the Cliosophic Society, instituted in the College of New Jersey, 1765. Princeton, NJ: John Bogart, printer, 1840. 39 p. MB; NjR; NN; PU; WM. 40-5562

Prindle's Almanac for 1841. By Charles Prindle. New Haven, CT: A. H. Maltby & Co. [1840] p. CtMW; MHi; MWA. 40-5563

Prison discipline. The Auburn and Pennsylvania systems copared. New York: s. l., 1840. PHi. 40-5564

Prize essays on a Congress of nations, for the adjustment of international disputes, and for the promotion of universal peace without resort to arms. Together with a sixth essay, comprising the substance of the rejected essays. Boston, MA: pub. by Whipple & Damrell, for the American Peace Society, 1840. 706 p. CtWM; MiD; OMC; VtU. 40-5565

Prize essays on the temporal advantages of the Sabbath, considered in relation to the working classes. Containing Heaven's antidote, the torch of time, and the pearl of days. Philadelphia, PA: Presbyterian Board of Publication [184-?] 298 p. MiU. 40-5566

Proceedings of the opponents of the present administration at public meetings. Held in the City of Washington, February 15 and 18, 1840. With the address of Philip R. Fendall, esq. [S. l.: n. p., 1840?] 35 p. NcU; OCHP; OClWHi. 40-5567

Proch, Heinrich, 1809-1878. Ah! mother dear. [Song. Accomp. for piano] Boston, MA: Ditson & Co. [184-?] 7 p. MB. 40-5568

Proch, Heinrich, 1809-1878. From the Alp Horn resounding. Das Alpenhorn. Composed by Heinrich Proch... New York: Firth & Hall, J. L. Hewitt [184-?] 6 p. ViU. 40-5569

Proctor, Robert J. The life and adventures of Robert J. Proctor, from the year 1821 to March, 1825... Portland, ME: printed for the author, 1840. 22 p. MeHi. 40-5570

Proffit, George H. Speech of Mr. Proffit, of Indiana, on the general appropriation bill. Delivered in the House of Representatives, April 27, 1840. Washington, DC: Gales & Seaton, 1840. 14 p. NNS; OClWHi; PHi; TxDaM; Vi. 40-5571

The progress of freedom. [With minor pieces] Savannah, GA: W. T. Williams, 1840. 71 p. MH; NcD. 40-5572

Proprietors of the Locks & Canals on the Merrimac River. Committee on the Subject of a New Canal. Report of the Committee on the Subject of a New Canal to the proprietors of the locks and canals of the Merrimac River. Boston, MA: E. N. Moore, 1840. 20 p. IU; NN. 40-5573

Protestant Episcopal Church in the U. S. A. Canons for the government of the Protestant Episcopal church in the United States of America...; also, the canons passed in general conventions A. D. 1835 and 1838. New York: Virginia Convention Union Depository, 1840. 40 p. DLC; MdBD; NcD; ViU. 40-5574

Protestant Episcopal Church in the U. S. A. Alabama Diocese. Journal of the Proceedings of the Ninth Annual Convention of the Protestant Episcopal church in the Diocese of Alabama. Held in the City of Mobile on Saturday, April 25th, and by adjournments to Wednesday, 29th April 1840. Mobile, AL: Printed by Langdon & Barker at the Office of the Advertiser and Chronicle, 1840. 32 p. MiD-B; MoWgT; NBuDD. 40-5575

Protestant Episcopal Church in the U. S. A. Book of Common Prayer. The book of common prayer and administration of the sacraments, and other rites and ceremonies of the Church, according to the use of the Prostentant Episcopal Church in the United States of America. Together with the Psalmster, or Psalms of David. New York: s. l., 1840. 250, 115 p. MW. 40-5576

Protestant Episcopal Church in the U. S. A. Book of Common Prayer. The book of common prayer and... rights and ceremonies of the Church, according to the use of the Protestant Episcopal Church in the United States of America... New York: Bible and Common Prayer Book Society, 1840. 296, 51, 48 p. MBeHi; NjPass. 40-5577

Protestant Episcopal Church in the U. S. A. Book of Common Prayer. The book of common prayer and administration of the sacraments, and other rites and ceremonies of the Church, according to the use of the Prostentant Episcopal Church in the United States of America. Together with the Psalmster, or Psalms of David. Philadelphia, PA: Female Protestant Episcopal Prayer Book Society of Pennsylvania, 1840. 567 p. IaHi; MdBD; MnHi; NNP; WNaE. 40-5578

Protestant Episcopal Church in the U. S. A. Book of Common Prayer. The book of common prayer and administration of the sacraments, and other rites and ceremonies of the Church, according to the use of the Prostentant Episcopal Church in the United States of America. Together with the Psalmster, or Psalms of David. Philadelphia, PA: Published by Henry F. Anners, 1840. 160 p. ScCoT. 40-5579

Protestant Episcopal Church in the U. S. A. Book of Common Prayer. The book of common prayer and administration of the sacraments, and other rites and ceremonies of the Church, according to the use of the Prostentant Episcopal Church in the United States of America. Together with the Psalmster, or Psalms of David. Philadelphia, PA: Henry F. Anners, 1840. 542 p. MBC. 40-5580

Protestant Episcopal Church in the U. S. A. Book of Common Prayer. The book of common prayer and administration of the sacraments, and other rites and ceremonies of the Church, according to the use of the Prostentant Episcopal Church in the United States of America. Together with the Psalmster, or Psalms of David. Philadelphia, PA: Published by Henry F. Anners, 1840. 327 p. NN. 40-5581

Protestant Episcopal Church in the U. S. A. Book of Common Prayer. The book of common prayer... Together with the Psalter or Psalms of David. Philadelphia, PA: Pub. by Hooker & Agnew; stereotyped by L. Johnson, King & Baird, printers [1840] 283 p. IaHi; InPchE. 40-5582

Protestant Episcopal Church in the U. S. A. Book of Common Prayer. The book of common prayer and administration of the sacraments, and other rites and ceremonies of the Church, according to the use of the Prostentant Episcopal Church in the United States of America. Together with the Psalmster, or Psalms of David. Philadelphia, PA: Published by Henry F. Anners, 1840. 314 p. PAtM. 40-5583

Protestant Episcopal Church in the U. S. A. Book of Common Prayer. The book of common prayer and administration of the sacraments... Together with the Psalter or Psalm of David. Philadelphia, PA: Henry F. Anners, 1840. 376 p. MBD. 40-5584

Protestant Episcopal Church in the U. S. A. Book of Common Prayer. The book of common prayer and administration of the sacraments, and other rites and ceremonies of the Church, according to the use of the Prostentant Episcopal Church in the United States of America. Together with the Psalmster, or Psalms of David. Philadelphia, PA: Thomas, Cowperthwait & Co., 1840. 531 p. AMob; CtHWatk; ICU. 40-5585

Protestant Episcopal Church in the U. S. A. Connecticut Diocese. Journal of the Proceedings of the Annual Convention of the Protestant Episcopal church in the Diocese of Connecticut. Held in Trinity Church and St. Paul's Chapel, June 9th and 10th, 1840. New Haven, CT: Stanley & Chapin, printers, 1840. 72 p. Ct; CtSoP; MBD; MiD-B; NBuDD. 40-5586

Protestant Episcopal Church in the U. S. A. Eastern Diocese. Journal of the Proceedings of the Annual Convention of the Protestant Episcopal church in the Eastern Diocese. Held in St. James' Church, Roxbury, Sept., 1840. With the Bishop's address. Boston, MA: James B. Dow, office of the Christian Witness, 1840. 27 p. MBD; MiD-MCh; RPB. 40-5587

Protestant Episcopal Church in the U. S. A. Eastern Diocese. Journal of the Proceedings of the Annual Convention... 1840. Boston, MA: Press of William A. Hall & Company, 1840. 30, 2 p. MBD; MiD-B; RPB. 40-5588

Protestant Episcopal Church in the U. S. A. Georgia Diocese. Journal of the Proceedings of the Eighteenth Annual Convention of the Protestant Episcopal Church in the Diocese of Georgia. Held in the Parish of Grace Church, Clarksville, Habersham County, on the 4th and 5th of May, 1840. Columbus, GA: Enquirer Printing Office, 1840. 25 p. MiD-B; NBuDD; NcWsM; NN; WHi. 40-5589

Protestant Episcopal Church in the U. S. A. Indiana Diocese. Journal of the proceedings of the second annual convention of the ... in the diocese of Indiana, held in Indianapolis, May 31-June 3, 1839. Indianapolis: Stacy & Williams, 1840. 40 p. CtHT; MB; NBuDD; NN; WHi. 40-5590

Protestant Episcopal Church in the U. S. A. Indiana Diocese. Journal of the proceedings of the third annual convention of the ... in the diocese of Indiana, held in Lafayette, July 10-12, 1840. Indianapolis: Stacy & Williams, 1840. 38 p. InID; MBD; NBuDD; NN; WHi. 40-5591

Protestant Episcopal Church in the U. S. A. Kentucky Diocese. Journal of the Proceedings of the Twelfth Annual Convention... Louisville... June 11th, 1840... Princeton, KY: Printed at the Examiner office, 1840. 24 p. MBD; MiD-B; NBuDD; NN. 40-5592

Protestant Episcopal Church in the U. S. A. Liturgy. Offices from the liturgy of the Protestant Episcopal Church in the United States of America. Philadelphia: Female Protestant Episcopal Prayer Book Society of Pennsylvania, 1840. 219, 567 p. CtHT; WNaE. 40-5593

Protestant Episcopal Church in the U. S. A. Louisiana Diocese. Journal of the proceedings of the second convention... In Christ Church in the City of New Orleans on Thursday, the 16th of January, 1840. New Orleans, LA: s. l., 1840. 6 p. CtHT; LU; MBD; NN. 40-5594

Protestant Episcopal Church in the U. S. A. Maine Diocese. Journal of the twenty-first convention... June 3, 1840; with an abstract of unpublished journals. Bangor: Printed by order of the convention, 1840. 16 p. ICU; MHi; MiD-MCh. 40-5595

Protestant Episcopal Church in the U. S. A. Maryland Diocese. Journal of a convention of the Protestant Episcopal Church of Maryland... Baltimore, MD: Printed by Joseph Robinson, 1840. 72 p. MBD; MdBD; MoWgT; NBuDD. 40-5596

Protestant Episcopal Church in the U. S. A. Massachusetts Diocese. Board of Missions. Resolve to make collections from the parishes in Boston "to enable the Board to meets its engagements," Boston, November 25, 1840. Boston, MA: s. l., 1840. 1 p. MHi. 40-5597

Protestant Episcopal Church in the U. S. A. Massachusetts Diocese. Journal... fiftieth annual convention... Held in Grace Church, Boston, June 17 & 18, 1840. With an appendix. Boston, MA: James B. Dow, office of the Christian Witness, 1840. 72 p. MBD; WHi. 40-5598

Protestant Episcopal Church in the U. S. A. Mississippi Diocese. Journal of the proceedings of the fifteenth annual convention of the Protestant Episcopal

Church in the Diocese of Mississippi. Held in the City of Vicksburg, Wednesday, May 6th, 1840. Natchez, MS: Printed at the Daily Courier Office, 1840. 24 p. ICU; MsJPED; NBuDD; NN. 40-5599

Protestant Episcopal Church in the U. S. A. New Hampshire Diocese. Journal of the proceedings of the fourteenth annual convention of the Protestant Episcopal Church in the State of New Hampshire. Held at Drewsville, in St. Peter's Church on Wednesday, June 24, 1840. Bellow Falls, NH: Printed by Moore & Fulton, 1840. 12 p. MBD. 40-5600

Protestant Episcopal Church in the U. S. A. New Jersey Diocese. Journal of the fifty-seventh annual convention of the Protestant Episcopal Church... Held in Grace Church and Trinity Church, Newark. Burlington, NJ: At the Missionary Press, 1840. 43 p. MiD-MCh; NBuDD; NjR. 40-5601

Protestant Episcopal Church in the U. S. A. New York Diocese. The Constitution of the Protestant Episcopal Church in the Diocese of New York. Together with the canons of said Church, as adopted at the Annual Convention, Oct. 2, 1834, and amended Oct. 4, 1839. Published by order of the Convention. New York: Printed for the convention, 1840. 16 p. MiD-MCh; NBuDD; NjR. 40-5602

Protestant Episcopal Church in the U. S. A. New York Diocese. Journal of the proceedings of the 56th convention... New York: Church Depository, 1840. 133 p. MBD; RPB. 40-5603

Protestant Episcopal Church in the U.

S. A. Ohio Diocese. Journal of the twenty-third annual convention of the Protestant Episcopal Church in the Diocese of Ohio... on the 6-8th day of August, 1840. Gambier, OH: T. R. Raymond, 1840. 68 p. MiD-B; Nj; NN. 40-5604

Protestant Episcopal Church in the U. S. A. Pennsylvania Diocese. Journal of the proceedings of the fifty-sixth convention of the Protestant Episcopal Church in the State of Pennsylvania. Held in St. Andrew's Church, in the City of Philadelphia, on Tuesday, May 19, Wednesday, May 20, and Thursday, May 21, 1841. Printed by order of the convention. Philadelphia, PA: Jesper Harding, printer 1840?. 99 p. MBD; MiD-MCh; NBuDD; TxU. 40-5605

Protestant Episcopal Church in the U. S. A. Pennsylvania Diocese. Journal of the proceedings of the fifty-seventh convention of the Protestant Episcopal Church in the State of Pennsylvania. Held in St. Stephen's Church, Harrisburg, on Tuesday, May 18, Wednesday, May 19, and Thursday, May 20, 1841. Printed by order of the convention. Philadelphia, PA: Jesper Harding, pritner, 1840?. RP; TxU. 40-5606

Protestant Episcopal Church in the U. S. A. Rhode Island Diocese. Journal of the proceedings of the fiftieth convention of the Protestant Episcopal Church in Rhode Island. Held in St. Paul's Church, North Providence, Tuesday, June 9 and Wednesday, June 10, A. D. 1840. Boston, MA: James B. Dow, office of the Christian Witness, 1840. 56 p. MBD; MiD-B; MiD-MCh; NBuDD; RWe. 40-5607

Protestant Episcopal Church in the U.

S. A. South Carolina Diocese. Journal of the proceedings of the fifty-first annual convention of the Protestant Episcopal Church in South Carolina. Held in the City of Charleston on the 12th, 13th, 14th, and 15th of February, 1840. With the parochial reports, the constitution and canons, and proposed amendments. Charleston, SC: Printed by A. E. Miller, 1840. 48 p. NBuDD. 40-5608

Protestant Episcopal Church in the U. S. A. Tennessee Diocese. Journal of the proceedings of the clergy and laity of the Protestant Episcopal Church in the Diocese of Tennessee. Held at Immanuel Church, Lagrange, on the 6th, 7th, 8th & 9th May, 1840. Nashville, TN: S. Nye & Co., printers, 1840. 30 p. MBD; MnHi; NN. 40-5609

Protestant Episcopal Church in the U. S. A. Vermont Diocese. Journal of the proceedings of the fiftieth annual convention of the Protestant Episcopal Church in the Diocese of Vermont, being the eighth annual convention since the full organization of the Diocese. Held in St. James Church, Woodstock, on the sixteenth and seventeenth days of September, 1840. Burlington, VT: Chauncey Goodrich, 1840. 35 p. MBD; NBuDD. 40-5610

Protestant Episcopal Church in the U. S. A. Virginia Diocese. Journal of the convention... in the Diocese of Virginia. Richmond: Printed by B. R. Wren, 1840. 44 p. MBD; NBuDD. 40-5611

Protestant Episcopal Church in the U. S. A. Virginia Diocese. Revised constitution of the Protestant Episcopal Church in the Diocese of Virginia, as finally adopted by the convention which met in

Fredericksburg in May, 1836. Canons adopted by the convention of 1836 and 1837; and resolutions adopted at different periods and renewed in May, 1839. New York: Virginia Convention, 1840. 12 p. MdBD; Vi; ViU. 40-5612

Protestant Episcopal Church in the U. S. A. Virginia Diocese. Revised constitution of the Protestant Episcopal Church in the Diocese of Virginia, as finally adopted by the convention which met in Fredericksburg in May, 1836. Canons adopted by the convention of 1836 and 1837; and resolutions adopted at different periods and renewed in May, 1839. New York: Union Depository, 1840. 47 p. MdBD. 40-5613

Protestant Episcopal Church in the U. S. A. Western New York Diocese. The Constitution of the Protestant Episcopal Church in the Diocese of Western New York. Together with the canons of said Church, as adopted at the Annual Convention, Oct. 1, 1840. Published by order of the Convention. Utica, NY: Printed for the convention, 1840. 16 p. N; NBuDD; NN. 40-5614

Protestant Episcopal Church in the U. S. A. Western New York Diocese. Journal of the proceedings of the third annual convention of the Protestant Episcopal Church in diocese of Western New York... Utica, NY: John P. Bush [1840] 124 p. MBD; MiD-MCh; MWA; NBu; NN. 40-5615

Protestant Episcopal Church in the U. S. A. Western New York Diocese. Proposed canons reported by a committee of the convention of the diocese of Western New York. Printed by order of the convention for the use of its members. Utica, NY: John P. Bush [1840] 29 p. NBuDD. 40-5616

Providence, R. I. Board of Assessors. A list of persons assessed in the City Tax of sixty-five thousand dollars, ordered by the City Council, June, 1840, with the amount of valuation and tax of each. Providence, RI: Published by H. H. Brown, 1840. 60 p. RHi. 40-5617

Providence, R. I. Third Baptist Church. A Sketch of the Third Baptist Church, Providence; with the Covenant and a list of Officers and Members. Providence, RI: printed by Isaac A. Pitman, 1840. 24 p. RHi. 40-5618

Providence. Mechanics and Apprentices' Library. Catalogue of the Mechanics' and Apprentices' Library, established by the Providence Association of Mechanics and Manufacturers in the year 1821. Providence, RI: s. l., 1840. 22 p. RPA. 40-5619

Providence. School Committee. By-laws of the school committee and regulations of the public schools in the City of Providence. Providence, RI: B. Cranston & Co., 1840. 31, 1 p. CtHT-W; RP. 40-5620

Providence. School Committee. By-laws of the school committee and regulations of the public schools... Providence, RI: Printed by Knowles and Vose [etc.] 1840-55. 3 v. CtHWatk; DLC. 40-5621

Providence. Universalist Chapel. Concert of oratory and music, by Prof. Bronson and M. Colburn... November 12, 1840. [Providence, RI: s. l., 1840] p. RPB. 40-5622

Prynne's Almanac for 1841. Adapted... for the Meridian of Albany, but will answer for any part of the State of New York. Albany, NY: s. l., 1840. 24 p. No Loc. 40-5623

Prynne's Almanac for 1841. By Arthur Prynne. Albany, NY: Erastus H. Pease [1840] p. MeHi; MHi; MWA; NAl; WHi. 40-5624

Public Buildings & Statuary of the Government. The public buildings and architectural ornaments of the capitol of the United States at the city of Washington. Washington, DC: P. Haas, 1840. 44 p. DLC; MB; NcD; NN; OOxM. 40-5625

Public documents of Maine; being the annual reports of the various public officers & instructions for the year. Augusta, ME: sl., 1840. Ct. 40-5626

Public School Society of New York. Remonstrance, to the honorable the Common Council of the city of New York. [New York, 1840] 8 p. DLC. 40-5627

Pucitta, Vicenzo, 1778-1861. Strike the cymbal. Composed by Pucitta. Baltimore, MD: G. Willig [184-?] 4 p. ViU. 40-5628

Pugni, Cezare, 1805-1870. La redowa polka. Danced by Meel. Cerito and Monsr. St. Leon. Baltimore, MD: F. D. Benteen [184-?] 6 p. ViU. 40-5629

Pulaski Co., Ark. Democratic Citizens. Address of the Democratic citizens of the County of Pulaski to the people of Arkansas. Adopted May 5, 1840. Little Rock, AR: Printed by Edward Cole, printer to the state, 1840. 16 p. TxU. 40-5630

Punchard, George, 1806-1880. A view of Congregationalism. By George Punchard, pastor of the Cong. Church, Plymouth, N. H. With introductory notice by R. S. Storrs, D. D. Salem; New York: Pub. by John P. Jewett; Gould, Newman and Saxton, 1840. 208 p. CtHC; InCW; NbCrD; PPiW; RPB. 40-5631

The pupils of the Locust St., P. School female department affectionately dedicate this little volume to their disinterested director and friend C. Smith, Esq... Philadelphia, PA: s. l., 1840. PPPM. 40-5632

Purcell, John Baptists. The crescent and the cross: a discourse, delivered before the Miami society, of Miami university, on the 11th of August, 1840... Oxford, OH: John B. Peat, 1840. 27 p. IaHA; ICU; NN; OCX; OClWHi; OUr. 40-5633

The Puritan. Salem, MA: Salem & Lynn, 1840-41. v. MBC. 40-5634

Purkitt, J. H. An address delivered before several temperance associations, on man's likeness to God, or the right exercise of his powers. By J. H. Purkitt... Boston, MA: Torrey & Blair, 1840. 23 p. MBAt; MBC; MiD-B; NNUT. 40-5635

Pusey, Edward Bouverie. Scriptural views of Holy Baptism, as established by the consent of the ancient church, and contrasted with the system of modern schools. By the Rev. E. B. Pussey, D. D. New York: Charles Henry, 1840. 313 p. IAIS; MsJPED; NHC-S; TSewU. 40-5636

Puseyism and episcopacy, by a Protestant Churchman, pseud. S. l.: s. l. [184-?] p. MB; NNUT. 40-5637

Putnam, Allen. An address before the Essex Agricultural Society, at Georgetown, September 26, 1839, by Allen Putnam. Salem: Salem Power Press, printed at the Gazette office, 1840. 36, 7 p. ICU; MWA. 40-5638

Putt, Charles. Hints for the establishment of an asylum for the reformation of persons who have been imprisoned for the first time. S. l.: n. pr. [1840] 8 p. MH. 40-5639

Q-R

Quincy, Josiah, 1772-1864. The history of Harvard University... Cambridge, MA: Published by John Owen, Folsom, Wells, and Thurston, printers to the University, 1840. 2 v. KU; MBBC; MBBC; MH-L; MiGr; MnHi. 40-5640

Quincy, Josiah, 1772-1864. Memoir of the life of John Quincy Adams. Boston: Phillips, Sampson & Co., 1840. 429 p. NGH. 40-5641

Quincy, Mass. First Church. Order of services, on the completion of the second century since the original incorporation of the Town. May 25, 1840. [S. l.: s. l., 1840?] p. MH. 40-5642

Rafinesque, Constantine Samuel, 1783-1840. Autikon Botanikon, or botanical illustrations by self figures of 2500 trees and plants, chiefly American. Second part, Centuries 6-10. [Philadelphia, PA: s. l., 1840?] 84 p. OMC; PHi. 40-5643

Rafinesque, Constantine Samuel, 1783-1840. The good book, and amenities of nature, or annals of historical and natural sciences. [Philadelphia, PA: Printed for Eleutherium of Knowledge, 1840] 84 p. ICU; MH; OMC; PPAN; WHi. 40-5644

Rafinesque, Constantine Samuel, 1783-1840. The pleasures and duties of wealth. By C. S. Rafinesque... Philadelphia, PA: Printed for the Eleutherium of knowledge, 1840. 32 p. CU; MH; PPM; OMC; WHi. 40-5645

Raguet, Condy, 1784-1842. A treatise on currency and banking... 2d ed. Philadelphia, PA: Grigg & Elliot, 1840. 328 p. ArCH; ICU; MdBJ; NNC; TxU; WaPS. 40-5646

Raiford, Alexander S. A reply to "A state rights' man of 1825" and the prsidential question considered in a series of numbers. By "Scrutator." First published in the Savannah, Georgian; republished at the request of and by the Democratic Republication Association of Chatham County. Savannah, GA: Purse, 1840. 38 p. GHi. 40-5647

Raleigh and Gaston Railroad Company. Memorial of the... to the general assembly of North Carolina, December, 1840. Raleigh: Raleigh Register, pr., 1840. 8 p. NcU. 40-5648

Ralph, Joseph. A private treatise on venereal disease. In two parts... By Joseph Ralph, M. D. Second edition, greatly enlarged. New York: s. l. [1840] 259 p. DNLM; MBM; NNN. 40-5649

Ramsay, David, 1749-1815. The life of George Washington, commander in chief of the United States of America, throughout the war which established their independence and first President of the United States. By David Ramsay, M. D. With notes and biographical sketch of the author. Ithaca, NY: Mack, Andrus & Woodruff, 1840. 274 p. CSmH; MnHi; NIDHi; NN; PHi. 40-5650

Ramsey, William Sterrett. Speech on the Independent treasury bill, in the House of Representatives, Saturday, Jun 6, 1840. [Washington, DC: s. l., 1840?] 7 p. IU; MdHi. 40-5651

Rand, Benjamin Howard. Rand's ornamental copies, containing the Italian hand, Roman and italic prints, ornamental prints, German texts, etc. Philadelphia: The author, 1840. [12] p. WHi. 40-5652

Rand, Benjamin Howard. Rand's piece book, for the use of schools, etc. Philadelphia: The author, 1840. [12] p. WHi. 40-5653

Randolph, James Fitz, 1791-1872. Speech of Mr. Randolph, of New Jersey, on the New Jersey contected election. Delivered in the House of Representatives, January 9, 1840. [Washington, DC: s. l., 1840?] 8 p. NjR; OClWHi; P. 40-5654

Randolph, Joseph Fitz, 1803-1873. Address of Joseph Fitz Randolph to his constituents, the people of New Jersey. New Brunswick, NJ: n. pub., n. pr., 1840. 24 p. DLC; NjR. 40-5655

Rankin, John, 1793-1886. A present to families: A practical work on the covenant of grace as given to Abraham. Designed to promote family religion. Ripley: C. Edwards, 1840. 160 p. CSmH; ICP; InCW; OClWHi; PPPrHi. 40-5656

Rankine, John. Address, delivered before the Ontario Agricultural Society at its first annual meeting, October 20, 1840. By John Rankins, Esq. Published at the request of the Society. Canandaigua,

NY: Printed by George L. Whitney, 1840. 11 p. A; N. 40-5657

Ranney, Darwin Harlow. The evangelical church; or, True grounds for the union of the saints... Woodstock, VT: Mercury Press, 1840. 144 p. CtHT; IaU; MiOC; MWA; NNUT. 40-5658

Rantoul, Robert, Jr. The introductory discourse, delivered before the American Institute of Instruction, at their annual meeting, in 1839. Boston, MA: Marsh, Capen, Lyon and Webb, 1840. 33 p. MB; MBevHi; MiD-B; MWA; NjR; RPB. 40-5659

Raquet, Condy, 1784-1842. The principles of free trade. Illustrated in a series of short and familiar essays. Originally published in the Banner of the Constitution, 1829-1832. By Condy Raquet. Philadelphia, PA: Printed for the author, 1840. 439 p. NcU. 40-5660

Rasche, F. Dewanna waltz. Composed for the piano and dedicated to Miss D. Sinclair, by F. Rasche. Philadelphia, PA; New Orleans, LA: Lee & Walker, successors to Geo. Willig; W. T. Mayo [184-?] 2 p. ViU. 40-5661

Rathbun, Jonathan, b. 1765. Narrative of Jonathan Rathbun, with accurate accounts of the capture of Groton Fort... By Rufus Avery and Stephen Hempstead, eye witnesses of the same. Together with an interesting appendix. [New London, CT: s. l., 1840] 80 p. Ct; IaDa; MiU-C; RWe; ViU. 40-5662

Rauch, Friedrich August, 1806-1841. Psychology; or, A view of the human soul; including anthropology, being the substance of a course of lectures, delivered to the junior class, Marshall college, Penn., by Fredrich A. Rauch. New York: M. W. Dodd, 1840. 388 p. CU; KKcBT; OO; ScCOT; ViRut. 40-5663

Ravina, Jean Henri, 1818-1906. Nocturne. Cincinnati, OH: Peters [184-] p. MB. 40-5664

Rawlings, James H., 1820?. An oration. Delivered before the Tau Chi Society of William and Mary College... 8th February, 1840. Richmond, VA: s. l., 1840. 16 p. CSmH; MHi; NcD; Vi. 40-5665

Rawlings, Thomas A., b. 1775. By the margin of fair Zurich's waters. Air a la Swisse. Arranged as a rondino for the piano forte... by T. A. Rawlings. Philadelphia, PA: Wilig [1840] 6 p. MB. 40-5666

Rawlings, Thomas A., b. 1775. Lilla's a lady! [Song. S. or T. Arranged] for the guitar by L. Meignen. [Anon.] Philadelphia, PA: Fiot, Meignen & Co. [184-?] 2 p. MB. 40-5667

Ray, Joseph, 1807-1855. Ray's eclectic arithmetic on the inductive and analytic methods of instruction. Designed for common schools and academies. 13th edition. Revised, corrected and stereotyped. Cincinnati:Truman and Smith, 1840. 239 [1] p. DAU; OC. 40-5668

Raybold, George A. Paul Perryman. New York: s. l. [1840?] p. MB. 40-5669

Raymond, Daniel, 1786-1849. The elements of constitutional law and political economy. 4th ed. Baltimore, MD: Cushing & brother, 1840. 300 p. CU; IGK; InU; MB; OCY. 40-5670

Raymond, F. L. Greene's quick step. Composed, arranged, and respectfully dedicated to His Excellency Marcus Morton, Governor of Mass., by F. L. Raymond. Boston, MA: Pub. by H. Prentiss, 1840. 3 p. M. 40-5671

Raymond, Samuel G. The political duties of scholars. An address, delivered before the alumni of Columbia college... October 7, 1840. By Samuel G. Raymond... New York: Carvill & co., 1840. 34 p. MBC; MoS; NNC; PPAmP; WHi. 40-5672

Rayner, Menzies. The Universalist manual; or, Book of prayers and other religious exercises: adapted to the use of both public and private devotion in churches, Sunday schools, and families... 3d ed. New York: P. Price, 1840. 191, 95 p. IaMp; MBUGG; NCaS; NRU; PPL-R. 40-5673

Read, J. Childe Martin, an epic poem. New York: Published for the author, 1840. 32 p. ICU; MB; MdHi. 40-5674

Reasons why Wm. H. Harrison should have the support of the Democracy in preference to Van Buren. Boston, MA: s. l., 1840. PPL. 40-5675

Rede, William Leman, 1802-1847. ... The flight to America; or, Ten hours in New York! A drama in three acts... New York: Turner & Fisher [184-?] 47 p. CSt; DLC; NcU; RP. 40-5676

Redesdale, John [Freeman] Mitford, 1748-1830. A treatise on the pleadings in suits in the Court of Chancery by English bill... With notes and references by Charles Edwards. 4th American ed. New

York: Halsted, 1840. 401 p. GU-L; ICLaw; Ky; OrsaW-L; PPB. 40-5677

Redler, C. Learning to dance. A set of quadrilles. Composed [for piano forte] Boston, MA: Ditson [184-?] 7 p. MB. 40-5678

Reed, Andrew, 1787-1862. The revival of religion. A narrative of the state of religion at Wickliffe Chapel, in 1839. Boston, MA: Crocker & Brewster, 1840. 94 p. ICP; MB; NjR; RPB. 40-5679

Reed, Anna C. Vie de George Washington; pris de l' anglais et dedie a la jeuvesse americaine... Dixieme edition. Philadelphia, PA; Boston, MA: Henry Perkins; Ives & Dennet, 1840. 320 p. MAm; MBAt; MiOC; PU; WHi. 40-5680

Reed, Fitch. Methodism Evangelicam in its means and influences: Substance of a Sermon Preached in Sands Street, Brooklyn, October 25, 1839... By the Rev. Fitch Reed, Stationed Minister in said Church. New York: Published by T. Mason and G. Lane. For the Methodist Episcopal Church, 1840. 28 p. IEG; MBNMHi; MsJS; RPB. 40-5681

Reed, Isaac. The Youth's Book, in Four Parts, by Isaac Reed. Indianapolis, IN: s. l., 1840. 230 p. IEG; In; InU. 40-5682

Reed, John, 1781-1860. Speech of Mr. Reed, of Massachusetts, on the Sub-treasury bill, delivered in the [House of Representatives] in committee of the whole, June 27, 1840. Washington, DC: Gales and Seaton, 1840. 16 p. CtHC; M; MB; MiD-B; MWA. 40-5683

Reed, John, 1781-1860. Speech of the

Hon. John Reed, of Massachusetts, on the general appropriation bill, delivered in the House of Representatives, April 22, 1840. Washington, DC: Printed at the Madisonian Office, 1840. 12 p. CtHC; MHi; MiD-B; MiU-C. 40-5684

Reed, Thomas C., d. 1833. A tribute to the memory of the late Edward Savage, Esq., Professor of natural philosophy in Union College, in discourse delivered before the faculty and students... July 20, 1840. Schenectady, NY: Riggs & Norris, 1840. 38 p. CtMW; ICMe; MBC; NAuT; PHi. 40-5685

Reed, William Bradford, 1806-1876. On the infancy of the Union. A discourse delivered before the New York historical society, Thursday, December 19, 1839. By William B. Reed. Published at the request of the Society. Philadelphia, PA: J. Crissy, printer, 1840. 50 p. LNH; MHi; PPAmP; RPB; TxDaM. 40-5686

Reed, William Bradford, 1806-1876. Oration delivered on the occasion of the reinternment of the remains of General Hugh Mercer... Philadelphia, PA: Press of A. Waldie, 1840. 44 p. DeWi; ICHi; MH; OMC; PPAmP. 40-5687

Reflections addressed to the sincere enquirers after truth. By a Virginia farmer. [Baltimore, MD: s. l., 184-?] 11 p. MH. 40-5688

Reformed Church in America. The acts and proceedings of the General Synod of the Reformed Protestant Dutch Church of North America, at New York, June, 1840. New York: Mercein & Post's Press, 1840. 325-440 p. NjR. 40-5689

Reformed Church in America. The acts

and proceedings of the General Synod of the Reformed Protestant Dutch Church of North America, convened in extra session, at Albany, on Tuesday, November 10, 1840. New York: Mercein & Post's Press, 1840. 11 p. IaPeC. 40-5690

Reformed Church in America. Addresses. Delivered at the inauguration of Rev. J. W. Nevin, D. D., as professor of theology in the Theological Seminary of the German Reformed Church, Mercersburg, Pa., May 20th, 1840. Chambersburg, PA: Printed at the Office of Publication of the Ger. Ref. Church, 1840. 28 p. KyDC; MoKU; NNUT; OClWHi; PHi. 40-5691

Reformed Church in America. The constitution of the Reformed Dutch Church of North America. With an appendix, containing formularies for the use of the churches; together with the rules and orders for the government of the general synod, the catechism, articles of faith, canons of the synod of Dordrecht, and liturgy. Philadelphia, PA: Published by G. W. Mentz & Son, 1840. 48, 131 p. CSansS; IaDu; NbOP; WNaE. 40-5692

Reformed Church in America. Particular Synod of New York. Minutes of the Particular Synod of New York, May, 1840. New York: n. pub., Mercein & Post's Press, 1840. 36 p. NjR. 40-5693

Reformed Church in America. The Psalms and hymns, with the Catechism, Confession of faith, and Liturgy, ... of the Reformed Dutch Church of North America. Selected at the request of the General Synod. By John H. Livingston, D. D. S. T. P....To which are added, The additional hymns, and the canons of the

Synod of Dordrecht. With a new and copious index. Philadelphia, PA: G. W. Mentz & Son, 1840. 690 p. WBeaHi. 40-5694

Reformed Church in the U. S. Verhandlungen einer Speciellen allgemeinen Synode der Hochdeutschen Reformirten Kirche in den Vereinigten Staaten. Gehalten zu Chambersburg, Pa., den 29ten und 30ten Januar, A. D. 1840. Chambersburg, PA: Gedruckt in der Druckerei der Hochdeutschen Reformirten Kirche, 1840. 7 p. MoWgT; MdBSHG; PLERCHi. 40-5695

A refutation of the calumnies of the British Whig Party in regard to the expenditures of the administration and the defalcation [sic] of its officers. [Washington, DC: s. l., 1840] 16 p. MH; MHi. 40-5696

Reid, Adam. Address at the funeral of Caleb Ticknor, M. D. of New York; delivered at Salisbury, Conn., Sept. 23, 1840, by Adam Reid... New York: Printed by John F. Trow, 1840. 31 p. MHi; MWiW; NjR; NNNAM. 40-5697

Reid, John, 1809-1849. An experimental investigation into the functions of the eighth pair of nerves; or, the glossopharyngeal, pneumogastric, and spinal accessory. Philadelphia, PA: Haswell, Barrington, and Haswell, 1840. 59 p. GU; KyLxT; PPM; RNR; WMAM. 40-5698

Reid, Mayne, 1818-1883. Desert home, or, The adventures of a lost family in the wilderness. Boston, MA: Ticknor & Fields, 1840. InValU. 40-5699

Reiersen, C. P. P. F. A treatise on scarlet fever... By Dr. C. P. P. F. Reiersen...

New York: Printed by William S. Dorr, 1840. 29 p. DLC; NNNAM, 40-5700

Reily, James, d. 1863. Address of Major James Reily on the occasion of laying the cornerstone of the Houston and Brazos Rail Road. Published by the Committee of Arrangements. Houston, TX: Printed at the Telegraph Office, 1840. 19 p. CtY; NHi; TxU; TxWFM. 40-5701

Reissiger, Carl Gottlich. Flowers of spring. Arranged for the piano by Fries. Boston, MA: Reed [184-?] 5 p. MB. 40-5702

Religious liberty in danger. A vindication of the Whig Party from the charge of hostility to Catholics and foreigners. By a Catholic layman... S. l.: n. pr., no. pub. [184-?] 16 p. MnHi; N; NCU. 40-5703

Remarks of Messrs. Buchanan, King and Brown, in reply to Messrs. Davis, Preston, and Clay, of Kentucky, on the subject of the currency. Senate, U. S. March 6, 1840. Washington, DC: Printed at the Globe Office, 1840. 13 p. T; TxU. 40-5704

Remarks of Mr. Hubbard and Mr. Calhoun on the right of petition. In the Senate of the United States, Thursday, February 13, 1840. Washington, DC: Globe Office, 1840. 8 p. MdHi; MiD-B; NcD; OClWHi; TxH. 40-5705

Remarks on banks and banking, and the skeleton of a project for a national bank, by a citizen of Boston. Boston, MA: Torrey and Blair, printers, 1840. 62 p. M; PPAmP; WHi. 40-5706

Remarks on the affairs of the Illinois Land Company. New York: George F. Nesbitt, printer, 1840. 12 p. NN. 40-5707

Remarks on the Apostolic Gospel. [By a believer] New York: Samuel Adams, 1840. 41 p. NjR. 40-5708

Remarks on the utility and necessity of asylums or retreats for the victims of Intemperance. Philadelphia, PA: Brown, Bicking & Guilbert, 1840. 21 p. DLC; MB; MiU-C; NN; PHi. 40-5709

A reminiscence of the bold and successful adventures of small scouting parties of revolutionary patriots against the British and Tories in South Carolina and Georgia during the Revolutionary War, as related by one who took an active part in many of the scenes. Embellished with several beautiful engravings. New York: s. l., 1840. 40 p. ICN; MH. 40-5710

Remonstrance of the citizens to the people of the U. S., etc., against oppressions suffered from the misrule of Congress, Aug., 1840. Washington, DC: s. l., 1840. MBAt. 40-5711

Renney, Robert. The prophetic blessings of Jacob and of Moses, respecting the Twelve Tribes of Israel, explained and illustrated. An argument for the truth of Divine Revelation... Philadelphia, PA: Presbyterian Board of Publication, James Russell, publishing agent, 1840. 135 p. GDecCT; PPPrHi; ViRut. 40-5712

Rennie, James, 1787-1867. Natural history of birds: their architecture, habits, and faculties... New York: Harper & Brothers, 1840. 308 p. GU; MB; NCaS; OCY; ScCC. 40-5713

Rennie, James, 1787-1867. Natural history of insects. New York: Harper, 1840. 2 v. InRch; MB-HP; MnU; OWoC; PPT. 40-5714

Rennie, James, 1787-1867. Natural history of quadrupeds. By James Rennie. New York: Harper & Brothers, 1840. 324 p. CtMW; MnU; NbOM; RP; OCY. 40-5715

Renwick, Henry Brevoort, 1817-1895. Lives of John Jay and Alexander Hamilton. New York: Published by Harper & brothers, 1840. 341 p. ArLP; CSf; MeB; MiU; PP. 40-5716

Renwick, James, 1790-1863. Applications of the science of mechanics to practical purposes. By James Renwick... New York: Harper & brothers, 1840. 327 p. GU; ICU; MH; NjR; PPL-R. 40-5717

Renwick, James, 1790-1863. Familiar illustrations of nautral philosophy. Selected principally from Daniell's ... philosophy. By James Renwick, LL. D. New York: Harper & brothers, 1840. 403 p. IEG; NNE; OCX; RJa; RPE; TJoV. 40-5718

Renwick, James, 1790-1863. First principles of chemistry; being a familiar introduction to the study of that science... by James Renwick... New York: Harper & brothers, 1840. 444 p. NjP; PPCP; RNR; ScNP. 40-5719

Renwick, James, 1790-1863. Life of Alexander Hamilton. New York: Harper & brothers, 1840. KyDC; OMC; PHi. 40-5720

Renwick, James, 1790-1863. Life of Dewitt Clinton, by James Renwick, LL.

D., professor of natural experimental philosophy and chemistry in Columbia college. New York: Harper & brothers, 1840. 334 p. LNH; MB; MnU; PAnL; RJa. 40-5721

Reply to a pamphlet entitles "Observations on the Suspensions of Specie Payments by the Banks of the Charleston." Charleston, SC: A. E. Miller, 1840. 16 p. A-Ar; NcD; ScC. 40-5722

Report... of the controversy between Georgia and Maine... for certain alleged fugitives from justice. Boston, MA: s. l., 1840. 41 p. MBC. 40-5723

Report of the Democratic Party, in relation to an outrage recently committed upon their rights by the Whig authorities of Mobile. [Mobile, AL: n. p., 1840] 8 p. MiU-C; TxU. 40-5724

Report of The Directors of the Maryland Penitentiary, made to the Executive and Communicated by His Excellency Governor Grason, To the Legislature at December Session, 1840. Baltimore, MD: James Lucas & E. K. Deaver, 1840. 17 p. No Loc. 40-5725

Republican. Vol. 1, July, 1840. Concord, MA: s. l., 1840. MCon. 40-5726

Republican extra... City of Cincinnati, Republican Office, Nov. 8, 11 A. M. [Election returns Harrison 7 Tyler] [S. l.: s. l., 1840] p. OClWHi. 40-5727

Republican Party. Tennessee. Central Corresponding Committee. Address to the Republican people of Tennessee. By the Central Corresponding Committee of the State. [No. 2] Nashville, TN:

printed for the Committee, 1840. 40 p. TxU. 40-5728

Republican Whig Association. South Boston. Constitution & by-laws. South Boston, MA: s. l., 1840. MB. 40-5729

The Restorator; or, Every man and women their own doctor. From the writings of celebrated physicians. Pawtucket, RI: s. l., 1840. 70 p. RHi. 40-5730

Review of the controversy in the Presbyterian Church, showing the points of difference and causes of division. By a member of the Synod of West Tennessee... Nashville, TN: Printed by B. R. M'Kennie, Whig and Steam Press, 1840. 40 p. CSmH; ICU; OCHP; PPPrHi; T. 40-5731

A review of the question of the outlet lock at Black's eddy. S. l.: s. l., 1840. DLC; MB; MH; PHi; PU. 40-5732

Revival hymns; chiefly designed to be used in prayer meetings. Compiled from various authors. 2nd edition. Exeter, NH: Published by A. R. Brown, 1840. 221 p. MHNotn. 40-5733

Reynolds, B. Charles. Washington, the nation's capital. With 200 illustrations. New York: Foster & Reynolds, 1840. 115 p. LNH. 40-5734

Reynolds, George William MacArthur, 1814-1879. Kenneth, a romance of the Highlands. New York: H. Long & Bro [184-?] 318 p. NN. 40-5735

Reynolds, John, 1789-1865. Letter of the Hon. J. Reynolds, of Illinois, to his constituents. City of Washington, June, 1840. [Washington, DC: Globe Office,

184o] 8 p. IGK; IHI; MdHi; MWA. 40-5736

Reynolds, John, 1788-1865. Necessary appropriations. Remarks... on the bill for the relief of Thomas Fillebrown, Jr., delivered in the House of Representatives, March 28, 1840. Washington, 1840.
Reynolds, John, 1788-1865. To the people of the First Congressional District in the state of Illinois. A letter in regard to the passage of an act to grant preemption rights to settlers on the public lands. [Washington: The Globe, 1840] 4 p. NN. 40-5737

Reynolds, John, 1788-1865. Remarks of Mr. Reynolds, of Illinois. In the House of Representatives, February 8, 1840. Washington, DC: Printed at the Globe Office, 1840. 8 p. IU; MdHi. 40-5738

Reynolds, John, 1788-1865. Remarks of Mr. Reynolds, of Illinois. In the House of Representatives, April 17, 1840. Washington, DC: s. l., 1840. 8 p. DLC; IU; MdHi; ViU. 40-5739

Reynolds, John, 1789-1865. Speech of Mr. Reynolds, of Illinois, on the subject of the public lands. Delivered in the House of Representatives, December 24, 1840. [S. l.: s. l., 1840] 8 p. MdHi; MHi. 40-5740

Reynolds, John, 1788-1865. To my constituents in Illinois. [Dated Washington City, May 23, 1840] [S. l.: s. l., 1840?] 8 p. IaHi; NN. 40-5741

Rhett, Robert Barnwell, 1800-1876. Address of Hon R. Barnwell Rhett to his constitutents, the Citizens of Beaufort, Colleton, Orangeburgh, and Barnwell

Districts [South Carolina] [Washington, DC: s. l., 184-?] 11 p. DLC; MH. 40-5742

Rhett, Robert Barnwell, 1800-1876. Speech... in the House on the independent treasury bill on June 22, 1840. [Washington?1840] 15 p. DLC; NNC; NRU. 40-5743

Rhode Island. General Assembly. At the General Assembly: Acts and resolves. [Providence, RI: s. l., 1840] p. PPL. 40-5744

Rhode Island. Laws, statutes, etc. An Act to regulate the Militia. Providence, RI: George W. Jackson, printer, 1840. 32 p. RPB. 40-5745

Rhode Island. Laws, statutes, etc. Acts passed by the General Assembly of Rhode Island. [Providence, RI: s. l., 1840-49] p. C; Ia. 40-5746

Rhode Island. Laws, statutes, etc. [Laws passed at the General Assembly, June-Oct., 1840] [Providence, RI?: n. p., 1840] 43, 72 p. Mi-L. 40-5747

Rhode Island. Laws, statutes, etc. [Public laws... passed since Jan., 1839-1840] [S. l.: n. p., 1840] 32 p. Mi-L. 40-5748

Rhode Island. Laws, statutes, etc. Public laws of the State of Rhode Island and Providence Plantation, passed since the General Assembly, January, 1840-42. [Providence, RI: s. l., 1840-42] p. In-SC; MdBB. 40-5749

Rhode Island almanac for the year 1841; being 1st after Bissextile or Leap Year and beginning of the 65th and latter part of the 66th year of Independence of United States. By Isaac Bickerstaff, Esq. Providence, RI: Pubished and sold by H. H. Brown, 1840. 24 p. CU; DLC; RNHi; WHi. 40-5750

Rhode Island Suffrage Association. Preamble and Constitution of the Rhode Island Suffrage Association. Adopted Friday evening, March 27, 1840. Providence, RI: B. T. Albro, 1840. 11 p. MiD-B; RHi; RP. 40-5751

Rhodes, William Barnes. Bombastes furioso; a burlesque tragic opera, in one act. New York: s. l. [184-?] 18 p. MB; MH. 40-5752

Ribbing, Adolphe, comte de. The postillion of Lonjumeau. A comic opera in three acts. The music by A. Adam. Adapted to the English stage by Mr. Wilson. New York: Nixon [1840] 24 p. MB; MH. 40-5753

Rice, Roswell, Jr. The orations and poetry of Professors Moffitt, Nott, Bascom, Griffen, Summerfield, and other modern stars of Christianity, by Roswell Rice, Jr. First edition. Albany, NY: Printed by C. Van Benthupen and Co. [ca. 1840?] 209 p. NcD; NNC. 40-5754

Rich, George. Report, Survey and Estimates of the Attica and Buffalo Railroad made to the Commissioners, July 1, 1840. By George Rich, Engr. Buffalo, NY: Faxon & Graves, printers, 1840. 20 p. NBuHI. 40-5755

Richardson, Samuel B. Observations on tenotomy or section of the tendons... a remedy for club-foot and other deformaties. Louisville, KY: Prince and Weissinger [1840] 41 p. DLC; PPC. 40-5756

Richmond, James Cook, 1808?-1866. No slur, else-slur. A dancing poem or satyr, by Nobody. New York: Published by Any-body, 1840. 12 p. ICU; MH; NBuG; NN; ViU. 40-5757

Richmond, James Cook, 1808?-1866. No slur, else-slur. A dancing poem or satyr, by Nobody. 2d ed. New York: Published by Any-body, 1840. 12 p. ICU; MH; NBuG; NN; RPB. 40-5758

Richmond, Legh, 1772-1827. The cottager's wife. By a clergyman of the Church of England [pseud.] New York: s. l. [1840?] 28 p. MB. 40-5759

Richmond, Legh, 1772-1827. The dairyman's daughter, an authentic and interesting narrative in five parts. Communicated by a clergyman of the Church of England. New York: Published by the Protestant Episcopal Tract Society, [P. Martin, printer, 184-?] 34 p. WHi. 40-5760

Richmond, Legh, 1772-1827. The Rev. Legh Richmond's letters and counsels to his children. Written by his daughter. New York: American Tract Society [184-?] 201 p. DLC; MB; MWA; PPL; TNJ. 40-5761

Richmond, Va. Mercantile Library Association. The Constitution and by-laws of... Adopted Jan. 15, 1840. Richmond, VA: Shepherd & Collins, pr., 1840. CSmH. 40-5762

Richmond polka. Arranged for the piano forte by Henri Cramer. Boston, MA: Ditson [184-?] 2 p. MB. 40-5763

Richter, Jean Paul Friedrich, 1763-1825. Jean Paul, Schones und Gedieg

enes ausseinen verschiedenen Schriften und Aufsatzen. New York: Radde, 1840. 52 p. CtMW; InGrD; MB; TNJU. 40-5764

Ricord, Elizabeth (Stryker) Elements of the philosophy of mind, applied to the development of thought and feeling. By Mrs. Elizabeth Ricord... Geneva, NY; New York: J. N. Bogert; Collins, Keese and co., 1840. 408 p. DLC; NjR; ODaB; OUrC; PPiW. 40-5765

Ricord, Philippe, 1800-1889. A practical treatise on venereal disorders, and more especially on the history and treatment of Chancre. By Philippe Ricord, M. D., Surgeon to the Venereal Hospital of Paris, etc. In a series of articles from the Edinburgh Medical and Surgical Journal, Nos., 135, 136 and 137. Philadelphia, PA; New Orleans, LA: Haswell, Barrington and Haswell; John J. Haswell & Co., 1840. 58 p. CoCsE; KyLxT; MdBM; NjP; PPHa. 40-5766

Riddell, John. Front elevation & plan of a single house [Fifth Street] Philadelphia, PA: s. l., 1840? p. PPL. 40-5767

Riddle, David Hunter, 1805-1888. The nation's alternative:a sermon, preached in Providence Hall, before the students of Jefferson college, August 2d, 1840... Pittsburgh, PA: A. Jaynes, 1840. 16 p. CSmH; ICP; MnHi; OOxM; PHi. 40-5768

Rider, Sidney Smith, 1833-1917. Documents relating to the political troubles in Rhode Island in 1842; consisting of private correspondence, prisoners letters, accounts against the state, and other papers. [Providence, RI: s. l., 1840] 153 documents. RPB. 40-5769

Riell, Henry E. An appeal to the voluntary citizens of the United States, from all nations... New York: Office of the Evening Post, 1840. 16 p. DLC; InHi; MBC; MH; PHi. 40-5770

Ries, Ferdinand, 1784-1838. The morning. A cantata in four vocal parts... By Ferdinand Ries. Boston, MA: printed by Kidder & Wright, 1840. 40 p. MBrigStJ. 40-5771

Rigby, Edward, 1804-1860. Memoranda for practitioners in midwifery, by Edward Rigby, M. D... With additions by S. C. Foster, M. D. First American edition. New York: L. W. Ransom, 1840. 63 p. MB; NNNAM; PPCP. 40-5772

Rimbault, Edward Francis, 1816-1876. Happy land! Tyrolienne. [With accompaniment for piano forte] Boston, MA: Keith's Music Publishing House [184-?] 3 p. MB. 40-5773

Rimbault, Stephen Francis. O dolce concento. Arranged with variations for the piano forte, by S. F. Rimbault. New York: Firth & Hall [184-?] 7 p. ViU. 40-5774

Rinaldo and Isabel; or, Count Roderic's castle. An Italian romance. New York: Nafis & Cornish, 1840? p. No Loc. 40-5775

Ripe cherries; or, the history of William and Jane. New York: Published by the American Tract Society, 184-? 15 p. WHi. 40-5776

Ripley, George, 1802-1880. The claims of the age on the work of the evangelist. A sermon preached at the ordination of Mr. John Sullivan Dwight, as pastor of the Second Congregational church in Northhampton, May 20, 1840... Boston, MA: Weeks & Jordan, 1840. 54 p. CBPac; DLC; ICMe; MiD-B; WHi. 40-5777

Ripley, George, 1802-1880. Defence of "The latest form of infidelity examined. "A third letter to Mr. Andrew Norton, occasioned by his defence of a discourse on "The latest form of infidelity," by George Ripley. Boston, MA: James Munroe and Company [1840] 154 p. MB; MBAU; MBC; MH. 40-5778

Ripley, George, 1802-1880. Defence of "The latest form of infidelity examined. "Examined in a second letter to Mr. Andrew Norton... by George Ripley. Boston, MA: James Munroe and Company [1840] 85 p. ICMe; MBAU; MeBa; MdBJ; MWA; PPL. 40-5779

Ripley, George, 1802-1880. A letter addressed to the Congregational church in Purchase street... Boston, MA: Freeman and Bolles, printers, 1840. 31 p. IEG; MB; NNUT; RPB; VtU. 40-5780

Ripley, George, 1802-1880. Letters on the latest form of infidelity, including a view of the opinions of Spinoza, Schleiermacher, and De Wette. By George Ripley. Boston, MA: James Munroe and Company [1840] 160, 85, 154 p. CBPac; DLC; MeBaT; MH; RPB. 40-5781

The rise and progress of the doctrines of abolitionism and a remedy for bigotry and superstition. Alexander, LA: Office of the Red River Whig, print., 1840. 23 p. PHi; TxU. 40-5782

Ritchie, Leitch, 1800-1865. Windsor Castle and its environs. By Leitch

Ritchie... with fifteen engravings by the first artists after original drawings. New York: Appleton and Co. [1840] 260 p. ICU; MB; MdBJ; NjP; WU. 40-5783

Ritchie, Thomas, 1778-1854. Interesting correspondence [between Thomas Ritchie and J. R. Poinsett, Secretary of War, concerning the reorganization of the militia] [Richmond, VA: s. l., 1840] 8 p. DLC; KyDC; NcD; Vi. 40-5784

Rives, Alexander. An address delivered February 22nd, 1840, before the Charlottesville Lyceum, by Alexander Rives. Published by order of the Lyceum. Charlottesville, VA: James Alexander, printer, 1840. 21 p. CSmH; MBC; NN; TxU; Vi. 40-5785

Rives, Alexander. An address delivered September tenth, 1840, before the Union society of Hampden Sidney college: By Alexander Rives, of Albermarle, Va. Richmond, VA: Peter D. Bernard, 1840. 21 p. MeB; MHi; PHi; ViU. 40-5786

Rives, William Cabell, 1793-1868. Letter from the Hon. William C. Rives, of Virginia [regarding the election of Harrison [Washington, DC: s. l., 1840] 13 p. MHi; WHi. 40-5787

Rives, William Cabell, 1793-1868. Letter from the Hon. William C. Rives, of Virginia. [Washington, DC: s. l., 1840] 15 p. DLC; GEU; NcD; NN; NNC; ViU. 40-5788

Rives, William Cabell, 1793-1868. Letter... in the United States' Senate, exposing in their true colors, the policy and measures of the present administration and proving which is the real Republicatin Party of the Union. New

Orleans, LA: Published by John Gibson, Editor, True American, 1840. 28 p. NN. 40-5789

Robbins, Chandler, 1810-1882. A feature of the times. A sermon preached at the Second Church in Boston, in November last. Boston, MA: S. G. Simpkins, 1840. 15 p. ICMe; MB; MH; MHi; MH-AH. 40-5790

Robbins, Chandler, 1810-1882. A sermon preached at the Second Church in Boston, in November last, by its minister, Chandler Robbins. Boston, MA: S. G. Simpkins, 1840. 15 p. CtHC; ICMe; MH; MWA; RPB. 40-5791

Robbins, Chandler, 1810-1882. A Thanksgiving sermon preached at the Second Church in Boston, on November 26, 1840, by its minister, Chandler Robbins. Boston, MA: Printed by I. R. Butts, 1840. 15 p. ICMe; MH; MMeT; RPB. 40-5792

Robbins, Chandler, 1810-1882. Two sermons, preached at the Second Church in Boston; the one thanksgiving day; the other in November last, occasional to the time... Boston, MA: S. G. Simpkins, 1840. 15 p. ICMe; MBAU; MH; MHi; MnHi. 40-5793

Robbins, Eliza, 1786-1853. Tales from American history... containing the principal facts in the life of Christopher Columbus, etc. For the use of young persons and schools. New York: Harper & Bros., 1840. 3 v. NcAs. 40-5794

Robbins, Samuel Dowse. The worship of the soul. Discourse to Third Congregational Society in Chelsea at dedication of Chapel, Sept. 13, 1840. Chelsea:

Bowen, 1840. 16 p. MBAU; MBC; MH. 40-5795

Robbins, Thomas, 1777-1856. Century sermon. Delivered at Danbury January 1, 1801, in which is exhibited a brief view of the most remarkable events of the eighteenth century. With a sketch of the history of the Town of Danbury, from the first settlement to the present time. 3d ed. Danbury, CT: s. l., 1840. 32 p. WHi. 40-5796

Robert & William; or, The beauties of nature. Northampton: John Metcalf, 1840. 24 p. MHa. 40-5797

Roberts, Daniel, 1658-1727. Memoir of John Roberts. Philadelphia, PA: Kimber, 1840. 72 p. PSC. 40-5798

Roberts, Daniel. Some account of the persecutions and sufferings of the people called Quakers... Memoirs of the life of John Roberts, 1665. Philadelphia, PA: Kimber & Sharpless, 1840. 72 p. CSmH; ICHi; InRchE; MWA; PPA. 40-5799

Robert's world of romance. Boston, MA: s. l., 1840. DLC. 40-5800

Robertson, William, 1721-1793. The history of the reign of the Emperor Charles V. By William Robertson, D. D. Complete in one volume. Abridged edition. New York: Harper & Brothers [184-?] 615 p. MB; MdBJ. 40-5801

Robertson, William, 1721-1793. The history of the reign of the Emperor Charles. With a view of the progress of society in Europe; from the subdivision of the Roman empire, to the beginning of the sixteenth century. New York: Harper &

Bros., 1840. 643 p. IJI; MB; NeW; NTEW; PAmL. 40-5802

Robinette, Josiah C. The woman... and the beast. Richmond, VA: s. l., 1840. 24 p. DLC; Vi. 40-5803

Robinson, Alexander C. Report of cases of delirium tremens occuring in the hospital of the Baltimore Alms House, with observations. To which is added an appendix containing an appeal in behalf of the insane poor of Maryland. By A. C. Robinson. Baltimore, MD: Printed by J. Murphy, 1840. 47 p. DLC; DNLM; MdBJ. 40-5804

Robinson, Conway, 1805-1884. An essay upon the constitutional rights as to slave property. Republished from the "Southern Literary Messenger" for Feb., 1840. Richmond, VA: Printed by T. W. White, 1840. 20 p. DLC; MH; RP. 40-5805

Robinson, Peter, d. 1841. Trial of P. Robinson for the murder of Abraham Suydan, Esq.; containing all the testimony and the charge of Chief Justice Hornblower and etc., by Wm. H. Attree. New York: s. l., 1840? 32 p. DLC; MH; MoU; NjR; PPL. 40-5806

Robinson, Peter, d. 1841. A true account of the murder of Abraham Suydam, late of New Brunswick, together with an accurate outline of the testimony, elicited on the examination of witnesses. New Brunswick, N. J.: Printed at the times office, [1840?] 8 p. DLC; MH; RPB. 40-5807

Robinson, Richard P. Life and conversation of Richard P. Robinson, the supposed murdered of Ellen Jewett. With an account of his trial. Together with an account of the life of Ellen Jewett. By Richard P. Robinson. 1 New Haven, CT: Printed for the Purchaser, 1840. 24 p. MHi; MNF. 40-5808

Rochester, New York. Anniversary of American Independence, July 4, 1840. Celebration in the City of Rochester. [Rochester, NY: s. l., 1840] p. NRHi. 40-5809

Rochester, New York. First Presbyterian Church. A catalogue of the members. Rochester: Printed by David Hoyt, 1840. 28 p. CtY; NRHi. 40-5810

Rochester, New York. Library Catalogue. Additional catalogue, Rochester city Library, under the case of the Young Men's Association. [Rochester, NY: s. l., 1840] 6 p. NRHi. 40-5811

Rochester Institute of Technology, Rochester, N. Y. Charter and the constitution, the by-laws and the regulations. With the names of members and subscribers of the Rochester Athenaeum Young Men's Association, 1840. Rochester, NY: s. l. [1840] p. WHi. 40-5812

Rockingham Mutual Fire Insurance Company. Circular... Andover, MA: From the Press of Gould, Newman & Saxton, 1840. 16 p. MH-BA. 40-5813

Rockport, Mass. By-laws of the Town of Rockport. Adopted March 28 to Sept. 19, 1840. Salem, MA: Salem Gazette Office, 1840. 12 p. M. 40-5814

Rockstro, William Smyth, 1823-1895. A year ago. Canzonet. Poetry by A. Proctor.

Music by W. S. Rockstro. [With accompaniment for piano forte] Boston, MA: Ditson & Co. [184-?] 5 p. MB. 40-5815

Rockwell, Henry W. Poem pronounced before the literary societies in Amherst college, August 26, 1840... Amherst, MA: J. S. & C. Adams, 1840. 24 p. ICN; MDeeP; MiD-B; NUt; OO. 40-5816

... Rode's favorite air... Philadelphia, PA: George Willig [184-?] 3 p. ViU. 40-5817

Rodman, Benjamin, 1794-1876. A voice from the prison, being articles addressed to the editor of the New Bedford Mercury... New Bedford: B. Lindsey, printer, 1840. 63 p. DLC; ICN; MHi; MWA; RP. 40-5818

Rodman, Thomas P. A discourse on Liberty. Delivered before an assembly of the Friends of Emancipation in the Chritial Chapel in Providence, July 4, 1840. By Thomas P. Rodman. Providence, RI: Printed by B. T. Albro, 1840. 15 p. DLC; MWA. 40-5819

Rodwell, George Herbert Buonaparte, 1800-1852. Ah! would our eyes had never met. Ballad. [Accomp. for piano forte] Boston, MA: s. l. [184-?] 5 p. MB. 40-5820

Rodwell, George Herbert Buonaparte, 1800-1852. The banks of the Blue Moselle. Ballad. Sung by Mrs. Knight. Written by E. Fitz Ball, Esq. Composed by G. H. Rodwell. Boston, MA: Bradlee [184-?] 3 p. ViU. 40-5821

Rodwell, George Herbert Buonaparte, 1800-1852. The banks of the Blue Moselle. Ballad. Sung by Mrs. Knight.

Written by E. Fitz Ball, Esqr. Composed by G. H. Rodwell. Boston, MA: Charles K. Keith [184-?] 3 p. ViU. 40-5822

Rodwell, George Herbert Buonaparte, 1800-1852. The banks of the Blue Moselle. Ballad. Sung by Mrs. Keeley. Written by E. Fritz Ball, Esq. Composed by G. H. Rodwell. New York: James L. Hewitt & Co. [184-?] 3 p. ViU. 40-5823

Rodwell, George Herbert Buonaparte, 1800-1852. The banks of the Blue Moselle. Ballad. Sung by Mrs. Wood. Composed by G. H. Rodwell. New York: Atwill's Music Saloon [184-?] 2 p. ICN; NN. 40-5824

Rodwell, George Herbert Buonaparte, 1800-1852. The banks of the Blue Moselle. Ballad. Sung by Mrs. Wood. Composed by G. H. Rodwell. Philadelphia, PA: Kemm & Brother [184-?] 2 p. ViU. 40-5825

Rodwell, George Herbert Buonaparte, 1800-1852. Beautiful blue violets. Philadelphia, PA: Kretschmar & Nunns [184-?] 5 p. MB. 40-5826

Rodwell, George Herbert Buonaparte, 1800-1852. Draw the sword Scotland. Ballad. [T.] Boston, MA: Bradlee [184-?] 3 p. MB. 40-5827

Rodwell, George Herbert Buonaparte, 1800-1852. Here's a health to thee Mary. An admired ballad. Written by B. Cornwell, Esq. Composed by C. H. Rodwell. Philadelphia, PA: A. Fiot [184-?] 2 p. ViU. 40-5828

Rodwell, George Herbert Buonaparte, 1800-1852. Last days of Pompeii. New York: Hewitt & Co. [184-?] 3 p. MB. 40-5829

Rodwell, George Herbert Buonaparte, 1800-1852. The tartar drum. Ballad. Sung by Mrs. Knight. Written by E. Fritz Ball, Esq. Composed by G. H. Rodwell. New York: Dubois & Stodart [184-?] 3 p. ViU. 40-5830

Rodwell, George Herbert Buonaparte, 1800-1852. A tear shall tell him all; a favorite song. Philadelphia: George Willig, [1840?] 2 p. NcD. 40-5831

Rodwell, George Herbert Buonaparte, 1800-1852. The toast be dear woman. The poetry by Edward Fitz Be.. Composed expressly for and dedicated to J. Wood, Esqr. by his friend G. Herbert Rodwell. Baltimore, MD: John Cole & Son [184-?] 3 p. NcD; ViU. 40-5832

Rodwell, James Gooderham, d. 1825. More blunders than one. Boston, MA: Spencer [184-?] 24 p. MB. 40-5833

Rogers, George. The pro and con of Universaliam, both as to its doctrines and moral bearings; in a series of original articles... Utica, NY: Published for the author by O. Hutchinson, 1840. 356 p. ICBB; LNB; MBUPH; OO; OSW. 40-5834

Rogers, Hester Ann, 1756-1794. A short account of the experience of Mrs. Hester Ann Rogers. Written by herself. With a brief extract from her diary. New York: T. Mason and G. Lane, 1840. 290 p. MH. 40-5835

Rogers, William Matticks, 1806-1851. A sermon, occasioned by the loss of the Harold and the Lexington, delivered at the Odeon, January 26, 1840. Boston, MA: C. A. Elliott, printer, 1840. 18 p. DLC; MBC; MH; NjR; RHi-RPB; WHi. 40-5836

Rogers, William Matticks, 1806-1851. A sermon, occasioned by the loss of the Harold and the Lexington, delivered at the Odeon, January 26, 1840. By William M. Rogers, Pastor of the Franklin Street Church. Second edition. Boston, MA: Printed by Perkins & Marvin, 1840. 18 p. CtSoP; MBB; MeBat; MiD-B; MWA; PHi. 40-5837

Rollin, Charles, 1661-1741. The ancient history of the Egyptians, Carthaginians, Babylonians, Medes, and Persians, Grecians, and Macedonians, including a history of the arts and sciences of the ancients. By Charles Rollin. New York: Published by Nafis & Cornish, 184-? 2 v. PWmpDS. 40-5838

Romance of Indian history; or, Thrilling incidents in the early settlement of America. New York: Kiggins & Kellog [184-?] p. DLC; NNC. 40-5839

Rome! Rome! The poetry by Mrs. Hemans. Arranged for one or two voices. With an accompaniment for the piano forte. Baltimore, MD: F. D. Benteen [184-?] 3 p. ViU. 40-5840

Romeo, pseud. Noel Ronello; a tale of the present century. Portland, ME: S. H. Colesworthy, 1840. DeU; MH; NBuG; NN. 40-5841

Romer, Frank, 1810-1889. Oh! would I were a boy again. Ballad. As sung by Mr. Giubilei. The music by F. Romer. Baltimore, MD: F. D. Benteen [184-?] 3 p. MNF; ViU. 40-5842

Romer, Frank, 1810-1889. The one we love. Ballad. [S. or T.] From the opera Fridolin. [Pianoforte accomp.] Philadelphia, PA: Willig [184-?] 2 p. MB. 40-5843

Ronaldson, James. Observations on the sugar beet & its cultivation. Philadelphia, PA: W. F. Geddes, 1840. 15 p. DLC; MBAt; PPAmP. 40-5844

Ronceray, C. de. The President's march. Arranged for the use of his juvenile pupils, by C. De Ronceray. Baltimore, MD: G. Willig [184-?] 1 p. ViU. 40-5845

Rooke, William Michael, 1794-1842. [Amilie] The most popular melodies of W. M. Rooke's opera Amilie, or the love test. Arranged for the flute by E. Manuel. Philadelphia, PA: Fiot, Meignen & Co. [184-?] 12 p. MB. 40-5846

Rooke, William Michael, 1794-1842. My boyhood's home. Air. Sung by Mr. Leguin in the grand romantic opera, Amilie; or, The love test. Performed at the Chestnut Street Theatre. The words by I. T. Haines. The music by W. M. Rooke. Philadelphia, PA: George Willig [184-?] 7 p. MB; ViU. 40-5847

Rooke, William Michael, 1794-1842. Oh! I remember; song in the grand opera of Amilie, or, The love test. The words by J. T. Haines. Philadelphia: G. Willig, [184-?] 7 p. DLC. 40-5848

Rooke, William Michael, 1794-1842. Thou art gone. Air. Sung by Miss Schirreff in the grand opera, Amilie; or, The love test. Performed at the Chestnut Street Theatre. The words by I. T. Haines. The music by W. M. Rooke.

Philadelphia, PA: George Willig [184-?] 7 p. ViU. 40-5849

Root, David. A farewell discourse: addressed to the First Church and Society, in Dover, N. H., by Rev. David Root, pastor, September 8, 1939. Published by request. Dover, NH: G. & E. Wadleigh, 1840. 14 p. MBC; MBNEH; MiD-B; MWA; Nh. 40-5850

[Rosa Lee] The favorite Negro song, Rosa Lee, or "Don't be foolish Joe..." "Arranged with chorus & accompaniment for the piano forte. 10th edition. Baltimore, MD: Willig [184-?] 5 p. MB. 40-5851

Rosborough, A. M. An oration. Delivered on the 22nd February, 1840, before the Chi Delta Society of East Tennessee University. By AM., a member of the society. Published by request. Knoxville, TN: Gifford & Eastman, 1840. 11 p. TU. 40-5852

Roscoe, Henry, 1800-1836. Digest of law of evidence in criminal cases. By George Sharswood. American ed. Philadelphia, PA: s. l., 1840. 914 p. MBS. 40-5853

Roscoe, Henry, 1800-1836. A digest of the law of evidence in criminal cases... 2d ed... Philadelphia, PA: T. & J. W. Johnson, 1840. 914 p. CSt; InHuP; MeBa; NNLI; TxU-L. 40-5854

Roscoe, Henry, 1800-1836. A treatise on the law of actions relating to real property. By Henry Roscoe, Esq.. Philadelphia, PA; New York: John S. Littell; Halsted and Voorhies, 1840. 2 v. CoU; MdUL; OO; PP; Sc-SC. 40-5855

Roscoe, Thomas, 1791-1871. Legends of Venice. Illustrated by J. R. Herbert... ed. by Thomas Roscoe... New York; London: Appleton and Co.; Longman, Orine, Brown, Green, and Longmans [etc., etc.] 1840. 52 p. DLC; LNP; MoS; OCU; PU. 40-5856

Rose, Daniel. O where will bonny Annly [sic] A favorite Scotch air. With variations for the piano forte by Daniel Rose. Philadelphia, PA: G. Willig [184-?] 3 p. ViU. 40-5857

The rose of Sharon: a religious souvenir for... Boston, MA: A. Tompkins and B. B. Mussey, 1840-57. 18 v. CSmH; MB; MnU; TxU; WU. 40-5858

Rosellen, Henri, 1811-1876. ... Le Mignonette... Boston, MA: Geo. P. Reed & Co. [184-?] 5 p. ViU. 40-5859

Rosellen, Henri, 1811-1876. ... La Romantique... Philadelphia, PA: George Willig [184-?] 5 p. ViU. 40-5860

Rosellen, Henri, 1811-1876. ... La Rose Blanche... Boston, MA: Geo. P. Reed & Co. [184-?] 5 p. ViU. 40-5861

Rosellen, Henri, 1811-1876. ... Souvenir de Bal. Philadelphia, PA: George Willig [184-?] 9 p. ViU. 40-5862

Rosellen, Henri, 1811-1876. ... Le Tremalo... Philadelphia, PA: George Willig [184-?] 5 p. ViU. 40-5863

Rosellen, Henri, 1811-1876. Variations on a favorite Cavatina in Doinzetti's opera, Parisina... Composed for the piano forte by Henry Rosellen. Op. 18. Philadelphia, PA: A. Fiot [184-?] 9 p. ViU. 40-5864

Rosenstein, I. G. Theory and practice of Homoeopathy, by I. G. Rosenstein, M. D. Louisville: Henkle & Logan, printers, 1840. 288 p. ICU; MWal; OMC; PP; PPL-R. 40-5865

Ross, D. Auld Lang Syne, with variations, for the piano or harp, by D. Ross. Baltimore, MD: F. D. Benteen [184-?] 4 p. ViU. 40-5866

Ross, D. .... Auld Lang Syne, with variations, for the piano forte or harp, composed by D. Ross. New York: Firth & Hall [184-?] 6 p. ViU. 40-5867

Ross, D. .... Auld Lang syne, with variations, for the piano forte or harp. Composed by D. Ross. New York: W. Dubois [184-?] 6 p. ViU. 40-5868

Rossini, Gioacchino Antonio, 1792-1808. Ah, that day I well remember! Ah quet [sic] giorno. Cavatina. Sung by Mrs. Alfred Shaw at the Royal Theatre Covent Garden in the opera Semiramide. Composed by Rossini... Philadelphia, PA; New York: A. Fiot; W. Dubois [184-?] 11 p. ViU. 40-5869

Rossini, Gioacchino Antonio, 1792-1808. "At length a brillant ray." [Belraggio lusinghier] Cavatina. Sung by Miss Adelaide Kemble at the Covent Garden in the opera Semiramide. Composed by Rossini... Philadelphia, PA; New York: A. Fiot; W. Dubois [184-?] 9 p. MB; ViU. 40-5870

Rossini, Gioacchino Antonio, 1792-1808. The celebrated Cinderella waltz. Composed by Rossini... Adopted for the piano forte by H. Herz. Philadelphia, PA: Geo. Willig [184-?] 2 p. ViU. 40-5871

Rossini, Gioacchino Antonio, 1792-1808. The celebrated Tyrolean waltz. Adopted for the piano forte by H. Herz. New York: Dubois & Son [184-?] 2 p. MB. 40-5872

Rossini, Gioacchino Antonio, 1792-1808. Dark day of horror. [Giorno d'amore.] Duetto [S. A. Accomp. for piano forte] in the opera Semiramide. Boston, MA: Ditson [184-?] 5 p. MB. 40-5873

Rossini, Gioacchino Antonio, 1792-1808. Grand waltz, from the Overture to the Opera of La Gazza Ladra. Composed by Rossini. Boston, MA: James L. Hewitt & Co. [184-?] 3 p. ViU. 40-5874

Rossini, Gioacchino Antonio, 1792-1808. The inflammatus, in Rossini's celebrated Stabat mater. Arranged for the piano forte by Henry Herz. Philadelphia, PA; New York: A. Fiot; W. Dubois [184-?] 7 p. ViU. 40-5875

Rossini, Gioacchino Antonio, 1868. L'invito, belero from Rossini's musical soirees; arranged for the piano forte by F. Kalkbrenner. Philadelphia: A. Fiot, [184-?] 7 p. ViU. 40-5876

Rossini, Gioacchino Antonio, 1792-1808. ... March in La Donna Del L'ago. Baltimore, MD: F. D. Benteen [184-?] 3 p. NcD. 40-5877

Rossini, Gioacchino Antonio, 1792-1808. ... March in La Donna Del L'ago. Philadelphia, PA: A. Fiot [184-?] 3 p. ViU. 40-5878

Rossini, Gioacchino Antonio, 1792-1808. [Moses in Egitto] 'Tis music that whispers. [Mi manca la voce. A celebrated quartet [S. S. T. T.] from the oratorio Mose in Egitto. Composed by G. Rossini. [Words by Tottola. With accompaniment for piano forte] Philadelphia, PA: Fiot [184-?] 7 p. MB. 40-5879

Rossini, Gioacchino Antonio, 1792-1808. Non piu mesta. Aria in La Cenerentola, by Rossini. Arranged as a rondo by F. Hunten. Boston, MA: Geo. P. Reed [184-?] 5 p. ViU. 40-5880

Rossini, Gioacchino Antonio, 1792-1808. Non piu mesta. Aria in La Cenerentola, by Rossini. Arranged as a rondo for the piano forte by F. Hunten. New York: Firth, Hall & Pond [184-?] 7 p. ViU. 40-5881

Rossini, Gioacchino Antonio, 1792-1808. O hear me Jehovah. Prayer [S. A. T. B.] in Moses in Egypt. [Pianoforte accomp.] Arranged by A. U. Hayter. Boston, MA: Ditson [184-?] 6 p. MB. 40-5882

Rossini, Gioacchino Antonio, 1792-1808. Overture of Tancred. Arranged for two performers on one piano forte. Composed by G. Rofsini. Philadelphia, PA: G. Willig [184-?] 13 p. ViU. 40-5883

Rossini, Gioacchino Antonio, 1792-1808. Overture to L'Italiana in Algieri. Arranged for the piano forte. Composed by G. Rossini. New York: E. Riley & Co. [184-?] 11 p. ViU. 40-5884

Rossini, Gioacchino Antonio, 1792-1808. La pastorella dell' Alpi. La pastourelle des Alpes [Ariette] from Les soirees musicales. Philadelphia, PA: Fiot, Meignen & Co. [184-?] 5 p. MB. 40-5885

Rossini, Gioacchino Antonio, 1792-1808. William Tell [Hofer the Tell of the Tyrol] Accompaniment for the piano forte. New York: Dubois & Stodart [184-?] 6 p. MB. 40-5886

Rotteck, Karl Wenzeslaus Rodecker von, 1775-1840. General history of the world from the earliest times until the year 1831. By Charles von Rotteck, LL. D. Translated from the German and continued to 1840. By Frederick Jones, A. M. Illustrated by twenty-four historical engravings, designed be Heideloff, Dalbou, and others, and engraved by J. Spittall... First American edition. Philadelphia, PA: C. F. Strollmeyer, 1840-41. 4 v. CtHC; MBBC; NcD; RWoH; ViRU. 40-5887

Rouget de Lisle, Claude Joseph, 1760-1836. The celebrated Marseilles hymn. Philadelphia, PA: A. Fiot [184-?] 4 p. ViU. 40-5888

Rouget de Lisle, Claude Joseph, 1760-1836. The celebrated Marseilles hymn. Arranged for the Spanish guitar, by Otto Torp. Philadelphia, PA: Klemm [184-?] 3 p. MB. 40-5889

Rouget de Lisle, Claude Joseph, 1760-1836. The celebrated Marseilles hymn. With French and English words. Arranged for the piano forte. [3-part chorus] Boston, MA: Ditson [184-?] 4 p. MB. 40-5890

The Rough-hewer. Devoted to the democratic principles of Jefferson. Albany, NY: Thomas M. Burt, 1840. ICU; DLC; PPL-R; TxDaM; WHi. 40-5891

Rouillon, de. The French companion; consisting of familiar conversations on every topic which can be useful to the continental traveller, etc. Revised and corrected for the use of schools, by P. Mouls. 1st American from the 10th London ed. New York: W. E. Dean, etc., 1840. MH. 40-5892

Roupell, George Leith, 1797-1854. A short treatise on typhus fever. By George Leith Roupell, M. D.... Philadelphia, PA: Printed and published by A. Waldie, 1840. 162 p. KyLxT; MBM; NBuU-M; OCIM; PU. 40-5893

Rousmaniere, H. A manual of phrenology; containing a brief sketch of the science of phrenology... by H. Rousmaniere. Boston, MA: S. N. Dickinson, 1840. 16 p. MBilHi. 40-5894

Rousseau, Victor Arthur. here let us rest dear maid. Dormez mes cheres amours. A celebrated duett. [S. A. With accompaniment for piano forte] By A. de Beauplan [pseud.] [Philadelphia, PA: Lee & Walker, 184-?] 2 p. MB. 40-5895

Rowe, Elizabeth Singer, 1674-1737. Devout exercises of the heart, in meditation and soliloquy, prayer and praise. Boston, MA: Sight., 1840. 188 p. MdHi; MH; NNUT; OO. 40-5896

Rowe, Nicholas. Jane Shore; a tragedy in five acts. New York: S. French [184-?] p. MB; MH; NN. 40-5897

Rowland, Henry Augustus, 1804-1858. The frame-work of Liberty. A sermon, delivered in the Pearl-Street Presbyterian Church, in the City of New York, July 5, 1840... By Henry A. Rowland... New York: William S. Dorr, printer, 1840. 28 p. MeBat; MH-AH; MiD-B; NcMHi; NHi. 40-5898

Rowson, Susanna [Haswell] 1762-1824. Charlotte Temple. A tale of truth. New York: N. C. Nafis, 1840. 140 p. CtY; DLC; NN; OU; PPL. 40-5899

Rowson, Susanna [Haswell] 1762-1824. Charlotte Temple. A tale of truth. New York: Richard Marsh [1840] 140 p. NBuG. 40-5900

Rowson, Susanna [Haswell] 1762-1824. Lucy Temple, one of the three orphans. A sequel to Charlotte Temple. By Susannah Rowson... New York: Nafis & Cornish [etc., etc., 184-?] 179 p. NN. 40-5901

Roxbury, Mass. Selectmen. List of voters in the Town of Roxbury... 1840. Roxbury, MA: Torrey, printer, 184?. p. ICN. 40-5902

Roxbury Artillery, Roxbury, Mass. Constitution of the Roxbury Artillery. Instituted August 16, 1798. Altered and revised Aug. 16, 1837. Boston, MA: s. l., 1840. 44 p. MHi. 40-5903

Roxbury Democrat. Horrible Doctrines!!!Loco Focoism Unmasked!! Read and ponder well! The sub-treasury has passed and here is what is to come next!!!! Roxbury, 1840. 8 p. MH; MiD-B; NN; OClWHi. 40-5904

Runnells, Eliza B. A reply to a letter addressed to Mr. Van Buren, president of the United States; purported to be written by Miss Lucy Kenny, the whig missionary. [Washington, 1840?] 14 p. DLC. 40-5905

Ruoff, A. Joseph Fridericus. Ruoff's repertory of homoepathaic medicine nosologically arranged. Translated from the German by Howard Okie, student of medicine. With additions and improvements, by Gideon Humphrey, M. D. &c. Philadelphia, PA: Published by J. Dobson, Kay & Brothers & H. Hooker, 1840. 254 p. CtY; DNLN; PPA. 40-5906

Rupp, Israel Daniel, 1803-1878. Orginal history of the religious denominations in the U. S.: rise, progress, statistics and doctrines. Philadelphia, PA: s. l., 1840. 734 p. NHC-S. 40-5907

Rush, William. Valedictory address to the graduates of the Medical Department of Pennsylvania College, by Wm. Ruch, M. D., Professor of the Theory and Practice of Medicine in the Medical Department of Pennsylvania College. Philadelphia, PA: Printed by Francis G. Grund, 1840. 16 p. DSG; MB; OOC; PPL; PWW. 40-5908

Rushing, Joseph. Original hymns. For use of Sunday schools. 2d ed. New York: Mason & Lane, J. Collord, print, 1840. 152 p. NNUT. 40-5909

Ruskin, John. Arrows of the Chase; being a collection of scattered letters. Published chiefly in the Daily Newspapers, 1840-1880. By John Ruskin. Boston, MA: Dana Estes & company, publishers, 1840-80. 416 p. IaAt; MWsp; OkOk; UPB. 40-5910

Russ, Horace. Headsman: a sketch... by H. R. New York: Van Norden, 1840. 78 p. DLC; MB; PU. 40-5911

Russell, Michael, 1781-1843. History and present condition of the barbary states. By Michael Russell. New York: Harper and Brothers, 1840. 339 p. MNF; Nh-Hi; PHatU; ViR. 40-5912

Russell, Michael, 1781-1843. ... Palestine, or the Holy land from the earliest period to the present time... New York: Published by Harper & Brothers, 1840. 330 p. InRch; MB; MnU; NBuDD; ViR. 40-5913

Rutgers College, New Brunswick, N. J. Addresses... delivered at the inauguration of the Hon. Abraham Bruyn Hasbrouck, as President of Rutgers college in New Brunswick, N. J.... New York: Robert Carter, n. pr., 1840. 39 p. MB; MH; NjR; PPL; PPPrHi. 40-5914

Rutgers College, New Brunswick, N. J. Catalogue of the officers and alumni of Rutgers College, New Brunswick, N. J. New Brunswick, NJ: John Terhune's Press, 1840. 26 p. IaHA; MH; NjR; PPPrHi. 40-5915

Rutgers College, New Brunswick, N. J. Report of a committee to the trustees of Rutgers College... New Brunswick, NJ: Terhune, 1840. PPPrHi. 40-5916

Rutherford, Samuel. The trial and triumph of faith. By Samuel Rutherford. Wheeling: Printed for William Wilson, 1840. 400 p. GAU; OClWHi. 40-5917

Rutty, John. Extracts from the spiritual diary of John Rutty. Falmouth: printed by J. Trathan, 1840. MH. 40-5918

Ryckman, L. W. The largest liberty defined. A treatise on the inherent rights and obligations of man. By L. W. Ryckman... New York: printed by W. Applegate, 1840. 26 p. NHi; P. 40-5919

Rziha, Francis. Susanna polka. For the piano forte. As played with unbounded applause by the Steyermark Musical

Company. Composed by Francis Rziha, leader of the company. Baltimore, MD; New Orleans, LA: F. D. Benteen; W. T. Mayo [184-?] 5 p. ViU. 40-5920

S

Sabbath occupations. A letter. [Boston, MA: N. Willis, 1840?] 4 p. MB. 40-5921

Saco Water Power Company, Saco, Me. By-laws... Boston, MA: Benjamin Loring & Co., 1840. 12 p. DLC; MH-BA. 40-5922

The sacred offering; a tableaux [!] of remarkable incidents in the Old and New Testament. Being a series of original articles by... American writers. Boston, MA: Whittemore, Niles & Hall [184-?] p. WU. 40-5923

The sailor's companion; or, Songs of the sea. Consisting of a well-selected collection of naval songs. New York: Leavitt and Allen, 1840? 160 p. MH. 40-5924

Sacred wreath; or, Characters and scenes of the Holy Sciprtures, illustrated by distinguished writers of Great Britain and America. Philadelphia, PA: Orrin Rogers, 1840. 210 p. CtSoP; NNUT. 40-5925

Sadler, L. L. An epitome of a discourse. Delivered in the North Second Street Methodist Episcopal Church, of the City of Troy, N. Y., on the evening of March 8, 1840, by Rev. N. Levings. Troy, NY: Alanson Cook, printer, 1840. 56 p. ICU; MMeT; NCaS; NN. 40-5926

Sadler, L. L. Improvement. An address. Delivered before the Franklin Debating Society of Troy, February 21, 1840...

West Troy, NY: W. Hollands, printer, 1840. 8 p. NN. 40-5927

Sailors' songster. [Philadelphia, PA: s. l., 184-?] 248 p. MB. 40-5928

Saint Ceran, Tullius, 1800-1855. Les Louisianoises. Poesies Nouvelles. Par M. Tullius St. Ceran. New Orleans, LA: J. L. Sallee, 1840. 90 p. AU; CtY; LU; NjP; RPB. 40-5929

Saint Clair, Henry. The United States criminal calendar; or, an awful warning to the youth of America: being an account of the most horrid murders, piracies, highway robberies... By Henry St. Clair. Boston, MA: Charles Gaylord, 1840. 356 p. CL; MH-L; MoU; OMC; VtU. 40-5930

Saint George, Julian. Leisure moments; containing Corla, and other poems... Baltimore, MD: N. Hickman, 1840. 152 p. MdBP; MdHi; NBuG. 40-5931

Saint Hilaire, Augustin Francois Cesar Prouvencal de, 1779-1853. Monographic des Primulacees et des Lentibulariees du Bresil meridional. Orleans: s. l., 1840. 48 p. NNBG; OCLloyd. 40-5932

Saint John, Percy Bolingbroke, 1821-1889. The trapper's bride: a tale of the Rocky Mountains. By Percy B. St. John. New York; Philadelphia, PA: E. Ferrett & Co. [184-?] 48 p. DLC. 40-5933

Saint Mary's College, Marion Co., Ky. Fourth Annual Commencement of St. Mary's College, Marion County, Ky., 1839-40. Louisville, KY: s. l., 1840. 16 p. MHi. 40-5934

Saint Paul's College, College Point, N. Y. Catalogue of the professors, instructors, and students of St. Paul's College and grammar school for the session of 1839-40. College Point, NY: s. l., 1840. 36 p. MdBD; NN. 40-5935

Saint Pierre, Jacques Henri Bernardin de, 1737-1814. St. Pierre's studies of nature. Translated by Henry Hunter, D. D. Philadelphia, PA: J. & J. L. Gihon [184-] 398 p. ArBaA; MeWa; MoU; NcAs; OClW; OO. 40-5936

Saint Thomas. The child's first lessons; containing the shortest method of learning reading, writing, grammar, history, geography & composition, by St. Thomas, esq. New Orleans, LA: True America Office, 1840. 24 p. DLC. 40-5937

Salem Charitable Mechanic Associaton. Constitution of the Salem Charitable Mechanic Association. Instituted Oct. 1, 1817. Incorporated June 14, 1822. Revised Oct. 2, 1839. Salem, MA: Printed at the Register Press, 1840. 36 p. DLC; MSaE; MWA. 40-5938

Salem County, N. J. Lyceum. Constitution and by-laws of the Salem County Lyceum, December 10, 1839. Philadelphia, PA: s. l., 1840. 8 p. PHi. 40-5939

Salem, Mass. Address of the Mayor. Delivered at the organization of the city government, March 23, 1840. Published by order of the City Council. Salem, MA:

printed at the Register Press, 1840. 38 p. DLC; MSa; MWA. 40-5940

Salem, Mass. School Committee. Regulations for the public schools of the City of Salem. Adopted by School Committee, April, 1840. Salem: printed at the Register Press, 1840. 29 p. DLC; MHi; MiD-B. 40-5941

Salem, Mass. Second Baptist church. Declaration of faith and covenant of the Second Baptist Church, Salem, Mass. Adopted 1840. Salem: Gazatte press, 1840. 20 p. NNUT. 40-5942

Salem, Mass. Tabernacle Church. The claims of the Tabernacle Church to be considered the Third Church in Salem: or the Church of 1735. Salem: Printed for the Tabernacle Church, 184-? 56 p. MHi. 40-5943

Sallustius, Crispus C. Sallust. Translated by William Rose, M. A. With improvements and notes. New York: Harper and brothers, 1840. 242 p. DLC; NjP; PMy; ViU; WStfSF. 40-5944

Salomon, Louis. The Mosaic system in its fundamental principles. By the Rev. Dr. Louis Salomon... Philadelphia, PA: F. G. Dorsey [1840] 215 p. CU; GS. 40-5945

Saltonstall, Leverett. Speech of Mr. Saltonstall, of Massachusetts, in reply to Mr. Parmenter, on the bill providing for the Civil and diplomatic expenses of the government for the year 1840. Delivered in the House of Representatives, April 21, 1840. Washington, DC: Printed by Gales and Seaton, 1840. 16 p. MB; MBAt; MWA; PHi. 40-5946

San Francisco. The United States of America, Territory of California, San Francisco District... [San Francisco, CA: s. l., 184-?] p. CSmH. 40-5947

Sanborn, Dyer H. Analytical grammar of the English language. 2d edition. Concord, NH: Marsh, Capen, Lyon and Webb, 1840. MH; MnU. 40-5948

Sanborn, Dyer H. Analytical grammar of the English language. 3d edition. Concord, NH: Marsh, Capen, Lyon and Webb, 1840. 288 p. MH; NbU. 40-5949

Sanborn, Peter E. The sick man's friend, shewing [sic] the medical properties and use of the most valuable medical roots and herbs... Boston, MA: s. l., 1840. 23 p. MBCo; WU-M. 40-5950

Sanders, Billington McCarter, 1789-1854. Valedictory address. Delivered before the trustees, faculty, students, and friends of the Mercer University, Greene County, Ga., Dec. 16, 1839. [Washington, GA] printed by M. J. Kappell, 1840. 15 p. GU; MH. 40-5951

Sanders, Charles Walton, 1805-1889. The primary school primer. By Charles W. Sanders, A. M. New York; Cincinnati, OH; Chicago, IL: American Book Company [1840] 48 p. ICBB; MH; MiKT; NNC; RPB. 40-5952

Sanders, Charles Walton, 1805-1889. Primary school primer... New York: Ivison & Phinney, etc., etc. [1840] p. CtHWatk; MH. 40-5953

Sanders, Charles Walton, 1805-1889. The primary school primer... Sandover, MA: Gould & Saxton, 1840. 48 p. RPB. 40-5954

Sanders, Charles Walton, 1805-1889. Sander's spelling book; containing a minute and comprehensive system of introductory orthography... Designed to teach a system of orthography & orthoepy... For the use of schools. By Charles W. Sanders. Cortland Village, NY: published by Speed, Sinclair & Co., R. A. Reed, printer, 1840. 166 p. CtY; MB; MH; NjR. 40-5955

Sanders, Charles Walton, 1805-1889. Sander's spelling book; containing a minute and comprehensive system of introductory orthography... Designed to teach a system of orthography and orthoepy... For the use of schools. By Charles W. Sanders. Andover, MA: Gould, Newman and Saxton; stereotyped by F. W. Ripley, 1840. 166 p. NjR. 40-5956

Sanders, Charles Walton, 1805-1889. The school reader. First Book. Boston, MA: Ives & Dennet, 1840. 120 p. NRHi. 40-5957

Sanders, Charles Walton, 1805-1889. The school reader. First Book. New York: Mark H. Newman & Company, 1840. 120 p. ICU; MLexHi; MH; NN. 40-5958

Sanders, Charles Walton, 1805-1889. The school reader. Second book. Andover, Mass.: Gould, Newman and Saxton, 1840. 180 p. DLC; NjR; NN; NR. 40-5959

Sanders, Charles Walton, 1805-1889. The school reader. Second book. New York: M. H. Newman, etc. [1840] 180 p. CSt; DLC; MH; MPiB; NjR. 40-5960

Sanders, Charles Walton, 1805-1889. The school reader. Second Book. New

York: Mark H. Newman & Co., 1840. 180 p. N; NjN. 40-5961

Sanford, David, 1801-1875. Influence of the ministry... Boston, MA: Perkins & Marvin, 1840. 32 p. DLC; MB; NN; RPB. 40-5962

Sanford, David. Influence of the Ministry. A sermon delivered before the Auxiliary Education Society of Norfolk County, at their annual meeting in South Braintree, June 10, 1840. By David Sanford, Pastor of the Village Church, Medway. Boston, MA: Printed by Perkins & Marvin, 1840. 32 p. MBC; MHi; MWA; NhD; RPB. 40-5963

Sanford, S. Poem. Suggested by A. F. Beard's picture of a Slave Mart. By S. Sanford. [Boston, MA: s. l., 184-?] 4 p. CSmH; MB. 40-5964

Sargent, John Turner, 1808-1877. A discourse preached at the dedication of Suffolk Street Chapel, February 5, 1840, by John T. Sargent, pastor of the Chapel. Published by request. Boston, MA: printed by Samuel N. Dickinson, 1840. 20 p. CBPac; MBAt; MiD-B; NNC; WHi. 40-5965

Sargent, Lucius Manlius, 1786-1867. As a medicine. Founded on fact. Boston, MA: s. l., 1840. MH. 40-5966

Sargent, Lucius Manlius, 1786-1867. Fritz Hazell. Founded on fact. Boston, MA: s. l., 1840. 98 p. MH. 40-5967

Sargent, Lucius Manlius, 1786-1867. Groggy harbor, or, A smooth stone from the brook and a shepherd's sling. Boston, MA: s. l., 1840. 76 p. MH. 40-5968

Sargent, Lucius Manlius, 1786-1867. I am afraid there ia a God. Founded on fact. Boston, MA: Whipple and Damrell, 1840. 47 p. DLC; ICN; MH. 40-5969

Sargent, Lucius Manlius, 1786-1867. An Irish heart. Founded on fact. Boston, MA: s. l., 1840. MH. 40-5970

Sargent, Lucius Manlius, 1786-1867. Kitty Grafton. Founded on fact. Boston, MA: s. l., 1840. MH. 40-5971

Sargent, Lucius Manlius, 1786-1867. The life-preserver. Founded on fact. Boston, MA: s. l., 1840. 51 p. MH. 40-5972

Sargent, Lucius Manlius, 1786-1867. My mother's gold ring. Founded on fact. Boston, MA: s. l., 1840. 24 p. MH. 40-5973

Sargent, Lucius Manlius, 1786-1867. Nancy Le Baron. Founded on fact. Boston, MA: s. l., 1840. 89 p. MH. 40-5974

Sargent, Lucius Manlius, 1786-1867. The prophets! Where are they? Founded on fact. Boston, MA: s. l., 1840. 36 p. MH. 40-5975

Sargent, Lucius Manlius, 1786-1867. Right opposite. Founded on fact. Boston, MA: s. l., 1840. 64 p. MH. 40-5976

Sargent, Lucius Manlius, 1786-1867. A sectarian thing. Founded on fact. Boston, MA: s. l., 1840. 48 p. MH. 40-5977

Sargent, Lucius Manlius, 1786-1867. Seed time and harvest. Founded on fact. Boston, MA: s. l., 1840. 24 p. MH. 40-5978

Sargent, Lucius Manlius, 1786-1867. The stage-coach. Founded on fact. Boston, MA: s. l., 1840. 288 p. MH. 40-5979

Sargent, Lucius Manlius, 1786-1867. Too fast and too far, or, The cooper and the currier. Founded on fact. Boston, MA: s. l., 1840. 34 p. MH. 40-5980

Sargent, Lucius Manlius, 1786-1867. Well enough for the vulgar. Founded on fact. Boston, MA: s. l., 1840. 99 p. MH. 40-5981

Sargent, Lucius Manlius, 1786-1867. What a curse! or, Johnny Hodges, the black-smith. Founded on fact. Boston, MA: s. l., 1840. 32 p. MH. 40-5982

Sargent, Lucius Manlius, 1786-1867. Wild Dick and good little Robin. Boston, MA: s. l., 1840. 41 p. MH. 40-5983

Sargent, Lucius Manlius, 1786-1867. A word in season, or, The sailor's widow. Founded on fact. Boston, MA: s. l., 1840. 36 p. MH. 40-5984

Sargent, Nathan, 1794-1875. Brief outline of the life of Henry Clay. [Washington, DC: s. l., 184-?] 16 p. CSmH; DLC; MB; MiD-B; MWA. 40-5985

Sartwell, H. P. Catalogue of plants, growing without cultivation in the vicinity of Seneca and Crooked Lakes in western New York. Penn: Yates Co., 1840. 273, 290 p. IaAS. 40-5986

Savannah, Ga. Map of the City of Savannah... With the extended limits, by C. Stephens... New York: P. A. Mesier & Co., 1840. GSDe. 40-5987

Sawyer, Frederic William. Merchant's and shipmaster's guide, in relation to their rights, duties and liabilities... By Frederic W. Sawyer. Boston, MA: published by Benjamin Loring & Co., 1840. 306 p. MBAt; MBS; MOrl; MSaP; NcD. 40-5988

Sawyer, Thomas Jefferson, 1804-1899. Funeral discourse. A sermon. Delivered May 3, 1840, occasioned by the death of Miss Elizabeth... New York: s. l., 1840. MH-AH. 40-5989

Sawyer, Thomas Jefferson. 1804-1899. A Sermon delivered on Sunday, May 3, 1840, occasioned by the death of Miss Elizabeth Tremby. New York: Printed by the Union Press, 1840. 34 p. MH-AH; MMeT; MMeT-Hi. 40-5990

Saxe, John Godfrey, 1816-1887. Poems. 5th ed. Boston, MA: Ticknor, 1840. 192 p. CoD. 40-5991

Say, Thomas, 1787-1834. Descriptions of some new terrestrial and fluviatile shells of North America, 1829, 1830, 1831. By Thomas Say... New Harmony, IN: s. l., 1840. 26 p. A-GS; DLC; DSG; In; InHi; InLPU; InNhW; MH-Z; NNM; OC; PHi; PPAN; PPAmP. 40-5992

Schabalje, Jan Philipsen, 1585-1656. The wandering soul; or, dialogues between the wandering soul and Adam, Noah, and Simon Cleophas. Comprising a "History of the World." Descriptive history from the Creation until the Destruction of Jerusalem from which may be seen how one Monarchy and Kingdom succeeded another...; and an extensive detail of the destruction of Jerusalem by John Phillip Schabalie. Originally written in the Holland language. Translated into German by Bernhart B. Brecknell. Translated from the 4th American ed. into English by I. Daniel Rupp. Harrisburg, PA: I. S. Rupp & John Winebrenner, 1840. 504 p. KyMay; P; PLT; PPe; Schw. 40-5993

Schabalje, Jan Philipsen, 1585-1656. The wandering soul; or, dialogues between the wandering soul and Adam, Noah, and Simon Cleophas. Originally written in the Holland language. Translated into German by Bernhart B. Brecknell. Woodstock, VA: Orgden, 1840. 471 p. InGo; NcD; Vi. 40-5994

Scheffmacher, R. P. A controversial Catechism, in which the various points of Catholic Doctrine are concisely explained. Translatd from the French of R. P. Scheffmacher, S. J. Baltimore, MD: F. Lucas, Jr. [1840] 201 p. MBBCHS; MdBS; MdW; MoSU; PV. 40-5995

Schiller, Johann Christoph Friedrich von, 1759-1805. A collection of select pieces of poetry by Schiller and Burger. Together with some characteristic poems of the most eminent German bards. Translated in the metre of the original by George Maurer. New York; W. & B. Lange [1840] 141 p. ViU. 40-5996

Schiller, Johann Christoph Friedrich von, 1759-1805. Schiller's Maria Stuart. New edition. Philadelphia, PA: Perkins, 1840. 232 p. ICU; MB; MH; MNe; PPA. 40-5997

Schiller, Johann Christoph Friedrich von, 1759-1805. The robbers... New York; s. l. [184-?] 57 p. DLC; MB; TNJU. 40-5998

Schiller, Johann Christoph Friedrich von, 1759-1805. William Tell, and other poems. From the German by William Peter. New edition. Philadelphia, PA: s. l., 1840. CtHT; MH; PPL-R; TJoV. 40-5999

Schlegel, Frederich [von] 1772-1829. The philosophy of life... New York: Harper, 1840. 549 p. NRU. 40-6000

Schlusstein Landirthschafts Calendar, 1841. Von Carl F. Egelmann. Philadelphia, PA: Wm. W. Walker [1840] p. MWA. 40-6001

Schmauk, John G. Erstes buch fur deutsche schulen. Philadelphia, PA: W. G. Mentz, 1840. CtY; DLC; InU; IU; MnU; 40-6002

Schmid, Christoph von, 1768-1854. The carrier pigeon. New York: E. Dunigin & Bro., 1840. 70 p. DLC; NN. 40-6003

Schmid, Christoph von, 1768-1854. Heinrich von Eichenfels, oder: Das geraubte kind, welches viele jahre von raubern in einer finstern hohle gefangen gehalten... Harrisburg, PA: Gedrucket bei T. F. Scheffer [184-?] 38 p. MnU. 40-6004

Schmidt, Daniel. Das allgemeine A-B-C buchstabier-und lesebuch, zum gebrauch deutscher... Lancaster, PA: J. Bar, 1840. 128 p. DLC; MiU-C; PLF; PPG; PSt. 40-6005

Schmidt, Henry. The hero's quick step, as performed by the Military bands. Composed by Henry Schmidt. Baltimore, MD: F. D. Benteen [184-?] 2 p. ViU. 40-6006

Schmidt, Henry. The Tippecanoe... quick step... Boston, MA: H. Prentiss, 1840. 3 p. ICN; NN. 40-6007

Schmidt, Paul, 1811-1876. Erstes lehr- und lesebuch fur deutsche... Pittsburgh, PA: V. Scriba, 1840. 186 p. DLC; NjNbS. 40-6008

Schmitz, Adolph. Sweetly falls the dew of night. A serenade [S. or T. The accomp.] ... arranged for the guitar... Philadelphia, PA: Fiot [184-?] 3 p. MB. 40-6009

Schmucker, Samuel Simon, 1799-1873. Appeal in behalf of the Christian Sabbath... New York: pub. by the American Tract Society, 184-?] 16 p. WHi. 40-6010

Schmucker, Samuel Simon. 1799-1873. Portraiture of Lutheranism: A discourse... By S. S. Schmucker, D. D. Baltimore, MD: Publication Rooms, 1840. 89 p. InCW; MBC; MH; PLERC-Hi; ScNC. 40-6011

Schroeder, John Frederick, 1800-1857. Circular of St. Ann's Hall, Flushing, Long Island, devoted to the education of young ladies. Rev. J. F. Schroeder, D. D., Rector. New York: Printed by Albert Hanford, 1840. 8 p. NSmb. 40-6012

Schroeder, R. A popular Swiss air. Arranged and varied for the piano forte. Boston, MA: Bradlee [184-?] 3 p. MB. 40-6013

Schubert, Franz Peter, 1797-1828. Adieu. Melodie de F. Schubert. Transcrite et variee pour le piano par Th. Dohler, op. 45... Boston, MA: G. P. Reed & Co. [184-?] 7 p. ViU. 40-6014

Schubert, Franz Peter, 1797-1828. Ave Maria. [Song. With accompaniment for piano forte] New York: Firth & Hall [184-?] 7 p. MB. 40-6015

Schubert, Franz Peter, 1797-1828. ... Last greeting. L'Adieu. L'Addio... Philadelphia, PA; Boston, MA; New York: J. E. Gould, successor to A. Fiot; Oliver Ditson; C. C. Clapp & Co.; T. S. Berry & Co. [184-?] 5 p. ViU. 40-6016

Schubert, Franz Peter, 1797-1828. ... The Serenade... Baltimore, MD: George Willig [184-?] 5 p. ViU. 40-6017

Schubert, Franz Peter, 1797-1828. Paris polka. Composed by P. Schubert. Boston, MA: Geo. P. Reed [184-?] 2 p. ViU. 40-6018

Schubert, Franz Peter, 1797-1828. Rubini polka. Composed & arranged for the piano forte by P. Schubert. Boston, MA: Geo. P. Reed [184-?] 2 p. ViU. 40-6019

Schubert, Franz Peter, 1797-1828. Der Wanderer. [Song, A. or Bar. With piano forte accomp.] Boston, MA: Ditson & Co. [184-?] 5 p. MB. 40-6020

Schuylkill Navigation Company. Account of the Schuylkill Navigation Company in the State of Pennsylvania, with its improvements. From the Commercial List. Philadelphia, PA: s. l., 1840. 6 p. PHi. 40-6021

Scot's Charitable Society, Boston, Mass. Celebration of the 182d anniversary at the Pavilion on St. Andrew's Day, Nov. 30, 1839. Boston, MA: s. l., 1840. 29 p. CtSoP; MB; MBC; MHi; MWA. 40-6022

Scott, Amey. Memoirs of Mrs. Amey Scott. Written by herself. Lowell, MA: Published by E. A. Rice and Co., 1840. MLow; RPB. 40-6023

Scott, John B. An Appeal to the People, from the Decision of the Senate, in the Case of the Removal of the Justices of the Marine Court... New York: Wm. G. Boggs, 1840. 29 p. InHi; MH; NN. 40-6024

Scott, John Work, 1807-1879. An address on femalr education. Delivered at the close of the summer session for 1840 of the Steubenville Female Seminary in presence of its pupils and patrons, by Rev. John W. Scott, one of the Board of Visitors. Steubenville, OH: s. l., 1840. 12 p. CtY; OClWHi. 40-6025

Scott, Walter, Sir, bart., 1771-1832. The complete works of Sir Walter Scott. With a biography and his last additiona and illustrations. Philadelphia, PA: Carey & Hart, 1840. 10 v. IaMed; KyLoP; OCX. 40-6026

Scott, Walter, Sir, bart., 1771-1832. The history of Scotland. By Sir Walter Scott. In two volumes. New York: Harper & Brothers, 1840. 2 v. LNH; NcWfC; NICLA; NWatt. 40-6027

Scott, Walter, Sir, bart., 1771-1832. The lady of the lake... Cincinnati, OH: U. P. James [1840] 286 p. DLC. 40-6028

Scott, Walter, Sir, bart., 1771-1832. Marmion. A poem in six cantos. By Sir Walter Scott. With notes and an appendix from the lastest Edinburgh edition. With biographical sketch by William M. Rossetti. New York: A. L. Burt Company [1840] 344 p. OkGoP. 40-6029

Scott, Walter, Sir, bart., 1771-1832. The poetical works of Sir Walter Scott. With a sketch of his life, by J. W. Lake. Complete in one volume. Philadelphia, PA: J. Crissy [1840] 443 p. CoU; CSt; PPL; ViU; WShe. 40-6030

Scott, Winfield, 1786-1866. ... Infantry tactics; or, Rules for the exercise and maneuvers of the United States' infantry. New ed. By Major-General Scott, U. S. army... New York: Harper & brothers, 1840. 3 v. Ct; DLC; ICU; NRHi; ViU. 40-6031

The ... Scottish journal of intelligence and literature. Vol. 1-, Feb. 22, 1840-. New York [J. B. Cumming] 1840-. DLC; OClWHi. 40-6032

Scoutetten, Henri, 1799-1871. Memoir on the radical cure of club-foot. By H. Scoutetten... With six plates. Translated from the French. By F. Campbel Stewart... Philadelphia, PA: printed by A. Waldie, 1840. 54 p. CSt; MdBM; NNN; OClM; PPAmP. 40-6033

The scrap book; a selection of humorous stories, interesting fables, and authentic anecdotes. New York: s. l. [1840] 288 p. MB; ViU. 40-6034

Scrap book of Rhode Island history and biography. Providence, RI: s. l. [1840-70] v. RPB. 40-6035

Scribe, Augustin Eugene, 1791-1861. The school for politicians; or, Noncommittal. A comedy in five acts. New York: Carvill and Co., 1840. 179 p. CSf; IaU; MH; NBuG; PPA. 40-6036

Scripture scenes illustrated. Boston,

MA: Mass. Sabbath School Society, 1840. 82 p. DLC; MWinchrHi. 40-6037

Scudder, John, 1793-1855. Knocking at the door; an appeal to youth. New York: Pub. by the Am. Tract Society [184-?] 20 p. WHi. 40-6038

Scudder, John, 1793-1855. Letters from Dr. Scudder, of Ceylon, addressed... to the young men in the colleges and seminaries or learning in the United States of America. [New York: s. l., 184-?] p. CtY; Vi. 40-6039

Seabrook, Whitemarsh Benjamin, 1795-1855. Report of special committee... Charleston, SC: s. l., 1840. 20 p. NN. 40-6040

The seals opened; or, a voice to the Jews... Philadelphia, PA: Perkins, 1840. 365 p. MB; NjR; OO; PPDrop. 40-6041

Sears, Robert, 1810-1892. Pictorial history of the American Revolution. With a skertch of the early history of the country, the Constitution of the U. S., and a chronological index. Boston, MA: Lee & Shepard [184-?] 433 p. W-MaMar. 40-6042

Seaver, Jaems Everett, 1787-1827. Narrative of the life of Mrs. Mary Jemison... to her death at the Seneca Reservation, near Buffalo, N. Y., 1833. Rochester, NY: s. l., 1840. 35 p. NBuHi; NCastiM; NRU. 40-6043

Sedgwick, Adam, 1786-1873. A discourse on classical metaphysical, moral, and... [In Discourses on the objects and uses of science 7 literature] New York: s. l. [1840] p. DLC; MB. 40-6044

Sedgwick, Catharine Maria, 1789-1867. Live and let live; or, Domestic service illustrating. By the author of "Hope Leslie" [and] "The Linwoods. " New York: Harper & Brothers, 1840. 216 p. NcU; NjP. 40-6045

Sedgwick, Catharine Maria, 1789-1867. Means and ends; or, self-training. Boston, MA: Marsh, Capen, Lyon & Webb, 1840. 264 p. MTop; NcWsS; PFa; PU. 40-6046

Sedgwick, Catharine Maria, 1789-1867. Means and ends; or, self-training. By the author of "Redwood, " "Hope Leslie" [etc., etc.] 4th ed. Boston, MA: Marsh, Capen, Lyon & Webb, 1840. 264 p. MH; InU; NcWsS; NR; PU. 40-6047

Sedgwick, Catharine Maria, 1789-1867. The poor rich man and the rich poor man. By the author of "Hope Leslie, " "The Linwoods, " etc. New York: Harper & Brothers, 1840. MH. 40-6048

Sedgwick, Catharine Maria, 1789-1867. Stories for young persons. [Anon.] New York: Harper and Brothers, 1840. DLC; MStoc; NN. 40-6049

Sedgwick, Theodore, Jr., 1780-1839. How shall the lawyers be paid? or, some remarks upon two acts recently passed on the subject of the cost of legal proceedings. In a letter to John Anthon. New York: A. S. Gould, 1840. 31 p. MH-L; NN; NNC; PPL. 40-6050

Selby, Charles. 1802?-1863. Boots at the Swan; a farce in one act. New York: Wm. Taylor & Co. [184-?] 29 p. MH; NIC; NN. 40-6051

Selby, Charles, 1802?-1863. ... Hunting

a turtle; an original farce in one act, by Charles Selby... Philadelphia, PA: Turner [184-?] 29 p. NNC. 40-6052

Selby, Charles, 1802?-1863. ... The married rake. A farce in one act, by Charles Selby, esq. Philadelphia, PA; New York: Turner & Fisher [184-?] 25 p. DLC; MH; PksL. 40-6053

Selby, Charles, 1802?-1863. Robert Macaire; or, the two murderers. A melodrama in two acts. New York: French [184-?] 38 p. ICU; MB; NIC; NN. 40-6054

Selby, Charles, 1802?-1863. The widow's victim. A farce in one act. New York: Turner & Fisher [184-?] p. MH; NIC. 40-6055

Selden, Richard Ely, 1797-1868. The newest keepsake for 1840; containing the best account of the March of Mind. Together with the speeches, circumstances and doings of the trundlebed. Convention in session at the Marlboro Chapel, January 8, 1840. New York: S. Adams, printer, 1840. 207 p. CtHWatk; MB; MsJPED; TxDaUr. 40-6056

Select airs. Baltimore, MD; New Orleans, LA: F. D. Benteen; W. T. Mayo [184-?] 7 p. ViU. 40-6057

Seneca Nation. Memorial of a number of the chief warriors and chiefs of the six Seneca nations of Indians, praying that the actions of the Senate on thr treaty with the Seneca Indians may be suspended &c., &c., December 31, 1839. Washington, DC: Blair & Rives, 1840? 2 p. NBu. 40-6058

Sentimental songs for the lady's

songster. Philadelphia, PA: s. l. [184-?] 56-113 p. MB. 40-6059

Sergeant, John, 1779-1852. Speech of Mr. Sergeant, of Pennsylvania, on the sub-treasury bill. Delivered in the House of Representatives, June 24, 1840. Washington, DC: Printed by Gales and Seaton, 1840. 39 p. MB; MeLewB; NjP; NNC; PHi. 40-6060

Sergeant, Thomas, 1782-1860. A treatise upon the law of Pennsylvania, relative to the proceedings by foreign attachment. Second edition, with additions and improvements. Philadelphia, PA: John S. Littell, 1840. 341 p. C; IaDmD-L; LNT-L; NcD; PPB. 40-6061

Sessions, Alexander Joseph, 1809-1892. Afflictions necessary. A sermon delivered before the Crombie Street Congregation, Salem, Mass... Salem, MA: Ives & Pease, Observer Press, 1840. 24 p. CtSoP; ICMe; MWA; NjR; WHi. 40-6062

Sessions, Alexander Joseph, 1809-1892. The religious experiences of Eunice Winchester Smith... Salem, MA: Ives & Pease, 1840. 70 p. DLC. 40-6063

Sessions, John. Address delivered before the board of common school visitors of Chenango county, N. Y., at their semi-annual meeting, held at the courthouse, Norwich, June 8, 1840, by John Sessions, pastor of the Presbyterian Church in Norwich. Utica, NY: R. Northway, printer, 1840. 22 p. MBC; NjR. 40-6064

Severance, Moses. The American Manual, or, New English Reader. Consisting of exercises in reading and speaking, both in prose and poetry. Selected from the best writers. To which are added a succinct history of the colonies, from the discovery of North America to the close of the War of the Revolution, the Declaration of Independence, the Constitution of the United States, and of the State of New York. For the use of schools. By Moses Severance. Bath, NY: R. L. Underhill & Co., 1840. 300 p. MiHi; NNiaD. 40-6065

Sevier, Ambrose Hundley, 1801-1848. Speech of Mr. Sevier, of Arkansas, in Executive session, on the treaty with New York Indians, delivered in Senate, U. S., March 17, 1840. Washington, DC: Printed at the Globe Office, 1840. 15 p. MdHi; NjR; PPL; TxU. 40-6066

Sewall, Thomas, 1786-1845. Address on the effects of intemperance... New York: American Tract Society [1840] 20 p. DLC. 40-6067

Sewall, Thomas, 1787-1845. Memoir of Dr. Dodman: being an introductory lecture... by Thomas Sewell, M. D. New York: Published for the tract society of the Methodist Episcopal church, 1840. 24 p. KHi; MdHi; PHi; RPB; WHi. 40-6068

Seward, William H. Gov. Seward's message; its misrepresentations and perversions exposed. Albany, NY: s. l., 1840. 20 p. MBC; NN. 40-6069

Seward Female Seminary, Rochester, N. Y. Catalogue of the Teachers and Pupils in the Seward Female Seminary, Rochester, 1839-40. Rochester, NY: Printed by Shepard and Strong, 1840. 8 p. CSmH. 40-6070

Shakespeare, William, 1564-1616. The complete works of William Shakespeare, with Dr. Johnson's preface; a glossery and an account of each play, and a memoir of the author. New York: G. F. Cooledge and Brother, 1840? 926 p. sNN. 40-6071

Shakespeare, William, 1564-1616. The dramatic works of Shakespeare. From the text of Johnson and Stevens. Complete in one volume. Philadelphia, PA: Printed for Thomas Wardle, 1840. 1062 p. IaHi, NPla. 40-6072

Shakespeare, William, 1564-1616. The dramatic works of Shakespeare... New York: Leavitt & Allen [184-?] 828 p. OSW. 40-6073

Shakespeare, William, 1564-1616. ... Julius Caesar. A tragedy in five acts. By William Shakespeare. With the stage business, cast of characters, costumes, relative positions, etc. New York: S. French [etc., etc., 184-?] 66 p. CSt; MB. 40-6074

Shakespeare, William, 1564-1616. ... Katherine and Petruchio; or, The taming of the shrew. A comedy in three acts. By William Shakespeare. With the stage business, cast of characters, costumes, relative positions, etc. New York: S. French [etc., etc., 184-?] 34 p. CSt. 40-6075

Shakespeare, William, 1564-1616. ... King Henry IV, Part I. A tragedy in five acts. By William Shakespeare. With the stage business, cast of characters, costumes, relative positions, etc. New York: S. French [etc., etc., 184-?] 65 p. CSt; MH; RPB; ViU. 40-6076

Shakespeare, William, 1564-1616. ...
King Henry VIII. An historical play in
five acts. By William Shakespeare. With
the stage business, cast of characters, costumes, relative positions, etc. New York:
S. French [etc., etc., 184-?] 60 p. CSt. 40-
6077

Shakespeare, William, 1564-1616. ...
King Henry VIII. An historical play in
five acts. By William Shakespeare. With
the stage business, cast of characters, costumes, relative positions, etc. New York:
W. Taylor & Co. [etc., etc., 184-?] 60 p.
ViU. 40-6078

Shakespeare, William, 1564-1616. ...
King John. A tragedy in five acts. By William Shakespeare. With the stage business, cast of characters, costumes,
relative positions, etc. Also, a list of
authorities for costumes, by Charles
Kean, esq., as produced with great splendor at the Park Theatre. New York: S.
French [etc., etc., 184-?] 68 p. CSt. 40-
6079

Shakespeare, William, 1564-1616. ...
Macbeth. A tragedy in five acts. By William Shakespeare. With the stage business, cast of characters, costumes,
relative positions, etc. New York: S.
French [etc., etc., 184-?] 60 p. CSt; MB;
NN. 40-6080

Shakespeare, William, 1564-1616. ...
The merchant of Venice. A comedy in
five acts. By William Shakespeare. With
the stage business, cast of characters, costumes, relative positions, etc. New York:
S. French [etc., etc., 184-?] 63 p. MH. 40-
6081

Shakespeare, William, 1564-1616. ...
The merry wives of Windsor. A comedy

in five acts. By William Shakespeare.
With the stage business, cast of characters, costumes, relative positions, etc.
New York: S. French [etc., etc., 184-?] 71
p. MB; NNC. 40-6082

Shakespeare, William, 1564-1616. ...
Much ado about nothing. A comedy in six
acts. By William Shakespeare. With the
stage business, cast of characters, costumes, relative positions, etc. New York:
S. French [etc., etc., 184-?] 61 p. CSt. 40-
6083

Shakespeare, William, 1564-1616. ...
Othello. A tragedy in five acts. By William Shakespeare. With the stage business, cast of characters, costumes,
relative positions, etc. New York: S.
French [etc., etc., 184-?] 74 p. CSt. 40-
6084

Shakespeare, William, 1564-1616. ...
Romeo and Juliet. A tragedy in five acts.
By William Shakespeare. With the stage
business, cast of characters, costumes,
relative positions, etc. New York: S.
French [etc., etc., 184-?] 67 p. CSt. 40-
6085

Shakespeare, William, 1564-1616. ...
Twelfth night; or, What you will. A comedy in five acts. By William Shakespeare.
With the stage business, cast of characters, costumes, relative positions, etc.
New York: S. French [etc., etc., 184-?] 63
p. CSt. 40-6086

Shakespeare, William, 1564-1616. ...
The two gentlemen of Verona. A comedy
in five acts. By William Shakespeare.
With the stage business, cast of characters, costumes, relative positions, etc. As
produced at the Park Theatre by Mr. and

Mrs. Charles Kean. New York: S. French [etc., etc., 184-?] 59 p. CSt. 40-6087

Shakespeare, William, 1564-1616. Two gentlemen of Verona. Campe's edition. New York: F. Campe and Co. [1840] 71 p. MH. 40-6088

Shamokin Coal Company. A brief sketch of the peculiar advantages of the Shamokin Coal and Iron Company, situated in Northumberland County, state of Pennsylvania. Philadelphia, PA: Brown, Bicking & Guilbert, printers, 1840. 12 p. DLC; PHi; PPAN. 40-6089

Shand, Alexander. Pastoral letter to the young people... Salem, NY: Office, Washington County Post, 1840. 16 p. PPiPT; PPiXT. 40-6090

Shanks, Asbury H. A discourse. Delivered in the Methodist Episcopal Church at Selma, Ala., possibility of apostasy. Montgomery, AL: Robert Nelson, 1840. 34 p. MWo. 40-6091

Sharp, Daniel, 1783-1853. Obedience to magistrates inculcated. A discourse delivered before the ancient and honorable artillery company, June 1, 1840... By Daniel Sharp... Boston, MA: Gould, Kendall and Lincoln, 1840. 28 p. Ct; ICU; MH; NCH; WHi. 40-6092

Sharp, Daniel, 1783-1853. Sermon before the ancient and honorable Artillery Company... by Daniel Sharp. Boston, MA: Gould, Kendall and Lincoln, 1840. 28 p. MiD-B. 40-6093

Sharpe Family [pseud.] The Scimitar. Containing well-tempered reflections, by the Sharpe family. Boston, MA: s. l., 1840. 32 p. No Loc. 40-6094

Shattuck, H. C. Miscellaneous poems, by Mrs. H. C. Shattuck, Andover. Lowell, MA: Aleijah Watson, printer, 1840. 48 p. MabD; MAnHi; MLow. 40-6095

Shaw, Oliver J. Metacorn's grand march. [For the piano forte] Boston, MA: Bradlee, 1840. 3 p. MB. 40-6096

Shaw, Oliver J. There's nothing true but heav'n. Poetry from Moore's sacred melodies. Music by O. Shaw. Baltimore, MD: F. D. Benteen [1840] 2 p. ViU. 40-6097

Shelley, Mary Wollstonecroft [Godwin] 1797-1881. Lives of the most eminent French writers. By Mrs. Shelley [and others] In two volumes. Philadelphia, PA: Lea and Blanchard, 1840. 2 v. KyHi; OrU; RNR; ScU; Vi. 40-6098

Shelley, Percy Bysshe, 1792-1822. Essays, letters from abroad... By Percy Bysshe Shelley... In 2 Vols. Philadelphia, PA: Lea and Blanchard, 1840. 2 v. ArBl; LNH; MdBD; PPA; ViL. 40-6099

Shepard, Charles Upham, 1804-1886. Reports of Professor Charles U. Shepard and Forrest Shepard, Esq., respecting mineral deposits in the states of Missouri and Illinois. Accompanied by a map. Boston, MA: s. l., 1840? 12 p. MB; MH-BA; MoSHi. 40-6100

Shepard, Daniel. An oration. Delivered at Delhi on the sixty-fourth anniversary of American independence, July 4, 1840. By Rev. Daniel Shepard, A. M. Published by request. Delhi: Printed by Anthony M. Paine, 1840. 12 p. NGH. 40-6101

Shepard, Isaac Fitzgerald, 1816-1889. Bubbles from Castalia. By I. F. Shepard.

Boston, MA: Whipple and Damrell, 1840. 160 p. ICU; MB; MNe; MoSM; TxU. 40-6102

Shepard, James Biddle. Speech delivered at the great Republican meeting, in the county of Granville, in the presidential canvass of 1840. Raleigh, NC: Standard, 1840. 37 p. NcU. 40-6103

Shepard, John. The science of double-entry bookkeeping simplified... Laningsburgh: Printed by W. B. Harkness, 1840. 216 p. DLC; IU; NNMer. 40-6104

Sheppard, William, d.1675. Sheppard's touchstone of common assurances; or, A plain and familiar treatise, opening the learning of the common assurances or conveyances of the kingdom. From the last London ed... also, an enlargement of the text &c. by the addition of various criticisms... by Richard Preston... Philadelphia, PA: Littell, 1840-41. 2 v. CoU; IU; KyLxT; OO; PU-L. 40-6105

Shepherd, William, 1768-1847. Memoir of the last illness and death of William Tharp Buchanan, esq....by the late William Shepherd, esq. Philadelphia, PA: Presbyterian Board of publication, 1840. 116 p. CtHC; GDecCT; NcMHi; OWoC; ViRut. 40-6106

Sherman, Thomas. Divine breathings; or, a pious soul thirsting after Christ. In one hundred meditations. Lowell, MA: Published at the Office of Zion's Banner, A. Watson, printer, 1840. 110 p. MBrZ; MLit; MLow. 40-6107

Sherwood, Adiel. Address delivered before the trustees, faculty, and students, of Mercer University, Penfield, Georgia,

on the 7th Feb., 1840. Washington, GA: printed by M. J. Kappel, 1840. 12 p. MH; NHC-S; PPPrHi. 40-6108

Sherwood, Henry Hall. The motive power of the human system... New York: Printed by J. W. Bell, 1840. 120 p. CtHT; NNNAM. 40-6109

Sherwood, Mary Martha Butt, 1775-1851. History of little Henry and his bearer. New York: Published by B. Waugh and T. Mason for the Sunday School Union of the Methodist Episcopal Church at the Conference Office, J. Collard, printer, 1840. 48 p. OO; WHi. 40-6110

Sherwood, Mary Martha Butt, 1775-1851. The lofty and the lowly way. By Mrs. Sherwood. New York: M. W. Dodd, 1840. 99 p. NbOP; OO. 40-6111

Sherwood, Mary Martha Butt, 1775-1851. Memoirs of Sergeant Dale... Philadelphia, PA: s. l. [184-?] p. MB. 40-6112

Sherwood, Reuben. The reviewer reviewed; or, Doctor Brownlee, versus the Bible; versus the Catholic church; versus the fathers, ancient and modern; versus his own creed; versus himself. By Philalethes... Poughkeepsie, NY: Jackson & Schram, 1840. 81 p. MBC; MH; NGH; NNC; NNUT. 40-6113

Shillitoe, Thomas, 1754?-1836. A brief sketch of the life and religious labours of Thomas Shillitoe. Philadelphia, PA: s. l. [184-?] 40 p. MH. 40-6114

Shinn, Asa, 1781-1853. On the benevolence and rectitude of the Supreme Being, by Asa Shinn... Baltimore, MA; Philadelphia, PA: Book committee of the Methodist Protestant church; James Kay, jun. & brothers, 1840. 403 p. CtMW; GEU-T; MdBS; PPiW; ScCOT. 40-6115

Short, Charles Wilkins, 1794-1863. A supplementary catalogue of the plants of Kentucky. By Professors Short and Peter. Louisville, KY: s. l., 1840. 6 p. MyDC; OCN; PPAN. 40-6116

A short abridgement of the Christian Doctrine. Newly revised and augmented for the use of the Catholic Church in the Diocese of Boston. First published with the approbation of the Rt. Rev. Benedict, Bishop of Boston. New York: Published by John Doyle, 1840. 64 p. MWA. 40-6117

Short biographies of distinguished men of modern times. New York: s. l., 1840. 2 v. UU. 40-6118

A short directory for religious societies. Drawn up by appointment of the Reformed Presbytery for the particular use of the several socities or christian people under their inspection at the desire of the said socieities. An address to them. New York: John W. Oliver, printer, 1840. 46 p. NBuG; NcMHi. 40-6119

Short method with Universaliam. Accomplised by simply proving the absolute eternity of the words "Everlasting" and "Forever. " Written for and published by a friend of the Universalist. New York: printed by Henry Spear, 1840. 24 p. MBC; MMet-Hi; MNtcA. 40-6120

A short narrative of the horrid massacre in Boston perpetrated... fifth day of March, 1770, by the soldiers of the 29th regiment... Printed by order of the town... and sold by Edes and Gill, 1770. Republished with notes and illustrations. New York: Re-published by Doggett, 1840. 122 p. PPFrankI. 40-6121

Shurtleff College, Upper Alton, Ill. Catalogue of the officers and students of Shurtleff College of Alton, Ill., and of Alton Theological Seminary. For the year ending July, 1840. Alton, IL: printed at Parks' Job Office, 1840. 16 p. IHi; MB; MH. 40-6122

Signourney, Lydia Howard Huntley, 1791-1865. The boy's reading book; in prose and poetry for schools... New York: Taylor & Clement, 1840. 321 p. KyLo; MLow; MnU; MS. 40-6123

Signourney, Lydia Howard Huntley, 1791-1865. The Christian keepsake... Edited by Mrs. L. H. Sigourney. New York: s. l., 184-? 262 p. IU. 40-6124

Signourney, Lydia Howard Huntley, 1791-1865. The Girls' reading book in prose and poetry. For schools. By Mrs. L. H. Sigourney. Ed. 12. New York: published by Taylor & Clement, 1840. 243 p. WyHi. 40-6125

Signourney, Lydia Howard Huntley, 1791-1865. Letters to mothers, by Mrs. S. H. Sigourney. Fourth edition. New York: Harper & Brothers, 1840. 297 p. GA; ICMcHi; NhPet; PPL-R; WDep. 40-6126

Signourney, Lydia Howard Huntley, 1791-1865. Letters to young ladies. 6th edition. New York, 1840. Union Potomac Company. Charters of the Union Potomac Company, and the

Union Company, with a description of their coal and iron mines, situate in Hampshire County, Virginia. Baltimore: Printed by J. Murphy, 1840. 52 p. DLC; ViU. 40-6127

Signourney, Lydia Howard Huntley, 1791-1865. The religious souvenir for Christmas and New Years presents; edited by Mrs. L. H. Sigourney. New York: Leavitt & Allen [1840?] p. KU; NAnge; OO; PPM; WU. 40-6128

Signourney, Lydia Howard Huntley, 1791-1865. Sketches... Amherst, MA: J. S. & C. Adams, 1840. 216 p. CSfCP; ICU; MiOC; MPiB; WGr. 40-6129

Silver Lake waltz. Arranged for the piano forte. Baltimore, MD; New Orleans, LA: F. D. Benteen; W. T. Mayo [184-?] 2 p. MB; ViU. 40-6130

Silvestre de Sacy, Antoine Isaac, Baron. Principles of general grammar. Adapted to the capacity of youth and proper to serve as an introduction to the study of languages... 3rd American from the 5th French edition. New York: s. l. [184-?] p. MH. 40-6131

Sime, William. History of the Inquisition, from the establishment till the present time. By William Sime. 1st American ed. Philadelphia, PA: Presbyterian Board of Publication. Printed by Wm. S. Martien, 1840. 243 p. ArCC; NcCq; PeaL; TxU. 40-6132

Simmonds, Peter Lund, 1814-1897. The arctic regions; a narrative of discovery and adventure. New York: s. l., 1840. No Loc. 40-6133

Simmons, Charles, d. 1856. A Scripture manual, containing four hundred and thirty-five questions on theological and moral subjects, alphabetically arranged, designed to facilitate the finding of proof texts. By Charles Simmons... Boston, MA; Providence, RI: Crocker & Brewster; I. Wilcox, 1840. 290 p. IRA; NeSalL; NNUT; OO; WHi. 40-6134

Simmons, George Frederick. Two sermons on the Kind Treatment and on the Emancipation of Slaves, preached at Mobile, on Sunday the 10th, and Sunday the 17th of May, 1840. With a Prefactory Statement. Boston, MA: William Crosby & Co., 1840. 30 p. A-Ar; CtSoP; MHi; RPB; TxU. 40-6135

Simms, William Gilmore, 1806-1870. Border beagles; a tale of Mississippi. By the author of "Richard Hurdis"... [1st ed.] Philadelphia, PA: Carey and Hart, 1840. 2 v. ICU; KU; MWA; PU; RPB. 40-6136

Simms, William Gilmore, 1806-1870. Confession; or, The Blind Heart, a domestic story... [anon.] The history of South Carolina, from its first European discovery to its erection into a republic: with a supplementary chronicle of events to the present time... Charleston, SC: S. Babcock & co., 1840. 355 p. AB; LU; NcD; ScC; ViRU. 40-6137

Simpson, Matthew, 1811-1884. Address delivered upon the Author's Installation as president of the Indiana Asbury University, September 16, A. D. 1840. By Rev. M. Simpson... Indianapolis, IN: Published by the Board of Trustees, printed by W. Stacy, 1840. 40 p. CSmH; ICJ; IU; In; InGrD; InU. 40-6138

Sinclair, Catherine, 1800-1864. Scotland and the Scotch: or, The western circuit. By Catherine Sinclair... Dedicated to the Highland society. New York: D. Appleton & Co., 1840. 346 p. CtHC; InCW; NBuG; PU; RPA. 40-6139

Sinclair, Catherine, 1800-1864. Shetland and the Shetlanders; or, The northern circuit. New York: D. Appleton & Co., 1840. 348 p. CU; ICMe; OCY; PPA; VtU. 40-6140

Sismondi, Jean Charles Leonard de. History of the Italian Republics; being a view of the rise, progress, and fall of Italian freedom. New edition. New York: Harper, 1840. 300 p. CSfMA; MB; NP; MoSW; NUt. 40-6141

Skinner, Dolphus. Read, Pause, Digest, Consider. The Final Salvation of All Mankind clearly demonstrated by the united voice of Reason and Revelation. Second edition. Utica, NY: Printed by C. C. P. Grosh, 1840. 36 p. MMeT; MMeT-Hi; NUT; NUt. 40-6142

Skinner, Otis Ainsworth. Child's catechism. Boston, MA: Abel Tompkins, 1840. No Loc. 40-6143

Skinner, Otis Ainsworth. The theory of William Miller, concerning the end of the world in 1843, utterly exploded. With some other essays on the same subject. Boston, MA: T. Whittemore, 1840. 210 p. MH; NCaS; PPL; VtU; WHi. 40-6144

Slade, William, b. 1786. Speech of Mr. Slade, of Vermont, on the right side of petition; the power of Congress to abolish slavery and the slave trade in the District of Columbia. Washington, DC: Gale & Seaton, 1840. 64 p. KyDC. 40-6145

Slave holding a disqualification for church fellowship. A letter to Joshua L. Wilson and the First Presbyterian Church, Cincinnati, by "A brother." S. l.: n. pr. [1840] 8 p. WHi. 40-6146

Smedley, Edward, 1788-1836. Sketches from Venetian history. New York: Harper & Bros., 1840. 2 v. CLCM; LNH; MCli; MSwan; Nh-Hi. 40-6147

Smellie, William, 1740-1795. The Philosophy of natural history. By William Smellie... With an introduction by John Ware, M. D... Boston, MA: Hilliard, Gray, and Company, 1840. 327 p. CSt; GAU; MH; OU; PU. 40-6148

Smiles, Samuel, 1812-1904. Self help. With illustrations of character and conduct... Boston, MA: Published by Ticknor and Fields, 1840. 408 p. PPF. 40-6149

Smiley, Thomas Tucker, d. 1879. A complete key to Smiley's New Federal Calculation, or Scholar's Assistant. By Thomas T. Smiley. Philadelphia, PA: Grigg & Elliott, publishers, 1840. 177 p. NcCQ. 40-6150

Smiley, Thomas Tucker, d. 1879. The New Federal Calculation, or Scholar's Assistant... Philadelphia, PA: Grigg & Elliott, 1840. 180 p. InU. 40-6151

Smith, Benjamin Bosworth. Facts and opinions of the fathers. A charge to the clergy of... Kentucky... by Rt. Rev. B. B. Smith... Lexington, KY: J. Virden, 1840. 14 p. ICU; MdBD; NcD; NNG; RPB. 40-6152

Smith, Daniel, 1806-1852. Life of

David. New York: Mason, 1840. 160 p. ICa; OO. 40-6153

Smith, Daniel, 1806-1852. The Life of Esther. Revised by the editors. New York: Published by T. Mason and G. Lane, 1840. 126 p. DLC; IaScW; NNMHi; TNT. 40-6154

Smith, Daniel, 1806-1852. The life of John the Baptist. Revised by the editors. New York: T. Mason and G. Lane, for the Sunday school union of the Methodist Episcopal Church, 1840. 103 p. DLC. 40-6155

Smith, Daniel, 1806-1852. The Life of Jonah. By Rev. Daniel Smith... New York: Published by T. Mason and G. Lane, 1840. 80 p. DLC. 40-6156

Smith, Daniel, 1806-1852. The Life of Joshua... New York: Published by T. Mason and G. Lane for the Sunday School Union of the Methodist Episcopal Church, 1840. 200 p. CtMW; DLC; NNMHi. 40-6157

Smith, Daniel, 1806-1852. The Life of St. Peter, Rev. Daniel Smith... New York: Published by T. Mason and G. Lane, 1840. 132 p. DLC. 40-6158

Smith, Daniel, 1806-1852. The life of Sampson. Revised by the editors. New York: T. Mason and G. Lane, for the Sunday school union of the Methodist Episcopal Church, 1840. 94 p. DLC; ODW. 40-6159

Smith, Daniel, 1806-1852. The Life of Solomon, King of Israel. By Rev. Daniel Smith... New York: Published by T. Mason and G. Lane, 1840. 168 p. DLC. 40-6160

Smith, Daniel, 1806-1852. The Life of the Apostle John... Revised by the editors. New York: Published by T. Mason and G. Lane, 1840. 222 p. CtMW; DLC. 40-6161

Smith, Eli, 1801-1857. An address on the missionary character... By Eli Smith. Boston, MA: printed by Perkins & Marvin, 1840. 34 p. CtHC; ICP; MeB; MWA; NjR. 40-6162

Smith, Eli, 1801-1857. The missionary character. An address delivered in the Theological Seminary in New Haven, April 1, 1840. New Haven, CT: B. L. Hamlen, pr., 1840. 38 p. IaGG; MB; MeB; MWA; TxU. 40-6163

Smith, Elias. The life, conversion, preaching, travels and sufferings of Elias Smith. Written by himself... Boston, MA: s. l., 1840. MB; MH; MMal. 40-6164

Smith, James, of Sing Sing, N. Y. The winter of 1840 in St. Croix, with an excursion to Tortola and St. Thomas. By James Smith, esq. New York: printed for the author, 1840. 124 p. ICU; MdBE; MLow; NBuG; NNS. 40-6165

Smith, James. A sermon. Delivered on the occasion of the death of the Rev. Joseph Rusling, in the Fifth Street Methodist Episcopal Church, Philadelphia, July 17, 1839. By the Rev. James Smith. Philadelphia, PA: Published by J. Harnstead, 1840. 34 p. ICBB. 40-6166

Smith, James, 1789-1850. Remarks on thorough draining & deep ploughing. Stirling, MA: Drummond, 1840. MB. 40-6167

Smith, Jerome Van Crowninshield,

1800-1879. The class book of anatomy, explanatory of the first principles of human organization, as the basis of physical education, designed for schools and families. 4th ed. Boston, MA: R. S. Davis [et. al.] 1840. 286 p. CtHWatk; OCGHM; PPCP. 40-6168

Smith, Jerome van Crowninshield, 1800-1879. A condensed historical examination of the wars of the Indians in past and present times, within the boundaries of the United States. With an appendix embracing the researches of antiquariums in relation to the first inhabitants of America. Designed for youth. Boston, MA: G. Clarke, 1840. 304 p. DLC; DSI; Nh-Hi; NN; TxU. 40-6169

Smith, John Augustine. Select discourses on the functions of the nervous system in opposition to phrenology, materialism, and atheism. New York: D. Appleton and company, 1840. 210 p. IEG; MWiW; NNNAM; PPCP; WBelo-C. 40-6170

Smith, John Calvin. Map of the State of New York showing railroads, canals, and stage roads. New York: J. Diturnell, 1840. 1 p. MH-BA; PHi; PPL. 40-6171

Smith, John Cross, 1803-1878. A sermon delivered at Lisbon, Maryland, October 14, 1839, by John C. Smith... at the ordination of Rev. Thomas L. Hammer by the Presbytery of the District of Columbia. Together with the charges delivered on the occasion by Rev. William McLain & Rev. John Mines. Washington, DC: Printed by J. Gideon, Jr., 1840. 20 p. DLC; PPPrHi. 40-6172

Smith, John Cross, 1803-1878. Shall we build? A sermon, delivered March 1st,

1840, in view of building a new church edifice. Washington, DC: Gideon, 1840. 16 p. Ct; MoWgT; MWA; NCH; PPPrHi. 40-6173

Smith, John N. Ramanzo, the conscience stricken brigand. A tragic play in five acts. By John N. Smith. New York: Printed for the Author, 1840. 74 p. NBuG. 40-6174

Smith, John Pye, 1774-1851. The Congrgational lecture. Sixth series: Scripture and Geology. By the Rev. Dr. Pye Smith, D. D., F. G. S., Divinity Tutor in the Protestant Dissenting College at Homerton... on the relation between the Holy Sciprtures and some parts of geological science. New York: D. Appleton & Co., 1840. 364 p. CU; KyU; MB; NNUT; PPA. 40-6175

Smith, John Pye, 1774-1851. Holy Scriptures and... geology. New York: D. Appleton & Co., 1840. 364 p. NN. 40-6176

Smith, John Pye, 1774-1851. On the relation between the Holy Scriptures and some parts of geological science. By John Pye Smith... New York: D. Appleton & co., 1840. 364 p. CU; LNB; MeBaT; NNF; OO. 40-6177

Smith, John Pye, 1774-1851. Relation between the Holy Scriptures and some parts of geological science. New York: D. Appleton & co., 1840. InCW; KyDC; MB; MdW; NbCrD; O. 40-6178

Smith, John William, 1809-1845. A selection of leading cases on various branches of the law, with notes. By John William Smith, Esq. Philadelphia, PA:

John S. Litell, 1840. 2 v. In-SC; LnL-L; MdUL; MsU; W. 40-6179

Smith, Oliver Hampton, 1794-1859. Speech on the report and resolutions relative to the non-assumption of state debts. In the Senate of the United States, Feb. 12, 1840, by Oliver Hampton Smith. [Washington, DC: s. l., 1840] 16 p. DLC; InU; KSalW; OClWHi. 40-6180

Smith, Penelope. A place in thy memory dearest. A favorite ballad. Sung by Mrs. Wood. Written by the author of "The Collegians." Composed and arranged by Miss Penelope Smith. Boston, MA: Oliver Ditson [184-?] 2 p. ViU. 40-6181

Smith, Penelope. A place in thy memory dearest. Song. The words by the author of "The Collegians." Composed by Miss Smith. Philadelphia, PA: J. C, Smith [184-?] 3p. ViU. 40-6182

Smith, Perry. Speech in opposition to the proposition of Mr. C. Johnson, of Tennessee, at the election of 1838. Washington, DC: s. l., 1840. 21 p. CtHC; PHi. 40-6183

Smith, Roswell Chamberlain, 1797-1875. Atlas. Designed to accompany the geography. Hartford, CT: Spalding and Storrs [1840?] p. CtY. 40-6184

Smith, Roswell Chamberlain, 1797-1875. Atlas. Designed to accompany the geography. New York: Paine & Burgess [184-?] p. ViU. 40-6185

Smith, Roswell Chamberlain, 1797-1875. English grammar on the productive system... A method... recently adopted. Hartford, CT: Spalding & Storrs, 1840. 192 p. DLC; MH. 40-6186

Smith, Roswell Chamberlain, 1797-1875. English grammar on the productive system... Designed for schools and academies, by Roswell C. Smith. One hundred fifieth ed. Philadelphia, PA: W. Marshall & Co., 1840. 192 p. DLC. 40-6187

Smith, Roswell Chamberlain, 1797-1875. English grammar on the productive system. One hundred fifty-fifth sixtieth ed. Philadelphia, PA: Marshall, Williams and Butler, 1840. 192 p. MH. 40-6188

Smith, Roswell Chamberlain, 1797-1875. English grammar on the productive system. A method of instruction recently adopted in Germany and Switzerland. Designed for schools and academies. By Roswell C. Smith... One hundred and sixtieth ed. Philadelphia, PA: Marshall, Williams and Butler, 1840. 192 p. INormN; MB; MH; PLFM; PPW; VtMidb. 40-6189

Smith, Roswell Chamberlain, 1797-1875. Geography on the productive system for schools, academies, and families. By Roswell C. Smith. New York: Published by Cady & Burgess, 1840. 312 p. PAtM; ViHaI. 40-6190

Smith, Roswell Chamberlain, 1797-1875. A key to the "Practical and mental arithmetic... "By Roswell C. Smith. Hartford, CT: Published by John Paine, 1840. 168 p. Ct; MeHi; MH; MLY; NNC; PPM. 40-6191

Smith, Roswell Chamberlain, 1797-1875. Practical and mental arithmetic, on a new plan, in which mental arithmetic is combined with the use of the slate, containing a complete system for all practical purposes. Stereotyped edition, revised and enlarged. St. Louis: S. W. Meech, 1840. 284 p. ICHi. 40-6192

Smith, Roswell Chamberlain, 1797-1875. Practical and mental arithmetic, on a new plan, in which mental arithmetic is combined with the use of the slate, containing a complete system for all practical purposes. 51st edition, revised and enlarged. Hartford: Spaulding and Storrs, 1840. 284 p. IU. 40-6193

Smith, Roswell Chamberlain, 1797-1875. Smith's geography. Geography on the productive system... By Roswell C. Smith. Hartford, CT: Spalding and Storrs, 1840. 312 p. MB; MH; MoS; NeGC; NNC; PU. 40-6194

Smith, Roswell Chamberlain, 1797-1875. Smith's new arithmetic; arithmetic on the productive system. Accompanied by a key and cubical blocks, by Roswell C. Smith, author of "Practical and Mental Arithmetic, " "The Productive Grammar, " "The Productive Geography, " &c., &c. Hartford, CT: D. Burgess and Spaulding & Storres, 1840. 386 p. DLC; ICBB. 40-6195

Smith, S. R. Pocket manual; containing selections from the Scriptures in proof of the salvation of all mankind. To which is added a brief explanation of several Scripture terms. By S. R. Smith. Albany, NY: printed by J. Munsell, 1840. 59 p. MMeT-Hi. 40-6196

Smith, Stephen Sanford, 1797-. Power from on high, a sermon, read before the Suffolk South Association, at their meeting, Jan. 14, 1840. Boston, MA: D. S. King, 1840. 23 p. CtHCl ICU; MeB; MWA; NNUT. 40-6197

Smith, Sydney, 1771-1845. The spinning wheel. La fileuse pour piano. Boston, MA: Ditson & Co. [184-?] 11 p. MB. 40-6198

Smith, Thomas Laurens, 1797-1882. A Historical Address... centennial anniversary of the settlement of Windham, by Thomas Laurens Smith. Portland: Arthur Shirley, printer, 1840. 32 p. DLC; MB; MeHi; Nh-Hi. 40-6199

Smith, Thomas Mather. A Discourse delivered at the North Congregational Church, New Bedford, May 12, 1840. At the funeral of Mrs. Esther Holmes, wife of the Rev. Sylvester Holmes. By Thomas M. Smith. New Bedford, MA: Printed by Banjamin Lindsey, 1840. 18 p. MBC; MBD; MNBedf; PPL; RPB. 40-6200

Smith, Truman, 1791-1884. New Jersey election. Speech of Mr. Smith, of Connecticut, in opposition to the proposition of Mr. C. Johnson of Tennessee, to instruct the Committee on elections "To report forthwith which five of the ten individuals claiming seats from the state of New Jersey received the greatest number of votes, " at the election of 1838... Delivered in the House of Representatives, February 25 and 26, 1840. Washington, DC: Gales and Seaton, 1840. 21 p. CU; MiD-B; MWA; NjR; VtBrt. 40-6201

Smith, W. F. The re-opening of the Tennessee River... Wilmington, DE: s. l. [184?] p. MB. 40-6202

Smith, Whiteford. A sermon on the occasion of the centenary of Wesleyan Methodism, preached in the Methodist Church, Athens, Ga., on the 25th Oct.

1839. [S. l.: s. l., 1840] 24 p. NcD; ScU. 40-6203

Smith, William Henry, 1806-1872. ... The drunkard; or, The fallen saved. A moral domestic drama in five acts. Adapted by W. H. Smith. With the stage business, cast of characters, costumes, relative positions, etc. New York: S. French [184-?] 64 p. CSt; IEN; MB; NIC; PU. 40-6204

Smith, William Henry, d. 1860. Review of that portion of the ninth section of Presidents Wayland's valuable treatise on the limitations of human responsibilities, in which he gives his views of our duty as citizens of the U. S., in relation to the slavery question. Providence, RI: n. pr., 1840. 20 p. ICN; NcD; NNC; RPB; TNF. 40-6205

Smith, William Henry, d. 1860. The similarity of Washington and Harrison as to the circumstances of their early lives, traits of character, kinds of talents, and the kind of services rendered their country. Traced from the most authentic sources of information. Providence, RI: Printed by Knowles and Vose, 1840. 16 p. CSmH; RPB. 40-6206

Smithville Seminary, Providence, R. I. Catalogue of the officers and students of Smithville Seminary, from the time it commenced operation, October 14, 1840, up to the end of the Summer Term, August 13, 1841, embracing the terms and one half. Providence, RI: Printed by H. H. Brown, 184?. 16 p. RHi; RPB. 40-6207

Smithville Seminary, Scituate, R. I. Stock and Transfer book, 1840-44.

Scituate, RI: s. l., 1840-44. 39 p. RPB. 40-6208

Smollett, Tobias George, 1721-1771. The history of England, from the Revolution in 1688 to the death of George the Second. Designed as a continuation of Hume. By T. Smollett, M. D. Philadelphia, PA: M'Carthy & Davis, 1840. 967 p. CU; DAU; IU; OClW. 40-6209

Smolnikar, Andreas Bernardus, 1795-1869. Treatise on the work has now appeared in the German language in three volumes complete, and of which the third volume has the following title: "Memorable events in the life of Andreas Bernardus Smolnikar. " New York: Printed with stereotype, 1840. 24 p. MH. 40-6210

Smyth, Thomas, 1808-1873. A Form of public Christian profession... Rev. Thomas Smyth... Charleston, SC: published by the Publication Fund of the Second Presbyterian Church, printed by B. B. Hussey, 1840. 47 p. CSansS; MBC; PPPrHi. 40-6211

Smyth, Thomas, 1808-1873. The last Charleston Union Presbytery; the occasion of its division fairly stated, and the action of Presbytery fully justified. By the Rev. Thomas Smyth. Charleston, SC: Observer Office Press, 1840. 80 p. CSmH; GDecCT; PPPrHi; ViRut. 40-6212

Smyth, Thomas, 1808-1873. Solace for bereaved parents; or, Infants die to live. With a historical account of the doctrine of infant salvation. By the Rev. Thomas Smyth... Charleston, SC: B. B. Hussey, 1840. 220 p. GDecCT. 40-6213

Smythies, Harriet Maria [Gordon] 1838-1883. Cousin Geoffrey, the old bachelor. A novel. Philadelphia, PA: Lea & Blanchard, 1840. 2 v. MBL; MH; OU. 40-6214

Snell, Thomas, 1774-1862. A conference between Iota and Omega, upon the mode of Christian baptism... sermon... Delivered March 8, 1840. Brookfield: E. & L. Merriam, 1840. 28 p. MBC. 40-6215

Snow, Erastus, 1818-1888. E. Snow's reply to the self-styled Philanthropist, of Chester County. [S. l.: s. l., 184-?] 16 p. MH. 40-6216

Snow, P. H. The American reader: containing selections in prose, poetry and dialogue... By P. H. Snow. Hartford, CT; Boston, MA; New York: Spalding and Storrs; Gould, Kindall and Lincoln; F. J. Huntington and co., 1840. MHad; NNC; TxU-T. 40-6217

Snow, P. H. The American reader: containing selections in prose, poetry and dialogue... Designed for the use of advanced classes in public schools, high schools, and academies. By P. H. Snow [and J. H. Temple] Hartford, CT: Spalding and Storrs, 1840. 324 p. CtHWatk; MH; MNBedf; MWHi; NCH. 40-6218

Snow, Theodore W. Address delivered before the New Bedford Port Society for the Moral Improvement of Seamen, at an adjournment of their annual meeting, November 7th, 1839. By Rev. Theodore W. Snow. New Bedford, MA: Printed by Banjamin Lindsay, 1840. 23 p. MNBedf. 40-6219

Social Fire Society. Constitution, Social Fire Society. Worcester, MA: Lewis Metcalf, printer, 1840. 12 p. WMWHi. 40-6220

Social Reform Society. Address to the Citizens of Rhode Island who are denied the right of suffrage. [New York: s. l., 1840] 8 p. MB. 40-6221

Society for Propogating the Gospel Among the Indians. A report of the Select Committee... November 5, 1840. Boston, MA: Torrey & Blair, printers, 1840. 24 p. CtHWatk; NBLiHi; WHi. 40-6222

Society Hill Library Society. Catalogue of books belonging to the Society Hill Library Society, 1840. Charleston, SC: Printed by A. E. Miller, 1840. 23 p. NcU. 40-6223

Society of the Sons of St. George, Philadelphia, Pa. Charter and by-laws... together with an historical sketch of the origin and progress of the society, list of officers, members, &c. Philadelphia, PA: Haswell, 1840. 54 p. IU; PHi; PPAmP; PPL-R. 40-6224

Sola, Charles Michael Alexis, b. 1786. The moonlit bower. Sung by Madame Vestris. Composed by C. M. Sola. New York: E. Riley [184-?] 3 p. ViU. 40-6225

Soldier's pocket-bible. Issued for the use of the Army of Oliver Cromwell, A. D. 1643. New York: Published by the American Tract Society [184-?] 32 p. WHi. 40-6226

Solomon's temple & grand sweeper. [Ballad] Boston, MA: s. l. [184-?] p. MB. 40-6227

Some account of Hannah H-----, deceased late assistant matron of Magdalen Asylum of Philadelphia. Philadelphia, PA: Kite, 1840. 11 p. No Loc. 40-6228

Somerset, Charles A. Zelina; or, the triumphs of the Greeks. A grand warlike Grecian drama in three acts. New York: S. French [184-?] 27 p. MB. 40-6229

Somerset County, N. J. Reports and surveys of the mining lands, townships of Bedminster, Somerset County, New Jersey. New York: Narine & Co. 's Print, 1840. 20 p. NNC. 40-6230

Songs for the people; or, Tippecanoe Melodies, original and selected. New York: J. P. Giffing, 1840. DLC; ICN; MB. 40-6231

Sonntagsschul Gesangbuchlein Herausgegeben von der Salems Sonntagsschul Gesellschaft in den Nordlichen Freiheiten von Philadelphia... Chambersburg, PA: Gedruckt in der Druckerei der Christlichen Zeitschrift, 1840. 228, 7 p. MoWgT. 40-6232

Sons of Temperance minstrel. Philadelphia, PA: Torr [184-?] 33, [1] p. MB. 40-6233

Sons of Temperance of North America. Grand Division of Virginia. Constitution... [Richmond, VA?: s. l. [184-?] 20 p. Vi. 40-6234

Sophocles, Evangelinus Apostolides, 1807-1883. A Greek grammar. For the use of learners... 2d ed. Hartford, CT; New York: H. Huntington, Jun.; F. J.

Huntington and Company, 1840. 284 p. CU; MB; MH; MnS; NNC. 40-6235

Sophocles, Evangelinus Apostolides, 1807-1883. A Greek grammar. For the use of learners. By E. A. Sophocles, A. M. 3d ed. Hartford, CT: H. Huntington, Jun. [etc., etc.] 1840. 284 p. ICU; MH; NN. 40-6236

Sophocles. Sophocles. Translated by Thomas Francklin, D. D. New York: Harper and brothers, 1840. 343 p. ICU; KMK; MH; OCX; PMy. 40-6237

Soule, Pierre, 1801-1870. Quelques notes prises pendant la plaidoirie de Mr. Soule, daus laffaire de la municipalite No. 2, contre La Campagnie de la Presse a Coton, de la Nouvelle-Orleans. New Orleans, LA: Impreme par Brusle & Lesseps, 1840. 42 p. L; MH-L. 40-6238

South Carolina. Court of Appeals. Cases argued and determined in the Court of Appeals of South Carolina [1839-1840] by L. Cheves. Charleston, SC: s. l., 1840-. v. Ct; F-SC; LNL-L; PU-L; Tx-SC. 40-6239

South Carolina. General Assembly. Reports on the Free School System to the General Assembly of South Carolina at the regular session of 1839. Printed by order of the Legislature. Charleston, SC: A. H. Pemberton, state printer, 1840. 88 p. CtHT-W; DHEW; NcD; ScU; TxU. 40-6240

South Carolina. General Assembly. House. Committee on the Military. The uniform of the militia of South Carolina as prescribed by the General Assembly at its regular session of 1839. Printed by order of the Legislature. Charleston, SC:

A. H. Pemberton, state printer, 1840. 20 p. NcD; NcWfC; NjR; ScC. 40-6241

South Carolina. Medical College. Annual announcement of the trustees and faculty of the Medical College of the State of South Carolina for 1840-41. Charleston, SC: Printed by Burges & James, 1840. 15 p. NcU. 40-6242

South Carolina. Medical College. Catalogue of the officers and students, 1839-40. Charleston, SC: s. l. [1840] 8 p. MHi. 40-6243

South Cove Corporation, Boston. Catalogue of 556 lots of land and 8 wharves in South Cove, with numbers, dimensions, contents and minimum price... affixed to each lot respectively. To be sold at auction. Boston: Crocker and Brewster, 1840. 26 p. DLC; MB; MH-BA; MMal; WHi.. 40-6244

South Cove Corporation, Boston. Catalogue of lots... from which purchases may make selection at auction, November 2, 1840. Boston: Crocker and Brewster, 1840. 8 p. DLC; MB; MH-BA. 40-6245

Southgate, Horatio, 1812-1894. Narrative of a tour through Armenia, Kurdistan, Persia, and Mesopotamia, with an introduction, and occasional observations upon the condition of Mohammedanism and Christianity in those countries. By the Rev. Horatio Southgate. New York: D. Appleton & co., 1840. 2 v. CtHC; IaU; LNT; OO; PPA. 40-6246

Southgate, Horatio, 1812-1894. A tour through Armenia, Persia, and Mesopotamia. The condition of Moham-

medanism and Christianity in these countries. New York: D. Appleton & Co., 1840. 2 v. IaFd; Md; MLen; OClW; UU. 40-6247

Southwark, Pa. Protestant Episcopal Mission Church. Parish statistics for the Protestant Episcopal Mission Church of the Evangelists, Southwark, 1840-41... Opened in Christian Street, March 11, 1837 - the Congregation removed to Fifth Street near Catharine, March 10, 1839 - Church consecrated April 14, 1839, by Bishop H. U. Onderdonk. Philadelphia, PA: J. Ashmead and Co., printers, 1840. 16 p. NNUT. 40-6248

Southworth, Tertius Dunning. Civil government on ordinance of God; a sermon... in Franklin, Mass., on the occasion of the annual state fast, April 2d, 1840. Boston, MA: Samuel N. Dickinson, 1840. 31 p. MBC; MH-AH; MnHi; MWelC. 40-6249

Sparks, Jared, 1789-1866. The library of American biography, conducted by Jared Sparks. New York: Harper & Bros., 1840. v. ICMe; IHi; NGlo; PU; ViW. 40-6250

Sparks, Jared, 1789-1866. The life and treason of Benedict Arnold. By Jared Sparks. New York: Harper & Bros., 1840. 335 p. AzU; MSbo; NGlc; NT; NWatt; RKi. 40-6251

Sparks, Jared, 1789-1866. Life of George Washington. Abridged by the author. Boston, MA: Tappan, 1840-42. 2 v. NNP; PU. 40-6252

Sparks, Jared, 1789-1866. Life of George Washington. By Jared Sparks. Boston, MA: Ferdinand Andrews, 1840.

2 v. ArCC; CU; MSha; NNS; OUr; PP. 40-6253

Speakman, John. Circular on the currency. S. l.: s. l., 1840. No Loc. 40-6254

Speakman, John. Circulars to the producers [Harrison campaign] Philadelphia, PA: s. l., 1840. PPL. 40-6255

Spear, John Murray. Address before the Universalist Anti-Slavery Convention at its 1st session, held in Lynn, Mass., Nov. 19, 1840. By J. M. Spear... Also minutes of said convention. Waltham, MA: printed at the Christian Freeman Office, 1840. 46 p. MMeT-HI; NNUT. 40-6256

Speculation; or, Making Haste to be Rich; the story of William Wilson, the Whistling Shoemaker. Boston, MA: George W. Light, 1840. 80 p. CtHC; DLC; NBuG; PU. 40-6257

Speeches in Congress on the furniture of the White House, the sub-treasury, the bank of U. S., the issue of treasury notes, the reduction of wages, the currency, the N. J. election, the branch mint in N. C., the expenditures of the public money, &c. Washington, DC: s. l., 1840. PPL. 40-6258

Spencer, Thomas, 1791-1811. Address to the graduates of the Medical Institution of Geneva College, delivered January 21, 1840... Geneva, NY: Pr. by Frazee, Book and Job Printers, 1840. NBuU-M; NGH; NN; PPHa. 40-6259

Spencer, Thomas, 1791-1811. Appeals to the heart; exhibiting the beauties of christian truth, in twenty-one discourses.

By Thomas Spencer. 1st Amer. ed. Boston, MA: Pub. by James Loring, 1840. 274 p. CStor; IU; LNH; MiU; OO; OSW. 40-6260

Spicer, Tobias. Beauties of Fletcher; being extracts from his checks to antinomianism, in a series of letters to Rev. Mr. Shirley and Mr. Hill, by Rev. T. Spicer. New York: Mason & G. Lane, 1840. 315 p. IEG; InNea; NjMD; PPWe; TxDaM. 40-6261

Spirit of democracy. Daily, tri-weekly. Daily, Apr. 25-July 31, 1840; tri-weekly, Sept. 2-Oct. 26?, 1840. Only one issue published in August, 1840. Baltimore, MD: s. l., 1840. v. MdBE. 40-6262

The spirit of popery. An exposure of its origin, character, and results. In letters from a father to his children. New York: American Tract Society [184-?] 378 p. CU; DLC; ICU; ViU. 40-6263

Spohr, Louis, 1784-1859. Spohr's cradle song. [The accomp. arranged for the Spanish guitar] Boston, MA: Ditson [184-?] 1 p. MB. 40-6264

Sporle, Nathan James, 1812-1853. Do you ever think of me. Ballad. Written by Charles Jeffreys, esq. Composed by N. J. Sporle. New York: F. Riley [184-?] 3 p. ViU. 40-6265

Sporle, Nathan James, 1812-1853. Ev'ry land my home, or, "life is not all a desert waste. " [Song. Accomp. for piano forte] Baltimore, MD: Benteen [184-?] 3 p. MB. 40-6266

Sporle, Nathan James, 1812-1853. The heart that's true. [Song. Accomp. for piano forte] Boston, MA: Marsh [184-?] 4 p. MB. 40-6267

Sporle, Nathan James, 1812-1853. In the days when we went gipsying. Composed & arranged for the piano forte by N. J. Sporle. Baltimore, MD: Saml. Carusi [184-?] 3 p. ViU. 40-6268

Sporle, Nathan James, 1812-1853. In the days when we went gipsying. [Song. The accompaniment] arranged for the guitar... by I. I. Worrell. Philadelphia, PA: Fiot [184-?] 2 p. MB. 40-6269

Sporle, Nathan James, 1812-1853. Think ere you speak. Sung by the composer. Miss Thornton, Miss Cubitt, Mr. George & Mr. Robinson. Written by James Simmonds. Composed by N. J. Sporle... Piano. Philadelphia, PA; New Orleans, LA: Lee & Walker, successors to George Willig; W. T. Mayo [184-?] 5 p. MB; ViU. 40-6270

Sprague, Peleg, 1793-1880. The argument... before the Committee of the legislature upon the memorial of Harrison G. Otis and others, Feb., 1838. 3d ed. Boston, MA: s. l., 1840. 22 p. NH-L; MWA; RP; WHi. 40-6271

Sprague, S. Contrast between true and false religion. New York: D. Appleton and Co., pub., 1840. 449 p. IaPeC. 40-6272

Sprague, William Buell, 1795-1876. A Mind in ruins. A sermon occasioned by the death of Richard Marvin... August 23, 1840... Albany, NY: Printed by C. Van Benthuysen, 1840. 24 p. MBAt; MBC; NjR; PPPrHi; RPB. 40-6273

Spring, Gardiner, 1785-1873. Essays on

the distinguishing traits of Christian character. By Gardiner Spring, D. D. 6th ed., rev. by the author. New York: J. A. Hoisington, 184?. 123 p. CSansS; GDecCT; MiD; NBu; PPPrHi. 40-6274

Spring Lane School, Boston. Annual catalogue of the pupils of Spring Lane School, to which are annexed remarks on its system of instruction and management. Boston, MA: s. l., 1840-42. p. MiD-B. 40-6275

Spring-Villa Seminary, Bordentown, N. J. Fourth Annual Catalogue of the Spring-Villa Seminary for young ladies, at Bordentown, N. J., under the direction of A. N. Girault. Philadelphia, PA: Printed by William Stavely & Co., 1840. 16 p. NHi. 40-6276

Sproat, Nancy, 1766-1827. Village poems. New York: s. l. [184-?] p. MB. 40-6277

Spurzheim, Johann Caspar, 1776-1832. Phrenology, or, The doctrine of the mental phenomena. 5th American from 3d London ed. New York: s. l., 1840. 2 v. MH. 40-6278

The Spy-glass. Edited by Fabricus Videns, Union College, July, 1840. Schenectady, NY: s. l., 1840. 32 p. NN; NRU; RPB. 40-6279

Squier, Miles Powell, 1792-1866. Reason and the Bible; or, the truth of religion. New York: Scribner, 1840. 340 p. PPPrHi. 40-6280

Stael, J. The celebrated polka dances. Arranged for the piano forte. Boston, MA: Oliver Ditson [184-?] 3 p. ViU. 40-6281

Stael-Holstein, Anne Louise Germaine Necker, 1766-1817. Corrine, ou, L'Italie, par Mme. La Baronne de Stael. Nouvelle edition, revue et corrigee. New York: Leavitt & Allen, 1840. 431 p. MB; NJost. 40-6282

Stainer, John. A dictionary of musical terms. Edited by J. Stainer, M. A., Mus. Doc., Madg. College, Oxford, and W. A. Barrett, Mus. Back, S. Mary Hall, Oxford. Boston, MA; New York; Philadelphia, PA; Chicago, IL: Oliver Ditson & Co.; Charles H. Ditson & Co.; J. E. Ditson & Co.; Lyon and Healy, 1840. 456 p. OWoC. 40-6283

Stamford, Conn. First Congregational Church. The confession of faith and covenant. Stamford, CT?: n. pr., 1840. 19 p. MBC. 40-6284

Stanley, Anthony D., 1810-1853. Tables of the logarithms of numbers... to seven places of decimals. New Haven, CT: Durrie, 1840. PPF. 40-6285

Stanley, Arthur Penrhyn, 1815-1881. The life and correspondence of Thomas Arnold, D. D., late head-master of Rugby School and Regius Professor of Modern History in the University of Oxford. Boston, MA: Published by Ticknor and Fields, 1840. 2 v. Nh-Hi; Nj; OCh; ViU. 40-6286

Stanly, Edward, 1808-1872. Letter from Mr. Stanly, of North Carolina, to Mr. Botts, of Virginia. [Washington, DC: s. l., 1840] 7 p. DLC; GEU; MdHi; Vi. 40-6287

Stanly, Edward, 1810-1872. Sketch of the remarks of Mr. Stanly, on the bill making appropriations for the civil and diplomatic expenses of the government for the year 1840. [Washington, 1840] 8 p. NRU. 40-6288

Stanly, Edward. 1810-1872. Sketch of the remarks of Mr. Stanly on the branch mint in North Carolina. Together with extracts from the speeches of Messrs. Everett, Morgan, and Reed... Washington, DC: Gales, 1840. 14 p. IaHi; M; MWA; NcU; PPL. 40-6289

Stanly, Edward, 1810-1872. Speech... establishing proofs that the abolitionists are opposed to Gen. Harrison, and that Gen. Harrison is opposed to their unconstitutional efforts. Delivered in the House of Representatives, April 13, 1840. [Washington, 1840. 24 p. DLC; ICN; NcU; OC; OOxM. 40-6290

Stanly, Edward, 1808-1872. Speech of Mr. Stanly of North Carolina on abolition petitions. Delivered in the House of Representatives, January 16, 1840. [Washington, DC: s. l., 1840] 16 p. MBAt; MH; PPL; TxU. 40-6291

Stanly, Edward, 1808-1872. To the People of the state of North Carolina. [Washington, DC: s. l., 1840] 7 p. DLC. 40-6292

Star of freedom. New York: William S. Dorr, printer [184-?] 96 p. DLC; MWA; RPB. 40-6293

The Star-spangled banner. New York: Firth & Hall [184-?] 1 p. ViU. 40-6294

The Star-spangled banner. [Song, S. or T. Accomp. for piano forte] Boston, MA: Wade [184-?] 2 p. MB. 40-6295

Starcks, Johann Friedrich. Tagliches

Handbuch in guten und bosen Tagen enthaltend Aufmunterungen, Gebete und Lieder... von M. Johann Jacob Starck... mit funf Holzschnitten... Philadelphia, PA: Herausgegeben von George W. Mentz und Sohn, 1840. 536, 104 p. PRea-Hi. 40-6296

Stark, Cordelia. A Female Wanderer; or, The remarkable disclosures of Coredlia and Edwin. Written by herself. Boston, MA: Thayer and Edlridge, 1840? p. PU. 40-6297

A statement of the expenditures of Gov't. exhibiting the prodigality of the present administration. Washington, DC: s. l., 1840. PPL. 40-6298

A statement of the facts and circumstances relative to the operation of the pilot laws of U. S., with particular reference to New York, June, 1840. Newark, NJ: Printed by M. S. Harrison & Co. [1840] 27 p. DLC; MH; PPL; RPB. 40-6299

A statement of the true gospel; designed for those who are in danger of embracing a false one. In a letter to a friend. Albany: Weare C. Little, 1840. 24 p. OC. 40-6300

A statement proving Millard Fillmore, the candidate of the Whig Party for the office of Vice President, to be an abolitionist, by a review of his course in the 25th, 26th, and 27th Congresses. Also, showing Gen. Taylor to be in favor of extending the ordinance of 1787 over the continent beyond the Rio Grande. In other words, to be in favor of the Wilmot Proviso. [S. l.: s. l., 184-?] 8 p. DLC; Vi. 40-6301

Staunton, William. A dictionary of the church, containing an exposition of terms, phrases, and subjects connected with external order... and usages of the Protestant Episcopal church... By Rev. Wm. Staunton... Second edition, revised, corrected and enlarged, by the author. Philadelphia, PA: Herman Hooker, 1840. 473 p. NNUT; RPB; WM; WNaE; VtStal. 40-6302

Staunton, William, Jr., 1803-1889. In happier hours. [Song, A.] Symphonies & accompaniments [for piano forte] by William Staunton, Jr. German air. Boston, MA: Hewitt & Co. [184-?] 3 p. MB. 40-6303

Staunton, William, Jr., 1803-1889. When I left the shores O Naxos. An original Greek air. Words by Byron; arranged by Wm. Staunton, Jr. Baltimore, MD: S. Carusi [184-?] 2 p. ViU. 40-6304

Stearns, John, 1770-1848. Philosophy of mind, developing new sources of ideas, designing their distinctive classes, and simplifying the faculties and operations of the whole mind. By John Stearns... New York: Printed by W. Osborn, 1840. 25 p. MBC; MBMS; MH; NCH; PPAmP. 40-6305

Steele's Almanck for the year of Our Lord 1841. being first after Leap Year; and of American Independence Till July 4th, the Sixty-fifth. Containing, besides the usual Astronomical calculations, a variety of useful political information and election tables. Calculared for the Meridian of Buffalo, N. Y., but will answer for any of the adjoining States or Upper Canada. Astronomical calculations by Geo. R. Perkins, Professor of Mathematics, Utica, N. Y. Buffalo, NY:

Published by W. B. & C. E. Peck [1840] 24 p. N; NAl; NCH. 40-6306

Steenrod, Lewis, 1810-1862. Speech of Mr. Steenrod, of Virginia, in Committee of the Whole, on the bill making appropriation for the civil and diplomatic expenditures of the Government for the year 1840. House of Representatives, April 17, 1840. Washington, DC: Printed at the Globe Office, 1840. 16 p. DLC; MdHi; MeB; NNC. 40-6307

Steinruck, Charles. Henry Clay's funeral march. Composed for the piano by Charles Steinruck. Boston, MA: Oliver Ditson [184-?] 2 p. ViU. 40-6308

Stephen, Henry John, 1787-1864. Summary of the criminal law. By Henry J. Stephen, Sergeant at Law. New York; Philadelphia, PA: John S. Littell, publisher, 1840. 207 p. DLC; FU-L; Mo; NN; PPB; WaU-L. 40-6309

Stephens, Ellen. The cabin boy wife; or, Singular and surprising adventures of Mrs. Ellen Stephens... New York: C. E. Daniels, 1840. 24 p. MoSM. 40-6310

Stephens, John Lloyd, 1805-1852. Incidents of travel in Egypt, Arabia Petraea and the Holy Land. By an American. With map and engravings. In two volumes. 10th ed., with additions. New York: Harper & Bros., 1840. 2 v. MiNaz-C; MnSS; NCaS; NcC; SE; TxAu. 40-6311

Stephens, John Lloyd, 1805-1852. Incidents of travel in Greece, Turkey, Russia, and Poland. 7th ed. New York: s. l., 1840. 2 v. MCli; MoS; NiCLA; OUrC; RPB. 40-6312

Sterne, Laurence, 1713-1768. The works of Laurence Sterne, in one volume... with a life of the author. Philadelphia, PA: Grigg & Elliot, 1840. 416 p. MB; MNan; MoK; Ms; WHi. 40-6313

Stetson, Caleb, 1793-1870. Intuition of God. A sermon, by Caleb Stetson. Boston, MA: William Crosby & Co., 1840. 11 p. MiD-B. 40-6314

Stetson, Caleb, 1793-1870. Two discourses preached before the first Congregational Society in Medford; one upon leaving the old church; and one at the dedication of the new. By Caleb Stetson, Minister of the society. Boston, MA: Printed by I. R. Butts, 1840. 59 p. CBPac; ICN; MBAU; PPAmP; RPB. 40-6315

Stevens, Abel, 1815-1897. Centenary reflections on the providencial character of Methodism. New York: T. Mason and G. Lane, 1840. 32 p. ICN; IEG; MBC; MH; RPB. 40-6316

Stevens, Abel, 1815-1897. Government of the M. E. Church. Boston, MA: Reid & Rand [184-?] 18 p. IEG; MB. 40-6317

Stevens, J. H. Indian guide to health, or valuable vegetable medical prescriptions. Lafayette, IN: J. Rosser, print. [1840] 247 p. NNC. 40-6318

Stevenson, I. M., Sir. Fall'n is they throne. Sung... at the oratorios. Air Martini. Arranged by Sir I. M. Stevenson. [With accompaniment for piano forte] New York: Hewitt & Jaques [184-?] 3 p. MB. 40-6319

Stevenson, John Andrew, 1760?-1833. Farewell! But whenever you welcome the hour. Written by Thos. Moore, Esqr. The music arranged by Sir John Stevenson. Baltimore, MD; New Orleans, LA: F. D. Benteen; W. T. Mayo [184-?] 2 p. ViU. 40-6320

Stevenson, John Andrew, 1760?-1833. Flow on thou shining river. A favorite Portuguese air. With symphony & accompaniment [for the piano forte] by Sir John Stevenson. Written by T. Moore. New York: Firth & Hall [184-?] 3 p. MB. 40-6321

Stevenson, John Andrew, 1760?-1833. Hark, the convent bells. A favorite song and trio. Adapted, composed and arranged to an admired Portuguese melody by Sir John Stevenson. Boston, MA: Oliver Ditson [184-?] 4 p. ViU. 40-6322

Stevenson, John Andrew, 1760?-1833. The Irish schoolmaster. A celebrated comic duett. The words by Lady Clarke. The music by J. Stevenson. [With accompaniment for the piano forte] Philadelphia, PA: Willig [184-?] 2 p. MB. 40-6323

Stevenson, John Andrew, 1760?-1833. Oft in the stilly night. [Song. With accompaniment for piano forte, from Moore's National Melodies] Arranged by Sir John Stevenson. Boston, MA: Reed [184-?] 3 p. MB; ViU. 40-6324

Stevenson, John Andrew, 1760?-1833. 'Tis the last rose of summer. Written by T. Moore, Esqr. Arranged by Sir John Stevenson. Baltimore, MD: F. D. Benteen [184-?] 2 p. ViU. 40-6325

Stevenson, John Andrew, 1760?-1833. 'Tis the last rose of summer. Written by T. Moore, Esqr. Arranged by Sir John

Stevenson. Boston, MA: Oliver Ditson [184-?] 2 p. ViU. 40-6326

Stevenson, John Andrew, 1760?-1833. 'Tis the last rose of summer. Written by Thomas Moore; arranged by Sir John Stevenson. New York: Firth, Pond & co. [184-?] 2 p. ViU. 40-6327

Stewart, Alexander. Stories from the history of Scotland. By the Rev. Alexander Stewart, a minister of that county. From the second Edinburgh edition. New York: Published by T. Mason and G. Lane, 1840. 159 p. NIC. 40-6328

Stewart, John. The stable book; being a treatise on the management of horses in relation to stabling, grooming, etc... by John Stewart. With notes and additions... by A. B. Allen. 3d ed. New York: Orange Judd & Co., 1840. 378 p. CULA; DNLM; NIC; NIC-A. 40-6329

Stewart, John, 1749-1822. The moral state of nations, or, travels over the most interesting parts of the globe, to discover the source of moral motion... In the Year of Man's retrospective knowledge by astronomical calculation 5000, year of the common era, 1790. Granville; Middletown, NJ: Reprinted by George H. Evans, 1840. 126 p. CSmH; DLC; NN. 40-6330

Stiff, Edward. The Texan emigrant; being a narration of the adventures of the author in Texas... together with the pricipal incidents of fifteen years revolution in Mexico... by Col. Edward Stiff. Cincinnati, OH: George Conclin, 1840. 367 p. CSmH; IEN; MdBJ; OClWHi; TxGR. 40-6331

Stirling, Edward, 1807-1894. The old

curiosity shop. A drama in two acts. New York: Samuel French [1840?] 39 p. OCl. 40-6332

Stirling, Edward, 1807-1894. The Pickwick Club, or The age we live in. A burletta extravaganza in three acts. Philadelphia, PA: F. Turner, etc., etc. [184-?] p. CSmH; MH. 40-6333

Stirling, Edward, 1807-1894. ... The ragpicker of Paris, and the dress-maker of St. Antoine. A drama in three acts and a prologue. By Edward Stirling, esq... As performed at the New York Theatres. New York: S. French & Son [etc., etc., 184-?] 35 p. CSt. 40-6334

Stockton, Robert Field, 1795-1866. Address of Captain Stockton to the people of New Jersey. Trenton, NJ: Sherman and Harron, 1840. 27 p. NjR; NjT; PHi; TxU. 40-6335

Stockwell, William. The eventful narrative of Capt. William Stockell... of his travels... Written by himself. Rev. and corrected for the press by Edwin A. Atlee, M. D. Cincinnati, OH: Printed by S. Ward & Co., 1840. 326 p. LNH; MH; OUr; TNP; WHi. 40-6336

Stohlmann, Karl Friedrich E. Was ist dem Christen die trubsal dieser zeit; predigt uber 2. Kor. 4, 17-5, 10, gehalten am 16. August 1840... New York: Ludwig, 1840. 15 p. PPLT. 40-6337

Stokes, William, 1804-1878. Lectures on the theory of physics. By William Stokes. With numerous notes, and twelve additional lectures, by John Bell. 2d. American ed. Philadelphia, PA; New York: Haswell, Barrington, and Haswell; J. & H. G. Langley, 1840. 672 p. ICU;

MdBJ; MdBJ-W; NcD; OrUM; ViU. 40-6338

Stokes, William, 1804-1878. Researches into state of the heart and use of wine in typhoid fever. Philadelphia, PA: s. l., 1840. NNMSCQ; OClM; PPHa. 40-6339

Stone, E. Purposes and responsibilities of the Ch. Ministry. East Bridgewater: s. l., 1840. MB. 40-6340

Stone, John Seely, 1795-1882. A sermon, occasioned by the Burning of the Steamer Lexington, preached in St. Paul's Church, Boston. By John S. Stowe, D. D. Boston, MA: Perkins & Marvin, 1840. 20 p. CtSoP; MBC; MiD-B; PHi; WHi. 40-6341

Stone, Richard. Christian ministry. A sermon. October 28, 1840, at the ordination of James L. Stone. East Bridgewater: George Henry Brown, printer, 1840. 17 p. RPB. 40-6342

Stone, Timothy Dwight Porter, 1811-1887. Sabbath School Infant Class. Written for the Mass. S. S. Society and approved by the Committee of Publication. Boston, MA: s. l., 1840. No Loc. 40-6343

Storer, Bellamy. An address on Christian education, delivered at the commencement of Woodward College, July 2, 1840, before the Woodward Literary Society. Cincinnai, OH: s. l., 1840. 12 p. MH; OCHP. 40-6344

Storey, Thomas. The whole human race restored to the favour of God ultimately is clearly proved from the Scriptures alone, out of which so much eternal punishment is palmed upon the people, by the money loving priest of the day. Manchester: printed by W. Willis & Co., 1840. 12 p. MMeT. 40-6345

Stories for the little one. Nos. 1, 2, 3, 4. Boston, MA: American Tract Society [1840] 8 p. MH. 40-6346

Storrs, Richard Salter, 1787-1873. Conversion of the world. Discourse delivered at anniv. of Palestine missionary soc. at Abington, South Parish, June 17, 1840. Boston, MA: Perkins and Marvin, 1840. 36 p. ICU; MB; MiD-B; MWiW; OO; PPPrHi. 40-6347

Story, Joseph, 1779-1845. Commentaries on equity pleadings, and the incidents thereof, according to the practice of the courts of equity of England and America. By Joseph Story... 2d ed., rev. cor., and enl. Boston, MA: C. C. Little and J. Brown, 1840. 745 p. LNT-L; NcD; OO; TU; WU-L. 40-6348

Story, Joseph, 1779-1845. Commentaries on the law of bailments, with illustations from the civil and the foreign law. Second edition. Boston, MA: C. C. Little and James Brown, 1840. 409 p. ArU; CU; OCLaw; Pu-L; WU-L. 40-6349

Story, Joseph, 1779-1845. Commentary on equity pleadings and the incidents thereof, according to the practice of the courts of equity of England and America. By Joseph Story. 2d ed. Boston, MA: Charles C. Little and James Brown, 1840. 745 p. DLC; MoU; NcU; NN OU; ViU. 40-6350

Story, Joseph, 1779-1845. Exposition of the Constitution of the United States. Boston, MA: Thomas H. Webb & Co.,

1840. 372 p. AAP; DLC; MB; MWA; NcD; NcGC; OO. 40-6351

The story of Little Mary, Child of the Regiment. New York: Huestis & Cozans [1840] 16 p. No Loc. 40-6352

Stow, Edward. Deposition of Edward Stow in relation to the claim of the New England Mississippi Land Company [Thomas L. Winthrop and others] on the United States. Sworn to in Boston, March, 14, 1840. [Boston, MA: s. l., 1840] 12 p. MB; TxU; WHi. 40-6353

Stowe, Calvin Ellis. Wisdom and knowledge the nation's stability; an address delivered at Crawfordsville, Ind., July 7, 1840, before the Euphonean society of Wabash College... [Cincinnati, OH: printed at the Cincinnati observer office, 1840] p. In; InU; PPPrHi. 40-6354

Strack, Louis. Baltimore hop waltz. Composed & arranged for the piano forte by Louis Strack. Philadelphia, PA: George Willig, 1840. 2 p. ViU. 40-6355

Strakosch, M., 1825-1887. Postillon polka. New York; W. Hall & Son, [184?] ICN; MB; MH; PPL. 40-6356

Strang, Robert, 1796-1854. An address delivered before the Peithessophian and Philoclean societies of Rutgers' University. By the Hon. Robert Strange... New Brunswick, NJ: John Terhune's Press, 1840. 36 p. N; NcU; NNC; NjR; PPL. 40-6357

Strang, Robert, 1796-1854. Speech of Mr. Strang of North Carolina, on the assumption, by the federal government, of the debts of the state and in reply to Messrs. Clay and Crittenden. Senate,

February 27, 1840. Washington, DC: Printed at the Globe office, 1840. 14 p. MdHi; MiD-B; NcU; OClWHi; TxDaM. 40-6358

Stratton, William F. The Penman's Paradise, both pleasant and profitable, etc. Boston, MA: s. l., 1840. Bo Loc. 40-6359

Strauss, Johann, 1825-1899. Baden Baden, or, De Joinville polka. Composed by Strauss. Arranged by H. Herz. [For piano forte] Boston, MA: Ditson, 184-? 2 p. ICN; MB; MH. 40-6360

Strauss, Johann, 1825-1899. Beauties of Strauss. Arranged for the piano forte. Boston, MA: C. Bradlee [184-?] 5 p. ViU. 40-6361

Strauss, Johann, 1825-1899. Duke of Reichstadt's waltz. Arranged by Le Carpentier. [For the piano forte] Boston, MA: Reed [184-?] 2 p. MB. 40-6362

Strauss, Johann, 1825-1899. Empress Anne's polka. Composed for the piano forte by Johann Strauss. Boston, MA: Oliver Ditson [184-?] 2 p. ViU. 40-6363

Strauss, Johann, 1825-1899. Strauss' much admired waltzes, as performed in Europe by his celebrated band and in America by the Prague C ompany. Book 2. Baltimore, MD: Frederick D. Benteen, 184-? 11 p. ViU. 40-6364

Strauss, Johann, 1825-1899. Tambour polka. For the piano forte. Composed by J. Strauss. Baltimore, MD; New Orleans, LA: F. D. Benteen; W. T. Mayo [184-?] 2 p. ViU. 40-6365

Street, Alfred Billings, 1811-1881. Na-ture: a poem, pronounced before the Euglossian society at the annual commencement of Geneva College, August 4, 1849. By Alfred B. Street. Geneva, NY: Stow & Frazee [1840] 21 p. CSmH; MH; NGH; TxU; WU. 40-6366

Street, Robert, 1843-1924. Catalogue of exhibition at the artists' fund ball... of upwards of 200 evil paintings. Philadelphia, PA: J. Young, pr., 1840. 16 p. PHi; PPM. 40-6367

Strickland, Agnes, 1796-1874. Tales of illustrious children. Boston, MA: Munroe and Francis, 184-? 276 p. TxD-T. 40-6368

Strickland, William, 1787-1854. Tomb of Washington at Mount Vernon. Philadelphia, PA: Carey and Hart, 1840. 76 p. DeWi; MiU; PPAmP; TxU. 40-6369

Strictures on Governor Morton's message. By a Democrat. Boston, MA: s. l., 1840. No Loc. 40-6370

Strobel, B. B. Essay on the subject of yellow fever, intended to prove its transmissibility. Charleston, SC: Printed by Asa J. Muir, 1840. 224 p. GEU-M; IU; MdBM; NcD; PU. 40-6371

Strong, Carl, 1745-1819. Memoir of the Hon. Caleb Strong, LL. D., Governor of Massachusetts. Originally published in the American Quarterly Register. [Boston, MA: s. l., 1840] 12 p. MB; MHi; MWA. 40-6372

Strong, Theron Rudd. Speech of Mr. Strong of New York, on the Independent Treasury Bill. In the House of Representatives, June 8th, 1840. In Committee of the Whole on the state of the Union, on the Independent Treasury bill. [Washington, DC: s. l., 1840] 7 p. DLC; MdHi; NNC. 40-6373

Stuart, John T. Speech of the Honorable Mr. Stuart, of Illinois, in the House of Representatives, April 21, 1840. In the committee of the Whole on the State of Union, on the Civil and Diplomatic Appropriation Bill. [Boston, MA: s. l., 1840] 15 p. M; MdHi; NN. 40-6374

Stuyvesant Institute of the City of New York. Exhibition of Leutze's great national fiction of Washington crossing the DelawareCatalogue description by R. G. W. New York: Bake Godwise & Co. [184-?] p. NN. 40-6375

Sue, Eugene, 1804-1857. Latreaumont; or, the conspiracy, historical romance of the days of Louis the 14th. By Sue... Cincinnati, OH: U. P. James [1840] p. NBUG. 40-6376

Sue, Eugene, 1804-1857. The wandering Jew... Philadelphia, PA: Henry T. Coates & Company [184-?] 2 v. MiD; RPB; ViLxW. 40-6377

Sullivan, George, Member of Congress, U. S. Supreme Court of the United States: J. [or rather S.] B. Stone, ads. the United States of America. Argument for defendant [in action for violation of the Act of Congress providing for the better security of the lives of passengers in Steam-vessels, etc.] New York: s. l., 1840. No Loc. 40-6378

Sullivant, William Starling, 1803-1873. A catalogue of plants, native or naturalized in the vicinity of Columbus, Ohio, by

Wm. S. Sullivant. Columbus, OH: Charles Scott, printer, 1840. 63 p. CtHWatk; MH; NBuG; OCHP; OU; WU. 40-6379

Summer dew drops. Philadelphia, PA; New York: Turner & Fisher [184-?] 14 p. MH. 40-6380

Summers, Thomas O., 1812-1882. God's love to the people called Methodists. A sermon. Preached in friendship, Anne Arundel County, Maryland, October 25, 1839, at the celebration of the centenary of Methodism, by the Rev. Thomas O. Summers, of the Baltimore Conference. New York: Published by T. Mason and G. Lane for the M. E. Church, at the conference office, J. Collard, printer, 1840. 22 p. ICP; N; NNC; RPB. 40-6381

The Sun-flower; or, poetical blossoms... New Haven, CT: Printed and published by S. Babcock, 1840. 16 p. CtY; NN. 40-6382

Sunday School hymn book. Designed for Universalist Sunday Schools throughout the United States. New York: P. Price, 1840. 54 p. PHi. 40-6383

Sunday school lessons. Designed to provide both teachers and scholars. With subjects for study and conversation. By a pastor. Boston, MA: B. H. Greene, 1840. 15 p. NNUT. 40-6384

The Sunday School pioneer, or, the best method of opening and conducting new Sunday Schools. Philadelphia, PA: American Sunday School Union [184-?] 69 p. PHi; PP; WHi. 40-6385

Sunday School Society annual reports.

1840 to 1846. Boston, MA: s. l., 1840-46. v. OCHP. 40-6386

The Sunday School teacher in earnest. [Boston, MA: s. l., 184-?] p. MB. 40-6387

Sunday School Teacher judged. Philadelphia, PA: American Sunday School Union, 1840. 61 p. GMi; LvC; MH. 40-6388

Surenne, Gabriel, d. 1858. The standard pronouncing dictionary of the French & English languages, by G. Surenne. New York: D. Appleton & Co., 1840. 843 p. DLC; MiNazC. 40-6389

Sutherland, Joel Barlow, 1791-1861. A manual of legislative practice and order of business in deliberative bodies. 2d edition. Philadelphia, PA: Hay and Co., 1840. 244, 144 p. PPF. 40-6390

Sutherland, Thomas Jefferson. A canvass of the proceedings on the trial of William Lyon Mackenzie for an alleged violation of the neutrality laws of the United States with a report of the testimony - the charge of the presiding judge, the jury - the arguments of the United States attorney - and a petitin to the President for his release. New York: s. l., 1840. 104 p. MH; MiD-B; NjR. 40-6391

Sutherland, Thomas Jefferson. Loose leaves, from the port folio of a late patriot prisoner in Canada. New York: W. H. Colyer, printer, 1840. 216 p. DLC; MH; RPB. 40-6392

Sutherland, Thomas Jefferson. Three political letters addressed to Dr. Wolfred Nelson, late of Lower Canada, now at

Plattsburgh, N. Y. New York: s. l., 1840. 64 p. InHi; MH; Mi; NIC; O. 40-6393

Swammerdam, Eustasius [pseud.] The Lash, or, Truths in rhyme. New York: Printed for the author, 1840. NBuG. 40-6394

Swart, Isaac. Peace for the troubled mind. A sermon. Preached in St. Paul's Church, Owego, Tioga County, New York, on the evening of the twenty-fourth day of December, 1840, by I. Swart. Owego, NY: Printed by A. H. Calhoun, 1840. 24 p. DLC; MdBD; MH; NNG. 40-6395

Swartara and Good Spring Creek Railroad. Charter of the Swatara and Good Spring Creek Railroad Company and Acts of Assembly of Pennsylvania. With the supplements relating thereto. Capital 100, 000 dollars-share 50 dollars each. Baltimore, MD: Printed by Lucas & Deaver, 1840. 20 p. MdHi. 40-6396

Swartzell, William. Mormonism exposed; being a journal of a residence in Missouri from May 28 to August 20, 1838. Together with an appendix containing the Golden Bible. With numerous extracts from the Book of Covenants, etc. Pekin, OH: The Author, 1840. 40 p. CtY; MiU-C; MoSHi; MoSM; NN; PPPrHi. 40-6397

Swedenborg, Emanuel, 1688-1772. Angelic Wisdom concerning the divine providence. 2d Am. ed. Boston, MA: Otis Clapp, 1840. 387 p. CtHT; KTW; MBoy; MCNC; NbOM; OUrC; PPL-R. 40-6398

Swedenborg, Emanuel, 1688-1772. Delights of wisdom concerning conjugal love; after which follow pleasures of insanity concerning scortatory [sic] love. Boston, MA: Clapp, 1840. 438 p. CtHT; MH-AH; PU. 40-6399

Swedenborg, Emanuel, 1688-1772. Divine providence. Boston, MA: Otis Clapp, pub., 1840. 387 p. NSyU. 40-6400

Swedenborg, Emanuel, 1688-1772. The doctrine of the New Jerusalem concerning charity. From the posthumous works of Emanuel Swedenborg. Translated from the Latin. 2d American from the 1st London edition. Boston, MA: O. Clapp, 1840. 41 p. MdBD; MH; OCHP; OUrC. 40-6401

Swedenborg, Emanuel, 1688-1772. Heavenly arcana, which are in the sacred scripture or word of the Lord, laid open. Together with wonderful things which were seen in the world of spirits and in the heaven of angels, Genesis. By Emanuel Swedenborg. Originally published in Latin at London, A. D. 1751. 2d American from the 1st London edition. Boston, MA: Otis Clapp, Freeman and Bolles, printers, 1840. 451 p. MA. 40-6402

Swedenborg, Emanuel, 1688-1772. Intercourse between soul and body. Boston, MA: s. l. [184-?] p. MB. 40-6403

Swedenborg, Emanuel, 1688-1772. The last judgment, and the Babylon destroyed; so that all the predictions in the Apocalypse are at this day fulfilled. From things heard and seen. Tr. from the Latin of Emanuel Swedenborg. Boston, MA: Otis Clapp, 1840. 112 p. CtHT; MiU; PPiW; ScC; ViL. 40-6404

Sweeny, J. W. Jenny get your hoe-cake

done. The celebrated banjo song. Suns... at the Broadway circus. New York: Firth & Hall, 1840. 2 p. WHi. 40-6405

Swinburne, Henry. Letters written at the end of the eighteenth century. By Henry Swinburne. Philadelphia, PA: George Barrie & Sons [1840] 2 v. in 1. MdBE. 40-6406

Swinklefritzer, S. Galvanus. The senior of Washington. A comedy. By S. Galvanus Swinklefritzer. Washington, PA: [n. pr., 1840] 8 p. PWW. 40-6407

The Swiss Family Robinson; or, Adventures of a father and mother and four sons on a desert island. The progress of the story forming a clear illustation of the first principles of natural history and many branches of science which most immediately apply to the business of life. In two volumes. From the seventh London edition. New York: Harper & Brothers, 1840-41. 2 v. No Loc. 40-6408

The Swiss shepherd's ranz des vaches. [Song, S. or T. With accomp.] Arranged for the guitar. Philadelphia, PA: Fiot [184-?] 2 p. MB. 40-6409

Sword's pocket almanack, churchman's calendar, and ecclesiastical register, for the year of Our Lord 1841. Consisting the lunations, eclipses, and rising and setting of the sun and moon and time of high water... New York: Swords, Stanford, and Co. [1840] 96 p. MWA; NNS. 40-6410

Sylph waltz. [For the piano forte] Boston, MA: Prentiss [184-?] 2 p. MB. 40-6411

Symington, William, 1795-1862. The

nature, extent, and results of the atonement. By the Rev. William Symington.
Philadelphia, PA: Board of Publication,
James Russell, publishing agent, 1840. 88
p. CtHC; MsSC; NCMHi. 40-6412

Symington, William, 1795-1862. The
necessity of atonement. By the Rev. William Symington. Philadelphia, PA:
Board of Publication, James Russell,
publishing agent, 1840. 48 p. CtHC. 40-
6413

Symington, William, 1795-1862. On the

intercession of Jesus Christ. By the Rev.
William Symington. Philadelphia, PA:
Board of Publication, James Russell,
publishing agent, 1840. 40 p. CtHC;
MeBAt; MsSC. 40-6414

Synod of South Carolina. Minutes of the
Synod of South Carolina and Georgia at
their session in Augusts [Ga.] Nov., 1839,
and Nov., 1840. With an appendix. Charleston, SC: Observer Office Press, 1840-
49. v. GDecCT. 40-6415

T

Tacitus, Caius Cornelius. C. Cornelii taciti Historiarum libri quinque: cum libro de Germania, et vita Agricolac. Ad fiden optimarium editoionum expressi cum notis Barbou. Philadelphia, PA: Uriah Hunt, 1840. 299 p. InStmaS; ODaU; OrCA. 40-6416

Tacitus, Caius Cornelius. Germania, Agricola, et De oratoribus dialogus. Accedunt notae Anglicae. Ex editione Oberliniana. Boston, MA: C. K. Dillaway, 1840. MCR; MH; TxU. 40-6417

Tacitus, Caius Cornelius. The works of Caius Cornelius Tacitus; with an essay on his life and genius, notes, supplements, etc. By Arthur Murphy. New ed. Philadelphia, PA: Thomas Wardle, 1840. 742 p. GAuY; GDecCT; IaCrC; MoS; MsCliM; NCH. 40-6418

Die Taglichen Loosungern und Lehrtexte der Brudergemeine fur Jahr 1841. Easton, PA: Gedruckt von Heinrich Held, 1840? 125 p. PNazMHi. 40-6419

Tales for the times; being a selection of interesting stories. By the author of Peter Parley. New York: Hafis & Cornish, 1840. 192 p. CtY; IaU; MBAt; MH; MWHi. 40-6420

Tales of humor. Containing 1. "The Lame Pig." 2. "A Night's Adventure." 3. "From the Journal of an Odd Fellow." 4. "Madame Brillant. "... By S. G. Goodrich.

Stereotyped at the Boston Type and Stereotype Foundry. Boston, MA: E. Littlefield, 1840. 192 p. MWA; NcU; NSmb. 40-6421

Talfourd, Thomas Noon, Sir. Ion; a tragedy in five acts. By T. N. Talfourd. Providence, RI: B. Cranston, 1840. 106 p. MH; NjP; RHi; RPB. 40-6422

Taliaferro, John. To the voters of the Congressional District in the State of Virginia, composed of the counties of Westmoreland, Richmond, Northumberland, Lancaster, King George, Stafford, and Prince William. S. l.: s. l., 184-? 8 p. MdHi. 40-6423

Tannehill, Wilkins. The Masonic manual; or, Freemasonry illustrated. By Wilkins Tannehill, P. G. M. K. T. & C. Louisville, KY: W. Harrison Johnston, printer, 1840. 382 p. NNFM; OCM. 40-6424

Tannehill, Wilkins. The Masonic manual; or, Freemasonry illustrated, by Wilkins Tannehill, P. G. M., K. T. &c. Second edition. Louisville, KY: W. Harrison Johnston, 1840. 390 p. IaCrM; ICU; NNFM; OCM; TxWFM. 40-6425

Tanner, Henry Schenck, 1786-1858. The American traveller; or, guide through the United States... With tables of distances... 6th ed. Philadelphia, PA: published by the author; Joseph and Wil-

liam Kite, printers, 1840. 144 p. MBevHi;
NjP; OCl; PHi; PPAmP. 40-6426

Tanner, Henry Schenck, 1786-1858. A
brief description of the canals and rail
roads of the United States; comprehending notices of all the most important
works of internal improvement
throughout the several states... Philadelphia, PA: Tanner, 1840. 63 p. PPA. 40-
6427

Tanner, Henry Schenck, 1786-1858.
Central traveller. New York: s. l., 1840.
NN. 40-6428

Tanner, Henry Schenck, 1786-1858. A
description of the canals and railroads of
the United States, comprehending
notices of all the works of internal improvement throughout the several states,
by H. S. Tanner. New York: T. R. Tanner
& J. Disturnell, 1840. 272 p. CU; ICU;
MHi; NNC; PP. 40-6429

Tanner, Henry Schenck, 1786-1858.
New picture of Philadelphia; or, The
stranger's guide to the city and adjoining
districts... Philadelphia, PA: Tanner,
1840. 156 p. CtY; MB; MBAt; PPAmP;
PP. 40-6430

Tanner, Henry Schenck, 1786-1858.
New universal atlas containing maps of
the various empires, kingdoms, states &
republics of the world. With a special
map of each of the United States, plans
of cities & c. Comprehended in seventy
sheets & forming a series of one hundred
& seventeen maps. Philadelphia, PA:
Published by the Author [184-?] 68 p. Ct.
40-6431

Tanner, Henry Schenck, 1786-1858.

Pocket map of Connecticut. New York:
s. l. [184-?] p. MBAt. 40-6432

Tanner, John. Sound thy guitar again.
Composed & arranged for the Spanish
guitar, by John Tanner. Philadelphia,
PA: George Willig [184-?] 1 p. ViU. 40-
6433

Tapliff, R. Ruth and Naomi, from Sabbath melodies. The words selected from
the Holy Scriptures; the music composed
by R. Tapliff... Baltimore, MD: Geo. Willig, Junr. [184-?] 7 p. ViU. 40-6434

Tapliff, R. Ruth & Naomi, from Sabbath melodies. The words selected from
the Holy Scriptures; the music composed
by R. Tapliff... Philadelphia, PA: George
Willig [184-?] 7 p. ViU. 40-6435

Tappan, Benjamin, 1773-1857.
Remarks of Mr. Tappan, of Ohio, on
abolition petitions. Delivered in Senate,
February 4, 1840. [Washington, DC: s. l.,
1840] 4 p. MdHi; MWA; OClWHi; PU;
TxU. 40-6436

Tappan, Henry Philip, 1805-1881. The
doctrine of the will determined by an appeal to consciousness. By Henry P. Tappan... New York: Wiley and Putnam,
1840. 318 p. CtMW; KyBC; MWiW; OO;
PPP. 40-6437

Tappan, William Bingham, 1794-1849.
Gift of remembrance, a present for all
seasons. Boston, MA: s. l., 184-? 124 p.
CtMW. 40-6438

Tappan, William Bingham, 1794-1849.
Poems. Boston, MA: s. l., 1840. DLC;
MWA. 40-6439

Tappan, William Bingham, 1794-1849.

The poet's tribute. Poems of William B. Tappan. Boston, MA: D. S. King and Crocker & Brewster, 1840. 325 p. CoU; IU; MB; RPB; TxU. 40-6440

Taylor, Alfred [Swaine] 1806-1880. On perforations of the stomach from poisoning and disease. By Alfred S. Taylor. [Philadelphia, PA: Published by A. Waldie, 1840] 243 p. DSG; OClM; MBM. 40-6441

Taylor, Alfred [Swaine] 1806-1880. Poisons and relation to medical jurisprudence and medicine. Philadelphia, PA: Lea and Blanchard, 1840] p. DSG; GEU-M; ICACS. 40-6442

Taylor, Emily. Tales of the Saxons. Boston, MA: Munroe and Francis, etc., etc. [184-?] p. MH. 40-6443

Taylor, Fitch Waterman, 1803-1865. The flag ship or a voyage around the world in the United States Frigate Columbia, attended by her consort, The sloop of War, James Adams, and bearing the broad penant of Commodore George C. Read. New York: D. Appleton & Co., 1840. 388 p. ICN; LMC; MdHi; RRu; TxDa. 40-6444

Taylor, Ida Scott. Selected hymns, texts and original verses. Cincinnati, OH: Crouston & Curtis, 1840. IBlow. 40-6445

Taylor, Isaac, 1787-1865. Ancient Christianity, and the doctrines of the Oxford tracts. By Isaac Taylor... Philadelphia, PA: H. Hooker, 1840. 554 p. ArBaA; ICU; NGH; ODefC; PWW. 40-6446

Taylor, James Barnett, 1804-1871. Memoir of Rev. Luther Rice, one of the first American missionaries to the East. By James B. Taylor. Baltimore, MD: Armstrong and Berry, 1840. 344 p. LNB; MWA; RPB; TxDaM; RiRU. 40-6447

Taylor, James D. The log-cabin song book, being a selection of popular, patriotic, and Tippicanoe songs. By Jas. D. Taylor. Cincinnati, OH: J. D. Taylor, 1840. 40 p. InHi; MBAt; MHi; MWA. 40-6448

Taylor, James Wicks. Address: delivered before the Hamilton Chapter of the Alpha Delta Phi Society, in the college chapel, Clinton, October 22, 1840, on the life and character of George Langford, Jr., by James W. Taylor. Utica, NY: Pub. by request of the society; press of John P. Bush, 1840. 11 p. ICP; MnHi; MWA; NGH; NUt. 40-6449

Taylor, Jane, 1783-1824. Contributions of the Q. & Q. By Jane Taylor. New York: Published by Robert Carter & Brothers, 1840. 295 p. PWaybu. 40-6450

Taylor, Jane, 1783-1824. Original poems, for infant minds. By the Taylor family... Philadelphia, PA: H. F. Anners, 1840. 180 p. CtB; DLC; MB; NNUT; TxDaM. 40-6451

Taylor, Jane, 1783-1824. Physiology for children, by Mrs. Jane Taylor. Stereotype edition. New York: Published by Taylor & Clement at the American Common School Depository, 1840. 91 p. MiK; NNC. 40-6452

Taylor, Jeremy, 1613-1667. Life of our blessed Lord and Savior, Jesus Christ. Indianapolis, IN: Stacy & Williams, 1840. 243 p. In; InGrD; InU. 40-6453

Taylor, John, 1790-1863. An answer to some false statements and misrepresentations made by the Rev. Robert Heys in an address to his Society in Douglas and its vicinity, on the subject of Mormonism. Douglas: Printed by Penrice and Wallace, 1840. 11 p. MH. 40-6454

Taylor, John, 1790-1863. Arator; being a series of agricultural essays, practical and political. By John Taylor... 7th ed. Petersburgh, VA: J. M. Carter, 1840. 772 p. MdBE. 40-6455

Taylor, John, 1790-1863. John Taylor vs. E. C. Delavan prosecuted for libel. Report of trial. Albany, NY: s. l., 1840. 48 p. MB; MH; MiD-B; MWA; PHi. 40-6456

Taylor, John, 1790-1863. ... A report of the trial of the cause of John Taylor vs. Edward C. Delavan, prosecuted for an alleged libel; tried at the Albany circuit, April, 1840. And Mr. Delavan's correspondence with the ex. committee of the Albany city temperance society, &c... Albany, NY: Printed by Hoffman, White & Visscher, 1840. 48 p. CSmH; DLC; MoU; NjR; PSC-Hi; WaU. 40-6457

Taylor, John, 1790-1863. The Scripture doctrine of atonement examined... S. l.: s. l., 1840. 136 p. MBC. 40-6458

Taylor, John Neilson, 1805-1878. A Treatise on the Law of Landlord and Tenant, in a series of letters addressed to a citizen of New York. By John N. Taylor, Esq., Counsellor at Law. New York: Charles Wells, 1840. 164 p. CoCsC; IaCr; MH; NBuG; NNU. 40-6459

Taylor, Richard B. Slow march for the

piano... Providence, RI: s. l., 1840. 2 p. RHi. 40-6460

Taylor, Richard Cowling, 1789-1851. Two reports on the coal lands, mines, and improvements... Philadelphia, PA: E. G. Dorsey, printer, 1840. 74 p. MH-BA. 40-6461

Taylor, Richard Cowling, 1789-1851. Two reports: on the coal lands, mines and improvements of the Dauphin and Susquehanna coal company, and of the geological examinations, present condition and prospects of the Stony Creek coal estate... Philadelphia, PA: E. G. Dorsey, printer, 1840. 74 p. DLC; IU; MnHi; MWA; WU. 40-6462

Taylor, Tom. The bottle; a drama, in two acts. Founded on the graphic illustration of George Cruikshank. By T. P. Taylor. New York: C. T. DeWitt [184-?] p. MH. 40-6463

The tea tax. Yankee comic song. Boston, MA: s. l. [184-?] p. MB. 40-6464

Teachers' Seminary and Classical Institution, Plymouth, N. H. Catalogue, 1840. Concord, NH: s. l., 1840. Nh. 40-6465

Tedesco polka. As played by Murray's band at the private parties. Arranged for the piano forte. Baltimore, MD; New Orleans, LA: F. D. Benteen; W. T. Mayo [184-?] 2 p. ViU. 40-6466

Tefft, Benjamin Franklin, 1813-1885. The shoulder knot; or, sketches of the three fold life of man. New York: Harper & Brothers, 1840. 305 p. RPA; RPB. 40-6467

Tefft, Benjamin Franklin, 1813-1885. The three elements of a perfect church... discourse... October 25, 1840. Bangoe, ME: Printed by Samuel S. Smith, 1840. 24 p. CSPSR; DLC; MnHi; RPB. 40-6468

Tegner, Esais, 1782-1846. Die Frithiofs-sage, aus dem schwedischen, uebers, von A. E. Wollheim. New York: J. Schuberth & Company [1840] 190 p. OCl. 40-6469

Telford, Charles L. The address on individuality of character, delivered before the Miami chapter of the Alpha Delta Phi society, at its fourth anniversary, held at Oxford, O., August 6th, 1839. By Charles L. Talford. Cincinnati, OH: Chronicle office, printer, 1840. 15 p. MdBJ; MWA; OClWHi; OHi; WHi. 40-6470

Temperance almanac, for the year of our Lord 1840... Boston, MA: published under the direction of the executive committee of the Massachusetts Temperance Union, by Whipple and Damrell [1840?] 36 p. MWHi; RNHi; WaSp. 40-6471

Temperance almanac... for the year 1841... calculated by G. R. Perkins... Albany, NY: n. pub., from the steam press of C. Van Benthuysen [1840] 36 p. MiD-B; MWA; NjR; THi; WHi. 40-6472

The Temperance almanac, of the Massachusetts Temperance Union for the year of our Lord 1841... Boston, MA: Published by Whipple & Damrell [1840] 36 p. MBNMHi; MWA; MWo; NjR; WHi. 40-6473

Temperance almanack. Boston, MA: Whipple & Damrell, 1840. MWA. 40-6474

The temperance movement in Ireland. From the Dublin Review, May, 1840. Philadelphia, PA: M. Kelly, 1840. 48 p. MB; MdW; OClWHi; PHi. 40-6475

The Tempest; or, an account of the nature, properties, dangers, and uses of wind in various parts of the world. New York: Carlton & Carter [184-?] p. NN. 40-6476

Temple, John B. Address delivered to the Graduates of the Erodelphian Society of Miami University, August 12, 1840. By John B. Temple, esq. Cincinnati, OH: Chronicle Office, print, 1840. 23 p. CSmH; OHi; OUr; PPiXT; PPPrHi. 40-6477

Tender grass. Boston, MA: s. l. [1840] p. MB. 40-6478

Tennessee. General Assembly. Preamble and Resolutions adopted by the Legislature of the State of Tennessee, November 14th, 1839, and the Reply and resignation of Hugh L. White, a Senator from said State, in the Congress of the United States. Delivered January 13th, 1840. Nashville, TN: S. Nye & Co., printers, 1840. 26 p. TKL-Mc. 40-6479

Tennessee. General Assembly. Joint Select Committee on the Penitentiary. Report of the Joint Select Committee, to whom was referred sundry resolutions and a memorial in relation to the penitentiary. Nashville, TN: J. Geo. Harris, public printer, 1840. 6 p. T. 40-6480

Tennessee. General Assembly. Joint Select Committee on the Public Mismanagement of the Superintendent of Public Instruction. Report of the Joint Select Committee, on the Official Mismanagement of the Superintendent of Public Instruction. Made January 7, 1840. Nashville, TN: J. Geo. Harris, public printer, 1840. 13 p. DE; T. 40-6481

Tennessee. General Assembly. Senate. Senate Journal of the first session of the Twenty-fourth General Assembly of the State of Tennessee. Begun and held in the city of Nashville, on Monday, the seventh day of October, 1839. Published by authority. Columbia, TN: Printed by J. H. Thompson for Lawson Gifford, printer to the state, 1840. 567 p. T; TMeC. 40-6482

Tennessee. Geological Survey. Fifth geological report to the twenty-third General Assembly of Tennessee, made November, 1839. By G. Troost, M. D., geologist to the state, professor of chemistry, minerology and geology in the Nashville University, and member of the Geological Societies of France and Pennsylvania of the American Philosophical Society, and of the Academy of Natural Sciences, Philadelphia. Nashville, TN: J. Geo. Harris, public printer, 1840. 75 p. CSmH; DLC; ICJ; Ia; MB; T; TU. 40-6483

Tennessee. Laws, statutes, etc. Acts passed at the first session of the the twenty-third General Assembly of the State of Tennessee, 1839-40. Published by authority. Nashville, TN: J. Geo. Harris, printer to the State, 1840. 291 p. IaU-L; L; Mi-L; Nb; Nj; T. 40-6484

Tennessee. Laws, statutes, etc. The militia law of the State of Tennessee. Passed January 28, 1840. Nashville, TN: J. Geo. Harris, printer to the State, 1840.

45 p. MH-L; Mi; Mo; T; TKL-Mc. 40-6485

Terry, Daniel, d. 1829. ... Guy Mannering; or, The gipsey's prophesy. A musical play in three acts, by Daniel Terry. Also the stage business, casts of characters, costumes, relative positions, etc. New York: S. French [184-?] 59 p. CSt; MB; MH. 40-6486

Teschemacher, James Englebert. A concise applicatin of the principles of structural botany to horticulture, chiefly extracted from the works of Lindley, Knight, Herbert, and others, with additions and adaptations to this climate. By J. E. Teschemacher. Boston, MA: C. C. Little and J. Brown, 1840. 90 p. DLC; GU; IU; ICBB; MBAt; MH. 40-6487

Testimonials of the qualifications of Richard S. McCulloh, late Professor of Jefferson College, Pa. Washington, PA: s. l., 1840-? 14 p. DLC. 40-6488

Testimony of Francis M. Fowler and Evan Poultney in the case of the Bank of Maryland vs. Samuel Poultney & William M. Ellocitt. Tried before Hartford County Court... 1836. Baltimore, MD: s. l., 1840. 63, 97 p. DLC; MdBLC; MdBP; MdHi; PHi. 40-6489

Testimony relating to the great election frauds of 1838, taken in the recorder's court, New York, in October, 1840. [S. l.: s. l., 1840?] 55 p. CtY; InHi; NN; NNC; PPM. 40-6490

Texas [Republic] An act altering the several acts to raise a public revenue by import duties. Also, An act to provide and establish the warehousing system in the ports of this republic. To which is added the President's Proclamation. Austin, TX: Sentinel Printing, 1840. 39 p. TWS. 40-6491

Texas [Republic] An act defining the duties of the officers of the Treasury Department. David S. Haufman. Approved February 5th, 1840. Mirabeau B. Lamar. [Austin, TX: n. pr., 1840] Broadside. Tx. 40-6492

Texas [Republic] An act to amend and reduce into one of the several laws regulating the Post Office Department. To which is added instructions and forms for the guidance of Post-Masters. Printed by Order of the Post Master-General. Austin, TX: Gazette Office, S. Whiting, printer, 1840. 48 p. TxU. 40-6493

Texas [Republic] Alcance al Semanario del gobierno de N. Leon, No. 88 del Jueves 4 de Noviembre de 1840. Paz de la frontera de los Departamentoe de Coahiula y Tamaulipas y fliz Union de las Mejicanos para combatis a los uswepadores de Tejos. Monterey: [En la Imprenta del Nivel, a cargo del C. Francisco Molina] 1840. 6 p. No Loc. 40-6494

Texas [Republic] Journals of the Senate of the Republic of Texas, Fifth Congress, First Session. By order of the Secretary of State. Houston, TX: Printed at the Telegraph Office [1840] 198 p. TxWFM. 40-6495

Texas [Republic] Report of Board of Traveling Commissioners, for detection of fraudulent land certificates, issued west of the Brazos. Printed by order of House of Representatives. [Austin, TX: Whiting's Printing, 1840] 8 p. DLC; TxWFM. 40-6496

Texas [Republic] Report of the Commissioner General Land Office, November 17, 1840. Printed by order of Congress. [Austin, TX: Sentinel Printing, 1840] 9 p. No Loc. 40-6497

Texas [Republic] ... Report of the Secretary of State... [portions of correspondence concerning the boundary line of Texas, British Negroes detained in Texas, Indian affairs, and the establishment and endowment of the universities] [Austin, TX] : s. l., 1840. 24 p. TxU. 40-6498

Texas [Republic] Report of the Secretary of War, November, 1840. Printed by order of the House of Representatives. [Austin, TX: Whiting's Printing, 1840] 32 p. WxWFM. 40-6499

Texas [Republic] Report [upon the "Bill to exempt certain lands from certain debts therein named"] [Austin, TX] : Whiting's Printing, 1840. 4 p. RPB. 40-6500

Texas [Republic] Laws, statutes, etc. Alphabetical index to the laws of Texas [1836-1840] Arranged by a member of the bar. S. l.: s. l., 1840. xiv p. WaU. 40-6501

Texas [Republic] Laws, statutes, etc. Laws of the Republic of Texas, passed at the Session of the Fourth Congress, 1840 [and at the Fifth Congress, 1840-41] Houston, TX: Telegraph Power Press, 1840-41. p. Mi-L; Nj; PHi; R; TxU-L. 40-6502

Texas in 1840; or, The emigrant's guide to the new republic; being the result of observations, enquiry, and travel in that beautiful country. By an emigrant, late of

the United States. With an introduction
by the Rev. A. B. Lawrence. New York:
W. W. Allen, 1840. 275 p. CU; IaU;
OFH; PU; TxDaM; WHi. 40-6503

Thackery, William Makepeace, 1811-
1863. The adventures of Philip, by Wm.
Thackery. New York: A. L. Burt Co.,
1840. 414 p. GDecA; MiMarc. 40-6504

Thackery, William Makepeace, 1811-
1863. Complete works. New York:
Thomas Y. Crowell & Co., 1840-61. 8 v.
NSyU. 40-6505

Thackery, William Makepeace, 1811-
1863. The great Hoggarty diamond. New
York: Harper Bros. [184-?] 84 p. NN. 40-
6506

Thackery, William Makepeace, 1811-
1863. Paris sketch book -- Eastern
sketches, Irish sketch books. Character
sketches. Boston, MA: Samuel E. Cas-
sino, 1840. 510 p. IaG. 40-6507

Thackery, William Makepeace, 1811-
1863. The Paris sketch book; Eastern
sketches; The Irish sketch book. New
York: Continental Press [1840] 443, 361
p. NR. 40-6508

Thackery, William Makepeace, 1811-
1863. Paris sketch book -- Irish sketch
book. By William M. Thackery. Boston,
MA: Published by Dana Estes and Co.,
1840. 2 v. MoKiT. 40-6509

Thackery, William Makepeace, 1811-
1863. Paris sketch book of Mr. M. A. Titmarsh, sketch book, and notes of a
journey from Cornhill for Grand Cairo.
Chicago, IL; Rahway, NJ: Published by
Donohue Henneberry & Co.; Printed by

ther Mershon Press, 1840? 768 p. IaChe;
OClUC. 40-6510

Thackery, William Makepeace, 1811-
1863. The Paris sketch book of Mr. M. A.
Titmarsh, and Eastern sketches of a journey from Cornhill to Grand Cairo, by
William Makepeace Thackery. With 85
illustrations by the author, Thomas R.
Macquoid, and J. P. Atkinson. Boston,
MA: Laughton, MacDonald & Co., 1840.
50 p. NJam. 40-6511

Thackery, William Makepeace, 1811-
1863. The Paris sketch book of Mr. M. A.
Titmarsh, The Irish sketch book, and
Notes of a journey from Cornhill to
Grand Cairo... [Adv. to 1st ed.] New
York: A. L. Burt [1840] 262, 298, 144, 69
p. WaPS. 40-6512

Thackery, William Makepeace, 1811-
1863. The Paris sketch book of Mr. M. A.
Titmarsh. The Irish sketch book and
notes of a journey from Cornhill for
Grand Cairo. Illustrated. By William
Makepeace Thackery. New York:
Metropolitan Publishing Company,
1840. 262, [2] 298, [2] 69 p. MPiB. 40-
6513

Thackery, William Makepeace, 1811-
1863. The Paris Sketch Book of Mr. M.
A. Titmarsh; Notes of a Journey. New
York: Hurst & Co., 1840. 262 p. IaPeC.
40-6514

Thackery, William Makepeace, 1811-
1863. The Paris Sketch Book of Mr. M.
A. Titmarsh; The Irish Sketch Book; and,
Notes of a Journey from Cornhill to
Grand Cairo. By William Makepeace
Thackery. With illustrations by the
Author. Chicago, IL; New York; San
Francisco, CA: Belford Clarke & Co.,

publishers, 1840. 819 p. KyLoYMH; ORAV. 40-6515

Thackery, William Makepeace, 1811-1863. The Paris sketch book of Mr. M. A. Titmarsh; The Irish sketch book; and Notes of a journey from Cornhill to Grand Cairo, by William Makepeace Thackery. With illustrations by the author. New York: Frank F. Lovell and Company, 1840. 821 p. CU; MiD; NcHy; OU; PHC. 40-6516

Thackery, William Makepeace, 1811-1863. The Paris sketch book of Mr. M. A. Titmarsh; The Irish sketch book; and Notes of a journey from Cornhill to Grand Cairo, by William Makepeace Thackery. New York: International Book Company [1840] 821 p. IaBo; NcSo; WaPS. 40-6517

Thackery, William Makepeace, 1811-1863. Roundabout Papers to which is added the second Funeral of Napoleon, Critical reviews, The Four Georges, The English Humorists of the Eighteenth Century. Sketches and travels in London, by William Makepeace Thackeray. New York: American Publishers Corporation, 1840. 825 p. No Loc. 40-6518

Thackery, William Makepeace, 1811-1863. Works. New York: T. Y. Crowell [1840-59] 10 v. IUr; NTR. 40-6519

Thatcher, Benjamin Bussey, 1809-1840. Indian traits: being sketches of the manners, customs, and character of the North American natives. By B. B. Thatcher. New York: Harper & brothers, 1840. 2 v. MB; MFi; MiD-B; MLow; P. 40-6520

Thayer, Thomas Baldwin. The Bible Class assistant, or scriptural guide for

Sunday Schools... By Thomas B. Thayer. Boston, MA: Thomas Whittemore, 1840. 180 p. DLC; ICU; MeT-Hi; MH-AH; NcD. 40-6521

There's not a word thy lips hath breath'd. An admired ballad for the guitar. Philadelphia, PA: Burns & Co. [184-?] 1 p. MB; ViU. 40-6522

Thetford, Vt. First Congregational Church. Confession of faith and covenant of the First Congregational Church in Thetford, Vt., adopted April 4, 1831... [S. l.: Thomas Mann, 1840] 45 p. MBD. 40-6523

Thiers, Louis Adolphe, 1797-1877. The history of the French revolution. By M. A. Thiers. Translated, with notes and ilustrations from the most authentic sources, by Frederick Sober... Philadelphia, PA: Carey and Hart, 1840. 3 v. GAuW; LNT; OClW; RPA; ScU. 40-6524

Tholuck, August, 1799-1877. Commentary on the Semon on the Mount, by Dr. A. Tholuck. Translated by Rev. R. Lundin Brown, M. A. Phildelphia, PA: Smith, English and Co., 1840. 443 p. IAIS; NAlf. 40-6525

Thomas, Abel C. Analysis and Confutation of Miller's theory of the End of the World in 1843... By Abel C. Thomas. Lowell, MA: Printed and published by A. Watson, 1840. 32 p. MMeT-Hi; MWA. 40-6526

Thomas, Cowperthwait and Company. Catalogue of law, medical, school, and miscellaneous books. Philadelphia, PA: Thomas, Cowperthwait & Co., 1840. 48 p. NcWsM. 40-6527

Thomas, Ebenezer Smith. Reminiscences of the last sixty-five years, commencing with the Battle of Lexington. Also, sketches of his own life and times. Hartford, CT: Case, Tiffany and Burnham, 1840. 2 v. ArCH; ICHi; MBBC; OClWHi; ScDuE. 40-6528

Thomas, Frederick William, 1808?-1866. Howard Pickney. A novel. By the author of "Clinton Bradshaw." Philadelphia, PA: Lea & Blanchard, 1840. 2 v. LNH; MWA; TJoT. 40-6529

Thomas, R. Christian index; containing an account of the life of Christ and His apostles, and Christian persecution... By R. Thomas. Hartford, CT: Published by Ezra Strong, 1840. 288 p. OUrC; TKimJ. 40-6530

Thomas, R. The life of Our Lord and Saviour Jesus Christ and His Apostles... By R. Thomas. Hartford, CT: Published by Ezra Strong, 1840. 288 p. MiD; NSherb. 40-6531

Thomaston Theological Institution, Maine. Catalogue of the officers and students of the Thomaston Theological Institution, 1839-40. Thomaston, ME: H. P. Coombs, 1840. 24 p. CBPSR. 40-6532

Thompson, Daniel Pierce, 1795-1868. The Green Mountain Boys; an historical tale of the early settlement of Vermont... [anon.] Montpelier, VT: s. l., 1840. 2 v. IGK. 40-6533

Thompson, George, 1804-1878. Lectures on British India, delivered in the Friends' meeting-house, Manchester, England, in October, 1839, by George Thompson; with a preface by Wm. Lloyd Garrison. Pawtucket, RI: W. and R.

Adams, 1840. 206 p. ICMe; MBC; MiD; PWW; RHi. 40-6534

Thompson, George, 1804-1878. State and prospects of British India; the substance of a lecture, Feb. 27th, 1840. Bradford, PA: s. l., 1840. 24 p. MB; NIC. 40-6535

Thompson, J. W. To the... the Postmaster Gen'l. [Washington, DC: s. l., 1840?] p. MB. 40-6536

Thompson, James Hedge, 1814-1886. Oration delivered before the associate alumni of Washington college in Christ church, Hartford, August 5, 1840. Hartford, CT: The Assoc., 1840. 23 p. CtHT; MB; NNC. 40-6537

Thompson, James William, 1805-1881. The doctrine of the cross. By Rev. J. W. Thompson. Boston, MA: pr. for the American Unit assoc., James Monroe & co., 1840. 32 p. DLC; ICMe; MBAU; MeBat; MH; N. 40-6538

Thompson, Joseph Parrish, 1819-1879. Habitual thankfulness; a discourse delivered in the Chapel street Congregational church, New Haven, November 19, 1840... by... pastor of that church. Hartford, CT: B. L. Hamlen, 1840. 23 p. CtSoP; MA; MB; MBC; NHC-S; OCl. 40-6539

Thompson, LaRue P. Two discourses, preached in the Brick Church, Canandaigua, June 23, 1839. Canandaigua, NY: George L. Whitney, 1840. 29 p. NCanHi; NCH; WBeloC. 40-6540

Thompson, Leander. The influence of memory. A sermon. Preached by Rev. Leander Thompson, missionary at

Beyroot, Syria. Boston, MA: Crocker and Brewster, 1840. 16 p. CtHC; MH; MiD-B; MWo; Nh. 40-6541

Thompson, Waddy, 1798-1868. Examination of the claims of Mr. Van Buren and Gen. Harrison to the support of the South. An address to his constituents. [Washington, DC?: s. l., 1840] 11 p. DLC; GEU; MBC; NcD. 40-6542

Thompson, Waddy, 1798-1868. ... General Waddy Thompson's address to his constituents. Remarks by Mr. Graves [of Kentucky] in Congress on the treasury note bill... With other important articles. [Tuskalooa, AL: Independent Monitor, 1840?] 16 p. GEU. 40-6543

Thompson, Waddy, 1798-1868. ... Speech of Waddy Thompson, of South Carolina, on the President's annual message to Congress. Delivered in the House of Representatives, December 30, 1839. [Washington, DC: s. l., 1840] 8 p. GEU; MWA; NNC. 40-6544

Thompson, Waddy, 1798-1868. To the Honorable the Senate... [Washington, DC: J. & G. S. Gideon, printer, 184-?] 11 p. DLC; ICN. 40-6545

Thompson, William, 1802-1852. Historical notices on the occurrence of inflammatory affections of the internal organs after external injuries and surgical operations. By William Thompson, M. D. Philadelphia, PA: Haswell, Barrinton, and Haswell, 1840. 309 p. Nh; OCGHM. 40-6546

Thompson, William, 1802-1852. Historical notices on the occurrence of inflammatory affections of the internal organs after external injuries and surgi-

cal operations. By William Thompson, M. D. Philadelphia, PA: Haswell, Barrinton, and Haswell, 1840. 31 p. CSt-L; LNT-M; NhD; NNNAM; PPL; WMAM. 40-6547

Thompson, William, 1802-1852. Historical notices on the occurrence of inflammatory affections of the internal organs after external injuries and surgical operations. By William Thompson, M. D. Philadelphia, PA: Haswell, Barrinton, and Haswell, 1840. 409 p. Nh. 40-6548

Thompson, William, 1802-1852. Inflammatory affections of the internal organs after external injuries and surgical operations. Philadelphia, PA: Haswell, Barrinton, and Haswell, 1840. 59 p. ScCMeS. 40-6549

Thomson, James, 1700-1748. The seasons. By James Thomson. With a life of the author and index, by George Kent. From the London edition of 1780, compared with the London octavo and Edinburgh editions. For the use of schools and academies. Brown's edition. Concord, NH: John F. Brown, 1840. 165 p. CoPuB. 40-6550

Thomson, James, 1700-1748. The seasons. A new edition. Boston, MA: Weeks, Jordan & Co., 1840. 154 p. KyDC; MAm; MB. 40-6551

Thomson, James, 1700-1748. The seasons: a poem. By James Thomson. With notes and an index. Improved edition. New York: Clark & Maynard, publishers, 1840. 168 p. ICMBI; NcD; NvHi; OU; ScNC. 40-6552

Thomson, Samuel, 1769-1843. Thomsonian Almanac. Boston, MA: S. Thompson [1840] p. MWA. 40-6553

Thomson, Samuel, 1769-1843. Thomson's Almanac for 1841. Bellows Falls, VT: J. A. Martin; Moore & Fulton, printers [1840] p. MWA. 40-6554

Thomson, Samuel, 1769-1843. Thomson's Almanac for 1841. By James Osgood. Boston, MA: D. L. Hale [1840] p. MWA. 40-6555

Thomson, Samuel, 1769-1843. United States Thomsonian almanac for 1840; being bissextile or leap year. By Samuel Thomson. Poughkeepsie, NY: published by Lapham and Plate, Kelley and Lossing, printers, 1840. 36 p. FNp. 40-6556

Thomson, Thomas, 1773-1852. Sketch of the progress of physical science... [New York: Greeley and McElrath, 184-?] 44 p. MnHi; NN. 40-6557

Thornton, Henry, 1760-1815. Family prayers; to which is added a family commentary upon the Sermon on the Mount. By the late Henry Thornton, Esq. Edited by the Rev. Manton Eastburn, D. D... 6th American edition. New York: Swords, Stanford & Company, 1840. 168, 160 p. GHi; InID; MoS; OMC. 40-6558

Thornton, Phineas. Southern gardener and receipt book. [n. p.] : Author, 1840. Baltimore. St. Peter's Protestant Episcopal Church. By-laws for the government of the vestry of St. Peter's Protestant Episcopal Church, and of the officers of the vestry and church. Baltimore: Printed by Richard J. Machett, 1840. 12 p. MdBD. 40-6559

Thornwell, James Henry. A tract on the

doctrines of election and reprobation. By J. H. Thornwell. Columbia: Printed and published by Samuel Weir, 1840. 56 p. CSansS; GDecCT; KyLx; MH-AH; PPPrHi. 40-6560

Thoughts on the laws, government and morals. By a citizen of Boston. Boston, MA: printed for the author, 1840. 24 p. MH; MiU-C; MMeT; NjR; NN. 40-6561

Three letters from a citizen of New York to the Governor of the State of Indiana, showing how the state may raise money to complete their internal improvements. New York: James Van Norden, printer, 1840. 8 p. DLC; MiD-B; NHi; NN. 40-6562

Three letters to the Governor of Indiana, showing how the states may raise money to complete their internal improvements. New York: s. l., 1840. PPL-R. 40-6563

Thucydides. History of the Peloponneisan War. Translated from the Greek of Thucydides. By William Smith... Philadelphia, PA: Thomas Wardle, 1840. 344 p. GDecCT; PLPM; TNL; ViU. 40-6564

Thurston, N. A tract. [Lowell, MA: s. l., 1840] p. MB. 40-6565

Ticknor, Caleb B., 1805-1840. The philosophy of living; or, The way to enjoy life and its comforts... New York: Harper & brothers, 1840. 3 p. InRch; MB; RPB; ScDuE; ViR. 40-6566

Ticknor, Caleb Bingham, 1804-1840. Letter to the Hon. --- with reasons for examining and believing the fundamental principles of homoeopathy. By C. Ticknor, M. D. New York: Henry Ludwig, printer [1840] 31 p. MBC; MHi; MoSpD; NNNAM; PU. 40-6567

Tidd, William, 1760-1847. The practice of the courts of King's Bench and Common Pleas, in personal actions & Ejectment; to which are added the law & practice of extents and the Rules of Court and Modern Decisions in the Exchequer of Pleas. By William Tidd. With notes of Recent English Statutes & Decisions by Frances J. Troubat. Philadelphia, PA: Robert H. Small, publisher, 1840. 2 v. GOgU; OCoSc; RPL; TU; VtU. 40-6568

Tieck, Johann Ludwig, 1773-1853. Blue Beard. A story in five acts. Translated from the German by J. L. Motley. New York: s. l., 1840. MB. 40-6569

Tieck, Johann Ludwig, 1773-1853. Die Klausenburg: eine gespensterge-schichte... New York: W. Radde, 1840. 84 p. CtMW; InGrD; MH; OU. 40-6570

Tillinghast, John L. A treatise on the principles and practice, process, pleadings, and entries, in cases of writs of error, writs in the nature of error, appeals, and proceedings, in the nature of appeals, by John L. Tillinghast and John V. W. Yates. Albany, NY: William & A. Gould & co., 1840. 2 v. C; CEu; NcU; NNLI; Nv. 40-6571

Timrod, Henry. Poems. Boston, MA: Ticknor-Fields, 1840. 130 p. AMob. 40-6572

Tinelli, L. An address delivered by L. Tinelli before an assembly of silk culturists, held at Levy's Saloon, in New York, on the 2nd of March, 1840. New York: printed by C. Vinton, 1840. 8 p. MB; MH; MWA; NN; PPL. 40-6573

Tip and Ty [Tippecanoe and Tyler too] A new comic Whig glee. Respectfully dedicated to the Louisiana Whig delegation to the Bunker Hill Convention. Boston, MA: Parker & Ditson [1840?] p. MBNEC. 40-6574

Tip and Tye. A favorite patriotic ballad, as sung at the Tippecanoe Associations. With great applause, arranged with an accompaniment for the piano forte. By a member of the Fifth Ward Club. S. l.: s. l. [184-?] 2 p. ViU. 40-6575

Tippecanoe almanac for 1841. Philadelphia: M'Carty and Davis, [1840] Picture of Cincinnati. The Cincinnati almanac, 1840. Cincinnati: Gleyen and Shepard, 1840. Freemasons. Alabama. Proceedings of the grand lodge of the state of Alabama, A. D. 1840. Tuscaloosa: J. D. Slade, [1840] 28 p. AMFM; IaCrM; ICS; MBFM. 40-6576

The Tippecanoe and log cabin almanac, 1841. New York: H. A. Chapin & Co., 1840. MWA; PHi. 40-6577

Tippecanoe Club, Alton, Ill. Harrisonians! Attention!! An adjourned meeting of the Tippecanoe Club of the City of Alton... on Monday evening, the 13th instant, at 8 o'clock... a general attendance of the Friends of Harrison and Reform is desired, July 11, 1840. [Alton, IL: Printed at the "Telegraph Office, "1840] p. IHi. 40-6578

Tippecanoe Club, Alton, Ill. The regular monthly meeting of the Tippecanoe Club of the City of Alton... this evening... March 28, 1840. Alton, IL:

Printed at the "Telegraph Office, "1840. Broadside. CSmH. 40-6579

Tippecanoe Club, Alton, Ill. Tippecanoe Club!! A special meeting of the Tippecanoe Club of the City of Alton will be held at the Old Court Room This Evening! at 7 o'clock. A general attendance is requested. By order of J. Hall, Sec'y, July 8, 1840. [Alton, IL: s. l., 1840] Broadside. ICHi. 40-6580

The Tippecanoe song book... Cincinnati, OH: W. P. James, 1840. 64 p. InHi; MB; OClWHi. 40-6581

Tippecanoe song book: a collection of log cabin and patriotic melodies... Philadelphia, PA: Marshall, Williams, and Butler, 1840. 180 p. NN; OClWHi; RPB. 40-6582

Tipp's invitation to Loc. A favorite patriotic glee, as sung at the Tippecanoe Associations with great applause. Written and arranged for the piano forte by a member of the Fifth Ward Club. New York: Thomas Birch, 1840. 3 p. ViU. 40-6583

To be sold by public auction, the parcels of real estate of John Foster, late of Cambridge, to wit: one pew in the New Church of the First Parish, also [several lots of land] etc. Cambridge, MA: s. l., 1840. Broadside. MH. 40-6584

To be sung at elections. [New York?: s. l., 1840?] Broadside. NN. 40-6585

To the freemen of Maryland, statement of the Annapolis Tippecanoe Club. Washington, DC: s. l., 1840. PPL. 40-6586

To the people of North Carolina in relation to a law of Ohio subjecting white citizens to sale. Washington, DC: s. l., 1840. 7 p. DLC; PPL. 40-6587

Tobin, John, 1770-1804. ... The honeymoon. A play in five acts. By John Tobin. With the stage business, cast of characters, costumes, relative positions, &c. New York [etc.] : S. French [184-?] 62 p. CSt; MH. 40-6588

Tocqueville, Alexis Charles Henri Maurice Clerel de, 1805-1859. Democracy in America. By Alexis de Tocqueville... Tr. by Henry Reeve, esq. With an original preface and notes by John C. Spencer... New York; Philadelphia, PA: J. & H. G. Langley; Thomas, Cowperthwaite & Co., etc., etc., 1840. 2 v. MDeeP; OClWHi; ViU. 40-6589

Tocqueville, Alexis Charles Henri Maurice Clerel de, 1805-1859. Report to Chamber of Deputies on abolition of slavery in French Colonies, July 23, 1839. Translated from the French. Boston, MA: s. l., 1840. 54 p. MB; NcD; OClWHi; PU; RPB. 40-6590

Todd, Charles Stewart, 1791-1871. Sketches of the civil and military services of William Henry Harrison. By Charles S. Todd... and Benjamin Drake... Cincinnati, OH: U. P. James, 1840. 165 p. CSmH; IHi; MWA; PHi; WHi. 40-6591

Tomlinson, R. Statement of Reasons; proceedings of the Old Colony Association. Boston, MA: Printed by J. N. Bang, 1840. 24 p. MMeT; MMet-Hi; MNBedf. 40-6592

Tonna, Charlotte Elizabeth (Browne) Phelan, 1790-1846. Floral biography; or

Chapters on Flowers. By Charlotte Elizabeth. First American from second London edition. New York: Published by M. W. Dodd, 1840. 321 p. IU; KyBC; MB; MSaP; RPA. 40-6593

Tonna, Charlotte Elizabeth (Browne) Phelan, 1790-1846. The flower garden; or, Chapters on flowers, a sequel to Floral biography... by [pseud.] New York: M. W. Dodd, 1840. 330 p. IU; KU; NbU; NjR; OU; PPL. 40-6594

Tonna, Charlotte Elizabeth (Browne) Phelen, 1790-1846. Personal recollections, by Charlotte Elizabeth. Abridged, chiefly in parts pertaining to political and other controversies prevalent at the time in Great Britain. New York: Published by the American Tract Society, 184-? 248 p. DLC; MH; RPB; ViU; WU. 40-6595

Torrey, H. The manner of preaching. By Rev. H. Torrey, Pastor of the First Universalist Church of Pittsburgh, Pa. Pittsburgh, PA: Printed by A. A. Anderson, 1840. 23 p. MMeT. 40-6596

Torrey, Henry Warren, 1814-1893. An English-Latin lexicon. Prepared to accompany Leverett's Latin-English lexicon. Boston, MA: s. l., 1840. MBC; MoSpD. 40-6597

Townson, Calvin. A chart of the history of England... New York: R. C. Valentine, 1840. 1 p. MiU. 40-6598

Tract Society of Friends, Philadelphia. Memoirs and essays on moral and religious subjects. Philadelphia, PA: Published at the Depostiroy, J. and W. Kite [184-?] 2 v. MH. 40-6599

Tracts for the times. By members of the University of Oxford. New York: Charles Henry, 1840. 3 v. ICP; InID; M; RBr. 40-6600

Tracy, Caleb B. Sermon at the funeral of Mrs. Betsy Cogswell. Concord, NH: s. l., 1840. 12 p. MBC. 40-6601

Tracy, Calvin. A new system of arithemetic... New Haven, CT: Durrie, 1840. 311 p. CtHWatk; ICA. 40-6602

Tracy, Joseph. History of the American Board of commissioners for foreign missions. Comp. chiefly from the published and unpublished documents of the board by Joseph Tracy. Worcester: Spooner & Howland, 1840. GEU; InCW; MdBP; OClW; RPA; TxDaM. 40-6603

Trail, William. A guide to Christian communicants in the exercise of self examination, by the Rev. Wm. Trail, A. M... Philadelphia, PA: Presbyterian Board of Publication, 1840. 112 p. GDecCT; NbOP; NCH; PPPrHi. 40-6604

Traill, Robert. A vindication of Protestant doctrine concerning justification, and its preachers and professors from the unjust charge of Antinonianism. In a letter from the author... Columbia: Weir, 1840. 35 p. CSansS; GDecCT; ICP; NcD; PPPrHi. 40-6605

The traveller, or the wonders of nature. New York: s. l., 1840. MB. 40-6606

Travers, John. In the court for the trial of impeachments and the correction of errors. John Travers, plaintiff in error, vs. Abraham Godwin, Jr., John Clark, Jr., Charles Danforth, Defendants in error... error book. New York: John W. Oliver, 1840. 3, 4, 44 p. NNC. 40-6607

Treffry, Richard. Memoirs of the life, character, and labours of the Rev. John Smith, late of Sheffield, by Richard Treffry, Jr. New York; T. Mason & G. Lane, 1840. 328 p. KyBvU; MnSH. 40-6608

Tremayne, Mrs. S. C. H. Florence Dalbiac, and other tales... New York: Printed by S. W. Benedict, 1840. 234 p. CL; DLC; RPB. 40-6609

The tribune almanac and political register... New York: s. l., 1840. CS; CSf; MoS. 40-6610

A tribute to the memory of Fitzhugh Smith, the some of Gerritt Smith, by the author of "Thoughts on a New Order of Missionaries," etc. Resurgam! New York: Wiley and Putnam, 1840. 284p. DLC; NFrf; NNC; OO; WHi. 40-6611

Trinity College, Hartford, Ct. Catalogue of the library and members of the Athenaeum Society, of Washington College. Hartford, CT: Case, Tiffany and Burnham, printers, 1840. 37 [1] p. MiD-B. 40-6612

Trinity College, Hartford, Ct. Catalogue of the officers and students of Washington College, Hartford. For the academic year 1839-40. Hartford, CT: Case, Tiffany and Burnham, printers, 1840. 16 p. Ct. 40-6613

Trist, Nicholas Philip, 1800-1874. Case of Captain Abraham Wendell, jr., of the brig Kremlin of New York, arising from an outragte perpetrated by him upon William Bell, first officer of said brig, in the port of Havana, July, 1838. [Being an extract from a document recently printed by order of the House of representatives.] .... [Washington, DC: s. l., 1840] 52 p. DLC; MB; MBAt; PPL; ViU. 40-6614

Trist, Nicholas Philip, 1800-1874. Case of the crew of the ship "William Engs," embracing the inquiry, Who is Richard Robert Madden? the friend, confederate, and witness of Ferdinand Clark. [Being an extract from a document recently printed by order of the House of representatives.] [Washington, DC: s. l., 1840] 68 p. CSmH; DLC; MB; MBAt; NN. 40-6615

Trist, Nicholas Philip, 1800-1874. Condition of American seamen at the port of Havana. Washington: s. l., 1840. CSmH; DLC; MH; NIC; PPL. 40-6616

Trist, Nicholas Philip, 1800-1874. Reply of Nicholas P. Trist to the resolutions at a meeting in Boston on subject of the cases of Captain Abraham Wendell, Jr., and the crew of the ship "William Eugs... "Printed by order of the House of Representatives. [Washington, DC: s. l., 1840?] 43 p. CSmH; DLC; MB; MBAt; MH; NN. 40-6617

Trist, Nicholas Philip, 1800-1874. Reply of Nicholas P. Trist, counsel at Havana, to the preamble and resolutions adopted by the meeting of Ship Master and ship owners, convened at the City of New York... Printed by order of the House of Representatives. [Washington, DC: s. l., 1840] 35 p. DLC; MB; NN. 40-6618

Triumph of Faith; or, memoir of Miss Nancy M. Clark, destined on a mission to Western Asia, under the direction of the American Board. Written for the Massachusetts Sabbath School Society and revised by the Committee of Publication. Boston, MA: Massachusetts Sabbath

School Society, 1840. 148 p. DLC; NN. 40-6619

Trollope, Frances Milton, 1780-1863. The Life and adventures of Michael Armstrong, the factory boy. New York: Harper and brothers, 1840. 2 v. CtHT; MCon; NN; NjP; NNS. 40-6620

The Troy Almanac. Sandy Hill, NY: G. Howland, 1840. MWA. 40-6621

The Troy Almanac for 1841. Troy, NY: Elias Gates [1840] p. CSmH; MWA; OCHP. 40-6622

Troy, N. Y. Mechanics' Mutual Insurance Company. The charter, revised by-laws, and classes of hazards and rates of premiums of the Mechanics' Mutual Insurance Company in the City of Troy. In pursuance of a resolution passed at the annual meeting, 1840. Troy, NY: N. Tuttle, 1840. 20 p. NAuT; NT. 40-6623

Troy, N. Y. Receipt and expenditures of the City of Troy, from the 2d of March, 1839 to the 2d of March, 1840. Troy, NY?: N. Tuttle, printer, 1840. 32 p. NT. 40-6624

Troy, Albany and New York Steam-Boat Line. The New Steam-boat Troy. Troy, NY?: N. Tuttle, printer, 1840. Broadside. NN. 40-6625

Troy Conference Academy, West Poultney, Vt. Catalogue of the corporation, faculty, and students of the Troy conference academy, West poultney, Vt. Form the academic year 1840. Middlebury, VT: R. P. H. Malham, printer [1840] 23 p. TU. 40-6626

True, Charles Kittredge, 1809-1878.

The elements of logic... Adapted to the capacity of younger students and designed for academies and the higher classes of common schools. By Charles K. True... Boston, MA: Crocker, 1840. 156 p. FDU; MH; MMal; NSyU. 40-6627

Trumbull, Henry. History of the discovery of America: of the landing of the Pilgrims at Plymouth and their most remarkable engagements with the Indians, in New England, from their first arrival, in 1620, until the final subjugation of the natives in 1679... Boston, MA: G. Clark, 1840. 304 p. CtMW; DLC; MBBC; TxU; WHi. 40-6628

Trumbull, Joseph, 1782-1861. Speech of the Hon. Mr. Trumbull, of Connecticut, on the Treasury note bill. Delivered in Committee of the whole House on the state of the Union, March 24, 1840. [Washington, DC?: s. l., 1840?] 16 p. IU; MdBJ. 40-6629

Tuckeman, Joseph. A letter reflecting Santa Cruz as a winter residence for invalids, addressed to Doctor John C. Warren, of Boston, Mass. Boston, MA: D. Clapp, Jr., 184-? 27 p. DLC; MB; MH; MHi; NN. 40-6630

Tucker, Nathaniel Beverley, 1784-1851. A discourse on the importance of the study of political science, as a branch of academic education in the United States... By Beverley Tucker. Richmond, VA: Peter D. Bernard, 1840. 28 p. A-Ar; MH; NcD; Vi. 40-6631

Tully, J. H. Love launched a fairy boat. Ballad. Written by Mark Lemon. Music by J. H. Tully. Baltimore, MD; New Orleans, LA: F. D. Benteen; W. T. Mayo [184-?] 3 p. ViU. 40-6632

Tupper, Martin Farquhar. Proverbial philosophy; being thoughts and arguments originally treated. [1st series] From the London edition. 2d edition. Boston, MA: s. l., 1840. ICP; MBAt; MH; OMC. 40-6633

Turner, Edward, 1798-1837. Elements of chemistry, including the recent discoveries and doctrines of the science. By the late Edward Turner, M. D. With notes and emendations, by Franklin Bache, M. D. Sixth American edition. Philadelphia, PA: Thomas, Cowperthwait & Co., 1840. 666 p. KyLxT; Nh; OCPhar; OO. 40-6634

Turner, Francois. Elements de grammaire francaise; or, Principles of the French language. 2nd edition, corrected and improved. New Haven, CT: A. H. Maltby, 1840. CtHWatk; KWiU; MH; NPV. 40-6635

Turner, Jacob. Truth against error; or, Universalism, the truth of the Gospel. By Jacob Turner. Lowell, MA: A. Watson, printer, 1840. 62 p. MMeT-Hi. 40-6636

Turner, Joseph W. Where'er I wander. Written and composd by Joseph W. Turner. Boston, MA: Oliver Ditson [184-?] 3 p. ViU. 40-6637

Turner & Hughes's North Carolina Almanac for 1841. Vol. 1, No. 2 2nd ed. Raleigh, NC: Turner & Hughes [1840] p. MWA; NcD. 40-6638

Turner's Comic Almanack. Boston, MA: J. Fisher, 1840. MWA. 40-6639

Turner's Comick Almanac. New York: Turner & Fisher, 1840. MWA. 40-6640

Tuttle, Henry. An historical collection, comprising important and interesting items in the history of the United States. Twelfth edition - with additions. Utica, NY: Henry Tuttle, publisher; C. C. P. Grosh, printer, 1840. 36 p. MH. 40-6641

Tweedie, Alexander, 1794-1884. A system of practical medicine comprised in a series of original dissertations. Arranged and ed. by Alexander Tweedie... Philadelphia, PA: Lea & Blanchard, 1840-41. 5 v. CSt; ICU; MdBJ-W; MoU; ViU. 40-6642

The twelve brothers or the history of Joseph. New Haven, CT: Published by S. Babcock, 1840. 8 p. MiHi. 40-6643

Twilight dews. A favorite song. Arranged with an accompaniment for the piano forte. New York: E. S. Mesier [184-?] 2 p. ViU. 40-6644

Twing, A. T. Liberty not licentiousness. An oration. Delivered on the fourth of July, 1840, in the First Reformed Dutch Church, West Troy. By the Rev. A. T. Twing, A. M. West Troy, NY: W. Hollands, printer, 1840. 16 p. NGH. 40-6645

The two widows. Philadelphia, PA: American Sunday School Union, 1840. 49 p. MB; ScCliTO. 40-6646

Tyas, Robert, 1811-1879. The sentiment of flowers; or, Language of flora. Embracing an account of nearly three hundred different flowers, with their powers in language... Philadelphia, PA: Lea & Blanchard, 1840. 276 p. CtWatk; MB; MH; MiD; MnU. 40-6647

Tyler, John, 1819-1896. An oration on the life and character of Benjamin

Franklin. Delivered before the Franklin Society of William and Mary College on the 17th January 1840. By John Tyler, Jr. Norfolk, VA: Printed by W. C. Shields, 1840. 27 p. MiU-C; Vi. 40-6648

Tyng, Stephen H. Memento of a pastor's affection. Phildelphia, PA: William Stavely & Co., 1840. 112 p. PPM. 40-6649

Tyson, J. Washington. The doctrines of the "abolitionists" refuted, in a letter from J. Washington Tyson, the Democratic Harrison candidate for Congress, in the first district, of Pennsylvania. Philadelphia, PA: [n. pr.] 1840. 8 p. CtSoP; MdHi; NhHi; RP. 40-6650

U

Uncle Sam's large almanack for 1841. Phildelphia, PA: Wm. W. Walker [1840] p. KHi; MWA. 40-6651

Underwood, James. Address and the proceedings of the Festival, held in the City of Cincinnati, January 29th, 1840, in commemoration of the Revolutionary Services of that wonderful advocate of civil liberty, Thomas Paine. by James Underwood. Cincinnati, OH: s. l., 1840. 12 p. NHi. 40-6652

Underwood, Joseph Rogers, 1791-1876. Speech of Mr. Underwood, of Kentucky, on the Sub-treasury bill, delivered in the [House of Representatives] June 8, 1840. Washington, DC: Sales and Seaton, 1840. 36 p. M. 40-6653

Underwood, Joseph Rogers, 1791-1876. Speech on the amendment proposed to the bill for the support of the army, appropriating 300, 000 dollars to carry on military operations in Florida, delivered in the [House of Representatives] July 13, 1840. Washington, DC: s. l., 1840. 19 p. DLC; ICN; M; NBu; WHi. 40-6654

Union Bank of Florida, Tallahasse, Fla. Reply to the board of directors of the Union bank of Florida, to the reports of the bank and judiciary committees of the House of Representatives, of the legislative council of Florida. Tallahassee, FL: B. F. Whitner, jr., printer, 1840. 98 p. LNH; NN; PHi. 40-6655

Union Benevolent Association, Philadelphia, Pa. Report of the ladies' branch of the Union Benevolent Association, for the months of October, November, December, January and February, 1839-40. Philadelphia, PA: King & Baird, printers, 1840. 21 p. PHi; PPL; PPM. 40-6656

Union College, Schenectady, N. Y. A Catalogue of the officers and pupils of the Young Ladies' Seminary, Schectady, N. Y., for the year ending April, 1840. Schenectady, NY: Riggs & Norris, printers, 1840. 12 p. NSchHi. 40-6657

Union College, Schenectady, N. Y. Catalogue of the officers and students in Union College, 1840. Published by the students. Schenectady, NY: Printed by E. M. Packard, 1840. 23 p. NGlf. 40-6658

Union College, Schenectady, N. Y. Equitable Union. Catalogue of the members. Schenectady, NY: s. l., 1840. DLC; NHi. 40-6659

Union College, Schenectady, N. Y. Philomathean Society. Catalogue of the Philomathean Society, instituted in Union College, 1795. Schenectady, NY: Riggs & Norris, printers to the College, 1840. 37 p. MdHi; N. 40-6660

Union College, Schenectady, N. Y. Senate. Circular, constitution, and rules of order... Schenectady, NY: Riggs &

Norris, printers, 1840. 11 p. MB; MBC; NHi; NN. 40-6661

Union Potomac Company, Hampshire County, Va. Charters of the Union Potomac Company and the Union Company, with a brief description of their coal and iron mines, situatated in Hampshire County, Maryland. Baltimore, MD: Printed by John Murphy, 1840. 52 p. IU; MdBp; MH-BA; MnHi; ViU. 40-6662

Union Potomac Company, Hampshire County, Va. The coal and iron mines, of the Union Potomac Company, [incorporated by Virginia] and of the Union Company [incorporated by Maryland] comprising upwards of Fifty-six thousand acres of land, situated in Alleghany County, Maryland, and in Hampshire County, Virginia. Baltimore, MD: Printed by John Murphy, 1840. 23 p. IU; MdHi; NNE; PPL; ViU. 40-6663

The U. S. almanac exhibiting returns of elections and other political information. New York: Collins, 1840. MWA; PPL. 40-6664

United States almanac for 1841. Calculations by Charles Frederick Egelmann. Philadelphia, PA: George W. Mentz, 1840. MWA. 40-6665

United States' historical and statistical index... from the administration of Washington... to... 1840. New York: s. l., 1840. CtY; MBC; MH-BA; NjR. 40-6666

United States Marine March. Composed & dedicated to the officers of the Marine Corps, by a Lady of Charleston, S. C. Baltimore, MD: F. D. Benteen [184-?] 2 p. ViU. 40-6667

U. S. Mint. Remarks of Mr. Stanley on the branch mint in North Carolina. Washington, DC: s. l., 1840. NcU; PPL. 40-6668

Universalist Year Book. The Universalist companion, with almanac and register containing the statistics of the denomination for 1841. A. B. Grosh, editor. Utica, NY; New York; Boston, MA: Orren Hutchinson; A. Tompkins; T. Whittemore; C. C. P. Grosh, printer [1840] 72 p. MH; MWA; NHi; OClWHi; WHi. 40-6669

Unknown murderer... Cincinnati, OH: s. l., 1840. PPL. 40-6670

Upham, Charles Wentworth, 1802-1875. The life of Washington, in the form of an autobiography, the narrative being to a great extent, conducted by himself, in extracts and selections from his own writings... By Rev. Chas. W. Upham. Boston, MA: Marsh, Capin, Lyon, Webb, 1840. 2 v. ICN; MiU-C; OHi; PP; TxU. 40-6671

Upham, Charles Wentworth, 1802-1875. The scripture doctrine of regeneration. By Rev. C. W. Upham. Boston, MA: pr. for the Amer. Unit. assoc.; James Munroe & co., 1840. 40 p. CBPac; DLC; ICMe; MBC; MMeT-Hi. 40-6672

Upham, Thomas Cogswell, 1799-1872. Elements of mental philosophy, abridged and designed as a text-book for academies and high schools. By Thomas C. Upham... New York; Harper & Brothers, 1840. 480 p. IaB; LU; PU; ScC; TxHut. 40-6673

Upham, Thomas Cogswell, 1799-1872. Mental philosophy, abridged. New York;

Harper & Brothers, 1840. 480 p. INorm-
N. 40-6674

Upham, Thomas Cogswell, 1799-1872.
Outlines of imperfect and disordered
mental actions... New York: Harper &
brothers, 1840. 399 p. CU; GU; MoK;
Nh; PPA. 40-6675

The Upper Mississippian. A weekly
paper published in Rock County, Illinois,
and for the Iowa Territory. Vol. 1, No. 1,
October 8th, 1840. S. l.: s. l., 1840-. v. NN.
40-6676

Upshur, Abel Parker, 1790-1844. A
brief enquiry into the true nature and
character of our federal government...
Petersburg, VA: Printed by E. and J. C.
Ruffin, 1840. 132 p. MDeeP; NcU; PHi;
Vi; WaU. 40-6677

Upshur, H. L. Sketch showing the route
of the military road from Red River to
Austin, Col. William G. Cooke, com-
manding, Wiliam H. Hunt, engineer,
1840. S. l.: s. l., 1840. TxU. 40-6678

Upton, Wheelock Samuel, 1811-1860.
Address delivered before the Tippecanoe Club of New York [against the
re-election of M. Van Buren as President
of the United States of America] [New
York: s. l., 1840] p. NN. 40-6679

The Ursuline manual; or, A collection
of prayers... interspersed with the various
instructions necessary for forming youth
to the practice of solid piety. Originally
arranged for the young ladies educated at
the Ursuline Convent, Cork. Revised
and improved. 2nd edition. Baltimore,
MD: Published by Fielding Lucas, Jr.,
1840. 578 p. MCE. 40-6680

Ursuline manual; or, A collection of
prayers, spiritual exercises, etc. Arranged for the young ladies at the Ursuline Convent, Cork. Revised by Rev.
John Power. New York; Edward
Dunigan, 1840. 520 p. CtHC; MWA;
NjR; PPL; ViU. 40-6681

Usher, Edward. The truth of the Bible,
and the Divinity of Christ Demonstrated
and Strictures on Infidelity and
Socinianism. By Edward Usher. Boston,
MA: s. l., 1840. IEG. 40-6682

Utica, N. Y. Neptune Fire Engine Company, No. 5. By-laws of the Utica Neptune Fire Engine Company, No. 5.
Revised and passed March, 1840. Utica,
NY: Bennett, Backus, & Hawley, 1840.
12 p. NUt. 40-6683

The Utica directory, 1840-41. Compiled
by William Richards, City Letter Carrier.
Utica, NY: John P. Bush, printer, 1840.
142 p. MWA; NN; NUt. 40-6684

Utility & necessity of asylums for vic-
times of intemperance. Philadelphia,
PA: s. l., 1840. MB. 40-6685

Uxbridge, Mass. Report of the town officers. Uxbridge, MA: s. l., 1840. M. 40-
6686

V

Valentine, Elliot. Mental arithmetic. For common schools. Designed to prepare the mind for the use of the slate. By Elliot Valentine. Bangor, ME: E. F. Duren, William Hyde, 1840. 80 p. DLC. 40-6687

Valentine, Thomas, 1790-1878. Aria Alla scozzese. Arranged with variations for the piano forte by T. Valentine. Boston, MA: Oliver Diston [184-?] 4 p. ViU. 40-6688

Valentine, Thomas, 1790-1878. Aria Alla scozzese. Con variazione. For the piano forte by T. Valentine. Baltimore, MD; Cincinnati, OH; Louisville, KY: W. C. Peters; Peter & Field; Peters & Webster [184-?] 4 p. ViU. 40-6689

Valentine, Thomas, 1790-1878. Aria Alla scozzese. Con variazione. For the piano forte by T. Valentine. New York: Jollie [184-?] 4 p. ViU. 40-6690

Valentine, Thomas, 1790-1878. The Highland ladder... New York: Dubois & Stodart [184-?] 3 p. MB. 40-6691

Valentine, Thomas, 1790-1878. Home! sweet home. With variations for the piano forte by T. Valentine. Baltimore, MD: F. D. Benteen [184-?] 5 p. ViU. 40-6692

Valentine, Thomas, 1790-1878. Variations... on believe me if all those, etc...

Baltimore, MD: s. l. [184-?] p. MB. 40-6693

Van Bergen, Anthony. Address delivered before the New York State Agricultural Society, at their annual meeting on the 5th February 1840... Albany, NY: Pr. by Charles Van Benthuysen, 1840. 29 p. CSmH; MW; N; NjR; NN. 40-6694

Van Buren, Martin, Pres. U. S., 1782-1862. Broadside headed "Democrats!!!" showing the plan of V. B. to raise a standing navy. Washington, DC: s. l., 1840. p. PPL. 40-6695

Van Buren, Martin, Pres. U. S., 1782-1862. ... Great town meeting held in Independence Square [under a call signed by between 5 and 6000 citizens] Van Buren and Johnson, regularly nominated Democratic Candidates for President and Vice President of the United States. S. l.: s. l. [1840] 32 p. MiD-B. 40-6696

Van Buren, Martin, Pres. U. S., 1782-1862. Interesting correspondence between citizens of Elizabeth City County, Virginia, and Mr. Van Buren. [Washington, DC: s. l., 1840] 8 p. MH; NcD. 40-6697

Van Buren, Martin, Pres. U. S., 1782-1862. Mr. Van Buren's letter to the committee of Elizabeth City County, Virginia. Elizabeth City County, VA:

New Era Office, 1840. 8 p. MiGr; NHi; NN; PPL. 40-6698

Van Buren, Martin, Pres. U. S., 1782-1862. To the farmers! and working men!! the democracy of the country. S. l.: n. pr., 1840. 15 p. PHi. 40-6699

Van Buren, Martin, Pres. U. S., 1782-1862. The votes and speeches of Martin Van Buren on the subjects of the right of suffrage, the qualifications of coloured persons to vote, and the appointment or election of justices of the peace... Albany, NY: Printed by T. Week, 1840. 24 p. DLC; MH; MiD-B; MnU; MWA. 40-6700

Van Cortlandt, Henry. Before the Circuit Judge of the Second Circuit... in the matter of proving the last will and testament... of Henry Van Cortlandt [formerly Henry White] late of the Town of Yonkers. New York: s. l., 1840. 316 p. NBLIHI. 40-6701

Van Ness, Cornelius P., 1782-1852. Speech of the Hon. C. P. Van Ness... at the late Democratic convention at Woodstick, Vt... Burlington, VT: printed at the Sentinel office, 1840. 16 p. InHi; MiD-B; MWFl; PPL; VtHi. 40-6702

Van Ness, John Peter, 1770-1846. Letter from General John P. Van Ness, in reply to an invitation to a Whig meeting in Washington, September, 1840. S. l.: s. l., 1840? 7 p. MdHi; MWA; N; PPL. 40-6703

Van Rensselaer, John Sanders. Address before the Whig and Conservative citizens of Schenectady County at Union Hall, Dec. 30, 1839. Schenectady, NY: s. l., 1840. p. DLC; MB; N; NHi. 40-6704

Van Tyne, J. P. Steamboat accidents, loss of life &c. Letter from J. P. Tyne to the Hon. J. R. Underwood. With a schedule of accidents to American steam vessels since the year 1830 &c., December 21, 1840. S. l.: s. l., 1840. 7 p. DLC; TxU. 40-6705

Vanderpoel, Aaron. Speech on the bill to authorize the issue of treasury notes. Washington, DC: s. l., 1840. 14 p. IU; MBC; MdHi. 40-6706

Vass, Charles. Agatha. [When the swallows homeward fly] Baltimore, MD: New Orleans, LA: F. D. Benteen; W. T. Mayo [184-?] 7 p. ViU. 40-6707

Vattemare, Alexandre, baron, 1796-1864. Letter from Alexandre Vattemare, asking the immediate action of the Senate on Bill [S. 365] "in addition to the acts now in force for the encouragement of learning, by securing the copies of maps, charts, and books, to the authors and proprietors of such copies during the times therein mentioned" and on the joint resolution [S. 17] "authorizing the exchange of duplicate works in the Library of Congress, June 15, 1840. Submitted to Mr. Benton and ordered to be printed. [Washington, DC: Blair & Rives, printers, 1840] 3 p. DLC; MiU; OO; PPL; RPB. 40-6708

Vattemare, Alexandre, baron, 1796-1864. Plan for international exchanges. [Washington, DC: Blair & Rives, printers, 1840] p. PPL. 40-6709

Vega Carpion, Lope Felix de, 1562-1635. La estrella de Sevilla de Vega Carpio. New York: H. Holt, 1840. 290 p. WaTC. 40-6710

Vega Carpion, Lope Felix de, 1562-1635. Seleccion de obras maestras de Lope de Vega 7 Calderon de la Barca. Con indice y observaciones escenciales al uso de los colegios y de las universidades. Nueva ed., rev. y mejorada. New York: H. Holt [1840] 292 p. AB; CoCor; LNX; MH; OCl. 40-6711

Velpeau, Alfred Armand Louis Marie, 1795-1867. A treatise on the diseases of the breast. By M. Velpeau... Translated from the French by S. Parkman, M. D. Philadelphia, PA: printed by A. Waldie, 1840. 83 p. IEN-M; MH-M; OClM; ViU; WMAM. 40-6712

Venn, Henry, 1725-1797. The complete duty of man; or, a system of doctrinal and practical Christianity. Designed for the use of families. Revised and corrected by Rev. H. Venn. New ed. New York: Pub. by the American Tract Society [184-?] 430 p. WHi. 40-6713

Venu, L. La. On the banks of Caudalquiver. Ballad. Song in the opera of Loretta. The music by L. La Venu. Baltimore, MD; New Orleans, LA: F. D. Benteen; W. T. Mayo [184-?] 2 p. ViU. 40-6714

Venzano, Luigi, 1814-1878. The forest fairy. Boston, MA: Ditson [184-?] 9 p. MB. 40-6715

Verdi, Giuseppe, 1813-1901. Ernani. Boston, MA: s. l. [184-?] p. MB. 40-6716

Verdi, Giuseppe, 1813-1901. In tears I pine for three. [La Mia Letizia infondere from Verdi's opera of I. Lombardi] Boston, MA: Oliver Ditson [184-?] 5 p. ViU. 40-6717

Verdi, Giuseppe, 1813-1901. Oh! wilt thou leave thy tranquil home. From the opera, Nebucadnezzar. Performed in London under the title of Nino. Words by P. Mordant, Esqr. Music by Verdi. Baltimore, MD; New Orleans, LA: F. D. Benteen; W. T. Mayo [184-?] 7 p. ViU. 40-6718

Vermont. General Assembly. House of Representatives. Journal of the House of Representatives of the State of Vermont, Oct. session, 1840. Published by authority. Montpelier, VT: E. P. Walton & Sons, 1840. 296 p. MH; MnU; VtMidSM; WHi. 40-6719

Vermont. Laws, statutes, etc. Acts and resolves passed by the legislature of the State of Vermont at their October session, 1840. Burlington, VT: Channcy Goodrich, 1840. 68 p. CU-Law; IaU-L; MdBB; Nj; R; TxU-L. 40-6720

Vermont. Laws, statutes, etc. The revised statutes of the State of Vermont, passed November 19, 1839. To which are added several public acts now in force; and to which are prefixed the Constitution of the United States and of the State of Vermont. Published by order of the Legislature. Burlington, VT: C. Goodrich, 1840. 676 p. CU; IU; OClW; PU; WHi. 40-6721

Vermont Medical College, Woodstock, Vt. Catalogues and announcements. Woodstock, VT: s. l., 1840. p. PPCP. 40-6722

Vermont year book for 1841... astronomical calculations by Zadock Thompson, A. M. Montpelier, VT: Published by E. P. Walton & Sons [1840]

132 p. MH; MHi; Mi; MWA; Nh-Hi. 40-6723

Vincent, Nathaniel, 1639?-1697. The spirit of prayer. By Rev. Nathaniel Vincent, A. M. Philadelphia, PA: Presbyterian Board of Publication, William S. Martien, publishing agent, 1840. 191 p. CtHC; GDecCT; ViRut. 40-6724

Vincent, Thomas, 1634-1678. Love to Christ. Chiefly extracted from "The true Christians' love of the Unseen Christ." By Thomas Vincent. Philadelphia, PA: s. l., 1840. 160 p. No Loc. 40-6725

The village green; or, Sports of youth. New Haven, CT: Babcock, 1840. 8 p. CtY; DLC; ICU. 40-6726

The village in the mountains; conversion of Peter Bayssiere and history or [!] a Bible. New York: American Tract Society [1840?] 108 p. DLC; ICU; NcD; NNC. 40-6727

The vine. New York: Published by the American Tract Society, 184-? 16 p. WHi. 40-6728

The vine. Philadelphia, PA: American Sunday School Union [184-?] 16 p. ViU. 40-6729

The violet; a Christmas and New Year's present. Edited by Miss Leslie. Philadelphia, PA: Carey and Hart, 1840. 216 p. DLC; GMWa; MH; MWA; WU. 40-6730

Virginia. General Assembly. Journal of the House of Delegates of the Commonwealth of Virginia, Session 1840-41... Richmond, VA: Printed by Samuel Shepherd, 1840. p. Vi. 40-6731

Virginia. General Assembly. Journal of the Senate of the Commonwealth of Virginia... Richmond, VA: Printed by John Warrock, 1840. p. Vi. 40-6732

Virginia. Governor [Thomas W. Gilmer] Message of the Governor of Virginia, communicating a correspondence between the governors of Virginia and New York, in relation to certain fugitives from justice. Printed by order of the House of Delegates of Virginia. Richmond, VA: Printed by S, Shepherd, 1840. 58 p. MB; MdBJ; TxU. 40-6733

Virginia. Laws, statutes, etc. Acts of the General Assembly of Virginia, session of December 2, 1839, to March 19, 1840, and in the sixty-fourth year of the Commonwealth. Richmond, VA: Samuel Shephard, printer, 1840. 199 p. IaU; Ky; MdBB; Mi-L; Tx. 40-6734

Virginia. University. Catalogue of the officers and students of the University of Virginia, Session of 1839-40. Charlottesville, VA: Printed by Robert C. Noel, 1840. 10 p. DLC; PHi; TxU. 40-6735

Virginia and North Carolina almanack for 1840. By David Richardson. Richmond, VA: Printed by John Warrock [1840] p. MWA. 40-6736

Virgulius Maro, Publius. Bucolica, Georgica, et Aeneis. Accedunt clavis. Metrics notulae Anglicae, et quaestiones. Cure B. A. Gould. In usum scholae Bostoniensis. Boston, MA: Sumptibus Hillliard, Gray, etc., 1840. p. MH; PLatS. 40-6737

Virgulius Maro, Publius. The eclogues. Translated by Wrangham. The Georgics, by Sotheby. And the Aeneid by Dryden.

New York: Harper and Bros. [1840] 2 v. MBeloC; MMontg; PPL; ScDuE; WStfSF. 40-6738

Virgulius Maro, Publius. Publii Virgilii Maronis Opera; or, The work of Virgil... 9th stereotype ed. New York: Robinson, Pratt and Co., 1840. 615 p. IP; MWH; NcEd; RPB; TxAuPT. 40-6739

Virgulius Maro, Publius. The works of Virgil, by John Dryden. New York: United States Book Company [1840?] 425 p. MWH. 40-6740

A visit to the celestial city. Philadelphia, PA: American Sunday School Union, 1840. 54 p. PAnL. 40-6741

A visit to the Lackawanna mines. New York, 1840. Newton, John, 1725-1807. The life of the Rev. John Newton. An authentic narrative written by himself, to which some further particulars are added. New York: The American Tract Society, 1840. 3 v. MNS; MoIn. 40-6742

Volksfreund und Hagerstauner Calendar 1841. Hagerstown, MD: Johann Gruber [1840] p. MWA. 40-6743

Volney, Constiatin Francois Chasseboeuf, 1757-1820. Ruins; or, Meditations on the revolutions of empires. A new translation from the 6th Paris edition. To which is added the law of nature and a short biographical notice by Count Daru... Boston, MA: Gaylord, 1840. 216 p. KyOw; NbU; PU. 40-6744

Voltaire, Francoise Marie Arouet de, 1694-1778. Histoire de Charles XII, roi de Suede. Nouvelle edition. New York: W. E. Dean, [184-?] 287 p. ViU. 40-6745

Voorhees, Richard. Oration. Delivered before the Democratic Association. Goshen, NY: Independent Republican [1840] 8 p. NN; OHi. 40-6746

Vose, Richard H. Oration delivered at East Wilton on the anniversary of American Independent, July 4, 1840. By Hon. Richard H. Vose. Augusta, ME: Severance & Dorr, printers, 1840. 24 p. DLC; MeHi. 40-6747

Voss, Charles, 1815-1882. The fatal reverie. Waltz. Boston, MA: s. l. [184-?] p. MB. 40-6748

Voss, Charles, 1815-1882. La sylphide parisienne. Boston, MA: Ditson [184-?] p. MB. 40-6749

Vox. Address [No. 1] By Vox, a Baptist layman. New York: Printed for the Author, 1840. 12 p. ICU. 40-6750

W

Waddel, Moses, 1770-1840. Memoirs of the life of Miss Caroline Elizabeth Smelt, who died Sept. 21, 1817, in the City of Augusta, Georgia, in the 17th year of her age. By Moses Waddel. New York: Gardiner, printer, 1840. 175 p. NcRA. 40-6751

Wade, Joseph Augustine, 1800-1845. Come see me at morning. New York: Hewit and Co. [184-?] p. MB. 40-6752

Wade, Joseph Augustine, 1800-1845. I've wandered in dreams. A favorite duett. Written & composed by J. A. Wade. Boston, MA: Ditson [184-?] 6 p. MB. 40-6753

Wade, Joseph Augustine, 1800-1845. I've wandere'd in dreams. A favorite duett. Written & composed by J. A. Wade. New York: Atwill [1840?] 6 p. MiU-C. 40-6754

Wade, Joseph Augustine, 1800-1845. I've wandere'd in dreams. A favorite duett. Written & composed by J. A. Wade. New York: E. Riley [184-?] 6 p. ViU. 40-6755

Wade, Joseph Augustine, 1800-1845. I've wandered in dreams. A favorite duett. Written & composed by J. A. Wade. New York: Hewitt & Jacques [184-?] 6 p. ViU. 40-6756

Wade, Joseph Augustine, 1800-1845. Meet me by moonlight. Ballad. Written & composed by I. Augustine Wade. New York: Riley [184-?] 2 p. MB. 40-6757

Wade, Joseph Augustine, 1800-1845. Meet me by moonlight. Ballad. Written & composed by I. Augustine Wade. New York: William Hall & Son [184-?] 3 p. ViU. 40-6758

Wagener, David D. Speech in the house of representatives, Jun 16, 1840... on the independent treasury bill. Washington, DC: s. l., 1840. 12 p. IaHi; MdHi; WHi. 40-6759

Waite, Josiah K. A discourse delivered in the first parish church, Gloucester, Sunday, December 22d, 1839, on the interment of eleven mariners, wrecked on Cape Ann, December 15th, 1839. By Josiah K. Waite. Gloucester: Henry Tilden, printer, Telegraph Press, 1840. 14 p. MB; MBAU; MBB. 40-6760

Wakeman, Thaddeus B. Address delivered at Trenton, before the New Jersey state agricultural society, Feb. 12, 1840. By T. B. Wakeman... Princeton, NJ: Printed by R. E. Hornor, 1840. 34 p. DLC; NjP; NjR; OClWHi; WM. 40-6761

Walden, John H. The scripture view of baptism and the Lord's Supper. S. l.: Brandon, 1840. VtHi. 40-6762

Walker, Alexander. Beauty; illustrated chiefly by an analysis and classification of beauty in woman. By Alexander Walker. New York: Langley, 1840. 390 p. FOA; NH; MiOC; NBuG; NjP; PPA; RNR. 40-6763

Walker, Alexander. Woman physiologically considered, as to mind, morals, marriage, matrimonial slavery, infidelity, and divorce. By Alexander Walker... With an appendix containing notes and additions. Edited by an American physician. New York: J. & H. G. Langley, 1840. 432 p. GU; MH; MiU; ODW; PPCP. 40-6764

Walker, Alexander. Woman Physiologically considered as to mind, morals, marriage, matrimonial slavery, infidelity and divorce. New York: J. & H. G. Langley, 1840. 432 p. DNLM; GU; MH; NcD; ODW. 40-6765

Walker, George, 1803-1879. The chess player... illustrated with engravings and diagrams; containing Franklin's essay on the morals of chess... Boston, MA: National Dearborn, etc., 1840. 155 p. NhD; OCl. 40-6766

Walker, James Barr, 1806-1887. Philosophy of the plan of salvation. A book for all times. By an American citizen. New York: s. l., 1840. 240 p. OO. 40-6767

Walker, John, 1732-1807. A critical pronouncing dictionary and expositor of the English language. 1st pocket ed. Hartford, CT: W. Andrus, 1840. MH. 40-6768

Walker, John, 1732-1807. A critical pronouncing dictionary and expositor of the English language... By John Walker... New York: Published by Collins, Keese and Company, 1840. 650 p. MoSU; TNP. 40-6769

Walker, Jonathan, 1790-1878. A picture of slavery for youth. By the author of "The Branded Hand" and "Chattelized humanity." Boston, MA: J. Walker and W. R. Bliss [184-?] 36 p. DLC; MH; NIC; OClWHi; TNF. 40-6770

Walker, Mrs. Alexander. Female beauty as preserved and improved by regimen, cleanliness and dress. New York: Scofield and Voorhies, J. & H. G. Langley, 1840. 400 p. CtHWatk; LNH; NN; PU; TxH. 40-6771

Walker, Robert James, 1801-1869. Speech of Mr. Walker, of Miss., on the bill to provide for the collection, safe-keeping and disbursement of the public moneys, Senate, Jan. 21, 1840. Washington, DC: s. l., 1840. 14 p. MdHi; NcD; TxU. 40-6772

Walker, Robert James, 1801-1869. Speech on the bill to provide for the collection, safe-keeping and disbursement of the public moneys, Senate, United States, Jan. 21, 1840. Baltimore, MD: s. l., 1840. 14 p. MdBJ; MsJS; WHi. 40-6773

Walker, Samuel. Atlas of the world. Boston, MA: s. l. [1840?] 25 p. WHi-Mss. 40-6774

Walker, W. A. Remarks on the Statements of Dr. Coffin and the New School Elders, [as published in the Rev. J. W. Cunningham's Pamphlet] together with a Statement of the Old School Elders, in relation to the Division of the Presbyterian Congregation at Rogersville, E.

Tenn. Knoxville, TN: Gifford & Eastman, 1840. 46 p. T. 40-6775

Wall, Garret D., 1788-1850. Speech in Senate May 12, 1840 on the bill to establish an uniform system of bankruptcy. [Washington, DC: s. l., 1840] 8 p. NjR; WHi. 40-6776

Wallace, David. An address delivered at the installation of President Simpson, of the Indiana Asbury University, September 16, 1840. By David Wallace. Indianapolis, IN: Printed by W. Stacy, 1840. 14 p. CSmH; ICJ; IEN-M; I-U; In. 40-6777

Wallace, William V. ... Les perles. Composed for the piano forte by Wm. V. Wallace. Baltimore, MD: F. D. Benteen [184-?] 5 p. ViU. 40-6778

Wallace, William V. Les perles. Deux valses. Pour le piano forte. Composees et dediees a Mme. I. M. Kennedy [de la Nouvelle Orleans] par W. V. Wallace. New York: James L. Hewitt & Co.; Firth & Hall [184-?] 5 p. MB; ViU. 40-6779

Wallace, William Vincent, 1812-1865. The Anna waltz... Boston, MA: Oliver Ditson [184-?] 5 p. ViU. 40-6780

Wallace, William Vincent, 1812-1865. Blue bells of Scotland. By Wm. Vincent Wallace. Baltimore, MD: F. D. Benteen & Co. [184-?] 7 p. ViU. 40-6781

Wallace, William Vincent, 1812-1865. The Blue bells of Scotland. Boston, MA: Ditson [184-?] 7 p. MB. 40-6782

Wallace, William Vincent, 1812-1865. Blue bells of Scotland. With variations for the harp or piano forte. Composed by

Nathl. Carusi. Baltimore, MD: Samuel Carusi [184-?] 5 p. ViU. 40-6783

Wallace, William Vincent, 1812-1865. Comin' thro' the Rye... A Scotch ballad. Sung by Jenny Lind. Arranged for the piano forte. Boston, MA: Oliver Ditson [184-?] 3 p. ViU. 40-6784

Wallace, William Vincent, 1812-1865. Comin' thro' the Rye... By Wm. Vincent Wallace. Baltimore, MD: F. D. Benteen & Co. [184-?] 9 p. ViU. 40-6785

Wallace, William Vincent, 1812-1865. La Deseoda. Valse. Pour piano forte. Composee et dediee a Madlle. Isidora dr Cyprey [de Mexique] Par W. V. Wallace. New York: James L. Hewitt & Co.; Firth & Hall [184-?] 7 p. MB; ViU. 40-6786

Wallace, William Vincent, 1812-1865. Hirondelle... Boston, MA: Oliver Ditson [184-?] 5 p. ViU. 40-6787

Wallace, William Vincent, 1812-1865. In happy moments. Ballad. Sung by Mr. H. Phillips in the grand opera Maritana. Composed by W. V. Wallace. Philadelphia, PA: Lee & Walker [184-?] 3 p. NN; ViU. 40-6788

Wallace, William Vincent, 1812-1865. Jack O'Hazeldean... By Wm. V. Wallace. Baltimore, MD: F. D. Benteen [184-?] 9 p. ViU. 40-6789

Wallace, William Vincent, 1812-1865. Jenny Lind polka. As played at the Baltimore Museum. Composed by A. Wallerstein. Baltimore, MD; New Orleans, LA: F. D. Benteen; Wm. T. Mayo [184-?] 2 p. MB; ViU. 40-6790

Wallace, William Vincent, 1812-1865.

Logie O'Buchan... By Wm. Vincent Wallace. Baltimore, MD: F. D. Benteen & Co. [184-?] 9 p. ViU. 40-6791

Wallace, William Vincent, 1812-1865. La Louisianaise. Valse brillant. Pour piano forte. Composee et dediee Mme. F. Johns [de la Nouvelle Orleans] par W. V. Wallace. New York: James L. Hewitt & Co.; Firth & Hall [184-?] 7 p. MB; NcD; ViU. 40-6792

Wallace, William Vincent, 1812-1865. La Mexicana. Valse. Pour piano forte. Composee par W. V. Wallace. New York: James L. Hewitt & Co.; Firth & Hall [184-?] 5 p. ViU. 40-6793

Wallace, William Vincent, 1812-1865. La Mexicana. Waltz. Composed for the piano forte by W. V. Wallace. Philadelphia, PA; New York: A. Fiot; W. Dubois [184-?] 5 p. ViU. 40-6794

Wallace, William Vincent, 1812-1865. National anthem. Dedicated to the American people. The words by Geo. P. Morris, esq.; the music composed by W. V. Wallace. New York: James L. Hewitt & Co. [184-?] 4 p. ViU. 40-6795

Wallace, William Vincent, 1812-1865. Nocturne. Pour le piano forte. New York: Hall [184-?] 9 p. MB. 40-6796

Wallace, William Vincent, 1812-1865. Pretty Mary. Baltimore, MD; New Orleans, LA: F. D. Benteen; W. T. Mayo [184-?] 5 p. ViU. 40-6797

Wallace, William Vincent, 1812-1865. Scenes that are brightest. Ballad. Sung by Miss Romer in the grand opera Maritana. Composed by W. V. Wallace.

Philadelphia, PA; New York: A. Fiot; W. Dubois [184-?] 5 p. ViU. 40-6798

Wallace, William Vincent, 1812-1865. Scots wha hae. By Wm. V. Wallace. Baltimore, MD: F. D. Benteen [184-?] 7 p. ICJ; ViU. 40-6799

Wallace, William Vincent, 1812-1865. Sleeping I dreamed love. Words by Mrs. M. E. Hewitt. Music by W. V. Wallace. S. l.: s. l. [184-?] 6 p. ViU. 40-6800

Wallace, William Vincent, 1812-1865. La sympathie. Valse favorite. Pour le piano forte. Composee et dediee a Melle. Rosario Warran [de Mexique] par W. V. Wallace. New York: James L. Hewitt & Co., Firth & Hall [184-?] 5 p. ViU. 40-6801

Wallace, William Vincent, 1812-1865. La sympathie. Valse favorite. Pour le piano forte. Composee et dediee a Melle. Rosario Marzan [de Mexico] par W. V. Wallace. Philadelphia, PA; New Orleans, LA: A. Fiot; W. Dubois [184-?] 5 p. MB; ViU. 40-6802

Wallace, William Vincent, 1812-1865. 'Tis the last rose of summer. An Irish melody. Arranged with variations for the piano forte by William Vincent Wallace. Boston, MA: Oliver Ditson [184-?] 9 p. ViU. 40-6803

Waller, Sidney. The sailor's tear. Written and composed by Sidney Waller. New York: Published by J. L. Hewitt, 1840. 6 p. KU. 40-6804

Walpole, Horace, 1717-1797. The castle of Otranto. A Gothic Story. Translated by William Marshal, gent. [pseud.] From the Italian of Onuphrio Moralto [pseud.] Philadelphia, PA: C. Sherman & Co., 1840. 204 p. ViU. 40-6805

Walpole, Horace, 1717-1797. The letters of H. Walpole, Earl of Oxford, including numerous letters now first published. From the original manuscripts. Philadelphia, PA: s. l., 1840. 6 v. PPL-R. 40-6806

Walter, William Joseph, d. 1846. Mary, queen of Scots: a journal of her twenty years' captivity, trial and execution: from state papers, and contemporary letters and documents. By W. Jos. Walter... Philadelphia, PA: Carey & Hart, 1840. 2 v. CSrD; LNL; OCX; PPA; ScCC. 40-6807

Walter, William Joseph, d. 1846. Sir Thomas More. His life and times, illustrated from his own writings, and from contemporary documents. By W. Jos. Walter. Baltimore, MD: F. Lucas, jr. [1840] 376 p. CStclU; DLC; IC; IU; MdBE; NUC; OCX. 40-6808

Walton, Izaak, 1593-1683. The complete angler; or, The contemplative man's recreation of Izaak Walton and Charles Cotton. Edited by John Major. From the 4th London ed. New York: Crowell [184-?] 418 p. CBPSR. 40-6809

The wandering pilgrim, or, the way to be happy. With a warning to the old and young. New York: Cornelius Gould & Co., 1840. 16 p. CSmH. 40-6810

War of the giants against James Gordon Bennett... New York: s. l., 1840. no. 1-. IU; NN. 40-6811

Ward, Henry Dana, 1797-1884. History and doctrine of the Millennium. A dis-

course. Delivered in the conference on the second advent near at Boston, Mass., Oct. 14, 1840. By Henry Dana Ward. Boston, MA?: s. l., 1840. 74 p. MH-AH; MWA; Nh; PPPrHi; RPB. 40-6812

Ward, Jonathan, 1769-1860. American slavery and the means of its abolition. By Rev. Jonathan Ward. Published by request. Boston, MA: printed by Perkins & Marvin, 1840. 26 p. MB; MBC; Nh; OClWHi. 40-6813

Ward, Milton, 1808-1874. Discourses on Christian faith and practice. By Rev. Milton Ward, M. D. Boston, MA: James B. Dow; printed by William A. Hall & Co., 1840. 354 p. CtHC; GMM; MiOC; MMal; NhD; RNR. 40-6814

Ware, Henry, jr., 1794-1843. A discourse preached at the ordination of Mr. Robert C. Waterston, as minister at large, Nov. 24, 1839. By Henry Ware, jr., Professor in Harvard College. Boston, MA: Isaac R. Butts, printer, 1840. 51 p. CtHC; DLC; ICU; MPiB; PPAmP; RPB. 40-6815

Ware, Henry, jr., 1794-1843. How to spend holy time, in two chapters. By Rev. Henry Ware, jr. Boston, MA: Jas. Munroe & co., 1840. 20 p. CBPac; ICMe; MDeeP; MeB; N; RP. 40-6816

Ware, Henry, jr., 1794-1843. Thoughts for the New Year on the duty of Improvement. Boston, MA: Printed by I. R. Butts, 1840. 16 p. ICMe; MBC; MeBat; MDeeP; NjR. 40-6817

Ware, Thomas, b. 1758. Sketches of the life and travels of Rev. Thomas Ware who have been an itinerant Methodist preacher for more than fifty years. Written by himself. Revised by the editor. New York: s. l., 1840. 264 p. GEU; IU; MHi; MoS; OClW; WHi. 40-6818

A warning voice from a watery grave! or A solemn proof of the uncertainty of life and importance of an early preparation for death! In the instance of the melancholy and untimely fate of the much esteemed and lamented Miss Sophia W. / Wheeler... who perished by the awful conflagration on board the ill-fated steamboat Lexington, on her passage from New York to Stonington, Jan. 13, 1840... New York: Printed for the publisher, by Sackett and Sargent, 1840. 24 p. DLC; MB. 40-6819

Warren, Edward, 1804-1878. On scrofula, rheumatism, and erysipelatous inflammation. By Edward Warren... Philadelphia, PA: A. Waldie, 1840. 122 p. InU-M; KyLxT; MB; MNF; PPA. 40-6820

Warren, Jonathan Mason, 1811-1867. Rhinoplastic operations. With some remarks on the autoplastic methods usually adopted for the restoration of parts lost by accident or disease. Boston, MA: Clapp, 1840. 28 p. DLC; MB; MBM; MH-M; NNC. 40-6821

Warren, Lott. Speech of Mr. Lott Warren, of Georgia, on the "Bill additional to the act on the subject of treasury notes. "Delivered in the House... March, 1840. Washington, DC: Printed by Gales and Seaton, 1840. 11 p. GEU; M. 40-6822

Warren, Owen Grenliffe. Dream of the highlands: a poem. New York: printed for private distribution [J. Mackellan, printer] 1840. 76 p. DLC; MH; NBuG. 40-6823

Warren, Samuel, 1807-1877. Passages from the diary of a late physician, by Samuel Warren. In three volumes. New York: published by Harper & Brothers, 1840. 3 v. MH; MLen; NjP. 40-6824

Warren, Samuel, 1807-1877. Ten thousand a year... In three volumes. By Samuel Warren, F. R. S. Boston, MA: Little, Brown & Co., 1840-41. 3 v. IaMc; IU-Law; NBuUL; OkOk. 40-6825

Warren, Samuel, 1807-1877. Ten thousand a year... Philadelphia, PA: Carey and Hart, 1840-41. 6 v. CtMW; MBAt; MH; NN; RBR. 40-6826

Warren, William, 1806-1879. Giving and receiving compared. Portland, ME: s. l. [184-?] 12 p. MB. 40-6827

The Warrenton waltz. Baltimore, MD: Geo. Willig [184-?] 1 p. ViU. 40-6828

Washburn, Emory, 1800-1877. Sketches of the judicial history of Massachusetts from 1630 to the revolution in 1775. Boston, MA: Little & J. Brown, 1840. 407 p. CU; MWA; MWCL; NcD; OClWHi; PHi. 40-6829

Washington City, D. C., June 1, 1840. Sir: on behalf of the Republican Committee of Seventy-six, appointed by the citizens of the District of Columbia friendly to the election of General William Henry Harrison to the Presidency of the United States... Washington, DC: s. l., 1840? p. ICHi. 40-6830

Washington College, Lexington, Va. Catalogue... Lexington, VA: Gazette Office, 1841? p. MBC; PPPrHi. 40-6831

Washington College, Washington, Pa.

Catalogue of the officers and students of Washington College, 1839-40. Washington, DC: Printed by John Bausman, 1840. 20 p. MBC; PWW. 40-6832

Washington Total Abstinence Society, Troy, N. Y. Certificate of membership. [Troy, NY: s. l., 184-?] p. MB. 40-6833

Washington's march. Boston, MA: Published by C. Bradlee [184-?] 1 p. MB. 40-6834

Washington's march. Boston, MA: Ditson [184-?] 1 p. MB. 40-6835

Washington's march. Boston, MA: Keith [184-?] 1 p. MB. 40-6836

Washington's march. Boston, MA: Reed [184-?] 1 p. MB. 40-6837

Washington's march. Philadelphia, PA: Ferrett & Co. [184-?] 1 p. MB. 40-6838

Washington's march & Washington's march at the battle of Trenton. Baltimore, MD: F. D. Benteen [184-?] 1 p. ViU. 40-6839

Washington, George, 1732-1799. Valedictory address to the people of the United States. Published in September, A. D. 1796. Harrisburg, PA: Holbrook, Henlock & Bratton, printers, 1840. 16 p. MB; MH; MiD-B; PHi. 40-6840

Washington, George, 1732-1799. Valedictory address to the people of the United States. Published in September, A. D. 1796. Harrisburg, PA: William D. Boas, printer, 1840. 16 p. CSmH; MB; MBAt; MH; MiD-B; NN. 40-6841

Waterbury, Jared Bell, 1799-1876. A

book for the Sabbath, in three parts... By J. B. Waterbury... Andover, MA; New York; Boston, MA: Gould, Newman & Saxton; Ives & Dennett, 1840. 222 p. CU; GDecCT; InCW; MiOC; PPPrHi. 40-6842

Waterman, Catherine Harbeson Waterman, b. 1812. Flora's Lexicon: an interpretation of the language and sentiment of flowers. With an outline of botany and a poetical introduction. By Catherine H. Waterman. Philadelphia, PA: published by Herman Hooker, 1840. 252 p. CU; IaDa; MsNC; MTop; OMC. 40-6843

Waterman, Henry. The Prosperity of the Church. A discourse, preached in St. Paul's Church, Pawtucket, being the Fiftieth Annual Convention of the Protestant Episcopal Church, in Rhode Island, June 9, 1840. By Henry Waterman, Rector of St. James's Church, Woonsocket. Providence, RI: B. Cranston & Co., 1840. 24 p. MiCMCh; MiD-B; RPB; RHi. 40-6844

Waterson. Who nominated Gen. William Henry Harrison? and who should be elected President of the United States? Columbus, GA: Printed at the office of the Georgia Angus, 1840. 14 p. A-Ar. 40-6845

Waterson, Robert Cassie, 1812-1893. Addresses. Boston, MA: s. l., 1840-. v. ICU. 40-6846

Waterson, Robert Cassie, 1812-1893. The diffusive nature of Christianity. An address... Boston, MA: Weeks, Jordan & Co., 1840. 24 p. DLC; MH; NN; OClWHi; PHi. 40-6847

Waterson, Robert Cassie, 1812-1893. "Watch and pray. "By Rev. R. C. Waterson. Printed for the American Unitarian Association. Boston, MA: James Munroe & Co. 1840. 14 p. CBPac; ICU; MeBat; MMeT-Hi; N. 40-6848

Watson, Richard, Bp. of Llandaff, 1737-1816. Erwiedening an Paine; oder, Schutzrede fur die Bibel. In briefen an Thomas Paine... New York: Amerikanische Tractatgesellschaft [184-?] 232 p. CBPSR. 40-6849

Watson, Richard, Bp. of Llandaff, 1737-1816. Reply to Paine; or, An apology for the Bible in letters to Thomas Paine... With notices of Hume's denial of miracles and Gilbert West's order of events in the resurrection. New York: American Tract Society [184-?] 222 p. CBPSR. 40-6850

Watson, Richard, 1781-1833. An apology for the Bible. In a series of letters, addresses to Thomas Paine... New York: R. Carter, 1840. 173 p. IaFayU; IEG; MiDU. 40-6851

Watson, Richard, 1781-1833. A Biblical Theological dictionary of story, manners & customs of the Jews and neighboring nations... by Richard Watson. [Revised American edition] New York: Published by T. Mason & G. Lane for Meth. Epis. Ch. at Conference Off., 1840. 1003 p. No Loc. 40-6852

Watson, Richard, 1781-1833. The life of the Rev. John Wesley... By Richard Watson. 1st American official ed. New York: G. Lane & C. B. Tippet, for the Methodist Episcopal church, 1840. 323 p. ABBS; CtMW; GHi; NjR; PP. 40-6853

Watson, Richard, 1781-1833. Sermons and sketches of sermons. By the Rev. Richard Watson. New York: Published by T. Mason and G. Lane, for the Methodist Episcopal church, at the conference office, 1840. 2 v. FTa; MdBD; MoS; OWoC; TJaL. 40-6854

Watson, Richard, 1781-1833. Theological institutes; or, a view of the evidences, doctrines, morals, and institutions of Christianity. By Richard Watson. New York: George Lane, 1840. 2 v. ArCH; KWiU; MsU; NbCrD; ODefC. 40-6855

Watts, A. L. Sermon on the final perseverance of the saints. Preached in the Presbyterian churches of Lincolnton and Long Creek. Greensboro, NC: Patriot, 1840. 29 p. NcU. 40-6856

Watts, Charles. Address of the Hon. Charles Watts. Delivered on the 8th January 1840 on the occasion of the visit of General Jackson to the City of New Orleans. By invitation of the citizens. [New Orleans, LA: J. C. de St. Romes, 1840?] 8 p. OClWHi. 40-6857

Way, Lewis, 1772-1840. Thoughts on the scriptural expectations of the Christian church, by Basilicus [pseud.] Philadelphia, PA: Orrin Rogers, 1840. 72 p. CBPSR; ICU; MWA; NjMD; WHi. 40-6858

The way of the cross... Philadelphia, PA: Published by Eugene Cummiskey, 1840. 90 p. No Loc. 40-6859

Wayland, Francis, 1796-1865. The elements of moral science. By Francis Wayland, D. D. Twelfth edition, revised and stereotyped. Boston, MA; Worcester, MA: published by Gould, Kendall and Lincoln, 1840. 398 p. CBPSR; IaMP; LNB; MeB; MDeeP. 40-6860

Wayland, Francis, 1796-1865. The elements of political economy. By Francis Wayland, D. D., Prsident of Brown University and Professor of Moral Philosophy. Boston, MA: Gould, Kendall and Lincoln, 1840. 441 p. GOgU; LNT; OMC; ScC. 40-6861

Wayland, Francis, 1796-1865. Elements of political economy. By Francis Wayland. 3rd edition. Boston, MA; Worcester, MA: published by Gould, Kendall and Lincoln; printed by E. W. Bartlett and co., 1840. 441 p. KyLxT; MH; NNA; OO; RPB; TJaU. 40-6862

Wayland, Francis, 1796-1865. Letters to Rev. I. C. Welch, April 6, 1840. Providence, RI: s. l., 1840. RPB. 40-6863

Wayland, Francis, 1796-1865. Review of... views of duties of citizens of the U. S. in relation to the slavery question by Moderatus. Providence, RI: s. l., 1840. 8 p. OCHP. 40-6864

Wayland, Francis, 1796-1865. Sermons. Delivered in the chapel of Brown University. 2d ed. Boston, MA: Gould, 1840. 328 p. PPP. 40-6865

Wayland, John. Causes of prevalent failures in pulpit eloquence; address before Rhetorical society of the Baptist theological institution, Thomaston, Maine, Aug. 5, 1840. Boston, MA: s. l., 1840. 28 p. ICMe; MAnP; MeHi; MH; RPB. 40-6866

Webb, Samuel. Speech of Samuel Webb, in the national anti slavery convention held at Albany, N. Y. on the first

day of August, 1839. Philadelphia, PA: Merrihew & Thompson, 1840. 20 p. PHC; PHi; OO. 40-6867

Weber, C. H. The Elm wood waltz. Composed & arranged for the piano forte and most respectfully dedicated to Miss Louisa Berry by C. H. Weber. Philadelphia, PA: George Willig, 1840. 2 p. ViU. 40-6868

Weber, Carl M. Favorite waltz, from Oberon. By C. M. de Weber. Philadelphia, PA: J. Edgar [184-?] 2 p. ViU. 40-6869

Weber, Carl M. L'invitation a la valse. Aufforderung Zum Tanze. Rondeau brillant. Compose pour le piano forte par Carl M. de Weber. Philadelphia, PA: Lee & Walker [184-?] 9 p. ViU. 40-6870

Weber, Carl M. Preciosa waltz. Composed by C. M. von Weber. Arranged by J. C. Viereck. Baltimore, MD: F. D. Benteen [1841] 2 p. ViU. 40-6871

Weber, Carl M. Say my heart whence comes thine anguish. A celebrated German air. The music composed & arranged for the piano forte by C. M. von Weber. Boston, MA: Oliver Ditson [1841] 2 p. ViU. 40-6872

Weber, Carl M. Weber's last waltz. Boston, MA: s. l. [1841] p. MB. 40-6873

Webster, Daniel, 1782-1852. Mr. Webster's remarks upon that part of the president's message which relates to the revenue and finances. Delivered in the Senate of the United States, December 16 and 17, 1840. Washington, DC: Intelligencer office, 1840. 12 p. CU; GEU; IU; MDeeP; TxU. 40-6874

Webster, Daniel, 1782-1852. Mr. Webster's speech at Saratoga, N. Y., Aug. 19, 1840. Boston, MA: Perkins and Marvin, 1840. 28 p. MBC; MH; MHi. 40-6875

Webster, Daniel, 1782-1852. Remarks of Mr. Webster and Mr. Wright, on the President's message, the finances and debts of the nation. [Washington? 1840] 16 p. ICN; IU; MH; MiU-C; OClWHi. 40-6876

Webster, Daniel, 1782-1852. Speech at the convention at Richmond, Va., on Oct. 5th, 1840. New York: Youngs & Hunt, 1840. 24 p. CSfCW; MH; MH-AH; M; PU. 40-6877

Webster, Daniel, 1782-1852. Speech at the great mass meeting at Saratoga, New York, on 19th August, 1840. [Nashville: B. R. M'Kennie, pr., 1840] 12 p. DLC. 40-6878

Webster, Daniel, 1782-1852. Speech... at the Great Whig gathering, at Saratoga, N. Y., Aug. 19, 1840. Taunton: Published at the Taunton Whig Office, 1840. 16 p. CSmH; DGU. 40-6879

Webster, Daniel, 1782-1852. Webster on the currency. Speech of Hon. Daniel Webster at the merchants' meeting in Wall Street, New York, on Monday, September 28, 1840. Reported in full by Arthur J. Stansbury. New York: E. French, 1840. 24 p. DLC; MH; NN; PHi; WHi. 40-6880

Webster, James, 1803-1854. Lecture: Introductory to the course of anatomy and physiology in Geneva Medical College, October, 1840, by James Webster, M. D., Professor of Anatomy and Physiology in Geneva Medical College, Corresponding member of the Medical Society of London, etc., Published by the medical class. Geneva, NY: Stow & Frazee, book and job printer [1840] 21 p. DLC; MBC; MiU; NBuU-M; NNN. 40-6881

Webster, Noah, 1758-1843. Elementary spelling book. Concord, NH: Roby, Kimball & Merrill, 1840. 168 p. CtSoP; IU; MH; NN; RPB. 40-6882

Webster, Noah, 1758-1843. The elementary spelling book. New Brunswick, NJ: J. Terhune, 1840. ICN; MH; NN. 40-6883

Webster, Noah, 1758-1843. Elementary spelling book... being an improvement on the American spelling book. New Haven, CT: S. Babcock, 1840. CtHWatk; CtY; NN. 40-6884

Webster, Noah, 1758-1843. Elementary spelling book. Being an improvement on the American spelling book. Portland, ME: Sanborn and Carter [184-?] 168 p. MB; NN. 40-6885

Webster, Noah, 1758-1843. The elementary spelling book... being an improvement on the American spelling book. By Noah Webster, LL. D. Pulaski, NY: C. D. Loomis and Company, stereotyped by J. S. Redfield, 1840. 168 p. MH; MPiB. 40-6886

Webster, Noah, 1758-1843. The Elementary spelling book. Being an improvement on the American spelling book. By Noah Webster, LL. D. New York: Published by George F. Coolidge & Brothers, 1840. 168 p. ICU; NIDHi; NN. 40-6887

Webster's Calendar; Howland's Albany Almanack for 1841. Sandy Hill, NY: G. & E. Howland [1840] p. MWA. 40-6888

Webster's Calendar; or, The Albany almanack for the year of our Lord, 1840, being [till July fourth] the sixty-fourth year of American Independence. Albany, NY: s. l. [1840-61] v. CLSR. 40-6889

Webster's Calendar, or the Albany Almanack for 1841. By Edwin E. Prentiss. Albany, NY: E. W. & C. Skinner [1840] p. NAI; NN; MWA; WHi. 40-6890

Wedgwood, William B. Wedgwood's science of numbers; containing rules for the application of the mind in acquiring knowledge, a complete system of arithmetic... a complete system of bookkeeping by double entry... also in introduction to algebra, sufficient to give the pupil a knowledge of simple equations... New York: Linen and Fennell, 1840. 216 p. CtHT; DAU; DLC; PPF; PU. 40-6891

The wedding gift; or, duties and pleasures of domestic life. Boston, MA: Gould, Kendall & Lincoln [184-?] 2 v. in 1. DLC; NN; NNC. 40-6892

The weekly pilot... Baltimore, MD: s. l., 1840-. v. DLC; ICU. 40-6893

Weeks, John Mosely, 1788-1858. The bee-keeper's guide to manage bees in the Vermont bee-hive. Middlebury, VT: Argus Office, 1840. 24 p. NIC; VtMidSM; VtMiM. 40-6894

Weeks, John Mosely, 1788-1858. A manual of an easy method of managing bees in the most profitable manner to their owner. With infallable rules to

prevent their destruction by the moth. New ed., rev. & enl. Boston, MA: Weeks, Jordan & Co., 1840. 128 p. AAP; DLC; IU; PPL; WU. 40-6895

Weeks, John Mosely, 1788-1858. A manual of an easy method of managing bees in the most profitable manner to their owner. With infallable rules to prevent their destruction by the moth. 5th ed. Akron, OH: Allison's Print., 1840. 78 p. CSmH. 40-6896

Weeks, William Raymond, 1783-1848. Letter to the Rev. Charles Fitch, on his views of sanctification. Newark, NJ: Guest, 1840. 24 p. MBC; MH-AH; NCH; NeMHi; PPPrHi. 40-6897

Weems, Mason Locke, 1759-1825. Hymen's recruiting sergeant; or, the new matrimonial tat-too for old bachelors. Bath, NY: R. L. Underhill, 1840. 59 p. DLC; MWA. 40-6898

Weems, Mason Locke, 1759-1825. The life of George Washington. With curious anecdotes equally honorable to himself and exemplary to his young countrymen... By M. L. Weems. Philadelphia, PA: J. Allen, 1840. 244 p. IU; LU; NcD; OkU; PHi. 40-6899

Weisenthal, T. V. Fading, still fading. Evening humn. Composed for & respectfully dedicated to the sisterhood of St. Joseph by T. V. Weisenthal. Baltimore, MD; Cincinnati, OH; Louisville, KY: W. C. Peters; Peters & Field; Peters, Webb & Co. [184-?] 2 p. ViU. 40-6900

Welcome home. Dedicated to the New England delegates to the Baltimore Whig Convention, by G. Forrester Barstew. Music by B. Hime. [Song with accompaniment for the piano forte] Salem, MA: Brown [1840] 3 p. MB. 40-6901

Weld, Allen Hayden, 1812-1882. Latin lessons and readers. With exercises for the writing of Latin. By Allen H. Weld. Portland, ME: Sanbron & Carter, 1840. 258 p. NCan. 40-6902

Weld, Theodore Dwight, 1803-1895. Persons held to service, fugitive slaves, &c. [Boston, MA: New England Anti-Slavery Tract Association, 184-?] 8 p. MH; MiU; MWA; NjP; NNC. 40-6903

Weller, John B., 1812-1875. Speech of Mr. Weller, of Ohio, in committee of the whole, on the general appropriation bill. House of Representatives, April 18, 1840. Washington, DC: printed by Blair and Rives, 1840. 16 p. IU; MdBJ; MdHi; OCHP; OClWHi. 40-6904

Wells and Webb. Specimen of plain and ornamental type cut by machinery, by Wells & Webb. New York: The Firm, 1840. NNC-Atf. 40-6905

Wells. Oh! Susanna. As sung by the Ethiopian Serenoders. Written by Wells; arranged for the piano forte. Baltimore, MD; New Orleans, LA: F. D. Benteen; W. T. Mayo [184-?] 5 p. ViU. 40-6906

Wely, Lefebure. Danse des oiseaux. [The dance of the birds] Bluette Lefebure-Wely. Op. 78. Baltimore, MD: George Willig, Junr. [184-?] 9 p. ViU. 40-6907

Wenck, A. H. Ach du lieber augustin. With variations for the piano forte by A. H. Wenck. Philadelphia, PA: Geo. Willig [184-?] 1 p. ViU. 40-6908

Wener, J. Russian quickstep. Composed for the piano forte by J. Werner. Boston, MA: Oliver Ditson [184-?] 2 p. ViU. 40-6909

Wenham, Mass. Congregational Church. Confession of faith and covenant of the Congregational Church in Wenham. With the names of surviving members, May 25, 1840. Boston, MA: Whipple & Damrell, 1840. 16 p. MBC; MBNEH; MiD-B; MWA. 40-6910

Wentworth, John. Banks and corporations. Letter of John Wentworth, Esq., editor of the Chicago Democrat, published at Chicago, State of Illinois, in reply to an invitation to deliver a lecture before The Bay State Democratic Association, at Boston, Mass. From the Boston Morning Post. Mr. Wentworth's Letter. [35 line quotation] Boston, MA: s. l. [1840] 8 p. MBC; MdHi. 40-6911

Wesley, John, 1703-1791. Human life a dream. A sermon. [New York: Tract Society of the Methodist Episcopal Church, 1840?] 12 p. IEG. 40-6912

Wesley, John, 1703-1791. The works of the Reverend John Wesley. Notes by John Emory. First American complete & standard edition... New York: T. Mason & John Lane, 1840. 7 v. CoDi; IaMvC; MBC; TNS; WvU. 40-6913

Wesleyan Methodist Church. The catechisms of the Wesleyan Methodists. Compiled and published by order of the British Conference. Revised and adapted to the use of families and schools connected with the Methodist Episcopal Church. New York: T. Mason and G. Lane, 1840. 72 p. MWbor; MWborHi. 40-6914

West, W. H. C. The Jenny Lind mania. Boston, MA: Ditson [184-?] p. CtY; MB. 40-6915

West, W. H. C. The Jenny Lind mania. A humorous song. Written by W. H. C. West. Baltimore, MD; New Orleans, LA: F. D. Benteen; W. T. Mayo [184-?] 2 p. ViU. 40-6916

West, Walter. The evergreen; or, stories for childhood and youth. Edited by Walter West. Second edition. Boston, MA: Monroe and Francis, 1840. 160 p. CtY; MB; NBuG. 40-6917

Western almanac; correctly calculated for Ohio, and the adjoining states. Turner's Comick Almanack. [Pictures of men and women cover entire page.] Cincinnati, OH: U. P. James, publisher, 1840. 36 p. OC. 40-6918

Western almanac and Franklin Calendar for 1841. Rochester, NY: William Alling [1840] p. MWA.. 40-6919

Western almanac and New York Farmers' Calendar for 1841. Ithaca, NY: Mack, Andrus & Woodruff [1840] p. MWA. 40-6920

Western almanac and New York Farmers' Calendar for 1841. Rochester, NY: William Alling [1840] 23 p. MWA; NCasti; NRU. 40-6921

Western almanac for the year of our Lord 1840: bissextile or leap year, and, till July 4th, the 63d of American Independence. Adapted to the meridian of Rochester, Monroe Co., N. Y. Lat. 43o 8' 17"-lon. 49' 12" W. of Wash. city. [woodcut] Rochester, NY: Published and sold

by William Alling, 1840. 24 p. MBNMHi; NRMA. 40-6922

Western counterfeit detector and bank note table. Vol. 1, 2, 1840, 1841. [Cincinnati, OH: s. l., 1840-41] 2 v. MnHi; OClWHi. 40-6923

The Western farmer and gardener devoted to agriculture, horticulture, and rural economy. Edited by E. J. Hooper. Cincinnati, OH: E. J. Hooper, publisher, 1840-. v. 1-. IaAS; LNH; NNNBG; OClWHi; TxU. 40-6924

The Western farmers' almanac for 1841, being the 65th-66th year of American independence. Calculated for the western part of New York, and will serve for the western part of Pennsylvania, and northern part of Ohio, Michigan, Upper Canada &c. By Professor George R. Perkins. Auburn, NY: Published and sold, wholesale and retail, by Oliphant & Skinner [1840] 32 p. FNp; ICHi; MWA' NCH. 40-6925

Western farmer's comprehensive almanac, for the year of Our Lord 1840... Louisville, KY: Printed & published by Morton & Griswould, 1840. 36 p. OO. 40-6926

The Western Journal of Medicine and Surgery. Edited by Daniel Drake and Lunsford P. Yandell... Louisville, KY: s. l., 1840-55. 32 v. IaAS; LU; MdBJ; MiU; TxU. 40-6927

Western Railroad Corporation. Proceedings of the annual meeting of the Western Railroad Corporation, held by adjournment in the City of Boston, March 12, 1840, including the report of the Committee investigating. Appointed by the stockholders. Boston, MA: Dutton and Wentworth, printers, 1840. 56 p. Ct; IU; MeHi; MYH-BA; WU. 40-6928

Western Railroad Corporation. Regulations for the government of the Transportation Department of the Western Railroad Corporation. Springfield, MA: Merriam Wood & Co., 1840. 23 p. NN. 40-6929

Western Railroad Corporation. Report of the delegation to Albany to the stockholders April [i. e., May] 12, 1840. Boston, MA: Dutton and Wentworth, printers, 1840. 19 p. DBRE; InU; MBAt; MH; MWA. 40-6930

Western Railroad Corporation. Report of the trial of the engine America, from Boston to Springfield, Aug. 19, 1840. Boston, MA: Clapp and Son, 1840. 8 p. CSmH; MiU; NN. 40-6931

The Western Reserve Almanac for 1841... Cleveland, OH: s. l. [1840?] p. OClWHi. 40-6932

Western Reserve University, Cleveland, O. Catalogue of the officers and students of the Western Reserve College, Hudson, Ohio, November, 1840-41. Hudson, OH: Printed by Charles Aikin, 1840. 23 p. CSmH; MWA; NN; O; OClW; WBeloC. 40-6933

Western world. Warsaw, IL: s. l., 1840. NN. 40-6934

Westlake, Thomas. A general view of baptism; embracing extracts from various authors. With remarks and observations on the mode, subjects, and history of baptism... New York: s. l., 1840. 4 p. RPB. 40-6935

Westminster Assembly of Divines. The explanatory catechism, being the shorter catechism... Philadelphia, PA: Presbyterian Board of Publication, 1840. 61 p. MBC; NNUT; PLERC-Hi. 40-6936

Westminster Assembly of Divines. The shorter catechism of the reverend Assembly of Divines, with the proofs thereof out of the Scriptures in words at length... For the benefit of Christians in general, and youth and children in understanding in particular... Auburn, NY: Henry Ivison, Jr., 1840. 51 p. NNUT. 40-6937

Westminster Assembly of Divines. The Westminister assembly's shorter catechism explained by way of question and answer. What man is to believe concerning God. By several ministers of the Gospel... Fourth Philadelphia edition, carefully compared with an early and corrected Scotch impression. Philadelphia, PA: William S. Young, 1840. 173, 218 p. IaPeC; KKcBT; MiU; PP; TBriK. 40-6938

Westminster Assembly of Divines. The Westminister assembly's shorter catechism explained by way of question and answer. What man is to believe concerning God. By several ministers of the Gospel... Fourth Philadelphia edition, carefully compared with an early and corrected Scotch impression. Philadelphia, PA: William S. Young, Robert Carter, 1840. 267 p. IaPeC; ICP. 40-6939

Weston, Daniel Corry, 1815-1903. Vindication of the minority of the Congrgational Church in the South Parish, Augusta, on the subject of dancing. Augusta, ME: W. R. Smith & Co., 1840. 40 p. CSmH; MeHi; MH; PPL. 40-6940

Weston, Edward Payson, 1819-1879. The Bowdoin poets. Edited by Edward P. Weston. Brunswick, ME: Published by Joseph Griffin, 1840. 188 p. CtMW; ICU; MeBa; MNBedf; OO. 40-6941

A wet sheet and a flowing sea. A nautical song... written by Allan Cunningham. Adapted & arranged by Thomas Walton. [With accompaniment for piano forte.] Boston, MA: Keith [184-?] 2 p. MB. 40-6942

Weymouth School Committee. Report of the School Committee of Weymouth... Boston, MA: published by Whipple & Damrell, 1840. 11 p. MWey. 40-6943

The whale and the perils of whale-fishery. New Haven, CT: S. Babcock, 1840. 16 p. MH; NN. 40-6944

Wharey, James, 1789-1842. Brief view of the proper subjects and true mode of Christian baptism. Philadelphia, PA: Presbyterian Board of Pub., 1840. 24 p. CtHC; IEG; MBC; PU; ViRut. 40-6945

Wharey, James, 1789-1842. Sketches of church history. Comprising a regular series of the most important and interesting events in the history of the church, from the birth of Christ to the nineteenth century. By the Rev. James Wharey. Philadelphia, PA: Presbyterian board of publication, 1840. 324 p. ArBaA; FDeS; ICP; ODaB; PPiW. 40-6946

Wharton, Thomas Isaac, 1791-1856. A memoir of William Rawle, LL. D., president of the Historical Society... By T. I. Wharton... Philadelphia, PA: s. l., 1840. 59 p. DLC; MiU; NjP; OFH; PPAmP. 40-6947

Wheaton, Henry, 1785-1848. Life of William Pinkney, by Henry Wheaton, LL. D. Life of William Ellery, by Edward T. Channing. Life of Cotton Mather, by William B. O. Peabody. New York: Harper & Brothers, 1840. 350 p. MSbo; RPB. 40-6948

Wheeler, Daniel, 1771-1840. Extracts from the letters and journal of Daniel Wheeler, while engaged in a religious visit to the inhabitants of some of the islands of the Pacific Ocean, Van Dieman's Land, New South Wales, and New Zealand, accompanied by his son, Charles Wheeler. Philadelphia, PA: Printed by J. Rakestraw, 1840. 324 p. CU; DeWi; PU; RPB; TxU. 40-6949

Wheeler, Sarah, 1807-1867. Some particulars of the last illness and death of Jane Wheeler. Falmouth: J. Trathan, 1840. 22 p. MH; MWA; PHC. 40-6950

Wheeling, W. Va. Merchants and Mechanics Bank. Condition of the Merchants and Mechanics Bank... January 18, 1841. [Doc. No. 26] Richmond: Samuel Shepherd, printer, 1840. 2 p. WHi. 40-6951

Wheeling, W. Va. Ordinances, etc. Ordinances of the City of Wheeling. To which are prefixed the acts of the Legislature of Virginia, relating to the city. Published by authority of the Council. Wheeling, WV: printed by J. E. Wharton, 1840. 151 p. CSmH; OClWHi. 40-6952

Whelpley, Samuel, 1766-1817. A compend of history, from the earliest times... With additions by Rev. Joseph Emerson... 11th ed. New York: Published by Collins, Keese & Co., 1840. 2 v. in 1.

ArCH; MH; OBerB; OSW; ScDuE. 40-6953

"Wherefore change?" More than one hundred reasons why W. H. Harrison should and will have the support of the democracy for President of the United States in preference to Martin Van Buren. By a workingman. Boston, MA: s. l., 1840. 16 p. MH; MH-BA. 40-6954

Whig gathering. Song and chorus respectfully dedicated to the Whigs of the United States. Boston, MA: Henry Prentiss, 1840. 2 p. MB; MNF. 40-6955

Whig Party. Alabama. Convention, 1840. Address of the committee of the Whig Convention to the people of Alabama. [Tuscaloos, AL: Printed at the Monitor Office, 1840?] 48 p. GEU; TxU. 40-6956

Whig Party. Alabama. Convention, 1840. Proceedings of the Whig Convention, held at the State-house, Tuscaloosa, Alabama, December 23, 24, 1840. Tuscaloosa, AL: Printed by M. D. J. Slade, 1840. 7 p. AB; GEU. 40-6957

Whig Party. Arkansas. Democratic Whig State Convention, Monday, March 16, 1840. [Little Rock, AR: s. l., 1840] 12 p. NHi. 40-6958

Whig Party. Arkansas. Young Men's Convention, 1840. Address of the Young Men's Whig Convention, held at Little Rock, July 13, 1840. To which is added an appendix, containing many important documents in relation to the life and services of Gen. W. H. Harrison. Printed by order of the convention. Little Rock, AR: Printed by Stone & McCurdy, 1840. 80 p. TxU. 40-6959

Whig Party. Cambridge [Mass.] Convention. Whig Republican Association of Cambridge Constitution and By-laws... Cambridge, MA: s. l., 1840. 8 p. MHi. 40-6960

Whig Party. Connecticut. Convention, 1840. Proceedings of a state convention of the Whic Young Men of Connecticut, assembled at Hartford, February 26, 1840. Hartford, CT: Courant Office, 1840. 16 p. Ct; MH. 40-6961

Whig Party. Connecticut. Fairfield County. First in war---First in peace---First in the hearts of their countrymen. New York? [1840] 40-6962

Whig Party. Maryland. Central Committee. Address to the people of Maryland by the Whig central committee of the state. Baltimore, 1840. 8 p. CtY; DLC; ViU. 40-6963

Whig Party. Massachusetts. Circular letter in regard to a general convention of Whigs of Mass., Boston, July 15th, 1840. Boston, MA: s. l., 1840. 1 p. MHi. 40-6964

Whig Party. Massachusetts. Cambridge Association. Constitution and by-laws of the Whig Republican Association of Cambridge. Instituted March 4, 1840. Cambridge, MA: Metcalf, Torry and Ballou, 1840. 8 p. No Loc. 40-6965

Whig Party. Massachusetts. Convention. 1840. Answer of Whig members of Massachusetts to address of Marcus Morton, delivered in convention of the two houses, January 22, 1840. Boston, 1840. 36 p. PHi; PPL. 40-6966

Whig Party. Massachusetts. Convention, 1840. Proceedings of the Whig State Convention at Worcester, Mass., June 17, 1840. Business Convention... Worcester, MA: s. l., 1840? p. WHi. 40-6967

Whig Party. Michigan. Matter for the people to read. The address of the Whig members of the legislature; and Thomas Corwin's eloquent defence of Gen. Harrison, against the attacks of Isaac E. Crary. [Detroit, 1840] 12 p. MiD. 40-6968

Whig Party. Missouri. Address to the people of Missouri. [Fayette? 1840] 46 p. MoHI 40-6969

Whig Party. National Executive Committee, 1840. To the Whigs and conservatives of the United States. Washington, DC: s. l., 1840. 3 p. OClWHi. 40-6970

Whig Party. New Jersey. Mr. Van Buren's standing army. Organization of the militia. [N. J. ?1840] 8 p. NjR. 40-6971

Whig Party. New York. Convention, 1840. Proceedings of the Whig state convention held at Utica, on the 12th and 13th August, 1840, for the purpose of nominating candidates for governor. Albany: Printed by Hoffman, White & Visscher, 1840. 16 p. ICU; NN. 40-6972

Whig Party. New York. Convention, 1840. To the Whigs of the Union, Albany, State of New York, July 20, 1840. Albany, NY: s. l., 1840? 4 p. WHi. 40-6973

Whig Party. Tennessee. Convention, 1840. Address to the People of Tennessee by the Whig Convention, which assembled at Knoxville, on Monday, the 10th of February, 1840. Knoxville, TN:

James C. Moses and Company, 1840. 42 p. TMeC. 40-6974

Whig Party. Tennessee. Facts for the people. The various charges against General W. H. Harrison briefly stated and refuted and some of the objections to the present administration enumberated. Jonesborough, TN: Brownlow and Garland Publishers, 1840. 40 p. DLC; T. 40-6975

Whig Party. Union of the Federal Whigs and British Tories. Boston, MA: s. l., 1840. PPL. 40-6976

Whig Party. Virginia. Address of the Whig Convention for the nomination of electors to the people of Virginia. [Richmond, VA?: s. l., 1840?] 40 p. DLC; ICU; MB; TU; ViU. 40-6977

Whig Party. Virginia. Convention, 1840. Address of the Whig convention, held at Richmond on the 5th October, 1840. To the people of Virginia. [Richmond?1840] Broadside. ViU. 40-6978

Whig Party. Virginia. Fauquier County. Address to the voters of the fifteenth electoral district of Virginia on the militia bill. [n. p., 1840. 16 p. CtY. 40-6979

Whig Party. Virginia. Fauquier County. Address of the Whig central commitee of vigilance of Fauquier County, Virginia. [Washington?1840] 16 p. DLC; NcD; ViU. 40-6980

Whig Party. Virginia. Fauquier County. Second address of the Central Committee of Fauquier, to the people of that county on the army bill. Washington, DC: Printed at the Madisonian Office, 1840.

34, 11 p. DLC; NBu; NcD; Vi; ViU. 40-6981

Whig Party. Virginia. Frederick County. To the people of Virginia. [Frederick County, Va., 1840. 14 p. NcD. 40-6982

Whig Party. Virginia. Hanover County. Address to the people of the county of Hanover. Richmond: John S. Gallaher, printer, 1840. Whig Party. Virginia. Powhatan County. Address of the Whig committee of vigilance to the people of Powhatan. Richmond: John S. Gallaher, printer, 1840. 14 p. ViW. 40-6983

The Whig song book. Columbus: I. N. Whiting [1840] 105 p. NN; OFH. 40-6984

Whig songs. Scrapbook of newspaper clippings. Boston? 1840. 24 p. Nh; RPB. 40-6985

Whig state convention. At a meeting of the committee appointed by the citizens of Richmond and Manchester to make all necessary arrangements for the Whig state convention. [Richmond:1840. Broadside. ViU. 40-6986

Whig Young Men of Connecticut. Proceedings of a state convention of the Whig Young Men of Connecticut, assembled at Hartford, February 26, 1840. Hartford, CT: printed at the Courant Office [1840] 16 p. CtY; DLC; NjP; NNC; OO. 40-6987

Whig Young Men of Massachusetts. Address of the Whig Young Men's Convention to the people of Massachusetts. [Boston, MA?: s. l., 1840?] 23 p. OClWHi. 40-6988

Whig Young Men of Massachusetts. Whigs of Boston... political poster in favor of Jonathan Chapman for mayor. [Boston, MA?: s. l., 1840?] p. MHi. 40-6989

Whitaker, John, 1776-1847. Oh! ask me not to be your bride. Written by T. H. Baylye, Esqr. Composed for the piano forte by John Whitaker. Philadelphia, PA: Geo. Willig [184-?] 2 p. ViU. 40-6990

White, Daniel Appleton, 1776-1861. An address, delivered at the consecration of the Harmony Grove Cemetery, in Salem, June 14, 1840. By Daniel Appleton White. With an appendix. Salem: printed at the Gazette Press, 1840. 33 p. CBPac; ICMe; RPB; WHi. 40-6991

White, Daniel T. White's New Cookbook, embracing temperate and economical receipts for domiestic liquors and cookery. Containing such condiments as most families can procure and nearly all selected to suit the general health as well as the palate. To which is added an appendix and miscellany, containing many valuable receipts in domestic economy, &c., &c., together with a catalogue of books, the knowledge and practice of the precepts in which will insure the old age and happiness of all. By Daniel T. White, Philanthropist. Cincinnati, OH: s. l., 1840. 96 p. KyU; OCHP. 40-6992

White, Edward Little, 1809-1851. The Melodeon; a collection of songs, duetts, trios & quartetts, original & selected. Adapted to sacred & moral words by Edward L. White. Part I. Boston, MA: W. H. Oakes [184-?] 34 p. NRES. 40-6993

White, Hugh Lawson, 1773-1840. Letter of the Hon. Hugh L. White, to the legislature of Tennessee, on declining to obey certain of their resolutions of instruction, and resigning the office of senator of the United States. Washington, DC: printed at the Madisonian office, 1840. 15 p. CU; MBAt; NcAS; OClWHi; WHi. 40-6994

White, Hugh Lawson, 1773-1840. Letter... to the Legislature of Tennessee, declining to obey certain of their resolutions of instruction and resigning the office of Senate of the United States. Washington, DC: s. l., 1840. 15 p. CtY; DLC; NRU; OClW; ViU. 40-6995

White, James, 1803-1862. Feudal times; or, the court of James the Third. A Scottish historical play. By Rev. James White. With the stage business, cast of characters, costumes, relative positions, etc. New York: S. French & Son [etc., etc., 184-?] 63 p. CSt. 40-6996

White, James, 1803-1862. The king of the commons. A play in five acts. With the stage business... New York: W. Taylor [184-?] 77 p. MB; MH; NN; NNC. 40-6997

White, James, fl. 1815-1818. A complete system of Farriery, and veterinary medicine. Containing a compendium of the veterinary art... With observations on stable management. Philadelphia: J. Kay, 1840. 216 p. OU. 40-6998

White, John, 1805-1845. Speech of Mr. John White, of Kentucky, delivered in the House of Representatives, on Friday, June 5, 1840, in committee of the whole on the state of the Union, in opposition to the sub-treasury bill. Washington, DC:

Printed at Gideon's office, 1840. 48 p. InU; MoS; NBu; NjR. 40-6999

White, William Spottswood, 1800-1873. The African preacher. An authentic narrative. By the Rev. William S. White. Philadelphia, PA: Presbyterian Board of Publication, 1840. 139 p. TKL-Mc. 40-7000

White, William Spottswood, 1800-1873. 4th of July reminiscences and reflections. A sermon. Preached in the Presbyterian Church, Charlottesville, July 5th, 1840, by William S. White. Charlottesville, VA: R. C. Noel, 1840. 19 p. CSmH; PHi; PPPrHi; ViU. 40-7001

White Water Canal Company. Report of the stockholders. Cincinnati, OH: s. l., 1840. OCHP. 40-7002

Whitecross, John. The assembly's shorter catechiam, illustrated by appropriate anecdotes; chiefly designed to assist parents and Sabbath school teachers, in the instruction of youth. By John Whitecross... Third American edition. New York: Robert Carter, 1840. 180 p. MH; TBriK; WBeloC. 40-7003

Whitehead, Charles, 1804-1862. Lives and exploits of the most noted highwaymen, robbers, and murderers of all nations, drawn from the most authentic sources and brought down to the present time. Hartford, CT: E. Strong, 1840. 422 p. CtSoP; MH; OCLaw; OClWHi; OU. 40-7004

Whitesboro Association. The constitution, confession of faith, and by-laws of Whitesboro Association, revised and adopted at its quarterly meeting held at Marshall, Oneida County, April 7, 1840.

Whitesboro, NY: Press of the Oneida Institute, 1840. 8 p. OClWHi. 40-7005

Whitewater, O. Congregational Church. The articles of faith, constitution and history of the Congregational Church of Whitewater, Morgan Township, Butler County, Ohio. Hamilton, OH: W. C. Howells, printer, 1840. 8 p. ICP. 40-7006

Whitman, Jason, 1799-1848. A letter to a friend on the duty of commencing at once a religious life. By Rev. Jason Whitman. Boston, MA: Christian Register Office, 1840. 14 p. ICME; MHi. 40-7007

Whitman, Jason, 1799-1848. Practical influence of the doctrine of total depravity. [Dover, DE: Unitarian Monitor, 184-?] 8 p. CBPac. 40-7008

Whitman, Jason, 1799-1848. Week-day religion. By Jason Whitman, Pastor of the Park Street Church, Portland. Portland, ME: Published by O. L. Sanborn, 1840. 320 p. CBPac; MB; MH; NhPet; RPB. 40-7009

Whitney, George, 1804-1842. A commemorative discourse pronounced at Quincy, Mass., 25 May, 1840, on the Second Centennial Anniversary of the Ancient Incorporation of the Town. By George Whitney. Boston, MA: James Munroe & Co., 1840. 71 p. CBPac; ICMe; MB; OClWHi; RPB; WHi. 40-7010

Whitney, George, 1804-1842. Voices of the Dead. A sermon, preached before the Jamaica Plain Parish... by Geroge Whitney. Boston, MA: printerd by I. R. Butts, 1840. 16 p. ICMe; MBC; MWA; NCH; RPB. 40-7011

Whittemore, Thomas, 1800-1861. Notes and illustrations of the parables of the New Testament, arranged according to the time in which they were spoken. Revised ed. Boston, MA: published by the Author, 1840. 381 p. MH; MMeT-Hi. 40-7012

Whittemore, Thomas, 1800-1861. Sermon on the end of the world. Boston, MA: s. l., 1840. PPL. 40-7013

Whittemore, Thomas, 1800-1861. The plain guide to Universalism. Designed to lead inquirers to the belive of that doctrine and believers to the practice of it. Ed. 15. Boston, MA: Usher, 1840. 408 p. CL; ICMBI; MWA; OClW; PPL. 40-7014

Whittemore, Thomas, 1800-1861. The plain guide to Universalism. Designed to lead inquirers to the belive of that doctrine and believers to the practice of it... By Thomas Whittemore. Boston, MA: The Author, 1840. 408 p. CtMW; IEG; MeBat; OO; PPL-R. 40-7015

Whittier, John Greenleaf, 1807-1892. Moll Pitcher, and The minstrel girl. Poems, by John G. Whittier. Rev. ed. Philadelphia, PA: J. Healy, 1840. 44 p. ICU; MB; MHa; PHC; PP. 40-7016

Whittier, John Greenleaf, 1807-1892. The north star: the poetry of freedom, by her friends... Philadelphia, PA: Merrihew and Thompson, 1840. 117 p. ICN; MB; MnU; OClWHi; PHC. 40-7017

Whittingham, William Rollinson, 1805-1879. Address... New York: s. l., 1840. PPL. 40-7018

Whittingham, William Rollinson, 1805-

1879. The annual sermon before the bishops, clergy and laity, constituting the board of missions of the Protestant Episcopal church in the United States... June 17, 1840. New York: published at the missionary rooms, 1840. 19 p. MBD; MdBD; NjR; OClWHi; PHi; WHi. 40-7019

Whittingham, William Rollinson, 1805-1879. Emanuel in the Euicharist. A sermon. Preached in St. Peter's Church, Baltimore, on the second Sunday in Advent. By William Rollinson Whittingham, Bishop of Maryland. Baltimore, MD: Knight & Colburn, 1840. 15 p. NGH. 40-7020

Whittingham, William Rollinson, 1805-1879. The ministry called to self-denial; a sermon, preached at the... Gen. theological seminary... Dec. 15, 1839... By W. R. Whittingham... New York: Xylographic press, 1840. 23 p. IEG; MdBD; NcU; NjR; NNG; PHi; RPB; TSewU. 40-7021

Whittingham, William Rollinson, 1805-1879. The order and duty of Bishops. A sermon. Preached in St. Paul's Church, Baltimore, September 17th, 1840, at the consecration of the Rev. Wm. R. Whittingham, D. D., as Bishop of the Protestant Episcopal Church. Baltimore, MD: Printed by Jos. Robinson, 1840. 19 p. MsJPED. 40-7022

Whittock, Nathaniel. The Oxford drawing book, or, the art of drawing, and the theory and practice of perspective... A new and improved edition. New York: Collins, Keese and company, 1840. 159 p. MH; NIDHi; OClStM; WMMD. 40-7023

Wickliffe, Robert, 1775-1859. Reply of Robert Wickliffe to Rev. R. J. Breckenridge. Delivered in Court House in Lexington... 1840. Lexington, KY: Observer & Reporter Print., 1840. 64 p. MsJS; PPPrHi. 40-7024

Wickliffe, Robert, 1775-1859. Speech of Robert Wickliffe in reply to the Rev. R. J. Breckenridge. Delivered in the Court House on Monday, the 9th November, 1840. Louisville, KY: Observer & Reporter Print., 1840. 55 p. CSmH; DLC; ICU; ViU. 40-7025

Wickliffe, Robert, 1775-1859. Speech of Robert Wickliffe in Senate of Kentucky in relation to Tariff and Internal Improvements... Frankfort, KY: s. l., 1840. 39 p. PHi. 40-7026

Wickliffe, Robert, 1775-1859. Speech of Robert Wickliffe upon resigning his seat as Senator, Aug. 10, 1840, more especially in reference to the "Negro Law." Lexington, KY: Observer & Reporter Print., 1840. 36 p. ICU. 40-7027

Wickliffe, Robert, 1815?-1850. Machiavel's political discourses upon the first decade of Livy... Louisville, KY: Prentice and Weissinger, 1840. 29 p. ICU; KyU; MBAt; MH; NGH. 40-7028

Wiesel, M. Cumberland guards' quick step. Boston, MA: Ditson [184-?] p. MB. 40-7029

Wiesel, M. Cumberland guards' quick step. Composed and respectfully dedicated to the officers & members of the corps, by M. Wiesel. Baltimore, MD: F. D. Benteen [184-?] 2 p. ViU. 40-7030

Wiesenthal, Thomas Van Dyke, 1790-1833. Ingle side. A popular Scotch song. Composed & arranged for the piano forte by T. V. Wiesenthal. Baltimore, MD: S. Carusi [184-?] 2 p. NcD. 40-7031

Wiesenthal, Thomas Van Dyke, 1790-1833. Ingle side. A popular Scotch song. Composed & arranged for the piano forte by T. V. Wiesenthal. Boston, MA: Keiths Music pub. House [184-?] 2 p. DLC. 40-7032

Wiesenthal, Thomas Van Dyke, 1790-1833. Ingle side. A popular Scotch song. Composed & arranged for the piano forte by T. V. Wiesenthal. Philadelphia, PA: John Marsh [184-?] 2 p. ViU. 40-7033

Wiggers, Gustav Friedrich, 1777-1860. ... Augustinism and Pelagianism; from the original sources, by G. F. Wiggers, D. D... translated from the German, with notes and additions by Rev. Ralph Emerson. Andover, MA: Gould, Newsman & Saxton, 1840. 383 p. MB; TxFwSB; TxMcK; WNaE. 40-7034

Wiggers, Gustav Friedrich, 1777-1860. An historical presentation of Augustinism and Pelagianism. From the original sources, by G. F. Wiggers, D. D. Translated from the German. With notes and additions by Rev. Ralph Emerson. Andover, MA: Published by Gould, Newman & Saxton, 1840. 383 p. CtY; DLC; NNUT; OrCS; ViRut. 40-7035

Wiggins, Francis S. The American farmers, instructor on practical agriculturist, comprehending the cultivation of plants, and husbandry of the domestic animals, and the economy of the farm... By Francis S. Wiggins. Philadelphia, PA:

printed by E. G. Dorsey, 1840. 504 p. MH; OUrC; PU-V; ScSch; ViL. 40-7036

Wightman, William May, 1808-1882. An address. Delivered before the Mutual Improvement Society of the South Carolina Conference, January 11, 1840, by Rev. Wm. M. Wightman, A. M., President of the Society. Published by request of the society. Charleston, SC: Burges & James, printers, 1840. 24 p. ScSp. 40-7037

Wilberforce, Samuel, 1805-1873. Agathos, and other Sunday stories. By Samuel Wilberforce. New York: General Protestant Episcopal Sunday School Union, 1840. 170 p. No Loc. 40-7038

Wilcox, Thomas, 1622-1682. Choice drops of honey from the rock Christ. With a sermon by Elder Knapp and revival hymns. Boston, MA: J. Loring [184-?] 96 p. NN. 40-7039

Wilder, Joshua. A Plea for Liberty of Conscience, and Personal Freedom from Military Conscription. In Letters to Thomas Loring, Esq., by Joshua Wilder. A place for every Member in the body, and also in the Body Politics-and every member in its place. Hingham: Printed by J. Farmer, 1840. 45 p. MB; Mh-AH; MWA. 40-7040

Wilkins, John Hubbard, 1794-1861. Elements of astronomy. By John H. Wilkins, A. M. Stereotype edition. Boston, MA: Published by Hilliard, Gray, and Company, 1840. 152 p. MH; MoS. 40-7041

Wilkins, M. An address. Delivered at the Reformed Dutch Church at West

Farms, July 4th, 1840, by Gouverneur M. Wilkins. New York: J. P. Wright, 1840. 23 p. NNG; PHi. 40-7042

Wilkinson, J. B. The annals of Binghamton, and of the country connected with it, from the earliest settlement. By J. B. Wilkinson... Binghamton, NY: Cooke & Davis, printers, 1840. 256 p. FDA; ICN; MWA; Nh-Hi; PMA; WHi. 40-7043

Wilks, Mark. Memoir of Clementine Cuvier, daughter of Baron Cuvier. With reflections by Rev. John Angell James. New York: s. l., 1840? 96 p. GMWa; NN. 40-7044

Will County, Ill. Anti-Slavery Society. Slave code of the State of Illinois; being an abstract of those laws now in force in this state which affect the rights of colored people, such as both bond and free. With notes. Joliet, IL?: Published by the Will Co. Anti-Slavery Society, 1840. 12 p. MH-L. 40-7045

Willard, Emma Hart, 1787-1870. Ancient atlas to accompany the universal geography. By William Channing Woodbridge and Emma Willard. Hartford, CT: Belknap & Hamersley [1840?] p. MH; OHi. 40-7046

Willard, Samuel, 1776-1859. The general class-book; or intersting lessons in prose and verse, with an epitome of English orthography and pronounciation. 19th ed. Greenfield, MA: s. l., 1840. MH. 40-7047

Willard, Samuel, 1776-1859. Secondary lessons, or the improved reader. Boston, MA; New York: Greenfield, 1840. MDeeP. 40-7048

Willcock, John William. The office of constable: compromising the laws relating to high, petty, and special constables, head-boroughs, tithingmen, borsholders, and watchmen, with an account of their institution and appointment. By J. W. Willcock, Esq... Philadelphia, PA: John S. Littell, 1840. 88 p. CoU; MH-L; OO; PP; ScSC. 40-7049

William and Mary College, Williamsburg, Va. Laws and regulations of the College of William and Mary, in Virginia. Petersburg, VA: printed by E. and J. C. Ruffin, 1840. 24 p. Vi. 40-7050

William College, Williamstown, Mass. Catalogue of the officers and students of Williams College and of the Berkshire Medical Institution connected with it, Oct., 1840. New York: W. E. Dean, printer, 1840. 16 p. MBC; NN; NNAM; PWW. 40-7051

William College, Williamstown, Mass. Catalogue of the Philotechnian Society, Williams College, 1840. Troy, NY: N. Tuttle, 1840. 15 p. IU; MBC; MWiW; OCHP. 40-7052

William College, Williamstown, Mass. Programme of juvenile exhibition, May 5, 1840... S. l.: s. l., 1840. OCHP. 40-7053

William Henry Harrison in Congress. [Washington, DC? published by the National Intelligencer, 1840] 32 p. PHi. 40-7054

Williams, H. Dearest! remember me. Philadelphia, PA: s. l. [184-?] p. MB. 40-7055

Williams, Henry, of Boston. Remarks on banks and banking and the skeleton of a project for a national bank. By a citizen of Boston. Boston, MA: Torrey & Blair, printers, 1840. 62 p. ICU; LNH; MHi; NNC; OClFRB; PPL. 40-7056

Williams, Henry, 1804-. Speech of Mr. Williams, of Massachusetts, on the independent treasury bill. In the House of Representatives, June 4, 1840... [Washington, DC: s. l., 1840] 15 p. MdHi; MeB; MWA; PPL; WHi. 40-7057

Williams, Jesse. A description of the United States lands in Iowa: being a minute description of every section and quarter section, quality of soil, groves of timber, praries, ledges of rock, coal banks, iron and lead ores, water-falls, mill-seats, etc... With an appendix. By Jesse Williams. New York: J. H. Colton, 1840. 180 p. CU; IaHA; MHi; NN; WHi. 40-7058

Williams, John, physician. Dr. John Williams' Last Legacy and Useful Family Guide. New and improved edition. Boston, MA: Published by S. Bates & Co., 1840. 24 p. MWA. 40-7059

Williams, John, 1789-1819. Life and actions of Alexander the Great. New York: Harper, 1840. 351 p. InRch. 40-7060

Williams, John D. An elementary treatise on algebra... Boston, MA: Hilliard, Gray & Co., 1840. 605 p. MB; MiU; RPB. 40-7061

Williams, Nathaniel West. A valedictory sermon to the First Baptist Church and Congregation... Beverly, April 19, 1840. Salem: published by request, printed at the register press, 1840. 16 p. MB; MBC; MBevHi; MH. 40-7062

Williams, Robert Folkstone. The youth of Shakespeare, by the author of "Shakespeare and his friends"... Philadelphia, PA: Lea and Blanchard, 1840. 3 v. InGrD; MH; NjN; PU; RPB. 40-7063

Williams, Thomas, 1779-1876. Centurial [sic] sermon on the revival of religion, 1740. Inscribed to the memory of N. Strong. Hartford, CT: s. l., 1840. 32 p. CSmH; CtY; MWA; Nh; OO. 40-7064

Williams, Thomas, 1779-1876. The Mercy of God. A centorial sermon, on the revival of religion, A. D. 1740. Inscribed to the memory of the Rev. Nathan Strong. Hartford, CT: Elihu Geer, 1840. 32 p. CtMW; MDeeP; MWA; MWiW; PHi; RPB. 40-7065

Williams, Thomas, 1779-1876. The official character of Rev. Nathanael Emmons, D. D., taught and shown in a sermon on his life and death. By Rev. Thomas Williams, A. M., of East Greenwich, R. I. Boston, MA: Published by Ferdinand Andrews, 1840. 80 p. CtY; ICMe; MiU-C; MWA; NBuG. 40-7066

Williams, Thomas, d. 1854. The bride's farewell. A favorite ballad. Written by Miss M. L. Beevor. Composed for the piano forte by Thomas Williams. Baltimore, MD: Geo. Willig, Junr. [184-?] 2 p. CtY; MB; ViU. 40-7067

Williamson, Isaac Dowd, 1807-1876. An expositon and defence of Universaliam, in a series of sermons delivered in the Universalist church, Baltimore, Md. New York: Price, 1840. 227 p. KyLoP; MB; NCaS; RPB. 40-7068

Willis, Nathaniel Parker, 1806-1867. American scenery; or, Land, lake, and river, illustrative of transatlantic nature. From drawings by W. H. Bartlett... by N. P. Willis. New York: Virtue & Yorston [1840-41] 2 v. MH; NWM. 40-7069

Willis, Nathaniel Parker, 1806-1867. Romance of travel, comprising tales of five lands, by the author of Pencillings by the way. New York: S. Colman, 1840. 300 p. CSt; DLC; MiU; NCH; PU. 40-7070

Willison, John, 1680-1750. The afflicted man's companion; or, a directory for persons and families afflicted with a sickness of any other distress. Revised edition. New York: Published by the American Tract Society [184-?] 343 p. WHi. 40-7071

Willson, James R. Hebrew literature. An introductory lecture. Delivered at the opening of the Allegheny Institute, Nov. 2nd, 1840. Newburgh, NY: J. D. Spalding, printer, 1840? p. N. 40-7072

Willson, Marcius, 1813-1905. ... A treatise on civil polity and political economy. With an appendix containing a brief account of the powers, duties, and salaries of national, state, county and town officers. For the use of schools and academies. By Marcius Willson. 3rd ed. New York: Taylor & Clement, 1840. NGH; NGlf; NjP. 40-7073

Wilmington & Raleigh Railroad Company. Proceedings of the fourth meeting of the stockholders of the Wilmington & Raleigh railroad company... [Wilmington, NC: printed at the Wilmington Chronicle Office, 1840] 7 p. NjR. 40-7074

Wilmington & Raleigh Railroad Company. Proceedings... of the Wilmington &

Raleigh railroad company... on April 13, 1840. [Wilmington, NC: printed at the Wilmington Chronicle Office, 1840] 4 p. WU. 40-7075

Wilmot, Robert. A new work, in favor of the Whig cause, and the election of General Harrison to the presidential chair... By R. Wilmot. Cincinnati, OH: Printed by J. B. & R. P. Conogh, 1840. 36 p. DLC; IU; OCHP; OClWHi. 40-7076

Wilmot, Robert. True democracy contrasted with false democracy; or, Gen'l Harrison's cause vindicated... by R. Wilmot. Cincinnati, OH: n. p., 1840. 36, [2] p. In. 40-7077

Wilson, Alexander, 1766-1813. Wilson's American ornithology, with notes by which is added a synopsis of American birds, including those described by Bonaparte, Audubon, Nuttall and Richardson, by T. M. Brewer. Boston, MA: Otis, Broaders, and Company, 1840. 746 p. CtHt; MB; MSaP; PPAN. 40-7078

Wilson, Caroline [Fry] 1787-1846. A word to women. The love of the world and other gatherings, being a collection of short pieces... Philadelphia, PA: Carey & Hart, 1840. 264 p. GMM; MWA; TBriK; WU. 40-7079

Wilson, J. Love wakes and weeps. Boston, MA: s. l. [184-?] p. MB. 40-7080

Wilson, Luther. A temperance discourse. Delivered in Westford on the day of the annual fast, April 5, 1838. Greenfield, MA?: Phelps & Ingersoll, 1840. 16 p. MH. 40-7081

Wilson, Margaret [Harries] 1797-1846.

Memoirs of Harriot, Duchess of St. Albans, by Mrs. Cornwell Baron-Wilson... Philadelphia, PA: Carey, 1840. 2 v. CtMW; FTa; MiD; OZeG; ScSoh. 40-7082

Wilson, Samuel, 1702-1750. A scripture manual; or, A plain representation of the ordinance of baptism. Philadelphia, PA: American Baptist Pub. and S. S. Society, 1840. 24 p. ICRL; RPB; WHi. 40-7083

Wilson, Samuel, 1702-1750. A scripture manual; or, A plain representation of the ordinance of baptism. Search the Scripture, John V. 39. By Samuel Wilson. Philadelphia, PA: Published by the American Baptist Publication and S. S. Society, 1840. 12 p. ICU. 40-7084

Wilson, Thomas, 1663-1755. The nature of sin. A sermon. By the late Thomas Wilson. New York: P. E. Tract Society [1840?] 11 p. NNG. 40-7085

Wilson, Thomas, 1663-1755. On delay of repentance. A sermon. By the late Thomas Wilson. New York: P. E. Tract Society [1840?] 8 p. NNG. 40-7086

Wilson, Thomas, 1663-1755. On fraud. A sermon. By the late Thomas Wilson. New York: P. E. Tract Society [1840?] 12 p. NNC. 40-7087

Wilson, Thomas, 1663-1755. On holiness. A sermon. By the late Thomas Wilson. New York: P. E. Tract Society [1840?] 12 p. NNG. 40-7088

Wilson, Thomas, 1663-1755. On self-examination. A sermon. By the late Thomas Wilson. New York: P. E. Tract Society [1840?] 12 p. NNG. 40-7089

Wilson, William, 1788-1857. The Blessedness of a nation whose God is Jehovah: a sermon. Pittsburgh, PA: William Allinder, 1840. 55 p. MBAt; MWiW; PPPrHi; TKC. 40-7090

Winans, William, 1788-1857. Sermon on the evidence of Christianity. Delivered by request at Woodville, Mississippi, 1839. By Rev. W. Winans. Published at the request of a committee of the church in Woodville. [Quotation] Cincinnati, OH: Printed at the Methodist Book Concern at, R. R. Thompson, printer, 1840. 55 p. MsJS; NcD. 40-7091

Winans, William, 1788-1857. The Substance of a discourse on our political advantages. Delivered at Midway, Miss., on the 4th of July, 1840. By the Rev. William Winans. Published by a Committee of the Audience. Cincinnati, OH: Printed at the Methodist Book Concern at, R. R. Thompson, printer, 1840. 24 p. KyLx; MsJS. 40-7092

Winans, William, 1788-1857. Substance of a funeral sermon on occasion of the Death of Simeon Gibson and his Infant Grand-child. Delivered at Pine Ridge Church, Miss., July 22, 1840. By Rev. W. Winans. "To die is gain," St. Paul. Cincinnati, OH: Printed at the Methodist Book Concern at, R. R. Thompson, printer, 1840. 17 p. KyLx. 40-7093

Winchester, B. The origin of the Spaulding story, concerning the manuscript found; with a short biography of Dr. P. Hulbert... So far as its connection with the Book of Mormon is concerned. By B. Winchester... Philadelphia, PA: Brown, Bickering and Guilbert, printers, 1840. 24 p. MiInRC; NBLiHi; USIC. 40-7094

Winchester, Samuel Gover, 1805-1841. The cheater. By S. G. Winchester. Philadelphia, PA: Wm. S. Martien, 1840. 239 p. NcMHi. 40-7095

Winchester, Samuel Gover, 1805-1841. The importance of doctrinal and instructional preaching. By the Rev. S. G. Winchester. Philadelphia, PA: Presbyterian Board of Publications,.1840. 32 p. CSansS; CtHC; IEG; PPPrHi; TxShA. 40-7096

Winchester, Samuel Gover, 1805-1841. The Spruce Street lectures. By several clergymen. Delivered during the years 1831-32. To which is added a lecture on the importance of creeds and confessions by Samuel Miller, D. D. Philadelphia, PA: Presbyterian Board of Publication, William S. Martien, publishing agent, 1840. 398 p. CSansS; ICP; GDecCT; MWiW; ViRut. 40-7097

Winchester, Samuel Gover, 1805-1841. The Sumner's inability is no excuse for his impenitency. By S. G. Winchester. Philadelphia, PA: Presbyterian Board of Publication, James Russell, publishing agent [1840] 24 p. CtHT; MB; MsJMC; PPM. 40-7098

Winchester, Samuel Gover, 1805-1841. The theatre. By Rev. S. G. Winchester. Philadelphia, PA: W. S. Martien, 1840. 239 p. LU; MsU; OWoC; PPiW; RPB. 40-7099

Winer, Georg Benedikt, 1789-1858. A grammar of the idioms of the Greek language of the New Testament. By Dr. Geo. Benedict Winer... Tr. by J. H. Agnew and O. G. Ebbeke. Philadelphia, PA: H. Hooker, 1840. 469 p. ArBaA; GDecCT; ICU; KyLoS; NjP. 40-7100

Winslow, Harriat Wadsworth [Lathrop] 1796-1833. Memoir of Mrs. Harriat L. Winslow, thirteen years a member of the American mission in Ceylon. By Rev. Miron Winslow. New York; American Tract Society [1840?] 479 p. GEU; KWiU; MBC; MiU; WHi. 40-7101

Winslow, Octavius, d. 1878. Experimental and practical views of the atonement. New York: M. W. Dodd, 1840. 248 p. ODaB. 40-7102

Winslow, Octavius, d: 1878. The inquirer directed to an experimental and practical view of the work of the Holy Spirit. By the Rev. Octavius Winslow... New York: R. Carter, 1840. 282 p. ICU; NbOP; ScDuE; TxU. 40-7103

Winter, George Simon. Wohlerfahrener pferde arzt... durchgesehen... von Valentin Tricher. Phialdelphia, PA: Schelly, 1840. 839 p. CtY; MiEN; PU-V. 40-7104

Winter, J. The Crocovienne waltz. Arranged for the piano forte by J. Winter. Baltimore, MD: F. D. Benteen [184-?] 2 p. ViU. 40-7105

Winthrop, Robert Charles, 1809-1894. An address delivered before the New England society, in the city of New York, December 23, 1839. Boston, MA; New York: Perkins & Marvin; Gould, Newman & Saxton, 1840. 60 p. ICU; MdBJ; MeB; MWA; PPL; ScCC; Vi. 40-7106

Winthrop, Robert Charles, 1809-1894. Question of order. Interested members... Commonwealth of Massachusetts... House of Representatives... Feb. 19... [Boston, MA: s. l., 1840] 4 p. MB; MBAt; MH. 40-7107

Wirt, William, 1772-1834. Sketches of the life and character of Patrick Henry. By William Wirt. Philadelphia, PA: Published by Thomas, Cowperthwait & Co., 184?. 306 p. IaCorn; IRA; MBerk. 40-7108

Wirt, William, 1772-1834. Sketches of the life and character of Patrick Henry. By William Wirt. Tenth edition, corrected by the author. Hartford, CT: Published by S. Andrus & Son, 1840. 468 p. KyOw. 40-7109

Wise, Daniel. A Summary View of All Religions... By D. Wise and J. Porter. Boston, MA: Stereotyped at the Boston Types and Stereotype Foundry, 1840. 24 p. IEG; MBC; MeLewB; MNtCA; Nh. 40-7110

Wise, Daniel. Why stand ye here all day idle? Personal effort explained and enforced. A sermon. Preached at Eastham Camp, meeting Aug. 14, 1840. Boston, MA: D. S. King, 1840. 50 p. MBNMHi. 40-7111

Wiseman, Nicholas Patrick Stephen, 1802-1865. The lives of St. Alphonsus Ligueri, St. Francis de Girclamo, St. John Joseph of the Cross, St. Pacificus of San Severin, and St. Veronica Giuliani; whose canonization took place on Trinity Sunday, May 26, 1839; to which are prefixed a treatise of the Abbe Gerbet on the invocation of saints, and an account of the proceedings and ceremonies used at their canonization. Philadelphia, PA: Michael Kelly, 1840. 267 p. IaDuCl; MBrigStJ; MoFloss; MoSU; NPStA; OCl. 40-7112

Withington, Leonard. The Bell of Zion. By the author of "The Puritan, or, Lay-es-

sayist." Boston, MA: Stereotyped by G. A. & J. Curtis, 1840. 243 p. CtY; MBC. 40-7113

Withington, Leonard, 1789-1885. A review of the late temperance movements in Massachusetts. By Leonard Withinton, Pastor of the First Church in Newburg, Massachusetts. Boston, MA: James Munroe and Company, 1840. 28 p. MeB; MiD-B; MnBedf; RPB; TxH; WHi. 40-7114

Wolff, Edouard. Souvenirs de Treport. Grand Valse brillante. Dediee a Madame de Lazareff nee Princesse Maunuck Bey, par Edouard Wolff. Philadelphia, PA; New Orleans, LA: Lee & Walker; W. T. Mayo [184-?] 11 p. ViU. 40-7115

Woman's mission... From the English Editor. Boston, MA: William Crosby & Co., 1840. 156 p. ICBB; MLow; NhPet; RPA. 40-7116

Woman's mission... From the English Editor. 2d American edition. New York: Wiley, 1840. 149 p. MH; NjP; NRAB; PCA; WM. 40-7117

Wood, Alphonso, 1810-1881. Class book of botany in two parts. By Alphonso Wood. Forty-first edition, revised and enlarged. Troy, NY: Merriam, Moore and CO., 1840. 645 p. KyLxT. 40-7118

Wood, Benjamin. A discourse occasioned by the death of Deacon Daniel Fisk: who died April 23, 1840, Aged LXIX. By Rev. Benjamin Wood, Pastor of the church in Upton. Boston, MA: Dutton and Wentworth's Print., 1840. 24 p. ICN; MBC; MiD-B; MWHi; OO; RPB. 40-7119

Wood, George Bacon, 1797-1879. Introductory lecture to the course of materia medica in the University of Pennsylvania. Delivered Nov. 3, 1840, by Geo. B. Wood, M. D. Philadelphia, PA: Haswell, Barrington, and Haswell, 1840. 30 p. DLC; NNNAM; PPCP; PU; Tx. 40-7120

Wood, George Bacon, 1797-1879. A late memoir of the life and character of the late Joseph Parrish, M. D. Philadelphia, PA: L. R. Bailey, 1840. 72 p. CtHT; ICU; KyLxT; PPM; RPB. 40-7121

Wood, George Bacon, 1797-1879. Syllabus of the course of lectures on materia medica and pharmacy... by George Bason Wood. Philadelphia, PA: Printed by L. R. Bailey, 1840. 69 p. GEU-M; NcU; NNN; PU; ViRA. 40-7122

Wood, Norman N. The duties and qualifications of deacons; [originally published as a circular letter of the Stephentown Baptist Association.] By N. N. Wood, pastor of the Baptist Church, at Lebanon Springs, N. Y. Hudson, NY: Printed by L. Van Dyck, 1840. 12 p. MB; N; NRAB; PCA. 40-7123

Wood, Thomas Newton. An address delivered before the two literary societies of the University of Alabama, in the Rotunda, July 4, 1840. Tuskaloosa, AL: M. D. J. Seade, 1840. MH; NcD; PPPrHi. 40-7124

Woodbridge, Sylvester. Historical discourse. Delivered November 29, 1840, at the dedication of "Christ's First Church" chapel in Raymor South, Hempstead, L. I. New York: pub. by John P. Haven, 1840. 22 p. CU; MBHi; NN; NSm. 40-7125

Woodbridge, William Channing, 1794-1845. Modern atlas on a new plan to accompany the system of universal geography. Hartford, CT: Belknap and Hamersley, 1840. 39 p. DLC. 40-7126

Woodbridge, William Channing, 1794-1845. System of universal geography. 9th ed. Hartford, CT: Belknap and Hamersley, 1840. 336, 96 p. IaDaM; ICU; MH; MWHi. 40-7127

Woodhouselee, Alexander Fraser Tytler, Lord, 1747-1813. Elements of general history, ancient and modern. 76th edition. Concord, NH: published by Horatio Hill & Co. [1840?] 527, 44 p. DLC; IaK; MnU; PWW; WvU. 40-7128

Woodman, Jabez C. Address, pronounced before the citizens of Minot [Me.] July 4, 1840. S. l.: n. pr. [1840] 32 p. MeHi; MH. 40-7129

Woodstock, Conn. Second Church of Christ. Confession of faith, covenant, historical notice & names of officers & members of the Second Church of Christ, in Woodstock, Conn. Approved & adopted July 2d, 1840... Hartford, CT: Case, Tiffany & Co., 1840. 16 p. Ct. 40-7130

Woodward, Henry. Essays on the millennium. By the Rev. Henry Woodward, A. M.... Philadelphia, PA: Orrin Rogers, E. G. Dorsey, printer, 1840. 25 p. ICP; MBC; MMeT-Hi; NbOP; TxH. 40-7131

Wooler, J. P. A man without a head. New York: French [184-?] p. MB; OCl. 40-7132

Woolman, John, 1720-1772. Extracts on the subect of slavery from the journal and writings of... Mount Holly, New Jersey... New York: M. Day & Co., 1840. 24 p. DLC; MH; MWA; NjJ; PHC. 40-7133

Woolman, John, 1720-1772. Journal of the life, gospel, labours, and Christian experiences of that faithful minister of Jesus Christ, John Woolman... Washington, DC: Thomas Hurst, 1840. 339 p. OSW; TxDaM. 40-7134

Woolsey, James L. The doctrine of christian baptism... by James J. Woolsey... Philadelphia, PA: Printed by I. Ashmead, 1840. 364 p. CtSoP; KKcBT; PCA; PPTU; RPB. 40-7135

Worcester, Henry Aikin. The Sabbath... Boston, MA: Otis Clapp, 1840. 126 p. MBAt; MH; NAlf: OUrC; PBa. 40-7136

Worcester, Joseph Emerson, 1784-1865. A comprehensive pronouncing and explanatory dictionary of the English language, with pronouncing vocabularies of classical, Scripture, and modern geographical names. Carefully revised and enlarged. Boston, MA; Philadelphia, PA: Jenks and Palmer; Thomas Cowperthwait & Co., 1840. 424 p. MdBS; MHi. 40-7137

Worcester, Joseph Emerson, 1784-1865. Elements of geography, modern and ancient, with a modern and ancient atlas. By J. E. Worcester. Improved ed. Boston, MA: D. H. Williams, 1840. 257 p. InCW; KWiU; MBAt; MH; NcAS. 40-7138

Worcester, Joseph Emerson, 1784-1865. Elements of history, ancient and modern. With a chart and tables of history included within the volume. By J. E.

Worcester... Boston, MA: Hilliard, Gray & Co., 1840. 386 p. MH. 40-7139

Worcester, Joseph Emerson, 1784-1865. Elements of history, ancient and modern. With a chart and tables of history included within the volume. By J. E. Worcester... Boston, MA: William J. Reynolds and Company, 184-? 386 p. IaHA; OUrC. 40-7140

Worcester, Joseph Emerson, 1784-1865. Historical atlas. Elements of history, ancient and modern. With a chart and tables of history included within the volume. By J. E. Worcester... 6th edition. Boston, MA: Hilliard, Gray, & Co., 1840? p. MH; NN. 40-7141

Worcester, Joseph Emerson, 1784-1865. Worcester's ancient classical and Scripture atlas. Improved edition. Boston, MA: Lewis and Sampson [184-?] p. CtY. 40-7142

Worcester, Samuel Melanchthon, 1801-1866. Hymns selected from various authors. With a key of musical expression. By Samuel Worcester, D. D., late pastor of the Tabernacle Church, Salem, Mass. New ed. Boston, MA: published by Crocker and Brewster, 1840. 776 p. MAnHi. 40-7143

Worcester Agricultural Society. Catalogue of the officers and members. Worcester, MA: s. l., 1840. 29 p. MWHi; N. 40-7144

Worcester County [Mass.] Common School Teachers Convention. Proceedings, Worcester, Dec. 12, 1840. Worcester, MA: s. l., 1840? p. CSmH; MH. 40-7145

The Workingman's advocate; a monthly publication to the political and social advancement of the masses. Vol. 1, No. 3-10, Aug., 1840-Jan., 1841. Washington, DC: F. S. Meyers, 1840-41. p. MdHi; MH-BA; PPL. 40-7146

Works on banking and currency; tables of contents of the financial register, and Quin's trade of banking. Washington: Printed for the publisher, 1840. 12 p. RPB. 40-7147

Worrell, Charles Flavel, 1805-1881. Catechism of the rudiments of music. Designed for the assistance of teachers. By Charles Flavel Worrell. 2d ed., enlarged. Princeton, NJ: Bogart, 1840. 114 p. NjP; PPPrHi. 40-7148

Worthington, George. An inquiry into the power of juries, to decide incidentially on question of law. Philadelphia, PA: John S. Littell, 1840. 62 p. CoU; IU; MdBB; Nj; OO; PP. 40-7149

Wright, A. E. A. E. Wright's Boston, New York, Philadelphia and Baltimore commercial directory and general advertising medium... to be continued annually. Philadelphia, PA: A. Wright, 1840. 401 p. ICU; MdHi; PPL; PPW. 40-7150

Wright, Aaron Kinne. An address delivered before the Society of Alumni of Western Reserve College, August 25, 1840. By Rev. A. K. Wright. Hudson: Ptd. by Charles Aikin, 1840. 16 p. CBPSR; MiD-B; NN; OCHP; OClW. 40-7151

Wright, Robert E. Constable's manual; a practical digest of the laws of Pennsylvania relative to the office and duties of constable. Philadelphia, PA: Small, 1840. 172 p. DeWi; PAlt. 40-7152

Wright, Silas, 1795-1847. Remarks of Mr. Wright in reply to Mr. Webster. In Senate, December 17, 1840. [Washington, DC?: s. l., 1840?] 16 p. MdBJ; MdHi; MH; N. 40-7153

Wright, Silas, 1795-1847. Speech of the Hon. Silas Wright at a mass meeting of the Democracy of Brooklyn, held at the Colonnade Garden, on Thursday evening, Sept. 29, 1840. New York: Published by Youngs & Hunt, 1840. 15 p. MBC; MdHi; NN; NSmb. 40-7154

Wyckoff, Isaac Newton, 1792-1869. Stability, an indispendable element of usefulness and greatness; an address delivered before the alumni of Rutgers college, July 14, 1840, inscribed to them by their consociate, Isaac N. Wyckoff, D. D. Albany, NY: Printed by Joel Munsell, 1840. 28 p. MH; MHi; NjR; NN; PHi. 40-7155

Wylie, Andrew, 1789-1851. Address to the citizens of Monroe County and to the members of the county lyceum, by Andrew Wylie, D. D. Bloomington, IN: printed in the old college building, 1840. InU. 40-7156

Wylie, Andrew, 1789-1851. Sectarianism is heresy. In three parts, in which are shown its nature, evils, and remedy. Bloomington, IN: s. l., 1840. 132 p. ICMe; ICP. 40-7157

Wylie, Andrew, 1789-1851. Sectarianism is heresy. In three parts, in which are shown its nature, evils, and remedy. Bloomington, IN: s. l., 1840. 148 p. ICU; In; InU; NN; OCLT; PPPrHi. 40-7158

Wyman, William. An address delivered

Wyman, William. An address delivered to the Voters in Manchester, N. H., June 25, 1840, in view of the approaching presidential election. By William

Wyman of Lowe.. Lowell, MA: Printed at the Literary Souvenir Office, 1840. 8 p. NN. 40-7159

X-Y-Z

Xenophon. The whole works of Xenophon. Translated by Ashley Cooper, Spelman, Smith, Fielding, and others. Philadelphia, PA: T. Wardle, 1840. 758 p. GAuY; GDecCT; IaCrC; MH; WM. 40-7160

Yale University. Catalogue of paintings, by Colonel Trumbell... New Haven, CT: Printed by B. L. Hamlen, 1840. 38 p. NNUT. 40-7161

Yale University. Catalogue of the officers and students in Yale College. New Haven, CT: B. L. Hamlen, 1840-90. 35 p. KHi; MdBP; MeB; MoS; NUtHi. 40-7162

Yale University. Commencement. Order of exercises. New Haven, CT: s. l., 1840-91. 3 v. MB. 40-7163

Yale University. Medical Institution. Annual circular of the medical institution of Yale College... New Haven, CT: Stanley & Chapin, printers, 1840. 8 p. OC. 40-7164

Yale University. Statistics of the class of 1837... Published by order of the class. New Haven, CT: s. l., 1840-50. 3 v. Ct; M. 40-7165

The Yankee: or Farmer's almanac for 1841. By Thomas Spofford. Boston, MA: Sold by Thomas Groom [1840] p. MWA. 40-7166

Yankee Doodle. Arranged with variations for the piano forte. Philadelphia, PA: George Willig [184-?] 2 p. ViU. 40-7167

Yankee Doodle. With variations composed by James Hewitt. New York: Firth & Hall [184-?] 5 p. ViU. 40-7168

Yankee Doodle as a dance & Over the hills and far away. Baltimore, MD; New Orleans, LA: F. D. Benteen; W. T. Mayo [184-?] 1 p. ViU. 40-7169

The Yankee Farmer and New England Cultivator, etc. Vol. 6, 1840. Boston, MA: s. l., 1840. v. MBHo. 40-7170

Yeomans, John William. A sermon delivered to the Presbyterian congregation of Trenton, New Jersey, at the dedication of their new house of worship, January 19, 1840. Trenton, NJ: William D. Hart, 1840. 26 p. DLC; ICP; MB; MWA; PHi. 40-7171

Young, Alexander, 1800-1854. Chronicles of the first planters of the Colony of Massachusetts Bay, from 1623-1636. Now first collected from original records and contemporaneous manuscripts... Boston, MA: C. C. Little and J. Brown, 1840. 571 p. O. 40-7172

Young, Alexander, 1800-1854. The church, the pulpit and the gospel. A discourse at the ordination of the Rev.

George Edward Ellis, as pastor of the Harvard church in Charlestown, March 11, 1840... Boston, MA: C. C. Little and J. Brown, 1840. 40 p. CtSoP; ICMe; MBAU; MWA; OClWHi; RPB. 40-7173

Young, Alexander, 1800-1854. A discourse on the life and character of the Reverend John Thornton Kirkland, D. D., LL. D... Delivered in the church on Church Green, May 3, 1840. By Alexander Young. Boston, MA: Charles C. Little and James Brown, 1840. 104 p. ICMe; KHi; MWA; NcU; OO. 40-7174

Young, Andrew White, 1802-1877. First lessons in civil government, including a comprehensive view of the government of the State of Ohio. Cleveland, OH: s. l., 1840. OCLaw. 40-7175

Young, Andrew White, 1802-1877. Introduction to the science of government... by Andrew W. Young. 4th edition. Albany, NY: from the press of C. Van Benthuysen, 1840. 336 p. CSfLaw; CtY; MiU; NmU. 40-7176

Young, David. The Indiana Almanac for 1841. No. 3. By David Young. Indianapolis, IN: Stacy & Williams [1840] p. In; MWA. 40-7177

Young, Edward, 1683-1765. The complaint; or, night thought. Exeter, NH: Published by J. and B. Williams, 1840. 216 p. NjR; PWbo. 40-7178

Young, Edward, 1683-1765. The complaint; or, night thought. Hartford, CT: Andrus & Judd [1840?] 324 p. NjR. 40-7179

Young, Edward, 1683-1765. The com-

plaint; or, night thought. New York: D. Appleton & Co. [1840] 324 p. DLC. 40-7180

Young, Edward, 1683-1765. The complaint; or, night thought. New York: Williams, 1840. 216 p. IaFairP. 40-7181

Young, Edward, 1683-1765. Night thoughts on life, death and immortality. By Edward Young, LL. D. Philadelphia, PA: James Kay and Brother, 1840. 301 p. No Loc. 40-7182

Young, John Radford, 1799-1885. An elementary treatise on algebra... by John Radford Young. A new American edition from the last London edition, revised and corrected by a mathematician. Philadelphia, PA: Hogan and Thompson, 1840. 324 p. NjMD. 40-7183

Young, Samuel, 1789-1850. Oration delivered at the Democratic-Republican celebration... July fourth, 1840... Pub. by request of the Democratic-Republican Convention. New York: J. W. Bell, 1840. 24 p. Nh; PPPrHi; TxU; WHi. 40-7184

The young Christian's pocket-book; or, Counsels, comforts and cautions conveyed in short striking sentences... General P. E. Sunday School Union. New York: General P. E. S. S. Union [1840?] 92 p. NNG. 40-7185

The young lady's book; a manual of elegant recreations, exercises, and pursuits. 7th ed. Boston, MA: C. A Wells, 1840. 504 p. NjR; WU. 40-7186

The young learner; a book for children and youth. By a teacher. Andover, MA; New York: Published by Gould, Newman & Saxton, 1840. 107 p. DLC; MHi; OC. 40-7187

Young Ladies Ass'n. P. L. M. C. I. Y. L.... Philadelphia, PA: s. l., 1840. PPL. 40-7188

The young mechanics library. [Baltimore, MD: Armstrong and Berry; Woods and Crane, printers, 1840] 208 p. NjR. 40-7189

Young Men's Association, Albany, New York. Catalogue of the Library of the Young Men's Association for Mutual Improvement... Albany, NY: s. l., 1840. 50 p. MHi. 40-7190

Young Men's Association of the City of Utica, N. Y. Catalogue of the Library of the Young Men's Association of the City of Utica, containing the acts of incorporation, constitution, and by-laws, April, 1840. Utica, NY: Press of E. Morrin [1840] 35 p. NUt. 40-7191

The young scholar's refrence book; being a collection of useful tables... by a teacher. Second edition, enlarged. Andover: Gould, Newman and Saxon [etc.] 1840. 72 p. MB; MHa; NjR; NNC; OClWHi. [Elssler quadrille. Arranged for the pianforte.] [Boston, MA?: s. l., 184-?] 7 p. MB. 40-7192

Youth's keepsake. A Christmas and

New Year's gift for young people. Boston, MA: Otis, Broaders & Co., 1840. 192 p. KyBC; MoS; MoSpD; WGr; WU. 40-7193

Zabriskie, James Cannon, 1804-1883. Reply to an address of Capt. R. T. Stockton, N. S. N... Trenton, NJ: s. l., 1840. PPL. 40-7194

Zaleucus. Herculean quick step. Composed and arranged for the piano forte by Zaleucus. Boston, MA: G. P. Reed [184-?] 4 p. MB; ViU. 40-7195

Zeuner, Charles. The ancient lyre, a collection of old, new and original church music, under the approbation of the Professional Music Society in Boston. Arranged and composed by Ch. Zeuner... 11th ed., rev. and improved, containing seventy new tunes. Boston, MA: Crocker and Brewster, 1840. 363 p. MAnP; MDeeP; MLei; NhD. 40-7196

Zimmerman, John George. Solitude, by John G. Zimmerman. With the life of the author. In two parts. New York: C. Wells, 1804. 296 p. MWelC; NR; OMC; WAsN. 40-7197

Zschokke, Heinrich. The dead guest. Translated from the German. New York, 1840. 58 p. MH. 40-7198